Food, Farming, and Sustainability

Nicholas J. Garcia

Food, Farming, and Sustainability

Readings in Agricultural Law

Susan A. Schneider

PROFESSOR OF LAW
UNIVERSITY OF ARKANSAS SCHOOL OF LAW

CAROLINA ACADEMIC PRESS
Durham, North Carolina

Library of Congress Cataloging-in-Publication Data

Schneider, Susan A.
  Food, farming, and sustainability : readings in agricultural law / Susan A. Schneider.
      p. cm.
  Includes bibliographical references and index.
  ISBN 978-1-59460-588-8 (alk. paper)
  1. Agricultural laws and legislation--United States. I. Title.

  KF1682.S36 2010
  343.73'076--dc22

                          2010035659

Carolina Academic Press
700 Kent Street
Durham, North Carolina 27701
Telephone (919) 489-7486
Fax (919) 493-5668
www.cap-press.com

Printed in the United States of America

Dedicated to my grandparents and my parents, for affording me the opportunity to be raised on a family farm; to my sister and her family for the care that they provide in preserving that farm; to my husband and colleague, Christopher Kelley for his advice, inspiration and dedication to excellence; and to our students in the LL.M. Program in Agricultural & Food Law, past, present, and future.

Contents

Preface

Agricultural law and policy, once of concern only to agricultural economists, farm commodity group lobbyists, and a handful of congressional aids is now a topic of everyday discussion. And, to be certain, it is a controversial topic.

After years of claiming responsibility for "feeding the world," farmers are caught between advice that their operations must be bigger, more efficient, and produce a more uniform product and criticism that they are too big and their practices unsustainable.

Some farm groups vigorously oppose any type of regulation; others clamor for additional regulatory protection.

Everyday news stories contrast the iconic image of the family farm with pictures of sheds that house tens of thousands of animals, manure lagoons, and watersheds threatened with runoff. Animal welfare advocates with secret video cameras film scenes that horrify the public. Food safety recalls seem common.

Our food system—with perhaps the cheapest and most abundant supply of a wide variety of food products in the world—is now linked to obesity and related diseases.

How can U.S. farm policy assure an adequate and healthy food supply in a manner that can be sustained for generations to come?

Food, Farming, and Sustainability: Readings in Agricultural Law attempts to make sense of these controversies by providing an issues-based study of some of the complex topics that make up the body of agricultural law. Each is presented in the context of one or more current policy issues. The readings raise difficult questions, provide contrasting information, and leave readers with the task of developing solutions for the future.

Because of the extent and variety of the legal issues involved in agricultural law today, many important issues are not included. These readings provide only a first step in an analysis that affects us all.

From its initial discussion of "agricultural exceptionalism" to its concluding remarks on food and agriculture, the book is written to spark thoughtful dialogue.

Some citations and footnotes have been eliminated from the original source in the editing process. Full original source citation is provided so that readers can view the original document in its complete form is so desired.

Food, Farming, and Sustainability

I

Agriculture and Agricultural Law

We have now lands enough to employ an infinite number of people in their culti-vation. Cultivators of the earth are the most valuable citizens. They are the most vig-orous, the most independant, the most virtuous, & they are tied to their country & wedded to it's liberty & interests by the most lasting bonds.

Excerpt from *Letter from Thomas Jefferson To John Jay*, Paris, Aug. 23, 1785, available at http://www.yale.edu/lawweb/avalon/jefflett/let32.htm through The Avalon Project at Yale Law School.

A. The Agrarian Ideal or the Agrarian Myth?

Richard S. Kirkendall
Up to Now: A History of American Agriculture from Jefferson to Revolution to Crisis
Agriculture and Human Values 4, 4–5 (Winter 1987)

American Agrarianism

Farming and farm people have always occupied special positions in the American mind. The belief that they deserve high status and that the nation should be based upon them was part of the American heritage from Europe, running back to Ancient Rome, the Renaissance, English writers of the seventeenth and eighteenth centuries, and the French physiocrats and other continental writers of the eighteenth century. This heritage main-tained that farming was the best way of life and the most important economic activity, that it conferred psychological as well as economic benefits, and that it produced the best citizens and soldiers. These ideas encouraged people to believe that America was a supe-rior place for it supplied more and better opportunities to farm than Europe did.

Americans both accepted and reshaped these ideas. In this development Thomas Jef-ferson was especially important. The greatest "agrarianizer" he tried to construct a na-tion with an agrarian base. He took ideas that had not been identified with democracy, at least not exclusively, and democratized them, arguing that to be democratic a nation must have a farm foundation. Although a planter himself, Jefferson emphasized the po-litical value of the family farm, a farm owned and worked by members of one family and large enough to supply their needs. In his view, such a farm conferred independence, since the people on it worked for themselves, not others, and it required self-reliance and hard work. Its most important product was the personality type required for a democracy, rather than the debased type that appeared to grow out of European urban conditions. With family farms as democracy's essential foundation, farming's importance transcended the economic goods produced by farmers.

Jefferson did not advocate fully self-sufficient non-commercial farms. He saw value for the United States in Europe's need for food. It meant that there would be many good opportunities to farm in America. To prosper, American farmers should produce a surplus; they should grow more than farm families needed and more than the nation needed. Thus the agrarian politician opposed obstacles to American trade with Europe, including protective tariffs and French control of the mouth of the Mississippi River.

Jefferson and other American agrarianizers saw western lands as even more valuable than the European market. More perhaps than any other feature, they distinguished the United States from Europe. They must be available to farmers, free of control by Indians and Europeans, and sold at a low price or given away. Their importance justified the purchase of Louisiana, for, by greatly enlarging the land possessed by the United States, the purchase guaranteed the success of American democracy and the continuation of American superiority....

Jefferson's democratic agrarianism achieved its most spectacular victory in 1862 with the passage of the Homestead Act. Giving 160 acres to those who would make farms out of them, this land policy seemed to be a way of making the lands truly valuable and the nation healthy and strong. And giving lands away seemed beneficial to urban workers as well as farmers, for it offered those workers a "safety valve." Giving them a way of escaping or avoiding oppression, it enabled them to develop a personality that differed from that of the European proletariat and was compatible with democracy. Or so it seemed to American agrarians....

———————

Kirkendall's article is based on three concepts—agrarianism, as excerpted above; the technological revolution in agriculture, which he refers to as the "Great American Agricultural Revolution;" and the farm crisis of the 1980s. Kirkendall argues that Jeffersonian agrarianism "gets in the way of realistic thinking about farming and rural life." His article presents an effective analysis of the historical development of U.S. agriculture as less and less farmers were needed to produce increasing amounts of food. In his conclusion, Kirkendall asks, "[n]ow that the number of farms and the size of the farm population have become so small, what difference does it make to the nation whether our farms are plantations, corporations, or family units? Certainly no one can longer argue convincingly that the survival of democracy depends upon the survival of the family farm."

Nevertheless, the image of an independent and self sufficient land owner, in direct contact with nature, perseveres. In the introduction to his 1969 book AGRARIANISM IN AMERICAN LITERATURE, M. Thomas Inge defines agrarianism according to three basic tenets.

- Cultivation of the soil provides direct contact with nature; through the contact with nature the agrarian is blessed with a closer relationship to God. Farming has within it a positive spiritual good; the farmer acquires the virtues of "honor, manliness, self-reliance, courage, moral integrity, and hospitality" and follows the example of God when creating order out of chaos.

- The farmer "has a sense of identity, a sense of historical and religious tradition, a feeling of belonging to a concrete family, place, and region, which are psychologically and culturally beneficial." The harmony of this life checks the encroachments of a fragmented, alienated modern society which has grown to inhuman scale.

- In contrast, farming offers total independence and self-sufficiency. It has a solid, stable position in the world order. But urban life, capitalism, and technology destroy our independence and dignity while fostering vice and weakness within us. The agricultural community can provide checks and balances against the imbalances of modern society by its fellowship of labor and cooperation with other agrarians, while obeying the rhythms of nature. The agrarian community is the model society for mankind.

Consider the history of U.S. Farm Policy in this context as described by Agricultural Economist, Anne Effland.

Anne B. W. Effland
U.S. Farm Policy: The First 200 Years

USDA Economic Research Service, Agricultural Outlook Special Article
available at
http://www.ers.usda.gov/publications/agoutlook/mar2000/ao269g.pdf

Reviews of the past as a backdrop for present and future policy often stop at the 1920s in their look backward. Although the last 70 years undoubtedly are critical for comprehending the rationale of current and recent policies, they mark a period when a single approach, one characterized by programs of farm income support, dominated farm policy. Since the founding of the national government more than 200 years ago, farmers have been supported by a series of markedly different approaches, which roughly coincide with four periods, all of which overlap through decades of debate and transition.

In the first period, roughly 1785–1890, the focus of "farm" policy was land distribution and expansion of settlement through numerous private farm operations. The second period, from about 1830 to 1914, focused on improving the productivity of farm operations, through support of research and education. The third period, approximately 1870–1933, ushered in limited regulation of markets, infrastructure improvements, and provision of economic information to help farmers compete. The fourth period, since 1924, focused on direct government intervention to provide farm income support. Whether we are currently in a time of transition toward a new type of policy remains to be seen, but over the last 15 years or so, debate about farm income support policies has accelerated. Movements toward more open global trade, an increasing emphasis on market-driven production decisions, and attention to environmental costs of agricultural production have all influenced current policy discussions.

Within each of these periods, public policy that addresses the needs of agriculture has faced conflicting interests, often grounded in the consequences of policies and developments of earlier periods. Although resolution of these conflicts has been different in each period, throughout the years a remarkably consistent public consensus has remained: that the problems inherent in farming warrant public support.

"… any person who is the head of a family … shall … be entitled to enter one quarter section or a less quantity of unappropriated public lands … for the purpose of actual settlement and cultivation."   The Homestead Act, 1862

Promoting Agriculture in the New Nation

For the first five or six decades after the U.S. became a nation, the focus of national government was expansion and development. As land transfers, purchases, and treaties added territory to the U.S., policies were formulated to encourage the movement of population and industry to fill the space. Policy developments in this period that led to widespread access to land for farming, in a sense laid the foundation for public policy toward the agricultural sector.

Early Federal land policy favored sale of large amounts of land at relatively high prices, to bring revenues to the new government and to transfer public lands into private hands as rapidly as possible. Slow sales, however, and pressure from interests that favored transfer of public lands to small, independent farmers led to progressively more liberal laws governing sale of public lands. Minimum prices per acre were reduced and credit terms eased by legislation in 1790 and 1800. Later laws in 1820, 1841, and 1854 reduced prices further, forgave outstanding debts for land, provided means for illegal settlers — "squatters" — to gain title to land they occupied, and eventually, through the Homestead Act of 1862, provided for free distribution of land to anyone who would settle and farm it. Land distribution on these terms continued in unsettled areas into the 20th century, but the bulk of American farmland had been claimed and the traditional American frontier declared closed by 1890.

Debate over these land distribution issues reflected the conflict between two political-economic philosophies. Those in favor of selling large parcels at high prices believed public lands were an asset that should be sold to bring the greatest revenues to the government, reducing the need for taxes and assuring that the landowners could afford to develop it constructively.

Those who favored lower prices and smaller minimum parcels believed the best use of public land was to foster as much settlement as possible by small, independent farmers. Widespread settlement would support further development by increasing population in new areas, fueling economic growth, and in the earliest years, securing the territorial claims of the new nation. It would also assure the development in the new territories of a reliable independent citizenry not beholden to the politically or economically powerful. These citizens would own their own land and depend only on the labor of their own families for their wellbeing, exemplifying the agrarian ideal.

Debate between the two points of view was also embedded in the regional politics of the day. In the first decades of the 19th century, older states along the eastern seaboard resisted relatively open access to land for farming in the West. Settlement in the new areas threatened their political dominance and threatened the national treasury through loss of potential revenues from land sales and increasing demands for transportation developments to link the old and new regions.

In the decades preceding the Civil War, proponents of the southern plantation system of agriculture began to oppose the increasingly open access to public land. They viewed it as public promotion of an agricultural system based on an agrarian ideal that was at odds with their own system. With secession of the southern states in 1860, southern political leaders left the U.S. Congress, leaving proponents of free distribution of public land and other forms of assistance to small farmers virtually unopposed. Success in embedding this agrarian ideal in land policy, symbolized by passage of the Homestead Act, laid the basis for continued influence of that ideal in farm policy debates into the future. The national government had used its resources — in this case land — to encourage and support expansion of an agricultural structure of independent family farms. Thus Federal land policy created a precedent of Federal support for an independent family farm system, which has continued to be a prominent public goal of farm policy.

Moving Agriculture Toward Efficiency

As land policy continued encouraging increasing numbers of independent farmers across the U.S., improving American farmers' productivity and quality of life became a goal among progressive farmers, journalists, educators, and producers of commercial farm inputs. In the 1820s, farmers began to organize into state and county agricultural societies and to promote the need for specialized training and scientific research to advance the productivity and professionalism of the industry.

Much of the support for these ideas came from older farming regions of the South and East, which had begun to suffer from competition with newly opened lands in the West. The availability of extensive, fertile lands on which staples like wheat, cotton, and livestock could be produced more cheaply forced farmers in older, settled regions to evaluate their production methods. Years of cultivation without attention to preserving fertility of the soil had led to falling yields and even abandonment of land, particularly in areas growing cotton and tobacco. Some of these farmers saw potential for greater competitiveness through, for example, improved fertilizers and better methods of preparing soil for planting. Agricultural education and scientific research would be the source of these potential improvements.

Agricultural leaders looked to government for support of education and research programs. To a certain extent, the call for Federal support for improved productivity in farming grew out of the consequences of earlier land policy — Federal distribution of public lands in the West increased competition for farmers in the older regions of the nation, making the Federal government partially responsible for helping farmers in the older regions improve their productivity. But arguments for public support of agricultural education and scientific research rested largely on the belief that to be effective, advancements in agricultural productivity needed to be broadly accessible to the large population of independent farmers on whom the nation depended for food and fiber.

The U.S. was maturing as a nation and experiencing rapid urban and industrial growth in cities along the eastern seaboard. As manufacturing developed, employing increasing numbers of people, agriculture became a distinct economic sector, working in tandem with other industries to help the nation grow. Improving the productivity of this sector would support the development of other industries, by releasing labor for emerging factories, and by providing food and fiber for the increasing urban population, as well as inputs for these new industries — textile mills, for example.

"... in order to aid in diffusing among the people of the United States useful and practical information on subjects relating to agriculture and home economics, and to encourage the application of the same ... there may be inaugurated ... agricultural extension work ... in cooperation with the United States Department of Agriculture." The Smith Lever Act, 1914

Federally supported agricultural education and scientific research eventually took four major forms: establishment of the U.S. Department of Agriculture, authorization of a national system of agricultural colleges, appropriation of Federal funds to support agricultural science research at state agricultural experiment stations, and organization of an adult education system, USDA's Cooperative Extension Service. The first two of these took place in 1862, the year the Homestead Act was passed. Federal support for agricultural research at state experiment stations began about a decade later in the 1870s, while the Cooperative Extension Service was established in 1914.

Agrarianism Clashes with Industrialism

As agriculture, manufacturing, and other industries continued to expand, the increasing consolidation and wealth of urban-based industries began to contrast with the relative poverty and unconsolidated nature of agriculture. Beginning in the 1870s and lasting through the 1890s, chronic national surpluses of farm products depressed prices, while on a regional level repeated droughts, grasshopper infestations, and other natural disasters compounded problems for farmers in the recently settled lands of the Great Plains and Far West. Repeated national financial panics throughout the period made credit scarce and expensive. Meanwhile, as farmers saw their incomes falter, they watched the rising revenues and increasing political influence of railroads, processors, and urban financial interests, apparently the beneficiaries of regional monopolies, high interest rates, and high tariffs that protected manufacturing and other industries at the expense of farmers.

Demands from farm interests for Federal action drew on the same ideology that had supported free distribution of public lands. Free land turned out to be insufficient, particularly as farmers moved beyond self-sufficient frontier farming and became increasingly dependent on markets. Having settled western lands with Federal government support, farmers on these lands looked to the Federal government for new kinds of support when they began to face decades of harsh conditions. Farmers, primarily in the West and South, organized to demand assistance in the form of Federal government regulation. Eventually forming the Populist Party in the 1890s, they advocated national government control of an expanded money supply, government ownership of transportation (railroads) and communication (telegraph) systems, an income tax to replace high tariffs as a source of Federal revenue, and continued government support for distribution of land to small, independent farmers.

The Populist assumption that fostering agriculture was a proper concern of government remained essentially unquestioned, although not all participants in the debate believed government regulation of markets was the proper form of assistance. As Populist ideas spread, particularly in the Plains, other farm organizations proposed expanding education and research programs to help individual farmers compete in free markets. During the 1910s and 1920s, these programs were administered particularly through the Cooperative Extension Service and USDA's new Bureau of Agricultural Economics, established in 1924. During the same period, legislation exempting agricultural cooperatives from antitrust regulation left farmers free to join together for the purpose of purchasing inputs or marketing their products. Market information services and infrastructure development, especially farm-to-market roads, through Department of Agriculture programs equipped small rural producers with market access and economic information that larger commercial interests acquired privately.

"… it is hereby declared to be the policy of Congress to promote the effective merchandising of agricultural commodities in interstate and foreign commerce, so that the industry of agriculture will be placed on a basis of economic equality with other industries, and to that end to protect, control, and stabilize the currents of interstate and foreign commerce in the marketing of agricultural commodities and their food products."   Federal Farm Board Act of 1929

Tackling Economic Depression & Chronic Overproduction

During the years 1910–14, the rise in population migration from rural areas to cities and the end of what had been a continual expansion of acreage in agricultural production led to slower growth in food production. With increased demand for food from growing U.S. urban populations and, during the second half of the decade, from a world embroiled in war, food prices reached levels at which farmers seemed to have achieved incomes on a par with other sectors of the economy. The U.S. farm population peaked around 1910 at about 32 million and the number of farms in the U.S. peaked around 1920 at about 6 1/2 million.

Soon after the war ended, however, international food demand plummeted as European production started to recover, and U.S. farm prices fell sharply. In response, farm leaders began laying out a proposal for a national program to support farm prices by controlling domestic supplies and using exports to absorb surpluses. Although Presidential vetoes held off the program during the 1920s, Congress twice passed measures providing for direct government intervention to lift farm prices by controlling supplies. The Federal government did implement some programs to regulate markets and to improve farm credit, but the limited intervention had little effect in improving the farm economy.

"It is hereby declared to be the policy of Congress ... To establish and maintain such balance between the production and consumption of agricultural commodities ... as will reestablish prices to farmers at a level that will give agricultural commodities a purchasing power ... equivalent to the purchasing power of agricultural commodities in ... the prewar period, August 1909–July 1914."
The First Agricultural Adjustment Act, 1933

It took a Depression to get the price supports farmers wanted. The demands of agriculture for an equal share of prosperity were swept up in a much broader package of direct Federal interventions as the economy at large faltered at the end of the 1920s. Beginning with Franklin Roosevelt's New Deal in 1933, the solution to rapidly falling farm incomes was primarily price supports, achieved through dramatic reductions in supply. Supply controls for staple commodities included payments for reduced planting and government storage of market-depressing surpluses when prices fell below a predetermined level. For perishable commodities such as milk and some specialty crops, supply control worked through a system of marketing orders that provided negative incentives for producing beyond specified levels.

The combination of price supports and supply management functioned as the essential outline of Federal farm policy from 1933 until 1996, and continues to figure in current debate, although the mechanisms and relative weights of the policies' components were modified by successive farm legislation. In some years, notably during World War II and postwar reconstruction, and again during the early 1970s and mid-1990s, global supplies tightened sharply, sending demand and prices soaring above farm price supports and rendering acreage reduction programs unnecessary. But for most of the period, repeated cycles of above-average production and/or reduced global demand put downward pressure on prices, keeping the programs popular and well funded.

Deepening distress in the agricultural economy in the 1920s and economic depression in the 1930s had fueled political support for a new direction in farm policy. Limited market regulation and programs to help farmers compete had not been enough to keep farm incomes from falling; the call for more direct intervention had gained support. Continued public support for direct intervention after World War II arose for different reasons.

Low prices and consequent low farm incomes of the 1920s and early 1930s had been the result of surpluses created by sharply reduced global and domestic demand, beginning with Europe's return to normal production after World War I and followed by the international economic depression of the 1930s. Surpluses in years following World War II resulted from rapidly increasing productivity, exacerbated by continuing high price supports that kept production above demand. The apparent success of production controls and price supports in raising and maintaining farm incomes by the mid-1930s, however, made a continuation of these policies publicly acceptable.

Nonetheless, intense debate between proponents of high price supports and those who believed farm prices should be allowed to fluctuate according to market demand continued from the mid-1950s to the mid-1960s. The debate was set in the context of large surpluses, low prices, and efforts led by the Eisenhower administration to return the U.S. economy and government bureaucracy to pre-New Deal, pre-World War II structures. Out of the debate—between advocates of very high price supports and mandatory production controls and those who wished to end direct government market intervention—came a compromise for farm policy. The Food and Agriculture Act of 1965 made most production controls voluntary and set price supports in relation to world market prices, abandoning the "parity" levels intended to support farm income at levels comparable to the high levels achieved during the 1910s. A system of direct income support ("deficiency") payments compensated farmers for lower support prices.

The debate over price supports and supply control recurred with enough intensity to divert the direction of policy in the mid-1980s. The new setting was the farm financial crisis and its aftermath, along with efforts by the Reagan presidency to end "big government" and place the American farm economy on a free-market footing. This time, with steadily increasing government stocks of program commodities and Federal budget deficits at record levels, the argument against continuing expensive government support of the farm economy gained support. At the same time, the farm crisis began to undermine some of the farm sector's confidence that domestic price supports and production controls were a very effective way to secure U.S. farm income in a global economy. Supported U.S. prices reduced international marketing opportunities and increasing global supplies undercut domestic production control efforts. Farm legislation passed in 1985 and 1990 maintained the traditional combination of price supports, supply controls, and income support payments, but introduced changes that moved farmers toward greater market orientation—i.e., lower price supports, greater planting flexibility, and more attention to developing export opportunities for farm products.

By the time of the Federal Agriculture Improvement and Reform Act of 1996, which legislated a dramatic shift in the character of Federal assistance to farmers, farm policy seemed to be again passing into a new period, pressed by the rising costs of farm income support programs and by the requirements of global agreements that farm income support programs keep production decisions tied to market signals. The new policy consensus behind the 1996 legislation held that farmers would be better equipped to compete in global markets under a system that allowed nearly complete planting flexibility and that promised continued government efforts to enhance access to international markets. To ease the transition from previous policy, the 1996 act offered a program of decreasing fixed income support payments no longer tied to production decisions.

Another Transition at Hand?

During the period of short supplies and high prices immediately following passage of the 1996 Farm Act, the consensus favoring the new policy direction held. With the return of low prices in 1998—the result of good weather and global financial crises—the debate has resumed about whether traditional policies of direct income support tied to price fluctuations are the most effective solution to farm income variability. But a host of post-World War II developments in agriculture has led to a markedly changed context for farm policy in the last decade and a half, and that new context has produced some new challenges.

Increasing productivity has reduced the number of people needed to work on farms and decreased profitability has reduced the number who can be supported by income from a single family farm. While many farm residents have left rural areas for employment in cities, others have stayed and found employment or developed businesses to supplement their household income. Sources of income to farm households have greatly diversified, complicating questions of how the appropriate level of farm income support should be calculated and how it should be delivered.

Also since World War II, the business of farming and food production has become increasingly consolidated and industrialized. Average farm size continues to grow. Contract production in poultry, hogs, and other commodities has become common. Consolidation is evident in the food processing, transportation, and trading sectors of the agricultural economy. Consumer preferences in diet and food preparation have changed dramatically. These and other developments have led to production processes and business relationships resembling other industries more than the traditional agrarian model of small independent producers—the model on which earlier periods of farm policy have been based.

International trade issues have grown in importance over the last 50 years, as soaring productivity of U.S. farms has created a need for additional outlets for U.S. goods, preferably in export markets. But these issues have gained increased significance in deliberations over domestic farm policy in the last 15 years as new global and regional agreements have been negotiated that require reduction in trade-distorting farm policies. Income support policies that have been traditionally used since the 1930s are limited in this trade environment because they can affect individual production decisions which in turn can affect global commodity markets.

Equally challenging will be integrating the increasingly complex and changing goals of environmental policy with agricultural policy. Conservation programs for agriculture began primarily as efforts to combat soil erosion, an objective driven largely by concern for improving productivity. More recently, efforts have focused on a broader array of issues—water and air quality, wildlife habitat, and open space and landscape preservation—not driven by concern for agricultural production, although they may offer such benefits. The goal, rather, has become controlling environmental impacts beyond the farm.

These postwar developments seem likely to produce some marked changes in the approach to farm policy, although they do not yet seem to have weakened public support for some kind of direct assistance to farmers. The tradition of public support for farmers has persisted through a long history of changing contexts and policy responses—from access to land to access to education and research and from marketing and information programs to income support programs.

All of these policies have been rooted in attempts to ensure opportunities for individuals and families to make a living at farming, beginning with Federal land policy. With its promise of virtually open access to land, the policy offered nearly anyone the chance to become a farmer with a minimal investment. Each period since has ushered in a new policy approach intended to help farmers improve their incomes in the face of ever-increasing production. Current challenges facing farm policymakers may test the strength of public support for the direct income support programs typical of the last 70 years, and will surely require creativity in crafting policies that function well in the new context of advanced structural change, global trade constraints, and new environmental goals.

Neither the United States nor its agricultural sector can be described in the terms espoused by Jefferson. The number of commercially viable farms has decreased significantly over the years. The number of U.S. farms peaked in 1935 at almost 7 million; there are now just over 2 million farms. Less than 2 percent of the U.S. population is now employed in agriculture. See, ROBERT A. HOPPE ET AL., USDA, STRUCTURE AND FINANCES OF U.S. FARMS: FAMILY FARM REPORT 4 (2007). The U.S. 2000 Census reported that 79 percent of the population lives in urban areas.

Is there any role for agrarianism in defining U.S. agriculture today? Do Jeffersonian ideals have any relevance to farm and food policy in a modern world? Consider the following thought-provoking excerpt discussing agrarianism in the context of a model for citizenship.

William P. Browne, Jerry R. Skees, Louis E. Swanson, Paul B. Thompson, and Laurian J. Unnevehr, SACRED COWS AND HOT POTATOES: AGRARIAN MYTHS IN AGRICULTURAL POLICY
8–11 (1992)

Jefferson and Citizenship Ideals

It is useful to think of citizenship as a role that we prepare for, as an actor studies a script. The founding fathers clearly believed that some people would be far better equipped than others for the part. A person's ability to play the role of citizen hangs on having sympathy with the part, on being able to motivate oneself to faithfully carry out the citizen's responsibilities. Performing as a citizen thus requires a certain kind of character. Jefferson argued that, in America, freeholding yeoman farmers would have that character because their farming would make it obvious that the state's ability to protect their lands served personal interests. Because they could not remove themselves (or their farms), they had to accept the need for resolving political differences in ways that did not endanger the stability of the state....

Jefferson notes that it is not the aristocrat but the common farmer who occupies the land in America. His remarks start from the idea that landowners, unlike other people, make a stronger identification between self-interest and the common good and hence are more virtuous *as citizens*. A landed population is therefore less apt to be tempted by short-term, unsustainable government policies. In America, however, the land was owned by small yeoman farmers. Jefferson's argument is a rationale for aligning political power with a previously existing pattern of land holdings. In the American context of the age, the argument favored democracy and undercut key premises of the antidemocratic themes of the Federalists.

Jefferson's statements about farms must be ready as part of his strategy to place government power in pursuit of the common good. Small farms were important to Jeffersonian democracy because they promised temporary relief from the threat of mob rule. Jefferson knew that the structure of society would eventually change. But, he hoped that, if it could be established on a democratic basis, new traditions would emerge to serve the public good.

For Jefferson, farmers were valuable as citizens because they would be well placed to see the convergence of personal interest and the public good. The idea of "public good" at work here is the stability and fiscal responsibility of the society. The ability to understand the link between public and private interest is a mark of citizenship.

* * *

Untold number of politicians and political commentators have quoted [Jefferson's] passages to bring forward the idea of a political duty to preserve and protect farms. But Jefferson's words are open to other interpretations. While they have a political message of preserving the farm basis of the American economy, they also and more aptly reconcile self-interest with the public good.

* * *

B. Agrarianism and the Development of U.S. Agricultural Law

Following up on the theme in Sacred Cows and Hot Potatoes, does agricultural law represent a "convergence of personal interest and the public good"?

Professor Grace Skogstad from the University of Toronto explained that the idea of agricultural exceptionalism in both the U.S. and the European Union was based on both the specific interests and needs of farmers and upon the broader national interest in a secure food supply. See, Grace Skogstad, *Ideas, Paradigms and Institutions: Agricultural Exceptionalism in the European Union and the United States*, 11 Governance 463, 468 (1998). In this sense, the dual rationales, the interests of farmers and the national interest, are reconciled by a support system of agricultural laws.

It seems that the "duty to preserve and protect farms" has been easier to translate into specific farm policy goals than the "reconciliation of self interest and the public good." Over the years, the agrarian ideal, in the form of support for the family farm has been used to justify a wide range of political support. As agricultural economist Don Paarlberg wrote, "[f]armers were considered uniquely worthy."

> Since farmers were unique, the country set up a group of unique institutions to serve them: a Department of Agriculture, a Homestead Act, a land grant college system, a network of Agricultural Experiment Stations, an Agricultural Extension Service, a Rural Electrification Administration, and a Bureau of Reclamation. Farmers were given preferred access to land and water. We voted price and income supports for farmers, but not for automobile manufacturers or hardware merchants. Don Paarlberg, Farm and Food Policies: Issues of the 1980s, 6 (1980).

The notion that farmers are different and that family farms are worthy of special treatment permeates the law.

> "Agricultural exceptionalism," i.e., the use of legal exceptions to protect the agricultural industry, is pervasive. This term is often used to reference its American

origins in labor law, where agricultural laborers are excluded from many of the protections afforded to other workers.[4] However the concept is evident throughout the law, with farmers protected from involuntary bankruptcy,[5] exempted from many environmental regulations,[6] and excepted from anti-trust restrictions.[7] The first use of the term is often credited to international trade scholarship, where special exceptions also are evident in other countries.[8]

Other laws, most notably the federal farm programs provide unique benefits for farmers, paying billions of dollars to farmers who produce certain favored crops.[9] Additional specialized laws include the federally subsidized system of crop insurance,[10] the special use valuation afforded to farmers for estate planning purposes,[11] the farm loan programs provided to farmers who cannot obtain credit elsewhere,[12] and Chapter 12 of the Bankruptcy Code, a powerful tool available only to "family farmers."[13] Of all industries, only agriculture has its own cabinet department, the U.S. Department of Agriculture (USDA).

Susan A. Schneider, *A Reconsideration of Agricultural Law: A Call for the Law of Food, Farming, and Sustainability*, 34 WM & MARY ENVT. L. REV. 935 (2010).

Admittedly, there are justifications beyond agrarianism that support the unique treatment of agriculture under the law. However, support for the family farm is often the political attraction. The authors of SACRED COWS AND HOT POTATOES express concern about the misuse of agrarianism in public policy development.

It is far from obvious how mythic values ought to be accommodated in policy. The farms of the agrarian ideal form a part of their cultural heritage for many Americans. The agrarian myths may be vitally important to our feeling of community and common purpose, and a failure to address them seriously could haunt society's attempts to address agricultural policy. As it stands, they are contested symbols, vague images of how agriculture ought to be, or once was. Their

---

4. The most notable current exceptions are that "agricultural laborers" are excluded the definition of "employee" for purposes of protection under the federal National Labor Relations Act, 29 U.S.C. § 152(3) (2006); and "any employee employed in agriculture" is exempt from the overtime pay requirements of the Fair Labor Standards Act, 29 U.S.C. § 213(b)(12) (2006). A limited exclusion for minimum wage protection still exists under the Fair Labor Standards Act; previously agricultural workers were completely excepted. 29 U.S.C. § 213(a)(6) (2006). *See, Farm Workers and the Fair Labor Standards Act: Racial Discrimination in the New Deal*, 65 TEX. L. REV. 1335 (1987).

5. 11 U.S.C. § 303(a) (2006).

6. *See,* J.B. Ruhl, *Farms, Their Environmental Harms, and Environmental Law*, 27 ECOLOGY L. Q. 263, 293–327 (2000) (describing the "active and passive safe harbors farms enjoy" under environmental law).

7. 7 U.S.C. § 291 (2006).

8. Grace Skogstad, *Ideas, Paradigms and Institutions: Agricultural Exceptionalism in the European Union and the United States*, 11 GOVERNANCE 463, 468 (1998) (explaining that agricultural exceptionalism is based both on the specific interests and needs of farmers and upon the broader national interest in a secure food supply).

9. 7 U.S.C. ch. 113—*Agricultural Commodity Support Programs*, §§ 8701–8793; *See,* Environmental Working Group Farm Subsidy Database Update, http://farm.ewg.org/farm/summary.php/. For a review of the history of the federal farm programs, *see* Allen H. Olson, *Federal Farm Programs— Past, Present And Future— Will We Learn From Our Mistakes?*, 6 GREAT PLAINS NAT. RESOURCES J. 1 (2001).

10. 7 U.S.C. ch. 36, subch. I, *The Federal Crop Insurance Act*, §§ 1501–1524 (2006).

11. 26 U.S.C. § 2032A (2006).

12. 7 U.S.C. ch. 50, *Agricultural Credit*, §§ 1921–1949 (2006).

13. 11 U.S.C. § 109(f) (2006).

lack of specificity means that competing political interests can easily appropriate them.

When farm policy advocates say that farming is a way of life worthy of public support, they draw upon an image of farming from times past. But how misleading is their claim?

William P. Browne, Jerry R. Skees, Louis E. Swanson, Paul B. Thompson, and Laurian J.
Unnevehr, *Agrarianism, Myth, and Public Policy,* in Sacred Cows and Hot Potatoes:
Agrarian Myths in Agricultural Policy 13–15 (1992).

Does an agrarian ideal advocate for a certain model of behavior or simply elevate one
occupation over others, rendering it worthy of special treatment? For a particularly critical look at agrarianism and its historical impact on farm policy, consider Dean Jim Chen's
analysis.

> Industrial conquest of production agriculture cannot come soon enough. The en-
> tire body of agrarian rhetoric touting the unproven virtues of the farming class
> exhibits nearly no sense of irony about the profoundly antidemocratic and an-
> timeritocratic elements of the American agricultural tradition. American agri-
> cultural law, fully and properly defined, began with the 1787 Constitution's
> acquiescence in the peculiar agrarian institution called slavery. Today, virtually
> every law regulating the terms by which farmland may be owned and restricting
> the types of business entities that may engage in farming may be distilled into
> the spirit of family farm preservation. What the Midwestern states' corporate
> farming statutes merely imply, the related battery of statutes banning alien own-
> ership of farmland blatantly articulates: No newcomers, domestic or foreign,
> need apply. New capital, new farmers, new ideas-nothing alien to the farming tra-
> dition as incumbent landowners know it need apply for entry into American
> agricultural markets. Early Supreme Court decisions upholding state-law re-
> strictions on alien involvement in farming all involved Japanese immigrants on
> the West Coast. In every case, the Japanese immigrant sought merely to farm as
> a tenant, not to acquire strategically valuable farmland. These statutes and de-
> cisions reflected the racial consciousness of the day, which was embodied in race-
> based limitations on eligibility for America citizenship and which would eventually
> subject the Isei and Nisei to a sort of legal mistreatment that transcended the
> initial denial of freedom to farm-involuntary wartime internment. Against this
> backdrop, agrarian arrogance reaches its apogee when farm advocates speak of
> their preferred lifestyles as though they were inalienable entitlements, undeni-
> ably worthy of positive legal protection and transcendently shielded by the moral
> imperatives of natural law.

Jim Chen, *The American Ideology*, 48 Vand. L. Rev. 809, 827–28 (1995).

A far more sympathetic discussion of the special treatment of agriculture under the law
is provided by Professor Don Pedersen in his introductory article to an agricultural law
symposium issue published by U.C. Davis Law Review in 1990. In addition to the impact of "the agrarian tradition, viewed as myth or reality," three other factors support the
separate legal treatment of agriculture.

> First there is the land. No other industry in the United States makes as extensive
> use of the land resource as agriculture does....
>
> Second, biological cycles govern production agriculture. Thus, programs and
> laws suited to other industries often cannot adequately facilitate or regulate pro-

duction agriculture. Seasonal patterns, rather than supply and demand dictates of the marketplace, govern many decisions and transactions......

Third, even in the contemporary era of fewer and larger farms and advancing vertical integration, agricultural production is still largely atomistic. Many producers, few of whom have any real control over prices paid for inputs or prices received for commodities characterize production agriculture. Add to this the periodic boom and bust cycles, and we begin to see the impetus for federal farm programs, marketing orders, special trade practices regulation, unique credit institutions, and favorable treatment of agricultural cooperatives.

Donald B. Pedersen, *Introduction*, 23 U.C. DAVIS L. REV. 401, 405–409 (1990).

Another factor that is implicit, but sometimes forgotten in the discussion of legal support for agriculture, is the production of food.

What justifies any special treatment for an industry that is increasingly an industrialized and financially powerful sector of the business economy? One word sets the stage for the future of agricultural law as a mature legal discipline — food.

The need for food is the most rational basis for agricultural law as a unique discipline. Food, as the most basic of human needs provides a compelling justification for a legal system that nurtures and guides its agricultural sector. A primary role of government is the assurance that its people have sufficient food. Agricultural law scholar Neil Hamilton referred to this as, "the fundamental nature of the production of food to human existence" and identified it as one of the primary reasons for the origins of agricultural law as a special discipline.[83]

This food-based agricultural law, however, cannot be driven solely by protectionism or exceptionalism, and it cannot be focused solely on assuring the economic vitality of the agricultural industry. A return to the agrarianism that reconciles the self interest of farmers with the public good of society should be the hallmark of the new food-based agriculture. Three unique attributes involved in agricultural production are themselves areas of significant public interest. These unique attributes, reflecting the public's interest in agricultural production should frame the outline of the new food-focused agricultural law.

First, agricultural production is the primary way that we obtain food — a product that is essential to human health and survival. Both farmers and the public at large have a fundamental interest in the production of healthy foods, in policies that assure the safety of those foods, and in the ready availability of healthy foods to all segments of society.

Second, agricultural production involves the production of living things, evoking ecological and moral issues that are completely different than the production of inanimate products. That these products are the food we eat accentuates this imperative.

Third, agricultural production is heavily dependent upon the natural world and its resources — in particular, land and water, and it has been both a significant consumer of natural resources and a significant source of environmental degradation. Moreover, it remains heavily dependent on human resources, resources

---

83. Neil D. Hamilton, *The Study of Agricultural Law in the United States: Education, Organization and Practice*, 43 ARK. L. REV. 503, 504 (1990).

that in the past have often not been adequately respected. Each of these attributes makes agriculture a unique industry, and each reflects an important societal concern.

These fundamental attributes provide policymakers with a new framework for analysis. The new agricultural law should be a system of agricultural laws and policies that promote an agricultural sector that produces healthy food in a sustainable manner. This requires a balancing of the needs of farmers with the needs of consumers, all within the context of protecting both the social fabric of society and the environment.

Susan A. Schneider, *A Reconsideration of Agricultural Law: A Call for the Law of Food, Farming, and Sustainability,* 34 Wm & Mary Envt. L. Rev. 935, 947 (2010).

C. Industrialization of Agricultural Production

The most recent U.S. Census of Agriculture reports that most agricultural production occurs on large commercial farms that employ an industrialized model of production. This model focuses on both economies of scale and upon the application of an industrial manufacturing model to an agricultural setting. Industrialized farming seeks to capture increased profitability through the standard incidents of the industrial model: reliance upon technology, the large scale production of a specialized product, and vertical integration. Vertical integration in this context means the control of the product from beginning to end through ownership and/or through contract.

Agricultural Economists Michael Boehlje and Otto Doering from Purdue described industrialization as follows:

> Industrialization of agriculture means the movement to larger scale production units that use standardized technology/management and are linked to the processor by either formal or informal arrangements. Size and standardization are important characteristics in lowering production costs and in producing products that fit processor specifications and meet consumers' needs for specific product attributes, as well as food safety concerns. Smaller operations not associated with an industrialized system will have increasing difficulty gaining the economies of size and the access to technology required to be competitive, except perhaps in niche markets. Access to input and product markets will be especially critical.... Technological advances, combined with continued pressures to control assets and improve quality, are expected to provide incentives for further industrialization of the industry.

Michael Boehlje and Otto Doering, *Farm Policy in an Industrialized Agriculture,* 18 Journal of Agribusiness, 53 (Special Issue March 2000).

The main goal of industrialized agriculture is increased productivity at reduced cost per unit produced. In this regard, American agriculture has been unparalleled in its success.

> Gains in productivity have been a driving force for growth in U.S. agriculture. The effects of these changes over the second half of the 20th century were dramatic: between 1950 and 2000, the average amount of milk produced per cow increased from 5,314 pounds to 18,201 pounds per year, the average yield of

corn rose from 39 bushels to 153 bushels per acre, and each farmer in 2000 produced on average 12 times as much farm output per hour worked as a farmer did in 1950....

There are many reasons for the impressive improvements in U.S. agriculture in the late 20th century. The greater use of agricultural inputs, such as more fertilizer and more machinery per acre of land, was one reason. But yield was also increased through the development of new technology, which made inputs more effective or allowed inputs to be combined in new and better ways....

Although the use of some inputs like fertilizer and machinery increased, these increases were more than offset by reductions in cropland and especially the amount of labor employed in agriculture. Overall, the amount of crop and animal output produced per unit of (aggregate) input ... increased 2.70 times....

Productivity growth in agriculture allows farm commodities to be grown and harvested more cheaply. This benefits not only farmers but also food and textile manufacturers and consumers. Most of these cost reductions are passed on to the nonfarm economy as lower commodity prices.... From 1948 to 2004, the prices paid for farm inputs rose at roughly the same rate as general producer price inflation. Prices of farm commodities, on the other hand, doubled in the 1970s but hardly changed at all afterward.... Productivity growth allowed more output to be produced from the same amount of inputs, reducing the average cost of production. The gains in productivity largely benefited agricultural processors and consumers in the form of lower real prices. Productivity growth in agriculture is a key reason why, on average, the American consumer spends a small and declining share of family income on food.

Agriculture is more dependent on improvements in technology as a source of growth than the rest of the economy.... Although the longrun rate of growth in agricultural output was fairly steady from 1948 through 2004, the nature of that growth has shifted in important ways. In the 1950s, 1960s, and 1970s, labor was exiting agriculture very quickly (falling by almost 4 percent per year), and the increased use of nonlabor inputs, such as new machinery and improved chemicals, helped to substitute for the loss of farm labor. This substitution was reflected in rising amounts of cropland, machinery, and other inputs employed per farmworker. The rising cost of labor relative to other inputs encouraged farmers to adopt technologies and farming methods that saved on labor and used more nonlabor inputs instead. In more recent decades, however, there was a shift to new technologies that saved nonlabor inputs as well as labor, even as output continued to expand.

Keith O. Fuglie, James M. MacDonald, and Eldon Ball, *Productivity Growth in U.S. Agriculture*, USDA Economic Research Report, Economic Brief No. 9 (September 2007).

1. Improved Agricultural Production Through Technology

Technology, when discussed in terms of increased agricultural production, includes synthetic chemicals, fertilizers, genetic improvements both through traditional breeding and genetic engineering, information technology, and the full range of advanced machinery. However, it also includes techniques such as integrated pest management that offer farmers a new tool for improving production. "Technological advancement [can be] broadly defined as any positive change in the way goods and services are produced." *Agricultural Productivity: An Engine of Development*, 6 in 21st Century Agriculture: A Critical Role for Science and Technology, USDA Foreign Agricultural Service, available at http://www.fas.usda.gov/icd/stconf/pubs/scitech2003/part1.pdf.

Thus, technological advances are not limited in applicability to the industrial model of agriculture. Indeed, many who criticize industrialized agriculture support a "technologically progressive" model of diversified family farming. *See*, Marty Strange, Family Farming: A New Economic Vision, 32–35 (1988). An industrialized model of agriculture, however, depends largely on technology, and much of the recent technological research and development for agricultural production has focused on the promotion of an industrialized model.

2. The Large Scale Production of a Specialized Product

The second component of an industrialized model of agriculture is the large scale production of a specialized product, an obvious attribute of an industrialized manufacturing system. Such a system allows for the efficient distribution of the costs of technology. For example, a monocultural cropping system makes it possible to spread the cost of the purchase of an expensive piece of specialized farm equipment over a large number of acres. In livestock production, specialized technology can play a similar role, rewarding expanded operations that are able to specialize the production of large numbers of animals in a concentrated area.

Competition within the farm sector, inelastic demand, and the production of fungible commodities result in a pricing system where most farmers have little if any control over farm prices. This has contributed to a production model that has focused almost exclusively on producing more for less. Cost-saving technology in this context offers the opportunity to increase production and to reduce per unit production costs. The connection between technology, the reduced cost of production, and an increase in farm size has been termed the "technology treadmill," and it was first described in 1958 by Professor Willard Cochrane.

> [F]armers constantly strive to improve their incomes by adopting new technologies. 'Early adopters' make profits for a short while because of their lower unit production costs. As more farmers adopt the technology, however, production goes us, prices go down, and profits are no longer possible even with the lower production costs. Average farmers are nonetheless forced by lower product prices to adopt the technology and lower their production costs if they are to survive at all. The 'laggard" farmers who do not adopt new technologies are lost in the price squeeze and leave room for their more successful neighbors to expand.

Richard A. Levins and Willard W. Cochrane, *The Treadmill Revisited*, 72 Land Economics 550 (1996).[1]

---

1. The *Treadmill Revisited* article updates the original technology treadmill theory and applies it to land ownership patterns, demonstrating increased land consolidation and increased ownership by those who do not farm the land.

> The treadmill as presented here shows how cost-reducing technology, government payments to support farmers, and a free market for a fixed amount of farmland work to keep farmers chasing an unattainable goal of higher lasting profits. Early adopters of technology may gain for a short while, but the long-term benefits go to landowners. There landowners need not be farmers; in fact, we have shown how the treadmill creates incentives for people to leave farming and become landowners.

New technology is dependent upon research and development funding. Who provides this funding and how it is directed influences what new technologies are developed and who they are designed to benefit. In the past, publicly funded land grant institutions were responsible for much of this development. However, multinational corporations now lead the effort. This not only affects the technology developed for U.S. markets, it has worldwide significance.

> With public investment lagging, multi-national corporations — Monsanto, Pioneer, and Dow Chemical, to name a few — have lured many of the most talented scientists to their private laboratories, which are better equipped and better funded than national and international research stations, particularly those in international countries.... The research now primarily pays off for large commercial farms. Public research tends to cast its benefits more widely, including to many traditional farmers, which it allows to make small but significant improvements such as adding nutrients to the soil or replacing draft animals with mechanical tillage. Together, diminished investments in agricultural research and the shift of the research from the public sector to the private sector have redirected the benefits to large, already successful commercial farmers.

Carlisle Ford Runge and Carlisle Piehl Runge, *Against the Grain: Why Failing to Complete the Green Revolution Could Bring the Next Famine*, 89 FOREIGN AFFAIRS 8, 12 (January/ February 2010).

Thus, in a circular fashion, the commercial developers of technology are most inclined to seek to serve the large industrial farm market as their most profitable clientele, increasing their economic advantage over smaller, more diversified operations.

3. Vertical Integration

The third attribute associated with industrialized agriculture is vertical integration, i.e., the control of the stages of production by a single entity. This is most easily illustrated by the complete vertical integration of much of the poultry industry. The company that processes and sells chicken and chicken products on the retail market most often owns the chickens on the farm where they are raised, with the "farmer" responsible only for providing care according to industry and contract standards. Vertical integration allows the integrated company the maximum amount of control over production. This is exemplified in the meat industry, as explained below.

> Vertical integration in the meat industry exists in two forms. In "pure" vertical integration, the integrator owns its animals and grows them itself. More commonly, integrators enter into contracts with growers who raise the animals for them. There are two forms of such contracts: production contracts and marketing contracts. Under production contracts, growers raise animals owned by the integrators. The growers are paid based on how efficiently they use feed (which the integrator provides) to raise the animals. Production contracts usually contain detailed conditions to which the growers must adhere. Integrators

---

Richard A. Levins and Willard W. Cochrane, *The Treadmill Revisited*, 72 LAND ECONOMICS 550 (1996). Government payments to landowners under the federal farm programs have also been associated with the consolidation of farmland ownership and with absentee landowners. These programs are presented *infra*, in Chapter II, *Economic Support to Agriculture*.

using such contracts often require that facilities be constructed to their specifications. The contracts tell growers how to feed, house, and medicate the animals, how to handle manure, and how to dispose of carcasses.[24] Under marketing contracts, growers agree in advance to sell their animals to integrators under an agreed price system.[25] Both production and marketing contracts commonly contain language purporting to shield the integrator from liability for the grower's actions.[26] Contracts are sometimes form contracts in which the only negotiable term is price.

Contracting has been the dominant model in the poultry industry for many years, with almost 90 percent of broilers sold under contract.[27] It is becoming increasingly common in the pork industry as well. In 2004, 69 percent of hogs were sold under marketing contracts, up from 2 percent in 1980.[28] The practice is much less common in the cattle industry. In 2005, packers acquired only about 29 percent of cattle under contracts, a figure down from a high of 35 percent in 2002.[29]

Paul Stokstad, *Enforcing Environmental Law in an Unequal Market: The Case of Concentrated Animal Feeding Operations*, 15 Mo. Envtl. L. & Pol'y Rev. 229, 234–36 (Spring 2008).

Vertical integration allows a manufacturer a variety of economic advantages that allow for greater profitability — greater control over the supply of the initial product, greater control over the characteristics of the product, enhanced market control over the price paid for the product, protection for intellectual property and trade secrets associated with production, and in some cases, a contractual shield for liability for environmental damage. Note, however that these advantages may present disadvantages for the individual farmer who often has little control over either the contracting relationship or the production process. *See* Chapter VI, *infra*, *The Regulation of Livestock Production and Sales*.

---

24. *See* Neil D. Hamilton, A Farmer's Legal Guide to Production Contracts (1995). *See also* Farmers' Legal Action Group, Inc., *Assessing the Impact of Integrator Practices on Contract Poultry Growers*, Sept. 2001, 3-3 to 3-18 (description and analysis of terms in two sample contracts).

25. *See* Tom Harkin, Economic Concentration and Structural Change in the Food and Agriculture Sector: Trends, Consequences and Policy Options 12 (2004). Production contracts are more common in the poultry sector, while marketing contracts are more common for cattle and hogs.

26. For example, a clause in a standard swine marketing contract Farmland uses in Iowa provides that: "[I]t is understood and agreed by the parties that this Agreement does not create a fiduciary relationship between them, that the producer is an independent contractor, and that nothing in this Agreement is intended to constitute either party an agent, legal representative, subsidiary, joint venturer, partner, employee, employer, joint employer, enterprise or servant of the other for any purpose whatsoever ... nor shall Farmland be deemed liable by reason of any act or omission of producer in the conduct of its business pursuant to this Agreement, or for any claim or judgment arising there from." Iowa Office of the Attorney General, Working for Farmers, Contracts, http://www.state.ia.us/government/ag/images/contracts/Farmlandl.pdf (last visited Feb. 20, 2008).

27. James Macdonald et al., Contracts, Markets, and Prices: Organizing the Production and Use of Agricultural Commodities, AER-837, AER-83, at 15 (Nov. 2004) (88 percent of poultry produced under production contracts, 7 percent under marketing contracts).

28. Steve Martinez & Kelly Zering, Pork Quality and the Role of Market Organization, AER-835 at 1 (Nov. 2004). In addition to the 69 percent of hogs raised under marketing agreements, some of the 17 percent of hogs owned by packers were raised under production contracts.

29. USDA, Grain Inspection, Packers and Stockyards Admin., 2006 Annual Report 54, *available at* http://archive.gipsa.usda.gov/pubs/06ar.pdf.

4. Industrialization in Animal Agriculture

The industrialized model is most pronounced and most controversial in the animal agriculture sector. The USDA Economic Research Service analyzed the changes in this sector in its report, *The Transformation of U.S. Livestock Agriculture.*

> Livestock agriculture has undergone a series of striking transformations. Production is more specialized — farms usually confine and feed a single species of animal, often with feed that has been purchased rather than grown onsite, and they typically specialize in specific stages of animal production. Today's livestock farms tend to be tightly linked to other stages of production and processing through formal contracts. While the farms are usually owned and operated by a family, they rely increasingly on hired labor. And the farms that account for most production are much larger than they were in the past.
>
> Strong financial pressures have driven the industrialization of U.S. livestock farms. Larger operations are able to realize lower costs and higher returns, while tighter coordination among farms at different processing stages can reduce financial risks. But growing to a more efficient scale also concentrates livestock in a limited area, and excess concentrations of manure-based nutrients can lead to increased air and water pollution. Large operations are also more prone to use antibiotics intensively in order to preempt the spread of animal disease and to accelerate animal growth. Extensive antibiotic use in livestock raises concerns about increased pathogen resistance and related risks to human health....

James M. MacDonald and William D. McBride, *The Transformation of U.S. Livestock Agriculture: Scale, Efficiency, and Risks,* iii, USDA Economic Research Service, EIB no. 43 (Jan. 2009).

Poultry production provides the clearest example of vertical integration in an industrialized model, with all aspects of production controlled by the ultimate processor.

> Firms called integrators own hatcheries, processing plants, and feed mills. Integrators then contract with farmers to "grow out" broiler chicks to market weight, and to produce replacement breeder hens for hatcheries. Under a production contract, the integrator provides the farmer/grower with chicks, feed, and veterinary and transportation services, while the farmer provides labor, capital in the form of housing and equipment, and utilities. The birds are sent to slaughter after 5–9 weeks on the farm, and the farmer is paid for the growing services provided.
>
> The organizational innovations developed in broiler production have been adopted in other commodities, but the methods of grower compensation remain distinctive. Growers receive a base payment for each flock of birds and an incentive. The incentive payment depends on the grower's performance, relative to other growers delivering birds to the integrator during the same period. Those growers who can convert feed to meat more efficiently, while having fewer birds die, realize higher payments.
>
> While contracts in other commodities may specify incentive payments, they are set against fixed standards and not relative performance. The industry's current form developed during the 1950s and 1960s as integrators devised grow-out contracts, built production complexes, and developed breeding flocks. Early grow-out farms weren't very large, but that changed. In 1959, farms producing at least 100,000 broilers in a year accounted for 28.5 percent of production. That share doubled by 1969 and

continued to grow rapidly until the 1990s. Today, hardly any commercial growers produce fewer than 100,000 broilers in a year. The industry's basic organization remains unchanged, but production continues to shift to larger operations, from a production locus of 300,000 broilers in 1987 to 520,000 in 2002 and 600,000 by 2006.

Id., at 6–7. Under this and other vertically integrated models, "[p]roducers are increasingly paid for the services that they provide, and not for the products that they sell." *Id.* at 1.

Changes in the hog industry as described below illustrate the adoption of the industrialized model in pork production. Note that the dairy industry shows similar patterns of consolidation and the adoption of the industrialized model, although vertical integration is not as common.

Nigel Key and William D. McBride
Technology, Larger Farm Size Increased Productivity on U.S. Hog Farms
USDA, Economic Research Service, AMBER WAVES (April 2008)

Today's hog sector bears little resemblance to the one that existed 15 years ago. There are fewer hog farms, and the average number of hogs per farm has increased substantially. Most production occurs under contracts with processors.

Technological innovation and shifts to larger, more specialized hog operations have led to increases in productivity, reduced production costs, and lower hog prices.

Under those arrangements, processors supply feed, feeder pigs, and veterinary services to growers who receive a fee for providing the capital, utilities, and labor used to grow the hogs to market weight. Production contracts encourage individual producers to specialize in a single phase of production rather than combining all phases on one hog farm, as in the traditional farrow-to-finish approach. The past 15 years have also seen substantial geographical movement of production into States outside of the Corn Belt, especially North Carolina, Oklahoma, and Utah.

The structural transformation of the hog sector has been driven in part by technological advances in livestock genetics, nutrition, housing and handling equipment, veterinary and medical services, and management. These changes have contributed to large increases in hog-farm productivity, which have exerted downward pressure on hog and pork prices. As the industry has changed, hog producers have adjusted the size, organizational structure, and technological base of their operations to remain competitive. Recent ERS research combines information from surveys of hog producers at three points in time to document how the hog sector changed between 1992 and 2004 and to measure the level and sources of the hog-farm productivity gains.

Industry Scale and Specialization Increasing

Although the number of farms with hogs dropped over 70 percent from more than 240,000 in 1992 to fewer than 70,000 in 2004, the U.S. hog inventory remained stable at about 60 million head. Thus, hog production consolidated considerably during this period as fewer and larger farms accounted for an increasing share of total output. Although this is not unusual for U.S. livestock production, consolidation in hog production was among the most rapid of all livestock types.

The average size of U.S. hog operations grew from 945 head in 1992 to 4,646 head in 2004. The share of the hog inventory on operations with 2,000 or more head increased from less than 30 percent to nearly 80 percent, with operations having 5,000 or more head accounting for more than 50 percent of the hog inventory by 2004.

Traditionally, individual hog farms, known as farrow-to-finish operations, managed all phases of hog production from breeding to slaughter. Today, farrow-to-finish operations have given way to large operations that specialize in one of the three major life-cycle phases of production: farrow-to-wean, wean-to-feeder pig, or feeder pig-to-finish. In 1992, 65 percent of hogs came from farrow-to-finish operations, while only 22 percent came from specialized hog-finishing operations. By 2004, only 18 percent came from farrow-to-finish operations, while 77 percent came from specialized hog finishers.

Changes in scale and specialization have been made possible, in part, by substantial growth in the use of production contracts. Hog operations with production contracts grew from 5 percent of operations in 1992 to 67 percent in 2004. Production contracts govern the relationship between hog growers and owners ("integrators" or "contractors"), specifying the inputs provided by each party and their compensation. Because contractors typically provide feeder pigs and feed to growers and handle the marketing, such an arrangement facilitates growers' specialization in one phase of production.

The increasing use of production contracts has also promoted farmers' specialization in the hog enterprise. Because contractors supply feed from off-farm sources to their growers, individual growers can use their time and financial resources to increase the scale of hog operations rather than expand crop acreage to produce feed. Between 1992 and 2004, hog production as a share of the total production value on hog farms increased from 46 to 71 percent. At the same time, hog farms grew a smaller share of their hog feed: the share of grain produced on their farms for hog feed fell from about half to below 20 percent.

Farm Productivity Gains Mean Lower Production Costs

Hog farms, particularly the specialized feeder pig-to-finish operations that are more likely to use production contracts, showed large increases in productivity between 1992 and 2004. The average quantity of feed required per hundredweight gain declined 44 percent for feeder pig-to-finish operations, and the average quantity of labor used fell 83 percent.

Farrow-to-finish operations exhibited smaller productivity gains than feeder pig-to-finish operations. For farrow-to-finish operations, the average quantity of feed required per hundredweight of gain declined by only 15 percent over the period, while the average quantity of labor used per hundredweight declined by 52 percent. The stronger productivity growth of feeder pig-to-finish operations, compared with farrow-to-finish operations, helps account for the growth in their share of finished hog output.

Productivity gains contributed to a decline in production costs between 1992 and 2004. For all farrow-to-finish hog producers, average production costs (in 2004 dollars) per hundredweight of gain were 28 percent lower in 2004 than in 1992. This change amounts to a 2.7-percent average annual rate of decline. Real costs declined faster for feeder pig-to-finish hog producers, falling 44 percent between 1992 and 2004, or 4.7 percent annually.

Structural change in the U.S. hog industry is the outcome of economic competition to increase farm productivity and lower production costs. If larger operations are more profitable than smaller ones, competitive pressures may be expected to result in a larger average farm size in the long run. Similarly, operations that are first to adopt a cost-saving technology, are in regions with lower input costs, or are closer to markets have a competitive advantage that makes them more likely to survive and grow. Business relationships between growers and processors also evolve to reflect productivity gains from increased specialization of the various phases of hog production on separate operations.

---

5. Unanticipated Costs

While the increased productivity associated with industrialized agricultural production is well established, many question whether the cost of this method of production is accurately assessed. *See, e.g.*, Doug Gurian-Sherman, *CAFO's Uncovered: The Untold Costs of Confined Animal Feeding Operations*, Union of Concerned Scientists (April 2008) (examining the hidden cost of concentrated animal feeding operations as well as the government policies that favor this production method and advocating for alternative production methods). *See also, Putting Meat on the Table: Industrial Farm Animal Production*, A Report of the Pew Commission on Industrial Farm Animal Production in America (A Project of The Pew Charitable Trusts and Johns Hopkins Bloomberg School of Public Health) (2008), available at http://www.ncIFAP.org/ (citing environmental problems, public health problems, and the social and economic decline of rural areas as all unanticipated costs associated with large scale industrialized animal production).

The most obvious omission from the per unit economic calculation is environmental degradation. Externalities such as pollution impose costs on others without being factored into the economic model or the decision making of the industry. These costs are eventually borne by others, primarily the taxpayer. Industrialized animal operations and the tremendous amount of concentrated waste produced have been associated with water pollution and air pollution, with costs spread throughout the community and not factored into the cost of production. *See, e.g., infra*, Chapter III, Section C.2, *The Regulation of Concentrated Animal Feeding Operations* (discussing the environmental problems associated with industrialized animal production).

In addition to pollution concerns associated with the generation of waste, industrialized agriculture's heavy reliance on fossil fuel-based inputs for its successful increase in production has been sharply criticized.

> [T]he 20th-century industrialization of agriculture has increased the amount of greenhouse gases emitted by the food system by an order of magnitude; chemical fertilizers (made from natural gas), pesticides (made from petroleum), farm machinery, modern food processing and packaging and transportation have together transformed a system that in 1940 produced 2.3 calories of food energy for every calorie of fossil-fuel energy it used into one that now takes 10 calories of fossil-fuel energy to produce a single calorie of modern supermarket food. Put another way, when we eat from the industrial-food system, we are eating oil and spewing greenhouse gases. This state of affairs appears all the more absurd when you recall that every calorie we eat is ultimately the product of photosynthesis — a process based on making food energy from sunshine. There is hope and possibility in that simple fact.

Michael Pollan, *Farmer-in-Chief*, New York Times Sunday Magazine (October 9, 2008).

The debate over the hidden costs of industrialized agriculture is not limited to the United States.

> The proclaimed economic and societal benefits of a worldwide industrial agriculture system wouldn't measure up when compared to a sustainable system if an evaluation honestly measured all of the "external costs" against claimed benefits. That is the primary point driven home by Jules Pretty, professor and director of the Centre for Environment and Society at the University of Essex in England. Pretty, who also is editor of the Journal of Sustainability, contends that "those who support industrialized agriculture measure its success in narrow economic terms of food price and availability and tend to ignore its costly unintended consequences to society and the environment." He adds, "They are not being seriously challenged to give a full accounting. We are trying at the center to change that by scientifically measuring or estimating in Britain what we call the 'externalities' of industrialized agriculture and also the full benefits of a sustainable ag system." In his study, some of the industrial ag externalities evaluated were: water pollution from farm waste, soil nutrients, erosion and pesticides; loss of landscape and biodiversity; food-borne diseases; air pollution from gaseous emissions; unnecessary transportation costs of food; human dislocation from rural to urban areas; rural community decline; poor human diets and obesity; and the cost of direct government subsidies.

> The study found that annual costs of these externalities during the 1990s totaled 1.54 billion pounds (approximately U.S. $2.6 billion). "Britain had to spend this to deal with the effects of industrial ag, so this cost is a hidden subsidy from the public to polluters," Pretty asserted.

Thayne Cozart, *Industrial vs. Sustainable Agriculture*, 33 Acres (December 2003).

Concerns regarding the human and economic costs of industrialization on rural America are similarly raised. These concerns are for the farmer and the overall rural community. With respect to the farmer, bargaining power as well as access to market may be severely limited:

> The essential problem with consolidation and vertical integration, when taken too far, is that such trends reduce choice in the marketplace. Problems arise when one player has choices and the other player does not. This lack of choice can lead to unequal bargaining power in business relationships. With unequal bargaining power, the more dominant firm will almost always take advantage of the more vulnerable party by squeezing price, shifting liabilities, demanding certain things without paying an associated price. Consolidation and vertical integration provide this type of setting.

Doug O'Brien, *Policy Approaches to Address Problems Associated with Consolidation and Vertical Integration in Agriculture*, 9 Drake J. Agric. L. 33, 34 (Spring 2004). *See infra*, Chapter VII, *Regulation of Livestock Sales* for a discussion of the government's attempts to address this issue pursuant to its authority under the Packers and Stockyards Act.

Beyond concern for the individual farmer, the impact of agricultural consolidation and industrialization on American rural communities as a result of depopulation and the associated decline of economic activity is well documented. *See, e.g., Putting Meat on the Table: Industrial Farm Animal Production*, Pew Commission on Industrial Farm Animal

Production in America (2008), available at http://www.ncIFAP.org/ (citing industrialized agriculture as one of the factors that has led to the economic decline of rural America).

It is alleged that U.S. government policies tip the scales in favor of industrialized animal production, making it more cost effective than it would otherwise be. These policies and their potential effects will be discussed in subsequent chapters.

- Although industrialized agriculture may model itself after manufacturing, its environmental effects are far less regulated than other industries. And, farm programs provide government funds for cost-share and remedial clean up activities. See *infra* Chapter III, *Agriculture and Environmental Law*.

- Farm subsidies are paid to produce corn, the majority of which is used for livestock feed. Arguably, this benefits feedlot operations more than operations that rely on pasture. *See* Michael Pollan, THE OMNIVORE'S DILEMMA: A NATURAL HISTORY OF FOUR MEALS, 65–84 (2006) (tracing the subsidized corn in Iowa to the feedlots of Kansas). *See infra* Chapter II, *Economic Support to Agriculture*.

- The federal Animal Welfare Act categorically excludes farm animals from its protection, as do many state anti-cruelty statutes. Industrialized animal operations are criticized for practices that would be illegal in other settings. *See infra* in Chapter VIII, *Animal Welfare*.

- An industrialized and globalized food system may have food safety and public health consequences that we are just beginning to understand. *See, infra,* Chapter X, *Food & Agriculture*.

Professor Neil Hamilton, in a thoughtful and forward-looking article written in 1997, addressed the industrialization issue as follows.

> A central question is whether the forces stimulating industrialization can be harnessed for the improvement of all parties affected by the food and agricultural sector—consumers, farmers, and businesses alike—or whether it will simply be another means to increase the profits and market shares of the companies promoting it, further eroding the role of farmers and compromising the interests of consumers.

Neil D. Hamilton, *Reaping What We Have Sown: Public Policy Consequences of Agricultural Industrialization and the Legal Implications of a Changing Production System*, 45 DRAKE L. REV. 289 (1997).

Notes

1. The different treatment of agriculture under the law is supported in part by a recognition that agricultural production is somehow different than other industries. Is it? How does the industrial model apply in this context? Consider the following analysis.

> Agriculture, however, is not simply manufacturing the proverbial widget. It is a unique industry in that it relies on the production of living things through use of natural processes and the consumption of natural resources. Being in the business of creating living things through an intertwined relationship with nature gives agricultural producers a special responsibility to confront ecological and ethical issues that arise. In contrast, under an industrialized model, the primary responsibility is mass production of a uniform product at the lowest price. Natural processes of life are not respected, but are to be controlled and modified

for improved efficiency. The intense specialization that is key to the industrial model — making a lot of one product very cheaply — runs counter to the forces of nature which reward, perhaps demand, such non-industrial attributes as genetic diversity and crop rotation.

Susan A. Schneider, *Reconnecting Consumers and Producers: On the Path Toward a Sustainable Food and Agriculture Policy,* 14 Drake J. Agric. L. 75, 78–79 (2009) (citing Wendell Berry, The Unsettling of America: Culture & Agriculture 43 (1977) (stating "food is a cultural product; it cannot be produced by technology alone.").

Can agriculture essentially have it both ways, enjoying special treatment under the law while employing industrial practices modeled after the manufacturing industry? What ethical considerations may be involved and should they be incorporated into public policy? If so, how?

2. Buoyed by financial success and concerned about increased regulation, U.S. agribusiness corporations, most notably Smithfield Farms are expanding industrialized animal operations overseas. Eastern European countries are struggling with the impact of Smithfield Farms' expansion of its industrialized hog operations into Poland and Romania. As was reported in the New York Times, "[i]n less than five years, Smithfield enlisted politicians in Poland and Romania, tapped into hefty European Union farm subsidies and fended off local opposition groups to create a conglomerate of feed mills, slaughterhouses, and climate-controlled barns housing thousands of hogs." Smithfield's chairman is quoted as describing its global approach as moving in a "very, very big way, very, very fast." Serious environmental problems, a devastating swine fever outbreak, and a dismantling of the traditional rural economy has resulted. In Romania, the number of hog farmers declined 90 percent between 2003 to 2007 (from 477,030 in 2003 to 52,100 in 2007). "In Poland, there were 1.1 million hog farmers in 1996. That number fell by 56 percent by 2008." Reduced pork prices benefit consumers but put farmers in local and in export markets out of business. Doreen Carvajal and Stephen Castle, *A U.S. Hog Giant Transforms Eastern Europe,* New York Times (May 6, 2009). As an example of the hostility generated, see the recently released anti-industrial hog farming European documentary, *Pig Business,* http://www.pigbusiness.co.uk.

3. From a consumer's perspective, Michael Pollan refers to "industrial eating," incorporating both the agricultural industrial model and ultimate retail sale of processed products by the food industry. He observes that it deliberately obscures the relationships and connections between people and the natural world. He references the "increasingly high walls of our industrial agriculture," noting that if we could see what lies on the other side of that wall, "we would surely change the way we eat." Michael Pollan, The Omnivore's Dilemma: A Natural History of Four Meals, 10 (2006).

4. In 2006, Time Magazine wrote about what it termed the "Grass Fed Revolution," and characterized the growth in the number of grass-fed beef operations as "part of a growing revolt against industrial agriculture." The article noted that between 2001–2006, more than 1,000 ranchers switched herds to an all-grass diet. "Pure-pasture raised beef still represents less than 1% of the nation's supply, but sales reached some $120 million last year and are expected to increase 20% a year over the next decade." *The Grass Fed Revolution,* Time Magazine (June 11, 2006). For a short documentary about a rancher's decision to switch to raising grass-fed beef, see *Cudd* (Southern Foodways Alliance 2009), available at http://www.whiteoakpastures.com. The USDA now has a grass-fed marketing claim certification program under its quality verification program at 7 C.F.R. pt. 62. *See* 72 Fed. Reg. 58,631 (Oct. 16, 2007).

D. Sustainability

Wendell Berry refers to farming, or at least "good farming" as "the proper use and care of an immeasurable gift." He describes "true agrarianism" as:

> Agrarian farmers see, accept, and live within their limits. They understand and agree to the proposition that there is 'this much and no more.' Everything that happens on an agrarian farm is determined or conditioned by the understanding that there is only so much land, so much water in the cistern, so much hay in the barn, so much corn in the crib, so much firewood in the barn, so much food in the cellar or freezer, so much strength in the back and arms—and no more.[30]

Does sustainable agriculture embody the "true agrarian"? Should sustainable production be the goal of U.S. agricultural policy? What does sustainability mean?

The term sustainability, now commonly used in many different contexts, is most often defined according to the 1987 United Nations World Commission on Environment and Development (WCED) publication, *Our Common Future*, also known as the *Brundtland Report*. The UN focus was on development, but the concept is applicable with respect to any activity that involves the use of resources.

The original WCED definition of sustainable development was, "development that meets the needs of the present without compromising the ability of future generations to meet their own needs." Some argue that American agriculture today is unsustainable and that we are on the verge of a dramatic realization of the extent to which our production practices fail the test of sustainability.

The rise of the "sustainable agriculture" movement, however, predates *Our Common Future* by decades. One of the earliest proponents of sustainable agriculture, at least in North America, was the Canadian organization The Land Fellowship, established in the early 1950s. *See,* Stuart B. Hill and Rod J. MacRae, *Organic Farming in Canada, Ecological Agriculture Projects*, EAP Publication No. 4, available at http://eap.mcgill.ca/publications/eap104a.htm.

In 1978, Wendell Berry published his book THE UNSETTLING OF AMERICA, questioning the American tradition of expanding and exploiting while being "unconscious of the effects of one's life or livelihood." He contrasts the "exploiter" with the "nurturer," using as his examples a strip-miner and "the ideal of a farmer."

> The exploiter is a specialist, an expert; the nurturer is not. The standard of the exploiter is efficiency; the standard of the nurturer is care. The exploiter's goal is money, profit; the nurturer's goal is health—his land's health, his own, his family's, his community's, his country's. Whereas the exploiter asks of a piece of land only how much and how quickly it can be made to produce, the nurturer asks a question that is much more complex and difficult; What is its carrying capacity? (That is—How much can be taken from it without diminishing it? What can it produce dependably for an indefinite time?) ...

WENDELL BERRY, THE UNSETTLING OF AMERICA, 7 (1978). Berry views the industrialization of agriculture as the movement of the farmer from nurturer to exploiter. And, he warns not only agriculture but society as a whole of the dangers of specialization and the loss of "any idea of personal wholeness." *Id.* at 19.

---

30. WENDELL BERRY, *The Agrarian Standard*, THE ESSENTIAL AGRARIAN READER, THE FUTURE OF CULTURE, COMMUNITY, AND THE LAND, 24 (Norman Wirbzba, ed., 2003).

Soon thereafter, Wes Jackson published NEW ROOTS FOR AGRICULTURE, arguing that the production of monocultural annual crops in reliance on chemical inputs was unsustainable and predicting the "failure of success."

> The plowshare may well have destroyed more options for future generations than the sword. Tillage has hastened the erosion of irreplaceable topsoil everywhere and a technology based on fossil fuels has increased yields for short-term profits, leaving crops ever more vulnerable to diseases, pests, and droughts.

WES JACKSON, NEW ROOTS FOR AGRICULTURE (1980).

In 1987, Miguel Altierri coined the term "agroecology" in his book, AGROECOLOGY: THE SCIENCE OF SUSTAINABLE AGRICULTURE. And in 1988, the National Academy of Sciences published ALTERNATIVE AGRICULTURE, describing profitable, ecologically-based alternatives to conventional, chemical input-based agricultural practices.

U.S. lawmakers responded by funding research initiatives, slowly at first, but with increasing emphasis. The 1985 Food Security Act authorized sustainable agriculture research. In 1989, the USDA Low-Impact Sustainable Agriculture (LISA) program was created. LISA later became SARE, the Sustainable Agriculture Research and Education program.

Given the economic success of conventional agriculture, the strength of the industries that support it, and the low cost of food, sustainable agriculture remained relatively politically insignificant. The 1990 farm bill provided the first legal definition.

"Sustainable agriculture" is defined under federal law as

> [A]n integrated system of plant and animal production practices having a site-specific application that will, over the long-term—

> (A) satisfy human food and fiber needs;

> (B) enhance environmental quality and the natural resource base upon which the agriculture economy depends;

> (C) make the most efficient use of nonrenewable resources and on-farm resources and integrate, where appropriate, natural biological cycles and controls;

> (D) sustain the economic viability of farm operations; and

> (E) enhance the quality of life for farmers and society as a whole.

Food, Agriculture, Conservation, and Trade Act of 1990 (FACTA), Public Law 101-624, Title XVI, Subtitle A, Section 1603, codified at 7 U.S.C. § 3103.

Note that sustainable agriculture is not organic agriculture, although most consider organic agriculture to be an environmentally sustainable system.

How is sustainable agriculture defined in terms of agricultural practices?

Gail Feenstra, Chuck Ingels, and David Campbell, with contributions from David Chaney, Melvin R. George, Eric Bradford, the staff and advisory committees of the UC Sustainable Agriculture Research and Education Program
What Is Sustainable Agriculture?

University of California Sustainable Agriculture Research and Education Program available at http://www.sarep.ucdavis.edu

Agriculture has changed dramatically, especially since the end of World War II. Food and fiber productivity soared due to new technologies, mechanization, increased chemical use, specialization and government policies that favored maximizing production. These changes allowed fewer farmers with reduced labor demands to produce the majority of the food and fiber in the U.S.

Although these changes have had many positive effects and reduced many risks in farming, there have also been significant costs. Prominent among these are topsoil depletion, groundwater contamination, the decline of family farms, continued neglect of the living and working conditions for farm laborers, increasing costs of production, and the disintegration of economic and social conditions in rural communities.

A growing movement has emerged during the past two decades to question the role of the agricultural establishment in promoting practices that contribute to these social problems. Today this movement for sustainable agriculture is garnering increasing support and acceptance within mainstream agriculture. Not only does sustainable agriculture address many environmental and social concerns, but it offers innovative and economically viable opportunities for growers, laborers, consumers, policymakers and many others in the entire food system.

*   *   *

Sustainable agriculture integrates three main goals—environmental health, economic profitability, and social and economic equity. A variety of philosophies, policies and practices have contributed to these goals. People in many different capacities, from farmers to consumers, have shared this vision and contributed to it. Despite the diversity of people and perspectives, the following themes commonly weave through definitions of sustainable agriculture.

Sustainability rests on the principle that we must meet the needs of the present without compromising the ability of future generations to meet their own needs. Therefore, stewardship of both natural and human resources is of prime importance. Stewardship of human resources includes consideration of social responsibilities such as working and living conditions of laborers, the needs of rural communities, and consumer health and safety both in the present and the future. Stewardship of land and natural resources involves maintaining or enhancing this vital resource base for the long term.

A systems perspective is essential to understanding sustainability. The system is envisioned in its broadest sense, from the individual farm, to the local ecosystem, and to communities affected by this farming system both locally and globally. An emphasis on the system allows a larger and more thorough view of the consequences of farming practices on both human communities and the environment. A systems approach gives us the tools to explore the interconnections between farming and other aspects of our environment.

A systems approach also implies interdisciplinary efforts in research and education. This requires not only the input of researchers from various disciplines, but also farmers, farmworkers, consumers, policymakers and others.

Making the transition to sustainable agriculture is a process. For farmers, the transition to sustainable agriculture normally requires a series of small, realistic steps. Family economics and personal goals influence how fast or how far participants can go in the transition. It is important to realize that each small decision can make a difference and contribute to advancing the entire system further on the "sustainable agriculture continuum." The key to moving forward is the will to take the next step.

Finally, it is important to point out that reaching toward the goal of sustainable agriculture is the responsibility of all participants in the system, including farmers, laborers, policymakers, researchers, retailers, and consumers. Each group has its own part to play, its own unique contribution to make to strengthen the sustainable agriculture community.

* * *

Water. When the production of food and fiber degrades the natural resource base, the ability of future generations to produce and flourish decreases. The decline of ancient civilizations in Mesopotamia, the Mediterranean region, Pre-Columbian southwest U.S. and Central America is believed to have been strongly influenced by natural resource degradation from non-sustainable farming and forestry practices. Water is the principal resource that has helped agriculture and society to prosper, and it has been a major limiting factor when mismanaged.

Water supply and use. In California, an extensive water storage and transfer system has been established which has allowed crop production to expand to very arid regions. In drought years, limited surface water supplies have prompted overdraft of groundwater and consequent intrusion of salt water, or permanent collapse of aquifers. Periodic droughts, some lasting up to 50 years, have occurred in California. Several steps should be taken to develop drought-resistant farming systems even in "normal" years, including both policy and management actions: 1) improving water conservation and storage measures, 2) providing incentives for selection of drought-tolerant crop species, 3) using reduced-volume irrigation systems, 4) managing crops to reduce water loss, or 5) not planting at all.

Water quality. The most important issues related to water quality involve salinization and contamination of ground and surface waters by pesticides, nitrates and selenium. Salinity has become a problem wherever water of even relatively low salt content is used on shallow soils in arid regions and/or where the water table is near the root zone of crops. Tile drainage can remove the water and salts, but the disposal of the salts and other contaminants may negatively affect the environment depending upon where they are deposited. Temporary solutions include the use of salt-tolerant crops, low-volume irrigation, and various management techniques to minimize the effects of salts on crops. In the long-term, some farmland may need to be removed from production or converted to other uses. Other uses include conversion of row crop land to production of drought-tolerant forages, the restoration of wildlife habitat or the use of agroforestry to minimize the impacts of salinity and high water tables. Pesticide and nitrate contamination of water can be reduced using many of the practices discussed later in the Plant Production Practices and Animal Production Practices sections.

Wildlife. Another way in which agriculture affects water resources is through the destruction of riparian habitats within watersheds. The conversion of wild habitat to agricultural land reduces fish and wildlife through erosion and sedimentation, the effects of pesticides, removal of riparian plants, and the diversion of water. The plant diversity in and around both riparian and agricultural areas should be maintained in order to support a diversity of wildlife. This diversity will enhance natural ecosystems and could aid in agricultural pest management.

Energy. Modern agriculture is heavily dependent on non-renewable energy sources, especially petroleum. The continued use of these energy sources cannot be sustained indefinitely, yet to abruptly abandon our reliance on them would be economically catastrophic. However, a sudden cutoff in energy supply would be equally disruptive. In sustainable agricultural systems, there is reduced reliance on non-renewable energy sources and a substitution of renewable sources or labor to the extent that is economically feasible.

Air. Many agricultural activities affect air quality. These include smoke from agricultural burning; dust from tillage, traffic and harvest; pesticide drift from spraying; and nitrous oxide emissions from the use of nitrogen fertilizer. Options to improve air quality include incorporating crop residue into the soil, using appropriate levels of tillage, and planting wind breaks, cover crops or strips of native perennial grasses to reduce dust.

Soil. Soil erosion continues to be a serious threat to our continued ability to produce adequate food. Numerous practices have been developed to keep soil in place, which include reducing or eliminating tillage, managing irrigation to reduce runoff, and keeping the soil covered with plants or mulch. Enhancement of soil quality is discussed in the next section.

Plant Production Practices

Sustainable production practices involve a variety of approaches. Specific strategies must take into account topography, soil characteristics, climate, pests, local availability of inputs and the individual grower's goals. Despite the site-specific and individual nature of sustainable agriculture, several general principles can be applied to help growers select appropriate management practices: Selection of species and varieties that are well suited to the site and to conditions on the farm; Diversification of crops (including livestock) and cultural practices to enhance the biological and economic stability of the farm; Management of the soil to enhance and protect soil quality; Efficient and humane use of inputs; and Consideration of farmers' goals and lifestyle choices.

Selection of site, species and variety. Preventive strategies, adopted early, can reduce inputs and help establish a sustainable production system. When possible, pest-resistant crops should be selected which are tolerant of existing soil or site conditions. When site selection is an option, factors such as soil type and depth, previous crop history, and location (e.g., climate, topography) should be taken into account before planting.

Diversity. Diversified farms are usually more economically and ecologically resilient. While monoculture farming has advantages in terms of efficiency and ease of management, the loss of the crop in any one year could put a farm out of business and/or seriously disrupt the stability of a community dependent on that crop. By growing a variety of crops, farmers spread economic risk and are less susceptible to the radical price fluctuations associated with changes in supply and demand.

Properly managed, diversity can also buffer a farm in a biological sense. For example, in annual cropping systems, crop rotation can be used to suppress weeds, pathogens and insect pests. Also, cover crops can have stabilizing effects on the agroecosystem by holding soil and nutrients in place, conserving soil moisture with mowed or standing dead mulches, and by increasing the water infiltration rate and soil water holding capacity. Cover crops in orchards and vineyards can buffer the system against pest infestations by increasing beneficial arthropod populations and can therefore reduce the need for chemical inputs. Using a variety of cover crops is also important in order to protect against the failure of a particular species to grow and to attract and sustain a wide range of beneficial arthropods.

Optimum diversity may be obtained by integrating both crops and livestock in the same farming operation. This was the common practice for centuries until the mid-1900s when technology, government policy and economics compelled farms to become more specialized. Mixed crop and livestock operations have several advantages. First, growing row crops only on more level land and pasture or forages on steeper slopes will reduce soil erosion. Second, pasture and forage crops in rotation enhance soil quality and reduce erosion; livestock manure, in turn, contributes to soil fertility. Third, livestock can buffer the negative impacts of low rainfall periods by consuming crop residue that in "plant only" systems would have been considered crop failures. Finally, feeding and marketing are flexible in animal production systems. This can help cushion farmers against trade and price fluctuations and, in conjunction with cropping operations, make more efficient use of farm labor.

Soil management. A common philosophy among sustainable agriculture practitioners is that a "healthy" soil is a key component of sustainability; that is, a healthy soil will produce healthy crop plants that have optimum vigor and are less susceptible to pests. While many crops have key pests that attack even the healthiest of plants, proper soil, water and nutrient management can help prevent some pest problems brought on by crop stress or nutrient imbalance. Furthermore, crop management systems that impair soil quality often result in greater inputs of water, nutrients, pesticides, and/or energy for tillage to maintain yields.

In sustainable systems, the soil is viewed as a fragile and living medium that must be protected and nurtured to ensure its long-term productivity and stability. Methods to protect and enhance the productivity of the soil include using cover crops, compost and/or manures, reducing tillage, avoiding traffic on wet soils, and maintaining soil cover with plants and/or mulches. Conditions in most California soils (warm, irrigated, and tilled) do not favor the buildup of organic matter. Regular additions of organic matter or the use of cover crops can increase soil aggregate stability, soil tilth, and diversity of soil microbial life.

Efficient use of inputs. Many inputs and practices used by conventional farmers are also used in sustainable agriculture. Sustainable farmers, however, maximize reliance on natural, renewable, and on-farm inputs. Equally important are the environmental, social, and economic impacts of a particular strategy. Converting to sustainable practices does not mean simple input substitution. Frequently, it substitutes enhanced management and scientific knowledge for conventional inputs, especially chemical inputs that harm the environment on farms and in rural communities. The goal is to develop efficient, biological systems which do not need high levels of material inputs.

Growers frequently ask if synthetic chemicals are appropriate in a sustainable farming system. Sustainable approaches are those that are the least toxic and least energy intensive, and yet maintain productivity and profitability. Preventive strategies and other alternatives should be employed before using chemical inputs from any source. However, there may be situations where the use of synthetic chemicals would be more "sustainable" than a strictly nonchemical approach or an approach using toxic "organic" chemicals. For example, one grape grower switched from tillage to a few applications of a broad spectrum contact herbicide in the vine row. This approach may use less energy and may compact the soil less than numerous passes with a cultivator or mower.

Consideration of farmer goals and lifestyle choices. Management decisions should reflect not only environmental and broad social considerations, but also individual goals and lifestyle choices. For example, adoption of some technologies or practices that promise profitability may also require such intensive management that one's lifestyle actually deteriorates. Management decisions that promote sustainability, nourish the environment, the community and the individual.

Animal Production Practices

In the early part of this century, most farms integrated both crop and livestock operations. Indeed, the two were highly complementary both biologically and economically. The current picture has changed quite drastically since then. Crop and animal producers now are still dependent on one another to some degree, but the integration now most commonly takes place at a higher level—between farmers, through intermediaries, rather than within the farm itself. This is the result of a trend toward separation and specialization of crop and animal production systems. Despite this trend, there are still many farmers, particularly in the Midwest and Northeastern U.S. that integrate crop and animal systems—either on dairy farms, or with range cattle, sheep or hog operations.

Even with the growing specialization of livestock and crop producers, many of the principles outlined in the crop production section apply to both groups. The actual management practices will, of course, be quite different. Some of the specific points that livestock producers need to address are listed below.

Management Planning. Including livestock in the farming system increases the complexity of biological and economic relationships. The mobility of the stock, daily feeding, health concerns, breeding operations, seasonal feed and forage sources, and complex marketing are sources of this complexity. Therefore, a successful ranch plan should include enterprise calendars of operations, stock flows, forage flows, labor needs, herd production records and land use plans to give the manager control and a means of monitoring progress toward goals.

Animal Selection. The animal enterprise must be appropriate for the farm or ranch resources. Farm capabilities and constraints such as feed and forage sources, landscape, climate and skill of the manager must be considered in selecting which animals to produce. For example, ruminant animals can be raised on a variety of feed sources including range and pasture, cultivated forage, cover crops, shrubs, weeds, and crop residues. There is a wide range of breeds available in each of the major ruminant species, i.e., cattle, sheep and goats. Hardier breeds that, in general, have lower growth and milk production potential, are better adapted to less favorable environments with sparse or highly seasonal forage growth.

Animal nutrition. Feed costs are the largest single variable cost in any livestock operation. While most of the feed may come from other enterprises on the ranch, some purchased feed is usually imported from off the farm. Feed costs can be kept to a minimum by monitoring animal condition and performance and understanding seasonal variations in feed and forage quality on the farm. Determining the optimal use of farm-generated by-products is an important challenge of diversified farming.

Reproduction. Use of quality germplasm to improve herd performance is another key to sustainability. In combination with good genetic stock, adapting the reproduction season to fit the climate and sources of feed and forage reduce health problems and feed costs.

Herd Health. Animal health greatly influences reproductive success and weight gains, two key aspects of successful livestock production. Unhealthy stock waste feed and require additional labor. A herd health program is critical to sustainable livestock production.

Grazing Management. Most adverse environmental impacts associated with grazing can be prevented or mitigated with proper grazing management. First, the number of stock per unit area (stocking rate) must be correct for the landscape and the forage sources. There will need to be compromises between the convenience of tilling large, unfenced fields and the fencing needs of livestock operations. Use of modern, temporary fencing may provide one practical solution to this dilemma. Second, the long term carrying capacity and the stocking rate must take into account short and long-term droughts. Especially in Mediterranean climates such as in California, properly managed grazing significantly reduces fire hazards by reducing fuel build-up in grasslands and brushlands. Finally, the manager must achieve sufficient control to reduce overuse in some areas while other areas go unused. Prolonged concentration of stock that results in permanent loss of vegetative cover on uplands or in riparian zones should be avoided. However, small scale loss of vegetative cover around water or feed troughs may be tolerated if surrounding vegetative cover is adequate.

Confined Livestock Production. Animal health and waste management are key issues in confined livestock operations. The moral and ethical debate taking place today regarding animal welfare is particularly intense for confined livestock production systems. The issues raised in this debate need to be addressed.

Confinement livestock production is increasingly a source of surface and ground water pollutants, particularly where there are large numbers of animals per unit area. Expensive waste management facilities are now a necessary cost of confined production systems. Waste is a problem of almost all operations and must be managed with respect to both the environment and the quality of life in nearby communities. Livestock production systems that disperse stock in pastures so the wastes are not concentrated and do not overwhelm natural nutrient cycling processes have become a subject of renewed interest.

The Economic, Social & Political Context

In addition to strategies for preserving natural resources and changing production practices, sustainable agriculture requires a commitment to changing public policies, economic institutions, and social values. Strategies for change must take into account the complex, reciprocal and ever-changing relationship between agricultural production and the broader society.

The "food system" extends far beyond the farm and involves the interaction of individuals and institutions with contrasting and often competing goals including farmers, researchers, input suppliers, farmworkers, unions, farm advisors, processors, retailers, consumers, and policymakers. Relationships among these actors shift over time as new technologies spawn economic, social and political changes.

A wide diversity of strategies and approaches are necessary to create a more sustainable food system. These will range from specific and concentrated efforts to alter specific policies or practices, to the longer-term tasks of reforming key institutions, rethinking economic priorities, and challenging widely-held social values. Areas of concern where change is most needed include the following:

Food and agricultural policy. Existing federal, state and local government policies often impede the goals of sustainable agriculture. New policies are needed to simultaneously promote environmental health, economic profitability, and social and economic equity. For example, commodity and price support programs could be restructured to allow farmers to realize the full benefits of the productivity gains made possible through alternative practices. Tax and credit policies could be modified to encourage a diverse and decentralized system of family farms rather than corporate concentration and absentee ownership. Government and land grant university research policies could be modified to emphasize the development of sustainable alternatives. Marketing orders and cosmetic standards could be amended to encourage reduced pesticide use. Coalitions must be created to address these policy concerns at the local, regional, and national level.

Land use. Conversion of agricultural land to urban uses is a particular concern in California, as rapid growth and escalating land values threaten farming on prime soils. Existing farmland conversion patterns often discourage farmers from adopting sustainable practices and a long-term perspective on the value of land. At the same time, the close proximity of newly developed residential areas to farms is increasing the public demand for environmentally safe farming practices. Comprehensive new policies to protect prime soils and regulate development are needed, particularly in California's Central Valley. By helping farmers to adopt practices that reduce chemical use and conserve scarce resources, sustainable agriculture research and education can play a key role in building public support for agricultural land preservation. Educating land use planners and decision-makers about sustainable agriculture is an important priority.

Labor. In California, the conditions of agricultural labor are generally far below accepted social standards and legal protections in other forms of employment. Policies and programs are needed to address this problem, working toward socially just and safe employment that provides adequate wages, working conditions, health benefits, and chances for economic stability. The needs of migrant labor for year-around employment and adequate housing are a particularly crucial problem needing immediate attention. To be more sustainable over the long-term, labor must be acknowledged and supported by government policies, recognized as important constituents of land grant universities, and carefully considered when assessing the impacts of new technologies and practices.

Rural Community Development. Rural communities in California are currently characterized by economic and environmental deterioration. Many are among the poorest locations in the nation. The reasons for the decline are complex, but changes in farm structure have played a significant role. Sustainable agriculture presents an opportunity to rethink the importance of family farms and rural communities. Economic development policies are needed that encourage more diversified agricultural production on family farms as a foundation for healthy economies in rural communities. In combination with other strategies, sustainable agriculture practices and policies can help foster community institutions that meet employment, educational, health, cultural and spiritual needs.

Consumers and the Food System. Consumers can play a critical role in creating a sustainable food system. Through their purchases, they send strong messages to producers, retailers and others in the system about what they think is important. Food cost and nutritional quality have always influenced consumer choices. The challenge now is to find strategies that broaden consumer perspectives, so that environmental quality, resource use, and social equity issues are also considered in shopping decisions. At the same time, new policies and institutions must be created to enable producers using sustainable practices to market their goods to a wider public. Coalitions organized around improving the food system are one specific method of creating a dialogue among consumers, retailers, producers and others. These coalitions or other public forums can be important vehicles for clarifying issues, suggesting new policies, increasing mutual trust, and encouraging a long-term view of food production, distribution and consumption.

Mary V. Gold
Sustainable Agriculture: Definitions and Terms, Background

USDA National Agricultural Library
available at http://www.nal.usda.gov/afsic/pubs/terms/srb9902.shtml#toc2

How have we come to reconsider our food and fiber production in terms of sustainability? What are the ecological, economic, social and philosophical issues that sustainable agriculture addresses?

The long-term viability of our current food production system is being questioned for many reasons. The news media regularly present us with the paradox of starvation amidst plenty — including pictures of hungry children juxtaposed with supermarket ads. Possible adverse environmental impacts of agriculture and increased incidence of foodborne illness also demand our attention. "Farm crises" seem to recur with regularity.

The prevailing agricultural system, variously called "conventional farming," "modern agriculture," or "industrial farming" has delivered tremendous gains in productivity and efficiency. Food production worldwide has risen in the past 50 years; the World Bank estimates that between 70 percent and 90 percent of the recent increases in food production are the result of conventional agriculture rather than greater acreage under cultivation. U.S. consumers have come to expect abundant and inexpensive food.

Conventional farming systems vary from farm to farm and from country to country. However, they share many characteristics: rapid technological innovation; large capital investments in order to apply production and management technology; large-scale farms; single crops/row crops grown continuously over many seasons; uniform high-yield hybrid crops; extensive use of pesticides, fertilizers, and external energy inputs; high labor efficiency; and dependency on agribusiness. In the case of livestock, most production comes from confined, concentrated systems.

Philosophical underpinnings of industrial agriculture include assumptions that "a) nature is a competitor to be overcome; b) progress requires unending evolution of larger farms and depopulation of farm communities; c) progress is measured primarily by increased material consumption; d) efficiency is measured by looking at the bottom line; and e) science is an unbiased enterprise driven by natural forces to produce social good."[31]

Significant negative consequences have come with the bounty associated with industrial farming. Concerns about contemporary agriculture are presented below.... While considering these concerns, keep the following in mind: a) interactions between farming systems and soil, water, biota, and atmosphere are complex — we have much to learn about their dynamics and long term impacts; b) most environmental problems are intertwined with economic, social, and political forces external to agriculture; c) some problems are global in scope while others are experienced only locally; d) many of these problems are being addressed through conventional, as well as alternative, agricultural channels; e) the list is not complete; and f) no order of importance is intended.

Ecological Concerns

Agriculture profoundly affects many ecological systems. Negative effects of current practices include the following:

---

31. Karl N. Stauber et al., *The Promise of Sustainable Agriculture*, in PLANTING THE FUTURE: DEVELOPING AN AGRICULTURE THAT SUSTAINS LAND AND COMMUNITY (Elizabeth Ann R. Bird, Gordon L. Bultena, and John C. Gardner, ed., Iowa State University Press 1995).

- Decline in soil productivity can be due to wind and water erosion of exposed topsoil; soil compaction; loss of soil organic matter, water holding capacity, and biological activity; and salinization of soils and irrigation water in irrigated farming areas. Desertification due to overgrazing is a growing problem, especially in parts of Africa.

- Agriculture is the largest single non-point source of water pollutants including sediments, salts, fertilizers (nitrates and phosphorus), pesticides, and manures. Pesticides from every chemical class have been detected in groundwater and are commonly found in groundwater beneath agricultural areas; they are widespread in the nation's surface waters. Eutrophication and "dead zones" due to nutrient runoff affect many rivers, lakes, and oceans. Reduced water quality impacts agricultural production, drinking water supplies, and fishery production.

- Water scarcity in many places is due to overuse of surface and ground water for irrigation with little concern for the natural cycle that maintains stable water availability.

- Other environmental ills include over 400 insects and mite pests and more than 70 fungal pathogens that have become resistant to one or more pesticides; stresses on pollinator and other beneficial species through pesticide use; loss of wetlands and wildlife habitat; and reduced genetic diversity due to reliance on genetic uniformity in most crops and livestock breeds.

- Agriculture's link to global climate change is just beginning to be appreciated. Destruction of tropical forests and other native vegetation for agricultural production has a role in elevated levels of carbon dioxide and other greenhouse gases. Recent studies have found that soils may be sources or sinks for greenhouse gases.

Economic and Social Concerns

Economic and social problems associated with agriculture can not be separated from external economic and social pressures. As barriers to a sustainable and equitable food supply system, however, the problems may be described in the following way:

- Economically, the U.S. agricultural sector includes a history of increasingly large federal expenditures and corresponding government involvement in planting and investment decisions; widening disparity among farmer incomes; and escalating concentration of agribusiness—industries involved with manufacture, processing, and distribution of farm products—into fewer and fewer hands. Market competition is limited. Farmers have little control over farm prices, and they continue to receive a smaller and smaller portion of consumer dollars spent on agricultural products.

- Economic pressures have led to a tremendous loss of farms, particularly small farms, and farmers during the past few decades—more than 155,000 farms were lost from 1987 to 1997. This contributes to the disintegration of rural communities and localized marketing systems. Economically, it is very difficult for potential farmers to enter the business today. Productive farmland also has been pressured by urban and suburban sprawl—since 1970, over 30 million acres have been lost to development.

Impacts on Human Health

Potential health hazards are tied to sub-therapeutic use of antibiotics in animal production, and pesticide and nitrate contamination of water and food. Farm workers are poisoned in fields, toxic residues are found on foods, and certain human and animal diseases have developed resistance to currently used antibiotics.

Philosophical Considerations

Historically, farming played an important role in our development and identity as a nation. From strongly agrarian roots, we have evolved into a culture with few farmers. Less than two percent of Americans now produce food for all U.S. citizens. Can sustainable and equitable food production be established when most consumers have so little connection to the natural processes that produce their food? What intrinsically American values have changed and will change with the decline of rural life and farmland ownership?

World population continues to grow. According to recent United Nations population projections, the world population will grow from 5.7 billion in 1995 to 9.4 billion in 2050, 10.4 billion in 2100, and 10.8 billion by 2150, and will stabilize at slightly under 11 billion around 2200. The rate of population increase is especially high in many developing countries. In these countries, the population factor, combined with rapid industrialization, poverty, political instability, and large food imports and debt burden, make long-term food security especially urgent.

Finally, the challenge of defining and dealing with the problems associated with today's food production system is inherently laden with controversy and emotion. "It is unfortunate, but true, that many in the agriculture community view sustainable agriculture as a personal criticism, or an attack, on conventional agriculture of which they are justifiably proud. 'I guess that the main thing people get defensive about when you say sustainable,' explained one agent, 'is that it implies that what they've been doing is not sustainable. And that's the biggest issue.'" [Judy Green, *Sustainable Agriculture: Why Green Ideas Raise a Red Flag*, Farming Alternatives Newsletter (Cornell) (Summer 1993).]

Notes

1. According to the National Sustainable Agriculture Coalition (NSAC), "[t]he basic goals of sustainable agriculture are environmental health, economic profitability, and social and economic equity (sometimes referred to as the "three legs" of the sustainability stool). *See* http://sustainableagriculture.net/about-us/what-is-sustainable-ag/.

How sustainable is the U.S. agricultural sector today? Which of the three 'legs' may present challenges? Are all of equal importance?

What will an increased emphasis on sustainability do to our supply of "cheap food"? How do concerns about adequate food production, affordability, and poverty intersect with agricultural sustainability?

Does the notion of a family farm or any other particular structure matter if the "three legs of the sustainability stool" are met? Why or why not?

2. NSAC's website states its vision of agriculture as one "where a safe, nutritious, ample, and affordable food supply is produced by a legion of family farmers who make a decent living pursuing their trade, while protecting the environment, and contributing to the strength and stability of their communities." It goes on to provide that:

> NSAC member groups advance common positions to support small and mid-size family farms, protect natural resources, promote healthy rural communities, and ensure access to healthy, nutritious foods by everyone. By bringing grassroots perspectives to the table normally dominated by big business, NSAC levels the playing field and gives voice to sustainable and organic farmers.

See http://sustainableagriculture.net/about-us.

What is a family farm, and how does it fit within the consideration of agrarianism, sustainability, and agricultural law and policy? What role should the family farm play in the overall food system?

E. What is a Family Farm?

Despite the changing face of agriculture, agrarianism is still apparent today in public statements that call for the continued support for the family farm. Consider the following passage from the United States Code.

UNITED STATES CODE
TITLE 7. AGRICULTURE
CHAPTER 55—DEPARTMENT OF AGRICULTURE

§ 2266. Congressional reaffirmation of policy to foster and encourage family farms; annual report to Congress

(a) Congress reaffirms the historical policy of the United States to foster and encourage the family farm system of agriculture in this country. Congress believes that the maintenance of the family farm system of agriculture is essential to the social well being of the Nation and the competitive production of adequate supplies of food and fiber. Congress further believes that any significant expansion of nonfamily owned large-scale corporate farming enterprises will be detrimental to the national welfare. It is neither the policy nor the intent of Congress that agricultural and agriculture-related programs be administered exclusively for family farm operations, but it is the policy and the express intent of Congress that no such program be administered in a manner that will place the family farm operation at an unfair economic disadvantage.

There is disagreement, however, regarding the definition of a "family farm system of agriculture."

The USDA Farm Service Agency (FSA), the agency charged with administering the USDA loan programs for family farms who need special access to credit, has a regulatory definition of family farm. It provides as follows:

Family farm is a farm that:

(1) Produces agricultural commodities for sale in sufficient quantities so that it is recognized as a farm rather than a rural residence;

(2) Has both physical labor and management provided as follows:

(i) The majority of day-to-day, operational decisions, and all strategic management decisions are made by:

(A) The borrower and persons who are either related to the borrower by blood or marriage, or are a relative, for an individual borrower; or

(B) The members responsible for operating the farm, in the case of an entity.

(ii) A substantial amount of labor to operate the farm is provided by:

(A) The borrower and persons who are either related to the borrower by blood or marriage, or are a relative, for an individual borrower; or

(B) The members responsible for operating the farm, in the case of an entity.

(3) May use full-time hired labor in amounts only to supplement family labor.

(4) May use reasonable amounts of temporary labor for seasonal peak workload periods or intermittently for labor intensive activities.

7 C.F.R. §761.2 (2010).

In the book FAMILY FARMING, published just over twenty years ago, Marty Strange described the difference between the "family farm" model of agriculture and the industrialized model. He described the family farming model as an "[o]wner-operated," "[f]amily centered" operation that is "[e]ntrepreneurial" and "[t]echnologically progressive" while still "[s]triving for production processes in harmony with nature" through "[d]iversified" production and "[r]esource conserv[ation]." Such a system is characterized by "[d]ispersed" ownership, equal access to markets, and with a view of "[f]arming as a way of life." Marty Strange, FAMILY FARMING: A NEW ECONOMIC VISION 32–39 (1988). Obviously, this holistic definition takes into consideration more than simple familial ties and family labor.

The Center for Rural Affairs in Nebraska provides a flexible definition.

We subscribe to the definition of a family farm or ranch as one on which the management and the majority of the labor are provided by the family or families that own the production and at least some of the productive assets.

However, we believe that it is more important to decide what system of agriculture we want than to define a category to decide who is in and who is out. We believe it is in the interest of rural America and all of America to have a strong family farm system of agriculture. By that we mean a system that:

- Provides genuine opportunity for those who work on farms and ranches to own the fruits of their labor and productive assets.

- Offers open opportunity for new people to enter the business even if they aren't rich.

- Fairly compensates those who produce food and provides a meaningful share of food system profit to agricultural producers.

- Maintains a substantial number of farms and ranches, sufficient to support healthy communities.

Within such a system, there will always be farms of varying sizes. The key threat to the family farm system today is the loss of our smaller commercial farms — our medium-size farms — and movement toward a system where production is dominated by a few very large farms with little opportunity for anyone else.

Center for Rural Affairs website, available at http://www.cfra.org/about.

The USDA Economic Research Service (ERS) uses a much broader definition of "family farm." A farm is defined "as any place that produced or sold — or normally would have produced or sold — $1,000 worth of agricultural products during a given year." And, "family farms" are defined as "operations organized as proprietorships, partnerships, or family corporations that do not have hired managers." Robert A. Hoppe, Penni Korb, Erik J.

O'Donoghue, David Banker, *Structure and Finances of Family Farms — Family Farm Report 2007 Edition*, iii, USDA, ERS, Bull. No. 24 (June 2007). Under the USDA ERS definition, there is no size limitation on family farms. Hired labor is also not a factor, so long as management is retained by the family. Method of farming is similarly not at issue.

> Under the ERS definition, 98 percent of farms in 2004 were family farms. Family farms produced 84.8 percent of the value of total farm production; nonfamily farms produced 15.2 percent.

See Robert A. Hoppe, Penni Korb, Erik J. O'Donoghue, David Banker, *Structure and Finances of Family Farms — Family Farm Report 2007 Edition*, USDA, ERS, Bull. No. 24 (June 2007).

The ERS divides family farms into categories. Large scale family farms are those with gross sales of $250,000 or more. This category is broken down into two sub-categories, large family farms with gross sales between $250,000 and $499,000, and very large family farms with gross sales of $500,000 or more.

Small family farms are defined as those with less than $250,000 in gross sales per year. The sub-categories of small family farms are somewhat more complex. This category includes limited resource farms, retirement farms, residential/lifestyle farms, and farming-occupation farms. These are defined as:

> *Limited resource farms.* Farms with gross sales less than $100,000 in 2003 and less than $105,000 in 2004. Operators of limited-resource farms must also receive low household income in both 2003 and 2004. Household income is considered low in a given year if it is less than the poverty level for a family of four, or it is less than half the county median household income. Operators may report any major occupation except hired manager.
>
> *Retirement farms.* Farms whose operators report they are retired.
>
> *Residential/lifestyle farms.* Farms whose operators report a major occupation other than farming.
>
> *Farming-occupation farms.* Farms whose operators report farming as their major occupation.

Robert A. Hoppe, Penni Korb, Erik J. O'Donoghue, David Banker, *Structure and Finances of Family Farms — Family Farm Report 2007 Edition*, USDA, ERS, Bull. No. 24 (June 2007). Within the category of farming-occupation farms, operations are categorized as either low-sales farms or medium-sales farms. Low sales farms are those with gross sales less than $100,000; medium-sales farms have gross sales between $100,000 and $249,999. *Id.*

The USDA ERS summarizes its findings as follows:

> **Small family farms account for most U.S. farms and farm assets.** Small family farms (sales less than $250,000) accounted for 90 percent of U.S. farms in 2004. They also held about 68 percent of all farm assets, including 61 percent of the land owned by farms. As custodians of the bulk of farm assets—including land—small farms have a large role in natural resource and environmental policy. Small farms accounted for 82 percent of the land enrolled by farmers in the Conservation Reserve and Wetlands Reserve Programs (CRP and WRP).
>
> **Large-scale family farms and nonfamily farms produce the largest share of agricultural output.** Large-scale family farms, plus nonfamily farms, made up only 10 percent of U.S. farms in 2004, but accounted for 75 percent of the value of

production. Nevertheless, small farms made significant contributions to the production of specific commodities, including hay, tobacco, wheat, corn, soybeans, and beef cattle.

The number of larger farms is growing. The number of farms with sales of $250,000 or more grew steadily between the 1982 and 2002 Censuses of Agriculture, with sales measured in constant 2002 dollars. The growth in the number of these larger farms was accompanied by a shift in sales in the same direction. The most rapid growth was for farms with sales of $1 million or more. By 2002, million-dollar farms alone accounted for 48 percent of sales, compared with 23 percent in 1982.

For the most part, large-scale farms are more viable businesses than small family farms. The average operating profit margin and rates of return on assets and equity for large and very large family farms were all positive in 2004, and most of these farms had a positive operating profit margin. Small farms were less viable as businesses. Their average operating profit margin and rates of return on assets and equity were negative. Nevertheless, some farms in each small farm group had an operating margin of at least 20 percent. In addition, a majority of each small farm type had a positive net farm income, although the average net income for each small-farm type was low compared with large-scale farms.

Small farm households rely on off-farm income. Small farm households typically receive substantial off-farm income and do not rely primarily on their farms for their livelihood. Most of their off-farm income is from wage and salary jobs or self-employment. Because of their off-farm work, small farm households are affected significantly by the nonfarm economy. Households operating retirement or limited-resource farms, however, receive well over half of their income from such sources as Social Security, pensions, dividends, interest, and rent, reflecting the ages of operators on such farms.

Payments from commodity-related programs and conservation programs go to different types of farms. The distribution of commodity related program payments is roughly proportional to the harvested acres of program commodities. As a result, medium-sales ($100,000–$249,999) and large-scale farms received 78 percent of commodity-related government payments in 2004. In contrast, CRP, which pays the bulk of environmental payments, targets environmentally sensitive land rather than commodity production. Retirement, residential/lifestyle, and low-sales small farms received 62 percent of conservation program payments in 2004. However, most farms—61 percent in 2004—receive no government payments and are not directly affected by farm program payments.

A growing number of farms operate under production and marketing contracts to guarantee an outlet for their production. About two-fifths of U.S. agricultural production is produced or marketed under contract, although the share varies by commodity and type of farm. Relatively few small family farms use production and marketing contracts, while 64 percent of very large family farms use contracts and, as a group, produce 61 percent of the value of production grown under contract.

Robert A. Hoppe, Penni Korb, Erik J. O'Donoghue, David Banker, *Structure and Finances of Family Farms—Family Farm Report 2007 Edition*, iv–v, USDA, ERS, Bull. No. 24 (June 2007).

F. A Survey of Current U.S. Agricultural Production

Every 5 years, the USDA National Agricultural Statistics Service (NASS) conducts a Census or survey of U.S. agriculture. NASS describes this census providing "a complete count of U.S. farms and ranches and the people who operate them" and it includes information about "land use and ownership, operator characteristics, production practices, income and expenditures, and many other areas."

The first agriculture Census was taken in 1840, and for the next 156 years (1840–1996) the U.S. Department of Commerce, Bureau of the Census conducted the Census of Agriculture. In 1997, responsibility for conducting the Census of Agriculture transferred to the USDA NASS. The 2007 Census of Agriculture is the 27th Federal Census of Agriculture and the third conducted by NASS.

The results of the 2007 Census of Agriculture were released February 4, 2009 and updated in December 2009. Although the number of farmers has diminished, the productivity and economic influence of American agriculture has not. The 2007 Census of Agriculture revealed a productive, largely industrialized agricultural sector that produces food, fiber, and fuel for the United States and for export. The data and the summary reports are available on the USDA NASS Ag Census website at http://www.agcensus.usda.gov/. The following summary of U.S. agriculture is based on the 2007 Census of Agriculture.

1. The Number of Farms

The USDA National Agricultural Statistics Service (NASS) defines a "farm" as any place that produced or sold — or normally would have produced or sold — $1,000 or more of agricultural products in a given year.

The 2007 Census of Agriculture counted 2,204,792 farms in the United States, up 4 percent from the previous census in 2002, showing an increase of 75,810. This increase represents a change, as the number of farms has previously declined each census since World War II.

The growth in the number of farms was not uniform across either size or type of farm. Most of the growth in U.S. farm numbers came from small farms, defined as farms with $250,000 or less in sales of agricultural commodities. In 2007, there were 18,467 more small farms counted than in 2002, for a total of 1,995,133 small farms, or 91 percent of all farms.

The 2007 Census of Agriculture shows a continuation in the trend towards more small and more very large farms, with mid-size farms declining in number.

However, the increase in the number of farms and the number of small farms was concentrated in the smallest of farms. Farms with sales less than $10,000 increased while small farms with sales of more than $10,000 decreased. U.S. farms with sales between $100,000 and $249,999 decreased by 7 percent.

Certain types of farms, including grains and oilseeds, horticulture, cattle and hog operations, declined in number, as increasing consolidation was evidenced. This comports with a continuation of the trend of an increase in both small and very large farms. For example, between 2002 and 2007, the number of the smallest size farms grew by 118,000 and the number of farms categorized as "very large," i.e., with sales of more than $500,000, grew by 46,000.

2. Agricultural Production

In 2007, U.S. farms sold $297 billion in agricultural products. This was an increase of 48% above the value of products sold in 2002. The average market value of products sold in 2007 was $134,807 per farm.

The average value is perhaps misleading, however, as there are extreme variations in production by crop, geographic area, and by size of farm or concentration in the sector. The largest farms, however, consistently produce the greatest share of overall production.

Type of Product. Grains, oilseeds and pulse crops accounted for 26 percent of all agricultural products sold in the United States during 2007. U.S. sales of grains, oilseeds and pulse crops totaled $77.2 billion, nearly double the value in 2002. Corn sales, at $39.9 billion dollars, accounted for 52 percent of sales in this category, while soybeans accounted for 26 percent, wheat for 14 percent and rice for 3 percent.

Total sales of cattle and calves accounted for 21 percent of all agricultural products sold in the United States during 2007. U.S. sales of cattle and calves totaled $61.2 billion, an increase of $16.1 billion, or 36 percent, from 2002.

Poultry and eggs sales accounted for 12 percent of all agricultural products sold in the U.S. in 2007. During 2007, sales totaled $37 billion, an increase of 55% over 2002.

The sale of milk and other dairy products totaled $31.8 billion in 2007 and accounted for 11 percent of all sales of U.S. agricultural products. This amount reflected an increase of $11.6 billion, i.e., 57 percent, over 2002 sales.

Hog and pig sales in 2007 were valued at $18.1 billion, compared to $12 billion in 2002 —an increase of 46%. These sales accounted for 6 percent of all agricultural products sold in the U.S. during 2007.

The value of cotton production also increased from 2002 to 2007. In 2002, cotton sales were valued at $4 billion, and in 2007, cotton sales were valued at almost $4.9 billion.

The category "specialty crops" includes fruits, tree nuts, berries, vegetables, potatoes, melons, pulse crops, nursery, greenhouse, floriculture, cut Christmas trees, short rotation woody crops and other specialty crops. Specialty crops as a separate category of production were surveyed for the first time in 2007, and the results are found in a separate report, the 2007 Census of Agriculture, Specialty Crops, Vol. 2, Subject Series, Pt. 8 (Nov. 2009). The value of specialty crop production totaled over $67 billion in 2007, thus accounting for approximately 21 percent of total agricultural production value.

Geographic Area. The value of agricultural production is generally concentrated in the Midwest, the Mississippi Delta, California and on the Atlantic Coast. The top five states and their share of total value are: California (11.4 percent), Texas (7.1 percent), Iowa (6.9 percent), Nebraska (5.2 percent) and Kansas (4.8 percent). Fifty percent of the total value of agricultural products comes from only 9 states—the top five plus four additional states,

Illinois, Minnesota, North Carolina, and Wisconsin. Fresno County in California was the largest single county in terms of agricultural products sold in 2007, with $3.7 billion, or 1.2 percent of the total U.S. value.

The production of grain, oil seeds and pulse crops are focused in five states—Illinois, Iowa, Nebraska, Minnesota, and Indiana. These states account for 49 percent of the total value of U.S. sales of these crops.

Cattle production is focused primarily in five states—Texas, Kansas, Nebraska, Iowa, and Colorado; these states provide more than 50 percent of the total value of U.S. sales of cattle and calves. Deaf Smith County in Texas was the largest single county in terms of cattle and calf sales during 2007 with $965 million, or 1.6 percent of the total U.S. value.

Poultry production is heavily concentrated in the southeast. More than 50 percent of poultry and egg sales come from six southern states—Georgia, North Carolina, Arkansas, Alabama, Mississippi, and Texas.

Milk and dairy production is more dispersed geographically, but more than 50 percent of the total value of U.S. sales comes from the top 5 states of California, Wisconsin, New York, Pennsylvania, and Idaho. Tulare County in California was the largest single county in terms of milk and other dairy product sales during 2007, with $1.685 million, or 5.3 percent of the total U.S. value.

Over fifty percent of the value of U.S. hog and pig sales comes from the states of Iowa, North Carolina, and Minnesota. One county in North Carolina was responsible for 4 percent of the total value of U.S. sales.

The production of specialty crops is heavily based in California where over $23 billion of specialty crops were produced and sold in 2007. This accounts for approximately 35 percent of the total production value. The next two states with the highest value of 2007 production are Florida, with $5.9 billion and Michigan, with $4.1 billon. Combined, these three states made up almost half of U.S. specialty crop production value in 2007.

Size of Farm and Concentration. In general, U.S. agricultural production has become more concentrated in the last five years, with a smaller number of larger farms producing most of the value. In 2002, 144,000 farms produced 75 percent of the value of U.S. agricultural production. In 2007, just 125,000 farms produced 75 percent of the value. In 2002, farms with more than $1 million in sales produced 47 percent of all production. In 2007, these largest of farms produced 12 percent more. Farms with more than $1 million in sales produced 59 percent of U.S. agricultural production in 2007.

Concentration is apparent in each sector of production, but to different degrees. The total number of farms that sold grains, oilseeds and pulse crops declined by 1 percent from 2002 to 2007. Farms with more than 2,000 acres accounted for 10 percent of the farms and more than 40 percent of sales.

Concentration in cattle production was more pronounced. In 2002, 45,000 farms produced 75 percent of cattle sales; by 2007, that number had decreased to 35,000. In 2007, corporations composed only 4 percent of all cattle operations, but they held 19 percent of inventory and 35 percent of sales.

In the dairy sector, concentration was also evident. In 2002, the largest 24 percent of dairy farms produced 74 percent of the total value of sales of dairy products. In 2007, these large farms produced 81 percent of dairy products. Of the $31.8 billion in dairy sales in 2007, over $13 billion of it came from dairies with a herd size of over 1,000 cows.

The hog sector continues the trend toward more specialization and concentration. The number of hog farms declined by 9%, while production and sales increased 46 percent from 2002.

3. Production Expenses

Although across the board, farm sale values rose from 2002 to 2007, farm production expenses also rose significantly. In 2007, production expenses for all farms totaled $241 billion, a 39 percent increase over 2002. The greatest increase (averaged for all farms) was for gasoline and other fuels, up 93 percent. Fertilizer costs rose 86 percent. Seed and feed costs both rose 55 percent.

4. Government Farm Program Payments

In 2007, a total of approximately $8 billion was paid to farmers under the federal farm programs. Of the 2.2 million farms in the U.S., 840,000, just 38 percent of farms received payments.

5. Demographics

The 2007 Census revealed a continuation of the long term trend of the aging of farm operators. The average age of the principal farm operator has increased roughly one year in each census cycle, from 50.3 in 1978 to 57.1 in 2007. The majority of all farm operators are between 45 and 64, but the fastest growing age group is those 65 years and older. The number of all farm operators under 45 years of age declined 14 percent from 2002 to 2007. The number of primary farm operators under 45 years of age declined 21 percent. The number of operators 75 years or older grew by 20 percent. The number of operators under 25 years of age declined by 30 percent.

The 2007 Census shows that U.S. farm operators are becoming somewhat more diverse. Of the 2.2 million farms in the United States, 1.83 million have a white male principal operator. However, since 2002, the growth in the number of non-white operators has outpaced overall growth in the industry. For example, the number of operators of Hispanic origin increased 10 percent since 2002.

One of the most significant demographic changes in the 2007 Census is the increase in female farm operators. There were 306,209 female principal operators counted in 2007, up from 237,819 in 2002 — an increase of almost 30 percent.

6. Off-farm Income and Part-time Farming

Of the 2.2 million principal farm operators in the nation, 1.2 million report something other than farming as their primary occupation. Almost 900,000 principal operators report working off the farm more than 200 days a year. The share of farmers working off-farm grew from 55 percent in 2002 to 65 percent in 2007.

The demographic characteristics of operators on larger farms, with sales over $250,000, differ from those of small farms. Operators of larger farms tend to be somewhat younger, are more likely to report farming as their primary occupation, and are less likely to work off the farm.

7. Organic Farming

The USDA NASS reports that it did a follow up to the 2007 Census of Agriculture and conducted an in-depth survey of organic farming in the United States, the 2008 Organic Production Survey. This was the first in-depth survey of organic agriculture performed by the USDA. Data was collected from operators of farms that were either USDA-certified as organic, were making the transition to organic production, or were exempt from USDA certification because of sales totaling less than $5,000.

The survey revealed 14,540 organic farms and ranches in the United States, comprising 4.1 million acres of land. Of those farms, 10,903 were USDA-certified and 3,637 were exempt from certification. Total sales were $3.16 billion—$1.94 billion in crop sales and $1.22 billion in sales of livestock, poultry and their products. Organic farms had average annual sales of $217,675, compared to the $134,807 average for U.S. farms overall.

Average production expenses are higher on organic farms than on all other farms. The organic farms surveyed incurred production expenses totaling $2.5 billion. The largest production expense was labor at $569 million followed by feed purchases at $480 million.

California has the most organic farms; almost 20 percent of the total number of organic farms are located there. The states with the highest number of organic farms and the number of certified and exempt organic farms located within the state are: California (2,714); Wisconsin (1,222); Washington (887); New York (887); Oregon (657); Pennsylvania (586); Minnesota (550); Ohio (547); Iowa (518); and,Vermont (467).

8. Structural Trends in Production

The data presented in the 2007 Census of Agriculture reveals a highly productive agricultural sector. It also reveals trending shifts in production from small and medium sized family farms to larger farms. The USDA Economic Research Service predicts this trend to continue.

James MacDonald, Robert Hoppe, and David Banker
Growing Farm Size and the Distribution of Farm Payments
USDA Economic Research Service Economic Brief No. 6 (March 2006)

Agricultural Production Is Shifting to Larger Farms

Family-operated farms continue to account for most U.S. agricultural production. The share of production held by nonfamily farms has grown over time, but still accounted for just 14 percent of the value of production in 2003. A more striking shift is toward very large family farms (sales of at least $500,000, in 2003 dollars), which accounted for nearly half (45 percent) of production in 2003, up from 32 percent in 1989. The number of those very large family farms also grew—from 39,700 in 1989 to 66,700 in 2003. Meanwhile, the share of production on smaller family farms ($10,000–$250,000 in sales) fell from 40 percent in 1989 to 26 percent in 2003.

The trend to larger farms is sectorwide. The shift to larger livestock operations is well-documented and pronounced. For example, family farms with at least $500,000 in production value held 61 percent of hog production and 75 percent of poultry and egg production in 2003, up from 16 percent and 48 percent in 1989. But important shifts are also occurring in crop production, where very large family farms hold rapidly growing shares of production in cash grains and soybeans, tobacco, cotton, and peanuts, crops traditionally covered by commodity programs and farm legislation.

We assess changes since 1989 because we have accurate and comparable data on farm production, farm household incomes, and farm payments starting in 1989. But changes in farm structure were clearly occurring before that time; the census of agriculture shows ongoing shifts of production to larger farms in the 1970s and 1980s, continuing after the dramatic decline of farm numbers that had occurred between 1935 and 1975 had run its course. We expect these changes in farm structure to continue, for two broad reasons.

Many small farm operators are nearing retirement. Among the principal operators of smaller commercial farms, those with sales between $10,000 and $250,000, the share who are age 65 or older has risen sharply since 1989, suggesting that many are near retirement and not simply transferring the farm to younger operators. More specifically, over 30 percent of operators in the $10,000–$99,999 sales class were at least 65 years old by 2003, versus 13 percent of the operators of very large family farms.

Larger farms realize higher profits, on average. Margins (the ratio of operating profit 1 to gross farm income) were negative, on average, for farms with sales below $250,000 in 2003, and they rose steadily as farm sales increased. The pattern (losses among small farms, and a strong relation between margins and farm size) holds in earlier years, and suggests that there are strong financial pressures driving production toward larger enterprises.

G. Consumer Awareness and Impact

In his essay *Food Democracy*, Neil Hamilton wrote of our changing food system and its impact on agriculture.

> [I]t is undeniable a major social transformation is underway in our nation's food, one that has the potential to reshape our food system, creating one more reflective of democratic values. The signs of this are all around us. You can see it in the foods we eat (Have you purchased anything organic lately?), in the issues being debated (Was obesity such a concern five years ago?), and in the discussions in farms and kitchens, boardrooms and dining rooms, in every corner of the land. You may be part of the social movement yearning for a food democracy, perhaps without realizing it. If you shop at the farmers' market, buy organic food, tend a garden, or eat at restaurants serving fresh local foods, then you are part of the food democracy movement. If you are a food democrat, or want to be, in reality you are joining a larger social movement, one resting on com-

munity involvement and personal creativity, in which our identity and values are reflected through the lives we lead. The growth in farmers markets, the demand for high quality, more satisfying foods, the influence of chefs in shaping our views of food, our passion for gardening, even our worries about food safety, nutrition, and health, all these key forces are driving changes in our food system. These developments are about more than just food. They are the visible expression of democratic tendencies in society and they are the evidence and the confirmation of an emerging food democracy.

Neil Hamilton, *Essay—Food Democracy and the Future of American Values*. 9 DRAKE J. AGRIC. L. 9, 24 (Spring 2004).

There is undeniably an increasing interest in food and food systems in the United States. It is seen in the popularity and numerosity of food and food system books such as OMNIVORE'S DILEMMA; IN DEFENSE OF FOOD; FAST FOOD NATION; TWINKIE DECONSTRUCTED; ANIMAL, VEGETABLE, MIRACLE; FOOD POLITICS; WHAT TO EAT; FOOD RULES; ALL YOU CAN EAT: HOW HUNGRY IS AMERICA?; EVERYTHING I WANT TO DO IS ILLEGAL; EATING ANIMALS; THE TASTE FOR CIVILIZATION: FOOD, POLITICS AND CIVIL SOCIETY and others that have come out in recent years. These books not only evidence consumer interest in food, they have played an important role in fueling this interest by disclosing many unknown aspects of the food system to consumers. Similarly, documentaries about food and agriculture are also abundant and have taken on the role of exposing consumers to a world of food production and food policy that is not what they expect. Examples include KING CORN; OUR DAILY BREAD; and the Academy Award nominee, FOOD INC.

Universities, anxious to build on student interest, are developing food studies programs. According to the Washington Post, such programs have now "[h]it the [a]cademic [m]ainstream." *See* Jane Black, *Field Studies*, WASH. POST, Aug. 20, 2008, at F01. As these programs are preparing the consumers of the future, it is likely that the disconnection that has marked our food system in recent years will become an historic anomaly.

For many consumers, there is a desire not only to know about their food, but to connect more personally with its source. This trend is evidenced by the increased number of consumers who seek to purchase their food directly from the producer. The 2007 Census of Agriculture reported $1.2 billion direct-to-consumer sales, compared with only $551 million in 1997. According to the USDA Agricultural Marketing Service, there were 5,274 farmers markets in 2009, up from 2,756 in 1998 and only 1,755 in 1994. The National Center for Appropriate Technology estimates that there were over 1400 community-supported agriculture (CSA) organizations in early 2010, but notes that the actual number may be much larger. There were only 400 CSAs counted in 2001. *See*, Steve Martinez, Michael Hand, Michele Da Pra, Susan Pollack, Katherine Ralston, Travis Smith, Stephen Vogel, Shellye Clark, Luanne Lohr, Sarah Low, and Constance Newman, *Local Food Systems: Concepts, Impacts, and Issues*, USDA, Economic Research Service (2010). Neil Hamilton refers to a growing consumer interest in "putting a face on our food." Neil D. Hamilton, *Putting a Face on Our Food: How State and Local Food Policies Can Promote the New Agriculture*, 7 DRAKE J. AGRIC. L. 407 (2002).

Reviewing some of the latest books on food and our food system and commenting on consumer interest, Michael Pollan wrote,

> Cheap food has become an indispensable pillar of the modern economy. But it is no longer an invisible or uncontested one. One of the most interesting social movements to emerge in the last few years is the "food movement," or perhaps I should say "movements," since it is unified as yet by little more than the recog-

nition that industrial food production is in need of reform because its so-cial/environmental/public health/animal welfare/gastronomic costs are too high.

Michael Pollan, *The Food Movement Rising*, New York Review of Books (June 10, 2010), available at http://www.nybooks.com/articles/archives/2010/jun/10/food-movement-rising/?pagination=false.

Pollan puts a variety of groups into his combined food movement—groups with concerns regarding not only local food and direct contact with the producer, but also child nutrition, animal welfare, environmental protection, food sovereignty, food safety, obesity, farmland preservation, and food security, to provide only a partial list. Pollan notes that it is a "big, lumpy tent" that houses these movements, but sees indications that these various voices may be coming together in something that looks more and more like a coherent movement." *Id.*

Consumers have not typically been involved in either farm policy or food policy. Is this about to change? If so, what might consumers do with their newfound power? What impact will there be on the global food system?

Consider the interests of the consumer both American and international, and consider the concerns of the advocacy groups described by Hamilton and Pollan, as the specific aspects of agricultural law unfold in the subsequent chapters.

II

Economic Support to Agriculture: The Federal Farm Programs, Federal Crop Insurance, and Disaster Assistance

The first business of the Hundred Days had been the banks. But another problem lay urgently on Roosevelt's mind that March: this was the problem of the farmers. No group in the population, except perhaps the Negro workers, was more badly hit by depression. The realized net income of farm operators in 1932 was less than one-third what it had been in 1929—a dizzying collapse in three years. Farm prices had fallen more than 50 per cent; and the parity ratio—the ratio of prices received by farmers to the prices they paid—had plummeted from 89 in 1929 down to 55 in 1932 (in terms of 1910–14 as 100). The seething violence in the farm belt over the winter—the grim mobs gathered to stop foreclosures the pickets along the highways to prevent produce from being moved to town—being moved to town—made it clear that patience was running out. In January 1933, Edward A. O'Neal the head of the Farm Bureau Federation, warned a Senate committee: "Unless something is done for the American farmer we will have revolution in the countryside within less than twelve months."

Arthur M. Schlesinger, Jr., THE COMING OF THE NEW DEAL, *Part I The Fight for Agricultural Balance*, 27–83 (1958).

The origins of the federal farm programs that continue to support U.S. agriculture are found in President Franklin Roosevelt's New Deal. The desperation facing farmers at that time, however, is in sharp contrast to the economic condition of many federal farm program participants today.

Farm subsidy programs in the 1930s were largely prompted by concern for the chronically low, and highly variable, incomes of U.S. farm households. Seventy years later, commodity-based support programs are still prominent, even though the income and wealth of the average farm household now exceed those of the average nonfarm household-wealth by a large margin. Carol A. Jones, Hisham El-Osta, and Robert Green, *Economic Well-Being of Farm Households*, Economic Brief No. 7, USDA Economic Research Service (March 2006).

Is this evidence of the success of federal farm policy or an indictment of it? Whether and to what extent these programs are a necessary component of a successful farm economy today is a much debated point, as is the impact of the programs on the structure of American agriculture and America's food system.

This chapter provides an overview of the types of economic support provided to farmers by the federal government through the farm programs, federal crop insurance, and disaster assistance. Due to the complexity of each of these programs, only an overview can be accomplished. However, the information provided, along with reference to the resources cited, should provide a framework for understanding for how this economic support is provided and what legal and policy issues are raised.

A. Federal Farm Programs

The USDA Economic Research Service reports that since the introduction of the 2002 Farm Act, farm program payments have averaged about $15 billion per fiscal year. Federal expenditures reached record highs in 2000 due to low crop prices in 1999 and 2000. In 2005–06, expenditures rose to over $20 billion in response to low commodity prices and a jump in disaster and emergency assistance. Because of the restructuring of the programs in 1996, however, about half of program payments are "direct payments" made regardless of crop prices, income received, or annual production.

These cost estimates do not include the costs to consumers of programs that restrict supplies and raise food costs, such as the sugar and dairy programs. Also excluded are certain conservation payments that provide economic support to farmers but that accomplish a conservation goal.

USDA's Economic Research Service estimates that about thirty-nine percent of all farms received government payments in calendar year 2008. Payments averaged $11,922 for those operations receiving payments, accounting for about 5 percent of gross cash income and 21 percent of net cash income in 2008 for those farms. Averages can be misleading, however. The largest 12.4 percent of farms in terms of gross receipts received 62.4 percent of all government payments.

See, Government Payments and the Farm Sector, Who Benefits and How Much? USDA Economic Research Service, Briefing Room: Farm and Commodity Policy available at http://www.ers.usda.gov/Briefing/FarmPolicy/gov-pay.htm.

Among the factors influencing the allocation of government payments are the types of commodities produced (only some crops are supported), farm size (acreage), historical production records, and operator characteristics. These factors have historically favored and thus encouraged large farming operations with minimal crop rotation, intensive production practices, and the production of specifically supported commodities, i.e., an industrialized model of commercial agricultural production focused on fungible commodity crops. This model is recognized for very successful and efficient short term production, but also recognized as problematic in terms of environmental sustainability.

> Farms generating 50 percent or more in total farm sales from a single commodity are classified as specialized commodity producers. Ninety-seven percent of all farms specializing in the production of wheat, corn, soybeans, and cotton receive government payments....
>
> •   In 1999–2001, government payments represented nearly all net cash income for wheat, corn, and soybean producers and over three-fourths for cotton producers.
>
> •   Since 2002, government payments have been half of net cash income for wheat, corn, soybean, and cotton producers. The ratio of government pay-

ments to net cash income appears to be more stable since the 2005 price spike generated by Hurricane Katrina.

Government Payments by Production Type 1999–2008, USDA Economic Research Service, Briefing Room: Farm Income and Costs: Farms Receiving Government Payments, available at http://www.ers.usda.gov/Briefing/FarmIncome/govtpaybyfarmtype.htm.

The specific crops that receive the most support under the federal farm programs are corn, wheat, cotton, soybeans, and rice, in descending order. These five crops lead other crops by a significant margin, with corn far above the rest. The number of farmer recipients is also significantly higher for corn. The farm programs are coming under increased scrutiny not only for the amount of subsidies provided but for their focus on and encouragement of these five crops, and in particular the emphasis on corn.

The data on the amount of support provided is maintained by the USDA. For a number of years, the Environmental Working Group has featured a "Farm Subsidy Database" that provides an analysis of USDA federal farm program data that is readily available to the public through its website at http://www.farm.ewg.org/. National data, state-by-state data, support categorized by crop, and even individual recipient information is available through this website.

Top Ten Ranking Crops EWG Estimated Receipt of Subsidies 1995–2009

	Recipients 1995–2009	Subsidy Total 1995–2009
Corn	1,639,547	$73,775,277,671
Wheat	1,374,499	$30,726,213,559
Cotton	264,850	$29,715,272,513
Soybeans	1,044,247	$22,776,514,081
Rice	69,990	$12,551,853,937
Sorghum	615,604	$5,904,106,527
Peanut	91,565	$3,402,012,935
Barley	352,891	$2,462,713,557
Tobacco	394,780	$944,104,224
Sunflower	61,675	$819,268,301

Source: Environmental Working Group estimates based on USDA data; ERW indicates that the estimates include crop insurance premiums paid by RMA but do not include Counter Cyclical Payments; omitted from the list published by EWG are the Conservation Reserve Program, disaster assistance, the dairy program subsidies (almost $4.8 billion) and livestock subsidies ($3.4 billion). *See* http://farm.ewg.org/region.php?fips+00000#topprogs.

1. The Statutory Framework: The Farm Bill

In introducing the federal farm program statutory scheme, Professor Christopher R. Kelley noted that:

> At their inception in the 1930s, the domestic commodity programs "were not implemented to establish the foundational superstructure for a permanent policy of income support for agriculture."[9] Nonetheless, perhaps because "[f]armers have long held hypnotic sway over politicians,"[10] domestic commodity programs have "taken on the appearance of a permanent fixture."[11] Not surprisingly, therefore, the Agricultural Adjustment Act of 1938[12] and the Agricultural Act of 1949[13] have become known as the "permanent" farm legislation.[14] Historically, these statutes have been amended every four to five years through the enactment of a "farm bill."[15]

Christopher R. Kelley, *Recent Federal Farm Program Developments*, 4 Drake J. Agric. L. 93, 95–96 (1999).

Each Farm Bill suspends or repeals the "permanent" acts and typically includes federal price and income support for certain agricultural commodities (the commodity programs), incentive programs for agricultural conservation and environmental clean up (the conservation programs), government subsidized lending programs (the farm credit programs), and risk management programs (crop insurance and disaster relief programs), as well as support for agricultural research, rural development programs, and all of the foreign and domestic food programs (including the nutrition programs).

Debate over the most recent farm bill was contentious, and the 2002 farm bill had to be extended under a series of temporary extensions to allow time for the House and Senate to resolve their differences. The *Food, Conservation, and Energy Act of 2008* was eventually passed over a presidential veto in June of 2008. Pub. L. 110-246, 122 Stat. 1651 (2008). The farm program provisions are codified at 7 U.S.C. ch. 113, §§ 8701–8793.

---

9. Gordon C. Rausser & David Nielson, *Looking Ahead: Agricultural Policy in the 1990s*, 23 U.C. Davis L. Rev. 415, 419 (1990). The domestic commodity programs are primarily intended to promote the economic welfare of producers of certain agricultural commodities. *See id.* at 418. They do so through direct income transfers, nonrecourse and recourse loans, quotas, allotments, commodity purchases, and disaster assistance, although not all of these mechanisms apply to all program commodities. *See id.* Some of these programs directly increase their beneficiaries' wealth by providing cash payments. *See id.* Others provide financial gains indirectly, such as by allowing the repayment of loans for a sum less than the amount borrowed. *See id.* at 419. In addition, all of the programs indirectly add to farm landowner wealth because their benefits are capitalized into the value of farmland. In fact, "[m]ost of the ultimate benefit from farm programs has gone to owners of farmland or other resources in inelastic supply." Daniel A. Sumner, Targeting and the Distribution of Program Benefits, in Agricultural Policies in a New Decade 125, 127 (Kristen Allen ed., 1990).

10. David Rapp, How the U.S. Got into Agriculture, and Why It Can't Get Out 7 (1988).

11. Rausser & Nielson, *supra* note 9, at 419.

12. Agricultural Adjustment Act of 1938, Pub. L. No. 75-430, 52 Stat. 31 (codified as amended in scattered sections of 7 U.S.C.).

13. Agricultural Act of 1949, Pub. L. No. 81-439, 63 Stat. 1051 (codified as amended in scattered sections of 7 U.S.C.).

14. *See* M.C. Hallberg, Policy for American Agriculture: Choices and Consequences 30 (1992).

15. *See id.* For a concise history of federal farm program legislation, *see* Kristen Allen & Barbara J. Elliott, The Current Debate and Economic Rationale for U.S. Agricultural Policy, in U.S. Agriculture in a Global Setting: An Agenda for the Future 9 (M. Ann Tutwiler ed., 1988).

Each of the Farm Bills, back to the original Agricultural Adjustment Acts of 1933 and 1938, along with research links can be found on the Farm Bills page of the National Agricultural Law Center website at http://aglawcenter.org/farmbills.

Renée Johnson, Coordinator[*]
The 2008 Farm Bill: Major Provisions and Legislative Action
Congressional Research Service Report No. RL34696, 5–7
November 6, 2008

Brief Overview of Provisions

The enacted 2008 farm bill contains 15 titles covering support for commodity crops, horticulture and livestock production, conservation, nutrition, trade and food aid, agricultural research, farm credit, rural development, energy, forestry, and other related programs. It also includes tax-related provisions that make certain changes to tax laws in order to offset new spending initiatives in the rest of the bill. The 2008 farm bill replaces many of the provisions of the 2002 farm bill (P.L. 107–171) and guides most federal farm and food policies through 2012.

The 2008 farm bill includes five new titles that were not in the 2002 farm bill, covering horticulture and livestock products, crop insurance and disaster assistance, commodity futures, and various tax and trade provisions.

The 2008 Farm Bill: Titles and Respective Programs and Policies

- Title I, Commodities: Income support to growers of selected commodities, including wheat, feed grains, cotton, rice, oilseeds, peanuts, sugar, and dairy. Support is largely through direct payments, counter-cyclical payments, and marketing loans. Other support mechanisms include government purchases for dairy, and marketing quotas and import barriers for sugar.

- Title II, Conservation: Environmental stewardship of farmlands and improved management practices through land retirement and working lands programs, among other programs geared to farmland conservation, preservation, and resource protection.

- Title III, Agricultural Trade and Food Aid: U.S. agriculture export and international food assistance programs, and various World Trade Organization (WTO) obligations.

- Title IV, Nutrition: Domestic food and nutrition and commodity distribution programs, such as food stamps and supplemental nutrition assistance.

- Title V, Farm Credit: Federal direct and guaranteed farm loan programs. Also specifies loan eligibility rules and other policies.

- Title VI, Rural Development: Business and community programs for planning, feasibility assessments, and coordination activities with other local, state, and federal programs, including rural broadband access.

---

[*] Other authors of this report are Geoffrey S. Becker, Tom Capehart, Ralph M. Chite, Tadlock Cowan, Ross W. Gorte, Charles E. Hanrahan, Remy Jurenas, Jim Monke, Jean M. Rawson, Randy Schnepf Joe Richardson Donald J. Marples, Mark Jickling, and N. Eric Weiss.

- Title VII, Research: Agricultural research and extension programs, including biosecurity and response, biotechnology, and organic production.
- Title VIII, Forestry: USDA Forest Service programs, including forestry management, enhancement, and agroforestry programs.
- Title IX, Energy: Bioenergy programs and grants for procurement of biobased products to support development of biorefineries and assist eligible farmers, ranchers, and rural small businesses in purchasing renewable energy systems, as well as user education programs.
- Title X, Horticulture and Organic Agriculture: A new farm bill title covering fruits, vegetables, and specialty crops and organic agriculture.
- Title XI, Livestock: A new farm bill title covering livestock and poultry production, including provisions that amend existing laws governing livestock and poultry marketing and competition, country-of-origin labeling requirements for retailers, and meat and poultry state inspections, among other provisions.
- Title XII, Crop Insurance and Disaster Assistance: A new farm bill title covering crop insurance and assistance previously included in the miscellaneous title (not including the supplemental disaster assistance provisions in the Trade and Tax title).
- Title XIII, Commodity Futures: A new farm bill title covering reauthorization of the Commodity Futures Trading Commission (CFTC) and other changes to current law.
- Title XIV, Miscellaneous: Other types of farm programs and assistance not covered in other bill titles, including provisions to assist limited-resource and socially disadvantaged farmers, agricultural security, and other provisions.
- Title XV, Trade and Tax Provisions: A new title covering tax-related provisions intended to offset spending initiatives for some programs, including those in the nutrition, conservation, and energy titles. The title also contains other provisions, including the new supplemental disaster assistance and disaster relief trust fund.

For commodities (Title I), the enacted 2008 farm bill generally continues the framework of the 2002 farm bill, but with changes to program eligibility criteria and payment limitations, and adjustments to target prices and loan rates for some commodities, covering the 2008 through 2012 crop years. The bill creates a new Average Crop Revenue Election (ACRE) program beginning in crop year 2009. It also adds new provisions to address horticulture and livestock issues, and creates two new titles to address these sectors (Title X and Title XI). The bill provides mandatory funding for specialty crop block grants and adds new provisions supporting pest and disease programs, new funding for growth of farmers' markets and for transitioning producers to organic production, and price reporting and organic data collection, among other provisions. New animal agriculture provisions include changes to existing laws governing livestock and poultry marketing and competition, and changes in country-of-origin labeling requirements and meat and poultry inspections.

The nutrition title (Title IV) reauthorizes and increases funding for most farm bill authorized programs. It increases benefits and makes more households eligible under in the Food Stamp program, which the farm bill conferees have renamed the Supplemental Nutrition Assistance program. The 2008 farm bill also provides new spending to increase purchases of commodities for The Emergency Food Assistance Program (TEFAP), expands the Fresh Fruit and Vegetable program, and adds funding for the Senior Farmers' Market Nutrition program (SFMNP). The bills' international food aid and trade provisions (Title III) reauthorize funding for USDA's international food aid export market development, export credits, and export guarantees, and also address barriers to U.S. agriculture exports.

Under the conservation (Title II), energy (Title IX), rural development (Title VI), and forestry titles (Title VIII), the 2008 farm bill reauthorizes, expands, and modifies many existing programs, creates new programs and initiatives, and allows some programs to expire. The bill also reauthorizes, expands, and modifies many of the existing provisions under the research title (Title VII) by requiring the reorganization of USDA's research, extension, and economic agencies.

The 2008 farm bill expands borrowing opportunities under USDA's Farm Service Agency loan program (Title V). It also creates a new farm bill title to modify crop insurance (Title XII), which provides significant savings to offset the cost of new spending in other parts of the bill. Provisions in the bill also provide ongoing disaster assistance (Title XV) and address agricultural security and animal quarantine inspections (Title XIV).

The bill includes revenue and offsetting cost provisions that are outside the jurisdiction of the agriculture committees. These provisions make certain changes to tax laws that are intended to offset additional spending in the farm bill, and were added by both chambers to comply with current pay-go budget rules (Title XV). The 2008 farm bill also includes the reauthorization of and modifications to the Commodity Futures Trading Commission (CFTC)....

---

2. USDA Implementation of the Farm Bill

The Farm Bill designates significant authority to the Secretary of Agriculture for rule-making and implementation of the federal farm programs. The economic support programs are primarily administered through the Farm Service Agency (FSA), under the supervision of the Under Secretary of Farm and Foreign Agricultural Services. Conservation programs will also involve the Natural Resources Conservation Service (NRCS), under the supervision of the Under Secretary for Natural Resources and the Environment. Regulations are promulgated under typical administrative law procedures, i.e., published in the Federal Register and then in the Code of Federal Regulations. Administrative interpretations, however, are set forth in detailed and extensive agency handbooks.

Note that farm programs depend upon the voluntary participation of the farmer. Although economically, farmers may have a great incentive to participate, an individual farmer is never required to do so. The voluntary decision to participate in a specific program, however, will bind the farmer to specific statutory and regulatory requirements that are imposed as conditions to participation. Participation is evidenced by a written contract signed by the farmer that recites the primary obligations of the farmer and the government and incorporates by reference the regulations governing the particular program. The terms of the contract are not negotiated by the parties but are standardized for each program.

a. The Farm Service Agency

Although regulations and overall administrative policy formation is done by Farm Service Agency officials in Washington, D.C., the implementation of the FSA programs is

---

Source of Law and Implementation Guidance

The statutory authority for the Agricultural Commodity Support Programs, as enacted under the *Food, Conservation, and Energy Act of 2008,* Pub. L. 110-246, 122 Stat. 1651 (2008) can be found at 7 U.S.C. ch 113, §§ 8701–8793.

The regulations implementing these programs are found at 7 C.F.R. pt. 1400 (2010).

The USDA Handbooks that contain the agency's interpretations of the regulations are available online on the USDA FSA website under the heading "Laws and Regulations." *See* http://www.fsa. usda.gov.

Note that some of the Handbook provisions may differ from the actual regulatory language. The federal courts have ruled that the provisions contained in the USDA Handbooks do not have the force and effect of law, as they are not promulgated as legislative rules under the Administrative Procedure Act (APA). *See* 5 U.S.C. § 553.

Nevertheless, FSA often treats the Handbook provisions as if they were legally binding rules. The courts are inclined to treat the provisions as interpretive rather than legislative, and to then defer to the agency's interpretation. *See* Christopher R. Kelley, *Recent Developments in Federal Farm Program Litigation,* 25 U. Mem. L. Rev. 1107, 1117–18 (1995).

---

the responsibility of field offices based in states and counties. There are more than 2,346 state and county FSA offices in the 48 continental states, with FSA representation as well in Hawaii and Puerto Rico. State offices are managed by a State Executive Director (SED) who presides over the State Committee. Each county office has a County Executive Director (CED) who presides over an elected Farmer County Committee (FCC).

> Committee members are the local authorities responsible for fairly and equitably resolving local issues while remaining dually and directly accountable to the Secretary of Agriculture and local producers though the elective process. They operate within official regulations designed to carry out Federal laws and provide a necessary and important voice in Federal decisions affecting their counties and communities.

> Committee members make decisions affecting which FSA programs are implemented county-wide, the establishment of allotment and yields, commodity price support loans and payments, conservation programs, incentive, indemnity, and disaster payments for commodities, and other farm disaster assistance.

USDA FSA website, *About FSA—Structure and Organization,* available at http://www.fsa. usda.gov/; *see also,* 7 C.F.R. pt. 7 (2010).

b. The Commodity Credit Corporation

The Commodity Credit Corporation (CCC) also has a role in the implementation of the federal farm programs.

> The CCC is a federally chartered corporation that acts as "an agency and instrumentality of the United States, within the Department of Agriculture, sub-

ject to the general supervision and direction of the Secretary of Agriculture."[28] The CCC is used by the Secretary to carry out the congressionally authorized farm commodity and related land use programs.[29] Specifically, a primary function of the CCC has been to fund the federal commodity and related land use programs. Thus, "the CCC has functioned as the fiscal agency of the U.S. government for commodity and other farm programs since its inception in 1933."[30] As more prosaicly [sic] described by the United States Supreme Court, the CCC "is simply an administrative device established by Congress for the purpose of carrying out federal farm programs with federal funds."[31]

In addition to its function as a fiscal agent, the CCC has been given a variety of specific powers including the authority to "[m]ake available materials and facilities required in connection with the production and marketing of agricultural commodities,"[32] to "procure agricultural commodities for sale,"[33] and to "remove and dispose of … surplus agricultural commodities."[34] These powers are intended to facilitate the Secretary's use of the CCC in carrying out the federal commodity and related land use programs.[35]

Christopher R. Kelley and John S. Harbison, *A Guide to the ASCS Administrative Appeal Process and to the Judicial Review of ASCS Decisions*, 36 S.D. L. Rev. 14, 20–21 (1991). Note that the FSA was previously named the Agricultural Stabilization and Conservation Service (ASCS).

The CCC has no operating personnel. Its price support, storage, and reserve programs, and its domestic acquisition and disposal activities are carried out primarily through the personnel and facilities of the Farm Service Agency (FSA).

---

28. 15 U.S.C. §714.… 15 U.S.C. §714g; *see also* W. Cochrane & M. Ryan, American Farm Policy, 1948–1973 121–27 (1976) [hereinafter Cochrane & Ryan] (explaining the functions and activities of the CCC, including the functions and activities of its board) … All of the officers of the CCC are employees of the USDA. *See Rainwater v. United States*, 356 U.S. 590, 591 (1958).

29. *See* H. Pickard, *Price and Income Adjustment Programs*, I Agricultural Law § 1.23, at 43 (J. Davidson, ed. 1981) [hereinafter Pickard] (noting that "[t]he secretary of agriculture is required to provide the price support authorized or mandated by law through the Commodity Credit Corporation and other means available to him") (citing 7 U.S.C. § 1421(a) (1982); 7 U.S.C. § 1782(a) (1982 & Supp. 1987)); *see also* 7 U.S.C. § 1424 (1982) (providing that the "Secretary … may utilize the services and facilities of the Commodity Credit Corporation").

30. Cochrane & Ryan, *supra* note 28, at 123. The CCC's financing of farm programs is accomplished through a combination of direct appropriations and borrowing. *See* 15 U.S.C. §714b(i); Linden, *An Overview of the Commodity Credit Corporation and the Procedures and Risks of Litigating Against It*, 11 J. Agric. Tax'n & L. 305, 308 (1990).

31. *Rainwater*, 356 U.S. at 592. Some might quarrel with such a summary description of the CCC's activities. For example, consider the following description:

In reality the CCC plays the role of an army general headquarters with an almost limitless budget in the operation of farm programs. It is here that information regarding new demand and supply developments is received; it is here that plans are discussed and decisions made to cope with those demand-supply developments within the terms of the existing legislation; and it is here that funds are dispensed to implement the program and actions decided upon.

Cochrane & Ryan, *supra* note 28, at 123; *see also* 15 U.S.C. §714c (setting forth the specific powers of the CCC); Pickard, *supra* note 29, at § 1.23 (describing the role of the CCC in the administration of federal farm programs); Linden, supra note [30], at 306–09 (describing the functions of the CCC); *Gibson v. U.S.*, 11 Cl. Ct.6, 7 (describing the functions of the CCC under the 1983 "Payment-In-Kind" (PIK) program).

32. 15 U.S.C. §714c(b).

33. 15 U.S.C. §714c(c).

34. 15 U.S.C. §714c(d).

35. *See Gibson*, 11 Cl. Ct. at 7.

The USDA describes the CCC mission as "to stabilize, support, and protect farm income and prices" … and to help "maintain balanced and adequate supplies of agricultural commodities and aid[] in their orderly distribution."

> The CCC is managed by a Board of Directors, subject to the general supervision and direction of the Secretary of Agriculture, who is an ex-officio director and chairperson of the Board. The Board consists of seven members, in addition to the Secretary, who are appointed by the President of the United States by and with the advice and consent of the Senate. All members of the Board and Corporation officers are USDA officials.

USDA FSA website, *About the Commodity Credit Corporation*, available at http://www.fsa.usda.gov; *see also*, 7 C.F.R. ch. XIV (2010).

c. The National Appeals Division

"Adverse decisions" that are made by FSA or another USDA agency that affect a farmer who participates in one of the USDA programs, such as the denial of program benefits, are appealable to another USDA agency, the National Appeals Division.

Karen R. Krub

USDA's National Appeals Division Procedures and Practice

National Agricultural Law Center (2003) available at
http://www.nationalaglawcenter.org/assets/articles/krub_nad.pdf

The National Appeals Division (NAD) of the United States Department of Agriculture (USDA) was established in late 1994[1] in the wake of a broader USDA reorganization mandated by the Federal Crop Insurance Reform and Department of Agriculture Reorganization Act of 1994.[2] NAD was assigned responsibility for program participant appeals of adverse decisions by certain agencies and offices within USDA, as assigned by the Secretary.

NAD is an organization within USDA that is formally independent from all other agencies and offices of the Department, including USDA officials at the state and local level.[3] This is a significant change from USDA's pre-NAD appeals systems, in which a disputed agency decision would be reviewed by an employee of the same agency, often a peer or supervisor of the original decisionmaker. In contrast, NAD is organizationally housed within USDA's Office of the Secretary and is therefore formally independent of other USDA agencies, including those whose decisions it reviews.[4] However, NAD remains subject to the general supervision of and policy direction by the Secretary of Agriculture.[5] The NAD Director is appointed by and reports directly to the Secretary of Agriculture, whose authority over NAD may not be delegated to any other USDA officer or employee.[6] …

---

1. *See* 59 Fed. Reg. 66,517, 66,518 (1994) (notice of department reorganization).
2. Pub. L. No. 103-354, tit. II, subtit. H, §§ 271–283, 108 Stat. 3178, 3228–3235 (codified at 7 U.S.C. §§ 6991–7002).
3. 7 C.F.R. § 11.2 (2003).
4. 7 U.S.C. § 6992(a); 7 C.F.R. § 11.2 (2003).
5. 7 U.S.C. § 6992(a), (c); 7 C.F.R. § 11.2 (2003).
6. 7 U.S.C. § 6992(b)(1), (c); 7 C.F.R. § 11.2 (2003). The NAD Director serves for a six-year term and may be removed only for cause. 7 U.S.C. § 6992(b)(2). The NAD Director cannot be a political appointee or noncareer employee. *Id.* § 6992(b)(3).

[The] NAD appeal process begins when a USDA program participant requests an appeal of an "adverse decision" issued by one of the USDA agencies whose program determinations are appealable to NAD. For some adverse decisions, the participant must first seek "informal review" by the deciding agency before appealing to NAD. In other cases, informal review and/or mediation are optional steps that a participant may pursue before requesting an appeal. After the appeal request is filed, a date will be set for an in-person evidentiary hearing before a NAD hearing officer. Shortly before this date, the hearing officer and the parties will have a prehearing conference, usually on the telephone.

Depending on the outcome of the hearing, either the participant or the agency may ask the NAD Director to perform a record review of the hearing officer's determination. If neither party requests Director review, the hearing officer's determination becomes the final administrative decision.

Final NAD determinations are subject to review in the federal district courts. A program participant who receives an unfavorable final NAD determination can also ask the Secretary of Agriculture to review that determination before or instead of seeking judicial review. A program participant may also seek review by the NAD Director of an agency determination that a particular adverse decision is not appealable....

***

Notes

1. After completing the NAD process, farmers may seek judicial review of an FSA decision that affected their rights under a farm program.

Judicial review is available in the federal district courts. 7 U.S.C. § 6999; *Deaf Smith County Grain Processors, Inc. v. Glickman*, 162 F.3d 1206 (D.C. Cir. 1998); *Farmers & Merchants Bank of Eaton, Georgia v. United States*, 43 Fed. Cl. 38 (1999). The judicial review provisions of the Administrative Procedure Act apply.

By statute, the USDA NAD appeal process must be completed before judicial review is available. 7 U.S.C. § 6912(e). This statutory exhaustion of administrative remedies requirement also applies to matters that are subject to a determination by the NAD Director as to whether they are appealable to NAD. In other words, the Director must determine that a matter is not appealable to NAD before such a matter may be presented for judicial review. *See Bastek v. Federal Crop Ins. Corp.*, 145 F.3d 90 (2d Cir. 1998). The Fourth Circuit, however, has permitted a facial challenge to a regulation to proceed in the absence of a Director's determination as to whether the challenge was appealable to NAD. *See Gold Dollar Warehouse, Inc. v. Glickman*, 211 F.3d 93 (4th Cir. 2000). In *McBride Cotton and Cattle Corp. v. Veneman*, 290 F.3d 973, 980–81 (9th Cir. 2002), the court ruled that the statute's exhaustion requirement was not jurisdictional, but courts should require compliance with it unless the suit alleges a constitutional claim which is "(1) collateral to a substantive claim of entitlement, (2) colorable, and (3) 'one whose resolution would not serve the purposes of exhaustion.'" (citations omitted).

Christopher R. Kelley, *The USDA National Appeals Division: An Outline of the Rules of Procedure* (Feb 2003), available at http://nationalaglawcenter.org/research/#nadoutline.

See also, Karen R. Krub, *USDA's National Appeals Division Procedures and Practice* (May 2003) available at http://www.nationalaglawcenter.org/assets/articles/krub_nad.pdf.

2. The articles referenced above were written prior to a change in the NAD regulations regarding the availability of attorneys fees under the Equal Access to Justice Act (EAJA). On November 6, 2009, the USDA published a final rule amending its regulations to allow for EAJA fees. Its explanation in the prefatory comments are as follows:

> Prior to publication of this final rule, the position of USDA was that EAJA (5 U.S.C. 504) and the provisions of the APA applicable to formal adjudicative proceedings (5 U.S.C. 554–557) did not apply to NAD proceedings except where required by judicial ruling. See 64 FR 33367, 33368 (June 23, 1999). At that time, only one U.S. Circuit Court of Appeals — the 8th — had issued a decision holding that EAJA applies to NAD proceedings. *See Lane v. USDA*, 120 F.3d 106 (8th Cir. 1997).

> Since then, the 7th and 9th Circuits also have issued decisions holding that EAJA applies to NAD proceedings. *See Five Points Rd. Joint Venture v. Johanns*, 542 F.3d 1121 (7th Cir. 2008); *Aageson Grain & Cattle v. USDA*, 500 F.3d 1038 (9th Cir. 2007). Additionally, on May 1, 2009, a U.S. District Court in the 5th Circuit entered a decision following the 7th, 8th, and 9th Circuits. *See Rosenbaum v. USDA*, No. 07–02808 (S.D. Tex. May 1, 2009) (final judgment).

> In light of the decisions in these four Circuits, USDA is no longer maintaining the position that the APA and EAJA do not apply to NAD proceedings except where required by judicial ruling. Effective immediately, EAJA and USDA's implementing regulations at 7 CFR part 1, subpart J, will apply universally to NAD proceedings regardless of the judicial Circuit in which the proceeding arises. While the four decisions cited above addressed only the issue of whether EAJA applies to NAD proceedings, the applicability of EAJA is derivative of the applicability of the APA and thus, by extension, the court rulings apply to the applicability of the APA as well. Therefore, the provisions of the APA generally applicable to agency adjudications (5 U.S.C. 554–557) also will apply generally to NAD proceedings regardless of the judicial Circuit in which the proceeding arises. However, it is the position of USDA that the applicability of the APA does not require any changes to existing NAD administrative procedures.

> This final rule applies to proceedings conducted under 7 CFR part 11, except for proceedings under § 11.5 (USDA agency informal reviews of adverse decisions) and § 11.6(a) (NAD Director reviews of USDA agency determinations of appealability).

74 Fed. Reg. 57,401 (Nov. 6, 2009) (codified at 7 C.F.R. § 11.4).

3. The Price and Income Support Programs Under the 2008 Farm Bill

Federal farm programs, excluding the crop and revenue insurance programs can be divided into categories roughly based on the underlying goal of the program. First, there are programs that provide direct or "fixed" payments based on historical cropping patterns and not linked to the operator's current production. These programs seek to provide consistent income support to program participants. Second, there are programs that provide payments dependent on market prices for enrolled commodities. These programs assist producers when commodity prices are low. These first two categories of programs are considered to be price and income support programs.

In addition, there are conservation programs that pay farmers for undertaking conservation or environmental clean-up actions. These programs and the "green payments" they provide are not included in this chapter's consideration but are discussed in Chapter III, *Agriculture and Environmental Law.*

The federal crop insurance program provides subsidized crop insurance to producers of many crops. And, there are emergency and disaster relief programs provided previously through frequent ad hoc special legislation, but now also available through a permanent disaster program. These programs are summarized in the discussion of *Crop Insurance and Disaster Assistance, infra,* sections B and C of this chapter.

There are also a number of special programs tailored to the needs of producers of certain distinctive products. These include the milk support program, the peanut and tobacco buy out programs, the sugar program, and a variety of small specialty programs. These programs are not covered herein, but analysis is available through the USDA Economic Research Service website, http://www.ers.usda.gov/ and program information for producers is found on the USDA Farm Service Agency website at http://www.fsa.usda.gov/. Informative Congressional Research Service (CRS) Reports can be found on the website of the National Agricultural Law Center at http://nationalaglawcenter.org/crs/. And, the Government Accountability Office (GAO) provides critical analysis in their reports, available at http://www.gao.gov.

Jim Monke
Farm Commodity Programs in the 2008 Farm Bill
Congressional Research Service No. RL-34594, 3–13, 20–26
September 30, 2008

Eligible Commodities

Federal support exists for about two dozen farm commodities representing nearly one-third of gross farm sales. Five crops (corn, cotton, wheat, rice, and soybeans) account for about 90% of these payments. About 66% of the payments go to 10% of recipients.

- The **"covered commodities"** are the primary crops eligible for support: wheat, corn, grain sorghum, barley, oats, upland cotton, rice, pulse crops (dry peas, lentils, small chickpeas, and large chickpeas), soybeans, and other oilseeds (including sunflower seed, rapeseed, canola, safflower, flaxseed, mustard seed, crambe, and sesame seed). Peanuts are supported similarly. Farmers receive constant "direct payments" tied to historical production (except pulse crops do not receive direct payments despite being a covered commodity). Farmers may also receive "counter-cyclical" and "marketing loan" payments that increase when market prices (or, in some cases, revenue) are low.

- **"Loan commodities"** include all of the "covered commodities" plus extra long staple cotton, wool, mohair, and honey. These commodities are eligible for the marketing loan program only.

- Dairy prices are indirectly supported through federal purchases of nonfat dry milk, butter, and cheese. Producers also receive a counter-cyclical "milk income loss contract" (MILC) payment when prices fall below a target price. *See* CRS Report RL34036, *Dairy Policy and the 2008 Farm Bill,* by Ralph M. Chite.

- Sugar support is indirect through import quotas and domestic marketing allotments. No direct payments are made to growers and processors. See CRS Report RL34103, *Sugar Policy and the 2008 Farm Bill, by Remy Jurenas.*

Meats, poultry, fruits, vegetables, nuts, hay, and nursery products (about two-thirds of farm sales) do not receive direct support or payments in the commodity title of the farm bill.

Eligible Producers

The 2008 farm bill defines a producer (for purposes of farm program benefits) as an owner operator, landlord, tenant, or sharecropper that shares in the risk of producing a crop and is entitled to a share of the crop produced on the farm. In addition, an individual must comply with certain conservation and planting flexibility rules. A term commonly used in federal regulations is "actively engaged in farming," which generally means providing significant contributions of capital (land or equipment) and labor and/or management, and receiving a share of the crop as compensation. Conservation rules include protecting wetlands, preventing erosion, and controlling weeds. Planting flexibility rules allow crops other than the program crop to be grown, but generally prohibit planting fruits or vegetables on subsidized acreage.

Modern farming enterprises usually involve some combination of owned and rented land. Two types of rental arrangements are common: cash rent and share rent.

- Under cash rental contracts, the tenant pays a fixed cash rent to the landlord. The landlord receives the same rent, bears no risk in production, and thus is not eligible to receive program payments. The tenant bears all of the risk, takes all of the harvest, and receives all of the government subsidy.

- Under share rental contracts, the tenant usually supplies most of the labor and machinery, while the landlord supplies land and perhaps some machinery or management. Both the landlord and tenant bear risk in producing a crop and receive a portion of the harvest.[5] Both are eligible to share in the government subsidy.

Even though tenants might receive all of the government payments under cash rent arrangements, they might not keep all of the benefits if landlords demand higher rent. Economists widely agree that a large portion of government farm payments passes through to landlords, and that government payments raise the price of land. About 60% of acres enrolled in the government commodity programs are rented.[6]

Farm Commodity Program Provisions

The farm commodity price and income support provisions in the 2008 farm bill include three primary types of payments:

- **Direct payments** unrelated to production or prices;
- **Counter-cyclical payments** which are triggered when
    (a) prices are below statutorily-determined target prices, or
    (b) revenue for a commodity falls below a historical guaranteed level, and

---

5. For example, a typical share rental arrangement in some regions is a 50–50 split of the crop harvested, with the landlord supplying all of the land and half of the cost of certain inputs such as fertilizer. The tenant supplies all of the labor and pays the remaining share of the input costs. Management decisions, such as crop diversification, are usually made jointly.

6. M. Burfisher and J. Hopkins, "Farm Payments," *Amber Waves,* USDA Economic Research Service, Feb. 2003.

- **Marketing assistance loans** that offer interim financing and, if prices fall below loan prices set in statute, additional income support, sometimes paid as **loan deficiency payments (LDP)**.

The first two types of payments are subject to payment limits on the size of payments. All three types of payments may be subject to income eligibility limits, depending on the size of farm and non-farm income.

The 2008 farm bill generally continues the farm commodity price and income support framework of the 2002 farm bill, with modifications. It continues the direct payment, counter-cyclical payment, and marketing loan programs for the 2008–2012 crop years, but adjusts target prices and loan rates for some commodities. The law also creates a pilot revenue-based counter-cyclical program ("ACRE") beginning with the 2009 crop year. It revises payment limitations by tightening some limits and relaxing others. The new law also has a pilot program for planting flexibility, new restrictions on base acres developed for residential use, and elimination of benefits to farms with fewer than 10 acres of program crops. For the 2008 crop year, the programs are essentially unchanged from the 2002 farm bill....

An important consideration for the farm commodity programs is how they are classified for trade purposes. As a member of the World Trade Organization (WTO), the United States made agricultural policy commitments under the WTOs Agreement on Agriculture. All WTO members agree to submit annual notifications of their farm program outlays to the WTO, and these outlays are subject to specific limits. For the United States, its total spending limit for programs that are considered to be trade distorting is $19.1 billion per year. Other types of payments are not subject to limits if they are "decoupled" or not considered to be trade distorting.

Direct Payments

Direct payments (DP) are fixed annual payments based on historical production; they do not vary with current market prices or yields. Recent high commodity prices and high farm incomes have made it difficult for some to justify the annual outlays for direct payments, which amount to $5 billion per year. Eligible commodities include wheat, corn, grain sorghum, barley, oats, upland cotton, rice, peanuts, soybeans, and other oilseeds (including sunflower seed, rapeseed, canola, safflower, flaxseed, mustard seed, crambe, and sesame seed).

A farm is eligible for direct payments in proportion to its "base acres" (which are a constant historical average of its planting history of a particular commodity). For many farms, base acres date to the 1980s, but for some farms base acres were updated in 2002. In addition to its base acreage, each farm has a "direct payment yield" for each commodity, which is also an unchanging historical average based on the farms actual yields over the 1981–1985 period.

A farmer is not obligated to grow the covered commodity to receive a direct payment for that commodity (e.g., a farm may plant soybeans on corn base acres, and receive the direct payment for corn). The rationale for this planting flexibility is to allow farmers to respond to market signals when choosing crops.

Because direct payments are constant and allow planting flexibility, they are arguably less distorting of production than prior farm programs that had greater government intervention.[7] Direct payments thus are thus known as "decoupled payments, and the United

---

7. Before planting flexibility was introduced in the early 1990s, farmers were required to grow the commodity for which they had base acres in order to participate in the government program. To con-

States has classified them as "green box" when reporting agricultural subsidies to the WTO. Green box payments help countries comply with international trade agreements because they do not count against subsidy ceilings.[8]

However, because the planting flexibility rules still have restrictions on planting fruits and vegetables (discussed later in this report), the direct payment program may be subject to challenge as to whether it qualifies as a green box payment.[9] This challenge was raised during the 2008 farm bill debate as a reason to revise the direct payment program or allow complete planting flexibility, but the program was not changed.

In the 2008 farm bill, the direct payment rates per commodity remain the same as in the 2002 farm bill..., but the overall formula to compute the payment contains a 2% reduction in direct payments for crop years 2009–2011. Conferees accomplished this by changing the ratio of base acres on which direct payments are made from 85% to 83.3%.[10] The 85% ratio is restored for the 2012 crop year to maintain a higher baseline for the next farm bill.

The law eliminates advance direct payments beginning in the 2012 crop year. This delays advance payment of 22% of the direct payment from the December before most crops are planted to the following October at or after harvest, and thus into a new fiscal year.[11] This scores budget savings of about $1.1 billion in FY2012. Although farmers will have to wait longer, they will receive their full payment.

Participants in the new ACRE counter-cyclical program will continue to receive direct payments, but their direct payment amount will be reduced by 20% as required by the 2008 farm bill.

Counter-Cyclical Payments

The traditional counter-cyclical payment (CCP) program makes automatic payments when market prices fall below target prices set in statute.[12] Historically, the farm commodity programs have focused on price, but producers have cited insufficient government support during years with natural disasters when yields are low and prices are high. In those years, they have little to sell and thus do not benefit from high market prices, but do not receive counter-cyclical support either. In response to this criticism, the 2008 farm bill creates a revenue-based counter-cyclical program called the Average Crop Revenue Election (ACRE). The ACRE program is an alternative to the traditional price counter-cyclical program, and

---

trol production when surpluses existed, the government often required farmers to "set aside," or not plant, part of their base acreage.

8. For a brief discussion about WTO procedures for classifying government support programs, see CRS Report RS20840, *Agriculture in the WTO: Limits on Domestic Support*, by Randy Schnepf.

9. In 2007, Canada and Brazil initiated WTO cases against the U.S. farm programs, charging that direct payments are inappropriately classified in the green box. See CRS Report RL34351, *Brazil's and Canada's WTO Cases Against U.S. Agricultural Support*, by Randy Schnepf.

10. The reduction in payment acres to 83.3% does not affect the counter-cyclical payment formula, but the lower percentage is used for planted acreage in the ACRE program.

11. For example, without the provision eliminating advance payments, an advance direct payment for crop year 2012 would have been paid in December 2011 (FY2012). With advance payments eliminated, farmers will need to wait until October 2012 (FY2013). This pattern continues thereafter, rolling advance direct payment amounts into later fiscal years.

12. This type of price support was first implemented in 1973 as the "deficiency payment," but was discontinued in the1996 farm bill. The 2002 farm bill reinstated counter-cyclical payments for wheat, feed grains, rice, and upland cotton and extended them to soybeans, other oilseeds, and peanuts. Dairy also has a direct counter-cyclical payment created in 2002 — the milk income loss contract (MILC) — but with a different payment mechanism.

is based on statewide cropspecific revenue data. ACRE makes payments when actual revenues from a commodity are less than a market-based, moving average revenue guarantee.

Eligible commodities for either counter-cyclical option include the covered commodities for the direct payment program (wheat, corn, grain sorghum, barley, oats, upland cotton, rice, peanuts, soybeans, and other oilseeds), plus four new pulse crops beginning in 2009 (dry peas, lentils, small chickpeas, and large chickpeas).

Traditional Counter-Cyclical Payments (CCP)

Traditional counter-cyclical payments compensate for the difference between a crop's target price and a lower effective market price.[13] When effective market prices exceed the target price, no payment is made.

As with direct payments, traditional counter-cyclical payments are proportional to a farm's base acres and "counter-cyclical payment yield," and do not depend on current production. Although the counter-cyclical program payment rate formula depends on market prices, it does not require the farmer to produce any of the commodity. Thus it is partially decoupled; it is decoupled from yield and acreage, but not from market prices. The United States has classified them as "amber box" when reporting agricultural subsidies to the WTO, and thus they are limited in size together with other amber box subsidies.

The 2008 farm bill continues the traditional price counter-cyclical program, although it adjusts target prices and adds new commodities. Six out of 10 ongoing commodities receive a target price increase (wheat, sorghum, barley, oats, soybeans, and minor oilseeds), one has a small decrease (cotton), three are unchanged (corn, rice, and peanuts), and four are new in 2009 (dry peas, lentils, small chickpeas, and large chickpeas).

Some commodity groups argued that their support levels were not high enough relative to other commodities in the 2002 farm bill (e.g., wheat and soybeans).

The decrease in the cotton target price is the only change in the 2008 crop year. The new crops are added in the 2009 crop year. None of the target price increases occur until the 2010 crop year.

The 2008 farm bill generally makes counter-cyclical payments after the October 1 that falls after the end of the marketing year[14] and eliminates advance counter-cyclical payments beginning with the 2011 crop year, both of which help score budget savings by delaying some payments compared to the 2002 farm bill.

Participants in ACRE are ineligible for traditional counter-cyclical payments.

Average Crop Revenue Election (ACRE)

Beginning with the 2009 crop year, farmers may choose either the traditional CCP or the new revenue-based ACRE option. Participants in ACRE will continue to receive

---

13. The effective price is the higher of (a) the national season-average market price or (b) the national loan rate, plus the direct payment rate. By adding the direct payment rate, the formula recognizes that farmers receive direct payments and avoids paying them more than the target price. The CCP compensates for lower market prices down to the loan rate, below which the marketing loan program supports.

14. A "marketing year" is the 12-month period after a commodity is harvested. A "crop year" refers to the calendar year in which a commodity is harvested. For example, corn harvested in the fall of 2008 is in the 2008 crop year. The marketing year for the 2008 crop of corn begins in October 2008 and continues until September 2009.

direct payments, but at a 20% reduced rate. Participants will also continue to be eligible for nonrecourse marketing loans, but with a 30% lower loan rate. Producers who choose ACRE (whether in 2009, 2010, 2011, or 2012) may not revert to the traditional CCP for the remainder of the farm bill. The ACRE program is available for the same crops as traditional counter-cyclical payments, but is based on planted acres rather than base acres.[15]

If market prices are expected to be high, ACRE might be preferred by many farmers because the traditional counter-cyclical payments would be zero or small. Even under high prices, ACRE may help farmers manage downside systemic risks — that is, manage the risks that are inherent in the market and cannot be diversified away. And, as market price falls, ACRE may make payments when traditional counter-cyclical programs would not. ACRE is expected to perform better than traditional counter-cyclical programs under high-price environments, in states with larger yield increase since the 1980s, in states with more variable yields, and in states that are outside the primary growing regions of a particular commodity.[16]

To receive an ACRE payment, two triggers need to be met:

- First, the actual state revenue for a supported crop during the crop year must be less than the state-level revenue guarantee amount.

- Second, an individual farm's actual revenue for a supported crop must be less than the farm's benchmark revenue.

The second trigger keeps farms from receiving payments when they did not have a sufficient loss, even if the state as a whole sustained a loss in revenue for the crop.

The state-level revenue guarantee amount and the individual farm benchmark revenue are determined by the product of a guaranteed price with a guaranteed level of production. Benchmark or guaranteed yields at the state and farm levels are Olympic averages of the most recent five years.[17] Price guarantees are averages of the higher of (a) the marketing year price or (b) the marketing loan rate as reduced under ACRE for the most recent two years. The revenue guarantee is 90% of the product of the average benchmark yield and the price guarantee. The 10% reduction allows for some variation in revenue before subsidy payments begin (similar to a deductible). Changes in the revenue guarantee are limited to plus or minus 10% from the previous year.

If both triggers are met, an individual farm will receive an ACRE payment that is based on the state-level difference between actual revenue and the ACRE guarantee per acre, multiplied by a percentage (83.3% in crop years 2009–2011, or 85% in crop year 2012) of the farm's planted acreage, but pro-rated based on the individual farm's yield history compared to the state's yield history. The maximum payment rate is 25% of the ACRE guarantee....

---

15. The total number of planted acres enrolled in ACRE cannot exceed the total number of base acres for all covered commodities on a farm.

16. Carl Zulauf, "Understanding ACRE: Breakeven Price With Traditional Programs, Corn Soybeans, Wheat," The Ohio State University, Department of Agricultural, Environmental, and Development Economics, AEDE-RP-0109-08, June 2008, 1 p., [http://aede.osu.edu/resources/docs/pdf/wegfsz 4y-ag7a-vxx7-j003psoreuml1a3f.pdf].

17. Olympic averages are averages computed after deleting the highest and lowest observations. Thus, an Olympic average over a five year period is an average of three data points, after deleting the highest and lowest observations during the five-year period.

New ACRE Program

Farmers can enroll in the new ACRE (Average Crop Revenue Election) Program as an alternative to the Counter-Cyclical Program (CCP). ACRE provides participating producers a *revenue guarantee* each year based on market prices and average yields for the respective commodities.

ACRE participants must enroll all covered commodities for a participating farm. Upon enrollment, the farm is enrolled for the remainder of the 2008 Farm Act, which ends with crop year 2012. Enrollment will reduce direct payments to 80 percent of the legislated direct payment rate, and marketing loan benefits will be reduced to 70 percent of the legislated national marketing loan rate.

The ACRE revenue guarantee is based on State-level planted yields and national market prices. ACRE payments can be triggered by a decrease in national average market prices or State planted yields.

See, Average Crop Revenue Election (ACRE), USDA, Economic Research Service, Briefing Room: Farm and Commodity Program Provisions, available at http://ers.usda.gov/Briefing/farmpolicy/acre.htm.

Marketing Loans and Loan Deficiency Payments

Marketing loans are nonrecourse loans[22] that farmers can obtain by pledging their harvested commodities as collateral. Traditionally, the loans provide interim financing by allowing farmers to receive some revenue for their crop when the loan is requested, while at the same time storing the commodity for later disposition when prices may be higher.[23] As an alternative to taking out a loan, the loan deficiency payment (LDP) is a cash payment option that allows farmers to sell grain in response to market signals without putting their commodity under loan, while receiving the price benefits of the loan program.

Marketing loans provide minimum price guarantees on the crop actually produced, unlike direct or counter-cyclical payments, which are tied to historical bases. They are not decoupled as they depend both on current production and market prices. The United States has classified them as "amber box" when reporting agricultural subsidies to the WTO.

National-level loan prices are set by the farm bill and are negotiated in the legislative process, rather than established based on formulas using historical market prices as was

---

22. "Nonrecourse" means that the collateral can be forfeited at the end of the term with no penalty. The government takes no recourse against the borrower beyond accepting the commodity as full settlement of the loan, even if the market price of the commodity is less than the loan.

23. The marketing loan program allows farmers to pay creditors with money from the USDA loan and not make marketing decisions based on the immediate need to pay creditors. Without the loan program, farmers sometimes would need to sell their crop at low harvest prices to pay operating expenses, and not be able to benefit from a cyclical rise in market prices. Market prices of covered commodities within a marketing year usually follow a predictable pattern. They are often lowest at harvest when a surge of new supply floods the market, and grain not stored on the farm is delivered to elevators. As the marketing year progresses, prices gradually rise to compensate for storing the commodity and to draw the commodity out of storage in response to new demand.

done in farm bills before 1990. USDA adjusts the national average loan rate to local (usually county) loan rates to reflect spatial difference in markets and transportation.[24]

Commodities eligible for marketing loans include all of the commodities that are eligible for direct and counter-cyclical payments, plus extra long staple (ELS) cotton, wool, mohair, and honey. However, ELS cotton is not eligible for loan deficiency payments. Sugar receives assistance through commodity loans, but under a separate provision with unrelated procedures. The 2008 farm bill continues the nonrecourse marketing loan program under the same framework as in the previous farm bill. The 2008 farm bill increases the loan rate for eight out of 20 commodities (wheat, barley, oats, minor oilseeds, graded wool, honey, cane sugar, beet sugar), decreases the loan rate for two commodities (dry peas, lentils), and adds one new pulse crop beginning with the 2009 crop year (large chickpeas).

Loan rates for the 2008 crop year are the same as under the 2002 farm bill. Increases in loan rates do not occur until the 2010 crop year, while changes for the pulse crops occur in the 2009 crop year.

Participants in the ACRE counter-cyclical program continue to be eligible for marketing loans and LDPs, but loan rates will be reduced by 30% as required in the farm bill.

Beneficial Interest

Beneficial interest generally refers to owning the commodity or having a stake in its disposition. Beneficial interest is lost when the commodity is sold. The [Bush]Administration had recommended that the farm bill change the "beneficial interest" rule,[25] but Congress did not change it. The rule allows farmers to lock in their LDP when market prices are low (usually at harvest), continue to own the commodity, and sell it at a future and possibly higher market price than when the LDP was determined. Policy makers said they wanted farmers to continue to have the flexibility to market their commodities in response to market signals and benefit from the program.

Advocates for change pointed out that if farmers can sell their crop for more than the support price, then government support should be unnecessary. More generally, if farmers can sell their crop for more than the market price at the time that the LDP was determined, the LDP would not need to be as large. These advocates for change wanted the determination of the LDP to be tied to when a farmer loses beneficial interest. Although the beneficial interest rules remain the same, the loan repayment rate (also known as the posted county price, or PCP) used to determine the LDP is to be computed using a 30-day average of market prices, rather than the daily repayment rate of the 2002 and prior farm bills. Using a 30-day average for the repayment rates will lessen, but not eliminate, the market timing strategies that some farmers have used to maximize LDPs.

Cotton Users Payment

Among the special marketing loan provisions for upland cotton (which continue the prior law policies of special import quotas and limited global import quotas), the 2008 farm bill also creates a new payment for domestic users of upland cotton. The payment is termed "economic adjustment assistance," and is only to be used to acquire, construct, modernize, develop, convert, or expand operations. Unlike the Step 2 cotton payment

---

24. Local loan prices are available at [http://www.fsa.usda.gov/FSA/webapp?area=home&subject=prsu&topic=lor].

25. USDA 2007 farm bill proposal, p. 22, at http://www.usda.gov/documents/fbcommodity_071.pdf.

that was eliminated following a WTO ruling against the U.S. cotton program,[26] the new cotton users payment is for upland cotton of domestic or foreign origin. The payment is 4 cents per pound from August 1, 2008, to July 31, 2012. Thereafter, the payment rate is 3 cents per pound....

Other Commodity Provisions

Eliminating Payments on Fewer than 10 Acres

The 2008 farm bill eliminates direct and counter-cyclical payments to farms with fewer than 10 base acres (combined across all crops). The exclusion, however, does not apply to farms owned by socially disadvantaged[36] or limited-resource farmers and ranchers. Moreover, Congress intended for farmers to be able to aggregate land across multiple farms they operate before USDA enforces the restriction.[37]

The justification for the prohibition on small payments and/or small farms is a desire by some to stop payments to non-farmers. Some landowners with small holdings receive payments but are not full-time farmers; they receive most of their income from non-farm jobs and are sometimes called hobby farmers. Supporters of the 10-acre restriction do not want to include these farmers as program beneficiaries. However, the restriction does not address payments to the non-farm landowners of larger farms who may still qualify for payments. Moreover, implementing the new provision may reduce the number of recipients (and the constituency) of the farm programs and increase the size of the average payment, which may have negative connotations.

Policy differences have arisen over congressional intent to allow farmers to combine parcels of land they farm before the 10-acre rule is enforced and the Administration's more restrictive interpretation of statute. The statute says:

> A producer on a farm may not receive ... payments if the sum of the base acres of the farm is 10 acres or less ... [but this provision] shall not apply to a farm owned by ... a socially disadvantaged farmer or rancher ... or a limited resource farmer or rancher. (P.L. 110-246, sec. 1101(d))

Strictly speaking, the statute does not mention aggregating or combining acreage. USDA chose to apply a direct interpretation of statute and does not give any weight to the conference report language that states:

> The Managers intend for the Department to allow for aggregation of farms for purposes of determining the suspension of payments on farms with 10 base acres or less. The Managers expect for the Department to review farms in this category on an annual basis rather than prohibiting payments to these farms for the life of the farm bill. (H.Rept. 110-627 for H.R. 2419, pp. 674–675).

The Administration's regulation to implement this provision for the 2008 crop year has caused some farmers or landowners to be denied participation in the commodity

---

26. For more information about the Step 2 program and the WTO ruling, see CRS Report RL32571, *Brazil's WTO Case Against the U.S. Cotton Program*, by Randy Schnepf.

36. Socially disadvantaged farmers are defined for other farm programs as women, African Americans, American Indians, Alaskan Natives, Hispanics, Asian Americans and Pacific Islanders.

37. The 2008 farm bill also requires USDA to track the use of land affected by the 10-acre requirement and issue a report on the impact on specialty crop producers. Some believe that more acres may go into production of fruits and vegetables if small acreages are disqualified from direct payments. Existing fruit and vegetable growers are wary of more acres competing with their specialty crops.

programs. USDA adopted a strict interpretation of the statute and its regulations prohibited reconstitutions of farms under 10 acres unless the tracts were under the same ownership:

> [T]o be assured that producers on farms with base acres of 10 acres or less are prohibited from receiving payments ... [FSA] will not approve requests for farm combination reconstitutions of farms having base acres of 10 acres or less ... However, as an exception to the above rule, a farm with a total of 10 base acres or less may combine with another farm if one of the farms undergoes a change in land ownership [and the ownership of the two farms is identical]."[38]

Constituents have complained to Congress, and Members have written to USDA to say that USDA is not following congressional intent as explained in report language. Because of this implementation issue, both the House and Senate passed a bill, H.R. 6849, to suspend enforcement of the 10-acre requirement for the 2008 crop year. [The President signed this bill October 13, 2008.] A longer-term fix is being left to the 111th Congress....

Planting Flexibility for Fruits and Vegetables for Processing

As described previously, under the direct payment program farmers may plant crops other than the program crop and still receive direct payments—this is known as planting flexibility. They are prohibited, however, from planting fruits, vegetables, and wild rice on program crop base acres. Limited exceptions have allowed growers with a history of planting fruits and vegetables to continue to do so, but direct and counter-cyclical payments were reduced acre-for-acre of fruits and vegetables.

The restriction on planting fruits and vegetables is a seemingly reasonable response to protect growers of unsubsidized fruits and vegetables who do not want competition from subsidized growers of program crops. The planting restriction on fruits and vegetables, however, jeopardizes the ability of the United States to classify direct payments as non-distorting, decoupled, or "green box" for WTO accounting. The WTO has determined that the restrictions are inconsistent with the rules of a minimally distorting subsidy.[46]

Another complication with the restriction on planting fruits and vegetables surfaced when soybeans became eligible for direct payments in the 2002 farm bill. This created a shortage of acres in some parts of the Midwest for growing fruits and vegetables for processing (canning and freezing). Some landlords stopped allowing fruits and vegetables to be grown in rotation in place of soybeans. Many growers and processors asked for flexibility to grow fruits and vegetables for processing on base acres without other penalties, in return for giving up payments on those acres while growing fruits and vegetables. Such proposals became known as "farm flex."

The 2008 farm bill creates a pilot planting flexibility program for fruits and vegetables for processing, while continuing the overall restriction on planting fruits and vegetables on base acreage. The pilot program begins in 2009, and allows farmers in seven Midwestern states to plant base acres in cucumbers, green peas, lima beans, pumpkins, snap beans, sweet corn, and tomatoes grown for processing. Their base acres are temporarily reduced for the year (resulting in lower direct and counter-cyclical payments), but restored for the next crop year. The states include Minnesota (34,000 acres), Wisconsin (9,000 acres), Michigan (9,000 acres), Illinois (9,000 acres), Indiana (9,000 acres), Ohio (4,000 acres), and Iowa (1,000 acres).

---

38. *Federal Register*, vol. 73, no. 126 (June 30, 2008), p. 36840, at [http://www.fsa.usda.gov/Internet/FSA_Federal_Notices/dcp.pdf].

46. CRS Report RL32571, *Brazil's WTO Case Against the U.S. Cotton Program*, by Randy Schnepf.

The 2008 farm bill continues the exceptions of prior law that allowed farms with a history of growing fruits and vegetables to plant them, but with a one-year reduction in direct and countercyclical payment acres. The pilot program is similar in that it reduces payments acres, but in the aggregate is in addition to the acreage allowed under the continuation of the exceptions.

The additional planting flexibility of the pilot program addresses the subset of concerns in the Midwest, but it does not address concerns over WTO compliance. Restrictions on planting fruits and vegetables remain on acreage outside the pilot program, and for all fresh fruits and vegetables. The [Bush]Administration had proposed eliminating the fruit and vegetable planting restriction completely. For more background, see CRS Report RL34019, *Eliminating the Planting Restrictions on Fruits and Vegetables in the Farm Commodity Programs*, by Renée Johnson and Jim Monke.

Eliminating Base Acres in Residential Development

The 2008 farm bill adopts a Senate provision that eliminates base acres on land that has been subdivided into multiple residential units or other non-farming uses. Prior farm bills have eliminated base acres only for land developed for nonagricultural commercial or industrial use. This provision addresses the issue raised in media stories about the farm programs making payments to non-farmers or for land that is not in production. A Washington Post article in 2006 identified the practice of non-farm homeowners receiving farm commodity payments on what had become known as "cowboy starter kits," which were residential developments in Texas on land with rice base acres. Developments of houses had been built on several acres each, and the few acres that were not directly in the yard of the house retained their rice base acreage and still qualified for direct payments, even though there was no intention by the homeowners to farm or maintain the land for agriculture.[47]

Limited Payments to Deceased Farmers' Estates

The 2008 farm bill requires USDA to reconcile the social security numbers of program recipients with a Social Security database twice a year. The purpose is to assure that program beneficiaries are alive, and that estates do not continue to qualify beyond a reasonable period. USDA must also issue regulations describing how long a deceased person's estate may continue to qualify for program benefits. Prior to 2008, a USDA regulation already specified a two-year period for estates to qualify, unless excepted individually by the Secretary (7 C.F.R. 1400.206). The farm bill provision will require USDA to reissue and update the regulation, and presumably to increase enforcement. The provision was in response to a 2007 GAO report showing that some farm commodity programs continued to be paid to deceased farmers or their estates beyond the two-year regulation.[48]

Cost of the Commodity Title

Because spending on the farm commodity programs is a combination of fixed decoupled payments and market-driven counter-cyclical payments, outlays may be highly variable from year to year.... [F]rom 1981 to 2007, commodity program outlays (in-

---

47. *Washington Post*, "Farm Program Pays $1.3 Billion to People Who Don't Farm," July 2, 2006, A01 [http://www.washingtonpost.com/wp-dyn/content/article/2006/07/01/AR2006070100962.html].
48. U.S. Government Accountability Office, *USDA Needs to Strengthen Controls to Prevent Improper Payments to Estates and Deceased Individuals*, GAO-07-818, July 2007 [http://www.gao.gov/new.items/d07818.pdf].

cluding dairy and sugar, but excluding disaster payments) have ranged from a low of $3.3 billion in 1981 to a high of $27 billion in 2000. The average over the period was $11.1 billion per year. From 1981–1990, the average annual outlay was $11.4 billion; from 1991–2002, the average was $10.6 billion, and from 2003 to 2007 (roughly the years of the 2002 farm bill), the average was $11.7 billion. The CBO forecast for the 2008–2017 period is about $7.4 billion annually, well below the historical averages due to the record high commodity prices at the time that the 2008 farm bill was enacted.…

Compared to the baseline of continuing the provisions of the 2002 farm bill, the Congressional Budget Office (CBO) cost estimate (score) of the new provisions in Title I of the farm bill is a five-year savings of $1.726 billion and a 10-year savings of $1.658 billion. If the scores of these changes are added to the 2007 baseline of budget outlays used to write the farm bill, then CBO's expected cost of Title I is $41.628 billion for FY2008–2012 and $85.521 billion over 10 years … This includes the program crop commodities, dairy, and sugar.

The 5- and 10-year savings that are scored for all of Title I are the net result of various provisions that both score savings or cost more than prior law. The largest savings is the result of a shift in the timing of direct payments. Making advance payments of a portion of direct payments is ended beginning with the 2012 crop year … This shifts about $1.1 billion of payments into a later fiscal year, which achieves savings in the budget window but does not reduce the total amount eventually paid to farmers. Other savings are scored by reducing the proportion of base acres on which direct payments are paid, reducing direct payments and marketing loan rates for participants in the new ACRE revenue counter-cyclical program, replacing some counter-cyclical payments with ACRE payments, eliminating advance counter-cyclical payments beginning in crop year 2011, and by tightening payment limits …

Some of these savings are offset with costs of the new ACRE payments, economic assistance for cotton users, and higher target prices and loan rates for certain covered commodities, dairy, and sugar. CBO combines the effect of some of these provisions into a single score (e.g., raising counter-cyclical target prices and eliminating traditional counter-cyclical payments for ACRE participants). Thus, a provision-by-provision score is not possible.

Notes

1. Farmers Legal Action Group, Inc. published a report that analyzes federal farm programs in the context of public health goals. Jill Krueger, Karen Krub, Lynn Hayes, PLANTING THE SEEDS FOR PUBLIC HEALTH: HOW THE FARM BILL CAN HELP FARMERS TO PRODUCE AND DISTRIBUTE HEALTHY FOODS (Farmers' Legal Action Group, Inc., Feb. 2010) (available for free download at http://www.flaginc.org). Chapter 2 of this report, *Commodity Programs*, provides a clear, concise explanation of the specific farm programs authorized by the 2008 Farm Bill. This chapter provides a helpful supplement for those new to the structure of the programs, and its analysis of the programs in light of overall nutrition policy is instructive.

2. The international trade implications of U.S. support for agricultural commodities is a critical issue that is beyond the scope of this survey of agricultural law. However, it should be recognized that some elements of U.S. farm program policy clearly violate World Trade Organization (WTO) trade agreements. This presents serious trade problems for both agricultural and non-agricultural goods in the future.

Traditional Commodity Programs and the 2008 Farm Act

Direct payments are made based on historical acreages and yields, called base acres and program yields. Direct payment rates, which vary from crop to crop, play a role in the calculation of other commodity program payments. Direct payments are similar to the production flexibility contract (PFC) payments that were made available in 1996–2001 for wheat, feed grains, rice, and upland cotton. The 2002 Farm Act replaced PFC payments with direct payments and added oilseeds to the list of eligible crops. The 2008 Farm Act leaves payment rates unchanged, but reduces eligible payment acres from 85 percent of base acres to 83.3 percent for crop years 2009–11.

The **Nonrecourse Loan Program** provides commodity-secured loans to producers for a specified period of time (typically 9 months), after which producers must either repay the loan and accrued interest (if market prices are above the loan rate) or transfer ownership of the commodity pledged as collateral to the Commodity Credit Corporation as full settlement of the loan, without penalty.

Instead of taking out a commodity loan, eligible farmers may choose to receive marketing loan benefits through **Loan Deficiency Payments (LDP)** when market prices are lower than commodity loan rates. The LDP option allows the producer to receive the benefits of the marketing loan program without having to take out and subsequently repay a commodity loan. The LDP rate is the amount by which the loan rate exceeds the loan repayment rate or prevailing world market price, and, thus, is equivalent to the marketing loan gain that could be obtained for crops under loan.

The 2008 Farm Act continues commodity loan programs for wheat, corn, grain sorghum, barley, oats, long- and medium- grain rice, soybeans, other oilseeds, upland cotton, extra-long staple cotton, peanuts, wool, mohair, honey, small and large chickpeas, lentils, and dry peas. The loan rates, specified in the legislation, are unchanged for crop year 2008, but will increase for wheat, barley, oats, other oilseeds, and wool for crop years 2010–12. Loan rates for dry peas and lentils will be lowered for crop years 2009–12.

Counter-cyclical payments (CCPs) were established as a commodity program under the 2002 Farm Act and were initially available for wheat, corn, grain sorghum, barley, oats, rice, upland cotton, soybeans, other oilseeds, and peanuts. The 2008 Act continues CCPs for these crops and adds dry peas, lentils, and chickpeas. The 2008 Act does not change the target prices through crop year 2009, for all commodities, except for upland cotton. For upland cotton, the target price will be lowered to 71.25 cents per pound for crop years 2008–12. Target prices will increase for wheat, grain sorghum, barley, oats, soybeans, and other oilseeds for crop years 2010–12.The amount of historical production to which the CCP rate is applied will remain at 85 percent for crop years 2008–12.

Source: Robert Dismukes and Edwin Young, "New Market Realities Affect Crop Program Choices," *Amber Waves* 3, 5 USDA Economic Research Service, Nov. 2008.

In 2005 and again in 2008, in response to charges brought by Brazil, the WTO held that specific elements of U.S. support for cotton producers violated WTO commitments. On August 31, WTO arbitrators issued arbitration awards that authorized $820 million in countermeasures, about $260 million of which could be cross-sectoral. On March 8, 2010

Brazil announced a list of products that would be subject to tariffs, but negotiations prevented these tariffs from being imposed. These negotiations resulted in a settlement described as follows by the USDA.

> [T]he United States agreed to work with Brazil to establish a fund of approximately $147.3 million per year on a pro rata basis to provide technical assistance and capacity building. Under terms to be agreed by the United States and Brazil in the Memorandum of Understanding, the fund would continue until passage of the next Farm Bill or a mutually agreed solution to the Cotton dispute is reached, whichever is sooner. The fund would be subject to transparency and auditing requirements.
>
> The United States also agreed to make some near term modifications to the operation of the GSM-102 Export Credit Guarantee Program, and to engage with the Government of Brazil in technical discussions regarding further operation of the program. The United States also agreed to publish a proposed rule by April 16, 2010, to recognize the State of Santa Catarina as free of foot-and-mouth disease, rinderpest, classical swine fever, African swine fever, and swine vesicular disease, based on World Organization for Animal Health Guidelines and to complete a risk evaluation that is currently underway and identify appropriate risk mitigation measures to determine whether fresh beef can be imported from Brazil while preventing the introduction of foot-and-mouth disease in the United States.

U.S., Brazil Agree upon Path Toward Negotiated Solution of Cotton Dispute Would Avoid Imposition of Countermeasures Against U.S. Exports, U.S. Intellectual Property Rights, USDA Press Release, Release No. 0168.10 (April 6, 2010).

Reaction against the settlement was voiced by some, with calls that the settlement money should be taken out of the cotton program funding.

> U.S. cotton farmers took in almost $2.3 billion dollars in government subsidies in 2009, and the top 10% of the recipients got 70% of the cash. Now Uncle Sam is getting ready to ask taxpayers to foot the bill for another $147.3 million a year for a new round of cotton payments, this time to Brazilian growers.

The Madness of Cotton, Wall Street Journal, Editorial Board Opinion (May 21, 2010)

3. For many years, U.S. farm programs, in particular the cotton program, have been criticized for their negative impact on developing countries who try to compete against U.S. farmers in world trade. This problem remains. *See e.g.,* Kimberly Ann Elliot, Delivering on Doha: Farm Trade And the Poor (2006); Roger Thurow and Scott Kilman, Enough: Why the World's Poorest Starve in an Age of Plenty (2009).

4. Advocates for a more healthful American diet criticize the farm programs' significant support for commodity crops, while fruits and vegetables receive no direct assistance. The prohibition against shifting production to fruits and vegetables under the farm program is an additional target of criticism.

4. Economic Analysis and the Payment Limitations Debate

Jim Monke
Farm Commodity Programs in the 2008 Farm Bill
Congressional Research Service No. RL-34594, 1–2
September 30, 2008

Economics Shape Perceptions of Farm Subsidies

The economic argument for the farm commodity price and income support programs is that markets do not efficiently balance commodity supply with demand. Imbalances develop because consumers do not respond to price changes by buying proportionally smaller or larger quantities (food demand is price inelastic). Similarly, farmers do not respond to price changes by proportionally reducing or increasing production (supply is price inelastic). These imbalances may contribute to volatile farm income, which can result in inadequate (or exaggerated) resource adjustments by farmers. Moreover, the long time lag between planting and harvest may magnify imbalances because economic and yield conditions may change.

The economic argument against the farm commodity programs is that, like any subsidy, the farm programs distort production, capitalize benefits to the owners of the resources, encourage concentration of production, and comparatively harm smaller domestic producers and farmers in lower-income foreign nations.

The objectives of federal commodity programs are to stabilize and support farm incomes by shifting some of the risks to the federal government. These risks include short-term market price instability and longer-term capacity adjustments. The goals are to maintain the economic health of the nation's farm sector so that it can utilize its comparative advantages to be globally competitive in producing food and fiber.

Federal law mandates support for a specific list of farm commodities. For most of these commodities, support began during 1930s Depression-era efforts to raise farm household income when commodity prices were low because of prolonged weak consumer demand. While initially intended to be a temporary effort, the commodity support programs survived, but have been modified away from supply control and management of commodity stocks into direct income support payments.

Critics of commodity programs usually acknowledge the underlying economic conditions that make stability more difficult to achieve for agriculture than for some other sectors. However, they argue that (1) current programs are highly distorting of world production and trade, (2) the levels of subsidies are high and have become capitalized into land prices and rents that raise the cost of production and make the United States less competitive in global markets,[2] 2 and (3) the benefits are concentrated among a comparatively small number of commodities produced on a small number of large farms.[3]

When farm programs were first authorized in the 1930s, most of the 6 million farms in the United States were small and diversified. Policymakers reasoned that stabilizing

---

2. Predictable government payments are capitalized into land values and rents. Since 60% of program acres are rented, the landowners receive many benefits (M. Burfisher and J. Hopkins, "Farm Payments," *Amber Waves*, USDA Economic Research Service, Feb. 2003).

3. J. MacDonald, R. Hoppe, and D. Banker, "Growing Farm Size and the Distribution of Commodity Program Payments," *Amber Waves*, USDA Economic Research Service, Feb. 2005.

farm incomes using price supports and supply controls would help a large part of the economy (25% of the population lived on farms) and assure abundant food supplies. In recent decades, the face of farming has changed. Farmers now comprise less than 2% of the population. Most agricultural production is concentrated in fewer, larger, and more specialized operations. About 8% of farms account for 75% of farm sales (these 175,000 farms had average sales over $1 million). Most of the country's 2 million farms are part-time, and many operators rely on off-farm jobs for most of their income.

Supporters of commodity subsidy programs may not contradict the critics, but do point out that other nations have distorting subsidy programs and/or trade barriers that should be eliminated if the United States is to make reforms. Landowners are concerned about a loss of rents and wealth if land prices drop in response to a reduction in the subsidies. Similarly, rural communities are concerned about any large decline in the real estate tax base that supports local schools, roads, and other community services. While large farms receive most of the production-linked subsidy payments, recipients argue that lower input costs and marketing efficiencies make large farms efficient and small farms uneconomic in the production of bulk commodities. Therefore, targeting subsidies to small farms, recipients say, would encourage inefficient production.

From July to December 2006, the WASHINGTON POST published *Harvesting Cash*, a series of nine investigative articles on the federal farm programs, along with related stories and a website complete with interactive maps, "identifying more than $15 billion in wasteful, unnecessary and redundant spending." The website with all of the articles posted is still available at http://www.washingtonpost.com/wp-srv/nation/interactives/farmaid/. *Harvesting Cash* forcefully articulated many of the rising complaints about the federal farm programs.

One of the articles revealed that the federal government paid "at least 1.3 billion in subsidies for rice and other crops since 2000 to individuals who do no farming at all." A suburban asphalt contractor and program recipient interviewed for the article noted, "They give all this money to landowners who don't even farm, while real farmers can't afford to get started. It's wrong." The article accuses the farm programs of having "altered the landscape and culture of the Farm belt, pushing up land prices and favoring large, wealthy operators." Dan Morgan, Gilbert M. Gaul and Sarah Cohen, *Harvesting Cash: Farm Program Pays $1.3 Billion to People Who Don't Farm*, WASHINGTON POST, July 2, 2006.

Another article characterizes farm program payments as "empathy payments" and begins with the following imagery.

> The cornerstone of the multibillion-dollar system of federal farm subsidies is an iconic image of the struggling family farmer: small, powerless against Mother Nature, tied to the land by blood.

> Without generous government help, farm-state politicians say, thousands of these hardworking families would fail, threatening the nation's abundant food supply.

Dan Morgan, Gilbert M Gaul and Sarah Cohen, *Harvesting Cash: The Myth of the Small Farmer—Federal Subsidies Turn Farms Into Big Business*, WASHINGTON POST, July 2, 2006. The article goes on to raise a variety of challenging policy questions. As the title implies, it observes that the bulk of our food and fiber is not produced on small farms.

> Today, most of the nation's food is produced by modern family farms that are large operations using state-of-the-art computers, marketing consultants and

technologies that cut labor, time and costs. The owners are frequently college graduates who are as comfortable with a spreadsheet as with a tractor. They cover more acres and produce more crops with fewer workers than ever before.

This observation does not actually support a specific criticism of the federal farm programs, although it suggests that with added business acuity and sophisticated techniques, government support may not be needed. And, as the American support for the "family farmer," with this term's associated agrarian image, has been used so successfully to rally political support for federal assistance, the more sophisticated image leaves some feeling duped. That said, business sophistication and advanced education do not change the fundamental vulnerabilities associated with farming.

The article then raises a different complaint—that the farm programs work against the interests of the small farming operations.

> The very policies touted by Congress as a way to save small family farms are instead helping to accelerate their demise, economists, analysts and farmers say. That's because owners of large farms receive the largest share of government subsidies. They often use the money to acquire more land, pushing aside small and medium-size farms as well as young farmers starting out.

Dan Morgan, Gilbert M. Gaul and Sarah Cohen, *Harvesting Cash: The Myth of the Small Farmer—Federal Subsidies Turn Farms Into Big Business*, Washington Post, July 2, 2006.

Harvesting Cash was widely publicized and both evidenced and fueled the Farm Bill debate regarding farm program payments. Who should receive payments, and how should these payments be capped or limited?

a. Limitations on Farm Program Payments

Jim Monke
Farm Commodity Programs in the 2008 Farm Bill
Congressional Research Service No. RL-34594, 14–18
September 30, 2008

Payment Limits

Two types of payment limits exist for the farm commodity programs. One sets the maximum amount of farm program payments that a person can receive per year. The other sets the maximum amount of income that an individual can earn and still remain eligible for program benefits (a means test). The farm commodity programs have had the first type of limit since 1970. The means test was added starting with the 2002 farm bill, and also is known as the adjusted gross income (AGI) limit.

The 2008 farm bill makes several changes to payment limits, some by tightening the limits and others by relaxing them.

- Limits are tightened by

    (a) reducing the AGI limit,

    (b) eliminating the "three-entity rule," which allowed individuals to double their payments by having multiple ownership interests, and

    (c) requiring "direct attribution" of payments to a living person instead of to a corporation, general partnership, etc.

- Limits are relaxed by eliminating any limit on marketing loans.

The new payment limit rules do not take effect until the 2009 crop year.

Factors Affecting Payment Limits

The payment limits issue is controversial because it directly addresses questions about what size farms should be supported, whether payments should be proportional to production or limited per individual, and who should receive payments. The effect of payment limits varies across regions. The South and West have more large farms than the Upper Midwest or Northeast, and are more affected by payment limits. Cotton and rice farms are affected more often than corn, soybean, or wheat farms since the former group's subsidies per acre are higher.

Supporters of payment limits use both economic and political arguments to justify tighter limits. Economically, they contend that large payments facilitate consolidation of farms into larger units, raise the price of land, and put smaller, family-sized farming operations at a disadvantage. Even though tighter limits would not redistribute benefits to smaller farms, they say that tighter limits could help indirectly by reducing incentives to expand, and could help small and beginning farmers buy and rent land. Politically, they believe that large payments undermine public support for farm subsidies and are costly. Newspapers have published stories critical of farm payments and how they are distributed to large farms, non-farmers, or landowners.[27] Limits are increasingly appealing to urban lawmakers, and have advocates among smaller farms and social interest groups.

Critics of payment limits (and thus supporters of higher limits or no limits) counter that all farms are in need of support, especially when market prices decline, and that larger farms should not be penalized for the economies of size and efficiencies they have achieved. They say that farm payments help U.S. agriculture compete in global markets, and that income testing is at odds with federal farm policies directed toward improving U.S. agriculture and its competitiveness.

Limits on the Size of Payments

Under the 2008 farm bill, the annual limit on payments that are directly attributed to a person is $105,000 for direct and counter-cyclical payments combined. The payment limit has two parts:

$40,000 for direct payments, and $65,000 for counter-cyclical payments. These amounts effectively can be doubled to a combined $210,000 for a sole proprietor's farm by having a spouse (Table 2). These amounts are the same as in the 2002 farm bill.

Corporations, partnerships, and trusts are eligible for payments, but the payments must be attributed to a living person by the fourth level of ownership. Payments for most commodities are combined toward a single limit, but a separate and equal payment limit applies to peanuts.

Marketing loan gains and LDPs are unlimited in the 2008 farm bill, a change from prior law that had imposed a $75,000 limit but that could be avoided legally by using

---

27. For example, see the *Washington Post* series "Harvesting Cash," published in 2006, at [http://www.washingtonpost.com/wp-srv/nation/interactives/farmaid/].

Table 2. Commodity Payment Limit Provisions in the Farm Bill

Type of Law	Prior Law	2008 Farm Bill		
	2002 Farm Bill	House-passed H.R. 2419	Senate-passed H.R. 2419	Enacted P.L. 110-246
Adjusted Gross Income (AGI) Limitation				
Ineligible for payments if AGI exceeds…	$2.5 million unless 75% from farming	$500,000 unless 67% from farming $1 million, firm (no exceptions)	2008: $2.5 m^a 2009: $1.0 m^a 2010: $750,000^a	Non-farm AGI: $500,000 (all pmts.) Farm AGI $750,000 (DP only)
Allocate AGI on joint return	No	No	Yes	Yes
Direct and Counter-Cyclical Payments (separate limit for peanuts)				
(a) Direct Payments	$40,000	$60,000	$40,000	$40,000^b
(b) Counter-Cyclical, ACRE	$65,000	$65,000	$60,000	$65,000^b
Doubling allowance	spouse, 3-entity	spouse	spouse	spouse
Subtotal, doubled	*$210,000*	*$250,000*	*$200,000*	*$210,000*
Marketing				
(c1) Marketing Loan Gains (c2) Loan Deficiency Pmt.	$75,000			
(c3) Commodity Certificates (c4) Loan Forfeiture Gains	Unlimited	Unlimited	Unlimited	Unlimited
Subtotal (c1) (c2), doubled	*$150,000*			
Subtotal (c1) through (c4)	*Unlimited*			
Sum of Direct, Counter-Cyclical, and Marketing Loan Payments				
Total of limited payments	*$360,000* *(a), (b), (c1), (c2)*	*$250,000* *(a), (b)*	*$200,000* *(a), (b)*	*$210,000* *(a), (b)*
Total including all payments	*Unlimited*	*Unlimited*	*Unlimited*	*Unlimited*

Source: CRS.

a. Unless 67% from farming.

b. For ACRE participants, the $40,000 direct payment limit is reduced by the amount of the 20% reduction in the individua's direct payment. The amount of the reduction is added to the $65,000 limit on counter-cyclical payments.

commodity certificates to repay marketing loans.[28] Both the House- and Senate-passed bills chose to eliminate limits on marketing loans altogether in the 2008 farm bill, rather than apply payment limits to the use of commodity certificates. This was in response to con-

---

28. Marketing loan benefits in the 2002 farm bill were essentially unlimited because producers could use commodity certificates without limit when other marketing loan options were limited. Cotton and, to a lesser extent, rice farms were the primary users of certificates. Corn, soybeans, and wheat used certificates minimally. The prior law allowed certificates (7 U.S.C. 7286), and farmers essentially bought certificates at a discount and used them to repay their loans. But, technically, a certificate exchange was a momentary forfeiture, followed by "in-kind" receipt of commodities in exchange for a certificate bought at a discounted price, and only available to marketing loan participants (USDA, Report of the Commission on the Application of Payment Limitations for Agriculture, Aug. 2003, pp. 80–83, at [http://www.usda.gov/oce/reports/payment_limits/paymentLimitsAll.pdf].

cerns from cotton and rice growers who did not want tighter limits, and who were already opposing reductions in the AGI limit. Since commodity certificates now are viewed by many as unnecessary, the farm bill terminates authority to use certificates to repay marketing loans after the 2009 crop year.

Because the 2008 farm bill eliminates any limit on marketing loans, it is difficult to compare the $210,000 limit of the 2008 farm bill with the $360,000 limit of the 2002 farm bill. The $360,000 limit was for three types of payments; the $210,000 limit is for only two types of payments.

Doubling the Limits

The 2008 farm bill continues the "spouse rule" that allows a husband and wife to be treated as separate persons to double a farm's payment limit. It repealed, however, the long-standing "three entity rule," which allowed an alternative means of doubling by letting one person receive payments on up to three entities, with second and third entities being eligible for one-half of the limits (one whole plus two halves results in doubling).

For the AGI limit, the 2008 farm bill allows a married couple to divide their income for the AGI test as if separate income tax returns had been filed. This effectively allows doubling if the income is divided in an exact manner (discussed below).

Direct Attribution

When the three-entity rule was repealed, it was replaced with "direct attribution." Rather than tying payment limits to farm organization, which sometimes promoted the creation of entities for the purpose of doubling payment limits, the 2008 farm bill allows payments to various types of entities. But it now requires that the payments be attributed to a living person based on ownership shares in the entities. If a payment to a business entity cannot be allocated to a living person after four levels of ownership, the payment to the overall entity is reduced proportionately. Thus, individual people may receive payments on any number or ownership arrangement of farms (not limited to three entities), but the total amount of payments attributed to each living person may not exceed the statutory limits.

Adjusted Gross Income (AGI) Limits

The 2008 farm bill adopts a slightly different approach from the 2002 farm bill for the AGI limit. Formerly, the AGI limit had an exception if 75% of AGI was earned from farming sources. The 2008 farm bill eliminates the exception and creates two new measures of AGI: adjusted gross non-farm income, and adjusted gross farm income.

First, if a three-year average of non-farm AGI exceeds $500,000, then no program benefits are allowed (direct, counter-cyclical, and marketing loan). Second, if a three-year average of farm AGI exceeds $750,000, then no direct payments are allowed (but counter-cyclical and marketing loan benefits are allowed for these higher-income farmers). Table 2 shows that program participants can have income from both sources, but the caps for each type are "hard" caps (that is, there are no exceptions to the cap as with "soft" caps, except that the cap on farm AGI applies only to direct payments).

For example, if a full-time farmer has non-farm AGI over $500,000, his/her program payments are eliminated regardless of his/her farm income. Another example is that a taxpayer may have AGI between $750,000 and $1.25 million and still receive program

---

**Defining Farm AGI
For Purposes of Payment Limitations Rules**

"Adjusted Gross Income" is the legal entity's or individual's IRS-reported adjusted gross income, or a comparable measure as determined by CCC.

"Adjusted Gross Farm Income" is broadly defined and specifically includes income from:

- Production of crops, including raw forestry products.

- Production, feeding, rearing, or finishing of livestock.

- Production of farm-based renewable energy. The term "renewable energy" means energy derived from a wind, solar, biomass, or geothermal source; or hydrogen derived from biomass or water using wind, solar, or geothermal energy.

- Sale of farm, ranch, or forest land or land that has been used as such (including easements and development rights) and water or hunting rights and environmental benefits.

- Processing, storing, or transporting of farm, ranch, and forestry commodities.

- Rental or leasing of farm, ranch, or forestry land and equipment, including water or hunting rights.

See, Payment Limitations, USDA, Economic Research Service, Briefing Room: Farm and Commodity Policy: Program Provisions; *see also, Average Adjusted Gross Income 2009–2012,* USDA, Farm Service Agency Fact Sheet.

---

benefits if the income is split in such a way as to remain below the caps on farm and non-farm income. Moreover, the 2008 farm bill adopts a Senate provision that allows the AGI of a married couple to be divided as if separate tax returns were filed. While this provision theoretically allows doubling of the AGI limits to $2.5 million for a married couple, the income needs to be legitimately allocated both between the spouses and by the types of income, likely by Social Security numbers or equivalent identifiers. Such doubling to $2.5 million would be more difficult than the $2.5 million AGI test of the 2002 farm bill.

How Many Farmers Are Affected?

Reliable national data on the effect of payment limits are rare, especially for the payment limit or AGI levels specified in the 2008 farm bill. However, data developed since enactment of the 2002 farm bill provide some guidance on the general magnitude of the effects.

According to the report of the Payment Limits Commission mandated by the 2002 farm bill,[29] about 1% of producers receiving payments in 2000 were affected by the $40,000 limit on what now are called direct payments. This amounted to 12,300 producers across 42 states. The reduction was $83 million, or 1.6% of the value of payments, with California and Texas accounting for 36% of the reduction.

---

29. USDA, Payment Limit Commission Report, pp. 65–75.

Under the 2002 farm bill's AGI limit of $2.5 million, annual data suggest that only about 3,100 (0.15%) farmers had AGI over $2.5 million. Since not all of these farm tax-payers receive commodity subsidy payments and some likely would have qualified for the 75% farm income exception, USDA estimated that the 2002 farm bill's AGI cap affected only a few hundred farmers.[30]

Masked by these data is the fact that limits could be avoided, usually legally, by reor-ganizing a farm.[31] In fact, one study in 2007 suggests that about 20% of rice farmers re-organized their business because of limits, despite only 1.2% appearing to be subject to the limit.[32] The 2008 farm bill's elimination of the three-entity rule and application of direct attribution to living persons should lessen reorganization of farm businesses solely for purposes of avoiding payment limits.

In terms of the 2008 farm bill, data are not yet available that are specific to the farm bill limits of $500,000 non-farm AGI and $750,000 farm AGI. During the debate over tighter limits, USDA data suggested that about 1.5% of farm operator households have AGI over $200,000 and received some farm program payments (1.1% of farm sole pro-prietorships, 2.5% of farm partnerships, and 9.7% of farm households involved in farm-ing through a corporation). About 8.5% of rice farms and 9.3% of cotton farms have AGI over $200,000 and receive program payments. This compares to 5.5% for corn farms and only 1.3% for soybean farms.[33]

The farms potentially affected by the AGI limit are not necessarily large farms, nor necessarily above the AGI limit because of high *farm* income. Supporters of the AGI pro-posal say farmers are skilled at managing income taxes and can keep taxable farm income lower using tax incentives and rules.[34] The portion of farmers affected by the relatively higher limits in the farm bill would be smaller than the percentages in the preceding paragraph.

The USDA Economic Research Service concurs that the 2008 Farm Bill changes will affect some program payment recipients, but not have widespread significance.

> The changes with regard to payment limits should affect a relatively small share of program payment recipients and payments. Since marketing loan ben-efits are unlimited, the primary impact will be on direct and counter-cyclical payments for unmarried producers that previously utilized the three-entity rule

---

30. Ron Durst, *Effects of Reducing the Income Cap on Eligibility for Farm Program Payments*, USDA-ERS Report EIB-27, Sept. 2007, [http://www.ers.usda.gov/publications/eib27/eib27.pdf].

31. USDA, pp. 31–39; and General Accountability Office, *Farm Program Payments: USDA Needs to Strengthen Regulations and Oversight to Better Ensure Recipients Do Not Circumvent Payment Lim-itations*, GAO-04-407, April 2004, pp. 20–26, at[http://www.gao.gov/new.items/d04407.pdf].

32. Barrett Kirwan (University of Maryland) "The Distribution of U.S. Agricultural Subsidies," May 2007, p. 19–22, at [http://www.aei.org/docLib/20070515_kirwanfinal.pdf].

33. Ron Durst, USDA-ERS, at [http://www.ers.usda.gov/publications/eib27/eib27.pdf].

34. AGI is a common measure of household taxable income, and combines income from all sources. AGI measures net income, and Schedule F farm income contributes to AGI on a net basis, that is, after farm business expenses. Farms overwhelmingly report losses for tax purposes (because of cash accounting, depreciation, and other practices), even though USDA farm income numbers are positive. For example, in 2004, two-thirds of all Schedule F tax returns showed a loss, resulting in a sector-wide net farm *loss* of $13 billion for all Schedule F returns. By comparison, USDA farm in-come data showed an $80 billion *profit*. Even for "large" farms with sales over $250,000, about one-third report a loss for tax purposes. Source: CRS analysis of IRS data at [http://www.irs.gov/taxstats/index.html], and USDA-ERS, *Effects of Federal Tax Policy on Agriculture*, by Ron Durst and James Monke, AER 800, April 2001, at [http://www.ers.usda.gov/publications/aer800/aer800.pdf].

to increase payments. Since over four of five payment recipients are married and average direct and counter-cyclical payments for the unmarried group averaged only $5,399 and $4,048 in 2004, respectively, few should be affected. The elimination of the three-entity rule should reduce the incentive to utilize multiple entities and complex organizational structures to maximize payments, while the direct attribution of payments to individuals rather than entities will limit opportunities to evade payment limits.

The abandonment of the overall income limit in favor of separate lower limits for the farm and nonfarm components of total income is unlikely to have a significant impact on eligibility for, or the distribution of, farm program payments. While the nonfarm limits are more restrictive, the ability to allocate income on a joint return among spouses effectively doubles the income limitations for many sources of income for payment recipients who are married. Consequently, few payment recipients with adjusted gross income below $1 million will be affected.

In addition, given the separate limits (farm/nonfarm) as opposed to an overall AGI limit, a husband and wife could have as much as $2.5 million in income ($1 million nonfarm and $1.5 million farm) and still be eligible for all farm program payments. In 2005, only 0.48 percent of farm sole proprietors and share rent landlords had an AGI above $1 million, and they received 0.87 percent of farm payments. Despite the broad definition of farm income, since over two-thirds of farmers report a farm loss and the remaining one-third report relatively low levels of farm profit, few payment recipients will be affected by the $750,000 farm income limit.

Payment Limitations, USDA, Economic Research Service, Briefing Room: Farm and Commodity Policy: Program Provisions, available at http://www.ers.usda.gov/Briefing/Farm policy/paylimits.htm.

Notes

1. Farm program compliance issues and business planning to maximize payments have been areas where producers need competent legal advice. Like tax attorneys, farm program attorneys have assisted producers in structuring their business operations so that they can receive the maximum amount of government support allowed. In so doing, they must comply with all of the eligibility requirements and not run afoul of the "scheme or device" rule. 7 U.S.C. § 1308-2.

Given the complexity of these issues and the amount of payments at stake, farm program litigation has been a specialty in itself. Many of the previous payment limitations cases involved the "three entity" rule that was eliminated in the 2008 Farm Bill. Some gained notoriety, such as the "Mississippi Christmas Tree" described in an episode of the television show, *60 Minutes* in the early 1990s involving a Mississippi farm that structured its business so that dozens of "persons" were eligible for payments. Many attorneys, however, have sought to guide their clients through the legal maze of business planning issues while staying well within the law. *See* Christopher R. Kelley and Alan Malasky, *Federal Farm Program Payments: A Lawyers Guide*, 17 Wm. Mitchell L. Rev. (1991). Litigation can arise if attorneys are over-zealous or incompetent, when clients fail to follow the rules and their business plan, when the government is suspicious, when an FSA official is vindictive, or for a variety of other reasons. The stakes may be very high, with an obligation to return money paid, future ineligibility, and even criminal sanctions possible.

The complexity of payment limitations law and farm program litigation is beyond the scope of any survey of agricultural law. Moreover, as the rules have changed under the 2008 Farm Bill, with new implementing regulations issued in December 2009, application of past litigation to current farm program planning is complex. Nevertheless, for a representative flavor of federal farm program litigation, see *Mages v. Johanns*, 431 F.3d 1132 (8th Cir. 2005).

b. An Overview of Farm Program Recipients

James MacDonald, Robert Hoppe, and David Banker
Growing Farm Size and the Distribution of Farm Payments
USDA Economic Research Service Economic Brief No. 6 (March 2006).

Commodity Program Payments Are Shifting to Larger Farms

Federal commodity programs have traditionally provided support to producers of selected commodities, principally grains and oilseeds. With production of "program commodities" shifting to larger farms, commodity payments are also shifting in that direction, since payments are linked to planting and yield histories.

Commodity payments include all commodity and disaster assistance payments, and exclude environmental payments, such as payments received under the Conservation Reserve Program (CRP) or the Environmental Quality Incentives Program (EQIP). Commodity payments reflect a farm's production history for certain commodities. Specific programs have applied to dairy, peanut, and tobacco production, while broader programs have applied to field crops such as barley, corn, cotton, oats, rice, sorghum, soybeans, and wheat. Payments are tied to the amount of a farm's cropland that has been enrolled in programs, as well as yield histories. As a result, farms that produce higher volumes of program commodities generally receive higher payments.

High-value crops, as well as fed cattle, hogs, and poultry, are not supported by traditional government price and income support programs, although they do receive disaster assistance and occasionally may benefit from an ad hoc support program. Consequently, farms that produce such commodities receive substantial commodity payments only if they also produce program commodities or have a history of producing them. Because production of fed cattle, hogs, poultry, and high-value crops tends to occur on very large farms, farms in that sales category have traditionally drawn relatively small shares of total commodity payments.

However, as production of traditional program commodity crops shifted to very large farms, commodity payments also shifted sharply. Farms with less than $250,000 in production value (2003$) received 63 percent of commodity payments in 1989; by 2003, they received 43 percent of payments. But farms with at least $500,000 of production received 32 percent of all commodity payments in 2003, up from 13 percent in 1989.

Operators of the Largest Farms Have Higher Incomes

Farm households are not, in general, poor. Mean household income among all U.S. farm operator households was $68,500 in 2003, which compares favorably to the nationwide mean household income of $59,100 (for more on how household incomes are distributed, see Economic Brief No. 7, *Economic Well-Being of Farm Households*). Moreover, mean incomes do not vary sharply with farm size among smaller farms, those with sales below $250,000. Operators of the smallest farms, those with less than $10,000 in sales, derive almost all of their household income from off-farm work and from unearned income, such as Social Security, pensions, and financial investments. About 75 percent of those operators report negative incomes from farming, but those losses are offset by enough off-farm income to raise their household incomes above the national average. Households that operate farms with annual sales up to $250,000 frequently combine a financially viable farm business with off-farm employment to generate household incomes that match or exceed national averages.

However, operators of very large family farms realize much higher incomes, on average, and as production shifts to those farms, it also shifts to much higher-income farm households. The principal operators of very large family farms reported a mean household income of $214,200 in 2003, well above the mean across all family farms, and well above the mean of $102,400 reported by principal operators in the next largest size class ($250,000–$500,000).

Commodity Payments Are Shifting to Higher-Income Households

In 1989, half of commodity payments went to principal operators whose households earned more than $45,808 (in 2003 dollars), and half went to principal operators whose households had incomes below that figure (table 1). To further summarize the distribution of payments in 1989, one quarter went to households earning more than $94,784 (also in 2003 dollars), while 10 percent went to households with incomes above $189,149.

Since then, payments have shifted sharply to higher-income farm households. By 2003, half of commodity payments went to households with income above $75,772. One quarter went to households earning more than $160,142, and 10 percent of payments went to households earning more than $342,918.

Because household incomes did not rise sharply with farm sales among operators of farms with less than $500,000 in sales, shifts in production to larger farms within these size classes did not shift commodity payments to noticeably higher income households. Rather, the apparent shift in commodity payments to higher income households is being driven by shifts of production to the largest class of farms (over $500,000 in sales), whose households have substantially higher incomes.

These shifts have far outpaced the growth in overall U.S. incomes. Between 1989 and 2003, median U.S. household income grew by just 1 percent, from $42,892 (2003 dollars) to $43,318. The median U.S. household income in 1989 was near the median of the farm payments distribution ($45,808). This was not so by 2003.

In the last two decades, incomes have grown most rapidly at the upper levels of the income distribution; at the 90th percentile (10 percent of households earn more), U.S. income grew by 10 percent between 1989 and 2003. The incomes of households receiving most commodity payments have grown even more sharply than this. In short, commodity payments are being shifted, through structural change, toward relatively high-income households.

Carol A. Jones, Hisham El-Osta, and Robert Green
Economic Well-Being of Farm Households
USDA Economic Research Service Economic Brief No. 7 (March 2006).

Farm subsidy programs in the 1930s were largely prompted by concern for the chronically low, and highly variable, incomes of U.S. farm households. Seventy years later, commodity-based support programs are still prominent, even though the income and wealth of the average farm household now exceed those of the average nonfarm household-wealth by a large margin.

Farm households continue to face variability in income due to weather and natural disasters. Household income is most variable for the small segment that operates commercial farms (above $250,000 in annual sales). Relative to small farms, these farms achieve greater economies of scale, generate higher profit margins, and their households realize a larger share of their income from farming. However, the substantial net worth of these households acts as a cushion against uncertain farm income, much as off-farm income does for households operating smaller farms.

In a variable-income/high-wealth sector such as farming, economic well-being measures based on both income and wealth can provide a better signal of household capacity to support a consistent living standard than income measures alone. In 2003, 5 percent of farm households had both income and wealth below the respective U.S. household medians, and those households, on average, spent more on basic consumption than they earned in income. Households with low income and low wealth are less likely to receive commodity payments; by contrast, only 3 percent of households receiving payments had income and wealth below the U.S. household medians for each.

Increasing Farm Household Participation in Off-Farm Employment and Investment is Key to Well-Being

The average income of farm households increased from half of non-farm household income (per capita) in the 1930s to relative parity by the 1970s. In every year since 1996, average income for farm households has exceeded the average U.S. household income by 5 to 17 percent. Today, the economic portfolios of most farm operator households are highly diversified. Off-farm sources of income (including employment earnings, other business activities, other investments, and transfer payments) provided 85–95 percent of household income over 1999–2003, up from around 50 percent in 1960.

Operators of family farms in all sales classes had average household income exceeding the 2003 U.S. average for all households ($59,083). However, farm households are following diverse paths to economic well-being. Commercial farms (annual sales above $250,000, representing about 7 percent of U.S. farms) produce about 70 percent of total farm sales and have an average operating profit margin[35] greater than 10 percent, with economic performance and farm share of household income increasing with farm size within the commercial segment. Very large commercial farms (sales greater than $500,000) average household income about four times the U.S. household average. Though farm income provided 80 percent of household income for the average commercial farm operator in 2003, off-farm income still contributed around $44,033 per year.

The other 93 percent of farm households have negative farm operating profits, on average, and draw most of their income from off-farm sources. Here, farm operating margins become more negative and share of household income from farm sources decreases as farm size diminishes. Households just below commercial farms ($100,000–$249,999

---

35. Operating profit refers to net farm income plus interest payments, minus the opportunity cost of operators' unpaid labor and management time.

in sales) represent 8 percent of U.S. farms and produce 17 percent of sales. Their average household income was $67,275 in 2003. The remaining 85 percent of farms produce around 15 percent of sales, and earn negligible income from farming. The operators of these smaller farms (particularly those with less than $10,000 in sales) disproportionately identify their primary occupation as "other than farming or ranching" or as "retired." The "other occupation" group, who operate 42 percent of all farms, is more integrated into the off-farm economy than the farmer/rancher or the retired, and relies primarily on earned income (off-farm wages and salaries and off-farm business income.)

Farm Household Income is Most Variable for Households with Highest Net Worth

Farm households as a group no longer experience chronically low incomes relative to non-farm households. On the other hand, farm households do continue to experience more variable income from year to year. However, it is the 7 percent of farm households operating commercial farms, who derive a majority of household income from the farm, that experience the greatest degree of variability in household income from year to year. The 8 percent of farm households operating the next size class of farms ($100,000–$249,999) also experience variability in household income, though the effect is dampened because about two-thirds of their income comes from off-farm activities.

Distribution of Income and Wealth Across Farm Households

Within a given year, the variability of income across farm households tends to mirror that for all U.S households. However, farm households tend to have lower incomes at the low end of the income spectrum than non-farm households, and higher incomes at the high end. The share of farm households with negative household income was 6 percent in 2003, versus 1 percent of all U.S. households.

In contrast to all U.S. households, where wealth is highly concentrated at the top end of the distribution, wealth is more equally distributed across farm households. Nonetheless, differences exist by farm size and by age/retirement status. Across size classes, the variation in farm household wealth roughly mirrors the variation in income levels: farm net worth and, to some extent, nonfarm net worth are higher for households operating larger farms. So the larger farms can counter their greater exposure to variable income with higher net worth—on average in excess of $1 million, and closer to $2 million for very large commercial farms.

Again, the households operating larger farms (sales greater than $100,000) are the ones more likely to experience the effects on household income from variability in farm income: in 2003, around 13 percent of households operating larger farms had negative household income, compared with 4 percent of households operating smaller farms (fig. 3). In contrast, the likelihood of incurring losses from farm operations is highest among the smaller farms (less than $100,000 in sales). But these latter households acquire virtually all of their income from off-farm sources, so negative farm earnings seldom translate into negative household income.

A Joint Income-Wealth Indicator is More Indicative of Farm Household Well-Being

In 2003, median wealth of farm households ($416,250) was five times the estimated median wealth of all U.S. households ($89,578). (By definition, 50 percent of households have wealth lower than the median—also known as the 50th percentile—of wealth). Seventy three percent of farm household net worth is in farm assets (plus an unknown share in non-farm business equity), whereas 17 percent of the net worth of U.S. households is in business equity. Farmland, which has appreciated greatly in recent years, particularly near urban centers, currently represents about 60 percent of farm household wealth. Excluding farm wealth, median non-farm wealth of farm households ($83,750) was almost as high as estimated median total wealth of all U.S. households.

Gauging what share of farm households has low economic well-being is challenging, because farming is characterized by variable income but also by high wealth. During periods of low income, farm households may be able to maintain living standards by borrowing against, or liquidating, assets. Consequently, household income for an individual year, the standard measure of economic well-being, is not necessarily a good indicator of a farm household's ability to support a given consumption level through time. And wealth is particularly important for the retired and near-retired, who may be drawing down wealth accumulated over their lifetime, rather than spending current income, to support their standard of living.

To create a well-being indicator that accounts for both income and wealth, we separate farm households by low and high income and low and high wealth, using the U.S. household medians for income and wealth as the dividing lines. By definition, 50 percent of U.S. households had income greater than the U.S. median income ($43,378) in 2003. In contrast, 54 percent of farm households had income greater than that level in 2003. However, the big difference is in the distribution of wealth across the groups: 92 percent of all farm households—in contrast to 50 percent of all U.S. households—had wealth greater than the U.S. median (estimated to be $89,578 in 2003).

So who is in the small group of low-wealth households? On average, the low-wealth group was younger (virtually none was retired), operated substantially fewer acres, and generated lower farm sales than the farm operator population as a whole. They reported substantial losses in the off-farm component of household wealth. Among low-wealth households, a major factor differentiating the high-income subgroup (3 percent of total households) from their low-income counterparts (5 percent of total households) is occupation: their primary occupation is disproportionately "other than farming/ranching," whereas the low-income group was more evenly split between operators declaring farming/ranching or "other" as their primary occupation.

Do households with variable income have sufficient equity to borrow against, or to liquidate, to maintain living standards when income is low? Among farm households with income lower than the U.S. median (46 percent), household wealth exceeded the U.S. median in 9 out of 10 households. Retired households are disproportionately represented in this low-income/high-wealth subgroup. Even in the low-wealth group, basic consumption expenditures exceeded income, though to a lesser extent than for the high-wealth group.

Farm Households that Receive Commodity Payments also Have High Incomes and Wealth

About 16 percent of all farm households receive commodity payments. (Commodity payments include all commodity and disaster payments and exclude environmental payments, such as those received under the Conservation Reserve Program and the Environmental Quality Incentives Program.) The share is lowest (7 percent) for households operating the smallest farms (sales less than $10,000); over 25 percent of households operating farms in each of the larger size classes receive payments. The high-income high-wealth group is more likely to be receiving commodity payments (16 percent) than the low-income, low-wealth group (10 percent). Among recipients, payment levels increase with production levels, and so payments disproportionately go to farm households operating larger farms, with their higher average incomes and wealth.

B. Federal Crop Insurance

Many of the protections afforded farmers in the law are "steeped in the concept of risk; farmers are caught in a risk-ridden enterprise."[1] Farmers produce living products relying on a combination of different natural resources, most often in an outdoor environment at the mercy of the weather. Hail damage alone is estimated to cause $1 billion of crop loss each year. Excessively wet conditions can drown plants, stunt growth, stimulate mold and fungus growth, and cause the loss of applied nitrogen. Drought, frost, or wind damage can all devastate a growing crop. The following news story could describe almost any region, any year, depending on the weather.

> Southwest wheat production could be off by 50 percent from last year, a victim of the double disasters of prolonged drought and late freezing temperatures.
>
> "A 50 percent crop loss is likely across the state," says Gaylon Morgan, Texas AgriLife Extension small grains specialist. He said the 60-million bushel crop estimate from the Texas Agricultural Statistics Service puts the crop about half of last year's.
>
> The situation is not much better is Oklahoma where Extension small grains specialist Jeff Edwards estimates the crop could be down 40 percent to 50 percent from last year's "bumper crop."
>
> "Farmers had some damage from the March freeze," Edwards says, "but not a lot. The April freeze hammered us."
>
> He says the real story in southwest Oklahoma was not the cold snap, but the drought that extended from late last summer through early spring.
>
> "The freeze just put it out of its misery."

Ron Smith, *Southwest Wheat Crop Hammered by Prolonged Drought, Late Freezes*, Southwest Farm Press (May 6, 2009). The USDA reported in 2009 that one-half to two-thirds of the counties in the United States had been designated as disaster areas in each of the past several years.[2] And, as weather impacts overall crop performance, the markets react with price fluctuations completely out of the control of any individual farmer.

Risk management strategies are critical to the success of the farm business. Insurance is perhaps the most obvious the risk management strategy. Yet, as noted on the website of the National Crop Insurance Services, the lobbying organization for the crop insurance companies that participate in the federal crop insurance programs, "[b]ecause of the inherent risks and potential for widespread catastrophic losses associated with agricultural production, insuring farmers and ranchers has always posed a challenge."

The challenge of insuring farmers is more complex than the risk of weather-related losses, however. Getting farmers to buy insurance, getting insurance companies to offer

---

1. *Matter of Armstrong*, 812 F.2d 1024 (7th Cir. 1987).
2. USDA, FSA Fact Sheet, *Emergency Disaster Designation and Declaration Process* (July 2009), available at www.fsa.usda.gov/Internet/FSA_File/disaster09.pdf.

multi-peril insurance policies in limited markets, and trying to minimize insurance fraud have all been challenges facing crop insurance. Yet, as agriculture is such a critical component of the economy and food such an essential product, farmers' collective risks become a risk to society as a whole. And many markets are too small or too prone to loss to be attractive to the private insurance agency without federal inducements.[3]

The federal government has been involved in crop insurance since the 1930's. And, this involvement is likely to continue. Chairman of the House Agriculture Committee, Collin Peterson, holding hearings in April 2010 in preparation for the 2012 Farm Bill negotiations predicted greater integration between crop insurance and the federal farm programs, with crop loss and revenue insurance eventually becoming the primary vehicle for providing support to farmers.[4]

1. Introduction to Federal Crop Insurance

Multi-peril federal crop insurance is provided through the Federal Crop Insurance Corporation (FCIC) as part of a complex public-private partnership with select companies in the insurance industry. The FCIC is a wholly-owned government corporation managed by the USDA's Risk Management Agency (RMA).

> The FCIC's mission is to encourage the sale of crop insurance—through licensed private agents and brokers—to the maximum extent possible. FCIC also provides reinsurance (subsidy) to approved commercial insurers which insure agricultural commodities using FCIC-approved acceptable plans. Since 1998, the private insurance companies reinsured by FCIC have sold and serviced all Multiple Peril Crop Insurance authorized under the Federal Crop Insurance Act.

USDA Risk Management Website available at http://www.rma.usda.gov.

A History of the Crop Insurance Program
USDA, Risk Management Agency
http://rma.usda.gov/aboutrma/what/history.html

Congress first authorized Federal crop insurance in the 1930s along with other initiatives to help agriculture recover from the combined effects of the Great Depression and the Dust Bowl. The Federal Crop Insurance Corporation (FCIC) was created in 1938 to carry out the program. Initially, the program was started as an experiment, and crop insurance activities were mostly limited to major crops in the main producing areas. Crop insurance remained an experiment until passage of the Federal Crop Insurance Act of 1980.

The 1980 Act expanded the crop insurance program to many more crops and regions of the country. It encouraged expansion to replace the free disaster coverage (compensation to farmers for prevented planting losses and yield losses) offered under Farm Bills cre-

---

3. Crop Hail policies are generally available in farming areas directly through private insurance providers. Multi-peril (MPCI) insurance policies are not; these are the policies covered by the federal crop insurance program.

4. Phillip Brasher, *Peterson Eyeing Major Overhaul of Crop Subsidies*, DesMoinesRegister.com (Apr. 21, 2010) available at https://blogs.desmoinesregister.com; see also, Keith Good, FarmPolicy Blog, *Report on House Agriculture Committee Hearing*, April 21, 2010, (providing notes and unofficial transcript) available at http://FarmPolicy.com.

ated in the 1960s and 1970s, because the free coverage competed with the experimental crop insurance program. To encourage participation in the expanded crop insurance program, the 1980 Act authorized a subsidy equal to 30 percent of the crop insurance premium limited to the dollar amount at 65 percent coverage.

Although more farmers took part in the program after passage of the 1980 Act, it did not achieve the level of participation that Congress had hoped for. Therefore, after a major drought in 1988, ad hoc disaster assistance was authorized to provide relief to needy farmers. Another ad hoc disaster bill was passed in 1989. A third one enacted in 1992 gave farmers the option of claiming disaster losses on a farm-by-farm basis for any year between 1990 and 1992. An extremely wet and cool growing season in 1993 caused more losses, and Congress passed yet another ad hoc disaster bill. However, dissatisfaction with the annual ad hoc disaster bills that were competing with the crop insurance program led to enactment of the Federal Crop Insurance Reform Act of 1994.

The 1994 Act made participation in the crop insurance program mandatory for farmers to be eligible for deficiency payments under price support programs, certain loans, and other benefits. Because participation was mandatory, catastrophic (CAT) coverage was created. CAT coverage compensated farmers for losses exceeding 50 percent of an average yield paid at 60 percent of the price established for the crop for that year. The premium for CAT coverage was completely subsidized. Participants paid $50 per crop per county subject to maximum amounts for multiple crops and counties insured by the same individual. Subsidies for higher coverage levels were increased.

In 1996, Congress repealed the mandatory participation requirement. However, farmers who accepted other benefits were required to purchase crop insurance or otherwise waive their eligibility for any disaster benefits that might be made available for the crop year. These provisions are still in effect.

In the same year, the Risk Management Agency (RMA) was created to administer FCIC programs and other non-insurance-related risk management and education programs that help support U.S. agriculture.

Participation in the crop insurance program increased significantly following enactment of the 1994 Act. For example, in 1998, more than 180 million acres of farmland were insured under the program. This is more than three times the acreage insured in 1988, and more than twice the acreage insured in 1993. According to estimates by the USDA National Agricultural Statistics Service, in 1998, about two-thirds of the country's total planted acreage of field crops (except for hay) was insured under the program. The liability (or value of the insurance in force) in 1998 was $28 billion, the largest amount since the inception of the program. The total premium, which includes subsidy, and the premium paid by insured persons (nearly $950 million) were also record figures.

In 2000, Congress enacted legislation that expanded the role of the private sector allowing entities to participate in conducting research and development of new insurance products and features.... Restrictions on the development of insurance products for livestock were removed [and a]uthority was added to allow the Board of Directors to create an expert review panel to provide assistance to the Board in evaluating new insurance products for feasibility and actuarial soundness. Premium subsidies were increased to encourage producers to purchase higher insurance coverage levels and to make the insurance program more attractive to prospective producers....

―――――――

Today, RMA works with fifteen private insurance companies that are authorized to sell and service the insurance policies to farmers. RMA approves and supports the insurance products that are sold, develops or approves the premium rate charged to the farmers who purchase the insurance, subsidizes the cost of the premium, provides administrative and operating (A&O) subsidies to the insurance companies, and reinsures the companies for losses.

The RMA Insurance Services division is responsible for managing the contracts with the private insurance companies. The Product Management division oversees insurance product development. And, the Risk Compliance division monitors program compliance by both farmers and the private insurance companies.

The Federal Crop Insurance Act, as amended, is found at 7 U.S.C. § 1501 et seq. and extensive administrative regulations promulgated by RMA are found at 7 C.F.R. pt. 400.

Lisa Shames
Crop Insurance: Continuing Efforts Are Needed to Improve Program Integrity and Ensure Program Costs Are Reasonable
Testimony Before the House Committee on Oversight and Government Reform
U.S. Government Accountability Office, GAO-07-819T, 5–7 (May 3, 2007)

* * *

RMA administers the program in partnership with private insurance companies, which share a percentage of the risk of loss and the opportunity for gain associated with each insurance policy written. RMA acts as a reinsurer—reinsurance is sometimes referred to as insurance for the insurance companies—for a portion of all policies the federal crop insurance program covers. In addition, RMA pays companies a percentage of the premium on policies sold to cover the administrative costs of selling and servicing these policies. In turn, insurance companies use this money to pay commissions to their agents, who sell the policies, and fees to adjusters when claims are filed.

Background

FCIC insures agricultural commodities on a crop-by-crop and county-by-county basis, considering farmer demand and the level of risk associated with the crop in a given region. Major crops, such as grains, are covered in almost every county where they are grown, while specialty crops such as fruit are covered in only some areas. Participating farmers can purchase different types of crop insurance and at different levels.

RMA establishes the terms and conditions that the private insurance companies selling and servicing crop insurance policies are to use through the [Standard Reinsurance Agreement] SRA. The SRA provides for the cost allowance intended to cover administrative and operating expenses the companies incur for the policies they write, among other things. The SRA also establishes the minimum training, quality control review procedures, and performance standards required of all insurance providers in delivering any policy insured or reinsured under the Federal Crop Insurance Act, as amended.

Under the crop insurance program, participating farmers are assigned (1) a "normal" crop yield based on their actual production history and (2) a price for their commodity based on estimated market conditions. Farmers can then select a percentage of their normal yield to be insured and a percentage of the price they wish to receive if crop losses exceed the selected loss threshold. In addition, under the crop insurance program's "prevented planting" provision, insurance companies pay farmers who were unable to plant the insured crop because of an insured cause of loss that was general to their surrounding area, such as weather conditions causing wet fields, and that had prevented other farmers in that area from planting fields with similar characteristics. These farmers are entitled to claims payments that generally range from 50 to 70 percent, and can reach as high as 85 percent, of the coverage they purchased, depending on the crop.

RMA is responsible for protecting against fraud, waste, and abuse in the federal crop insurance program. In this regard, RMA uses a broad range of tools, including RMA's compliance reviews of companies' procedures, companies' quality assurance reviews of claims, data mining, and FSA's inspections of farmers' fields. For example, insurance companies must conduct quality assurance reviews of claims that RMA has identified as anomalous or of those claims that are $100,000 or more to determine whether the claims the companies paid comply with policy provisions.…

[F]ederal crop insurance plays an invaluable role in protecting farmers from losses due to natural disasters, and the private insurance companies that participate in the program are integral to the program's success. Nonetheless, … we identified crop insurance as an area for oversight to ensure that program funds are spent as economically, efficiently, and effectively as possible.…

RMA has made progress in addressing fraud, waste, and abuse, but the weaknesses we identified in program management and design continue to leave the crop insurance program vulnerable to potential abuse. Furthermore, as our work on underwriting gains and losses has shown, RMA's effort to limit cost allowances and underwriting gains by renegotiating the SRA has had minimal effect. In fact, it offers insurance companies and their agents a windfall. We believe that the crop insurance program should be delivered to farmers at a reasonable cost that does not over-compensate insurance companies participating in the program. A reduced cost allowance for administrative and operating expenses and a decreased opportunity for underwriting gains would potentially save hundreds of millions of dollars annually, yet still provide sufficient funds for the companies to continue delivering high-quality service while receiving a rate of return that is closer to the industry benchmark.

---

2. Types of Insurance Available to Farmers

Multi-peril crop insurance policies are purchased prior to planting and have typically covered crop yield losses due to all types of natural causes such as drought, frost, disease, and excessive moisture. In recent years, coverage available now includes policies that protect farmers from a loss in revenue, whether due to yield or pricing.

Dennis A. Shield
Federal Crop Insurance: Background and Issues
Congressional Research Service Report No. R40532
Jan. 20, 2010

In purchasing a policy, a producer growing an insurable crop selects a level of coverage and pays a portion of the premium, which increases as the level of coverage rises. The remainder of the premium is covered by the federal government (nearly 60% of total premium, on average, is paid by the government). In the case of catastrophic coverage, the government pays the full premium. In the absence of subsidies, farmer participation in the crop insurance program would be substantially lower.

In 2009, crop insurance policies covered 265 million acres. Major crops are covered in most counties where they are grown. Four crops—corn, cotton, soybeans, and wheat—accounted for more 73% of total enrolled acres. For these major crops, a large share of plantings is covered by crop insurance: corn at 83% of plantings; cotton, 94%; soybeans, 83%; and wheat, 82%.

Policies for less widely produced crops are available in primary growing areas. Examples include dry peas, blueberries, citrus, and walnuts. In total, policies are available for more than 100 crops (including coverage on a variety of fruit trees, nursery crops, pasture, rangeland, and forage).

Crop insurance is not necessarily limited to crops; livestock coverage has recently become available. Relatively new or pilot programs protect livestock and dairy producers from loss of gross margin or price declines.

The availability of crop insurance for a particular crop in a particular region is an administrative decision made by USDA. The decision is made on a crop-by-crop and county-by-county basis, based on farmer demand for coverage and the level of risk associated with the crop in the region, among other factors. In areas where a policy is not available, farmers may request that RMA expand the program to their county. The process usually starts with a pilot program in order for RMA to gain experience and test the program components before it becomes more widely available.

Current law requires that RMA strive for actuarial soundness for the entire federal crop insurance program (that is, indemnities paid out should equal total premiums, including premium subsidies).

Federal crop insurance policies are generally either yield-based or revenue-based. For most yield-based policies, a producer can receive an indemnity if there is a yield loss relative to the farmer's "normal" (historical) yield. Revenue-based policies were developed in the mid-1990s to protect against crop revenue loss resulting from declines in yield, price, or both. The most recent addition has been products that protect against losses in whole farm revenue rather than just for an individual crop....

Two million crop insurance policies were sold in 2009, with yield-based policies accounting for 48% of the total, and the remainder being revenue-based policies.

Yield-Based Insurance

When purchasing a crop insurance policy, a producer is assigned (1) a "normal" crop yield based on the producer's actual production history, and (2) a price for his commodity based on estimated market conditions. The producer can then select a percentage of his normal yield to be insured and a percentage of the price he wishes to receive when crop losses exceed the selected loss threshold. The level of crop yield coverage is viewed by farmers as a critical feature of crop insurance, and a major determinant of whether a farmer will purchase insurance.

In determining what a normal production level is for an insurable farmer, USDA requires the producer to present actual annual crop yields (usually stated on a bushel-per-acre basis) for the last 4 to 10 years. The simple average of a producer's annual crop yield over this time period then serves as the producer's actual production history (APH). If a farmer does not have adequate records, he can be assigned a transition yield (T-yield) for each missing year of data, which is based on average county yields for the crop.

The most basic policy is called catastrophic (CAT) coverage. The premium for this level of coverage is completely subsidized by the federal government. The farmer pays an administrative fee for CAT coverage ($300 per crop per county under the 2008 farm bill, up from $100 previously), and in return can receive a payment on losses in excess of 50% of normal yield, equal to 55% of the estimated market price of the crop (called 50/55 coverage). [Limited Resource farmers can have the administrative fee waived.]

Coverage levels that are higher than CAT are called "buy-up" or "additional" coverage.[8] For an additional premium paid by the producer, and partially subsidized by the government, a producer can "buy up" the 50/55 catastrophic coverage to any equivalent level of coverage between 50/100 and 75/100 (i.e., up to 75% of "normal" crop yield and 100% of the estimated market price). In limited areas, production can be insured up to the 85/100 level of coverage.

The producer's premium increases as the levels of insurable yield and price coverage rise, and the premium on buy-up coverage is subsidized by the government at amounts ranging from 38% to 67%, depending upon the coverage level. While the subsidy rate declines as the coverage level rises, the total premium subsidy in dollars increases because the policies are more expensive.

APH policies account for more than 90% of yield-based policies sold. The remaining policies, including the Group Risk Plan and Dollar Plan (see box on page 5), are not widely used but can be important for certain crops. Some of these policies use an area-wide index—county-level yield in the case of the Group Risk Plan—to measure losses.

Revenue-Based Insurance

Revenue insurance is another major type of crop insurance, accounting for just over one-half of all crop insurance policies. It began in 1997 as a buy-up option on a pilot basis for major crops. By 2003, acreage under revenue-based insurance exceeded acreage covered by APH policies. Revenue insurance combines the production guarantee component of crop insurance with a price guarantee to create a target revenue guarantee.

Under revenue insurance programs, participating producers are assigned a target level of revenue based on market prices for the commodity and the producer's production history. A farmer who opts for revenue insurance can receive an indemnity payment when his actual farm revenue (crop-specific or entire farm, depending on the policy) falls below a certain percentage of the target level of revenue, regardless of whether the shortfall is caused by low prices or low production levels. The two most popular revenue plans are Revenue Assurance and Crop Revenue Coverage, which together account for slightly more than one-half of all yield- and revenue-based policies sold....

---

3. Loss Claims and the Payment of Indemnities

When a federal crop insurance policyholder experiences a loss, the insurance policy itself will largely govern the rights and duties of the parties to the contract. The Federal

---

8. Participation at the CAT level has steadily decreased, particularly since subsidies on buy-up levels were increased in the Agriculture Risk Protection Act (ARPA) of 2000. In 2008, only about 11% of insured acres were insured at the CAT level.

Source of Law and Implementation Guidance

The statutory authority for the Agricultural Commodity Support Programs, as enacted under the *Food, Conservation, and Energy Act of 2008,* Pub. L. 110-246, 122 Stat. 1651 (2008) can be found at 7 U.S.C. ch 113, §§ 8701–8793.

The regulations implementing these programs are found at 7 C.F.R. pts. 400, 402, 407, 412, and 457. (2010). Approved insurance contract provisions for various types of insurance are included in the regulations.

RMA is required by law to respond to requests for interpretation of any part of the Federal Crop Insurance Act as amended or the regulations promulgated thereunder. However, RMA will not apply the law to a specific set of facts or an individual case. The Final Agency Determinations (FAD) and the process making requests are provided on the RMA website at http://www.rma.usda.gov/regs/533/section533.html.

Farmers Legal Action Group, Inc. has a variety of current legal information involving crop insurance and disaster relief including an extensive handbook posted on their website at http://www.flaginc.org/topics/disaster/index.php. *See* Karen R. Krub, Jill E. Krueger, and Jennifer A. Jambor, *Federal Crop Insurance*, in FARMERS GUIDE TO DISASTER ASSISTANCE, Farmers Legal Action Group, Inc. (6th ed. 2008).

Crop Insurance Act, as amended, and the federal crop insurance regulations promulgated by RMA will be incorporated into the contract terms. Legal issues are likely to arise from disputes regarding these rights and duties.

Only losses caused by natural disaster are covered, and several other causes are specifically excluded from coverage. If neglect or malfeasance by the farmer caused the loss, coverage is excluded under the federal statute. 7 U.S.C. § 1508(a)(3)(A). The insurance policy may specifically exclude coverage for losses caused by "neglect, mismanagement, or wrongdoing." *See* 7 C.F.R. § 457.8 (2010).

Similarly, losses will not be covered if the farmer is found to have failed to follow "good farming practices." *See* 7 C.F.R. § 457.8 (2010). "Good farming practices" are defined as follows:

> The production methods utilized to produce the insured crop and allow it to make normal progress toward maturity and produce at least the yield used to determine the production guarantee or amount of insurance, including any adjustments for late planted acreage, which are: (1) For conventional or sustainable farming practices, those generally recognized by agricultural experts for the area; or (2) for organic farming practices, those generally recognized by the organic agricultural industry for the area or contained in the organic plan. We may, or you may request us to, contact FCIC to determine whether or not production methods will be considered to be "good farming practices."

7 C.F.R. § 457.8, Common Crop Insurance Policy, Definitions (2010).

Recognizing the potential difficulty in accurately assessing "good farming practices," an informal appeal process has been established to allow farmers to seek a review of a decision on this issue. 7 C.F.R. § 400.98 (2010).

The farmer who has experienced a crop loss will be responsible under the contract for protecting the crop to prevent further damage, giving prompt notice to the insurance provider, allowing the provider access to the crop (including leaving representative samples that show the damage), and cooperating with any investigation. The farmer may need to seek permission before taking certain actions such as destroying or abandoning the crop. A written claim will have to be submitted along with harvest and sale records.

See 7 C.F.R. § 457.8 (2010); *see also,* Karen R. Krub, Jill E. Krueger, and Jennifer A. Jambor, *Federal Crop Insurance in* Farmers Guide to Disaster Assistance, Farmers Legal Action Group, Inc. (6th ed. 2008).

Legal disputes may arise if the insurance company denies the claim or reduces the indemnity below the covered level of losses. Mediation can be used to settle disputes between the insurance company and the farmer, if both parties agree. Unless mediation resolves the dispute, it must be resolved through arbitration under the rules of the American Arbitration Association. Either party can seek judicial review of the arbitration findings. FCIC decisions may be appealed to the National Appeals Division (NAD), and after this process has been exhausted, judicial review can be sought. Strict time limits set forth in the regulations and in the contracts apply to preserve all of the aforementioned rights.

Notes

1. Rising government costs associated with the federal crop insurance program have caused Congress and the USDA to consider cost-saving changes.

> Government costs for crop insurance have increased substantially in recent years. After ranging between $2.1 and $3.6 billion during FY2000–FY2006, costs rose to $5.7 billion in FY2008 and $7.9 billion in FY2009 as higher policy premiums from rising crop prices drove up premium subsidies to farmers and expense reimbursements (which are based on total premiums) to private insurance companies.

Dennis A. Shield, *Federal Crop Insurance: Background and Issues,* 2 CRS Report No. R40532 (Jan. 20, 2010).

Of particular concern are the administrative and operating cost (A&O) reimbursements provided to industry. *See,* Lisa Shames, *Crop Insurance: Continuing Efforts Are Needed to Improve Program Integrity and Ensure Program Costs Are Reasonable,* Testimony Before the Committee on Oversight and Government Reform, House of Representatives, U.S. Government Accountability Office, GAO-07-819T, 5–7 (May 3, 2007) (noting that from 1996–2007, more than forty cents of every government dollar spent on the crop insurance program went to the insurance companies). As A&O reimbursements have been based on a percentage of premiums, the amounts have gone up significantly as higher crop prices have increased premiums.

> The A&O reimbursement increased from an average of $881 million during FY2004–FY2006 to $1.7 billion in 2009, after reaching $1.3 billion in FY2007 and $2.0 billion in FY2008. Some observers argue that reimbursements should be pegged to something other than premiums, such as a flat fee per policy sold, to better reflect actual costs and to help reduce federal expenditures. The insurance industry contends that reimbursements are currently less than actual delivery expenses.

> Similarly, company underwriting gains (the amount by which a company's share of retained premiums exceeds its indemnities) have increased substantially in recent years, as weather has been generally favorable for growing crops.

Some have argued that if the government share of gains is increased in exchange for a larger government share of losses, average taxpayer costs would decline....

Dennis A. Shields, *Renegotiation of the Standard Reinsurance Agreement (SRA) for Federal Crop Insurance*, 2, CRS Report No. R40966 (Dec. 9, 2009).

The 2008 Farm Bill reduced the A&O reimbursement by 2.3% as well as several other efforts to trim costs. In addition, the RMA is authorized to renegotiate the Standard Reinsurance Agreement (SRA) with the crop insurance companies for the 2011 insurance year. As noted, the SRA defines the A&O expense reimbursements and risk sharing between the government and the private insurance companies, and as such, is key to the overall cost of the program.

Renegotiation of the SRA with the insurance companies was contentious. Insurance companies reacted negatively to many of the changes proposed and launched a campaign against the new proposal. Fears were raised in the farm community that crop insurance would no longer be affordable or as readily available.[9] RMA fought back with its "Myths vs. Facts" statement available at http://rma.usda.gov/news/2010/04/myth-fact2.pdf. After a number of drafts, final agreement regarding a revised SRA was reached in June of 2010. The new agreement includes significant cost saving. It is available at http://www.rma.usda.gov/news/2009/12/sra.html.

2. The significant subsidies provided to the insurance companies have been used to support the argument that the government would save money by replacing the current federal crop insurance system with a simplified county-based loss payment following the model of the new ACRE program. Professor Bruce Babcock of Iowa State University made this proposal in his testimony to Congress on May 13, 2010.

The crop insurance program has cost taxpayers $37 billion since 2000. Of the $13 billion in support over the last two years more than $7 billion flowed to companies. Farmers received indemnity payments (net of premium) totaling $4.5 billion in 2008 and $1.5 billion in 2009. A large proportion of the 2008 net payments came about because the price guarantees were so high that even the modest price drops that we saw in 2008 generated lots of indemnity payments. Nobody should begrudge farmers these indemnity payments because they were made as a result of an insurance contract, but should the government really be in the business of running a program that makes payments to farmers even when farm income is at an all-time record high? If the price drop in 2008 had not occurred, then the crop insurance industry would have been paid an additional $2 billion in 2008 to run the program. It just does not make sense to see such a large portion of farm program costs going to a middleman.

The crop insurance program can also cause environmental problems. The ability of farmers to transfer yield histories on productive ground to high-risk grass-

---

9. A visit to the National Crop Insurance Services website during the negotiations was likely to produce a pop up window with the following message, "Crop insurance currently protects over 265 million acres and 80 billion dollars of America's food supply. With the financial uncertainties and volatilities facing today's farmers and ranchers, crop insurance is more important now than ever before. But severe funding reductions proposed by USDA will impair many of the fifteen private insurance companies preventing them from efficiently providing coverage and leaving farmers financially vulnerable." Easy access to a draft letter to Congress is provided. *See* http://www.cropinsuranceinamerica.org.

land that is prone to crop loss can dramatically increase the profitability of planting on susceptible ground. The Government Accountability Office documents how subsidizing risk on susceptible land can lead to loss of native grassland. *See Farm Program Payments Are an Important Factor in Landowners' Decisions to Convert Grasslands to Cropland*, U.S. Government Accountability Office, GAO-07-1054 (September 2007).

Professor Babcock proposes elimination of direct payments as they are now structured and modification of the ACRE program so that it would cover county revenue losses. He argues that "[f]or approximately the same cost as the direct payment program, 100% of planted acres could be covered at a 95% coverage level. Accounting for county ACRE payments before crop insurance payments are made could easily reduce the cost of the crop insurance program by more than $4 billion per year." Professor Bruce A. Babcock, *Costs and Benefits of Moving to a County ACRE Program*, CARD Policy Brief 10-PB 2, Center for Agriculture and Rural Development, Iowa State University (May 2010) available at www.card.iastate.edu/publications/DBS/PDFFiles/10pb2.pdf.

3. The focus of the federal crop insurance program on traditional commodity crops may discourage farmers from shifting production to fruit and vegetable crops. While the RMA has expanded its insurance coverage recently, many fruits and vegetable crops are not yet covered, particularly in areas where commodity crops have been concentrated. And, NAP does not provide the same level of extensive protection. *See* Jill E. Krueger, Karen R. Krub, and Lynn A. Hayes, PLANTING THE SEEDS FOR PUBLIC HEALTH: HOW THE FARM BILL CAN HELP FARMERS TO PRODUCE AND DISTRIBUTE HEALTHY FOODS, 3-3–3-7 (Farmers' Legal Action Group, Inc., Feb. 2010). The crops and products for which federal crop insurance is available are listed on the RMA website at http://www.rma.usda.gov/policies/ by reference to the crop year available.

4. Organic crops present complex crop insurance issues as generally accepted practices of farming are different and the crop is produced at a significant price premium. For guidance, see Karen R. Krub, Jill E. Krueger, and Jennifer A. Jambor, *Disaster Readiness and Recovery: Considerations for Organic Farmers*, Appendix A in FARMERS GUIDE TO DISASTER ASSISTANCE, Farmers Legal Action Group, Inc. (6th ed. 2008) available at http://www.flaginc.org/topics/disaster/index.php.

The 2008 Farm Bill included the following directive to the FCIC:

> The Corporation shall submit to the Committee on Agriculture of the House of Representatives and the Committee on Agriculture, Nutrition, and Forestry of the Senate an annual report on progress made in developing and improving Federal crop insurance for organic crops, including—
>
> (I) the numbers and varieties of organic crops insured;
>
> (II) the development of new insurance approaches; and
>
> (III) the progress of implementing the initiatives required under this paragraph, including the rate at which additional price elections are adopted for organic crops.

The Farm Bill further requires that the report include "recommendations as the Corporation considers appropriate to improve Federal crop insurance coverage for organic crops."

The RMA submitted a report to Congress on March 19, 2010. It is available on the RMA website at www.rma.usda.gov/pubs/2010/organics.pdf.

C. Disaster Assistance

Farmers who are not eligible for crop insurance may participate in the Noninsured Crop Disaster Assistance Program (NAP). And, in addition to crop insurance protection and NAP, Congress has frequently been willing to approve funding for ad hoc disaster assistance. The 2008 Farm Bill included a new permanent disaster assistance program, the Supplemental Revenue Assistance Program, termed SURE. All three of these programs are administered by USDA Farm Service Agency (FSA) instead of RMA, the agency that administers crop insurance. A brief overview of each of these programs is provided, with additional resources referenced.

1. The Non-Insured Disaster Assistance Program (NAP)

The Noninsured Crop Disaster Assistance Program (NAP) provides crop loss assistance to farmers whose crops are ineligible for federal crop insurance. It provides minimal yield loss protection—50% of historical yield at 55% of expected market price, the same level of protection as catastrophic risk coverage (CAT). NAP is administered by the FSA under regulations found at 7 C.F.R. pt. 1437. An administrative handbook for NAP explains the agency's interpretations of the program. The handbook is available at http://www.fsa.usda.gov/FSA/webapp?area=home&subject=lare&topic=hbk.

The following fact sheet prepared by FSA for producers explains the requirements for NAP participation. The reporting requirements, the administrative fee, and the low level of coverage in the event of loss have caused some farmers to refrain from participating. This is understandable in that many of the farmers who are eligible for NAP have not been eligible for many of the other federal farm programs, as they raise non-commodity crops such as fruits and vegetables.

Congress encourages participation, generally by linking other benefits to participation in NAP. For example, farmers must have obtained coverage under either federal crop insurance or NAP in order to be eligible for new Supplemental Revenue Assistance Payment Program; the new Livestock Forage Disaster Program; the new Tree Assistance Program; and the new Emergency Assistance for Livestock, Honeybees, and Farm Raised Fish Program. *See* 7 C.F.R. § 760.104.

Noninsured Crop Disaster Assistance Program (NAP) Fact Sheet
USDA Farm Service Agency
Disaster Assistance Programs
March 2009

USDA's Farm Service Agency's (FSA) Noninsured Crop Disaster Assistance Program (NAP) provides financial assistance to producers of noninsurable crops when low yields, loss of inventory or prevented planting occur due to natural disasters.

Eligible Producers
An eligible producer is a landowner, tenant or sharecropper who shares in the risk of producing an eligible crop. As authorized by the Food, Conservation, and Energy Act of 2008 (2008 Act), effective May 22, 2008, the average nonfarm adjusted gross income (AGI) limitation of the eligible producer cannot exceed $500,000 to be eligible for NAP.

Eligible Crops

To be eligible for NAP, crops must be noninsurable and commercially-produced agricultural commodity crops for which the catastrophic risk protection level of crop insurance is not available, and must be any of the following:

- crops grown for food;
- crops planted and grown for livestock consumption, including, but not limited to grain and forage crops, including native forage;
- crops grown for fiber, such as cotton and flax (except for trees);
- crops grown in a controlled environment, such as mushrooms and floriculture;
- specialty crops, such as honey and maple sap;
- value loss crops, such as aquaculture, Christmas trees, ginseng, ornamental nursery and turfgrass sod;
- sea oats and sea grass; and
- seed crops where the propagation stock is produced for sale as seed stock for other eligible NAP crop production.

Eligible Natural Disasters

An eligible natural disaster is any of the following—damaging weather, such as drought, freeze, hail, excessive moisture, excessive wind or hurricanes; an adverse natural occurrence, such as earthquake or flood; or a condition related to damaging weather or an adverse natural occurrence, such as excessive heat, disease or insect infestation.

The natural disaster must occur before or during harvest and must directly affect the eligible crop.

Applying for Coverage

Eligible producers must apply for coverage of noninsurable crops using Form CCC-471, "Application for Coverage," and pay the applicable service fees at their local FSA office. The application and service fees must be filed by the application closing date as established by the producer's FSA state committee.

The service fee is the lesser of $250 per crop or $750 per producer per administrative county, not to exceed a total of $1,875 for a producer with farming interests in multiple counties. This fee is authorized by the 2008 Act. It replaces the previous service fee of the lesser of $100 per crop or $300 per producer per administrative county, not to exceed a total of $900 for a producer with farming interest in multiple counties.

Limited resource producers may request a waiver of service fees. To qualify for an administrative service fee waiver, the producer must meet both of the following criteria:

- earn no more than $100,000 gross income in farm sales from each of the previous two years (to be increased starting in FY 2004 to adjust for inflation, using the prices paid by farmers index as compiled by the National Agricultural Statistics Service (NASS);
- have a total household income at or below the national poverty level for a family of four, or less than 50 percent of county median household for both of the previous two years.

Limited resource producer status can be determined using the USDA Limited Resource Farmer and Rancher Online Self Determination Tool at http://www.lrftool.sc.

egov.usda.gov/tool.asp. The automated system calculates and displays adjusted gross farm sales per year and the higher of the national poverty level or county median household income.

Coverage Period for NAP

The coverage period for NAP may vary depending on whether the producer grows annual, perennial or value-loss crops.

The coverage period for annual crops begins the later of 30 days after application for coverage and the applicable service fees have been paid or the date the crop is planted (cannot exceed the final planting date). [Coverage] ends the earlier of the date the crop harvest is completed; the normal harvest date for the crop; the date the crop is abandoned; or the date the entire crop acreage is destroyed.

The coverage period for perennial crops, other than those intended for forage, begins 30 calendar days after the application closing date and ends the earlier of 10 months from the application closing date; the date the crop harvest is completed; the normal harvest date for the crop; the date the crop is abandoned; or the date the entire crop acreage is destroyed....

Information Required to Remain Eligible for NAP

To remain eligible for NAP assistance, the following crop acreage information must be reported annually:

- name of the crop (lettuce, clover, etc.);
- type and variety (head lettuce, red clover, etc.);
- location and acreage of the crop (field, sub-field, etc.);
- share of the crop and the names of other producers with an interest in the crop;
- type of practice used to grow the crop (irrigated or non-irrigated);
- date the crop was planted in each field; and
- intended use of the commodity (fresh, processed, etc.).

Producers should report crop acreage shortly after planting (early in the risk period) to ensure reporting deadlines are not missed and coverage is not lost.

In addition, producers must annually provide the following production information: the quantity of all harvested production of the crop in which the producer held an interest during the crop year; the disposition of the harvested crop, such as whether it is marketable, unmarketable, salvaged or used differently than intended; and verifiable or reliable crop production records (when required by FSA).

Producers must provide production records in a manner that can be easily understood by the FSA county committee. Questions regarding acceptable production records should be directed to your local FSA office. Failure to report acreage and production information may result in reduced or zero NAP assistance. Be aware that acreage reporting and final planting dates vary by crop and by region....

FSA Use of Reported Acreage and Production

FSA uses acreage reports to verify the existence of the crop and to record the number of acres covered by the application. The acreage report and the production report are combined to calculate the approved yield (expected production for a crop year). The approved yield is the average of your actual production history (APH) for a minimum of 4 to a maximum of 10 crop years (5 years for apples and peaches). To calculate your APH, FSA divides your total production by your crop acreage.

Your approved yield may be calculated using substantially reduced yield data if you do not report acreage and production, or report fewer than 4 years of crop production.

Applying for NAP Assistance When a Natural Disaster Strikes

When a crop or planting is affected by a natural disaster, you must notify your local FSA office and complete Part B, (the Notice of Loss portion) of the application, which is Form CCC-576, the Notice of Loss and Application for Payment. This must be completed within 15 calendar days of the natural disaster occurrence; final planting date if your planting was prevented by a natural disaster; date damage to the crop or loss of production becomes apparent to you.

To receive NAP benefits, producers must complete Form CCC-576, Notice of Loss and Application for Payment, parts D, E, F as applicable, and G, no later than the immediately subsequent crop year acreage reporting date for the crop. The CCC-576 requires producers to provide evidence of production and note whether the crop was marketable, unmarketable, salvaged or used differently than intended.

Amount of Production Loss to Receive a NAP Payment

The natural disaster must have either reduced the expected unit production of the crop by more than 50 percent; or prevented the producer from planting more than 35 percent of the intended crop acreage.

Expected production is the amount of the crop produced in the absence of a natural disaster. FSA compares expected production to actual production to determine the percentage of crop loss.

Defining a NAP Unit

The NAP unit includes the specific crop acreage in the county in which the producer has a unique crop interest. A unique crop interest is either [a] 100 percent interest; or a shared interest with other producers.

How Much Loss NAP Covers

NAP covers the amount of loss greater than 50 percent of the expected production based on the approved yield and reported acreage.

Information FSA Uses to Calculate Payment

The NAP payment is calculated by unit using crop acreage; approved yield; net production; 55 percent of an average market price for the specific commodity established by the FSA state committee; [and,] a payment factor reflecting the decreasing cost incurred in the production cycle for the crop that is harvested, unharvested or prevented from being planted.

Payment Limitation

NAP payments received, directly or indirectly, will be attributed to the applicable individuals or entities and limited to $100,000 per crop year per individual or entity.

Risk Management Purchase Requirement

Noninsurable commodities on a farm are required to have NAP coverage in order for producers on that farm to be eligible for the Supplemental Revenue Assistance Payments (SURE) Program, Tree Assistance Program (TAP) and the Emergency Assistance for Livestock, Honey Bees, and Farm-raised Fish Program (ELAP).

For additional information on NAP see Karen R. Krub, *Noninsured Crop Disaster Assistance Program (NAP)*, materials prepared for Federation of Southern Cooperatives, Farmers Legal Action Group, Inc. (Sept. 11, 2009) available at http://www.flaginc.org/topics/disaster/index.php.

2. Ad Hoc Disaster Assistance

While federal crop insurance for eligible crops or NAP for ineligible crops is the primary form of risk management assistance provided by the government, disaster assistance payments have also been frequently provided.

For at least thirty years, Congress has attempted to rein in this spending by encouraging the purchase of crop insurance. In 1980, when it passed the Federal Crop Insurance Act, its goal was to replace the costly disaster assistance programs. In 1980, 1994, and 2000, premium subsidy levels were increased to encourage farmers to purchase coverage.[1] Coverage has greatly increased, along with government costs.

Crop insurance is sometimes linked to other benefits as an additional inducement. For the 1995 crop year, farmers were required to obtain at least CAT coverage to be eligible for the federal farm programs and certain other USDA programs. Still, in the face of weather disasters, Congress continued to pass emergency assistance, and the requirement was softened. Farmers were allowed to waive any future claim to disaster assistance instead obtaining crop insurance.[2]

In 1998 and 1999, however, Congress extended emergency crop loss assistance benefits to producers despite any prior waiver.[3] To receive these benefits, these producers were required to purchase CAT or additional coverage in the subsequent two years for all crops of economic significance produced by such person for which insurance is available.[4]

To this day, however, as is suggested in the following article, providing assistance to farmers in the face of a disaster remains politically compelling.

---

1. Robert Dismukes and Joseph Glauber, "Why Hasn't Crop Insurance Eliminated Disaster Assistance," *Amber Waves*, USDA Economic Research Service, June 2005.

2. Christopher R. Kelley, *The Agricultural Risk Protection Act of 2000: Federal Crop Insurance, the Non-insured Crop Disaster Assistance Program, and the Domestic Commodity and Other Farm Programs*, 6 Drake J. Agric. L. 141, 145 (2001) (explaining the newly enacted crop insurance provisions and citing 7 U.S.C. § 1508(b)(7)(a) (1994)).

3. *Id.*, citing The Agriculture, Rural Development, Food and Drug Administration, and Related Agencies Appropriations Act, 2000, Pub. L. No. 106-78, tit. VIII, § 801, 113 Stat. 1135, 1175–76; Consolidated Appropriations Act, 2000, Pub. L. No. 106-113, App. E, tit. I, 113 Stat. 1501, 1537 (appropriations for 1999 crop losses); Omnibus Consolidated and Emergency Supplemental Appropriations Act of 1999, Pub. L. No. 105-277, tit. X, §§ 1101–1103, 112 Stat. 2681, 2681-44 to 2681-45 (appropriations for 1998 crop losses and losses in at least three of the years from 1994 through 1998).

4. *See* 65 Fed. Reg. 7,942, 7,964 (2000) (to be codified at 7 C.F.R. pt. 1498.7(a)) (1999 crop loss assistance); 7 C.F.R. § 1477.108(a) (1999) (1998 crop loss assistance).

Dennis A. Shields and Ralph M. Chite
Agricultural Disaster Assistance
Congressional Research Service Report No. RS21212
March 11, 2010

* * *

Emergency Supplemental Farm Disaster Assistance

In virtually every crop year between 1988 and 2007, Congress provided ad hoc disaster assistance to farmers and ranchers with significant weather-related production losses. Ad-hoc assistance has been made available primarily through emergency supplemental appropriations to a wide array of USDA programs.[10]

While disaster programs authorized in the 2008 farm bill are meant to replace the need for ad hoc payments, it is an open question whether Congress will continue to pass additional emergency payments for producers. This is particularly true for crop losses, because of the potential time lag between actual losses and government payments.[11] The sections below describe the most recent emergency funding, beginning with 2005 losses and ending with congressional action in March 2010 for 2009-crop losses.

2005–2007 Supplemental Assistance

Title IX of the FY2007 Iraq war supplemental appropriations act (P.L. 110-28) provided emergency agricultural disaster assistance, primarily for crop and livestock losses in any one of years 2005, 2006, or 2007 (for crops planted before February 28, 2007). Subsequently, Congress extended the assistance for crop and livestock losses in all of 2007 in the FY2008 Consolidated Appropriations Act (P.L. 110-161, Division A, Section 743). Both laws limited payments to one of the three years, as selected by the producer. The cost of 2005–2007 assistance was $2.45 billion, including $2.03 billion for crop loss assistance and $383 million for livestock feed and mortality losses.[12] The following is a description of the major agricultural disaster provisions.[13] The producer signup period for 2005–2007 crop years ended on February 27, 2009.

Crop Loss Assistance

P.L. 110-28, as amended by P.L. 110-161, provided such sums as necessary to fund a crop disaster payment program for 2005, 2006, or 2007 production losses. Payments under the crop loss provisions were $2.03 billion. In order to contain program costs, a pro-

---

10. For a history of the congressional response to agricultural disasters, see CRS Report RL31095, *Emergency Funding for Agriculture: A Brief History of Supplemental Appropriations*, FY1989–FY2009, by Ralph M. Chite.

11. In contrast to crop disaster payments under the 2008 farm bill, the method for determining loss under the livestock programs is more streamlined, and livestock payments arrive more quickly. Livestock death losses for individual producers immediately trigger Livestock Indemnity Program payments, while the weekly publication "U.S. Drought Monitor" is used to determine payments for grazing losses under the Livestock Forage Disaster Program. As of early January 2010, USDA had made more than $175 million in disaster payments under both programs.

12. Payment figures in this section are from U.S. Department of Agriculture, Economic Research Service, *Agricultural Outlook: Statistical Indicators*, Table 35 — CCC Net Outlays by Commodity and Function, http://www.ers.usda.gov/ publications/agoutlook/aotables/2009/11Nov/aotab35.xls.

13. For more information on these disaster programs, see various USDA fact sheets accessed at http://www.fsa.usda.gov/FSA/webapp?area=home&subject=diap&topic=landing.

ducer could not receive a payment for more than one crop year. Eligible producers could receive a payment on losses in excess of 35% of normal crop yields. The payment rate was 42% of the established market price for the commodity. The act also prohibited any crop disaster payments to a producer who either waived crop insurance or did not participate in the Noninsured Crop Disaster Assistance Program in the year of the loss. Also, the sum of disaster payments, crop insurance indemnities, and crop marketings could not exceed 95% of what the value of the crop would have been in the absence of losses. P.L. 110-28 also required USDA to make payments to farmers who experienced quality losses to their 2005–2007 crops, as well as for quantity losses.

Livestock Assistance

P.L. 110-28, as amended by P.L. 110-161, contained necessary sums to fund a Livestock Compensation Program (LCP) to reimburse livestock growers for feed losses caused by a natural disaster. Payments under the LCP provision were $341 million. Payments were made to producers of beef, dairy, poultry, hogs, sheep, goats, and catfish, in any county that was declared a disaster area by the President or Secretary of Agriculture between January 1, 2005, and December 31, 2007, with payments limited to one year of losses. To contain costs, the act limited the payment rate to 61% of the payment rate used in previous years. For the same time period, P.L. 110-28, as amended, contained necessary funds (payments totaled $42 million) for a Livestock Indemnity Program to reimburse producers for replacing livestock killed by a natural disaster, at a payment rate of at least 26% of the market value of the livestock prior to death. The statute also included payments to dairy producers for production losses in disaster-designated counties (payments totaled $12 million).

Conservation

P.L. 110-28 contained $16 million in additional funding for the Emergency Conservation Program (ECP) to assist farmers in the cleanup and restoration of farmland damaged by a natural disaster. Separately, P.L. 110-28 in effect provided additional funds for the Emergency Forestry Conservation Reserve Program, a program that helps restore forest lands in the South that were damaged by the 2005 hurricanes. The act removed statutory language that prohibited any spending beyond calendar year 2006, which CBO estimated at $115 million for FY2007.

2008 Supplemental Assistance

Primarily in response to the 2008 Midwest floods, the FY2008 Supplemental Appropriations Act (P.L. 110-252) contained a total of nearly $480 million in emergency funding to eligible farmers to defray the cost of clean-up and rehabilitation of farmland and watersheds following a disaster. Of the total amount available, $89.4 million was for the Emergency Conservation Program (ECP), which assists farmers in the cleanup and restoration of farmland damaged by a natural disaster, and $390.5 million was for the Emergency Watershed Protection Program (EWPP), which is designed to relieve imminent hazards created by natural disasters and to alleviate future flood risk. Second supplemental amounts of $115 million for ECP and $100 million for the EWPP were provided under the Consolidated Security, Disaster Assistance, and Continuing Appropriations Act of 2009 (P.L. 110-329).[14] No emergency supplemental disaster assistance was authorized

---

14. U.S. Department of Agriculture, Farm Service Agency, *FY2010 USDA Budget Explanatory Notes for Committee on Appropriations*, Farm Service Agency, June 3, 2009, p. 68, http://www.obpa. usda.gov/18fsa2010notes.pdf

for 2008 crop and livestock losses, since new programs were authorized and funded through the 2008 farm bill, as described above....

Potential Disaster Assistance for 2009-Crop Losses

Following losses to 2009 crops due to excessive rain across much of the country, legislation was introduced in late 2009 in both chambers (S. 2810 and H.R. 4177) to make emergency payments to producers for losses in calendar year 2009. The bills were referred to committees in both chambers. Subsequently, the Senate Finance Committee attached emergency agricultural assistance to the House-passed version of the Tax Extenders Act of 2009 (H.R. 4213), which does not contain provisions for agricultural disaster payments.[17] The Senate passed the amended bill on March 10, 2010.

The legislation would provide a supplemental "direct payment" to producers in counties designated as primary natural disaster areas (i.e., excluding contiguous counties) who receive direct payments for 2009 crops under Section 1103 of the 2008 farm bill (wheat, corn, grain sorghum, barley, oats, upland cotton, long grain rice, medium grain rice, soybeans, and other oilseeds) and under Section 1303 (peanuts). The yield threshold for loss due to a natural disaster is 5%, much lower than historical norms, and the payment would be 90% of a farm's direct payment in 2009. At 5%, the proposed loss threshold is much lower than previous disaster programs that paid for losses in excess of 35% at 65% of established prices.

Provisions in the Senate bill are also included for payments to specialty crop producers ($300 million), producers and first handlers of cottonseed ($42 million), and aquaculture producers ($25 million) for high feed costs in 2009. USDA is also directed to make a $21 million payment to an agricultural transportation cooperative in Hawaii for assistance to maintain and develop employment. Additional provisions authorize $75 million in no-interest emergency loans to poultry producers who have suffered financial losses associated with the termination or nonrenewal of a contract with a poultry company that has filed under Chapter 11 of the U.S. Bankruptcy Code. Finally, provisions that trigger payments for 2009 losses under the existing Livestock Forage Disaster Program are loosened. The Congressional Budget Office estimates the total cost at $1.48 billion.

To avoid paying a producer twice for the same loss, the legislation stipulates that any payments would be included in the calculation of farm revenue for a producer's payment under the SURE program (see "Supplemental Revenue Assistance Payments Program (SURE)").

Some Members of Congress are concerned that payments under the legislation could be too generous because of the low loss threshold. Normal variation in crop yields can be more than 5%. As a result, payments could go to producers and landowners (receiving direct payments) who had not experienced weather-related disasters.

———————

Given that the last ad hoc disaster legislation that was enacted, the Disaster Assistance for 2009 Crops was passed *after* Congress created a new permanent disaster program, it seems likely that ad hoc disaster assistance will continue to be enacted in the future.

———————

17. Senate Finance Committee, "Baucus, Reid Introduce Package to Restore Aid for Out-of-Work Americans, Improve Tax Certainty for Families, Businesses to Bolster Job Creation," press release, March 1, 2010, http://finance.senate.gov/press/Bpress/2010press/prb030110b.pdf. The proposed legislation is at http://finance.senate.gov/sitepages/leg/LEG%202010/030110_Workers_State_Business_Relief_Act.pdf.

3. Supplemental Revenue Assistance Payments (SURE)

The 2008 Farm Bill created a new set of five disaster programs called "Supplemental Agricultural Disaster Assistance." These standing disaster programs outline the support that will be provided to farmers experiencing disasters, allowing farmers a degree of certainty regarding a "safety net" to protect them in an emergency. The programs are designed to supplement crop insurance coverage and to provide disaster assistance for crops as well as livestock (including aquaculture and honey bees), forage, and tree and nursery crops.

> The largest component of Supplemental Agricultural Disaster Assistance is a new crop disaster program called the Supplemental Revenue Assistance Payments Program (SURE). The program pays producers for crop revenue losses due to natural disaster or adverse weather. It essentially compensates eligible producers for a portion of losses that are not eligible for an indemnity payment under a crop insurance policy. The program departs, however, from both traditional disaster assistance and crop yield insurance by calculating and reimbursing losses using total crop revenue for the entire farm (i.e., summing revenue from all crops for an individual farmer)....
>
> On December 28, 2009, USDA issued regulations for SURE. [74 Fed. Reg. 68,480 (Dec. 28, 2009).] Previously, farm groups had been calling for their publication so that farmers could learn program details, sign up, and consider related business issues such as appropriate insurance coverage levels. USDA officials say that this is the most complex program USDA's Farm Service Agency has undertaken, and the Department has faced a number of issues as it implements the program.

Dennis A. Shields, *A Whole-Farm Crop Disaster Program: Supplemental Revenue Assistance Payments (SURE)*, Congressional Research Service Report No. R40452 (Jan. 28, 2010).

The USDA Economic Research Service explains the mechanics of SURE payments as follows:

> **Supplemental Revenue Program (SURE)** makes payments to eligible producers on farms in disaster counties that incurred crop production or crop-quality losses or both during the crop year. SURE provides payments of 60 percent of the difference (greater than zero) between the disaster assistance program guarantee revenue and actual total farm revenue.
>
> The disaster assistance program guarantee is the sum of:
>
> - 115 percent of the insured value of each insurable commodity
>   - insured value = 100 percent of price election × acres insured × coverage level × yield, where yield is the higher of the adjusted actual production history yield or the counter-cyclical payment (CCP) program yield
> - 120 percent of value of noninsurable commodity(ies) = 100 percent of NAP price × acres planted × the higher of the adjusted NAP yield or the CCP program yield
>
> Actual total farm revenue is the sum of:
>
> - Acres harvested × estimated actual yield × national average market price
> - 15 percent of any direct payments
> - All CCP and Average Crop Revenue Election Program payments and marketing loan benefits

- Any prevented plantings payments
- Crop insurance indemnities and NAP payments
- Any other related Federal natural disaster payments.

Natural Disaster and Emergency Assistance Programs, USDA Economic Research Service, Briefing Room: Farm and Commodity Policy: Program Provisions, available at http://www.ers.usda.gov/Briefing/Farmpolicy/disaster.htm.

While many support the certainty promised by a standing, i.e., permanent disaster program, the complexity of the program has been criticized.

> The purpose of SURE is to provide supplemental whole-farm coverage to provide payments when crop insurance deductibles are not exceeded. The problem with SURE is that it is so complicated that almost nobody knows when a payment will be triggered. To calculate SURE guarantees and payments requires knowledge of what crop insurance a farmer buys, a farmer's crop insurance yield, a farmer's countercyclical base yield, direct payment levels, crop insurance indemnity payments, countercyclical payments, marketing loan payments, and ACRE payments. The complexity of the program is caused by the need to make sure that farmers are not over paid for crop losses. It is ironic that such an effort is expended to ensure that a farmer suffers a whole-farm loss before a SURE payment is received when direct payments will flow to the same farmer even in the most profitable years.

Professor Bruce A. Babcock, *Costs and Benefits of Moving to a County ACRE Program,* CARD Policy Brief 10-PB 2, Center for Agriculture and Rural Development, Iowa State University (May 2010) available at http://www.card.iastate.edu/publications/DBS/PDFFiles/10pb2.pdf.

The USDA ERS describes the other four components of the standing disaster assistance program as follows:

> [The] **Livestock Indemnity Program** makes payments available to eligible producers for livestock death losses in excess of normal mortality due to adverse weather. The indemnity payment rate is 75 percent of market value of applicable livestock on the day before death, as determined by the Secretary of Agriculture.

> [The] **Livestock Forage Disaster Program** payments are available to eligible producers of covered livestock for grazing losses due to drought or fire on public managed land. Payment rates are based on monthly feed costs.

The monthly feed cost equals the product of:

- 30 days
- The feed-grain equivalent of:
    - 15.7 pounds of corn per day for an adult beef cow, or
    - For any other weight of livestock, a value that represents the average number of pounds of corn per day necessary to feed the livestock as determined by the Secretary of Agriculture
- A payment rate that is equal to the corn price per pound: 56 pounds per bushel multiplied by the higher of the national average corn price per bushel for the 12-month or 24-month period immediately preceding March 1 of the year for which the disaster assistance is calculated

[The] **Emergency Assistance Program for Livestock, Honey Bees, and Farm-Raised Fish** provides emergency relief to eligible producers of livestock, honey bees, and farm-raised fish for losses due to disease, adverse weather, or other conditions not covered by the Livestock Indemnity Program or by the Livestock Forage Disaster Program. Total payments are limited to $50 million per year.

[The] **Orchard and Nursery Tree Assistance Program** provides assistance to eligible orchardists and nursery tree growers for trees lost to natural disasters. Assistance includes reimbursement of 70 percent of the cost of replanting trees in excess of normal mortality and reimbursement of 50 percent of the cost of salvaging damaged trees and preparing land to replant trees.

Natural Disaster and Emergency Assistance Programs, USDA, Economic Research Service, Briefing Room: Farm and Commodity Policy: Program Provisions, available at http://www.ers.usda.gov/Briefing/Farmpolicy/disaster.htm.

Notes

1. The Farmers Legal Action Group, Inc. report, PLANTING THE SEEDS FOR PUBLIC HEALTH: HOW THE FARM BILL CAN HELP FARMERS TO PRODUCE AND DISTRIBUTE HEALTHY FOODS (Farmers' Legal Action Group, Inc., Feb. 2010) (available for free download at http://www.flaginc.org) provides an overview of federal crop insurance and disaster assistance mechanisms. *See* Chapter 3: *Crop Insurance and Disaster Assistance Programs.* The report also analyzes the ways in which these programs as implemented influence the overall food system.

D. Farm Programs and the Food System

In the past, it seemed that only those involved directly in the agricultural industry paid attention to the federal farm programs. The crafting of the farm program sections of the farm bill often seemed to be primarily a matter of negotiation between commodity groups.

In recent years, however, there has been increasing interest in considering the impact of federal farm policy on the structure of our food system and its impact on the actual food that Americans consume. Michael Pollan[18] is largely credited with leading this inquiry and providing a critical analysis of the impact.

What our food system does well is precisely what it was designed to do, which is to produce cheap calories in great abundance. It is no small thing for an American to be able to go into a fast-food restaurant and to buy a double cheeseburger, fries and a large Coke for a price equal to less than an hour of labor at

---

18. Pollan is a contributing writer to the NEW YORK TIMES MAGAZINE and the Knight Professor of Journalism at University of California, Berkeley. He is the author of THE OMNIVORE'S DILEMMA: A NATURAL HISTORY OF FOUR MEALS, named one of the ten best books of the year by both the NEW YORK TIMES and the WASHINGTON POST. A young readers' version of THE OMNIVORE'S DILEMMA: THE SECRETS BEHIND WHAT YOU EAT is now also available. Pollan also authored IN DEFENSE OF FOOD: AN EATER'S MANIFESTO, winner of the James Beard Award. His new book FOOD RULES: AN EATER'S MANUAL was released in December 2009. Previous books include SECOND NATURE, THE BOTANY OF DESIRE, and A PLACE OF MY OWN. Pollan appears in *Food, Inc*, a documentary on the food industry.

the minimum wage—indeed, in the long sweep of history, this represents a re-markable achievement.

It must be recognized that the current food system—characterized by mono-cultures of corn and soy in the field and cheap calories of fat, sugar and feedlot meat on the table—is not simply the product of the free market. Rather, it is the product of a specific set of government policies that sponsored a shift from solar (and human) energy on the farm to fossil-fuel energy.

Michael Pollan, *Open Letter to the Next Farmer in Chief*, THE NEW YORK TIMES MAGA-ZINE, (Oct. 12, 2008), available at http://www.nytimes.com/2008/10/12/magazine/12policy-t.html?_r=1&pagewanted=2.

In the *Open Letter to the Next Farmer in Chief*, and in greater depth in OMNIVORE'S DILEMMA, Pollan describes the transformation of agriculture from a diversified system of production to an industrialized system of monocultural production. He attributes the transformation to the government's encouragement of the "conversion of the munitions in-dustry to fertilizer—ammonium nitrate being the main ingredient of both bombs and chemical fertilizer—and the conversion of nerve-gas research to pesticides. " He also blames the structure of federal farm program subsidies for commodity crops, subsidies that encouraged farmers to grow "all the corn, soybeans, wheat and rice they could produce."

> The chief result ... was a flood of cheap grain that could be sold for substan-tially less than it cost farmers to grow because a government check helped make up the difference. As this artificially cheap grain worked its way up the food chain, it drove down the price of all the calories derived from that grain: the high-fructose corn syrup in the Coke, the soy oil in which the potatoes were fried, the meat and cheese in the burger.

Pollan connects the cheap corn that is produced under government subsidies to the de-velopment of the current industrialized model in animal agriculture and to the wide-spread use of corn in an astounding array of products. Consider the vast number of products containing processed corn products such as high fructose corn syrup, corn oil, and corn starch. Government policies favoring corn based ethanol have further encour-aged agricultural production of corn, to the exclusion of a more diversified cropping pat-tern. The environmental effects of the extensive production of corn are addressed in Chapter IV, *Agriculture and Environmental Law*.

The USDA Economic Research Service Briefing Room, *Corn*, describes the predomi-nance of corn in current production.

- Corn is the most widely produced feed grain in the United States, accounting for more than 90 percent of total value and production of feed grains.

- Around 80 million acres of land are planted to corn, with the majority of the crop grown in the Heartland region.

- Most of the crop is used as the main energy ingredient in livestock feed.

- Corn is also processed into a multitude of food and industrial products including starch, sweeteners, corn oil, beverage and industrial alcohol, and fuel ethanol.

- The United States is a major player in the world corn trade market, with approx-imately 20 percent of the corn crop exported to other countries.

> Corn is grown in most U.S. States, but production is concentrated in the Heart-land region (including Illinois, Iowa, Indiana, eastern portions of South Dakota and Nebraska, western Kentucky and Ohio, and the northern two-thirds of Mis-

souri). Iowa and Illinois, the top corn-producing States, typically account for slightly more than one-third of the U.S. crop.

USDA, Economic Research Service Briefing Room: Corn, available at http://www.ers.usda.gov/Briefing/corn/.

Theoretically, the use of Direct Payments that are de-coupled from actual production should have freed farmers from planting program crops such as corn, potentially reinstituting crop diversity. A variety of factors, however, including other farm policies, have produced the opposite effect. Increased farm size, with larger, more specialized and more expensive equipment favors limiting crop production to one or two crops. Much of the livestock industry is now dependent upon a continuing supply of corn-based feed. Research, often at land grant universities, continues to develop new uses for the very versatile corn crop, increasing demand.

> Corn acreage in the United States has increased from a government-mandated low of 60.2 million planted acres in 1983 due to provisions in the Federal Agriculture Improvement and Reform Act of 1996. The Act permitted farmers to make their own crop planting decisions based on the most profitable crop for a given year. While the number of feed grain farms (those that produce corn, sorghum, barley, and/or oats) in the United States has declined in recent years, the acreage per corn farm has risen. Moreover, the number of large corn farms (those with more than 500 acres) has increased over time, while the number of small corn farms (those with less than 500 acres) has fallen.
>
> Corn production has risen over time, as higher yields followed improvements in technology (seed varieties, fertilizers, pesticides, and machinery) and in production practices (reduced tillage, irrigation, crop rotations, and pest management systems).
>
> Strong demand for ethanol production has resulted in higher corn prices and has provided incentives to increase corn acreage. In many cases, farmers have increased corn acreage by adjusting crop rotations between corn and soybeans, which has caused soybean plantings to decrease. Other sources of land for increased corn plantings include cropland used as pasture, reduced fallow, acreage returning to production from expiring Conservation Reserve Program contracts, and shifts from other crops, such as cotton.

USDA, Economic Research Service, Briefing Room: Corn, available at http://www.ers.usda.gov/Briefing/corn/.

Beyond the focus on corn and its impact on food in the United States, the government policy of subsidizing crops in order to promote and sustain "cheap food" through its farm programs has been under recent attack as promoting an unhealthy diet and leading to the current obesity epidemic. Neil Hamilton identified obesity as one of a number of the hidden costs of "cheap food" in his essay, *Food Democracy II: Revolution or Restoration?*, stating that "much of the real cost of cheap food is shifted out of the market and onto society in other ways—poor diets, obesity, environmental damage, exploited workers, and underpaid farmers."[19]

At a minimum, support for commodity crops has allowed the cost of grain starches, oils, and sweeteners to remain low while the more healthy and largely unsubsidized fruits and vegetables are more expensive.

---

19. Neil D. Hamilton, 1 J. Food L. & Pol'y 13, 30 (2005)

Increasing U.S. consumption of fruits and vegetables has been a major theme of Federal dietary guidelines for over a decade. A diet rich in fruits and vegetables is associated with higher intakes of key nutrients, such as folate, potassium, and vitamins A and C. Because these foods tend to have fewer calories per serving than other foods, they can also play an important part in reducing incidence of overweight and obesity. Yet, despite clear health benefits and consistent Federal recommendations, most Americans fall short of their recommended fruit and vegetable intake.

Dietary Patterns, Diet Quality, and Obesity, USDA, Economic Research Service, Briefing Room: Diet Quality and Food Consumption, available at http://www.ers.usda.gov/Briefing/DietQuality/DietaryPatterns.htm.

While increasing fruit and vegetable consumption is a "major theme," the federal farm programs continue to subsidize commodities to the general exclusion of fruits and vegetables, with disincentives to convert acreage to fruit and vegetable production built into the programs.

Moreover, the introduction of additional processed foods into the average American diet has been eased by the low cost of the sweeteners and oils made from supported crops.

Americans are consuming more calories per day than they did over 30 years ago. In 1970, Americans consumed an estimated 2,172 calories per person per day whereas in 2007, they consumed an estimated 2,704 calories (after adjusting for plate waste, spoilage, and other food losses). Of this 533-calorie increase, added fats and oils accounted for 210 calories; grains (mainly refined grains), 194 calories; caloric sweeteners, 58 calories; meats, 28 calories; fruits and vegetables, 28 calories; and dairy fats, 18 calories. Only dairy products declined (3 calories).

According to this data, the average American consumed more calories from added fats and oils per day than any other food group.

Added fats and oils	639 calories
Flour and cereal products	626 calories
Meat, eggs, and nuts	476 calories
Caloric sweeteners	459 calories
Dairy	284 calories
Fruit and vegetables	220 calories

Dietary Trends From Food and Nutrient Availability Data, USDA, Economic Research Service, Briefing Room: Diet Quality and Food Consumption, available at http://www.ers.usda.gov/Briefing/DietQuality/Availability.htm.

In *A Fair Farm Bill for Public Health*, the Institute for Agricultural Trade and Policy argued that:

The current obesity crisis has increased the focus on the prevalence of high-fat, high-sugar foods in the U.S. diet—and on the commodities used to make them. Although the relationship between commodity prices and use of these commodities in the U.S. food system is not completely clear, low-priced commodities have become ubiquitous in food processing.

Many food industry companies have developed successful business models based on current agricultural policies and existing cropping systems. Corn, soybeans and other low-cost commodities have proliferated in the U.S. food system, likely because the food industry has found using these crops to be very profitable. For example, high fructose corn syrup and hydrogenated vegetable oils—products that did not even exist a generation ago—are now prevalent in foods, probably due to inexpensive corn and soybeans.

By keeping prices for these crops artificially low, U.S. farm policy allows food processors to purchase commodities at a fraction of their true cost. This market deviation has dramatically increased the amount of cheap, processed and fast food in the U.S. diet and put healthier foods like fruits and vegetables at a competitive disadvantage.

The gains of these industries come at the direct expense of traditional meals. Effectively reducing the consumption of fast foods and other unhealthy options cannot be done without creating a level playing field for healthier foods.

Heather Schnoover, *A Fair Farm Bill for Public Health*, Institute for Agriculture and Trade Policy (May 2007). For the supporting analysis linking food trends including obesity to agricultural policies, see Mark Muller, Heather Schnoover, and Dr. David Wallinga, *Considering the Contribution of U.S. Food and Agricultural Policy to the Obesity Epidemic: Overview and Opportunities*, Institute for Agriculture and Trade Policy (Feb. 2007), available at http://www.agobservatory.org/library.cfm?RefID=99608.

The article, *A Reconsideration of Agricultural Law: A Call for the Law of Food, Farming, and Sustainability* argues that agriculture should receive special treatment as a protected and supported industry, but calls for "a reconsideration of the framework of agricultural law and the development of an agricultural policy that supports and encourages a sustainable food policy." The article advocates for "a policy that supports the economic welfare of the agricultural industry but only in the context of the universal societal goal that justifies its special treatment—the production of food." The article goes on to recognize that "not all food is created equal."

> Some serves as healthy fare; other food can actually contribute to health problems. Because food production is a limited resource, choices should be made wisely. Although, as a mature industry, much of agriculture can and should flourish without government intervention, to the extent that government policies influence the production of food this influence should be focused on the production of healthy food. "Agricultural law" should be recast as the law of food, farming, and sustainability, with the sustainable production and delivery of healthy food to consumers as its central goal.

Susan A. Schneider, *A Reconsideration of Agricultural Law: A Call for the Law of Food, Farming, and Sustainability*, 34 Wm. & Mary Envtl. L. & Pol'y Rev. 935, 937 (2010).

Whether there will be the widespread popular support and the political will necessary to make any significant redirection in the federal farm programs remains an open question. As noted by an agricultural economist in testimony before the House Agriculture Committee as it prepares for the next Farm Bill, "[c]alls for reform of farm commodity programs have a history as long as farm programs themselves."[20]

---

20. Professor Bruce A. Babcock, *Costs and Benefits of Moving to a County ACRE Program*, CARD Policy Brief 10-PB 2, Center for Agriculture and Rural Development, Iowa State University (May 2010) available at www.card.iastate.edu/publications/DBS/PDFFiles/10pb2.pdf.

III

Agriculture and Environmental Law

In a well-researched critique of agriculture and environmental law published in 2000, Professor J.B. Ruhl noted agriculture's "dramatic impact on our planet's landscape and environmental systems."[1] Ruhl coined the term "anti-law" to characterize the lack of agricultural law and regulation to address the environmental consequences of agricultural production.

> Farms are one of the last uncharted frontiers of environmental regulation in the United States. Despite the substantial environmental harms they cause—habitat loss and degradation, soil erosion and sedimentation, water resources depletion, soil and water salinization, agrochemical releases, animal wastes, nonpoint source water pollution, and air pollution—environmental law has given them a virtual license to do so. When combined, the active and passive safe harbors farms enjoy in most environmental laws amount to an "anti-law" that finds no rational basis given the magnitude of harms farms cause.

J.B. Ruhl, *Farms, Their Environmental Harms, and Environmental Law*, 27 Ecology L.Q. 263 (2000). Ruhl's stinging analysis of the variety of ways in which agriculture damages the environment remains even more poignant ten years later. Yet, Ruhl is not anti-agriculture, nor is he anti-farmer.

> To acknowledge that farms pollute and degrade the environment should neither indict farming as a way of life nor denigrate the ideals farmers hold. Farming in America is a deeply-rooted cultural institution with many noble qualities and important economic and social benefits, but it is also an industry with much in common with other industries, their owners, and their workers. Acknowledging that industries cause environmental damage has not generally been regarded as an attack on the people or the institutions involved. Nor should it be so for farms. The plain truth is that farms pollute ground water, surface water, air, and soils;

---

1. J.B. Ruhl, *Farms, Their Environmental Harms, and Environmental Law*, 27 Ecology L.Q. 263, 265 (2000) (citing A.M. Mannion, Agriculture and Environmental Change 227 (1995) ("Agriculture, to state the obvious, has had a profound influence on the Earth's surface and the processes that operate thereon. There are few parts of the globe that remain unaffected by agriculture."); P.A. Matson et al., *Agricultural Intensification and Ecosystem Properties*, 277 Sci. 504, 504 (1997) ("Expansion of agricultural land is widely recognized as one of the most significant human alterations to the global environment."); Peter M. Vitousek et al., *Human Domination of Earth's Ecosystems*, 277 Sci. 494, 494 (1997) ("The use of land to produce goods and services represents the most substantial human alteration of the Earth system.").

they destroy open space and wildlife habitat; they erode soils and contribute to sedimentation of lakes and rivers; they deplete water resources; and they often simply smell bad. These effects are and always have been consequences of farming in general.[2] What is amazing is that these consequences have escaped serious regulatory attention even through the recent decades of environmental awakening.

This chapter presents an introduction to the environmental affects of the agricultural industry and provides an overview of the exceptions made for agriculture in U.S. environmental law. It then singles out two areas of environmental law that are unique to agriculture and are of particularly current interest. Other areas are referenced with resource suggestions.

A. Agriculture's Environmental Effects

J.B. Ruhl
Farms, Their Environmental Harms, and Environmental Law
27 Ecology L.Q. 263 274–293 (2000)

The Inventory of Environmental Harms that Farms Cause

Consider the typical farming process: first, remove all existing vegetation from the land and level it; second, deploy a single-species regime of crop or livestock; third, cultivate the crop or livestock with water and chemicals; finally, remove the crop or livestock and associated waste products from the land and start over. A number of environmental harms flow directly and necessarily from that basic reality of farming: (1) habitat loss and degradation; (2) soil erosion; (3) water resources depletion; (4) soil salinization; (5) chemical releases; (6) animal waste disposal; (7) water pollution; and (8) air pollution.[36] In each of these categories, farms are a significant source of environmental harm.

---

2. Farming has caused widespread environmental degradation for centuries. For example, the January 1849 Scientific American included a report of the practice, common in England at the time, of steeping wheat in an arsenic solution before sowing it to prevent loss of the crop to worms and birds. Although successful in achieving its intended agricultural purpose, the magazine condemned the practice for the adverse effect it had on partridges and pheasants, concluding "we can afford to feed both men and birds." *See 50, 100, and 150 Years Ago — Biocides for Agriculture*, Sci. Am., Jan. 1999, at 14. Six thousand years ago, Sumerian irrigation practices salinized water and soils to the point of inhibiting food production, a factor many historians believe contributed to the decline of the Sumerian culture. *See* Mohamed T. El-Ashry et al., *Salinity Pollution From Irrigated Agriculture*, 40 J. Soil & Water Conservation 48, 48 (1985). For comprehensive histories of agriculture from the perspectives of its effects on the environment and vice versa since the dawn of agriculture, see generally Mannion, *supra* note 1, at 31-226 and Daniel E. Vasey, An Ecological History of Agriculture, 10,000 B.C.–A.D. 10,000 (1992).

36. To some extent these eight categories interrelate and overlap. For example, farm irrigation practices lead to water resource depletion and soil salinization; the pollutants carried in nonpoint source water runoff from farms include chemicals, animal waste, and eroded soils; farms release nitrogen into the environment through chemical applications and animal waste. Nevertheless, the literature on the impacts of farming on the environment tends to break the problem down into these discrete topics, each of which is susceptible to measurement and study....

1. Habitat Loss and Degradation

The consequences of modern agriculture on wildlife habitat are undeniable, from habitat elimination to more direct effects on water and wildlife species.[37] The "structure and diversity of the agroecosystem can also influence the movement of wildlife between natural and agricultural systems and affect their use of such systems."[38] Despite the ability of perennial, vegetationally diverse agro-ecosystems with complex structure to provide important habitats for many birds and other animals typically found in undisturbed habitats,[39] farms pose an enormous net negative to wildlife.

Farming no longer poses a significant direct threat of habitat loss. Most direct loss of habitat resulting from conversion of land areas to farming has already occurred.[40] In fact, the United States loses a small portion of its available farmland each year, mainly to urban and suburban land uses.[41] But the magnitude of the historical transformation of undisturbed habitat to farming was immense—after all, at one time virtually all of the 930 million acres currently in farming uses were undisturbed habitat. The fact that these habitat losses were experienced in the past does not obviate the seriousness of their continuing impacts to wildlife in the present.[42] Further, habitat losses to farms have not been geographically uniform throughout the nation.[43]

The continuing loss of valuable habitat on farms themselves is often overlooked. The amount of undisturbed grass-dominated cover and non-cropped areas on farms has decreased, resulting in lower availability of habitat and higher losses to predators of many species of wildlife.[44] In many agricultural areas, crucial wildlife habitat components such

---

37. *See* National Biological Serv., U.S. Dep't of the Interior, *Our Living Resources: A Report to the Nation on the Distribution, Abundance, and Health of U.S. Plants, Animals, and Ecosystems* 424 (1995) [hereinafter Our Living Resources].

38. Matson et al., *supra* note 1, at 507.

39. *See id.*

40. For example, "conversion of wetlands to agricultural land has declined steadily since the 1950s." *Geography of Hope* [USDA Natural Resource Conservation Serv., *Geography of Hope* 7 (1996)] at 52. Over 790,000 acres of wetland were lost on non-Federal lands between 1982 and 1992, for a yearly loss estimate of 70,000 to 90,000 acres. Agriculture was responsible for 87% of the loss of wetlands from the mid-1950s to the mid-1970s, but only 54% of the loss from the mid-1970s to the mid-1980s. *See* National Water Quality Inventory, [Office of Water, U.S. Envtl. Protection Agency, *National Water Quality Inventory 1994 Report to Congress* (1994)] at 28–29.

41. Between 1992 and 1997, farmland in the United States fell from 946 million acres to 932 million acres, a loss of about 1.5% in five years. In 1964, land in farming was about 1.1 billion acres, about 18% more than we have today. *See* Census, [1997 Census of Agriculture, United States Data] at 10, tbl.1. Between 1982 and 1992, 3 million acres of cropland were converted to commercial or residential uses. *See Geography of Hope,* [*supra* note 40] at 30; …

42. For example, reduced habitat is the most common threat to endangered species. *See* William Stolzenburg, *Habitat Loss Affects 88 Percent of Species*, NATURE CONSERVANCY, Nov.–Dec. 1997, at 6; David S. Wilcove et al., *Quantifying Threats to Imperiled Species in the United States*, 48 BioSci. 607 (1998). The effects of habitat loss on species viability may not be fully manifested for decades or centuries, see Michael L. Rosenzweig, *Heeding the Warning in Biodiversity's Basic Law*, 284 Sci. 276, 277 (1999), and for many endangered species, habitat restoration is a necessary ingredient for recovering the species from the path toward extinction, see Theodore C. Foin et al., *Improving Recovery Planning for Threatened and Endangered Species*, 48 BioSci. 177, 179–80 (1998).

43. *See Geography of Hope,* [*supra* note 40] at 23 (map of farmland distribution in the United States). For example, the Mississippi River ecosystem, which covers almost 40% of the contiguous United States, has lost over 75%, and in some places 95%, of its floodplain to farmland, urban development, and impoundments. *See 500,000 Acres Will Shield Waterways from Farm Runoff*, EDF NEWSLETTER, June 1998, at 1, 3 (discussing plans to restore some of the converted floodplain).

44. *See Our Living Resources, supra* note 37 at 424. Harvested cropland has increased by 20 million acres since 1987. *See* Census, [*supra* note 41] at United States Data 19, tbl.7.

as undisturbed grassland have been dissected into small, isolated patches.[45] Habitat diversity on farms has also declined drastically as a consequence of the elimination of hay and pasture once needed by draft animals and a shift to crop monocultures.[46] In addition, wetland drainage, consolidation of fields and farms, and elimination of fence-rows and idle areas have reduced habitat diversity even further, thereby diminishing the populations of wildlife that once co-existed with crops on farms.[47] Increased agrochemical use has also been implicated in the long-term decline of species that relied on farmland as part of their habitat base.[48]

Despite these losses, the truly pernicious effects of farming on habitat today occur offsite.[49] For example, gaseous and dissolved nitrogen oxide and ammonia emitted from agricultural ecosystems are transported to and deposited in downwind and downstream terrestrial and aquatic ecosystems. This deposition causes inadvertent fertilization, which can lead to acidification, eutrophication, shifts in species diversity, and effects on predator and parasite systems.[50] Transport of pesticides beyond farm boundaries also causes severe damage to wildlife and habitat functions.[51] Similarly, because evaporation and concentration effects cause irrigation return-flows to carry greater concentrations of salt and minerals than found in irrigation water sources, fish and wildlife populations downstream often suffer.[52] Also, high erosion rates associated with cultivated agriculture can lead to sedimentation in reservoirs and lakes, which reduces the lifetime of these water systems as aquatic habitat.[53] Overall, therefore, farming has caused and continues to cause significant habitat degradation both on the farm and off.[54]

2. Soil Erosion and Sedimentation

Converting natural ecosystems to permanent agriculture results in a loss of soil organic matter, thus increasing the erosion potential of the soils.[55] As a result, farms are by far the leading national cause of soil erosion.[56] In 1997, for example, there were 375 million acres of cropland in the United States, of which 103.5 million acres were considered "highly erodible."[57] In 1982, forces of erosion moved almost 3.1 billion tons of soil from

45. *See Our Living Resources, supra* note 37 at 424.

46. *See id.*

47. *See id.*

48. *See id.*

49. *See* Matson et al *supra* note 1 at 507 ("Although agroecosystems are typically managed in isolation from other ecosystems within a region, the physical, ecological, and biogeochemical changes that take place within them have numerous consequences for adjacent, and even distant, ecosystems.").

50. *See id.*

51. *See* [James Stephen] Carpenter, [*Farm Chemicals, Soil Erosion, and Sustainable Agriculture,* 13 Stan. Envtl. L.J. 190 (1994); *Report Links Wildlife Decline to Chemical Exposure,* 30 ENV'T REP. (BNA) 718 (1999)] at 213–18.

52. *See id., supra* note 1 at 508.

53. *See id.*; Carpenter, *supra* note [51], at 218–19.

54. When land conversion, farm practices, and the offsite effects of pesticides and fertilizers are combined, farming has significantly affected 38% of the listed endangered species. *See Wilcove* et al., *supra* note 42, at 610–12. For additional economic and legal analysis of the relation between farming and habitat, see Jan Lewandrowski & Kevin Ingram, *Policy Considerations for Increasing Compatibilities Between Agriculture and Wildlife,* 39 NAT. RESOURCES J. 229 (1999).

55. *See* Matson et al., *supra* note 1, at 506.

56. For example, 90% of all the soil erosion that happens in Illinois, about 158 million tons per year, occurs on farms. *The Nature of Illinois Found. & Ill. Dep't of Energy and Natural Resources,* THE CHANGING ILLINOIS ENVIRONMENT: CRITICAL TRENDS 59 (1994).

57. *See* Natural Resources Conservation Serv., U.S. Dep't of Agric., 1997 National Resources Inventory—Summary Report tbl.14, ... [hereinafter 1997 National Resources Inventory]. Highly erodi-

America's cropland, 1.4 billion by wind and 1.7 billion by water.[58] This loss of topsoil is replenished at a rate of less than one inch in 200 years.[59]

Depending on a variety of factors,[60] between 25 and 40% of soil that erodes from a field will reach a water body.[61] Erosion thus leads directly to sedimentation in reservoirs and lakes.[62] Yearly soil discharge from agricultur[al] land to waterways in the United States is estimated at over 1 billion tons of sediments and 447 million tons of total dissolved solids.[63] The Mississippi River alone carries 331 million tons of topsoil to the Gulf of Mexico annually.[64]

Sediments not only reduce the lifetime and uses of water systems,[65] but also carry significant amounts of pollutants. Both "instream suspended sediment and bedload are, by volume, the largest category of pollutants in the United States."[66] "High levels of suspended sediments can also reduce net primary production in freshwater and marine systems, ultimately affecting" the feeding and reproduction of fish and aquatic invertebrates.[67] Farming also releases nutrients and other chemicals that are absorbed by the sediment soil particles entering streams and rivers as a result of soil erosion.[68] Bottom sediment contaminated with pesticides and other agricultural chemicals is an increasing problem in watersheds around the nation.[69]

Through improved soil management technology and practices, soil erosion is to some extent on the mend.[70] Average cropland erosion rates in tons per acre per year for 1997

---

ble cropland is generally steeper and less fertile, requires more inputs to maintain production, and can be damaged by high erosion rates. *See* Carpenter, *supra* note [51], at 204–05 (explaining protocol for evaluating highly erodible land).

58. *See Geography of Hope*, *supra* note 34, at 36.

59. *See* Charles M. Cooper & William M. Lipe, *Water Quality and Agriculture: Mississippi Experiences*, 47 J. Soil & Water Conservation 220 (1992).

60. "[T]he rate and amount of [soil organic matter] loss depends on a number of factors, including climate and soil type as well as numerous factors directly influenced by cropping systems, such as the amount of organic inputs, crop coverage of the soil, tillage practice, and length and type of fallow." Matson et al., *supra* note 1, at 506.

61. *See* David Zaring, *Federal Legislative Solutions to Agricultural Nonpoint Source Pollution*, 26 Envtl. L. Rep. (Envtl. L. Inst.) 10,128, 10,129 (1996).

62. *See* Matson et al., *supra* note 1, at 508. Wind erosion contributes to the aerosol content of the atmosphere, playing a large role in climate and air pollution. *See id.*

63. *See* Cooper & Lipe, *supra* note 59, at 220.

64. *See id.*

65. *See* Carpenter, *supra* note [51], at 210 ("[T]he hundreds of millions of tons of eroded soils deposited in waterways disrupts navigation, fills reservoirs, increases the costs of water treatment, and limits recreational uses.").

66. Cooper & Lipe, *supra* note 59, at 220; *see also* Carpenter, *supra* note [51], at 210–11.

67. Matson et al., *supra* note 1, at 508.

68. *See Geography of Hope*, *supra* note [40], at 40.

69. For example, EPA recently delivered to Congress a report entitled The Incidence and Severity of Sediment Contamination in Surface Waters of the United States, identifying 7% of watersheds sampled as containing areas of probable concern because of contaminated bottom sediment, and including agricultural runoff as one of the leading causes. *See* Notice of Availability of Report to Congress, 63 Fed. Reg. 2237, 2238 (1998).

70. Between 1982 and 1997, total erosion on all cropland decreased by 42%. In 1982, erosion totaled 3.07 billion tons, and by 1997 it had been reduced to 1.9 billion tons. *See* 1997 Natural Resources Inventory, *supra* note 57, fig.3. Some controversy has developed over whether the picture looks even better than that. Most of the erosion figures discussed in the text are derived from large scale models of erosion rates. A recent study based on a watershed-specific survey of historical "markers" of soil loss and sedimentation suggests that erosion rates have fallen dramatically from the 1970s to the 1990s, though the study is not without its critics. *See* James Glanz, *Sharp Drop Seen in Soil Erosion Rates*, 285 Sci. 1187 (1999); R. Monastersky, *Erosion: Dustup over Muddy Waters*, 156 Sci. News 116 (1999).

were substantially lower than erosion rates for 1982.[71] Most of this improvement, however, occurred by 1992, with little additional performance improvement since that time.[72] Moreover, even these improved rates are 12 times higher than soil formation rates, meaning net losses of cropland soils each year at an annual cost to society in excess of $29 billion.[73] Indeed, some new "good farming" practices actually increase soil erosion rates.[74] Soil erosion associated with farming thus continues to reduce soil productivity and substantially affect water quality and atmospheric resources.[75]

3. Water Resources Depletion

Farms use vast quantities of water. In 1992, for example, farmers in the United States irrigated 49 million acres of agricultural land,[76] and by 1997, that number had soared to 55 million acres.[77] Over 40% of the energy used by agriculture is devoted to irrigation.[78] Although irrigation acreage in the western states declined from 1982–1992 as the use of groundwater for irrigation became increasingly uneconomical,[79] irrigation acreage in the eastern United States has expanded in that time period as farmers attempt to reduce the risk of drought.[80]

Overpumping of groundwater sources for irrigation is a serious concern in many regions,[81] leading to effects such as water table drawdown, land subsidence, desertification, destruction of natural springs and associated wildlife habitats, and saltwater intrusion.[82] Yet as old surface water reservoirs lose capacity due to siltation and new ones become increasingly difficult or impracticable to site,[83] increases in agricultural production will raise the demand for irrigated water from groundwater sources. Irrigation water for farms, from all sources, can be expected to become more scarce "as competition for withdrawals

---

71. *See* 1997 National Resources Inventory, *supra* note 57, at 7 (noting that combined water and wind erosion rates fell from 7.4 in 1982 to 5.0 in 1997).

72. *See id.* tbls.10 & 11 (showing rates of water and wind erosion for cropland in each state for years 1982, 1987, 1992, and 1997). The amount of highly erodible land in cropland production, which fell significantly from 1982 to 1992, has also leveled off through 1997. *See id.*

73. *See* David Pimentel & Edward L. Skidmore, *Rates of Soil Erosion*, 286 Sci. 1477 (1999).

74. For example, farmers who use impermeable plastic sheet mulch, which is better than vetch-covered rows at retaining soil moisture and temperature, experience higher soil erosion rates. *See Plastic Mulch's Dirty Secrets*, 156 Sci. News 207 (1999).

75. *See Geography of Hope, supra* note [40], at 34.

76. *See* Census, *supra* note [41], United States Data at 10, tbl.1.

77. *See id.* On a global scale, 40% of crop production comes from the 16% of agricultural land that is irrigated. *See* Matson et al., *supra* note 1, at 506.

78. *See* Lindsey McWilliams, *Groundwater Pollution in Wisconsin: A Bumper Crop Yields Growing Problems*, Env't, May 1984, at 25, 27.

79. For a comprehensive history and future prognosis of irrigated farming in western states, see Council for Agricultural Science and Technology, *Future of Irrigated Agriculture* (1996).

80. *See Geography of Hope, supra* note [40], at 31.

81. For example, intensive irrigation has drawn down the huge Ogallala aquifer that stretches across Kansas, Nebraska, and Colorado, posing the possibility of future shortages and reduced productivity. *See* Sandra Postel, *When the World's Wells Run Dry*, World Watch, Sept.–Oct. 1999, at 30, 32; [C. Ford] Runge [Environmental Protection from Farm to Market, in Thinking Ecologically: The Next Generation of Environmental Policy 200 (Marian R. Chertow & Daniel C. Esty eds., 1997)], at 204; Robert R.M. Verchick, *Dust Bowl Blues: Saving and Sharing the Ogallala Aquifer*, 14 J. Envtl. L. & Litig. 13 (1999); Erla Zwingle, *Ogallala Aquifer: Wellspring of the High Plains*, Nat. Geo., Mar. 1993, at 83.

82. *See* Barton H. Thompson, Jr., Water Allocation and Protection: A United States Case Study, in Earth Systems: Processes and Issues 476 (W.G. Ernst ed., 2000).

83. *See* Matson et al., *supra* note 1, at 506.

increases with human population growth and development."[84] Complicating this problem are massive federal subsidies for existing and expanded farm irrigation infrastructure and supply.[85] Agricultural demand for water thus appears to be headed upward on a collision course with competing uses.

4. Soil and Water Salinization

In addition to being a significant user of limited water supplies, irrigated farming continually degrades its surrounding environment in arid and semi-arid areas through the salinization of soils and water.[86] Irrigating arid and semi-arid soils leaches salts and other minerals from the soil, causing them to accumulate in the plant root zone and retard plant growth.[87] Highly salinized soil is useless for agriculture, and reclaiming it is economically difficult, if not impossible.[88] Over 570 million acres of the continental United States have a moderate to severe potential for soil and water salinity problems,[89] and an estimated 20 to 25% of all irrigated land in the United States suffers from saline-induced yield reductions.[90] At least 48 million acres of cropland and pastureland are categorized as saline, and recent surveys indicate that this number is growing at a rate of 10% a year.[91]

For farmers, the solution to salinized soil is to flush the salinized soils with more high quality water than is needed for the crops so that the excess water carries away the leached salts.[92] Often this flushing process is accomplished through installation of an underground drainage tile system, which captures the irrigation water as it percolates through the soils, collects it into an underground drainage pipe network, and then efficiently moves the saline-rich waters away from the farmland in a drainage ditch system.[93] The salts that have been flushed from the irrigated farmlands end up in irrigation return flows which typically carry substantially higher concentrations of salt and minerals than their original surface or groundwater sources.[94] This salinized water has potentially devastating ef-

---

84. *Id.* Irrigation also leads to significant alteration of surface water systems and habitat, as large surface storage reservoirs must be constructed to convert seasonal stream flows to permanent water supplies. The effects of such projects have been tremendous and irreversible in many areas of the nation, particularly in the West. *See* Harrison Dunning, *Confronting the Environmental Legacy of Irrigated Agriculture in the West: The Case of the Central Valley Project*, 23 ENVTL. L. 943, 944–54 (1993). The classic discussion of the issue is found in MARC REISNER, CADILLAC DESERT (1986).

85. The Bureau of Reclamation has spent billions of dollars developing sources of economically inefficient irrigation water for western farmers. *See* Thompson, *supra* note 82, at 483 (noting the irony that this subsidized water encourages western farmers to grow crops that other federal subsidy programs pay midwestern and southern farmers not to grow, even though the latter could grow them more economically).

86. *See* Matson et al., *supra* note 1, at 506.

87. *See* El-Ashry et al., *supra* note 2, at 49 ("Repeated application of water to land for irrigation results in the accumulation of salts in the upper layers of soil."). Saline soils are those that contain sufficient salts to adversely affect plant growth. *See Geography of Hope*, *supra* note [40], at 33.

88. *See Geography of Hope*, *supra* note [40], at 33.

89. *See id.*

90. *See* El-Ashry et al., *supra* note 2, at 48.

91. *See Geography of Hope*, *supra* note [40], at 33.

92. *See* El-Ashry et al., *supra* note 2, at 49 ("To maintain agricultural productivity, these salts must be leached out of the crop root zone.").

93. *See* Gary Bobker, *Agricultural Point Source Pollution in California's San Joaquin Valley*, 9 NAT. RESOURCES & ENV'T 13, 13 (1995) (noting that hundreds of thousands of farmland acres in the San Joaquin Valley employ such tile systems).

94. The "leaching fraction" of the irrigated water—the excess needed for leaching away the salts —will contain unnaturally high salt concentrations because of the intended "salt loading" effect and

fects on downstream aquatic systems.[95] Indeed, "[i]rrigation-related salinity is the major water quality problem in the semiarid western states, where significant quantities of salts occur naturally in rocks and soils."[96]

5. Agrochemical Releases

Farms are massive users of chemicals, including insecticides, herbicides, and fungicides.[97] Every year, over "750 million pounds of pesticides are applied to agricultural crops yearly" in the United States.[98] Since 1979, agriculture has been responsible for about 80% of all pesticide use in the United States,[99] and pesticide use on farms has nearly tripled since 1964.[100] "Four of the most prevalent herbicides—atrazine, simazine, alachor, and metolachlor—are applied nationwide, and grain belt states receive large shares of the estimated 135 million pounds" of herbicides used annually.[101] Although pesticides have undoubtedly improved agricultural efficiency and human living conditions immensely,[102] their adverse environmental impacts are also undeniable.

A significant fraction of pesticides applied to agricultural systems fails to reach its target pests and moves into the soil where it poses immediate and long-term environmental threats.[103] For example, chlorinated hydrocarbons such as DDT can persist in the

---

because the irrigation return water is further concentrated by evaporation. *See* El-Ashry et al., *supra* note 2, at 48–49.

95. One of the most tragic examples is the Kesterson National Wildlife Refuge, which was created when financial troubles caused a planned irrigation return flow "regulation" project to become a terminal reservoir for return flow waters in California's Central Valley. Seen as a potential waterfowl haven, selenium-laden return flow water collected in the vegetation and invertebrates, eventually causing tremendous damage to the waterfowl. *See* Dunning, *supra* note 84, at 953–54; Bobker, *supra* note 93, at 14–15.

96. El-Ashry et al., *supra* note 2, at 49.

97. The Federal Insecticide, Fungicide, and Rodenticide Act (FIFRA) defines pesticides to include nitrogen stabilizers and "substances intended for preventing, destroying, repelling, or mitigating any pest ... [or] for use as a plant regulator, defoliant, or desiccant." 7 U.S.C. § 136(u) (1994). The pesticide industry involves about 30 major manufacturing companies, 100 smaller companies marketing the active ingredients of pesticides, 3,300 product formulators who take the raw pesticide ingredients and produce finished pesticide products, and over 29,000 pesticide distributors. About 600 distinctive groups of active ingredients are found in the 45,000 pesticide products that are marketed in the United States. About 1.2 billion pounds of pesticides, valued at over $6.5 billion, are sold each year in the United States, over 70% of which are used in farming. *See* P.S.C. Rao et al., Inst. of Food and Agricultural Sciences, Fact Sheet SL-53, *Regulation of Pesticide Use* 1–2 (rev. ed. 1997)....

98. Zaring, *supra* note 61, at 10,129.

99. *See Geography of Hope, supra* note [40], at 45. About 25% of pesticide use in the United States is in California. *See* James Liebman et al., Pesticide Action Network and Californians for Pesticide Reform, *Rising Toxic Tide-Pesticide Use in California,* 1991–1995, ... Pesticide applications on farms in the United States have risen dramatically since the 1960s, while land in cultivation has remained about the same. See Carpenter, supra note 4, at 191.

100. *See* Zaring, *supra* note 61, at 10,129.

101. Penny Loeb, *Very Troubled Waters*, U.S. NEWS & WORLD REPORT, Sept. 28, 1998, at 43.

102. For an aggressive defense of the use of pesticides, arguing that this and other technology-intensive farming practices will allow the Earth easily to support the projected population of 10 billion, see DENNIS T. AVERY, SAVING THE PLANET WITH PESTICIDES AND PLASTIC (1995).

103. *See, e.g., Plastic Mulch's Dirty Little Secrets, supra* note 74, at 207 (measuring and comparing chemical runoff from fields using different kinds of mulch). Even when pesticides reach their target, long-term environmental effects remain, for example, the problem of increasing pest resistance. *See* MATSON et al., *supra* note 1, at 505. Once pests develop resistance to pesticides, farmers typically respond by increasing the quantity of the pesticide applied or shifting to other pesticides, fueling the pests' resistance buildup mechanisms. Today, nearly 1,000 major agricultural insect, disease, and weed pests are immune to common pesticides. *See* LESTER R. BROWN et al., VITAL SIGNS 1999, at 124 (1999).

environment for decades after their use, while organophosphates and carbamates are short-lived but acutely toxic.[104] As urban areas increasingly encroach upon farmlands or even encompass them, the danger that residents will be exposed to harmful levels of pesticide increases.[105]

Pesticides from farm applications have also infiltrated adjacent ecosystems through a multitude of pathways, including discharges and runoff to surface waters,[106] leaching to ground water,[107] and aerial drift.[108] These unwanted pesticide migrations can have significant adverse impacts on the diversity and abundance of nontarget species as well as complex effects on ecosystem processes and trophic interactions.[109] The threat also extends to human health; more than 14 million Americans drink public water obtained from river sources that contain herbicides,[110] and millions more ingest pesticides in drinking water obtained from groundwater sources.[111]

---

104. *See* Matson et al., *supra* note 1, at 508.

105. For example, in 1999, the New Jersey Historic Pesticide Contamination Task Force estimated that 5% of the state's land is affected by agricultural pesticides and recommended that areas formerly used for agricultural purposes should be tested for pesticide residue before they are developed. Some local jurisdictions in New Jersey already impose such a requirement. See Task Force Urges Sampling of Farm Areas for Pesticide Residues Before Development, 29 *Env't Rep.* (BNA) 1896 (1999). Recent studies indicate that humans, and even fetuses, continue to be exposed to pesticides that have long been banned in the United States. *See Pesticide Exposure Begins Early*, 156 Sci. News 47 (1999).

106. *See* text accompanying notes 48–51.

107. A soil's vulnerability to leaching of pesticides and other agricultural chemicals depends upon three principal factors: (1) the propensity of soils to leach pesticides and nitrates; (2) the amount and timing of rainfall; and (3) the extent of chemical use. The coastal plains stretching from Alabama, Florida, and Georgia, as well as the Corn Belt and the Mississippi River Valley all have the highest vulnerability to leaching agrochemicals. *See* Robert L. Kellogg et al., *The Potential for Leaching of Agrichemicals Used in Crop Production: A National Perspective*, 49 J. Soil & Water Conservation 294, 294–97 (1994). Not surprisingly, pesticides from every major chemical class have been detected in groundwater. *See Geography of Hope, supra* note [40], at 48. The United States Geological Survey's 1999 National Water Quality Assessment report, which analyzes 5,000 water samples from 20 major river and groundwater areas of the country, found at least one pesticide at detectable levels in more than 90% of water and fish samples from all streams. *See* U.S. Geological Survey, U.S. Dep't of the Interior, USGS Circ. 1225, *The Quality of Our Nation's Waters: Nutrients and Pesticides* (1999); *see also Chemicals Widely Present in Stream, Potential Threats Uncertain, Study Finds*, Daily Env't Rep. (BNA), Mar. 22, 1999, at A-3. In 1992, the EPA reported that 132 pesticide-related compounds, 117 parent pesticides, and 16 pesticide degradates had been found in ground water in 42 states. See Natural Resources Defense Council, *Trouble on the Farm, Growing up with Pesticides in Agricultural Communities* 28 (1998) [hereinafter Trouble on the Farm].

108. *See infra* text accompanying notes 174–77.

109. *See* Matson et al., *supra* note 1, at 508. For example, evidence is mounting that the presence of certain pesticides in water bodies is linked to increasing rates of amphibian deformities. *See* J. Raloff, *Thyroid Linked to Some Frog Defects*, 156 Sci. News 212 (1999). Ironically, the unintended effects of pesticide use have direct ramifications for farms. For example, farmers must compensate for reduced pollination resulting from declining honeybee populations lost to pesticides, and must apply excess pesticides when pesticides kill the pests' natural predators. *See generally* Carpenter, *supra* note [51], at 213.

110. *See* Loeb, *supra* note 101, at 43. Indeed, several water supply systems recently sued the manufacturer of the herbicide atrazine for the costs of removing the chemical from their water supplies. *See No Class Action for Herbicide Cleanup Costs: Water Systems Have No Standing, Court Says*, Daily Env't Rep. (BNA), Apr. 9, 1999, at A-2. For a detailed review of the impact of farm chemical releases on groundwater and some of the legal instruments that can be used to regulate *those practices, see* Debbie Sivas, *Groundwater* Pollution from Agricultural Activities: Policies for Protection, 7 Stan. Envtl. L.J. 117 (1987–1988).

111. The State of California reported that 22 pesticides were detected in a total of 436 groundwater wells in 1996. *See Trouble on the Farm, supra* note 107, at 28. A 1997 survey of water contamination

Fertilizers are another major agrochemical pollutant.[112] Farmers apply nitrogen, phosphorous, and potassium to promote crop growth; however, when applied inappropriately or in excessive amounts the excess nutrients are carried from farmlands into waterways. Fertilizer application rates have increased dramatically.[113] American agriculture now discharges 1.16 million tons of phosphorous and 4.65 million tons of nitrogen into waterways annually.[114] Land use models identify agriculture as the leading source of nitrogen and phosphorus in the environment, accounting for 76 and 56%, respectively.[115] These nutrients, so beneficial on the farm, threaten associated water resources by fostering excessive plant growth.[116] Nutrient runoff from farms thus influences the health of natural systems by stimulating eutrophication of estuaries and coastal marine environments, resulting in anoxic conditions that are toxic to aquatic animal populations.[117]

6. Animal Waste

Driven by economies of scale and new production and processing technologies, industrialization of the livestock production sector[118] has produced unprecedented livestock concentrations in the United States.[119] As a result, the United States produces 200 times more livestock waste than human waste.[120] "Livestock in the United States produce approximately 1.8 billion metric tons of wet manure per year, much of which reaches surface water after being applied to fields as fertilizer."[121]

Although many farming operations contain their animal waste in on-site structures, spills occur frequently and with drastic effects. For example, a 100,000 gallon spill in Minnesota killed almost 700,000 fish along 19 miles of a major stream. As a result, a downstream dairy operation had to dump 3,000 pounds of milk after cows drank infected water and half the pregnant animals aborted.[122] The Missouri Department of Natural Resources found that 63% of all large animal feeding operations had spills between 1990 and 1994.[123] In North Carolina, a 25 million gallon hog-waste spill is the biggest on

---

found that about 4.3 million Americans in 245 communities are exposed to levels of carcinogenic herbicides in drinking water that exceed the EPA's benchmark of "acceptable" cancer risk. *See id.*

112. *See* Carpenter, *supra* note [51], at 201–03.

113. In 1987, 1.38 million farms spent $6.7 billion applying fertilizer to 211 million acres; ten years later 1.2 million farms spent $9.6 billion applying fertilizers to 233 million acres. *See* Census, *supra* note [41], at United States Data 23, tbl.15; *see also* Zaring, *supra* note 61, at 10,129.

114. *See* Cooper & Lipe, *supra* note 59, at 221.

115. *See* Carpenter, *supra* note [51], at 201 (seven million tons per year in 1960; nineteen million tons per year in 1994).

116. *See generally* Geography of Hope, *supra* note [40], at 41.

117. *See* Matson et al., *supra* note 1, at 507; Zaring, *supra* note 61, at 10,129. Although most attention regarding the environmental impacts of fertilizer runoff has been devoted to its nutrient loading effect, recent studies have suggested that fertilizers may pose toxicity threats as well. *See* Office of Solid Waste, U.S. Envtl. Protection Agency, *Estimating Risk from Contaminants Contained in Agricultural Fertilizers* 1-1 (1999) (draft report); J. Raloff, *Fertilizer: Hiding a Toxic Pollutant?*, 156 Sci. News 245 (1999).

118. For further discussion of these industry trends, *see infra* text accompanying notes 386–90.

119. *See* Geography of Hope, *supra* note [40], at 41.

120. *See* Ted Williams, *Assembly Line Swine*, Audubon, Mar.–Apr. 1998, at 26, 31.

121. Zaring, *supra* note 61, at 10,129.

122. *See* Williams, *supra* note 120, at 28.

123. *See id.*

record, and killed 10 million fish and closed 364,000 acres of coastal wetlands to shellfishing in 1995.[124] The Illinois Environmental Protection Agency reported that 15 out of 22 randomly inspected manure lagoons in western Illinois were illegally discharging wastewater into streams in 1998.[125] In Iowa, 60 spills have been recorded since 1992. One of those, a 1.5 million gallon spill in 1995, killed 8,861 fish, polluted thirty miles of river, and closed a primary recreation area.[126] Recently, several cases involving intentional bypasses of manure holding ponds have resulted in substantial criminal fines.[127]

Spills and illegal discharges are merely the tip of the iceberg, however. Even proper farm waste management releases immense amounts of waste and waste-related pollutants. For example, California's Central Valley is home to 1,600 of the state's 2,400 dairies, and its 891,000 cows create as much waste as 21 million people.[128] Creeks in that area often contain 200 times more ammonia than the level that is poisonous for fish.[129] Dairy manure pollution in California is a significant cause of fishery depletion.[130]

Cows are not the only source of waste management problems on farms. For example, chicken manure contains twice as much phosphorous as human waste.[131] The 625 million chickens raised annually in the Delmarva area, which includes portions of Delaware, Maryland, and Virginia, produce 3.2 billion pounds of waste annually, the constituents of which include 13.8 million pounds of phosphorous and 48.2 million pounds of nitrogen.[132]

Hogs are a major pollution source as well. In North Carolina, the significant progress made by municipal and industrial sources of pollution has been largely offset by agricultural pollution, primarily runoff from hog production facilities. North Carolina has been the fastest growing swine-producing state in the country, as the number of hogs has increased from 3.7 million in 1991 to more than 10 million in 1998.[133] In 1998, the North Carolina Department of Environment, Health and Natural Resources investigated 1,595 drinking water wells located on property adjacent to hog and poultry production facilities and found that 10.2% of the wells tested were contaminated with nitrate levels above current drinking water standards, and 34.2% of the wells tested exhibited detectable nitrate levels.[134] According to EPA estimates, in 1995 agriculture in eastern North Carolina was responsible for airborne emissions of 179 million pounds

---

124. *See id.* at 27.

125. *See* Natural Resource Defense Council & Clean Water Network, *America's Animal Factories: How States Fail to Prevent Pollution from Livestock Waste* 26 (1998) [hereinafter America's Animal Factories].

126. *See id.* at 34.

127. *See* Carolyn Whetzel, *Dairy Farm Ordered to Pay $250,000 for Polluting California River in CWA Case*, 29 Env't Rep. (BNA) 2572 (1999); Pamela Najor, *Iowa Hog Farm Pleads Guilty to Discharge in First Criminal Manure Discharge Case*, Daily Env't Rep. (BNA), June 29, 1999, at A-4.

128. *See* America's Animal Factories, *supra* note 125, at 15. A mature dairy cow produces as much waste as 34 people, or an average of 114 pounds of waste per day, or 22.5 tons of manure per year. *See id.*

129. *See id.* at 16.

130. *See id.* (noting that salmon and steelhead fisheries are down more than 90% from their historic levels).

131. *See id.* at 50.

132. *See New NPDES Permit Condition to Hold Chicken Producers Accountable for Waste*, Daily Env't Rep. (BNA), Mar. 22, 1998, at A-2.

133. *See* America's Animal Factories, *supra* note 125, at 73.

134. *See id.* at 76.

of ammonia nitrogen per year. Hog operations alone were responsible for 73% of these emissions.[135] Indeed, current scientific studies find that at least 67% and perhaps as much as 95% of the total nitrogen produced by swine is actually volated to the atmosphere as ammonia nitrogen,[136] making land and water pollution control measures largely a moot point.

7. Nonpoint Source Water Pollution

In addition to pollutants released in irrigation return flows, farms release massive quantities of pollutants through runoff from fields and livestock operations. These releases are collectively known as nonpoint source water pollution.[137] Nonpoint source pollution from all sources accounts for 65–75% of the pollution in the nation's most polluted waters.[138] In 33 states, nonpoint source pollution is the most significant form of pollution affecting streams and rivers.[139] In Iowa, Missouri, Montana, Nebraska, and Wisconsin, nonpoint source pollution accounts for over 90% of stream and river pollution.[140] In 42 states, nonpoint sources are the predominant source of pollution in lakes,[141] and in six states nonpoint source pollution accounts for 100% of lake pollution.[142]

Farms are the major source of nonpoint water pollution nationally,[143] with farm runoff acting as a primary transport mechanism for fertilizers, animal wastes, pesticides, sediments, and bacteria.[144] For example, commercial fertilizers in farm runoff have wide-

---

135. *See id.*

136. *See id.* at 77.

137. EPA defines nonpoint water pollution as "water pollution caused by rainfall or snowmelt moving over and through the ground and carrying natural and human-made pollutants into lakes, rivers, streams, wetlands, estuaries, coastal waters, and ground water." Section 319 Federal Consistency Guidance, 63 Fed. Reg. 45,504, 45,504 (1998). Agricultural nonpoint source pollution thus includes "runoff from manure disposal areas, and from land used for livestock and crop production." Federal Water Pollution Control Act (Clean Water Act), 33 U.S.C. § 1288(b)(2)(F) (1994). By legislative decree, if not physical reality, agricultural nonpoint source pollution also includes "return flows from irrigated agriculture." …

138. *See* Zaring, *supra* note 61, at 10,128.

139. *See id.* at 10,128–29.

140. *See id.*

141. *See id.* at 10,128–29.

142. *See id.* at 10,129.

143. *See* [Drew L.] Kershen, [*Agricultural Water Pollution: From Point to Nonpoint and Beyond*, 9 NAT. RESOURCES & ENV'T 3 (1995)]at 3 ("Near unanimous agreement exists that agricultural nonpoint source pollution is the largest contributor."). EPA's 1994 National Water Inventory ranks agriculture, defined as crop production, pastures, rangeland, feedlots, and other animal holding areas, as the leading source of water quality impairment in lakes and rivers, in both cases by wide margins, and the third leading cause of impairment in estuaries. *National Water Quality Inventory*, supra note [40], at ES-11 to ES-12, ES-15 to ES-18. Federal government efforts to control agricultural nonpoint source runoff have proven costly. For example, since fiscal year 1994, the federal government has spent $3 billion annually to address nonpoint source runoff. USDA spent a total of $11 billion in that period, primarily on farm soil conservation programs designed to reduce sedimentation loading of streams. EPA, which spent $225 million in fiscal year 1998 funding state and regional programs to control nonpoint source pollution, has estimated that it will cost $9.4 billion annually to control what it says are the three main sources of nonpoint pollution: agriculture, silviculture, and animal feeding operations. *See* U.S. General Accounting Office, GAO/RCED-99-45, *Water Quality: Federal Role in Addressing—and Contributing to—Nonpoint Source Pollution* 4–5 (1999); *Methodology Used to Calculate Costs of Nonpoint Pollution Inadequate, GAO Says*, DAILY ENV'T REP. (BNA), Mar. 16, 1999, at A-10.

144. *See* Cooper & Lipe, *supra* note 59, at 220–22.

spread and pernicious effects,[145] leading to eutrophication as the nutrient laden runoff promotes rapid algal and plant growth, and attendant consequent depletion of oxygen resources.[146] Overall, nitrate concentrations from fertilizer runoff have increased three-to tenfold in our nation's surface waters since the early 1900s.[147] Commercial fertilizers today are the dominant nonpoint source pollutant in the western, central, and southeastern United States,[148] and their effects can be felt far from the farm source. For example, hundreds of thousands of tons of agricultural fertilizers applied in the enormous Mississippi River watershed reach Louisiana's Gulf Coast estuaries, contributing to an offshore hypoxic "dead zone."[149] Eighty percent of the nitrogen delivered to the Gulf originates more than a thousand miles upstream above the confluence of the Ohio and Mississippi Rivers—almost all of it from cropland runoff.[150] Agriculture is also a major source of nutrient discharge into the watershed of the Chesapeake Bay, where inputs of nitrogen and phosphorous have led to excessive plankton production and the demise of submerged aquatic vegetation.[151] Other coastal regions have experienced similar hypoxia problems.[152]

Animal waste is another major component of farm runoff, accounting for one-third of all water impairments attributable to agriculture.[153] "Livestock in the United States

---

145. For example, commercial fertilizers, animal manure, and atmospheric deposition, in that order, are the primary nonpoint sources of nitrate in surface water and groundwater. *See Geography of Hope, supra* note [40], at 48.

146. *See* National Water Quality Inventory, *supra* note [40], at ES-9; *Geography of Hope, supra* note [40], at 41–45; Matson et al., *supra* note 1, at 507. The eutrophication effect is also discussed *supra* at the text accompanying note 50.

147. *See* Matson et al., *supra* note 1, at 507.

148. *See Geography of Hope, supra* note [40], at 48.

149. *See id.* at 44; Runge, *supra* note [81], at 205.

150. The Harmful Algal Bloom and Hypoxia Research and Control Act of 1998 directs a newly formed federal task force on the hypoxia issue to assess the ecological and economic impacts of hypoxia in the Gulf and develop a plan for controlling the effects by 2000. *See* Coast Guard Authorization Act of 1998, Pub. L. No. 105-383, § 604(a)-(b), 112 Stat. 3411, 3449 (1998). The Department of Commerce's National Oceanic and Atmospheric Administration (NOAA) recently released reports on a series of comprehensive studies it had funded on the Gulf hypoxia effect. *See* National Center for Coastal Ocean Science, NOAA, U.S. Dep't of Commerce ... One report concludes that "[t]he principal source areas for the nitrogen that discharges to the Gulf are watersheds draining intense agricultural regions in southern Minnesota, Iowa, Illinois, Indiana, and Ohio." "Nonpoint sources contribute about 90% of the nitrogen and phosphorous discharging to the Gulf. Agricultural activities are the largest contributors of both nitrogen and phosphorous." Donald A. Goolsby et al., FLUX AND SOURCES OF NUTRIENTS IN THE MISSISSIPPI-ATCHAFALAYA RIVER BASIN 14 (1999); *see also Clean Water Act Should Be Strengthened to Address Nutrient Reduction, Group Says*, DAILY ENV'T REP. (BNA), Mar. 30, 1999, at A-10. The task force has finalized the assessment phase of its mission and has begun to develop an action plan proposal. *See* Notice of Fifth Meeting of the Mississippi River/Gulf of Mexico Watershed Nutrient Task Force, 64 Fed. Reg. 56,788 (1999) (notice of availability of the report and public comment period, and of task force decision to begin work on action plan).

151. *See Water Quality Policies Must Be Integrated Among Air, Water, Land, USGS Official Says*, DAILY ENV'T REP. (BNA), Mar. 8, 1999, at A-2. The United States Geological Survey's National Water Quality Assessment found that 85% of nitrogen contributed to the Chesapeake Bay is from groundwater and the atmosphere, suggesting that integrated management will be needed to address watershed degradation, nonpoint source pollution, total maximum daily loads, and wetlands protection. Id.; *see also* Thomas E. Jordan et al., *Effects of Agriculture on Discharges of Nutrients from Coastal Plain Watersheds of Chesapeake Bay*, 26 J. ENVTL. QUALITY 836, 836 (1997).

152. *See* Oliver A. Houck, *TMDLs IV: The Final Frontier*, 29 ENVTL. L. REP. (Envtl. L. Inst.) 10,469, 10,470 (1999).

153. *See* [Larry C.] Frarey & [Staci J.] Pratt, [*Environmental Regulation of Livestock Production Operations*, 9 NAT. RESOURCES & ENV'T 8 (1995)], at 8. Farm animal waste management is discussed in more detail *supra* at the text accompanying notes 118–36.

produce approximately 1.8 billion metric tons of wet manure per year, much of which reaches surface water supplies after being applied to fields as natural fertilizer."[154] In 1996, the Maryland Department of Environment reported that approximately 93% of Maryland waters that fail to meet state water quality standards do so because of excessive nutrient pollution.[155] The Department also estimated that 326 million pounds of nitrogen and 19 million pounds of phosphorous enter the Chesapeake Bay every year.[156] The effect of these nutrient loads goes beyond eutrophication of aquatic habitat; entire ecological processes are affected. For example, Pfiesteria piscicida, a one-celled organism that lives in many estuaries and rivers and under certain conditions eats away at fish's scales, has been implicated in massive fish kills in rivers leading to the Chesapeake Bay and other Atlantic and Gulf Coast estuaries, forcing the closing of many rivers to commercial and recreational uses.[157] According to scientists, the Pfiesteria piscicida outbreaks are correlated with increased nitrate levels in rivers caused by chicken waste, which, when applied to crops as "natural" fertilizer, runs into the watershed.[158]

Overall, runoff of topsoil, silt, sediment, manure, nutrients, chemicals, and other pollutants from agricultural nonpoint sources is the leading source of impairment in the Nation's rivers,[159] affecting 60% of the impaired river miles.[160] Agriculture is the leading source of impairment in lakes as well, affecting 50% of impaired lake acres, or 2 million lake acres.[161] Agriculture also pollutes 34% of impaired estuarine waters.[162] Groundwater, on which half of the U.S. population and most rural communities depend,[163] is also substantially threatened from polluted farm runoff.[164]

---

154. Zaring, *supra* note 61, at 10,129.

155. *See America's Animal Factories, supra* note 125, at 50.

156. *See id.*

157. *See generally* JoAnn M. Burkholder, *The Lurking Perils of Pfiesteria*, Sci. Am., Aug. 1999, at 42; Carol Jouzaitis, *Fish-Killing Microbe Found in Fourth River*, USA Today, Sept. 15, 1997, at 3A.

158. *See, e.g.*, John P. Almeida, *Nonpoint Source Pollution and Chesapeake Bay Pfiestera Blooms: The Chickens Come Home to Roost*, 32 Ga. L. Rev. 1195 (1998); ... Burkholder, *supra* note 157, at 46.

159. From 1984 through 1996, the percentage of rivers designated as "impaired," meaning that they cannot support aquatic life and are unsafe for fishing and swimming, grew from 26% to 36%. *See Loeb, supra* note 101, at 42.

160. *See Geography of Hope, supra* note [40], at 40; *National Water Quality Inventory, supra* note [40], at ES-14; Zaring, *supra* note 61, at 10,129.

161. *See National Water Quality Inventory*, supra note [40], at ES-19; Zaring, *supra* note 61, at 10,129.

162. *See National Water Quality Inventory, supra* note [40], at ES-25.

163. More than 97% of the nation's rural drinking water comes from underground aquifers, and over 50% of the nation's population relies on groundwater as its source of drinking water. *See* Erik Lichtenberg & Lisa K. Shapiro, *Agriculture and Nitrate Concentrations in Maryland Community Water System Wells*, 26 J. Envtl. Quality 145, 145 (1997).

164. Groundwater is especially susceptible to nitrate contamination from the nitrogen sources in commercial inorganic fertilizer and manure. *See id.* at 145–47; *see also* Carpenter, supra note [51], at 202–03; Runge, *supra* note [81], at 204. Nitrogen is present in water as nitrate-nitrogen (known as NO_3-N) and converts to nitrites, which have acute toxic effects at high concentrations. Nitrates and nitrites are also suspected to have carcinogenic effects either through secondary conversion to other compounds or in synergistic effects with pesticides also found in contaminated waters. *See generally* Lichtenberg & Shapiro, *supra* note 163, at 145; Carpenter, *supra* note [51], at 202. Rising use of commercial fertilizer has been suspected as a primary source for increasing NO_3 concentrations found in groundwater, which at some locations reaches levels deemed unhealthy for human consumption. *See* N.R. Kitchen et al., *Impact of Historical and Current Farming Systems on Groundwater Nitrate in Northern Missouri*, 52 Soil & Water Conservation 272, 272 (1997) ("Nitrates attributable to fertilizers and manure have been found in the groundwater of every agricultural region of the nation."); Zaring, *supra* note 61, at 10,129. Water in one-fourth of the wells in many agricultural areas has become unsafe to drink because of high levels of nitrates. *See Loeb, supra* note 101, at 43.

8. Air Pollution

Although farms are often associated with unpleasant odors, many people overlook the fact that farms are significant sources of chemical air pollution. Fertilizer is a source of several greenhouse gases, including carbon dioxide, nitrous oxide, and methane,[165] and leads to increased emissions of gases that play critical roles in tropospheric and stratospheric chemistry and air pollution.[166] Worldwide, agricultural soils emit nitrogen oxides (commonly known as NOx) at estimated rates of up to 25% of the emissions from global fossil fuel combustion.[167] Once in the atmosphere, NOx is a critical regulator of tropospheric ozone, a key component of smog, and a threat to human health, agricultural crops, and natural ecosystems.[168] NOx is also "transported and deposited in gaseous or dissolved solution forms to downwind terrestrial and aquatic ecosystems," leading to acidification, eutrophication, shifts in species diversity, and changes in predator and parasite systems.[169] Wind erosion also contributes to the aerosol content of the atmosphere, which plays a critical role in climate change as well as air pollution.[170]

Animal waste is another major source of air pollution. In Minnesota, large-scale feedlots emit hydrogen sulfide at levels vastly exceeding state air quality standards for other industries.[171] According to EPA estimates, agriculture in eastern North Carolina was responsible for airborne emissions of 179 million pounds of ammonia nitrogen in 1995, with hog operations responsible for 73% of these emissions.[172]

Pesticide dispersal in the air is also often overlooked in comparison to more visible and documented pollution problems, but it is significant. Sources include fumigants, wind erosion of pesticide-laden soil particles, and aerial drift from spraying.[173] In California, two weeks of ambient air monitoring near sugar beet and potato fields for the carcinogen fumigant Telone II measured ambient air levels that exceeded the safe level for chronic inhalation exposures,[174] and 19 of 26 monitored pesticides have been detected in and around California communities between 1986 and 1998.[175] Fog samples gathered in suburban Maryland and in agricultural regions of California revealed up to 16 different agricultural pesticides.[176] Thus, farms pose a substantial threat to air quality.

---

165. *See* Matson et al., *supra* note 1, at 507–08. EPA estimates that agricultural activities were responsible for seven percent of total U.S. greenhouse gas emissions in 1997. *See* Office of Policy, U.S. EPA, *Inventory of U.S. Greenhouse Gas Emissions and Sinks: 1990–1997*, at 5-1 (1999).

166. *See* Matson et al., *supra* note 1, at 507.

167. *See id.*

168. *See id.*

169. *Id.* For example, air pollution is the leading cause of water quality impairment in the Great Lakes, with pesticides and nutrients being significant components of that impairment. *See National Water Quality Inventory, supra* note [40], at ES-20 to ES-22.

170. *See* Matson et al., *supra* note 1, at 508.

171. *See America's Animal Factories, supra* note 125, at 53. "[T]he Minnesota Pollution Control Agency ... confirmed through a testing program that half of the CAFOs tested were exceeding state standards for hydrogen sulfide, some by up to 50 times," and "[v]iolations occurred on a frequent basis, with one operation exceeding the half-hour standard 32 times over 19 days." *Id.*

172. *See id.* at 76.

173. *See Trouble on the Farm, supra* note 107, at 29.

174. *See id.*

175. *See* Zev Ross & Jonathan Kaplan, *Californians for Pesticide Reform, Poisoning the Air* 1 (1998), available at (visited Apr. 8, 1999) ... (compilation of state government testing data).

176. *See Trouble on the Farm, supra* note 107, at 30.

Notes

1. Updated data analyzed by the USDA supports much of Professor Ruhl's analysis. "Agriculture is a major user of ground and surface water in the United States, accounting for 80 percent of the Nation's consumptive water use and over 90 percent in many Western States." USDA Economic Research Service, Briefing Room, Irrigation and Water Use, available at http://www.ers.usda.gov/Briefing/WaterUse/.

The USDA Economic Research Service's 2006 report, *Agricultural Resources and Environmental Indicators* 2006 report confirms agriculture's continued role in water quality degradation.

> The production practices and inputs used by agriculture can result in a number of pollutants entering water resources, including sediment, nutrients, pathogens, pesticides, and salts. Farmers, when making production decisions, often do not consider offsite impacts associated with runoff or leaching. Documenting the links between agriculture and water quality can help policymakers provide appropriate incentives to farmers for controlling pollution that originates on farms.

> Agriculture is widely believed to have significant impacts on water quality. While no comprehensive national study of agriculture and water quality has been conducted, the magnitude of the impacts can be inferred from several water quality assessments. A general assessment of water quality is provided by EPA's 2000 Water Quality Inventory. Based on State assessments of 19 percent of river and stream miles, 43 percent of lake acres, and 36 percent of estuarine square miles, EPA concluded that agriculture is the leading source of pollution in 48 percent of river miles, 41 percent of lake acres (excluding the Great Lakes), and 18 percent of estuarine waters found to be water-quality impaired, in that they do not support designated uses. This makes agriculture the leading source of impairment in the Nation's rivers and lakes, and a major source of impairment in estuaries. Agriculture's contribution has remained relatively unchanged over the past decade.

> The significance of water pollutants commonly produced by agriculture is suggested by information on impaired waters provided by States, tribes, and territories to EPA in accordance with Section 303(d) of the Clean Water Act. These are waters that do not meet water quality standards, and cannot meet those standards through point-source controls alone. The most recent information (2005) indicates that 25,823 bodies of water (stream reaches or lakes) are impaired nationwide. Pathogens, sediment, and nutrients are among the top sources of impairment, and agriculture is a major source of these pollutants in many areas.

Marc Ribaudo and Robert Johansson, *Water Quality: Impacts of Agriculture*, in AGRICULTURAL RESOURCES AND ENVIRONMENTAL INDICATORS, USDA Economic Research Service, available at http://www.ers.usda.gov/publications/arei/eib16/.

EPA's latest report to Congress on water quality includes the following summary of its preliminary findings.

Rivers and Streams

This report includes states' assessments of 16% of the nation's 3.5 million miles of rivers and streams for the 2004 reporting cycle. Of these assessed waterbodies, 44% were reported as impaired, or not clean enough to support at least one of their designated uses (e.g., fishing, swimming). The states found the remaining 56% to be fully supporting all assessed uses. Pathogens, habitat alterations, and organic enrichment/oxygen depletion were cited as the leading causes of impairment in rivers and streams, and the top sources of impairment included agricultural activities, hydrologic modifications (e.g., water diversions, channelization), and unknown/unspecified sources.

Lakes and Reservoirs

This report includes states' assessments of 39% of the nation's 41.7 million acres of lakes, ponds, and reservoirs during the 2004 reporting cycle. Of these assessed waterbodies, 64% were reported as impaired and 36% were fully supporting all assessed uses. Mercury, polychlorinated biphenyls (PCBs), and nutrients were cited as the leading causes of impairment in lakes. The top sources of pollutants to lakes, ponds, and reservoirs included atmospheric deposition, unknown/unspecified sources, and agriculture.

Environmental Protection Agency, *National Water Quality Inventory: Report to Congress*, 2004 Reporting Cycle (Jan. 2009) (available at http://www.epa.gov/owow/305b/2004report/).

2. Concerns with respect to animal waste have increased since publication of Ruhl's analysis as concentrated animal feeding operations have grown in size and concentration.

According to the Environmental Protection Agency (EPA), the release of waste from animal feedlots—the portion of the livestock industry that involves large, intensive animal raising and feeding operations—to surface water, groundwater, soil, and air is associated with a range of human health and ecological impacts and contributes to degradation of the nation's surface waters. The most dramatic ecological impacts are massive fish kills, which have occurred in a number of locations in the United States. A variety of pollutants in animal waste can affect human health in several ways, such as causing infections to the skin, eye, ear, nose, and throat. Contaminants from manure can also pollute drinking water sources. Data collected for the EPA's 2000 National Water Quality Inventory report identified agriculture as the leading known contributor to water quality impairments in rivers and lakes. Animal feeding operations are only a subset of the agriculture sector, but 29 states specifically identified animal feeding operations as contributing to water quality impairment. Federal efforts to control these sources of water pollution have accelerated in recent years, but they have been highly controversial. The primary pollutants associated with animal wastes are nutrients (particularly nitrogen and phosphorus), organic matter, solids, pathogens, and odorous/volatile compounds. Animal waste also contains salts and trace elements, and to a lesser extent, antibiotics, pesticides, and hormones. Pollutants in animal waste can impact waters through several possible pathways, including surface runoff and erosion, direct discharges to surface waters, spills and other dryweather discharges, leaching into soil and groundwater, and releases to air (including subsequent deposition back to land and surface waters). Pollutants associated with animal waste can also originate from a variety of other sources, such as cropland, municipal and industrial discharges, and urban runoff.

Claudia Copeland, *Animal Waste and Water Quality: EPA's Response to the WaterKeeper Alliance Court Decision on Regulation of CAFOs*, Congressional Research Service Report, No. RL33656 (Feb. 17, 2010).

In September of 2008, the Government Accountability Office issued a report, *Concentrated Animal Feeding Operations: EPA Needs More Information and a Clearly Defined Strategy to Protect Air and Water Quality from Pollutants of Concern*. The Report notes that "[w]hile CAFOs may have improved the efficiency of the animal production industry, their increased size and the large amounts of manure they generate have resulted in concerns about the management of animal waste and the potential impacts this waste can have on environmental quality and public health." The Report references a wide range of studies and summarizes the environmental concerns associated with CAFOs as follows:

> The amount of manure that a large farm raising animals can generate depends on the types and numbers of animals being raised at a specific operation; such farms can produce from over 2,800 tons to more than 1.6 million tons of manure annually. For example, a layer farm that meets EPA's minimum large CAFO threshold of 82,000 laying hens could produce more than 2,800 tons of manure a year, while a farm with 10,000 beef cattle (cattle fattened with feed) could produce about 117,000 tons of manure a year. In fact, some large farms can produce more raw waste than the human population of a large U.S. city. For example, a very large hog farm, with as many as 800,000 hogs, generates more than 1.6 million tons of manure annually — more than one and a half times the sanitary waste produced by the about 1.5 million residents of Philadelphia, Pennsylvania in 1 year. Furthermore, while manure is a valuable resource often used as fertilizer, agricultural experts and government officials have raised concerns about the large amounts of manure produced by animal feeding operations that are increasingly clustered within specific geographic areas within a state. For example, five contiguous North Carolina counties had an estimated hog population of over 7.5 million hogs in 2002 and the hog operations in these counties could have produced as much as 15.5 million tons of manure that year. According to agricultural experts and government officials that we spoke to, such clustering of operations raises concerns that the amount of manure produced could result in the over application of manure to croplands in these areas and the release of excessive levels of some pollutants that could potentially damage water quality.

> At least 68 government-sponsored or peer-reviewed studies have been completed on air and water quality issues associated with animal waste since 2002 and 15 of these studies have directly linked pollutants from animal waste to specific health or environmental impacts. Of the remaining 53 studies, 7 found no impacts, 12 made indirect linkages between these pollutants and health and environmental impacts, and 34 of the studies focused on measuring the amount of water or air pollutants emitted by animal feeding operations. However, EPA has not yet assessed the extent to which air and water pollution from CAFOs may be impairing human health and the environment because it lacks key data on the amount of pollutants that CAFOs are discharging. Of the 15 studies we found directly linking pollutants from animal waste to human health or environmental impacts, 8 focused on water pollutants and 7 on air pollutants. Most of the water studies found that nutrients or hormones released from animal feeding operations were causing environmental harm, such as reproductive disorders in fish and degraded water quality. One water study found that animal feeding operations were causing pathogens such as E. coli to contaminate drinking water, which were then causing gastrointestinal illnesses in humans. Similarly, all seven air studies linked air emissions from animal feeding operations to adverse human health effects. Specifically, six found exposure to these emissions caused respi-

ratory inflammation and one found an increased incidence of headaches, eye ir-ritation, and nausea in people working at or living near these operations. Ac-cording to EPA officials, although the agency has long recognized the potential impacts that water pollutants from CAFOs can have on human health and the environment, it has not yet assessed these impacts because it lacks information on the extent to which water pollutants are actually being discharged by CAFOs. According to other officials at EPA, the agency does not have the resources needed to conduct a study that would provide this information. Likewise, EPA has not yet assessed the air quality impacts from animal feeding operation emissions be-cause, according to agency officials, it lacks key data on the extent to which these operations are emitting pollutants. To gather this information, EPA entered into a series of agreements with animal feeding operations to implement a national air emissions monitoring study that is currently ongoing and is being funded by the industry and will measure and quantify air emissions from animal feeding operations.

U.S. Government Accountability Office, *Concentrated Animal Feeding Operations: EPA Needs More Information and a Clearly Defined Strategy to Protect Air and Water Quality from Pollutants of Concern,* GAO-08-944, September 2008.

The Pew Commission on Industrial Farm Animal Production in America, a joint ef-fort between the Pew Commission and John Hopkins Bloomberg School of Public Health, issued a particularly critical report in 2009 that raised concerns about "Industrialized Farm Animal Production" (IFAP) in four areas: public health, impact on rural commu-nities, environment, and animal health and well-being. The environmental concerns are summarized as follows:

> As with the public health impact, much of IFAP's environmental impact stems from the tremendous quantities of animal waste that are concentrated in and around IFAP facilities. Animal waste in such volumes may exceed the capacity of the land to absorb the nutrients and attenuate pathogens. Thus, what could be a valuable byproduct becomes a waste that must be disposed of in an appro-priate manner. In addition, many IFAP facilities have not been sited in areas that are best able to cope with these enormous amounts of nutrients and pathogens. Many are found in vulnerable locations, such as on flood plains or close to com-munities that utilize well water.

> The annual production of manure produced by animal confinement facilities ex-ceeds that produced by humans by at least three times (EPA, 2007). Manure in such large quantities carries excess nutrients, chemicals, and microorganisms that find their way into waterways, lakes, groundwater, soils, and airways. Excess and inappropriate land application of untreated animal waste on cropland contributes to excessive nutrient loading and, ultimately, eutrophication of surface waters.

> IFAP runoff also carries antibiotics and hormones, pesticides, and heavy metals. Pesticides are used to control insect infestations and fungal growth. Heavy met-als, especially zinc and copper, are added as micronutrients to the animal diet. Tylosin, a widely used antibiotic (macrolide) for disease treatment and growth promotion in swine, beef cattle, and poultry production, is an example of a vet-erinary pharmaceutical that decays rapidly in the environment, but can still be found in surface waters of agricultural watersheds (Song et al., 2007).

> Air quality degradation is another problem in and around IFAP facilities, due to localized releases of toxic gases, odorous substances, particulates, and bioaerosols

containing a variety of microorganisms and human pathogens (Merchant et al., 2008).

Other environmental issues associated with IFAP include high levels of resource use. IFAP requires a large amount of water for irrigation of animal feed crops, as well as cleaning of many buildings and waste management systems. Much of this water comes from finite groundwater sources that recharge slowly or not at all, and are in demand for human needs. Greenhouse gas emissions from all livestock operations, including IFAP facilities, account for 18 percent of all human-caused greenhouse gas emissions, exceeding the emissions caused from the transportation sector (Steinfeld et al., 2006). Greenhouse gases, primarily methane, carbon dioxide, and nitrous oxide, are produced by the animals during the digestion process in the gut. Additional emissions result from degradation processes occurring in uncovered waste lagoons and digesters.

Putting Meat on the Table: Industrial Farm Animal Production, A Report of the Pew Commission on Industrial Farm Animal Production in America (2009), available at http://www.ncIFAP.org/.

B. Exceptions for Agricultural Operations Under Environmental Laws

Despite the environmental problems associated with agricultural production, farms enjoy a wide variety of exceptions from the laws that seek to protect the environment. Almost every major environmental law provides for special treatment of agricultural operations. Professor Ruhl outlines the "safe harbors" that agriculture has historically enjoyed in the excerpt provided below. Updates with respect to the Clean Water Act and the EPA's efforts to regulate CAFOs follow.

J.B. Ruhl
Farms, Their Environmental Harms, and Environmental Law
27 Ecology L.Q. 263 293–327 (2000)

Environmental Law Safe Harbors That Farms Enjoy

Getting a handle on the environmental law of farms is difficult. There is no unified code of environmental law for farms. Federal environmental law is scattered throughout many statutes, making it difficult to piece together the various provisions that could apply to farms. Although the general theme at the federal level is hands-off, no express or implied preemption prevents states from more aggressively regulating farms. To date, however, states have generally not chosen to regulate the environmental impacts of farming in any comprehensive manner.[177] We are left, therefore, with a collection of provisions, spread throughout many different laws, which combine to form what I call the "anti-law" of farms and the environment. There are few exceptions to this anti-law.

---

177. *See id.* On a global scale, 40% of crop production comes from the 16% of agricultural land that is irrigated. *See* Matson et al., *supra* note 1, at 506.

A. An Inventory of Safe Harbors for Farming

The anti-law of farms and the environment comes in two forms. Some laws, while not expressly exempting or even mentioning farms, are structured in such a way that farms escape most if not all of the regulatory impact. Other laws expressly exempt farms from regulatory programs that would otherwise clearly apply to them. Together, these passive and active exemptions provide a large safe harbor for farms from the impact of environmental law.

1. Clean Water Act

The Clean Water Act (CWA)[178] prohibits the "discharge of any pollutant by any person"[179] into waters of the United States and establishes a series of permit programs designed to regulate the discharge of pollutants provided certain conditions are met. Though seemingly straightforward, this prohibition is riddled with important exemptions for farms. Although the CWA defines "pollutant" to include "agricultural waste discharged into water,"[180] other provisions of the statute put discharges of agricultural wastewater, stormwater, and fill material largely beyond regulatory reach.

a. Wastewater Permits

Section 402 of the CWA establishes a permitting program, known as the National Pollutant Discharge Elimination System (NPDES), to regulate the discharge of pollutants.[181] NPDES permits may be issued only if, among other conditions, the permittee satisfies a set of technology-based[182] and water quality-based[183] limitations on the amount and quality of discharged effluent. For almost twenty years, the NPDES program focused on discharges of wastewater effluent from "industrial" processes — that is, water which had come into contact with process wastes or which was used as a waste disposal medium.

Many wastewater discharges from agriculture, such as the collected return flow from irrigated fields, appear to fit within the NPDES permit program as generally described. Indeed, EPA knew that this interpretation was inescapable under the CWA as it was originally enacted.[184] Awed by the prospect of issuing NPDES permits to two million farms, EPA thus promulgated an administrative exemption from the statute's unambiguous terms.[185] The courts struck down that exemption as contrary to the clear intent and meaning of the CWA,[186] but in 1977 Congress overruled the courts and codified EPA's farm ex-

---

178. 33 U.S.C. §§ 1251–1387 (1994). For an overview of the CWA programs, see THE CLEAN WATER ACT HANDBOOK (Parthenia B. Evans ed., 1994).

179. 33 U.S.C. § 1311(a) (1994).

180. *Id.* § 1362(6).

181. *See id.* § 1342.

182. *See id.* §§ 1311, 1316–1317.

183. *See id.* §§ 1312–1315.

184. See Kershen, supra note [143], at 3 (explaining that EPA took a broad view of its CWA jurisdiction, leading the agency to conclude that farm irrigation return flows channeled in ditches and other conveyances were covered).

185. *See* 38 Fed. Reg. 18,000, 18,003 (1973) (previously codified at 40 C.F.R. § 125.4). The regulation provided that "the following do not require an NPDES permit: ... (j) Discharges of pollutants from agricultural and silvicultural activities, including irrigation return flow and runoff from orchards, cultivated crops, pastures, rangelands, and forest lands," with an exception for discharges from large confined animal feeding operations and large irrigation projects. *Id.*

186. *See* NRDC v. Costle, 568 F.2d 1369 (D.C. Cir. 1977). EPA argued that the regulatory exemption was necessary to allow the agency to avoid the "administrative infeasibility" of issuing and administering millions of farm NPDES permits. *See id.* at 1374. Although the court rejected EPA's position, it explained that EPA could accomplish most of its objectives by promulgating a general

emption. The original version of the CWA defined discharge of a pollutant as "any addition of any pollutant to navigable waters from any point source."[187] To exempt farm irrigation return flows from the reach of NPDES wastewater discharge permits, Congress adopted the fiction that "these sources were practically indistinguishable from any other agricultural runoff"[188] and simply redefined "point source" to exclude "return flows from irrigated agriculture."[189] Congress drove home the point in Section 402 as well, dictating that EPA may not "require a permit under this section for discharges composed entirely of return flows from irrigated agriculture,"[190] and, leaving nothing to doubt, elsewhere described irrigation return flows as "agriculturally ... related nonpoint sources of pollution."[191] Through this exemption, therefore, farms that discharge soils, animal wastes, fertilizers, and pesticides via return flows into waters of the United States need no authorization for such discharges under the CWA.[192]

b. Stormwater Permits

Although EPA's focus for the first twenty years of the NPDES program was on process wastewater, the CWA always provided EPA the authority, under certain conditions, to require permits for stormwater discharged through point sources. In 1987, Congress renewed EPA's attention to polluted stormwater through a series of amendments outlining in detail a framework for NPDES permitting of municipal and industrial stormwater discharges.[193] In the course of doing so, however, Congress made it clear that the stormwater NPDES program would not extend to farm stormwater runoff. As it had in 1977 for irrigation return flows, Congress defined "point source" so as to exclude "agricultural

---

permit describing and authorizing the classes of discharges it had sought to exempt entirely. *See id.* at 1380–82. EPA later accepted the court's invitation. *See* 42 Fed. Reg. 6846 (1977).

187. 33 U.S.C. § 1362(12) (1994). The "point" in point source refers to the requirement that the discharge be from "any discernible, confined and discrete conveyance, including but not limited to any pipe, ditch, channel, tunnel, conduit, well, discrete fissure, container, rolling stock, concentrated animal feeding operation, or vessel or other floating craft, from which pollutants are or may be discharged." *Id.* § 1362(14).

188. S. Rep. No. 95-370, at 35 (1977), *reprinted in* 1977 U.S.C.C.A.N. 4326, 4360.

189. Clean Water Act of 1977, Pub. L. No. 95-217, § 33(b), 91 Stat. 1566, 1577 (1977) (codified at 33 U.S.C. § 1362(14) (1994)).

190. Pub. L. No. 95-217, § 33(c), 91 Stat. 1566, 1577 (1977) (codified at 33 U.S.C. § 1342(l)(1) (1994)).

191. *Id.* § 33(a) (codified at 33 U.S.C. § 1288(b)(2)(F) (1994)) (emphasis added).

192. It is through this exemption, for example, that hundreds of thousands of acres of California farm lands using subsurface drainage tile fields discharge polluted wastewater to the San Joaquin Valley watershed. *See* Bobker, *supra* note 93, at 14–16. The exemption does not apply to other wastewater discharges a farm might produce, such as animal waste collected from feed lots, or manure distributed from spreaders onto farm lands, when ultimately discharged through a point source. *See* Concerned Area Residents v. Southview Farm, 34 F.3d 114 (2d Cir. 1994); *see also,* Kershen, *supra* note [143], at 4; Susan E. Schell, *The Uncertain Future of Clean Water Act Agricultural Pollution Exemptions After* Concerned Area Residents for the Environment v. Southview Farms, 31 LAND & WATER L. REV. 113 (1996). Recently, for example, state and local prosecutors in California joined in filing four lawsuits against dairy operators in San Joaquin County for allegedly allowing cattle manure runoff to pollute waterways. *See Carolyn Whetzel, Attorney General, County District Attorney File Civil Complaints Against Dairy Operators,* DAILY ENV'T REP. (BNA), May 6, 1999, at A-9. Also, a court recently held that wastes removed from NPDES-regulated manure holding ponds and spread on land as fertilizer remain subject to the continuing jurisdiction of the NPDES permit, meaning that unpermitted discharges of nonpoint runoff from the manure are illegal. *See* Community Ass'n for Restoration v. Henry Bosma Dairy, 65 F. Supp. 2d 1129 (E.D. Wash. 1999) (granting motion for summary judgment); Susan Bruninga, *Land Application of Manure Subject to CWA Requirements, Court Says,* 30 ENV'T REP. (BNA) 173 (1999).

193. *See* Water Quality Act of 1987, Pub. L. No. 100-4, Title IV, §§ 401–405, 101 Stat. 65, 65–69 (1987) (codified at 33 U.S.C. § 1342 (1994)).

stormwater discharges."[194] Hence, like irrigation return flows, stormwater from farms collected in ditches, canals, and other conveyances, and the pollutants carried in it, are beyond NPDES stormwater program coverage.[195]

c. Dredge and Fill Permits

The third major CWA water pollutant discharge permitting program, found in Section 404 of the statute, covers "the discharge of dredged or fill material into the navigable waters."[196] This so-called dredge-and-fill permit program has been the nation's principal vehicle for wetlands protection.[197] Prominently excluded from the program, however, are discharges "from normal farming … activities such as plowing, seeding, cultivating, minor drainage, harvesting for the production of food, … or upland soil and water conservation practices."[198] A significant limitation on this "normal farming" exemption is that it does not apply to activities intended to bring a wetlands area into a use to which it was not previously subject.[199] Hence, "normal farming" does not include the conversion of a natural wetlands area to a rice farm or the conversion of farmed wetlands into upland cultivated farmlands.[200] Nevertheless, continued farming in wetlands, or activities de-

---

194. Pub. L. No. 100-4, Title V, § 503, 101 Stat. 75, 75 (1987) (codified at 33 U.S.C. § 1362(14) (1994)). Congress believed these activities "have no serious adverse impact on water quality," that regulating them under the dredge and fill permit program would produce "no countervailing environmental benefit," and that they would be "more properly controlled by State and local agencies." S. Rep. No. 95-370, at 76, 77 (1977), *reprinted in* 1977 U.S.C.C.A.N. 4326, 4401; *see also* 123 CONG. REC. 26,707 (1977) (remarks of Sen. Anderson) ("The exemption of these activities from permit requirements will greatly simplify the administrative process and reduce the potential redtape burden.").

195. *But see, supra* note 192 (discussing cases applying NPDES program to irrigation and stormwater runoff carrying pollutants from manure piled onto farmlands).

196. 33 U.S.C. § 1344 (1994).

197. For a history of how Section 404, which does not mention the word "wetlands," has become associated primarily with wetlands protection, see Jason Perdion, *Protecting Wetlands Through the Clean Water Act and the 1985 and 1990 Farm Bills: A Winning Trio*, 28 U. TOL. L. REV. 867, 869–73 (1997).

198. 33 U.S.C. § 1344(f)(A) (1994). Additional exemptions apply to "construction or maintenance of farm or stock ponds or irrigation ditches," *id.* § 1344(f)(1)(C), and "construction or maintenance of farm roads," id. § 1344(f)(1)(E). *See generally* Perdion, *supra* note 197, at 874–77.

199. *See* 33 U.S.C. § 1344(f)(2) (1994). This so-called "recapture" provision has generally been construed broadly by courts and administrative agencies, making the normal farming exemption narrow and tricky for farmers. *See, e.g.*, U.S. Army Corps of Engineers, Section 404 and Agriculture Information Paper (1990) (addressing various scenarios under the normal farming exemption and recapture provision); *see also* Perdion, *supra* note 197, at 877–83.

200. The recapture provision addresses only those conversions of wetlands to farming accomplished through discharges subject to Section 404. Two important limitations on the scope of that jurisdiction apply to farms. First, farm wetland areas converted to cropland uses before December 25, 1985 — so-called "prior converted croplands" — are not subject to Section 404. See 58 Fed. Reg. 45,008 (1993). Second, a recent court decision holding that the Section 404 program does not reach draining and clearing activities that do not involve more than incidental redischarge of small amounts of debris opens the door to relatively easy conversion of many wetlands to farming free of any Section 404 consequences. *See* National Mining Assoc. v. United States Army Corps of Engineers, 145 F.3d 1399 (D.C. Cir. 1997); *see also Revisions to the Clean Water Act Regulatory Definition of "Discharge of Dredged Material,"* 64 Fed. Reg. 25,120 (1999) (codified at 33 C.F.R. pt. 323 and 40 C.F.R. pt. 232) (revising regulations to correspond to National Mining decision and explaining background thereof). Some farmers already have attempted to take advantage of this turn of events by draining wetlands for conversion to crop uses. *See, e.g., In re Slinger Drainage, Inc.*, CWA App. No. 98-10, 1999 WL 778576 (EPA App. Bd. 1999) (finding that a farmer who drained wetlands after National Mining decision violated Section 404 because installation of drainage tiles involved more than incidental redischarge). Such conversions may nonetheless have undesirable consequences to farmers under farm subsidy programs and thus may not be widely implemented. …

signed to reclaim historically farmed wetlands, has accounted for substantial loss and degradation of wetland ecosystems since the enactment of the CWA [201]

2. Nonpoint Source Water Pollution

In a classic example of passive nonregulation, the repeated references in the CWA to "point source" as an essential criterion for application of the NPDES program create one of the largest safe harbors in environmental law for farms — the failure to regulate nonpoint sources of water pollution. The size of this harbor and its effects have not gone unnoticed.[202] It has, however, remained largely open, particularly for farms.[203]

Efforts to address nonpoint source water pollution in the CWA and other statutes have been feeble, unfocused, and underfunded. For example, Section 208 of the CWA required states to develop area-wide waste treatment management plans that were to include a process for identifying nonpoint sources and establishing feasible control measures.[204] Upon EPA's approval of a state's plan, the state could receive federal assistance for the planning process.[205] With high expectations, Congress used the program as the rationale for moving irrigation return flows from the point source side of the CWA to the nonpoint source side[206] and for excluding normal farming from the Section 404 dredge-and-fill permit program.[207] Similarly, in the 1987 amendments, Congress added Section 319 to the statute, requiring states to prepare "state assessment reports" that identify waters which cannot reasonably be expected to meet water quality standards because of non-

---

201. *See* National Water Quality Inventory, *supra* note 7, at ES-27 to ES-29 (noting that agriculture was responsible for 54% of national wetland losses from the mid-1970s to the mid-1980s, and remains the leading source of wetland degradation). One of the murkiest issues involving wetlands and farming is the delineation of wetlands on farms and the determination of which such areas are prior converted croplands for purposes of Section 404 and farm subsidy programs. *See* Justin Lamunyon, *Wetlands and the Swampbuster Provisions: The Delineation Procedures, Options, and Alternatives for the American Farmer*, 73 NEB. L. REV. 163 (1994). Recently, environmental groups have alleged that USDA, the lead agency for delineation of wetlands on farms, has used poor delineation methodology and undercounted wetlands on farming land. *See* Susan Bruninga, *Group Says Oversight Inadequate in Delineations on Farmland Tracts*, 30 ENV'T REP. (BNA) 313 (1999); Susan Bruninga, *Group Charges EPA Overlooks Failings in Farmland Delineation, Seeks Review*, DAILY ENV'T REP. (BNA), June 14, 1999, at A-6.

202. *See* Scott D. Anderson, *Watershed Management and Nonpoint Source Pollution: The Massachusetts Approach*, 26 B.C. ENVTL. AFF. L. REV. 339, 339–40 (1999) ("[T]he control of nonpoint source pollution continues to frustrate the [Clean Water Act's] stated goal to 'restore and maintain the chemical, physical, and biological integrity of the Nation's waters.'"); Kershen, *supra* note [143], at 3 (recounting descriptions of nonpoint source pollution as "'the neglected legacy and unfinished agenda' of federal water pollution laws").

203. For a comprehensive overview of federal regulation of nonpoint source water pollution from farms, see Zaring, *supra* note 61; George A. Gould, *Agriculture, Nonpoint Source Pollution, and Federal Law*, 23 U.C. DAVIS L. REV. 461 (1990).

204. *See* 33 U.S.C. § 1288(a) (1994); *see also* [K. Jack] Haugrud, [*Agriculture*, in SUSTAINABLE ENVIRONMENTAL LAW 451–574 (Celia Campbell-Mohn et al. eds., 1993) (environmental law treatise chapter covering agriculture)] § 8.2(C)(3)(b)(i), at 540–41.

205. *See* 33 U.S.C. § 1329(f) (1994); *see also* Haugrud, *supra* note [204] at § 8.2(C)(3)(b)(ii), at 541–42.

206. *See* S. Rep. No. 95-370, at 35 (1977), *reprinted in* 1977 U.S.C.C.A.N. 4326, 4360 ("All such sources, regardless of the manner in which the flow was applied to the agricultural lands, and regardless of the discrete nature of the entry point, are more appropriately treated under the requirements of section 208(b)(2)(F)."); *see also supra* text accompanying notes 185–93.

207. *See* S. Rep. No. 95-370, at 76 (1977), *reprinted in* 1977 U.S.C.C.A.N. 4326, 4401 (noting that Section 404 need not extend to normal farming activities because they will be "controlled by State and local agencies under section 208(b)(4)").

point source pollution.[208] States must prepare "state management programs" prescribing the "best management practices" to control sources of nonpoint pollution.[209] When EPA approves a state's assessment reports and management plans, the state is eligible for federal financial assistance to implement its programs.[210]

In the absence of any concrete, enforceable federal blueprint for addressing nonpoint source pollution, the success of Sections 208 and 319 depended largely on state initiative. It is little surprise, then, that neither Section 208 nor Section 319 produced meaningful results.[211] Congress thus took a more aggressive step in Section 6217 of the Coastal Zone Act Reauthorization Amendments of 1990,[212] amending the Coastal Zone Management Act[213] (CZMA) to add a requirement that any state with a federally approved coastal zone management plan[214] must develop a Coastal Nonpoint Pollution Program subject to federal review and approval.[215] States must identify land uses leading to nonpoint source pollution and develop measures to apply "best available nonpoint pollution control practices, technologies, processes, siting criteria, operating methods, or other alternatives."[216] When EPA and the National Oceanic and Atmospheric Administration approve a state's Coastal Nonpoint Pollution Program, the federal government agrees not to fund, authorize, or carry out projects inconsistent with the state's plan.[217] For coastal states, this requirement can serve as an impetus for more aggressive regulation of nonpoint source pollution, but federal funding assistance is woefully short of the expected cost of plan preparation and implementation.[218]

Another federally-based incentive for state regulation of nonpoint source pollution derives from the CWA's program for determining Total Maximum Daily Load (TMDL)

208. *See* 33 U.S.C. § 1329(a) (1994).

209. *See id.* § 1329(b).

210. *See id.* § 1329(h).

211. An EPA Advisory Committee recently summed up the weakness of the Section 208 and 319 programs by explaining that "EPA had no 'hammer' provision for States not adopting programs and no ability to establish a program if a State chose not to." EPA TMDL Federal Advisory Committee, *Discussion Paper, Nonpoint Source-Only Waters* 5 (1997) (on file with author). *See generally* Anderson, *supra* note 202, at 344 (noting that "the section 208 program failed to make any significant progress" and under Section 319 "EPA continues to lack the authority to require the states to take any affirmative action"); Kershen, *supra* note [143], at 4 (noting that "section 208 gave states great discretion … and carried no enforcement penalties" and under Section 319 "the states have been slow to act and EPA has limited enforcement authority to make states act."); Zaring, *supra* note 61, at 10,130, 10,132 (noting that Section 208 was "toothless" and Section 319 suffered from "not enough carrot, not enough stick"). EPA continues nonetheless to devote considerable resources to the Section 319 program, largely in the form of increased funding for states that EPA is proposing be tied to the requirement that states follow "key elements" EPA is in the process of developing. *See Chances for Clean Water Bill Dim; EPA to Use Existing Authorities on Nonpoint Sources*, DAILY ENV'T REP. (BNA), Jan. 20, 1999, at S-18.

212. Pub. L. No. 101-508, Title VI, § 6217 (1990), 104 Stat. 1388-314.

213. 16 U.S.C. §§ 1451–1464 (1994).

214. For a description of the CZMA coastal management plan provisions, *see infra* text accompanying note 431.

215. *See* 16 U.S.C. § 1455b (1994). *See generally* Clare Saperstein, *State Solutions to Nonpoint Source Pollution: Implementation and Enforcement of the 1990 Coastal Zone Amendments Reauthorization Act Section 6217*, 75 B.U. L. Rev. 889 (1995).

216. 16 U.S.C. § 1455b(g)(5) (1994).

217. *See id.* § 1455b(k). EPA has recently outlined the guidelines for federal consistency determinations. *See* Section 319 Federal Consistency Guidance, 63 Fed. Reg. 45,504 (1998).

218. *See* Robert v. Percival et al., ENVIRONMENTAL REGULATION 973 (2d ed. 1996) (noting that EPA estimated the cost of implementing the measures contemplated in the program at $390 million to $590 million, whereas only $50 million in grant money was available).

waste load allocations under Section 303(d) of the CWA.[219] Where application of the technology-based NPDES permit discharge limits does not bring a water body within ambient water quality standards,[220] the TMDL program implements a procedure to impose more restrictive discharge limits on the NPDES permittees.[221] Under the TMDL program, states must identify impaired water bodies, calculate the total maximum daily loading of pollutants that the water body can tolerate while still meeting water quality goals, and then allocate the necessary reduction in total discharges among NPDES dischargers and, theoretically, nonpoint source dischargers of that pollutant.[222] States must include TMDL

---

219. *See* 33 U.S.C. § 1313(d) (1994).

220. Water quality standards are based on two components: (1) designated uses of the water body, such as recreation or water supply, and (2) water quality criteria, which set concentration levels for individual pollutants designed to attain particular designated uses. Water quality standards thus are designed to regulate ambient water pollution concentrations for identified pollutants in different classes of waters. *See* 33 U.S.C. § 1313(c) (1994); *see also* Percival et al., *supra* note 218, at 937. One of the difficulties facing efforts to apply the water quality standards program to water pollution from farming is that, at present, no federally-promulgated water quality criteria exist for nutrients from nitrogen and phosphorous discharges. EPA, however, is in the process of developing them. *See* Office of Water, U.S. Envtl. Protection Agency, *Nutrient Criteria Technical Guidance Manual: Rivers and Streams* (review draft of Sept. 1999); Office of Water, U.S. Envtl. Protection Agency, *Nutrient Criteria Technical Guidance Manual: Lakes and Reservoirs* (review draft of Apr. 1999); U.S. Envtl. Protection Agency, Notice of National Strategy for the Development of Regional Nutrient Criteria, 63 Fed. Reg. 34,648 (1998); *see also* Susan Bruninga, *Effort to Set Nutrient Criteria Premature, Too Burdensome on POTWs, Officials Say*, 30 Env't Rep. (BNA) 172 (1999); Susan Bruninga, *Regulating Nutrients, Implementing Controls Focus of EPA Meeting on Draft Criteria*, 30 Env't Rep. (BNA) 310 (1999); Karen L. Werner, *Project to Guide States in Development of Limits for Pesticides in Impaired Waters*, 30 Env't Rep. (BNA) 1284 (1999). In the meantime, some states have developed their own nutrient criteria in the absence of federal guidelines, though the process has often been contentious. *See* Pamela S. Clarke & Stacey M. Cronk, *The Pennsylvania Nutrient Management Act: Pennsylvania Helps to "Save the Bay" Through Nonpoint Source Pollution Management*, 6 Vill. Envtl. L.J. 319 (1995); Alfred R. Light, *The Myth of Everglades Settlement*, 11 St. Thomas L. Rev. 55, 62–65 (1998) (discussing litigation over Florida's water quality criteria for phosphorous); McElfish, *supra* note 232, at 10,197. The Ecological Sciences Division of the Department of Agriculture's Natural Resources Conservation Service is also developing policies for providing nutrient management technical assistance in connection with programs protecting highly erodible lands and wetlands. See 64 Fed. Reg. 19,122 (1999).

221. The TMDL program thus represents the intersection of the CWA's technology-based and water quality-based components of regulation. For comprehensive explanations of the TMDL program, see Robert W. Adler, *Integrated Approaches to Water Pollution: Lessons from the Clean Air Act*, 23 Harv. Envtl. L. Rev. 203, 215–30 (1999); Office of the Administrator, U.S. EPA, *Report of the Federal Advisory Committee on the Total Maximum Daily Load (TMDL) Program* (1998); ... Oliver A. Houck, *TMDLs: The Resurrection of Water Quality Standards-Based Regulation Under the Clean Water Act*, 27 Envtl. L. Rep. (Envtl. L. Inst.) 10,329 (1997); Oliver A. Houck, *TMDLs, Are We There Yet?: The Long Road Toward Water Quality-Based Regulation Under the Clean Water Act*, 27 Envtl. L. Rep. (Envtl. L. Inst.) 10,391 (1997); Oliver A. Houck, *TMDLs III: A New Framework for the Clean Water Act's Ambient Standards Program*, 28 Envtl. L. Rep. (Envtl. L. Inst.) 10,415 (1998); Oliver A. Houck, *TMDLs IV: The Final Frontier*, 29 Envtl. L. Rep. (Envtl. L. Inst.) 10,469 (1999). The TMDL program lay dormant for almost twenty years before a series of lawsuits against states and EPA in the early 1990s resulted in court-imposed deadlines for completing the TMDL process in many states. *See* Adler, *supra*, at 221; Houck, *TMDLs, Are We There Yet?, supra*. As the weight of litigation turned against them, EPA and the states worked to develop a plan to carry out the TMDL program nationally over a twelve year period beginning in 1998. For current information on this development and the status of the TMDL program, see Office of Water, U.S. Envtl. Protection Agency, Total Daily Maximum Load (TMDL) Program [visited June 3, 2010 http://www.epa.gov/owow/tmdl/].

222. *See* 33 U.S.C. § 1313(d) (1994). EPA recently distributed proposed TMDL regulations designed to include many nonpoint sources in the full scope of the TMDL program. *See* Proposed Revisions to the Water Quality Planning and Management, 64 Fed. Reg. 46,011 (1999) (to be codified at 40 C.F.R. § 130.33(b)(6)); Revisions to the National Pollutant Discharge Elimination System Program and Federal Antidegradation Policy in Support of Revisions to the Water Quality Planning and

implementation as part of "continuing planning process" programs that EPA must approve in order for a state to retain delegation to administer the NPDES permit program within its boundaries.[223]

The TMDL program stops there, however, providing no independent source of authority for enforcing load reduction allocations.[224] Enforcing allocations for NPDES permit dischargers is a straightforward matter of tightening NPDES permits to reduce total discharges of the pollutants of concern.[225] For nonpoint sources, however, the most EPA can say is that TMDL load allocations are to be "enforced" through the Section 319 program,[226] which, as pointed out above, fails to secure real gains in control of nonpoint source discharges from farms.

EPA has recognized the obstacle this dichotomy poses to TMDL program implementation. In waters impaired primarily or exclusively by nonpoint sources, EPA has proposed a policy that allows states that promulgate demonstrable means of reducing nonpoint source pollution in a given water body to ease the burdens on NPDES permittees.[227] Where

---

Management Regulation, 64 Fed. Reg. 46,057 (1999) (proposed rule amending various provisions of 40 C.F.R. pt. 122). *See generally* Lisa E. Roberts, *Is the Gun Loaded This Time? EPA's Proposed Revisions to the Total Maximum Daily Load Program*, 6 ENVTL. LAW. 635 (2000). Nevertheless, there is far from universal agreement as to whether the CWA allows allocation of a portion of the pollutant load to nonpoint sources. Indeed, farming groups have initiated litigation challenging EPA's authority to implement the TMDL program so as to assign allocations to nonpoint sources. See Susan Bruninga, *Suit Challenging EPA Authority to Set TMDLs for Nonpoint Sources Concerns Cities*, DAILY ENV'T REP. (BNA), May 27, 1999, at A-2; Houck, *TMDLs IV, supra* note 152, at 10,474. Some members of Congress have also questioned EPA's authority in this regard. *See* Susan Bruninga, *House Panel Members Question EPA Authority to Issue TMDL Proposal*, 30 ENV'T REP. (BNA) 1241 (1999). EPA's Federal Advisory Committee on TMDL's declined to address these legal issues in its final report. *See* Office of the Administrator, U.S. Envtl. Protection Agency, *Report of the Federal Advisory Committee on the Total Maximum Daily Load (TMDL) Program* 42 (1998) (visited Feb. 8, 2000) http://www.epa.gov/ OWOW/tmdl. In the first judicial opinion on the question, a California federal district court held that agricultural nonpoint source pollution must be included in TMDL determinations, but that states have discretion as to the load reduction allocation between point and nonpoint sources. *See* Pronsolino v. Marcus, No. C99-01828WHA (N.D. Cal. Mar. 30, 2000). Given the complexities involved in the TMDL and waste load allocation calculations, it appears likely that the implementation process will continue to face litigation challenges at virtually every stage. *See* Dana A. Elfin, *Challenges to Total Maximum Daily Loads Possible Following Upcoming EPA Regulation*, 30 ENV'T REP. (BNA) 311 (1999) (reporting that discharger groups are filing "pre-litigation type comments" on proposed TMDL allocations).

223. *See* 33 U.S.C. § 1313(e)(3)(C) (1994).

224. *See* Office of Water, U.S. Envtl. Protection Agency, Total Maximum Daily Load (TMDL) Program, Memorandum from Robert Perciasepe, EPA Assistant Administrator, to Regional Administrators and Regional Water Division Directors Re: New Policies for Establishing and Implementing Total Maximum Daily Loads (Aug. 8, 1997) (visited Feb. 1, 2000) http://www.epa.gov/OWOW/tmdl/ ratepace.html [hereinafter Perciasepe Memorandum] ("A TMDL improves water quality when the pollutant allocations are implemented, not when a TMDL is established.... Section 303(d) does not establish any new implementation authorities beyond those that exist elsewhere in State, local, Tribal, or Federal law."). Because the TMDL program is limited in this respect, establishing TMDLs "trigger[s] no additional obligations on the part of any [nonpoint source]." Federal Advisory Committee, *supra* note 211, at 5.

225. *See* 33 U.S.C. § 1312(a) (1994); *see also* Perciasepe Memorandum, *supra* note 224 ("[P]oint sources implement the wasteload allocations within TMDLs through enforceable water quality-based discharge limits in NPDES permits authorized under section 402 of the CWA.").

226. *See* Perciasepe Memorandum, *supra* note 224 ("[P]rograms and efforts for control of nonpoint sources should be described in the State nonpoint source management program under section 319.").

227. For example, one of EPA's proposed policies is designed to prevent degradation of existing water quality levels by requiring that new significant point sources in a watershed offset their pollu-

that approach does not work, EPA suggests that states simply declare, presumably as a matter of state law, that offending nonpoint sources are actually point sources and require state-issued NPDES permits and full TMDL compliance.[228] Nonpoint source pollution, a significant contributor to water quality degradation, has been unregulated for decades. Substantial gains in water quality thus could be achieved through such an intense focus on nonpoint source pollution. In addition, the marginal costs of pollution reduction for nonpoint sources might be well below those that NPDES permittees would bear to achieve the same reductions in pollutant loads. Although it is questionable whether the EPA can use the TMDL program in such a manner or require states to do the same, the program may allow states to do so in order to balance the costs of water quality improvement between point and nonpoint sources.[229]

The problem with relying on the CZMA's program and CWA's TMDL program as the foundations for regulating farm nonpoint pollution is that neither program addresses farms specifically at the federal level. States, in other words, will have the discretion to achieve the general goal of nonpoint source pollution control in ways that do not place serious burdens on farms, or leave farms entirely unregulated.[230] Some states have done exactly that in their initial TMDL implementation policies.[231] Indeed, in a recent series of com-

---

tant load with reductions in the existing baseline load by a ratio of less than one-to-one. Where the reductions are made to nonpoint source pollution sources, EPA has explained that "the discharger's NPDES permit would need to contain any conditions necessary to ensure that the load reductions from the nonpoint source will be realized." 64 Fed. Reg. 46,057, 46,071 (1999); *see also* Perciasepe Memorandum, *supra* note 224 (noting that under the TMDL program, "where any wasteload load allocation to a point source is increased based on an assumption that loads from nonpoint sources will be reduced, the State must provide 'reasonable assurances' that the nonpoint source load allocations will in fact be achieved"); Office of Water, U.S. EPA, *Ensuring That TMDLs Are Implemented—Reasonable Assurance* (visited Oct. 10, 1999) http://www.epa.gov/ OWOW/tmdl/ensure.html ("In allocating reductions to nonpoint sources, States must provide reasonable assurance that those nonpoint sources will meet their allocated amount of reductions.").

228. *See* Office of Water, *supra* note 227 ("Reasonable assurance is satisfied by designating these [nonpoint] sources as point sources and issuing them an NPDES permit.").

229. EPA cannot mandate the methods by which states accomplish this balancing, but the agency has suggested that states may institute "regulatory, non-regulatory, or incentive-based [measures], depending on the program." Perciasepe Memorandum, *supra* note 224. The use of incentive-based measures could, for example, allow NPDES dischargers to pay for nonpoint source dischargers' reductions in discharge loads and thereby ease restrictions in their NPDES permits. The irony is that farms, the leading source of water pollution in America, would be paid to stop polluting. This prospect is likely to pit farms and other nonpoint sources against NPDES dischargers, which are more likely to support EPA's suggestion that reasonable assurance can also be demonstrated through the direct regulation of nonpoint sources. EPA has essentially left it to each state to decide how to resolve the debate, but it has made clear that a state's failure to resolve the debate will result in federal imposition of TMDLs and load allocations. See Office of Water, *supra* note 227 ("Because reasonable assurance is a required element of a TMDL, EPA may then disapprove that State's TMDL. If EPA disapproves a TMDL, EPA must establish the TMDL.").

230. Even if the CWA allows EPA to include nonpoint sources directly in the TMDL program, in the end "states have discretion in allocating pollution loads among sources as long as the allocations will meet TMDL targets." Report of the Federal Advisory Committee, *supra* note 211, at iii. States will be free to leave farms out of the picture even if other nonpoint sources such as urban runoff are covered. Indeed, although EPA's proposed TMDL rules aggressively invite states to cover more farm animal feeding operations as point sources, see 64 Fed. Reg. 46,057, 46,074 (1999), the proposed rules are otherwise silent with respect to farms. For further discussion of the animal feeding operations issue, see *infra* text accompanying notes 307–26.

231. For example, Florida recently enacted a TMDL implementation statute that subjects only nonagricultural nonpoint source pollution to load allocations by the Florida Department of Environmental Protection, leaving agricultural sources subject to voluntary best management practices

prehensive studies of state law, the Environmental Law Institute identified few states with any meaningful program regulating farm nonpoint source pollution, much less an actively enforced one.[232] Most states have followed the federal lead and focused on point source pollution; of those that have ventured into addressing nonpoint source pollution, most leave farms out of the picture.[233] EPA remains fundamentally powerless to require otherwise.[234] Hence, while the impetus for state regulation of nonpoint pollution is growing under the CZMA and the CWA, farms appear poised to slip through the process once again. Although states could reverse this continuation of past practice, farms appear likely to retain a safe harbor for their nonpoint source discharges.

3. Clean Air Act

The Clean Air Act (CAA) provides a complex and comprehensive regulatory framework covering stationary and mobile sources of air pollution.[235] Although farms do not enjoy the range of express exemptions under the CAA that they do under the CWA, they generally escape most CAA regulatory programs by virtue of de minimus discharge exceptions. By limiting their emphasis to "major sources" emitting more than threshold quantities of regulated pollutants, CAA regulatory programs essentially give farms yet another safe harbor, this one for air pollution.[236] By contrast, other sectors of the agriculture economy upstream and downstream of farms are heavily regulated by the CAA.[237]

---

developed by the Florida Department of Agriculture. *See* Fla. Stat. Ann. §403.067(7)(c) (nonagricultural sources) & 403.067(7)(d) (agricultural sources).

232. *See* Environmental Law Institute, *Enforceable State Mechanisms for the Control of Nonpoint Source Water Pollution* (1997); Environmental Law Institute, *Research Report: Almanac of Enforceable State Laws to Control Nonpoint Source Water Pollution* (1998); James M. McElfish, *State Enforcement Authorities for Polluted Runoff*, 28 Envtl. L. Rep. (Envtl. L. Inst.) 10,181, 10,195–99 (1998).

233. *See* Environmental Law Institute, *Enforceable State Mechanisms*, *supra* note 232, at iii ("Agriculture is the most problematic area for enforceable [nonpoint source water pollution] mechanisms. Many laws of general applicability ... have exceptions for agriculture. Where state laws exist, they often defer to incentives, cost sharing, and voluntary programs."); McElfish, *supra* note 232, at 10,182. Although "no state is entirely without any enforceable authority relevant to nonpoint source discharges ... some states have few such authorities [and] others have adopted a bewildering array of enforceable tools ... paired with equally bewildering arrays of exemptions and exclusions." *Id.*

234. For example, EPA has explained that for water bodies impaired primarily or exclusively by nonpoint source pollution, the primary implementation mechanism for the TMDL program "will generally be the State section 319 nonpoint source management program coupled with State, local, and Federal land management programs and authorities. For example, voluntary, incentive-based approaches at the State and local level can be used...." Perciasepe Memorandum, *supra* note 224.

235. *See* 42 U.S.C. §§7401–7671q (1994). For an overview of the CAA programs, see The Clean Air Act Handbook (Robert J. Martineau, Jr. & David P. Novello eds., 1998).

236. *See, e.g.*, 42 U.S.C. §7412(a)(1) (1994) (defining major source of hazardous air pollutants as a source emitting 10 tons per year of any such pollutant or 25 tons per year of any combination of such pollutants); id. §7479(1) (defining major source for purposes of permits designed to prevent significant deterioration of air quality generally as any source emitting 250 tons per year of any air pollutant; farms are not included in the list of specifically identified sources requiring only 100 tons per year to qualify as major); id. §7602(j) (defining major source generally for the CAA to mean any source emitting 100 tons per year of any pollutant, unless otherwise specified). One exception is the CAA program for standards of performance for new stationary sources, which establishes no "major source" threshold. *See id.* §7411. However, the new source emission limits apply only to categories of sources EPA has designated and for which it has promulgated such standards. EPA has not done so for farms generally, though grain terminal elevators storing over 2.5 million bushels are subject to gas emission opacity and particulate matter emission limits. *See* 40 C.F.R. subpt. DD, §60.300 (1999) (standards of performance for grain elevators).

237. *See, e.g.*, 64 Fed. Reg. 33,550 (1999) (to be codified at 40 C.F.R. pts. 9 & 63) (EPA final rule regulating emissions of hazardous air pollutants from pesticide manufacturers); 64 Fed. Reg. 31,358

A significant CAA regulatory program not tied to minimum emission quantity thresholds leaves the fate of farms open to the states and thus largely beyond direct federal control. Under Sections 108 and 109 of the CAA, EPA must designate "criteria" air pollutants that may reasonably be anticipated to endanger public health or welfare, and then establish nationally uniform ambient air quality standards.[238] Section 110 of the CAA allows states, if they elect to do so, to develop State Implementation Plans (SIPs) prescribing the enforceable measures the state will implement to achieve the NAAQS.[239] Within the SIP framework, the details are left to state discretion. The criteria pollutants are federally designated, but the questions of whom and what to regulate in order to achieve the federal standards are left to the states.[240] Although states could regulate air pollutant emissions from farms within that scope of discretion,[241] most states do not do so rigorously, and EPA actively dissuades them from doing so.[242]

(1999) (to be codified at 40 C.F.R. pts. 9 & 63) (EPA final rule regulating emissions of hazardous air pollutants from fertilizer manufacturers).

238. *See* 42 U.S.C. §§ 7408–7409 (1994). For a thorough overview of the NAAQS program, comparing its operation to that of the CWA water quality protection programs, see Adler, *supra* note 221, at 230–34

239. *See* 42 U.S.C. § 7410 (1994). *See generally* Adler, *supra* note 221, at 234–50. If a state elects not to prepare a SIP, or prepares one that does not meet EPA approval, EPA must prepare a Federal Implementation Plan for the area in question. *See* 42 U.S.C. § 7410(c) (1994).

240. *See* United Electric Co. v. EPA, 427 U.S. 246, 267, 269 (1976) ("[T]he State has virtually absolute power in allocating emissions limitations so long as the national standards are met.... Congress plainly left the States, so long as the national standards were met, the power to determine which sources would be burdened by regulation and to what extent.").

241. EPA has explained that "the degree to which ambient air emissions from farming practices —such as prescribed burning—are allowed are location-specific (specific to a geographic area) within each State Implementation Plan." National Agric. Compliance Assistance Ctr., U.S. Envtl. Protection Agency, Laws & Policies—Clean Air Act 3....

242. For example, faced with the prospect that its new regulations establishing NAAQS for fine particulate matter could extend to farm emissions of soil and particulates from tilling, prescribed burning, and other practices, EPA is currently devising policies to allow farms to escape regulation. EPA has contended that farms do not constitute major sources of the fine particulates, though data to support that claim appear to be nonexistent. Farm industry advocates are concerned that states could nonetheless attempt to regulate farm emissions through the state SIPs, so EPA is developing "guidance" for states that will reflect the purportedly small contribution farms make to fine particulate emissions. These and other issues are the subject of the Agricultural Air Quality Task Force EPA and USDA jointly established in 1997. *See* Alec Zacaroli, *Agencies Develop MOU Addressing Agricultural Impacts on Air Quality*, 28 ENV'T REP. (BNA) 1282 (1997). The issue has been complicated by a recent court decision striking down EPA's new rule on the ground that it violates the nondelegation doctrine. *See* American Trucking Ass'n v. EPA, 195 F.3d 4 (D.C. Cir. 1999); *see also* Alec C. Zacaroli, *Court Rulings Imperil EPA's Efforts to Clamp Down on Ozone Pollution*, 30 ENV'T REP. (BNA) 325 (1999). A related program designed to protect visibility in and near national parks and other vista areas may provide states with another opportunity to regulate farm emissions. Section 169A of the CAA establishes this so-called "regional haze" regulatory program, new regulations which EPA recently promulgated to require all states to develop regional haze SIPs to achieve clear visibility for protected areas by the year 2064. *See* Regional Haze Regulations, 64 Fed. Reg. 35713 (July 1, 1999) (to be codified at 40 C.F.R. pt. 51); *see also* Eric L. Hiser, *Regional Haze and Visibility: Potential Impacts for Industry*, 29 ENV'T REP. (BNA) 2597 (1999). Although few protected areas lie close to heavily farmed areas, the farm industry has expressed concerns that states may implement regional haze SIPs so as to restrict emissions from tilling and prescribed burning, which could be transported in the atmosphere to distant protected areas. Farming groups have suggested that they would seek congressional intervention should states focus on farms with that objective. *See* James Kennedy, *Farmers Fear Haze Rule Implementation, Could Seek Congressional Help, Group Says*, 29 ENV'T REP. (BNA) 2558 (1999). As of yet there is no evidence that states are moving toward regulation of farms under regional haze SIPs any more than they have under the NAAQS SIPs.

Under the CAA's program for prevention of significant deterioration (PSD) of air quality, in areas where the NAAQS is met for a regulated pollutant, states must establish "increments" of maximum air quality degradation and administer permits for major sources of the covered pollutant.[243] States may exclude from the increment "concentrations of particulate matter attributable to the increase in emissions from ... temporary emission-related activities."[244] This provision would probably cover prescribed seasonal agricultural burning. Hence, although farms would not normally be regulated under the PSD permitting program as they would not meet the "major source" threshold,[245] the exclusion of seasonal burning removes any incentive a state may have to restrict such farming practices in order to protect the area's increment for other economically valuable sources of emissions.

Beyond the general omission of farm regulation from the CAA framework, several specific exemptions for farms apply, or are proposed to apply, under programs that might otherwise capture some farming emissions. For example, Section 112 of the CAA requires sources of designated hazardous air pollutants to comply with specified prevention, control, and reporting conditions. Facilities that use the chemicals in quantities above specified thresholds must prepare and file a "risk management plan" with EPA prescribing measures for prevention of and response to accidental releases.[246] Farms do not enjoy a blanket exemption from these requirements; rather, the program allows EPA wide discretion to set threshold quantities and "exempt entirely" any substance that is used as a nutrient in agriculture.[247] EPA has done so for ammonia, exempting it "when held by farmers."[248] EPA also has raised the quantity threshold for propane, widely used on farms for heating, cooling, drying grain, and powering irrigation systems, to a level that effectively removes farms from the scope of the planning requirement.[249]

Regulation of emissions from mobile source fuels and engines under Subpart II of the CAA[250] also takes a hands-off approach to farms. For example, Section 209 of the CAA

---

243. *See* 42 U.S.C. §§ 7470–7478 (1994).

244. *Id.* § 7473(c)(1)(C).

245. *See supra* note 237 (discussing the major source feature of the PSD and other CAA programs).

246. *See* 42 U.S.C. § 7412 (1994).

247. *See id.* § 7412(r)(5).

248. 40 C.F.R. § 68.125 (1999). EPA has explained that the ammonia exemption applies "as long as it is used on that [farm] establishment. It would not be exempt if resold or used on another establishment." National Agric. Compliance Assistance Ctr., U.S. Envtl. Protection Agency, Laws & Policies — Clean Air Act 6 ... Congress added the nutrient exemption option because it believed "the imposition of costly and burdensome regulation on routine use of ammonia emissions associated with the production of crop nutrients would place an undue economic burden on an already beleaguered farm economy," and because "America's farmers have learned to live with and handle ammonia safely." *See* S. Rep. No. 228, 101st Cong., 1st Sess. (1989), *reprinted in* 1990 U.S.C.C.A.N. 3385.

249. *See Browner Signs Administrative Stay to Exempt Fuels from Risk Management Requirements,* DAILY ENV'T REP. (BNA), May 25, 1999, at A-4. In response to a court-ordered stay issued in connection with litigation challenging EPA's authority to extend the program to fuel-related uses of propane, see National Propane Gas Assoc. v. EPA, No. 96-1278 (D.C. Cir. Apr. 27, 1999), EPA simultaneously stayed the risk management program for propane, see 64 Fed. Reg. 29,168 (1999), and proposed a regulation raising the propane threshold quantity to a level that effectively will exclude farms even if the litigation challenging coverage of propane does not succeed, *see* 64 Fed. Reg. 29,171 (1999) (to be codified at 40 C.F.R. pt. 68).

250. *See* 42 U.S.C. §§ 7521–7590 (1994).

preempts states from controlling emissions from "new engines ... used in farm equipment or vehicles and which are smaller than 175 horsepower."[251] Farms also are exempt from the requirement that centrally-fueled fleets of vehicles use lower-polluting fuels.[252]

A recent example of the clout the farm industry has in securing safe harbors in the air pollution realm comes at the international environmental policy level. The production and consumption of methyl bromide, a colorless gas used as a pesticide on more than 100 crops, has been banned both domestically and internationally because it depletes the stratospheric ozone layer.[253] International protocols will ban methyl bromide in 2010.[254] Originally, the CAA specified a domestic phase-out date of 2001;[255] however, under tremendous farm industry lobby pressure, Congress extended the implementation date.[256] Hence, where the CAA's "passive" safe harbors for farms do not suffice to protect farms, Congress often provides targeted "active" safe harbors. Although there have been efforts by a few states to regulate farm air pollutant emissions more aggressively, they are trivial by comparison to the overall negligence in this area.[257]

4. Agrochemical Regulation Laws

Farms purchase pesticides and fertilizers, apply them to crops and soils, and any excess is removed by water runoff and air dispersal. As demonstrated above, the CWA and CAA do not purport to reach this "disposal" of chemicals in any meaningful way. Consistent with that theme, the nation's core agrochemical regulation statute, the Federal Insecticide, Fungicide, and Rodenticide Act (FIFRA),[258] does little to regulate farm applications of pesticides and leaves fertilizers untouched. FIFRA is primarily a product-licensing statute under which no one may sell, distribute, or use a pesticide unless it has been registered with EPA.[259] The registration process for new pesticides involves testing designed

---

251. *Id.* § 7543(e)(1).

252. *See id.* §§ 7586 (application of clean fuels requirement to centrally fueled fleets) & 7581(5) (exemption of farm vehicles).

253. For background on methyl bromide and the phase-out bans, see U.S. General Accounting Office, GAO/RCED-96-16, *The Phaseout of Methyl Bromide in the United States* (1995): Sondra Goldshein, *Methyl Bromide: The Disparity Between the Pesticide's Phaseout Dates Under the Clean Air Act and the Montreal Protocol on Substances that Deplete the Ozone Layer*, 4 ENVTL. LAW. 577 (1998).

254. *See* Goldshein, *supra* note 253, at 587–92.

255. *See id.* at 585–86

256. *See* Omnibus Consolidated Appropriations Act, Pub. L. No. 105-277, § 764(a), 112 Stat. 2681, 2681–36 (1998) (codified at 42 U.S.C. § 7671c(h) (1994)). EPA had indicated its receptiveness to the extension, and USDA lobbied outright in its favor. *See* Goldshein, *supra* note 253, at 599–601.

257. *See* Kip Betz, *Agricultural Coalition Asks Court to Void, Block Enforcement of Odor Regulations*, 30 ENV'T REP. (BNA) 952 (1999) (discussing dispute over attempt by Missouri to promulgate ambient air standard for hydrogen sulfide); Kip Betz, *State's Largest Hog Producer Submits Plan to Control Odors, Risk of Waste Spills*, 30 ENV'T REP. (BNA) 1338 (1999) (large hog farm agrees to odor control measures as part of consent agreement in settlement of state environmental law violations); Trevor Oliver, *Fighting Corporate Pigs: Citizen Action and Feedlot Regulation in Minnesota*, 83 MINN. L. REV. 1893, 1901–04 (1999) (discussing Minnesota's ambient air standard for hydrogen sulfide from feedlots, which has no federal counterpart).

258. 7 U.S.C. §§ 136–136y (1994). For an overview of the FIFRA program, see WILLIAM H. RODGERS, ENVIRONMENTAL LAW ch. 5 (2d ed. 1994). For an excellent summary of how FIFRA applies to farms, see Michael T. Olexa, Institute of Food and Agricultural Sciences, Fact Sheet FRE-71, *Laws Governing Use and Impact of Agricultural Chemicals: Registration, Labeling, and the Use of Pesticides* (rev. ed. 1995).

259. *See* 7 U.S.C. § 136a(a) (1994). EPA reviews about 15,000 pesticide registration applications annually, most of which involve new formulations containing active ingredients which have already been registered. Only about 15 new active ingredients are registered each year. *See* Rao et al., *supra*

to detect the harmful effects a product may have on the environment.[260] Approved pesticides must be periodically re-registered, which involves a thorough review of available data about the pesticide.[261] The end result of FIFRA's registration program, assuming the pesticide is approved and retains its registration, is a label describing, among other things, how the pesticide must be used.[262]

By regulating which pesticides can be made and sold, FIFRA clearly has a direct effect on farm pesticide use.[263] Direct regulation of farms, however, is not a main concern of FIFRA; the statute does little more than require that pesticides be applied by certified persons and consistent with their label instructions. Pesticides are approved for either "general use," in which case anyone can apply them,[264] or "restricted use," which requires application by a certified applicator.[265] For purposes of restricted pesticide use on farms, FIFRA divides users into "private applicators" who use or supervise the use of restricted pesticides for agricultural commodity production on property owned or leased by them or their employers,[266] and "commercial applicators" who are hired to apply restricted pesticides or otherwise do not qualify as private applicators.[267] Commercial applicators must pass a rigorous certification test administered by EPA or a state-approved program;[268] private applicators must also obtain certification, but may not be required to take an examination.[269] In addition to following worker safety rules,[270] all certified applicators — private and commercial — must maintain records of restricted pesticide applications,

---

note 97, at 2. FIFRA allows states to register pesticides for use in their respective boundaries, subject to EPA review. *See* 7 U.S.C. § 136v(c) (1994).

260. *See* 7 U.S.C. § 136a(c)(5) (1994) (EPA must find that the pesticide "will perform its intended function without unreasonable adverse effects on the environment.").

261. *See id.* § 136a-1.

262. *See id.* § 136a(c)(1)(C). It is a violation of FIFRA "to use any registered pesticide in a manner inconsistent with its labeling." *Id.* § 136j(a)(2)(G).

263. *See* [J.W.] Looney, [*The Changing Focus of Government Regulation of Agriculture in the United States*, 44 MERCER L. REV. 763, 771 (1993)] at 796–97. EPA can take its product restriction authority one step further toward direct regulation of farm practices by conditioning the legal use of a pesticide. A current example is EPA's proposed rule to restrict the legal sale and use of five pesticides that are in common use on farms — alachlor, atrazine, cyanazine, metolachlor, and simazine — except in compliance with an EPA-approved state management plan outlining measures farms must employ for groundwater protection. *See* 61 Fed. Reg. 33,260 (1996) (to be codified at 40 C.F.R. pts. 152 & 156).

264. *See* 7 U.S.C. § 136a(d) (1994).

265. *See id.* § 136a(d)(1)(C)(i). A pesticide must be classified as restricted if EPA determines that it "may generally cause, without additional regulatory restrictions, unreasonable adverse effects on the environment, including injury to the applicator." *Id.* § 136a(d)(1)(C).

266. *See id.* § 136e(2).

267. *See id.* § 136e(3).

268. *See id.* § 136i. EPA has promulgated rules for states to use in administering the certified applicator tests. *See* 40 C.F.R. pt. 171 (1999).

269. *See* 40 C.F.R. § 171.5 (1999).

270. Thousands of farm workers have become ill or died from exposure to pesticides in the farm workplace. *See generally* Carpenter, *supra* note 4, at 191–95 (summarizing studies of farming occupational health threats). Regulations to protect farm workers from the dangers of exposure to pesticides have been controversial, though ultimately limited in effect, for over twenty-five years. *See* Haugrud, *supra* note [204], § 8.2(C)(2)(h), at 366–67. Most such regulation at the federal level is channeled through EPA's authority to regulate the uses of pesticides under the Federal Insecticide, Fungicide, and Rodenticide Act, under which EPA has promulgated rules regarding hazard notification to workers and restriction of workers from areas where pesticides have recently been applied. See 40 C.F.R. pt. 170 (1999). EPA continues to explore other ways of directly and indirectly ensuring farm worker protection through this and other authorities. *See, e.g., Setting Residue Limits Not Way to Reduce Farm Children's Exposure, Industry Says,* DAILY ENV'T REP. (BNA), Dec. 22, 1998, at A8 (discussing

showing product, amount, date, location, and area of application, and comply with any additional state recordkeeping requirements,[271] but they need not report the applications to anyone unless a federal agency (acting through the USDA), state agency (acting through a designated lead state agency), or health professional administering medical treatment so requests or state law requires regular disclosure.[272]

In short, so long as the label instructions are followed, the applicator is properly certified and the applicator follows worker safety and recordkeeping requirements, FIFRA imposes no direct restrictions or requirements on farms. While this does not amount to a complete safe harbor for farm use of pesticides, FIFRA's hands-off approach to farms—the primary users of pesticides—pales in comparison with the CAA and CWA's regulatory approach to their targeted industries. Under FIFRA, with regard to farmers, no permits are required, no environmental or efficiency performance standards are imposed, no technology-based standards are applied, no regular public reporting of pesticide applications is required, and no monitoring of pesticide levels in soils, runoff, or groundwater is required. Although some states regulate pesticide applications more aggressively than does FIFRA, it is fair to say that the nation has no comprehensive regulatory framework governing farm use of pesticides.

Farm use of fertilizers is subject to even less federal and state control. The Toxic Substances Control Act (TSCA)[273] requires pre-manufacture registration of the chemical ingredients of fertilizers;[274] however, TSCA imposes no use restrictions equivalent to FIFRA's labeling, certification, worker safety, or recordkeeping provisions, and few states impose more rigorous controls.[275] As previously explained, the CWA and CAA offer a mixture of active and passive safe harbors for pollution that results from farm use of fertilizers. Other federal environmental laws contain numerous express exemptions for "normal application of fertilizers."[276] Overall, then, fertilizers are simply not in the sights of federal environmental laws.

5. Chemical Storage and Release Reporting Laws

One of the most prominent trends that has unfolded with the proliferation of federal environmental statutes is the use of information disclosure devices as an adjunct to direct regulation of pollution behavior.[277] These measures range from the requirements in

---

issue of whether EPA should establish food pesticide residue limits as a way of reducing risks to children in farm occupational settings).

271. *See* 7 U.S.C. § 136i-1(a) (1999).

272. *See id.* § 136i-1(b) to (c). Certified commercial applicators must provide copies to the person for whom the application was performed. See id. § 136i-1(a)(2). USDA and EPA must also survey certified applicator records to develop a database sufficient to compile annual reports concerning pesticide use. *See id.* § 136i-1(f).

273. 15 U.S.C. §§ 2601–2692 (1994).

274. *See id.* § 2604(a).

275. Washington recently enacted fertilizer registration legislation that imposes restrictions on the metals content of fertilizers. *See* Nan Netherton, *Governor Signs Bill on Dairy Farms, Changes to Commercial Fertilizer Rules*, 30 ENV'T REP. (BNA) 186 (1999).

276. *See, e.g., infra* notes 284 (hazardous substance release reporting), 286 (chemical storage reporting), and 299 (contaminated site remediation liability).

277. *See* Paul R. Kleindorfer & Eric W. Orts, *Informational Regulation of Environmental Risks*, 18 RISK ANALYSIS 155 (1998) (describing the regulatory impact of several environmental information disclosure programs). The growing importance of information disclosure and other "right-to-know" mechanisms to environmental regulation and enforcement is evidenced by EPA's recent decision to create a new Office of Information. *See* Sara Thurin Rollin, *New Information Office to Focus On TRI, Confidential Information, FOIA Rule Changes*, DAILY ENV'T REP. (BNA), June 16, 1999, at AA-1.

Superfund[278] and the Emergency Planning and Community Right-to-Know Act (EPCRA)[279] that persons who release designated hazardous substances in specified quantities must report such events to public authorities,[280] to EPCRA's broader emergency planning and toxic release inventory (TRI) programs.[281] These programs have significantly increased the information available to the government and citizens about the sources and magnitude of chemical releases to the environment.[282] But not surprisingly, farms have been left out of the information revolution in environmental law.

Superfund, for example, excludes "the normal application of fertilizer" from the definition of release[283] and excludes from reporting requirements any application of a FIFRA-registered pesticide.[284] EPCRA excludes from the definition of hazardous chemicals subject to emergency planning and storage notification any substance in "routine agricultural operations,"[285] and the EPCRA TRI emission reporting regulations specifically incorporate the CERCLA exemption for FIFRA-registered pesticides.[286] Farms also are outside the categories of facilities subject to the TRI program.[287] Information transfer from farms to the public concerning agrochemical use and release is simply not a part of the CERCLA and EPCRA programs.

6. Hazardous Waste Management Laws

Farms handle large volumes of chemicals, much of which are disposed either directly as spent or residue materials or indirectly as excess fertilizer or pesticide. Most industries in this position must deal with the mind-numbing complexity of the Resource Conservation and Recovery Act (RCRA), the nation's principal hazardous waste management and disposal regulation law.[288] Farms, however, do not.

For example, EPA has not classified solid wastes generated from growing and harvesting crops and from raising livestock as hazardous wastes subject to RCRA's compre-

---

278. Superfund is the shorthand name for the Comprehensive Environmental Response, Compensation, and Liability Act, 42 U.S.C. §§ 9601–9675 (1994). For an overview of the Superfund remediation and liability programs, see Rodgers, *supra* note 258, ch. 8.

279. 42 U.S.C. §§ 11001–11050 (1994). For an overview of the EPCRA program, see James M. Kuszaj, THE EPCRA COMPLIANCE MANUAL (1997).

280. *See* 42 U.S.C. §§ 9603(a) (1994) (Superfund) & 11004 (EPCRA).

281. *See id.* §§ 11022 (emergency planning) & 11023 (toxic releases).

282. One of the most innovative uses of the information derived from the TRI and other information disclosure programs is found at the Environmental Defense Fund's "Scorecard" web page where a wealth of information about reporting facilities and the chemicals they emit can be obtained on a site-specific basis in a matter of seconds. *See* Environmental Defense Fund, *Scorecard* [visited June 4,2010] http://www.scorecard.org. As previously noted, *See supra* note 272, although FIFRA requires recordkeeping for restricted pesticide applications, there is no equivalent to the TRI public disclosure requirement under FIFRA.

283. *See* 42 U.S.C. § 9601(22)(D) (1994).

284. *See id.* § 9603(e)

285. *See id.* § 11021(e)(5).

286. *See* 40 C.F.R. § 355.40(2)(iv) (1999).

287. *See* 42 U.S.C. § 11023(b)(1)(A) (1994) (limiting the TRI requirements to "facilities ... that are in Standard Industrial Classification Codes 20 through 39"). Courts have also ruled that EPA may not designate chemicals, including fertilizer components such as phosphoric acid, as toxic under the EPCRA TRI program based on their environmental effects; rather, only inherent toxicity may be considered. *See* Fertilizer Inst. v. Browner, 1999 U.S. Dist. LEXIS 9298 (D.D.C. Apr. 15, 1999). Although farms would not be required to report their applications of such fertilizers in any event, fertilizer manufacturers would be subject to reporting their emissions in manufacturing the chemicals.

288. *See* 42 U.S.C. §§ 6901–6992k (1994). For an overview of the RCRA program, *See* American Bar Association, THE RCRA PRACTICE MANUAL (Theodore L. Garrett ed., 1994).

hensive "cradle-to-grave" regulations.[289] Similarly, farm irrigation return flows are not considered solid waste and are not subject to RCRA regulation, notwithstanding the fact that such return flows carry significant quantities of fertilizers, pesticides, contaminated soil, and animal wastes.[290] Farms disposing of waste pesticide from their own use are exempt from RCRA waste management regulations so long as empty containers are triple rinsed and the pesticides are disposed of consistent with label instructions.[291] Farms generating less than 25 gallons per month on average of used oil are exempt from RCRA's used oil management and disposal regulation,[292] and farms generating less than 100 kilograms per month on average of specified "universal wastes," which include obsolete or unused pesticides, enjoy exemptions from a variety of hazardous waste regulations.[293] Finally, wind dispersal of chemicals used in pesticides is generally not considered a RCRA problem, but instead is handled under the Clean Air Act—which does not regulate it in any meaningful way.[294] Although a farm that engages in hazardous waste management not related to farming would fall squarely within RCRA's scope, farms that stick to farming are outside that scope, notwithstanding the large volume of chemicals they dispose.

7. Contaminated Site Remediation Laws

Superfund's enactment in 1980 acknowledged that we had begun the process of beefing up environmental law too late to prevent the proliferation of thousands of contaminated properties around the country. While laws such as the CWA, CAA, and RCRA helped to stem the tide, Superfund was designed to establish a remedial program focused primarily on the contaminated sites that had been created before those laws were promulgated.[295]

While the administrative, legal, and remedial costs of Superfund have grown difficult to justify under any cost-benefit calculus,[296] the farm industry has not paid its share in any way. Despite the persistence of many agrochemicals in soils and sediments and the growing realization that urban expansion into converted farmland contains those latent chemical threats,[297] Superfund does not impose liability for any response costs resulting from application of FIFRA-registered pesticides,[298] and excludes the "normal application of fertilizer" from remediation and liability provisions.[299] Farms also enjoy a significant exemption under the related program for the remediation of petroleum product releases from underground storage tanks.[300]

---

289. *See* 40 C.F.R. § 261.4 (1999).

290. *See* 42 U.S.C. § 6903(27) (1994).

291. *See* 40 C.F.R. §§ 261.4, 262.70 (1999)

292. *See id.* § 279.20(a)(4).

293. *See* 40 C.F.R. §§ 273.3, 273.10 to 273.20 (1999).

294. *See* RCRA Practice Manual, *supra* note 288, at 9 ("Although air emissions from industrial facilities may exhibit hazard characteristics..., they ordinarily would not be 'solid wastes' within the meaning of RCRA, thus avoiding an overlap in the Clean Air Act and RCRA regulatory programs.").

295. For a discussion of Superfund's objectives and an overview of its remedial and liability program, see Rodgers, *supra* note 258, ch. 8.

296. One recent study found that each case of cancer that Superfund-led remediations have purported to avoid in the future has carried a median cost of $418 million. *See Study Says Faulty Risk Perceptions, Political Influences Bias Site Remediation*, DAILY ENV'T REP. (BNA), June 1, 1999, at A-5.

297. *See supra* text accompanying note 105.

298. *See* 42 U.S.C. § 9607(i) (1994).

299. *See id.* § 9601(22).

300. The underground storage tank program is found in subchapter IX of RCRA. *See* 42 U.S.C. §§ 6991–6991i (1994). The program exempts from the definition of underground storage tank any "farm or residential tank of 1,100 gallons or less capacity used for storing motor fuel for non-commercial purposes." Id. § 6991(1)(A). For an overview of the underground storage tank program, see Richard

8. Common Law Nuisance and Statutory "Right-to-Farm" Laws

It has often been said that the statutory form of modern environmental law is built on the backbone of the common law of nuisance.[301] Given the extent to which modern environmental law is prevented from reaching farms, it is no surprise that nuisance law continues to play an important role in efforts to control the environmental impact of farms. Particularly in areas where suburban development has encroached upon existing farm operations, new residents are likely to object to the resulting dust, noise, and odors, and nuisance provides an obvious cause of action.

It should also be no surprise that farms enjoy a substantial safe harbor even on this front. All states have enacted so-called "right-to-farm" laws, which generally exempt farms from common law nuisance attack.[302] Although the degree of protection afforded by these laws varies,[303] the basic theme is to protect farms from private nuisance actions by codifying the "comes to the nuisance" rule.[304] Although the tide is turning against such laws in some areas,[305] they remain a significant obstacle to the use of common law environmental remedies against farms.

B. Significant Exceptions to the General Rule of Safe Harbor

The breadth and depth of the safe harbor that farms enjoy from environmental regulation make it all the more remarkable that three regulatory programs have managed to levy a significant degree of environmental controls on farming. The three programs represent three different approaches to environmental regulation. First, the regulation of concentrated animal feeding operations under the Clean Water Act NPDES program constitutes direct regulation of a limited class of farms; second, the Endangered Species Act is a general environmental protection program that has no safe harbor exceptions for farming; and third, the so-called "Swampbuster" provisions of the 1985 and 1990 Farm Bills indirectly regulate environmental impacts of farms through the manipulation of farm subsidy policies. In each case, farms have felt the unaccustomed pinch of environmental law.

P. Fahey, Underground Storage Tanks: A Primer on the Federal Regulatory Program (2d ed. 1995).

301. *See*, e.g., Rodgers, *supra* note 258, ch. 2.

302. *See generally* Neil D. Hamilton, *Right-To-Farm Laws Reconsidered: Ten Reasons Why Legislative Efforts to Resolve Agricultural Nuisances May Be Ineffective*, 3 Drake J. Agric. L. 103 (1998); McElfish, *supra* note 232, at 10,190–91; Alexander A. Reinert, *The Right to Farm: Hog-Tied and Nuisance-Bound*, 73 N.Y.U. L. Rev. 1694 (1998). Prior to the advent of these laws in the past two decades, it was not uncommon for farms to be declared a nuisance. *See* Hank W. Hannah, *Farming in the Face of Progress*, Prob. & Prop., Sept.–Oct. 1997, at 9, 9–11.

303. *See generally* McElfish, *supra* note 232, at 10,191 (explaining variation among state laws); Hannah, *supra* note 302, at 11–13 (discussing plaintiff tactics for circumventing right-to-farm laws); Haugrud, *supra* note [204], §8.2(B)(1), at 485–87 (dividing the laws into three models based on scope of covered farms and scope of the safe harbor). Most of the right-to-farm laws deny the protection when the farm is operated negligently in violation of federal or state laws or so as to cause water pollution or soil erosion.

304. *See* Hamilton, *supra* note 302, at 104; Haugrud, *supra* note [204], §8.2(B)(1), at 484–85; McElfish, *supra* note 232, at 10,191.

305. Most significantly, the Iowa Supreme Court recently found that Iowa's right-to-farm law constituted an illegal taking of property adjacent to protected farms, and the United States Supreme Court let the decision stand. *See* Bormann v. Board of Supervisors, 584 N.W.2d 309 (Iowa 1998), *cert. denied sub nom.* Girres v. Bormann, 525 U.S. 1172 (1999). *But see* Pure Air and Water, Inc. v. Davidsen, 246 A.2d 786 (N.Y. App. Div. 1998) (differing result from *Bormann*); Jeff Feirick, *Upholding the New York Right to Farm Law*, Agric. L. Update, Aug. 1999, at 1 (discussing *Davidsen*).

1. Regulation of Concentrated Animal Feeding Operations

Only 190,000 of the 640,000 farms in the United States that raise or keep livestock rely on pasture land to feed the livestock.[306] The remaining farms use animal feeding operations (AFOs) known as confined feedlots—food is brought to animals kept in confined quarters.[307] The size of an AFO is measured by the number of cows, hogs, chickens, or turkeys translated into "animal units" (AUs).[308] Many AFOs squeeze an impressive number of AUs into confined feedlots, resulting in what is known as a concentrated AFO (CAFO) and, consequently, a point source within the meaning of the Clean Water Act.[309] There were about 6,600 such CAFOs holding more than 1000 AUs each in operation in the United States in 1992.[310]

Anyone who has visited a CAFO is unlikely to forget the odoriferous experience. Most CAFOs handle their massive quantities of animal waste by collecting the manure and urine in large impoundments and applying it to farmland as crop fertilizer or simply as a method of disposal.[311] This practice results not only in an intensely unpleasant odor, but it also increases the potential for environmental degradation and the transport of pathogens to human populations.[312] Given their intense and pernicious impacts on surrounding communities, CAFOs have become lightning rods for local land use controversy.[313]

Although regulation of CAFOs is a significant exception to the general rule that farms enjoy a safe harbor, the story has two sides. In 1998—over 25 years after Congress included

---

306. *See* Office of Enforcement and Compliance Assurance, U.S. Envtl. Protection Agency, Compliance Assurance Implementation Plan for Concentrated Animal Feeding Operations 2 (1998) ...

307. In their joint policy on AFOs, EPA and USDA explain that AFOs "congregate animals, feed, manure and urine, dead animals, and production operations on a small land area. Feed is brought to the animals rather than the animals grazing or otherwise seeking food in pastures, fields, or rangeland." USDA/U.S. Envtl. Protection Agency, Unified National Strategy for Animal Feeding Operations P 2.1 ... [hereinafter Unified National Strategy]. To qualify as an AFO, the confined feeding must occur at least 45 days per year and prevent any sustained vegetative production on the lot. *See* 40 C.F.R. § 122.23(b)(1) (1999).

308. One AU is equal to roughly 1 beef cow, 2.5 hogs, 5 horses, 10 sheep, 55 turkeys, or 100 chickens. *See* 40 C.F.R. pt. 122, app. B (1999).

309. *See* 33 U.S.C. § 1362(14) (1994) (including "concentrated animal feeding operation" within the CWA definition of point source). Generally any AFO is a CAFO if it either (1) confines at least 1000 AUs, (2) confines at least 300 AUs and discharges pollutants through a point source, or (3) confines under 300 AUs but is designated a CAFO on a case-by-case basis by the relevant permitting authority because it is a significant source of water pollution. However, such operations are not CAFOs if they discharge pollutants only in the event of a 25-year, 24-hour storm event. *See id.* The more technical details of deciding whether an AFO is a CAFO requiring an NPDES permit took EPA ten pages to explain in a recent draft guidance document on CAFO permits. *See* Office of Waste Management, U.S. Envtl. Protection Agency, Guidance Manual and Example NPDES Permit for Concentrated Animal Feeding Operations 2-1 to 2-10 (1999) (review draft) (on file with author).

310. *See* Unified National Strategy, *supra* note 307, P 4.5. EPA and USDA estimate that the number of large CAFOs has grown to 10,000 since the 1992 figure was compiled. *See id.* The vast majority of AFOs confine fewer than 250 AUs. *See id.* P 2.1. Nevertheless, the proliferation of large CAFOs has boosted livestock production even as the total number of AFOs has decreased, indicating that the industry is consolidating into fewer, but larger, AFOs. *See id.*

311. For vivid descriptions of AFO operations, see generally Frarey & Pratt, *supra* note 15, at 8; Oliver, *supra* note 257, at 1895–97.

312. *See* Unified National Strategy, *supra* note 307, P 2.2. Recent studies suggest that CAFOs present a measurable public health threat to surrounding communities. *See* Terry Hammond, Study Finds Hog Lagoon Neighbors Report Higher Levels of Respiratory Illness, Daily Env't Rep. (BNA), May 14, 1999, at A-5.

313. *See generally* Williams, *supra* note 120; Fern Shen, *Md. Hog Farm Causing Quite a Stink*, WASH. POST, May 23, 1999, at A1; William Claiborne, *Despite Stink, Hog Farm Proceeds on Tribal Land*, WASH. POST, Apr. 4, 1999, at A3.

CAFOs in the CWA's definition of point source—only 2,000 of the nation's 450,000 AFOs had NPDES permits or state equivalents.[314] One large safe harbor for AFOs from the CWA, of course, is the regulatory definition of a CAFO and its relatively high AU threshold. Even those AFOs which attain CAFO status through sufficient AUs or because of the nature of their discharge have another safe harbor in the exclusion of AFOs that only discharge pollutants through a point source in significant storm events. These two filters winnow the nation's 450,000 AFOs down to the 2,000 presently required to follow NPDES permitting requirements.

Clearly, the AFO issue encompasses more than the 2,000 farms presently under the thumb of NPDES permitting requirements. That reality has become a major focus of federal and state regulators in the past several years. The federal focus recently culminated in the issuance by USDA and EPA of a Unified National Strategy for Animal Feeding Operations (Unified National Strategy).[315] The cornerstone of the Unified National Strategy is a "national performance expectation" that all AFOs will develop and implement technically sound and economically feasible nutrient management plans addressing such operational matters as feed management, manure handling and storage, and land application of manure.[316] Because the Unified National Strategy imposes no new regulatory requirements, preparation of a plan for most AFOs will be purely voluntary unless state law requires one.[317] On the regulatory front, the Unified National Strategy outlines provisions for CAFOs that will effectively expand the coverage of permitting controls. For example, the Unified National Strategy will expand the number of AFOs requiring NPDES permits to 15,000–20,000 by including most large (over 1000 AUs) operations as well as AFOs that are either operating under unacceptable conditions or are otherwise contributing to water quality impairment, regardless of their size.[318] Moreover, all AFOs needing an NPDES permit may be required to prepare nutrient management plans and comply with feedlot effluent standards.[319] EPA has begun to implement these proposals through TMDL rules[320] and guidance documents.[321]

---

314. *See* Unified National Strategy, *supra* note 307, P 4.2.

315. *See* Unified National Strategy, *supra* note 307. The Clinton Administration's 1998 Clean Water Action Plan called for USDA and EPA to compile the National Uniform Strategy as one of 111 specific action plans. *See id.* P 1.1. The agencies released a draft for public comment in September 1998. *See* 63 Fed. Reg. 50,192 (1998). For a detailed overview of the proposal, describing it as a sign that "AFOs and CAFOs are now entering the meat grinder of regulatory politics," *See* Gregory Blount et al., *The New Nonpoint Source Battleground: Concentrated Animal Feeding Operations*, 14 Nat. Resources & Env't 42 (1999). For a comprehensive overview of the Unified National Strategy, *See* Dana R. Flick, *The Future of Agricultural Pollution Following USDA and EPA Drafting of a Unified National Strategy for Animal Feeding Operations*, 8 Dickinson J. Envtl. L. & Pol'y 61 (1999).

316. *See* Unified National Strategy, *supra* note 307, PP 3.1–3.5.

317. *See id.* P 4.1.

318. *See id.* P 4.5. The Unified National Strategy envisions that the permitting program will be implemented over several phases and will rely on general permits for all but the larger (over 1,000 AUs) CAFOs, which will need to obtain individual permits. *See id.* P 5.0 (Strategic Issue #3).

319. *See id.* P 4.6. The effluent guidelines presently impose a "zero discharge" condition on CAFO feedlots with NPDES permits. *See* 40 C.F.R. pt. 412 (1999). EPA has announced plans to revise the standards, including measures to address phosphorous levels in runoff. *See* 63 Fed. Reg. 62,469 (1998) (codified at 40 C.F.R. §§ 412 & 122.23 (1999)). Farming interests have vociferously opposed EPA's efforts. *See USDA Proposal to Include Phosphorous in Nutrient Plans Concerns Farm Group*, 29 Env't Rep. (BNA) 610 (1998) (quoting American Farm Bureau official).

320. *See supra* note 223.

321. For example, EPA has issued a draft NPDES permit for CAFOs and other AFOs subject to permitting. *See* Office of Wastewater Management, U.S. Envtl. Protection Agency, Draft Guidance Manual and Example NPDES Permit for Concentrated Animal Feeding Operations....

Predictably, reaction to the Unified National Strategy has been mixed, with few interest groups fully in favor. Environmental groups contend the measures do not reach far enough, while farm groups assert that a purely voluntary program will be sufficient.[322] Many state government representatives have expressed the concern that the Unified National Strategy will constrain state efforts to respond to the CAFO issue with locally-designed measures,[323] even though environmental groups have argued that past state efforts have been weak and poorly implemented.[324] Moreover, some congressional representatives have questioned whether EPA and USDA have the legal authority to issue and implement the National Uniform Strategy as a "strategy" without following rulemaking procedures.[325] In any event, issuance of and debate on the Unified National Strategy signals continuing federal and state commitment to retain the lone exception to farming's safe harbor from

---

322. *See Environmentalists Fault Feedlot Plan While Farmers Want Voluntary Approach*, DAILY ENV'T REP. (BNA), Sept. 17, 1998, at A-6; Susan Bruninga, *Farmers, Public Interest Groups Debate Merits of Animal Runoff Control Strategy*, 29 ENV'T REP. (BNA) 1645 (1998); Susan Bruninga, *Ranchers and Farmers in the West Sound Off on Pollution Control Strategy*, 29 ENV'T REP. (BNA) 1646 (1998). Farm groups have pointed to several significant voluntary efforts initiated by different farm sectors to improve nutrient management. *See, e.g.*, Registration and Agreement for Clean Water Act Section 301 Compliance Audit Program for the Pork Production Industry, 63 Fed. Reg. 69,627 (1998) (recommending that EPA and pork producers agree to initiate voluntary third party compliance audit program for hog farms in return for reduced penalties and increased EPA educational support). Environmental groups contend that such efforts, while salutary, should not deter efforts to regulate CAFOs more stringently. *See Millions to Be Spent on Training, Oversight of EPA Agreement with Pork Producers*, DAILY ENV'T REP. (BNA), Nov. 30, 1998, at A-9.

323. EPA has compiled a comprehensive summary of state laws dealing with CAFOs, proving the states' claims that they are addressing CAFOs in ways that often go beyond EPA's regulations. *See* U.S. Envtl. Protection Agency, State Compendium: Programs and Regulatory Activities Related to Animal Feeding Operations (1999).

324. In the time it took for the Unified National Strategy to go from draft to final stages, a flurry of initiatives to address AFOs through increased regulation were passed by a variety of states. *See, e.g.*, Michael Blogna, *State Adopts New Reporting Rules for Spills from Livestock Waste Lagoons*, DAILY ENV'T REP. (BNA), Feb. 17, 1999, at A-3 (Illinois); Thomas R. Head, III, *Local Regulation of Animal Feeding Operations: Concerns, Limits, and Options for Southeastern States*, 6 ENVTL. LAW. 503 (2000) (canvassing federal law and the law of eight southeastern states); Theresa Heil, *Agricultural Nonpoint Source Runoff—The Effects Both On and Off the Farm: An Analysis of Federal and State Regulation of Agricultural Nonpoint Source Pollutants*, 5 WIS. ENVTL. L.J. 43, 50–63 (1998) (Wisconsin); Drew Kershen, *Clean Water and Concentrated Animal Feeding Operations, Looking Ahead*: ABA Section of Natural Resources, Energy, & Envtl. L. Newsletter, Mar.–Apr. 1999, at 2 (Oklahoma, Colorado, and Mississippi); Oliver, *supra* note 257 (Minnesota); Carolyn Whetzel, *Regulators Issue Waste Discharge Plan for Dairy Farms in Southern California*, DAILY ENV'T REP. (BNA), Apr. 13, 1999, at A-4 (California); *Large Hog Farms to Have Releases Regulated by Water, Multimedia Permits*, 30 ENV'T REP. (BNA) 71 (1999) (Mississippi); *Proposed Rules for Corporate Hog Farms Ready for Comment, State Official Says*, 29 ENV'T REP. (BNA) 1215 (1998) (Missouri). Indeed, the Unified National Strategy recognizes that many states have already implemented permitting programs for CAFOs that equal or exceed the federal NPDES program requirements and has invited such states to seek delegation of authority to administer the NPDES program. *See* Unified National Strategy, *supra* note 307, P 5.0 (Strategic Issue #3); Susan Bruninga, *Nonpoint Sources: Animal Waste Strategy to Recognize State Programs, Hold Corporations Liable*, 29 ENV'T REP. (BNA) 2225 (Mar. 12, 1999). Nevertheless, state water regulators maintain that the Unified National Strategy will be too expensive to implement fully and have proposed an AFO initiative that relies more on incentives and voluntary measures. *See State Group Seeks More Flexibility in Regulation of Livestock Waste*, DAILY ENV'T REP. (BNA), Feb 26, 1999, at A-4; Susan Bruninga, *Faulting EPA-USDA Livestock Strategy, States Say Their Programs Already Work*, 29 ENV'T REP. (BNA) 1757 (1999). Environmental groups charge that the state programs are inconsistent and ineffective. *See, e.g.*, America's Animal Factories, *supra* note 125, at ix–xii (identifying 15 major deficiencies in the existing state-level regulation of AFOs).

325. Susan Bruninga, *Small Livestock Facilities May Get More Time to Comply with AFO Strategy*, 29 ENV'T REP. (BNA) 2131, 2132 (1999).

water pollution regulation and suggests that at least some components of the farming industry are amenable to direct, concerted environmental regulation.

2. Endangered Species Act

The Endangered Species Act (ESA)[326] is a rare example of an environmental law with sharp teeth and no safe harbor for farms. Once designated as endangered or threatened,[327] a species is protected through several provisions with virtually no federal, state, local, or private actor beyond the ESA's reach. Given their pervasive impact on wildlife habitat, farms have increasingly been at the center of ESA controversy.

Most of the ESA's land use battles begin through the application of one of two regulatory provisions. Section 9 of the ESA prohibits any federal, state, local, or private entity from "taking" a listed animal species,[328] which has been construed to prohibit "significant habitat modification or degradation where it actually kills or injures wildlife by significantly impairing essential behavioral patterns, including breeding, feeding or sheltering."[329] As farming can involve both the conversion of habitat to farm uses and the degradation of farm and non-farm habitat through pollution, sedimentation, water resource depletion, and other farming impacts, the ESA's habitat modification restriction has increasingly become an issue for farming practices.[330]

---

326. 16 U.S.C. §§ 1531–1544 (1994). For an overview of the ESA programs, see Michael J. Bean & Melanie J. Rowland, THE EVOLUTION OF NATIONAL WILDLIFE LAW 193–281 (3d ed. 1997).

327. For a discussion of the listing process and criteria, see J.B. Ruhl, *Section 4 of the ESA — The Cornerstone of Species Protection Law*, 8 NAT. RESOURCES & ENV'T 26 (1993); Holly Doremus, *Listing Decisions Under the Endangered Species Act: Why Better Science Isn't Always Better Policy*, 75 WASH. U. L.Q. 1029, 1049–50, 1117–29 (1997).

328. 16 U.S.C. § 1538(a) (1994). For an overview of the take prohibition as implemented, see Frederico M. Cheever, *An Introduction to the Prohibition Against Takings in Section 9 of the Endangered Species Act of 1973: Learning to Live with A Powerful Species Preservation Law*, 62 U. COLO. L. REV. 109 (1991); Albert Gidari, *The Endangered Species Act: Impact of Section 9 on Private Landowners*, 24 ENVTL. L. 419 (1994). Section 9(a) species protections vary according to whether a species is plant or animal and whether it is listed as endangered or threatened. Thus, Section 9(a)(1), the cornerstone of ESA regulation, applies only to "endangered species of fish or wildlife," making it unlawful for "any person subject to the jurisdiction of the United States to ... take any such species within the United States or territorial sea of the United States." 16 U.S.C. § 1538(a)(1) (1994). Threatened species of fish or wildlife receive the same level of protection by regulations authorized under Section 4(d) of the ESA. *See id.* § 1533(d); 50 C.F.R. § 17.31(a) (1999); *see also* Keith Saxe, *Regulated Taking of Threatened Species Under the Endangered Species Act*, 39 HASTINGS L.J. 399 (1988). Plants receive less protection under Section 9(a) than do fish and wildlife species and are not in any circumstance protected from take in the broad sense used in the context of fish and wildlife species. Rather, Section 9(a)(2)(B) provides that endangered plants on federal lands are protected from being removed, maliciously damaged, or destroyed. *See* 16 U.S.C. § 1538(a)(2)(B) (1994). Endangered plants on non-federal lands are protected only if removing, damaging, or destroying them would constitute "a knowing violation of any law or regulation of any State or ... violation of a State criminal trespass law." Id. § 1538(a)(2)(B). Hence, farming implicates the ESA's take prohibition primarily through its effects on terrestrial and aquatic wildlife species.

329. 50 C.F.R. § 17.3 (1999). The Supreme Court recently upheld the regulation defining take to include habitat modification, albeit emphasizing the narrow criteria of actual death or injury required to make habitat modification into a prohibited take. *See* Babbitt v. Sweet Home Chapter of Communities for a Great Oregon, 515 U.S. 687 (1995). For a description of the controversial administrative and judicial developments leading up to and culminating in the Sweet Home case, see Steven G. Davison, *Alteration of Wildlife Habitat as a Prohibited Taking Under the Endangered Species Act*, 10 J. LAND USE & ENVTL. L. 155 (1995).

330. A current and highly controversial example is the black-tailed prairie dog, which is under consideration for listing as a threatened species. *See* 64 Fed. Reg. 14,424 (1999) (proposed to be codified at 50 C.F.R. pt. 17). Most of the reasons contributing to the species' impaired status relate to

While the Section 9 "take" prohibition applies directly to private actions, including farming, Section 7 of the ESA adds another layer of regulation for farms by restricting the practices of federal agencies that fund, carry out, or grant approvals to state, local, and private actions. Federal agencies must ensure that their actions conserve listed species[331] and do not jeopardize the continued existence of any listed species.[332] As farming in the United States depends heavily on federal support through subsidies and access to federal public resources, Section 7 conditions have also become major battlegrounds between farming and the ESA.[333]

Although the restrictions in Sections 9 and 7 of the ESA are mitigated by the availability of permits for "incidental take" of listed species,[334] farms have no special status under the relevant permitting provisions and enjoy no general exemptions from Sections 9 and 7. Moreover, neither Section 9 nor Section 7 contains any threshold criteria or gaps in coverage that would allow farms to escape regulatory consequences covertly. While a farm that poses no on-site or off-site consequences to listed species need not take affirmative conservation steps to promote a listed species,[335] the ESA stands virtually alone

---

farming—for example, conversion of habitat to farming; sport and varmint shooting; competition and predation from species introduced through farming; habitat fragmentation through farming; and poisoning. *See id.* at 14,426–28. Farming interests have decried the potential listing of the species as "propaganda" and contend that the Section 9 prohibitions that would come with listing the species will destroy "the agricultural way of life ... because it is not compatible with uncontrolled prairie dog populations." Jake Cummins, Target on Prairie Dogs ... (statement of Montana Farm Bureau official); *see also Prairie Dog Receives Positive Petition Finding,* Endangered Species & Wetlands Rep., Apr. 1999, at 13. Recognizing the potential constraints Section 9 places on farming practices after a species is listed, the Farm Bureau has become active in challenging species listings. *See, e.g.,* Idaho Farm Bureau Fed'n v. Babbitt, 58 F.3d 1392 (9th Cir. 1995) (upholding listing of a small snail deemed endangered because of water depletion through farm irrigation and other farming practices).

331. Conservation is defined in the ESA as "the use of all methods and procedures which are necessary to bring any endangered species or threatened species to the point at which the measures provided pursuant to this chapter are no longer necessary." 16 U.S.C. § 1532(3) (1994). Section 7(a)(1) of the ESA directs federal agencies to "utilize their authorities in furtherance of the purposes of this chapter by carrying out programs for the conservation of endangered species and threatened species." Id. § 1536(a)(1). Though mandatory on its face, agencies and courts have construed the conservation provision as a discretionary guideline for agency action. *See J.B. Ruhl, Section 7(a)(1) of the "New" Endangered Species Act: Rediscovering and Redefining the Untapped Power of Federal Agencies' Duty to Conserve Species,* 25 Envtl. L. 1107 (1995).

332. Section 7(a)(2) of the ESA initiates a complicated set of procedures implementing the duty of federal agencies to "insure that any action authorized, funded, or carried out by such agency ... is not likely to jeopardize the continued existence of endangered or threatened species or result in the destruction or adverse modification of habitat of such species which is determined ... to be critical." 16 U.S.C. § 1536(a)(2) (1994). Section 7(a)(2) has by far been the dominant ESA provision affecting federal agencies. *See* Ruhl, *supra* note 331, at 1119–20.

333. *See, e.g.,* Bennett v. Spear, 520 U.S. 154 (1997) (involving application of the Section 7(a)(2) "no jeopardy" provision to a federal agency granting ranching interests access to federal irrigation water); Sierra Club v. Glickman, 156 F.3d 606 (5th Cir. 1998) (involving application of the Section 7(a)(1) conservation duty to federal agency subsidization of farm irrigation water supplies).

334. Section 7(b)(4) provides for issuance of "incidental take statements" allowing projects that are carried out, funded, or authorized by federal agencies to obtain permission to commit take of listed species. 16 U.S.C. § 1536(b)(4) (1994). Section 10(a)(1)(B) of the ESA provides "incidental take permit" procedures and standards for all other projects. Id. § 1539(a)(1)(B). Both permitting paths involve complicated and expensive procedures and impact mitigation requirements. *See generally* J.B. Ruhl, *How to Kill Endangered Species, Legally: The Nuts and Bolts of Endangered Species Act "HCP" Permits for Real Estate Development,* 5 Envtl. Law. 345 (1999).

335. Section 7(a)(1) is the only provision of the ESA that imposes a conservation duty. By its terms it applies only to federal agency programs and thus does not extend to private actors whose actions do not require funding or approval from federal agencies.

among the major federal environmental laws as offering farms no safe harbor from its prohibitions and permitting requirements.[336]

3. Subsidy-Based Conservation Programs

Given the size of the farm economy, even without its related agricultural industries, federal farm policy has been a centerpiece of national politics since its emergence in the New Deal. The primary objectives of federal farm policy have been stabilizing commodity prices and supporting farm income.[337] Indeed, even what passes today as the "conservation" component of federal farm policy began as a means of controlling farm commodity production.[338] Nevertheless, the important role federal farm programs play today in the economics of farming[339] has created opportunities to influence environmental performance through means other than direct regulation.

For many decades the core of federal farm policy, and the feature that provides leverage for influencing farms' environmental record, has been a complicated web of commodity and income support programs.[340] These rely on a mixture of loan support and forgiveness measures, crop set-aside payments, government purchases, marketing agreements, low-cost insurance, benefit payments, price support payments, and import restrictions. When combined, these and other price and farm income supports create a remarkably convoluted and inconsistent set of incentives and disincentives with respect not only to farm production decisions[341] but also to the environment.[342] Notwithstanding recent changes in some federal farm commodity and income subsidy programs,[343] determining the amount and methods of federal support for farming through these and other mechanisms remains an annual rite of passage for American politics,[344] and the bill to taxpayers remains massive.[345]

---

336. *See generally* Lewandrowski & Ingram, *supra* note 54, at 252–55, 261–62.

337. For an excellent overview and history of these objectives, see AGRICULTURAL POLICY REFORM IN THE UNITED STATES (Daniel A. Sumner ed., 1995).

338. *See* Charles E. Grassley & James J. Jochum, *The Federal Agriculture Improvement and Reform Act of 1996: Reflections on the 1996 Farm Bill*, 1 DRAKE J. AGRIC. L. 1, 4 (1996). For a concise history of the conservation side of federal farm policy, see Christopher R. Kelley & James A. Lodoen, *Federal Farm Program Conservation Initiatives: Past, Present, and Future*, 9 NAT. RESOURCES & ENV'T 17 (1995).

339. Farm income attributable to government payments exceeded $5 billion in 1997. *See* Census, *supra* note 17, at United States Data 66, tbl.47.

340. *See* Grassley & Jochum, *supra* note 340, at 3 ("The commodity title is the heart of any farm bill."). For a brief history of these programs, *See* Haugrud, *supra* note[204], §8.1(B)(3), at 465–70.

341. For example, crop set-aside payments reduce supply to increase commodity prices, but commodity price support programs provide incentive to increase supply, which reduces prices. *See* Kelley & Lodoen, *supra* note 338, at 19.

342. For example, commodity price support programs generally focus on crops with high agrochemical input and soil erosion impacts and discourage farmers from crop rotation. *See* [Margaret Rosso] Grossman, *Agriculture and the Environment in the United States*, 42 AM. J. COMP. L. 291(1994)] at 332–34; Kelley & Lodoen, *supra* note 338, at 19. For a thorough review of the environmental impact of the crop payment subsidy programs, *See* Walter N. Thurman, *Assessing the Environmental Impact of Farm Policies* (1995).

343. Ostensibly to move closer to a market-based farming economy, in 1996 Congress overhauled the subsidy programs to wean farmers from their reliance on fixed, guaranteed payments by reducing subsidy levels in return for relaxing crop restrictions. *See* Freedom to Farm Act, Federal Agriculture Improvement and Reform Act of 1996, Pub. L. No. 104-127, 110 Stat. 888 (1996).

344. See, e.g., *Farmers' Plight Takes Campaign Spotlight*, USA TODAY, Aug. 9, 1999, at 4A (describing the politics behind the 1999 bill).

345. Notwithstanding Congress's professed theme of moving toward a market-based farm economy, the federal government will spend $15 billion in 1999 on direct payments to farmers, the highest of any fiscal year on record. *See* Published Comments by Glickman on the Future of Agriculture,

A relatively recent appendage to these "crop payment" programs is a grab-bag of four major "green payments" programs designed to pay farmers not to put land into commodity production, with an ancillary objective being conservation of soil and wildlife resources.[346] The Conservation Reserve Program (CRP) pays farmers to take highly erodible land out of production for extended periods.[347] The Wetlands Reserve Program (WRP) pays farmers to remove wetlands from production for extended periods or permanently.[348] The Wildlife Habitat Incentives Program (WHIP) pays farmers to restore and develop wildlife habitat.[349] And finally, the Environmental Quality Incentives Program (EQIP) consolidates and expands financial incentives to farmers who agree to participate in conservation plans prescribing structural, vegetative, and land management practices.[350]

Almost no one is completely satisfied with the crop payment/green payment system of farm conservation policy. Although an impressive amount of farmland has been placed in temporary or permanent conservation status as a result of the four programs,[351] the results have come only at huge taxpayer cost.[352] Moreover, the crop payment and green payment programs have not dovetailed as completely as intended in terms of recipients.[353] Evidence suggests that farmer participation in the green payment programs is highly sen-

---

Agric. L. Update, Aug. 1999, at 7 (published speech of USDA Secretary Dan Glickman). Moreover, the combination of sagging export markets, bumper domestic and worldwide crops, increased domestic harvested cropland, and domestic droughts and floods led Congress to approve $6 billion in emergency farm support in 1998 and an $8.7 billion bailout in 1999. *See generally Congress Passes a Record $8.7B Farm Bailout Package*, USA TODAY, Oct. 14, 1999, at 4A; James Cox, *Farmers' Tough Row to Hoe*, USA TODAY, Aug. 24, 1999, at 1B; Debbie Howlett, *Farmers' Crops, Worries, Pile Up*, USA TODAY, Aug. 2, 1999, at 1A; Judy Keen, *In Iowa, a Full Harvest of Political Discontent*, USA TODAY, Aug. 9, 1999, at 4A.

346. Some commentators condemn the green payment programs, which are "putatively designed to protect the environment," as being "more honestly described as programs for boosting commodity prices and farm incomes by restricting output." Chen, *supra* note 4, at 343.... The four major programs discussed here were introduced through the 1985, 1990, and 1996 Farm Bills. *See* Federal Agriculture Improvement and Reform Act of 1996, Pub. L. No. 104-127, 110 Stat. 888 (1996); Food, Agriculture, Conservation, and Trade Act of 1990, Pub. L. No. 101-624, 104 Stat. 3359 (1990); Food Security Act of 1985, Pub. L. No. 99-198, 99 Stat. 1354 (1985)

347. *See* 16 U.S.C. §§ 3831–3836 (1994); *See also* Haugrud, *supra* note [204], § 8.2(B)(2)(a), at 493–99.

348. *See id.* §§ 3837–3837f.

349. *See id.* § 3836a.

350. *See id.* §§ 3839aa–3839aa-8.

351. Total acreage conserved under the CRP and WRP combined was 29.5 million acres in 1997, divided among 225,000 farms. *See* Census, *supra* note [41], United States Data at 19, tbl.7.

352. There is considerable debate over whether the green payment programs are the most cost-efficient means of attaining lasting farm conservation progress. *See generally* Grossman, *supra* note [342], at 324; Ralph E. Heimlich & Roger Claassen, *Paying for Wetlands: Benefits, Bribes, Taxes*, NAT. WETLANDS NEWSLETTER, Nov.–Dec. 1998, at 1. Indeed, many commentators are quick to point out that the green payment programs violate the polluter pays principle that provides a common thread to most of environmental law—that is, while most landowners must obtain permits and pay mitigation costs to develop their land for productive purposes, farmers are paid not to develop their land. *See* Chen, *supra* note 4, at 344. The green payment programs are not an anomaly in this respect. For example, in 1999 federal agencies doled out $144 million to help CAFOs better manage their livestock wastes. *See Large Scale, Intensive Livestock Operations Getting USDA Help with Waste Management*, 30 ENV'T REP. (BNA) 661 (1999).

353. For example, many farms favored by and thus heavily invested in the crop payment programs are not located in areas where the green payment programs are likely to focus. *See* Kelley & Lodoen, *supra* note 338, at 67.

sitive to market commodity prices and does not reflect any newly found farm steward-ship ethic.[354] Farmers, like most of us, follow the money.

Hence, rather than relying entirely on an incentive-based approach to farm conserva-tion policy, the so-called Swampbuster and Sodbuster programs add a punitive element to farm conservation policy. The Swampbuster program makes farmers ineligible for all crop payment program benefits if a farmer converts certain wetlands to agricultural pro-duction.[355] Meanwhile the Sodbuster program imposes the same sanctions on farmers who put any highly erodible land into production without an approved conservation plan.[356] Unlike the green payment programs, these payment ineligibility provisions work close to the core of federal farm policy. Indeed, the subsidy programs have been so im-portant to the farming industry that farmers may perceive any prerequisites to receiving subsidies as regulatory requirements.[357] Nevertheless, because the Swampbuster and Sod-buster programs remain coupled to crop payment subsidy programs, they depend on the subsidy programs for their force and thus do little to alter the fundamental incentives in federal farm policy.[358] Moreover, through a litany of exemptions from ineligibility and a lackluster enforcement record, the programs no doubt have accomplished less than they could have even given their inherent limits[359]. Including the Swampbuster and Sodbuster programs as the third major exception to the general rule of safe harbor for farms thus illustrates how paltry the universe of environmental regulations is for farms.[360] ...

––––––––––––

Professor Ruhl identifies three factors that have influenced the development of the fa-vorable treatment of agriculture under environmental laws. First, "geographic dimen-sions"—including the large number of farms, their wide distribution, and their diversity—are factors that make any effort to regulate the farming industry "a daunting prospect." Second, are "economic dimensions." Ruhl notes that:

––––––––––––

354. *See* Tina Adler, Prairie Tales, 149 Sci. News 44, 45 (1996) (discussing research showing "com-modity prices determine the popularity of the [CRP] program among farmers").

355. *See* 16 U.S.C. §§ 3821–3824 (1994); *see also* Grossman, *supra* note [342], at 323–24; Haugrud, *supra* note [204], § 8.2(A)(2)(c), at 480–81; Linda A. Malone, *Reflections on the Jeffersonian Ideal of an Agrarian Democracy and the Emergence of an Agricultural and Environmental Ethic in the 1990 Farm Bill*, 12 Stan. Envtl. L.J. 3 (1993).

356. *See* 16 U.S.C. §§ 3811–3813 (1994); *see also* Grossman, *supra* note [342], at 322–23; Haugrud, *supra* note [204], § 8.2(C)(1)(d), at 518–20; Karen R. Hansen, *Agricultural Nonpoint Source Pollu-tion: The Need for an American Farm Policy Based on an Integrated Systems Approach Recoupled to Eco-logical Stewardship*, 15 Hamline J. Pub. L. & Pol'y 303 (1994).

357. *See* Percival et al., *supra* note 218, at 970; *see also* Looney, *supra* note [263], at 799.

358. *See* Kelley & Lodoen, *supra* note 338, at 67. Of the 78 million acres of wetlands in the United States, only 17 million acres are suitable for conversion to croplands, and of those only 6 million acres would depend heavily on crop program payments to make production viable. *See* Econ. Res. Serv., USDA, Agric. Info. Bull. No. 587, The U.S. Farming Sector Entering the 1990's 27 (1990) [hereinafter U.S. Farming Sector].

359. *See* Kelley & Lodoen, *supra* note 338, at 67.

360. Some commentators point to the CRP, WRP, and Swampbuster programs as providing "ex-tensive evidence of agriculture's greatly improved [environmental] performance in recent years." Neil D. Hamilton, *Agricultural Production and Environmental Policy: How Should Producers Respond?*, 1 Drake J. Agric. L. 141, 142 (1996). Yet CRP, WRP, and Swampbuster are but small specks in the sea of environmental policy, under which farms stand out as one of the dirtiest of America's dirty in-dustries. Even if farming has improved its overall environmental performance record in recent years, an assertion that finds little support in the data presented *supra*, it clearly has not improved its posi-tion relative to other industries.

Farms in the United States have tremendous economic value and are a critical economic link to vast supplier and consumer industries. Part of the economic potency of farms has to do with the dispersal of the farm economy among many small farms. But the economic climate for farms is highly volatile today in terms of both individual farm profitability and industry-wide structure. Both factors will play an important role in shaping environmental policy for farms.

Ruhl also credits "political dimensions" and observes that "any proposal for comprehensive environmental regulation of farming faces stiff political opposition."

J.B. Ruhl, *Farms, Their Environmental Harms, and Environmental Law*, 27 ECOLOGY L.Q. 263 328–333 (2000).

Rather than advocating for the prescriptive regulation of agriculture, Ruhl proposes a unique model for controlling the environmental problems associated with agriculture. This model combines the increased regulation of some areas of agriculture, such as CAFOs, with additional reporting efforts to obtain reliable information about the impacts of farming; the taxation of agrochemical inputs; the increased use of incentive programs such as the Conservation Reserve Program; and area-based planning in combination with market-based trading mechanisms. *Id.* at 333–349. There has been some movement in line with Ruhl's proposals since this article was published. CAFOs are now subject to at least some increased regulation, and there are new initiatives to incentivize farmers to adopt more sustainable farming practices. However, "any proposal for comprehensive environmental regulation of farming" continues to face "stiff political opposition."

C. Unique Aspects of Environmental Law As Applied to Agriculture

Two areas of environmental law that apply specifically to agricultural operations have been selected for special study: USDA conservation programs and the regulation of Concentrated Animal Feeding Operations (CAFOs).

1. USDA Conservation Programs

The importance of agricultural conservation is illustrated by the share of U.S. land currently in use by the agricultural industry. It is estimated that about 440 million acres, almost 20 percent of the total U.S. land area is agricultural cropland. Combined agricultural use including cropland, pasture, range, and grazed forests, increases the number to 1.2 billion acres, over 52 percent of total U.S. land area.

The USDA divides its conservation programs into four categories: compliance provisions, land retirement programs, working-land conservation programs, and farmland and grazing land protection programs.

a. Compliance Provisions: Sodbuster, Swampbuster, and Conservation Compliance

The compliance provisions are statutory eligibility criteria that link the federal commodity programs with conservation goals, requiring farmers to meet a minimum standard of environmental protection on environmentally sensitive land as a condition of eligibility for farm programs. Beginning with the 1985 Food Security Act, Congress required farmers to engage in conservation activities in order to receive government payments. These compliance provisions apply to cropland that is designated as highly erodible land (HEL) and to wetlands. The USDA estimates that about 25 percent of U.S. cropland, or just over 100 million acres, is designated HEL. It is estimated that there are about 90 million acres subject to swampbuster, although only 12.9 million are adjacent to existing cropland and easily converted to cropping.

"Conservation compliance" requires producers to apply and maintain approved conservation plans on HEL cropland that was already in crop production in 1985 or risk losing farm income support, price support, and conservation payments from voluntary programs. "Sodbuster" requires producers to refrain from bringing new HEL under cultivation as a condition to farm program eligibility. 16 U.S.C. §3811. "Swampbuster" requires producers to refrain from converting wetlands into cropland as an eligibility condition. 16 U.S.C. §3821.

Conservation Policy: Compliance Provisions for Soil and Wetland Conservation

USDA, Economic Research Service, Briefing Room: Conservation Policy available at http://www.ers.usda.gov/Briefing/ConservationPolicy/compliance.htm

Under current compliance requirements, farm program eligibility can be denied to producers who:

- Fail to implement and maintain a Natural Resources Conservation Service (NRCS)-approved soil conservation system on highly erodible land (HEL) that is currently in crop production and was cropped before 1985 — a provision known as conservation compliance;

- Convert HEL to crop production without applying an approved soil conservation system — referred to as sodbuster; or,

- Produce an agricultural commodity on a wetland converted after December 23, 1985, or convert a wetland after November 28, 1990, in a way that makes the production of an agricultural commodity possible — referred to as swampbuster.

Producers who violate compliance requirements risk losing all Federal farm programs payments — not just those payments that were (or might have been) made on the HEL or wetland in question.

Sodbuster and swampbuster provisions became effective on December 23, 1985, when the Food Security Act became law. Conservation compliance was implemented over a period of years. By 1990, producers growing crops on HEL were required to have an approved conservation plan. Plans were developed site by site to account for the broad diversity of resource conditions, cropping patterns, and producer preferences. By 1995, producers were required to be actively applying the conservation systems specified in their conservation plan. All three types of compliance have been continued in subsequent Farm Acts (1990, 1996, 2002, and 2008)....

Compliance mechanisms can also leverage farm program payments for environmental gain — without additional payments — to the extent that producers adopt conservation practices to retain farm program eligibility. Compliance mechanisms are a unique policy tool, distinct from — and in some ways more effective than — conservation payment incentives (e.g., cost sharing). In particular, compliance may be more effective than payments in deterring environmentally harmful actions. For example, a hypothetical subsidy program designed to prevent wetland drainage would require policymakers to pay for protection of all wetlands on agricultural land—a potentially expensive proposition—or decide which wetlands are sufficiently vulnerable to agricultural conversion as to warrant protection—a potentially difficult task. In contrast, swampbuster penalties are assessed only when a violation occurs, eliminating the need for broad-based subsidies or the need to anticipate the potential for a violation to occur on any given wetland. No direct costs are imposed on producers who comply, although there may be an opportunity cost associated with production forgone on wetlands....

U.S. v. Dierckman
201 F.3d 915 (7th Cir. 2000)

Before Cudahy, Coffey and Easterbrook, Circuit Judges.

Cudahy, Circuit Judge.

In 1993, the United States Department of Agriculture (USDA) declared Jerry Dierckman[1] ineligible for all USDA farm program benefits, retroactive to the 1991 crop year. Ineligibility was based on Jerry's violation of the Swampbuster provisions of the Food Security Act of 1985 (FSA), as amended by the Food, Agriculture, Conservation, and Trade Act (FACTA). The United States sued to recover the $92,703.00 in farm benefits paid to Jerry from 1991 to 1993. In that lawsuit, Jerry challenged the constitutionality of certain portions of the FSA and the validity of certain USDA regulations promulgated under the FSA, and he requested a declaration that his eligibility for benefits be reinstated. Both parties filed cross-motions for summary judgment, and on October 21, 1998, the district court granted summary judgment in favor of the government. Jerry appeals, and we affirm.

I. Legal Background

Congress adopted the Food Security Act on December 23, 1985 [FSA]. Pub. L. No. 99-198 (1985) (codified at 16 U.S.C. § 3801 et seq. (1986)). By enacting the FSA, Congress intended to "discourage the draining and cultivation of wetland that is unsuitable for agricultural production in its natural state." To further this goal, Congress included the Swampbuster provision of the FSA, which, in its initial form, stated that "following December 23, 1985, any person who in any crop year produces an agricultural commodity on converted wetland shall be ineligible for" various USDA farm benefit programs. 16 U.S.C. § 3821 (1986).

In 1990, Congress decided to toughen up Swampbuster in the Food, Agriculture, Conservation, and Trade Act [FACTA]. While retaining the original 1985 provision, FACTA added a new provision which provided that "any person who in any crop year subsequent to November 28, 1990, converts a wetland by draining, dredging, filling, leveling, or any other means for the purpose, or to have the effect, of making the production of an agri-

---

1. The opinion will refer to the defendant-appellant Jerry Dierckman as Jerry because Jerry's father, Milton Dierckman, figures substantially into the story. Jerry's father will be referred to as Milton. This should prevent any confusion.

cultural commodity possible on such converted wetland shall be ineligible for" USDA farm benefits. 16 U.S.C. § 3821(b)(1994).[2] After the 1990 Swampbuster amendments, a person could become ineligible for USDA farm benefits either by (1) converting wetland and growing crops on the land if the conversion was accomplished after December 23, 1985, or (2) merely converting wetland after November 28, 1990, so that crops could be grown on the land. *See* 16 U.S.C. § 3821 (1994); 7 C.F.R. § 12.4 (1994).

The ineligibility determination under the Swampbuster provisions involves multiple agencies within the USDA. The Soil Conservation Service (SCS)[3] determines whether a wetland or converted wetland exists on a particular farm and whether production of a crop is possible on any converted wetland. *See* 7 C.F.R. § 12.6(c). The initial SCS determination is made by the district conservationist. The district conservationist's decision is appealable to the area conservationist, then to the state conservationist, and finally to the Chief of the SCS at USDA headquarters in Washington, D.C. After the SCS makes its technical determination regarding the existence or conversion of a wetland, another USDA agency, the Agricultural Stabilization and Conservation Agency (ASCS),[4] determines whether any exemptions apply to the conversion of the wetland. *See* 7 C.F.R. § 12.6(b). The ASCS then determines the eligibility of any farmer who applies to the ASCS for USDA farm benefits. *See* 7 C.F.R. § 12.6(a). These ASCS determinations are first made by an ASCS county committee. An appeal can be taken to the appropriate state committee, then to the Deputy Administrator for State and County Operations (DASCO) and finally to the National Appeals Division (NAD) of the ASCS. *See* 7 C.F.R. § 12.6(b).

II. Factual Background

The facts of this case can be nicely segmented into three phases. In the first phase, the SCS determined that wetlands and converted wetlands were present on Jerry's farm but that no Swampbuster violation existed as of early 1991. In the second phase, the SCS determined that additional conversions took place in 1991 in violation of the Swampbuster provision prohibiting the conversion of a wetland after November 28, 1990. In the third phase, the ASCS determined that both Jerry and Milton were ineligible for all USDA farm benefits as a result of the conversion.

A. The Wetland Determination

Jerry Dierckman is a farmer who grows crops both on his own land and on land that he rents from others, including his father, Milton Dierckman. The land relevant to this

---

2. In amending 16 U.S.C. § 3821 in 1990, Congress renumbered the original Swampbuster provision as § 3821(a). Congress has since amended § 3821 again. See Pub. L. No. 104-127, Title III, Subtitle C, § 321 (1996). The original Swampbuster provision in the FSA, as amended, is still codified as § 3821(a). The 1990 Swampbuster provision added by FACTA is now codified as § 3821(c) instead of § 3821(b), as it was originally codified. All further references to Swampbuster provisions and all citations in this opinion will be to the 1994 editions of the United States Code and Code of Federal Regulations, which contain the versions of the statute and regulations in effect at all times relevant to this appeal.

3. The SCS has since been abolished, and its functions have been transferred to the Natural Resources Conversation Service. See Pub. L. No. 103-354, § 246 (1994) (codified at 7 U.S.C. § 6962). However, because the SCS was operating during all times relevant to this appeal, the opinion will refer to the SCS throughout.

4. The ASCS has been replaced by the Farm Service Agency. See Pub. L. No. 103-354, § 226 (1994) (codified at 7 U.S.C. § 6932) (replacing the ASCS with the Consolidated Farm Service Agency (CFSA)); 60 Fed. Reg. 56,392 (Nov. 8, 1995) (renaming the CFSA as the Farm Service Agency). The ASCS was operative during all times relevant to this appeal, and the opinion will refer to the ASCS throughout.

appeal is located in Franklin County, Indiana, and Jerry rented it from his father. In 1986, Milton cut down the trees on roughly the eastern two-thirds of the northern portion of this property. The stumps were left in the ground for a number of years afterwards—thus continuing to preclude farming on that portion of the farm—but in August of 1990, Gunter Excavating Company (Gunter) was hired to dig up the stumps, fill the holes and haul the stumps away. On September 3, 1990, Gunter issued a written proposal to Jerry concerning the work, and Gunter began work shortly thereafter.Gunter issued a bill for its work to Jerry on September 25. The bill shows "work ordered by" Jerry, but Milton paid this bill on October 10. Due to heavy rains in October of 1990, the excavating machinery bogged down, and Gunter could not continue its work of removing tree stumps. For the next several months, the land remained in the same condition, with some holes filled, some stumps remaining in the ground, other stumps scattered about the property and some holes left unfilled.

Jerry wanted USDA farm benefits for the land that he had rented from his father. In order to receive these farm benefits from the USDA for the 1991 crop year, Jerry was first required to get his eligibility certified. On January 7, 1991, Jerry completed ASCS Form AD-1026, entitled "Highly Erodible Land and Wetland Conservation Certification." On this form, Jerry indicated that he intended to convert "wet areas" and intended to grow crops on converted "wet areas" on his farm.[6] Needless to say, these responses attracted the attention of the ASCS, which referred the matter to the SCS. After receiving the referral, the SCS set out to determine if any of Jerry's "wet areas" were wetlands protected by the Swampbuster provisions of the United States Code. In March of 1991, an SCS district conservationist determined that the northern portion of Jerry's farm contained both wetlands and converted wetlands. The district conservationist determined that the conversion of the wetlands had begun in August of 1990 but had ended before the more stringent Swampbuster provision went into effect on November 28, 1990. Thus, with respect to the already converted wetlands, Jerry was not in violation of Swampbuster because no crops had been planted on them. The district conservationist informed Jerry that any additional conversion of any additional wetlands, however, would be a Swampbuster violation, whether crops were grown or not. After the district conservationist's determination, Jerry filed another Form AD-1026, this time stating that he had no plans to convert wet areas on the land.[7] On March 19, 1991, however, Jerry had appealed to the area conservationist the determination that the farm contained wetlands, stating: "I request a redetermination and permission to continue to clear the area in question.... Intended land use will be hayland, permanent pasture."

On May 17, 1991, the area conservationist denied the appeal, and on July 11, the area conservationist's determination was affirmed by the state conservationist after members of the state conservationist's wetland appellate review team visited the farm and performed some field tests. In September of 1991, the administrative appeal process for the wetland determination ended with the affirmance by the SCS of the state conservation-

---

6. Question 5 on Form AD-1026 read: "Will an agricultural commodity be produced on any land, including wet areas, on the farm(s) listed on AD-1026A that was or will be improved, maintained, drained, modified, or converted after December 23, 1985? If 'YES', check the appropriate Tract Number in column 13 of attached AD-1026A." And Question 6 read: "Do you plan to convert any land, including wet areas, for the production of an agricultural commodity this year or during the term of a requested USDA loan or other program benefit? If 'YES', check the appropriate Tract Number in column 14 of attached AD-1026A." Jerry Dierckman answered "YES" to each of these questions.

7. He indicated this by answering "NO" to questions regarding conversion of wet areas on a new Form AD-1026 dated April 26, 1991. The format of the AD-1026 had changed, but the substance of the questions remained the same.

ist's determination. In a letter to Jerry Dierckman dated September 27, the Chief of the SCS explained its conclusions: "We have determined that the areas in standing trees and stumps are wetlands (W), and the areas where the stumps have been removed are converted wetlands (CW). This decision supports the earlier decision of the SCS State Conservationist...." The Chief also explained that because the converted wetlands had been converted before November 28, 1990, and crops had not been grown on those converted wetlands, there had been no Swampbuster violation as of that time. The Chief further made clear that any additional conversion activity would result in USDA ineligibility.

B. The Conversion Determination

On December 18, 1991, the district conservationist and an SCS technician visited the part of Jerry's farm previously designated as wetlands and noticed changes to the property. Since their visit the prior spring, some additional stumps had been removed from the ground and moved into rows, the holes had been filled and the land appeared to have been root raked. The ground was now farmable. The visitors concluded that this work had occurred after November 28, 1990, and constituted a conversion of a wetland. They designated the land "CW+91," signifying that a Swampbuster violation had taken place in 1991, and notified Jerry of the finding by letter on January 31, 1992. Jerry responded by phone on February 3, for the first time making an argument that he would repeat throughout the administrative appeals process and still repeats in this court: Jerry told the district conservationist that his father, Milton Dierckman, owned the tract and that Milton was going to continue to "improve" the land. Jerry added, in an obvious attempt to exonerate himself, "I have no control over the ground. Dad owns it. I just rent it."

In July of 1992, Jerry met with SCS officials at the farm. Further conversion had taken place, and only a small wooded section remained untouched. Jerry (and his mother, who was also present) again explained that the conversion was Milton's doing. The notes of the meeting indicate that the SCS agent asked Jerry "if he had checked with the ASCS office to see if the records could be changed to only show him ... as the renter[] of the cropland." Jerry responded that he had "had no dealings with the ASCS office."[8]

Although he supposedly had no control over the wetlands, Jerry pursued an appeal that was rejected by the area conservationist on July 17, 1992. The determination that wetlands had been converted after November 28, 1990, was subsequently affirmed by the state conservationist. In its letter of September 15, 1992, the SCS again urged Jerry to contact his local ASCS office to discuss his status as operator with respect to USDA program benefits. Finally, on October 28, 1993, the Acting Chief of the SCS rejected Dierckman's final appeal. Jerry was advised that any conversion taking place after November 28, 1990, that made agricultural production possible would result in the loss of eligibility until the area designated CW+91 was restored.

C. Ineligibility Determination

The SCS referred the matter to the Franklin County ASCS Office, explaining that its wetlands and conversion inquiries were complete with its having found that Jerry Dier-

---

8. The agent's notes continue: "I checked with the Jennings County ASCS when I returned[, and] they said that the farm could be [reconstituted] by an operator to only show him as operator of the cropland and the owner could be shown as the owner and operator of the wooded part." However, rather than pursuing reconstitution, Jerry had continued to list himself as the "operator" of the farm and filed another Form AD-1026 with the ASCS, this time for the 1992 crop year. On that form, dated March 2, 1993, Jerry indicated that he had converted or he would convert wetland to make it farmable.

ckman had converted wetlands after November 28, 1990. At a regular session meeting on November 17, 1993, the county ASCS committee discussed the SCS's final determinations in the Dierckman matter, and determined that both the owner, Milton Dierckman, and the operator, Jerry, were the producers responsible for the conversion. Therefore, both were declared ineligible for USDA farm benefit payments on all land that they owned and operated. Jerry asked the committee to reconsider on the grounds that he was not the operator of the land constituting converted wetlands and that any work he performed had ended before the November 28, 1990, trigger date for the more stringent Swampbuster provision. The committee rejected this argument in January of 1994, stating that, after reviewing all the facts, it determined that Jerry was the operator of the farm—which "means the total farm, not just the cropland"—and was therefore ineligible.

Jerry appealed to the state ASCS, and received his first favorable decision. The committee determined that "although Jerry may have been associated with the conversion of the wetland, he had no control over his father's decision to finish clearing the wetland after he was told to stop by the SCS. The state body requested that the county grant Jerry's requested relief, but the county committee refused to reverse its determination, and the appeal continued up the chain. The Deputy Administrator for State and County Operations found Jerry ineligible for subsidies "because there is evidence that Jerry Dierckman was in general control of the operation on the wetland area in question...." Jerry appealed this decision to the ASCS National Appeals Division, but the NAD denied his appeal by letter on January 17, 1995. Thus, Jerry was ineligible for USDA subsidies retroactive to the 1991 crop year.

D. Proceedings Below

The United States sued Jerry to recover the benefit payments it had made during the 1991, 1992 and 1993 crop years, totaling $92,703.00. Jerry challenged the United States' claim on the ground that the wetland at issue is not covered by the FSA. He also challenged the ineligibility determination because: (1) the agency fails to provide a rational basis for its conclusion that Jerry violated the Swampbuster provisions of the FSA, (2) the USDA regulation mandating his ineligibility is void because it is inconsistent with the FSA and (3) the FSA and its implementing regulations violate substantive due process. The district court upheld all of the administrative determinations and found for the United States on summary judgment. *See United States v. Dierckman*, 41 F.Supp.2d 870 (S.D.Ind.1998). This appeal followed.

III. Discussion

In his appeal to this court, Jerry Dierckman makes basically the same challenges as he did in the district court. He argues that the wetland in question is outside the reach of the FSA. He also argues that the agency regulation on which the USDA based its decision is outside the scope of the FSA and that the agency failed to provide a rational basis for its conclusion that Jerry violated the Swampbuster provision of the FSA. Finally, Jerry argues that the FSA and its implementing regulations violate substantive due process.

A. The Reach of the FSA

Jerry asserts that because the wetland on his farm is isolated and has no connection to interstate commerce, it cannot be regulated under the Food Security Act. His argument centers on an analogy to the Clean Water Act (CWA), 33 U.S.C. §1251 et seq. (1999), which prohibits the discharge of pollutants into the waters of the United States. Because the "wetlands" regulated by the FSA are a subset of the waters of the United States regulated by the CWA, Jerry argues, regulation of an intrastate wetland is only valid if the appropriate agency has determined that the wetland in question had at least some relationship to interstate commerce. Therefore, he concludes, because no agency has determined that the wetlands on his farm had a connection to interstate commerce, no federal agency has proper jurisdiction. But this analogy between the FSA and the CWA lacks force because, as the district court explained, "the language in the Clean Water Act on which he relies is not parallel to the Food Security Act." Further, Jerry's argument overlooks the difference between direct congressional regulation under the Commerce Clause, which requires a connection to interstate commerce, and indirect regulation under the spending power, which does not.

The CWA directly regulates the chemical, physical and biological integrity of the Nation's waters, and "the geographical scope of the Act reaches as many waters as the Commerce Clause allows." Therefore, Jerry is entirely correct that any potential target of CWA regulation must have some connection to interstate commerce. But, Jerry fails to provide a plausible reason why the limitations that narrow the application of the CWA should also limit the FSA.

Jerry's argument falters because it assumes that the FSA is a creature of the Commerce Clause. The FSA is not an exercise of direct regulatory power; instead, the FSA conditions the receipt of USDA farm benefits on the preservation of wetlands. This is indirect regulation invoking the spending power and is not limited by the enumeration of Congressional powers in Article I, section 8 of the Constitution. As the Supreme Court has explained:

> "[T]he power of Congress to authorize expenditure of public moneys for public purposes is not limited by the direct grants of legislative power found in the Constitution." Thus, objectives not thought to be within Article I's "enumerated legislative fields," [like the Commerce Clause,] may nevertheless be attained through the use of the spending power and the conditional grant of federal funds.

South Dakota v. Dole, 483 U.S. at 207, 107 S.Ct. 2793 (quoting *United States v. Butler*, 297 U.S. 1, 66, 56 S.Ct. 312, 80 L.Ed. 477 (1936)).

Even though Congress may lack the authority to regulate directly a strictly intrastate wetland, the incentive provided by the Food Security Act is a valid exercise of the spending power....

B. The Implementing Regulations

Jerry next argues that the USDA regulation which mandates his ineligibility—namely 7 C.F.R. § 12.4(e)—is void because it is inconsistent with the FSA. Jerry characterizes the regulation as extending liability to a farm "operator" who has played no role in the wetland conversion; he further argues that the plain language of the Swampbuster provision prohibits this extension.[10] After a thorough consideration of Jerry's argument, we find that the regulations easily survive his challenge.

We review USDA regulations under the Administrative Procedure Act, and we may set aside the agency action only if the regulations are "arbitrary, capricious, an abuse of

---

10. Jerry's argument, so stated, has both a legal and a factual predicate. He claims as a fact that he had nothing to do with the conversion, and then states that to hold him liable, given his innocence, is legally beyond the scope of the FSA. We first address the legal aspect of his argument because, if the regulation is invalid, the agency's findings of fact are irrelevant, and Jerry wins. However, if the regulation employs a valid method for determining ineligibility, then we must decide if the agency followed the regulation faithfully in finding Jerry ineligible. If it did, he loses.

discretion, or otherwise not in accordance with law." 5 U.S.C. § 706(2)(A)(1999). Because Congress expressly authorized the USDA to promulgate regulations on ineligibility, see 16 U.S.C. § 3844 (1994),[11] we review the USDA's regulations within the framework established by the Supreme Court in *Chevron U.S.A., Inc. v. Natural Resources Defense Council*, 467 U.S. 837, 104 S.Ct. 2778, 81 L.Ed.2d 694 (1984). The starting point of this analysis is, of course, the language of the statutory Swampbuster provisions,[12] and if "the plain meaning of the text of the statute either supports or opposes the regulation," the inquiry ends, and this court applies the statute's plain meaning. If the statute is silent or ambiguous, "the court must defer to the agency interpretation so long as it is based on a reasonable reading of the statute."

Jerry's challenge to the regulation depends on defining the scope of the phrase "any person who converts a wetland."[13] Jerry argues that this phrase is unambiguous and demonstrates clearly that Congress intended "[o]nly the person who converts the wetland" to be ineligible for USDA benefits. He claims that the person who converts the wetland must be the person who actually brings about the conversion—e.g., by draining, dredging, filling or leveling—or any person who hires another to perform the conversion. This interpretation strikes us as a plausible reading, but nothing in the statutory text unambiguously compels such a reading.

The most obvious reading of the phrase "any person who converts a wetland" may denote an individual who physically converts wetlands—i.e., who digs up the stumps, fills in the holes, etc. With that reading, only the excavation company—in this case Gunter—would be deemed ineligible for USDA farm benefits. Congress certainly intended to cover more than an excavator, but the precise contours of the phrase "any person who converts a wetland" do not leap from the text of the statute. Congress leaves us only with this ambiguous phrase; therefore, "the question for the court is whether the agency's answer is based on a permissible construction of the statute." *Chevron*, 467 U.S. at 843, 104 S.Ct. 2778.

The regulations addressing ineligibility for farm benefits are found at 7 C.F.R. § 12.4. Jerry challenges 7 C.F.R. § 12.4(e), which provides that the statutory phrase "any person who converts a wetland" covers the operator of a wetland that is converted to farmland. The regulation states:

---

11. This section stated, in part:
  [T]he Secretary shall issue such regulations as the Secretary determines are necessary to carry out this chapter, including regulations that . . .
  (2) govern the determination of persons who shall be ineligible for program benefits . . . , so as to ensure a fair and reasonable determination of ineligibility. . . .
16 U.S.C. § 3844 (1994) (since omitted in general revision to statute by Pub.L. No. 104-127, Title III, Subtitle E, § 341 (1996)).
  12. The first step of *Chevron* focuses on the text of the statute, leaving legislative history for the second step. *See* Bankers Life & Casualty Co. v. United States, 142 F.3d 973, 983 (7th Cir.1998) ("While this circuit has examined legislative history during the first step of Chevron, we now seem to lean toward reserving consideration of legislative history and other appropriate factors until the second Chevron step.") (citations omitted).
  13. At the time relevant to this action, the statute stated, in full:
  Except as provided in section 3822 of this title and notwithstanding any other provision of law, any person who in any crop year subsequent to November 28, 1990, converts a wetland by draining, dredging, filling, leveling, or any other means for the purpose, or to have the effect, of making the production of an agricultural commodity possible on such converted wetland shall be ineligible for those payments, loans, or programs specified in subsections (a)(1) through (3) of this section for that crop year and all subsequent crop years. 16 U.S.C. § 3821(b) (1994).

For the purposes of paragraph (a)[14] of this section, a person shall be determined to have produced an agricultural commodity on a field in which highly erodible land is predominant or to have designated such a field as conservation use, to have produced an agricultural commodity on converted wetland, or to have converted a wetland, if:

(1) SCS has determined that—

(i)Highly erodible land is predominant in such field, or

(ii)All or a portion of the field is converted wetland; and

(2) ASCS has determined that the person is or was the owner or operator of the land, or entitled to share in the crops available from the land, or in the proceeds thereof.

7 C.F.R. §12.4(e). The regulations defined an "operator" as "the person who is in general control of the farming operations on the farm during the crop year." 7 C.F.R. §12.2(a)(20). In this case, the SCS determined that a portion of the field was converted wetland under §12.4(e)(1)(ii) of the regulations.[15] Then the ASCS found that Jerry was the person who was in general control of the farming operations during the 1991 crop year. See §§12.4(e)(2), 12.2(a)(20). On this basis, Jerry was deemed to have converted the land.

This regulatory interpretation of the phrase "any person who converts a wetland" is broad but not unreasonable. Jerry argues to the contrary because the regulations impose "strict and vicarious" liability on an "innocent" operator, and he points toward legislative history as supportive of his argument. We, however, find little to help him there. The legislative history does not do much more than repeat, mantra-like, the phrase "any person who converts a wetland." *See, e.g.*, S. Rep. No. 101-357 at 236 (1990), *reprinted in* 1990 U.S.C.C.A.N. 4656, 4890 ("This new provision holds a person who converts a wetland ..."). Based on the legislative history, neither Jerry's nor the USDA's reading is unreasonable.

But Jerry further claims that an operator should not be charged with the actions of an owner because the owner has "ultimate" control over the land. However, under the regulations, before one can be considered an operator of a piece of land, such a person "must be in general control of the farming operations on the farm during the crop year." 7 C.F.R. §12.2(a)(20). Thus, a measure of control over the land, even with respect to the owner, is explicit in the definition of "operator." It is, therefore, not unreasonable for the USDA to hold such a person in "control" responsible for the conversion of a wetland. If the operator is in fact in "control," he must at least have acquiesced in the conversion and to that extent is responsible for it. *See* 7 C.F.R. §12.10.[17] On the present facts, to escape liability, Jerry must at least have done or said something to negate clearly his acquiescence in his father's actions and to put himself in opposition to them.

---

14. Section 12.4(a) echoes the language found in §3821(b) of the statute, stating that "a person shall be ineligible for all USDA program benefits" if "[a]fter November 28, 1990, the person converts a wetland...." 7 C.F.R. §12.4(a)(2).

15. Jerry apparently does not challenge the SCS's determination in this appeal. Thus, it is beyond doubt that there were converted wetlands that violated Swampbuster on the farm.

17. Although not cited by either of the parties, the USDA regulations explicitly suggest that acquiescence is grounds for ineligibility:

All or any part of the [USDA benefits] may be withheld or required to be refunded if the person adopts or participates in adopting any scheme or device designed to evade, or which has the effect of evading, the provisions of this part. Such acts shall include ... acquiescence in, approval of or assistance to acts which have the effect of, or the purpose of, circumventing these regulations.

7 C.F.R. §12.10.

The effect of the regulation is to make one who is in control of the farm and is seeking USDA benefits responsible for the conversion. Congress acknowledged that "[p]articipation in federal programs is voluntary, and participation has always carried with it certain responsibilities, obligations, and conditions." S. Rep. No. 101-357 at 231, *reprinted in* 1990 U.S.C.C.A.N. at 4885. The regulations serve to align the benefits with the burdens: one who seeks USDA benefits must make certain to meet the conditions which encumber them. In light of all these considerations, the regulations are not "unreasonable or contrary to the purposes of the statute or to clearly expressed legislative intent on the point in issue." Therefore, under *Chevron*, we uphold the agency regulation....

Although Jerry characterizes himself as helpless and punished for the whims of his father, there were several paths he could have chosen to avoid the ineligibility sanction. As we have noted, Jerry should have done what he could to stop his father's conversion activities and to negate his acquiescence in those activities. Also, he could have declined to seek USDA benefits for this particular farm, thus dodging the USDA's authority to deny him benefits on his other farmland. And had Jerry wanted to effectively disclaim control over the wetlands in question, he could have requested reconstitution of the farm, separating the wetlands and the cropland into separate administrative units. 7 C.F.R. pt. 719 (1994). But instead of negating acquiescence, foregoing benefits or requesting reconstitution, Jerry continued to pursue USDA benefits and continued to label himself the "operator" of the undivided farm, pursuing administrative appeals of the wetland determination to the national level. And, while it is true that Jerry repeatedly told the SCS that he had no control over his father's actions, he produced little or no evidence that he actually tried to stop the conversion.[20] Thus, it was not arbitrary or capricious for the ASCS to find that Jerry was the "operator" of the wetland when it was converted. On that basis, he is ineligible for farm benefits under 7 C.F.R. § 12.4(e).

D. Substantive Due Process

Jerry finally challenges the assessment of liability on the grounds that the FSA and its implementing regulations violate substantive due process because they irrationally penalize the operator even though it was the owner who did the conversion. This is a most unpromising argument because "[i]t is by now well established that legislative Acts adjusting the burdens and benefits of economic life come to the Court with a presumption of constitutionality, and that the burden is on one complaining of a due process violation to establish that the legislature has acted in an arbitrary and irrational way." Jerry claims that it is irrational to attempt to deter wetlands conversion through an ineligibility sanction imposed on an operator. Jerry contends that because an owner would be undeterred by an operator's loss of benefits, sanctioning an operator is a vain exercise. We must disagree.

The owner and the operator share control of the land, and, to the extent each is penalized for the conversion of wetlands, the purposes of Swampbuster will be furthered. Sanctions fall on owners and operators who could potentially benefit from agricultural conversion of their land, thus providing both with incentives to prevent conversion. The legislation and regulations have a rational basis, and they survive Jerry's substantive due process challenge.

---

20. We also note that Jerry produced no evidence that his father has thwarted any attempts to restore the converted wetlands. Apparently, Jerry has made no such attempt even though he could regain some benefits by restoring the land. *See* 7 C.F.R. § 12.5(b)(7). Again, this suggests acquiescence in the conversion.

IV. Conclusion

In conclusion, we hold that (1) the Swampbuster provisions of the United States Code are a proper exercise of Congress' spending power and can therefore reach an intrastate wetland with no connection to interstate commerce; (2) 7 C.F.R. §12.4(e) is a reasonable interpretation of the underlying statute and therefore valid; (3) the ASCS properly determined that Jerry was the operator of the wetland when it was converted; and (4) the statute and regulations as applied in this case satisfy the requirements of substantive due process.

The decision of the district court is AFFIRMED.

Source of Law and Implementation Guidance

The statutory authority for the general conservation compliance requirements are found in Title 16, chapter 58 of the U.S. Code. Conservation plans are required under 16 U.S.C.§3812a. The requirements with respect to highly erodible lands are at 16 U.S.C. §3811. The wetlands requirement is at 16 U.S.C. §3821. The regulations applicable to highly erodible lands and wetlands are found at 7 C.F.R. pt. 12 (2010).

The relevant Handbooks for these programs are found on the USDA Farm Service Agency webpage at htp://www.fsa.usda.gov under the Laws and Regulations tab.

Notes

1. For an analysis of the effectiveness of the compliance programs, see Roger Claassen, *Have Conservation Compliance Incentives Reduced Soil Erosion?* USDA AMBER WAVES 1 (June 2004) available at http://www.ers.usda.gov/amberwaves/june04/features/HaveConservation.htm.

2. A new provision in the 2008 Farm Bill could affect producers who till "native sod" in Prairie Pothole National Priority areas, which span Iowa, Minnesota, Montana, North Dakota, and South Dakota. Native-sod acreage that has been tilled for production of an annual crop could be ineligible for crop insurance and non-insured disaster assistance for the first five years of its planting. The provisions would be implemented only with the approval of individual Governors in those five States. 7 U.S.C. §§1508(o), 7333(a)(3)(C); 7 C.F.R. §407.9(1), §457.8.

3. The effectiveness of the compliance programs is dependent upon farm program payments that are worth more to a producer than what could be gained from farming sensitive land. Efforts to reduce or eliminate farm program payments without other means of preserving highly erodible land or wetlands could result in the cultivation of that sensitive acreage. For example, the USDA estimates that between 1.5 million and 3.3 million acres of wetlands could be profitably converted to crop production under favorable market conditions. *See, Conservation Policy: Compliance Provisions for Soil and Wetland Conservation*, USDA, Economic Research Service, Briefing Room: Conservation Policy, available at http://www.ers.usda.gov/Briefing/ConservationPolicy/compliance.htm

4. Section 404 of the Clean Water Act (CWA) gives the Environmental Protection Agency and the Army Corps of Engineers authority to regulate wetland drainage. 33 U.S.C. §1344.

However, a divided Supreme Court has struggled to define "navigable waters" and has limited CWA regulation of isolated wetlands. *See Rapanos v. United States*, 547 U.S. 715 (2006). While some State and local governments have wetland laws and regulations, many heavily agricultural States have little wetland regulation. In these states, swampbuster may be the only remaining policy disincentive to wetland drainage.

b. Land Retirement Programs

Conservation Policy: Land Retirement Programs

USDA, Economic Research Service, Briefing Room: Conservation Policy available at http://www.ers.usda.gov/Briefing/ConservationPolicy/retirement.htm

In 2007, USDA's land retirement programs accounted for almost half of all the Department's conservation expenditures. Under these programs, USDA offers rental payments and other incentives to farmland owners who convert land from agricultural production to land covers deemed more environmentally beneficial. In 2007, USDA spent over $1.82 billion in rental payments and other incentives on the Conservation Reserve Program (CRP) to retire over 36.8 million acres of cropland. In addition, $139 million spent on the Wetlands Reserve Program (WRP) increased protected wetland acreage to over 1.88 million acres. The Food, Conservation, and Energy Act of 2008 continued a trend started in 2002, of shifting conservation support towards working lands programs. However, land retirement is still economically and environmentally important.

The Conservation Reserve Program (CRP)

The Conservation Reserve Program (CRP) was established by the Food Security Act of 1985 and began enrolling farmland in 1986. The program uses contracts with agricultural producers and landowners to retire highly erodible and environmentally sensitive cropland and pasture from production for 10–15 years. Enrolled land is planted to grasses, trees, and other cover, thereby reducing erosion and water pollution and providing other environmental benefits (as well as reducing the supply of agricultural commodities).

Enrollment in CRP increased rapidly once the program got underway, with nearly all eligible applicants accepted. Approximately 34 million acres were enrolled during the first 9 signups (between 1986 and 1989). In the early years, CRP eligibility was limited to about 100 million acres of land with highly erodible soils, with per-acre payments based on a regional average of cropland rental rates (along with half the cost of establishing permanent cover)....

The Food, Agriculture, Conservation, and Trade Act of 1990 expanded eligibility for CRP beyond highly erodible land. The 250 million acres of eligible land included several "Conservation Priority Areas" (the Chesapeake Bay, Long Island Sound, and Great Lakes watersheds), State water quality priority areas, and smaller plots of land adopting high-priority conservation practices.

USDA also made two significant changes to program enrollment criteria:

- An environmental benefits index (EBI) that accounts for multiple environmental concerns was used to rank offers. The EBI weights a number of different concerns, including water quality, air quality, and soil erodibility.

- Maximum allowable rental rates were based on a soil-specific estimate of the rent earned on comparable local cropland. Use of soil specific maximum rental rates enabled USDA to enroll environmentally sensitive, but highly productive, land into the program.

Following passage of the Federal Agriculture Improvement and Reform Act of 1996, wildlife habitat was added to the EBI. A continuous signup was initiated for acreage devoted to specific conservation practices, such as filter strips, riparian buffers, grassed waterways, field windbreaks, shelterbelts, living snow fences, salt-tolerant vegetation, shallow water areas for wildlife, and wellhead protection. Enrollment was capped at 36.4 million acres. In 1997, continuous signups were augmented by the Conservation Reserve Enhancement Program (CREP), a Federal-State partnership designed to encourage farm conservation practices that meet specific State and national conservation and environmental objectives. These include impacts to water supplies, loss of critical habitat for threatened and endangered wildlife, soil erosion, and reduced habitat for fish populations.

With early contracts expiring, signups conducted in 1997 and 1998 enrolled over 22 million acres. Unlike the early signups, competition was keen, with all bids ranked using the EBI. Because the bid process meant that already enrolled lands were not automatically re-enrolled, the distribution of CRP enrollment shifted somewhat during the 1990s.

Although a roughly equal number of counties (about 23%) gained and lost CRP acreage between 1990 and 2002, there was little redistribution of acreage across ERS's Farm Resource Regions. The Northern Great Plains gained slightly, at the expense of the Heartland (probably due to the lower rental rates requested by Plains bidders) and the Southern Seaboard (where many CRP acres planted in trees were not offered for re-enrollment).

Under the terms of this wave of contracts, between 2007 and 2010 over 75 percent (28 million acres) of existing CRP contracts were scheduled to expire. For several reasons, including distributing the administrative burden over time, in 2006 FSA offered holders of expiring CRP contracts a chance to re-enroll or extend their contracts. Approximately 82 percent (22.9 million acres) of these acres were re-enrolled or extended. Hence, expiring acres will vary between 3.9 and 5.6 million acres per year over the next 5 years.

The Food, Conservation, and Energy Act of 2008 continued the CRP, but reduced the enrollment cap to 32 million acres. However, because of the number of contracts scheduled to expire, the cap leaves room for a steady stream of new enrollments.

Overall, the CRP started as a program with a soil conservation and commodity-reduction agenda, in a time when the farm sector was weathering a severe economic downturn. As conservation effects were identified and quantified, other stakeholders recognized CRP's potential for generating multiple environmental benefits, and CRP evolved beyond soil conservation, with greater weight given to wildlife habitat, air and water quality, and carbon sequestration.

The amount of land enrolled in CRP does not necessarily reflect the amount of land removed from production. First, "slippage," the reallocation of lands outside the program (such as pastureland) to cropland uses, may occur. Second, land enrolled in CRP might have left production even without the program.

The Wetlands Reserve Program

The Wetlands Reserve Program (WRP) was established by the Food, Agriculture, Conservation, and Trade Act of 1990. The stated emphasis of WRP is to protect, restore, and enhance the functions and values of wetland ecosystems to attain:

- Habitat for migratory birds and wetland-dependent wildlife, including threatened and endangered species,

- Protection and improvement of water quality,
- Attenuation of water flows to reduce flooding,
- Recharge of ground water,
- Protection and enhancement of open space and aesthetic quality,
- Protection of native flora and fauna contributing to the Nation's natural heritage, and
- Contribution to educational and scientific scholarship.

In 1991 and 1992, WRP enrollment consisted of pilot projects in a limited number of States. The program was fully operational in 1994, has continually increased wetland acreage to the present, and has been legislated to continue wetland restoration through 2012. The WRP has sought the greatest wetland functions and values, along with optimum wildlife habitat, on every acre enrolled. In pursuing these goals, WRP has undergone some changes. Most importantly, in the earlier years a "walk away" strategy was often used: parcels were allowed to return to their wetland condition with no other intervention. However, this strategy led to poor wetland function. So, a "full restoration" strategy was adopted in the late 1990s. Full restoration implies considerably more site preparation (for example, undoing land leveling). At least 70 percent of each project must be restored to the original natural condition (to the extent practicable). The remaining 30 percent can be restored to "other than natural" conditions.

With enrollment approaching 2 million acres, the Food, Conservation, and Energy Act of 2008 reauthorized the WRP, increasing the area cap to 3.041 million acres through 2012.

Source of Law and Implementation Guidance

The statutory authority for the conservation compliance requirement can be found at 16 U.S.C. §§ 3831–3835a. The CRP regulations are found at 7 C.F.R. pt. 1410 (2010).

The statutory authority for the WRP is found at 16 U.S.C. §§ 3837–3837f. The regulations are found at 7 C.F.R. pt. 1467 (2010).

The relevant Handbooks for these programs are found on the USDA Farm Service Agency webpage at http://www.fsa.usda.gov, under the Laws and Regulations tab.

Notes

1. The CRP imposes specific contractual obligations on the farmer during the term of the land retirement, incorporating all relevant statutory and regulatory requirements. *See* 7 C.F.R. §§ 1410.20, 1410.32. If the farmer violates any of these duties, the USDA can terminate the contract and impose penalties. *See* 7 C.F.R. § 1410.52. For an example of the judicial review of a CRP dispute, see *Payton v. USDA*, 337 F.3d 1163 (10th Cir. 2003).

2. Wildlife and environmental organizations support the land retirement programs because of the associated increase in wildlife habitat. Ducks Unlimited, a non-profit orga-

nization devoted to wetlands and waterfowl conservation, describes the impact of the CRP on wildlife and habitat as follows:

> Across the plains states of the central United States, grassland loss continues at alarming rates. In the U.S. Prairie Pothole Region (which includes portions of Minnesota, South Dakota, Iowa, Nebraska, North Dakota, Montana, and Wyoming), 56 million acres (62 percent) of the original 90 million acres of native grassland has been converted to other land uses. The 4.7 million acres of CRP within this landscape has helped to recapture the wildlife, soil and water quality values of grassland on this landscape, but more grassland restoration through CRP is needed to achieve a level of sustainability of these public benefits.
>
> CRP is a proven, results-oriented conservation program that has accomplished a variety of positive outcomes for wildlife habitat. Research has proven that putting land in to CRP has resulted in measurable benefits to wildlife populations in many areas of the country....
>
> During 1992–1997, nest success of five common duck species were 46 percent higher with CRP on the landscape in the Prairie Pothole Region (PPR) of North Dakota, South Dakota and Montana compared to a simulated scenario where existing CRP was replaced with cropland (Reynolds et al. 2001). This study concluded that an additional 12.4 million recruits were added to the waterfowl fall flight as a result of CRP from 1992–1997.
>
> During 1990–1994, nest success of female pheasants in north central Iowa was 40 percent higher in large blocks of CRP than in smaller fragmented nesting cover types like roadsides and fence lines (Clark and Bogenschutz 1999). When CRP acreage was enrolled in large fields, pheasant populations were 53 percent greater compared to no CRP (Clark and Bogenschutz 2001).
>
> Based on densities of 12 grassland songbird species in CRP fields compared to adjacent croplands, Johnson and Igl (1995) predicted that populations of at least five of these species would decline statewide in North Dakota by 17 percent or more if CRP was greatly reduced on the state's landscape.
>
> These studies document positive impacts of CRP on wildlife populations. After precipitation returned to the prairies in 1993, CRP proved to be a major contributor to the rebounds of many species of waterfowl. This impact of CRP on waterfowl populations is further substantiated by comparisons with the Canadian prairies where waterfowl nest success and population growth remains low and CRP and other conservation cover programs are lacking. CRP has resulted in a boom to pheasant and white-tailed deer populations throughout the plains states and the Midwest. Non-game grassland birds, one of the fastest declining groups of birds in the country, have also responded positively to the habitat afforded by CRP, staving off declines that could lead to increased listings of threatened and endangered species.

Ducks Unlimited website, *Conservation Reserve Program*, available at http://www.ducks.org/ Conservation/GovernmentAffairs/1617/ConservationReserveProgram.html.

2. Increased crop prices and the associated increase in farmland rental values may diminish the financial draw of the CRP at a time when Congress has also reduced the acreage capacity.

> After a period of relative stability, the CRP faces a number of changes. The 2008 Farm Act reduced the CRP's maximum enrollment to 32 million acres—4.6 mil-

lion acres less than the program's peak acreage in 2007. Moreover, increases in agricultural commodity prices since 2006 not only increase CRP costs, but may decrease landowner interest in the CRP if further increases are expected in the future. And, if program goals evolve in response to emerging environmental concerns, such as climate change, the location and types of practices installed on CRP lands may change, possibly affecting wildlife habitat and other environmental services provided by the program....

As of October 1, 2009, the CRP is capped at 32 million acres—nearly 20 percent below the cap of 39.2 million acres allowed under the 2002 Farm Act. To meet the new cap, USDA allowed approximately 2 million acres in contracts that expired on or before September 30, 2009, to leave the program without an offer to renew or extend the contracts. However, even under the lower CRP acreage cap, USDA will have continuing opportunities to add new enrollments or to seek modifications on currently enrolled acres, since contracts on 3.3 million to 6.5 million acres are scheduled to expire annually between 2010 and 2014.

Beginning in 2006, prices for many commodity crops rose, nearly doubling by the summer of 2008. While prices have since dropped, they are still high by historical standards, which will increase program costs as CRP rental rates increase to remain competitive with market returns.

High price expectations may also affect incentives to enroll. While CRP rental rates on new enrollments are based on yearly estimates of market rates provided by USDA's National Agricultural Statistics Service (NASS), to the extent that these estimates fail to capture expectations of future price increases, offered acreage could decline.

Daniel Hellerstein, *Challenges Facing USDA's Conservation Reserve Program*, USDA AMBER WAVES (June 2010). In response to these challenges, Hellerstein recommends that "[i]mproved targeting of benefits, encouragement of better conservation practices, and heightened competition among bidders could hold promise for increasing the environmental benefits and lowering the cost of the Conservation Reserve Program." *Id.*

3. Other resources that explore both the workings of the land retirement programs include Jeffrey Ferris and Juha Siikamäki, *Conservation Reserve Program and Wetland Reserve Program: Primary Land Retirement Programs for Promoting Farmland Conservation*, Resources for the Future (Aug. 2009); Tadlock Cowan, *Conservation Reserve Program: Status and Current Issues*, Congressional Research Service Report No. RS21613 (Jan. 22, 2010).

4. There are a number of additional smaller USDA programs that offer land retirement opportunities. The USDA Farm Service Agency website has information on all conservation programs available. See http://fsa.usda.gov. A helpful review of the authorized programs as reflected in the 2008 Farm Bill is also provided in Megan Stubbs, *Agricultural Conservation: A Guide to Programs*, Congressional Research Service Report No. R40763 (Mar. 25, 2010); and, in Tadlock Cowan and Renee Johnson, *Conservation Provisions of the 2008 Farm Bill*, Congressional Research Service Report No. RS34557 (July 2, 2008).

c. *Working Land Conservation Programs*

Congress has also sought to address environmental problems on the farm by direct funding of clean up and conservation activities. The USDA refers to these programs as the "working land conservation programs," as they apply to ongoing farming operations and land that will continue to be in an agricultural use. The two most significant such programs are the Environmental Quality Incentives Program and the Conservation Stewardship Program.

Conservation Policy: Working-Land Conservation Programs

USDA, Economic Research Service, Briefing Room: Conservation Policy available at http://www.ers.usda.gov/Briefing/ConservationPolicy/workingland.htm

The Environmental Quality Incentives Program—EQIP

EQIP was established under the 1996 Federal Agriculture Improvement and Reform (FAIR) Act, replacing the Agricultural Conservation Program. EQIP's principal objective is to provide producers with assistance that promotes production and environmental quality as compatible goals, optimizes environmental benefits, and helps farmers and ranchers meet Federal, State, and local regulatory requirements.

EQIP provides producers with financial and technical assistance for implementing and managing a wide range of conservation practices consistent with crop and livestock production. Sixty percent of overall EQIP funding is targeted to natural resource concerns related to poultry and livestock production. The remainder is directed toward practices that address conservation priorities on working cropland.

Farmers seeking to participate in EQIP complete an application indicating which land will be enrolled, which resource concerns will be addressed, and what practices will be used. Enrollment decisions are made at the State or local level. Each State or local Natural Resources Conservation Service (NRCS) office ranks applications based on the treatment of priority natural resource concerns; treatment of multiple resource concerns; use of conservation practices that provide long-term environmental enhancements; compliance with Federal, State, local, or tribal regulatory requirements; and the relative cost-effectiveness of the proposed conservation practice. Applications receiving the highest environmental benefit scores based on the ranking criteria are approved for funding.

EQIP uses two types of financial assistance to encourage implementation and management of conservation practices: cost-share and incentive payments. Cost-sharing applies to structural and vegetative practices and payments can be up to 75 percent of installation costs, although a 50-percent cost-share is more typical. Examples of eligible practices are grassed waterways, filter strips, waste storage facilities, and fencing. Incentive payments encourage producers to adopt land management practices they may not have otherwise used. Eligible practices include nutrient management, integrated pest management, irrigation water management, and wildlife habitat management.

Key Changes in the 2008 Farm Act

The Food, Conservation, and Energy Act of 2008 (2008 Farm Act) made some changes to EQIP relating to:

- increased funding,
- eligibility requirements,
- overall payment limitations,
- payment terms for groups defined by USDA as "traditionally underserved,"
- offer ranking procedures, and
- the ground and surface water conservation fund.

Increased funding. EQIP is slated to receive the largest share of new conservation funding under the 2008 Farm Act, a total of $1.15 billion. This increase would bring EQIP spending to about $7.25 billion for fiscal years (FY) 2008–12. Funding authorized in the 2008 Farm Act increases from $1.2 billion in FY 2008 to $1.75 billion in FY 2012.

Eligibility requirements. The 2008 Farm Act provides clarification regarding lands eligible for EQIP participation. Eligible lands include cropland, grassland, rangeland and pasture land, nonindustrial private forestland, and other agricultural land (e.g., cropped woodland, marshes, incidental land that is part of the agricultural operation, and agricultural land used for the production of livestock) on which resource issues could be addressed. Conservation practices related to organic production and transition to organic production are also now eligible for funding. Organic practices are subject to payment limitations of $20,000 annually and $80,000 over 6 years.

Overall payment limitations. Aggregate payment limitations are reduced from $450,000 to $300,000 for any individual or legal entity during the ensuing 6 years. However, the $450,000 cap established under the 2002 Farm Act is maintained for projects of special environmental significance.

Payment terms for groups defined by USDA as "traditionally underserved." Payment terms are improved and expanded for beginning, limited-resource, and socially disadvantaged farmers and ranchers. In the 2002 Farm Act, beginning and limited-resource farmers and ranchers benefited from a provision that provided greater financial assistance (up to 90 percent of the estimated cost of certain conservation practices) than that provided to other farmers and ranchers (up to 75 percent of the cost). The 2008 Farm Act extends the higher payment rates to socially disadvantaged producers as well, and establishes that the rates for these three groups of farmers be increased no less than 25 percent above otherwise applicable rates (up to the 90-percent maximum rate). Another provision eases potential liquidity constraints to conservation program participation. EQIP payments are typically made upon completion of the practice installation. The 2008 Farm Act allows traditionally underserved participants to qualify for advance payments of up to 30 percent for purchasing materials or services. Beginning and socially disadvantaged farmers also benefit from the "Conservation Access" provision, which requires that a total of 10 percent of EQIP funds be initially set aside to enroll these targeted individuals.

Offer ranking procedures. Changes in EQIP's procedures for ranking contract offers under the 2008 Farm Act include consideration of how comprehensively and completely a proposed conservation project would address resource issues and whether the project would improve or complete a conservation system. The legislation encourages the grouping of "similar" contract offers for ranking purposes.

Ground and surface water conservation fund. This fund, established in 2002, is replaced by the Agricultural Water Enhancement Program. The 2008 Farm Act expands the program's purpose from ground and surface water conservation to include improving water quality on agricultural lands. In addition to signing contracts with individuals, the Secretary of Agriculture may enter into agreements with partners, including producer associations or other groups of producers, State or local governments and Indian tribes, to collectively address water quality or quantity concerns on a regional basis.

Features maintained from the 2002 Farm Act. Several changes enacted with the 2002 Farm Act are maintained, including allocating 60 percent of funding for livestock-related practices, relaxing the requirement to maximize environmental benefits per dollar of program expenditure, and disallowing the use of competitive bidding. The latter precludes the Secretary of Agriculture from assigning higher priority to an application based on a producer's offer to accept a lower payment rate for installing a given practice, when comparing contract offers that would provide similar environmental values.

Economic Implications of 2008 Farm Act Changes

The changes made to EQIP have some implications for the economic performance of the program.

Expanded funding for EQIP. The funding increases authorized in the 2008 Farm Act will allow more producers to enroll in EQIP but may not be sufficient to enroll all producers who are interested in participating. Historically, producer interest in enrolling in EQIP has outweighed the available funding by a large margin. Even though EQIP received a significant funding boost in the 2002 Farm Act, so many producers applied that in 2003, the offers exceeded the $691 million in funds obligated that year by an estimated $3 billion. In 2007, $993 million was obligated in EQIP but an estimated $865 million in offers remained unfunded due to budget constraints.

$300,000 payment limitation. The reduction in the limit on EQIP payments from $450,000 to $300,000 over 6 years could reduce the attractiveness of EQIP to some producers. However, the sizes of EQIP payments typically made to individuals or entities suggest that very few producers are likely to be affected by a $300,000/6-year limit. Analysis of EQIP administrative data suggests that less than 0.5 percent of those receiving payments would be directly affected by the reduced limit. About three-quarters of those getting payments over the 2004–07 period received them in a single year, and the vast majority—about 90 percent—received $50,000 or less.

Improved payment terms for traditionally underserved groups. Increases in payment rates for certain farmer groups may increase participation of those groups in EQIP. Higher rates reduce the cost to farmers of investing in conservation improvements. Allowing beginning and socially disadvantaged farmers to be eligible for higher cost share rates may encourage some farmers to enroll in EQIP who otherwise might not have participated because they faced financial constraints. Or some participants may make additional conservation investments because they are now less costly. Lastly, participants who become eligible for the higher cost share rate may make the same investments as they would have without the higher rates, but shift a portion of the costs to the Government.

Setting aside of funds for beginning and socially disadvantaged farmers is another way of increasing enrollment. Given the same selection criteria for all farmer groups, setting aside funds (in EQIP) or acres (in CStP) for beginning and socially disadvantaged farmers can increase participation of those farmers if some eligible farmers' applications are unlikely to be accepted without the set aside, and the set-aside funds or acres exceeds the amount currently claimed by eligible farmers.

EQIP contract data suggests a 5-percent set-aside of EQIP funds may have little effect on participation, at least for beginning farmers. Payments to beginning farmers accounted for 12 percent of all EQIP payments in 2006. This suggests the 5-percent set-aside funds would likely go to beginning farmers who are able to participate in EQIP even when funds are not set aside.

The 5-percent set-aside funds for beginning farmers in EQIP may have more of an impact if administered at the regional level. For example, payments to beginning farmers in the Lake States region (including Michigan, Minnesota, and Wisconsin) totaled less than 5 percent of all EQIP payments in the region in 2006. Some beginning farmers in this region who could not previously participate in EQIP may be able to enroll with a regional 5-percent set-aside. See a listing of the States included in each region.

Continuation of ban on competitive bidding. In the 2002 Farm Act, a change in EQIP bid assessment procedures discontinued the option of competitive bidding, and the 2008 Farm Act does not restore the option. Disallowing bidding likely reduced the overall level of environmental benefits per dollar of program expenditure that could be achieved in EQIP. ERS analysis of EQIP contract data revealed that cost-sharing and incentive payments were much lower than the maximum rates when bidding was allowed in 1996–2002. During that period, the average bid on cost-shared structural practices was 35 percent of practice cost, compared with the 50–75-percent rates allowed. For management practices, bids averaged 43 percent of the maximum rate, which was established by practice and by county.

Continuation of fund set-aside for livestock practices. The continuing requirement in the Farm Act that 60 percent of EQIP funds be allocated to livestock-related practices could impact the types of practices that get funded, particularly if livestock-related practices would not have received funding in the absence of the set-aside. EQIP has always had a set aside, which makes it difficult to discern if livestock-related practices would have been funded in the absence of a constraint. Over the 1997–2000 period when at least 50 percent of EQIP funds had to be devoted to addressing concerns arising from livestock production, at least 60 percent of funds went to livestock-related practices. In 2002, the set aside was raised to 60 percent. Between 2004 and 2007, 65–68 percent of funds went to livestock-related practices. While the 60-percent set-aside is specified and achieved nationally, not all regions achieve this allocation to livestock-related practices. The Southern Plains, Mountain, Northeast, and Appalachia regions allocated over 70 percent of funds to livestock-related practices in 2007, while the Pacific and Delta regions allocated less than 50 percent.

The Conservation Stewardship Program — CStP

The 2008 Farm Act replaced the Conservation Security Program (CSP) with the Conservation Stewardship Program (CStP). Existing contracts, entered into under the old CSP will continue in force. Beginning in 2009, USDA will begin entering into contracts under the new CStP.

Producers can enroll cropland, grazing land, and (within limits) forest land located on their farms. To participate in the new CStP farmers and rancher must, at minimum: (1) have already addressed at least one resource concern throughout their farm and (2) agree to address at least one additional priority resource concern (priorities set by USDA) during the 5-year contract term. Resource concerns can include water quality, air quality, soil quality and other aspects of environmental quality. Producers who have already addressed more resource concerns, or agree to address more resource concerns during the contract term, are more likely to be selected for enrollment. The likelihood of enrollment is also higher when environmental benefits are provided at least cost, although producers cannot improve their chances by offering to take lower payments.

Conservation Stewardship Program payments can compensate producers for installing and adopting conservation activities, improving or maintaining existing conservation activities, or adopting resource-conserving crop rotations. Payment amounts are to be based on out-of-pocket cost of these activities, income forgone by producer, and expected environmental benefits. Total CStP payments to a single producer cannot exceed $200,000 during any 5-year period. Payments cannot be made for expenses associated with animal-waste storage or treatment facilities or related waste transport or transfer devices for animal feeding operations.

To the extent that it can be done, the 2008 Farm Act directs USDA to enroll 12.77 million acres per year in CStP at an average cost of $18 per acre per year. Program acreage is to be allocated to States based primarily on each State's proportion of total national eligible acres, but also taking into account conservation needs, the degree to which CStP can help address these needs, and equity in the distribution of funds. Five percent of acres are to be made available to beginning farmers, and another 5 percent to socially disadvantaged producers.

EQIP and CStP — Different Approaches to Similar Concerns

Both EQIP and CStP are designed to address similar resource concerns on working lands, both are administered by NRCS, and in both, payment levels largely determine which eligible producers are willing to participate. Another similarity is that program managers review producers' proposals and decide which ones to accept for program enrollment. This step allows program managers to gather information on potential environmental performance and benefits (and, perhaps, potential to meet other program objectives) and costs directly from farmers—information that can be critical where determining which proposals best contribute to achieving program objectives. EQIP and CStP are distinguished, however, by the details of program design, including budget, eligibility, enrollment screens (ranking criteria), and participation incentives.

In combination, these programs provide a very flexible set of incentives for conservation on working lands and on livestock operations. These programs complement land retirement by rounding out the conservation policy portfolio. Many environmental problems, such as pesticide and nutrient runoff, can be cost-effectively addressed on working lands. Because land remains in production, specific environmental benefits can often be achieved at a lower cost per acre than through land retirement.

———————

New final regulations for the Conservation Stewardship Program were published in the Federal Register on June 3, 2010.

USDA Issues Final Rule for Conservation Stewardship Program

USDA, Natural Resources Conservation Service, News (June 3, 2010), available at http://www.nrcs.usda.gov/news/releases/2010/csp_final_rule_6.03.10.html

Agriculture Secretary Tom Vilsack today announced that USDA published the final regulations governing the Conservation Stewardship Program (CSP). Authorized in the 2008 Farm Bill, CSP is a voluntary program that offers payments to producers who exercise good land stewardship and want to improve their conservation performance.

"Voluntary conservation practices by private landowners and producers are an essential part of our effort to improve soil and water quality," said Vilsack. "Broad and diverse participation in the CSP program will provide producers with many benefits such as enhancing wildlife habitat and helping to mitigate the impact of climate change." ...

Administered by the Natural Resources Conservation Service (NRCS), CSP is available to all producers regardless of operation size, crops produced, or geographic location. Eligible lands include cropland, pastureland, rangeland, non-industrial private forest land, and agricultural land under the jurisdiction of an Indian tribe. Under the final rule published today and effective immediately, the program retains the broad features outlined in the interim final rule, including:

- CSP pays participants for conservation performance—the higher the performance, the higher the payment.

- Producers get credit both for conservation measures they have already implemented and for new measures they agree to add.
- CSP is offered in all 50 states, the District of Columbia, and the Pacific and Caribbean areas through continuous sign-up, with announced cut-off dates for ranking and funding applications.

The experience gained during the program's first year, and comments received from partners and the public during the 90-day public comment period, have contributed to a number of important changes in the program rules. The program's new features include the following:

- Higher payment rate for additional conservation performance. USDA is implementing a split payment structure, with one payment rate for existing conservation activities and a higher payment rate for new activities. This is expected to encourage producers to apply more new activities and thereby generate greater environmental benefits.
- Higher payment limit. The total contract limitation for joint operations is increased from $200,000 to $400,000, with annual payment limits increased from $40,000 to $80,000 to fairly compensate joint operations that produce environmental benefit levels needed to earn the payments.
- New minimum payment. To directly encourage participation by small-scale, historically underserved producers, the rule establishes a minimum payment of $1,000.
- Pastured cropland. "Pastured cropland" is added as a new designation with a higher payment than "pastureland" because of the greater income foregone by producers who maintain a grass-based livestock production system on land suitable for cropping.
- Enhancements. Some conservation enhancements work better when implemented as a system and under the new rule are offered as enhancement "bundles." Participants who implement such comprehensive bundles get higher rankings and higher payments.
- Resource-conserving crop rotation. In response to extensive public comment, the definition of "resource-conserving crop rotation" is revised to require the use of grass and/or legumes. Since resource-conserving crops receive supplemental payments under CSP, the rule change ensures that the crops provide a sufficient level of environmental benefit.

Other changes in the regulation give producers greater flexibility in establishing their eligibility to apply for CSP and in certifying their control of the land. . . .

Notes

1. The EQIP has been strongly criticized for the use of federal funds in support of concentrated animal operations. *See, e.g.,* Elanor Starmer, *Industrial Livestock at the Taxpayer Trough: How Large Hog and Dairy Operations are Subsidized by the Environmental Quality Incentives Program*, A Report to the Campaign for Family Farms and the Environment (Dec. 2008), available at http://www.inmotionmagazine.com/ra08/tgibbons_subsidies08.html. This report analyzes EQIP funding from 2003–2007 and criticizes the program for providing a

---

Source of Law and Implementation Guidance

The statutory authority for EQIP can be found at 16 U.S.C. §§ 3839aa–3839aa-9. The EQIP regulations are found at 7 C.F.R. pt. 1466 (2010).

Information about the EQIP is available at http://www.nrcs.usda.gov/programs/eqip/.

The statutory authority for the Conservation Security Program is found at 16 U.S.C. §§ 3838–3838c and the authority for the new Conservation Stewardship Program is found at 16 U.S.C. §§ 3838d–3838g. The regulations that governed the Conservation Security Program were found at 7 C.F.R. pt 1469. The new regulations were published in the Federal Register at 75 Fed. Reg. 31,610 (2010) (to be codified at 7 C.F.R. pt. 1470).

Information about the CStP is available at http://www.nrcs.usda.gov/programs/new_csp/csp.html.

Both programs are administered by the Natural Resources Conservation Service (NRCS) of the USDA.

---

disproportionate share of funding to large industrialized operations. It estimates that during this time period, approximately 1,000 industrialized hog and dairy operations received at least $35 million per year in EQIP funding.

Critics of industrialized animal operations complain that the alleged economic efficiency of these operations is based largely on the fact that external costs such as environmental harm are not considered. EQIP provides government support to pay these costs.

2. There are a number of additional cost-share USDA programs that offer assistance to farmers. The USDA Farm Service Agency website has information on all conservation and environmental clean-up programs available. See http://fsa.usda.gov. A helpful review of the authorized programs as reflected in the 2008 Farm Bill is also provided in Megan Stubbs, *Agricultural Conservation: A Guide to Programs*, Congressional Research Service Report No. R40763 (Mar. 25, 2010); and, in Tadlock Cowan and Renee Johnson, *Conservation Provisions of the 2008 Farm Bill*, Congressional Research Service Report No. RS34557 (July 2, 2008).

d. The Farmland and Grazing Land Protection Programs

Conservation Policy: Farmland and Grazing Land Protection Programs

USDA, Economic Research Service, Briefing Room: Conservation Policy available at http://www.ers.usda.gov/Briefing/ConservationPolicy/farmland.htm

Conversion of agricultural and rural lands to urban uses—including residential, commercial, and industrial development—is on the rise. Data from the National Resources Inventory indicate that developed land increased 2.1 million acres per year, on average, between 1992 and 2002, versus 1.4 million acres per year during the previous decade. However, this annual rate represents barely 0.2 percent of the Nation's 1.03 billion acres of cropland, grassland, pasture and range, suggesting little threat to the Nation's capacity to produce food and fiber. Nevertheless, about a third of the value of U.S. agricultural output is produced on the 16 percent of cropland that is subject to urban development pressure.

Though the conversion of agricultural and rural lands to urban uses does not threaten our Nation's capacity for agricultural production, some localities face reduced agricultural production capacity as well as losses in amenities associated with agriculture due to farmland conversions.

Farmland provides a number of rural amenities, including open space, scenic views, rural agrarian character, wildlife habitat, and other environmental services. These non-market benefits are not typically accounted for in the land market, as landowners are seldom able to extract payment from anyone for providing these amenities. Consequently, landowners may not take the social value of these amenities into account when considering whether to develop land for urban-related purposes. Though land moves into and out of different uses for a variety of reasons, cropland conversion to urban uses tends to be permanent, as it is typically economically infeasible to revert back to farming. Thus, the losses of amenities are irreversible.

Similarly, the ecological benefits that are lost when native grasslands and rangelands are converted to cropping uses have raised awareness of the need for intervention to protect these environmental services. Grazing lands support a rich biodiversity of plant and animals species, while providing important ecological functions involving hydrologic systems and carbon sequestration. Besides supporting livestock production, ecosystem services provided by grazing lands can support other activities that contribute to rural economies, such as hunting and fishing, wildlife viewing, and other ranch-based recreation.

Rising cropland conversion rates have motivated growing public financial support for farmland protection at the Federal level to supplement State and local efforts. Grazing land protection has also been gaining attention as a Federal conservation priority, to protect native grasslands from conversion to cropland or urban uses. Federal funding for farmland protection occurs primarily through two programs—the Farmland Protection Program and the Grassland Reserve Program.

Farmland Protection Program

Despite State and local prerogatives in land use management and a growing number of farmland protection programs administered at State and local levels, the Federal Government is increasingly engaging in efforts to protect farmland from conversion to urban uses. Federal efforts to protect farmland began with the Agriculture and Food Act of 1981, which required Federal agencies to evaluate the impact of federally funded programs that converted farmland to nonagricultural uses, and to consider alternative actions that would lessen the adverse impacts. Direct Federal involvement in permanent farmland protection did not begin until 1996, when the USDA Farmland Protection Program (FPP) was established. Through FPP, the Federal government provided matching funds to eligible entities (State, tribal and local governments) to purchase agricultural conservation easements to protect prime topsoil. The easements restrict the land from being converted to non-agricultural uses. The FPP distributed about $53 million in matching funds across 28 States over 1996–2001.

The 2002 Farm Security and Rural Investment Act (2002 Farm Act) reauthorized the FPP (renaming it the Farm and Ranch Lands Protection Program), and provided matching funds up to 50 percent of the appraised fair market value of easements on qualified, privately owned agricultural land (with the remainder of the value contributed through payments from the eligible entity and donations of part of the easement value by landowners). It also expanded the set of entities eligible to sponsor applications for funding to include nongovernmental organizations (primarily land trusts). Farm and Ranch Lands Protection funding for the 5-year period 2003–2007 was $448 million, with eligible entities in 49 States receiving funding.

The Food, Conservation, and Energy Act of 2008 (2008 Farm Act) authorized further increases in spending, with mandated funding set at $743 million over the 5-year period from 2008–2012. If actual spending is realized at authorized levels, annual spending will increase more than 75 percent annually. Also, FPP's purpose for limiting nonagricultural uses was broadened from its original focus on protecting topsoil, to preserving the agricultural uses and conservation values of land. FPP continues to provide matching funds of up to 50 percent of the fair market value of the easement, and allows more flexible terms regarding payments from eligible entities and landowner donations. Previous limitations on impervious surfaces of 2 percent of the easement area (up to 6 percent under certain conditions) were also relaxed in the 2008 Farm Act; eligible entities can now specify limits on impervious surfaces with the approval of the Secretary of the Department of Agriculture.

The agency administering the program, USDA's Natural Resources Conservation Service (NRCS), allocates program funding to its State offices. The criteria used in making the FPP allocations have historically included the overall loss and percent loss of total farmland and farmland with prime, unique, and important farmland soils in the State, the degree of development pressure, estimates of demand for the funds, and the contributions and performance of eligible entities. Cooperating entities submit parcels for consideration to the individual State offices. The NRCS State offices score the parcels based on National and State ranking criteria. The ranking criteria include factors that assess the parcel's land quality, farm and ranch viability, county-level development pressure and other State-specific factors. The State offices rank the scored parcels and select the highest ranked parcels for which the State office has funding. NRCS State offices then develop cooperative agreements obligating the funds with the cooperating entities associated with the selected parcels. The cooperating entities are responsible for administering the easement acquisition process, monitoring the easement, and enforcing the conservation easement deed.

Grassland Reserve Program

The Grassland Reserve Program (GRP), first authorized in 2002 and extended under the 2008 Farm Act, is the primary Federal program for grazing land conservation. The program is designed to protect grasslands for livestock grazing and other uses from conversions to cropland and urban uses, and promote sustainable grazing practices. Under the current legislation, participating landowners voluntarily sell cropping and/or development rights under permanent easements, or via long-term rental agreements (10, 15, and 20 years) with annual payments. An approved grazing management plan is required for all enrolled lands, with cost-sharing provided for use of approved restoration practices, when applicable. Program funding of $230 million was spent over FY 2002–07, with a total enrollment cap of 2 million acres nationwide. The 2008 Farm Act authorizes an additional 1.22 million acres of enrollment during FY 2009–12.

Historically, GRP has enrolled eligible grassland under rental agreements of 10, 15, 20, or 30 years, 30-year easements, or easements of maximum duration allowed under State law. Under the 2008 Farm Act, 30-year rental agreements and 30-year easements are no longer authorized. The 2008 Farm Act also changes cost-share rates for grassland restoration practices. Prior to 2008, GRP participants could receive cost-sharing of up to 75 percent of restoration costs on restored grassland and up to 90 percent on virgin grassland. Under the 2008 Act, restoration cost shares are capped at 50 percent, with an annual payment limitation of $50,000. The 2008 Farm Act also removed the prohibition to disturb the soil.

Like FPP, GRP funds grazing land protection through a two-stage process. In the first stage, NRCS allocates GRP program funding to States, which in most years has been based on the number of grazing operations, pasture and range acres under threat of conversion, and biodiversity considerations. Once funds are allocated to States, State NRCS offices award funds to eligible entities for easement purchases based on State criteria....

State Trends in Farmland Protection

State and local governments spend millions of dollars annually on voluntary programs to protect farmland, with most attention given to protecting farmland from conversion to developed uses. Direct government outlays occur through State and county purchase of development rights (PDR) programs (otherwise known as purchase of agricultural conservation easement, or PACE, programs). Twenty-one States have funded easement purchases in State-level PDR programs, and at least 57 local jurisdictions operate separate programs in 18 States. The average easement cost in State PDR programs was over $2,300 per acre, and over $3,000 per acre in local PDR programs. PDR expenditures are generally one-time expenditures to restrict development permanently or for an extended (25–30 year) period, with some programs allowing landowners to elect payments in installments.

The most active State and local PDR programs exist in the Northeast. Maryland, Massachusetts, New Jersey, and Pennsylvania account for 92 percent of State-level PDR expenditures to date and 71 percent of the acres preserved in State programs through May 2008 (up from 76 percent and 58 percent in 2004, respectively). Especially active programs elsewhere include county-level programs in Sonoma County, CA; Gallatin County, MT; and Douglas County, CO.

On a cumulative basis, State PDR programs have preserved nearly 1.8 million acres of farmland at a cost of nearly $4 billion since the late 1970s. Local PDR programs have independently preserved an additional 326,000 acres of farmland for about $1.2 billion (in 2000 dollars). These cost estimates exclude the income tax benefits that landowners may qualify for if they sold development rights at less than their market value....

The amount of land preserved through PDR programs represents only about 2 percent of the 94.7 million acres of cropland that ERS estimated to be subject to some degree of development pressure in 1995. ERS estimated the total cost of preserving this cropland subject to development pressure to be as much as $130 billion, in 1995 dollars.

In addition to direct purchases of easements, States forgo over $1 billion in annual tax receipts through preferential assessment programs. ERS estimated that when capitalized at 4 percent, the total value of U.S. public expenditures on preferential assessment was $27 billion (1995 dollars). These implicit subsidies (from forgone tax revenues) ranged from about $25,000 annually in Wyoming to $218 million annually in California.

The high costs of permanently preserving farmland through government funded easement programs have generated support for locally sponsored transfer of development rights (TDR) programs, largely in places where urban development pressures are the major driver in land use change. While the sponsoring jurisdiction faces fewer costs, garnering taxpayer support in areas targeted to receive the urban densities being transferred is difficult, as is balancing the supply of and demand for development rights. Almost 100 local jurisdictions have passed TDR ordinances through 2007 (up from 50 in

2000), but not all of these jurisdictions have been actively preserving land. A survey of 64 of these TDR programs revealed that only 27 have individually preserved more than 100 acres.

In some regions, land trusts are particularly engaged in preserving farmland. These private, nonprofit organizations accept donations of conservation easements on farmland and environmentally sensitive land. The donations benefit landowners in the form of Federal and, for some, State income tax deductions. In Colorado, South Carolina, and Virginia, formal markets are developing that allow a landowner who donates an easement but cannot use the State tax credit to sell the unused credit to a third party. In addition, private land trusts often assist in administering public and private funding for land easement acquisition.

Are Easement Programs Effective?

Because they result in permanent (or long-term, i.e., 25–30 year) restrictions on non-farm development, easement programs are considered to be more effective in preserving agricultural lands and providing intended benefits than agricultural zoning, preferential assessment, or other land use management tools. However, the actual effect of these programs on land conversion rates and patterns is uncertain. While the number of acres preserved can be counted, these programs may simply shift development pressures—and cropping pressures in the case of virgin grasslands—elsewhere. Also, issues concerning compliance with and enforcement of easement restrictions over the long term can arise.

An often-cited argument in support of PDR programs to protect farmland from development is that they help keep farmland affordable for new farmers. In theory, once the development rights have been sold, the market value of the preserved land will reflect only its value in a farming use, and may be significantly lower than its residential market value. However, a recent study found little evidence that easement restrictions significantly lowered preserved farmland prices. It could be that landowners who farm as a recreational pursuit are outbidding "traditional" farmers for the land.

To help counter urban development pressures on farmland, States have begun to implement "smart growth" strategies. Smart growth is a catch-all phrase to describe a number of land use policies for influencing the pattern and density of new development. Without prohibiting development outside designated areas, smart growth policies use incentives and disincentives to direct new development to existing urban areas with appropriate infrastructure. PDR programs are one tool used to meet these goals. The effectiveness of smart growth will depend on how the incentive effects of new policies differ from pre-existing policies.

Source of Law and Implementation Guidance

The statutory authority for the GRP can be found at 16 U.S.C. §§ 3838n–3838q. The GRP regulations are found at 7 C.F.R. pt. 1415 (2010).

The statutory authority for the FPP is found at 16 U.S.C. §§ 3838h–3838j. The regulations are found at 7 C.F.R. pt. 1491.

Information about the CStP is available at http://www.nrcs.usda.gov/programs/new_csp/csp.html.

Notes

1. Private non-profit farmland preservation organizations such as American Farmland Trust (AFT) are active in promoting farmland preservation. AFT partners with the NRCS in hosting the farmland preservation website at http://www.farmlandinfo.org/ offering access to farmland loss statistics, laws designed to protect farmland, and other resources.

2. The rising interest in local foods has increased interest in farmland preservation, as the availability of local food is often less than current demand. Farmland near metropolitan areas is needed to serve the local food markets. Neil D. Hamilton, *Preserving Farmland, Creating Farms, and Feeding Communities: Opportunities to Link Farmland Protection and Community Food Security,* 19 N. ILL. U. L. REV. 657 (1999). *See also*, Steve Martinez, Michael Hand, Michelle Da Pra, Susan Pollack, Katherine Ralston, Travis Smith, Stephen Vogel, Shellye Clark, Luanne Lohr, Sarah Low, and Constance Newman, *Local Food Systems Concepts, Impacts, and Issues,* USDA Economic Research Service, (May 2010) available at http://www.ers.usda.gov/Publications/ERR97/ERR97.pdf.

2. The Regulation of CAFOs

The Clean Water Act (CWA) prohibits the discharge of pollutants from any point source into waters of the United States without a "national pollution discharge elimination system" (NPDES) permit issued by the EPA or an authorized state agency. 33 U.S.C. § 1311(a). The CWA expressly defines concentrated animal feeding operations (CAFOs) as point sources. 33 U.S.C. § 1362(14). Nevertheless, as noted by Professor Ruhl, "[i]n 1998 — over 25 years after Congress included CAFOs in the CWA's definition of point source, only 2,000 of the nation's 450,000 [animal feeding operations] had NPDES permits."

There have been a number of important developments since that time, beginning with a new definition of terms. An *"Animal Feeding Operation"* (AFO) is defined as

> [A] lot or facility (other than an aquatic animal production facility) where the following conditions are met: (i) Animals (other than aquatic animals) have been, are, or will be stabled or confined and fed or maintained for a total of 45 days or more in any 12-month period, and (ii) Crops, vegetation, forage growth, or post-harvest residues are not sustained in the normal growing season over any portion of the lot or facility.

40 C.F.R. § 122.23(b)(1) (2010).

A *"Concentrated Animal Feeding Operation"* (CAFO) is defined as

> [A]n AFO that is defined as a Large CAFO or as a Medium CAFO by the terms of this paragraph, or that is designated as a CAFO in accordance with paragraph (c) of this section. Two or more AFOs under common ownership are considered to be a single AFO for the purposes of determining the number of animals at an operation, if they adjoin each other or if they use a common area or system for the disposal of wastes

40 C.F.R. § 122.23(b)(2) (2010).

A *"Large Concentrated Animal Feeding Operation"* (Large CAFO) is defined as

> [an AFO that] stables or confines as many as or more than the numbers of animals specified in any of the following categories:

(i) 700 mature dairy cows, whether milked or dry;

(ii) 1,000 veal calves;

(iii) 1,000 cattle other than mature dairy cows or veal calves. Cattle includes but is not limited to heifers, steers, bulls and cow/calf pairs;

(iv) 2,500 swine each weighing 55 pounds or more;

(v) 10,000 swine each weighing less than 55 pounds;

(vi) 500 horses;

(vii) 10,000 sheep or lambs;

(viii) 55,000 turkeys;

(ix) 30,000 laying hens or broilers, if the AFO uses a liquid manure handling system;

(x) 125,000 chickens (other than laying hens), if the AFO uses other than a liquid manure handling system;

(xi) 82,000 laying hens, if the AFO uses other than a liquid manure handling system;

(xii) 30,000 ducks (if the AFO uses other than a liquid manure handling system); or

(xiii) 5,000 ducks (if the AFO uses a liquid manure handling system).

40 C.F.R. § 122.23(b)(4) (2010).

A "*Medium Concentrated Animal Feeding Operation*" (Medium CAFO) "includes any AFO with the type and number of animals that fall within any of the ranges listed [below] and which has been defined or designated as a CAFO."

(i) The type and number of animals that it stables or confines falls within any of the following ranges:

(A) 200 to 699 mature dairy cows, whether milked or dry;

(B) 300 to 999 veal calves;

(C) 300 to 999 cattle other than mature dairy cows or veal calves. Cattle includes but is not limited to heifers, steers, bulls and cow/calf pairs;

(D) 750 to 2,499 swine each weighing 55 pounds or more;

(E) 3,000 to 9,999 swine each weighing less than 55 pounds;

(F) 150 to 499 horses;

(G) 3,000 to 9,999 sheep or lambs;

(H) 16,500 to 54,999 turkeys;

(I) 9,000 to 29,999 laying hens or broilers, if the AFO uses a liquid manure handling system;

(J) 37,500 to 124,999 chickens (other than laying hens), if the AFO uses other than a liquid manure handling system;

(K) 25,000 to 81,999 laying hens, if the AFO uses other than a liquid manure handling system;

(L) 10,000 to 29,999 ducks (if the AFO uses other than a liquid manure handling system); or

(M) 1,500 to 4,999 ducks (if the AFO uses a liquid manure handling system); and

(ii) Either one of the following conditions are met:

(A) Pollutants are discharged into waters of the United States through a man-made ditch, flushing system, or other similar man-made device; or

(B) Pollutants are discharged directly into waters of the United States which originate outside of and pass over, across, or through the facility or otherwise come into direct contact with the animals confined in the operation.

40 C.F.R. § 122.23(b)(6) (2010). The regulation further provides that [t]he appropriate authority (i.e., State Director or Regional Administrator, or both ...) may designate any AFO as a CAFO upon determining that it is a significant contributor of pollutants to waters of the United States. 40 C.F.R. § 122.23(c) (2010).

In 2000, EPA proposed significant revisions to its regulation of CAFOs, seeking to bring more within the CWA permitting system, and in February 2003, the final regulations revising these rules were published. 68 Fed. Reg. 7175–7274 (2003). Under these 2003 regulations, the NPDES permitting requirements and the Effluent Limitation Guidelines (EFLs) were amended, and the regulation of discharges of manure and wastewater from CAFOs was revised. The new regulations required all CAFOs to apply for an NPDES permit. EPA estimates suggested that this would mean that about 15,500 of the largest confined animal facilities would be subject to permitting. The new regulations became effective April 14, 2003, and they were almost immediately challenged by both representatives from the agricultural industry and environmental groups.

The cases were consolidated and eventually heard by the Second Circuit Court of Appeals. On February 28, 2005, court issued its decision. *Waterkeeper Alliance et al. v. EPA*, 399 F.3d 486 (2nd Cir. 2005). The court provided a partial victory for all of the parties, as it either upheld or did not address significant parts of the regulation, but agreed with some of the challenges raised by each side of the petitioners. It vacated parts of the regulation and remanded others for clarification. The lengthy and complex decision is summarized as follows.

Summary of the Second Circuit's Decision in the CAFO Litigation

U.S. Environmental Protection Agency, Animal Feeding Operations Publications available at http://www.epa.gov/npdes/pubs/summary_court_decision.pdf

The February 2003 CAFO regulations revise previous regulations from 1974 and 1976. Those regulations made changes to the NPDES regulations that define which facilities are CAFOs and included changes to the CAFO effluent guidelines, which set the technology-based limitations for CAFO NPDES permits. The 2003 revised regulations expanded the number of operations covered by the CAFO regulations to an estimated 15,500 and included requirements to address the land application of manure from CAFOs. The rule became effective April 14, 2003 and States were required to modify programs by February 2005 and develop State technical standards.

After EPA issued the 2003 regulations, petitions for judicial review were filed by CAFO industry organizations (American Farm Bureau Federation, National Pork Producers Council, National Chicken Council, and National Turkey Federation) and by environmental groups (Waterkeeper Alliance, Natural Resources Defense Council, Sierra Club, and American Littoral Society). The petitions for review, which were originally filed in several different circuit courts of appeal, were consolidated into one proceeding before the Second Circuit.

On February 28, 2005, the U.S. Court of Appeals for the Second Circuit issued its decision in *Waterkeeper Alliance et al. v. EPA*, 399 F.3d 486. In its decision, Second Circuit addressed a range of issues raised by the litigants. The Court both upheld many of the basic tenets of the regulations promulgated by EPA but also overturned certain sections.

Issues Upheld

Land application regulatory approach and interpretation of "agricultural storm water"

The Court upheld EPA's authority to regulate, through NPDES permits, the runoff to the waters of the U.S. containing manure that CAFOs have applied to crop fields. It rejected the Industry Petitioners' claim that land application runoff must be channelized before it can be considered to be a point source discharge subject to permitting. It noted that the CWA expressly defines the term "point source" to include "any … concentrated animal feeding operation … from which pollutants are or may be discharged," and found that the Act "not only permits, but demands" that land application discharges be construed as discharges "from" a CAFO.

The Court also upheld EPA's determination in the CAFO rule that storm water runoff of manure from a CAFO's crop fields qualifies as "agricultural storm water," which is exempt from regulation under section 502(14) of the Act, only where the CAFO has applied the manure to its crops at rates that represent "appropriate agricultural utilization" of the manure nutrients. EPA's interpretation of the Act in this regard was reasonable, the Court found, in light of the legislative purpose of the agricultural storm water exemption and given the precedent set in an earlier Second Circuit case, *Concerned Area Residents for the Environment v. Southview Farm*, 34 F.3d 114 (2d Cir. 1994).

Effluent guidelines

The Court upheld the CAFO effluent guidelines in all respects against challenges from the environmental organizations. Three areas upheld in particular are listed below. The areas that were remanded to EPA are listed in the following section.

Identification of best available technologies. The Court rejected the environmental organizations' claim that when EPA chose the pollution control technologies on which to base effluent guidelines for CAFOs, the Agency did not meet its duty to identify the single CAFO with the best-performing technology. The Court found that EPA had collected extensive data on the waste management systems at CAFOs and had considered approximately 11,000 public comments on the proposed CAFO rule, and on those bases, EPA had adequately justified its selection of "best available technologies" on which to base the regulations. This includes the zero discharge requirement from production areas when there is a very large storm event.

Ground water controls. The Court upheld EPA's decision not to include controls in the national regulations on CAFO discharges that reach surface waters through a ground water connection. EPA had determined that because such discharges depend greatly on local geology and other site-specific factors, the need for permit controls on ground water discharges was a matter to be evaluated by the permitting agency in each individual case rather than established in a national regulation.

Economic methodologies. The Court upheld the financial methodologies that EPA used for determining whether the technology-based permit requirements for CAFOs set in the new effluent guidelines would be economically achievable by the industry as a whole.

Issues Vacated by the Court

Nutrient Management Plans

The Court vacated rule provisions that allow permitting authorities to issue permits to CAFOs without including the terms of the CAFO's Nutrient Management Plan ("NMP" or "Plan") in the permit and without the Plan being reviewed by the permitting agency and available to the public. The Court relied on provisions of the Act that authorize discharges only where NPDES permits "ensure that every discharge of pollutants will comply with all applicable effluent limitations and standards," citing CWA sections 402(a)(1), (a)(2), and (b). Because the rule allows CAFOs to write their own nutrient management plans and because those plans are not required to be reviewed by the permitting agency or made available to the public, the Court found, the rule does not ensure that each Large CAFO has developed a satisfactory Plan. The Court analogized to the Ninth Circuit's decision in *Environmental Defense Center, Inc. v. EPA*, 344 F.3d 832 (9th Cir. 2003), in which the Court held that the failure to require permitting authority review of storm water management plans under EPA's Phase II storm water rule violated the Act. The Court also found that the terms of the NMPs themselves are "effluent limitations" as that term is defined in the Act and therefore must be made part of the permit. In addition, the Court found that by not making the NMPs part of the permit and available to the public, the CAFO rule violated public participation requirements in sections 101(e) and 402 of the Act.

Duty to Apply

The Court vacated the "duty to apply" provisions of the new CAFO rule. These provisions require all CAFOs to apply for an NPDES permit unless they can demonstrate that they have no potential to discharge. The Court found that the duty to apply, which the Agency had based on a presumption that all CAFOs have at least a potential to discharge, was invalid, because the CWA subjects only actual discharges to regulation rather than potential discharges. The Court acknowledged EPA's strong policy considerations for seeking to impose a duty to apply — "EPA has marshaled evidence suggesting that such a prophylactic measure may be necessary to effectively regulate water pollution from large CAFOs, given that Large CAFOs are important contributors to water pollution and that they have, historically at least, improperly tried to circumvent the permitting process" — but found that the Agency nevertheless lacked statutory authority to do so.

Issues Remanded by the Court

The Court also remanded other aspects of the CAFO rule to EPA for further clarification and analysis:

BCT effluent guidelines for pathogens

The Court held that the CAFO rule violated the CWA because EPA had not made an affirmative finding that the BCT-based ELGs — i.e. the "best conventional technology" guidelines for conventional pollutants such as fecal coliform—do in fact represent BCT technology. The Court remanded this issue to EPA to make such a finding based on the BAT/BPT technologies EPA studied or to establish specific BCT limitations for pathogens based on some other technology.

NSPS—100-year storm standard

The CAFO rule set the new source performance standards for swine and poultry CAFOs at a level of "absolute" zero discharge. As an alternative to meeting this standard, however, the rule allowed a CAFO in these categories to show that either (1) its production area was designed to contain all wastewater and precipitation from the 100-year, 24-hour storm, or (2) it would comply with "voluntary superior performance standards" based on innovative technologies, under which a discharge from the production area would be allowed if it was accompanied by an equivalent or greater reduction in the quantity of pollutants released to other media (e.g., air emissions). The Court found that EPA had not justified either of these alternatives in the record and that EPA had not provided adequate public participation with respect to either provision. As a result, the Court remanded these provisions to EPA to clarify, via a process that adequately involves the public, the statutory and evidentiary basis for allowing either of these alternative provisions.

Water quality-based effluent limits

The Court agreed with EPA that agricultural storm water is exempt from NPDES regulation and therefore is not subject to water quality-based effluent limitations in permits. However, the Court directed EPA to "clarify the statutory and evidentiary basis for failing to promulgate water quality-based effluent limitations for discharges other than agricultural storm water discharges, as that term is defined in 40 C.F.R. § 122.23(e)," and to "clarify whether States may develop water quality-based effluent limitations on their own."

Claudia Copeland
Animal Waste and Water Quality: EPA's Response to the Waterkeeper Alliance Court Decision on Regulation of CAFOs
Congressional Research Service Report No. RL33656, pp. 3–5
February 17, 2010

In response to the ruling, EPA proposed revisions to the 2003 rule in June 2006.[7] … EPA officials indicated in the 2006 proposal that they expected to promulgate revised regulations by June 2007. Earlier in 2006, EPA had extended compliance dates in the 2003 rule for facilities that were affected by the *Waterkeeper Alliance* decision until July 31, 2007.[8] This extension affected the date for newly defined CAFOs (facilities not defined as

---

7. U.S. Environmental Protection Agency, "Revised National Pollutant Discharge Elimination System Permit Regulation and Effluent Limitation Guidelines for Concentrated Animal Feeding Operations in Response to Waterkeeper Decision; Proposed Rule," 71 Federal Register 37744–37787, June 30, 2006.

8. U.S. Environmental Protection Agency, "Revised Compliance Dates for National Pollutant Discharge Elimination System Permit Regulation and Effluent Limitation Guidelines for Concentrated Animal Feeding Operations," 71 *Federal Register* 6978–6984, February 10, 2006.

CAFOs as of April 14, 2003—the effective date of the 2003 rule) to seek NPDES permit coverage and the date by which all CAFOs must develop and implement nutrient management plans.

In May 2007, EPA announced that it was still considering comments on the 2006 proposal and did not expect to complete work on a final rule until 2008. Thus, EPA extended the July 31, 2007, compliance deadline until February 27, 2009—giving livestock operators another 19 months to obtain discharge permits and to develop and implement manure management plans.[9] The compliance deadline extension did not apply to new livestock operations (which were required by the 2003 rule to comply with those rules when they begin operations) or to existing CAFOs that were covered by permits prior to 2003 (which also were required to comply when the 2003 rule became effective).

In March 2008, EPA released a supplement to the 2006 proposal, modifying it in two respects by proposing additional options to respond to the *Waterkeeper Alliance* ruling, but not reopening the entire 2006 proposal for additional public comment. EPA provided a 30-day public comment period on the supplementary proposal.[10] Even with the supplementary proposal, EPA expected to promulgate a final revised regulation by the summer of 2008 and would not need to extend the February 2009 compliance date.

Several hundred public comments on EPA's regulatory proposal were submitted by individual citizens, environmental advocacy groups, state agencies (environmental, public health, and agricultural departments), individual livestock and poultry producers, and groups that represent livestock and poultry producers.[11] Public comments addressed a number of general and specific technical points, with particular focus on the "duty to apply" and agricultural stormwater exemption provisions of the proposal ... Industry's comments were generally supportive of the proposal, approving deletion of the previous "duty to apply" provision and also of EPA's efforts to provide flexibility regarding nutrient management plan modifications—especially to limit review and public participation requirements to only those changes that are substantial. Environmental groups, on the other hand, strongly criticized the proposal, arguing that the *Waterkeeper Alliance* court left in place several means for the agency to accomplish much of its original permitting approach, but instead EPA chose not to do so. State environmental and resource agencies, the primary implementers of CWA permitting, also had a number of criticisms. They focused on key parts that they argued would greatly increase the administrative and resource burden on states.

A final revised regulation was issued by EPA on October 31, 2008.[12] The final rule substantially adopted the 2006 proposal and the 2008 supplementary proposal, with some mainly editorial modifications. According to EPA, the revised rule applies to about

---

9. U.S. Environmental Protection Agency, "Revised Compliance Dates Under the National Pollutant Discharge Elimination System Permit Regulations and Effluent Limitations Guidelines and Standards for Concentrated Animal Feeding Operations," 72 *Federal Register* 40245–40250, July 24, 2007.

10. U.S. Environmental Protection Agency, "Revised National Pollutant Discharge Elimination System Permit Regulations for Concentrated Animal Feeding Operations; Supplemental Notice of Proposed Rulemaking," 46 *Federal Register* 73, March 7, 2008, pp. 12321–12340.

11. Materials in the EPA docket for this rulemaking, No. EPA-HQ-OW-2005-0037, including EPA documents and public comments on the proposal, can be found at http://www.regulations.gov/fdms public/component/main.

12. U.S. Environmental Protection Agency, "Revised National Pollutant Discharge Elimination System Permit Regulation and Effluent Limitations Guidelines for Concentrated Animal Feeding Operations in Response to the *Waterkeeper* Decision, Final Rule," 73 *Federal Register* 225, November 20, 2008, pp. 70417–70486. See http://www.epa.gov/npdes/regulations/cafo_final_rule_preamble2008.pdf

15,300 CAFOs that will need permit coverage (74% of the 20,700 CAFOs operating in 2008).[13] The agency estimated that 9,000 CAFOs currently were covered by existing permits as of 2008.

———————

The 2008 EPA final rule now appears in the Code of Federal Regulations at 40 C.F.R. pts. 9, 122, and 412 (2010). The EPA has selected those provisions applicable to animal feeding operations and published them as a separate document, *Consolidated CAFO Regulations* on their website at http://www.epa.gov/npdes/regulations/cafo_final_rule2008_comp.pdf.

Concentrated Animal Feeding Operations
Final Rulemaking—Fact Sheet
U.S. Environmental Protection Agency (October 2008)
available at http://www.epa.gov/npdes/pubs/cafo_final_rule2008_fs.pdf

The final rule includes two key changes that address the Waterkeeper court decision. First, it revises the requirement for all CAFOs to apply for NPDES permits and instead requires only those CAFOs that discharge or propose to discharge to apply for permits. In the discussion accompanying the revised rule, EPA is providing additional clarification on how operators should evaluate whether they discharge or propose to discharge. As explained in the final rule, this evaluation calls for a case-by-case determination by the CAFO owner or operator as to whether the CAFO does or will discharge from its production area or land application area based on an objective assessment of the CAFO's design, construction, operation, and maintenance. The final rule also provides a voluntary no discharge certification option for CAFOs that do not discharge or propose to discharge. A properly certified CAFO demonstrates to the permitting authority that it is not required to seek permit coverage.

Second, the rule adds new requirements relating to NMPs for permitted CAFOs. CAFO operators were already required to develop and implement NMPs under the 2003 rule; the new rule requires CAFOs to submit the NMPs along with their NPDES permit applications. Under the new rule, permitting authorities are then required to review the NMPs and provide the public with an opportunity for meaningful review and comment on the plans. Permitting authorities are also required to include the terms of the NMP as enforceable elements of the permit. The final rule lays out a process for including these facility-specific provisions in both individual and general permits.

The final rule also addresses other aspects relating to the Waterkeeper court decision. First, EPA is clarifying that water quality-based effluent limitations (WQBELs) may be required in any CAFO permit with respect to production area discharges and discharges from land application areas that are not exempt agricultural stormwater. Second, EPA removed the provision that allowed new source swine, poultry, and veal calf CAFOs to use containment structures designed for the 100-year, 24-hour storm to fulfill the no discharge requirement. Such CAFOs may now meet the no discharge requirement with site-specific best management practice effluent limitations. Finally, the final rule affirms that

———————

13. U.S. Environmental Protection Agency, "Revised National Pollutant Discharge Elimination System Permit Regulation and Effluent Limitations Guidelines for Concentrated Animal Feeding Operations in Response to the Waterkeeper Decision, Final Rule," 73 Federal Register 225, November 20, 2008, pp. 70417–70486. See http://www.epa.gov/npdes/regulations/cafo_final_rule_preamble2008.pdf.

the Best Conventional Technology (BCT) limitations established in 2003 do in fact represent the Best Conventional Control Technology for achieving fecal coliform reductions.

Environmental Benefits and Public Costs of the Regulation

The February 2003 CAFO rule presented an extensive discussion of the environmental benefits associated with updating the CAFO regulations. This final rule does not alter these benefits since the technical requirements for CAFOs that discharge are not affected and all facilities will still need to control nutrient releases from production and land application areas. Since the final rule does not alter these technical requirements, CAFO operators and State permitting authorities will only experience a minor change to the existing regulatory burden under the CAFO NPDES regulations as revised in the final rule. This change in regulatory burden arises exclusively from the amended administrative processes associated with the final rule, and EPA estimates that the final rule will add less than one percent to the total current administrative burden.

Notes

1. In 2009, agricultural industry groups and environmental organizations again challenged the CAFO CWA regulations. The cases were consolidated in the Fifth Circuit Court of Appeals in *National Pork Producers Council v. Environmental Protection Agency*, case No. 08-61093 (5th Cir.).

On May 5, 2010, the environmental groups announced a settlement with EPA. One concern voiced by these groups was that CAFOs would be able to escape government regulation by claiming—without government verification—that they do not discharge into CWA protected waterways. According to press release issued by one of the petitioners, the Natural Resources Defense Counsel (NRDC), "[u]nder today's settlement, EPA will initiate a new national effort to track down factory farms operating without permits and determine for itself if they must be regulated. The specific information that EPA will ultimately require from individual facilities will be determined after a period of public comment. But the results of that investigation will enable the agency and the public to create stronger pollution controls in the future and make sure facilities are complying with current rules." *EPA, Environmental Groups Reach Settlement on Factory Farm Pollution Lawsuit—Agency to Initiate Investigation of Industry that has Chronically Skirted Accountability for Animal Waste*, NRDC press release available at http://www.nrdc.org/media/2010/100526.asp.

2. The Government Accountability Office (GAO) has also expressed concerns about the lack of information available regarding CAFOs. *Concentrated Animal Feeding Operations: EPA Needs More Information and a Clearly Defined Strategy to Protect Air and Water Quality*, Report No GAO-08-1177T (Sept. 24, 2008).

3. Developing Issues

There are a variety of important developing issues that will affect the future of the environmental regulation of agricultural production. While a full review of these issues is beyond the scope of a survey of agricultural law, this section highlights several of these issues and provides resource citations for further exploration.

a. Liability for Environmental Harm from CAFOs

The contracting arrangement common to the poultry industry raises challenging environmental liability issues. While the farmer cares for the birds and has contractual ownership and responsibility for the waste that is produced, the integrated poultry processing company owns the birds and controls their care. *See, e.g.*, Neil D. Hamilton, *Broiler Contracting in the United States—a Current Contract Analysis Addressing Legal Issues and Grower Concerns*, 7 Drake J. Agric. L. 43 (2002).

In the case of *Sierra Club v. Tyson Foods, Inc.*, 299 F. Supp. 2d 693 (W.D. Ky. 2003), the court held that the integrator was nonetheless the "responsible party" under the Comprehensive Environmental Response Compensation Liability Act (CERCLA)).

In long-running and ongoing litigation, the state of Oklahoma brought suit against thirteen poultry companies in Arkansas seeking to hold them liable for contamination of the Illinois River Watershed that flows through Northwest Arkansas and into Oklahoma. The farmers who care for the birds were not named as plaintiffs. *Oklahoma v. Tyson Foods, Inc.*, Case No. 4:05-cv-00329. Closing arguments were held in February 2010, but a decision has not been entered, and appeals are anticipated.

b. Air Quality

In January 2005, the EPA announced the *Air Compliance Agreement*, a negotiated agreement with prominent representatives of the animal agriculture industry. 70 Fed. Reg. 4958, (Jan. 31, 2005). The agreement was intended to produce air quality monitoring data on AFO emissions, while at the same time protecting the participating farms from liability under a "safe harbor." *See Air Quality Issues and Animal Agriculture: EPA's Air Compliance Agreement*, Congressional Research Service Report No. RL32947 (Apr. 9, 2008).

In December 2008, the EPA published a notice, *Administrative Reporting Exemption for Air Releases of Hazardous Substances From Animal Waste at Farms*, exempting farms from certain notification requirements under the Comprehensive Environmental Response Compensation and Liability Act (CERCLA). 73 Fed. Reg., 76,948 (Dec. 18, 2008).

For background information on this topic, see *Animal Waste and the Environment: EPA Regulation of Concentrated Animal Feeding Operations (CAFOs)*, Congressional Research Service Report No. RL31851 (Nov. 28, 2008); *Air Quality Issues and Animal Agriculture: A Primer*, Congressional Research Service Report No. RL32948 (Nov 24, 2009).

c. Effect of Pesticide Use

Concerns about the health and environmental effects associated with pesticide use continue. For example, new research regarding the popular pesticide Atrazine renews concerns about its environmental effects. *See, e.g, Pesticide Atrazine Can Turn Male Frogs Into Females*, Science Daily, Mar. 10, 2010, available at http://www.sciencedaily.com/releases/2010/03/100301151927.htm.

Atrazine is reported to be one of the most commonly used pesticides in the United States, with significant use in corn production. Agricultural pesticides such as Atrazine are regulated under the Federal Insecticide, Fungicide and Rodenticide Act (FIFRA) and cannot be sold until they are approved, i.e, registered with the EPA. 7 U.S.C. ch. 6, § 136a. Atrazine was first registered for use in 1958 and re-registered after a review in 2003. The

EPA found "risks of concern" particularly with respect to drinking water contamination, but decided to address these concerns only through labeling restrictions. *See, Atrazine in Drinking Water*, LEGAL PLANET: THE ENVIRONMENTAL LAW AND POLICY BLOG, Bekeley-Law/UCLA (Aug. 23, 2009) (providing links to EPA, NRDC, Academy of Sciences and other studies), available at http://legalplanet.wordpress.com/2009/08/23/atrazine-in-drinking-water/. Atrazine use has continued to generate controversy, and its use is banned in the European Union.

From the Natural Resources Defense Council (NRDC):

> Approximately 75 percent of stream water and about 40 percent of all ground-water samples from agricultural areas tested in an extensive U.S. Geological Survey study contained atrazine.... Atrazine was found in 80 percent of drinking water samples taken in 153 public water systems. All twenty watersheds sampled in 2007 and 2008 had detectable levels of atrazine, and sixteen had average concentrations above the level that has been shown to harm plants and wildlife.

NRDC Atrazine website available at http://www.nrdc.org/health/atrazine.

From the manufacturer of Atrazine, Syngenta:

> Levels of atrazine in U.S. waters are well within the federal lifetime drinking water standard of 3 parts-per-billion—a level containing a 1,000-fold safety buffer. In 2008, none of the 122 Community Water Systems monitored in 10 states exceeded the federal standards set for atrazine in drinking water or raw water.

Syngenta Atrazine website available at http://www.atrazine.com/water.

In late 2009, EPA announced that it was undertaking a new review of Atrazine. EPA Press Release, *EPA Begins New Scientific Evaluation of Atrazine*, Oct. 7, 2009; see EPA Atrazine website at http://www.epa.gov/opp00001/reregistration/atrazine/atrazine_update.htm.

Pesticide residues in municipal drinking water are monitored and regulated by the EPA pursuant to the Safe Drinking Water Act. 42 U.S.C. §§ 300f–300j26. *See* http://www.epa.gov/safewater/sdwa/index.html.

Pesticide residues in food are regulated jointly by the EPA and the Food & Drug Administration (FDA) pursuant to FIFRA and the Food, Drug and Cosmetic Act as amended. 21 U.S.C. § 346a. The EPA determines whether a pesticide is approved for use on a food product under its FIFRA authorities, and it establishes pesticide tolerance levels for any pesticide used on a raw agricultural commodity. The FDA then enforces the limits for pesticide residues in food. *See,* Richard A. Merrill & Jeffrey K. Francer, *Organizing Federal Food Safety Regulation*, 31 SETON HALL L. REV. 61, 86–88 (2000); Neal D. Fortin, FOOD REGULATION: LAW, SCIENCE, POLICY & PRACTICE 212–14 (2009). See also, FDA's pesticide website at http://www.fda.gov/Food/FoodSafety/FoodContaminantsAdulteration/Pesticides/default.htm.

d. Nuisance and Right to Farm Laws

Most states have a "right to farm" law that protects farming operations by providing a legislative defense to nuisance actions brought by farm neighbors. While initially these laws were designed to protect farms from urban encroachment, many question the appropriate limits of such protection in light of expanded livestock operations. Professor Neil Hamilton analyzed these types of laws and the concerns raised as follows:

The laws give a legal priority to the farmer if certain conditions are met, such as being located there first, operating reasonably, or complying with "generally accepted agricultural practices." The question for society is, should farmers be given such special protections to carry on activities which have adverse social consequences? The same question can be asked about laws passed in several states, referred to as "right to spray" laws, to protect farmers from suits for cleaning up water pollution if they used farm chemicals according to the label. Passage of these laws indicates society has answered the question affirmatively, at least for now. But the change to an industrialized agriculture, from the traditional model of independent family farms, may mean the question of whether there is a right to farm is reopened for legitimate inquiry....

Neil D. Hamilton, *Feeding Our Future: Six Philosophical Issues Shaping Agricultural Law*, 72 Neb. L. Rev. 210, 212 (1993).

Given the questions raised by Professor Hamilton *in 1993*, one might be surprised that communities are still struggling with finding appropriate answers. Livestock operations continue to grow in size, and while some operations find protection in right to farm laws, suits against others are successful. In March 2010, a Missouri jury awarded $11 million to the neighbors of a large hog operation owned by Premium Standard Farms, a subsidiary of Smithfield Foods. The operation at issue houses 80,000 hogs at a time, roughly 200,000 per year in 80 barns, each holding 1,000 hogs. The facility is a "finishing farm" where swine are placed at about 60 lbs and raised in confinement until they reach approximately 260 lbs and are ready for slaughter. It is estimated that 83 million gallons of waste are generated each year from the facility. The plaintiffs, all family farmers and some with farms owned for generations, alleged that the relentless and extreme odors were so intense that they were sometimes unable to spend any time outdoors. Evidence at trial showed that methane, ammonia, and hydrogen sulfide were detected in the air for miles. Premium Standard Farms continues under a 1999 settlement agreement with the state of Missouri where it was ordered to develop pollution controls. *See Missouri Jury Awards Residents $11 Million in Damages from Living Under a Cloud of Stench Caused by Industrial Hog Farms*, PR Newswire, March 5, 2010.

For an instructive article on nuisance law that analyzes the Wisconsin right to farm law in light of the changing livestock industry, see Andrew C. Hanson, *Brewing Land Use Conflicts: Wisconsin's Right to Farm Law*, Wisconsin Lawyer, Wisc. Bar Assoc. (Dec. 2002), available at http://www.wisbar.org/AM/Template.cfm?Section=Wisconsin_Lawyer&template=/CM/ContentDisplay.cfm&contentid=53190. *See also*, Terence J. Centner, *Governments and Unconstitutional Takings: When Do Right-to-farm Laws Go Too Far?* 33 B.C. Envtl. Aff. L. Rev. 87 (2006); and, Neil D. Hamilton *Right-to-farm Laws Reconsidered: Ten Reasons Why Legislative Efforts to Resolve Agricultural Nuisances May Be Ineffective* 3 Drake J. Agric. L. 103 (Spring 1998). For information about the right to farm laws enacted in each state, see Elizabeth Springsteen, *States' Right-To-Farm Statutes*, National Agricultural Law Center, at http://www.nationalaglawcenter.org/assets/righttofarm/index.html.

e. Sustainability and Conventional Agricultural Practices

Although proponents of sustainable agriculture have criticized the practices of conventional agriculture for years, a greater recognition of the environmental problems associated with current farming practices has led sustainability concerns into the mainstream. With respect to intensive monocultural cropping systems, Michael Pollan argues that we have replaced the natural systems of production that relied on solar energy for photo-synthesis with a fossil fuel-based system that wrecks havoc on the environment. Michael Pollan, *Open Letter to the Next Farmer in Chief*, THE NEW YORK TIMES MAGAZINE, (Oct. 12, 2008), available at http://www.nytimes.com/2008/10/12/magazine/12policy-t.html?_r=1&pagewanted=2.

And, with regard to concentrated animal feeding operations, Pollan observed that,

> [I]f taking the animals off farms made a certain kind of economic sense, it made no ecological sense whatever: their waste, formerly regarded as a precious source of fertility on the farm, became a pollutant—factory farms are now one of America's biggest sources of pollution. As Wendell Berry has tartly observed, to take animals off farms and put them on feedlots is to take an elegant solution—animals replenishing the fertility that crops deplete—and neatly divide it into two problems: a fertility problem on the farm and a pollution problem on the feed-lot. The former problem is remedied with fossil-fuel fertilizer; the latter is reme-died not at all.

Id. For more on Pollan's analysis, view his lecture, *Deep Agriculture*, broadcast on FORA TV at http://fora.tv/2009/05/05/Michael_Pollan_Deep_Agriculture.

IV

Financing the Farming Operation

Agriculture is a highly vulnerable sector with a relatively low rate of return on assets, befitting a sector in perfect competition in an economic sense. Agriculture also has a relatively heavy dependence on debt capital and a relatively high level of capital intensity.

NEIL HARL, THE FARM DEBT CRISIS OF THE 1980S, xvii (1990).

Nowhere is the diversity of American agriculture more easily observed than in the analysis of the financing of the farming operation. Consider the financial situation of the beginning farmer in contrast to the established commercial operation with significant land holdings. Consider as well the diverse needs with respect to different crops and different types of farming operations—the direct marketer who sells produce at the local farmers market will have a very different financial situation than the large scale industrialized fruit or vegetable farm. A crop farmer may be able to rent acreage and build a farming operation slowly while a contract poultry producer will need to erect a chicken house that may cost several hundred thousand dollars in order to begin his or her operation.

Nevertheless, several aspects of farm finance unite these disparate ends of the financial spectrum. This chapter first considers these unique features of farm finance, those factors that generally apply to the interests of farm operations, big and small, and that make agricultural finance unique. It then presents an overview of the current farm finances followed by an overview of the federal credit assistance provided to the agricultural sector. The chapter concludes with an introduction to one area of commercial law with specific agricultural attributes—secured transactions involving farm assets.

A. Distinct Attributes of Farm Finance

The financing of a farming operation raises unique considerations involving 1) the nature of the inputs needed; 2) the special risks associated with production; 3) the typical merger of personal and business assets associated with family farming; and 4) society's basic need for food production. Each makes farm finance somewhat different than the financing of other businesses.

1. The Nature of Farm Production Inputs

As noted in the preface to the agricultural law casebook published in 1984, "[a]griculture is the only industry where land is the predominant production input. Unlike other resources, land is neither mobile nor fungible." KEITH G. MEYER, DONALD B. PEDERSEN, NORMAN

W. Thorson, and John H. Davidson, Agricultural Law: Cases and Materials, xix (1984). Indeed, the acquisition of land for farming has always been central to agriculture, with land serving both as an essential component to farming and also as a central asset that could be mortgaged for operating and expansion financing. Farm land serves as the most basic farm asset, and it continues to be a costly and the most valuable ingredient to the farming operation.

> Farmland occupies a uniquely important role in the financial performance of U.S. production agriculture because of its dominance in the farm sector balance sheet. Farm real estate accounts for roughly 80 percent of the total value of farm sector assets and is thus a major component of farm wealth.

J. Michael Harris, Kenneth Erickson, James Johnson, Mitch Morehart, Roger Strickland, Ted Covey, Chris McGath, Mary Ahearn, Tim Parker, Steve Vogel, Robert Williams, and Robert Dubman, *Agricultural Income and Finance Outlook*, 29, USDA, Economic Research Service, No, AIS-88 (December 2009) (hereinafter, *Agricultural Income and Finance Outlook*).

Although average farmland values decreased somewhat in 2009, land values have increased every prior year since 1987. In 2009, U.S. farmland values averaged $2,100 an acre; crop land averaged $2,650 per acre. These averages represent a wide regional disparity, with crop land in densely populated areas such as land on both the coasts being significantly higher than elsewhere. The highest farmland real estate value is found in the Northeast where land has an average value of $4,830 per acre. The least expensive farmland is found in the Mountain region where the average value is $922 per acre. *See, Land Values and Cash Rents, 2009 Summary*, 2, USDA, National Agricultural Statistics Service (August 2009).

Farmers' business mobility is obviously restricted by their dependence on land as an input. And, the value of their land assets is generally outside of their control.

> The most important factor affecting real estate values is "location, location, location," and this is accurate for farmland as well. Farm owners in the Northeast see their land values greatly influenced by urban development. In other regions (e.g., Midwest, Plains States) land values are buoyed by Government payments. And in the Rocky Mountain region, people pay extra for the amenity values associated with mountain properties. Many factors affect farm investors' returns on their portfolios across regions and over time, including: (1) the productivity of land when in agricultural production, (2) urban influence, (3) policy effects (such as Government payments, conservation programs, and credit policy), (4) amenity effects, (5) capital gains taxation, and (6) inflation. To this list, one might add two additional factors: the globalization of world input and commodity markets, and increased market volatility.

Agricultural Income and Finance Outlook at 31.

In addition, agricultural economists observe a particular volatility to farmland valuation that can be particularly problematic when financing is at issue.

> It has been well documented that farmland values increase more than would be appropriate in response to an increase (decrease) in returns. These periods of overreaction are referred to as "boom-bust cycles." A boom (bust) is a period of time in which farmland increases (decreases) in value above (below) its fundamental value (i.e., the present value of expected future returns to farmland). Sustained periods of either overvaluation or undervaluation are inconsistent with efficient markets for farmland. Since farmland values account for about 80

percent of U.S. farm assets, boom-bust cycles have a profound effect on farm operation wealth and access to credit. As a result of boom-bust cycles, some of the more efficient and profitable producers may be forced to exit, business risks (including borrowing costs) may rise, and rural communities may experience increased financial difficulties.

Agricultural Income and Finance Outlook at 29–30.

Many beginning and limited resource farmers cannot afford to own their own land and must lease acreage in order to farm. At times, leasing can present a financial advantage, and many established farmers supplement their acreage by renting land in addition to what they own. Although long term control over this land cannot be assured, the financial risk associated with a purchase is avoided.

> Renting land allows the farm operator to expand by controlling additional land without the debt and commitment of capital associated with ownership. For about two-thirds of medium- and large-scale farms, farm operators own part of the land they operate and rent the rest. Also, 14 percent of large-scale farms— versus 6 percent of all farms—are run by tenants who own none of the land they farm. About three-quarters of large-scale tenants specialize in crops, compared with two-fifths of farms in general....

> Nearly one-third of U.S. farmland is operated under some form of lease, according to the 2007 Census of Agriculture. The most common form of lease, the cash rental agreement, is a fixed payment negotiated before planting. Share rental agreements, by contrast, vary with the amount of product harvested. Under cash rental leases, the tenant bears all of the production and market-price risk; share rental arrangements divide production and market risks between tenant and landlord.

> Cash rents are usually considered a short-term indicator of the return to a landowner's investment. To tenants, however, cash rents are a major expense and, like farm real estate values, have been increasing for a number of years. Because rents reflect the income-earning capacity of the land, they vary widely across the country. Cropland rents tend to be highest in areas where higher value crops are grown. The highest average cash rents in 2008 were reported for irrigated land in California, at $360 per acre. Cropland most suitable for corn and soybean production, principally in the Midwest, also commands high rents. The highest rents for nonirrigated cropland in 2008 were $180 per acre in Iowa and $170 per acre in Illinois.

Agricultural Income and Finance Outlook at 32–33.

Livestock farming carries the additional costs associated with the specialized buildings affixed to the farm real estate. For example, in the poultry industry, broiler houses are a major expense that the grower must incur in order to contract with a major poultry integrator. A pair of new broiler houses "can cost from $350,000 to $750,000, depending on size and location." James M. MacDonald and William D. McBride, *The Transformation of U.S. Livestock Agriculture: Scale, Efficiency, and Risks,* 7, USDA Economic Research Service, EIB no. 43 (Jan. 2009).

In addition to land, water is a critical natural resource component to the farming operation. In many areas, irrigated land may be essential to farming and the cost of irrigation will be factored into the real estate value. Increasingly, however, the concern is raised that water availability and cost will be a major limiting factor for farming in a wide range of areas.

> As global population grows, the demand for food and fiber also grows, thereby increasing the water demand for household, community, industrial, and energy

purposes. Rising standards of living throughout the world also impact water requirements. Despite current uncertainty about the United States' economic future, most reports suggest that growth will resume and competition for freshwater will continue. An abundant, reliable supply of water to meet these demands cannot be taken for granted. Overall, public water supplies account for approximately 10% of all freshwater withdrawals in the United States, whereas irrigation accounts for nearly 40% (USGS 2004). The strong dominance of agriculture compared with municipal consumption of freshwater also is consistent with worldwide statistics.

As one of the largest users of water in the United States, agriculture will be impacted significantly by changes in water availability and cost. The water withdrawn from U.S. surface and groundwater sources for agriculture is used to irrigate more than 63 million acres of cropland. The increase in agricultural water use in some areas of the country coincides with fixed or diminishing water supplies.

Several trends challenge water managers and users. Population continues to grow rapidly; by 2050, the population is expected to increase by 25% in the United States and by 50% globally. Some areas experience a scarcity of water compared with demand. In these and other locations, relic groundwater is being mined, resulting in declining water tables and associated problems that increase the costs of water withdrawal and result in the deterioration of water quality. In some areas—most notably the Western states—long-term drought conditions have greatly decreased surface water flows. Climate change predictions include higher temperatures, decreases in snowpack, shifts in precipitation patterns, increases in evapotranspiration, and more frequent droughts. How water managers and users respond to these challenges will determine, in part, the long-term availability of water for municipal, agricultural, and other uses, including those of riparian systems.

Sharon Megdal, Richard Hamann, Thomas Harter, James W. Jawitz, and J. Michael Jess, *Water, People, and the Future: Water Availability for Agriculture in the United States*, Cast Issue Paper No. 44 (November 2009).

Thus, agriculture's special dependency on finite natural resources, land and water, raise unique issues for financing an agricultural operation.

2. The Special Risks Associated with Agricultural Production

Agriculture's dependency on natural forces, in particular, the weather, combined with the raising of living products brings special risks that are not usually encountered in other industries. Adverse weather, pests, and diseases all threaten production quantity and quality.

Bankruptcy courts have frequently discussed these risks, often combined and categorically termed as "the inherent risk of farming," and risk has been considered to be an essential factor determining whether or not a debtor was a farmer and thus subject to special bankruptcy protection.

With the enactment in 1986 of Chapter 12 of the Bankruptcy Code, it appears that two main methods have evolved in determining whether a particular enterprise constitutes a *farming operation*. One view concentrates on whether the operation is subject to "traditional risks of farming," ... while the other employs a "totality of the circumstances test" of which the risks of farming is but one factor to be considered....

In re Teolis, 419 B.R. 151, 156 (Bankr. D.R.I. 2009). Similarly, an Oklahoma bankruptcy court addressing farmer status questioned whether the debtor's activities were "subject to the inherent risks of farming such as being subject to drought or other temporary, uncontrollable circumstances." *In re Cluck*, 101 B.R. 691, 695 (Bankr. E.D. Okla. 1989). Thus, risk due to factors outside of the control of the farmer is perceived to be a primary element of what it means to be a farmer. Viewing this from a lender's perspective, financing presents special considerations.

Moreover, agriculture's traditional role as a "price taker" makes farmers particularly vulnerable to market fluctuations beyond their control. Farmers are generally unable to set the price for the commodity that they produce, but rather must accept the price that the market determines. At times, this price may even be below the farmer's cost of production. Again, this calls for special consideration when seeking financing.

These special risks are passed along to any creditor that agrees to finance the farming operation, often making the collateral offered as security of particular significance.

3. The Typical Merger of Personal and Business Assets Associated with Family Farming

Built into the family farm system of agriculture is the overlap, even merger, of the family and business interests. The farm family lives and works together on the farm, so the success or failure of the farm has significance even beyond the immediate source of income. The family home is located on the farm, and it is often mortgaged to secure the farm debt. The land may have been passed down from prior generations of farmers, adding historical and personal significance. And, the business success or failure of the farming operation is often obvious for friends, neighbors, and passers-by to see. When failure comes, it comes at a high personal cost for everyone in the family. It may mean not only losing a job and losing a business, it may well mean losing a home and a heritage.

> Hidden from national consciousness are the social and cultural realities of farmers who found the price of protest too exacting or the cost of publicity too much to bear. For every news clip of activists protesting the forced sale of a family farm, tens of thousands of farm families avoided the spotlight, settled out of court, or suffered for years in silence behind closed doors. Economic failure is a stigma in virtually all walks of life, but it is especially discrediting in rural townships, where viable farms remain in the family for generations. A pioneering spirit runs deep in the hearts of those who till the land, and these settlers of the prairie have never looked kindly upon those who succumb to adversity, blame their troubles on others, or start crying for help with the going gets tough., When the names of neighboring families began to appear in the local paper—foreclosures, bankruptcies, auctions, tax delinquencies—there was often little sympathy for the individuals involved and a general consensus that anyone who lost a farm had done something to deserve it.

Kathryn Marie Dudley, Debt and Dispossession: Farm Loss in America's Heartland (1994).

4. Society's Basic Need for Food Production

Given the importance of an adequate food supply, and recognizing the need for adequate capital for production, the government has enacted a variety of measures to support and encourage farm financial investment and to assure the success of farming ventures. Federal farm programs provide greater income stability and enhanced farm income. The payments received from these programs provide a critical asset that can be offered as collateral for farm loans. Farm financial institutions and lending programs have been created specifically to increase credit opportunities for farmers. *See*, subsection C, *The Special Lenders Created to Serve the Financial Needs of the Agricultural Sector*, *infra*. And, special laws to protect farm borrowers have been enacted to soften the personal toll of farm failure. Thus, agricultural finance and credit is often governed by a unique set of policies, programs, and laws.

B. Overview of Current Farm Finances

As American agriculture has evolved, the need for capital has risen dramatically. Most farmers need significant amounts of capital to fund their operations. The USDA Economic Research Service reports that farm debt for 2008 totaled approximately $240 billion, with nominal farm debt showing a "near steady annual increase" over the past twenty years. J. Michael Harris, James Johnson, John Dillard, Robert Williams & Robert Dubman, *The Debt Finance Landscape for U.S. Farming and Farm Business*, USDA Economic Research Service, AIS-87, 7 (November 2009).

The capital-intensive nature of farming today has been criticized as linked to the "industrialization" of agriculture. "Industrialized farms would rather employ capital — land, machinery, and technology — than labor." Marty Strange, Family Farming: A New Economic Vision, 37 (1988). The relatively low cost of fossil fuels, spurring the creation of new chemical inputs and an expanding biotechnology industry, have assisted in the development of a farming industry increasingly dependent on capital. Nevertheless, even for farmers that adhere to a traditional family farm model, farming can be an expensive business.

Production costs for major commodities are high and have generally been on the rise. Total production expenses totaled a record high of $307 billion in 2008; expenses in 2007 were $284 billion, a 19.2 percent increase over 2006. Farm machinery costs led the increase with tractors and self-propelled machinery up 32.6 percent and other machinery up 34.1 percent. Fertilizer, lime, and soil conditioners were up 27.1 percent; seeds and plants were up 19.8 percent; fuels were up 18.5 percent; and rent was up 13.7 percent. Interest rates and livestock and poultry purchase prices were down. *See, Farm Production Expenditures: 2008 Summary*, 3, USDA Economic Research Service (August 2009).

Production costs vary significantly by type of farm and size of farm. The total averages, however, reflect the capital-intensive nature of commercial farming today.

In 2008, the average per farm U.S. Total Farm Expenditure was $140,075 compared with $129,062, an increase of 8.5 percent over 2007. On average, U.S. farm operations spent: $21,398 on Feed, $17,337 on Farm Services, $13,550 on Labor, $12,912 on Livestock and Poultry Purchases, $10,265 on Fertilizer, Lime, and Soil Conditioners, and $10,220 on Rent. Revised estimates for 2007 indicate U.S. farms spent an average of: $19,073 on Feed, $16,752 on Farm Services, $15,022 on Livestock and Poultry Purchases, $13,019 on Labor, and $8,968 on Rent.

Average 2008 Total Expenditures for the largest economic class of farms ($5 million and Over) were $11.4 million, 6.4 times larger than the next largest economic class with farms $1,000,000–$4,999,999 averaging $1.8 million followed by the $500,000–$999,999 economic class of farms averaging $0.7 million. The average Total Expenditure for a Crop farm was $175,141 compared with $113,390 per Livestock farm....

The Midwest region contributed the most to U.S. Total Farm Production Expenditures with expenses of $91.2 billion or 30 percent, up from $80.7 billion in 2007. The other regions ranked by Total Expenditures are: Plains at $74.2 billion (24 percent); West at $68.7 billion (22 percent); Atlantic at $39.0 billion (13 percent); and South at $34.0 billion (11 percent)....

Crop Farms expenditures increased to $165.9 billion and Livestock Farms expenditures increased to $141.1 billion. The largest expenditures for Crop Farms were Farm Services at $21.9 billion and Labor at $20.4 billion, accounting for 25 percent of their total expenses. Combined crop inputs (chemicals, fertilizer, and seed) were $43.2 billion, accounting for 26 percent of Crop Farms total expenses. The largest expenditures for Livestock Farms were Feed at $43.3 billion, accounting for 31 percent of total expenses, followed by Livestock and Poultry Purchases, at $25.1 billion accounting for 18 percent of total expenses. Together they accounted for 48 percent of Livestock Farms total expenses.

Farm Production Expenditures: 2008 Summary, 3, USDA Economic Research Service (August 2009).

Although some farms are able to use profits from one year to pay production expenses for the next, most farms rely on financing of some sort to pay annual production expenses, and the vast majority need financing for land purchases. Levels of farm debt are still characterized in comparison to the farm financial crisis of the 1980s, a landmark financial period marked by devastating farm losses. In this regard, there are mixed views on farm debt. For those who experienced the farm financial crisis of the 1980s, debt represents the ultimate risk of loss of the farming operation. Following on the heels of an agricultural boom in the 1970s, the "agricultural depression" that marked the 1980s has been said to "rival that of the 1930s in terms of its impacts on farmers." S. Rep. No. 100-230, 14 (1987). Farmers saw their net worth decline by more than half as land values, machinery values, and crop prices all declined dramatically. *Id.* at 21. Farmers who had expanded their operations (as was recommended by most agricultural economists and agricultural lenders) or who recently entered farming and purchased land all found themselves with obligations that greatly exceeded the value of their assets. Economic forces outside of the agricultural economy caused a similarly dramatic rise in credit costs as interest rates soared. Neil E. Harl, The Farm Debt Crisis of the 1980s, 13–17 (1990). Thousands of farms were lost to foreclosure and rural communities were devastated. The farmers who had little debt survived the crisis and may have even benefitted from the downturn.

Others view farm equity as essentially wasted if it is not used to capacity, with borrowing against real estate assets viewed as a positive way to leverage that asset for creating additional wealth. Which view provides the best guidance at any given time will likely be determined by overall economic forces that are difficult to predict.

> Since undergoing a multiyear retrenchment in the 1980s, with debt for farm purposes bottoming out at $131 billion in 1989, nominal farm debt has exhibited a near steady annual increase over the past two decades. As a result, year end debt levels reached new nominal records in 2005 and in each year thereafter through 2009.
>
> U.S. farm sector debt reached an estimated $238.9 billion by year end 2008 and is forecast at about the same amount for 2009. Debt classified by lenders as being for real estate purposes accounted for 50.5 percent of total farm sector debt in 2008, down from 52.6 percent in 2007. Real estate debt is now projected to rise to around 56 percent of farm sector debt in 2009, reflecting an increase in real estate debt of about $2 billion over 2008 in combination with a reduction in non-real estate debt. The relatively stable share of real estate and non-real estate debt in recent years likely reflects farmers' ongoing need to use debt financing for a wide range of purposes—from acquiring increasingly expensive machinery, equipment, and inputs to the purchase of farmland, buildings, and other structures.

Agricultural Income and Finance Outlook at 29–30.

Today, fewer farm operators rely on borrowed funds, but farm debt is increasingly concentrated in larger farms.

Debt Use Is Concentrated Among Fewer Operators

According to USDA's Agricultural Resource Management Survey (ARMS), a joint effort by ERS and the National Agricultural Statistics Service, the distribution of farm debt reveals several trends. First, the share of farm businesses that end the year with unpaid debt has declined. While many farm businesses use credit cards and lines of credit to finance input purchases during the year, most pay off their loans during the current production cycle, normally by year's end. The debt discussed in the remainder of this article comprises loans with balances carried on the farm business balance sheet from one year to the next.

In 1986, nearly 60 percent of U.S. farm operators reported outstanding debt at the end of the year; by 2007, this figure had dropped to 31 percent. Larger farms, with a greater asset base and higher revenues, are now much more likely to use debt than are smaller farms. The majority of smaller farms surveyed indicated that they have sufficient funds to finance their operations.

Poultry, hog, dairy, and cash grain farms tend to require more capital-intensive production practices and facilities, and their operators are more likely than other farmers to use debt to finance these enterprises. Over two-thirds of poultry and dairy operators owed debt at year-end 2007, as did 56 percent of hog farmers. Overall, dairy operations totaled about 3 percent of U.S. farms in 2007, but owed 13 percent of debt. Corn and general cash grain farms together accounted for 10 percent of farms and about 23 percent of debt.

At the end of 2007, 50 percent of farm business debt was held by 15 percent of farmers, compared with 30 percent held by farmers at the end of 1986 ... Farm debt is also concentrated geographically, with the Corn Belt, the Northern Plains, and the Southeast having relatively high levels of debt due to their larger share of grain, hog, poultry, and dairy operations.

J. Michael Harris, Robert Dubman, Robert Williams & John Dillard, *Debt Landscape for U.S. Farms Has Shifted,* AMBER WAVES (USDA, ERS) Dec. 2009, available at http://www.ers. usda.gov/AmberWaves/December09/Features/DebtLandscape.htm.

> An increase in the level of debt used in farming may be perceived as drawing down the farm sector's credit reserve. And depending on the prevailing view of prospective farm earnings and underlying collateral values, growth in debt out-standing may be regarded as financially troublesome. But debt, by itself, is only part of the story. Debt levels need to be examined relative to the value of equity contributed by farmers and other stakeholders, and relative to the amount of income available to meet debt service and other funding requirements. Asset values are important in the broader view of farm debt. The relationship between debt and its underlying collateral base indicates both the degree of leverage in U.S. agriculture and the share of total assets provided by creditors, farm owners, or other stakeholders engaged in agriculture. The increase in the value of assets and equity has altered the farm sector's capital structure. Debt relative to the total value of assets used in agriculture has fallen in recent years, particularly between 2003 and 2007 when sectorwide asset values were experiencing substantial an-nual increases in nominal terms. Thus, creditors' claims on assets have fallen from more than one dollar out of five during the 1980s, to around one dollar out of eight in 2009. As a result, the risk exposure of both farm asset owners and farm lenders has been reduced....

> Debt in relation to both equity and assets has dropped significantly to less than half the level it was when farm-level balance sheets were first estimated. The farm-level debt-to-asset ratio was estimated to be 0.22 in 1986, but stood at 0.08 in 2008, a drop of nearly two-thirds. The drop in debt volume in relation to the amount of assets owned means that farm operators are providing a much larger share of the capital used in farming, and that farms have become significantly less leveraged. Consequently, across all farmers, lenders have a smaller stake in farm assets and both farmers and lenders have less financial risk exposure from farm business debt than was the case when farm businesses emerged from the 1980s' crisis years and throughout the 1990s.

Agricultural Income and Finance Outlook at 38.

Financial distress, however, is evident in some segments of agriculture. Debt to eq-uity relationships is one measure of financial strength and weakness.

> Even though a smaller proportion of farms rely on debt than in the past, some farms remain highly leveraged. The 2008 ARMS [Agricultural Resource Man-agement Survey] indicates that 0.3 percent of farms owed more debt than they had assets, which is similar to the level in 1991. Farms with more debt than as-sets in 2008 owed 4.1 percent of total farm business debt, versus 2.4 percent in 1991. Farms that either held debt equal to 71 to 100 percent of asset values or that were technically insolvent (with debt levels in excess of the current market value of assets) include all sizes and types of farms. Poultry, dairy, and other field crop farms had a larger than proportional share of insolvent farms in 2008. Farms with debt equal to 71 to 100 percent of asset values included a more than proportional share of hog, dairy, poultry, and beef cattle operations. General livestock farms, which tend to be among the smallest farms both in terms of the acreage operated and value of production, also reported a larger than proportional share of highly leveraged and technically insolvent farms in 2008.

Id. at 42.

Overall financial vulnerability, however, incorporates more than debt to asset ratio. The ability of a farming operation to "cash flow," i.e., to maintain a level of net income profitability, is also essential to financial success. The USDA defines financial vulnerability as having "debts in excess of 40 percent of the value of their assets and negative farm income."

> Farms in a favorable financial position have debts less than 40 percent of their assets and positive farm income. Marginal solvency refers to positive-income, high-debt farms, while marginal income refers to negative-income, high-debt farms.

Id. at 48.

> On December 31, 2008, the overall measure of financial performance indication classified 3.6 percent of farms as being in a vulnerable position, having both negative net cash income and a debt-to-asset ratio over 0.40. On a net farm income basis, which includes all sources of non-money income such as change in inventories and charges for capital items like tractors or buildings, approximately 3.1 percent of farms were classified as vulnerable. Use of a cash income measure shifts about 10,000 more farms into the vulnerable class moving farms largely from a position of high leverage and positive income to a negative earnings circumstance on a cash basis. At the lower debt end of the spectrum, more farms are also classified as being in a marginal income position as a result of having negative net cash incomes, but relatively low debt levels....

> Of the nearly 69,000 farms classified as vulnerable in early 2008, 67 percent were rural residence farms while 15 percent were commercial-size farm businesses. For farms with over $100,000 in sales, 60 to 73 percent were classified in a favorable position in 2008. Hogs, general livestock, dairy, and beef cattle were farm types that ended 2008 with the largest share of farms in a vulnerable position with from 3 to 7 percent of farms being classified as vulnerable. Dairy farming also had the largest share of farms in a favorable position, at 75 percent, while hog farms were at the low end with 48 percent in a positive income, low-debt position. Over 70 percent of corn and soybean farms were also in a favorable position in early 2009.

Id. at 48.

As noted in Chapter II, *Economic Support to Agriculture, supra,* the federal farm programs provide a significant amount of income support to certain types of farming operations. Changes to the farm programs not only affect farmer decision making but can have a significant effect on farm finances. Similarly crop insurance and related programs serve to compensate for losses, evening out volatile farm income.

Another varied, but extremely important source of income is "off-farm" or non-farm income. About 46 percent of all farm households are "dual-career," with a spouse working off the farm, and many full-time farm operators also hold off-farm jobs to further supplement household income. While some of these farming operations are not the main support for the household, a significant number of farm families hold non-farm jobs in order to maintain the farming operation. This is particularly the case for small to mid-sized farming operations. *See,* Robert A. Hoppe, Penni Korb, Erik J. O'Donoghue, David E. Banker, *Structure and Finances of U.S. Farms: Family Farm Report,* 2007 Edition, 22–25 USDA Economic Research Service, EIB-24 (June 2007).

Notes

1. The central feature of off-farm income in the financial viability of small to mid-sized family farms has led many to complain that our "cheap food" may be too cheap, or at least that too little of the food dollar is returned to the farmer. USDA ERS estimates that just "19 cents of every dollar spent on U.S. grown food went to the farmer for the raw food inputs, while 81 cents covered the cost of transforming these inputs into food products and getting them to the grocery store shelves and restaurants. of food purchased flows to the farmer for the actual food produced." *See, Food Marketing System in the U.S.: Price Spreads from Farm to Consumer*, USDA, Economic Research Service Briefing Room, Food Marketing in the U.S., available at http://www.ers.usda.gov/Briefing/FoodMarketingSystem/ pricespreads.htm.

2. Peggy Bartlett, in her thoughtful book, AMERICAN DREAMS AND RURAL REALITIES: FAMILY FARMS IN CRISIS presents an interesting twist in suggesting that part-time farming may offer a solution to what she portrays as a clash of values between an agrarian and an industrial definition of success. "[P]art time farmers are able to conform to the dominant industrial values concerning affluence and the meaning of personal success, while also gaining some of the satisfactions of the agrarian ethic." Peggy F. Bartlett, AMERICAN DREAMS AND RURAL REALITIES: FAMILY FARMS IN CRISIS, 93 (1993).

C. Federal Credit Assistance Provided to the Agricultural Sector

Farmers settling the West in the early 1900s experienced difficulties in obtaining access to the credit that they needed. Both a commission appointed by President Taft and a private commission studied the problem and considered the rural credit assistance provided to farmers in Europe, particularly in Germany. Three proposals were generated from the commissions' work: 1) obtaining funds to loan to farmers through the sale of bonds to non-farm investors; 2) organizing lending cooperatives; and, 3) making direct government loans to farmers. Christopher R. Kelley and Barbara J. Hoekstra, *A Guide to Borrower Litigation Against the Farm Credit System and the Rights of Farm Credit System Borrowers*, 66 N.D. L. REV. 127, 132–33 (1990).

Each of these three proposals found their way into American federal credit assistance to the agricultural sector, and each is still apparent today. The Farm Credit System is a network of cooperatively owned entities that obtain loan funds for their members through the sale of bonds. And, the USDA Farm Service Agency provides direct loans to farmers that meet specific criteria.

Farmers today obtain loans from a variety of sources, public and private. Commercial banks provide the largest percentage of farm loans, lending 45% of the farm sector's total indebtedness. The Farm Credit System provides the second largest percentage of farm loans, lending 34% of the farm sector's total indebtedness. Individuals and others, including merchants, credit card companies, and dealers lend 10% of farm debt; and life insurance companies provide large long-term real estate financing that comprises 5 percent of the total farm loan volume. The USDA Farm Service Agency provides less than 3 percent of the total farm loan volume through direct loans, although it guarantees about 4 percent of the loans made by other lenders. The USDA loan programs are targeted to borrowers that need special financial assistance.

1. The Farm Service Agency

The USDA's Farm Service Agency is considered to be the "lender of last resort" as it makes direct and guaranteed loans only when credit is not available at reasonable terms from other lenders. Previously, it was called the Farmers Home Administration (FmHA), and in that capacity had a rather storied history that included serving a tremendous need while also engaging in careless lending and ultimately being involved in landmark litigation based on its reluctance to help farmers facing foreclosure during the farm financial crisis of the 1980s. *See Coleman v. Block*, 562 F. Supp 1353, 1367 (D. N.D. 1983) (recognizing class and granting preliminary injunction). That litigation eventually resulted in a national foreclosure moratorium that was portrayed in the movie *Country*.

a. The History of the USDA's Lending Programs

The 1970s were historic for the expansion of agricultural operations. Crop losses in Russia led to an unanticipated increase in commodity exports, raising farm prices. In order to fuel trade and lower food prices in the U.S., the Nixon administration adopted agricultural policies that encouraged farmers to plant from "fence row to fence row" and to "get big or get out." These policies, guided by Purdue University Agricultural Economist, Earl Butz, President Nixon's Secretary of Agriculture, are credited with transforming farm policy. *See*, Michael Pollan, The Omnivore's Dilemma: A Natural History of Four Meals, 51–52 (noting that Butz "probably did more than any other single individual to orchestrate [… the] plague of cheap corn").

The FmHA was a significant lender to the agricultural industry during this time period, providing low cost loans to farmers who were unable to obtain credit elsewhere. FmHA's clientele included beginning farmers, limited resource farmers, and minority farmers. Although FmHA borrowers were encouraged to "graduate" to commercial credit, many remained FmHA borrowers for long periods of time.

Several factors contributed to major problems with FmHA's loan portfolio in the 1980s. First, the economic fragility of FmHA borrowers made them particularly vulnerable to the dramatic downturn in the farm economy in the 1980s.

Second, the "get big or get out" advice had also been given to FmHA borrowers, and large loans were made to borrowers for expansion of their farming operations. When the farm economy collapsed, these loans were dramatically under-secured.

Third, FmHA was an important lender when crop or livestock disasters affected a borrower's access to credit, and in the late 1970s and early 1980s there were a large number of FmHA Emergency Loans given to farmers experiencing natural disasters. At the time, these loans were given to eligible borrowers based on only "minimal projected cash flow margins" and with no maximum limit on the total amount of emergency loan debt that a farmer could incur. The number of emergency loans peaked in 1981 at 138,990, and while some were small loans, some were for hundreds of thousands of dollars. The combined factors of farm losses from the underlying disasters, unmanageable debt loads, and stresses from the farm economy proved catastrophic for many of these borrowers.

By the end of December 1986, almost seventy percent of outstanding FmHA farm debt was delinquent. By November 1987, it was estimated that over 90,000 FmHA borrowers were delinquent on their loans.

"When you are farming for a living, you make your money from the ground—
You take it to the bankers, and there ain't enough to go around." Willie Nelson,
"Farm Aid: A Song for America"

See Emergency Disaster Farm Loans—Government's Financial Risk Could Be Reduced, U.S.
General Accounting Office, GAO/RCED 96-80 (Mar. 29, 1996) (available at 1996 WL
244743); *Farmers Home Administration: Billions of Dollars in Farm Loans Are at Risk*, U.S.
General Accounting Office, GAO/RCED-92-86 (Apr. 3, 1992); *Farmers Home Adminis-*
tration: Problems and Issues Facing the Emergency Loan Program, U.S. General Accounting Office, GAO/RCED-8 (Nov. 30, 1987).

Despite its social welfare mission, during the farm financial crisis, the USDA was resistant to implementing any program of assistance for FmHA's financially distressed borrowers. Political struggles were readily apparent. Congress at this time was controlled by
Democrats that expressed strong support for the social welfare mission of the FmHA.
President Reagan was in office, and his budget director, David Stockman, took the position that there were too many farmers, and that the financial crisis would serve the function of weeding out the least profitable farmers, eventually strengthening and concentrating
the farm sector. Associated with this position was the argument that fewer farmers would
mean less production, and less production would raise prices. This argument has since
been recognized as erroneous, as when one farmer goes out of business, other farmers generally purchase the land, and production remains the same or increases. In his testimony
to Congress, Stockman once said that farmers had been greedy and were suffering the
consequences. Taxpayers, he said, ought not be required to refinance the bad debt incurred by those farmers. President Reagan attempted to distance himself from these comments, even though there were many in his administration that agreed. *See,* NEIL E. HARL,
THE FARM DEBT CRISIS OF THE 1980s (1990).

This resistance was most notable with regard to the USDA's failure to implement the
loan deferral provisions enacted by Congress in its 1978 amendments to the Consolidated
Farm and Rural Development Act. 7 U.S.C. § 1981a (1982 Supp.). The USDA interpreted
these provisions as permissive, allowing the agency to determine if and when to implement a deferral program, and they declined to implement it.

Curry v. Block

541 F.Supp. 506 (D. S.D. Ga. 1982)

Alaimo, Chief Judge.

I. Introduction

Plaintiffs, acting on their own behalf and on behalf of a class defined as:

all persons in Georgia who have farm operating, ownership, or emergency loans
financed under the Consolidated Farm and Rural Development Act, P.L. 87-128,
whose loans were, are, or will be held by the Farmers Home Administration of
the United States Department of Agriculture, and whose farm loans have been
foreclosed, are in foreclosure, are threatened with foreclosure, or shall be foreclosed upon or threatened with foreclosure,

have brought this action seeking declaratory and injunctive relief in a challenge to the
procedures used by the Farmers Home Administration (FmHA) in implementing a 1978

amendment to the Consolidated Farm and Rural Development Act entitled "Loan moratorium and policy on foreclosures." 7 U.S.C. § 1981a (1982 Supp.). Specifically, the plaintiffs seek a declaration by the Court that the members of the class must be given personal notice of the availability of deferral relief under s 1981a and must be granted the opportunity to apply for the same before any acceleration action is commenced. Plaintiffs also pray that the Court enjoin the defendants from foreclosing on the applicable FmHA loans without first providing the borrowers with personal notice of and an opportunity to apply for s 1981a deferral relief. A declaration is also sought that the FmHA has a duty to promulgate regulations implementing s 1981a consistent with the underlying Congressional intent. Further, plaintiffs ask the Court to enjoin the failure of the FmHA to promulgate these regulations. Finally, plaintiffs seek an Order enjoining the defendants from foreclosing on all consolidated rural housing and farm loans until they have complied with a consent Order entered in a similar case. *See Williams v. Butz*, No. 176-153 (S.D.Ga. Oct. 7, 1977). In that case, the FmHA agreed to provide certain rural housing program borrowers with personal notice of the availability of moratorium relief under the Rural Housing Act, 42 U.S.C. s 1475 (that Act's functional equivalent of § 1981a). Plaintiffs claim that the refusal of the FmHA to provide consolidated farm and rural housing borrowers with the rights due to rural housing borrowers (personal notice of moratorium rights) violates the *Williams v. Butz* consent Order.

II. Factual Basis

The named plaintiffs and the class they represent are farmers in rural Georgia. One way or another, each of them has become eligible for and received agricultural credit through the FmHA under the Consolidated Farm and Rural Development Act. 7 U.S.C. § 1921 *et seq.*

It is apparent that most if not all of these farmers began experiencing financial difficulty in 1977 due in large part to adverse weather and economic conditions. As a result, the farmers have found it desirable to maximize their use of loan servicing devices and have attacked the FmHA's implementation of § 1981a.

At this point in the litigation, it is clear that the only real issue between the parties is legal in nature. Accordingly, the parties have filed extensive cross-motions for summary judgment, and the case is now ready for final adjudication.

III. Background

The legal issue in this case basically involves the interpretation and construction of a section of a Congressional enactment-section 1981a. In such situations, it is "the conventional judicial duty to give faithful meaning to the language Congress adopted in light of the evident legislative purpose in enacting the law in question." Thus, a cursory review of the history of federal involvement in agricultural credit through 1978, and a summary of the statutory and regulatory framework, are necessary to aid this Court in determining the legislative purpose.

A. History of federal involvement in agricultural credit

The federal government has been involved in extending agricultural credit for some 120 years. The first such involvement was initiated in 1863 with the passage of the Homestead Act; an act designed to provide farming opportunities for small-scale, family farmers—still a goal for federal intervention in agricultural credit. Although this aspect of federal involvement remained basically the same over the next 72 years, credit to farmers was also made available through the Federal Land Banks (1916), the Federal Intermediate Credit Banks (1923), and the Banks for Cooperatives (1933). The federal government was also making "natural disaster" loans available pursuant to a presidential directive issued in 1918 in response to a severe drought.

Then, in 1935, the earliest predecessor to the FmHA, the Resettlement Administration, was created by Executive Order. This agency was authorized to make small loans to farmers with the goal toward helping families settle in the rural areas. Soon thereafter, Congress again entered the agricultural credit market, this time by passing the Bankhead-Jones Farm Tenant Act of 1937. This Act created the Farm Security Administration to administer a program of supervised, long-term farm ownership loans to be made to farmers without alternative credit sources—a basic duty of the present-day FmHA. Thus, the concepts of the present farm loan programs are rooted in that mass of social legislation arising out of the Depression years.

The Bankhead-Jones Farm Tenant Act of 1937 was reenacted in 1946 as a part of the Farmers Home Administration Act of 1946. This latter Act did not change the nature of federal involvement in agricultural credit; instead it was enacted "to simplify and improve credit services to farmers and promote farm ownership." (1946) U.S. Code Cong. Service 1028. As implied by its title, the act abolished the ten year old Farm Security Administration and replaced it with the Farmers Home Administration.

Fifteen years after the Farmers Administration Act of 1946 was passed, changing conditions in the agricultural section of this country forced Congress to update its program for agricultural credit:

> (T)he revolution occasioned by the mechanization of farming operations generally, the change in character and extent of resources necessary to successful operation of family farms, and the increase in farming technology have made tremendous differences in the credit needs of farmers. While amendments have been made since 1946 to modify the Secretary's lending authority as these changes were taking place, many of the provisions of earlier loans have ceased to serve their initial purpose and are unworkable as a basis for a Federal supplement to the financing of our Nation's agricultural production.

(1961) U.S. Code Cong. & Ad. News 2243, 2306. As a result, Congress passed the Consolidated Farmers Home Administration Act of 1961 (as Title III of the Agricultural Credit Act of 1961). The Act, in response to the "increase in farming technology" and the "tremendous differences in the credit needs of farmers," was designed as "a consolidation and modernization of the Secretary's authority to make available to eligible farmers who cannot obtain credit elsewhere direct and insured loans necessary to finance their acquisition, improvement and operation of farms." *Id.* at 2305. Thus, the 1961 Act placed under one more modern roof the already existing authority of the Secretary to loan money for three purposes—real estate acquisitions and improvement (Subtitle A), operating expenses (Subtitle B) and emergencies (Subtitle C).

Contemporaneously with its intervention in the farmer program loans, the federal government was also involved in extending credit, through the FmHA, to farm owners to enable them to construct, improve, alter or repair their farm dwellings. *See* 42 U.S.C. § 1471, 63 Stat. 432 (1949). This program was a part of the Congressional action on a national housing policy designed to assist in the "elimination of substandard and other inadequate housing…, and the realization of the goal of a decent home and a suitable living environment for every American family." The Housing Act of 1949, 63 Stat. 413, 413 (1949).

In 1972, the farmer loan program and the rural housing loan program were consolidated through an amendment to the Consolidated Farms Home Administration Act of 1961. This amendment changed the name of the 1961 Act to the Consolidated Farm and Rural Development Act and adopted provisions relevant to Rural Housing loans. It did not, however, change the nature of the farmer loan program; thus this program stands today basically as it has for almost half a century.

In summary, federal intervention in agricultural credit shows a long history of farmer loans designed to aid the family farmer who cannot obtain credit from a different source. Thus, as with most programs spawned in the Depression years (the roots of today's program lie in the Bankhead-Jones Tenant Act of 1937 and not the Homestead Act of 1863), the object of the legislation is to aid the "underprivileged" farmer, and is therefore a form of social welfare legislation.

B. The Statutory and Regulatory Framework

The Consolidated Farm and Rural Development Act as it existed in 1978 (and presently) is divided into four subtitles. The first three subtitles contain the substantive provisions of the Act while the fourth contains the administrative provisions.

Subtitle A, headed "Real Estate Loans," authorizes the Secretary to make or insure loans to eligible persons "for (1) acquiring, enlarging, or improving farms, including farm buildings, land and water development, use and conservation, (2) recreational uses and facilities, (3) enterprises needed to supplement farm income, (4) refinancing existing indebtedness, and (5) loan closing costs." 7 U.S.C. § 1923(a). Those persons eligible for these loans include "family farmers" unable to obtain sufficient credit elsewhere. 7 U.S.C. § 1922. To insure repayment, the Secretary is directed to take such security interest (generally the land) "as he may determine to be necessary." 7 U.S.C. § 1927.

Subtitle B, headed "Operating Loans," authorizes the Secretary to make or insure loans to eligible persons for, inter alia, "(1) paying costs incident to reorganizing the farming system for more profitable operation, (2) purchasing livestock, poultry, and farm equipment (including equipment which utilized solar energy), (3) purchasing feed, seed, fertilizers, insecticides, and farm supplies and to meet other essential farm operating expenses including cash rent, ... (7) refinancing existing indebtedness ..." 7 U.S.C. § 1942. Those persons eligible for these loans, as with Subtitle A, include operators of "family farms" unable to obtain sufficient credit elsewhere. 7 U.S.C. § 1941. The Secretary has the discretion to make these loans "upon the full personal liability of the borrower upon such security as the Secretary may prescribe." 7 U.S.C. § 1946(a)(1). The Secretary is further authorized to consolidate or reschedule outstanding loans. 7 U.S.C. § 1946(b). Interestingly, the conditions under which the consolidation or rescheduling can occur are not prescribed by statute.

Subtitle C, headed "Emergency Loans," authorizes the Secretary to make and insure loans where the applicant's operations "have been substantially affected by a natural disaster in the United States or by a major disaster or emergency designated by the President under the Disaster Relief Act of 1974." 7 U.S.C. § 1961(a). Loans can also be made based on extreme production losses. 7 U.S.C. § 1970. The emergency loans can be made for any purpose consistent with Subtitle A or Subtitle B, 7 U.S.C. § 1963. The persons eligible for these emergency loans, unlike under Subtitle A and Subtitle B, include those able to obtain credit elsewhere,[3] although it is apparent that there must be a "reasonable

---

3. For those able to obtain sufficient credit elsewhere, however, "three years after the loan is made or insured, and every two years thereafter for the term of the loans, the Secretary shall review the loan; and if ... the borrower is able to obtain a loan from non-Federal sources at reasonable rates and

prospect for successful operation with the assistance of such a loan." 7 U.S.C. § 1961(a)(b). Again, the Secretary is directed to try to insure repayment by taking adequate security interests. Loans are made "upon the full personal liability of the borrower and upon the best security available.... Provided that the security is adequate to assure repayment of the loans, except that if such security is not available because of the disaster, the Secretary shall (1) accept as security such collateral as is available, ... together with the Secretary's confidence in the repayment ability of the applicant." 7 U.S.C. § 1964(d).

Subtitle D, headed "Administrative Provisions," outlines the various procedures to be used by the Secretary in implementing the three loan programs and supplies miscellaneous grants of authority. For example, one section authorizes the creation of national, area, state and local offices to aid in administration. 7 U.S.C. § 1981(a). For the purposes of this case, however, only two sections are relevant. Section 1981(d) provides the source authority for many of the loan servicing devices used by the FmHA and provides that "(t)he Secretary may ... (d) compromise, adjust, or reduce claims, and adjust and modify the terms of mortgage, leases, contracts and agreements entered into or administered by the Farmers Home Administration under any of its programs, as circumstances may require, ..." 7 U.S.C. § 1981(d). The other section, § 1981a, the interpretation of which is the subject of this litigation, provides in pertinent part:

> In addition to any other authority that the Secretary may have to defer principal and interest and forego foreclosure, the Secretary may permit, at the request of the borrower, the deferral of principal and interest on any outstanding loan made, insured or held by the Secretary under this chapter, or under the provisions of any other law administered by the Farmers Home Administration, and may forego foreclosure of any such loan, for such period as the Secretary deems necessary upon a showing by the borrower that due to circumstances beyond the borrower's control, the borrower is temporarily unable to continue making payments of such principal and interest when due without unduly impairing the standard of living of the borrowers.

7 U.S.C. § 1981a. A comparison between § 1981a and § 1981(d) reveals important differences. First, the fact that the former establishes authority "in addition to any other authority ... to defer principal and interest and forego foreclosure," necessitates the conclusion that § 1981a provides a loan servicing mechanism above and beyond that provided for in § 1981(d). Second, and more importantly, while § 1981(d) contains broad language of discretion—"as circumstances may require"—§ 1981a contains no such provision. In fact, § 1981a lists eligibility criteria that must be met before the deferral benefits of that section can be enjoyed. The importance of these differences will become apparent later.

Beyond this statutory framework, there are certain administrative regulations placing obligations on the FmHA. For example, a major obligation of the FmHA is to provide "management assistance to individual borrowers and applicants." 7 C.F.R. Part 1924, Subpart B. This assistance, which includes credit counseling, planning, recordkeeping, supervision, review and evaluation, is designed to assist the FmHA borrower to move in a positive direction toward a better financial position so that he may no longer require government agricultural credit.

While "management assistance" regulations tend to indicate that the loan program is a form of social welfare legislation, the extensive regulations governing security interests

---

terms..., the borrower shall on request by the Secretary, apply for and accept such non-Federal loan in sufficient amount to repay the Secretary." 7 U.S.C. § 1964(d).

are a reminder that the government has become a lending institution desirous of receiving adequate repayment of its loans. Without recounting the regulations governing security interests, it is sufficient to note that these regulations cover farm ownership loans, operating loans, emergency loans and the disposition of security....

C. Nature of the Program

The foregoing recitation of the history of and the statutory and regulatory framework of the Consolidated Farm and Rural Development Act, while seemingly long and superfluous, is actually necessary to aid this Court in properly construing the mandates, if any, of section 1981a. "Reference to the entire statutory scheme is necessary in analyzing a statute.... A court must look to the legislation as a whole in order to discern its statutory purpose." An examination of the prefatory material reveals that the farmers loan program is a unique mixture of social welfare legislation and legislation carefully designed to supplement the business needs of high credit risk farmers.

Despite this obvious mixture of objectives, it is the position of the government that this Court should interpret s 1981a with the notion that the FmHA is in the business of making loans and is not a social welfare organization. The loans are made with the expectation that they will be repaid and must be adequately secured to assure such repayment. Since the government is catering to high-risk borrowers, and since the borrower must be able to generate income in order to pay back the loan, the FmHA must get involved in virtually all aspects of the farmer's operation. Thus, for its own protection, management assistance must be rendered that includes planning, reviewing and evaluating. Yet it must be recognized that, at some point, the government must protect its own interest in the funds expended and, if the farmer is experiencing severe financial problems, it must attempt to collect the debt or liquidate the collateral. Thus, it is argued, the Court must look at the statutory scheme with a business bias.

The plaintiffs, on the other hand, argue that the farmer loan program is a type of social welfare legislation designed to lift the living standards of lower echelon farmers, and that the legislation should be interpreted accordingly (i.e., liberally in favor of the farmers). As support, the plaintiffs cite to *United States v. Kimbell Foods, Inc.*, 440 U.S. 715, 99 S.Ct. 1448, 59 L.Ed.2d 711 (1979) wherein it was noted that:

> The overriding purpose of the tax law statute obviously is to ensure prompt revenue collection. The same cannot be said of the SBA and FHA lending programs. They are a form of social welfare legislation, primarily designed to assist farmers and businesses that cannot obtain funds from private lenders on reasonable terms.

Id. at 734–35, 99 S.Ct. at 1461–62 (emphasis added). Further, Congress, in commenting on the use of qualified personnel by the Department of Agriculture, refutes the notion that the program is strictly a business venture.

> It is the sense of Congress that in carrying out the provisions of the Consolidated Farm and Rural Development Act, the Secretary of Agriculture should ensure that—
>
> 1) only officers and employees of the Department of Agriculture who are adequately prepared to understand the particular needs and problems of farmers in an area are assigned to such area; and
>
> 2) a high priority is placed on keeping existing farm operations operating.

Pub.L. No. 95-334, Title I § 126, 92 Stat. 429 (August 4, 1978), *reprinted in*, Congressional Findings, 7 U.S.C. § 1921 (Supp.1982).

It is obvious to this Court from an examination of the above materials that the interpretation of § 1981a should reflect the fact that the farmers loan program is predominately a form of social welfare legislation. Accordingly, in interpreting § 1981a, this Court will attempt to implement the social welfare goals of Congress as well as its directive to keep "existing farm operations operating" by placing a liberal, but not a strained, gloss on that section.

IV. Discussion

As stated, the plaintiffs have brought this suit to challenge the procedures used by the FmHA in implementing the provisions of 7 U.S.C. § 1981a. This section, added in 1978 as an amendment to the Consolidated Farm and Rural Development Act, provides:

> In addition to any other authority that the Secretary may have to defer principal and interest and forego foreclosure, the Secretary may permit, at the request of the borrower, the deferral of principal and interest on any outstanding loan made, insured, or held by the Secretary under this chapter, or under the provisions of any other law administered by the Farmers Home Administration, and may forego foreclosure of any such loan, for such period as the Secretary deems necessary upon a showing by the borrower that due to circumstances beyond the borrower's control, the borrower is temporarily unable to continue making payments of such principal and interest when due without unduly impairing the standard of living of the borrower. The Secretary may permit interest that accrues during the deferral period on any loan deferred under this section to bear no interest during or after such period: Provided, that if the security instrument securing such loan is foreclosed such interest as is included in the purchase price at such foreclosure shall become part of the principal and draw interest from the date of foreclosure at the rate prescribed by law.

7 U.S.C. § 1981a. The plaintiffs desire the initiation of two procedures not presently being used by the FmHA. First, they desire personal notice of their right to apply for this deferral relief and an opportunity to be heard. Second, they desire the promulgation of regulations concerning the eligibility criteria similar to that used by the FmHA for the Rural Housing loan moratorium statute, 42 U.S.C. § 1475.[6]

The government argues that since § 1981a is permissive in nature, the plaintiffs have no legal basis on which to demand such relief. Also, it argues that even if such relief could be demanded, the present practices of the FmHA provide sufficient compliance with any statutory or constitutional mandates.

Thus, it is left to this Court to decide whether § 1981a creates a mandatory duty on the Secretary to provide FmHA borrowers with personal notice of the substantive provisions of that section. In finding that such personal notice is required, this Court must then de-

---

6. 42 U.S.C. § 1475 provides:
   During any time that such loan is outstanding, the Secretary is authorized under regulations to be prescribed by him to grant a moratorium upon the payment of interest and principal on such loan for so long a period as he deems necessary, upon a showing by the borrower that due to circumstances beyond his control, he is unable to continue making payments of such principal and interest when due without unduly impairing his standard of living. In cases of extreme hardship under the foregoing circumstances, the Secretary is further authorized to cancel interest due and payable on such loans during the moratorium. Should any foreclosure of such a mortgage securing such a loan upon which a moratorium has been granted occur, no deficiency judgment shall be taken against the mortgagor if he shall have faithfully tried to meet his obligation.

termine whether the present practices of the FmHA are sufficient to provide FmHA borrowers with the requisite notice. Finally, this Court must also decide whether the regulatory scheme utilized by the FmHA to implement its loan deferral program is consistent with the Congressionally mandated program for loan deferral contained in § 1981a. The latter issue will be discussed first.

A. Is the present deferral procedure used by the FmHA consistent with the Congressional mandates of § 1981a ?

It is the position of the government that § 1981a is entirely permissive and therefore leaves the final decision as to the promulgation of regulations with the Secretary of Agriculture. Thus, it is argued, the use of the deferral mechanism already present in the statute for real estate loans and operating loans is a sufficient implementation of the provisions of § 1981a.

The plaintiffs, on the other hand, argue that § 1981a creates an affirmative duty on the Secretary to implement a deferral program comparable to the moratorium procedure used in the rural housing scheme. *See* 7 C.F.R. § 1951.17. They argue that the practices and regulations used by the FmHA, being inconsistent with this mandate, must be restrained. In finding for the plaintiff, this Court will look not only to the plain meaning of the statute but also to the legislative history of § 1981a (in conjunction with the history of federal intervention in agricultural credit as hereinbefore described) as well as at the regulations promulgated pursuant to the comparable provision of the Rural Housing Act.

1. Language of the Statute

* * *

The government argues that the inclusion in the statute of the phrases "the Secretary may permit ... the deferral of principle and interest," "may forego foreclosure" and the like, unambiguously shows this Court that Congress did not intend to impose that duty on the Secretary as requested by the plaintiffs, but that instead the decision as to how to implement s 1981a was left to his discretion. As support, the government cites cases enunciating the general rule that the word "may" is permissive "and will be construed to vest discretionary power unless the context of its use clearly indicates a purpose to use it in a mandatory sense."

As plaintiffs point out, and as the cases establish, the existence of the word "may" in a statute does not necessarily render the procedural implementation of that statute by the appropriate agency discretionary....

In this case, a reading of the language of § 1981a does not leave this Court with the impression that Congress intended to permit the Secretary to decide whether and what regulations to prescribe in implementing the deferral mechanism. Instead, the Secretary would appear to have discretion only whether to either grant a deferral or forego foreclosure once the eligibility criteria established by the statute have been met, and for what period of time....

[B]efore diving into the murky waters of the legislative history behind the passage of § 1981a, two points concerning the "plain language" of the act should be made. First, the government contends that the regulations implemented pursuant to the FmHA's already existing authority to defer loan payments (i.e., those used pursuant to s 1981(d)) are also sufficient to implement s 1981a. Yet, s 1981a expressly provides that its authority is "(i)n addition to any other authority that the Secretary may have to defer principal and interest." Thus, it is apparent that Congress intended that s 1981(d) (which is discretionary) and s 1981a should operate in different ways. Second, while Congress indicated in s 1981(d) that the FmHA could use these loan servicing devices "as circumstances may require" with insignificant limitations on that discretion (see note 4, supra), in s 1981a Congress has established explicit criteria of eligibility for FmHA borrowers seeking payment deferrals. Thus, it can be again concluded that these two sections were intended to operate differently and that while s 1981(d) is discretionary, s 1981a imposes a mandatory duty on the Secretary to implement it through regulations consistent with its underlying purposes.

2. Legislative History of s 1981a

* * *

The first substantive legislative discussion of the proposed s 1981a meriting consideration by this Court is found in H.R. Rep. No.986, 95th Cong., 2d Sess. (1978), U.S. Code Cong. & Admin. News 1978, p. 1106. After noting that the purpose of proposed § 1981a was to "clarify" the Secretary's authority with respect to moratoriums on loan payments, *id.* at 4, the report discussed the proposal:

> In another amendment to Title I, Mr. Moore proposed that the Secretary should have explicit authority to provide a moratorium on payment of principal and interest and to forego foreclosure on Farmers Home Administration loans, upon a showing by the borrower that due to circumstances beyond his control he was temporarily unable to meet an installment when due without unduly impairing his standard of living. *Comparable language appears in the Housing Act with respect to housing loans by the Farmers Home Administration and was recommended by Mr. Moore in order to clarify the Secretary's authority.* The amendment was accepted by the committee with a change offered by Mr. Moore to provide that this would be in addition to any authority the Secretary may have under existing law, so that the Secretary's authority under current law would not be reduced or impaired by the proposed amendment.

Id. at 27, U.S. Code Cong. & Admin. News 1978, p. 1132 (emphasis added). This language would appear to be ambivalent with respect to a conclusion that s 1981a should be interpreted as imposing a mandatory duty upon the Secretary. However, the reference to "comparable language ... in the Housing Act" indicates a Congressional intent to have the programs implemented in the same manner. It should be noted at this point that the regulations implementing the Housing Act's moratorium provision (42 U.S.C. § 1475)—the same regulations for which the plaintiffs desire to be promulgated for § 1981a—were initially adopted on July 10, 1974 and finalized on October 13, 1977. Thus, in drafting s 1981a Congress knowingly used language "comparable" to that found in s 1475 at a time when the latter section was being implemented pursuant to regulations prescribing the type of eligibility criteria that the plaintiffs desire be promulgated under § 1981a. Congress, therefore, impliedly intendeds 1981a to be implemented in a similar manner.

The government responds to the assertion of comparability on two levels. First, it argues that the language of the two acts, while containing some similarities, is not comparable. Second, the government argues that the rural housing and the farmer loan programs are not comparable and therefore should not be accorded similar treatment. With respect to the latter argument, the government notes that Rural Housing loans are generally one-time personal loans designed to assist the borrower in obtaining shelter and are paid back from an income source not generated by the borrowed funds. Farmer program loans, on the other hand, consist of a series of loans to assist the borrower in purchasing a farm and operating the enterprise. These funds become the investment capital from which the income to pay back the loan is generated. Thus, if a farmer has a bad year or is hurt by "disaster" conditions, there is a ripple effect. Not only does he lose the income to pay back prior loans, but he must borrow a sufficient amount more to generate enough income to pay off the old loans as well as the new loan. If these "disaster" years string together, at some point the farmer will be unable to generate sufficient income to pay off all of the loans. Thus, it is argued, not only does § 1981a give the Secretary greater discretion in implementing the deferral under the Farm Program loans, but it should provide him with greater discretion.

The distinction between the programs is enlightening and points out important differences. However, it does not change the language of sections 1475 and 1981a, nor the fact that Congress knew said language was comparable. Further, the Secretary does have discretion under § 1981a. Once the eligibility criteria are met, the Secretary can control the length of the deferral period and even deny the use of deferral if it is determined that the borrower lacks "clean hands." ... Thus, it is apparent that through § 1981a, Congress is demanding that the FmHA strike a balance between the business nature of the loans and the predominant social welfare nature of the legislation by buying those farmers crippled by circumstances beyond their control a little time to get back on their feet.

With respect to the first argument, despite the government's contentions to the contrary, the language of sections 1475 and 1981a is comparable. The provisions of both sections permit the FmHA borrower to apply for moratorium relief upon request and upon a showing that due to circumstances beyond his control, the borrower is unable to continue making payments without unduly impairing his standard of living. In fact, the obvious similarities between the language used in sections 1981a and 1475 implicates a rule of statutory construction in support of the plaintiffs' position....

The fact that § 1981a contains comparable language to that used in s 1475, when coupled with the rules of statutory construction providing that similar language should be given similar treatment and that legislators are deemed to be aware of the existing law on the subject, strongly supports a conclusion by this Court that Congress intended that FmHA would implement s 1981a pursuant to regulations fashioned after those used to implement § 1475. Thus, H. R. Rep. No. 986 supports the position of the plaintiffs that the FmHA has not been properly implementing the § 1981a deferral mechanism....

4. Conclusion

It is the opinion of this Court, based on the foregoing discussion of the plain language of § 1981a and the legislative history behind its enactment (as well as the use of standard rules of statutory construction), that Congress intended § 1981a to impose a mandatory duty upon the FmHA to implement a deferral program similar in nature to that already in use under the Rural Housing Act, 42 U.S.C. § 1475 ... It is also the opinion of this Court that the FmHA did not comply with this Congressional mandate when it chose to implement s 1981a through the use of already existing regulations on deferral ... Accordingly, the FmHA is hereby enjoined from failing to implement § 1981a through regulations consistent with those in use pursuant to § 1475. The FmHA is further enjoined from foreclosing on farm program mortgages in Georgia created pursuant to 7 U.S.C. § 1921 *et seq.* until such time as those regulations are in full force and effect.

B. Must the FmHA Provide Borrowers with Personal Notice of the Substantive Provisions of s 1981a?

The plaintiffs want this Court to issue an Order requiring the FmHA to give borrowers under the farmers loan program personal notice of their right to apply for deferral relief under s 1981a, and an opportunity to be heard upon such an application. The government asserts that no notice is required by the section (since it is permissive in nature); and that even if notice is required, publication in the Code of Federal Regulations of the availability of deferral relief and the proposed notice regulations for s 1981a provide sufficient notice of that section's provisions.

1. Notice is Required

Due process considerations aside, it is the opinion of this Court that the plain meaning of the statute coupled with the effect of the *Williams v. Butz*, (No. 176-153, S.D.Ga., October 7, 1977) consent order, mandates a finding that personal notice of the § 1981a deferral mechanism is required. The language of the statute expressly provides that the deferral mechanism is triggered "at the *request* of the borrower." Further, no deferral relief will be forthcoming absent "*a showing* by the borrower that due to circumstances beyond the borrower's control, the borrower is temporarily unable to continue making payments of such principal and interest when due without unduly impairing the standard of living of the borrower." 7 U.S.C. § 1981a (emphasis added). Logically, the borrower is unable to request the deferral relief and show his eligibility to receive the same unless he has notice of the contents of s 1981a and an opportunity to be heard.

As mentioned, *Williams v. Butz* is also relevant in deciding whether personal notice of § 1981a is required. In that case, the plaintiffs brought suit for declaratory and injunctive relief to declare unconstitutional all nonjudicial foreclosures of mortgages financed under the Rural Housing Act, and to enjoin all foreclosures where the mortgagee has not had personal notice of the availability of moratorium relief under 42 U.S.C. § 1475 and an opportunity to be heard. Pursuant to the consent decree entered therein, the parties—the defendants are the same in the case at bar—agreed that under the language of § 1475, FmHA borrowers had the right to personal notice of the availability of the moratorium relief. This notice was to consist of "a letter at loan closing explaining moratorium and interest credit and strongly recommending that the borrowers make an appointment with the county supervisor to discuss these matters so that they will understand these provisions," *Williams v. Butz, supra* at 4, and the inclusion of the following paragraph in a letter sent to borrowers guilty of missed payments or other breaches of the loan covenants:

> If you are behind because of something beyond your control, like having less income or unexpected bills, we may be able to help. You may qualify for "Moratorium Relief" which would make it possible for you to miss some payments and still keep your home. Or you may qualify for "Interest Credit" which should make your payments smaller for a while. YOU CANNOT GET "MORATORIUM RELIEF" OR "INTEREST CREDIT" UNLESS YOU APPLY FOR IT. Please contact me immediately and let us see if you qualify or if there is something else we can do to help you keep your home.

Id. The FmHA also agreed to inform applicants during pre-loan approval interviews of the availability of moratorium relief through county office personnel. *Id.*

The *Williams v. Butz* consent order is important to a resolution of this case for two reasons. First and foremost, the FmHA agreed that the language of § 1475, found by this

Court to be comparable to the provisions of § 1981a, required the agency to give FmHA borrowers personal notice of the loan servicing mechanism contained therein. This is contrary to the present position of the FmHA that the language does not mandate giving personal notice. Second, since legislators are "presumed to act with knowledge of existing law on the subject," ... and since Congress knew that in enacting § 1981a it was using "comparable language" to that found in the Rural Housing Act, H.R. Rep. No.986, 95th Cong., 2d Sess. at 27 (1978), it can reasonably be concluded that Congress intended s 1981a also to require that the FmHA provide its farmer program borrowers with personal notice of the provisions of § 1981a....

3. Conclusion

It is the conclusion of this Court that § 1981a imposes a duty on the FmHA to provide borrowers with personal notice of its provisions. This notice will be given through a properly drafted paragraph, fashioned after that in use by the FmHA in implementing the moratorium provision of the Rural Housing Act, placed under a separate heading in a document to be given or sent to the borrower during the process of the loan making, and in a document to be given or sent to delinquent or problem borrowers at the beginning of the production season. Accordingly, the FmHA is enjoined from failing to implement the above notice requirement through appropriately drafted regulations. Further, the FmHA is enjoined from foreclosing on any farmer program loans in Georgia created under 7 U.S.C. §§ 1921 *et seq.* until the beneficiary of that loan has received the appropriate notice....

Notes

1. The holding in *Curry v. Block* was used in Missouri, with the Eighth Circuit Court of Appeals eventually holding that the deferral statute was not permissive, but required agency implementation. *Allison v. Block*, 723 F.2d 631, 635 (8th Cir. 1983). The challenge was then brought in the North Dakota case of *Coleman v. Block*, a national class action case. A moratorium on foreclosures was also ordered. *Coleman v. Block*, 562 F. Supp 1353, 1367 (D. N.D. 1983) (recognizing class and granting preliminary injunction). The *Coleman* litigation went on for years as the attorneys for the plaintiff farmers battled with the FmHA over the form and content of the notice regulations. The litigation was eventually mooted by Congress' passage of the Agricultural Credit Act of 1987, containing explicit provisions for debt restructuring.

2. FmHA remained a separate USDA agency until passage of the Federal Crop Insurance Reform and Department of Agriculture Reorganization Act of 1994, Pub. L. 103-354, 108 Stat. 3178. Under this Act, FmHA was merged with the Agricultural Stabilization and Conservation Service (ASCS), the agency that administered the federal farm programs. The new agency was first called Consolidated Farm Service Agency, but subsequently was renamed as Farm Service Agency (FSA).

3. A Congressional Research Service Report recently described FSA's current role in agricultural finance.

> The USDA Farm Service Agency (FSA) is a lender of last resort because it makes direct farm ownership and operating loans to family-sized farms that are unable to obtain credit elsewhere. FSA also guarantees timely payment of principal and interest on qualified loans made by commercial lenders such as commercial banks

and the FCS. Permanent authority exists in the Consolidated Farm and Rural Development Act (CONACT, 7 U.S.C. 1921 et seq.). FSA makes and guarantees about $3.5 billion of farm loans each year with about $150 million in appropriations for loan subsidies and $330 million for salaries and expenses to administer the program.

Direct loans are limited to $300,000 per borrower; guaranteed loans to $1,094,000 per borrower (adjusted annually for inflation). Direct emergency loans are available for natural or other disasters. Some guaranteed loans have a subsidized interest rate. Part of the FSA loan program is reserved for beginning farmers and ranchers (7 U.S.C. 1994 (b)(2)). For direct loans, 75% of the annual funding for farm ownership loans and 50% of direct operating loans are reserved for the first 11 months of the fiscal year. For guaranteed loans, 40% is reserved for ownership loans and farm operating loans for the first half of the fiscal year. Funds are also targeted to "socially disadvantaged" farmers based on race, gender, and ethnicity (7 U.S.C. 2003).

Jim Monke, *Agricultural Credit: Institutions and Issues*, 2, Congressional Research Service, Rep. No. RS21977 (January 27, 2009).

b. Farm Service Agency Direct Loans

As is evidenced by the *Curry v. Block* case, FSA loan programs are specifically authorized by statute and implemented by regulation. The eligibility criteria for a loan; the approved purposes for which a loan can be obtained; the terms of the loan; and the limitations on loan availability are all specified by statute and further implemented by regulation. Administrative notices further define the parameters of each aspect of the loan. Adverse decisions can be appealed to the National Appeals Division, and after exhausting that process, to federal district court.

Farm ownership loans are available for the purchase or improvement of farm land or fixtures; a special down-payment loan program is available to assist beginning farmers in purchasing farmland; and operating loans are available for farm production expenses. Loan limitation provisions and graduation requirements are in place to focus the program on temporary assistance.

Source of Law and Implementation Guidance

The statutory authority for the FSA Direct Loan programs are set forth according to the loan category. Farm Ownership Loans are authorized by 7 U.S.C. §§ 1922–1925; Operating Loans are authorized by 7 U.S.C. §§ 1941–1943; and Emergency Loans by 7 U.S.C. §§ 1961–1964.

The general program regulations are found at 7 C.F.R. pt. 761 (2010); specific direct loan making regulations are at 7 C.F.R. pt. 764 (2010). Loan servicing regulations are found at 7 C.F.R. pts. 765, 766 (2010).

Information about the FSA loan programs are found on the FSA website at http://www.fsa.usda.gov/FSA/webapp?area=home&subject=fmlp&topic=landing. This information includes a video *The Path to Success* that showcases eight farmers who have worked successfully with the FSA loan program.

Financial distress, loan servicing, and foreclosure defense continue to be areas where FSA direct loan borrowers still need legal advice and attorneys need specific expertise.

The FmHA debt restructuring legislation that ended the *Coleman* litigation and eventually lifted the foreclosure moratorium was part of the Agricultural Credit Act of 1987. Pub. L. No. 100-233, tit. VI, 101 Stat. 1568 (1987), amending the Consolidated Farm and Rural Development Act (CONACT), (codified in scattered sections of title 7 U.S.C.). Although amended over the years, this Act still provides the basic guidelines for the assistance provided to FSA direct loan farm borrowers who experience financial distress. It directs the Secretary of Agriculture to modify the terms of delinquent farmer program loans to the maximum extent possible to effectuate two competing goals.

The first goal is "to avoid losses to the Secretary on such loans," although "priority consideration" should be "placed on writing-down the loan principal and interest…, and debt set-aside…, whenever these procedures would facilitate keeping the borrower on the farm or ranch, or otherwise through the use of primary loan service programs …" 7 U.S.C. § 2001(a)(1).

The second goal is to "ensure that borrowers are able to continue farming or ranching operations." 7 U.S.C. § 2001(a)(2).

Given the documented failure of the agency to implement the deferral program, the statutory requirements imposed by Congress in the FmHA debt restructuring provisions of the Agricultural Credit Act of 1987 were mandatory and detailed. A specific formula is set forth for computing the net recovery value that the government would obtain upon the foreclosure and liquidation of a delinquent loan. Subject to certain basic eligibility criteria, the USDA is directed to offer to restructure a farmer's loan if the borrower can afford to pay an amount that is greater than or equal to what the agency would acquire in foreclosure.

Review the governing statute, 7 U.S.C. § 2001, set forth as follows:

United States Code
Title 7. Agriculture
Chapter 50 — Agricultural Credit
Subchapter IV — Administrative Provisions

§ 2001. Debt restructuring and loan servicing

(a) In general

The Secretary shall modify delinquent farmer program loans made or insured under this chapter, or purchased from the lender or the Federal Deposit Insurance Corporation under section 1929b of this title, to the maximum extent possible

> (1) to avoid losses to the Secretary on such loans, with priority consideration being placed on writing-down the loan principal and interest (subject to subsections (d) and (e) of this section), and debt set-aside (subject to subsection (e) of this section), whenever these procedures would facilitate keeping the borrower on the farm or ranch, or otherwise through the use of primary loan service programs as provided in this section; and

> (2) to ensure that borrowers are able to continue farming or ranching operations.

(b) Eligibility

To be eligible to obtain assistance under subsection (a) of this section

(1) the delinquency must be due to circumstances beyond the control of the borrower, as defined in regulations issued by the Secretary, except that the regulations shall require that, if the value of the assets calculated under subsection (c)(2)(A)(ii) of this section that may be realized through liquidation or other methods would produce enough income to make the delinquent loan current, the borrower shall not be eligible for assistance under subsection (a) of this section;

(2) the borrower must have acted in good faith with the Secretary in connection with the loan as defined in regulations issued by the Secretary;

(3) the borrower must present a preliminary plan to the Secretary that contains reasonable assumptions that demonstrate that the borrower will be able to–

(A) meet the necessary family living and farm operating expenses; and

(B) service all debts, including those of the loans restructured; and

(4) the loan, if restructured, must result in a net recovery to the Federal Government, during the term of the loan as restructured, that would be more than or equal to the net recovery to the Federal Government from an involuntary liquidation or foreclosure on the property securing the loan.

(c) Restructuring determinations

(1) Determination of net recovery

In determining the net recovery from the involuntary liquidation of a loan under this section, the Secretary shall calculate

(A) the recovery value of the collateral securing the loan, in accordance with paragraph (2); and

(B) the value of the restructured loan, in accordance with paragraph (3).

(2) Recovery value

For the purpose of paragraph (1), the recovery value of the collateral securing the loan shall be based on—

(A)(i) the amount of the current appraised value of the interests of the borrower in the property securing the loan; plus

(ii) the value of the interests of the borrower in all other assets that are—

(I) not essential for necessary family living expenses;

(II) not essential to the operation of the farm; and

(III) not exempt from judgment creditors or in a bankruptcy action under Federal or State law; less

(B) the estimated administrative, legal, and other expenses associated with the liquidation and disposition of the loan and collateral, including

(i) the payment of prior liens;

(ii) taxes and assessments, depreciation, management costs, the yearly percentage decrease or increase in the value of the property, and lost interest income, each calculated for the average holding period for the type of property involved;

(iii) resale expenses, such as repairs, commissions, and advertising; and

(iv) other administrative and attorney's costs; plus

(C) the value, as determined by the Secretary, of any property not included in subparagraph (A)(i) if the property is specified in any security agreement with respect to such loan and the Secretary determines that the value of such property should be included for purposes of this section.

(3) Value of the restructured loan

(A) In general

For the purpose of paragraph (1), the value of the restructured loan shall be based on the present value of payments that the borrower would make to the Federal Government if the terms of such loan were modified under any combination of primary loan service programs to ensure that the borrower is able to meet such obligations and continue farming operations.

(B) Present value

For the purpose of calculating the present value referred to in subparagraph (A), the Secretary shall use a discount rate of not more than the current rate on 90-day Treasury bills.

(C) Cash flow margin

For the purpose of assessing under subparagraph (A) the ability of a borrower to meet debt obligations and continue farming operations, the Secretary shall assume that the borrower needs up to 110 percent of the amount indicated for payment of farm operating expenses, debt service obligations, and family living expenses.

(4) Notification

Within 90 days after receipt of a written request for restructuring from the borrower, the Secretary shall

(A) make the calculations specified in paragraphs (2) and (3);

(B) notify the borrower in writing of the results of such calculations; and

(C) provide documentation for the calculations.

(5) Restructuring of loans

If the value of the restructured loan is greater than or equal to the recovery value, the Secretary shall, within 45 days after notifying the borrower of such calculations, offer to restructure the loan obligations of the borrower under this chapter through primary loan service programs that would enable the borrower to meet the obligations (as modified) under the loan and to continue the farming operations of the borrower. If the borrower accepts such offer, within 45 days after receipt of notice of acceptance, the Secretary shall restructure the loan accordingly.

(6) Termination of loan obligations

The obligations of a borrower to the Secretary under a loan shall terminate if—

(A) the borrower satisfies the requirements of paragraphs (1) and (2) of subsection (b) of this section;

(B) the value of the restructured loan is less than the recovery value; and

(C) not later than 90 days after receipt of the notification described in paragraph (4)(B), the borrower pays (or obtains third-party financing to pay) the Secretary an amount equal to the current market value.

(7) Negotiation of appraisal

(A) In general

In making a determination concerning restructuring under this subsection, the Secretary, at the request of the borrower, shall enter into negotiations concerning appraisals required under this subsection with the borrower.

(B) Independent appraisal

If the borrower, based on a separate current appraisal, objects to the decision of the Secretary regarding an appraisal, the borrower and the Secretary shall mutually agree, to the extent practicable, on an independent appraiser who shall conduct another appraisal of the borrower's property. The average of the two appraisals that are closest in value shall become the final appraisal under this paragraph. The borrower and the Secretary shall each pay one-half of the cost of the independent appraisal.

(d) Principal and interest write-down

(1) In general

(A) Priority consideration

In selecting the restructuring alternatives to be used in the case of a borrower who has requested restructuring under this section, the Secretary shall give priority consideration to the use of principal and interest write-down, except that this procedure shall not be given first priority in the case of a borrower unless other creditors of such borrower (other than those creditors who are fully collateralized) representing a substantial portion of the total debt of the borrower held by such creditors, agree to participate in the development of the restructuring plan or agree to participate in a State mediation program.

(B) Failure of creditors to agree

Failure of creditors to agree to participate in the restructuring plan or mediation program shall not preclude the use of principal and interest write-down by the Secretary if the Secretary determines that this restructuring alternative results in the least cost to the Secretary.

(2) Participation of creditors

Before eliminating the option to use debt write-down in the case of a borrower, the Secretary shall make a reasonable effort to contact the creditors of such borrower, either directly or through the borrower, and encourage such creditors to participate with the Secretary in the development of a restructuring plan for the borrower.

(e) Shared appreciation arrangements

(1) In general

As a condition of restructuring a loan in accordance with this section, the borrower of the loan may be required to enter into a shared appreciation arrangement that requires the repayment of amounts written off or set aside.

(2) Terms

Shared appreciation agreements shall have a term not to exceed 10 years, and shall provide for recapture based on the difference between the appraised values of the real security property at the time of restructuring and at the time of recapture.

(3) Percentage of recapture

The amount of the appreciation to be recaptured by the Secretary shall be 75 percent of the appreciation in the value of such real security property if the recapture occurs within 4 years of the restructuring, and 50 percent if the recapture occurs during the remainder of the term of the agreement.

(4) Time of recapture

Recapture shall take place at the end of the term of the agreement, or sooner —

  (A) on the conveyance of the real security property;

  (B) on the repayment of the loans; or

  (C) if the borrower ceases farming operations.

(5) Transfer of title

Transfer of title to the spouse of a borrower on the death of such borrower shall not be treated as a conveyance for the purpose of paragraph (4).

(6) Notice of recapture

Beginning with fiscal year 2000 not later than 12 months before the end of the term of a shared appreciation arrangement, the Secretary shall notify the borrower involved of the provisions of the arrangement.

(7) Financing of recapture payment

  (A) In general

  The Secretary may amortize a recapture payment owed to the Secretary under this subsection.

  (B) Term

  The term of an amortization under this paragraph may not exceed 25 years.

  (C) Interest rate

    (i) In general

    The interest rate applicable to an amortization under this paragraph may not exceed the rate applicable to a loan to reacquire homestead property less 100 basis points.

    (ii) Existing amortizations and loans

    The interest rate applicable to an amortization or loan made by the Secretary before October 28, 2000, to finance a recapture payment owed to the Secretary under this subsection may not exceed the rate applicable to a loan to reacquire homestead property less 100 basis points.

(D) Reamortization

  (i) In general

  The Secretary may modify the amortization of a recapture payment referred to in subparagraph (A) of this paragraph on which a payment has become delinquent by using loan service tools under section 1991(b)(3) of this title if—

    (I) the default is due to circumstances beyond the control of the borrower; and

(II) the borrower acted in good faith (as determined by the Secretary) in attempting to repay the recapture amount.

(ii) Limitations

(I) Term of reamortization

The term of a reamortization under this subparagraph may not exceed 25 years from the date of the original amortization agreement.

(II) No reduction or principal or unpaid interest due

A reamortization of a recapture payment under this subparagraph may not provide for reducing the outstanding principal or unpaid interest due on the recapture payment.

(f) Determination to restructure

If the appeal process results in a determination that a loan is eligible for restructuring, the Secretary shall restructure the loan in the manner consistent with this section, taking into consideration the restructuring recommendations, if any, of the appeals officer.

(g) Prerequisites to foreclosure or liquidation

No foreclosure or other similar actions shall be taken to liquidate any loan determined to be ineligible for restructuring by the Secretary under this section

(1) until the borrower has been given the opportunity to appeal such decision, and

(2) if the borrower appeals, the appeals process has been completed, and a determination has been made that the loan is ineligible for restructuring.

(h) Time limits for restructuring

Once an appeal has been filed under section 1983b of this title, a decision shall be made at each level in the appeals process within 45 days after the receipt of the appeal or request for further review.

(i) Notice of ineligibility for restructuring

(1) In general

A notice of ineligibility for restructuring shall be sent to the borrower by registered or certified mail within 15 days after such determination.

(2) Contents

The notice required under paragraph (1) shall contain

(A) the determination and the reasons for the determination;

(B) the computations used to make the determination, including the calculation of the recovery value of the collateral securing the loan; and

(C) a statement of the right of the borrower to appeal the decision to the appeals division, and to appear before a hearing officer.

(j) Independent appraisals

An appeal filed with the appeals division under section 1983b of this title may include a request by the borrower for an independent appraisal of any property securing the loan.

On such request, the appeals division shall present the borrower with a list of three appraisers approved by the country supervisor, from which the borrower shall select an appraiser to conduct the appraisal, the cost of which shall be borne by the borrower. The results of such appraisal shall be considered in any final determination concerning the loan. A copy of any appraisal made under this paragraph shall be provided to the borrower.

(k) Partial liquidations

If partial liquidations are performed (with the prior consent of the Secretary) as part of loan servicing by a guaranteed lender under this chapter, the Secretary shall not require full liquidation of a delinquent loan in order for the lender to be eligible to receive payment on losses.

(l) Disposition of normal income security

For purposes of subsection (b)(2) of this section, if a borrower—

(1) disposed of normal income security prior to October 14, 1988, without the consent of the Secretary; and

(2) demonstrates that—

(A) the proceeds were utilized to pay essential household and farm operating expenses; and

(B) the borrower would have been entitled to a release of income proceeds by the Secretary if the regulations in effect on November 28, 1990, had been in effect at the time of the disposition,

the Secretary shall not consider the borrower to have acted without good faith to the extent of the disposition.

(m) Only 1 write-down or net recovery buy-out per borrower for a loan made after January 6, 1988

(1) In general

The Secretary may provide for any one borrower not more than 1 write-down or net recovery buy-out under this section with respect to all loans made to the borrower after January 6, 1988.

(2) Special rule

For purposes of paragraph (1), the Secretary shall treat any loan made on or before January 6, 1988, with respect to which a restructuring, write-down, or net recovery buy-out is provided under this section after such date, as a loan made after such date.

(n) Liquidation of assets

The Secretary may not use the authority provided by this section to reduce or terminate any portion of the debt of the borrower that the borrower could pay through the liquidation of assets (or through the payment of the loan value of the assets, if the loan value is greater than the liquidation value) described in subsection (c)(2)(A)(ii) of this section.

(o) Lifetime limitation on debt forgiveness per borrower

The Secretary may provide not more than $300,000 in principal and interest forgiveness under this section per borrower.

Notes

1. An explanation of the debt restructuring process and the actual notices provided to farm borrowers in default is set forth at 7 C.F.R. pt. 766, subpart C, Appendices, B, and C. Note that this debt restructuring process only applies to borrowers with direct loans from FSA. The process does not apply to any other lending situation.

2. Borrowers who cannot restructure an FSA direct loan on their homestead and are facing foreclosure may be eligible to lease their home and up to ten acres of land under the homestead protection program. *See* 7 C.F.R. pt 766, subpart D.

3. The shared appreciation requirement associated with the write-down of real estate debt produced a great deal of controversy when the original ten-year trigger on recapture first began to affect borrowers. Many borrowers alleged that FSA loan officers had assured them that the recapture amount would be written off at the end of the ten year term. Capital improvements to the property were not fairly considered, and a number of confusing changes to the regulations were made. *See* Susan A. Schneider, *Shared Appreciation Agreements: Confusion and Mismanagement Threaten Family Farms*, 7 Drake J. Agric. L. 107 (Spring 2002).

4. Farmers Legal Action Group, Inc. (FLAG), a non-profit law center "dedicated to providing legal services to family farmers and their rural communities in order to help keep farmers on the land," has long been a source for analysis of the FSA loan programs. FLAG attorneys, along with Sarah Vogel, former Commissioner of Agriculture for the State of North Dakota, brought the *Coleman v. Block* case. And, FLAG has published a series of excellent "Farmers' Guides," including the original, Farmers' Guide to FmHA, targeting various FSA loan issues. *See* http://flaginc.org for additional information.

c. Farm Service Agency Guaranteed Loans

Until the early 1970s, USDA's social welfare lending mission for family farmers was met only through its direct loan programs. To supplement the direct loan program, The Rural Development Act of 1972 authorized FmHA to guarantee farm loans made by private commercial lenders.

An early description of the program is still accurate today, although now FSA is the agency responsible.

> The guaranteed loan program is designed to make credit available to family farm owners or operators who are unable to qualify for adequate credit from commercial agricultural lenders without a loan guarantee. Their financial conditions are normally slightly better than FmHA direct loan program eligibility criteria, which stipulate that borrowers must not be able to obtain private financing at reasonable rates and terms. In guaranteeing loans, FmHA agrees to reimburse the lending institution for a specified percentage (up to 90 percent) of any loss—principal. interest, and liquidation costs—it may incur if the borrower defaults on the loan. Lenders may sell loans with guarantees, in whole or in part, to secondary market investors. FmHA insures loans sold to secondary market investors against loss of principal and interest at the original guarantee percentage.

Farmers Home Administration: Implications of the Shift From Direct to Guaranteed Farm Loans, Government Accountability Office, GAO/RCED 89-86 (Sept. 1989).

In 1984, as FmHA's deteriorating direct loan portfolio began to generate negative political sentiments, the agency shifted its emphasis toward guaranteed farm operating and ownership loans as an alternative to direct lending. All subsequent Farm Bills and agricultural appropriations bills have steadily supported this shift in USDA lending.

Guaranteed loans allow the government to leverage federal funds, receiving a program benefit that far exceeds what it could afford with a direct outlay. The government pays nothing up front, but simply promises to pay if and when the borrower defaults. Moreover, all loan making and servicing is done by the commercial lender, reducing government costs and responsibilities.

The USDA Farm Service Agency administers the guaranteed loan program for loans to farmers. Rural development loans for rural businesses, including eligible farm businesses, provide a complementary service that is administered by the USDA Rural Development Agency.

The implementation of any type of guaranteed loan program has always involved a balancing between ensuring fiscal responsibility through careful regulation with encouraging lender participation. In the late 1990s, USDA responded to complaints from commercial lenders that its paperwork burdens for the farm loan program were discouraging lenders from participating. After extensive consultation with commercial banking interests, in February 1999, FSA promulgated new regulations designed to "streamline" FSA's procedures for implementing the guaranteed loan program. In the prefatory comments to the new regulations, the agency predicted:

> By making FSA's guaranteed loan program more consistent with standard practices used within the lending industry, use by lenders will be simplified and they will be more willing to use the program. This will increase the availability of commercial credit for family size farmers.

> FSA currently guarantees repayment on approximately 65,000 farm loans to 40,000 farmers. Each year, FSA receives 15,000 requests for new loans. By reducing the application burden on lenders, and making FSA rules more consistent with industry practices, we expect lenders will increase requests for loan guarantees by 25 percent, or an additional $395 million. This means an additional 3,000 farmers will be able to receive commercial credit. These farmers would otherwise have gone without credit or required assistance through FSA's direct loan programs.

64 Fed. Reg. 7357, 7358 (Feb. 12, 1999). As part of its attempt to streamline the new regulations, the FSA put many of the practical details implementing the Program into an extensive Handbook. In addition, the agreement between the lender and the FSA is specifically defined by the written contract between the lender and the agency. The agency Handbook is available through the FSA website at http://www.fsa.usda.gov/dafl/guaranteed.htm.

i. Eligible Lenders

The FSA regulations divide eligible commercial lenders into three program categories, the Preferred Lender Program (PLP), the Certified Lender Program (CLP), and the Standard Eligible Lenders (SEL). 7 C.F.R. §762.101 (2010). Applications for each category are to be submitted to the FSA State Executive Director in the State where the lender's headquarters are located. The FSA maintains a current list of lenders who express a desire to participate in the guaranteed loan program, and this list is made available to farmers upon request. 7 C.F.R. §762.101(b) (2010).

The FSA describes the PLP as follows:

The Preferred Lender Program, or PLP, is the top status that a lender can hold in the FSA guaranteed loan program. PLP was developed to reward experienced lenders by (1) streamlining and adding flexibility to the loan application and servicing requirements; (2) expediting loan approval and other FSA decisions; and (3) allowing lenders to originate and service guaranteed loans the way they do other loans in their portfolio. Lenders with "Preferred" status have broad authority in making and servicing FSA guaranteed loans and can utilize their own underwriting and servicing policies. Lenders who apply for PLP outline the manner in which they intend to process and service FSA loan guarantees. This "credit management system" becomes the basis for approval decisions on applications they submit.

FSA Guaranteed Loan Program, Lender Types website available at http://www.fsa.usda.gov/FSA/webapp?area=home&subject=fmlp&topic=gfl-lt.

In order for a lender to achieve PLP status, the lender must meet all of the CLP eligibility criteria; and in addition—

- Have guaranteed loan losses—net of recovery—that do not exceed 3 percent;
- Have closed a minimum of 20 FSA guaranteed farm ownership, soil and water, and operating loans/lines of credit in the past 5 years;
- Demonstrate a consistent, above average ability to process and service guaranteed loans; and
- Have an acceptable credit management system (CMS), approved by FSA, for originating and servicing guaranteed loans.

See, 7 C.F.R. § 762.106 (2010) (providing a more detailed explanation of and additional required characteristics).

PLP lenders are afforded several significant administrative advantages. A PLP lender is allowed to use its own standard polices to administer its loans as opposed to adopting mandated FSA standards. Only an application form and loan narrative is required when a PLP applies for an FSA loan guarantee. 7 C.F.R. § 762.110 (2010). And, the regulations provide that FSA must act upon PLP loan requests within 14 calendar days; otherwise, the loan will be approved automatically. 7 C.F.R. § 762.130(a)(2)(ii) (2010). PLP status normally extends for a 5-year period, with renewal available based on a review of the lender's performance. 7 C.F.R. § 762.106 (2010).

The next level of priority for lenders is the CLP. In order to fit within this category, the lender must:

- Provide evidence of being a Standard Eligible Lender.
- Have closed a minimum of 10 FSA guaranteed loans (farm ownership, soil and water, and operating loans/lines of credit); 5 of which must have been closed within the past 2 years.
- Have guaranteed loan losses—net of recovery—that do not exceed 7 percent.
- Demonstrate the capacity to process and service FSA guaranteed operating loans/lines of credit.
- Certify that the person designated to process and service FSA guaranteed loans has attended FSA loan processing and servicing training within the previous 12 months or will attend training within the next 12 months.
- Agree to send to annual training the designated person from each of the lender's offices who is responsible for processing guaranteed loans.

- Agree to use forms acceptable to FSA for processing, analyzing, securing and servicing FSA guaranteed loans/lines of credit. (Lenders should submit copies of financial statements, cash flow plans, loan agreements, analysis sheets, security agreements, and promissory notes with their request for CLP status.)

CLP lenders have the flexibility of using their own forms and many of their own processes with some FSA involvement in administering the guaranteed loans.

See, 7 C.F.R. § 762.106 (2010).

The third category, SEL, refers to lenders with experience making farm loans, but with little or no experience with FSA guaranteed loans. This status is granted for the purpose of allowing these lenders the opportunity to make and service guaranteed loans with a greater degree of FSA supervision. After a lender gains experience with the guaranteed loan program, it can apply for CLP or PLP status. *See*, FSA Guaranteed Loan Program, Lender Types website available at http://www.fsa.usda.gov/FSA/webapp?area=home&subject=fmlp&topic=gfl-lt.

ii. The Obligation of the Government

When a loan is guaranteed by the USDA under the Guaranteed Loan Program, this guarantee "constitutes an obligation supported by the full faith and credit of the United States." The government's obligation to honor the guarantee can only be contested with allegations of "fraud or mismanagement" in which:

(1) The lender or holder had actual knowledge of the fraud or misrepresentation at the time it became the lender or holder, or

(2) The lender or holder participated in or condoned the fraud or misrepresentation.

7 C.F.R. § 762.103 (2010). However, the regulations are clear that in the event of certain "[l]ender violations" the guarantee "cannot be enforced by the lender." *Id.* This may occur "regardless of when the Agency discovers the violation" if the loss on the loan is a result of:

(1) Violation of usury laws;

(2) Negligent servicing;

(3) Failure to obtain the required security; or,

(4) Failure to use loan funds for purposes specifically approved by the Agency.

Id.

In the usual circumstances, the loan guarantee will remain in place until the underlying loan is paid in full; a final loss claim is paid to the holder of the loan; or upon written notice from the lender to the Agency that a guarantee is no longer desired. 7 C.F.R. § 762.101(e) (2010).

The USDA guaranteed loan programs provide significant benefits to the rural and agricultural communities, benefits that could never be achieved through direct lending because of the costs. Administration of the programs, however, have not been without problems. If the guaranteed lender does not treat the borrower fairly, what responsibility does the government have to the borrower?

Given the special mission underlying the FSA loan programs, many farm borrowers assume that FSA has an obligation to ensure that a lender with a FSA guaranteed farm loan offers a borrower some opportunity for assistance if he or she runs into financial difficulty. In general, however, borrowers have been unsuccessful in their attempts to involve FSA in the loan servicing process. FSA has consistently taken the position that it has no obligations whatsoever to the guaranteed loan borrower. FSA views the guaranteed loan transaction as reflecting two independent contracts: a loan agreement between the borrower and the lender, and a guaranteed agreement between FSA and the lender. This position is reflected in the following case. Although some of the regulations have changed since it was decided, the USDA's position regarding its role under the guaranteed loan program remains the same.

Fleet Bank of Maine v. Harriman
721 A.2d 658 (Me. 1998)

Before Wathen, C.j., and Clifford, Rudman, Dana, Alexander, and Calkins, JJ.

Calkins, J.

Gregory and Kathryn Harriman appeal from a judgment of foreclosure entered in favor of Fleet Bank of Maine after a nonjury trial in the Superior Court ... On appeal, the Harrimans contend that Fleet was not entitled to foreclose under the terms of its guaranty contract with the federal government. We affirm the judgment.

The Harrimans are dairy farmers who reside in Troy. In 1990, having sold their previous farm, they sought a loan to finance the purchase of the farm in Troy. They initially requested a direct loan from the Farmer's Home Administration (FmHA), now called the Farm Services Agency (FSA), of the United States Department of Agriculture. FmHA was not making direct loans, so they applied for an FmHA-guaranteed loan from Fleet. Fleet applied to FmHA for a guaranty, and FmHA issued a Conditional Commitment for Guarantee dated June 12, 1990. Attached to that document was Schedule A, which stated, in part:

> The lender agrees that, if liquidation of the account becomes imminent, the lender will consider the borrower for an Interest Rate Buydown under Exhibit D of Subpart B of 7 CFR Part 1980, and request a determination of the borrower's eligibility by FmHA. The Lender may not initiate foreclosure action on the loan until 60 calendar days after a determination has been made with respect to the eligibility of the borrower to participate in the Interest Rate Buydown Program.

Fleet and Gregory Harriman signed the Conditional Commitment for Guarantee on June 15, 1990. On the same day, in consideration of a $155,000 loan from Fleet, the Harrimans executed a promissory note secured by a mortgage on the farm.

The Harrimans stipulated at trial that they defaulted on the note and mortgage by failing both to make required payments and to pay real estate taxes on the property. Apparently no effort was made to investigate the Harrimans' eligibility for the Interest Rate Buydown Program (IRBP). In November 1995 Fleet brought this foreclosure action.

The Harrimans resist foreclosure solely on the grounds that Fleet had not considered them for the IRBP as required by the guaranty contract. They contend that they were parties to the contract. The trial court found, and we agree, that the contract is unambiguous. Its interpretation, therefore, is a question of law.

The Harrimans were not parties to the guaranty contract; it was solely between FmHA and Fleet. We have held that "[t]he undertaking of a guarantor is his own separate and independent contract, distinct from the principal debtor." ... "A guaranty contract is an undertaking collateral to a principal obligation and binds only those who are parties to the guaranty contract itself." At least two federal courts interpreting guaranty contracts for FmHA-guaranteed private loans similar to the one here have concluded that the borrowers were not parties to the guaranty.... In light of these precedents, the language of the guaranty contract in this case, and the very nature of a guaranty contract, the trial court did not err in its conclusion that the Harrimans were not parties to the guaranty.

The Harrimans also argue that they are third-party beneficiaries of the guaranty contract. In determining whether a party is entitled to enforce a contract as a third-party beneficiary we have utilized the definition of "intended beneficiary" in the Restatement:

> (1) Unless otherwise agreed between promisor and promisee, a beneficiary of a promise is an intended beneficiary if recognition of a right to performance in the beneficiary is appropriate to effectuate the intention of the parties and either

> (a) the performance of the promise will satisfy an obligation of the promise to pay money to the beneficiary; or

> (b) the circumstances indicate that the promisee intends to give the beneficiary the benefit of the promised performance.

> (2) An incidental beneficiary is a beneficiary who is not an intended beneficiary.

Restatement (Second) of Contracts § 302 (1981) ...

This means the Harrimans must demonstrate that in order to effectuate the intention of Fleet and FmHA, it is appropriate to recognize that the Harrimans have a right to performance and the circumstances indicate that FmHA, as the promisee, intended to give the Harrimans the benefits of the promised performance. The "promised performance" at issue here is the promise of forebearance by Fleet of foreclosure for a period of 60 days while the eligibility of the Harrimans for the IRBP is determined. The intention of FmHA is ascertained from the written instrument and the circumstances under which it was executed. The Harrimans must show more than that they benefitted from the contract; they must show that FmHA had a "clear and definite" "intent that they receive an enforceable benefit under the contract[ ]." *Id.* We have explained:

> In assessing the relevant circumstances, courts must be careful to distinguish between the consequences to a third party of a contract breach and the intent of a promisee to give a third party who might be affected by that contract breach the right to enforce performance under the contract. If consequences become the focus of the analysis, the distinction between an incidental beneficiary and an intended beneficiary becomes obscured. Instead, the focus must be on the nature of the contract itself to determine if the contract necessarily implies an intent on the part of the promisee to give an enforceable benefit to a third party.

Devine v. Roche Biomedical Labs, 659 A.2d 868, 870 (Me.1995).

The record contains no evidence about the intent of either Fleet or FmHA. Indeed, the federal regulations supply the terms of the guaranty contract.... Neither FmHA nor Fleet could deviate from those terms, and therefore, to an extent, the intention of the parties is substituted by the legislative and regulatory intentions. It was the intention of Congress and the Department of Agriculture to assist family farms by providing incentives to banks to loan money for family farms and by providing mechanisms to assist farmers in meeting those loan obligations. *See* 7 U.S.C.A. § 1998 (1988).

The Harrimans were beneficiaries of the guaranty because it allowed them to get a loan they could not have otherwise obtained. They were also beneficiaries of the foreclosure forebearance condition because they would have benefitted, if only by delaying the inevitable, had Fleet requested from FmHA a determination of their eligibility for the IRBP before commencing foreclosure. There is, however, no indication that either FmHA or Fleet had a "clear and definite" intent to give the Harrimans an enforceable benefit. In fact, had Congress intended to give borrowers a mechanism to enforce the condition it could have given them a cause of action, but it has not done so. The terms of the guaranty prevent FmHA from paying on its guaranty when the forebearance condition is breached by the bank, but it does not "necessarily impl[y] an intent on the part of the promisee to give an enforceable benefit to a third party." A breach by Fleet could give FmHA or its successor a defense to an action by Fleet to enforce the guaranty, but it gives the Harrimans no defense to the foreclosure.

That conclusion is consistent with the holdings of other courts that have found that borrowers are not intended third-party beneficiaries of federally-guaranteed private loans. *See Parker v. United States Dep't of Agric.,* 879 F.2d 1362, 1366 (6th Cir.1989) (FmHA-guaranteed loan); *United States v. Healy,* 923 F.Supp. 1424, 1428–29 (D.Kan.1996) (loan guaranteed by Small Business Administration); *United States v. Martin,* 344 F.Supp. 350, 356 (E.D.Mich.1972) (SBA-guaranteed loan); *Alder v. First Nat'l Bank & Trust,* 241 Neb. 873, 491 N.W.2d 686, 689 (Neb.1992) (SBA-guaranteed loan). In a case interpreting the same Conditional Commitment for Guarantee involved in this case, the Court of Federal Claims came to the opposite conclusion and held that the borrowers were entitled to enforce the conditions in the contract between FmHA and the Bank. *See Schuerman v. United States,* 30 Fed.Cl. 420, 427–433 (1994). To reach that conclusion, the *Schuerman* court abandoned its precedents and held that a third-party beneficiary can enforce performance if the parties intended the contract to benefit him, whether or not they intended to give him an enforceable right to that benefit. [footnote omitted] *See id.* That holding is directly contrary to the legal standard enunciated by this Court … and we decline to adopt it in this case.

Judgment affirmed.

Notes

1. Problems with the guaranteed loan program have been observed with respect to the financing of poultry houses for raising broiler chickens and turkeys under production contracts. These houses can cost several hundred thousand dollars to construct, and this cost is the responsibility of the farmer or "grower." The processing company, the "integrator," will have significant discretion regarding the number of flocks of birds placed with the grower. Some production contracts have literally been "flock to flock," i.e., the grower has no assurance of any income beyond the current birds in his or her control. Yet, the debt incurred for construction of the poultry houses will be secured by a mortgage on the underlying real estate, with long term repayment obligations to perform. Most lenders would not make a loan with this level of risk. FSA, however, has often stepped in to provide either a direct loan or a guaranteed loan for the construction of the poultry houses.

The involvement of the FSA loan program in poultry house construction has caused some to question 1) whether the risk of loss to the taxpayer is too great; 2) whether the government should be encouraging production contracting arrangements that are not financially viable without the guarantee; 3) whether the loan programs are encouraging the industrialization of agricultural production; and, 4) whether the guaranteed loan program is actually encouraging turnover in the industry as existing growers are edged out in favor of new growers with newly constructed poultry houses. The Rural Advancement Fund International, USA stated that in 2009, "Based on USDA data, FSA direct and guaranteed loans for new hog and poultry building construction for FY 2008 and 2009 totaled $264,466,341. *See,* http://www.rafiusa.org/.

In response to the concern about existing growers being displaced, the USDA issued a directive on June 9, 2009, *Guidance for Making and Servicing Direct and Guaranteed*

Loans to Poultry Producers, Notice FLP-540 that tightens the requirements for FSA involvement and questions whether a "flock to flock" contract can be considered a "dependable source of income." The notice encourages contracts that are for a minimum of 3 years. *See* Chapter VII *Livestock Production and Sales, infra* for more information on production contracting.

The specific problems of Hmong farmers who migrated from Minnesota and California to Oklahoma, Arkansas, and Missouri in order to enter into poultry contracts has been well documented. See, Chao Xiong, *Hmong Are Moving Again, This Time to Poultry Farms — Oft-Displaced Laotians Find New Start in Rural South; New Cultural Jolt as Well*, THE WALL STREET JOURNAL (January 26, 2004) (describing the difficult transition experienced and the significant financial investment involved). These farmers, completely new to poultry production, often obtained guaranteed loans to fund their purchase of older poultry houses, some in need of repair and improvement. For a number of these farmers, the projected contract income that they were to receive, even assuming that they were to continue to receive birds, was insufficient to pay the mortgage payments on the property.

> Across Arkansas, Oklahoma and southern Missouri, more than a dozen Hmong poultry farmers — most of them uneducated Vietnam-era refugees with little command of English — have filed for bankruptcy protection this year. Hmong community leaders and advocacy groups estimate that scores of others are in financial trouble.

> All of the farmers in bankruptcy appear to have paid far more for their farms than they were worth and are saddled with large mortgages they cannot repay. Most say they were told to sign loan documents they didn't understand that seemed to greatly overstate the income potential of their farms and understate their expenses....

> All the loans have one feature in common: They are guaranteed by the U.S. Department of Agriculture's Farm Service Agency program to assist minority farmers, which pays off up to 95 percent of each loan if the farmer defaults, thus relieving the banks of nearly all risk.

Howard Witt, *Hmong Poultry Farmers Cry Foul, Sue — Fraud Questions Arise from Loans to Refugees in Ozark Region*, CHICAGO TRIBUNE (May 15, 2006).

In response to criticism, the USDA's position was that under the guaranteed loan program, PLP lenders have almost complete autonomy to determine whether to make a loan. FSA's only role is to determine whether to honor the guarantee if and when there is a loss claim. There is no duty owed to the farm borrower.

2. In some circumstances, the FSA may refuse to honor a loan guarantee, using its authority under the regulations and the contract with the lender. Because the USDA wants to encourage commercial lender participation, however, this authority is not used often. For an example, *see Farmers Bank of Hamburg, Arkansas v. USDA*, 495 F.3d 559 (2007).

3. As reported by the Congressional Research Service:

The 2008 farm bill authorizes the FSA farm loan program at $4.226 billion for each of FY2008–FY2012, including $1.2 billion for direct loans. Actual funding is determined in annual appropriations acts.

In addition, the farm bill:

- Increases lending limits per farmer to $300,000 for direct farm ownership loans and $300,000 for direct operating loans, up from $200,000 each.

- Further prioritizes lending for beginning and socially disadvantaged farmers by increasing the amounts reserved for these groups (see above).

- Extends the term of the beginning farmer down-payment loan program, raises the lending limit, and lowers the interest rate. Adds eligibility for socially disadvantaged farmers.

- Makes permanent and nationwide the guarantee program for seller-financed land loans to beginning and socially disadvantaged farmers.

- Suspends until December 31, 2010, the enforcement of "term limits" on guaranteed loans that require farmers to graduate to commercial lenders.

- Adds eligibility for emergency loans to equine farmers; conferees noted that horses for racing, showing, and recreation should not be eligible.

- Creates a beginning farmer "Individual Development Account" pilot program. Farmers receive up to a 2:1 match, up to $6,000/year.

- Creates direct loans and loan guarantees for conservation projects.

- Extends the right of first refusal to reacquire a homestead property to the family of a socially disadvantaged borrower-owner.

- Adds socially disadvantaged farmers to beginning farmers as preferred groups when the USDA sells or leases property.

Jim Monke, *Agricultural Credit: Institutions and Issues*, 6–7, Congressional Research Service, Rep. No. RS21977 (January 27, 2009).

2. The Farm Credit System

The Farm Credit System (FCS) is a network of financial institutions and related service entities that specialize in providing credit and related services to individuals and businesses involved in agriculture. The overall system is considered to be the first Government Sponsored

Enterprise (GSE)[1] created in the United States.[2] It is characterized by three distinct attributes. First, lenders within the FCS system are federally chartered entities that are not under the control of the usual financial regulators, but rather, are subject to regulation

---

1. A "Government Sponsored Enterprise" is defined as "[a]ny of several enterprises created by Congress to improve credit availability and financial market competition to specific sectors of the economy, including farming and rural areas, housing, and education." Robert N. Collender & Audrae Erickson, *Farm Credit System Safety and Soundness* (USDA, Econ. Res. Serv., Agric. Bull. No. 722, Jan. 1996) at 28 [hereinafter Collender & Erickson]. Other GSEs include those serving housing concerns: the Federal National Mortgage Association (Fannie Mae), the Federal Home Loan Banks, and the Federal Home Loan Mortgage Corporation (Freddie Mac); those serving higher education needs: the Student Loan Marketing Association (Sallie Mae) and the College Construction Loan Insurance Corporation (Connie Lee); and the Federal Agricultural Mortgage Corporation (Farmer Mac) serving agricultural and rural areas.

2. David Freshwater, *Can Continuation of GSE Status for the Farm Credit System be Justified?* 11 J.Pub. Budgeting, Acct. & Fin. Mgmt. 35 (Spring 1999).

by the Farm Credit Administration, an independent federal agency. Second, it is organized as a borrower-cooperative. The FCS institutions are not owned or managed by either the federal government or private investors—they are owned on a cooperative basis by the member-borrowers. Third, as a creation of Congress, FCS lenders must operate exclusively within the confines of the lending authority granted to them by statute.

This chapter is divided into three components. First, it considers the history and purpose of the Farm Credit System. Second, it provides information regarding the current structure of the Farm Credit System. Third, FCS borrowers' rights are discussed.

a. The History and Purpose of the Farm Credit System

Christopher R. Kelley and Barbara J. Hoekstra
A Guide to Borrower Litigation Against the Farm Credit System and the Rights of Farm Credit System Borrowers
66 N.D. L. Rev. 127, 131-13 (1990)

The objective of the Farm Credit System has been defined as the satisfaction of " ... the peculiar credit needs of American farmers and ranchers while encouraging those farmers and ranchers to participate through management, control, and ownership of the system."[9] The Congressional expression of the policy and objectives of the Farm Credit System is as follows:

> (a) It is declared to be the policy of the Congress, recognizing that a prosperous, productive agriculture is essential to a free nation and recognizing the growing need for credit in rural areas, that the farmer-owned cooperative Farm Credit System be designed to accomplish the objective of improving the income by furnishing sound, adequate, and constructive credit and closely related services to them, their cooperatives, and to selected farm-related businesses necessary for efficient farm operations.

> (b) It is the objective of this chapter to continue to encourage farmer- and rancher-borrowers participation in the management, control, and ownership of a permanent system of credit for agriculture which will be responsive to the credit needs of all types of agricultural producers having a basis for credit, and to modernize and improve the authorizations and means for furnishing such credit and credit for housing in rural areas made available through the institutions constituting the Farm Credit System as herein provided.

> (c) It is declared to be the policy of Congress that the credit needs of farmers, ranchers, and their cooperatives are best served if the institutions of the Farm Credit System provide equitable and competitive interest rates to eligible borrowers, taking into consideration the creditworthiness and access to alternative sources of credit for borrowers, the cost of funds, including any costs of defeasance under section 4.8(b), the operating costs of the institution, including the costs of any loan loss amortization under section 5.19(b), the cost of servicing loans, the need to retain earnings to protect borrowers' stock, and the volume of net new borrowing. Further, it is declared to be the policy of Congress that Farm Credit System institutions take action in accordance with the Farm Credit Act Amend-

---

9. Daley v. Farm Credit Admin., 454 F. Supp. 953, 954 (D. Minn. 1978).

ments of 1986 in such manner that borrowers from the institutions derive the greatest benefit practicable from the Act: Provided, That in no case is any borrower to be charged a rate of interest that is below competitive market rates for similar loans made by private lenders to borrowers of equivalent creditworthiness and access to alternative credit.[10]

The policy and objectives assigned to the Farm Credit System reflect that the System was created as a result of a need by farmers for "dependable sources of adequate credit, on terms suited to the particular needs of agriculture, from lenders who understood their problems."[11] ...

B. The Federal Land Banks (FLB)

Congress, in 1916, enacted the Federal Farm Loan Act of 1916[19] authorizing the establishment of federal land banks for the purpose of making long-term loans secured by real estate.[20] Each federal land bank was initially capitalized by federal government subscription of the institution's stock, and supervision of the banks was placed in a five-member Federal Farm Loan Board serving under the Treasury Department.[21] However, the Act provided that the government owned stock was to be eventually retired through farmer-borrower purchases so that the federal loan banks would eventually be solely owned by farmers.[22] Since 1947, the federal land banks have been completely farmer owned.[23]

Pursuant to the Farm Loan Act of 1916, the Federal Farm Loan Board created twelve federal land bank districts.[24] In addition, national farm loan associations, later renamed federal land bank associations, were established to act as agents for the regional federal land bank associations.[25] Farmer-borrower purchases of stock in local federal land bank associations which, in turn, purchased stock in the federal land banks, ultimately achieved farmer ownership of both entities.[26]

C. The Federal Intermediate Credit Banks (FICB)

In 1923, pursuant to the Agricultural Credit Acts,[27] the federal intermediate credit banks were created to discount the notes of other lenders made for short or intermediate term farm

---

10. 12 U.S.C.A. § 2001 (West 1989).

11. W. HOAG, THE FARM CREDIT SYSTEM: A HISTORY OF FINANCIAL SELF-HELP 1 (1976) [herinafter HOAG]. *See also* McGowan & Noles, *The Cooperative Farm Credit System,* 4 MERCER L. REV. 263, 263 (1953) [hereinafter McGowan & Noles] ("[The System] is a complete, dependable and permanent system for the furnishing to farmers on a cooperative basis of various types of sound agricultural credits at reasonable rates of interest and costs."). *See generally* 11 N. HARL, AGRICULTURAL LAW, ch. 100 (1986) (describing the purposes of the System); 2 J. DAVIDSON, AGRICULTURAL LAW, ch. 10 (1981) (same); K. MEYER, D. PEDERSON, N. THORSON & J. DAVIDSON, AGRICULTURAL LAW: CASES AND MATERIALS, 269–74 (1985) (same); J. JUERGENSMEYER & J. WADLEY, AGRICULTURAL LAW § 14.3 (1982)(same).

19. Pub. L. No. 64-158, ch. 245, 39 Stat. 360 (1916)(repealed 1923).

20. *Id.* at 362–63.

21. *Id.* at 360–63.

22. *Id.* at 364–65.

23. Hoag, *supra* note 11, at 254.

24. *Id.* at 214.... *See also* 12 U.S.C.A. §§ 2002(b), 2252(a)(West 1989) (providing that there shall not be more than twelve farm credit districts and authorizing the merger of districts).

25. *Id.* at 216.

26. Brake, [*A Perspective On Federal Involvement In Agricultural Credit Programs,* 19 S.D.L. REV. 567, 570–72 (1974)]; HOAG, *supra* note 11, at 213–17.

27. Pub. L. No. 67-503, ch. 252, 42 Stat. 1454 (1923) (repealed 1933).

loans.[28] Although initially capitalized by the federal government in a manner similar to the capitalization of the federal land banks, the federal intermediate credit banks did not make direct loans to farmers as did the federal land banks.[29] Rather, the initial function of the federal intermediate credit banks was to purchase notes made by other lenders.[30]

D. The Production Credit Associations (PCA)

Because existing lenders did not make substantial use of the federal intermediate credit banks, regional production credit corporations were authorized in 1933.[31] The Farm Credit Act of 1933[32] created twelve regional production credit corporations, twelve regional banks for cooperatives, and the Central Bank for Cooperatives.[33] The banks for cooperatives were established to make loans to farmer cooperatives.[34]

The Farm Credit Act of 1933 also authorized the establishment of local production credit associations modeled after the federal land bank associations.[35] However, unlike federal land bank associations, the production credit associations were not merely agents of the regional production credit corporations.[36] Rather, they made direct loans that were discounted by the regional corporations.[37] Later, in 1956, the federal intermediate credit banks assumed the discounting function for production credit associations, and the assets of the twelve regional production credit corporations were transferred to the federal intermediate credit banks.[38]

E. The Farm Credit Administration and the Department of Agriculture

The Farm Credit Act of 1933 created the Farm Credit Administration to coordinate all federal lending activities.[39] For the first six years of its existence, the Farm Credit Administration operated as an independent agency of the executive branch.[40] However, in 1939, an executive order placed the agency in the Department of Agriculture.[41] The Farm

---

28. *Id.* at 1455–56.

29. HOAG, *supra* note 11, at 25. The Federal Intermediate Credit Banks stopped using government capital in 1956. *Id.*

30. Brake, supra note [26], at 572; HOAG, *supra* note 11, at 231–43.

31. HOAG, *supra* note 11, at 237.

32. Pub. L. No. 73-75, 48 Stat. 257 (1933)(repealed 1953).

33. *Id.* at 257–64.

34. *See* Brake, *supra* note [26], at 572–73; HOAG, *supra* note 11, at 231–43.

35. Farm Credit Act of 1933, Pub. L. No. 73-76, 48 Stat. 257, 259 (1933) (repealed 1953).

36. HOAG, *supra* note 11, at 46–48.

37. *Id.* at 50–53.

38. Brake, *supra* note [26], at 569. For a detailed account of the early history of the Farm Credit System, see McGowan & Noles, *supra* note 11.

39. Farm Credit Act of 1933, Pub. L. No. 73-76, 48 Stat. 257, 262–64 (1933) (repealed 1953). *See also,* HOAG, *supra* note 11, at 233, 234 (discussing the Farm Credit Act of 1933). The functions and powers transferred to the Farm Credit Administration included the following: the Federal Land Bank, National Farm Association and Federal Intermediate Credit Bank supervision from the Federal Farm Loan Board in the Treasury Department; loans to cooperatives from Agricultural Marketing Revolving Fund from the Federal Farm Board; Regional Agricultural Credit Corporations supervision from the Reconstruction Finance Corporation; Crop Production and Seed Loan Offices supervision from the Secretary of Agriculture; and the Fund for Investments in Stock of Agricultural Credit Corporations from the Secretary of Agriculture. *Id.* at 234.

40. HOAG, *supra* note 11, at 233.

41. Reorganization Plan No. 1 of 1939, 53 Stat. 1423, 1429 (April 25, 1939) (repealed 1953).

Credit Administration remained within the Department of Agriculture until the Farm Credit Act of 1953[42] re-established its independent status.[43]

F. Decentralization of the System — The Farm Credit Act of 1953

Not only did the Farm Credit Act of 1953 re-establish the independent status of the Farm Credit Administration, it redefined and redirected the Farm Credit System, moving it toward decentralization, farmer ownership and control, and cooperative development.[44] The 1953 Act created the Federal Farm Credit Board as the policy making body of the Farm Credit Administration.[45] In addition, the Farm Credit Administration, with its Governor responsible to the Board rather than the President, was accorded supervisory authority over the regional banks, the federal land banks hereinafter FLBs and federal intermediate credit banks hereinafter FICBs, and their local associations, the federal land bank associations hereinafter FLBAs, and production credit associations hereinafter PCAs respectively.[46] Farmer participation and control was increased by giving farmer members the authority to elect six of the seven members on each of the twelve district farm credit boards.[47] Also, recommendations were sought for retiring all of the remaining government capital in the system.[48] Further, the impetus of the Farm Credit Act of 1953 contributed to the repayment of all government capital in the Farm Credit System by the end of 1968.[49]

G. The Modern System — The Farm Credit Act of 1971

The Farm Credit Act of 1971[50] continued the trend toward decentralization by authorizing that more decisions be made at local district levels.[51] To implement decentralization, lending authority was expanded in three areas by the authorization of the following: long term mortgage loans for rural housing;[52] loans to persons furnishing custom ser-

---

42. Pub. L. No. 83-202, 67 Stat. 390 (1953) (repealed 1971).

43. *Id.* at 390–94.

44. *See generally* HOAG, *supra* note 11, at 231–43 (identifying and describing the broad themes of the Farm Credit Act of 1953).

45. Farm Credit Act of 1953, Pub. L. No. 83-202, 67 Stat. 390 (1953) (repealed 1971).

46. HOAG, *supra* note 11, at 257–58. The restoration of the Farm Credit Administration to the status of an independent agency after fourteen years as an agency within the United States Department of Agriculture was primarily motivated by a desire to insulate it from political influence. *Id.*

47. *Id.* at 121.

48. *Id.* at 259.

49. Brake, *supra* note 18, at 574–76; HOAG, *supra* note 11, at 257–61.

50. Pub. L. No. 92-181, 85 Stat. 583 (1971) (codified as amended at 12 U.S.C.A. §§ 2001–2279aa-14 (West 1989 & Supp. 1990).

51. *Id.* at 584–86 (FLBs), 590–97 (FICBs). *See generally* Kayl, [*Farm Credit Amendments Act of 1985: Congressional Intent, FCA Implementation, and Courts' Interpretation (And the Effect of Subsequent Legislation on the 1985 Act)*, 37 DRAKE L.REV. 271, 275–77 (1987–88)] (discussing the major features of the Farm Credit Act of 1971).

52. 12 U.S.C.A. §§ 2014, 2018 (West 1980). In amending the Farm Credit Act of 1971, the Agricultural Credit Act of 1987, Pub. L. No. 100-233, 101 Stat. 1568, 1572–1662 (1988), restructured the system. The previously separate FLBs and FICBs were required to merge into district farm credit banks. Although FLBAs and PCAs were permitted, with limited exceptions, to remain separate, the 1987 Act also allowed FLBAs and PCAs to merge as agricultural credit associations. *See infra* notes 125–27 and the accompanying text. However, the authority of the farm credit banks and the PCAs to make loans for rural housing was retained. 12 U.S.C.A. §§ 2019(b), 2075(b) (West 1989). See also 12 C.F.R. § 613.3040 (1990) (rural resident loan program); 55 Fed. Reg. 24,861, 24,878 (1990) (to be codified at 12 C.F.R. § 613.3040) (same). A FLBA can also make direct loans for rural housing if that author-

vices to farmers;[53] and financial services to farmers including financial management, record keeping, and estate planning.[54]

1. FLBs and FLBAs

After the Farm Credit Act of 1971, the Farm Credit System was entirely farmer owned for the last government subscription had been retired in 1968.[55] Long-term mortgage credit was provided through the FLBs and the FLBAs.[56] Although each FLB and each FLBA were separate corporations, each FLBA owned a portion of the stock of the regional FLB.[57] Farmers who sought FLB funds made application through their local FLBA.[58]

The farmer borrower of FLB funds was required to purchase capital stock in the FLBA in an amount at least equal to five percent of the face value of his loan.[59] With the purchase of stock, the borrower became a voting member of the FLBA, and the FLBA purchased a like amount of stock in the regional FLB.[60] Each stockholder was

---

ity has been delegated to it by the district farm credit bank. *See* 12 U.S.C.A. § 2013(18) (West 1989); 55 Fed. Reg. 24,861, 24,881 (1990) (to be codified at 12 C.F.R. 614.4030(a)(3)).

53. 12 U.S.C.A. § 2016 (West 1980). As with the authority to make housing loans to rural residents, the authority to make loans for persons furnishing custom services to farmers has been retained under the current amended version of the Farm Credit Act of 1971. 12 U.S.C.A. §§ 2019(c), 2075(a)(3) (West 1989). *See also* 12 C.F.R. § 613.3050 (1990) (farm-related businesses); 55 Fed. Reg. 24,861, 24,878 (1990) (to be codified at 12 C.F.R. § 613.3050) (same).

54. 12 U.S.C.A. §§ 2019, 2076 (West 1980). Under the current version of the Farm Credit Act of 1971, "technical assistance" may be provided by System lenders to their borrowers. 12 U.S.C.A. §§ 2020(a), 2076 (West 1989). *See also* 12 C.F.R. § 618.8000 (1990) (technical assistance); 55 Fed. Reg. 24,861, 24,888 (1990) (revising the authority for 12 C.F.R. § 618).

55. *See supra* note 49 and the accompanying text.

56. 12 U.S.C.A. § 2093 (West 1980). Currently, as a result of the Agricultural Credit Act of 1987, the authority formerly possessed by FLBs is held by the district farm credit banks (FCBs). 12 U.S.C.A. § 2015(a) (West 1989). *See also* 55 Fed. Reg. 24,861, 24,800 (1990) (to be codified at 12 C.F.R. § 614.4000) (long-term real estate lending authority of farm credit banks). Lending for long-term real estate purposes is still provided through a FLBA unless there is not an active association in the lending area. 12 U.S.C.A. § 2021(a)-(b) (West 1989). *See also* 55 Fed. Reg. 24,861, 24,881 (1990) (to be codified at 12 C.F.R. § 614.4030) (long-term real estate lending authority of federal land credit associations). However, a farm credit bank may delegate its direct lending authority to an association. 12 U.S.C.A. § 2013(18) (West 1989). When direct lending authority for long-term real estate loans is transferred to a FLBA, the association is referred to as a "federal land credit association." 55 Fed. Reg. 24,861, 24,889 (1990) (to be codified at 12 C.F.R. § 519.9155). *See also infra* notes 119–27 and the accompanying text (discussing the changes in lending authority occasioned by the 1987 Act).

57. 12 U.S.C.A. § 2093 (West 1980). Under the current version of the Farm Credit Act of 1971, FLBAs still subscribe to the stock of their respective farm credit bank. 12 U.S.C.A. § 2093(10) (West 1989).

58. 12 U.S.C.A. § 2020 (West 1980). Currently, borrowers seeking long-term loans for real estate purposes still apply for those funds through a FLBA if there is an association serving the prospective borrower's area. To obtain the funds, the prospective borrower must purchase stock in the association. 12 U.S.C.A. § 2017 (West 1989). If there is not an association serving the prospective borrower's area, the loan may be obtained directly from the district farm credit bank, and stock must be purchased in the district farm credit bank. 12 U.S.C.A. § 2021(b), (c) (West 1989).

59. 12 U.S.C.A. § 2034(a) (West 1980). For a discussion of current requirements regarding the amount of stock that must be purchased, see infra notes 131 and 132 and the accompanying text. *See also In re* Massengill, 100 Bankr. 276, 278 & n. 1 (E.D. N.C. 1988) (describing in detail the stock purchase requirements under the Farm Credit Act of 1971 prior to its amendment by the Agricultural Credit Act of 1987).

60. 12 U.S.C.A. § 2034 (West 1980). The voting shareholders of each FLBA continue to elect the association's board of directors. 12 U.S.C.A. § 2092 (West 1989). *See also supra* note 58 (discussing the current requirements for the purchase of stock). Under current law, when a FLBA has merged with

entitled to only one vote.[61] Further, the FLB and FLBA held a first lien on the borrower's stock.[62]

The primary source of FLB funds was derived from the sale of consolidated federal land bank bonds which were joint obligations of the twelve district FLBs.[63] However, the United States bears no liability on the bonds.[64]

2. FICBs and PCAs

PCAs under the Farm Credit Act of 1971 made short and intermediate term loans that were, in turn, discounted by the regional FICBs.[65] The capital stock of the FICBs was owned by PCAs.[66] The FICBs obtained funds through the sale of consolidated debentures.[67] As was required of FLBA and FLB borrowers, PCA borrowers also were required to purchase stock in an amount equal to at least five percent of the face value of the loan.[68]

3. Board of Directors

Each PCA and FLBA had a board of directors elected by its members.[69] Similarly, each of the twelve farm credit districts had a board of directors consisting of seven

---

a PCA, the stock purchased would be that of the agricultural credit association formed as a result of that merger. *See infra* notes 125–27 and the accompanying text.

61. *Id.* The one vote principle still applies. Thus, irrespective of the number of shares owned, a shareholder in a System institution has only one vote. *See* 12 C.F.R. § 615.5230(a)(1)(i) (1990).

62. 12 U.S.C.A. § 2054 (West 1980). Under the current law, FLBAs continue to be entitled to a first lien on borrower's stock and participation certificates issued by the association. 12 U.S.C.A. § 2097 (West 1989).

63. 12 U.S.C.A. § 2155 (West 1980). See also 12 U.S.C.A. §§ 2153, 2155 (West 1989) (the System continues to issue notes, bonds, debentures, and other obligations for which each bank in the System is jointly liable).

64. 12 U.S.C.A. § 2155(c) (West 1989). For an extensive and highly critical study of the Farm Credit System's funding of loans with long-term, non-callable, fixed rate bonds during the early 1980's, *see* General Accounting Office, Pub. No. GGD-86-150 Br, *Farm Credit System: Analysis of Financial Condition* (1986). *See also* Barry, *Financial Stress For the Farm Credit Banks: Impacts On Future Loan Rates For Borrowers*, 46 AGRIC. FINANCE REV. 27 (1986) (discussing the effect on loan rates resulting from the financial distress experienced by the System in the mid-1980s).

65. 12 U.S.C.A. §§ 2096, 2072(6) (West 1980). Under the Farm Credit Act of 1971, as currently amended, PCAs largely retain the same status and function that they assumed under the 1971 Act. PCAs continue to extend short- and intermediate-term credit. 12 U.S.C.A. § 2075(a) (West 1989). However, the functions formerly performed by FICBs are now the responsibility of the district farm credit banks. Those functions include the discounting of PCA loans. 12 U.S.C.A. § 2015(b)(A) (West 1989). See also infra notes 119–27 and the accompanying text (discussing the lending authority of System lenders under the Agricultural Credit Act of 1987).

66. 12 U.S.C.A. § 2073 (West 1980). Currently, PCAs continue to subscribe to stock in the "upstream" bank. However, that bank is now the district farm credit bank rather than the district FICB. 12 U.S.C.A. § 2073(7) (West 1989).

67. 12 U.S.C.A. § 2094 (West 1980). As a result of the Agricultural Credit Act of 1987, the successors to the district FICBs, the farm credit banks, are responsible for obtaining funds through the sale of obligations for which all of the System banks are liable. 12 U.S.C.A. §§ 2013(10), 2153, 2155(a) (West 1989).

68. 12 U.S.C.A. § 2094 (West 1980). Currently, prospective borrowers still must purchase stock in the PCA making the loan. 12 U.S.C.A. § 2017 (West 1989). For a discussion of the current requirements regarding the amount of stock that must be purchased, *see infra* notes 131–32 and the accompanying text.

69. 12 U.S.C.A. §§ 2092, 2032 (West 1980). Under the current law, each PCA's shareholders continue to elect the PCA's board of directors. 12 U.S.C.A. § 2072 (West 1989).

members.[70] Prior to the enactment of the Farm Credit Amendments Act of 1985,[71] one director was appointed by the Governor of the Farm Credit Administration and the remaining six were elected by the district's FLBAs, PCAs, and borrowers from the bank of cooperatives, with each of the three System institutions electing two directors.[72] Under the 1985 Act, the seventh member of the district board was elected by the "borrowers at large in a district," a phrase defined as follows:

(i) a voting shareholder of a Federal land bank association and a direct borrower, and a borrower through an agency, from a Federal land bank;

(ii) a voting shareholder of a production credit association; and

(iii) a voting shareholder or subscriber to the guaranty fund of a bank for cooperatives.[73]

H. The Farm Credit Amendments of 1985

The Farm Credit Amendments Act of 1985[74] also made structural changes in levels above the district board of directors. Prior to the 1985 Act, the Federal Farm Credit Board was a part-time board consisting of thirteen members, one nominated by each of the twelve districts and appointed by the President and one appointed by the Secretary of Agriculture as his representative.[75] The 1985 Act renamed the board the Farm Credit Administration Board and reduced its membership to three full-time members.[76] The three members are appointed by the President with the advice and consent of the Senate.[77]

The shift in the responsibilities of the Farm Credit Administration was a second major structural change caused by the 1985 Act.[78] Under prior law, the Farm Credit Administration directly participated in the supervision and management of the System.[79] Under the 1985 Act, the Farm Credit Administration assumed the function of an independent regulatory agency.[80] The enumerated powers of the Farm Credit Administration included

---

70. 12 U.S.C.A. § 2222 (1980). Currently, the number of directors serving on the board of directors of the district farm credit banks is dictated by the respective bank's bylaws. See 12 U.S.C.A. § 2012 (West 1989). *See also* 12 C.F.R. §§ 611.310–611.340 (1990) (relating to the election of bank and association directors).

71. *See infra* notes 74–92 and the accompanying text.

72. 12 U.S.C.A. § 2223 (West 1980) (repealed 1988).

73. 12 U.S.C.A. § 2223(a) (West Supp. 1986) (repealed 1988). Currently, the only statutory requirement concerning the qualification of a director is that "at least one member shall be elected by the other directors, which member shall not be a director, officer, employee, or stockholder of a System institution." 12 U.S.C.A. § 2012 (West 1989). A concise description of the System as it existed under the 1971 Act is found in Rosantrater, *Farm Credit: An Overview*, 15 Colo. Law. 1594 (1981).

74. Pub. L. No. 99-205, 99 Stat. 1678 (1985) (codified as amended in scattered sections of 12 U.S.C.A. (West 1989 & Supp. 1990)).

75. 12 U.S.C.A. § 2242 (West 1980).

76. 12 U.S.C.A. § 2242 (West 1989).

77. *Id.*

78. The significance of this change and its consequences are analyzed in Kayl, *supra* note 6, at 279–94, and Dewey, *supra* note 6, at 287–89.

79. *See* Dewey, [*The Farm Credit System*, 36 Fed. B. News & J. 287 (1987), at 287 (describing the selection process for the former, part-time, Federal Farm Credit Board, a process in which twelve of the thirteen members were nominated by the twelve farm credit districts, as a "process in which directors could place allegiances to their individual district's interests above their responsibilities to the federal regulatory body"). *See also* Kayl, *supra* note [51], at 288 ("the situation was the classic 'tail wagging the dog' wherein the FCA was intimidated by the FCS members").

80. See 12 U.S.C.A. §§ 2243, 2252 (West 1989) (setting forth the authority of the FCA board and the powers and duties of the FCA). See also Dewey, *supra* note 6, at 287–88 ("The 1985 Amendments recognized the wisdom in establishing the FCA as a non-captive agency which could carry out its governmental functions free of institutions' influence."); Kayl, *supra* note 6, at 286 ("Stronger indepen-

the power to modify the boundaries of farm credit districts, approve the merger of districts, and promulgate regulations.[81] In addition, the Farm Credit Administration was directed to examine System institutions in the same manner as followed by examiners under the National Bank Act, the Federal Reserve Act, and the Federal Deposit Insurance Act.[82] Further, the Farm Credit Administration was given broad enforcement powers under the 1985 amendments including the authority to issue cease and desist orders[83] and to suspend or remove System institution directors and officers.[84] Finally, the chairman of the Farm Credit Administration Board also serves as the chief executive officer of the Farm Credit Administration under the 1985 Act.[85]

The Farm Credit Amendments Act of 1985 also centralized the power to raise and distribute funds within the System.[86] The Act created the Farm Credit System Capital Corporation which, in turn, was granted the authority to require all of the System institutions to purchase its stock, to pay assessments to it, and to contribute to its capital.[87] The purposes of the Capital Corporation included the following functions:

1. provide financial assistance to System institutions;

2. acquire from and participate with other System institutions the nonperforming assets of those institutions;

3. "hold, restructure, collect, and otherwise administer nonperforming assets required from or participated in with other Farm Credit System institutions, and guarantee performing and nonperforming assets held by other Farm Credit institutions"; and

4. provide technical and other services to other System institutions relating to their loan portfolios.[88]

Probably the most controversial of the powers accorded to the Capital Corporation was the authority to draw funds from stronger districts to buttress weaker ones.[89] The Corporation's attempts to exercise that authority spawned numerous lawsuits initiated by district banks and local associations.[90]

The Farm Credit Amendments Act of 1985 also gave the Secretary of the Treasury the authority to provide financial assistance to the system on a "certification ... [of] need" by

---

dent regulation is an euphemism for greater control of the FCS by the FCA."); Bailey v. Federal Intermediate Credit Bank, 788 F.2d 498, 499 n. 3 (8th Cir. 1986) ("the concern of Congress was with decreasing the FCA's day-to-day involvement and increasing its role as an 'arm's length' regulator of the farm credit system" (citations omitted)), cert. denied, 479 U.S. 915 (1986); In re HOAG Ranches, 846 F.2d 1225, 1229 (9th Cir. 1988) ("The role of the Farm Credit Administration has been changed from supervisor to arms-length regulator").

    81. 12 U.S.C.A. § 2252(a)(1), (2), (9) (West 1989).
    82. 12 U.S.C.A. § 2254(a) (West 1989).
    83. 12 U.S.C.A. §§ 2261–63 (West 1989).
    84. 12 U.S.C.A. §§ 2264–74 (West 1989).
    85. 12 U.S.C.A. § 2244 (West 1989).
    86. One of the goals of the 1985 amendments was to "[g]ive the Farm Credit System broader authority to use its own resources to shore up weak system units". Kayl, *supra* note [51], at 285 (citing H.R. REP. NO. 425, 99th Cong., 1st Sess, reprinted in 1985 U.S. Code Cong. & Admin. News 2587).
    87. 12 U.S.C.A. §§ 2216–16k, 2152 (West Supp. 1986) (repealed 1988).
    88. 12 U.S.C.A. § 2216 (West Supp. 1986) (repealed 1988).
    89. 12 U.S.C.A. § 2216(f)(a)(14) (West Supp. 1986) (repealed 1988).
    90. *E.g.,* Federal Land Bank of Springfield v. Farm Credit Admin., 676 F. Supp. 1239 (D. Mass. 1987); Sikeston Production Credit Ass'n v. Farm Credit Admin., 647 F. Supp. 1155 (E.D. Mo. 1986). For general discussions of the issues presented in the litigation, see Webster, *Joined in Battle: Who Will Control the Farm Credit System?* AGRIFINANCE, March 1987, at 6; Taylor, *Big Trouble at Farm Credit,* FARM J., Nov. 1986, at 20; Kayl, *supra* note [51], at 289–305 (citing additional cases).

the Farm Credit System.[91] Finally, as will be discussed in greater detail later in this article, the 1985 Act granted to System borrowers certain rights not previously afforded to them.[92]

I. The Farm Credit Act Amendments of 1986

The mid-1980s saw continuing deterioration in the financial condition of the Farm Credit System.[93] The Congressional response, contained in the Farm Credit Act Amendments of 1986,[94] was to partially decentralize authority by giving district banks the power to set interest rates and to implement new "regulatory accounting practices" (RAP) that, among other things, allowed System institutions to amortize for up to twenty years the additions to their loss reserves.[95]

---

91. 12 U.S.C.A. § 2216 (West Supp. 1986). A good, but brief, discussion on the structural changes mandated by the 1985 Act is contained in *Note, The Congressional Response To A Crisis In Agricultural Credit: The 1985 Farm Credit Amendments*, 31 S.D.L. Rev. 471 (1986). *See also* Duncan, *Farm Credit System—Current Matters*, 38 Ala. L. Rev. 537, 539 (1987) (discussing the 1985 Act); Kayl, *supra* note [51] at 279–305 (same). *See generally* General Accounting Office, Pub. No. RCED-86-126BR, *Farm Finance: Farm Debt, Government Payments, and Options to Relieve Financial Stress* (1986) (discussing the agricultural economy at the time of the 1985 Act and the options available to improve that economy).

92. 12 U.S.C.A. § 2199(a) (disclosure of interest rates), 2199(b) (forbearance), 2200 (access to loan documents and other information), 2201 (prompt action on loan applications), 2202 (reconsideration of action on loan applications)(West Supp. 1986)(some of the borrower rights currently found in sections 2199–2202 were added by the Agricultural Credit Act of 1987, Pub. L. No. 100-233, tit. I, 101 Stat. 1568, 1572–85 (1988)) ... In addition to the codified protections for System borrowers, the 1985 Act also contained an uncodified provision mandating that System lenders review all loans that had been placed in "non-accrual" status "based on changes in the circumstances of such institutions as the result of this Act and the amendments made by this Act." Borrowers were to be notified in writing of the results of that review. Farm Credit Amendments Act of 1985, Pub. L. No. 99-205, 307, 99 Stat. 1678, 1709 (1985). Perhaps the most significant of the borrower protections contained in the 1985 Act was the requirement that System lenders develop forbearance policies. 12 U.S.C.A. § 2199(b) (West Supp. 1986). Previously, there had been no statutory requirement for such policies. Rather, the only directive for such policies was contained in the regulations at 12 C.F.R. § 614.4510 (1985). Section 614.4510 merely required that the banks and associations have policies providing a "means of forbearance for cases when the borrower is cooperative, making an honest effort to meet the conditions of the loan contract, and is capable of working out of the debt burden."

The imposition of a statutory mandate for the development of forbearance policies, though itself not specific regarding the availability and means of forbearance, reflected Congressional displeasure with the System's prior procedures and attitudes toward forbearance. *See* H.R. Rep. No. 99-425, 99 Cong., 1st Sess., *reprinted in* 1985 U.S. Code Cong. & Admin. News 2587, 2598. *See* also Kayl, *supra* note [51], at 287 ... Later, with the passage of the Agricultural Credit Act of 1987, Congress became more specific in its directives to the System regarding its treatment of its member-borrowers ...

93. General Accounting Office, Pub. No. Rced-89-33br, *Farm Finance: Financial Condition of American Agriculture as of December 31, 1987*, 66–73 (1988); General Accounting Office, Pub. No. Rced-88-26br, *Farm Finance: Financial Condition of American Agriculture as of December 31, 1986*, 64–71 (1987). *See also* Guebert, *Confessions of a Farm Credit Regulator*, Top Producer, June–July 1987, at 15 (discussing the deteriorating financial condition of the System); Taylor, *Day of Reckoning for Farm Credit*, Farm J., March 1987, at 26 (same).

94. Pub. L. No. 99-509, 1031–1037, 100 Stat. 1874, 1877–79 (1986) (codified as amended in scattered sections of 12 U.S.C.A. (West 1989 & Supp. 1990)).

95. *Id.*, 1035–1037, 100 Stat. at 1878–79. *See* generally Banner & Barry, *Rapping The Farm Credit System: Spreading Costs to the Future*, Choices, First Quarter 1988, at 31 (discussing the economics of the new regulatory accounting practices); *How the Farm Credit System Could Harvest a Big Profit*, Wash. Post Nat. Weekly Ed., Oct. 27, 1986, at 20, col. 1 (same); Kayl, *supra* note [51], at 309–10 (discussing the 1986 Act in general). The "regulatory accounting practices" regulations are currently found at 12 C.F.R. § 624 (1990).

J. The Agricultural Credit Act of 1987

The Agricultural Credit Act of 1987[96] was signed by the President on January 6, 1988.[97] The 1987 Act operates in two ways that have resulted or will result in structural changes to the System. First, it makes available up to four billion dollars of federal funds to improve the financial condition of System institutions.[98] Second, it mandates the merger of certain System institutions and provides for the voluntary consolidation of others.[99]

1. Financial Assistance to System Institutions

Under the 1987 Act, the Farm Credit Administration remains the regulatory authority over System institutions.[100] However, a new threefold approach to financial assistance is undertaken. First, the Capital Corporation, a creation of the 1985 Act, has been abolished.[101] In its place, an entity known as the Farm Credit System Assistance Board has been created to certify financially distressed institutions.[102] Once certified, an institution

---

96. Pub.L. No. 100-233, 101 Stat. 1568–1718 (1988) (codified in scattered sections of Titles 7, 12, & 14 of 12 U.S.C.A. (West 1988, 1989 & Supp. 1990)).

97. The 1987 Act substantially changed the loan servicing procedures for the loan programs administered by the Farmers Home Administration (FmHA) and made minor changes to other agricultural programs, including the Conservation Reserve Program. *See generally* Hayes, *Farmers Home Administration: What the New Law Provides*, 3 FARMERS' LEGAL ACTION REP. 6 (1988) (discussing, in detail, the changes made by the 1987 Act to FmHA loan servicing procedures); Hertzler, Jr., *The Agricultural Credit Act of 1987—A View from the Farmers Home Administration*, 2 J. AGRIC. LENDING 17 (1988) (briefly describing how the 1987 Act affected the FmHA); McEowen & Harl, *A Look at the Conservation Reserve Program (CRP) and How It Affects Owners and Tenants of Marginal Land*, 12 J. AGRIC. TAX'N & L. 121 (1990) (discussing the Conservation Reserve Program).

98. 12 U.S.C.A. § 2278b-6 (West 1989).

99. An uncodified provision of the 1987 Act required the merger of the FLB and FICB in each district within six months of the Act's enactment. Pub. L. No. 100-203, 410, 101 Stat. 1568, 1637 (1988). *See also* 12 U.S.C.A. § 2011 (West 1989) (setting forth in the annotations the terms of section 410). *See generally* 12 U.S.C.A. §§ 2279a–2279a-3 (West 1989) (authorizing the merger of banks within a district).

In addition, another uncodified provision of the 1987 Act required each FLBA and PCA sharing substantially the same geographic territory to submit to their respective shareholders a plan for merging the associations within six months after the merger of the district FLB and FICB. Pub. L. No. 100-203, 411, 101 Stat. 1568, 1638 (1988). *See also* 12 U.S.C.A. § 2071 (West 1989) (setting forth in the annotations the terms of section 411). *See generally* 12 U.S.C.A. § 2279c-1 (West 1989) (authorizing the merger of associations). Finally, the 1987 Act also required the development of a proposal for the consolidation of farm credit districts, Pub. L. No. 100-203, 412, 101 Stat. 1568, 1638–39 (1988), and the voluntary merger of the banks for cooperatives, Pub. L. No. 100-203, 413, 101 Stat. 1568, 1639–42 (1988). *See also* 12 U.S.C.A. §§ 2221, 2121 (West 1989) (setting forth in the annotations the terms of sections 412 and 413, respectively).

100. *See generally* Dewey, [*The Farm Credit System*, 36 FED. B. NEWS & J. 287, 289] (1987) (discussing the role of the FCA under the 1987 Act).

101. Pub. L. No. 100-233, 207(a)(3), 101 Stat. 1568, 1607 (1988). The assets and liabilities of the Capital Corporation were assumed by the Farm Credit System Assistance Board, 12 U.S.C.A. § 2278a-9 (West 1989).

102. 12 U.S.C.A. § 2278a (West 1989). The mission of the Assistance Board is to protect borrower's stock and "to assist in restoring System institutions to economic viability" 12 U.S.C.A. § 2278a-1 (West 1989). The Board has three directors, one appointed by the Secretary of the Treasury, one by the Secretary of Agriculture, and the third member, who is to be an agricultural producer "experienced in financial matters", is appointed by the President with the advice and consent of the Senate. 12 U.S.C.A. § 2278a-2 (West 1989). The Assistance Board is granted broad powers with which to fulfill its mission. *See* 12 U.S.C.A. § 2278a-3 (West 1989). Those powers include the authority to issue regulations without complying with the Administrative Procedure Act, and the Board is not subject to regulation by the FCA. 12 U.S.C.A. § 2278a-10(a), (b) (West 1989).

can issue preferred stock and receive financial assistance.[103] If the book value of the stock of a System institution is less than seventy-five percent of the par value of the stock, that is, if its value is less than $3.75 per share, the institution is required to seek certification.[104]

Second, the 1987 Act also created an entity known as the Financial Assistance Corporation.[105] That entity is authorized to issue federally guaranteed bonds and to purchase the preferred stock of System institutions that have been certified as eligible to issue preferred stock, thereby funnelling the federal "bail-out" funds to those institutions.[106] The Financial Assistance Corporation will terminate on the maturity and full payment of its bonds.[107] The bonds will have a fifteen year maturity period.[108]

In addition to creating an "assistance fund" through the issuance of federally guaranteed bonds, the 1987 Act created a "trust fund" funded solely from the proceeds from a one-time required purchase of Financial Assistance Corporation stock by the PCAs and Farm Credit Banks.[109] The creation of the "trust fund" already has been challenged as an unconstitutional taking under the fifth amendment.[110]

Third, the 1987 Act also creates the Farm Credit System Insurance Corporation.[111] The Corporation's function is to create an insurance fund by assessing and collecting premiums from System institutions.[112] The fund is intended to protect System institutions, investors, and stockholders beginning in 1993 by satisfying defaults on payments of bonds, preferred stock, and borrower stock.[113]

---

103. 12 U.S.C.A. § 2278a-4, 2278a-5 (West 1989). The preferred stock issued by certified institutions is purchased by the Financial Assistance Corporation using funds the Corporation obtained by issuing federally guaranteed bonds ...

104. 12 U.S.C.A. § 2278a-4(b) (West 1989). The $3.75 per share figure assumes that the stock had a par value of $5.00, which it usually did prior to the 1987 Act. *See* 12 U.S.C.A. §§ 2034(a), 2094(f) (West 1980). *See also In re* Massengill, 100 Bankr. 276, 278 & n. 1 (E.D. N.C. 1988) (discussing the stock purchase requirements in effect prior to the 1987 Act).

105. 12 U.S.C.A. § 2278(b) (West 1989). The purpose of the Financial Assistance Corporation is the provision of capital to financially distressed System institutions. 12 U.S.C.A. § 2278b-1 (West 1989). The board of directors of the Financial Assistance Corporation consists of the Board of Directors of the Federal Farm Credit Banks Funding Corporation. 12 U.S.C.A. § 2278b-2(a) (West 1989).

106. 12 U.S.C.A. §§ 2278b-6(a), 2278b-7(b) (West 1989). Interest must be paid on the federally guaranteed bonds. *See* 12 U.S.C.A. §§ 2278b-6(c), 2278b-8 (West 1989). Although the Secretary of the Treasury bears some initial responsibility for interest payments, the System is ultimately obligated to repay the Secretary up to the sum of $2,000,000,000 for interest payments. 12 U.S.C.A. §§ 2278b-6(c), 2278b-8(b) (West 1989).

107. 12 U.S.C.A. § 2278b-11 (West 1989). The System is required to pay the bond obligations. 12 U.S.C.A. § 2278b-6(c) (West 1989).

108. 12 U.S.C.A. § 2278b-6(a) (West 1989). For an excellent discussion of the federal "bailout" provisions of the 1987 Act, see Massey, *Farm Credit System: Structure and Financing Under the New Act,* 3 FARMERS' LEGAL ACTION REP. 52, 58–64 (1988) [hereinafter Massey] (includes flow chart diagrams of the "bailout" mechanisms).

109. 12 U.S.C.A. §§ 2278b-5(b), 2278b-9 (West 1989 & Supp. 1990). The purpose of the "trust fund" is to provide intermediate security for each System institution's share of interest and principal repayment on the "assistance fund" bonds. *See* Massey, *supra* note 108, at 63–64.

110. Colorado Springs Production Credit Ass'n v. Farm Credit Admin., 695 F. Supp. 15 (D.D.C. 1988) (order denying in part and granting in part motion to dismiss).

111. 12 U.S.C.A. § 2277a-1 (West 1989).

112. *Id. See* also Massey, *supra* note 108, at 65–68 (discussing purposes and functions of the Farm Credit System Insurance Corporation); Federal Farm Credit Banks Funding Corp. v. Farm Credit Admin., 731 F. Supp. 217, 219–20 (E.D. Va. 1990) (briefly describing the Insurance Corporation and the Insurance Fund).

113. *See* 12 U.S.C.A. § 2277a-9(a), (c) (West 1989).

The 1987 Act also created, as part of the Farm Credit System, the Federal Agricultural Mortgage Corporation to oversee a new agricultural mortgage secondary market.[114] Lenders other than System lenders will be eligible to participate in the secondary market.[115]

In addition, the Federal Farm Credit Banks Funding Corporation was created as the System's fiscal agent for the marketing of System bonds. In addition to marketing System bonds, the Funding Corporation will determine the terms and other conditions of those bonds.[116]

Questions have already been raised about the efficacy of the federal "bail-out."[117] Moreover, on Friday, May 20, 1988, the Federal Land Bank of Jackson was closed and placed in a receivership by the Farm Credit Administration after examiners determined that an additional infusion of federal funds would be "futile."[118]

2. Merger of System Institutions

The 1987 Act mandated the merger of the federal land bank and the federal intermediate credit bank in each district within six months after January 6, 1988.[119] The merged FLB and FICB within each district are now known as the Farm Credit Banks.[120]

---

114. 12 U.S.C.A. §§ 2279aa–2279aa-14 (West 1989). *See generally* Pariser, *Agricultural Real Estate Loans and Secondary Markets*, IV AGRIC. & HUMAN VALUES 29 (1987) (discussing the possible effects of the secondary market on the Farm Credit System); GENERAL ACCOUNTING OFFICE, Pub. No. RCED-90-118, *Federal Agricultural Mortgage Corporation: Secondary Market Development and Risk Implications* (1990) (discussing a variety of issues presented by the secondary market); GENERAL ACCOUNTING OFFICE, Pub. No. RCED-88-55FS, *Farm Finance: Provisions for Secondary Markets for Farm Real Estate Loans in H.R. 3030* (1987) (same); AMERICAN BANKERS ASSOC., FINANCING FARM REAL ESTATE: A COMPREHENSIVE TRAINING MANUAL FOR THE SECONDARY MARKET FOR AGRICULTURE (1988) (a lender's guide to the secondary market created by the 1987 Act); D. Freshwater & D. Trechter, *New Approaches to Financing Long-term Farm Debt* (Econ. Res. Serv., USDA, Agric. Info. Bull. No. 511, March 1987) (discussing secondary agricultural mortgage markets in general); Killebrew, *The Case for the Secondary Market,* 1 J. AGRIC. LENDING 6 (1987) (a commercial lender's argument for a secondary agricultural mortgage market).

115. 12 U.S.C.A. § 2279aa-5(2) (West 1989).

116. 12 U.S.C.A. § 2160 (West 1989).

117. Bullock & Dodson, *The Farm Credit System: It Was A New Lease On Life, But…*, CHOICES, First Quarter 1988, at 32.

118. 53 Fed. Reg. 18,812 (1988) (order appointing receiver) (the order has been amended at least twice, 53 Fed. Reg. 47,762 (1988), 55 Fed. Reg. 3,644 (1990)). *See also* WALL ST. J., May 23, 1988, at 4, col. 1 (reporting on the receivership order); GENERAL ACCOUNTING OFFICE, PUB. NO. GGD-90-16, *Farm Credit: Basis for Decision Not to Assist Jackson Federal Land Bank* (1989) (critical study of the decision to place the Jackson FLB in receivership); *Behind The Takeover of Jackson Farm Credit*, AGRI-FINANCE NEWS, July 1988, at 1 (discussing the Jackson FLB receivership); Hughes, Jackson, *FLB In Receivership*, AGRIC. OUTLOOK, July 1988, at 20 (same). Subsequently, the loans of the Jackson FLB were sold to the Farm Credit Bank of Texas, and the three states formerly served by the Jackson FLB, Alabama, Mississippi, and Louisiana, are now served by the Farm Credit Bank of Texas. FARM CREDIT ADMIN., 4 FCA BULL. 2–3 (1989). Some of the events leading up to the placing of the Jackson FLB in receivership are discussed in Federal Land Bank of Jackson in Receivership v. Federal Intermediate Credit Bank (of Jackson), 727 F. Supp. 1055, 1056–57 (S.D. Miss. 1989). *See also* Grant v. Federal Land Bank of Jackson, 559 So.2d 148, 150–55 (La. Ct. App. 1990) (discussing the Jackson FLB's receiver's liability under the "D'Oench doctrine" [D'Oench, Duhme & Co. v. Federal Deposit Insurance Corp., 315 U.S. 676 (1942)] in a lender liability action), *cert. denied,* 563 So.2d 886, 887 (La. 1990); *Note, Borrower Beware: D'Oench, Duhme and Section 1823 Overprotect the Insurer When Banks Fail*, 62 S. CAL. L. REV. 253 (1988) (discussing the "D'Oench doctrine").

119. Pub. L. No. 100-233, 401, 101 Stat. 1568, 1622 (1988). See also *supra* note 99 (discussing the mandatory merger of district FLBs and FICBs into district farm credit banks).

120. 12 U.S.C.A. § 2011 (West 1989).

The Farm Credit Banks, acting through FLBAs, will continue to provide real estate loans.[121] However, the Farm Credit Banks can transfer direct loan making authority to an FLBA.[122]

PCAs will continue to provide short and intermediate term loans.[123] Those loans may be discounted by the Farm Credit Banks, and associations, including both federal land bank and production credit associations, will continue to be supervised by the Farm Credit Banks.[124]

Under the 1987 Act, a PCA and an FLBA may merge.[125] If a merger occurs, the Farm Credit Banks must transfer the direct lending authority for long-term real estate mortgage loans to the FLBA.[126] Further, merged associations are referred to as "agricultural credit associations" (ACAs).[127]

The Act also required the twelve banks for cooperatives and the Central Bank for Cooperatives to consider consolidation into one national bank for cooperatives.[128] The St. Paul, Springfield, Jackson, and Spokane Banks recently voted not to consolidate; the remaining eight banks will consolidate into one national bank.[129]

The 1987 Act removed the requirement that a borrower must purchase stock in the amount of five percent of the face value of the loan.[130] A borrower now must purchase stock in an amount as set by the lender, subject to FCA regulation.[131] The FCA has issued regulations providing that the amount of stock required to be purchased must be not less than two percent of the loan amounts or $1,000, whichever is less.[132]

---

121. 12 U.S.C.A. §§2015, 2013(18), 2021(a), 2091, 2093(9) (West 1989). Where there is no active association, the Farm Credit Bank may make the loan directly. 12 U.S.C.A. §2021(b) (West 1989).

122. 12 U.S.C.A. §2013(18) (West Supp. 1989). When the direct lending authority has been delegated to a FLBA, the association is referred to as a "Federal land credit association". 55 Fed. Reg. 24,861, 24,889 (1990) (to be codified at 12 C.F.R. §619.9155). See also 55 Fed. Reg. 24,861, 24,881 (1990)(to be codified at 12 C.F.R. §614.4030) (lending authority for federal land credit associations).

123. 12 U.S.C.A. §§2073(13), 2075 (West 1989).

124. 12 U.S.C.A. §§2013(6), (13), (17)–(21) (West Supp. 1989). See also 55 Fed. Reg. 24,861, 24,882–83 (to be codified at 12 C.F.R. subpt. C) (final rules relating to the farm credit bank/association relationship) (The FCA still has not adopted in final form other rules relating to loan policies and operations proposed on November 3, 1988, at 53 Fed. Reg. 44,438–44,456 (1990)). See 55 Fed. Reg. 24,861, 24862 (1990)).

125. 12 U.S.C.A. §2279c-1 (West 1989). The 1987 Act directed that, not later than six months after the merger of the FLBs and FICBs into district farm credit banks, the board of directors of the FLBAs and PCAs were to submit to their respective association's shareholders a proposal to merge the FLBAs and PCAs serving the same geographical area. Pub. L. No. 10-233, 411, 101 Stat. 1568, 1368 (1988). See also 12 U.S.C.A. §2071 (West 1989) (setting for section 411 in the annotations). The 1987 Act also permits "like" associations to merge, i.e., a PCA may merge with another PCA. 12 U.S.C.A. §2279f-1 (West 1989).

126. 12 U.S.C.A. §2279b(b) (West 1989). See also 55 Fed. Reg. 24,861, 24,882 (1990) (loan authority for the "agricultural credit associations" formed by the merger of "unlike" associations).

127. 55 Fed. Reg. 24,861, 24,888 (1990) (to be codified at 12 C.F.R. §619.9015).

128. Pub. L. No. 100-233, 413, 101 Stat. 1568, 1639–42 (1988). See also 12 U.S.C.A. §2121 (West 1989) (setting forth the terms of section 413 in the annotations).

129. National Bank for Cooperatives Formed by Merger Vote, AGRIFINANCE NEWS, August 1988, at 4. A bank for cooperatives may merge with district farm credit bank. 12 U.S.C.A. §2279f(a) (West 1989). When such a merger occurs, the resulting bank is known as an "agricultural credit bank". 55 Fed. Reg. 24,861, 24,888 (1990) (to be codified at 12 C.F.R. §619.9020). See generally Hopkin, Sporleder, Padberg & Knutson, Evaluation of Restructuring Alternatives for the Banks for Cooperatives, 3 J. AGRIC. COOPERATION 71 (1988) (discussing the consolidation alternatives for the banks of cooperatives).

130. 12 U.S.C.A. §§2034, 2294 (West 1980). See supra notes 59 & 68 and the accompanying text.

131. 12 U.S.C.A. §§2074, 2094 (West Supp. 1989).

132. 12 C.F.R. §614.5220(d) (1990).

Finally, the 1987 Act also requires the Farm Credit Administration to propose a plan for the merger of the twelve districts into no less than six districts.[133] The various Farm Credit Banks are to submit the proposed merger affecting it to its members for their approval.[134]

b. The Current Structure of the FCS

Jim Monke
Farm Credit System
Congressional Research Service, Rep. No. RS21278
(June 12, 2007)

The FCS is authorized by statute to lend to farmers, ranchers, and harvesters of aquatic products. Loans may also be made to finance the processing and marketing activities of these borrowers, for home ownership in rural areas, certain farm- or ranch related businesses, and agricultural, aquatic, and public utility cooperatives. The FCS is not a lender of last resort. FCS is a commercial, for-profit lender.

Borrowers must meet creditworthiness requirements similar to those of a commercial lender. FCS has "young, beginning, and small" (YBS) farmer lending programs, but does not have particular targets or numerical mandates for such loans. The FCS holds about 31 percent of the farm sector's total debt (second to the 40 percent share of commercial banks) and has the largest share of farm real estate loans (38 percent). As of September 2006, FCS had $115 billion in loans outstanding, of which about 47 percent was in long-term agricultural real estate loans, 24 percent in short- and intermediate-term agricultural loans, 15 percent in loans to agribusinesses, 5 percent in energy loans, 3 percent in rural home loans, and 6 percent in communications, export financing, leases, and water and waste disposal loans.

A Government-Sponsored Enterprise (GSE). As a GSE, FCS is a privately owned, federally chartered cooperative designed to provide credit nationwide. It is limited to serving agriculture and related businesses and homeowners in rural areas. Each GSE is given certain benefits such as implicit federal guarantees or tax exemptions, presumably to overcome barriers faced by purely private markets. FCS is the only direct lender among the GSEs; other GSEs such as Fannie Mae are secondary markets. FCS is not a government agency and its debt instruments and loans are not explicitly guaranteed by the U.S. government.

The tax benefits for FCS include an exemption from federal, state, municipal, and local taxation on the profits earned by the real estate side of FCS (12 U.S.C. 2098). Income earned by the non-real estate side of FCS is subject to taxation. The exemption originated in the 1916 act. Commercial bankers estimate that the annual value of these tax benefits amounted to at least $425 million in 2004. For investors who buy FCS bonds on Wall Street, the interest earned is exempt from state, municipal, and local taxes. This makes FCS bonds more attractive to the investing public and helps assure a plentiful supply of funds for loans. Commercial bankers say that the tax benefits let FCS offer lower interest rates to borrowers, and thus give FCS an operating advantage since they compete in the same retail lending market.

A Cooperative Business Organization. FCS associations are owned by the borrowers who purchase stock, required as part of their loan (the smaller of $1,000 or 2 percent of

---

133. Pub. L. No. 100-203, 412, 101 Stat. 1568, 1638–39 (1988). See also 12 U.S.C.A. § 2002 (West 1989) (setting forth the terms of section 412 in the annotations).

134. *Id.*

the loan amount). FCS stockholders elect the boards of directors for banks and associations. Each has one vote, regardless of the loan size. Most directors are members, but federal law requires at least one from outside.

If an association is profitable, the directors may choose to retain the profits to increase lending capital, or distribute some of the net income through dividends or patronage refunds, which are proportional to the size of loan. Patronage refunds effectively reduce the cost of borrowing. Some associations tend to regularly pay patronage while others prefer to retain their earnings or charge lower interest rates.

A National System of Banks and Associations. FCS is composed of five regional banks that provide funds and support services to 95 smaller Agricultural Credit Associations (ACAs), Federal Land Credit Associations (FLCAs), and Production Credit Associations (PCAs). These associations, in turn, provide loans to eligible borrowers. The most common operating structure (due to favorable tax and regulatory rules) is a "parent ACA" with FLCA and PCA subsidiaries. There are 86 ACAs and nine stand-alone FLCAs

One of the regional banks, CoBank, has a nationwide charter to finance farmer owned cooperatives and rural utilities. It finances agricultural exports and provides international services for farmer-owned cooperatives through three international offices.

Capitalized with Bonds and Stock, Not the U.S. Treasury. The Federal Farm Credit Banks Funding Corporation ([http://www.farmcredit-ffcb.com]) uses capital markets to sell FCS bonds and notes. These debts become the joint and several liability of all FCS banks. The funding corporation allocates capital to the banks, which provide funds to associations, which lend to borrowers. Profits from loans repay bondholders. FCS also raises capital through two other methods. Borrowers are required to buy stock (the lesser of $1,000 or 2% of the loan amount) and become cooperative members. FCS also retains profits that are not returned as patronage to borrowers.

With the exception of seed money that was repaid by the 1950s and a temporary U.S. Treasury line of credit in the 1980s,6 FCS operates without any direct federal money. FCS banks and associations do not take deposits like commercial banks, nor do they receive federal appropriations to fund their loan program.

Types of Loans and Borrowers

The FCS provides three types of loans: (1) operating loans for the short-term financing of consumables such as feed, seed, fertilizer, or fuel; (2) installment loans for intermediate-term financing of durables such as equipment or breeding livestock; and (3) real estate loans for long-term financing (up to 40 years) of land, buildings, and homes. The FCS has a statutory mandate to serve agriculture, and certain agribusinesses and rural homeowners. Borrowers must meet certain eligibility requirements in addition to general creditworthiness. Eligible borrowers and their scope of their financing can be grouped into four categories. Full-time farmers. For individuals with over 50% of their assets and income from agriculture, FCS can lend for all agricultural, family, and non-agricultural needs (including vehicles, education, home improvements, and vacation expenses).

- **Part-time farmers.** For individuals who own farmland or produce agricultural products but earn less than 50% of their income from agriculture, FCS can lend for all agricultural and family needs. However, non-agricultural lending is limited.

- **Farming-related businesses.** FCS can lend to businesses that process or market farm, ranch, or aquatic products if more than 50% of the business is owned by farmers who provide at least some of the "throughput." FCS also can lend to businesses that provide services to farmers and ranchers (but not aquatic producers), such as crop spraying and cotton ginning. The extent of financing is based on the amount of the business's farm-related income.

- **Rural homeowners.** FCS can lend for the purchase, construction, improvement, or refinancing of single-family dwellings in rural areas with populations of 2,500 or less.

Consolidation

The number of banks and associations has been declining for decades through mergers and reorganizations. This consolidation accelerated, however, in 1999 when the Farm Credit Administration (FCA), the system's regulator, approved the "parent ACA" structure and the Internal Revenue Service declared FLCA subsidiaries tax-exempt. In the mid-1940s, there were over 2,000 lending associations, nearly 900 in 1983, fewer than 400 by 1987, 200 in 1998, and only 95 in 2006. The system operated with 12 districts into the 1980s, 8 districts in 1998, and 5 regional banks (districts) since 2004. Twenty years ago, the typical FCS association covered several counties and specialized in either land or farm production loans. Today, the typical FCS association covers a much larger region, delivers a wide range of farm and rural credit programs and services, and has an extensive loan portfolio. FCS benefits when consolidation creates more diversified portfolios. Customers may benefit if greater institutional efficiency is passed along through lower interest rates. However, consolidation may weaken the original cooperative concept of local borrower control and close many local offices at which farmers had established relationships.

Charter Territories

Each association within FCS has a specific "charter territory." If an association wants to lend outside its charter territory, it first must obtain approval from the other territory's association. For example, associations within U.S. AgBank's region (the southern Plains and West) can compete for loans, but associations in the AgFirst region (the East and Southeast) cannot. Charter territories help ensure that borrowers are served locally and maintain local control of the association. Charter territories and any changes must be approved by FCA.

In 2001, FCA proposed allowing national charters so that associations would not be restricted by geographical boundaries. The FCA board later dropped the idea after opponents raised concerns that national charters would weaken FCS's mission by pitting associations against each other for prime loans and reducing commitments to local areas.

Federal Regulation

Congressional Oversight. Congressional oversight of FCS is provided by the House and Senate Agriculture Committees. The most recent hearings on FCS include one in the House on June 2, 2004, concerning Farmer Mac, and another in the House on September 29, 2004, over the proposed sale of an FCS association.

Farm Credit Administration (FCA). The FCA (http://www.fca.gov) is an independent agency and the federal regulator responsible for examining and ensuring the safety and soundness of all FCS institutions. Regulations are published in 12 C.F.R. 600 et seq. FCA's operating expenses are paid through assessments on FCS banks and associations. Even though FCA does not receive an appropriation from Congress, the annual agriculture appropriations act in recent years has put a limit on FCA's administrative expenses ($44.25 million in FY2006).

FCA is directed by a three-member board nominated by the President and confirmed by the Senate. Board members serve a six-year term and may not be reappointed after serving a full term or more than three years of a previous member's term. The President designates one member as chairman, who serves until the end of that member's term.

Other FCS Entities

The Farm Credit System has several other entities besides those previously discussed.

Federal Agricultural Mortgage Company (Farmer Mac). Farmer Mac (http://www.farmermac.com) was established in the Agricultural Credit Act of 1987 to serve as a secondary market for agricultural loans—purchasing and pooling qualified loans, then selling them as securities to investors. Farmer Mac increases the capacity for agricultural lenders to make more loans; for example, if a lender makes a 30-year loan and sells it to Farmer Mac, the proceeds can be used to make another loan. This is similar to the much larger secondary market for housing loans, such as Fannie Mae.

Although Farmer Mac is part of FCS and regulated by FCA, it has no liability for the debt of any other FCS institution, and the other FCS institutions have no liability for Farmer Mac debt. It is considered a separate GSE. Farmer Mac is organized as an investor-owned corporation, not a member-owned cooperative. Voting stock may be owned by commercial banks, insurance companies, other financial organizations, and FCS institutions. Nonvoting stock may be owned by any investor. The board of directors has 15 members: five elected from the FCS, five elected from commercial banks, and five appointed from the public at large.

Farmer Mac operates two programs: Farmer Mac I (loans not guaranteed by USDA) and Farmer Mac II (USDA-guaranteed loans).

- A majority of **Farmer Mac I** volume comes from the sale of "long-term standby purchase agreements" (LTSPC). Farmer Mac promises to purchase specific agricultural mortgages, thus guaranteeing the loans against default risk while the participating lender retains interest rate risk.

- Under **Farmer Mac II**, the company purchases the portion of individual loans that are guaranteed by USDA. On these purchases, Farmer Mac accepts the interest rate risk but carries no default risk. Farmer Mac continues to hold most of the loans it purchases, a potentially more profitable activity for the company, but also more risky.

Farm Credit System Insurance Corporation. The Insurance Corporation (http://www.fcsic.gov) was established by statute in 1988 to ensure timely payment of principal and interest on FCS debt securities. The FCA board comprises its board of directors. Annual premiums are paid by each bank through an assessment based on loan volume until the secure base amount of 2 percent of total outstanding loans is reached. Farm Credit Council.

The Farm Credit Council (http://www.fccouncil.com) is the national trade association of FCS. FCC has offices in Washington, DC, and Denver, CO, and lobbies on behalf of FCS. FCC also provides support services.

c. Borrowers' Rights
Harper v. Federal Land Bank of Spokane
878 F.2d 1172 (9th Cir. 1989)

Before TANG, SKOPIL and KOZINSKI, Circuit Judges.

SKOPIL, Circuit Judge:

The primary issue on appeal is whether there is an implied private right of action to enforce the Agricultural Credit Act of 1987 ("1987 Act"), 12 U.S.C. §§ 2001–2279aa-14. The district court held that the 1987 Act creates such an action and found that the Federal Land Bank ("FLB") and Willamette Production Credit Association ("WPCA") violated the statute. *Harper v. Federal Land Bank of Spokane,* 692 F.Supp. 1244, 1252–53 (D.Or.1988). We hold there is no implied private right of action for the 1987 Act. We reverse.

FACTS AND PRIOR PROCEEDINGS

Myron and Jane Harper ("the Harpers") own and operate a farm in Oregon encumbered by mortgages held by FLB and WPCA. The Harpers began having difficulty with loan repayments in the early 1980's. In May 1984 WPCA rejected the Harpers' loan renewal request and filed a foreclosure action against them five months later in state court. In February 1985 the Harpers filed a complaint against numerous institutions and officers of the Farm Credit System seeking, *inter alia,* an order enjoining WPCA's state foreclosure proceeding. The district court denied the Harpers' motion for an injunction and dismissed the action. *Harper v. Farm Credit Admin.,* 628 F.Supp. 1030, 1033–34 (D.Or.1985).

After several continuances of the state court's foreclosure trial, the Harpers entered into a settlement agreement to restructure the WPCA debt. Instead of performing the settlement, however, the Harpers filed a Chapter 11 bankruptcy petition on May 30, 1986. In July 1986 WPCA obtained relief from the automatic stay, and the state foreclosure action was reinstated.

In September 1986 FLB obtained relief from the automatic stay and filed a foreclosure complaint against the Harpers in January 1987. In June 1987 the Harpers asked FLB about possible forbearance on their FLB loans. FLB supplied them an application form and requested financial information but received neither an application for forbearance nor financial data from the Harpers until April 21, 1988.

On September 3, 1987 the state court entered a default judgment of foreclosure in favor of FLB. On October 9, 1987 WPCA secured a judgment of foreclosure by stipulation. FLB scheduled a sheriff's sale for November 17, 1987. On November 13, 1987 the Harpers filed a Chapter 12 bankruptcy petition, thereby staying the sheriff's sale. In February 1988, on the Harpers' motion, the bankruptcy court dismissed the petition. The sheriff's sale was held in March 1988.

The Harpers thereafter moved to set aside the judgments. The state court found that the judgments were authorized by the Harpers' prior attorney, denied the Harpers' motion to set aside the judgments, and ruled that the order confirming the sale could be entered.

The Harpers then filed this action in federal district court seeking an injunction barring continuation of the state court process. The district court granted a preliminary injunction and enjoined FLB and WPCA (together "the Lenders") from transferring the property pending resolution of the Harpers' claims. After a court trial the district court held that the Lenders violated the 1987 Act. The court concluded that the Lenders had a duty under federal law to "weigh the costs of foreclosure against the costs of restructuring prior to proceeding with the sheriff's sale." The Lenders were enjoined from evicting the Harpers from their property. The district court also issued an order directing the parties to apply to state court for an order rescinding the sheriff's sale.

On appeal, the Lenders contend the 1987 Act does not provide an implied private right of action. Alternatively, they argue (1) they have not violated the 1987 Act; (2) the actions taken by the district court were prohibited by the Anti-Injunction Act, 28 U.S.C. § 2283 (1982); (3) the district court did not have the authority to command the parties to stipulate in state court to an order rescinding a completed sheriff's foreclosure sale or to restrain the purchasers from taking possession of the property; and (4) the district court's findings as to WPCA are clearly erroneous. We decide only that there exists no private right of action and therefore we do not reach the alternative arguments.

DISCUSSION
I.

In *Cort v. Ash*, 422 U.S. 66, 78, 95 S.Ct. 2080, 2087–88 (1975), the Supreme Court set forth four factors to determine whether Congress intended to imply a private cause of action in a federal statute.

> First, is the plaintiff one of the class for whose *especial* benefit the statute was enacted—that is, does the statute create a federal right in favor of plaintiff? Second, is there any indication of legislative intent, explicit or implicit, either to create such a remedy or to deny one? Third, is it consistent with the underlying purposes of the legislative scheme to imply such a remedy for the plaintiff? And finally, is the cause of action one traditionally relegated to state law, in an area basically the concern of the States, so that it would be inappropriate to infer a cause of action based solely on federal law?

Id. at 78, 95 S.Ct. at 2088 (emphasis in original). Subsequent to *Cort*, the Court has indicated that the second and third factors are determinative of whether a court should imply a private right of action from a statutory scheme. Moreover, it is now clear that the focal point of our inquiry is the second factor—the intent of Congress. Nevertheless, we look to all four factors "[a]s guides to discerning that intent."

1. Especial Benefit of Plaintiffs

The district court concluded that the Harpers satisfied the first factor as "one of the class for whose especial benefit the statute was enacted" because Title I of the 1987 Act, entitled "Assistance to Farm Credit System Borrowers," established broad rights for borrowers and mandatory duties for lenders. We agree that one of the purposes of the 1987 Act was to provide borrowers with certain limited rights, including the right to restructure distressed loans and the right of first refusal by the previous owner when the lenders elect to sell acquired property. We look at the overall purpose of the 1987 Act, however, and conclude that the major impetus for the legislation was the financial crisis of the Farm Credit System. "[The bill] is necessary to reassure both American farmers and our financial markets that the Farm Credit System will remain a viable entity next year and into the 21st century." 133 Cong.Rec.S. 16831 (Dec. 1, 1987) (remarks of Sen. Leahy). "[The bill] has two major objectives: First, provide meaningful assistance to the system; and second, minimize to the greatest extent possible exposure to the Federal budget." 133 Cong.Rec.S. 16833 (Dec. 1, 1987) (remarks of Sen. Boren).

Our conclusion that the financial crisis of the Farm Credit System was the primary purpose of the 1987 Act is further reinforced by the fact that a borrower's right to restructure a delinquent loan is limited to situations in which the cost of restructuring is less than or equal to the cost of foreclosure. 12 U.S.C. § 2202a(e)(1). In other words, restructuring is not always available to borrowers but is limited to situations involving no additional expense to the system.

2. Legislative Intent

The district court concluded that the legislative history supports an implied right of action, even though Congress considered enacting an express private right of action and later deleted that section. The court reasoned that the express provision was eliminated because some members of Congress "were under the misperception that the farmers already had the right to sue." Senators Pryor, Cochran, Fowler, and Sanford, for example, sought to include an express private right of action "to affirm that borrowers have a right to sue." S. 1156, 100th Cong. 1st Sess. 133 Cong.Rec. 6105 & 6107 (May 6, 1987). One version of the Senate bill included an express private right of action. S. 1665, 100th Cong., 1st Sess., 133 Cong.Rec. 11750 (August 7, 1987).

A proposed House bill also contained an express private right of action. Representative Watkins said he believed that "the right to sue is implied within the bill itself" but an express provision was necessary "to make sure that there is no question that the borrower has that right." H.R. 3030, 100th Cong., 1st Sess., 133 Cong.Rec. 7638, 7692 (September 21, 1987). In response to a question whether farmers currently had the right to sue, Representative Watkins responded that in some states they did, and Representative De La Garza said "I think basically they have that right now."

Prior to a conference committee on the bills, Senator Burdick questioned whether the House bill's inclusion of a private right of action "actually restricts the right to sue." S. 1665, 100th Cong. 1st Sess., 133 Cong.Rec. 16993, 16995 (December 2, 1987). Senator Boren responded with a plan to "oppose that House provision in the conference committee." *Id.* The Senate opposed the House provision and it was deleted from the final 1987 Act. H.R. 3030, 100th Cong., 1st Sess., 133 Cong.Rec. 11820 (December 18, 1987).

The district court concluded from that legislative history that "[b]oth the House and Senate intended that the borrower have the right to bring a private action in federal court to enforce the Act." citing *Cannon v. University of Chicago,* 441 U.S. 677, 711, 99 S.Ct. 1946, 1965 (1979) ("the relevant inquiry is not whether Congress correctly perceived the then state of the law, but rather what its perception of the law was."). It is abundantly clear, however, that there existed no implied private right of action under the various predecessor statutes or regulations in force prior to the 1987 Act. *See, e.g., Bowling v. Block,* 785 F.2d 556, 557 (6th Cir.) (Farm Credit Act of 1971), *cert. denied,* 479 U.S. 829, 107 S.Ct. 112, 93 L.Ed.2d 60 (1986); *Smith v. Russellville Prod. Credit Ass'n,* 777 F.2d 1544, 1548 (11th Cir.1985) (Farm Credit Act of 1971 and regulations); *Redd v. Federal Land Bank of St. Louis,* 661 F.Supp. 861, 864 (E.D.Mo.1987) (1985 amendments), *aff'd,* 851 F.2d 219, 223 (8th Cir.1988); *Mendel v. Production Credit Ass'n,* 656 F.Supp. 1212, 1216 (D.S.D.1987) (1985 amendments), *aff'd,* 862 F.2d 180, 182 (8th Cir.1988). *But cf. Federal Land Bank of St. Paul v. Overboe,* 404 N.W.2d 445, 449 (N.D.1987) (allowing use of 1985 amendments as an affirmative defense in state foreclosure action).

"The normal rule of statutory construction is that if Congress intends for legislation to change the interpretation of a judicially created concept, it makes that intent specific." Here, an express private right of action was proposed in both houses of Congress but deleted in the final conference version. "'Because the conference report represents the final statement of the terms agreed to by both houses, next to the statute itself it is the most persuasive evidence of congressional intent.'" We conclude that the district court gave inappropriate weight to remarks made by members of Congress. "To permit what we regard as clear statutory language to be materially altered by such colloquies, which often take place before the bill has achieved its final form, would open the door to the inadvertent, or perhaps even planned, undermining of the language actually voted on by Congress and signed into law by the President."

Even if the congressional statements are ambiguous on the creation of a private right of action, our review of the administrative remedies provided by the 1987 Act convinces us that Congress intended administrative review to be the exclusive remedy.

Here the administrative scheme provides for "Credit Review Committees" which must include farmer-director representatives. 12 U.S.C. § 2202(a). The applicant/borrower is entitled to prompt written notice of any action taken with respect to the denial or reduction of a loan or the denial of loan restructuring. 12 U.S.C. § 2201(a).

If a loan application or loan restructuring proposal is denied, the applicant/borrower is entitled to learn the reason for the denial and to receive notice of the applicant's/borrower's right to seek review of the adverse decision. 12 U.S.C. § 2201(b). The applicant/borrower has the right to seek review of the adverse decision and to bring counsel or other representation to seek a reversal of the denial. 12 U.S.C. §§ 2202(b) & (c). In addition, 12 U.S.C. § 2261–2274 grants extensive enforcement powers to the Farm Credit Administration ("FCA"). The FCA has the power to issue cease and desist orders against any institutions or persons who violate the statute or applicable regulations, as well as the power to suspend or remove Farm Credit System officers and directors. 12 U.S.C. §§ 2266(b), 2264. The FCA is further empowered to assess civil and criminal sanctions to enforce these provisions. 12 U.S.C. §§ 2268(a), 2269.

The Harpers nevertheless contend that the remedies available are not comprehensive enough to preclude an implied private cause of action under the 1987 Act. First, they claim there is no procedure for filing charges or for compelling FCA to commence an investigation. Second, they argue that FCA's enforcement apparatus is inadequate to enforce the borrower's rights. Third, they assert that FCA's authority to issue temporary cease and desist orders is limited to violations likely to cause insolvency and that FCA's issuance of permanent cease and desist orders is extremely time consuming. Finally, they argue there is no provision in the statute guaranteeing any remedy for the individual borrower; thus borrowers will be without a remedy for lender violations.

We do not dispute that an implied private right of action would enhance the administrative remedies provided under the 1987 Act. We have previously rejected, however, enhancement as a factor in the analysis of implied remedies. Moreover, the argument that a private right of action must be implied or else borrowers will be without a remedy overlooks the apparent right in some states of a borrower to allege the failure to afford restructuring rights as an affirmative defense to foreclosure. *See Federal Land Bank of St. Paul v. Bosch,* 432 N.W.2d 855, 858–59 (N.D.1988) (allowing use of 1986 regulations as an affirmative defense in state foreclosure action); *Overboe,* 404 N.W.2d at 449 (allowing use of 1985 Act as an affirmative defense in state foreclosure action). *But see Federal Land Bank of St. Louis v. Hopmann,* 658 F.Supp. 92, 94 (E.D.Ark.1987) (rejecting defense).

3. *Consistency with Legislative Purpose*

The district court concluded that a private right of action strengthens the Farm Credit System because it forces lenders to make cost effective decisions concerning the possibility of restructuring loans. While we do not disagree with that conclusion, we do conclude that the primary purpose of the 1987 Act was to restore financial integrity to the Farm Credit System. Allowing a private right of action undermines that objective by involving the Farm Credit System in costly litigation. Although the statute provides borrowers with limited rights, the major purpose of the 1987 Act was to provide financial stability to the Farm Credit System at a minimum cost to taxpayers. 133 Cong.Rec.S. 16833 (Dec. 1, 1987) (remarks of Sen. Boren).

4. *Cause of Action Relegated to State Law*

The district court concluded that the rights created under the 1987 Act were exclusively federal because Congress's goal of keeping farmers on their land is not a traditional state concern. *Harper,* 692 F.Supp. at 1249. The district court, however, addressed only sections 2202a(c) and (d) regarding loan restructuring and ignored section 2202a(b)(3) which prohibits lenders from continuing foreclosure proceedings. We have held that the latter is traditionally controlled by state law.

5. *Summary*

We conclude that none of the four *Cort* factors supports an implied private cause of action under the 1987 Act. Because Congress provided administrative remedies to borrowers and we find the legislative history to be ambiguous, "we are compelled to conclude that Congress provided precisely the remedies it considered appropriate." *Middlesex,* 453 U.S. at 15, 101 S.Ct. at 2623. "The federal judiciary will not engraft a remedy on a statute, no matter how salutary, that Congress did not intend to provide." *California v. Sierra Club,* 451 U.S. 287, 297, 101 S.Ct. 1775, 1781,(1981). Thus we join the several other courts which have also rejected an implied right of action under the 1987 Act. *See, e.g., Wilson v. Federal Land Bank of Wichita,* No. 88-4058-R (D.Kan. Jan. 30, 1989) (1989 WL 12731); *Neth v. Federal Land Bank of Jackson,* 717 F. Supp. 1478 (S.D.Ala. 1988); *Zajac v. Federal Land Bank of St. Paul,* No. 88-A3-88-115 (D.N.D. July 19, 1988) 1988 WL 166 118, appeal pending, No. 88-5353 (8th Cir.). *But see Griffin v. Federal Land Bank of Wichita,* 708 F.Supp. 313 (D.Kan.1989) (allowing a private right of action but finding no violation); *Leckband v. Naylor,* 715 F. Supp. 1451 (D.Minn. May 17, 1988) (allowing a private right of action to enforce right of first refusal), appeal pending, No. 88-5301 (8th Cir.); *Martinson v. Federal Land Bank of St. Paul,* No. A2-88-31 (D.N.D. Apr. 21, 1988) (same), appeal pending, No. 88-5202 (8th Cir.)....
REVERSED.

Notes

1. For a thorough analysis of the FCS borrowers' rights issues, see Christopher R. Kelley and Barbara J. Hoekstra, *A Guide to Borrower Litigation Against the Farm Credit System and the Rights of Farm Credit System Borrowers,* 66 N.D. L. Rev. 127 (1990).

2. Commercial banks and the Farm Credit System are continually in competition for well-qualified borrowers. And, sometimes FCS attempts to extend its loanmaking authority have been met with litigation. *See, e.g.,* Independent Bankers Association of America v. Farm Credit Administration, 164 F.3d 661 (D.C. Cir.) (1999) (challenging regulations that extended FCS loan making).

3. During the Farm Bill negotiations, the FCS lobbied Congress for additional statutory lending authorities, with the commercial banking industry in strong opposition. The 2008 Farm Bill as enacted did not include any expanded authority. It does, however, include several changes that impact the system. The Farm Bill:

- Allows rural utility (electric or telephone facility) loans to qualify for the agricultural mortgage secondary market (Farmer Mac). Provides for separate consideration of rural utility loans when determining credit risk.

- Makes technical changes in the payment of insurance premiums by FCS banks to the FCS Insurance Corporation.

- Makes more borrowers able to own Bank for Cooperatives voting stock.

- Equalizes lending authorities for associations in Alabama, Mississippi, and Louisiana by allowing Federal Land Bank Associations to make shorter-term loans, and Production Credit Associations to make longer-term loans. Requires board and shareholder votes. Effective Jan. 1, 2010.

Jim Monke, *Agricultural Credit: Institutions and Issues*, 6–7, Congressional Research Service, Rep. No. RS21977 (January 27, 2009).

D. Agricultural Commercial Law: Secured Transactions Involving Farm Assets

The agricultural loans that are made to cover input expenses, equipment purchases, livestock purchases, and other general operating expenses are generally secured by an Article 9 consensual security interest.

Article 9 of the Uniform Commercial Code sets forth the recommended rules for security interests in personal property. State legislatures have adopted Article 9 for the most part, although there are some individual differences between states. Because of the unique nature of some agricultural assets, and because of the special position that agriculture has traditionally had under the law, there are state deviations from the official version of Article 9 that have been adopted by several states. This chapter discusses the uniform provisions of Article 9.

Explore Article 9 of the UCC by using the following list of questions. Each answer references one or more specific sections or subsections of Revised Article 9 of the UCC or the Official Comments accompanying the article.

1) "Goods" is a major type of personal property under Article 9. What are the four different categories of goods under Article 9? Can something be in more than one category? What categories of goods are most likely to apply in a farm setting?

2) What are "farm products" under Revised Article 9?

3) Can something be a "farm product" at one point and not at another?

4) Will a cow always be a "farm product"?

5) Is a farm tractor a "farm product"?

6) What category of goods will the farm pick-up truck be?

7) How are farm-raised catfish categorized?

8) Is raising poultry under a poultry production contract a "farming operation" under Revised Article 9?

9) Under the former version of Article 9, certain goods were "farm products" if they were "in the possession of a debtor engaged in raising, fattening, grazing or other farming operations." What is the parallel qualifier in Revised Article 9, and what difference does this make?

10) Are "crops" defined under Revised Article 9?

11) Under what circumstances might crops change character and no longer be a "farm product"?

12) If state statutory law provides that a repair-person who repairs a piece of equipment will be granted an automatic lien on the equipment in order to secure payment of the cost of repair, will this lien be covered under Revised Article 9? Does it make a difference if the equipment repaired is farm equipment?

13) If state statutory law provides that a veterinarian who treats an animal will be granted an automatic lien on the animal in order to secure payment of the cost of care, when will the vet's interest be covered under Revised Article 9?

14) Many states have a statute that gives a farm landlord an interest in the crops grown on the rented property, securing payment of the rent. Is this an interest that would be covered under Revised Article 9?

15) If a creditor has a security interest in a crop, and that crop is sold, what interest does the creditor have?

16) Consider a production contract arrangement whereby a seed company contracts with a farmer to raise seed grain. The company provides the seed, and pursuant to contract, claims title to the crop. Does the farmer's creditor, with a valid interest in growing crops, have a security interest in the crop?

17) Can a purchase money security interest be taken in cattle? If so, how? If not, why not?

18) Can a seed supplier take a purchase money security interest in crops? Why or why not?

1. Crop Financing: Defining Crop Proceeds

Crop financing can be subject to all the risks associated with crop production. A security interest in crops is typically taken when financing is provided. Does this security interest extend to the federal farm programs that the farmer receives?

When a farmer seeks operating credit for crop input expenses, federal farm program payments are a particularly attractive asset for creditors seeking security for a loan. How should these payments be described as collateral? Consider how different courts analyze these farm program payments under the former version of Article 9.

Pombo v. Ulrich (Matter of Munger)
495 F.2d 511 (9th Cir.1974)

ALFRED T. GOODWIN, Circuit Judge:

In a contest between the trustee in bankruptcy and the holder of an assignment of an agreement to assign farm subsidy payments 'upon receipt' and several security agreements covering crops and proceeds, the referee in bankruptcy and the district court found for the trustee. We reverse.

Appellant claims the funds under ... security agreements executed between 1966 and 1969 between appellant's predecessor in interest, the Stockton Production Credit Association, and the bankrupt, Munger....

One of [t]he issues raised [is] whether perfected security agreements held by the Association covering 'all crops' and the 'proceeds' thereof included within their term certain federal farm subsidy payments to which the debtor may become entitled ...

Munger, a sugar-beet farmer, gave as collateral for a loan several statutory security interests, covering his farm equipment, the crops to be grown on his land over the next five years, and the proceeds or products from these crops. The financing statements covering these security agreements satisfied California law....

Prior to his bankruptcy, Munger abandoned a part of a crop and applied for abandonment payments. After his bankruptcy, he applied for other subsidy payments. Eventually, Munger became entitled to the funds here in dispute, and they were paid to the trustee. Meanwhile, the Association had assigned to appellant its interest in the payments.

Only the most basic description of property deemed to be collateral for a security interest under Division 9 of the California Commercial Code (hereinafter C.C.C.) is required by C.C.C. § 9402. The test of the sufficiency of the description is whether it would indicate to an interested third party the possible existence of prior encumbrances on the collateral. Using this standard, we conclude that the term 'proceeds' used in the security agreements and financing statements includes the federal subsidy payments in question here.

C.C.C. § 9306(1) defines proceeds broadly as including 'whatever is received when collateral or proceeds is sold, exchanged, collected or otherwise disposed of.' To us, such a definition indicates that the word 'proceeds' is to be given a flexible and broad content. Furthermore, we assume that the security agreements were drafted with an awareness of the importance of the various forms of federal subsidy payments to the realities of financing a farming operation based upon sugar beets, and that an interested third party could also be expected to know that the crops described were sugar beets and entitled to various conditional subsidy payments under the Sugar Act of 1948. Some of these payments are closely connected with the sale of the sugar beets, being computed on the basis of the amount of sugar in the sugar beets grown on the farm and marketed, and paid to the farmer by the Department of Agriculture in addition to any payment from the purchaser. 7 U.S.C. §§ 1131, 1132. These payments would be 'proceeds' under the most grudging interpretation of the security agreement. The other payments are 'abandonment payments' based upon the acreage abandoned because of disease. Such payments depend upon the size of the subsidy pool available in a given year and locality. 7 U.S.C. §§ 1131, 1133. Although resembling insurance payments, these subsidy payments flow not from private contract between the debtor and a third party but rather from a government program designed to protect both the United States sugar industry and the welfare of sugar producers. Abandonment payments, like the subsidy payments based on sugar content, are an integral part of the sugar-beet farming business and, when received, are within a broad reading of 'proceeds.' Not to include such payments within the term 'proceeds' would be to raise distinctions of form over the realities underlying this financing transaction, a result contrary to the intent of the Uniform Commercial Code. *See* Uniform Commercial Code § 9-110; C.C.C. § 9110; Biggins v. Southwest Bank, 490 F.2d at 1308.

The order of the district court upholding the decision of the referee in bankruptcy is reversed.

In the Matter of Schmaling
783 F.2d 680 (7th Cir. 1986)

CUDAHY, Circuit Judge.

In this case, we consider whether corn received under the federal government's Payment-in-Kind ("PIK") program—under which farmers receive surplus grain in exchange for an agreement not to plant their intended crop—constitute crop "proceeds" under the Uniform Commercial Code. The Bankruptcy Court for the Northern District of Illinois determined that PIK payments are proceeds and the District Court affirmed. We reverse.

Leland and Mary Schmaling (the "Schmalings" or the "debtors") are farmers in Jo Daviess and Carroll Counties, Illinois. On May 5, 1982, the Schmalings and the First National Bank of Freeport (the "Bank") entered into a security agreement.

The agreement covered the following collateral:

> All of the farm machinery and equipment, livestock and the young and products thereof, corn and all other crops grown or growing, and the feed, seed, fertilizer, and other supplies used in connection with the foregoing which are now owned or existing, and which are now located on the [Schmalings'] real estate..., together with all property of a similar nature or kind to that therein described which may be hereafter acquired....

In 1983, the Schmalings entered into a contract to participate in the United States Government's PIK program. Under that program, a farmer agrees to remove a specified percentage of his farm's acreage base and designated crops from production. He also agrees to follow certain soil conservation procedures. If the farmer takes these steps, the government transfers to him a commodity equal in quantity to a percentage of what his diverted or nonproducing acreage would normally yield. 7 C.F.R. § 770 et seq. (1984).

The debtors assigned their PIK rights to three parties: Esther Schmaling, the Carroll Service Company and the State Bank of Pearl City. Esther Schmaling was assigned the right to receive 22,960 bushels of PIK corn. In reliance on this assignment, she loaned the debtors $47,537.92 in 1983. The State Bank of Pearl City loaned the debtors $12,000 in 1983 for operating and rent expenses and received the right to 6,612 bushels of PIK corn as collateral. Later, Pearl City loaned the debtors an additional $3,300, using the PIK corn as collateral. Carroll Service Company sold the debtors supplies for the 1982 farming season worth over $40,000. By September 1983, the debtors still owed $13,972.44 on their 1982 bill and assigned Carroll Service 6,200 bushels of PIK corn toward payment. Later, expenses from the 1983 season came due and the debtors owed Carroll Service $32,196.03.

In October 1983, Esther Schmaling presented the document entitling her to the PIK corn to Johnston's Feed Service for payment. Payment was denied on the basis of a claim by the Bank of Freeport stating that it was entitled to the PIK payment because of its security agreement with the Schmalings. Thereafter, upon agreement of the parties to the dispute, the total amount of the proceeds that the debtors were entitled to receive under the PIK program—$99,343.44—was deposited in a trust account with the debtors' attorneys pending resolution of the respective priorities of the parties.

On March 9, 1984, the Schmalings filed a voluntary petition for relief under Chapter 11 of the Bankruptcy Code. On March 30, 1984, they filed a complaint in the Bankruptcy Court for the Northern District of Illinois under § 544(a) of the Bankruptcy Code[1] to set aside a lien against them in favor of the First National Bank of Freeport. Esther Schmaling, the Carroll Service Company and the State Bank of Pearl City intervened as parties plaintiff.

The Bankruptcy Court found for the Bank. It concluded that, "although the agreement did not contemplate the not-as-yet-commenced Payment-in-Kind program and its proceeds specifically, its coverage was intended to be broad so as [sic] cover all of the debtor's farm-related assets."

The United States district court affirmed. It found that because PIK payments are based on debtors' prior growing history, participants in the program in essence "'exchanged' their own corn for the PIK corn," thus making the PIK payments "proceeds."[2] A contrary result, the court found, would create a potential for fraud, as farmers could avoid a security agreement in crops merely by abandoning their farming activities and participating in a Payment-in-Kind program. We disagree.

I.

Because the Bankruptcy court found the Schmalings' intent to grant the Bank a security interest in all farm-related assets to be clear, it eschewed engaging in a "hypothetical bout over the meaning of the word 'crops.'" However, a security interest granted by a debtor to a creditor is limited strictly to the property or collateral described in the security agreement. Here, the security agreement does not refer to all farm-related assets. Rather, it grants the bank a security interest in certain specific assets pertaining to the debtors' farm, including "corn and all other crops grown or growing." Crops are "products of the earth which are the result of annual labor and cultivation ... by the person in possession of realty."

For something to be "proceeds" of crops, therefore, it must be received upon their "sale, exchange, collection or other disposition." U.C.C. § 9-306(2) ... But in the instant

---

1. Section 544(a)—the "strong arm clause" of the Bankruptcy Code—states:
    (a) The trustee shall have, as of the commencement of the case, and without regard to any knowledge of the trustee or of any creditor, the rights and powers of, or may avoid any transfer of property of the dealer or any obligation incurred by the debtor that is voidable by—
    (1) a creditor that extends credit to the debtor at the time of the commencement of the case, and that obtains, at such time and with respect to such credit, a judicial lien on all property on which a creditor on a simple contract could have obtained a judicial lien, whether or not such a creditor exists....
    Under section 544(a), the trustee takes the position of a hypothetical lien creditor and can avoid any unperfected security interest. In their complaint against the Bank of Freeport, the Schmalings stated that even if PIK revenues were proceeds, the Bank's interest in them was unperfected, as proceeds paid in tangible property require the filing of a financing statement for perfection under § 9-306(3) of the U.C.C. As the Bank never filed a financing statement specifically mentioning the in-kind payments, the Schmalings contended, the Bank's interest was subordinate to the interest of the Schmalings' assignees.
    2. Under the U.C.C., a security interest will continue in proceeds of collateral described in the security agreement unless the agreement or the secured party specifies otherwise. § 9-306(2) states:
    Except where this Act otherwise provides, a security interest continues in collateral notwithstanding sale, exchange or other disposition thereof unless the disposition was authorized by the secured party in the security agreement or otherwise, and also continues in any identifiable proceeds, including collections received by the debtor.

case there was never a crop of which to dispose. No corn was grown on the Schmalings' real estate. One condition for participating in the PIK program was that individuals *not* plant a crop.

As a consequence, most courts have concluded that inkind payments do not constitute proceeds of crops. As the court held in *In re Mattick,* 45 B.R. 615, 617 (Bankr.D.Minn.1985), "Under the PIK programs involved in this case, the Debtors were paid for agreeing to forego planting any crop. They were not paid a subsidy. The right to the PIK entitlement was a general intangible, not proceeds of an existing, failed crop — or proceeds of anything." Similarly, in *Matter of Binning,* 45 B.R. 9 (Bankr.S.D.Ohio 1984), a case similar to the one before us, debtors granted the bank a security interest in crops and afterwards enlisted in a payment-in-kind program. The security agreement made no reference to government entitlements as collateral. In finding that the bank had no right to the PIK payments, the court held, "Since the [bank's] security agreement does not list government entitlements as collateral, either specifically or generally under the category of 'accounts' or 'general intangibles,' their after-acquired security interest cannot be found to extend to these entitlements." ...

Cases finding PIK and like payments to be proceeds of crops are generally distinguishable. In *In re Kruse,* 35 B.R. 958 (D.Kan.1983) the court determined that PIK payments were proceeds where they substituted for crops that had been originally planted but were plowed under. However, the court found that PIK revenues were general intangibles and not proceeds where they were paid with respect to fields that had never been planted. In *Matter of Munger,* 495 F.2d 511 (1974), the Ninth Circuit found federal subsidy payments to be proceeds of crops, but there the farmer had abandoned his sugar beet crop in order to take advantage of the subsidy. Similarly, in *In re Nivens,* 22 B.R. 287 (Bankr.N.D.Tex.1982), Department of Agriculture disaster relief payments for cotton were found to be proceeds of crops. There, too, however, the subsidy was paid in compensation for already existing plants that had been cultivated through the recipient's effort.

Some cases have concluded that because the PIK payments substitute for crops that would have been grown but for the participation in the program, PIK receipts are proceeds. *See In re Judkins,* 41 B.R. 369 (Bankr.D.Tenn.1984); *In re Lee,* 35 B.R. 663 (Bankr.N.D.Ohio 1983). This argument has a certain appeal from an economic perspective since the government based its PIK calculations on the farmer's past and anticipated yields and intended the program to reduce production of certain crops. This appeal is perhaps even greater where the farmer is paid in the commodity he would have planted. But the fact that the farmer ended up with bushels of corn to distribute cannot obscure the fact that PIK corn is not a "crop" from that farmer's land. Nor should the federal government's intent in managing its agricultural programs or the broad economics of the transaction override the plain language of a security agreement which extends only to crops. The rationale of the transaction cannot cure clear deficiencies in the description of the collateral.

We also cannot accept the district court's contention that finding for the debtors will create an unintended potential for fraud. The court stated, "If PIK payments were not proceeds, a farmer could abandon all farming activities in favor of program participation, thereby allowing him to dissipate the proceeds of the programs without any regard for his creditors' interests." This argument can be made anytime a farmer finds a substitute use of his land, such as using his fields for a rock concert or a fair ground instead of for the growing of crops. Clearly, income derived from such alternative uses could not be considered crop proceeds. Moreover, banks can easily avoid such potential losses of collateral by careful drafting, ... and we see no good reason to apply unjustifiably loose constructions to documents of this kind. Even if this particular PIK program was new, land diversion programs and federal subsidies of this sort to farmers have been commonplace for years. *Cf.* Matter of Binning, 45 B.R. 9, 12–13 (Bankr.S.D. Ohio 1984) ("Land diversion programs have been in existence in one form or another since at least 1949. As a federally chartered instrumentality, operating under the auspices of the farm credit administration ... the [bank] could hardly claim to be ignorant as to be the existence or nature of these programs; nor could it claim to be unversed in drafting security agreements which adequately describe government entitlements as collateral.") The bank could presumably have acquired an interest in PIK revenues either by referring to government entitlements directly or by including a reference to general intangibles or to contract rights. Since the Bank did none of these things, the district court was incorrect in granting it the right to the Schmaling's PIK payments.

The decision below is therefore REVERSED.

Kingsley v. First American Bank of Casselton
865 F.2d 975 (8th Cir. 1989)

Before LAY, Chief Judge, PECK, Senior Circuit Judge, and JOHN R. GIBSON, Circuit Judge.

JOHN R. GIBSON, Circuit Judge.

The central issue in this case is whether farm deficiency and diversion payments under the federal price support and production adjustment programs are "proceeds" of crops under North Dakota law and therefore covered by a security agreement applying to crops and their proceeds. Truman and Connie Kingsley appeal from an order of the district court reversing the bankruptcy court and upholding as enforceable First American Bank of Casselton's claimed security interest in the Kingsleys' 1986 crops, cash proceeds thereof, and federal deficiency and diversion payments. We are convinced that these payments, arising from contracts between the Kingsleys and the federal Commodity Credit Corporation, are not proceeds of the 1986 crops and therefore are not covered by First American's security agreement. Accordingly, we reverse the judgment of the district court and remand the case to the bankruptcy court for further proceedings....

The Kingsleys farm in Cass County, North Dakota. In 1986, they owned two tracts of land and rented eight others, and their farming activities included raising cattle, wheat, soybeans, corn, and barley. On April 10, 1986, the Kingsleys entered into contracts with the U.S. Department of Agriculture's Commodity Credit Corporation (CCC) to participate in the 1986 price support and production adjustment programs for their wheat, corn, and barley crops. With respect to production adjustment, the Kingsleys agreed to devote specified percentages of their cropland to "approved conservation uses" rather than planting, and in return they would receive "diversion payments" in the form of commodity certificates from the CCC. With regard to price support, the CCC would make "deficiency payments" to the Kingsleys. These payments would be calculated using a complex formula; one element, the deficiency payment rate being based on the amount by which the Department of Agriculture's target price for each crop exceeded the Department's national market price or loan rate, whichever was higher.

On April 15, 1986, the Kingsleys and First American entered into an agreement including provisions for a $200,000 loan. On April 23, the Kingsleys gave First American a promissory note for the loan, secured in part by a separate agreement granting the bank a security interest in "[a]ll crops of every type and description grown and/or harvested" by the Kingsleys on the various tracts of land in 1986 and "[a]ll proceeds and products of all the foregoing." *Id.* at 46. The Kingsleys also assigned $20,000 of their 1986 deficiency and diversion payments to the bank.

The Kingsleys fell behind in payments on the loan, and on October 31, 1986, they filed for reorganization under Chapter 11 of the bankruptcy code. On November 26, the Kingsleys filed an adversary proceeding in the bankruptcy court to determine the validity of First American's security interest in their 1986 crops and farm program payments. The Kingsleys alleged that First American did not have a perfected security interest in the government payments because they failed to perfect by proper filing of a requisite financing statement and therefore its lien was subject to avoidance powers of the debtor in possession under the Bankruptcy Code....

On appeal, the Kingsleys argue that the district court erred in ruling that the government payments are "proceeds" of the 1986 crop....

II.

Under North Dakota law, proceeds include "whatever is received upon the sale, exchange, collection, or other disposition of collateral or proceeds." N.D.Cent.Code § 41-09-27(1) (1983) (U.C.C. § 9-306(1)). The Supreme Court of North Dakota has not decided whether federal deficiency and diversion payments are crop proceeds. However, the relevant provisions of North Dakota law are enactments of the Uniform Commercial Code. While we may therefore consider U.C.C. decisions from other jurisdictions material to our analysis, as the bankruptcy and district courts did, we are confronted with a division of authority based substantially on differences among the various types of government farm payment programs. We therefore look to the specific features of the two programs involved here to determine whether diversion and deficiency payments, respectively, are proceeds of crops under section 41-09-27(1). The Kingsleys signed a "contract to participate in the 1986 price support and production and adjustment programs," the terms and conditions of which were contained in a ten page appendix to the contract also requiring their signature. Accordingly, resolution of the issues before us require that we analyze these documents, as well as the statutory and regulatory framework on which they are based.

A.

The Secretary of Agriculture is authorized to make land diversion payments to producers of wheat and feed grains, including corn and barley, who "devote to approved conservation uses an acreage of cropland on the farm in accordance with land diversion contracts entered into by the Secretary with such producers." 7 U.S.C. §§ 1444e(f)(5)(A) (feed grains), 1445b-3(f)(5)(A)(i) (wheat) (Supp. IV 1986). The Secretary may regulate the amounts payable to producers under these contracts through bids or "such other means as the Secretary determines appropriate."

Here the Kingsleys entered into a series of land diversion contracts with the Secretary through the CCC for their 1986 wheat, corn, and barley crops. The appendix to these contracts requires the Kingsleys to devote 2.5% of their land for each crop to conservation uses. The appendix also provides a formula for determining the amount of the diversion payments, which is essentially based on the past yield of the diverted acres and calculated at a rate which is roughly 25% of the government's 1986 target price for each crop. Further details of these arrangements are not necessary to the issues before us. Their basic effect is to compensate the Kingsleys for converting cropland to conservation uses as part of a general program for regulating the total national acreage of the crops they produce....

In the recent case of *In re Schmaling*, the Seventh Circuit thoroughly reviewed the decisional authority governing in-kind diversion payments and concluded that such payments are not crop proceeds. It observed that unlike a subsidy, diversion payments result from a farmer's agreement not to plant certain crops. The court also distinguished diversion payments from abandonment and disaster relief payments, which result when a planted crop is plowed under or fails. *Id.* The court reasoned that in the latter instances, the government payments might be considered "substitutes" for the original crops (although it did not decide the issue), but that this rationale did not extend to crops which were never planted.

It is not necessary to repeat here the careful analysis of precedents undertaken by the *Schmaling* court. Suffice it to say that we are persuaded by the court's reasoning and convinced that it should be applied to this case. The Kingsleys entered the federal diversion program on April 10, 1986, five days before First American agreed to extend them a loan and nearly two weeks before the Kingsleys granted the bank a security interest in their crops. First American was aware of the limited planting the Kingsleys would undertake in 1986, and sought assignment of the 1986 diversion payments. The bank failed, however, to perfect this assignment, or to seek a security agreement specifically covering the payments, although it could readily have done so. In these circumstances, it would be particularly inappropriate to rule that the diversion payments are proceeds or "substitutes" for the 1986 crops. There is simply no sense in which the Kingsleys received the diversion payments "upon the sale, exchange, collection or other disposition" of their crops, as section 41-09-27(1) requires. Accordingly, we conclude that the district court erred in interpreting the definition of "proceeds" in section 41-09-27(1) as including the Kingsleys' diversion payments. *Osteroos* was not appealed to this court, and is not persuasive to us. We decline to apply its analysis of PIK payments to the Kingsleys' diversion payments.

B.

Whether the Kingsleys' deficiency payments are proceeds of their 1986 crops is a more difficult question. These payments are part of the federal price support program. Under this program, producers of wheat and feed grains, including corn and barley, are compensated under a formula using a deficiency payment rate. This rate is the amount by which the target price for the crop exceeds the higher of the national weighted average market price received by farmers for the crop during the first five months of the marketing year, or the national average loan rate for the crop before reduction to maintain the crops competitive market position. The Secretary sets the target price after considering a variety of factors related to the crop's supply and demand. Under certain limited circumstances the deficiency payments can take into consideration a percentage of the preceding year farm program payment yield. Finally, the combined total of deficiency and diversion payments under these provisions in 1986 cannot exceed $50,000.

This complex price support system was incorporated into the Kingsleys' contract with the CCC, including the Secretary's specific target prices for each crop. Again, we need not delve into this system in any further detail. Like the land diversion program, the price support program is part of a larger, general system for regulating national production of basic agricultural commodities.

We believe that deficiency payments, like the diversion payments, are not proceeds within the meaning of the statute, as they were not received by the Kingsleys upon the sale, exchange or other disposition of their 1986 crops, but resulted solely from the Kingsleys' contracts with the CCC. First American argues that the term "proceeds" should be interpreted broadly and that deficiency payments should be treated as proceeds or "substitutes" for proceeds, because they are part of the minimum return the Kingsleys expected on their crops. *See, e.g., In re Munger,* 495 F.2d 511, 513 (9th Cir.1974); *In re Nivens,* 22 B.R. 287, 291–92 (Bankr.N.D.Tex. 1982). While this approach has significant appeal, it does not withstand close analysis and we are convinced that it should not be applied here. A study of the documents upon which the payments are made convincingly demonstrates that the payments are based on contract rights having origin in the statutory and regulatory fabric of the farm support program, rather than upon marketing the crop.

The deficiency and diversion programs are closely interrelated, and both are described in detail in the same ten-page appendix attached to the contract which the farmer must sign. The deficiency payments are keyed to the permitted acreage, defined as part of the agreement to devote land to conservation usages, which is in turn the essence of the diversion program. The two types of payment are subject to a common overall limit, and the CCC contracts and appendix indicate that farmers agreeing to participate in one program must also participate in the other. The appendix specifies particular dates on which the deficiency payments are to be made without any reference to when the crop is marketed. As the deficiency and diversion programs are part and parcel of the same program, it is nearly impossible to make a useful distinction between the payments. Following *Schmaling,*, we could perhaps emphasize that deficiency payments subsidize the farmer's return on planted crops, while diversion payments compensate the farmer for not planting. We are not dealing with a simple crop subsidy, however, and consistent application of this approach would require a further distinction between those deficiency payments based on planted acreage and those based on diverted land. In either case, we would necessarily increase the complications in this area and thereby frustrate one of the overriding aims of North Dakota's commercial code — to simplify and clarify the law governing commercial transactions. Such a result is, of course, to be avoided. A study of the contract documents upon which the diversion and deficiency payments are based convinces us that the diversion payments are not proceeds, and while the deficiency payments may fall closer to the definition, the difficulty of distinguishing deficiency and diversion payments satisfies us that we should not expand the definition of proceeds in section 41-09-27(1) to include the deficiency payments.

In these circumstances, we simply cannot dismiss the fact that the deficiency payments do not fall within the definition of proceeds. The wide variety and changing forms of federal farm payment programs have continued to generate difficulties for farmers, farm lenders and courts in determining the extent of security interests in crops and their proceeds, as this case amply demonstrates. In contrast, there appears to be no dispute with our ruling in *Sunberg,* 729 F.2d at 562–63, that rights to government farm payments are either accounts or general intangibles under the U.C.C., and that security interests in these rights may be created through a security agreement applying specifically to such collateral.

Accordingly, we conclude that the definition of proceeds set forth in N.D.Cent.Code §41-09-27(1) should not be expanded to include the Kingsleys' federal deficiency payments under the 1986 price support program.

Bank of North Arkansas v. Owens

884 F.2d 330 (8th Cir. 1989)

Before JOHN R. GIBSON, Circuit Judge, FLOYD R. GIBSON, Senior Circuit Judge, and BOWMAN, Circuit Judge.

JOHN R. GIBSON, Circuit Judge.

The Bank of North Arkansas appeals from a district court order affirming the bankruptcy court's decision that North Arkansas did not possess a perfected security interest in dairy termination payments received by debtor Jimmy Owens. Owens, who had pledged his dairy herd to secure a loan with North Arkansas, contracted with the federal government to stop producing milk for five years, in return for the termination payments. This agreement also required Owens to sell his dairy cows for slaughter or export. The cattle were sold, with the sale price being prorated between North Arkansas and the Bank of Salem, which also held a perfected security interest in the herd. North Arkansas argues that it, rather than Salem, is entitled to the termination payments, either as "proceeds" from the cattle sale, or as "contract rights, accounts or general intangibles." We affirm the judgment of the district court.

I.

The facts in this case are not disputed. On May 17, 1983, Owens borrowed $175,254.75 from North Arkansas, granting a security interest that North Arkansas promptly perfected.[2] He borrowed an additional $52,500 from Salem on January 15, 1984, securing the debt with an interest in 75 head of Holstein cattle and other general intangibles. The Salem debt was further secured with an additional 50 head of Holstein heifers on July 22, 1985.[3] Owens was unable to meet his debts, and sought protection in Chapter 11 bankruptcy proceedings.

Before the Chapter 11 filing, however, Owens had successfully applied to participate in the "Dairy Termination Program" run by the United States Department of Agriculture, Agricultural Stabilization and Conservation Service (ASCS). This program, dis-

---

2. North Arkansas' security agreement covered specific items of Owens' farm property, including 70 head of Holstein heifers, 78 head of dairy cattle, and certain pieces of farm machinery. The property covered by the agreement included:

    (a) All … property specifically listed and, if a general description is used (whether or not any specific property is listed), in all … property fitting the general description; and (b) all benefits which arise from the described property, including cash or non-cash proceeds, insurance benefits, interest, dividends, stock splits, and voting rights and,

    (c) any property which is now or hereafter becomes attached to, a part, or results from the described property.

Record at 75–76.

3. Owens used broader language in each of his contracts with Salem. These agreements granted:

    All my cattle, and the increase, produce and products thereof, now owned or hereafter acquired, whether by purchase or natural increase, (together with all rights of payment of money now owed or hereafter owed to debtor, whether due or to become due and whether or not earned by performance, including, but not limited to accounts, contract rights, chattel paper, instruments and general intangibles, all of which are hereafter called receivables. (sic).

Record at 77.

cussed at length in the next section, provided him with total payments of $92,296.05, eighty percent of which he received immediately. Owens executed an assignment of these payments to the Farmers Home Administration (FmHA), as partial satisfaction of debts he owed to that agency. As required by the dairy program, Owens sold his 148 head of cattle, prorating the proceeds between North Arkansas and Salem. Owens continued to owe North Arkansas a balance of $107,279.76. In a separate but related action, North Arkansas was awarded equipment valued at $15,000, leaving a balance owed of approximately $92,000.

North Arkansas considered itself entitled to the dairy payments to pay the remaining debt, and it brought the present claim in bankruptcy court, naming Owens, Salem, and the FmHA as adversary parties. Salem answered that it too claimed a security interest in the payments, and that its claim was superior to that of North Arkansas. FmHA's answer admitted inferior priority to that of Salem, but alleged that North Arkansas' security agreement did not include any of the payments. Thus, if North Arkansas' security agreement covered the dairy termination payments, it had the superior claim. If the agreement did not encompass these payments, Salem was entitled to the money, followed by the FmHA.

North Arkansas advanced two theories as to why its agreement with Owens applied to the dairy payments. First, it argued that the payments were proceeds from the disposition of Owens' cattle. Second, it stated that even if the payments were not proceeds, they were at least contract rights or general intangibles, and the security agreement in question sufficiently described them to create a valid security interest. The bankruptcy court rejected both arguments. [I]t concluded that the dairy payments were made by the government in return for an agreement to refrain from milk production, not for the cattle. Additionally, the bankruptcy court found no other language in the agreement that might cover the dairy payments. North Arkansas appealed to the district court, but that court affirmed on the basis of the same analysis. The present appeal followed.

II.

We first consider whether Owens' dairy termination payments constitute proceeds from the sale of his cattle. Arkansas law adopts the Uniform Commercial Code definition of proceeds as "whatever is received upon the sale, exchange, collection, or other disposition of collateral or proceeds." Ark.Code Ann. § 4-9-306(1) (1987). The Arkansas courts have not decided how this section applies to dairy payments, and courts interpreting the laws of other states have split in their results. *See, e.g., Lisbon Bank and Trust Co. v. Commodity Credit Corp.,* 679 F.Supp. 903 (N.D.Iowa 1987) (payments not proceeds of livestock under Iowa law); *In re Hofstee,* 88 B.R. 308 (Bankr.E.D.Wash.1988) (payments are cattle proceeds under Washington law). Our recent decision of *In re Kingsley,* 865 F.2d 975 (8th Cir.1989), holding that federal diversion and deficiency payments are not crop proceeds under North Dakota law, requires us to begin our analysis by thoroughly examining the government program involved.

The Dairy Termination Program is designed to reduce the amount of commercially available milk, in the hopes of stabilizing milk prices. Participation is voluntary; every producer desiring to enter the program must submit a bid to the Commodity Credit Corporation (CCC). These bids reflect the price that each producer would demand to remain outside the dairy business for five years. The CCC evaluates each bid, considering both the price requested and the amount of milk that would be removed from the market. The CCC then notifies each chosen participant of approval, and executes a contract binding the producer to the restrictions of the program.

These restrictions are designed to cut nationwide milk availability in two ways. First, the individual producer is totally barred from the dairy business during the contract period. This ban extends to his immediate family, and forbids the acquisition of any personal interest in any phase of the milk production process. Second, the equipment and facilities of the contractor are prohibited from producing any milk. All dairy cattle must be sold for slaughter or export, to ensure that they produce no further domestic milk. Moreover, the contractor must prevent his facility from being used by others to produce milk during the contract period, even if the premises are sold. Breach of any of these provisions subjects the contractor to penalties under the program.

Viewing these regulations in light of *Kingsley*, we conclude that the dairy payments do not constitute proceeds from the sale of the cattle, but instead "are based on contract rights having origin in the statutory and regulatory fabric of the [Dairy Termination Program]...." The government agrees to pay a certain sum of money based on the milk producer's estimated potential milk income over the next five years. In consideration for these payments, the producer agrees to take three steps to leave the dairy business: he must sell his current herd for either slaughter or export, agree to abandon the dairy business for five years, and prevent other dairy producers from using his production facilities.

The question asked by *Kingsley* is whether these government payments are earned through the sale of secured property, or by other means. It is evident that the Dairy Termination Program does not compensate producers for the loss of their cattle, but instead for their agreement to abandon the milk business for five years. The government does not take possession of the dairy herd, but merely requires that it be sold for slaughter or export. The funds received from that sale go to the producer or his assignees, not to the government, and in this case those funds were prorated between North Arkansas and Salem. Further, the payments "are calculated and based upon factors which are particular to the business production of the farmer and not to the cows themselves." These factors are related to the producer's facilities and past skill at milk production.

Under these circumstances, we have no difficulty in concluding that the dairy payments were not proceeds from the sale of the dairy herd. The term "proceeds" in North Arkansas' security agreement entitled it to the sale price of the cows, and that is what they received. Since the cows were sold for slaughter or export, rather than for domestic dairy use, it is possible, indeed probable, that the actual sale price was below the fair market value for dairy cattle. North Arkansas has made no claim that it is entitled to the dairy termination payments to the extent that they may reflect the differential between the sale price and the fair market value, *i.e.,* the prejudice from forced sale conditions. Had such a claim been raised, a number of difficult issues might have been presented to the bankruptcy court, but as it was not asserted or considered by the bankruptcy court or district court, it is inappropriate that we consider such hypothetical but unasserted and unlitigated questions in reaching our decision.

III.

Finally, we consider whether North Arkansas is entitled to the dairy termination payments through some other portion of its security agreement. We conclude that it is not. North Arkansas argues that its security agreement is so broadly worded that the parties intended contract rights or general intangibles to be included, and that the dairy payments fall within this category. We agree with the district court that the other language in the agreement is too vague to reasonably describe the dairy termination payments.[7]

---

7. North Arkansas points to language in its security agreement entitling it to all "benefits" and "results" from the cattle. We have already stated, however, that Owens' dairy payments had nothing

We therefore reject North Arkansas' arguments, and affirm the judgment of the district court.

BOWMAN, Circuit Judge, concurring.

As the opinion of the Court points out, North Arkansas has made no claim that it is entitled to the dairy termination payments to the extent that they may reflect a differential between the sale price of the dairy cattle and their fair market value. The Court therefore correctly declines to consider the merits of this hypothetical claim. Had North Arkansas asserted such a claim, however, I believe it might well have been meritorious. The Dairy Termination Program encourages the reduction of milk production by giving producers a substantial incentive to abandon the milk business. To qualify for the program, a dairy farmer must sell his herd for slaughter or export. This feature of the program raises the possibility that the actual sale price may be below the price that could have been obtained had the herd been sold for domestic dairy use. Viewed from the perspective of a lender who has a security interest in the herd and in proceeds from the sale of the herd, a sale for slaughter or export thus may result in an impairment of collateral—an impairment of collateral that the program encourages the farmer to bring about. In this way, there may be what amounts to an uncompensated "taking" of a portion of the collateral for a public purpose. Such uncompensated takings could be avoided by treating Dairy Termination Program payments as "proceeds" from the sale of the herd to the extent that the sale for slaughter or export is made at a price below the price the herd would bring if sold for domestic dairy use. The views expressed herein are of course only tentative, since we have not had the benefit of briefing or argument on this issue.

FLOYD R. GIBSON, Senior Circuit Judge, dissenting.

I respectfully dissent. While I agree with much of what is written in the majority and concurring opinions, I believe that this panel should reach the issue of whether North Arkansas has a claim to the Dairy Termination Payments due to the forced sale of its collateral. As the concurring opinion ably notes, this forced sale undoubtedly impaired the rights of North Arkansas in the collateral. While neither the majority nor the concurring opinion felt that this panel should decide this question, I disagree and would decide it in the manner described in Judge Bowman's concurrence. Therefore, I would allow North Arkansas to assert an interest in the Dairy Termination Payments to the extent of the difference in the fair market value of the cattle when used for dairy production and the proceeds from the sale of the cattle for slaughter or export.

Accordingly, I dissent.

———————

Many commercial lenders that provide overall operating financing now include the "general intangible" category in their security agreements as well as referring specifically to farm program payments, crops and their proceeds. That said, there are still lenders who provide crop input financing and landlords who seek to secure their rental payments who only have a security interest in "crop proceeds." Farm programs have changed over the years, as has the UCC definition of proceeds. What is the proper characterization of today's farm program payments? Can they ever be considered crop proceeds?

---

to do with his cattle. By comparison, Salem's comprehensive language of "accounts, contract rights, chattel paper, instruments and general intangibles" provides an excellent example of how North Arkansas could have expanded the scope of its security interest.

Revised Article 9, although drafted in an attempt to clarify the law of secured transactions, may have further clouded the issue. Consider the following excepts from Revised Article 9 and its comments.

§ 9-102 Proceeds

"Proceeds" … means the following property:

(A) whatever is acquired upon the sale, lease, license, exchange, or other disposition of collateral;

(B) whatever is collected on, or distributed on account of, collateral;

(C) rights arriving out of the collateral;

(D) to the extent of the value of collateral, claims arising out of the loss, nonconformity, or interference with the use of, defects or infringement of rights in, or damage to, the collateral; or

(E) to the extent of the value of collateral and to the extent payable to the debtor or the secured party, insurance payable by reason of the loss of nonconformity of, defects or infringement of rights in, or damage to, the collateral.

§ 9-102 Official Comment 4(I)

This Article does not contain a defined term that encompasses specifically rights to payment or performance under the many and varied government entitlement programs. Depending on the nature of a right under a program, it could be an account, a payment intangible, a general intangible other than a payment intangible, or another type of collateral. The right also might be proceeds of collateral (e.g., crops).

Even aside from federal farm programs, crop proceeds can be a difficult and controversial category of collateral. Consider the issue of "hauling fees" that are paid in connection with contracts for the sale of farm products.

Western Farm Service, Inc. v. Lynn J. Olsen, II
90 P.3d 1053 (Wash. 2004)

MADSEN, J.

Key Bank National Association (Key Bank) challenges a Court of Appeals decision reversing the trial court's grant of summary judgment in its claim for conversion against J.R. Simplot Co. (Simplot). Key Bank, which held a security interest in potato crops purchased by Simplot, claims that Simplot converted proceeds when it failed to designate Key Bank as a copayee on a check issued to the seller as a hauling allowance. We hold that the hauling allowance constitutes proceeds and reinstate the judgment of the trial court.

Facts

Lynn Olsen is a potato and onion farmer, farming approximately 4,000 acres of land. Key Bank financed Olsen's farming operation between 1996 and 1998 and had a perfected security interest in Olsen's assets, including all general crops and proceeds thereof as well as instruments arising out of sales or other disposition of crops. Key Bank's security interest in crops and the proceeds was perfected by filing a financial statement on April 1,

1996. There were no prior filings. Pursuant to the Food Security Act of 1985, 7 U.S.C. § 1631(e), Key Bank sent a notice to buyer alerting Simplot, with which Olsen contracted for as many potatoes as he had grown, of its security interest in Olsen's crops in 1996 and 1997. The notice to buyer stated that all proceeds shall be paid jointly to Olsen and Key Bank.

In one of the contracts between Olsen and Simplot, Olsen was to deliver his potatoes to a place designated by Simplot at Olsen's own expense. However, the contract also provided that Simplot was to give Olsen a hauling allowance, along with payment for the sale of the potatoes, once Olsen completed delivery. After the delivery, Simplot issued a check to Olsen for $160,607.44 representing a hauling allowance, made payable only to Olsen, not to Key Bank.

For reasons unrelated to the issue under consideration here, Simplot sued Key Bank for breach of contract. Key Bank then filed a counterclaim against Simplot for conversion, alleging that Simplot converted money by issuing a check payable only to Olsen. Both Key Bank and Simplot filed motions for summary judgment. Key Bank asserted that Simplot should have designated Key Bank as a copayee of the check because Key Bank's security interest covered the hauling allowance as proceeds of the potato crop. The trial court granted summary judgment in favor of Key Bank.

Simplot appealed and the Court of Appeals reversed, concluding that there was no conversion because the hauling allowance was not proceeds of the potato crops.

Analysis

The issue presented here is whether a payment for hauling potatoes, made pursuant to a contract for the sale of potatoes, constitutes crop proceeds that are subject to a security interest in the potato crops. Key Bank claims that Simplot converted proceeds when it failed to name Key Bank as a joint payee on the check it paid Olsen for hauling potatoes.

The legislature has defined the term "proceeds" broadly. Former RCW 62A.9-306(1) (1995) provided that proceeds include "whatever is received upon the sale, exchange, collection or other disposition of collateral or proceeds." Key Bank argues that the trial court correctly applied the statute and relevant case law when it held that the hauling allowance paid to Olsen constituted proceeds. We agree.

As this court has noted, the broad statutory definition of proceeds is intended to ensure that the term will be all-encompassing and will be given "'a flexible and broad content.'" *Rainier Nat'l Bank v. Bachmann* 111 Wash.2d 298, 302, 757 P.2d 979 (1988) (quoting *In re Munger,* 495 F.2d 511, 513 (9th Cir.1974)). In *Rainier National Bank,* the bank held a security interest in the debtors' collateral, including their dairy cattle and the proceeds. Under the Food Security Act of 1985, the debtors received payments from the federal government in exchange for selling all of their cattle for slaughter or for export and an agreement not to acquire any interest in dairy cattle or in the production of milk. The debtors refused to assign the payments from the government to the bank, claiming that the bank's security interest did not cover the government payments, although it covered the cash gained through the sale of their cattle. In concluding that the payments were included in proceeds, the court noted that, by including the words "whatever is received" in the statutory definition of proceeds, the legislature clearly intended to include more than the usual cash proceeds received in a normal sale of collateral.

We employed an expansive reading of proceeds again in *Central Washington Bank v. Mendelson-Zeller, Inc.,* 113 Wash.2d 346, 779 P.2d 697 (1989). In that case, the bank financed the debtor's expenses for their crops. As collateral, the bank retained a perfected security interest in the apple crops and the proceeds. Pursuant to the bank's requirements, the debtors contracted with Premium Packing and Storage, Inc. (Premium) to operate as a commission merchant. In turn, Premium had a sales agent agreement with Mendelson-Zeller to perform marketing functions for a commission. Mendelson-Zeller sold the apples and advanced funds to Premium for picking, hauling, and packing expenses. Premium retained the packing advances and distributed the picking and hauling expenses to the debtors and other growers. When Mendelson-Zeller sold the debtors' crops, it retained a part of the gross proceeds as sales commission and brokerage fees and repayment of advances made to Premium, remitting the remaining proceeds to Premium. In turn, Premium deducted its commission and forwarded the remaining amount to the bank. The bank brought a conversion action against Premium and Mendelson-Zeller, claiming a right to all proceeds. In its defense, Mendelson-Zeller argued that the bank's proceeds included only payments received by the debtors after payment of the costs of handling and marketing. The court rejected this claim, finding that the term "proceeds" includes "whatever is received," including proceeds that were not actually received by the debtor. In reaching this conclusion, the court quoted language from *Johanson Transportation Service v. Rich Pik'd Rite, Inc.*, where the court held that "[p]roceeds 'includes all economic components that go into the total amount received for the product.'" 164 Cal.App.3d 583, 592, 210 Cal.Rptr. 433 (1985)....

The *Johanson* case ... is particularly germane. There, Wells Fargo and Rich Pik'd Rite had a security interest in strawberries and proceeds grown by a farmer. Johanson Transportation Service (Johanson) advanced freight charges to the farmer, who failed to repay. The freight charges were included in the sale price to the fruit buyer. The farmer deposited all the checks he received for the sale of the strawberries in the deposit account at Wells Fargo. Johanson sued Wells Fargo and Rich Pik'd Rite for conversion and unjust enrichment. Johanson claimed that the freight charges were not included in proceeds. The court rejected Johanson's claim, stating that the term "proceeds" is to be construed broadly.

Simplot, however, urges that *Johanson* is distinguishable and that the court should instead follow *Thompson v. Danner*, 507 N.W.2d 550 (N.D.1993). In *Thompson*, a bank had a security interest in potato crops grown by growers Thompson and Danner. The growers sold their potato crops to Simplot. The potatoes-sales contracts between Simplot and Danner contained a section for storage payments to Danner because those contracts called for delayed deliveries of Danner's potatoes to Simplot. The bank claimed that the storage payments were included within proceeds of the potato crops, which Simplot protested. On review, the court held that the storage payments were not included within proceeds, noting that the storage payment was received as an additional compensation for a service provided by Danner to Simplot rather than in consequence of the disposition of the crops.

In contrast to *Johanson*, Simplot points out that here, as in *Thompson*, there is a separate contract section providing payment for hauling potatoes. However, the decision in *Thompson* stems from the court's view that the nature of storage payments is significantly different from a hauling allowance. The court noted that the term "proceeds" includes whatever is received upon disposition of collateral. It then reasoned that Danner received storage payments because the disposition of his crops was delayed and the storage payments were additional compensation for the storage service. The court concluded the storage payments fell outside the scope of the term "proceeds" even though the crops were subject to a security interest ... In contrast, a hauling allowance, including the allowance in this case, is a payment received upon the sale of crops. Thus, a hauling allowance is an integral part of the disposition of the crops.

Simplot also urges a more flexible approach to defining proceeds that looks to the language of the sales contracts between the parties. Simplot points out the hauling allowance is provided in a separate contract clause and this indicates that the parties did not intend the allowance to be a part of the sales price of the potatoes. However, if we conclude that the hauling allowance is not proceeds in this case because it is mentioned in a separate clause, brokers and carriers will be encouraged to create contract sections for freight allowances, commissions, or brokerage fees and the like, separate from the main sales section, lowering the value of the collateral. By doing so, the contracting parties can effectively undermine the interest of a secured party and could allow a creditor with subordinate rights to defeat a secured interest in collateral.... Simplot's position is contrary to our determination that the term "proceeds" includes all economic components that go into the total amount received for the product.

Additionally, Simplot would not prevail under the approach it suggests. Here, the hauling allowance was an integral part of the potato-sales contract between Olsen and Simplot. According to the contract, Olsen was required to deliver his potatoes to a place designated by Simplot at Olsen's own expense. Although he was entitled to the hauling allowance along with the payment for potatoes, Olsen could collect these sums only after the potatoes were delivered. Plainly, these sums were "received upon the sale, exchange, collection or other disposition" of Olsen's potatoes and thus properly viewed as proceeds.

We hold that the hauling allowance in this case constitutes proceeds of the potato crops and that Key Bank's security interest covers the check Simplot gave to Olsen for that purpose....

Conclusion

We hold that the hauling allowance paid as a part of the sale of crops is proceeds as defined in former RCW 62A.9-306(1). Accordingly, we conclude that the trial court did not err in granting a motion for summary judgment in Key Bank's favor. We reverse the judgment of the Court of Appeals and reinstate the trial court's summary judgment.

ALEXANDER, C.J., JOHNSON, BRIDGE, OWENS and FAIRHURST, JJ., concur.

SANDERS, J., (dissenting).

J.R. Simplot Co. contracted with farmer Lynn Olsen to buy potatoes. The price was computed per ton and varied depending on the quality of potatoes Olsen delivered. The terms of the contract required Olsen to bear the cost of delivering the potatoes to a site chosen by Simplot if within eight miles. ("Said potato crop shall be harvested and delivered field run to the Company *at the expense of the Grower.*" (emphasis added)). Only when Simplot instructed Olsen to deliver the potatoes outside an eight mile radius did the provision central to this case become relevant:

> The Company [Simplot] shall pay to the Grower [Olsen] a haul allowance of Sixteen Cents ($.16) per ton mile for all usable potatoes to which the Eighty Dollars ($80.00) base price applies for each mile one way, over eight (8) miles and limited to forty (40) miles (maximum payable mileage thirty-two (32) miles) from the public road nearest the Grower's field as described in Section II above to the point of delivery designated by the Company. Payments will

be made at the same time as the first payment to Grower as set forth in Section VII below.

Stated another way, while the cost of shipping the crops up to eight miles was included in the price of crops, Simplot agreed to compensate Olsen in addition to the agreed price for an added service Olsen would provide. Such compensation would increase or decrease depending not on the value of the potatoes delivered but rather on the distance traveled. But despite the parties' express contract that this hauling allowance was solely payment for a service separate from the price of the goods, the majority broadly holds the payment constitutes "proceeds," defined by former Article 9 of the Uniform Commercial Code (U.C.C.) as adopted in Washington as "whatever is received upon the sale, exchange, collection or other disposition of collateral or proceeds." However since this payment was given in consideration of a service, not the collateral, I would hold the hauling allowance was not "proceeds" for the sale of the collateral and affirm the Court of Appeals.

I. Contract for Services, Not Crops

Thompson v. Danner, 507 N.W.2d 550 (N.D.1993) is instructive, though the majority attempts to distinguish it. Similar to these facts the creditor bank there held a perfected security interest in the debtor's potato crops and proceeds thereof. The debtors received storage payments from Simplot (who was the buyer in that case as well) because the sales contracts called for delayed deliveries of the potatoes. Simplot would pay the debtors an amount which varied depending on how much time the potatoes were left in storage....

> Contrary to the Bank's assertion that these payments are merely "a premium added to the agreed upon price," the amount of the storage payment is directly related to the length of time the potatoes are held in storage. *The payment is not received in consequence of the disposition of the crop, but is additional compensation for a service provided by the Danners to Simplot.*

Thompson, 507 N.W.2d at 558 (emphasis added). The same is true here. Olsen was to bear the cost of transporting the potatoes to a site designated by Simplot within eight miles. However if Simplot instructed the grower to ship the potatoes to a site farther than eight miles away from Olsen's farm, it compensated Olsen a separate sum for the added cost of transportation, not an additional sum for the potatoes themselves. Thus, like in *Thompson*, this hauling allowance "is not received in consequence of the disposition of the crop, but is additional compensation for a service provided by [Olsen] to Simplot." The amount which Simplot paid Olsen for hauling the potatoes had nothing to do with the value of the collateral transferred but rather varied by the distance traveled from origin to destination. There is no meaningful distinction between *Thompson* and this case.

II. Proceeds Must Be Received for the Collateral, Not Services

The majority disregards the contractual language, holding "a hauling allowance is an integral part of the disposition of the crops." However I know of no legal principle which states any farmer must, ipso facto, bear the cost of hauling his crops to a remote location without additional compensation for transportation. If that were the rule farmers would sell only to local customers, losing the potential benefits of a national market. For the same reason the secured party would also lose the potential to maximize the price of the collateral.

But rather than hinge my analysis on arbitrary notions of what a black robed judge might opine is an "integral" part of a sales contract, majority at 1056, I direct my attention exactly where a court should: the statutory language and the text of the contract. The statutory language here at issue provides "proceeds" "are whatever is received upon the sale, exchange, collection or other disposition of collateral or proceeds."

If the statute said nothing more than "whatever is received," the majority would have a point. But the remainder of the definition requires the whatever to be "received *upon* the sale, exchange, collection or other disposition of collateral." Former RCW 62A.9-306(1) (emphasis added). In other words, "whatever" received is the value received from the sale of the collateral, not from the sale of something else. My reasons follow.

The revised code does not explicitly define "upon," thus compelling analysis of the dictionary definition. *Webster's* defines "upon" two separate ways which could be applied to former RCW 62A.9-306(1). The first option defines "upon" as "immediately following on [ ] very soon after." WEBSTER'S THIRD NEW INTERNATIONAL DICTIONARY 2518 (1993) (using as example sentence "[upon] his death, she went on the ... stage"). But certainly here "upon" cannot mean something temporal. For example, were we to follow this definition, we would be forced to include in "proceeds" any lottery winnings received by the debtor contemporaneously with income from the sale of collateral. This is absurd.

This leaves the alternative definition of "upon," which means "in answer to [ ] in satisfaction of." WEBSTER'S, (using as example sentence "transcripts are sent [upon] the request of the particular student"). This definition is consistent with the purpose behind extending security interests to the proceeds of collateral, namely to protect the creditor's ability to secure repayment of the debt owed notwithstanding the debtor's transfer of the collateral to a third party ... Property in the debtor's possession still secures the debt owed to the creditor, even though the original collateral is now in someone else's possession.[3] This makes sense, for if "proceeds" were merely whatever the debtor receives during the time his or her property is subject to a security interest, the collateral's value would grow exponentially beyond that contemplated by the debtor and secured creditor identified in the security agreement.

Consequently, a payment must be received "in answer to" or "in satisfaction of," ..., the "sale, exchange, collection or other disposition of collateral" to constitute proceeds. Former RCW 62A.9-306(1). The payment must therefore be the bargained-for consideration received by the debtor in direct exchange for the transfer of collateral.

But this hauling allowance was paid in addition to the price of the collateral. It was not merely a reimbursement of included shipping costs, which under the terms of the sales agreement Olsen was to bear, but rather extraordinary shipping costs for which additional compensation would be due. Simplot compensated for a service Olsen provided that was separate and distinct from the sale of the crops. The allowance was not "in answer to" or "in satisfaction of" the *sale* of the potato crops, but rather for a trucking expense unrelated to the value of the potatoes.

III. "Whatever" Must Be Limited to its Facts

The majority claims *Rainier National Bank* supports its definitional construction, centering its analysis on the court's statement, "[T]he expansive statutory definition of 'proceeds' [should] be given 'a flexible and broad content.'" ... Closer scrutiny of that factual context reveals the majority's reliance is misplaced.

---

3. Of course the security interest remains attached to the original collateral *and* its proceeds if the debtor fails to obtain the creditor's authorization to transfer the collateral free of the security interest, thereby protecting the creditor even further.

The creditor bank there held a perfected security interest in the debtor's livestock and all proceeds thereof. The debtor took advantage of a federal program instituted to maintain milk prices, which required the sale of all livestock for auction or slaughter and an agreement to leave the milk production industry for a period not less than five years. The debtor elected to sell his cattle for slaughter, and in consideration he received over $670,000 from the federal government. The court quoted the dictionary definition of "whatever," noting its broad scope includes "'anything ... everything ... no matter what ... anything at all.'" Reasoning the sale of the livestock for slaughter under the federal program was within the statutory phrase "or other disposition" and noting the payments were received for such disposition, the court held the government payments constituted proceeds of the livestock.

But the issue here is not as it was in *Rainier National Bank*, namely whether the transfer of collateral between Simplot and Olsen was a sale or other disposition covered by former RCW 62A.9-306(1); certainly it was. Rather our issue is whether Simplot's payment to Olsen for a trucking service additional to the transfer was "received upon" that transaction. The "whatever" component, despite its expansive nature, references the immateriality of the *types* of consideration given in exchange for collateral, which is evidenced by former RCW 62A.9-306(1)'s explicit recognition that both cash and noncash consideration constitute proceeds.... But it does not and cannot eliminate the requirement that the consideration be given *in response* to the debtor's transfer of collateral. Therefore payment, "whatever" its nature must still be received by the debtor "in answer to" or "in satisfaction of" the transfer of the collateral to a third party to qualify as proceeds under the U.C.C. *Rainier National Bank* does not negate this principle.

I further take issue with the majority's willingness to disregard the language of the actual sales contract because of its fear debtors and third-party buyers might engage in creative contracting to defeat a creditor's security interest. Such a fear is unfounded, especially since both the common law and equity supplement the U.C.C. and each gives the creditor a remedy should a debtor and third party act tortiously to defeat the creditor's property right ... Moreover, such a view disregards *Rainier National Bank's* instruction to consider these cases in "the factual context presented." Here "the factual context presented" by this contract encourages Olsen to sell to Simplot for an $80 base price by not risking uncompensated remote delivery. If anything, removal of this contingency benefits the creditor by encouraging the sale without giving Simplot any incentive to require delivery any further than necessary because Simplot has to pay for the delivery *in addition to* the potatoes.

My view is further supported by the far more expansive definition of "proceeds" in the revised secured transactions article adopted by the legislature in 2000. In addition to the language of former RCW 62A.9-306(1), now proceeds may also be "[w]hatever is collected on, or distributed on account of, collateral," RCW 62A.9A-102(64)(B), as well as "[r]ights arising out of collateral," RCW 62A.9A-102(64)(C). If former RCW 62A.9-306(1) is as broad as the majority claims, then the legislature needlessly expanded the definition. This cannot be the case as "'[t]he legislature does not engage in unnecessary or meaningless acts, and we presume some significant purpose or objective in every legislative enactment.'"

The cases relied on by the majority are not to the contrary. In *Central Washington Bank v. Mendelson-Zeller, Inc.*, 113 Wash.2d 346, 348–49, 779 P.2d 697 (1989), the creditor bank owned a perfected security interest in the debtor's apple orchard crops and its proceeds. The creditor bank filed a conversion action against a third party who had performed marketing services on behalf of the debtor and retained a percentage of the gross proceeds from the sale of the apple crop. At issue was whether the "[b]ank's security interest extend[ed] to the gross proceeds or only the net proceeds after costs of processing and sale." Relying on both *Johanson Transportation Service v. Rich Pik'd Rite, Inc.* and *In re Estate of Philp,*, we held the U.C.C. definition of proceeds included gross proceeds and not just the net benefit earned as a result of the sale.

Likewise in *Johanson Transportation* the debtor business had sold its strawberry crops which were subject to a security interest on a "sold delivered" or "delivered price" basis, meaning "the freight charges were included in the total cost to the fruit buyer and not charged separately." When payment for the strawberries arrived, the debtor deposited the sales revenue in an account controlled by the creditor bank. The debtor failed to repay the transportation broker for funds it advanced to the truckers for shipping the strawberries, inducing the broker to sue the creditors for conversion. Holding the gross proceeds received by the debtor for the sales were "proceeds" of the strawberries, the California Court of Appeal concluded:

> To us it seems illogical to agree that the cost of the seed, fertilizer, other agri-chemicals, water, picking, packaging, etc., are included within the term "proceeds" but the cost of transporting the product to market is not. Such an argument exalts form over substance and should be rejected. "Proceeds" includes all economic components that go into the total amount received *for the product.*

(emphasis added). The most one can say about both *Central Washington Bank* and *Johanson Transportation* is that a security interest will attach to gross proceeds, not just the net benefit the debtor derives from the sale of collateral, because there the product was sold at its point of destination. It would have been a different case had the buyer arranged to purchase the strawberries in California and then entered into a separate arrangement to truck them to the east coast. The former is an expense absorbed by the farmer, i.e., part of the gross; however the latter is not part of the gross but compensation for an additional service. In sum, neither case displaces the unambiguous statutory requisite that consideration received by the debtor must be in direct exchange for the sale or other disposition of collateral.

Had Simplot designated a delivery location within an eight mile radius of Olsen's farm, Olsen would not have been entitled to any additional compensation. The entire sum received by Olsen would have been *for* the potatoes and the transportation costs subsumed in the gross price, rendering such sum proceeds. But, unlike the situation in *Johanson Transportation* where there was no additional service provided by the debtor in addition to the sale of the strawberries, Olsen provided Simplot with a supplemental service of delivering the potatoes outside the normal eight mile radius contemplated by the contract. The hauling allowance was not "in answer to" or "in satisfaction of" the sale of potatoes to Simplot. It therefore was not "received [by Olsen] upon the sale" of the potato crop and consequently not proceeds.

CONCLUSION

Simplot paid Olsen $160,607.44 to transport potato crops, not for the crops themselves. It therefore does not constitute "proceeds" from the sale of the crops and is not subject to the bank's security interest. To hold otherwise discourages commerce and ultimately works to the disadvantage of all concerned. I would therefore follow the sound reasoning of *Thompson* and affirm the Court of Appeals.

CHAMBERS and IRELAND, J., concur.

2. Livestock Sales and Purchase Money Security Interests

From the early days of "cattle rustling" in the West, interests in livestock have produced conflicts. The complexities of today's livestock industry raise a variety of new conflicts. When a creditor advances funds and takes a security interest in "all livestock now owned or hereafter acquired," the extent of this creditor's interest and what control this interest gives the creditor may become issues in conflict.

Consider the following questions:

1) Presumably, the farmer is raising the livestock for eventual sale. Under what circumstances will a sale violate the terms of the security agreement and be an act of conversion against the creditor's interest? To answer this question, consider the sample security agreement that was provided earlier. How does this agreement protect the creditor's interest and protect the farmer from being charged with conversion?

2) Under the terms of that security agreement, can a farmer elect to use the proceeds from the sale of livestock to purchase new livestock?

3) If so, will the creditor have a security interest in the new livestock?

4) What provisions of Revised Article 9 apply to these questions?

5) Given that livestock may be goods that are "held by a person for sale," when will they be "farm products" and when will they be "inventory"?

Most cattle are born on farms or ranches and later transferred to large concentrated feeding operations. They may be sold to these feeding operations, but more likely, they will be held by the feeding operation, with ownership held by another—either the original farmer or rancher or a third party investor. Feedlot owners may buy and sell cattle, sometimes financing the sale themselves, and almost always relying upon significant credit or other financial backing. Thus, a concentrated feed lot operation may involve tens of thousands of cattle owned by a number of different people and claimed as security by many creditors. Ownership may change hands based on contract, typically without the owner ever taking possession of the cattle or even seeing the cattle. And, the end result of the feeding operation is, of course, the sale of the cattle for food, most often with commingled proceeds.

Under such circumstances, the opportunities for fraud are evident. Owners of cattle in the feedlot, creditors of those owners, and creditors of the feedlot operator may all believe that the cattle in the feedlot are subject to their claimed interest, when in fact, multiple entities may claim conflicting interests in the same cattle. Consider the involuntary bankruptcy case in Missouri of George L. Young and his corporation, Professional Business Services, Inc. The bankruptcy court reported that although at the time of filing there were approximately 28,000 cattle of various ages and stages of production under the care of the debtors, prior to the bankruptcy, they had apparently sold interests to others in more than 343,000 cattle. As the court noted, the debtors were "short some 315,000 cattle." *In re* Young, 269 B.R. 816, 826 (Bankr. W.D.Mo. 2001). Sorting out financial interests in these types of cases can be difficult, time consuming, and expensive.

"Purchase Money Security Interests" (PMSI) often come into play in these types of livestock financing arrangements, and litigation may involve a creditor with an underlying blanket security interest in livestock (or inventory) pitted against another creditor claiming a purchase money security interest that takes a priority position.

As a good introduction to the concept and workings of PMSIs, consider the following excerpt from an article by Professor Keith Meyers of the University of Kansas School of Law.

Keith G. Meyer
A Primer on Purchase Money Security Interests Under Revised Article 9 of the Uniform Commercial Code
50 U. Kan. L. Rev. 143, 150–155 (Nov. 2001)

II. Purchase Money Security Interests (PMSIs) in General

A. Introduction

Whether a security interest is a PMSI, as defined in revised section 9-103, is important in several contexts.[38] One is perfection.[39] Most PMSIs in consumer goods are "automatically" perfected upon attachment;[40] no filing or possession by the secured party is required.[41] A number of special priority rules apply to conflicts between other creditors and PMSI holders. For example, a PMSI perfected by filing "before or within 20 days after the debtor receives delivery of the collateral"[42] has priority over certain buyers', lessees' and lien creditors' interests "which arise between the time the security interest attaches and the time of filing."[43] Another special rule applies to conflicts between PMSI holders and other secured parties. The normal priority rule dealing with more than one secured party claiming the same collateral is set forth in revised section 9-322, which provides that the

---

38. Kan. Stat. Ann. § 16a-5-103 (1995).

39. *Id.* § 9-309(1). *See also supra* note 7 (explaining perfection as defined in revised section 9-309).

40. U.C.C. Rev. § 9-203(b). Attachment requires that the secured party give value, that the debtor have rights in the collateral, and that a security agreement exist. Id. "Value" is defined very broadly in section 1-201(44). "Rights" are not generally defined, but revised section 9-203(b)(2) provides that the debtor must have rights or "the power to transfer rights in the collateral to a secured party." The debtor can obtain this power through any of the traditional bodies of law mentioned in section 1-103, or through specific Code provisions as in section 2-403(1)(b). The third requirement is that the debtor must have authenticated a security agreement unless the secured party has possession of the collateral, or the collateral must be a certificated security in registered form delivered to the secured party pursuant to a security agreement, or the collateral must be deposit accounts, electronic chattel paper, investment property or letter-of-credit-rights over which the secured party has control under revised section 9-104, 9-105, or 9-107 pursuant to the debtor's security agreement. "Security agreement" is defined in revised section 9-102(a)(73), and the definition of "agreement" is in revised section 1-201(3). Under R9, "authentication" of a "record" is the key to attachment rather than the signing of a piece of paper entitled "Security Agreement." "Authenticate" is defined in section 9-102(a)(7) as meaning: "(A) to sign; or (B) to execute or otherwise adopt a symbol, or encrypt or similarly process a record in whole or in part, with the present intent of the authenticating person to identify the person and adopt or accept a record." "'Record,' except as used in 'for record,' 'of record,' 'record or legal title,' and 'record owner,' means information that is inscribed on a tangible medium, or which is stored in an electronic or other medium and retrievable in perceivable form." *Id.* § 9-102(a)(69).

41. *Id.* §§ 9-309(1), 9-310(b), 9-313(a). This rule does not apply to vehicles required to be registered and subject to a certificate of title. *Id.* §§ 9-309(1), 9-311. It is very important to note that Kansas' version of R9 does not continue the $3000 limitation that was applied to a PMSI in consumer goods under F9. Kan. Stat. Ann. § 84-9-302(1)(d) (Supp. 2000).

42. U.C.C. Rev. § 9-317(e).

43. *Id.*

first to file wins unless another rule applies.[44] Revised section 9-324 provides a number of exceptions to revised section 9-322. For example, a qualifying PMSI holder in equipment, inventory, or livestock may achieve priority over security interests perfected earlier in time of filing. Finally, under 11 U.S.C. § 522(f)(1)(B), a debtor in bankruptcy can avoid a nonpossessory, nonpurchase money security interest to the extent it would impair the debtor's ability to claim an exemption in certain assets. These special rules apply only if a secured party can qualify as a PMSI holder. Thus, it is appropriate to first examine the definition of a PMSI.

B. PMSI Defined and the Tracing Requirement

A PMSI is a special type of security interest for which the normal attachment[47] requirements, as well as the special purchase money definitional elements in revised section 9-103, must be satisfied.[48] In general, a PMSI can be obtained only in goods or some types of software [49] but not intangibles; and like under former section 9-107, it is created when a secured party provides the credit that enables the debtor to obtain the collateral.[50]

Revised section 9-103(b)(1) contains the basic definition, which provides: "A security interest in goods is a purchase money security interest ... to the extent that the goods are

---

44. U.C.C. Rev. §§ 9-322(a), 9-322(f)(1), 9-322 cmt. 4 ...

47. *See* U.C.C. F. § 9-203 (2000) (setting forth the formal requisites for the attachment and enforceability of security interests under F9); U.C.C. Rev. § 9-203 (giving the formal requisites for the attachment and enforceability of security interests under R9) ...

48. U.C.C. Rev. § 9-103.

49. *Id.* § 9-103(a)(1) ... Again, under R9, a PMSI cannot be obtained in an intangible. *See id.* § 9-103 cmt. 5 (explaining that "[s]ubsections (b) and (c) limit purchase-money security interest to security interests in goods, including fixtures, and software."). Revised section 9-102(a)(75) provides that "'[s]oftware' means a computer program and any supporting information provided in connection with a transaction relating to the program The term does not include a computer program that is included in the definition of goods."

50. Former section 9-107 provided:
A security interest is a "purchase money security interest" [PMSI] to the extent that it is
    (a) taken or retained by the seller of the collateral to secure all or part of its price; or taken by a person who by making advances or incurring an obligation gives value to enable the debtor to acquire rights in or the use of collateral if such value is in fact so used.
U.C.C. F. § 9-107.
Revised section 9-103(a)-(b) defines a PMSI as follows:
    (a) [Definitions.] In this section: [Definitions.]
        (1) "purchase-money collateral" means goods or software that secures a purchase-money obligation incurred with respect to that collateral; and
        (2) "purchase-money obligation" means an obligation of an obligor incurred as all or part of the price of the collateral or for value given to enable the debtor to acquire rights in or the use of the collateral if the value is in fact so used.
    (b) [Purchase-money security interest in goods.] A security interest in goods [Purchase-money security interest in goods.] is a purchase-money security interest:
        (1) to the extent that the goods are purchase-money collateral with respect to that security interest;
        (2) if the security interest is in inventory that is or was purchase-money collateral, also to the extent that the security interest secures a purchase-money obligation incurred with respect to other inventory in which the secured party holds or held a purchase-money security interest; and
        (3)also to the extent that the security interest secures a purchase-money obligation incurred with respect to software in which the secured party holds or held a purchase-money security interest.
U.C.C. Rev. § 9-103.

purchase-money collateral with respect to that security interest."[51] "Purchase money collateral"[52] means goods or software that secures a "purchase-money obligation," which is defined as "an obligation of an obligor[53] incurred as all or part of the price of the collateral, or for value given to enable the debtor to acquire rights in or use of the collateral if the value is in fact so used."[54] Under these definitions, like under former section 9-107, two types of PMSIs in goods or software can exist. One is held by sellers to secure the buyer's obligation to pay, and the other is held by a qualifying lender.[55]

While a seller can normally establish the PMSI without difficulty, lenders must show that the loan "enabled" the debtor to acquire the good and that the money was in fact used to purchase the good; i.e., the funds must be traced.[56] The tracing problem is solved by the lender issuing a check to the seller of the good or a joint payee (debtor and seller) check. The enabling requirement can present an issue if the purchase is made a long time after the loan or if the debtor purchases the good before the loan is in fact made. For example:

> July 1 Farmer's tractor breaks irreparably during harvest and must be replaced immediately. He calls his banker, who tells him that the bank will loan him the money but that it will take about five days to process everything. After this conversation, Farmer purchases a new tractor from Dealer on an unsecured basis.
>
> July 6 Farmer obtains a loan and signs the security agreement granting Lender a security interest in the equipment as of July 6. Lender immediately issues Seller a check to pay for Debtor's purchase.

Did this loan enable Debtor to purchase the equipment? Would it make any difference if Farmer told Seller that the bank would loan him the money for the purchase on July 1 but that it would not be available until at least July 6?

Comment 3 to revised section 9-103 provides:

> The concept of "purchase-money security interest" requires a close nexus between the acquisition of collateral and the secured obligation. Thus, a security interest does not qualify as a purchase-money security interest if a debtor acquires property on unsecured credit and subsequently creates the security interest to secure the purchase price.[57]

Notwithstanding the comment, it appears that the enabling requirement raises a question of fact to be determined on a case-by-case basis. Moreover, the enabling requirement should not be rigidly construed to exclude all transactions where the debtor first acquired

---

51. *Id.* §9-103(b)(1).

52. *Id.* §9-103(a)(1).

53. Revised Article 9 uses two terms: "debtor" and "obligor." Revised section 9-103 refers to an obligor. "Obligor" is defined in part to mean "a person that, with respect to an obligation secured by a security interest ... (i) owes payment or other performance of the obligation...." *Id.* §9-102(a)(59). "Debtor" is defined in part to mean "a person having an interest, other than a security interest or other lien, in the collateral, whether or not the person is an obligor...." *Id.* §9-102(a)(28)(A).

54. *Id.* §9-103(a)(2). *See supra* note 50.

55. U.C.C. F. §9-107 (2000). *See supra* note 50.

56. It would appear that the cases construing former section 9-107 are still relevant here. U.C.C. Rev. §9-103 cmt. 3. *See, e.g., Chrysler Credit Corp. v. B.J.M., Jr., Inc.,* 834 F. Supp. 813, 830–31 (E.D. Pa. 1993) (finding a security interest not perfected when it was filed improperly), *aff'd,* 30 F.3d 1485 (3d Cir. 1994); *In re Freeman,* 956 F.2d 252, 255 (11th Cir. 1992) (holding that a "first in first out" payment allocation method is insufficient to determine which goods "secure their own purchase price"); *MBank Alamo Nat'l Ass'n v. Raytheon Co.,* 886 F.2d 1449, 1452 (5th Cir. 1989) (finding that a credit advance does not create an interest in accounts receivable as collateral under the U.C.C.).

57. U.C.C. Rev. §9-103 cmt. 3.

the collateral on an unsecured basis. This is particularly true if the seller would not have made the sale without the lender's commitment to make the loan. Certainly, the nexus between the purchase and the loan must be very close-months and years cannot pass. One of the architects of original Article 9, the late Grant Gilmore, argued in his treatise about Article 9 that "[i]f the loan transaction appears to be closely allied to the purchase transaction, that should suffice."[58] While it is not clear what kind of proof would be required to tie the loan and the sale together, it would seem that a lender should be able to make its case if the loan and sale were virtually contemporaneous and both Seller and Debtor understood that the sale would not happen without the loan.[59] From a strategic standpoint, the lender should make the loan directly to the seller and before the acquisition.

Consider the following recent case involving a Texas cattle feeding operation. The case provides an example of commercial livestock financing, conflicting interests in the cattle, and an interesting twist to the PMSI notice requirement.

First National Bank in Munday v. Lubbock Feeders
183 S.W.3d 875 (Ct. App. Tex. 2006)

Panel consists of: WRIGHT, C.J., and McCALL, J., and STRANGE, J.

OPINION

TERRY McCALL, Justice.

In this appeal, First National Bank in Munday and Lubbock Feeders, L.P., claim competing security interests in the same cattle. The trial court granted summary judgment to Lubbock Feeders, holding that it had a purchase money security interest in the cattle and the proceeds from the sales of the cattle with priority over the Bank's security interest in the cattle. In three appellate issues, the Bank argues that the trial court erred in granting summary judgment. Because Lubbock Feeders met its summary judgment burden of establishing that it had a perfected purchase money security interest in the cattle, we affirm the judgment of the trial court.

Background Facts

The Bank sued Briscoe Cattle Exchange Corp. and John William Cox for sums due and owing on various notes. The Bank alleged that Cox had defaulted on nine notes and that he had guarantor liability on two Briscoe Cattle Exchange notes. The Bank alleged that it had a security interest in all livestock owned by Cox, wherever located and whenever acquired. The Bank sought a writ of sequestration for all of Cox's livestock, including any livestock located in Lubbock County, Texas. Lubbock Feeders intervened in the suit, alleging claims against Cox for sums due and owing on various loans. Lubbock Feed-

---

58. 2 Grant Gilmore, Security Interests in Personal Property § 29.2 (1965).

59. Former section 9-107(b) had the same enabling requirement as revised section 9-103(a)(2) and therefore should be considered. U.C.C.F. § 9-107(b); U.C.C. Rev. § 9-103(a)(2); *supra* note 50. *See, e.g., Valley Bank v. Estate of Rainsdon*, 793 P.2d 1257, 1262 (Idaho Ct. App. 1990) (finding the loan not enabling because Rainsdon already owned the cows); *N. Platte State Bank v. Prod. Credit Ass'n*, 200 N.W.2d 1, 5 (Neb. 1972) (finding that a loan given a month and a half after sale is not enabling).

ers also sought a declaratory judgment that it had a superior purchase money security interest in Cox's Lubbock County cattle.[1]

The Bank and Lubbock Feeders moved for summary judgment. Both parties claimed a superior security interest in Cox's Lubbock County cattle. The Bank did not claim that it had a purchase money security interest in Cox's Lubbock County cattle. Lubbock Feeders argued that the summary judgment evidence established the following: (1) that it had a purchase money security interest in the cattle under Section 9.103(a) of the Uniform Commercial Code (UCC) because its loans to Cox enabled him to acquire his interests in the cattle; (2) that it perfected its security interest in the cattle under Sections 9.310 and 9.313 of the UCC by taking possession of the cattle and by filing financing statements covering the cattle; (3) that it was not required to give the Bank notice of its security interest under Section 9.324(d) of the UCC to obtain priority status; and (4) that, even though it was not required to give the Bank notice of its security interest, it gave the Bank notice of its security interest complying with Section 9.324(d). In response, the Bank asserted the following: (1) that Lubbock Feeders failed to perfect its security interest and (2) that Lubbock Feeders failed to give the Bank the required notice of its security interest under Section 9.324(d) of the UCC. Therefore, the Bank argued that it had the superior security interest in the cattle …

Issues Presented

* * *

[T]he Bank asserts that the summary judgment evidence created a fact issue as to (1) whether Lubbock Feeders had a perfected purchase money security interest in the cattle and (2) whether Lubbock Feeders complied with requirements for priority of a purchase money security interest in livestock.…

* * *

Affidavit of Kyle Williams

Lubbock Feeders presented an affidavit from its yard manager, Kyle Williams, in support of its motion for summary judgment. Williams stated that he had familiarity with Lubbock Feeders's financed accounts with its customers and that his job duties required him to stay familiar with the accounts.

Williams explained that Lubbock Feeders operates a commercial feed yard and offers its customers feeding programs with several different payment options, including a cattle and feed financed option. Under the cattle and feed financed option, Lubbock Feeders advances a line of credit to its customer to finance the customer's purchase of cattle and makes subsequent periodic loan advances for financing feed costs and yardage. Customers choosing the cattle and feed financed option execute a loan and security agreement granting Lubbock Feeders a security interest in the customer's cattle. Lubbock Feeders documents each money advance to its customers with a loan certificate.

Williams explained in detail Cox's relationship with Lubbock Feeders. Cox fed cattle at Lubbock Feeders's feedlot under the cattle and feed financed option. If Cox wanted to purchase cattle and place those cattle with Lubbock Feeders, then Lubbock Feeders would finance 80% of the purchase price of Cox's interest in the cattle and reasonable feeding costs.

---

1. Lubbock Feeders had possession of Cox's Lubbock County cattle on its feedlot. Pursuant to an agreed order, Lubbock Feeders sold the cattle and deposited the sales proceeds, less feeding costs and yardage costs due to Lubbock Feeders, into the registry of the court. That amount totaled $104,886.43.

In 2002 and 2003, Cox fed cattle on the following lots, among others, at Lubbock Feeders's feed yard: Lot 101, Lot 151, Lot 277, and Lot 282. Cox and Lubbock Feeders executed feeding agreements covering all four lots. Cox had a revolving line of credit with Lubbock Feeders enabling him to borrow the money necessary to purchase his interests in the cattle. Cox signed loan and security agreements evidencing the loans. The security agreements gave Lubbock Feeders a security interest in Cox's cattle then owned or thereafter acquired.

Cox purchased all of the cattle from third party vendors at sale barn auctions. When Cox wanted to purchase a group of cattle, he submitted an invoice to Lubbock Feeders identifying the cattle by a specific head number, sex, pay weight, and price. As Cox purchased each set of cattle, Lubbock Feeders prepared a loan certificate relating to that set of cattle and showing the amount of the loan advance. All of the cattle were delivered directly to Lubbock Feeders. Cox never had possession of the cattle. After Cox and Lubbock Feeders signed a loan certificate relating to a set of cattle and Lubbock Feeders received the set of cattle, Lubbock Feeders made an advance to Cox enabling him to complete the purchase of the cattle from the third party vendor. Lubbock Feeders made 20 loan advances to Cox on the four lots. Each advance related to a specific set of cattle.

Lot 101

Lubbock Feeders and Cox, each as 50% owners, placed 102 heifers with Lubbock Feeders for feeding and growing. Lubbock Feeders received and placed the 102 heifers at its feedlot as follows: (1) 70 head on June 28, 2002, and (2) 32 head on July 1, 2002. Lubbock Feeders made money advances to Cox on June 19, 2002 and July 9, 2002. The advances totaled $16,680.94. All of the cattle in Lot 101 were sold to packers.

Lot 151

Flintrock Cattle Company as a 50% owner, Harve Williams as a 25% owner, and Cox as a 25% owner placed 107 steers with Lubbock Feeders for feeding and growing. Lubbock Feeders received and placed the 107 steers at its feedlot as follows: (1) 21 head on September 30, 2002; (2) 28 head on October 3, 2002; (3) 21 head on October 7, 2002; (4) 3 head on October 9, 2002; (5) 6 head on October 10, 2002; and (6) 28 head on October 14, 2002. Lubbock Feeders made money advances to Cox on October 8, 2002; October 9, 2002; October 14, 2002; and October 18, 2002. The advances totaled $12,418.36. All of the Lot 151 cattle were sold to packers.

Lot 277

Flintrock Cattle Company and Cox, each as 50% owners, placed 86 steers with Lubbock Feeders for feeding and growing. Lubbock Feeders received and placed the 86 steers at its feedlot as follows: (1) 6 head on January 9, 2003; (2) 29 head on January 16, 2003; (3) 2 head on January 20, 2003; (4) 4 head on January 24, 2003; and (5) 45 head on January 30, 2003. With respect to the Lot 277 cattle, Lubbock Feeders made money advances to Cox on January 27, 2003, and January 31, 2003. The advances totaled $22,625.77. All of the Lot 277 cattle were sold to packers.

Lot 282

Flintrock Cattle Company and Cox, each as 50% owners, placed 94 heifers with Lubbock Feeders for feeding and growing. Lubbock Feeders received and placed the 94 heifers at its feedlot as follows: (1) 43 head on January 15, 2003; (2) 25 head on January 20, 2003; (3) 4 head on January 24, 2003; and (4) 22 head on

January 30, 2003. With respect to the Lot 282 cattle, Lubbock Feeders made money advances to Cox on January 27, 2003, and January 31, 2003. The advances totaled $21,691.62. All of the Lot 282 cattle were sold to packers.

Loan Documents

Williams attached copies of documents detailing Lubbock Feeders's loans to Cox as exhibits to his affidavit, including the feeding agreements, loan and security agreements, loan certificates, and checks showing money advances to Cox. The documents detailed each transaction in which Lubbock Feeders advanced money to Cox for his purchase of cattle from the sale barns. Williams's affidavit, along with the attached documents, traced Cox's purchase of each set of cattle that Lubbock Feeders placed into Lots 101, 151, 277, and 282....

Security Interest Issues

Lubbock Feeders had the summary judgment burden of establishing each of the following: (1) that it had a purchase money security interest in the subject cattle, (2) that it perfected its security interest in the cattle, and (3) that its security interest in the cattle had priority over the Bank's security interest. Lubbock Feeders argues that it had a purchase money security interest in the cattle under Section 9.103 of the UCC. Section 9.103 defines purchase money security interest in part as follows:

(a) In this section:

(1) "Purchase-money collateral" means goods or software that secures a purchase-money obligation incurred with respect to that collateral.

(2) "Purchase-money obligation" means an obligation of an obligor incurred as all or part of the price of the collateral or for value given to enable the debtor to acquire rights in or the use of the collateral if the value is in fact so used.

(b) A security interest in goods is a purchase-money security interest:

(1) to the extent that the goods are purchase-money collateral with respect to that security interest.

Thus, when a creditor makes a loan enabling a debtor to acquire an interest in goods, the creditor may obtain a purchase money security interest in the goods. Section 9.103(a)(2).

Lubbock Feeders asserts that it had a purchase money security interest in the cattle because its loans to Cox enabled him to acquire his interests in the cattle. The summary judgment evidence established that Lubbock Feeders made 20 money advances to Cox with respect to the cattle involved in the four lots. Williams's affidavit and the loan certificates demonstrated that each money advance related to a specific set of cattle. Cox purchased the cattle from third party vendors at sale barn auctions before receiving loan proceeds from Lubbock Feeders. Based on the timing of the loans, the Bank asserts that Cox acquired interests in the cattle before receiving the loan proceeds from Lubbock Feeders. Therefore, the Bank argues that the loans from Lubbock Feeders did not enable Cox to acquire interests in the cattle.

Section 9.103 of the UCC does not contain a requirement that the debtor receive the loan proceeds before purchasing the collateral. Instead, Section 9.103(a)(2) requires that the loan "enable the debtor to acquire rights in or the use of the collateral." Although the Texas courts have not addressed this issue, courts from other jurisdictions have held that a creditor may obtain a purchase money security interest when the debtor receives the loan proceeds after purchasing the collateral.... Thus, the timing of the loan does not determine whether the creditor receives a purchase money security interest in the collateral. Rather, the key consideration is whether the loan enables the debtor to acquire rights in the collateral....

The summary judgment evidence established that Lubbock Feeders's loans to Cox enabled him to purchase the cattle. Each loan advance related to a specific set of cattle. Lubbock Feeders made each of the 20 loan advances to Cox within a short time after receiving the related set of cattle at its feed yard. This time period ranged from the day Lubbock Feeders received a set of cattle until 18 days after receiving a set of cattle. Cox signed a loan certificate with respect to each set of cattle. The loan certificates showed the loan advance amount and the specific cattle relating to the loan advance. The loans were "closely allied" to Cox's purchase transactions. Lubbock Feeders met its summary judgment burden of establishing that it had a purchase money security interest in the cattle.

Lubbock Feeders argues that it perfected its purchase money security interest in the cattle by taking possession of the cattle and by filing financing statements covering the cattle. A secured party may perfect a security interest in goods by taking possession of the goods or by filing a financing statement. Sections 9.310(a), (b)(6), 9.313(a)); *see also Kunkel v. Sprague Nat'l Bank*, 128 F.3d 636, 644 (8th Cir.1997)(Feed yard perfected its purchase money security interest in cattle by taking possession of the cattle) ...

Cox purchased all of the subject cattle from third party vendors at sale barn auctions. Lubbock Feeders received delivery of the cattle at its feed yard. Cox never had possession of the cattle. Thus, the summary judgment evidence established that Lubbock Feeders perfected its security interest in the cattle by taking possession of the cattle. Sections 9.310(b)(6) and 9.313(a). Therefore, we need not address Lubbock Feeders's contention that it also perfected its security interest by filing financing statements nor the Bank's contention that the financing statements filed by Lubbock Feeders were insufficient to perfect its security interest.

The Bank argues that Lubbock Feeders's security interest did not have priority over its security interest because Lubbock Feeders failed to comply with the notice requirements set forth in Section 9.324(d) of the UCC. In response, Lubbock Feeders argues that, because Cox never had possession of the cattle, Section 9.324(d) of the UCC did not require it to give the Bank notice of its security interest to maintain priority status. Section 9.324(d) provides as follows:

> Subject to Subsection (e) and except as otherwise provided in Subsection (g), a perfected purchase-money security interest in livestock that are farm products has priority over a conflicting security interest in the same livestock, and, except as otherwise provided in Section 9.327, a perfected security interest in their identifiable proceeds and identifiable products in their unmanufactured states also has priority, if:
>
> (1) the purchase-money security interest is perfected when the debtor receives possession of the livestock;
>
> (2) the purchase-money secured party sends an authenticated notification to the holder of the conflicting security interest;
>
> (3) the holder of the conflicting security interest receives the notification within six months before the debtor receives possession of the livestock; and
>
> (4) the notification states that the person sending the notification has or expects to acquire a purchase-money security interest in livestock of the debtor and describes the livestock.

The issue is whether the notification requirement in Section 9.324(d) applies when the creditor maintains possession of the livestock. While Texas courts have not decided this issue, the Eighth Circuit Court of Appeals decided it in the *Kunkel* case. *Kunkel* involved facts similar to the facts in this case. A feedlot perfected a purchase money security interest in cattle by taking possession of the cattle. *Kunkel,* 128 F.3d at 644. The issue was whether the feedlot's purchase money security interest in the cattle had priority over a bank's security interest in the same cattle. *Kunkel,* 128 F.3d at 641. The Kansas UCC applied in *Kunkel.* Under the Kansas UCC, the subject cattle were classified as "inventory." *Kunkel,* 128 F.3d at 639. A creditor with a purchase money security interest in inventory could acquire priority lien status by sending notice of its security interest to holders of competing security interests within five years before the debtor received possession of the inventory. *Kunkel,* 128 F.3d at 644.

In *Kunkel,* the feedlot argued that the UCC's notice provision did not apply to its purchase money security interest because the debtor never received possession of the collateral. Therefore, the feedlot asserted that it could maintain priority status without providing notice of its security interest to holders of competing security interests. The Eighth Circuit Court of Appeals interpreted the UCC's notification requirement "to be triggered by actual possession of the inventory by the debtor." *Kunkel,* 128 F.3d at 645. Because the *Kunkel* debtor never obtained possession of the cattle, the feedlot could maintain its priority status without notifying the bank of its security interest. *Kunkel,* 128 F.3d at 645–46.

We agree with the reasoning of the *Kunkel* court. Section 9.324(d)(3) provides that the holder of the conflicting security interest must receive the notice of the purchase money security interest within six months before the debtor receives possession of the livestock. Cox never possessed the cattle. Because Cox never received possession of the cattle, the notification requirement in Section 9.324 was not triggered. Therefore, Lubbock Feeders was not required to give the Bank notice of its security interest to maintain priority status.

Based on our holding, we need not address Lubbock Feeders's alternative contention that it provided the Bank notice of its security interest complying with Section 9.324(d).

Lubbock Feeders met its summary judgment burden of establishing a superior purchase money security interest in the cattle and in the proceeds from the sales of the cattle. The trial court properly granted summary judgment to Lubbock Feeders. We overrule the Bank's first and second issues.

The judgment of the trial court is affirmed.

Notes

1. The Conservation Reserve Program (CRP) has raised an interesting issue. Are the payments received under this land retirement program rental payments from the real estate or are they a type of personal property under Revised Article 9? *FDIC v. Hartwig*, 463 N.W. 2d 2 (Iowa 1990) (CRP payments are rental payments); *Contra, Brown v. FmHA (In re Koerkenmeier)*, 107 B.R. 195 (Bankr. W.D. Mo. 1989) (CRP payments are not rents; they are contract rights akin to other farm program payments).

2. Although non-possessory statutory liens are generally excluded from the coverage of Article 9, the special category of "agricultural liens" was brought within Article 9 coverage by Revised Article 9. U.C.C. Revised Article 9, §9-109. An "Agricultural lien" is defined broadly as

[A]n interest, other than a security interest, in farm products:

(A) which secures payment or performance of an obligation for:

(i) goods or services furnished in connection with a debtor's farming operation; or

(ii) rent on real property leased by a debtor in connection with its farming operation;

(B) which is created by statute in favor of a person that:

(i) in the ordinary course of its business furnished goods or services to a debtor in connection with a debtor's farming operation; or

(ii) leased real property to a debtor in connection with the debtor's farming operation; and

(C) whose effectiveness does not depend on the person's possession of the personal property.

U.C.C. Revised Article 9, § 9-102(a)(5). Note that this definition does not apply to liens created to protect producers of farm products.

Section 9-322 provides the general rule that conflicting perfected security interests and perfected agricultural liens rank in priority according to time of filing. This general rule gives priority to pre-existing security interests, undercutting the special treatment previously afforded statutory lienholders.

However. § 9-322(g) provides that a "perfected" agricultural lien will have priority over a conflicting security interest in the same collateral "if the statute creating the agricultural lien so provides." This exception allows the lienholder's interest to "trump" a pre-existing security interest, but only if two requirements are met. First, the lien must be perfected, and second, the lien statute must establish the priority. U.C.C. Revised Article 9, § 9-322(g).

3. Section 9-315 provides that a security interest "continues in collateral notwithstanding sale, lease license, exchange or other disposition thereof unless the secured party authorized the disposition free of the security interest." Under this general rule, buyers are at risk of having to pay for their purchase twice — once to the seller and once to his or her unsatisfied secured creditor. In order to encourage commercial transactions, other sections of the Code soften the potentially harsh impact of the general rule. Under § 9-320(a) a "buyer in the ordinary course of business" will take free of the security interest. However, a person "buying farm products from a person engaged in a farming operation" is specifically excepted from the 9-320 protection. U.C.C. Revised Article 9, § 9-320.

Congress intervened in 1986 by passing a federal law governing the sale of farm products and the underlying security interests. The law preempts state law with regard to the sale of farm products. The rule is codified at 7 U.S.C. § 1631, with regulations published at 9 C.F.R. pt. 205. It provides for either direct notice or the creation of a central filing system to be used to put buyers on notice of underlying security interests. If a secured creditor does not comply with the notice or filing requirements, the buyer will take free of the security interest.

4. Although Revised Article 9 extended the special treatment of purchase money lenders to livestock financing through the PMSI priorities at § 9-324, the recommended uniform provisions do not include any opportunity for a lender to take a purchase money security interest in crops. The drafters prepared a sample provision for a Production Money Security Interest, and it is found in the Appendix to Revised Article 9.

5. Anne Kanten, Minnesota farmer, farm organizer, and former Minnesota Commissioner of Agriculture is an outspoken advocate for economic justice for farm families. She has argued that farmers should have an exemption, similar to a wage or salary exemption that recognized their labor in producing a crop. She quoted the biblical verse from Timothy that is inscribed on the USDA headquarters in Washington, D.C.: "The husbandman that laboreth must be the first partaker of the fruits." Kanten translated this as, "The farmer who gives his labor has the first claim on the crop." The UCC does not adopt this approach. Putting this in commercial law terms, should a farmer's labor be compensated in a way similar to a purchase-money security interest or agricultural input lien?

V

"Forty Acres and a Mule" — Discrimination in Agriculture

The 2007 Census of Agriculture indicates that U.S. farm operators have become more diverse in the last five years. That said, U.S. agriculture does not come close to reflecting the demographics of the U.S. population. The Census reveals that ninety-six percent (96%) of the 2,204,792 farms in the United States have a principal operator who is white. Eighty-six percent (86%) of principal farm operators are men.

As described in Chapter III, the increased capitalization of American agriculture has made access to financial credit key to the viability of farming operations. Credit is particularly important for beginning farmers and for farmers who wish to expand their operations. The groups identified as having most difficulty in obtaining credit are beginning farmers and farmers in under-represented groups.

Discrimination in lending has been a continued struggle for minority and women farmers. This chapter focuses on a consideration of African American farmers, although references to discrimination against other "socially disadvantaged" farmers is also provided. The chapter concludes with reference to current USDA efforts to address the problems.

A. History of African American Farmers in the United States

Christopher R. Kelley
Notes on African American Farmers
Agricultural Law Update, p. 4
August 1999

With estimates of the current numbers of African American farmers as low as 15,000,[1] it is ironic that Africans were brought to and held in this country for their "ability to work the land...."[2] Although blacks have been closely attached to the land for much of their his-

---

1. Spencer D. Wood & Jess Gilbert, *Re-entering African-American Farmers: Recent Trends and a Policy Rationale* (Land Tenure Center, Univ. of Wis., Mar. 1998) at 2 [Wood & Gilbert]. The most recent USDA estimates indicate that in 1992 there were 18,800 black farmers. Anne B. W. Effland et al., *Minority & Women Farmers in the U.S., Agric. Outlook* (USDA, Econ. Research Serv., May 1998) at 16, 16 [Effland et al.].
2. Peter Kolchin, American Slavery: 1619–1877, 29 (1993) [Kolchin].

tory in America, American farming today is overwhelmingly dominated by whites. "American agriculture's entrepreneurial class is roughly ninety-eight percent white–a higher concentration of whites than in almost any other economic endeavor in the United States."[3] Moreover, while the numbers of farmers who are members of other under-represented groups, including Hispanics and women, have stabilized or increased, the number of black farmers continues to decline.[4]

That blacks have labored on farms since they were first brought to America as slaves is well-known.[5] Less well-known is the fact that blacks have operated their own farms for almost as long. Since no other group of farmers has faced greater obstacles to their advancement in this country, the history of this nation's black farm operators is extraordinary. The notes that follow offer a brief chronology of the gains and losses of black farmers in America.

Black Farmers Before the Civil War

Until the end of the Civil War, farm ownership by blacks was almost exclusively limited to blacks who were free. Though the number of free blacks was always relatively small, the path from slavery to freedom was never entirely blocked. The first blacks imported as slaves in this country during the seventeenth century were brought to the southern mainland British colonies, initially Maryland, Virginia, and South Carolina, and later North Carolina and Georgia. Few in number, "they were allowed a large measure of autonomy" working on small farms or "isolated cowpens."[6] Some were able to use this autonomy to acquire cash and to purchase themselves. In the Virginia colony, some of the first blacks to arrive apparently came to the colony as indentured servants, and they received their freedom after serving their indenture. Others were freed by their masters or had their freedom purchased by missionary and religious organizations or previously freed relatives.[7]

By the 1650s, a small number of free blacks in Virginia had become landowners. Notably industrious, they raised tobacco, corn, wheat, vegetables, and livestock and used the proceeds to acquire more land. Some also acquired slaves and were not hesitant to assert their rights as property owners and slaveholders. For example, in 1655, Anthony Johnson, a black owner of a 250-acre Virginia farm successfully sued his white neighbor for the return of a runaway slave.[8] In the 1660s, after Virginia began to restrict the activ-

---

3. Jim Chen, *Of Agriculture's First Disobedience and Its Fruit*, 48 VAND. L. REV. 1261, 1306–07 (1995)(footnotes omitted)(also noting that "[t]he civilian occupations with the most comparable racial profiles are geologists and geodesists." *Id.* at 1307 n. 324).

4. Effland et al, *supra* note 1, at 16. In 1992, there were 20,956 Hispanic farm operators and 145,156 female farm operators. *Id.* at 20. A current trend in American agriculture is an increase in the number of immigrants from Asia and elsewhere who have become farmers. *See* Scott Kilman & Joel Millman, *Field of Dreams: Immigrants Find Hope In a Life of Farming As Others Sour On It*, WALL STREET J., Aug. 12, 1999, at A1.

5. Also well-known is the considerable contribution of black slaves to the development of American agriculture. Less well known is that the slave trade stimulated the growth of agriculture in coastal Africa in response to the need for supplies for slave ships and slave prisons. *See* Hugh Thomas, THE SLAVE TRADE 796 (1997).

6. Loren Schweninger, BLACK PROPERTY OWNERS IN THE SOUTH, 1790–1915, 11–12 (1997) [Schweninger].

7. *Id.* at 15.

8. *Id.* at 16. *See also* Peter Kolchin, AMERICAN SLAVERY: 1619–1877, 99 (1993) [Kolchin] (noting that a small number of freed blacks owned slaves and that the "leaders of the Cherokee, Chickasaw, Choctaw, and Creek nations consciously appropriated the culture of white Americans — including the ownership of black slaves").

ities of free blacks, he moved his family to Maryland. There, both his son and his grand-son acquired farms. By 1677, "fifty-eight years after the arrival of the first slaves on Amer-ican soil," the Johnson family could boast of three generations of farm ownership.[9] As illustrated by Mr. Johnson's willingness to sue a white neighbor, free "black farmers in early Virginia considered themselves equal to white colonists."[10] As more slaves arrived, however, whites became increasingly fearful of freed slaves, and in 1691 the Virginia Assembly prohibited future manumissions. Thereafter, the number of free blacks declined in Virginia and elsewhere in the South. By 1770, only 1.5 percent of Southern blacks were free.[11]

The American Revolution reversed this decline. Both during and following the Revolution, a substantial number of slaves gained their freedom. Some were freed by the British while others were freed for fighting the British. In 1782, Virginia repealed its prohibition against private manumissions and over the next eight years over 12,000 Virginia slaves were freed. Slaves were also freed elsewhere in the South, but in substantially smaller numbers in the Lower South. Nonetheless, by 1800, "the number of free blacks had grown an astonishing 1,700 percent; one out of every twelve blacks in the South was free."[12]

In the 1780s and 1790s, freed slaves began acquiring land in the Lower South. Some even acquired large plantations. By 1786, for example, James Pendarvis, a former slave, had acquired a 3,250 acre plantation in South Carolina and owned 113 black slaves, placing him "among the largest individual black slave owners in American history."[13] Like Pendarvis, whose father was a white planter and his mother a black slave, most of those who acquired farms in South Carolina "were direct descendants of whites who had granted them large tracts of land...."[14] Freed slaves, usually of French or Spanish and black ancestry, also entered the planter class in Louisiana.[15]

Prior to the end of the Civil War, however, most blacks remained slaves. Rarely were slaves able to acquire land, though many acquired livestock and other personal property through the widespread practice of allowing slaves to tend a portion of their masters' lands for their own use. While this practice began to permit slaves to supplement their meager diet, in some locations it expanded into a "domestic slave economy" that allowed slaves to produce cash crops which were sold to the slaves' masters or local merchants.[16]

Livestock and other property was also acquired through self-hire. "Self-hire had a long tradition in American slavery, stretching back to the earliest colonial period when some slaves, usually the most skilled and trustworthy, were allowed to contact a potential employer, make arrangements for wages and working conditions, and secure their own food and lodging."[17] Despite laws forbidding self-hire throughout the South, the practice persisted because both slaves and masters benefitted from it. Even though self-hired slaves

---

9. Schweninger, *supra* note 6, at 16.

10. *Id*. at 16.

11. *Id*. at 17.

12. *Id*. at 18.

13. *Id*. at 23. James Pendarvis' father was white and his mother was black. Under the so-called "one-drop rule" in effect at the time, he would have been deemed to be black. *See* Jim Chen, *Unloving*, 80 Iowa L. Rev. 145, 159 (1994)(noting that the "one-drop rule" traces its origins to American slave law, which adopted the civil law maxim of partus sequitur ventrem (the offspring follows the mother) for defining ownership interests not only in farm animals but also in human slaves").

14. Schweninger, *supra* note 6, at 20, 23.

15. *Id*. at 21.

16. *Id*. at 30–36.

17. *Id*. at 39.

usually paid their master a portion of their earnings, the arrangement gave them a degree of autonomy as well as income. Slave masters benefitted because they "did not have to pay for the slave's clothing or lodging and also saved the 5 to 8 percent fee charged by a hiring broker as well as the aggravation of taking care of the matter themselves."[18]

Some black farm operators were "quasifree," or "virtually free" slaves. While still nominally slaves, "quasi-free" slaves included those who were illegally manumitted or simply left unsupervised by their owners.[19] Most of these slaves resided in cities and towns where it was easier to avoid detection, but a few occupied and farmed land owned by their masters or took up residence on deserted farms.[20] A small number of "quasi-free" slaves acquired land by posing as free.[21]

Despite laws prohibiting property ownership by slaves throughout the South, by the eve of the Civil War "considerable numbers of slaves had become property owners."[22] The ownership of livestock was particularly widespread. Indeed, in commenting on the General Sherman's confiscation and consumption of most of the livestock his army encountered in its advance on Georgia, an historian has observed that "little did he realize ... that some of the possessions and livestock being seized [by his troops] belonged to the very slaves he had marched to the sea to liberate."[23]

Black Farmers Following the Civil War

Notwithstanding the extraordinary rise of some blacks from slaves to farm owners during the antebellum period, most blacks were landless at the end of the Civil War. In 1880, 75 percent lived in the former Confederate states and were primarily engaged in agricultural work as sharecroppers or tenants.[24] Though the distinction between a sharecropper and a tenant is sometimes blurred in accounts of both, sharecroppers were wage laborers. "The courts in every southern state came to the same conclusion: the cropper was a wage laborer, his wages being a portion of what he produced paid to him by the landlord. The tenant was a renter who paid to the landlord for use of the land; it did not alter the relationship if the rent was a portion of the crop produced...."[25] In theory at least, sharecropping offered the possibility of higher income than fixed wages.[26] While the question of whether this theory matched reality remained subject to debate, sharecropping predominated in places like the Arkansas Delta until World War II.[27]

Even those blacks who had the capital to purchase farmland found that whites, who "looked upon land as their only important capital investment, ... were reluctant to sell

---

18. *Id.*

19. *Id.* at 44–47

20. *Id.*

21. *Id.* at 47

22. *Id.* at 59

23. *Id.* at 60.

24. John Hope Franklin & Alfred A. Moss, Jr., FROM SLAVERY TO FREEDOM: A HISTORY OF AFRICAN AMERICANS 277 (7th ed. 1994)[Franklin & Moss].

25. Harold D. Woodman, NEW SOUTH—NEW LAW: THE LEGAL FOUNDATIONS OF CREDIT AND LABOR RELATIONS IN THE POSTBELLUM AGRICULTURAL SOUTH 68–69 (1995)(footnotes omitted).

26. Fon Louise Gordon, CLASS & CASTE: THE BLACK EXPERIENCE IN ARKANSAS, 1880–1920, 66 (1995).

27. Donald Holley, THE PLANTATION HERITAGE: AGRICULTURE IN THE ARKANSAS DELTA IN THE ARKANSAS DELTA: LAND OF PARADOX 238, 251–53 (Jeanine Whayne & Willard B. Gatewood eds., 1993). See generally, Jeanine M. Whayne, A NEW PLANATION SOUTH: LAND, LABOR, AND FEDERAL FAVOR IN TWENTIETH-CENTURY ARKANSAS (1996)(discussing sharecropping and tenant farming in Arkansas); H.L. Mitchell, MEAN THINGS HAPPENING IN THIS LAND: THE LIFE AND TIMES OF H.L. MITCHELL, COFOUNDER OF THE SOUTHERN TENANT FARMERS UNION (1979) (same).

land to blacks, whom they did not want to enjoy the power that came from the owner-ship of land in the South."[28] Remarkably, however, some blacks were able to work up the "agricultural ladder," a phrase used to describe the transition from "landless laborer to sharecropper to renter to landowner."[29] The patterns of black farmland ownership varied across the South, but almost invariably blacks were able only to acquire land deemed un-desirable by whites:

> [t]he proportions of black farmers who owned land were greatest in the Upper South, along the coastal regions, and in the trans-Mississippi states. Very few blacks owned land in the Black Belt that cut across the region. Black landown-ing was the greatest, in other words, where the concentration of cotton was low-est and where blacks made up a relatively small part of the population. Blacks owned farms where land was cheap, where railroads had not arrived, and where stores were few; they got the "backbone and spare ribs" that white farmers did not value.[30]

Black landownership in 1910 embraced an estimated 15 million acres.[31] Most of that land was in the South, where 91 percent of all African Americans lived.[32] In 1910 blacks constituted one-half of the South's population, and owned 158,479 farms. Southern whites, on the other hand, owned 1,078,635 farms.[33] Black-operated farms totaled 212,972.[34]

The number of black-operated farms stood at about 926,000 in 1920. Black farmers, including sharecroppers and tenants, constituted one-seventh of all of the nation's farm-ers.[35] However, nearly one-half of all farms in the South in 1920 were less than fifty acres. "Tenancy remained at 50 percent for the white farmers, and tenancy rates for African-American farmers reached as high as 90 percent in some areas."[36]

Though the peak of black landownership roughly coincided with World War I, "[t]he outbreak of World War I marked the beginning of the long and tragic decline of black agri-culture and land tenure in the South."[37] When European nations ceased importing cot-ton, cotton prices collapsed. "The cotton disaster of 1914 ruined many thousands of black and white farmers, and affected agriculture for years to come."[38] The boll weevil was even more destructive, since few black sharecroppers or owner-operators could afford insec-ticides.[39] Added to these problems were worsening race relations, soil erosion and deple-

---

28. Franklin & Moss, *supra* note 24, at 277.

29. Edward L. Ayers, THE PROMISE OF THE NEW SOUTH: LIFE AFTER RECONSTRUCTION 195 (1992).

30. Edward L. Ayers, SOUTHERN CROSSING: A HISTORY OF THE AMERICAN SOUTH, 1877–1906, 35 (1995)(also noting that "[b]lack farmers and their families often had to rent from neighboring planters additional land for cash crops or to work off the farm to bring in enough money to keep the place; black landholding may have been so much higher in predominantly white counties in part because wage-paying jobs for blacks were more plentiful there").

31. Leo McGee & Robert Boone, INTRODUCTION IN THE BLACK RURAL LANDOWNER—ENDAN-GERED SPECIES, xvii (Leo McGee & Robert Boone eds., 1979)[McGee & Boone].

32. *Id.* at xviii.

33. Franklin & Moss, *supra* note 24, at 277.

34. Manning Marable, *The Land Question in Historical Perspective: The Economics of Poverty in the Blackbelt South 1865–1920*, in THE RURAL BLACK LANDOWNER—ENDANGERED SPECIES 3, 3 (Leo McGee & Robert Boone eds., 1979)[Marable].

35. McGee & Boone, *supra* note 31, at xvii.

36. R. Douglas Hurt, AMERICAN AGRICULTURE: A BRIEF HISTORY 225 (1994)[Hurt].

37. Marable, *supra* note 34, at 15.

38. *Id.* at 16. World War I was generally a boon for farmers who did not raise cotton. *See* Willard W. Cochrane, THE DEVELOPMENT OF AMERICAN AGRICULTURE: A HISTORICAL ANALYSIS 100 (2d ed. 1993).

39. Marable, *supra* note 34, at 17.

tion, and the monopolistic control that white planters and their allies held over credit and other factors of agricultural production.[40] "Given the structure of the domestic economy, it was inevitable that black farmers would be forced off the land and evicted from their homes to work at factory jobs in the cities of the New South and the urban ghettos of the North."[41]

The farm programs of the New Deal did little to help black farmers. Some successes were achieved by the efforts of the Resettlement Administration and the loan programs administered by the Farm Security Administration,[42] although the successes of these programs were diluted by racial discrimination in their administration.[43] In the main, however, the New Deal programs worked against black farmers by protecting white planters and shifting the risks to tenants, white and black:

> [U]nder the [Agricultural Adjustment Act (AAA)] the government actually assumed most of the landowners' risks and shifted them to tenants. The owners were protected from overproduction by fixed quotas with rents for their retired lands, while the tenants, whose share was pitifully small or nil carried most of the reduced acreage burden. The risks of price fluctuation for the owners was met with loans of ten cents a pound or more to help maintain prices; and the government credit production corporations and the [Farm Credit Administration] offered them credit at a rate unavailable to the tenant unless the landlord waived his first lien on the crop. The owner's likelihood of losing the equity in his farm also was lessened by the opportunities available to him to refinance and scale down debts owed them by croppers and share-tenants. The only way a tenant could escape assuming risks under the AAA and the existing system, in other words, was by becoming a landowner.[44]

In the years following the Great Depression blacks lost their land for a host of reasons, including "legal trickery perpetuated by southern white lawyers, land speculators, and county officials taking advantage of unsophisticated rural blacks."[45] The failure to devise land by will also resulted in the loss of land by making it vulnerable to sale through forced partition actions.[46] Tax sales, eminent domain, and voluntary sales also eroded black farmland ownership.

---

40. *Id.* at 18–19.

41. *Id.* at 19.

42. Theodore Saloutos, The American Farmer and the New Deal 190 (1982) [Saloutos]. For a discussion of the long-term effects of these programs, see Lester M. Salamon, *The Future of Black Land in the South* in The Rural Black Landowner—Endangered Species 167–85 (Leo McGee & Robert Boone eds., 1979). For a discussion of a relatively small program, the Tenant Purchase Program, and its modest success in Claiborne County, Mississippi, see David Crosby, *"A Piece of Your Own": The Tenant Purchase Program in Claiborne County*, Southern Cultures (Summer 1999) at 46.

43. *See* Farmers' Legal Action Group, Inc., *A Brief Historical Perspective on Discrimination in Farmer Credit Programs at USDA* in USDA Investigator's Standard Operating Procedure Manual: FSA Credit Discrimination (1997) (unpublished internal USDA manual).

44. Saloutos, *supra* note 42, at 188–89.

45. Carl H. Marbury, *The Decline in Black-Owned Rural Land; Challenge to the Historically Black Institutions of Higher Education* in The Rural Black Landowner—Endangered Species 97, 101 (Leo McGee & Robert Boone eds., 1979).

46. *See, e.g.*, John Casagrande, *Acquiring Property Through Forced Partition Sales: Abuses and Remedies*, 27 B.C. L. Rev. 755 (1986); Christopher R. Kelley, *Stemming the Loss of Black Owned Farmland Through Partition Actions—A Partial Solution*, 1995 Ark. L. Notes 35.

Following World War II, changes in Southern agriculture caused it to lose its distinctiveness and to become "more like farming elsewhere in the nation ... [with an emphasis] on capitalization, mechanization, and labor efficiency."[47] This change had a profound effect on black farmers. As one observer has noted, "most black farmers were forced off the land by technology in the form of cotton pickers and tractors, science in the form of herbicides, and government programs that favored landowners. They simply were not needed in the fields anymore."[48] The migration that followed this change in Southern agriculture was captured in a remark attributed by Anthony Walton to his father. Noting that the tracks of the Illinois Central Railroad run through the agricultural lands of the Mississippi Delta, Mr. Walton recounts that his father used to say, "It wasn't Lincoln who freed the slaves, it was the Illinois Central...."[49]

Discrimination by the USDA also impeded the ability of many black farmers to flourish or even to survive as farmers. In addition to the USDA's lack of attention to black farmers during the New Deal,[50] much of the public agricultural infrastructure largely ignored the plight of the black farmer for decades thereafter:

> [d]uring the late twentieth century, the USDA, agricultural colleges, and state experiment stations remained devoted to helping the most capital-intensive and economically viable farmers, and those agriculturalists were invariably white. The USDA ignored black farmers because they had neither the land nor capital to maintain productive, efficient, and profitable agricultural operations, nor did the agency provide educational and developmental programs to help those unneeded and often displaced farmers to build a new life.[51]

For its part, the USDA compounded its inattention to black farmers by discriminating against them. In 1965, the U.S. Civil Rights Commission concluded that the USDA treated white and black farmers differently, to the disadvantage of black farmers.[52] Subsequent reports of the Commission found that the USDA had not made significant improvement.[53] In 1990, following hearings, the House Government Operations Committee found that as many as two-thirds of all black farmers received loans from the USDA and concluded that discrimination by the USDA in its loan programs had been "a catalyst in the decline of minority farming."[54]

Between 1920 and 1969, a 90 percent decrease in the number of black farmers had occurred. By 1992, this decrease had risen to 98 percent. The number of white farmers also decreased, but for the same period, 1920 to 1992, the decline of white farmers was 65 percent.

The decline in the number of black farmers can only be described as dramatic. For every decade following World War II, the loss of black farmers approached 50 percent. That

---

47. Hurt, *supra* note 36, at 332. *See generally* Jack Temple Kirby, RURAL WORLDS LOST: THE AMERICAN SOUTH, 1920–1960 (1987).
48. Hurt, *supra* note 36, at 332–33.
49. Anthony Walton, MISSISSIPPI: AN AMERICAN JOURNEY 224–25 (1996).
50. Saloutos, *supra* note 42, at 179–90.
51. Hurt, *supra* note 36, at 333.
52. United States Commission on Civil Rights, *Equal Opportunity in Farm Programs* (1965).
53. *E.g.*, United States Commission on Civil Rights, *Cycle to Nowhere* (1970).
54. *The Minority Farmer: A Disappearing American Resource: Has the Farmers Home Administration Been the Primary Catalyst?*, House Committee on Government Operations, H.R. 101-984, 101st Cong., 2d Sess., 1990, at 41.

race was a factor is supported by the finding that "[b]lack-operated farms have decreased at a faster rate than white-operated farms regardless of size...."[55]

Black farmers today are mostly Southern farmers. In 1992, 94 percent of all black-owned farms were in seventeen Southern states. The largest number were in Texas (2,861), followed by Mississippi (2,480); North Carolina (1,866); South Carolina (1,765); Alabama (1,381); Virginia (1,298); Louisiana (1,097); and Georgia (1,080). These eight states accounted for 75 percent of the nation's African American farmers. The remaining Southern states had fewer than 1,000 black-owned farms.[56]

"[M]ost black-operated farms engage primarily in livestock production, with some field crops and cash grains."[57] Livestock production appears to be favored because of its relatively flexible labor requirements that allow time for an off farm job.[58]

Most black-operated farms are smaller than 140 acres and generate gross sales less than $10,000. In the eight Southern states accounting for 75 percent of all black farmers, the average farm size in 1992 was 117 acres, up seven acres from the 1987 average of 110 acres. Except in North Carolina and Virginia, the majority of the income of black farm operators is derived from off-farm sources.[59]

In 1992, the overwhelming majority of black farmers were male, and their average age was 59. Thirty-eight percent of all black farmers were 65 years or older.[60]

Based on 1966 data, black farm households have an average household income of $19,600. This figure is substantially lower than the average household income of white farmers, $52,300. About 43 percent of black farmers operate limited resource farms, compared to 13 percent of white farmers.[61]

The future of black farmers in America is uncertain. Some promise is offered by the success of cooperatives such as the Indian Springs Farmers Association in Mississippi which helps its black farmer members market their fruits and vegetables,[62] the efforts of the Federation of Southern Cooperatives/Land Assistance Fund to expand its marketing efforts into the international arena,[63] and the recent settlement of a discrimination action against the USDA.[64] The trend represented by the decline in the numbers of black farmers, however, is not favorable to the survival of black farming in this country. By all accounts, the emergence of black farm operators before and after the Civil War is a tribute to their collective industriousness and skill. Whether this industriousness and skill will remain a part of this nation's agricultural sector is a question faced by all who ponder the full scope of the future of American agriculture.

---

55. Wood & Gilbert, *supra* note 1, at 2.

56. *Id.* at 2, 4.

57. *Id.* at 9.

58. *See* Effland et al., *supra* note 1, at 19.

59. Wood & Gilbert, *supra* note 1, at 6.

60. Effland et al., *supra* note 1, at 19.

61. USDA, Econ. Research Serv., *Rural Conditions and Trends*, Feb. 1999, at 111. A "limited resource farm" is "any small farm with (1) gross sales less than $100,000, (2) total farm assets less than $150,000, and (3) total operator household income less than $20,000." *Id.* at 108.

62. Donna F. Abernathy, *A Legacy Lives On: Cooperative Approach Helps Black Growers Succeed*, Rural Cooperatives (USDA, Rural Bus. — Coop. Serv., May–June 1998) at 4.

63. Donald Washington & Kurt Seifarth, *Federation of Southern Cooperatives Makes Big Move To Become an International Player*, AgExporter (USDA, Foreign Agric. Serv., May 1999) at 4.

64. *See Pigford v. Glickman*, 185 F.R.D. 82 (D.D.C. 1999).

B. USDA Discrimination Against African American Farmers

It is ironic that the USDA, "the people's department," and its agency, the Farmers Home Administration (now renamed the Farm Service Agency), an agency charged with assisting borrowers who are unable to get credit elsewhere, have been guilty of a pattern of persistent racial discrimination.

In 1998, the The Wall Street Journal published a front page article by Roger Thurow describing the plight of several African American farmers who experienced discrimination in the administration of the USDA loan programs.

> A tattered screen, dangling from a window of his shabby trailer home here, waves goodbye as [Eddie Ross] jumps off the front stoop to begin the 17-hour drive to Washington. Not long into the journey, he picks up fellow Mississippian Lloyd Shaffer, whose hair is falling out in clumps as eviction nears. In Alabama, they add George Hall, who's already gone bankrupt. Lucious Abrams, who can see the whites of his creditors' eyes, jumps aboard in Georgia. In North Carolina, they all make room for Tim Pigford, whose family sat in a dark house for one year and 12 days when there was no money to pay the light bill.
>
> They don't look like much when they hit Washington, toting their lunch in paper bags and squeezing into one hotel room. But together, this group of angry, desperate, determined men has pushed the government into settlement talks over a $2.5 billion federal discrimination suit by 400 black farmers against the U.S. Department of Agriculture....
>
> When Mr. Shaffer applied for an equipment loan, a USDA county official told him: "All you need is a mule and a plow." USDA investigators looking into the denial of Mr. Hall's application for crop-disaster relief found a county loan officer referring to a black community as a "baby factory." In a complaint that is part of the suit, Abraham Carpenter, an Arkansas farmer, says a county official deemed his disaster-relief request "too much money for a nigger to receive."
>
> Much of the alleged discrimination hasn't been so blunt; instead it occurred under the guise of paper shuffling by county and state USDA authorities: delaying loans until the end of the planting season, approving only a fraction of loan requests, denying crop-disaster payments that white farmers got routinely.

Roger Thurow, *Soiled Legacy: Black Farmers Hit The Road to Confront A 'Cycle of Racism'—Many Lost Lands, Dignity As USDA Denied Loans Whites Routinely Got*, THE WALL STREET JOURNAL (May 1, 1998).

The Equal Credit Opportunity Act (ECOA) provides in part that "[i]t shall be unlawful for any creditor to discriminate against any applicant, with respect to any aspect of a credit transaction—(1) on the basis of race, color, religion, national origin, sex or marital status, or age (provided the applicant has the capacity to contract)." 15 U.S.C. §1691.

It cannot be disputed that the treatment of many African American farmers was in violation of this provision. Proving past discrimination, however can be difficult, and for many, the two year statute of limitations for bringing litigation passes before a suit is initiated. Tim Pigford was a named plaintiff in a class action case filed on behalf of African American farmers, but the case was destined to fail under these burdens. In 1999, with the support and encouragement of the Clinton administration, Congress passed legislation lifting the statute of limitations, allowing the USDA to settle the case. What resulted was one of the largest class action civil rights settlements in U.S. history. It did not, however, conclude the story.

Pigford v. Glickman

United States District Court, District of Columbia
185 F.R.D. 82 (1999)

OPINION

PAUL L. FRIEDMAN, District Judge.

Forty acres and a mule. As the Civil War drew to a close, the United States government created the Freedmen's Bureau to provide assistance to former slaves. The government promised to sell or lease to farmers parcels of unoccupied land and land that had been confiscated by the Union during the war, and it promised the loan of a federal government mule to plow that land. Some African Americans took advantage of these programs and either bought or leased parcels of land. During Reconstruction, however, President Andrew Johnson vetoed a bill to enlarge the powers and activities of the Freedmen's Bureau, and he reversed many of the policies of the Bureau. Much of the promised land that had been leased to African American farmers was taken away and returned to Confederate loyalists. For most African Americans, the promise of forty acres and a mule was never kept. Despite the government's failure to live up to its promise, African American farmers persevered. By 1910, they had acquired approximately 16 million acres of farmland. By 1920, there were 925,000 African American farms in the United States.

On May 15, 1862, as Congress was debating the issue of providing land for freed former slaves, the United States Department of Agriculture was created. The statute creating the Department charged it with acquiring and preserving "all information concerning agriculture" and collecting "new and valuable seeds and plants; to test, by cultivation, the value of such of them as may require such tests; to propagate such as may be worthy of propagation, and to distribute them among agriculturists." An Act to establish a Department of Agriculture, ch. 71, 12 Stat. 387 (1862). In 1889, the Department of Agriculture achieved full cabinet department status. Today, it has an annual budget of $67.5 billion and administers farm loans and guarantees worth $2.8 billion.

As the Department of Agriculture has grown, the number of African American farmers has declined dramatically. Today, there are fewer than 18,000 African American farms in the United States, and African American farmers now own less then 3 million acres of land. The United States Department of Agriculture and the county commissioners to whom it has delegated so much power bear much of the responsibility for this dramatic decline. The Department itself has recognized that there has always been a disconnect between what President Lincoln envisioned as "the people's department," serving all of the people, and the widespread belief that the Department is "the last plantation," a department "perceived as playing a key role in what some see as a conspiracy to force minority and disadvantaged farmers off their land through discriminatory loan practices."

For decades, despite its promise that "no person in the United States shall, on the ground of race, color, or national origin, be excluded from participation in, be denied the benefits of, or be otherwise subjected to discrimination under any program or activity of an applicant or recipient receiving Federal financial assistance from the Department of

Agriculture," 7 C.F.R. § 15.1, the Department of Agriculture and the county commissioners discriminated against African American farmers when they denied, delayed or otherwise frustrated the applications of those farmers for farm loans and other credit and benefit programs. Further compounding the problem, in 1983 the Department of Agriculture disbanded its Office of Civil Rights and stopped responding to claims of discrimination. These events were the culmination of a string of broken promises that had been made to African American farmers for well over a century.

It is difficult to resist the impulse to try to undo all the broken promises and years of discrimination that have led to the precipitous decline in the number of African American farmers in the United States. The Court has before it a proposed settlement of a class action lawsuit that will not undo all that has been done. Despite that fact, however, the Court finds that the settlement is a fair resolution of the claims brought in this case and a good first step towards assuring that the kind of discrimination that has been visited on African American farmers since Reconstruction will not continue into the next century. The Court therefore will approve the settlement.

I. BACKGROUND OF THE CASE

The plaintiffs in this case allege (1) that the United States Department of Agriculture ("USDA") willfully discriminated against them and other similarly situated African American farmers on the basis of their race when it denied their applications for credit and/or benefit programs or delayed processing their applications, and (2) that when plaintiffs filed complaints of discrimination with the USDA, the USDA failed properly to investigate and resolve those complaints. Plaintiffs allege that defendant's actions violated a number of statutes and the Constitution, but both sides agree that this case essentially is brought under the Equal Credit Opportunity Act, 15 U.S.C. § 1691 ("ECOA").

The Court certified this case as a class action on October 9, 1998, and preliminarily approved a Consent Decree on January 5, 1999. After a hearing held on March 2, 1999, the parties made some revisions to the proposed Consent Decree and filed a revised proposed Consent Decree with the Court on March 19, 1999. The Court now concludes that the revised proposed Consent Decree is fair, adequate and reasonable.

A. Factual Background

Farming is a hard way to make a living. Small farmers operate at the whim of conditions completely beyond their control; weather conditions from year to year and marketable prices of crops to a large extent determine whether an individual farmer will make a profit, barely break even or lose money. As a result, many farmers depend heavily on the credit and benefit programs of the United States Department of Agriculture to take them from one year to the next. For instance, if an early freeze kills three-quarters of a farmer's crop one year, he may not have sufficient resources to buy seeds to plant in the following season. Or if a farmer needs to modernize his operations and buy a new grain harvester in order to make his operations profitable, he often cannot afford to buy the harvester without an extension of credit. Because of the seasonal nature of farming, it also is of utmost importance that credit and benefit applications be processed quickly or the farmer may lose all or most of his anticipated income for an entire year. It does a farmer no good to receive a loan to buy seeds after the planting season has passed.

The USDA's credit and benefit programs are federally funded programs, but the decisions to approve or deny applications for credit or benefits are made locally at the county level. In virtually every farming community, local farmers and ranchers elect three to five member county committees. The county committee is responsible for approving or denying farm credit and benefit applications, as well as for appointing a county executive who is supposed to provide farmers with help in completing their credit and benefit applications. The county executive also makes recommendations to the county committee regarding which applications should be approved. The salaries of the county committee members and the county executives are paid from federal funds, but they are not considered federal government employees. Similarly, while federal money is used to fund the credit and benefit programs, the elected county officials, not federal officials, make the decision as to who gets the federal money and who does not.

The county committees do not represent the racial diversity of the communities they serve. In 1996, in the Southeast Region, the region in the United States with the most African American farmers, just barely over 1% of the county commissioners were African American (28 out of a total of 2469). In the Southwest region, only 0.3% of the county commissioners were African American. In two of the remaining three regions, there was not a single African American county commissioner. Nationwide, only 37 county commissioners were African American out of a total of 8147 commissioners—approximately 0.45%.

Throughout the country, African American farmers complain that county commissioners have discriminated against them for decades, denying their applications, delaying the processing of their applications or approving them for insufficient amounts or with restrictive conditions. In several southeastern states, for instance, it took three times as long on average to process the application of an African American farmer as it did to process the application of a white farmer. Mr. Alvin E. Steppes is an African American farmer from Lee County, Arkansas. In 1986, Mr. Steppes applied to the Farmers Home Administration ("FmHA") for an operating loan. Mr. Steppes fully complied with the application requirements, but his application was denied. As a result, Mr. Steppes had insufficient resources to plant crops, he could not buy fertilizer and crop treatment for the crops he did plant, and he ended up losing his farm.

Mr. Calvin Brown from Brunswick County, Virginia applied in January 1984 for an operating loan for that planting season. When he inquired later that month about the status of his loan application, a FmHA county supervisor told him that the application was being processed. The next month, the same FmHA county supervisor told him that there was no record of his application ever having been filed and that Mr. Brown had to reapply. By the time Mr. Brown finally received his loan in May or June 1984, the planting season was over, and the loan was virtually useless to him. In addition, the funds were placed in a "supervised" bank account, which required him to obtain the signature of a county supervisor before withdrawing any funds, a requirement frequently required of African American farmers but not routinely imposed on white farmers.

In 1994, the entire county of Greene County, Alabama where Mr. George Hall farmed was declared eligible for disaster payments on 1994 crop losses. Every single application for disaster payments was approved by the Greene County Committee except Mr. Hall's application for four of his crops. Mr. James Beverly of Nottaway County, Virginia was a successful small farmer before going to FmHA. To build on his success, in 1981 he began working with his FmHA office to develop a farm plan to expand and modernize his swine herd operations. The plan called for loans to purchase breeding stock and equipment as well as farrowing houses that were necessary for the breeding operations. FmHA approved his loans to buy breeding stock and equipment, and he was told that the loan for farrowing houses would be approved. After he already had bought the livestock and the equipment, his application for a loan to build the farrowing houses was denied. The livestock and equipment were useless to him without the farrowing houses. Mr. Beverly ended up having to sell his property to settle his debt to the FmHA.

The denial of credit and benefits has had a devastating impact on African American farmers. According to the Census of Agriculture, the number of African American farmers has declined from 925,000 in 1920 to approximately 18,000 in 1992. The farms of many African American farmers were foreclosed upon, and they were forced out of farming. Those who managed to stay in farming often were subject to humiliation and degradation at the hands of the county commissioners and were forced to stand by powerless, as white farmers received preferential treatment. As one of plaintiffs' lawyers, Mr. J.L. Chestnut, aptly put it, African American farmers "learned the hard way that though the rules and the law may be colorblind, people are not."

Any farmer who believed that his application to those programs was denied on the basis of his race or for other discriminatory reasons theoretically had open to him a process for filing a civil rights complaint either with the Secretary of Agriculture or with the Office of Civil Rights Enforcement and Adjudication ("OCREA") at USDA. USDA regulations set forth a detailed process by which these complaints were supposed to be investigated and conciliated, and ultimately a farmer who was unhappy with the outcome was entitled to sue in federal court under ECOA. All the evidence developed by the USDA and presented to the Court indicates, however, that this system was functionally nonexistent for well over a decade. In 1983, OCREA essentially was dismantled and complaints that were filed were never processed, investigated or forwarded to the appropriate agencies for conciliation. As a result, farmers who filed complaints of discrimination never received a response, or if they did receive a response it was a cursory denial of relief. In some cases, OCREA staff simply threw discrimination complaints in the trash without ever responding to or investigating them. In other cases, even if there was a finding of discrimination, the farmer never received any relief.

In December of 1996, Secretary of Agriculture Dan Glickman appointed a Civil Rights Action Team ("CRAT") to "take a hard look at the issues and make strong recommendations for change." In February of 1997, CRAT concluded that "[m]inority farmers have lost significant amounts of land and potential farm income as a result of discrimination by FSA [Farm Services Agency] programs and the programs of its predecessor agencies, ASCS [Agricultural Stabilization and Conservation Service] and FmHA [Farmers Home Administration].... The process for resolving complaints has failed. Minority and limited-resource customers believe USDA has not acted in good faith on the complaints. Appeals are too often delayed and for too long. Favorable decisions are too often reversed."

Also in February of 1997, the Office of the Inspector General of the USDA issued a report to Secretary Glickman stating that the USDA had a backlog of complaints of discrimination that had never been processed, investigated or resolved. The Report found that immediate action was needed to clear the backlog of complaints, that the "program discrimination complaint process at [the Farm Services Agency] lacks integrity, direction, and accountability," and that "[s]taffing problems, obsolete procedures, and little direction from management have resulted in a climate of disorder within the civil rights staff at FSA."

The acknowledgment by the USDA that the discrimination complaints had never been processed, however, came too late for many African American farmers. ECOA has a two year statute of limitations. *See* 15 U.S.C. § 1691e(f). If the underlying discrimination alleged by the farmer had taken place more than two years prior to the filing of an action in federal court, the government would raise a statute of limitations defense to bar the farmer's claims. For instance, some class members in this case had filed their complaints of discrimination with the USDA in 1983 for acts of discrimination that allegedly occurred in 1982 or 1983. If the farmer waited for the USDA to respond to his discrimination complaint and did not file an action in court until he discovered in 1997 that the USDA had stopped responding to discrimination complaints, the government would argue that any claim under ECOA was barred by the statute of limitations.

In 1998, Congress provided relief to plaintiffs with respect to the statute of limitations problem by passing legislation that tolls the statute of limitations for all those who filed discrimination complaints with the Department of Agriculture before July 1, 1997, and who allege discrimination at any time during the period beginning on January 1, 1981 and ending on or before December 31, 1996. *See* Agricultural, Rural Development, Food and Drug Administration, and Related Agencies Appropriations Act, 1999, Pub.L. No. 105-277, §741, 112 Stat. 2681 (codified at 7 U.S.C. §2297, Notes)....

II. CLASS CERTIFICATION

* * *

The newly certified class is defined as:

All African American farmers who (1) farmed, or attempted to farm, between January 1, 1981 and December 31, 1996; (2) applied to the United States Department of Agriculture (USDA) during that time period for participation in a federal farm credit or benefit program and who believed that they were discriminated against on the basis of race in USDA's response to that application; and (3) filed a discrimination complaint on or before July 1, 1997, regarding USDA's treatment of such farm credit or benefit application....

The ultimate settlement of this action envisions the creation of a mechanism on a class-wide basis that will then be utilized to resolve the individual claims of class members outside the traditional litigation process, most of them (Track A) in a rather formulaic way.

Most members of the class lack documentation of the allegedly discriminatory transactions at issue. Without any documentation of those transactions, it would be difficult if not impossible for an individual farmer to prevail in a suit in federal court under a traditional preponderance of the evidence standard. The parties acknowledge, however, that it is not the fault of class members that they lack records. Since class members' lack of documentation is at least in part attributable to the passage of time which has been exacerbated by the USDA's failure to timely process complaints of discrimination, there is a common issue of whether and how best to provide relief to class members who lack documentation, and that common issue "predominate[s] over any questions affecting only individual members." *See* Rule 23(b)(3), Fed.R.Civ.P. This class action and its settlement as proposed in the Consent Decree provide a mechanism to address that common issue.

In addition to the lack of documentation making individual adjudication of most claims so difficult, the sheer size of the class makes the prospect of individual adjudication of damages virtually unmanageable. For this or any other court to adjudicate the individual claims of the 15,000 to 20,000 African American farmers now estimated to be members of the class would take years or perhaps even a decade or more. Any "fair and efficient" resolution of the claims therefore necessitates the implementation of some sort of class-wide mechanism such as the creative and speedy Track A/Track B procedures proposed by the parties in the Consent Decree. The Court therefore finds that "a class action is superior to other available methods for the fair and efficient adjudication of the controversy." *See* Rule 23(b)(3), Fed.R.Civ.P. The Court concludes that this action appropriately is certified for resolution pursuant to Rule 23(b)(3) of the Federal Rules of Civil Procedure. The remaining question is whether the proposed Consent Decree is fair, adequate and reasonable under Rule 23(e).

III. PROVISIONS OF PROPOSED CONSENT DECREE

The proposed Consent Decree, as revised after the fairness hearing and jointly filed by the parties on March 19, 1999, is a negotiated settlement that resolves all of the claims raised by plaintiffs in the Seventh Amended Complaint. The purpose of the Consent Decree is to ensure that in the future all class members in their dealings with the USDA will "receive full and fair treatment" that is "the same as the treatment accorded to similarly situated white persons." As with all settlements, it does not provide the plaintiffs and the class they represent with everything they sought in the complaint. Instead it is a negotiated settlement intended to achieve much of what was sought without the need for lengthy litigation and uncertain results. It is impossible to know precisely how much the overall settlement in this case will cost the government, in part because the exact size of the class has not been determined and because the Consent Decree provides for debt relief that is dependent on the amount of debt that individual class members owe to the USDA, but plaintiffs estimate that the settlement is worth at least $2.25 billion, the largest civil rights settlement in the history of this country.

The Consent Decree accomplishes its purposes primarily through a two-track dispute resolution mechanism that provides those class members with little or no documentary evidence with a virtually automatic cash payment of $50,000, and forgiveness of debt owed to the USDA (Track A), while those who believe they can prove their cases with documentary or other evidence by a preponderance of the evidence — the traditional burden of proof in civil litigation — have no cap on the amount they may recover (Track B). Those who like neither option provided by the Consent Decree may opt out of the class and pursue their individual remedies in court or administratively before the USDA. The essential terms of the proposed Consent Decree and settlement are summarized below.

Under the terms of the proposed Consent Decree, any class member has the right to opt out of the class and pursue his remedies either administratively before the USDA or in a separate court action. A class member who opts out of the class cannot collect any relief under the settlement, but he retains all of his legal rights to file his own action against the USDA. In other words, if a class member opts out of the class, nothing in this settlement affects him. Any class member who wishes to opt out of the class must file a written request with the facilitator within 120 days of the date on which the Consent Decree is entered.

Those who choose to remain in the class have 180 days from the entry of the Consent Decree within which to file their claim packages with the facilitator.[The Court may grant an extension of this 180 day period "where the claimant demonstrates that his failure to submit a timely claim was due to extraordinary circumstances beyond his control."] When a claimant submits his claim package, he must include evidence that he filed a discrimination claim with the USDA between January 1, 1981 and July 1, 1997. In the absence of documentation that a complaint was filed with the USDA, a claimant may submit a declaration from "a person who is not a member of the claimant's family" stating that he or she has first-hand knowledge that the claimant filed the complaint.[7] A claimant also must

---

7. For purposes of the proposed Consent Decree, a "discrimination complaint" means either a communication directly from the class member to the USDA or a communication from the claimant to a member of Congress, the White House, or a state, local, or federal official who forwarded the com-

include a certification from an attorney stating that the attorney has a good faith belief in the truth of the factual basis of the claim and that the attorney will not require compensation from the claimant for his or her assistance.[8]

At the time that they submit their claim packages, claimants asserting discrimination in credit transactions also must choose between two options: adjudication of their claims under the Track A mechanism or arbitration of their claims under the Track B mechanism.[9] The choice made between Track A and Track B has enormous significance. Under Track A, the class member has a fairly low burden of proof but his recovery is limited. Under Track B, there is a higher burden of proof but the recovery is unlimited. The claims facilitator, the Poorman-Douglas Corporation, has 20 days after the filing of a claims package within which to determine whether the claimant is a member of the class and, if he is, to forward the materials to counsel for the USDA and to the appropriate Track A or Track B decision-maker.

Under Track A, a claimant must submit "substantial evidence" demonstrating that he or she was the victim of race discrimination. Substantial evidence means something more than a "mere scintilla" of evidence but less than a preponderance. Put another way, substantial evidence is such "relevant evidence as a reasonable mind might accept to support [the] conclusion," even when "a plausible alternative interpretation of the evidence would support a contrary view." *Secretary of Labor v. Federal Mine Safety and Health Review Comm'n,* 111 F.3d 913, 918 (D.C.Cir.1997).[10]

A claimant asserting discrimination in a credit transaction can satisfy this burden by presenting evidence of four specific things: (1) that he owned or leased, or attempted to own or lease, farm land; (2) that he applied for a specific credit transaction at a USDA county office between January 1, 1981 and December 31, 1996; (3) that the loan was denied, provided late, approved for a lesser amount than requested, encumbered by restrictive conditions, or USDA failed to provide appropriate loan service, and such treatment was less favorable than that accorded specifically identified, similarly situated white farmers; and (4) that USDA's treatment of the loan application led to economic damage to the class member. A claimant asserting discrimination only in a non-credit benefit program can satisfy his burden by presenting evidence (1) that he applied for a specific non-credit benefit program at a USDA county office between January 1, 1981 and December 31, 1996, and (2) that his application was denied or approved for a lesser amount then requested and that such treatment was less favorable than that accorded to specifically identified, similarly situated white farmers.

The USDA has sixty days after it receives notice of a Track A referral to provide the adjudicator and class counsel with any information relevant to the issues of liability and damages. After receiving any material from the USDA, the facilitator will either make a recommendation with respect to whether the claim should be approved or indicate its inability to make a recommendation. The entire packet of material, including the submissions

---

munication to the USDA asserting that the USDA had discriminated against the claimant on the basis of race in connection with a federal farm credit transaction or benefit application. Consent Decree at ¶ 1(h)

8. Class counsel is available to perform these services without charge to the claimant.

9. Claimants asserting discrimination in non-credit benefit programs are only entitled to proceed under Track A. Consent Decree at ¶ 5(d).

10. The Consent Decree defines "substantial evidence" as "such relevant evidence as appears in the record before the adjudicator that a reasonable person might accept as adequate to support a conclusion after taking into account other evidence in the record that fairly detracts from that conclusion." Consent Decree at ¶ 1(l).

by the claimant and the USDA and the recommendation of the facilitator, then is referred to a member of JAMS-Endispute, Inc., for a decision which is to be made within 30 days. That decision is final, except that the Monitor, whose responsibilities are discussed further below, shall direct the adjudicator to reexamine the claim if he determines that "a clear and manifest error has occurred" that is "likely to result in a fundamental miscarriage of justice."

If the adjudicator finds in the claimant's favor and the claim involves discrimination in a credit transaction, the claimant will receive (1) a cash payment of $50,000; (2) forgiveness of all debt owed to the USDA incurred under or affected by the program that formed the basis of the claim; (3) a tax payment directly to the IRS in the amount of 25% of the total debt forgiveness and cash payment; (4) immediate termination of any foreclosure proceedings that USDA initiated in connection with the loan(s) at issue in the claim; and (5) injunctive relief including one-time priority loan consideration and technical assistance. If the adjudicator finds in the claimant's favor and the claim involves discrimination in a benefit program, the claimant will receive a cash payment in the amount of the benefit wrongly denied and injunctive relief including one-time priority loan consideration and technical assistance.

Track B arbitration is the option for those who have more extensive documentation of discrimination in a credit transaction. Under Track B, an arbitrator will hold a one day mini-trial and then decide whether the claimant has established discrimination by a preponderance of the evidence. Class counsel will represent any claimant who chooses Track B, or a claimant may be represented by counsel of his choice if he so desires. Track B is designed to balance the need for prompt resolution of the claim with the need to provide adequate discovery and a fair hearing. The entire Track B process will take a maximum of 240 days. During the first 180 days, there is a mechanism for limited discovery and depositions of witnesses. Following the one day mini-trial, the arbitrator will render a decision within 30 to 60 days.

If the arbitrator finds that the claimant has demonstrated by a preponderance of the evidence that he was the victim of racial discrimination and that he suffered damages from that discrimination, the claimant will be entitled to actual damages, the return of inventory property that was foreclosed and other injunctive relief, including a one-time priority loan consideration. As with Track A claims, the decision of the arbitrator is final except that the Monitor shall direct the arbitrator to reexamine the claim if he determines that "a clear and manifest error has occurred" that is "likely to result in a fundamental miscarriage of justice."

The proposed Consent Decree also provides for an independent Monitor who will serve for a period of five years following the entry of the decree. The Monitor will be appointed by the Court from a list of names proposed by the parties and cannot be removed "except upon good cause." The Monitor is responsible for making periodic written reports to the Court, the Secretary of Agriculture, counsel for the government and class counsel, reporting on the good faith implementation of the Consent Decree and efforts to resolve disputes that arise between the parties under the terms of the decree. He or she will be available to class members and members of the public through a toll-free telephone number to facilitate the lodging of Consent Decree complaints and to expedite their resolution.

The Court retains jurisdiction to enforce the Consent Decree through contempt proceedings. If one side believes that the other side has violated the terms of the Consent Decree, there is a mandatory procedure for attempting to resolve the problem with the assistance of the Monitor that the parties must follow before filing a contempt motion with the Court, but the Court remains available in the event that the terms of the decree are violated. Finally, the Consent Decree provides that class counsel shall be entitled to reasonable attorneys' fees and costs under ECOA, 15 U.S.C. § 1691e(d), and under the Administrative Procedure Act, 28 U.S.C. § 2412(d), for the filing and litigation of this action and for implementation of the Consent Decree.

IV. FAIRNESS OF PROPOSED CONSENT DECREE

Under Rule 23 of the Federal Rules of Civil Procedure, no class action may be dismissed, settled or compromised without the approval of the Court. Before giving its approval, the Court must provide adequate notice to all members of the class, conduct a "fairness hearing," and find, after notice and hearing, that the "settlement is fair, adequate and reasonable and is not the product of collusion between the parties." In performing this task, the Court must protect the interests of those unnamed class members whose rights may be affected by the settlement of the action.

In this circuit there is "no obligatory test" that the Court must use to determine whether a settlement is fair, adequate and reasonable. Instead the Court must consider the facts and circumstances of the case, ascertain what factors are most relevant in the circumstances and exercise its discretion in deciding whether approval of the proposed settlement is fair.[13] By far the most important factor is a comparison of the terms of the compromise or settlement with the likely recovery that plaintiffs would realize if the case went to trial.... Having carefully considered all of the objections that have been filed with the Court or expressed at the fairness hearing in relation to the strength of plaintiffs' case, the Court concludes that the settlement is fair, adequate and reasonable and is not the product of collusion between the parties.[14]

---

13. The Third Circuit has adopted a nine-factor test for determining the fairness of a settlement of a class action, *see Girsh v. Jepson*, 521 F.2d 153 (3rd Cir.1975), while the Tenth Circuit has adopted a four factor test, *see Gottlieb v. Wiles*, 11 F.3d 1004, 1014 (10th Cir.1993), and the Eleventh Circuit has developed a six factor test. *See Bennett v. Behring Corp.*, 737 F.2d 982 (11th Cir.1984). Other circuits, including ours, have not imposed such rigid sets of factors, instead recognizing that the relevant factors may vary depending on the factual circumstances. *See Thomas v. Albright*, 139 F.3d at 231; *Torrisi v. Tucson Elec. Power Co.*, 8 F.3d 1370, 1375–76 (9th Cir.1993), cert. denied sub nom. *Reilly v. Tucson Elec. Power Co.*, 512 U.S. 1220, 114 S.Ct. 2707, 129 L.Ed.2d 834 (1994). To the extent that the factors enumerated by the other circuits are at all relevant to the determination of whether this Consent Decree is fair, adequate and reasonable, however, the Court has considered and addressed those factors in this Opinion.

14. The Court has received written objections or comments from the following organizations: Black Farmers and Agriculturists Assoc.; Black Farmers of North Carolina; Central Piedmont Economic Assoc.; Concerned Black Farmers of Tennessee, Arkansas, Mississippi, Georgia and North Carolina; Coordinating Council of Black Farm Groups; Kansas Black Farmers Assoc.; Land Loss Prevention Project; Federation of Southern Cooperatives Land Assistance Fund; Lawyers' Committee for Civil Rights Under Law; NAACP; National Black Farmers; National Council of Community Based Organizations in Agriculture; National Family Farm Coalition; Oklahoma Black Farmers and Agriculturalists Assoc.; and United States Dept. of Agriculture Coalition of Minority Employees.

The Court has received written objections or comments from the following individuals (on behalf of themselves and/or on behalf of other class members): Theodore F.B. Bates; Robert R. Binion; Abraham Carpenter, Jr.; Leonard C. Cooper; Harold M. Dunkelberger; George and Larry Ephfrom; Percy Gooch, Sr.; Estell Green, Jr.; Patricia Gibson Green; Brown J. Hawkins; Clarence Hardy; George and Patricia Hildebrandt; George Hobbs; Dave J. Miller; Jessie Nimmons; Timothy C. Pigford; Amelia Roland Washington; Roy L. Rolle, Jr.; Luis C. Sanders; Herbert L. Skinner, Jr.; Gregory R. Swecker; V.J. Switzer; George M. Whitehead; Gladys R. Todd and Griffin Todd, Sr.; Andrew Williams; Jerome Williams; and Eddie and Dorothy Weiss. All of the organizations and most of the individuals who had submitted written comments or objections spoke at the hearing on March 2, 1999. In addition,

A. The Process of Settlement

Preliminarily, the Court considers those objections that address the fairness of the way in which the settlement negotiations were conducted, the amount of discovery completed at the time of settlement, the definition of the class, whether there is any evidence of collusion between class counsel and counsel for the government, and whether class members have had adequate notice and opportunity to be heard on the proposed settlement.

1. Timing of Settlement and Extent of Discovery Completed

Some of the objectors maintain that settlement came too early and that class counsel undertook insufficient discovery in this case before settling it. A review of the history of the case, however, reveals that "[t]here has been a literal mountain of discovery provided and reviewed." Less than three months after the case was filed, the Court ordered the USDA to open its files to plaintiffs within fifteen days.

On the fifteenth day, the government provided plaintiffs with ten boxes of documents containing approximately 35,000 to 40,000 pages of records related to approximately 105 pending claims of race discrimination. Three days later, the government delivered an additional 20,000 pages related to another 30 pending cases of discrimination. At the time, the government represented that it was continuing to search for files, many of which had already been sent to a federal records repository. Since that time, the government has continued to provide plaintiffs with the files of class members.

The problem for plaintiffs has been that files simply do not exist for many class members. Providing additional time for discovery would not have solved that problem. As class counsel has pointed out, on the issue of liability of the USDA, the government's own documents and own admissions are the most damning evidence. *See* Transcript of Hearing of March 2, 1999 at 184 (Comments of Mr. Alexander Pires) ("I have an office full of admissions. I have tape recordings of Mr. Glickman. I have tape recordings of Government officials. I've interviewed everybody there is to interview. I have documents. I have the CRAT Report annotated. I have all the [Office of the Inspector General] Reports"). There really was no other discovery that could have made a difference. The same is true on the issue of damages. The government delivered to class counsel all of the files it had on individual class members. But without documentary evidence that does not exist, an individual farmer would be hard-pressed to provide evidence beyond his own testimony, and additional discovery from the government would not be helpful.

In addition, a relatively extensive amount of litigation had occurred by the time the parties agreed to a settlement. The issue of class certification had been extensively briefed by the parties and decided by the Court. Plaintiffs' motion for summary judgment on the issue of the statute of limitations was fully briefed when the statute of limitations was tolled by legislative action. The government also had filed a motion for judgment on the pleadings and for partial summary judgment that was fully briefed. In sum, the discovery, investigation and legal research conducted by class counsel before entering into settlement was thorough and supports the fairness and reasonableness of the settlement.

---

the following individuals spoke at the hearing: Mattie Mack; Kevin Pyle; Sherman Witchler; Eddie Slaughter; Ridgeley Mu'Min Muhammed; Willie Frank Smith; John Bender; Troy Scroggins; and Willie Head.

All of the objections and comments, whether received in the form of letters to the Court or as formal filings, have been filed as part of the official record of this case. To the extent possible, the Court has attempted to address all of the objections that have been raised. Whether or not specifically mentioned in this Opinion, the Court has carefully considered the objections and appreciates the extent to which the objectors have shared their thoughts and views.

2. Class Definition

The class is defined to include all African American farmers who (1) farmed, or attempted to farm, between January 1, 1981 and December 31, 1996; (2) applied to the United States Department of Agriculture (USDA) during that time period for participation in a federal farm credit or benefit program and who believed that they were discriminated against on the basis of race in USDA's response to that application; and (3) filed a discrimination complaint on or before July 1, 1997, regarding USDA's treatment of such farm credit or benefit application. Some characterize this class definition as too narrow. They claim that the class should be broadened to include all African American farmers who claim to have faced discrimination in credit transactions or benefit programs with the USDA, regardless of whether they filed a complaint of discrimination with the USDA.

The legal issues for those who never have filed a discrimination complaint, however, are much more difficult than those facing the members of the class as currently defined. The statute of limitations issue still exists for those who never have filed complaints of discrimination because Congress tolled the statute of limitations only for those who filed discrimination complaints by July 1, 1997. Moreover, from the beginning, plaintiffs' complaint only sought relief for those who had filed discrimination complaints with the USDA. Accordingly, the Consent Decree in this case cannot provide relief for those who never purported to complain to the USDA in any way about the alleged discrimination. . . .

The Consent Decree also requires each class member to provide proof that he filed a "discrimination complaint" with the USDA. The term "discrimination complaint" is defined broadly to include "a communication from a class member directly to USDA, or to a member of Congress, the White House, or a state, local or federal official who forwarded the class member's communication to USDA, asserting that USDA had discriminated against the class member on the basis of race in connection with a federal farm credit transaction or benefit application." In the absence of specified documents, a class member may submit an affidavit from a non-family member stating that he or she has personal knowledge that a discrimination complaint was filed and describing the way in which it was filed.

Some objectors maintain that it is unfair to require an affidavit from someone who is not a family member because, as Mr. Vernon Breckinridge put it, "getting loans from USDA is just like you go to a normal bank and get a loan. You don't normally go around and tell everybody in the neighborhood that you've gone to the bank to secure a loan." While it may be that some will be precluded from obtaining relief because they cannot use affidavits from family members, the class membership determination is designed to be mechanistic so that it can be done quickly by the facilitator. If family members were permitted to submit affidavits, the facilitator would be required to make credibility determinations that inevitably would slow the process of determining class membership.

3. Asserted Collusion

The Court finds that there is absolutely no evidence of collusion between the class counsel and counsel for the government. From the outset, all settlement negotiations were conducted in the presence of the mediator, Mr. Michael Lewis, a neutral and detached mediator with twenty-five years of experience who has mediated many complex class action cases including employment and environmental cases. Mr. Lewis has stated quite emphatically that there was no collusion in this case: "If this case represented collusion or the negotiations in this case represented collusion I as a mediator never ever want to mediate a case in which the parties are at each others' throats. To term this negotiation intensive ... understates the difficulty. This was an arduous negotiation. It took a year. It was hard fought."

Nor has the Court has seen any evidence of collusion or other impropriety on the part of counsel on either side. From the day this case was filed, Mr. Alexander Pires has tenaciously asserted that his clients had a right to receive relief from the government. Even faced with difficult statute of limitations issues and a serious lack of documentation, he has never wavered from his fundamental position that the government had wronged generations of African American farmers and must provide compensation. Even when settlement negotiations were ongoing, both sides maintained their positions and continued to assert the interests of their respective clients in every filing and at every status conference. At the status hearing on March 20, 1998, for example, Mr. Chestnut pleaded for a trial date because he had no faith that the case would settle and he wanted to protect the interests of the class. Government counsel continued to file motions and protect the legal interests of the USDA. Certainly the Court can attest to the fact that the parties litigated vigorously all of the issues that were or logically could have been raised.

4. *Notice, Opportunity to Be Heard and Reaction of the Class*

When a class is certified and a settlement is proposed, the parties are required to provide class members with the "best notice practicable under the circumstances." Rule 23(c)(2), Fed.R.Civ.P. The Court concludes that class members have received more than adequate notice and have had sufficient opportunity to be heard on the fairness of the proposed Consent Decree.

First, the timing and breadth of notice of the class settlement was sufficient under Rule 23. Notice was mailed to all known class members by January 15, 1999, nearly six weeks before the fairness hearing and a month before the deadline for comments, providing class members with ample time to submit their objections.[15] The parties also exerted extraordinary efforts to reach class members through a massive advertising campaign in general circulation and African American targeted publications and radio and television stations.

Second, the content of the notice was sufficient because it "fairly apprise[d] the ... members of the class of the terms of the proposed settlement and of the options that are open to them in connection with [the] proceedings." The notice provided class members with information on the class, the purpose and timing of the fairness hearing, opt-out procedures and deadlines, and the deadline and process for filing claims packages. In addition, it provided telephone numbers for the facilitator and for class counsel to the extent that anyone had any questions.

Third, the Court gave objectors ample opportunity to present their objections to the Consent Decree. As noted above, the Court considered all of the written objections that were filed and provided objectors with an opportunity to present their objections orally at the fairness hearing. While the Court denied a request for an evidentiary hearing made by one group of objectors, ... the Court is not obligated to hold an evidentiary hearing, especially in view of the fact that it accepted and considered affidavits in place of testimony....

Finally, because the Court has received a number of objections, it is clear that class members do not unanimously support the settlement. It is significant, however, that there

---

15. One objector maintains that notice was insufficient because the facilitator did not advertise in the United States Virgin Islands. With the exception of that one objection, no one appears to believe that the scope of the notice provided was insufficient.

are relatively few objections to the settlement in comparison with the size of the class. This is a large class. As of March 26, 1999, 16,559 farmers had requested claims packages from the facilitator, and the facilitator already has received 1686 completed claim packages. By contrast, only 85 farmer class members have elected to opt out of the class. Given the low rate of opt-outs and the relatively small percentage of class members objecting to the Consent Decree, the Court concludes that those objections do not warrant rejecting the Consent Decree.[16]

B. Substantive Fairness: Likely Recovery at Trial Compared with Terms of Proposed Settlement

As our court of appeals has said, in considering a proposed class action settlement, the Court first must compare the likely recovery that plaintiffs would have realized if they had gone to trial with the terms of the settlement. *See Thomas v. Albright,* 139 F.3d at 231. The Court must look at the settlement as a whole and should not reject a settlement merely because individual class members claim that they would have received more at trial. The Court should scrutinize the terms of the settlement carefully, but the discretion of the Court to reject a settlement is restrained by the "principle of preference" that encourages settlements. The Court has received approximately sixty written submissions from forty-three groups or individuals objecting to or commenting on the fairness of the settlement.

The Court also heard from numerous individuals and organizations at the fairness hearing on March 2, 1999. Some of the objectors have argued persuasively that the settlement could have included broader relief, but that is not the test. *See Stewart v. Rubin,* 948 F.Supp. at 1087 ("the Court [should not] make the proponents of the agreement justify each term of settlement against a hypothetical measure of what concessions might have been gained"). The question is whether the structure of the settlement and the substantive relief including the amount of money provided are fair and reasonable when compared to the recovery that plaintiffs likely would have realized if the case went to trial. The Court concludes that they are.

The settlement provides a measure of certainty for most class members. The vast majority of class members probably will be entitled almost automatically to recovery under Track A, while Track B, which has no cap on the amount of damages available, provides those with stronger cases with the opportunity to realize greater recoveries. It is clear from the structure and terms of the settlement that class counsel were trying to strike a delicate balance between ensuring that as many class members as possible would receive compensation and ensuring that any compensation was adequate for the harm suffered. In striking this balance, class counsel were forced to recognize that most of the members of the class had little in the way of documentation or proof of their claims and likely would have recovered nothing if they were required to prove their cases by the traditional preponderance of the evidence standard. Track A was devised to provide a set amount of compensation for those class members who could meet only a minimal burden of proof, while Track B was not so limited. The Track A/Track B mechanism also ensures that this compensation is distributed as promptly as possible.

---

16. Certain of the original named plaintiffs, including both Mr. Timothy Pigford and Mr. Cecil Brewington, have objected to the terms of the settlement. The Court has carefully considered their objections but nonetheless concludes that the settlement is fair, adequate and reasonable. *See Thomas v. Albright,* 139 F.3d at 232 (fact that named class representatives object to proposed settlement does not preclude court from finding that settlement is fair).

The Court is sympathetic to the reasons that various class members would have wanted class counsel to strike the balance differently in their negotiations. Nonetheless, the Court is not persuaded that striking a different balance would have been either achievable in the negotiating process or more favorable to all or even most members of the class. It certainly is not convinced that a better result would have been achieved by taking this case to trial where a substantial number of class members would have been unable to prove their claims by a preponderance of the evidence and thus would have recovered nothing. While each class member understandably wants the settlement to provide the greatest possible compensation to himself, the Court cannot conclude that the final balance struck by class counsel is anything but fair.

1. *Likely Recovery If Case Had Proceeded to Trial*

If the case had proceeded to trial, plaintiffs would have had in their possession strong evidence that the USDA discriminated against African American farmers. The reports of the Inspector General and the Civil Rights Action Team provide a persuasive indictment of the civil rights record of the USDA and the pervasive discrimination against African American farmers. There does not appear to be much dispute that racial discrimination has occurred throughout the USDA and that the USDA and the county committees discriminated against African American farmers for decades in evaluating their applications for farm credit and benefits. In addition, when Congress took the unprecedented action of tolling the statute of limitations for ECOA, one of plaintiffs' major obstacles to establishing defendant's liability to the class was removed.

The problem is that even with that evidence, 80 to 90 percent of the class members lack any documentary evidence of the alleged discriminatory denial of credit or benefits to them. *See* Pls' Response to Written Objections at 11; Transcript of Hearing of March 2, 1999 at 180 (Mr. Alexander Pires) ("What would happen … in this case if we went to trial? 90 percent of our clients do not have files.… 90 percent do not have files"). In order to recover damages under ECOA at a trial, a class member would have to be able to establish by a preponderance of the evidence a discriminatory denial of loans or terms of credit, the extent of the injury to him caused by the denial and the amount of damages he suffered. Absent any documentation, this would have been an impossible burden for the majority of class members. In addition, many class members lack any documentation to prove that they ever filed a complaint of discrimination with the USDA and therefore would have encountered great difficulty in even establishing their membership in the class. With no documentary evidence that they fall within the parameters of the class, it is not at all clear that those plaintiffs would have been able to recover anything.

Some objectors have suggested that the issue of damages could have been resolved by trying the claims of representative members of the class. As Mr. Alexander Pires explained, however, "I would never take the thousands of clients we have now and say bet your claim on those 12 or 13 cases that are your lead cases. Even though we helped pick them. I know what's in those 12 cases, and that's risky." In fact, class counsel discovered during the process of negotiating the settlement that mediating the cases individually was risky. When the parties were in the initial stages of settlement negotiations, they agreed to mediate twelve individual test cases: six chosen by the government and six chosen by plaintiffs. The lack of documentation presented serious obstacles to the resolution of those cases. The parties worked for an entire month trying to settle eight of those twelve cases, and at the end of that month, not one case had been resolved.

Moreover, bringing this case to trial likely would have been a very complex, long and costly proposition. Practically speaking, prevailing class members likely would not have obtained relief for many years. Trial on the issue of liability was scheduled to last the month of February 1999. Trial probably would have involved a number of experts, and the government probably would have raised a number of legal issues for the Court to resolve. Even if the Court devoted all of its resources and time to deciding the issue of liability, it is unlikely that a decision would have been issued before the summer of 1999. If the Court had found the USDA liable, it then would have had to resolve the issue of remedy for each farmer. A mechanism for establishing class or subclass membership and for resolving issues of individual damages for each farmer in the class or subclass would have been necessary. If the remedy phase were tried on an individual basis for each farmer— as the government might have urged again as it has in the past, because of the acknowledged lack of documentation in so many cases—the remedial process would have dragged on for years. If the remedy phase were not tried on an individual basis for each farmer, it is not inconceivable that a mechanism much like that negotiated in this settlement ultimately would be utilized. Even barring the inevitable appeal that the government would have taken in the event that plaintiffs prevailed, it is unlikely that any class member would have received any recovery for his injury for many years.

By contrast, the settlement negotiated by the parties provides for relatively prompt recovery. The claim of a claimant who chooses Track A will be resolved within 110 days of the date that the claim is filed. For those who choose Track B, the wait is a little longer because of discovery and trial, but the total time required is at most 240 days from the date that the claim is filed. Because neither side may appeal, the claimant will receive his compensation long before he would have if the case had gone to trial.

2. Overall Structure of Settlement: Track A and Track B

As currently structured, class members have three options: they have 120 days after the entry of the Consent Decree within which to notify the facilitator if they want to opt out of the class altogether, they may remain in the class and choose Track A or they may remain in the class and choose Track B. Those who do not opt out have 180 days from the entry of the decree within which to file their claim packages and, for those who choose Track A, to submit their proof.

A number of class members complain that they lack sufficient information to select among these three options and that the settlement is structured to force class members to choose Track A. At meetings throughout the country, class counsel currently is making every effort to reach all class members, to explain the options and to sit down with individual class members to provide advice. The turnout for these meetings has been overwhelming and has far exceeded everyone's expectations: literally hundreds of farmers show up for each meeting. It has become clear that there are more class members than anyone had anticipated and some class members contend that although they show up at the meetings, class counsel does not have time to meet with them. Class counsel is in the midst of scheduling more meetings and providing more time for each meeting, and they have assured the Court that they will be able to meet with all class members prior to the deadline for filing claim packages.

Those who assert only discrimination in non-credit, benefit transactions, rather than discrimination in credit transactions, do not have the option of proceeding under Track B, and one objector complains that those who have faced discrimination in the USDA's benefit programs ought to be allowed to proceed under Track B. The problem is that programs that do not involve credit transactions are not subject to ECOA. The cause of action for those who allege discrimination in benefit programs arises solely under the Administrative Procedure Act, 5 U.S.C. § 706, which does not provide for the same measure of damages as is provided under ECOA. For that reason, those who allege only that they have suffered discrimination in a benefit program are afforded a slightly different form of relief than the relief provided for those who suffered discrimination in a credit transaction with the USDA. In other words, the different statutory predicates for the two different kinds of claims restricted the solutions that counsel could negotiate in each context.

A class member who selects Track A must submit "substantial evidence" demonstrating that he was a victim of race discrimination in a credit or benefit transaction with the USDA. Some have objected that the "substantial evidence" standard is too high a burden of proof. Part of that concern stems from a misunderstanding of the "substantial evidence" standard. While the phrase "substantial evidence" makes it sound as though the burden of proof is high, the substantial evidence standard actually is one of the lowest possible burdens of proof known to the law. A "substantial evidence standard" is significantly easier for the claimant to meet than a "preponderance of the evidence" standard. A "preponderance of the evidence" standard means that the claimant has to show that it is more likely than not that discrimination happened, while under a "substantial evidence" standard, the claimant only has to provide a reasonable basis for the adjudicator to find that discrimination happened. The substantial evidence standard therefore should not be a bar to the claims of most class members.

In order for a claimant to prevail under Track A, he must present specified evidence, including evidence that he was treated less favorably than a "specifically identified, similarly situated" white farmer. Some objectors contend that it will be too difficult for some claimants to present evidence of a specific, similarly situated white farmer who received more favorable treatment, especially since there is no right to discovery under Track A. At this point, however, class counsel has amassed a significant amount of material regarding the treatment by the USDA of both African American farmers and white farmers, and claimants will be able to call upon that material in completing their claim packages. Class counsel should be able to provide most claimants with the evidence they need.

Under Track B, after limited discovery the claimant has a one day mini-trial before an arbitrator, and the claimant has the burden of establishing by a preponderance of the evidence that the USDA discriminated against him in a credit transaction. There are a number of objections to the Track B mechanism. First, the original Consent Decree defined Track B arbitrators as Michael Lewis and "any other person or person who he assigns to decide Track B claims." Some objectors contended that the definition of arbitrator was too vague and that those who were thinking about choosing Track B would have no way of knowing who the arbitrator might be. As Mr. James Morrison put it, "If Mr. Lewis chooses to have distinguished jurists, lawyers, former judges, I think he has that right as the four corners of the document gives him the authority. But if he wishes to choose Mickey Mouse, he could choose Mickey Mouse." The parties addressed this concern in the revised Consent Decree by defining arbitrators as either Michel Lewis or "other person or persons selected by Mr. Lewis who meet qualifications agreed upon by the parties and by Mr. Lewis and whom Mr. Lewis assigns to decide Track B claims. . . ." The parties have specified that Mr. Lewis will "develop a single list of alternates which the parties would pre-approve and from which Mr. Lewis can select an arbitrator for any arbitration that he is unable to handle himself." While a claimant may not know the identity of the arbitrator at the time that the claimant chooses Track B, he will know who the potential candidates are and that they were not unilaterally selected by Mr. Lewis. In addition, class counsel can provide background information about the people on the list so the claimant will be able to make a more informed decision about whether he wants to select Track B.

Track B provides for limited discovery prior to the one day mini-trial. Discovery is limited essentially to an exchange of lists of witnesses and exhibits and depositions of the opposing side's witnesses. Some contend that discovery should be much broader. While it undoubtedly is true that the Track B mechanism anticipates less discovery than is ordinarily provided in the course of civil litigation, the Track B mechanism also resolves the claim much more quickly than an ordinary civil case would be resolved, in large part because of the shortened discovery period. Expanding the scope of discovery would take significantly more time, and class counsel in their judgment reasonably weighed the possible benefits of additional discovery against the delays that would ensue and determined that this was an adequate amount of discovery.[19]

A hearing on a Track B claim lasts eight hours. There is no live direct testimony. All direct testimony is submitted in writing. The eight hours at the hearing are comprised entirely of cross-examinations: each side is allotted four hours to cross-examine any witness of the opposing side. Several objectors contend that the claimant should be able to present live direct testimony, rather than presenting it only in written form. As with the Track B discovery issue, class counsel clearly was trying to balance the need for expedition with the need to ensure that the process produces just results. Again, the Court cannot conclude that the balance that counsel ultimately struck renders the terms of the settlement unfair.

In order to prevail on his claims, a Track B claimant must prove by a preponderance of the evidence that "he was the victim of racial discrimination and that he suffered damages therefrom." One objection maintains that this standard is too high and that claimants will be unable to meet this standard. To the extent that a claimant is concerned that he lacks sufficient evidence to meet the preponderance of the evidence standard, the traditional standard in civil litigation in all states and federal courts in this country, Track A provides a safer option. A claimant who cannot meet the preponderance of the evidence standard is not barred from all relief; instead, he is required to choose Track A rather than choosing Track B. Another objector also contends that a Track B claimant should not be required to establish economic damage in order to prevail on a Track B claim, and that the claimant should be able to prevail even if he can only establish emotional injury. As class counsel has pointed out, however, the economic damage requirement stems from ECOA, which provides the cause of action for all Track B claimants.

Some objectors complain about the Track A/Track B structure because those claimants who select Track B and fail to demonstrate by a preponderance of the evidence that they were the victims of race discrimination and that they suffered economic harm as a result will recover nothing under the settlement, rather than being permitted to proceed under Track A if they lose under Track B. The decision whether to proceed under Track A or under Track B therefore takes on a great deal of significance. If a claimant who has sufficient evidence to meet Track A requirements but insufficient evidence to prevail in Track B nonetheless chooses Track B, he will receive nothing.

As class counsel and counsel for the government have pointed out, however, there simply is no way that those who fail on a Track B claim could be permitted to proceed under Track A without entirely undermining the settlement. The settlement is designed to re-

---

19. In fact, several objectors contend that the Track B mechanism, even with the shortened discovery period, takes too long to resolve claims. It is clear from the tensions between these two sets of objections that class counsel had to strike a delicate balance between resolving Track B claims expeditiously and obtaining the necessary discovery, and the balance finally struck appears eminently reasonable to the Court.

solve the claims of all class members as promptly as possible. Because of the absence of documentary proof in most cases, the vast majority of claimants will select Track A, and Track A is designed to be a mechanistic way to deal with claims very quickly. Track B, by contrast, involves a much lengthier, fact-specific inquiry, but it is anticipated that very few class members will opt for Track B. If there were a fallback mechanism to provide relief for claimants who failed in their Track B claims, every class member would choose Track B and the settlement structure would collapse under its own weight ...

Finally, the decisions of the adjudicators on Track A claims and the decisions of the arbitrators on Track B claims are final; there is no right to appeal those decisions, except that the Monitor shall direct the arbitrator or adjudicator to reexamine the claim if he determines that a "clear and manifest error has occurred" that is "likely to result in a fundamental miscarriage of justice." Many objectors contend that the absence of appeal rights renders the settlement structure unfair and/or that it gives the arbitrators and adjudicators too much power. As Mr. Willie Head expressed it, "[w]ould you send your sons and daughters off to war with one bullet." While the objection has force, class counsel made a strategic decision not to press for appeal rights because the government would have insisted that any appeal rights be a two-way street. Any appeal process inevitably would delay payments to those claimants who prevailed on their claims. Since it is anticipated that most class members will prevail under the structure of the settlement, the Court concludes that the forfeit of appeal rights was a reasonable compromise.

3. *Track A Relief: The $50,000 Objection*

Any claimant who prevails on a Track A claim for discrimination in a credit transaction will receive: (1) a cash payment of $50,000; (2) forgiveness of all debt owed to the USDA incurred under or affected by the program that formed the basis of the claim; (3) a tax payment directly to the IRS in the amount of 25% of the total of the debt forgiveness and cash payment; (4) immediate termination of any foreclosure action that USDA initiated in connection with the loan(s) at issue in the claim; and (5) injunctive relief including one-time priority loan consideration and technical assistance. This relief package is the source of two objections.

Many objectors claim that a $50,000 cash award is insufficient to compensate them for the losses they sustained as a result of the USDA's discrimination. As Mr. Willie Head expressed it, "imagine that your home has been taken, your land has been taken, your automobile has been taken, and then you can make a decision and see if $50,000 will be enough for you." Putting a monetary value on the damage done to someone who has experienced discrimination at the hands of the government obviously is no easy matter, and it is probable that no amount of money can fully compensate class members for past acts of discrimination. It is quite clear, as the objectors point out, that $50,000 is not full compensation in most cases.

To the extent that a specific value can be put on such compensation, however, class counsel have thoroughly researched the issue and provided persuasive evidence that the amount is fair.[21] As class counsel points out, every claimant who prevails under Track A

---

21. To the extent that objectors are claiming that class counsel had no economic basis for agreeing to settle the case for the amount they did, that argument is belied by the fact that class counsel consulted a number of economists. Moreover, while one objector submitted affidavits from other economists that contend that the value of class members' claims may have been worth more than $50,000, those economists do not take into account the breadth of relief provided by the settlement. Class counsel also conducted an extensive study of the settlement of four previous civil rights actions in which plaintiffs alleged egregious violations of civil rights, including the case brought by Japanese Americans interned during World War II and the *Tuskegee* case involving the claims of African Amer-

will receive not $50,000 but at least $62,500 (the sum of a $50,000 cash payment plus $12,500 in tax relief). And most who prevail under Track A will receive much more than that. The government estimates that the average African American farmer carries government debt of approximately $100,000, and those debts will be forgiven under Track A; in addition, the settlement provides for a tax payment of 25% of the debt forgiveness. The average cash value of relief for a claimant who prevails under Track A therefore totals $187,500. Class members undoubtedly would have liked to have received a larger settlement. But $187,500 is a significant amount of money, especially in view of the fact that a claimant who lacks the detailed records required in a normal civil action to prove his case by a preponderance of the evidence need only establish his claim by substantial evidence in order to receive that compensation. The Court therefore concludes that class counsel had an adequate basis for agreeing to this amount and that it is fair and reasonable.

Some objectors also contend that the tax relief provided under Track A is insufficient because it may not cover all the federal taxes owed on the settlement and because it does not cover state taxes. Any effort to determine the exact amount of federal tax owed on a settlement, however, would have required scores of auditors and inevitably would have resulted in delays. The logistical problems presented by a provision covering state taxes would have been even more complicated, since every state has a different method of assessing income taxes and different tax rates. Again, class counsel in its judgment determined that a flat tax payment was in the best interests of the class and in assuring a prompt resolution of the claims, and the Court is unwilling to second-guess that judgment.

4. *Other Objections to Individual Relief*

The failure of both Track A and Track B to include certain measures of individual relief also has led to objections. First, some contend that the USDA should provide relief from loans owed to creditors other than the USDA. They argue that because the USDA discriminated in its credit programs, many African American farmers either had to obtain loans from private banks at very high interest rates or had to buy their equipment and supplies on credit from private companies at high interest rates. They therefore seek to have all of those loans forgiven or at least to have loans that were guaranteed by the USDA forgiven. Class counsel clearly tried to negotiate for as much debt forgiveness as possible. But as Mr. J.L. Chestnut put it, "There is no likelihood the United States government is going to go around to … commercial banks paying off private loans of black farmers, whether it relates to discrimination or not. Nobody is going to be able to negotiate that with the United States government. How do I know that? Because I tried."

Second, some have objected that the Consent Decree does not contain a provision to protect a class member's settlement award from his bankruptcy estate. The parties to this action cannot, however, determine whether the bankruptcy estate has a right to a claimant's settlement award. Those matters are controlled by operation of the bankruptcy laws and will turn on issues such as whether the claim is considered the property of the estate. Those matters properly are resolved in bankruptcy court between the parties to those actions and cannot be resolved by the parties to this action.

Third, a claimant who prevails under Track B is entitled to "any USDA inventory property that was formerly owned by the class member but which was foreclosed in connection with the ECOA claim(s) resolved in the class member's favor by the arbitrator." With

---

icans injected with syphilis as part of government experiments. Class counsel reasonably concluded that this settlement, which affords class members greater monetary relief than that afforded to individuals in those four cases, was fair and adequate.

that one exception, however, the Consent Decree has no provision for returning land to prevailing claimants. A number of objectors have stated the need for more extensive land return provisions. Again, this was a matter that class counsel clearly tried to negotiate, and they obtained the best possible resolution they could.

Finally, one objector expressed concern that the credit records of many claimants have been damaged by the discrimination they experienced at the hands of the USDA and that it therefore will be difficult for those farmers to obtain credit from the USDA or others in the future. In response to that objection, the parties agreed to revise the Consent Decree to include a provision stating that "outstanding debt discharged pursuant to [Track A or Track B] shall not adversely affect the claimant's eligibility for future participation in any USDA loan or loan servicing program." In sum, while some class members clearly would have liked the terms of the settlement to be slightly different, the terms of the settlement are fair when compared with the likely recovery plaintiffs would have obtained at trial.

C. Monitoring and Enforcement Provisions

Some objectors contend that at the very least the enforcement and monitoring provisions of the Consent Decree must be strengthened. The Consent Decree provides for the appointment of a Monitor for a period of five years to track and report on the USDA's compliance with the terms of the Consent Decree. Under the original proposed Consent Decree, the Monitor was appointed by the Secretary of Agriculture, subject to class counsels' approval. A number of objections noted that the USDA did not have any incentive to appoint a strong and independent Monitor, and that the Monitor provision therefore needed to be changed. In response to those concerns, the parties revised the Monitor provision so that the Court now appoints the Monitor from a list of names submitted by the parties. The Monitor is removable only for "good cause."

A number of objections also noted that the original proposed Consent Decree appeared to prevent the Court from exercising jurisdiction in the event that the USDA did not comply with the terms of the decree. The law is clear that the Court retains jurisdiction to enforce the terms of the Consent Decree.... The parties also have clarified that the Court retains jurisdiction to enforce the terms of the Decree.

D. Absence of Provisions Preventing Future Discrimination

The stated purpose of the Consent Decree is to "ensur[e] that in their dealings with the USDA, all class members receive full and fair treatment that is the same as the treatment accorded to similarly situated white persons." The Consent Decree does not, however, provide any forward-looking injunctive relief. It does not require the USDA to take any steps to ensure that county commissioners who have discriminated against class members in the past are no longer in the position of approving loans. Nor does it provide a mechanism to ensure that future discrimination complaints are timely investigated and resolved so that the USDA does not practice the same discrimination against African American farmers that led to the filing of this lawsuit. In fact, the Consent Decree stands absolutely mute on two critical points: the full implementation of the recommendations of the Civil Rights Action Team and the integration and reform of the county committee system to make it more accountable and representative. The absence of any such provisions has led to strong, heart-felt objections. It also has caused the Court concern. After comparing the terms of the settlement as a whole with the recovery that plaintiffs likely would have received after trial, however, the Court cannot conclude that the absence of any such prospective injunctive relief renders the settlement as a whole unfair.

There are several legal responses to the objections about the lack of forward-looking injunctive relief. First, while plaintiffs sought both declaratory and monetary relief in the complaint, they never sought an injunction requiring the USDA to restructure or to fire people who may have engaged in discrimination. All of the objectors who seek to have the USDA restructured therefore are going beyond the scope of the complaint in this case. The role of the Court in approving or disapproving a settlement is limited to determining whether the settlement of the case before it is fair, adequate and reasonable. The Court cannot reject the Consent Decree merely because it does not provide relief for some other hypothetical case that plaintiffs could have but did not bring.

Second, nothing in the Consent Decree authorizes the USDA to engage in illegal conduct in the future, and the Consent Decree therefore should not be rejected for its failure to include such prospective injunctive relief....

Third, even if plaintiffs had prevailed on their ECOA claims at trial, it is not at all clear that the Court could have or would have granted the broad injunctive relief that the objectors now seek. The injunctive relief that the objectors seek, essentially an injunction requiring the USDA to change the way it processes credit applications, may be authorized where plaintiffs prove a constitutional violation, ... but plaintiffs in their Seventh Amended Complaint do not allege a constitutional violation and they have not undertaken to prove one. Moreover, while ECOA authorizes the Court to "grant such equitable and declaratory relief as is necessary to enforce the requirements imposed under this subchapter," 15 U.S.C. § 1691e(c), in employing its broad equitable powers the Court must exercise "the least possible power adequate to the end proposed."...

Those legal responses, however, provide little comfort to those who have experienced discrimination at the hands of the USDA and who legitimately fear that they will continue to face such discrimination in the future. The objections arise from a deep and overwhelming sense that the USDA and all of the structures it has put in place have been and continue to be fundamentally hostile to the African American farmer. As Mr. Leonard Cooper put it, "You cannot mediate ... institutionalized racism." Another class member expressed it more personally: "They have humiliated me and my family since [1989].... And I was just wondering if there couldn't be something put in the provisions that would stop these FSA agents from humiliating and degrading [us] as they do.... my wife has almost had a nervous breakdown by dealing with our agent and he continues to do the same things that he has done in the past and I just wish there was some way for you to put something in that provision that would stop some of that stuff."

Most fundamentally, these objections result from a well-founded and deep-seated mistrust of the USDA. A mistrust borne of a long history of racial discrimination. A mistrust that is well-deserved. As Mr. Chestnut put it, these objections reflect "fear which reaches all the way back to slavery.... That objection, you heard it from many today, it really asks you to retain jurisdiction over this case in perpetuity. Otherwise they say USDA will default, ignore the lawful mandates of this Court, and in time march home scot-free while blacks are left holding the empty bag again." The Court cannot guarantee class members that they will never experience discrimination at the hands of the USDA again, and the Consent Decree does not purport to make such a guarantee. But the Consent Decree and the Court do provide certain assurances.

First, under the terms of this Consent Decree, the USDA is obligated to pay billions of dollars to African American farmers who have suffered discrimination. Those billions of dollars will serve as a reminder to the Department of Agriculture that its actions were unacceptable and should serve to deter it from engaging in the same conduct in the future.

Second, the USDA is not above the law. Like many of the objectors, the Court was surprised and disappointed by the government's response to the Court's modest proposal that the Consent Decree include a simple sentence that in the future the USDA shall exert "best efforts to ensure compliance with all applicable statutes and regulations prohibiting discrimination." Whether or not the government explicitly states it in this Consent Decree, however, the Constitution and laws of the United States continue to forbid discrimination on the basis of race, *see, e.g.,* U.S. Const. amend. V; 15 U.S.C. § 1691; 42 U.S.C. § 2000d, as do the regulations of the USDA. *See* 7 C.F.R. §§ 15.1, 15.51. The actions of the USDA from now into the future will be scrutinized closely—by class members, by their now organized and vocal allies, by Congress and by the Court. If the USDA or members of the county committees are operating on the misapprehension that they ever again can repeat the events that led to this lawsuit, those forces will disabuse them of any such notion.

Most importantly, the farmers who have been a part of this lawsuit have demonstrated their power to bring about fundamental change to the Department of Agriculture, albeit more slowly than some would have wanted. Each individual farmer may feel powerless, but as a group they have planted seeds that are changing the landscape of the USDA. As a group, they spurred Secretary Glickman in 1996 to look inward at the practices of the USDA and to examine African American farmers' allegations that the discrimination of the USDA was leading them to the point of financial ruin. As a group, they led Secretary Glickman to create the Civil Rights Action Team, a team that recommended sweeping changes to the USDA and to the county committee system. Indeed, in February 1997, the USDA Civil Rights Action Team itself recommended that the county committee system be revised by converting all county non-federal positions, including the county executive directors, to federal status, that the committee selection process by changed, that voting members of underrepresented groups be appointed to state and county committees, and that county committees be removed from any farm loan determinations.

As a group, the farmers mobilized a broad coalition within Congress to take the unprecedented action of tolling the statute of limitations. As a group, they brought Secretary Glickman to the negotiating table in this case and achieved the largest civil rights settlement in history. And as a group, they have made implementation of the recommendations of the CRAT Report a priority within the USDA. *See* Statement of February 9, 1999, by Secretary Dan Glickman, Before the Subcommittee on Agriculture, Rural Development, and Related Agencies Committee on Appropriations, United States Senate ("I also want to emphasize the importance that the President and I have placed on USDA civil rights issues; this priority is reflected in the [FY 2000] budget. The President's budget provides the necessary funding to continue to carry out the recommendations of the Civil Rights Action Team (CRAT) as well as the recommendations of the National Commission on Small Farms which supports our civil rights agenda"). While the USDA landscape has remained resistant to change for many seasons, the labors of these farmers finally are beginning to bear fruit. This settlement represents one significant harvest. It is up to the Secretary of Agriculture and other responsible officials at the USDA to fulfill its promises, to ensure that this shameful period is never repeated and to bring the USDA into the twenty-first century.

V. CONCLUSION

Forty acres and a mule. The government broke that promise to African American farmers. Over one hundred years later, the USDA broke its promise to Mr. James Beverly. It promised him a loan to build farrowing houses so that he could breed hogs. Because he was African American, he never received that loan. He lost his farm because of the loan that never was. Nothing can completely undo the discrimination of the past or restore lost land or lost opportunities to Mr. Beverly or to all of the other African American farmers whose representatives came before this Court. Historical discrimination cannot be undone.

But the Consent Decree represents a significant first step. A first step that has been a long time coming, but a first step of immeasurable value. As Mr. Chestnut put it, "Who really knows the true value, if there is one, for returning a small army of poor black farmers to the business of farming by the year 2000 who otherwise would never make it back? I am not wise enough to put a dollar value on that and I don't think anybody on this planet is wise enough to reduce that to dollars and cents." The Consent Decree is a fair, adequate and reasonable settlement of the claims brought in this case. It therefore will be approved and entered.

SO ORDERED.

Notes

1. Judge Friedman's optimistic approval of the consent decree in *Pigford v. Glickman* in no way foretold the distressing divide that followed. On one side were prominent members of the African-American community, including Tim Pigford himself, who had opposed the settlement from the beginning, arguing that it was insufficient to correct past wrongs and did nothing to prevent future wrongs. On the other side, it appears that neither the attorneys representing the USDA nor the Bush administration that implemented the settlement completely shared the perspectives of Secretary Glickman and President Clinton regarding the case. Some believed that many of the class member's claims were unfounded and the settlement a mistake; others simply viewed their job as protecting the government's financial interests by minimizing plaintiff recovery and working aggressively to weed out those who could not prove their claims.

Heightening the animosity, there were far more claims filed under the *Pigford* consent decree than anyone had anticipated. Some viewed this as even stronger evidence of the magnitude of the problem of discrimination at the USDA. Others viewed it as an effort to unfairly take advantage of the settlement offering. The government aggressively fought each class member's claim, making even Track A relief unattainable for many class members. Particularly problematic was the plaintiff's need to show the benefits received by similarly situated white farmers. Despite previous assurances to the court, the necessary documentation was simply not available in some cases.

With the number of claims and the adversarial nature of the proceedings, the lead attorneys for the class were not up to the daily work of representing the thousands of individual claimants. Errors, missed deadlines, incorrect filings, and other problems ensued. The news media picked up on the continued problems with the settlement.

> For a second time, a federal judge has strongly criticized plaintiffs' lawyers for the way they are handling the last stages of a settlement involving black farmers who alleged that the government discriminated against them.

> Judge Paul L. Friedman of the District of Columbia pointed to a dramatic increase in the rate at which class counsel has withdrawn petitions and he noted a failure by class counsel to respond to a large percentage of the government's petitions for monitor review—the appeals process. He also wrote that the lawyers'

"cursory" efforts to communicate with the class members did not constitute full, fair and adequate representation.

"The Court still fears that class counsel may be withdrawing meritorious petitions because of time constraints, threatened financial penalties and a lack of the resources required," Friedman wrote in a recent opinion.

Elizabeth Amon, *Class Counsel Blasted-again: Federal Judge Takes Lawyers to Task in Record Civil Rights Case,* 23 Nat'l L. J., Aug. 6, 2001.

Judge Friedman ordered a review of a number of the petitions; the monitor took on a greatly enhanced role, examining cases one-by-one; the facilitator was directed to communicate with the claimants to advise them when the government challenged their claims; appeal time lines were extended; and plaintiffs' counsel was admonished. The Judge also ordered class counsel to work with pro bono attorneys on the remaining appeals. A group of 15 firms in the D.C. area took up the challenge.

2. The *Pigford* Monitor reported that as of March 2, 2010, there were 22,721 farmers found to be eligible *Pigford* class members. Ninety-nine percent (99%), or 22,550, chose Track A relief. Fifty-nine percent (59%) of the Track A claims were initially denied, but after reexamination, that number increased to sixty-nine percent (69%) of claimants. Track A relief was thus available to 15,638 farmers and relief was denied to 6,912 farmers. The total relief provided is summarized in the following table.

Track A relief provided to 15,638 farmers under *Pigford v. Glickman* settlement

Type of relief provided	Total amount of relief provided
Cash awards to claimants ($50,000)	$ 767,450,000
Non-credit awards to claimants ($3,000)	1,512,000
IRS payments made on behalf of claimants	191,862,500
Debt relief provided to claimants	39,180,011
IRS payments for debt relief	6,690,517
Total Track A Relief	**$1,006,695,028**

Data derived from the *Pigford* Monitor statistics at http://pigfordmonitor.org/stats/ (May 14, 2010)

The payment of over one billion dollars to claimants, however, does not end the story. Indeed, while Judge Friedman had stated that Track A provided claimants with a "virtually automatic cash payment of $50,000, and forgiveness of debt owed to the USDA," even after significant monitor assistance, only 69% of Track A claimants were awarded relief.

Moreover, the 69% success rate is based upon the 22,550 farmers found to be eligible class members. Over 73,000 farmers filed claims past the filing deadline, with 2,116 allowed to proceed under a late claims procedure. The rest were denied as untimely. Including these farmers in the statistics transforms the success rate to as low as 14%. *See, Obstruction of Justice: USDA Undermines Historic Civil Rights Settlement with Black Farmers,* Environmental Working Group (EWG), available at http://www.ewg.org/reports/blackfarmers. As compelling as the story of these farmers may be, with claims denied without review solely because of their late filing, the sheer number of claims filed raised concerns that not all claims were meritorious. The stage was set for a continuing battle.

Tadlock Cowan & Jody Feder
The Pigford Case: USDA Settlement of a Discrimination Suit by Black Farmers
Congressional Research Service Report RS-20430
April 21, 2010

* * *

In general, there seems to be a consensus that many of the issues surrounding the implementation of *Pigford* can be attributed to the gross underestimation of the number of claims that would actually be filed.[11] At the same time, many in Congress and those closely associated with the settlement agreement have voiced much concern over the large percentage of denials, especially under Track A the "virtually automatic cash payment." Interest groups have suggested that the poor approval percentages (59%) can be attributed to the consent decree requirement that claimants show that their treatment was "less favorable than that accorded specifically identified, similarly situated white farmers, which was exacerbated by poor access to USDA files.[12] ..."

More alarming for many, however, is the large percentage of farmers who did not have their cases heard on the merits because they filed late—so-called *Pigford II* claimants. Approximately 73,800 *Pigford II* petitions (66,000 before the September 15, 2000, late-filing deadline) were filed under the late filing procedure, of which 2,116 were allowed to proceed.[14]

Many claimants who were initially denied relief under the late filing procedures requested a reconsideration of their petitions. Out of the approximately 20,700 timely requests for reconsideration, 17,279 requests had been decided, but only 113 had been allowed to proceed by the end of 2005, according to the most recent compilation of individual case data.[15] Many argued that the large number of late filings indicated that the notice was "ineffective or defective."[16] Others countered these claims by arguing that the *Pigford* notice program was designed, in part, to promote awareness and could not make someone file.[17] Some also suggested—including many of the claimants—that the class counsel was responsible for the inadequate notice and overall mismanagement of the settlement agreement.[18] Judge Friedman, for example, cautioned the farmers' lawyers for their failure to meet deadlines and described their representation, at one point, as "border[ing] on legal malpractice."[19]

---

11. *See* Status of the Implementation of the Pigford v. Glickman Settlement, hearing Before the House Committee on the Judiciary, Subcommittee on the Constitution, 108th Cong. at 1595 (2004) (letter from Michael K. Lewis, Arbitrator).

12. Environmental Working Group, Obstruction of Justice, USDA Undermines Historic Civil Rights Settlement with Black Farmers, Part 4 (July 2004) available at http://www.ewg.org/reports/blackfarmers/execsumm.php [hereinafter EWG Report].

14. Arbitrators Ninth Report on the Late-Claim Petition Process (November 30, 2005).

15. *Id.*

16. Notice Hearing, 1–4. *See also* EWG Report, at Part 3.

17. Notice Hearing, at 10 (statement of Jeanne C. Finegan, consultant to Poorman-Douglas).

18. Tom Burrell, President, Black Farmers and Agriculturalists Association, Inc., *Tom Burrell Lays out the Case of why Al Pires, Class Counsel, Must be Fired!*, available at http://www.bfaa.net/case_layout.pdf; see also EWG Report, at Part 3.

19. *Pigford v. Glickman*, No. 97-1978 and No. 98-1693 (D.D.C. April 27, 2001); *see also Pigford v. Veneman*, 292 F.3d 918, 922 (D.C. Cir. 2002).

Judge Friedman also declared that he was "surprised and disappoint[ed]" that the USDA did not want to include in the consent decree a sentence that in the future the USDA would exert "best efforts to ensure compliance with all applicable statutes and regulations prohibiting discrimination."[20] The judge's statements apparently did not go unnoticed, as the Black Farmers and Agriculturalists Association (BFAA) filed a $20.5 billion class action lawsuit in September 2004 on behalf of roughly 25,000 farmers against the USDA for alleged racial discriminatory practices against black farmers between January 1997 and August 2004. The lawsuit, however, was dismissed in March 2005 because BFAA failed to show it had standing to bring the suit.[21]

In the 110th Congress, the Pigford Claims Remedy Act of 2007 (H.R. 899; S. 515) and the African-American Farmers Benefits Relief Act of 2007 (H.R. 558) were introduced to provide relief to many of these claimants who failed to have their petitions considered on the merits. The provisions of these bills were incorporated into the 2008 farm bill (P.L. 110-246, Section 14012), providing up to $100 million for potential settlement costs. The Administration requested an additional $1.15 billion for these potential settlement costs in its FY2010 budget. Appropriators did not provide additional funding in the FY2010 appropriations bill (P.L. 111-80). On May 5, 2009, Senator Charles Grassley and Senator Kay Hagan introduced S. 972, a bill that would amend the 2008 farm bill to allow access to an unlimited judgment fund at the Department of Treasury to pay successful claims.[22] The legislation also allows for legal fees to be paid from the fund in addition to anti-fraud protection regarding claims. The bill was referred to the Committee on Agriculture, Nutrition, and Forestry. A related bill in the House (H.R. 3623) was introduced by Representative Arthur Davis on September 9, 2009, and referred to the Subcommittee on the Constitution, Civil Rights, and Civil Liberties on October 19, 2009.

On February 18, 2010, Attorney General Holder and Secretary of Agriculture Vilsack announced a $1.25 billion settlement of the *Pigford II* claims.[23] The Administration requested $1.15 billion in an emergency appropriation, to remain available until expended, for the *Pigford II* claimants. When combined with the $100 million authorized in the 2008 farm bill (P.L. 110-246, Section 14012), this appropriation, if authorized by Congress, would make $1.25 billion available to settle the *Pigford II* claims.

Senator Inouye introduced an amendment (S.Amdt. 3407) to H.R. 4213, the Tax Extenders Act of 2009, to provide the requested $1.15 billion. On March 10, 2010, the Senate voted 66-34 to invoke cloture on the bill and limit debate on the substitute being considered for amendment purposes. The vote blocked S.Amdt. 3407 as non-germane. No funding has yet been appropriated.

The *Pigford II* settlement is final and may not be appealed. A provision of the settlement permits the claimants to void the settlement should Congress not make the $1.15 billion appropriation by March 31, 2010. Congress did not make this deadline before leaving for the Easter recess. The settlement is clearly a priority of both the USDA and the White House, suggesting that the plaintiffs are unlikely to exercise the right to void the settlement in the near term. Unlike the original *Pigford* decision, the *Pigford II* settlement does not include a suggested settlement amount for individual claimants, although it does

---

20. *Pigford v. Glickman*, 185 F.R.D. 82, 112 (D.D.C. 1999).

21. *Black Farmers and Agriculturalists Assoc. v. Veneman*, 2005 U.S. Dist. LEXIS 5417 (D.D.C. March 29, 2005).

22. The U.S. Treasury fund is established under 31 U.S.C. 1304.

23. *In Re Black Farmers Discrimination Litigation*, Case Number 08-mc-00511 in the United States District Court for the District of Columbia.

provide for higher payments to claimants who go through a more rigorous review process. Claimants can seek fast-track payments of up to $50,000 plus debt relief, or choose a longer process for damages of up to $250,000. Payments to successful claimants could begin in the middle of 2011.

The 2008 farm bill provision also mandated a moratorium on all loan acceleration and foreclosure proceedings where there is a pending claim of discrimination against [the] USDA related to a loan acceleration or foreclosure. This provision also waives any interest and offsets that might accrue on all loans under this title for which loan and foreclosure proceedings have been instituted for the period of the moratorium. If a farmer or rancher ultimately does not prevail on her claim of discrimination, then the farmer or rancher will be liable for any interest and offsets that accrued during the period that the loan was in abeyance. The moratorium terminates on either the date the Secretary of Agriculture resolves the discrimination claim or the date the court renders a final decision on the claim, whichever is earlier. *The Pigford II* settlement reiterates these provisions.

C. USDA Discrimination: Native American, Hispanic and Women Farmers

In addition to the *Pigford* case, three other major class action cases were filed against the Secretary of Agriculture alleging discrimination. *See* Jody Feder and Tadlock Cowan, *Garcia v. Vilsack: A Policy and Legal Analysis of a USDA Discrimination Case*, Congressional Research Report R-40988 (Mar. 30, 2010).

1. Native American Farmers

Native American farmers and ranchers brought the *Keepseagle* case alleging systemic discrimination at the USDA from 1981–1999. Their complaint alleges that they were denied the opportunities to obtain farm loans and farm loan servicing that were routinely provided to white farmers, in violation of the Equal Credit Opportunity Act. They also alleged that they were denied the opportunity to obtain redress for this discrimination because of a disfunctional and sometimes non-existent office of civil rights at the USDA.

In 2001, the *Keepseagle* plaintiffs were granted class certification; certification was upheld on appeal in 2002. The class was certified for purposes of declaratory and injunctive relief only, however, and the district court deferred the question certification with respect to monetary damages until the completion of discovery. After a number of procedural battles, the discovery process began in July 2004 and continued into 2009.

At the conclusion of discovery, the plaintiffs filed a motion seeking class certification for their claims for damages. They then agreed with the USDA to enter into court-approved discussions. On October 19, 2010, Secretary Vilsack and Attorney General Holder announced a settlement of the case. Like *Pigford*, the settlement provides for individual financial compensation through two different tracks, debt forgiveness, and programmatic changes. Congressional approval is not required. *See*, http://www.usda.gov/wps/portal/usda/usdahome?contentidonly=true&contentid=2010/10/0539.xml.

For additional information about the legal issues affecting Native American farmers and ranchers, see Jessica A. Shoemaker, *Farm and Ranch Issues in Indian Country*, Farmers Legal Action Group, Inc. (June 2006), available at http://flaginc.org/topics/pubs/civilrights.php.

2. Hispanic Farmers

In 2000, the case of *Garcia v. Vilsack* was filed on behalf of Hispanic farmers, alleging that the USDA unlawfully discriminated against them, in violation of the Equal Credit Opportunity Act. While there has been no decision on the merits of the claims, in 2002, the district court denied class certification, holding that the plaintiffs did not make the requisite showing that there were questions of law or fact common to the class or that the claims were typical of the class. The plaintiffs appealed this decision, but the Court of Appeals for the D.C. Circuit affirmed. The Supreme Court declined to review the decision. Updates on the *Garcia* case can be found in the press releases of the law firm representing the plaintiffs at http://www.howrey.com.

3. Women Farmers

The plaintiffs in *Love v. Vilsack* alleged discrimination on the basis of gender in connection with farm loans from the USDA, in violation of the Equal Credit Opportunity Act. *Garcia* and *Love* were initially heard by the same district court judge and were eventually consolidated on appeal. In 2004, the court denied the plaintiffs' class certification. On appeal, the D.C. Circuit affirmed this denial and the Supreme Court declined to review. The Washington, D.C. law firm handling the *Love* case, Arent Fox, has updates available at a case website, http://www.womenfarmers.com/.

In December 2009, Representative Rosa DeLaura proposed the *Equality for Women Farmers Act* (H.R. 4264) to provide a remedy for the *Love* plaintiffs. The bill would create a mechanism for resolving allegations of gender discrimination against USDA by establishing a procedure for submitting and processing claims for damages and by placing a moratorium on foreclosures against farmers who have complained of gender discrimination. The bill has been referred to the Judiciary, Agriculture, and Ways and Means Committees. Further updates on this legislation can be tracked on the Library of Congress site, http://www.thomas.gov.

D. Current USDA Policy and Issues

The *Pigford*, *Keepseagle*, *Garcia* and *Love* cases all seek redress for discriminatory practices that took place more than a decade ago. The USDA has remedied some of its structural problems, e.g., loan-making decisions are no longer made by county committee members, and there is now a functioning USDA office responsible for receiving and resolving discrimination complaints. Congress created a priority category for USDA lending that targets loans to "socially disadvantaged" groups. This category is defined as "a group whose members have been subjected to racial, ethnic, or gender prejudice because of their identity as members of a group, without regard to their individual qualities." 7 U.S.C. § 2003. The USDA further defines this category in its regulations, providing that it "consists of American Indians or Alaskan Natives, Asians, Blacks or African Americans, Native Hawaiians or other Pacific Islanders, Hispanics, and Women." 7 C.F.R. § 761.2 (2009). Information on the loan programs available is set forth on the USDA Farm Service Agency Loan Programs website at http://fsa.usda.gov.

However, other discrimination problems have persisted. The following testimony presented to Congress on April 29, 2009, describes the Government Accountability Office's assessment and its suggestions.

Lisa Shames
U.S. Department of Agriculture: Recommendations and Options Available to the New Administration and Congress to Address Long-Standing Civil Rights Issues

Testimony Before the Subcommittee on Department Operations, Oversight, Nutrition and Forestry, Committee on Agriculture, House of Representatives U.S. Government Accountability Office, GAO-09-650T
April 29, 2009

I am pleased to be here today to discuss the U.S. Department of Agriculture's (USDA) progress in addressing long-standing civil rights issues. For decades, USDA has been the focus of federal inquiries into allegations of discrimination against minorities and women both in the programs it administers and in its workforce. Numerous reports and congressional testimony by officials of the U.S. Commission on Civil Rights, the U.S. Equal Employment Opportunity Commission, USDA's Office of Inspector General (OIG), GAO, and others have described extensive concerns about discriminatory behavior in USDA's delivery of services to program customers—in particular, minority farmers—and its treatment of minority employees. Many of these reports and testimonies described serious weaknesses in USDA's management of its civil rights programs—in particular, weaknesses in providing minorities with access to USDA programs and in resolving discrimination complaints. In addition, USDA has been the subject of several large class-action lawsuits claiming discriminatory behavior on the part of the department. For example, the *Pigford v. Glickman* case has resulted in the payment of about $1 billion in claims to African-American farmers.

The Farm Security and Rural Investment Act of 2002 (2002 Farm Bill) authorized the Secretary of Agriculture to create the new position of Assistant Secretary for Civil Rights, elevating responsibility within USDA for carrying out USDA's civil rights efforts. Under the 2002 Farm Bill, the Secretary may delegate responsibility to the Assistant Secretary for Civil Rights for ensuring that USDA complies with all civil rights-related laws and considers civil rights matters in all USDA strategic planning initiatives. In 2003, the position of Assistant Secretary for Civil Rights was created with these and other delegated responsibilities, and these responsibilities are carried out through the Office of the Assistant Secretary for Civil Rights (ASCR). In addition, the 2002 Farm Bill and subsequent legislation require USDA to report annually on minority participation in USDA programs.

The new Administration has indicated its commitment to improve the management of civil rights at USDA. For example, the new Secretary of Agriculture testified in March

2009 that improving this management is one of his top priorities and he will dedicate the resources necessary to achieve this improvement. And earlier this month, USDA's new Assistant Secretary for Civil Rights was confirmed. This official, who brings to the position prior civil rights experience, also has pledged to improve this management. Furthermore, on April 21, 2009, the Secretary issued a memorandum to all USDA employees reiterating that civil rights is one of his top priorities and stating that he intends to take definitive action to improve USDA's record on civil rights and move USDA to a new era as a model employer and premier service provider. Thus, this oversight hearing is particularly timely: it provides an opportunity to briefly restate the scope of civil rights problems at USDA, but more importantly it offers an opportunity to discuss possible solutions to these problems for the benefit of these new officials.

I will focus my testimony today on three primary issues: ASCR's (1) resolution of discrimination complaints, (2) reporting on minority participation in USDA programs, and (3) strategic planning for ensuring USDA's services and benefits are provided fairly and equitably. I will also discuss lessons learned from the experiences of other federal agencies to develop options for addressing USDA's long-standing problems. My statement is based primarily on our May 2008 testimony on management deficiencies in ASCR and our October 2008 report on recommendations and options to address these deficiencies.[1] To perform that work, we interviewed officials representing ASCR, USDA's OIG, USDA's agency level civil rights offices, the Equal Employment Opportunity Commission, community-based organizations, and minority groups. We examined ASCR's strategic plan and other relevant planning documents, USDA documents about efforts to resolve discrimination complaints, and USDA's reporting on minority participation in its programs. In addition, we analyzed data provided by ASCR and found it to be unreliable; we made recommendations accordingly. We also considered our own guidance and reporting on results-oriented management[2] and reviewed our experience in addressing the problems of high-risk, underperforming agencies.[3] We conducted this work in accordance with generally accepted government auditing standards. Those standards require that we plan and perform the audit to obtain sufficient, appropriate evidence to provide a reasonable basis for our findings and conclusions based on our audit objectives. We believe the evidence obtained provides this reasonable basis.

In summary, I would like to make two observations. First, we found numerous deficiencies in ASCR's management of civil rights, and we offered a number of recommendations to address them. In April 2009, ASCR officials said that USDA has begun to take steps to implement each of these recommendations. Specifically:

- Regarding discrimination complaint resolution, we reported that ASCR had not achieved its goal of preventing backlogs of complaints and that this effort was undermined by ASCR's faulty reporting and disparities in ASCR data. Also, some

---

1. GAO, *U.S. Department of Agriculture: Management of Civil Rights Continues to Be Deficient Despite Years of Attention*, GAO-08-755T (Washington, D.C.: May 14, 2008) and *U.S. Department of Agriculture: Recommendations and Options to Address Management Deficiencies in the Office of the Assistant Secretary for Civil Rights*, GAO-09-62 (Washington, D.C.: October 22, 2008).

2. GAO, Executive Guide: Effectively Implementing the Government Performance and Results Act, GAO/GGD-96-118 (Washington, D.C.: June 1996); Agencies' Strategic Plans Under GPRA: Key Questions to Facilitate Congressional Review, GAO/GGD-10.1.16 (Washington, D.C.: May 1997); The Results Act: An Evaluator's Guide to Assessing Agency Annual Performance Plans, GAO/GGD-10.1.20 (Washington, D.C.: April 1998); and Results-Oriented Government: GPRA Has Established a Solid Foundation for Achieving Greater Results, GAO-04-38 (Washington, D.C.: Mar. 10, 2004).

3. For example, see most recently GAO, *High-Risk Series: An Update*, GAO-09-271 (Washington, D.C.: January 2009).

steps ASCR took to speed up its work may have adversely affected the quality of its work. Consequently, we recommended that USDA prepare and implement an improvement plan for resolving discrimination complaints; develop and implement a plan to ensure the accuracy, completeness, and reliability of ASCR's databases on complaints; and obtain an independent legal examination of a sample of USDA's prior investigations and decisions on civil rights complaints. ASCR officials said that the department is taking steps to set timeframe goals and establish proper management controls; move data from ASCR's three complaint databases into one; and obtain independent legal advice on its program complaints.

• Regarding minority participation in USDA programs, we reported that much of the data that USDA provided to Congress and the public on minority farmers' participation in farm programs are unreliable because they are, for the most part, based on visual observation of program applicants. Data gathered in this manner are considered unreliable because individual traits, such as race and ethnicity, may not be readily apparent to an observer. To address this inherent shortcoming, USDA said it needs to collect standardized data directly from program participants, which requires approval from the Office of Management and Budget (OMB). Accordingly, we recommended that USDA work expeditiously to obtain such approval from OMB. ASCR officials indicated that a draft Federal Register notice requesting OMB's approval to collect these data is being reviewed within the department.

• Regarding strategic planning, we reported that ASCR's planning was limited and did not reflect the views of relevant stakeholders, such as community-based organizations and minority interest groups; did not link to the plans of other USDA agencies or the department; could better measure performance to gauge its progress; did not discuss the potential for using performance information for identifying USDA's performance gaps; and did not link funding with anticipated results. Consequently, we recommended that USDA develop a results-oriented department-level strategic plan for civil rights that unifies USDA's departmental approach with that of ASCR and the newly created Office of Advocacy and Outreach and that is transparent about USDA's efforts to address stakeholder concerns. ASCR officials said they plan to implement this recommendation during the next department-wide strategic planning process.

Moving forward, my second observation is that the experience of other agencies in addressing significant performance issues provides options that are relevant for addressing certain long-standing ASCR issues. We identified three options that are relevant for consideration.

• Option 1: Congress could require USDA's Assistant Secretary for Civil Rights to be subject to a statutory performance agreement. Congress previously required executives at several other federal agencies to be subject to these agreements. Such an agreement can be transmitted to congressional committees and made public, and the office in question can be required to report to Congress annually on its performance, including the extent to which it met its performance goals. Such an agreement for ASCR could assist in achieving specific expectations by providing additional incentives and mandatory public reporting.

• Option 2: Congress could authorize an oversight board for USDA civil rights activities. Oversight boards have been used for a wide variety of purposes by the federal government, including oversight of public accounting, intelligence matters, civil liberties, and drug safety. A USDA civil rights oversight board could be authorized to independently monitor, evaluate, approve, and report on USDA's administration of civil rights activities, thereby identifying weaknesses that need to be addressed and providing transparency.

- Option 3: USDA could explore establishing an ombudsman office to address customer and employee concerns about civil rights, including determining whether legislation is a prerequisite for an ombudsman to be effective at USDA. Many other agencies have created ombudsman offices for addressing employees' concerns. A USDA ombudsman who is independent, impartial, fully capable of conducting meaningful investigations and who can maintain confidentiality could assist in resolving civil rights concerns at USDA.

In October 2008, we suggested that Congress consider (1) making USDA's Assistant Secretary for Civil Rights subject to a statutory performance agreement and (2) establishing a USDA civil rights oversight board. USDA initially disagreed with these suggestions; in April 2009, however, ASCR officials said that, while the department no longer disagrees with these suggestions, they hope that the actions they are taking or planning to improve the management of civil rights at USDA will preclude the need for these mechanisms. In addition, we recommended that USDA explore the potential for an ombudsman office to contribute to addressing the civil rights concerns of USDA customers and employees. In April 2009, ASCR officials indicated that the Assistant Secretary for Civil Rights has convened a team to study the ombudsman concept and to make recommendations by September 30, 2009, to the Secretary of Agriculture for establishing an ombudsman office.

Problems in Resolving Discrimination Complaints Persist

The credibility of USDA's efforts to correct long-standing problems in resolving customer and employee discrimination complaints has been undermined by faulty reporting of complaint data, including disparities we found when comparing various ASCR sources of data. When ASCR was created in 2003, there was an existing backlog of complaints that had not been adjudicated. In response, the Assistant Secretary for Civil Rights at that time called for a concerted 12-month effort to reduce this backlog and to put lasting improvements in place to prevent future complaint backlogs. In July 2007, ASCR reported that it had reduced its backlog of 690 complaints and held the complaint inventory to manageable levels through fiscal year 2005.[4] However, the data ASCR reported lack credibility because they were inconsistent with other complaint data it reported a month earlier to a congressional subcommittee. The backlog later surged to 885 complaints, according to ASCR data. Furthermore, the Assistant Secretary's letter transmitting these data stated that while they were the best available, they were incomplete and unreliable. In addition, GAO and USDA's OIG have identified other problems with ASCR's data, including the need for better management controls over the entry and validation of these data.

In addition, some steps that ASCR took to speed up its investigations and decisions on complaints in 2004 may have adversely affected the quality of its work. ASCR's plan called for USDA's investigators and adjudicators, who prepare agency decisions, to nearly double their normal pace of casework for about 12 months. ASCR's former Director, Office of Adjudication and Compliance, stated that this increased pace led to many "summary"

---

4. USDA, *First 1,000 Days, 2003–2006* (Washington, D.C.: July 2007).

decisions on employees' complaints that did not resolve questions of fact, with the result that many decisions were appealed to the Equal Employment Opportunity Commission. This official also said these summary decisions "could call into question the integrity of the process because important issues were being overlooked." In addition, inadequate working relationships and communications within ASCR, as well as fear of retaliation for reporting management-related problems, complicated ASCR's efforts to produce quality work products. In August 2008, ASCR officials stated they would develop standard operating procedures for the Office of Adjudication and Compliance and had provided USDA staff training on communication and conflict management, among other things. While these are positive steps, they do not directly respond to whether USDA is adequately investigating complaints, developing thorough complaint decisions, and addressing the problems that gave rise to discrimination complaints within ASCR.

The Food, Conservation, and Energy Act of 2008 (2008 Farm Bill), enacted in June 2008, states that it is the sense of Congress that all pending claims and class actions brought against USDA by socially disadvantaged farmers and ranchers should be resolved in an expeditious and just manner. In addition, the 2008 Farm Bill requires USDA to report annually on, among other things, the number of customer and employee discrimination complaints filed against each USDA agency, and the length of time the agency took to process each complaint.

In October 2008, we recommended that the Secretary of Agriculture take the following actions related to resolving discrimination complaints:

- Prepare and implement an improvement plan for resolving discrimination complaints that sets time frame goals and provides management controls for resolving complaints from beginning to end.

- Develop and implement a plan to ensure the accuracy, completeness and reliability of ASCR's databases on customer and employee complaints, and that provides for independent validation of ASCR's data quality.

- Obtain an expert, independent, and objective legal examination of the basis, quality, and adequacy of a sample of USDA's prior investigations and decisions on civil rights complaints, along with suggestions for improvement.

USDA agreed with the first two recommendations, but initially disagreed with the third, asserting that its internal system of legal sufficiency addresses our concerns, works well, and is timely and effective. Given the substantial evidence of civil rights case delays and questions about the integrity of USDA's civil rights casework, we believe this recommendation remains valid and necessary to restore confidence in USDA's civil rights decisions. In April 2009, ASCR officials said that USDA now agrees with all three of the recommendations and that the department is taking steps to implement them. These steps include hiring a consultant to assist ASCR with setting timeframe goals and establishing proper management controls; a contractor to help move data from ASCR's three complaint databases into one; and a firm to provide ASCR with independent legal advice on developing standards on what constitutes a program complaint and actions needed to adjudicate those complaints.

Reports on Minority Participation Are Unreliable and of Limited Usefulness

As required by the 2002 farm bill, ASCR has published three annual reports on the participation rate of socially disadvantaged farmers and ranchers in USDA programs. The reports are to provide statistical data on program participants by race and ethnicity, among other things. However, much of these data are unreliable because USDA lacks a uniform method of reporting and tabulating race and ethnicity data among its component agencies. According to USDA, to collect standardized demographic data directly from participants in many of its programs, it must first obtain OMB's approval. In the meantime, most of USDA's demographic data are gathered by visual observation of program applicants, a method that is inherently unreliable and subjective, especially for determining ethnicity. To address this problem, ASCR published a notice in the Federal Register in 2004 seeking public comment on its plan to collect standardized data on race, ethnicity, gender, national origin, and age for all its programs. However, while it received some comments, ASCR has not moved forward to finalize this rulemaking and obtain OMB's approval to collect these data.

The 2008 Farm Bill contains several provisions related to reporting on minority farmers' participation in USDA programs. First, it requires USDA to annually compile program application and participation rate data for each program serving those farmers. These reports are to include the raw numbers and participation rates for the entire United States and for each state and county. Second, it requires USDA to ensure, to the maximum extent practicable, that the Census of Agriculture and studies by USDA's Economic Research Service accurately document the number, location, and economic contributions of minority farmers in agricultural production.

In October 2008, to address underlying data reliability issues, as discussed, and potential steps USDA could take to facilitate data analysis by users, we recommended that the Secretary of Agriculture work expeditiously to obtain OMB's approval to collect the demographic data necessary for reliable reporting on race and ethnicity by USDA program. USDA agreed with the recommendation. In April 2009, ASCR officials indicated that a draft Federal Register notice requesting OMB's approval to collect these data for Farm Service Agency, Natural Resources Conservation Service, and Rural Development programs is being reviewed within USDA. These officials said they hoped this notice, which they considered an initial step toward implementing our recommendation, would be published and implemented in time for USDA's field offices to begin collecting these data by October 1, 2009. According to these officials, USDA also plans to seek, at a later time, authority to collect such data on participants in all USDA programs.

Strategic Planning is Limited and Lacks Needed Components

In light of USDA's history of civil rights problems, better strategic planning is vital. Results-oriented strategic planning provides a road map that clearly describes what an organization is attempting to achieve and, over time, it can serve as a focal point for communication with Congress and the public about what has been accomplished. Results-oriented organizations follow three key steps in their strategic planning: (1) they define a clear mission and desired outcomes, (2) they measure performance to gauge progress, and (3) they use performance information for identifying performance gaps and making program improvements.

ASCR has started to develop a results-oriented approach as illustrated in its first strategic plan, Assistant Secretary for Civil Rights: Strategic Plan, Fiscal Years 2005–2010, and its ASCR Priorities for Fiscal Years 2007 and 2008. However, ASCR's plans do not include fundamental elements required for effective strategic planning. In particular, we found that the interests of ASCR's stakeholders—including representatives of community-based organizations and minority interest groups—are not explicitly reflected in its strategic plan. For example, we found that ASCR's stakeholders are interested in improvements in (1) USDA's methods of delivering farm programs to facilitate access by underserved producers; (2) the county committee system, so that stakeholders are better represented in local decisions; and (3) the diversity of USDA employees who work with minority producers. A more complete list of these interests is included in the appendix.

In addition, ASCR's strategic plan does not link to the plans of other USDA agencies or the department and does not discuss the potential for linkages to be developed. ASCR could also better measure performance to gauge progress, and it has not yet started to use performance information for identifying USDA performance gaps. For example, ASCR measures USDA efforts to ensure USDA customers have equal and timely access to programs by reporting on the numbers of participants at USDA workshops rather than measuring the results of its outreach efforts on access to benefits and services. Moreover, the strategic plan does not make linkages between levels of funding and ASCR's anticipated results; without such a discussion, it is not possible to determine whether ASCR has the resources needed to achieve its strategic goal of, for example, strengthening partnerships with historically black land-grant universities through scholarships provided by USDA.

To help ensure access to and equitable participation in USDA's programs and services, the 2008 Farm Bill provided for establishing the Office of Advocacy and Outreach and charged it with, among other things, establishing and monitoring USDA's goals and objectives to increase participation in USDA programs by small, beginning, and socially disadvantaged farmers and ranchers. As of April 2009, ASCR officials indicated that the Secretary of Agriculture plans to establish this office, but has not yet done so.

In October 2008, we recommended that USDA develop a results-oriented department-level strategic plan for civil rights that unifies USDA's departmental approach with that of ASCR and the newly created Office of Advocacy and Outreach and that is transparent about USDA's efforts to address stakeholder concerns. USDA agreed with this recommendation. In April 2009, ASCR officials said they plan to implement this recommendation during the next department-wide strategic planning process, which occurs every 5 years. Noting that the current plan runs through 2010, these officials speculated that work on the new plan will start in the next few months.

Lessons Learned Could Benefit USDA's Civil Rights Performance

Our past work in addressing the problems of high-risk, underperforming federal agencies, as well as our reporting on results-oriented management, suggests three options that could benefit USDA's civil rights performance. These options were selected based on our judgment that they (1) can help address recognized and long-standing problems in USDA's performance, (2) have been used previously by Congress to improve aspects of agency performance, (3) have contributed to improved agency performance, and (4) will result in greater transparency over USDA's civil rights performance. These options include (1) making USDA's Assistant Secretary for Civil Rights subject to a statutory performance agreement, (2) establishing an agriculture civil rights oversight board, and (3) creating an ombudsman for agriculture civil rights matters.

A Statutory Performance Agreement Could Help Define Accountability for Results

Our prior assessment of performance agreements used at several agencies has shown that these agreements have potential benefits that could help improve the performance of ASCR.[5] Potential benefits that performance agreements could provide USDA include (1) helping to define accountability for specific goals and align daily operations with results oriented programmatic goals, (2) fostering collaboration across organizational boundaries, (3) enhancing use of performance information to make program improvements, (4)

---

5. GAO, *Managing for Results: Emerging Benefits from Selected Agencies' Use of Performance Agreements*, GAO-01-115 (Washington, D.C.: Oct. 30, 2000).

providing a results-oriented basis for individual accountability, and (5) helping to maintain continuity of program goals during leadership transitions.

Congress has required performance agreements in other federal offices and the results have been positive. For example, in 1998, Congress established the Department of Education's Office of Federal Student Aid as the government's first performance-based organization.[6] This office had experienced long-standing financial and management weaknesses and we had listed the Student Aid program as high-risk since 1990. Congress required the office's Chief Operating Officer to have a performance agreement with the Secretary of Education that was transmitted to congressional committees and made publicly available. In addition, the office was required to report to Congress annually on its performance, including the extent to which it met its performance goals. In 2005, because of the sustained improvements made by the office in its financial management and internal controls, we removed this program from our high-risk list. More recently, Congress has required statutory performance agreements for other federal executives, including for the Commissioners of the U.S. Patent and Trademark Office and the Under Secretary for Management of the Department of Homeland Security.[7]

A statutory performance agreement could benefit ASCR. The responsibilities assigned to USDA's Assistant Secretary for Civil Rights were stated in general terms in both the 2002 Farm Bill and the Secretary's memorandum establishing this position within USDA. The Secretary's memorandum stated that the Assistant Secretary reports directly to the Secretary and is responsible for (1) ensuring USDA's compliance with all civil rights laws and related laws, (2) coordinating administration of civil rights laws within USDA, and (3) ensuring that civil rights components are incorporated in USDA strategic planning initiatives. This set of responsibilities is broad in scope, and it does not identify specific performance expectations for the Assistant Secretary. A statutory performance agreement could assist in achieving specific expectations by providing additional incentives and mandatory public reporting.

In October 2008, we suggested that Congress consider the option of making USDA's Assistant Secretary for Civil Rights subject to a statutory performance agreement. USDA initially disagreed with this suggestion, in part stating that the Assistant Secretary's responsibilities are spelled out in the 2002 and 2008 farm bills. In response, we noted, in part, that a statutory performance agreement would go beyond the existing legislation by requiring measurable organizational and individual goals in key performance areas. In April 2009, ASCR officials indicated that the department no longer disagrees with this suggestion. However, these officials expressed the hope that the actions they are taking or planning to improve the management of civil rights at USDA, such as obtaining an independent external analysis of program delivery, will preclude the need for this mechanism.

An Oversight Board Could Improve ASCR Management

Congress could also authorize a USDA civil rights oversight board to independently monitor, evaluate, approve, and report on USDA's administration of civil rights activities, as it has for other federal activities. Oversight boards have often been used by the federal

---

6. Higher Education Amendments of 1998, Pub. L. No. 105-244 § 101(a), 112 Stat. 1581 (amending 20 U.S.C. § 1018).

7. Pub. L. No. 106-113, § 1000(a)(9) (§ 4713), 113 Stat. 1501, 1536, 1501A-21, 1501A-575 (1999)(amending 35 U.S.C. § 3); Implementing Recommendations of the 9/11 Commission Act of 2007, Pub. L. No. 110-53 § 2405(b), 121 Stat. 266, 548 (amending 6 U.S.C. § 341(c)).

government—such as for oversight of public accounting, intelligence matters, civil liberties, and drug safety—to provide assurance that important activities are well done, to identify weaknesses that may need to be addressed, and to provide for transparency.

For example, Congress established the Internal Revenue Service (IRS) Oversight Board in 1998 to oversee IRS's administration of internal revenue laws and ensure that its organization and operation allow it to carry out its mission. At that time, IRS was considered to be an agency that was not effectively serving the public or meeting taxpayer needs. The board operates much like a corporate board of directors, tailored to fit the public sector. The board provides independent oversight of IRS administration, management, conduct, and the direction and supervision of the application of the internal revenue code. We have previously noted the work of the Internal Revenue Service Oversight Board—including, for example, the board's independent analysis of IRS business systems modernization.[8] Currently, there is no comparable independent oversight of USDA civil rights activities.

In October 2008, we suggested that Congress consider the option of establishing a USDA civil rights oversight board to independently monitor, evaluate, approve, and report on USDA's administration of civil rights activities. Such a board could provide additional assurance that ASCR management functions effectively and efficiently. USDA initially disagreed with this suggestion, stating that it would be unnecessarily bureaucratic and delay progress. In response, we noted that a well-operated oversight board could be the source of timely and wise counsel to help raise USDA's civil rights performance. In April 2009, ASCR officials said that the department no longer disagrees with this suggestion. However, these officials expressed the hope that the actions they are taking or planning to address our recommendations to improve the management of civil rights at USDA will preclude the need for this mechanism.

An Ombudsman Could Address Concerns of USDA Customers and Employees

An ombudsman for USDA civil rights matters could be created to address the concerns of USDA customers and employees. Many other agencies have created ombudsman offices for addressing employees' concerns, as authorized by the Administrative Dispute Resolution Act. However, an ombudsman is not merely an alternative means of resolving employees' disputes; rather, the ombudsman is a neutral party who uses a variety of procedures, including alternative dispute resolution techniques, to deal with complaints, concerns, and questions.

Ombudsmen who handle concerns and inquiries from the public—external ombudsmen—help agencies be more responsive to the public through impartial and independent investigation of citizens' complaints, including those of people who believe their concerns have not been dealt with fairly and fully through normal channels. For example, we reported that ombudsmen at the Environmental Protection Agency serve as points of contact for members of the public who have concerns about certain hazardous waste cleanup activities. We also identified the Transportation Security Administration ombudsman as one who serves external customers and is responsible for recommending and influencing systemic change where necessary to improve administration operations and customer service.[9]

---

8. GAO, *Business Systems Modernization: Internal Revenue Service Needs to Further Strengthen Program Management*, GAO-04-438T (Washington, D.C.: Feb. 12, 2004).

9. GAO, *Transportation Security Administration: Actions and Plans to Develop a Results-Oriented Culture*, GAO-03-190 (Washington, D.C.: Jan. 17, 2003).

Within the federal workplace, ombudsmen provide an informal alternative to existing and more formal processes to deal with employees' workplace conflicts and other organizational climate issues. USDA faces concerns of fairness and equity from both customers and employees—a range of issues that an ombudsman could potentially assist in addressing. A USDA ombudsman who is independent, impartial, fully capable of conducting meaningful investigations and who can maintain confidentiality could assist in resolving these civil rights concerns. As of April 2007, 12 federal departments and 9 independent agencies reported having 43 ombudsmen. In October 2008, we recommended that USDA explore the potential for an ombudsman office to contribute to addressing the civil rights concerns of USDA customers and employees, including seeking legislative authority, as appropriate, to establish such an office and to ensure its effectiveness, and advise USDA's congressional oversight committees of the results. USDA agreed with this recommendation. In April 2009, ASCR officials indicated that the Assistant Secretary for Civil Rights has convened a team to study the ombudsman concept and to make recommendations by September 30, 2009, to the Secretary of Agriculture for establishing an ombudsman office.

Concluding Observations

USDA has been addressing allegations of discrimination for decades and receiving recommendations for improving its civil rights functions without achieving fundamental improvements. One lawsuit has cost taxpayers about a billion dollars in payouts to date, and several other groups are seeking redress for similar alleged discrimination. While ASCR's established policy is to fairly and efficiently respond to complaints of discrimination, its efforts to establish the management system necessary to implement the policy have fallen short, and significant deficiencies remain.

Unless USDA addresses several fundamental concerns about resolving discrimination complaints—including the lack of credible data on the numbers, status, and management of complaints; the lack of specified time frames and management controls for resolving complaints; questions about the quality of complaint investigations; and concerns about the integrity of final decision preparation—the credibility of USDA efforts to resolve discrimination complaints will be in doubt. In addition, unless USDA obtains accurate data on minority participation in USDA programs, its reports on improving minority participation in USDA programs will not be reliable or useful. Furthermore, without better strategic planning and meaningful performance measures, it appears unlikely that USDA management will be fully effective in achieving its civil rights mission.

Given the new Administration's commitment to giving priority attention to USDA's civil rights problems, various options may provide a road map to correcting long-standing management deficiencies that have given rise to these problems. Specifically, raising the public profile for transparency and accountability through means such as a statutory performance agreement between the Secretary of Agriculture and the Assistant Secretary for Civil Rights, a civil rights oversight board, and an ombudsman for addressing customers' and employees' civil rights concerns would appear to be helpful steps because they have proven to be effective in raising the performance of other federal agencies. These options could lay a foundation for clarity about the expectations USDA must meet to restore confidence in its civil rights performance.

**Appendix: Interests of Selected USDA Stakeholders in
Civil Rights-Related Matters as Identified by GAO in 2007 and 2008**

Category of Interest	Stakeholder Interests
Outreach programs	USDA outreach programs for underserved producers could be much better. Systematic data on minority participation in USDA programs are not available. The 10708 Report and Minority Farm Register have been ineffective. Partnerships with community-based organizations could be better used.
Program delivery	Methods of USDA program delivery need to better facilitate the participation of underserved producers and address their needs. USDA could do more to provide assistance in accessing markets and programs. USDA could better address cultural and language differences for providing services. Some USDA program rules and features hinder participation by underserved producers. Some USDA employees have little incentive to work with small and minority producers. County offices working with underserved producers continue to lack diversity, and some have poor customer service or display discriminatory behaviors toward underserved producers. USDA lacks a program that addresses farmworker needs. There continue to be reports of cases where USDA has not processed loans for underserved producers. Some Hmong poultry farmers with guaranteed loans facilitated by USDA are experiencing foreclosures.
County system	The county committee system does not represent minority producers well. Minority advisers are ineffective because they have no voting power. USDA has not done enough to make underserved producers fully aware of county committee elections, and underserved producers have difficulties winning elections.
Investment	There is a lack of USDA investment in research and extension services that would determine the extent of minority needs.
Census of Agriculture	The Census of Agriculture needs to better count minority producers.
Foreclosure	USDA may continue to be foreclosing on farms belonging to producers who are awaiting decisions on discrimination complaints.
Authority	ASCR needs authority to exercise leadership for making changes at USDA.
Resources	USDA and ASCR need additional resources to carry out civil rights functions.
Diversity	Greater diversity among USDA employees would facilitate USDA's work with minority producers.
Access	Producers must still access services through some USDA employees who discriminated against them.
Management structure	The Office of Adjudication and Compliance needs better management structure and function. Backlogs of discrimination complaints need to be addressed. Alternative dispute resolution techniques to resolve informal employee complaints should be used consistently and documented. Civil rights compliance reviews of USDA agencies are behind schedule and should be conducted.
General Counsel Review	USDA's Office of General Counsel continues to be involved in complaint cases.

E. The Face of Agriculture Today

On February 4, 2009, USDA Secretary Tom Vilsack stated that "[i]n the spirit of President Obama's call to make government more transparent, inclusive, and collaborative, I will be directing my team at USDA to review the findings of the 2007 Census and propose ambitious, measureable goals to make sure that the People's Department is hard at work for all the people—our diverse customers and the full diversity of agriculture."

The USDA provides a website for the results of the 2007 Census of Agriculture and summarizes the data on fact sheets by category of information. See http://www.agcensus.usda.gov. It reports "increasing diversity" and notes the following:

> The Census of Agriculture collects data on both the race and ethnic background of farm operators. The 2007 Census shows that U.S. farm operators are becoming more diverse. Of the 2.2 million farms in the United States, 1.83 million have a white male principal operator. The number of principal operators of all races and ethnic backgrounds has increased 4 percent since 2002, but the growth in the number of non-white operators has outpaced this overall growth. The number of operators of Hispanic origin has also increased 10 percent since 2002. Hispanic origin operators can be of any race. One of the most significant changes in the 2007 Census of Agriculture is the increase in female farm operators, both in terms of the absolute number and the percentage of all principal operators. There were 306,209 female principal operators counted in 2007, up from 237,819 in 2002—an increase of almost 30 percent.

The definition of a "farm" for purposes of the census is broad. "A farm is any place from which $1,000 or more of agricultural products were, or normally would be, produced and sold during the Census year." The concept of a "farm operator" has changed somewhat, and the term "principal operator" is relatively new.

> Before 2002, the Census of Agriculture collected detailed demographic data on only one operator per farm. Since 2002, the census has taken a more comprehensive approach, counting all operators and collecting detailed demographic information on up to three operators per farm. The principal operator is the person in charge of day-to-day decisions for the farm or ranch.

1. African American Farmers

With respect to "Black or African-American Farm Operators," the USDA reports:

> The 2007 Census counted a total of 41,024 black operators on 32,938 farms and ranches across the United States. The number of black operators grew 9 percent from 2002, outpacing the 7 percent increase in U.S. farm operators overall.

> There were a total of 39,697 black operators who reported black or African-American as their only race in 2007. Of these, 30,599 were principal operators, up 5 percent from 2002....

> When compared to all farms nationwide, those with black principal operators tend to be smaller both in terms of size and sales. These operations are also less likely to have Internet access.

Farm/Ranch Operations	All Farms	Black-Operated Farms
Average Size of Farm	418 acres	104 acres
Average Value of Sales	$134,807	$21,340
Sales & Government Payments <$10,000	58%	79%
Farms with Internet Access	57%	34%

The number of black farm operators who are women grew 53 percent from 2002, outpacing the 29 percent increase in the number of female farm operators overall. Women now comprise 14 percent of all black or African-American principal farm operators.

Black farm operators tend to be older than their counterparts nationwide, with an average of 60.3 years, as compared to 57.1 years for U.S. farmers overall. A total of 37 percent of all black farmers are 65 or older, compared to 30 percent of all farmers nationwide. ...

Almost half (46 percent) of all black-operated farms are classified as beef cattle farms and ranches, compared to 30 percent of all farms nationwide. Another 20 percent are classified as "all other crop farms," compared to 23 percent of farms overall. This category includes hay farms and farms where no single crop comprised more than 50 percent of sales. And, while 15 percent of farms overall are classified as grain and oilseed farms, only 8 percent of black-operated farms fall into this category. ...

The percentage of black principal operators is highest in the Southern United States. The states with the highest percentage of black principal operators are Mississippi (12.6 percent), South Carolina (8.1 percent), Louisiana (6.4 percent), Alabama (5.6 percent) and Georgia (4.3 percent). Texas has 6,124 Black principal farm operators, the largest number in any state. Blacks make up 2.5 percent of the total farm operators in Texas. In 35 states, blacks or African Americans comprise less than 1 percent of all principal farm operators.

2. Native American Farmers

With respect to "American Indian or Alaska Native Farm Operators," the USDA reports:

The 2007 Census counted a total of 79,703 American Indian or Alaska Native operators on 61,472 farms and ranches across the United States. More than a quarter of these operators also reported another race. The count of American Indian or Alaska Native operators grew 88 percent from 2002, significantly outpacing the 7 percent increase in U.S. farm operators overall.

Part of the reason for the dramatic increase in the number of American Indian farmers is a change in the way the 2007 Census of Agriculture counted farm operators on reservations in the Southwestern United States. In 2002, the U.S. Department of Agriculture's National Agricultural Statistics Service conducted a pilot program to count American Indian operators on reservations in three states—North Dakota, South Dakota and Montana—rather than simply counting a single reservation as a single farm operation. In 2007, the pilot program was extended throughout the United States. The majority of the increase in the number of American Indian operators occurred in just two states: Arizona and New Mexico, where the count increased from 694 in 2002 to 12,929 in 2007.

There were a total of 55,889 American Indian operators who reported American Indian or Alaska Native as their only race in 2007. Of these, 34,706 were principal operators, up 124 percent from 2002....

When compared to all farms nationwide, those with American Indian or Alaska Native principal operators tend to be smaller in terms of sales but significantly larger in size. These operations are also less likely to have Internet access.

Farm/Ranch Operations	All Farms	American Indian-Operated Farms
Average Size of Farm	418 acres	1431 acres
Average Value of Sales	$134,807	$40,331
Sales & Government Payments <$10,000	58%	78%
Farms with Internet Access	57%	42%

Since 2002, the number of American Indian principal operators who are women grew 318 percent, to 29 percent of the total number of American Indian principal operators. All women American Indian operators increased 169 percent, to 41 percent of the total number of American Indian operators.

American Indian farm operators are more likely than their counterparts nationwide to report farming as their primary occupation and they are likely to derive a larger portion of their overall income from farming. They are also more likely to own all of the land that they operate, rather than renting or leasing land....

38 percent of all American Indian-operated farms are classified as beef cattle farms and ranches, compared to 30 percent of all farms. Another 13 percent are classified as sheep and goat farms, compared to 3 percent of farms overall. And, while 15 percent of farms overall are classified as grain and oilseed farms, only 3 percent of American Indian-operated farms fall into this category....

The percentage of American Indian principal operators is highest in the Western United States. The states with the highest percentage of American Indian principal operators are Arizona (53.9 percent), New Mexico (21.5 percent), Nevada (12.5 percent), Oklahoma (8.1 percent) and Montana (5.0 percent).

In 33 states, American Indians and Alaska Natives comprise less than 1 percent of all principal operators.

3. Hispanic Farmers

The USDA reports the following with respect to "Farm Operators of Spanish, Hispanic or Latino Origin."

The 2007 Census counted a total of 82,462 Hispanic operators on 66,671 farms and ranches across the United States. The number of Hispanic operators grew

14 percent from 2002, significantly outpacing the 7 percent increase in U.S. farm operators overall. A total of 55,570 U.S. farms had a principal operator of Spanish, Hispanic or Latino origin in 2007, up 10 percent from 2002....

When compared to all farms nationwide, those with Hispanic or Latino principal operators tend to be smaller both in terms of size and sales. These operations are also less likely to have Internet access.

Farm/Ranch Operations	All Farms	Hispanic-Operated Farms
Average Size of Farm	418 acres	307 acres
Average Value of Sales	$134,807	$119,634
Sales & Government Payments <$10,000	58%	67%
Farms with Internet Access	57%	44%

Hispanic or Latino principal farm operators themselves are predominantly male, as are principal operators overall. However, the total number of female farm operators of Hispanic or Latino origin grew 20 percent from 2002. Women now comprise 12 percent of Hispanic operators, up from 10 percent in 2002.

Hispanic farmers and ranchers tend to be slightly younger on average than their counterparts nationwide. They are significantly more likely to own all of the land that they operate, rather than renting or leasing land. They are more likely to have worked at least some days in an off-farm job. And, a higher-than-average percentage of Hispanic or Latino operators report that they've been on their present farm or ranch for 4 years or less....

More than one-third of all Hispanic-operated farms and ranches are classified as beef cattle operations. Another 16 percent are classified as fruit and nut farms, compared to 4 percent of farms overall. And, while 15 percent of farms overall are classified as grain and oilseed farms, only 3 percent of Hispanic-operated farms fall into this category.

Texas, New Mexico and the Pacific Coast states saw the largest increases in Hispanic or Latino farm operators from 2002 to 2007. Overall, the percentage of Hispanic principal operators is highest in the Western United States. The states with the highest percentage of Hispanic principal operators are New Mexico (30.9 percent), California (11.3 percent), Texas (8.2 percent), Florida (6.7 percent) and Hawaii (5.9 percent).

In 29 states, people of Hispanic or Latino origin comprise less than 1 percent of all principal operators....

4. Women Farmers

The USDA reports the following with respect to women farmers.

Of the 3.3 million U.S. farm operators counted in 2007 Census, 30.2 percent — or more than 1 million — were women. The total number of women operators increased 19 percent from 2002, significantly outpacing the 7 percent increase in the number of farmers overall. The number of women who were the principal operators of a farm or ranch increased by almost 30 percent, to 306,209. Women are now the principal operators of 14 percent of the nation's 2.2 million farms....

When compared to all farms nationwide, those with female principal operators tend to be smaller both in terms of size and sales. However, women are more likely to own all of the farmland that they operate.

Farm/Ranch Operations	All Farms	Male-Operated Farms	Female-Operated Farms
Average Size of Farm	418 acres	452 acres	210 acres
Average Value of Sales	$134,807	$150,671	$36,440
Sales & Government Payments <$10,000	58%	55%	75%
Average Age of Principal Operator	57.1	56.8	58.8
Farming as Primary Occupation	45%	46%	40%
Operator Owns All Farm Acres	69%	66%	85%

Like farm operators overall, the majority of women farm operators are white. However, a growing percentage of female farmers are of other races or ethnicity. The largest number of women minority operators is American Indian, followed by operators of Hispanic origin....

Women-operated farms tend to be diverse. Women are much more likely than their male counterparts to operate farms classified as "other livestock farms," a category that includes horse farms, or "all other crops," which includes hay farms. Men, meanwhile, are much more likely to run grain and oilseed farms and beef cattle operations....

The percentage of women principal operators is highest in the West and in New England. The states with the highest percentage of women principal operators are Arizona (38.5 percent), New Hampshire (29.7 percent), Massachusetts (28.9 percent), Maine (25.1 percent) and Alaska (24.5 percent).

The states with the lowest percentages of women principal operators are in the Midwest. Women make up less than 10 percent of all farm operators in four Midwestern states: South Dakota (7.7 percent), Nebraska (8.4 percent), Minnesota (9.1 percent) and Iowa (9.1 percent).

VI

Agricultural Labor Law

Each year, over 1.3 million migrant farmworkers and their families labor in Amer-ica's fields and orchards. They stoop among long rows of vegetables, filling buckets of produce under the stark heat of the summer sun and the bitter cold of late au-tumn. They climb ladders in orchards, piling fruit into sacks slung across their shoul-ders. They prune vines, tie plants, remove weeds, sort, pack, spray, clean, and irrigate. They travel across the nation, drifting from one field to another, crossing state lines and international borders. Farmworkers labor in every region of the coun-try, wherever there are fields to be planted, tended, or harvested—in isolated rural communities, within the shadows of great cities, scattered among suburban tracts.

Few Americans know much about the world of farmworkers—their struggles, their travels, the key role they play in our lives. Farmworkers provide the hand labor nec-essary to produce and harvest the fruits and vegetables we eat, and in this sense, they are bound to every consumer in a direct, almost visceral manner. Every or-ange, peach, tomato, or watermelon we purchase was handpicked by a farmworker. Every pepper, apple, head of lettuce, or bunch of grapes—pulled from the earth, plucked from a bush, or picked from a tree—was harvested by a farm laborer, a member of the poorest and most disadvantaged class of American workers.

Daniel Rothenberg, With These Hands: The Hidden World of Migrant Farm-workers Today, 1 (2000).

Agricultural labor issues present some of the most complex and troubling legal and pol-icy issues within the study of agricultural law. Agricultural labor needs are extensive, par-ticularly with respect to certain crops. The living product that distinguishes agriculture from other industries, makes labor needs variable and extremely time-sensitive. The de-mand for cheap food, low-cost imported food, and hard bargaining on the part of food processors pressure farmers to lower their cost of production. Farmworkers, with little po-litical or economic power, remain among the most economically disadvantaged working groups in the United States.

The study of agricultural labor and employment law is characterized by three over-arching challenges.

- First, it is difficult to obtain accurate information about exactly how many agri-cultural workers are employed, how many are available for employment, how they are treated as employees, or how they and their families fare. Much of the work they perform is seasonal, thus the workforce is largely migrant. It is estimated that over half of the workforce are undocumented workers. Some are categorized as in-dependent contractors, putting them outside the employment classification. Some are minors, working illegally.

- Second, agricultural workers are treated very differently than any other category of worker. Most federal and state labor laws contain provisions that either exclude agricultural workers from protection or limit the applicability of the law. One law, the Migrant & Seasonal Agricultural Protection Act, applies only to agricultural workers.

- Third, there is widespread recognition that the laws that apply to agricultural workers are often not enforced. Widely dispersed employment locations, short term employment, insufficient regulatory staffing, as well as political and economic pressure to ignore violations all contribute to an underground culture that is largely outside the bounds of labor laws.

This chapter provides an introduction to agricultural labor law by reviewing information about the agricultural workforce. It introduces three of the major federal labor laws as applied to agriculture and raises concerns about the enforcement of these laws.

A. Who Are America's Farm Workers?

A variety of factors make it difficult to assemble accurate information about the agricultural workforce. Terminology and categorization of workers complicate the task.

In some studies, the category "agricultural worker" may include farmers and their family members, if they are all engaged in farm work. Indeed, one of the hallmarks of a "family farm" is that most of the labor is performed by family members. On the other hand, many loosely (and incorrectly) use the term "agricultural worker" to refer only to hired agricultural workers.

The term "hired farmworker" generally applies to all workers who are employed for compensation for agricultural work, excluding the farm operator, but also potentially including paid family members. However, even excluding family members, the category "hired farmworker" encompasses a wide range of workers performing vastly different jobs. Both crop workers and livestock workers are included in the hired farmworker category, even though their job situations may be significantly different. Particularly in large industrialized operations, livestock workers may work regular hours on a set schedule. Crop workers are generally seasonal workers with hours based on weather and harvest conditions. Migrant farmworkers are typically crop workers. Their work will depend largely on the weather and the development of the crop.

Some workers may not be hired directly by the farmer, but may be employed by a farm labor contractor or may themselves be an independent contractor. In some industries, distinct categories of work have moved from employment to contracting. For example, in the poultry industry, "chicken catchers," i.e., the workers who go into the large chicken houses at night to collect birds for delivery to the processor, used to be employed by the processor but now are often independent contractors.

There is general agreement that a significant number of agricultural workers are foreign citizens that are working without proper legal documentation. There is also agreement that there are a significant number of children who work in violation of child labor laws.

The diverse nature of agricultural work, the widely dispersed employment locations, the seasonal nature of the work, the migratory pattern of many in the workforce, and the illegality of some of the employment relationships contribute to the difficulties in obtaining accurate information about the workforce.

How the data is collected may also influence the survey results. Household surveys may not count workers who live in temporary labor camps, who are homeless, or who are in frequent migration. Unauthorized workers will likely be reluctant to respond to surveys. Similarly, interviewing farmers for data may not produce accurate results if unauthorized workers are employed or if conditions of employment violate existing laws.

In 2008, the USDA Economic Research Service updated its profile of hired farmworkers, updating its year 2000 analysis of the 1998 Current Population Survey (CPS) using current data from a variety of sources and providing expanded sections on legal status, poverty, housing, and use of social services.

William Kandel
Profile of Hired Farmworkers: A 2008 Update
USDA Economic Research Service, Economic Research Report No. 60
(July 2008)

Introduction

Hired farmworkers make up an estimated third of the total U.S. agricultural labor force and are critical to U.S. agricultural production, especially for labor-intensive agricultural sectors such as fruits and vegetables. A steadily increasing U.S. population, growing demand for labor-intensive crops, and a continually consolidating farm sector have stabilized the demand for hired farm labor in the past decade.

Changing geographic patterns of immigrant settlement in rural areas have increased the visibility of immigrants. Changing production methods now permit year-round production for some farm enterprises, which has helped increasing numbers of formerly migratory workers settle permanently in nonmetropolitan counties.

The hired-farmworker labor market is unique in several respects:

1. Many farmworkers are mobile, traversing State and national boundaries. However, only an estimated 12 percent are "follow-the-crop" farmworkers who follow well-established migrant streams corresponding to agricultural production cycles.

2. Roughly half of all hired farmworkers in the United States lack legal authorization according to the U.S. Department of Labor, making their employment status tenuous and work circumstances and conditions more difficult.

3. Hired farmworkers face a challenging work environment that may include hazardous work conditions, low pay, and substandard housing conditions.

Consequently, while critical to many agricultural sectors, hired farmworkers remain among the most economically disadvantaged working groups in the United States. This relative position within the U.S. occupational structure has changed little over time. Safety improvements notwithstanding, agriculture remains one of the most hazardous industries in the Nation, and farmworkers encounter relatively unique risks from pesticides as well as conventional hazards from heavy equipment operation and physically strenuous labor. Moreover, unauthorized workers fail to qualify for some social programs or choose not to use them for fear of deportation.

Total Estimates of Hired Farmworkers

In 2006, an average of 1.01 million hired farmworkers made up a third of the estimated 3 million people employed in agriculture. The other 2.05 million included self-employed farmers and their unpaid family members. This report focuses exclusively on the characteristics and well-being of hired farmworkers. The 1.01 million figure is one of several cross-sectional estimates—ranging from 691,000 to as much as 1.4 million depending on the data source—for the average number of hired farmworkers employed at any point throughout the year. Depending on the month or agricultural cycle, such estimates can change substantially. Moreover, high employment turnover means that an estimated 2.0 to 2.5 unique workers fill each farmworker job slot over the course of a year....

Labor occupies a prominent place as the third largest production expense (considering all cash and noncash expenses, such as capital depreciation), behind feed and capital depreciation for the agricultural sector as a whole. For 2007, employee compensation for hired labor is forecast to be $22.8 billion. After declining for decades, labor's share of U.S. farm expenses began increasing in the mid-1980s. Consequently, any factors affecting the farm labor supply—such as minimum wage increases, changes in labor demand from other industries employing low-skilled workers (e.g., construction, manufacturing), or new immigration policies—will alter farm profitability and viability among agricultural sectors heavily reliant on farm labor. Growers who specialize in vegetables, fruits and nuts, and horticultural products, for which labor costs range from 30 to 40 percent of total expenses, are especially sensitive to fluctuations in the cost and availability of labor.

Growing reliance on foreign-born, hired farmworkers became firmly institutionalized at the outset of World War II with the Bracero Program, an immigration-related farm labor policy that allowed agricultural growers to hire Mexican workers to make up for war-induced labor shortfalls. This program lasted 22 years, from 1942 until 1964, when several factors including public concern over abusive labor practices, the rising use of unauthorized labor, and the growing farm labor movement convinced Congress to terminate it.

During the Bracero Program and following its demise, unauthorized immigration to the United States grew, becoming an established trend by the 1980s. The Immigration Reform and Control Act of 1986 (IRCA), which was intended to reduce unauthorized immigration, regularized the legal status of over 1 million hired farmworkers between 1986 and 1989, but also increased penalties to employers who hired unauthorized workers. Nevertheless, after a brief respite, unauthorized immigration increased and continues to occur in substantial numbers.

Agricultural producers have become accustomed to having a large pool of hired farmworkers available, and they continue to utilize a largely immigrant workforce that includes many who lack authorization to work in the United States. Despite increased border and employer enforcement policies, close to half of all farmworkers are unauthorized. While agricultural tasks for some crops have been automated, some growers contend that the expense of mechanization for other, currently labor-intensive products such as tree fruit and horticulture would prevent them from remaining competitive with foreign producers. Other research suggests that growers could adjust to smaller workforces with labor-efficient technologies and management practices. Both arguments remain untested because growers have relied upon a relatively ample labor supply.

Geography of Farm Labor

The geographic distribution of the hired farm labor force reflects the total quantity of agricultural production and the kind of crops grown in an area. Certain crops are more labor intensive. One way to put this in context is to compare labor expenses to cash receipts. For the United States, the total farm labor expense in 2006 was $24.4 billion—amounting to 10.2 percent of total agricultural commodity cash receipts. But, in California, which has the highest cash receipts of any State and produces many labor-intensive products (such as dairy, grapes, and greenhouse/nursery), total farm labor expense amounted to 22.3 percent of the total value of agricultural cash receipts for 2006. In contrast, in Iowa, farm labor expense totaled 2.5 percent of cash receipts. Iowa has the third highest total cash receipts, but grows primarily non-labor-intensive agricultural commodities (such as corn, hogs, and soybeans).

Since 1980, the geographic distribution of farmworkers has shifted, with proportions declining in both the South and Midwest and increasing in the West and Southwest. Roughly 60 percent of all hired farmworkers currently work in crops and 40 percent work in livestock. Most hired crop farmworkers are located disproportionately in the Southwest, with California and Texas accounting for almost a third of the $22 billion spent on hired farm and contract farm labor expenses in the United States in 2002.

Demographic Characteristics

The demographic profile of hired farmworkers contributes to their economic disadvantage relative to most other wage and salary workers in the United States. On average, they are younger, less educated, more likely to be foreign-born, and less likely to be citizens or authorized to work in the United States. The extent of this disadvantage depends on which data are used to represent the hired-farmworker population. We used CPS data to compare hired farmworkers with all wage and salary workers, but these data reflect characteristics of more established residents willing to respond to formal, repeated home-based interviews. To obtain an additional measure of relative disadvantage among unauthorized farmworkers, we present figures for each group by citizenship status. Presenting characteristics by citizenship status is not equivalent to presenting them by legal status, because many noncitizens possess legal authorization to work in the United States. Nevertheless, given the lack of complete legal status information, citizenship status roughly approximates the degree to which differences in authorized versus unauthorized status differentiate the farmworker population.

Hired farmworkers differ from other wage and salary workers, as a group, due to the gender imbalance of the hired farm workforce. Obstacles to international migration and the close living and working conditions of most U.S. farmworkers often present difficult or untenable circumstances for potential female migrants and their families. Hence, most hired farmworkers are men.

Approximately 1 of every 5 hired farmworkers is female, compared with gender parity found among wage and salary workers in general. Farm labor is physically demanding, and hired farmworkers tend to be younger than other wage and salary workers, in general. Visible differences between these two groups appear at the ends of the age distribution: the proportion of farmworkers in the youngest age group exceeds that of wage and salary workers in general, while the proportion in the oldest age group trails that of other wage and salary workers. Despite youth and gender imbalance, over half of all farmworkers are married, and in this respect they closely resemble all wage and salary workers.

The racial and ethnic makeup of the hired farm labor force has changed significantly in recent decades, the most consequential transformation being the increasing proportion of Hispanic farmworkers. According to 2006 CPS data, 43 percent of all hired farmworkers are Hispanic: for hired crop and hired livestock workers, the figures are 56 and 26 percent Hispanic, respectively. Almost all noncitizen farmworkers are Hispanic. Yet, since noncitizens comprise only about a third of all farmworkers, the total CPS figure of 43 percent continues to differ substantially from the 2006 NAWS figure of over 80 percent for hired crop farmworkers. Survey methodology explains the discrepancy between these two national data sets. CPS data are collected from households each month over a 16-month period and, therefore, reflect characteristics of more established residents. NAWS data, on the other hand, are collected at the worksite and are therefore more likely to capture persons who have less stable living arrangements and who tend to avoid participation in more formal data collection efforts....

Legal Status

Legal status influences economic and social well-being through its impact on outcomes ranging from social service eligibility, employment, residential mobility, working conditions, and wages. Legal status is a perpetual concern for farmworkers and growers alike. For farmworkers, unauthorized status means facing a greater likelihood of unfair labor practices and deportation. Growers, in turn, are concerned about having sufficient numbers of workers during critical work periods as well as complying with Federal and State administrative requirements to ensure workers are authorized to work in the United States....

The unauthorized proportion of foreign-born workers tends to be higher in agriculture than in other industries because agriculture has served as a point-of-entry into the U.S. labor market for unauthorized immigrants....

Unauthorized workers have fewer avenues for economic mobility outside of agricultural work, and their own perceptions of the U.S. labor market reflect these circumstances.

The H-2A visa program, operated cooperatively by the U.S. Department of Labor (DOL) and the U.S. Citizenship and Immigration Services Division of the Department of Homeland Security (DHS), processed over 64,000 agricultural worker applications in 2006 (DOL, 2007). This class of nonimmigrant admission that originated in 1943 was converted into a specific Federal legal provision in 1952, revised by IRCA, and amended by subsequent legislation. It permits employers to hire temporary foreign-born workers for up to 1 year with possible extensions for up to 3 years.

In addition to describing populations, demographic characteristics effectively predict economic outcomes. Age, educational attainment, employment experience, English language ability, and legal status all strongly influence earnings and occupational mobility. The disadvantaged demographic profile described earlier for hired farmworkers relative to all wage and salary workers in the U.S. labor force often translates into less favorable employment characteristics.

Farmworkers typically have more gaps in employment than nonfarm wage and salary workers and fewer opportunities to earn additional compensation. They are twice as likely to have schedules that either vary or exceed 50 hours per week, corresponding to sudden requirements of agricultural production. Yet among farmworkers, noncitizens are more likely to be employed 40 hours per week and less likely to have more flexible or more demanding work schedules. Noncitizen farmworkers are also more likely to be employed full-time. Part-time farmworkers who are citizens have a median age (18) that is half that of noncitizen part-time farmworkers (37), suggesting a greater presence of high-school or college-age workers among part-time workers with citizenship.

Farmworkers are about as likely as other wage and salary workers to earn hourly wages and, despite low earnings, are also about as likely to have only one job at any given time. Yet, because of the seasonal nature of farmwork, they are more likely to have a succession of jobs over a given time period. Hired farmworkers are less likely to earn overtime pay,

The H-2A Visa Program for Temporary Agricultural Workers

H-2A visa holders are considered non-immigrants because they are admitted temporarily to perform work; immigrants by contrast are admitted to the United States as legal permanent residents. To hire these workers, employers must demonstrate they lack a sufficient and timely supply of locally available qualified U.S. workers, and that using foreign workers would not adversely affect wages and working conditions of comparably employed U.S. workers. H-2A workers must earn the higher of the prevailing industry wage, the Federal or State minimum wage, or an Adverse Effect Wage Rate (AEWR) which is an average hourly wage rate based on data collected by USDA, and employers must provide them with detailed earnings statements when paid.

Employers are required to provide H-2A workers with a series of benefits, including housing that meets Federal standards for noncommuting workers, transportation for commuting workers, transportation to workers' home countries or next employment locations, either food preparation facilities or three meals per day, and workers' compensation insurance. U.S. workers must be offered the same benefits as H-2A workers.

Employers must apply to the DOL and their State Workforce Agency 45 days prior to hiring. After employers have met certain working condition stipulations, the DOL "certifies" within 7 days that there are not enough U.S. workers to fill these positions through State and employer recruitment during this period and that the presence of H-2A workers will not adversely affect local wages. Once filed, over 90 percent of employer applications are approved for most of the jobs requested. Following successful certification, the employer next petitions the Citizenship and Immigration Services Division of DHS. Approved petitions are sent to the appropriate consulates where workers apply for visas. At the port of entry, a Customs and Border Protection officer authorizes a traveler's admission into the United States and the period of time that the individual bearer of the nonimmigrant visa is allowed to remain in the United States for that visit.

Although less than 5 percent of all hired farmworkers are hired through the program, it remains controversial. Obstacles for farm operators wishing to use the H-2A visa program include:

- Complicated paperwork
- Requirements to try domestic worker recruitment before utilizing the program
- Requirements to anticipate future labor demand
- The requirement to pay the higher of the prevailing industry wage, the Federal or State minimum wage, or the AEWR; and
- Unwanted attention from advocacy groups and unions viewing publicly accessible H-2A requests

Farmworker advocates and unions have also been critical of the program, arguing that it lacks fundamental protections to prevent foreign workers from being mistreated and exploited....

tips, or commissions, or to join labor unions. NAWS data (not shown) also indicate a low proportion of union coverage for hired farmworkers.

CPS data indicate that when farmworkers are employed, they have relatively stable work schedules. However, due to the seasonal nature of their work, hired farmworkers, on average, experience rates of unemployment double those of wage and salary workers, in general, a difference that varies by demographic and economic characteristics. For instance, the unemployment rate of female farmworkers exceeds by threefold that of all female wage and salary workers. This relative disadvantage also accrues to workers who are over age 44, Hispanic, noncitizen, and foreign-born. Farmworkers with at least 9 years of schooling, on the other hand, experience unemployment rates that are comparable to those of all wage and salary workers. A number of these characteristics overlap. Recent international migrants, who are also likely to be younger, Hispanic, less educated, and unauthorized, face the greatest challenges obtaining employment.

Among hired farmworkers, unemployment rates also vary by sector and occupation. Those working in field crops have average unemployment rates more than quadruple those of livestock workers, owing to the more seasonal nature of field crop work. Nonsupervisory farmworkers have 2.5 times the unemployment rate of managers and supervisors. Unemployment characteristics also reflect greater employment instability over the course of a year. Hired farmworkers are more likely to have terminated employment due to layoffs or the conclusion of a temporary job and less likely to have quit or previously been employed full-time prior to searching for work.

Lower unemployment durations of farmworkers reflect several factors, including low barriers to entry for farm labor and the inability of hired farmworkers to remain unemployed for extended periods. Longer unemployment spells among hired farmworkers, many of whom are foreign-born, increase the chance that some of these workers will return to their countries of origin. When that occurs, such workers effectively remove themselves from the pool of potential survey respondents and, consequently, any and all resulting official statistics.

The unemployment rate for hired farmworkers was among the highest for all major occupations in 2006 and stems mainly from farmwork's seasonality. When employed, hired farmworkers work for roughly the same number of hours per week as other workers, yet total employment levels for hired farmworkers vary according to season. For example, NASS data for 2006 indicate that 1,195,000 hired farmworkers were employed in mid-July, compared with 796,000 in mid-January. Hired farmworkers have historically earned relatively low wages.

According to CPS data, median weekly earnings of full-time farmworkers are 59 percent of those for all wage and salary workers. The earnings gap between the two groups is smaller in the Midwest where farmworker earnings exceed the national farmworker median. The gap is greater for farmworkers in the Northeast whose earnings trail the national farmworker median, while those of all wage and salary workers exceed the national median. Within the farmworker population, supervisory and managerial personnel earn 57 percent more than nonsupervisory workers, and livestock workers, who often have more stable employment, earn roughly 24 percent more than crop workers.

Over time, wages and earnings of hired farmworkers vary as immigration policies tighten or loosen the labor supply. Between the end of the Bracero Program in 1964 and passage of IRCA in 1986, unauthorized migration steadily increased and hired farmworker real wages either stabilized or dropped in response. Following IRCA, real wages increased only slightly until increased border enforcement policies in the mid-1990s restricted the flow of unauthorized workers. Average real wages increased 10 percent between 1995 and 2000. Since the events of 9/11, real wages have continued to increase as the number of hired farmworkers declined. Hired-farmworker hourly wages, which are measured in NASS's Farm Labor Survey, the CPS, and the NAWS, would be substantially higher if they did not include a large proportion of unauthorized workers whose average wages are lower than those of authorized workers.

Hired farmworkers not only earn less, on average, than wage and salary workers as a group, but crop farmworkers also earn less than workers in similar low-skill occupations. Wages remain low in spite of the fact that labor analysts consider farmwork among the most arduous and hazardous occupations. Factors accounting for the relatively low earnings of farmworkers, include: a high proportion of unauthorized workers who have fewer options to seek employment in other industries; the use of farm labor contractors who reduce the hourly pay of hired farmworkers in exchange for arranging employment with growers; and, in the case of small farms, exemption from Federal minimum wage laws.

Demographic characteristics also influence hired-farmworker earnings and their relative difference compared to earnings of other wage and salary workers. The earnings gap shrinks for people who are similarly disadvantaged, namely the youngest, least-educated, and unauthorized workers. Otherwise, the average earnings gap does not vary substantially across most demographic characteristics. Based on the characteristics of race and ethnicity, Hispanics incur the smallest wage differences and Asians the largest for farm versus nonfarm employment.

Another way to compare hired-farmworker earnings with the rest of the U.S. labor force is to place them in the context of an earnings distribution. The range of earnings for all wage and salary employees, divided into 10 even deciles, serves as the baseline for this comparison. If the distribution of hired-farmworkers' earnings is then superimposed over that of all wage and salary workers, we can see that while supervisory farmworker earnings roughly mimic those of all wage and salary workers, nonsupervisory farmworker earnings concentrate at the lower end, with over 80 percent falling within the first four deciles of the U.S. workforce.

Migration Patterns

Hired farmworkers further differentiate themselves from most other wage and salary workers because they include large numbers of mobile or migrant workers. The NAWS data set includes information on migration patterns of hired crop farmworkers, and it distinguishes between six different migrant types based on settlement, international orientation, and number of work locations.

Settled workers, the largest group of hired crop farmworkers, represent nonmigratory hired farmworkers. Shuttler migrants migrate between their homes and a single location. To qualify as shuttler migrants, they must travel at least 75 miles to reach their location and must work only within a 75-mile radius of that location. NAWS further distinguishes between shuttler migrants within the United States and international shuttler migrants who have crossed an international border within 12 months since they were surveyed. Thus, workers who have homes near Philadelphia but travel to Lancaster County in central Pennsylvania for 3 months to harvest vegetables are classified as U.S. shuttler migrants.

Although follow-the-crop migrants embody the popular conception of hired farmworkers, they actually comprise less than 12 percent of this workforce. Follow-the-crop workers travel to multiple U.S. farm locations for work, frequently migrating in consistent geographic patterns according to agricultural season requirements. Like shuttler migrants, follow-the-crop migrants travel more than 75 miles to a work location, but unlike shuttler migrants, they travel to multiple U.S. farm locations. NAWS also distinguishes between U.S. and international follow-the-crop migrants. Finally, newcomers, which NAWS classifies as international migrants, are foreignborn farmworkers residing in the United States less than 1 year and whose shuttler or follow-the-crop migration patterns remain undetermined at the time of the NAWS survey.

After 1989, the proportion of migrant crop farmworkers increased following the passage of IRCA and then declined in the late 1990s. IRCA effectively legalized large numbers of hired farmworkers, who consequently gained sectoral and geographic mobility to seek better paying jobs. Yet, increasing use of year-round production techniques and greater border enforcement starting in the mid-1990s have reduced the proportion of migrating farmworkers.

Migrating hired farmworkers exhibit different demographic and employment profiles from settled farmworkers: they are younger, more likely to be male, and more often Hispanic. Disadvantages in the U.S. labor market include fewer years of education, less U.S. experience, less knowledge of English, and greater likelihood of being unauthorized (66 percent versus 27 percent). In addition, migrant farmworkers are twice as likely to work for labor contractors, who, in turn, must be reimbursed. Migrant farmworkers consequently earn less than settled farmworkers. In 2006, the most recent year for which NAWS data are available, average hourly wages for migrant and nonmigrant crop farmworkers were $7.52 and $8.53, respectively, a 13-percent difference. Low wages of migrant farmworkers are compounded by an annual work schedule that includes half as many workweeks as for settled farmworkers.

Farmworker poverty, like low wages, has been documented extensively. According to the U.S. Bureau of Labor Statistics, the poverty rate for farming, fishing, and forestry exceeds that of all other general occupation categories. This is the case for both men and women, as well as across four racial and ethnic categories.

Morever, when this poverty rate is disaggregated by occupation category and citizenship status, the rate for noncitizen hired farm laborers jumps to 25.3 percent and 27.2 percent for men and women, respectively, compared with 9.7 percent and 8.7 percent for citizen male and female farm laborers. Disadvantages from migrant status extend beyond monetary compensation to health vulnerability. Less than a tenth of migrant farmworkers have health insurance, which partly explains low health service utilization rates compared with settled migrants. Another reason for lower rates may be that fewer migrant farmworkers report health problems—about half the percentage of settled migrants— owing to their relative youth and fewer years of farm labor experience.

Children of migrant workers also face numerous challenges. In addition to growing up in households with higher rates of poverty and substandard housing, they are also much more likely than the average child to move from their home schools to new schools with different curricula, testing requirements, and credit accrual rates. Migrant children must constantly adjust to new environments, and American schools do not use a viable national system for transferring records. Despite over 30 years of concerted investment by the U.S. Department of Education's Office of Migrant Education, which facilitates educational attainment for this target population, rural migrant students continue to confront some of the most daunting learning challenges of any student population in the Nation.

Many studies have documented substandard housing conditions for hired farmworkers. Farmworkers earn relatively little and either cannot afford or choose not to purchase more expensive temporary housing, relying on what is provided for them by farm operators and Federal and State government agencies. They often confront substandard housing quality, crowding, deficient sanitation, proximity to pesticides (which is especially harmful for children), and lack of inspection and enforcement. CPS data indicate that housing for hired farmworkers differs from that of all workers as a group. Because hired farmworkers earn less, work shorter periods, and move frequently, they are more likely to live in crowded conditions, less likely to own their own homes, more likely to receive free housing, and more likely to live in mobile homes. Differences in housing tenure by citizenship status are particularly striking.

Farmworker housing studies that capture unauthorized workers more accurately portray more substantial differences. For example, data from a national survey of 4,600 housing units by the Housing Assistance Council (2001), a nonprofit housing research and advocacy organization, records aspects of housing conditions that affect hired farmworkers, but are not captured by other datasets, such as residential exposure to pesticides.

Because of lower earnings and a greater likelihood of remitting earnings to family members in their countries of origin, unauthorized workers are more likely to conserve earnings by living in overcrowded housing. Housing Assistance Council data suggest that half of all hired crop farmworkers live in overcrowded conditions compared with 3 percent of all wage and salary workers. NAWS data on hired crop farmworkers from 1989 to 2006 indicate this figure stands at 85 percent. The data also indicate that the prevalence and degree (number of people sharing a room) of overcrowding vary according to legal status, with unauthorized workers experiencing higher rates than authorized and citizen workers.

A limited housing supply hinders those wishing to purchase homes, particularly in rural agricultural areas and where large groups of farmworkers have settled with their families to become year-round residents. Migrant workers may be unable to meet credit checks, provide requested deposits, or engage in extended contracts. Landlords may be reluctant to rent to hired farmworkers out of fear that they may overcrowd rental units as an economic strategy. In some cases, housing may be in such short supply that hired farmworkers must remain homeless for extended periods, obtaining shelter wherever they can—including in fields, in cars, or under bridges.

Migrant housing is regulated under the Migrant and Seasonal Agricultural Worker Protection Act (MSPA), whose rules are enforced by the Wage and Hour Division of the U.S. Department of Labor's (DOL) Employment Standards Administration. States also have their own housing laws, and farm operators must abide by the more stringent of the laws. Farm operators are not required to provide farmworker housing, but if they do, they are required to ensure that their housing complies with substantive Federal and State safety and health standards. Yet, according to these same regulations, such protections apply only to farmworkers hired directly by farm operators, not to individuals hired through labor contractors.

From the farm operator perspective, migrant housing represents a considerable capital investment to meet temporary housing demands during labor intensive processes such as planting or harvesting. Farmers are more likely to make such investments for year-round workers. In one government survey, growers cited the H2-A visa program's housing provision requirement for their lack of program participation. Farmworker housing, therefore, remains a contentious issue, encompassing ongoing challenges for both farm operators—who may invest in it and are required to meet Federal and State farmworker housing guidelines if they do—and farmworkers and their advocates, who contend that much of it is substandard.

USDA administers a well-established Federal program known as the Section 514/516 Farm Labor Housing Program which provides funding to buy, build, improve, or repair housing for farm laborers. In addition, some States with the largest populations of hired farmworkers, such as Florida and California, have created model programs and led efforts to provide affordable housing and workable housing code enforcement. Assessments of farmworker housing in agricultural areas offer thorough descriptions of local conditions and policy recommendations for improvements.

Health

Agriculture is among the more hazardous industries in the United States, and farmworker health remains a considerable occupational concern for this sector. While farmworkers face workplace hazards similar to those found in other industrial settings, such as working with heavy machinery and hard physical labor, they also confront factors more common to agricultural production such as pesticide exposure, sun exposure, inadequate sanitary facilities, and crowded and/or substandard housing. Young farmworkers face greater risks of agricultural industry accidents because of their lack of experience.

A number of Federal and State programs serving the general public and/or farmworkers provide medical care as well as financial support for disabled workers. These include Medicaid, Social Security, State farmworker housing programs, and the Migrant Health Program. Yet, inadequate enforcement of Federal regulations and lack of program participation put farmworkers, particularly migrant farmworkers, at greater health risk. Apart from government programs, hired farmworkers typically cannot afford quality health care and often work in locations with limited access to medical facilities.

Two key indicators measuring occupational health risk include fatalities and the incidence of injuries and illnesses. Data from the 1996 and 2006 Department of Labor's Census of Fatal Occupational Injuries indicate that in many industrial sectors, fatalities have declined following general improvements in occupational safety. The data, however, do not indicate the same degree of improvement for the agricultural sector, where fatality rates have increased. This outcome is consistent with other government research on fatalities among foreign-born workers, whose increasing incidence of occupational fatalities exceeds their increasing proportion in the U.S. labor force. As a result, between 1996 and 2001, the agriculture, forestry, and fishing sector, which employed less than 2 percent of the U.S. workforce, accounted for a disproportionate 13 percent of all fatal occupational injuries.

The agricultural sector also exhibits some of the highest rates of occupational injuries and illnesses of all industrial sectors. These incidents have declined consistently over time, following similar patterns in other industrial sectors.

Data from NAWS illustrate the pervasiveness of some physical ailments, although comparisons are complicated by the lack of data for the U.S. employed population. Some rates, such as 8 percent of respondents reporting skin problems or 20 percent reporting musculoskeletal problems within the past year, are above national averages. Twelve percent of all farmworkers responding to the survey indicated they had worked with pesticides in the previous 12 months. Even relatively low levels of incidents, such as treatment for pesticide exposure, have considerable implications for long-term health. About 3 percent of those using pesticides were under age 18, making the consequences of such occupational hazards longer lasting over the course of these workers' lives.

The absence of adequate plumbing facilities at agricultural worksites poses health hazards for workers who constantly work in soiled conditions, particularly those who work with pesticides. Lack of drinking water poses a significant health threat to farmworkers who face hazards of dehydration and heat stroke. When NAWS data were first collected, 15 percent of all workers cited a lack of toilets and 20 percent a lack of washing water. Those rates have declined significantly in subsequent years. While 1 in 4 workers complained about the lack of at least one of the three sanitary facilities noted in 1989, the figure had fallen to 1 in 10 by 2006. NAWS data also indicate that workers lacking legal status are about 50 percent more likely to lack access to a sanitary facility than workers with legal status.

NAWS data also report what crop farmworkers cited as obstacles to their obtaining health care. Two-thirds of all farmworkers cited costs, and almost a third cited language barriers to explain their inability to obtain health care when needed. Within the hired crop farmworker population, unauthorized workers were almost twice as likely as authorized workers and three times as likely as citizen workers to report such obstacles. NAWS data indicate that almost three-quarters of crop farmworkers possess some type of health insurance in case of injury, and almost half receive some compensation from their employer while recuperating if injuries prevent them from working. Few workers receive health insurance for nonwork-related injuries or illnesses. Access to programs varies according to legal status, a reflection of U.S. experience and the ability to obtain employment with firms that offer such benefits.

Health insurance benefits provided in case of an injury should be distinguished from general health insurance. Only a fourth of crop farmworkers surveyed by NAWS between 2000 and 2006 stated that they had general health insurance. Farmworkers estimated the health insurance coverage of their spouses at roughly the same proportion, and farmworkers' children, who are often eligible for government support, were twice as likely to have health insurance.

Other farmworker health concerns not addressed in this report include dental health, tuberculosis, and mental illness. Health practitioners also cite HIV/AIDS as a growing concern among the farmworker population that may have repercussions in countries of origin. Several studies indicate that farmworkers are less likely than other wage and salary employees to receive financial or disability support from the Social Security program when they retire or become disabled.

Use of Social Services

Given their health hazards and substantially lower wages, hired farmworkers would be expected to utilize public services at higher rates than nonagricultural wage and salary workers. However, roughly half of all crop farmworkers and an undetermined yet substantial proportion of livestock farmworkers lack legal authorization, which limits their access to certain Federal public services. States may have eligibility requirements for their programs that permit unauthorized resident participation or that differ significantly from those of Federal programs. In all cases, previous research shows that unauthorized U.S. residents utilize public services less than authorized residents or citizens because of concerns about possible deportation.

Yet, according to CPS data, which capture only a small portion of the unauthorized population, utilization is more prevalent among hired farmworkers and their households than for all wage and salary workers. In addition, utilization is more prevalent among noncitizens than citizens for both groups of workers. Farmworker households, on average, have 50 percent more children under age 15, and those children are twice as likely to receive Medicaid and qualify for free/reduced-price school lunch. One benefit of the School Lunch Program is that farmworkers' children apparently enjoy the benefits of regular hot school meals at least as much as children of other wage and salary workers. Farmworker households do not appear to benefit more than the broader employed population from housing assistance programs and Medicare. They are far more likely to receive food stamps, WIC, and Medicaid owing, in part, to eligibility of citizen children for these programs. Receipt of unemployment, workers', and disability compensation is roughly 50 percent higher for hired farmworkers than for wage and salary employees in general.

One cannot make inferences about the utilization rates of unauthorized workers from CPS data because the noncitizen category includes authorized and unauthorized workers. NAWS data, however, provide evidence of clear differences in public service utilization by legal status. According to these data, which capture unauthorized, authorized, and citizen legal statuses, authorized crop farmworkers show above-average participation in five social welfare programs captured in the NAWS data compared with unauthorized workers who show below-average participation. Citizen farmworkers, whose poverty rates are a third of noncitizen farmworkers, utilize these programs less than authorized workers.

Findings and Implications

In the past several decades, the U.S. economy has undergone enormous changes, including broad-based industrial restructuring, service sector growth, technological innovation, and expanding globalization. Within the agricultural sector, technological change has increased productivity while reducing the use of farm labor. Future demand for hired farm labor depends on the relative weights of several opposing trends:

- Increased mechanization, technological advances and growing acceptance and consumption of imported food, reducing demand for hired farm labor; and

- Increased farm consolidation and greater consumer demand for year-round fresh fruits, vegetables, and more labor-intensive organic produce, maintaining or increasing the demand for hired farmworkers.

Contrasting these dynamic trends are the conditions and circumstances for hired agricultural workers who, as a group, remain among the most disadvantaged employees in the United States. Compared with workers in other sectors of the economy, a substantial proportion of farmworkers are foreign born and lack legal status, English language facility, and U.S. working or living experience. They are also younger and possess less education than most U.S. workers.

Agricultural work often serves as an entry point into the U.S. labor market and one from which significant numbers of workers exit when other more remunerative, less arduous, and more stable employment becomes available. Compared with many other wage and salary workers, hired farmworkers face more physically grueling and hazardous working conditions and substandard living conditions.

Despite improvements in policy and labor enforcement, numerous studies demonstrate that farmworkers continue to be subjected to a range of unfair labor practices. Hired farmworkers use social services at higher rates than other wage and salary workers, as a group, although access is limited by the unauthorized legal status of many.

Demands for changes to current immigration policies in the wake of a rapidly growing and geographically diverse foreign-born population, the events of 9/11, and discussions surrounding agricultural legislation such as the 2008 Farm Bill have increased the visibility of the hired-farm labor population among policymakers and the general public.

As of early 2008, several proposed immigration law reforms had been offered, notably *AgJobs* which is directly related to agricultural workers. Representing a compromise between growers, farm labor advocates, and Federal legislators, the *AgJobs* legislation would provide farmworkers with temporary citizenship status and the possibility of obtaining permanent legal residence in the United States.

AgJobs would also restructure the existing H-2A visa program to reduce administrative burdens for growers, while increasing legal protections for workers. The H-2A visa program, which in 2005 involved 64,000 workers out of an estimated 2.5 million engaged in hired farmwork (less than 2 percent), remains the only legally sanctioned guestworker program. According to both growers and worker advocates, however, the program remains flawed. Growers object to what they consider cumbersome administrative requirements, while farmworker advocates contend that the program invites pervasive abuses through a lack of regulatory enforcement. To address border security and immigration challenges, President Bush recently issued a directive to the Department of Labor to review H-2A program regulations and institute changes that tackle concerns of both growers and farm labor advocates.

Current legislative and public debates on immigration reform underscore the importance of unauthorized workers to certain sectors of the U.S. economy, particularly agriculture. Several studies based on the experience with IRCA estimate that if unauthorized workers were granted legal status, their agricultural wages would increase significantly, and they may be less likely to take seasonal agricultural production jobs. Hence, those employing seasonal workers would face the greatest financial challenges resulting from labor market constriction due to immigration reform. Owner operators are likely to adjust over time by acquiring additional capital equipment, switching commodities, or possibly ceasing agricultural production.

Hired crop farmworkers, on the other hand, display consistency regarding their expectations for future farmwork. NAWS data suggest that over 80 percent of all workers expect to continue doing farmwork for 4 or more years from the time they were surveyed. Except for a decline during 1995–2000, these expectations have remained stable over the entire 17-year NAWS data collection span. This suggests that, while a portion of hired farmworkers cycle through agricultural employment, using farm labor as a stepping stone to other opportunities within the U.S. labor market, most expect to remain in the agricultural sector for the foreseeable future.

Implications for change in farm labor and immigration policy extend beyond U.S. borders. An estimated 8 of every 10 hired farmworkers are foreign-born. Many have families in their countries of origin that they support through remitted earnings. Consequently, changing employment conditions for farmworkers in the United States can have economic consequences for communities in other countries.

One important finding relates to the shift from seasonal to year-round agricultural employment. Results show that migrant hired farmworkers work half as many weeks per year as nonmigrant hired farmworkers. Current research and industry trends indicate a growing tendency to switch from seasonal to year-round workers, corresponding in part to growing year-round domestic demand for fresh fruits and vegetables. In turn, migrant workers are settling permanently in places where they previously worked temporarily.

As seasonal workers transition into year-round workers by performing other tasks, both farm operators and hired farmworkers benefit—the former from a more stable and available workforce and the latter from improved economic conditions. The Department of Labor reports a correlation between the number of years worked for a single employer and the likelihood of working year round. Year-round workers also report higher rates of pay and greater benefits.

While this report attempts to provide a reasonably broad overview of the hired-farmworker population, an exhaustive survey of all issues related to this population is beyond its scope. Topics not mentioned include farmworker mental health; food security of farmworker families; nutrition, given the pervasiveness of fast food diets among farmworkers; substance abuse, gangs, and sexually transmitted diseases in migrant farmworker communities; farmworker youth education and health outcomes; and State variation in workers' compensation coverage.

Six States—California, Florida, Washington, Texas, Oregon, and North Carolina—account for half of the Nation's expenditure on hired labor. Any innovative or "best practices" and regulations that these States develop regarding hired farmworkers may provide lessons and set standards and innovations for the rest of the country.

Notes

1. For a real-world introduction to agricultural labor issues and the experiences of migrant farmworkers, see DANIEL ROTHENBERG, WITH THESE HANDS: THE HIDDEN WORLD OF MIGRANT FARMWORKERS TODAY (2000). Rothenberg presents the varied perspectives of workers, contractors, growers, coyotes, lobbyists, organizers, and others through interviews with members of each group. As the San Diego Union Tribune reported, "There are hands at both ends of the food chain. That is what Daniel Rothenberg strives so mightily and successfully to show us in this book, an engrossing and often surprising collection of oral histories."

2. Many farmworkers have long term health problems associated with their frequent pesticide exposure. *See, A Life Engulfed by Pesticides*, THE ATLANTIC (June 10, 2010) (reporting on the extensive problems experienced by workers who harvested in the Lake Apoka area of Florida in previous years). The Worker Protection Standards regulate the time period prior to entry into an area where pesticides have been sprayed. 40 C.F.R. pt. 170 (2010). It is widely conceded that the standards are difficult to enforce.

B. An Overview of Federal Labor and Employment Law

This section presents an overview of three of the main federal labor laws as they are applied to agricultural workers, the National Labor Relations Act, The Fair Labor Standards Act, and the Migrant & Seasonal Agricultural Worker Protection Act.

1. The National Labor Relations Act

A worker's right to organize with other workers was recognized in 1935 with the passage of the National Labor Relations Act (NLRA), ch. 372, 49 Stat. 449 (codified as amended at 29 U.S.C. §§ 151–169).

§ 157. **Right of employees as to organization, collective bargaining, etc.**

Employees shall have the right to self-organization, to form, join, or assist labor organizations, to bargain collectively through representatives of their own choosing, and to engage in other concerted activities for the purpose of collective bar-

gaining or other mutual aid or protection, and shall also have the right to refrain from any or all of such activities except to the extent that such right may
be affected by an agreement requiring membership in a labor organization as a
condition of employment as authorized in section 158(a)(3) of this title.

29 U.S.C. § 157.

In order to protect the rights granted by § 157, the NLRA defines various employer
actions as "unfair labor practices" that are disallowed. Employer's unfair labor practices
include:

§ 158. Unfair Labor Practices.

(a) **Unfair labor practices by employer.** It shall be an unfair labor practice for an
employer—

> (1) to interfere with, restrain, or coerce employees in the exercise of the rights
> guaranteed in section 157 of this title;

> (2) to dominate or interfere with the formation or administration of any labor
> organization or contribute financial or other support to it . . .

> (3) by discrimination in regard to hire or tenure of employment or any term
> or condition of employment to encourage or discourage membership in any
> labor organization . . .

> (4) to discharge or otherwise discriminate against an employee because he
> has filed charges or given testimony under this subchapter;

> (5) to refuse to bargain collectively with the representatives of his employees.

29 U.S.C. § 158.

In the case of *N.L.R.B. v. Jones & Laughlin Steel Corp.*, 301 U.S. 1 (1937) the Supreme
Court rejected a challenge to the law, recognizing a worker's right to organize and bargain collectively as a "fundamental right." The court reasoned,

> Employees have as clear a right to organize and select their representatives for law-
> ful purposes as the respondent [corporate employer] has to organize its busi-
> ness and select its own officers and agents. Discrimination and coercion to prevent
> the free exercise of the right of employees to self-organization and representa-
> tion is a proper subject for condemnation by competent legislative authority.
> Long ago we stated the reason for labor organizations. We said that they were or-
> ganized out of the necessities of the situation; that a single employee was help-
> less in dealing with an employer; that he was dependent ordinarily on his daily
> wage for the maintenance of himself and family; that, if the employer refused to
> pay him the wages that he thought fair, he was nevertheless unable to leave the
> employ and resist arbitrary and unfair treatment; that union was essential to
> give laborers opportunity to deal on an equality with their employer.

Id. at 33.

Nevertheless, the NLRA does not extend this right to all workers. In order to fall within
the protection of this statute, a worker must fall within the statutory definition of "employee."

Section 2 of the NLRA, codified at 29 U.S.C. § 152, sets forth the relevant definitions.
Subsection 3 provides the definition of employee. It provides as follows:

> (3) The term "employee" shall include any employee, and shall not be limited to
> the employees of a particular employer, unless this subchapter explicitly states oth-

erwise, and shall include any individual whose work has ceased as a consequence of, or in connection with, any current labor dispute or because of any unfair labor practice, and who has not obtained any other regular and substantially equivalent employment, *but shall not include any individual employed as an agricultural laborer*, or in the domestic service of any family or person at his home, or any individual employed by his parent or spouse, or any individual having the status of an independent contractor, or any individual employed as a supervisor, or any individual employed by an employer subject to the Railway Labor Act [45 U.S.C.A. § 151 et seq.], as amended from time to time, or by any other person who is not an employer as herein defined [emphasis added].

29 U.S.C. § 152(3).

Therefore, under federal law, agricultural workers do not have a protected right to collectively bargain with their employers. Some states, most notably California, have state statutes that provide agricultural workers with some comparable rights, but there is no federal protection for agricultural worker organizations, and the majority of agricultural workers are not represented by collective bargaining.

Because of the exception for agricultural laborers under the NLRA, employers have had an incentive to claim their workers as "agricultural laborers." While in many traditional farm settings, this categorization is not controversial, in less traditional settings many questions are raised. What is agriculture for purposes of defining the agricultural laborer exception?

The definition of agriculture for purposes of the agricultural laborer exception has been at the center of several disputes pursued all the way to the United States Supreme Court. For example, integrated poultry operations have resulted in two significant Supreme Court opinions, the most recent of which is the case of *Holly Farms Corp. v. National Labor Relations Board*. In this case, a sharply divided Court addressed the complex relationships and the definition of agriculture.

Holly Farms Corporation v. National Labor Relations Board
517 U.S. 392 (1996)

GINSBURG, J., delivered the opinion of the Court, in which STEVENS, KENNEDY, SOUTER, and BREYER, JJ., joined. O'CONNOR, J., filed an opinion concurring in the judgment in part and dissenting in part, in which REHNQUIST, C. J., and SCALIA and THOMAS, JJ., joined, post, p. 1406.

Justice GINSBURG delivered the opinion of the Court.

This controversy stems from a dispute concerning union representation at the Wilkesboro, North Carolina, headquarters facility of Holly Farms, a corporation engaged in the production, processing, and marketing of poultry products. The parties divide, as have federal courts, over the classification of certain workers, described as "live-haul" crews —teams of chicken catchers, forklift operators, and truckdrivers, who collect for slaughter chickens raised as broilers by independent contract growers, and transport the birds to Holly Farms' processing plant. Holly Farms maintains that members of "live-haul" crews are "agricultural laborer[s]," a category of workers exempt from National Labor Relations Act coverage. The National Labor Relations Board disagreed and approved a Wilkesboro plant bargaining unit including those employees. Satisfied that the Board reasonably aligned the "live-haul" crews with the corporation's processing operations, typing them covered "employee[s]," not exempt "agricultural laborer[s]," we affirm the Court of Appeals' judgment, which properly deferred to the Board's determination.

I
A

Petitioner Holly Farms Corporation, a wholly owned subsidiary of Tyson Foods, Inc., is a vertically integrated poultry producer headquartered in Wilkesboro, North Carolina.[1] Holly Farms' activities encompass numerous poultry operations, including hatcheries, a feed mill, an equipment maintenance center, and a processing plant.

"Broiler" chickens are birds destined for human food markets.[2] Holly Farms hatches broiler chicks at its own hatcheries, and immediately delivers the chicks to the farms of independent contractors. The contractors then raise the birds into full-grown broiler chickens. Holly Farms pays the contract growers for their services, but retains title to the broilers and supplies the food and medicine necessary to their growth.

When the broilers are seven weeks old, Holly Farms sends its live-haul crews to reclaim the birds and ferry them to the processing plant for slaughter. The live-haul crews — which typically comprise nine chicken catchers, one forklift operator, and one live-haul driver — travel in a flat-bed truck from Holly Farms' processing plant to the farms of the independent growers. At the farms, the chicken catchers enter the coops, manually capture the broilers, and load them into cages. The forklift operator lifts the caged chickens onto the bed of the truck, and the live-haul driver returns the truck, with the loaded cases and the crew, to Holly Farms' processing plant. There, the birds are slaughtered and prepared for shipment to retail stores.

B

In 1989, the Chauffeurs, Teamsters and Helpers, Local 391 (Union), filed a representation petition with the National Labor Relations Board (Board or NLRB), seeking an election in a proposed unit that included live-haul employees working out of Holly Farms' Wilkesboro processing plant. Over Holly Farms' objection, the Board approved the bargaining unit, ruling that the live-haul workers were "employee[s]" protected by the National Labor Relations Act (NLRA or Act), 49 Stat. 449, as amended, 29 U.S.C. § 151 et seq., rather than "agricultural laborer[s]" excluded from the Act's coverage by § 2(3) of the NLRA, 29 U.S.C. § 152(3).[3] After further proceedings not relevant here, the Board ordered the corporation to bargain with the Union as the representative of the unit.

The United States Court of Appeals for the Fourth Circuit enforced the Board's order. The court held that the Board's classification of the live-haul workers as "employee[s]," rather than "agricultural laborer[s]," rested "on a reasonable interpretation of the Act." The Board's reading, the court added, was consistent with the NLRB's prior decisions …[4]

---

1. Holly Farms maintains various facilities throughout the United States, but this controversy concerns only its Wilkesboro operation.

2. Holly Farms' operations also involve birds called "pullets," young chickens destined to serve as laying hens. The live-haul workers whose classification is at issue in this case work exclusively with broilers.

3. Board member Oviatt dissented from the Board's classification of the live-haul employees. He viewed the crew members as "agricultural laborer[s]," and therefore unprotected by the NLRA. *Holly Farms Corp.*, 311 N.L.R.B., at 287.

4. Judge Niemeyer dissented in relevant part; like dissenting Board member Oviatt, *see supra*, at 1400, n. 3, he ranked the live-haul employees as "agricultural laborer[s]" unprotected by the NLRA. 48 F.3d, at 1373.

Other Federal Courts of Appeals, in conflict with the Fourth and Eighth Circuits, have held that live-haul workers employed by vertically integrated poultry producers are engaged in "agriculture." ... We granted certiorari to resolve the division of authority.

II

The NLRA's protections extend only to workers who qualify as "employee[s]" under §2(3) of the Act. 29 U.S.C. §152(3). The term "employee," NLRA §2(3) states, "[does] not include any individual employed as an agricultural laborer." No definition of "agricultural laborer" appears in the NLRA. But annually since 1946, Congress has instructed, in riders to Appropriations Acts for the Board: "[A]gricultural laborer," for NLRA §2(3) purposes, shall derive its meaning from the definition of "agriculture" supplied by §3(f) of the Fair Labor Standards Act of 1938 (FLSA). *See Bayside Enterprises, Inc. v. NLRB*, 429 U.S. 298, 300, and n. 6, 97 S.Ct. 576, 578, and n. 6, 50 L.Ed.2d 494 (1977).[5]

Section 3(f) of the FLSA provides:

"'Agriculture' includes farming in all its branches and among other things includes the cultivation and tillage of the soil, dairying, the production, cultivation, growing, and harvesting of any agricultural or horticultural commodities (including commodities defined as agricultural commodities in section 1141j(g) of title 12), the raising of livestock, bees, fur-bearing animals, or poultry, and any practices (including any forestry or lumbering operations) performed by a farmer or on a farm as an incident to or in conjunction with such farming operations, including preparation for market, delivery to storage or to market or to carriers for transportation to market." 29 U.S.C. §203(f).

This definition, we have explained, "includes farming in both a primary and a secondary sense." *Bayside,* 429 U.S., at 300, 97 S.Ct., at 579. "Primary farming" includes the occupations listed first in §3(f): "the cultivation and tillage of the soil, dairying, the production, cultivation, growing, and harvesting of any agricultural or horticultural commodities ... [and] the raising of livestock, bees, fur-bearing animals, or poultry." 29 U.S.C. §203(f). "Secondary farming" has a broader meaning, encompassing, as stated in the second part of §3(f): "any practices ... performed by a farmer or on a farm as an incident to or in conjunction with such farming operations, including preparation for market, delivery to storage or to market or to carriers for transportation to market." *Ibid.; see Bayside,* 429 U.S., at 300, n. 7, 97 S.Ct., at 579, n. 7; *Farmers Reservoir & Irrigation Co. v. McComb,* 337 U.S. 755, 763, 69 S.Ct. 1274, 1278, 93 L.Ed. 1672 (1949) (secondary farming embraces "any practices, whether or not themselves farming practices, which are performed either by a farmer or on a farm, incidently to or in conjunction with 'such' farming operations").

If a statute's meaning is plain, the Board and reviewing courts "must give effect to the unambiguously expressed intent of Congress." *Chevron U.S.A. Inc. v. Natural Resources Defense Council, Inc.,* 467 U.S. 837, 843, 104 S.Ct. 2778, 2781, 81 L.Ed.2d 694 (1984). When the legislative prescription is not free from ambiguity, the administrator must choose between conflicting reasonable interpretations. Courts, in turn, must respect the judgment of the agency empowered to apply the law "to varying fact patterns," *Bayside,* 429 U.S., at

---

5. The most recent congressional rider states: "[N]o part of [the Board's] appropriation shall be available to organize or assist in organizing agricultural laborers or used in connection with investigations, hearings, directives, or orders concerning bargaining units composed of agricultural laborers as referred to in section 2(3) of the [NLRA] ... and as defined in section 3(f) of the [FLSA]." Pub.L. 103-333, Tit. IV, 108 Stat. 2569–2570.

304, 97 S.Ct., at 581, even if the issue "with nearly equal reason [might] be resolved one way rather than another," *id.*, at 302, 97 S.Ct., at 580 (citing *Farmers Reservoir*, 337 U.S., at 770, 69 S.Ct., at 1282 (Frankfurter, J., concurring)). We note, furthermore, that administrators and reviewing courts must take care to assure that exemptions from NLRA coverage are not so expansively interpreted as to deny protection to workers the Act was designed to reach. *See* 48 F.3d, at 1370 (citing *NLRB v. Cal-Maine Farms, Inc.*, 998 F.2d 1336, 1339 (C.A.5 1993));[6] *cf. Arnold v. Ben Kanowsky, Inc.*, 361 U.S. 388, 392, 80 S.Ct. 453, 456, 4 L.Ed.2d 393 (1960) (exemptions from the FLSA "are to be narrowly construed against the employers seeking to assert them"); *Mitchell v. Kentucky Finance Co.*, 359 U.S. 290, 295, 79 S.Ct. 756, 759, 3 L.Ed.2d 815 (1959) ("It is well settled that exemptions from the Fair Labor Standards Act are to be narrowly construed.").

III

Primary farming includes the raising of poultry. *See Bayside,* 429 U.S., at 300–301, 97 S.Ct., at 578–579. All agree that the independent growers, who raise Holly Farms' broiler chickens on their own farms, are engaged in primary agriculture. But we confront no contention that Holly Farms' live-haul employees are themselves engaged in raising poultry.[7] Thus, the only question we resolve is whether the chicken catchers, forklift operators, and truckdrivers are engaged in secondary agriculture—that is, practices "performed by a farmer or on a farm as an incident to or in conjunction with such farming operations." 29 U.S.C. § 203(f).

We take up, initially, the "performed by a farmer" strand of FLSA § 3(f). We do not labor over the point, for our decision in Bayside securely leads us to the conclusion that the live-haul activities are not performed "by a farmer." In *Bayside*, we considered the application of § 3(f)'s "by a farmer" specification to integrated agricultural companies that contract out farming work. We upheld the Board's rejection of the contention that "all of the activity on a contract farm should be regarded as agricultural activity of an integrated farmer" such as Holly Farms. 429 U.S., at 302, 97 S.Ct., at 580. When an integrated poultry producer "contracts with independent growers for the care and feeding of [its] chicks, [its] status as a farmer engaged in raising poultry ends with respect to those chicks." *Id.*, at 302, n. 9, 97 S.Ct., at 580, n. 9 ... Accordingly, when the live-haul employees arrive on the independent farms to collect broilers for carriage to slaughter and processing, Holly

6. The legislative history suggests that Congress, in linking the definition of "agricultural laborer" in NLRA § 2(3) to § 3(f) of the FLSA, intended to cabin the exemption. The version of the appropriations rider first adopted by the House incorporated the definition of "agricultural laborer" contained in the Social Security Act Amendments of 1939, 53 Stat. 1377. *See* 92 Cong. Rec. 6689–6692 (1946). Some lawmakers, however, objected that the amendment contained a "very broad definitio[n] of agricultural laborer excluding a great number of processing employees" from NLRA coverage. *See id.*, at 9514 (statement of Sen. Ball). After some debate—and upon consultation with a Board member and Board counsel—the Conference Committee agreed to substitute the "much narrower definition" supplied by § 3(f) of the FLSA. *See ibid.* The dissent's reading of § 3(f), while a plausible construction of a text we, the Board, and the Secretary of Labor find less than crystalline, *see infra*, at 1406, is inharmonious with a congressional will to create a slim exemption from the encompassing protection the NLRA and the FLSA afford employees in our Nation's commercial enterprises.

7. Holly Farms, it is true, ultimately argues that the catching and loading of broilers slated for slaughter constitute primary agriculture because those activities are best viewed as the "harvesting" of chickens. *See* Brief for Petitioners 29–30. But Holly Farms failed to advance this argument before the Court of Appeals, and it did not home in on this contention in its petition for certiorari. Because we "generally do not address arguments that were not the basis for the decision below," *Matsushita Elec. Industrial Co. v. Epstein*, 516 U.S. 367, 379, 116 S.Ct. 873, 880, 134 L.Ed.2d 6 (1996), we decline to entertain Holly Farms' primary farming argument.

Farms does not resume its status as "farmer" with respect to those birds, the status Holly Farms had weeks before, when the birds were hatched in its hatcheries. This conclusion, we note, entirely disposes of the contention that the truckdrivers are employed in secondary agriculture, for Holly Farms acknowledges that these crew members do not work "on a farm."

We turn, now, to the nub of the case for the chicken catchers and forklift operators: the "on a farm" strand of FLSA § 3(f).

A

Holly Farms argues that under the plain language of the statute, the catching and loading of broilers qualifies as work performed "on a farm as an incident to" the raising of poultry. The corporation emphasizes that § 3(f) of the FLSA enumerates "preparation for market" and "delivery to storage or to market" among activities that count as "agriculture." The live-haul employees' work, Holly Farms concludes, thus falls within the domain of the FLSA exemption and, accordingly, enjoys no NLRA protection.

We find Holly Farms' position to be a plausible, but not an inevitable, construction of § 3(f). Hence, we turn to the Board's position, examining only its reasonableness as an interpretation of the governing legislation.

B

While agreeing that the chicken catchers and forklift operators work "on a farm," the Board contends that their catch and cage work is not incidental to farming operations. Rather, the work is tied to Holly Farms' slaughtering and processing operations, activities that do not constitute "farming" under the statute. We conclude, as we next explain, that the Board's position "is based on a reasonable interpretation of the statute, is consistent with the Board's prior holdings, and is supported by the Secretary of Labor's construction of § 3(f)." Bayside, 429 U.S., at 303, 97 S.Ct., at 580 (footnotes omitted).

1

The Board underscores the statutory words "such farming operations." It does not suffice that the alleged secondary agriculture consists of "preparation for market," or "delivery to storage or to market," the Board maintains; to qualify for the statutory exemption, the Board urges, the work must be incidental to, or conjoined with, primary farming operations.[8] As just explained, see supra, at 1402, at the growing stage in the short life of a

---

8. As we noted in *Farmers Reservoir & Irrigation Co. v. McComb*, 337 U.S. 755, 69 S.Ct. 1274, 93 L.Ed. 1672 (1949), Congress specifically added the words "or on a farm" to FLSA § 3(f) to address some Senators' objections that the exemption otherwise would not cover "the threshing of wheat or other functions necessary to the farmer if those functions were not performed by the farmer and his hands, but by separate companies organized for and devoted solely to that particular job." *See id.*, at 767, 69 S.Ct., at 1280–1281 (citing 81 Cong. Rec. 7653 (1937)). Nothing in the Board's decision detracts from the application of § 3(f), based on the "on a farm" language, to employees of "separate companies organized for and devoted solely to" auxiliary work in aid of a farming enterprise. Hence, the words "on a farm" do the work intended, and are not redundant. *But see post*, at 1408.

Holly Farms presses the argument that its live-haul employees are analogous to the wheat threshers who figured in FLSA § 3(f)'s legislative history. The Board reasonably responds, however, that any worker—whether a wheat thresher, a feed-haul driver, or a chicken catcher—must perform his or her work "as an incident to or in conjunction with such farming operations" in order to fall under the agricultural exemption. If the chicken catching crews were employed by the independent growers, rather than by Holly Farms' processing operation, those crews would more closely resemble the wheat threshers contemplated by the framers of § 3(f).

broiler, Holly Farms is not involved in primary farming, but the contract growers are. The essential question, then, is whether the live-haul employees' activities are inevitably "incident to or in conjunction with" the farming operations of the independent growers.[9] The Board answers this question in the negative. *See Imco Poultry*, 202 N.L.R.B., at 261 (Because chicken catching crews "have no business relationship with the independent farmers, we conclude that the employees' activities were not incidental to the independent farmers' poultry raising operations.").

We find the Board's answer reasonable. Once the broilers have grown on the farm for seven weeks, the growers' contractual obligation to raise the birds ends, and the work of the live-haul crew begins. The record reflects minimal overlap between the work of the live-haul crew and the independent growers' raising activities. The growers do not assist the live-haul crews in catching or loading the chickens; their only responsibilities are to move certain equipment from the chicken coops prior to the crews' arrival, and to be present when the crews are on the farms. Nor do the live-haul employees play any role in the growers' performance of their contractual undertakings.

The record, furthermore, supports the Board's conclusion that the live-haul crews' activities were conjoined with Holly Farms' processing operations, rather than with farming.[10] The chicken catchers, forklift operators, and truckdrivers work as a unit. They all "work out of the processing plant" in Wilkesboro, located three miles from the hatcheries. Crew members begin and end each shift by punching a timeclock at the processing plant and are functionally integrated with other processing-plant employees. *See also* App. to Pet. for Cert. A-396 (correlation between Holly Farms' slaughter rate and work available for live-haul crews); App. 29a (live production manager for Holly Farms' Wilkesboro facility described catching and delivery of grown broilers as the first step in the producer's processing operations). The Board's determination, in sum, has the requisite "warrant in the record." *Bayside*, 429 U.S., at 304, n. 14, 97 S.Ct., at 581, n. 14.

We think it sensible, too, that the Board homed in on the status of the live-haul crews' employer. The employer's status respecting the particular activity at issue accounts for the Board's determination that Holly Farms' "egg haulers" (who transport eggs from the laying houses to the hatcheries), and "pullet catchers" (who collect the breeding-destined birds on the farms of independent growers) rank as "agricultural laborer[s]." As the record shows, the pullet catchers and egg haulers work in Holly Farms' hatchery operations, while the live-haul employees—who deal only with broilers—work out of the process-

---

9. To this question, the dissent asserts "there can be only one answer." *Post*, at 1409. In the dissent's view, activities "directly related to the farming operations that occurred on that very farm"— in this case, removing chickens from the independent growers' farms to make room for more—inescapably satisfy the statute. *Post*, at 1409. FLSA § 3(f), all agree, does not apply absent a connection between the activity in question and the primary farming operations conducted "on a farm." But the statutory language—"incident to or in conjunction with"—does not place beyond rational debate the nature or extent of the required connection. *See* 29 CFR § 780.144 (1995) (recognition by the Secretary of Labor that the "line between practices that are and those that are not performed 'as an incident to or in conjunction with' such farming operations is not susceptible of precise definition").

10. Holly Farms argues, and the dissent agrees, post, at 1409, that the Board's conclusion rests on the assumption that a given activity can be incidental to one thing only—in this case, either processing or farming, but not both. At oral argument, counsel for the Board stated that Holly Farms had not accurately conveyed the Board's position. Tr. of Oral Arg. 33, 38. The Board apparently recognizes, as do we, that an activity can be incidental to more than one thing. To gain the agricultural exemption, however, farming must be an enterprise to which the activity at issue is incidental. The relevant question under the statute, therefore, is whether the work of the live-haul crews qualifies as incidental to farming.

ing plant. "There is no interchange between these classifications. Broiler haulers do not haul pullets and pullet haulers do not haul broilers." Accordingly, the Board reasonably aligned the pullet catchers and egg haulers with Holly Farms' poultry-raising operation, and the live-haul employees with the corporation's slaughtering and processing activities.

2

The Board's decision regarding Holly Farms' live-haul crews adheres to longstanding NLRB precedent. For more than 23 years, the NLRB has maintained that vertically integrated poultry producers' employees who "handl[e] and transpor[t] chicks on the farms of independent growers only after [the poultry producers'] farming operations have ended ... cannot be performing practices incident to, or in conjunction with, [their employer's] farming operations." *Imco Poultry*, 202 N.L.R.B., at 260. Rather, such employees, the Board has repeatedly ruled, perform work "incident to, or in conjunction with, a separate and distinct business activity of [their employer], i.e., shipping and marketing." *Id.*, at 261. *See also Draper Valley Farms, Inc.*, 307 N.L.R.B., at 1440 ("We think it follows plainly from Imco that the Employer's chicken catchers are not, when working on the farms of independent growers who have concluded their 'raising' activities, exempt as agricultural laborers."); *Seaboard Farms of Kentucky, Inc.*, 311 N.L.R.B. No. 159 (1993) (same).[11]

3

In construing the agricultural laborer exemption, the Board endeavors to "follow, whenever possible, the interpretations of Section 3(f) adopted by the Department of Labor, the agency which is charged with the responsibility for and has the experience of administering the Fair Labor Standards Act." ... The Board has not departed from that endeavor here.[12] The Department of Labor's regulations do not address the precise situation of the live-haul workers before us, nor are the regulations free from ambiguity. We agree with the Board, however, that they are consistent with "employee" characterization of the crews that catch grown chickens for carriage to Holly Farms' processing plant.

On contract arrangements for raising poultry, the Department of Labor has issued an interpretative regulation, which we noted in *Bayside*, 429 U.S., at 303–304, n. 13, 97 S.Ct., at 580–581, n. 13, as follows:

> "Feed dealers and processors sometimes enter into contractual arrangements with farmers under which the latter agree to raise to marketable size baby chicks supplied by the former who also undertake to furnish all the required feed and

---

11. Our decision in *Maneja v. Waialua Agricultural Co.*, 349 U.S. 254, 75 S.Ct. 719, 99 L.Ed. 1040 (1955), does not cast doubt on the Board's view of operations like Holly Farms. In that case, which did not involve a Board ruling, we held that railroad workers employed by an integrated sugar cane producer were exempt, as "agricultural laborer[s]," from FLSA overtime provisions. The employer in *Maneja,* unlike Holly Farms, grew and cultivated its sugar cane autonomously, without the aid of independent growers; hence, we concluded that the activities of the railroad workers, who hauled the freshly cut cane from the sugar fields to the processing plant, were incidental to the employer's primary farming operations. *Id.*, at 262–263, 75 S.Ct., at 724–725.

12. *Coleman v. Sanderson Farms, Inc.*, 629 F.2d 1077 (C.A.5 1980), which determined that chicken catching crews were employed in "agriculture" under § 3(f), involved a dispute over applicability of the FLSA's overtime provisions, not over union representation. Thus, the court in that case was not required to respect the position of the Board. See id., at 1081, n. 4. We note, however, that the Coleman court did not advert to the Secretary of Labor's interpretations of § 3(f).

possibly additional items. Typically, the feed dealer or processor retains title to the chickens until they are sold. Under such an arrangement, the activities of the farmers and their employees in raising the poultry are clearly within section 3(f). The activities of the feed dealer or processor, on the other hand, are not 'raising of poultry,' and employees engaged in them cannot be considered agricultural employees on that ground. Employees of the feed dealer or processor who perform work on a farm as an incident to or in conjunction with the raising of poultry on the farm are employed in 'secondary' agriculture (*see* §§ 780.137 et seq. [explaining that work must be performed in connection with the farmer-employer's own farming to qualify as 'secondary' agriculture by a farmer] and *Johnston v. Cotton Producers Assn.*, 244 F.2d 553)." 29 CFR § 780.126 (1995).

This regulation suggests that live-haul crews surely are not engaged in a primary farming operation. The crews could rank as workers engaged in "secondary" agriculture if they "perform[ed] work on a farm as an incident to or in conjunction with the raising of poultry on the farm." Ibid. As we developed earlier, see supra, at 1403–1404, in the Board's judgment, the crews do not fit that bill. The live-haul crew members perform their work, as the Board sees it, not "as an incident to" poultry raising by independent growers, but "incident to" and "in conjunction with" the slaughter and processing of chickens at Holly Farms' Wilkesboro plant. In the Board's words, the crews are tied to "a separate and distinct business activity," the business of processing poultry for retail sale, *see Imco Poultry*, 202 N.L.R.B., at 261, not to the anterior work of agriculture.[13]

Other Department of Labor regulations are in harmony with the Board's conclusion that the live-haul crews do not engage in secondary farming because their work, though "on a farm," is not performed "as an incident to or in conjunction with" the independent growers' poultry-raising operations. Thus, 29 CFR § 780.129 (1995) reiterates that the work "must be performed 'as an incident to or in conjunction with' the farming operations," and § 780.143 adds:

> The fact that a practice performed on a farm is not performed by or for the farmer is a strong indication that it is not performed in connection with the farming operations there conducted. *Ibid.*

The same regulation, § 780.143, further states that, in determining whether a practice is performed "for" a farmer, it is "highly significant" whether the practice involves property to which the farmer has title or for which the farmer otherwise has responsibility. Ibid. Holly Farms retains title to the chicks and, once the live-haul crew undertakes its catch and remove operation, the independent grower "divest[s] himself of further responsibility with respect to the product." *Ibid.*[14]

---

13. The Department of Labor's interpretative regulation, 29 CFR § 780.126 (1995), includes a citation to Johnston v. Cotton Producers Assn., 244 F.2d, 553, 554 (C.A.5 1957). That case is readily distinguishable from the case before us. In *Johnston*, the Court of Appeals held that an employee of a rural farm supply store was exempt from FLSA minimum wage and overtime requirements as an agricultural laborer. The supply store sold baby chicks to farmers, while "retain[ing] title to the chicks as security for the purchase price and for advances for feed, supplies, or equipment." *Ibid.* While the supply store employee caught, cooped, and loaded chickens onto trucks for delivery to processors—entities independent of the supply store—that employee also "supervise[d] the growing of chicks by [independent] growers on their farms." Ibid. By contrast, in this case there is no contention that any of the live-haul employees similarly assist the independent growers in their chick-raising activities.

14. Petitioners point to 29 CFR § 780.151(k) (1995), which defines the FLSA § 3(f) words "preparation for market" to include "[c]ulling, grading, cooping, and loading" of poultry. See Brief for Petitioners 23. As another regulation emphasizes, however, "'preparation for market,' like other practices,

The Department of Labor candidly observed that "[t]he line between practices that are and those that are not performed 'as an incident to or in conjunction with' such farming operations is not susceptible of precise definition." § 780.144. This acknowledgment accords with our recognition that the meaning of FLSA § 3(f) is not so "plain" as to bear only one permissible construction in the context at hand.

IV

In sum, we find persuasive the Board's conclusion that the collection of broilers for slaughter was an activity serving Holly Farms' processing operations, and not Holly Farms' own or the independent growers' farming operations. Again, we stress that "the reviewing court's function is limited." *Bayside*, 429 U.S., at 304, n. 14, 97 S.Ct., at 581, n. 14. For the Board to prevail, it need not show that its construction is the best way to read the statute; rather, courts must respect the Board's judgment so long as its reading is a reasonable one. "[R]egardless of how we might have resolved the question as an initial matter," *Bayside*, 429 U.S., at 304, 97 S.Ct., at 581, the Board's decision here reflects a reasonable interpretation of the law and, therefore, merits our approbation. The judgment of the Court of Appeals is accordingly

Affirmed.

Justice O'CONNOR, with whom THE CHIEF JUSTICE, Justice SCALIA, and Justice THOMAS join, concurring in the judgment in part and dissenting in part.

Today the Court concludes that three categories of workers fall outside the definition of "agricultural laborer" supplied by § 3(f) the Fair Labor Standards Act of 1938 (FLSA) and § 2(3) of the National Labor Relations Act (NLRA): (1) Holly Farms' chicken catchers, who labor on a farm manually rounding up, catching, and caging live chickens, (2) forklift operators, who then load the caged chickens onto the bed of a flatbed truck, and (3) live-haul drivers, who drive the loaded trucks to Holly Farms' processing plants, where the chickens are slaughtered and prepared for market. I concur in the Court's judgment with respect to the live-haul drivers, since their work is neither performed "by a farmer" nor "on a farm." But the Court's conclusion that Holly Farms' chicken catchers and forklift operators do not perform agricultural work runs contrary to common sense and finds no support in the text of the relevant statute. Because the definition supplied by Congress makes clear that the chicken catchers and forklift operators are agricultural workers exempt from the reach of the NLRA, I respectfully dissent.

The Court devotes the bulk of its opinion to an analysis of the reasonableness of the National Labor Relations Board's (Board) interpretation of the statute, but gives remarkably short shrift to the statute itself. The Court dismisses Holly Farms' claim that the plain language of the statute covers the chicken catchers and forklift operators with the conclusory remark that Holly Farms' reading of the statute is "a plausible, but not an inevitable, construction of § 3(f)." *Ante*, at 1402. In my view, however, the language of the statute is unambiguous.

As we said in *Chevron U.S.A. Inc. v. Natural Resources Defense Council, Inc.*, 467 U.S. 837, 104 S.Ct. 2778, 81 L.Ed.2d 694 (1984): "First, always, is the question whether Congress has directly spoken to the precise question at issue. If the intent of Congress is clear, that is the end of the matter; for the court, as well as the agency, must give effect to the unambiguously expressed intent of Congress." *Id.*, at 842–843, 104 S.Ct., at 2781. None

---

must be performed 'by a farmer or on a farm as an incident to or in conjunction with such farming operations' in order to be within [FLSA] section 3(f)." 29 CFR § 780.150 (1995).

of our precedents sanction blind adherence to the Board's position when it is directly contrary to the plain language of the relevant statute. See, e.g., *NLRB v. Brown*, 380 U.S. 278, 291, 85 S.Ct. 980, 988, 13 L.Ed.2d 839 (1965) ("Reviewing courts are not obliged to stand aside and rubber-stamp their affirmance of administrative decisions that they deem inconsistent with a statutory mandate or that frustrate the congressional policy underlying a statute"); *American Ship Building Co. v. NLRB*, 380 U.S. 300, 318, 85 S.Ct. 955, 967, 13 L.Ed.2d 855 (1965) ("The deference owed to an expert tribunal cannot be allowed to slip into a judicial inertia …"). Section 3(f) of the FLSA defines agriculture as "farming in all its branches," including "the raising of … poultry," as well as "any practices … performed by a farmer or on a farm as an incident to or in conjunction with such farming operations." 29 U.S.C. §203(f) (emphasis added). The coverage intended by Congress under both the FLSA and the NLRA is best determined by consulting the language of the statute at issue. Because the relevant portions of §3(f) are perfectly plain and "directly [speak] to the precise question at issue," *Chevron, supra*, at 842, 104 S.Ct., at 2781, I would hold that the chicken catchers and forklift operators are agricultural laborers and that the Board's contrary conclusion does not deserve deference.

The Court's determination rests largely upon a misreading of the statute in two respects. First, the Court tethers the "or on a farm" clause of §3(f) to the employment relationship (or lack thereof) between the chicken catchers and forklift operators and the independent farmer who is charged with raising the chickens. And second, the Court decides that the secondary farming activities performed by the chicken catchers and forklift operators must not only be "incident" to the independent farmer's primary farming activities, but must be "mainly" or "most tightly" tied thereto. Neither conclusion finds support in the language of §3(f).

The Court's first error stems from its adoption of the Board's focus on the lack of a direct employment relationship between the live-haul workers and the independent growers. But the "or on a farm" clause nowhere mentions the nature of the employment relationship. Instead, it is plainly concerned only with the nature of the work performed by the worker. The Board's interpretation must be rejected, as it would read the "or on a farm" clause out of the statute entirely.

The Court relies on the legislative history underlying the "or on a farm" clause, which we described in *Farmers Reservoir & Irrigation Co. v. McComb*, 337 U.S. 755, 763, 69 S.Ct. 1274, 1278, 93 L.Ed. 1672 (1949). That history reveals that the clause was intended to include within the statutory definition work performed on a farm that was "necessary to" the farming operations but not performed by the farmer himself. *Id.*, at 767, 69 S.Ct., at 1280. One example figures prominently in the legislative history: a wheat thresher who travels from farm to farm performing wheat threshing chores for small farmers on a contract basis. The Court reasons that Holly Farms' employees are unlike the fictional wheat thresher, however, in that they are employed by Holly Farms, rather than by the independent growers themselves. *See ante*, at 1403, n. 8 ("If the chicken catching crews were employed by the independent growers, rather than by Holly Farms' processing operation, those crews would more closely resemble the wheat threshers contemplated by the framers of §3(f)").

The Court and the Board emphasize formal contractual arrangements to the virtual exclusion of practical realities. The fact that Holly Farms supplies the services of the chicken catchers and forklift operators seems entirely beside the point; the work performed by these employees is precisely the same whether they are hired by Holly Farms or by the independent growers. And the notion that Congress intended the status of the chicken catchers and forklift operators to turn on such a readily manipulable criterion strains credibility. If the live-haul crew's status depends only upon who "hires" them to perform the work, Holly Farms can simply charge the independent growers with raising and catching, caging, and cooping the chickens, and require the independent growers to hire Holly Farms' own live-haul workers to perform those tasks.

The Court's quotation from *Imco Poultry, Div. of Int'l Multifoods Corp.*, 202 N.L.R.B. 259 (1973), reveals precisely where the Board and the Court have gone astray: The Board takes the position that live-haul workers "'cannot be performing practices incident to, or in conjunction with, [their employer's] farming operations.'" Ante, at 1404 (quoting Imco Poultry, supra, at 260). But the statute does not require that work be performed "incident to or in conjunction with" one's employer's farming operations, but only incident to or in conjunction with "such" farming operations—the antecedent for which term is plainly the first clause of § 3(f), to wit, "farming in all its branches," including "the raising of ... poultry." If the sine qua non of status as an agricultural laborer is employment by the farmer or the independent grower, the "or on a farm" clause is redundant, because chicken catching crews that are agents or employees of the farmers themselves fall within the "by a farmer" clause. Ordinarily, "terms connected by a disjunctive [are] given separate meanings, unless the context dictates otherwise." ... The "or on a farm" clause has independent significance only if the work encompassed by that clause is performed by someone other than a farmer or the farmer's own agents or employees. Chevron deference is not owed to a Board construction of the statute that effectively redacts one of the statute's operative clauses.

The Court also cites with approval a Department of Labor (DOL) interpretive regulation that addresses contractual arrangements for raising poultry such as those between Holly Farms and the independent growers. The DOL regulation declares that "[e]mployees of [a] feed dealer or processor who perform work on a farm as an incident to or in conjunction with the raising of poultry on the farm are employed in 'secondary' agriculture." 29 CFR § 780.126 (1995). The Court thus accepts as reasonable a DOL regulation that plainly suggests that even workers employed by a poultry processor such as Holly Farms can be engaged in secondary agriculture and also accepts as reasonable a Board interpretation of § 3(f) that, in essence, dictates that employees of a processor cannot be employed in secondary agriculture. See ante, at 1404 ("We think it sensible ... that the Board homed in on the status of the live-haul crews' *employer*") (emphasis in original). The Court cannot have it both ways, and it need not, since the "or on a farm" clause is plainly indifferent to the nature of the employment relationship.

The Court's second misstep likewise derives from its deference to a Board construction that lacks foundation in the statute. Section 3(f) exempts work performed "as an incident to or in conjunction with" primary farming operations. The statutory language manifestly does not disqualify the work from agricultural status if it also "serve[s]," or is "tied to," some other enterprise. Even accepting the Court's conclusion that the work of the chicken catchers and forklift operators is "incident to" Holly Farms' processing operations, those workers fall within the § 3(f) definition so long as their work is also "incident to or in conjunction with" the farming operations performed by the independent growers.

As Holly Farms points out, the Board's contrary position hinges on the premise that a given activity can only be incident to one thing—either processing or farming, but not both. But the Board's position cannot be squared with the statute itself, which places no conditions upon the statutory prerequisite that work be "incident to or in conjunction with" covered farming operations. Indeed, the wheat thresher of the legislative history was clearly performing work "incident to" the business operations of the wheat threshing enterprise as well as "incident to" the farmer's farming operations. The statutory requirement is simple, and the imposition of a more stringent prerequisite must be rejected as contrary to the statute itself.

When the chicken catchers and forklift operators arrive at the farm of an independent grower to catch, cage, and load the live chickens in preparation for their delivery to market, they are certainly doing work that is directly related to the farming operations that occurred on that very farm during the preceding weeks: the raising of poultry. As Holly Farms points out, unless the chickens are caught, caged, and removed from the farm, the independent grower's farming operations will have been for naught. The independent grower must see to it that the chickens grow to the designated age and are caught, removed, and replaced with new chicks for the next growing cycle. And the fact that § 3(f) lists "preparation for market" as one of the activities that customarily is "incident to or in conjunction with" covered farming operations buttresses petitioners' argument.

The Court's response relies on the facts that the independent grower's contractual duties have ended, that the workers punch a timeclock in Holly Farms' processing plant rather than in Farmer Brown's barn, and that Holly Farms rather than the independent grower signs their paychecks at the end of the day. But these facts are irrelevant to the statutory definition. Section 3(f) asks only whether the chicken catchers and forklift operators perform work "on a farm" (which all parties concede they do) and whether that work is "incident to or in conjunction with such farming operations"—that is, whether the activities of the chicken catching crews are "incident to" the covered farming operations that take place on the farms of the independent growers, the raising of poultry for slaughter. To that question, there can be only one answer.

Because the Court today defers to an NLRB interpretation that runs directly contrary to the statutory language, I respectfully dissent from the Court's conclusion with respect to the chicken catchers and forklift operators.

Notes

1. As noted in *Holly Farms*, Congress reaffirms the exemption of agricultural laborers from the NLRA each year when it passes the appropriations bill that funds the National Labor Relations Board. The following language is included:

Departments of Labor, Health and Human Services, and Education, and Related Agencies Appropriations Act, 2006
Pub. L. No. 109–149 (2005)

Making appropriations for the Departments of Labor, Health and Human Services, and Education, and related agencies for the fiscal year ending September 30, 2010, and for other purposes.

H. R. 3293
Report No. 111–220

NATIONAL LABOR RELATIONS BOARD
SALARIES AND EXPENSES

For expenses necessary for the National Labor Relations Board to carry out the functions vested in it by the Labor-Management Relations Act, 1947, and other laws, $283,400,000: *Provided, That no part of this appropriation shall be available*

> *to organize or assist in organizing agricultural laborers or used in connection with investigations, hearings, directives, or orders concerning bargaining units composed of agricultural laborers as referred to in section 2(3) of the Act of July 5, 1935, and as amended by the Labor-Management Relations Act, 1947, and as defined in section 3(f) of the Act of June 25, 1938*, and including in said definition employees engaged in the maintenance and operation of ditches, canals, reservoirs, and waterways when maintained or operated on a mutual, nonprofit basis and at least 95 percent of the water stored or supplied thereby is used for farming purposes (emphasis added).

2. Labor law scholars and farmworker advocates have criticized the exclusion of agricultural laborers from the NLRA protection as unfair. *See, e.g.*, Michael H. LeRoy & Wallace Hendricks, *Should "Agricultural Laborers" Continue to Be Excluded From the National Labor Relations Act?* 48 EMORY L.J. 489 (1999).

2. The Fair Labor Standards Act

The Fair Labor Standards Act (FLSA), at 29 U.S.C. §§ 201–219, includes provisions requiring the payment of a minimum wage and the payment of enhanced overtime wages; restrictions on the employment of children; and requirements for employer record keeping. Coverage of the statute is broadly linked to either the employee's interstate commerce connection, the sale of the goods produced in interstate commerce, or with some limitations, the enterprise's involvement in interstate commerce. 29 U.S.C. § 206.

Federal Law vs. State Law

The FLSA expressly requires compliance with all other federal, state, and local laws that are not conflicting. 29 U.S.C. § 206. If any of these laws provide standards or employment requirements that exceed those required under FLSA, the higher standard is enforceable. In some instances, state or local laws provide additional protections for workers, and sometimes, the exemptions provided to agricultural employers are not as broad. The more stringent requirements will apply.

Employment Under the FLSA

The FLSA provides protections for workers by requiring "employers" to treat their "employees" in certain ways. Therefore, key to a determination as to whether FLSA requirements are applicable is a determination as to whether an employment relationship exists. The FLSA provides that:

> "Employer" includes any person acting directly or indirectly in the interest of an employer in relation to an employee and includes a public agency, but does not include any labor organization (other than when acting as an employer) or anyone acting in the capacity of officer or agent of such labor organization.

29 U.S.C. § 203(d).

Subject to certain exceptions, the term "employee" means "any individual employed by an employer." 29 U.S.C. § 203(e)(1). To "employ" is broadly defined as "to suffer or permit to work." 29 U.S.C. § 203(g).

When a farming operation has seasonal labor needs, the farm operator may hire workers directly or make arrangements with a "farm labor contractor" (FLC) to supply the farm with the needed crew of laborers. The arrangements with an FLC may raise questions regarding the relationships between the farmer, the FLC and the workers.

If the FLC is an employee of the farmer, it follows that the workers recruited by the FLC are also employees of the farmer. *See, e.g.,* 29 C.F.R. § 500.20(h)(4). If, however, the FLC is an independent contractor, the farmer may argue that the workers are not his or her employees, that they are employed by the FLC. If they are not the farmer's employees, arguably, the FLSA requirements may not apply to the farmer. The only person potentially liable would be the FLC. Similarly, either the farmer or the FLC may argue that the workers themselves are actually working as independent contractors and are not employees under the FLSA.

The courts and the Department of Labor regulations have attempted to articulate a standard for determining whether an independent contractor relationship exists, keeping in mind that there has been substantial abuse among employers seeking to use this characterization as a means for avoiding labor laws. Both have agreed that the test for independent contractor status should be based on the "economic reality" of the relationship, that is, "whether there is economic dependence" upon the farmer. *U.S. Dept. of Labor v. Lauritzen*, 835 F.2d 1529, 1538 (7th Cir. 1987), cert. denied, 488 U.S. 898 (1988); *Beliz v. McLeod*, 765 F.2d 1317, 1329 (5th Cir. 1985); *Castillo v. Givens*, 704 F.2d 181, 192 (5th Cir.), cert. denied, 464 U.S. 850 (1983); *Real v. Driscoll Strawberry Associates, Inc.*, 603 F.2d 748, 756 (9th Cir. 1979); *See also*, 29 C.F.R. § 500.20(h)(4). Note that the characterization of employment relationships and of independent contracting relationships under the FLSA may not be the same as under other areas of law such as tax law.

Even if the farmer can establish that the FLC was acting as an independent contractor and that the workers on the farm were the employees of the FLC, however, the farmer may still be liable. This result is based on the concept of "joint employment." The regulations define this concept as "a condition in which a single individual stands in the relation of an employee to two or more persons at the same time. *See,* 29 C.F.R. § 500.20(h)(5).

If it is found that a joint employment situation exists, both the FLC and the farmer will be liable for any violations of FLSA requirements.

Minimum Wage Provisions

The minimum wage provision of FLSA is perhaps the most widely known employer requirement. 29 U.S.C. § 206. It requires every employer, unless exempt, to pay a set minimum wage to each employee. Section 213(a)(6) of FLSA, however, provides a very large exemption for agricultural employers. It provides that the minimum wage requirement does not apply to five different categories of employees "employed in agriculture."

Exemptions for Employees Employed in Agriculture

The FLSA sets forth five specific exemptions to the minimum wage requirement that are applicable to those who are employed in agriculture. The first exemption applies to farming operations that do not rely upon a significant amount of non-family labor. The minimum wage requirement does not apply if the employer "did not use more than five hundred man-days of agricultural labor" during any calendar quarter during the preceding year. 29 U.S.C. § 213(a)(6)(A). A "man-day" is defined as a day in which an employee performs any agricultural labor for an hour or more. 29 U.S.C. § 203(e)(3). The employment of immediate family members does not count for purposes of reaching the 500 man-days threshold. 29 U.S.C. § 203(u).

The second minimum wage exemption applies to agricultural employees who are members of the farmer's immediate family. 29 U.S.C. §213(a)(6)(B). These employees need not receive the minimum wage under FLSA.

The third exemption applies to certain hand harvest laborers. Workers included in this exemption must be paid on a piece rate basis, and "in an operation which has been, and is customarily and generally recognized as having been, paid on a piece rate basis in the region of employment." The worker must commute daily from a permanent residence to the farm on which he or she is employed and must have been employed in agriculture less than thirteen weeks during the preceding calendar year. 29 U.S.C. §213(a)(6)(C).

The fourth category of exemption applies to employees who are sixteen years of age or under and are employed as hand harvest laborers on a piece rate basis "in an operation which has been, and is customarily and generally recognized as having been, paid on a piece rate basis in the region of employment." These workers fit within the exemption if they are employed on the same farm as a parent or person standing in the place of a parent, and are paid at the same piece rate as employees over age sixteen are paid on the same farm. 29 U.S.C. §213(a)(6)(D).

The fifth agricultural exemption applies to employees who are principally engaged in the range production of livestock. The employers of these workers are also exempt from the minimum wage requirement. 29 U.S.C. §213(a)(6)(E). As the regulations explain, this exemption is dependent upon the type of work that the employee does and where this work is done. 29 C.F.R. §780.323. As to the work that the employee does, he or she must be "principally engaged" in the production of livestock. This means that the employee's "primary duty" must be "to take care of the animals actively or to stand by in readiness for that purpose." 29 C.F.R. §780.325(a) Ordinarily, primary duty means that this activity will take up more than 50% of the employee's time. *Id.* If this test is met, the employee may spend the rest of the employment time doing other unrelated activities. 29 C.F.R. §780.325(b). As to the location of the work, the term "range" is defined generally as "land that is not cultivated." The regulations also identify it as "land that produces native forage for animal consumption, and includes land that is revegetated naturally or artificially to provide a forage cover that is managed like range vegetation." 29 C.F.R. §780.326. The regulations specifically provide that this exemption cannot be relied upon by feedlot operators. 29 C.F.R. §780.329(c).

Although in many contexts, aquaculture falls within the definition of farming, under the FLSA exemptions, in addition to the general agricultural provision discussed above, there is a specific section that exempts many aquaculture operations. Section 213(a)(5) exempts:

> any employee employed in the catching, taking, propagating, harvesting, culti-
> vating, or farming of any kind of fish, shellfish, crustacea, sponges, seaweeds,
> or other aquatic forms of animal and vegetable life, or in the first processing,
> canning or packing such marine products at sea as an incident to, or in con-
> junction with, such fishing operations, including the going to and returning
> from work and loading and unloading when performed by any such employee.
>
> 29 U.S.C. §213(a)(5).

Overtime Pay

The FLSA requires many employers to pay an enhanced rate of pay, termed "overtime pay," for work that totals more than 40 hours per week. 29 U.S.C. §207(a). The FLSA contains a broad-based overtime pay exemption for agriculture. Section 213(b) provides that the overtime pay requirement does not apply to "any employee employed in agriculture." 29 U.S.C. § 213(b)(12). There is no small farm/large farm distinction, nor is there any additional requirement for the exemption to apply. Section 213 also exempts certain irrigation and ditch work, 29 U.S.C. § 213(b)(12); certain livestock auction workers, 29 U.S.C. § 213(b)(13); certain county elevator employees, 29 U.S.C. § 213(b)(14); employees engaged in the processing of maple sap into sugar, 29 U.S.C. § 213(b)(15); certain workers involved in the in-state transportation of fruits and vegetables, 29 U.S.C. § 213(b)(16); and employees employed in planting or tending trees or involved in forestry and timber operations provided that there are less than eight employees, 29 U.S.C. § 213(b)(28). There is a special exemption with a time limitation that is applicable specifically to cotton ginning, 29 U.S.C. § 213(i), and to the processing of sugar beets, sugar beet molasses, and sugar cane, 29 U.S.C. § 213(j). There is also a limited exemption for workers involved in the production, harvest, and sale of tobacco. 29 U.S.C. § 207(m).

Enforcement of Wage and Hours Violations

The FLSA authorizes the Administrator of the Wage & Hour Division to investigate and inspect employers' payment records in connection with the FLSA requirements. 29 U.S.C. § 211. If a wage violation occurs, the FLSA authorizes an employee to sue his or her employer for unpaid minimum wages or for overtime pay that was not paid. 29 U.S.C. § 216(b). The court, in its discretion, can award liquidated damages of an amount equal to the wages owed to the employee and an award of reasonable attorneys fees and costs. *Id.* The Secretary of Labor is also authorized to sue on behalf of aggrieved employees and/or can also sue to enjoin the FLSA violations. *Id.* Criminal penalties can be imposed for willful and repeated violations. 29 U.S.C. § 216(a).

Child Labor Provisions

Section 212 of the Fair Labor Standards Act makes it unlawful to use "oppressive child labor" in the production of goods for commerce. This section provides:

> No employer shall employ any oppressive child labor in commerce or in the production of goods for commerce or in any enterprise engaged in commerce or in the production of goods for commerce.

29 U.S.C. § 212(c).

What constitutes "oppressive child labor" depends upon the age of the child that is employed, the industry that the employment is in, and the type of work that the child will perform.

Section 203 of FLSA defines "oppressive child labor" as follows:

> (l) "Oppressive child labor" means a condition of employment under which (1) any employee under the age of sixteen years is employed by an employer (other than a parent or a person standing in place of a parent employing his own child or a child in his custody under the age of sixteen years in an occupation other than manufacturing or mining or an occupation found by the Secretary of Labor to be particularly hazardous for the employment of children between the ages of sixteen and eighteen years or detrimental to their health or well-being) in any occupation, or

> (2) any employee between the ages of sixteen and eighteen years is employed by an employer in any occupation which the Secretary of Labor shall find and by order declare to be particularly hazardous for the employment of children

between such ages or detrimental to their health or well-being; but oppressive child labor shall not be deemed to exist by virtue of the employment in any occupation of any person with respect to whom the employer shall have on file an unexpired certificate issued and held pursuant to regulations of the Secretary of Labor certifying that such person is above the oppressive child-labor age. The Secretary of Labor shall provide by regulation or by order that the employment of employees between the ages of fourteen and sixteen years in occupations other than manufacturing and mining shall not be deemed to constitute oppressive child labor if and to the extent that the Secretary of Labor determines that such employment is confined to periods which will not interfere with their schooling and to conditions which will not interfere with their health and well-being.

The FLSA authorizes the Secretary of Labor to establish regulations that require employers to obtain proof of age from their employees. 29 U.S.C. §212(d).

Agricultural employment is treated differently than other forms of employment, with children allowed to work at earlier ages.

Section 213 of FLSA provides in part as follows:

(c) Child labor requirements

(1) Except as provided in paragraph (2) or (4), the provisions of section 212 of this title relating to child labor shall not apply to any employee employed in agriculture outside of school hours for the school district where such employee is living while he is so employed, if such employee—

(A) is less than twelve years of age and (i) is employed by his parent, or by a person standing in the place of his parent, on a farm owned or operated by such parent or person, or (ii) is employed, with the consent of his parent or person standing in the place of his parent, on a farm, none of the employees of which are (because of subsection (a)(6)(A) of this section) required to be paid at the wage rate prescribed by section 206(a)(5) of this title,

(B) is twelve years or thirteen years of age and (i) such employment is with the consent of his parent or person standing in the place of his parent, or (ii) his parent or such person is employed on the same farm as such employee, or

(C) is fourteen years of age or older.

(2) The provisions of section 212 of this title relating to child labor shall apply to an employee below the age of sixteen employed in agriculture in an occupation that the Secretary of Labor finds and declares to be particularly hazardous for the employment of children below the age of sixteen, except where such employee is employed by his parent or by a person standing in the place of his parent on a farm owned or operated by such parent or person....

29 U.S.C. §213(c).

At the specific request of groups of strawberry and potato growers, the FLSA was amended in 1977 to provide an additional exemption for the use of child labor in agriculture. This provision, referred to as the "strawberry amendment," provides:

(4)(A) An employer or group of employers may apply to the Secretary for a waiver of the application of section 212 of this title to the employment for not more than eight weeks in any calendar year of individuals who are less than twelve years of age, but not less than ten years of age, as hand harvest laborers in an agricultural operation which has been, and is customarily and generally recognized as being, paid on a piece rate basis in the region in which such individuals would be employed. The Secretary may not grant such a waiver unless he finds, based on objective data submitted by the applicant, that—

(i) the crop to be harvested is one with a particularly short harvesting season and the application of section 212 of this title would cause severe economic disruption in the industry of the employer or group of employers applying for the waiver;

(ii) the employment of the individuals to whom the waiver would apply would not be deleterious to their health or well-being;

(iii) the level and type of pesticides and other chemicals used would not have an adverse effect on the health or well-being of the individuals to whom the waiver would apply;

(iv) individuals age twelve and above are not available for such employment; and

(v) the industry of such employer or group of employers has traditionally and substantially employed individuals under twelve years of age without displacing substantial job opportunities for individuals over sixteen years of age.

(B) Any waiver granted by the Secretary under subparagraph (A) shall require that—

(i) the individuals employed under such waiver be employed outside of school hours for the school district where they are living while so employed;

(ii) such individuals while so employed commute daily from their permanent residence to the farm on which they are so employed; and

(iii) such individuals be employed under such waiver (I) for not more than eight weeks between June 1 and October 15 of any calendar year, and (II) in accordance with such other terms and conditions as the Secretary shall prescribe for such individuals' protection.

29 U.S.C. § 213(d).

Notes

1. Because the NLRA definition of "agriculture" is based on the Fair Labor Standards Act (FLSA) definition, the holding in *Holly Farms* has been extended to FLSA worker protections. *Herman v. Tyson Foods, Inc.*, 82 F. Supp.2d 631 (2000) (holding that chicken catchers are not agricultural workers and thus are not exempt from FLSA overtime pay requirements). The industry has reportedly switched to a system of hiring independent contractor crews to perform these tasks. That characterization was rejected in *Heath v. Perdue Farms*, 87 F.Supp.2d 452 (D. Md. 2000) (rejecting the characterization of chicken catching crews as independent contractors and penalizing the company for a willful violation of the Fair Labor Standards Act).

2. The presence of so many children, as workers or as companions to their farmworker-parents, has raised serious concern about pesticide exposure.

Pesticides: Improvements Needed to Ensure the Safety of Farmworkers and Their Children

U.S. Government Accountability Office, GAO/RCED-00-40 (March 2000)

Although pesticides play a significant role in increasing food production by reducing the number of crop-destroying pests, exposure to pesticides can be harmful to humans. The ill effects may follow from short- or long-term exposure through skin contact, inhalation, or ingestion. Acute symptoms range from relatively mild headaches to fatigue, nausea, skin rashes, eye irritation, burns, paralysis, and even death. Chronic illnesses and those with delayed onsets, such as cancer, which may only appear years after exposure to pesticides, can also occur. Some chronic illnesses linked to pesticide exposure may be subtle—such as neurological disorders or reduced cognitive skills.

EPA has reported that of the 1.2 billion pounds of pesticides used in the United States annually, 76 percent, or about 950 million pounds, is used in the agriculture industry. According to EPA, farmworkers are among the primary populations exposed to these pesticides. Children may be exposed to pesticides by doing farm work, by eating fruits and vegetables directly from the fields, by being caught in the drift from field applications of pesticides, or by direct contact with treated plants and soil. Children are more vulnerable than adults are to the effects of pesticides. For example, some pesticides pose a greater risk to infants and children because they breathe more and eat more than adults per unit of body weight, and their bodies and internal organs are still developing, which makes them much more susceptible to the effects of pesticides.

The Department of Labor estimates that there are about 2.5 million hired farmworkers and that about 1.8 million of them work on crops. The number of children who work in agriculture is not reliably known. In 1998, we reported that recent estimates from the Department of Labor's National Agricultural Workers Survey (the Survey) indicated that about 129,000 14- to 17-year-olds were being hired to work on crops in the United States, although this number may be an underestimate.[1] The Department did not survey workers under 14 years of age, but the Survey does contain limited information on children of farmworkers from interviews conducted with their parents. For example, the Survey indicated that, in 1996 and 1997, 7 percent of farmworkers with children 5 years of age or younger took their children with them, at least sometimes, when they worked in the fields. In this connection, on the basis of thousands of inspections of agricultural establishments, the Department of Labor's Wage and Hour Division reported in 1999 that "farmworker children [are] forced to suffer long

---

1. We reported that information collected by the Bureau of the Census indicated that the number of 15- to 17-year-old agricultural workers may be as high as 290,000. This number included workers who work on crops, with livestock, or in services related to agriculture, such as mechanical repairs. These young workers may be hired, self-employed, or unpaid family workers. We also reported that the Fair Labor Standards Act and state laws provide less protection for children working in agriculture than for children working in other industries. For example, children as young as 16 may work in agriculture in any capacity, including in some occupations declared hazardous by the Secretary of Labor, while in nonagricultural industries, children generally may not perform such tasks until age 18. The report also stated that the Congress may wish to reevaluate whether the Fair Labor Standards Act adequately protects children who are hired to work as migrant and seasonal farmworkers. *See Child Labor in Agriculture: Changes Needed to Better Protect Health and Educational Opportunities* (GAO/HEHS-98-193, Aug. 21, 1998).

hours in the fields with both parents working and [virtually] no day care alternatives."

———————

Castillo v. Givens
704 F.2d 181 (5th Cir. 1983)

Before THORNBERRY, JOHNSON and HIGGINBOTHAM, Circuit Judges.

JOHNSON, Circuit Judge:

Plaintiffs, thirty-nine Mexican and Mexican-American migrant farm laborers who chopped cotton in defendant's fields during the summers of 1977 and 1978, brought this action under section 216(b) of the Fair Labor Standards Act (FLSA) for unpaid minimum wages and liquidated damages.... The district court entered judgment for defendant.... Plaintiffs appeal from the court's denial of their motions for judgment n.o.v. and alternatively for a new trial. With regard to the FLSA claim, this Court reverses and remands for a new trial on the number of hours worked by the individual plaintiffs and for a finding by the Court as to an award of liquidated damages....

I. Facts

Defendant Ercell Givens, President of the First State Bank of Abernathy for twenty-six years, owned a farm of approximately 4000 acres, of which about 1800 acres in 1977 and 2000 acres in 1978 were devoted to cotton production. Defendant employed five fulltime "hands" to run his farm as well as seasonal temporary hands to perform jobs such as operating tractors and feeding cattle. Defendant himself made the decisions of when and where to prepare the fields, when to plough, when to plant, when to cultivate, and when to harvest. In order to produce a good cotton crop, cotton should be chopped in the summertime[1] —the job simply involves chopping or hoeing the weeds out of the rows of growing cotton. It is a menial, unskilled task which requires no aptitude, no training, and no ability to reason. It is a work of drudgery which can be performed by persons ranging from very young to quite old; it is accomplished with a simple instrument—the hoe. Defendant employed Manuel Tonche to furnish him with a crew of field workers and to chop his cotton.[2] Defendant knew that Tonche was registered with the Department of Labor (DOL) as a farm labor contractor, and defendant required Tonche to show him his identification card from the DOL at the beginning of each season. Tonche, an illiterate with only a second-grade education who "junked" cars (cut up the bodies and sold the metal as scrap iron) in the winter, worked only for the defendant. In search of field work, the workers contacted Tonche. Tonche provided transportation to the fields for most of the workers in his used school bus, but some came in their own vans or pickups. Tonche's son brought the hoes to the fields in his pickup.

Tonche provided defendant with workers to chop his cotton for four years ending in 1978.[3] The crew varied in size, ranging from around thirty or forty up to fifty persons on any one day. In addition to Tonche's crew, defendant also hired the wives, children, and friends of his fulltime hands to chop cotton. Although defendant always paid his bank em-

———————

1. The cotton chopping season in the area involved runs from around June 20 to mid-August.
2. Although defendant claims that he "contracted with" Tonche only to chop his cotton—not to furnish him with cotton choppers—defendant admitted at trial that Tonche could not chop the cotton on a 2000-acre farm all by himself.
3. Plaintiffs ask for unpaid minimum wages for the years 1977 and 1978.

ployees minimum wage, he paid his cotton choppers, including Tonche, $1.65 an hour in 1977 and $1.75 an hour in 1978. The minimum wage was $2.20 an hour in 1977 and $2.65 an hour in 1978. Although defendant was aware of the minimum wage law and the amount of the minimum wage in 1977 and 1978, he stated that he did not realize that the law required him to pay minimum wage to his farm workers as well as to his bank employees.

On each Friday, defendant would give Tonche a check based on the number of hands and the number of hours Tonche reported to him had been worked. Tonche would then mete out the wages to the individual workers in cash. Tonche kept track of the number of hands and the number of hours worked on a daily basis and brought these figures to defendant on a piece of a paper sack.[4] Defendant would then copy Tonche's figures into his own record book. Significantly, defendant did not keep any further records other than his cancelled paychecks to Tonche. In particular, defendant did not keep any records of the individual plaintiffs' names, their hours of work, or their wages.

Both the exigencies of running a farm and his serving as bank president prevented defendant from physically supervising the work of his farm employees at all times. Nevertheless, defendant went to the fields three or four times a week to make sure the workers were in the right fields (his fields), to check up on the number of hands working, and to make sure how his entire farming operation was progressing. It was defendant who made the decision on when to start chopping in the season, on which fields to chop, and in what order the fields were to be chopped. Moreover, defendant directed Tonche which weeds were to be chopped and which weeds were not to be chopped; defendant determined when a job was finished.

In September 1978, the DOL investigated defendant's farming operation and determined that defendant owed back FLSA minimum wages to nine members of Tonche's crew who chopped cotton in defendant's fields in 1977 and 1978; defendant paid those nine workers....

In addition to Tonche, the plaintiffs who filed the instant action on February 14, 1980,[5] were members of Tonche's crew who did not receive back minimum wages.[6]

The case was tried to a jury. At the close of all the evidence, plaintiffs moved for a directed verdict on all issues except the calculation of the number of hours of work performed by plaintiffs. The jury found against plaintiffs on each of nine special issues submitted to it.[7] On June 19, 1981, the court entered judgment for defendant on both claims. Plaintiffs moved for judgment n.o.v. with respect to all issues and alternatively for a new trial with regard to the hours they worked. In an order of October 7, 1981, the court denied both the motion for judgment n.o.v. and the motion for a new trial. With respect to the FLSA claim, the court concluded that the jury's finding that plaintiffs were not engaged in the production of goods for commerce was not supported by the evidence. The court stated, however, that the jury could have reasonably found that defendant was not plaintiffs' employer....

---

4. Tonche, with the help of his own children, kept a notebook of the individual workers' names (many were listed by nickname) and the number of hours they worked. The names and figures were often but not always transcribed into this notebook from loose pieces of paper where Tonche, his son, or daughter had written them while in the fields.

5. These plaintiffs include those who were later added by filing a written consent.

6. Tonche, who was not a plaintiff under the FLCRA claim, died at the age of fifty-six before the trial began on June 15, 1981. Tonche's wife was substituted as his representative.

7. In response to the special issues relating to the FLSA claim, the jury found that (1) plaintiffs were not engaged in the production of goods for commerce, (2) plaintiffs were not employees of defendant, and (3) defendant's failure to pay the minimum wage was not willful in 1977 or in 1978. Special Issues 4 and 5 related to the number of hours the individual plaintiffs worked in 1977 and 1978....

II. FLSA Claim

The issues this Court must address concerning the FLSA claim relate to the status of plaintiffs vis-a-vis defendant, the willfulness of any violation of section 16(b), and the number of hours plaintiffs worked.

A. Plaintiffs' Status

1. A Question of Law

This Court has repeatedly held that the ultimate conclusion that an individual is an "employee"within the meaning of the FLSA is a legal determination rather than a factual one.[8] ...

Given the record testimony in the instant case, there are no unresolved issues of fact which would alter this Court's conclusion that plaintiffs were employees of defendant. The sole question is whether the facts satisfy the statutory standard for an "employee"under the FLSA. Since employee status was established as a matter of law, the district court erred in submitting it to the jury.

2. Employee Status

In order to resolve the question whether plaintiffs were employees of defendant, this Court will examine the relationship between Tonche and defendant. If Tonche was an employee of defendant, the plaintiff field workers were also defendant's employees. Even in the event that Tonche were an independent contractor, this Court could conclude that Tonche was a joint employer with the defendant; in this instance, the field workers would still be employees of the defendant. *Hodgson v. Griffin & Brand*, 471 F.2d 235, 237 (5th Cir.), cert. denied, 414 U.S. 819, 94 S.Ct. 43, 38 L.Ed.2d 51 (1973). In this hypothetical situation, the Court could, of course, conclude that Tonche was not a joint employer with the defendant. Since this Court concludes that Tonche was an employee of defendant, we do not examine the possibility of a joint employer status.

Defendant maintains that he hired Tonche as an independent contractor to chop his cotton[9] and that plaintiff field workers were therefore employees of Tonche. In determining an individual's status as "employee"within the meaning of the FLSA, however, defendant's intent or the label that he attaches to the relationship is meaningless unless it mirrors the "economic realities"of the relationship. *Rutherford Food Corp. v. McComb*, 331 U.S. 722, 67 S.Ct. 1473, 1476, 91 L.Ed. 1772 (1947)[additional citations omitted]. Employee/independent contractor status under federal social welfare legislation is determined in light of the purposes of the legislation:[10] "[E]mployees are those who as a mat-

---

8. Any subsidiary factual issues leading to this conclusion are, of course, questions of fact for the jury.

9. Defendant argues that he contracted with Tonche to chop his cotton—not to furnish him with cotton choppers. This verbal distinction represents nothing more than an attempt at label attachment; the distinction is significant only insofar as it mirrors the economic reality of the relationship. *See Donovan v. Tehco*, 642 F.2d at 143. Not surprisingly, defendant admitted at trial that he expected Tonche to get the cotton chopped and that Tonche could not do the chopping all by himself, that he had to get others to chop.

10. The Supreme Court in *Rutherford*, 331 U.S. at 727, 67 S.Ct. at 1475 explained the purpose of the FLSA:

> The Fair Labor Standards Act was passed by Congress to lessen, so far as seemed then practicable, the distribution in commerce of goods produced under subnormal labor conditions. An effort to eliminate low wages and long hours was the method chosen to free commerce from the interferences arising from production of goods under conditions that were detrimental to the health and well-being of workers. It was sought to accomplish this

ter of economic reality are dependent upon the business to which they render service." *Bartels v. Birmingham*, 332 U.S. 126, 67 S.Ct. 1547, 1550, 91 L.Ed. 1947 (1947).[11] As this Court noted in *Fahs v. Tree-Gold Co-Op Growers*, 166 F.2d 40, 44 (5th Cir.1948):

> Under these decisions, the act is intended to protect those whose livelihood is dependent upon finding employment in the business of others. It is directed toward those who themselves are least able in good times to make provisions for their needs when old age and unemployment may cut off their earnings. The statutory coverage is not limited to those persons whose services are subject to the direction and control of their employer, but rather to those who, as a matter of economic reality, are dependent upon the business to which they render service.

Although defendant acknowledges that the common-law control test is not conclusive, defendant argues that the common-law control factors are material in defining an individual's status for purposes of the FLSA. Defendant places great weight on various specific control elements—defendant did not decide how many or which workers to hire and fire,[12] did not supervise the details of their work,[13] did not furnish the hoes, did not provide transportation, did not decide when the workers arrived at the fields and when they quit, and, defendant argues, did not determine their rate of pay.[14]

---

purpose by the minimum pay and maximum hour provisions and the requirement that records of employees' services be kept by the employer.

11. The critical decisions interpreting the term "employee" in federal social welfare legislation are as follows: *NLRB v. Hearst*, 322 U.S. 111, 64 S.Ct. 851, 88 L.Ed. 1170 (1944) (for purposes of the National Labor Relations Act); *United States v. Silk*, 331 U.S. 704, 67 S.Ct. 1463, 91 L.Ed. 1757 (1947), and Bartels v. Birmingham, 332 U.S. 126, 67 S.Ct. 1547, 91 L.Ed. 1947 (1947) (for purposes of employment taxes on employers under the Social Security Act, as amended); and *Rutherford Food Corp. v. McComb*, 331 U.S. 722, 67 S.Ct. 1473, 91 L.Ed. 1772 (1947) (for purposes of the Fair Labor Standards Act).

12. Defendant conceded at trial that he had the authority to fire a crew of workers.

13. Although defendant did not supervise the minor, regular tasks, the record demonstrates that he did exercise control over the significant aspects of the farming operations. Defendant showed Tonche where the fields were located; defendant determined which fields would be hoed and in what order; he gave instructions regarding which weeds to chop and which to leave in the ground; he determined when the workers had finished a job. Defendant went to the fields three to four times a week to check up on Tonche and the workers. He would make sure that they were in the right fields and he would often doublecheck Tonche's count of the number of workers in the fields on a particular day. Defendant admitted that it is the nature of the farming business that the farmer has to depend on his workers—the farmer cannot be in the fields supervising at all times.

14. Defendant argued at trial that Tonche set the workers' wages. Defendant testified that he asked Tonche how he wanted to "figure it" and Tonche replied he would figure $1.65 an hour (in 1977). Defendant also testified that he had no agreement with Tonche as to how much Tonche would pay the workers and that defendant had no idea how much Tonche did in fact pay them. Defendant also testified, however, as follows: "We [the farmers in the community] paid them the same amount all over the place for hoeing. All community-wide, it was the same.... I know what they [the farmers who were customers of defendant's bank] do. I know what they pay. They ask me what I am paying, and we are all the same." In addition, defendant testified that he gave money to Tonche for each day according to the number of hands he had listed as working on that day and the number of hours they worked. That is, defendant multiplied the number of workers times the number of hours worked times $1.65 an hour and on Fridays gave Tonche one check for the total number of hours worked. Moreover, defendant testified as follows:

Q. You also hired friends of the wives of your full-time hands to hoe cotton, didn't you?
A. Sometimes they would have a girl with them.
Q. And you paid them $1.65 in 1977?
A. I paid them the same.
Q. And you paid them $1.75 in 1978?
A. Right.

By focusing on selected and isolated control factors, however, defendant loses sight of the circumstances of the whole activity. This Court has on several occasions found employment status even though the defendant-employer had no control over certain aspects of the relationship, e.g., the right to set hours, hire and fire, or determine wages. *Usery*, 527 F.2d at 1312 (finding that "[i]n the total context of the relationship neither the right to hire employees nor the right to set hours"indicated such lack of control by [defendant] as would show that the laundry operators were independent contractors); *Mednick v. Albert Enterprises, Inc.*, 508 F.2d 297, 301 (5th Cir.1975) (stating that "the courts have had little difficulty in finding employment status though the employee could hire others within his own discretion"); *Fahs*, 166 F.2d at 43 (concluding that contractors at defendant's packing house were employees of defendant even though defendant had no right to control the number of employees, their wages or the hours they worked). As this Court stated in *Mednick*, 508 F.2d at 300, the "ultimate criteria"for the determination of employee status are found in the purposes of the Act. The presence of some indications of independent contractor status, however, must not obscure the focal inquiry—is the individual whose status is in question the "kind of person "meant to be protected by the FLSA? *Id.* at 301.

The presence of certain elements of control is not necessarily determinative. Whether Tonche was exposed "to the evils the statute [FLSA] was designed to eradicate,"*see id.* at 300, hinges upon whether he was dependent upon defendant's farming operation. Indeed, "[t]he touchstone of 'economic reality' in analyzing a possible employee/employer relationship for purposes of the FLSA is dependency." *Weisel*, 602 F.2d at 1189. The determinative question is whether the person is "dependent upon finding employment in the business of others." *Fahs*, 166 F.2d at 44.

Two factors have emerged as critically significant in answering this question: (1) how specialized the nature of the work is, and (2) whether the individual is "in business for himself." *Mitchell v. John R. Cowley & Brothers, Inc.*, 292 F.2d 105, 108 (5th Cir.1961). The first factor looks to whether the individual "regularly performs tasks essentially of a routine nature and that work is a phase of the normal operations of that particular business." If so, the Act ordinarily regards him as an employee. *Id.* The record unquestionably demonstrates the rote nature of Tonche's work. Cotton chopping involves one piece of equipment and one task: taking a hoe and chopping the weeds out of cotton. It is such a simple task that even children can do it—it requires no aptitude, no training, no skill, and no experience. Moreover, the evidence demonstrates that cotton chopping was merely a phase of the normal operation of defendant's cotton farming business. Cotton chopping constituted a part of an "integrated economic unit"devoted to the growing of cotton. Chopping the cotton made it grow and produce better, and made it easier to harvest. Chopping the cotton was an integral phase of defendant's entire farming operations. Although the chopping season only runs from mid-June to mid-August, the work is recur-

---

Q. In fact, you paid all your cotton hoers $1.65 in '77 and $1.75 in '78, isn't that true?
A. That's true.
Q. I believe, though, in your deposition you said that there was one person you felt sorry for a little bit and you had given her $2.00 an hour?
A. Well, there may be.
Q. Do you recall that?
A. I won't doubt but what that is true. I think that's right. I think I have. I don't remember it offhand, who it was. But may have a special daughter-in-law or son-in-law or something that you give $2.00 to. I don't know. I don't know. I paid $2.00 maybe to somebody.

Assuming, arguendo, the existence of an issue of fact concerning who set the workers' wages, this Court would still come to the same legal conclusion even if the jury resolved the issue in favor of defendant.

ring and of relative permanence—it has to be done every year during the growing season in order to harvest a good cotton crop. In addition to chopping cotton, Tonche supervised the workers in the field, provided transportation for some, kept what records there were of the number of workers and their hours, received a check from defendant every Friday, and meted out the earnings to the individual workers. All of these tasks were routine. The first inquiry, therefore, points strongly to employee status for Tonche and therefore for the field workers.

The second factor is the "focal inquiry in the characterization process": "whether the individual is or is not, as a matter of economic fact, in business for himself." *Donovan v. Tehco*, 642 F.2d at 143. The record here does not indicate that Tonche had anything that could be called an independent business as distinguished from personal labor. Tonche was an illiterate with only two years of schooling. He could not read or write in either Spanish or English; he only knew how to write his name and numbers and how to figure. He kept his "records"of the number of field workers and the number of hours they worked on parts of paper sacks which he brought to defendant's bank. Some of these "records"were later transcribed into Tonche's record book by Tonche's son or daughter. The workers were often listed in Tonche's book by nicknames or by families. Tonche had "no experience or qualifications to distinguish him from the general run of workers." *See Mednick*, 508 F.2d at 303. Although Tonche did exercise some control over the field workers, there was no "economic substance" behind his power. *See id.* at 302. The fact that Tonche supervised minor, routine tasks cannot be "bootstrapped into an appearance of real independence." *See Usery*, 527 F.2d at 1312. Neither minor record keeping nor rote work, even if the work requires industriousness, is indicative of independence and nonemployee status. *Id.* at 1314. Any decisions involving judgment, initiative, or basic control were made by defendant, not Tonche. Tonche did not exert control over any meaningful part of defendant's business such that Tonche's "part"stood as a separate economic entity. *See id.* at 1312–13. Given the rate of pay and method of payment (by the hour) there was no real opportunity for Tonche to make any profit or loss. Except for the one simple and virtually indestructible instrument utilized—the hoe—all investment or risk capital was provided by defendant. Tonche's investment in hoes was "minimal in comparison with the total investment in land, heavy machinery and supplies necessary for growing"cotton. Tonche's relationship with defendant was of limited duration but of a permanent nature, recurring every year. Significantly, Tonche did not work or provide workers for any grower other than defendant. The record here does not supply any indicia whatsoever of a business operated by Tonche whereby he offered crews of workers to other growers. Indeed, Tonche did not recruit the workers as an independent businessman would. Instead, the workers, who were Hispanic, called Tonche from South Texas to inquire about work. Tonche did not operate with recognizable or consistent crews in that the hands varied in number from day-to-day. In short, Tonche had little to transfer but his own labor....

Of particular importance is the fact that defendant did not pay Tonche enough for Tonche himself to pay the workers minimum wage; it was therefore impossible for Tonche to comply with the FLSA. [citation omitted] Tonche, as an economic entity, was not capable of doing business elsewhere. [citation omitted] The economic reality of the situation was that the workers were dependent upon defendant—not Tonche—to pay them the minimum wage. They were dependent upon defendant's cotton growing business—not any "business"of Tonche's.[23] As this Court stated in *Mednick*, 508 F.2d at 303:

---

23. Of course, these facts also support the conclusion that the field workers were employees of defendant. Since this Court has concluded that Tonche was an employee of defendant, we do not separately discuss the relationship of the employees to defendant.

> An employer cannot saddle a worker with the status of independent contractor, thereby relieving itself of its duties under the F.L.S.A., by granting him some legal powers where the economic reality is that the worker is not and never has been independently in the business which the employer would have him operate.

This approximately fifty-four year old illiterate cotton chopper cannot be said to be an independent businessman in any meaningful sense.

One last point is in order. Defendant cannot rely on Tonche's registration as a "farm labor contractor" to establish independent contractor status for Tonche for purposes of the FLSA, thereby insulating himself from the FLSA requirements. As the Court in *Marshall v. Presidio Valley Farms, Inc.*, 512 F.Supp. 1195, 1197 (W.D.Tex.1981), stated: "This interpretation would permit wholesale evasion of the requirements of the F.L.S.A...." The answer to the question of employee status lies in the "economic realities" of the situation. In the case at hand, those economic realities allow only one conclusion: Tonche was an employee of defendant....

C. Number of Hours Worked

Defendant failed to keep records of the hours worked by the individual plaintiffs[26] as required by 29 U.S.C. §211(c).[27] This section places on the employer the obligation of keeping accurate records of the hours worked by his employees; the employer cannot transfer his statutory duty to his employees.

Defendant argues on appeal that his failure to keep records was mitigated by the fact that Tonche kept records which were introduced into evidence. Tonche's records were clearly incomplete and insufficient to satisfy the record keeping provisions of the Act. Moreover, this Court in *Goldberg, id.*, stated that "while there is nothing to prevent an employer from delegating to his employees the duty of keeping a record of their hours, the employer does so at his peril. He cannot escape the record keeping provisions of the Act by delegating that duty to his employees."

In *Anderson v. Mount Clemens Pottery Co.*, 328 U.S. 680, 66 S.Ct. 1187, 1192, 90 L.Ed. 1515 (1946), the Supreme Court specified the burden of proof in cases where the employer has failed to maintain the records required by the FLSA:

> In such a situation, we hold that an employee has carried out his burden if he proves that he has in fact performed work for which he was improperly compensated and if he produces sufficient evidence to show the amount and extent of that work as a matter of just and reasonable inference. The burden then shifts to the employer to come forward with evidence of the precise amount of work performed or with evidence to negative the reasonableness of the inference to

---

26. The only records kept by defendant were his weekly paychecks to Tonche and a notebook which contained a tally of the hours worked each week (listing the number of hands and the number of hours worked) in 1978.

27. 29 U.S.C. §211(c) provides as follows:

   (c) Every employer subject to any provision of this chapter or of any order issued under this chapter shall make, keep, and preserve such records of the persons employed by him and of the wages, hours, and other conditions and practices of employment maintained by him, and shall preserve such records for such periods of time, and shall make such reports therefrom to the Administrator as he shall prescribe by regulation or order as necessary or appropriate for the enforcement of the provisions of this chapter or the regulations or orders thereunder.

be drawn from the employee's evidence. If the employer fails to produce such evidence, the court may then award damages to the employee, even though the result be only approximate.

A number of Fifth Circuit cases have applied this standard. *See, e.g., Skipper v. Superior Dairies, Inc.*, 512 F.2d 409, 419–20 (5th Cir.1975); *Brennan v. General Motors Acceptance Corp.*, 482 F.2d 825, 829 (5th Cir.1973); *Shultz*, 432 F.2d at 261.

In formulating this standard, the Court was concerned that employees not be penalized by an employer's failure to comply with its statutory duty to maintain accurate records:

> When the employer has kept proper and accurate records the employee may easily discharge his burden by securing the production of those records. But where the employer's records are inaccurate or inadequate and the employee cannot offer convincing substitutes a more difficult problem arises. The solution, however, is not to penalize the employee by denying him any recovery on the ground that he is unable to prove the precise extent of uncompensated work. Such a result would place a premium on an employer's failure to keep proper records in conformity with his statutory duty; it would allow the employer to keep the benefits of an employee's labors without paying due compensation as contemplated by the Fair Labor Standards Act.

Anderson, 66 S.Ct. at 1192....

C. Conclusion

This Court has concluded that Tonche was an employee of defendant and that therefore plaintiffs were defendant's employees, that defendant's failure to pay minimum wage was willful, and that the district court's erroneous instruction which failed to specify the burden of proof necessitates a new trial on the number of hours worked by the individual plaintiffs....

3. The Migrant and Seasonal Agricultural Worker Protection Act

Susan A. Schneider
Notes on the Migrant and Seasonal Agricultural Worker Protection Act
2001 Arkansas Law Notes 57

The Migrant & Seasonal Agricultural Worker Protection Act (MSPA) provides legal protections for migrant and seasonal farm workers. 29 U.C.S. §§ 1801–1864.

The Applicability of the MSPA

Workers Covered Under the MSPA

The MSPA provides basic employment protections for migrant and seasonal farm workers that are employed in agriculture. 29 U.S.C. § 1802(3) The statute defines a migrant agricultural worker as someone who is "employed in agricultural employment of a seasonal or other temporary nature, and who is required to be absent overnight from his permanent place of residence." 29 U.S.C. § 1802(8)(A). A seasonal worker is defined as "an individual who is employed in agricultural employment of a seasonal or other temporary nature and is not required to be absent overnight from his permanent place of residence." 29 U.S.C. § 1802(10)(A).

Excluded from both definitions are the immediate family member of either an agricultural employer or a farm labor contractor. Also excluded are workers hired under the H-2A Program. 29 U.S.C. §§ 1802(8),(10).

Employers Covered Under the MSPA

"Agricultural employers," "agricultural associations," and "farm labor contractors" are subject to the MSPA requirements unless specifically exempted. An "agricultural employer" is a person who "owns or operates a farm, ranch, processing establishment, cannery, gin, packing shed or nursery, or who produces or conditions seed, and who either recruits, solicits, hires, employs, furnishes, or transports any migrant or seasonal agricultural worker." 29 U.S.C. § 1802(2).

An "agricultural association" is defined as "any nonprofit or cooperative association of farmers, growers, or ranchers, incorporated or qualified under applicable State law, which recruits, solicits, hires, employs, furnishes, or transports any migrant or seasonal agricultural worker." 29 U.S.C. § 1802(1).

A "farm labor contractor"(FLC) is defined as a person who performs any farm labor contracting activity for consideration. 29 U.S.C. § 1802(7). Agricultural employers, agricultural associations, and their employees are exempted. *Id.* "Farm labor contracting activity" is defined as "recruiting, soliciting, hiring, employing, furnishing, or transporting any migrant or seasonal agricultural worker." 29 U.S.C. § 1802(6).

Exemptions to the MSPA Requirements

The MSPA provides for several important exemptions. Individuals who qualify under either the "family business exemption" or the "small business exemption" are not subject to the MSPA requirements. 29 U.S.C. § 1803.

The family business exemption

If all farm labor contracting activities are performed by either the farmer or a member of the farmer's immediate family, that farming operation is completely exempted from the MSPA requirements. 29 U.S.C. § 1803(a)(1). If someone other than a member of the immediate family recruits a farm worker in any way or performs any other activity that falls within the definition of "farm labor contracting," the exemption is lost for that business.

The small business exemption

Farm operations that fall within the "five hundred man-days" exemption set forth in the Fair Labor Standards Act are also exempted from the MSPA requirements. 29 U.S.C. § 1803(a)(2). This exemption applies to farming operations that do not use a significant amount of non-family labor. It applies if the employer "did not use more than five hundred man-days of agricultural labor" during any calendar quarter during the preceding year. 29 U.S.C. § 213(a)(6)(A). A "man-day" is defined as a day in which an employee performs any agricultural labor for an hour or more. 29 U.S.C. § 203(e)(3).

Other specific exemptions

The MSPA also lists a variety of other, more narrow exemptions. It provides exemptions for common carriers that transport workers, labor organizations, and educational institutions. Any person who engages in any farm labor contracting activity solely within a twenty-five mile intrastate radius of that person's permanent place of residence and for not more than thirteen weeks per year is also exempt. Custom combine, hay harvesting, sheep shearing operations are exempt, as are custom poultry harvesting, breeding, debeaking, desexing, and animal health service operations, provided that the employees are not regularly required to be away from their permanent place of residence other than during their normal working hours. There are also limited exemptions that apply to the employment of students doing corn detasseling and certain tobacco work. *See* 29 U.S.C. § 1803(a)(3)(A)-(H).

Basic Requirements Included in the MSPA

The MSPA sets forth a number of specific standards for agricultural employment. These standards are in addition to those that may be imposed by any other state or federal law. 29 U.S.C. § 1871.

Registration Requirements

The MSPA requires that anyone who works as a "farm labor contractor" (FLC) must register with the Department of Labor.

Any agricultural employer that uses an FLC is required to verify the registration status of the FLC. The Wage & Hour Division of the Department of Labor provides a toll free telephone number for verification purposes and provides an Internet listing of FLCs that have been deemed ineligible because of past MSPA violations.

Terms of Employment

The MSPA provides that each person that employs an agricultural worker must pay all wages that are due. 29 U.S.C. § 1822(a). This requirement incorporates employment conditions that may be mandated by other statutes. For example, if an employer is obligated to pay a worker the federal minimum wage under the Fair Labor Standards Act, the failure to do so would violate that Act as well as being a violation of the MSPA requirement to pay all wages that are due.

The MSPA prohibits the practice of requiring a worker to purchase goods or services from the employer or the farm labor contractor. Such sales can be made, but only on a voluntary basis. 29 U.S.C. § 1822(b).

The MSPA also requires compliance with the terms of any working arrangement agreed upon. Specifically, it provides that no FLC, agricultural employer, or agricultural association shall violate the terms of the employment arrangement "without justification." 29 U.S.C. § 1822(c).

Disclosure and Informational Requirements

The MSPA contains several informational requirements that are intended to promote agricultural workers' understanding of the nature of their employment and their legal rights. Disclosure of the terms and conditions of employment must be made at the time that the worker is recruited for the job. A Department of Labor poster describing workers' MSPA rights and protections must be displayed in a conspicuous place. If housing is provided to migrant workers, a poster explaining the terms and conditions of occupancy must also be displayed. Written disclosures are to be provided in English, or "as necessary and reasonable" in the language of the workers who are not fluent or literate in English. 29 U.S.C. § 1821 (applicable to migrant workers); 29 U.S.C. § 1831(applicable to seasonal workers).

Employment records for each employee must be made, kept, and preserved for three years. These records must include the basis on which wages are paid, the number of hours worked, the total pay period earnings, the amounts withheld, and the net pay earned. Each worker must be provided with an itemized written statement setting forth this information each pay period. 29 U.S.C. § 1821(d) (applicable to migrant workers); 29 U.S.C. § 1831(c) (applicable to seasonal workers).

In addition to these affirmative requirements, the MSPA specifically prohibits any FLC, agricultural employer, or agricultural association from knowingly providing false information to any worker regarding the terms, conditions, or existence of agricultural employment. 29 U.S.C. § 1821(f)(applicable to migrant workers); 29 U.S.C. § 1831(e) (applicable to seasonal workers).

Housing Requirements

Each person who "owns or controls" property that is used as housing for migrant workers is responsible for ensuring that the housing complies with substantive federal and state safety and health standards. The housing must be inspected and certified to be in compliance. Persons who provide housing on a commercial basis to the general public are exempted from these requirements. 29 U.S.C. § 1823.

Vehicle Safety Requirements

If migrant and seasonal workers are transported, the transport vehicles must conform to Department of Labor safety regulations as well as other applicable federal and state safety standards. Agricultural employers, associations and FLCs must ensure that each person driving has a valid driver's license, as provided by state law. An insurance policy or liability bond must be in effect. These transportation requirements do not apply in situations where a migrant or seasonal agricultural worker is using a "tractor, combine, harvester, picker, or other similar machinery and equipment while such worker is actually engaged in the planting, cultivating, or harvesting of any agricultural commodity or the care of livestock or poultry." 29 U.S.C. § 1841.

Discrimination

The MSPA prohibits any action taken to "intimidate, threaten, restrain, coerce, blacklist, discharge, or in any manner discriminate against any migrant or seasonal agricultural worker" because actions taken to enforce the protections set forth in the MSPA. 29 U.S.C. § 1855(a).

Enforcement

The MSPA provides for enforcement through the Wage & Hour Division of the Department of Labor 29. U.S.C. §§ 1851–1853. It also creates a private cause of action for any person "aggrieved by a violation." 29 U.S.C. § 1854(a). Criminal sanctions, judicial injunctions, administrative sanctions, and damages awards are all authorized. 29 U.S.C. §§ 1851–54.

Any person who "willfully and knowingly" violates a requirement under the MSPA can be fined "not more than $1,000 or sentenced to prison for a term not to exceed one year, or both." 29 U.S.C. § 1851(a). A subsequent violation can result in a $10,000 fine and/or a three year prison term. *Id.* The Secretary of Labor can seek and obtain temporary or permanent injunctive relief to remedy violations of the statute. 29 U.S.C. § 1852(a). Civil monetary penalties of not more than $1000 per violation can be assessed. 29 U.S.C. § 1853(a). The MSPA also includes an administrative and judicial review process for appealing the assessment of civil sanctions. 29 U.S.C. § 1853(b)-(c).

Any person aggrieved by a violation of the MSPA may bring an action under the statute in any federal district court having jurisdiction over the parties. 29 U.S.C. § 1854(a).

Federal jurisdiction is provided without regard to diversity of citizenship or amount in controversy. Exhaustion of any alternative administrative remedies is not required. *Id.* If the court finds intentional violations of the MSPA or any regulation promulgated thereunder, it may award damages "up to and including an amount equal to the amount of actual damages, or statutory damages of up to $500 per plaintiff per violation, or other equitable relief." Multiple infractions of a single statutory or regulatory provision will only constitute one violation for purposes of determining the amount of statutory damages. Class action awards are limited to the lesser of up to $500 per plaintiff per violation, or up to $500,000 or other equitable relief. 29 U.S.C. § 1854(c). This section also authorizes the court to consider "whether an attempt was made to resolve the issues in dispute before the resort to litigation." *Id.* Special provisions are set forth for limiting damages in certain cases in which workers' compensation benefits are available. 29 U.S.C. § 1854(d)-(e).

The Employment Relationship: Independent Contracting and Joint Employment

Farmers may attempt to avoid the difficulties associated with hired labor by working with an FLC. At least in theory, the FLC can be hired as an independent contractor. The independent contractor then hires the agricultural employees and assumes the responsibilities associated with the MSPA. However, neither the parties' characterizations nor the parties' intentions will control the legal determination of the relationship between the farmer and the agricultural laborer.

The courts have attempted to articulate a standard for determining whether an independent contractor relationship exists, keeping in mind that there has been substantial abuse among employers seeking to use this characterization as a means for avoiding labor laws. Both have agreed that the test for independent contractor status should be based on the "economic reality" of the relationship, that is, "whether there is economic dependence" upon the farmer. The true nature of this relationship will be determined based upon the "economic reality" of the situation. *See Castillo v. Givens, supra.*

Proving the independent contractor status of the farm labor contractor may not end the analysis, however. Under the doctrine of "joint employment," the farmer may still be liable as an agricultural employer. Under the MSPA regulations, "joint employment means a condition in which a single individual stands in the relation of an employee to two or more persons at the same time." 29 C.F.R. § 500.29(h)(5). Of particular importance is the determination of whether the workers are economically dependent upon both the farmer and the FLC. Similar to the independent contractor analysis, the regulations provide that "the ultimate question to be determined is the economic reality—whether the worker is so economically dependent upon the agricultural employer/association as to be considered its employee." *Id.* The regulations provide a listing of factors to be used as "analytical tools" in determining economic dependency, although this listing is not a "checklist" and no one factor is dispositive. How the factors are to be weighed depends on the facts and circumstances of each case. The factors set forth in the regulations are listed as follows.

> (A) Whether the agricultural employer/association has the power, either alone or through control of the farm labor contractor to direct, control, or supervise the worker(s) or the work performed (such control may be either direct or indirect, taking into account the nature of the work performed and a reasonable degree of contract performance oversight and coordination with third parties);

(B) Whether the agricultural employer/association has the power, either alone or in addition to another employer, directly or indirectly, to hire or fire, modify the employment conditions, or determine the pay rates or the methods of wage payment for the worker(s);

(C) The degree of permanency and duration of the relationship of the parties, in the context of the agricultural activity at issue;

(D) The extent to which the services rendered by the worker(s) are repetitive, rote tasks requiring skills which are acquired with relatively little training;

(E) Whether the activities performed by the worker(s) are an integral part of the overall business operation of the agricultural employer/association;

(F) Whether the work is performed on the agricultural employer/association's premises, rather than on premises owned or controlled by another business entity; and

(G) Whether the agricultural employer/association undertakes responsibilities in relation to the worker(s) which are commonly performed by employers, such as preparing and/or making payroll records, preparing and/or issuing pay checks, paying FICA taxes, providing workers' compensation insurance, providing field sanitation facilities, housing or transportation, or providing tools and equipment or materials required for the job (taking into account the amount of the investment).

Id.

Almost all of the cases brought under the MSPA arise in situations where there is an undisputed violation of the protections provided under the law. The issue that is litigated involves assessing responsibility—is the defendant an employer under the statute? If so, does one of the exemptions apply, freeing the defendant from any liability under the statute? The following two cases provide examples.

Charles v. Burton
169 F.3d 1322 (11th Cir. 1999)

Before HATCHETT, Chief Judge, and RONEY and CLARK, Senior Circuit Judges.

PER CURIAM:

Roney, Senior Circuit Judge, concurred in part and dissented in part with opinion.

In this case involving the Agricultural Workers Protection Act, 29 U.S.C. §§ 1801–1872 (1994) (AWPA), fifteen migrant farm workers challenge the district court's grant of summary judgment in favor of the appellees John Burton, Felix Burton, Little Rock Produce Company and Bobby Hall. The district court found that the appellees were not joint employers of the farm workers under the AWPA and did not award the farm workers actual damages for a violation of the AWPA's registration provision. We affirm in part, reverse in part and remand.

I. BACKGROUND

John Burton and Felix Burton (collectively, the Burtons) operated a farm in Brooks County, Georgia. The Burtons principally grew cotton, corn, soy beans and peanuts on their farm.

In 1990, the Burtons decided to grow other vegetables—snap beans and cucumbers—and contracted with Little Rock Produce Company (Little Rock), a produce packinghouse, and its president and principal stockholder, Bobby Hall, to subsidize these new crops and to advance money for labor costs. Both were to share in the profits. Little Rock also agreed to supply the seeds for the snap bean and cucumber crops, boxes for the harvest and a trailer to transport the beans, and the Burtons in turn agreed to market these crops through Little Rock.

Pursuant to the contract, Little Rock required the Burtons to fertilize the snap bean crop and to obtain labor for its harvest. In 1990, the Burtons contacted the Georgia Department of Labor to obtain workers for the snap bean crops, and Paul Emile Paul and Wilner Luxama, farm labor contractors (FLC), agreed to supply them with workers for the snap bean harvest. The Burtons eventually agreed to pay Luxama a set amount of money per box of snap beans that his crew picked, and Luxama paid each worker a set amount per box.[1] The 1990 harvest occurred too late in the snap bean season, and consequently, Luxama's workers spent a total of one-half of a day working on the Burtons' farm that year.

The next year, Luxama and his crew returned to the Burtons' farm to harvest the 1991 snap bean crop. Luxama transported the 25 to 35 members of his Florida-based crew between the Burtons' farm and their temporary housing in Ashburn, Georgia.[2] The Burtons would direct Luxama to a particular snap bean field, and his crew picked all of the field's beans. Luxama directed and supervised the harvest of the snap beans, and the Burtons observed the progress of the workers approximately two to three times a day. As they picked the snap beans, the workers placed them in the boxes that Little Rock provided. At the end of the day, Luxama weighed all of the boxes of snap beans, and a crew member placed the boxes onto a trailer that Little Rock owned. The Burtons then transported the snap beans to Little Rock's packinghouse, where a broker selected and sold them.

The Burtons failed to earn a substantial profit from the 1991 snap bean crop, but they decided to plant and harvest them for the next year.[3] In 1992, Luxama returned with his crew to harvest the crop. Luxama's registration as a farm labor contractor with the Department of Labor (as the AWPA requires) had lapsed in 1991 because he had failed to pay a fine that the Department of Labor had imposed. See 29 U.S.C. § 1811. As a result of this lapse and his inability to pay the fine, Luxama failed to purchase liability insurance for the vehicles used to transport his crew as the AWPA requires. See 29 U.S.C. § 1841.[4] The Burtons failed to check Luxama's certification as an FLC, and failed to learn that Luxama no longer carried the required insurance. See 29 U.S.C.

---

1. According to Luxama's deposition testimony, the Burtons agreed to pay him between $3.75 and $4 per box. Luxama in turn paid his workers $2.50 per box for the first picking, and then $3 per box for the second and additional pickings. Luxama provided his workers a ticket for each box they picked, and then paid them for each ticket the worker returned to him.

2. Luxama recruited his workers (Haitian immigrants) from Miami to pick crops, including snap beans, in Georgia. He also helped the workers find housing when they arrived in Georgia, although the crew paid for all of its housing expenses.

3. Since the 1991 crop failed to make a profit, the Burtons did not reimburse Little Rock's advancements for their labor costs.

4. Section 1841(b) of the AWPA provides:

(1) When using, or causing to be used, any vehicle for providing transportation ... each agricultural employer, agricultural association, and farm labor contractor shall ...

(C) have an insurance policy or a liability bond that is in effect which insures the agricultural employer, the agricultural association, or the farm labor contractor against liability for damages to persons or property arising from the ownership, operation, or the causing to be operated, of any vehicle used to transport any migrant or seasonal agricultural worker. See 29 U.S.C. § 1841(b)(1)(C).

§§ 1841(b) (duty to carry insurance of liability bond), 1842 (duty to check registration). On the morning of June 3, 1992, one of Luxama's trucks overturned while transporting the workers to the fields, killing the driver and two workers and seriously injuring others.[5]

In December 1992, the appellants sued John Burton, Felix Burton, Little Rock and Hall for violations of the AWPA, the Fair Labor Standards Act (FLSA), 29 U.S.C. § 201 et seq. and Georgia's common law of negligence. The appellants alleged, in part, that the appellees violated the "registration, vehicle safety, vehicle insurance, record keeping, wage statement and wage payment provisions of the AWPA," and the appellees moved for summary judgment. After conducting an evidentiary hearing, the district court held that the appellees did not "employ" the workers within the meaning of the AWPA and the FLSA, and granted the appellees summary judgment. This conclusion precluded the appellants from recovering any damages for the appellees' failure to ensure that Luxama's truck carried either insurance or a liability bond.

Thereafter, the appellees moved for summary judgment on the remaining claims, with (1) Little Rock and Hall arguing that they had not "utilized" the services of Luxama pursuant to the 29 U.S.C. § 1842; and (2) the Burtons alleging that although they had utilized Luxama's services and violated the registration verification provisions under 29 U.S.C. § 1842, the workers were entitled only to statutory damages under 29 U.S.C. § 1854(c)(1). The district court granted Little Rock's and Hall's motions for summary judgment, finding that they had not "utilized" the services of Luxama and his crew.[6] The district court later found the Burtons liable for $350 in statutory damages per worker for the violation of section 1842, but refused to award actual damages because the workers' injuries were "too far removed" from the Burtons' failure to verify Luxama's registration.[7]

II. ISSUES

The issues we discuss are: (1) whether the district court erred in finding that the appellees were not "joint employers" of the appellants, and were thus not liable under section 1841 of the AWPA (Part III); (2) whether the district court erred in finding that appellees Little Rock and Hall did not "utilize" the services of the appellants under section 1842 of the AWPA (Part IV); and (3) whether the district court erred in failing to award the appellants actual damages for the Burtons' violation of that provision (Part V).[8]

---

5. The accident killed appellant Jean J. Maissoneuve (Avelie Maissoneuve appears as the personal representative of his estate), rendered appellant Edner Phillipe a paraplegic, and caused various injuries to appellants Nicolas Charles, Charite Asseigne, Miguel Aubout, Samson Germain, Marcel Jean-Baptiste, Alexandre Joseph, Marcel Joseph, Fito Pierre, Frankel Pierre, Fatami Saint Fleur, Gerard Simeon, Lavius Dit Servius Vil and Jean Jacques Vytelle. We shall refer to these workers collectively as the appellants.

6. Appellee Bobby Hall died in October 1995, and the district court treated the appellants' motion for substitution of party as a motion to substitute Bobby Hall, Jr. (the administrator of Bobby Hall's estate) as a defendant, and granted the appellants' motion.

7. In August 1995 the appellants also filed diversity lawsuits alleging common law negligence claims against Little Rock and the Burtons. The district court consolidated those claims with the AWPA and FLSA claims and granted summary judgment in favor of Little Rock and the Burtons on the common law negligence claims.

8. The appellants raise for the first time the issue of whether the appellees formed a partnership or joint venture under Georgia law. This court, however, will not consider on appeal issues not raised before the district court.

III. JOINT EMPLOYMENT

In 1983, Congress enacted the AWPA "to remove the restraints on commerce caused by activities detrimental to migrant and seasonal agricultural workers; to require farm labor contractors to register under this chapter; and to assure necessary protections for migrant and seasonal agricultural workers, agricultural associations, and agricultural employers." 29 U.S.C. § 1801. Included in the AWPA are requirements (1) that an FLC obtain a certificate from the Secretary of Labor authorizing it to perform its duties, see 29 U.S.C. § 1811(a); 29 C.F.R. § 550.40 (1997); (2) that a person utilizing the services of an FLC verify the existence of such certificate, see 29 U.S.C. § 1842; and (3) that an FLC and an agricultural employer carry either an insurance policy or liability bond covering any vehicle used to transport agricultural workers, *see* 29 U.S.C. § 1841; 29 C.F.R. 500.120.

The appellees contend, and the district court agreed, that they did not "employ" the appellants, that they were not "agricultural employers" or "joint employers" within the meaning of the AWPA and that the AWPA did not require them to carry insurance or a liability bond under section 1841.[9] The definition of "employ" is the same under the AWPA and the FLSA. See 29 U.S.C. § 203(1); 29 U.S.C. § 1802(2). An entity "employs" a person under the AWPA and the FLSA if it "suffers or permits" the individual to work. See 29 U.S.C. § 203(g); 29 C.F.R. § 500.20(h)(1). "An entity 'suffers or permits' an individual to work if, as a matter of economic reality, the individual is dependent on the entity."

The AWPA's concept of "employ" also includes "the joint employment principles applicable under the [FLSA]."[10] According to the AWPA regulations,

> joint employment means a condition in which a single individual stands in the relation of an employee to two or more persons at the same time. A determination of whether the employment is to be considered joint employment depends upon all the facts in a particular case. If the facts establish that two or more persons are completely disassociated with respect to the employment of a particular employee, a joint employment situation does not exist.

29 C.F.R. § 500.20(h)(5). The issue in joint employment cases "is not whether the worker is more economically dependent on the independent contractor or grower, with the winner avoiding responsibility as an employer." *Antenor*, 88 F.3d at 932. Instead, the AWPA "envisions situations where a single employee may have the necessary employment relationship with not only one employer but simultaneously such a relationship with an employer and an independent contractor." *Antenor*, 88 F.3d at 932 (quoting H.R.Rep. No. 97-885, 97th Cong., 2d Sess. (1982) 7, 1982 U.S.C.C.A.N. 4547, 4553).

---

9. The AWPA defines "agricultural employer" as "any person who owns or operates a farm, ranch, processing establishment, cannery, fin, packing shed or nursery, or who produces or conditions seed, and who either recruits, solicits, hires, employs, furnishes, or transports any migrant or seasonal agricultural worker." 29 U.S.C. § 1802(2). The AWPA defines "migrant agricultural worker" as "an individual who is employed in agricultural employment of a seasonal or other temporary nature, and who is required to be absent overnight from his permanent place of residence." 29 U.S.C. § 1802(8)(A).

10. In 1997, the Department of Labor amended the AWPA regulations, attempting to remedy the misconceptions surrounding the definition of "joint employment." This clarification of joint employment focuses more closely on the "economic dependence" test that federal courts had previously established. *See* Migrant and Seasonal Agricultural Worker Protection Act, 62 Fed.Reg. 11734, 11745–46 (1997) (codified at 29 C.F.R. pt. 500 (1997)). This court accords significant weight to the statutory interpretation of the executive agency charged with implementing the statute being construed, particularly when that interpretation is incorporated in a formally published opinion.

This court, and the AWPA regulations, have considered the following regulatory factors as guidance in determining economic dependence, and ultimately, whether an employment relationship exists: (1) whether the agricultural employer has the power, either alone or through the FLC, to direct, control or supervise the workers or the work performed (such control may be either direct or indirect, taking into account the nature of the work performed and a reasonable degree of contract performance oversight and coordination with third parties); (2) whether the agricultural employer has the power, either alone or in addition to another employer, directly or indirectly, to hire or fire, modify the employment conditions, or determine the pay rates or the methods of wage payment for the workers; (3) the degree of permanency and duration of the relationship of the parties, in the context of the agricultural activity at issue; (4) the extent to which the services that the workers rendered are repetitive, rote tasks requiring skills that are acquired with relatively little training; (5) whether the activities that the workers performed are an integral part of the overall business operation of the agricultural employer; (6) whether the work is performed on the agricultural employer's premises, rather than on premises that another business entity owns or controls; and (7) whether the agricultural employer undertakes responsibilities in relation to the workers that employers commonly perform, such as preparing and/or making payroll records, preparing and/or issuing pay checks, paying FICA taxes, providing workers' compensation insurance, providing field sanitation facilities, housing or transportation, or providing tools and equipment or materials required for the job (taking into account the amount of the investment). *See* 29 C.F.R. § 500.20(h)(5)(iv)(A)-(G); *see also Antenor*, 88 F.3d at 932; *Aimable*, 20 F.3d at 439.

We will consider all of the enunciated factors as guidance, with "the weight of each factor [depending] on the light it sheds on the farmworkers' economic dependence (or lack thereof) on the alleged employer, which in turn depends on the facts of the case." Antenor, 88 F.3d at 932–33 (citing Aimable, 20 F.3d at 440). A determination of employment status under the AWPA and the FLSA is a question of law subject to de novo review. *See Antenor*, 88 F.3d at 929; Aimable, 20 F.3d at 440.

1. Whether the appellees had the power to direct, control or supervise the appellants (directly or indirectly).

Prior to 1997, the AWPA regulations split this factor into two concepts: first, the nature and degree of control over the workers; and second, the degree of supervision over their work. The district court also considered these two concepts separately. As for the nature and degree of control of the appellants, the district court found that "there is absolutely no indication ... that defendants [Hall] and Little Rock retained the 'right to dictate the manner in which the details of the harvesting function [were] executed.'" *Charles*, 857 F.Supp. at 1580 (quoting *Donovan v. Brandel*, 736 F.2d 1114, 1119 (6th Cir.1984)). The district court also found that "although defendants John and Felix Burton retained a degree of control over the harvest in that they directed which fields would be picked, they maintained no control over the manner in which the beans were picked. The details of the harvest were left to [Luxama]." *Charles*, 857 F.Supp. at 1580.

In *Aimable*, this court found that the focus of this concept "is more properly limited to specific indicia of control (for example, direct employment decisions such as whom and how many employees to hire, whom to assign to specific tasks, and how to design the employee's management structure)." *Aimable*, 20 F.3d at 440. *Antenor* identified several other indicia of control, including: when work should begin on a particular day; whether a worker should be disciplined; whether the agricultural employers were free to delay or stop the workers directly from continuing their work; and whether the agricultural employers could assign work to specific workers indirectly. *See Antenor*, 88 F.3d at 933–34. The evidence presented demonstrated that while Little Rock supplied boxes to the Burtons to be used for the appellants, neither Hall nor Little Rock engaged in direct or indirect control over the appellants. The Burtons, however, exhibited some control. For example, the Burtons determined the particular fields that they wanted the appellants to cultivate, determined when the appellants would begin picking each field and supplied appellants with boxes that Little Rock provided. They did not, however, tell Luxama when to commence picking each day and did not determine whether a specific worker should be disciplined. *See Hodgson v. Griffin & Brand of McAllen, Inc.*, 471 F.2d 235, 237 (5th Cir.) (finding that agricultural worker exercised sufficient control in determining when the workers were to commence harvesting each day to be an "employer" under the AWPA), cert. denied, 414 U.S. 819, 94 S.Ct. 43, 38 L.Ed.2d 51 (1973). Therefore, although we agree with the district court that this aspect of the first factor weighs against finding that the appellants were economically dependent on Hall and Little Rock, we find that the Burtons exercised some aspects of control that weigh in favor of finding that the appellants were economically dependent on the Burtons.

The second aspect of this factor concerns the degree of direct or indirect supervision that the agricultural employer enjoyed over the workers. The necessary supervision under this factor "includes overseeing the pickers' work and providing direction," while keeping in mind "special aspects of agricultural employment." *Antenor*, 88 F.3d at 934–35. In an agricultural setting, "the grower is not expected to look over the shoulder of each farm-worker every hour of every day. Thus, it is well settled that supervision is present whether orders are communicated directly to the laborer or indirectly through the contractor." *Antenor*, 88 F.3d at 935. "Infrequent assertions of minimal oversight," however, fail to satisfy the supervision necessary under this factor. *See Aimable*, 20 F.3d at 441.

The workers alleged, and the record reveals, that the Burtons directed Luxama to tell the appellants to harvest certain areas of their farm and monitored their harvesting several times per day.[11] The Burtons, however, entrusted most of the direct supervision and oversight over the appellants in Luxama. We believe that the Burtons' supervision overcomes *Aimable's* "infrequent assertions of minimal oversight" and instead resembles Antenor's definition of indirect control. The workers, however, have not presented any evidence that Little Rock or Hall directly or indirectly supervised their work in any fashion. We therefore find that this first factor favors a conclusion that the appellants were economically dependent on the Burtons, based on their indirect control and supervision. We also find that this factor weighs against such a conclusion as for Little Rock and Hall.

2. Whether the appellees had the direct or indirect power to hire, fire, modify the employment conditions or determine the pay rates or the methods of wage payment for the appellants.

The district court also considered aspects of this factor separately. First, the appellants argued that the appellees ultimately shared responsibility for their wages, because the appellees controlled the amount of seeds planted and fields harvested and paid Luxama a specific price for each box of beans harvested, and that Luxama then paid the appellants a set price for each box that they individually harvested. The appellees rely on *Rutherford*

---

11. Appellant Asseigne observed the Burtons near their worksite often, and noticed that they talked to Luxama. See Asseigne Dep. at 31. Appellant Aubout stated that he observed the Burtons talking to Luxama, and since most of the appellants did not speak English, Luxama then instructed the appellants in their native language what the Burtons needed. See Aubout Dep. at 17–18.

Food Corp. v. McComb, where the Supreme Court found the operator of a slaughterhouse exerted indirect influence over the pay rates for the boners when he controlled the number of cattle slaughtered and boned. 331 U.S. 722, 730, 67 S.Ct. 1473, 91 L.Ed. 1772 (1947). The district court found that *Aimable* precluded the reliance on *McComb*, finding this "leap of logic"—since the appellees controlled the amount of money Luxama received, and since Luxama controlled the amount the appellants received, that the appellees therefore controlled the amount the appellants received—to be unfounded. *See Aimable*, 20 F.3d at 442 ("Unfortunately for appellants, the laws that bind the Euclidian world do not apply with equal force in federal employment law."); *Charles*, 857 F.Supp. at 1580. The appellants presented no other convincing evidence to show that the appellees exercised direct or indirect power to determine their pay rates or the methods of payments. In fact, Luxama controlled their pay rates, determined how they received their pay and when they received payment.

The appellants also argue that the Burtons, on behalf of their enterprise with Hall and Little Rock, delegated the task of assembling a picking crew to Luxama and therefore indirectly enjoyed the rights to hire, fire or modify the employment conditions of the appellants. In *Antenor*, this court found that evidence showing that the agricultural employers "dictated the workers' hours, a condition of employment, by deciding when the work was to begin ... [and] forcing the pickers to stop picking when prices were bad[,]" indicated that they enjoyed these rights. See Antenor, 88 F.3d at 935. The Burtons planted and fertilized the snap bean crop and directed Luxama to have the appellants harvest it on certain dates. While the Burtons did not enjoy a "veto" power over Luxama's hiring decisions and did not modify such employment conditions as the picker's daily hours, they decided ultimately when the appellants would begin picking their snap bean crop, where they would pick it and for how long. Thus, elements of this factor weigh in favor of the appellants being economically dependent on the Burtons. Again, though, the appellants present no evidence that either Hall or Little Rock directly or indirectly enjoyed this power.

3. The degree of permanency and duration of the relationship of the parties.

The district court did not consider this factor, following *Aimable's* holding that this factor is irrelevant in analyzing joint employment. *See Aimable*, 20 F.3d at 443–44; *Charles*, 857 F.Supp. at 1579. The Aimable court found that this factor helped determine whether the FLC, as opposed to any other putative agricultural employer, employed the farm workers. *See Aimable*, 20 F.3d at 444. We note that the Aimable court nonetheless analyzed this factor, and, given its inclusion in the AWPA's regulations, feel that its analysis should provide this court guidance in determining "the economic reality of all the circumstances concerning whether the putative employee is economically dependent upon the alleged employer." 29 C.F.R. 500.20(h)(5)(iv)(C); *Antenor*, 88 F.3d at 933.[12]

---

12. The Department of Labor additionally commented on this issue, stating that, despite Aimable, the great weight of the case law supports consideration of the degree of permanency and exclusivity in the relationship between the workers and the putative employer in the context of the agricultural operation in question. The duration of that operation necessarily affects the duration or permanency of that relationship. Where an FLC and the workers are engaged for the duration of the operation and are obligated to work only for or be available to the agricultural employer/association at his/her discretion during that period, that information bears directly on the question of the workers' economic dependence. Other courts have found this factor relevant and the Department believes that duration of the relationship should be one of the factors considered in determining joint employment.

Agricultural Workers Protection Act, 62 Fed.Reg. at 11,740 (citations omitted).

The appellants allege that they had an ongoing relationship with the appellees because they spent most of their time during the 1992 snap bean harvest season working for them. Additionally, they contend that Luxama's relationship with the appellees was longstanding in that he had provided workers for their snap bean harvests between 1990 and 1992. The appellees allege, pursuant to Aimable, that the evidence showed that only Luxama, not the appellees, had the ongoing relationship with the appellants. The appellees also argue that no evidence indicated that the appellants harvested the snap bean crop in 1990 or 1991, and that the evidence showed that some of the appellants may have worked at a different farm during the snap bean harvest, and others may have chosen to stay home on certain days during the harvest.

Other courts have considered this issue and have found that "[h]arvesting of crops is a seasonal industry, without much permanence beyond the harvesting season. However temporary the relationship may be ... the relationship is permanent ... [if] the migrants work only for [the] defendants during that season." *Haywood v. Barnes*, 109 F.R.D. 568, 589 (E.D.N.C.1986) (quoting *Donovan v. Gillmor*, 535 F.Supp. 154, 162 (N.D.Ohio), appeal dismissed, 708 F.2d 723 (6th Cir.1982)). Another court has found that "[o]ne indication of permanency ... is the fact that it is not uncommon for the migrant families to return year after year." *Secretary of Labor v. Lauritzen*, 835 F.2d 1529, 1537 (7th Cir.1987), cert. denied, 488 U.S. 898, 109 S.Ct. 243, 102 L.Ed.2d 232 (1988). Luxama and the appellants harvested snap beans on the Burtons' farm in 1992. While this harvest was seasonal, the Burtons expected Luxama's crew to harvest the entire snap bean crop. Luxama and the appellants also worked for another farm during this snap bean harvest.[13] While Luxama returned between 1990 and 1992 to harvest the Burton's snap bean crop, the appellants presented no evidence to show that all of them picked snap beans for the Burtons during these dates. Therefore, we find that the appellants have failed to meet the permanency and exclusivity factor, and this factor weighs against a determination that the appellants were economically dependent on the appellees.

4. The extent to which the services that the appellants rendered are repetitive, rote tasks requiring skills that are acquired with relatively little training..

The district court also failed to consider this factor in determining that the appellees were not joint employers of the appellants, and the *Aimable* court found that an analysis of this factor fails to aid in this determination. See *Aimable*, 20 F.3d at 444. We, however, choose to analyze this factor, since it is included in the AWPA's regulations.[14] It is unquestionable that the services that the appellants rendered—picking snap beans—is a repetitive and rote task requiring relatively little training. Therefore, we find that this

---

13. Luxama stated that at times he would send some of the appellants to pick snap beans at a nearby farm in Tifton, Georgia. Luxama Dep. at 56.

14. The Department of Labor explained:

[C]ourts have considered the worker's degree of skill to be a relevant and probative factor in the determination of [economic] dependence. In common experience in the agricultural industry and other contexts, there is a reasonable correlation between the worker's degree of skill and the marketability and value of his/her services. In the free market place, an unskilled task may easily be learned and performed by almost any worker is a task for which many workers (both trained and untrained) can realistically compete, and is also a task for which the competing workers would not be able to demand or expect high wages. The lower the worker's skill level, the lower the value and marketability of his/her services, and the greater the likelihood of his/her economic dependence on the person utilizing those services.

Agricultural Worker Protection Act, 62 Fed.Reg. at 11,740–41.

factor weighs in favor of concluding that the appellants were economically dependent on the appellees.

5. Whether the activities that the appellants performed are an integral part of the appellees' overall business operation.

This factor is "probative of joint employment because a worker who performs a routine task that is a normal and integral phase of the grower's production is likely to be dependent on the grower's overall production process." *Antenor*, 88 F.3d at 937. The district court held that this factor favored the appellants, finding that they "performed a line-job integral to the harvesting and production of salable vegetables." *Charles*, 857 F.Supp. at 1581 (quoting *Aimable*, 20 F.3d at 444). While the Burtons contend that their snap bean harvest comprised a small percentage of their overall farming operations, we find that this factor weighs in favor of determining that the appellants were economically dependent on the Burtons, Little Rock and Hall because the appellants' picking of snap beans was integral to both harvesting and producing snap beans—the appellees' business.

6. Whether the work is performed on the appellees' premises, rather than on premises that another business entity owns or controls.

This factor is probative of joint employment because "without the land, the worker might not have work, and because a business that owns or controls the worksite will likely be able to prevent labor law violations, even if it delegates hiring and supervisory responsibilities to labor contractors." *Antenor*, 88 F.3d at 937 (citing *Gulf King Shrimp Co. v. Wirtz*, 407 F.2d 508, 513–14 (5th Cir.1969)).

The district court correctly found that the appellants picked snap beans on the Burtons' property, which provides indicia that the Burtons employed the workers. The district court also found, however, that no party presented any evidence that the appellants performed any work on the property of either Little Rock or Hall. Thus, we find that this factor weighs in favor of finding that the appellants were economically dependent on the Burtons, but were not economically dependent on either Little Rock or Hall.

7. Whether the appellees undertook responsibilities in relation to the appellants that employers commonly perform.

The district court did not consider this factor, finding that one of its considerations, "investment in equipment and facilities," to be irrelevant pursuant to *Aimable*. *Aimable*, 20 F.3d at 443; *Charles*, 857 F.Supp. at 1579. Once again, because this factor is enunciated in the AWPA's regulations, and considered in *Antenor*, we consider it as guidance in our determination of "economic dependence" and "joint employment."[15] The evidence, viewed in the light most favorable to appellants, demonstrates that neither Little Rock, Hall nor the Burtons had any responsibility in preparing or making payrolls, paying FICA taxes, or providing workers compensation insurance for the appellants. Little Rock issued checks to Luxama for the number of boxes his crew picked, but these payments were

---

15. The Department of Labor commented:

Where a putative employer provides materials or services, undertakes functions normally performed by an employer (such as providing workers' compensation, paying FICA taxes, transporting or housing workers, providing the tools and equipment necessary to the work), such behavior indicates that it is his/her interest to perform such functions that are commonly performed by employers rather than rely on the FLC. Further, workers who use the services, materials or functions are in a very tangible way economically dependent on the entity performing these functions.

Agricultural Workers Protection Act, 62 Fed.Reg. at 11,741–42.

advances to the Burtons for their labor costs. Luxama paid the appellants for the number of boxes they picked and provided housing and transportation for the appellants. Little Rock also provided the Burtons with boxes for the appellants to place the picked snap beans in and provided a trailer for the Burtons to transport the snap beans to Little Rock's packing shed. Although the appellees provided certain materials useful in the appellants' work, which is probative of the appellants' economic dependence on the appellees, the appellees did not undertake any other functions that an employer normally performed. Thus, we find that this factor weighs in favor of determining that the appellants were not economically dependent on the appellees.

In considering all of these factors, we realize that "no one factor is determinative," and that the existence of joint employment "depends on the economic reality of all the circumstances." *Antenor*, 88 F.3d at 932 (quotations and citations omitted). We note that "the absence of evidence on any one or more of the criteria listed does not preclude a finding that an ... agricultural employer was a joint employer along with the crewleader." *Antenor*, 88 F.3d at 933 (quotations and citations omitted). We also note that since the AWPA is a remedial statute, we must construe it broadly. *See Caro-Galvan*, 993 F.2d at 1505 ("AWPA is a remedial statute and should be construed broadly to effect its humanitarian purpose."). Based on our analysis of the factors, we hold that the appellants were economically dependent on the Burtons, and, as a matter of law, that the Burtons employed the appellants under the AWPA. The Burtons enjoyed a sufficient degree of indirect supervision and control over the appellants, supplied the land and ultimately decided when, where and how long the appellants would harvest their snap bean crop. Further, the appellants performed services that required little training, yet were integral to the Burtons' farming operation. Because we hold that the Burtons employed the appellants, they are liable as joint employers for violations of section 1841 of the AWPA. We also hold that, based on our analysis of these factors, Little Rock and Hall did not employ the appellants within the meaning of the AWPA.[16]

IV. UTILIZATION OF SERVICES

The next issue we discuss is whether the appellees "utilized" Luxama's services. *See* 29 U.S.C. § 1842. According to section 1842, unless a person utilizes the services of a farm labor contractor to supply an agricultural worker, there is no responsibility to be concerned about the farm labor contractor's certificate of registration. *See* 29 U.S.C. § 1842. Even though Little Rock and Hall did not "employ" appellants, they can be liable under section 1842 because it speaks only of a person who utilizes the services of an FLC, not an "employer."

The district court granted Little Rock's and Hall's motions for summary judgment on this issue, finding that neither Little Rock nor Hall "utilized" Luxama's services because the Burtons exercised the discretion to hire Luxama, and exercised subsequent control over Luxama and the appellants.

We find that the district court did not err in granting summary judgment for Hall and Little Rock, based on our analysis of "joint employment" and "economic dependence."

---

16. We note the district court's holding that to find the Burtons joint employers under the AWPA, "every farmer who hired a farm labor contractor would become for purposes of the AWPA ... a joint employer of the contractor's employees." Charles, 857 F.Supp. at 1581–82. We disagree, finding that the economic reality of the facts in this case indicate that the Burtons employed the appellants. We caution district courts to analyze each of these enunciated factors as guidance, taking into account the facts of each case, and the economic reality of each situation, to determine whether a farm worker is economically dependent on an agricultural employer.

The appellants presented no evidence that Little Rock or Hall engaged in directing, controlling or supervising the appellants. Further, Little Rock and Hall did not hire Luxama, but instead delegated the decision of hiring and paying for snap bean labor to the Burtons. Therefore, we agree with the district court that neither Little Rock nor Hall "utilized" the services of Luxama and the appellants. The Burtons however, concede that they utilized Luxama's services. We agree with the district court that the Burtons "utilized" the services of Luxama and the appellants, based on this same analysis.

V. DAMAGES

Having utilized the services of appellees, there was a statutory obligation on the part of John and Felix Burton to "first take[ ] reasonable steps to determine that the farm labor contractor possesse[d] a certificate of registration which [was] valid and which authorize[d] the activity for which the contractor [was] utilized." 29 U.S.C. § 1842. The Burtons concede they failed to determine if the farm labor contractor had a valid certificate authorizing him to transport agricultural workers. ("The Burtons did not check to see if [Luxama] had a certificate of registration when he came to the Burton's farm with the Haitian crew to pick beans.").

The district court granted the Burtons' motion for summary judgment in part, finding that the AWPA's legislative history failed to adopt a position on strict liability, and finding that the Burtons were not liable for the appellants' actual damages because their failure to check Luxama's certificate of registration was "too far removed from the type of harm complained of" to attribute actual damages to the Burtons. The district court therefore found that it should only award statutory damages of up to $500. *Charles v. Burton*, No. 7:92-cv-150 (M.D.Ga. Sept. 8, 1995). The district court later awarded the appellants $350 in statutory damages, finding the Burtons' violations to be "technically intentional." *See* 29 U.S.C. 1854(c)(1).

The district court erred by holding that the Burtons' failure to verify Luxama's registration, in violation of 29 U.S.C. § 1842, was too far removed from the appellants' injuries to warrant actual damages under 29 U.S.C. § 1854(c). Appellants do not claim the Burtons are responsible for the accident or their resulting physical injuries. Instead, they claim an inability to obtain medical care and a lack of compensation for lost wages because Luxama had no insurance coverage. Such a lack of access to insurance proceeds is an injury separate and distinguishable from appellants' physical injuries.... This is true even though appellants do not claim that the Burtons' actions caused them to be uninsured, but instead claim that the Burtons' actions precluded them from having access to insurance coverage which another person, in this case Luxama, was required to maintain. *See, e.g., Lippincott v. Exotica Imports, Inc.*, 413 So.2d 66, 67 (Fla.Dist.Ct.App.1982) (Defendant, an automobile dealer, sold a vehicle to a purchaser who did not have insurance coverage, dealer failed to verify that purchaser had insurance coverage, plaintiff was involved in an automobile accident while a passenger in purchaser's vehicle, plaintiff sued dealer, and court held that dealer "should be responsible to" plaintiff because it "did cause injury to [plaintiff] in that [plaintiff] was without the protection of [insurance] benefits at the time of the accident."). The Burtons' failure to check Luxama's certificate of registration was not far removed from the appellants' inability to obtain medical care and compensation for lost wages at all.

Luxama did not possess a certificate of registration and had no insurance to cover the damages that resulted from plaintiffs' physical injuries. To obtain a certificate of registration, Luxama, like any other farm labor contractor, would have had to produce documentation showing that he had an insurance policy or liability bond which insured "against liability to persons ... arising from the ownership, operation, or the causing to be operated, of any vehicle used to transport any migrant or seasonal agricultural worker." 29 U.S.C. § 1841(b)(1)(C); *see* 29 U.S.C. § 1812(2).

If the Burtons had utilized a farm labor contractor with a valid certificate of registration, there would have been insurance to cover appellants' physical injuries. See 29 U.S.C. §§ 1812(2); 1841(b)(1)(C). This uncontested fact is contrary to the district court's decision that "defendants' failure to check Mr. Luxama's certificate of registration is simply too far removed from the type of harm complained of for actual damages to be attributable to defendants." The Burtons' failure to determine whether Luxama had a valid certificate of registration was a proximate cause of the appellants' damages, not their physical injuries, but the damages that accrued because there was no insurance to cover their medical care and lost wages.

VI. CONCLUSION

Based on the foregoing, we reverse the district court's holding that the Burtons did not employ the appellants, affirm the district court's finding that neither Little Rock nor Hall employed the appellants or utilized their services, and remand this case to the district court to consider damages for the Burtons' failure to ensure that the automobiles transporting the appellants carried insurance or a liability bond, in violation of 29 U.S.C. § 1841, and to consider damages for the Burtons' failure to verify Luxama's certificate of registration before utilizing his services, in violation of 29 U.S.C. § 1842....

AFFIRMED IN PART, REVERSED IN PART and REMANDED. RONEY, Senior Circuit Judge, concurring in part and dissented in part.

Flores v. Rios
36 F.3d 507 (6th Cir. 1994)

Before: ENGEL, RYAN, and NORRIS, Circuit Judges.

ENGEL, J., delivered the opinion of the court, in which ALAN E. NORRIS, J., joined. RYAN, J.delivered a separate opinion concurring in the judgment.

ENGEL, Circuit Judge.

This case involves the proper interpretation of 29 U.S.C. § 1803(a)(1), which exempts family farms from regulations generally applied to agricultural employers under the Migrant and Seasonal Agricultural Worker Protection Act ("AWPA"), 29 U.S.C. §§ 1801 *et seq.* Defendant Gibsonburg Canning Co. ("GCC") is a tomato farm and cannery operated by John and Jerry Schuett. Defendant Reyes Rios is a farm worker employed by GCC. In 1989, plaintiff Jose Flores asked Rios to call the Schuetts and ask if farm work was available for the Flores family. Through Rios, Jerry Schuett instructed Flores to relocate his family from Santa Rosa, Texas to Gibsonburg, Ohio to harvest tomatoes for GCC. Flores brings this action individually and on behalf of his wife and children, claiming that GCC violated AWPA by failing to compensate them properly, failing to provide adequate housing, and failing to make certain required disclosures. GCC concedes non-compliance, but insists that as a family farm, it is exempt from AWPA regulation.

Immediately prior to their scheduled trial date, Flores and GCC agreed to 28 stipulations of fact. In response to the parties' joint motion for the entry of judgment based upon their stipulated facts, the district court concluded that GCC qualified for AWPA's family business exemption, and consequently dismissed the suit. For the following reasons, we REVERSE the judgment of the district court.

I. Background

AWPA protects migrant workers by establishing safety, compensation, and disclosure requirements with which all agricultural employers and labor contractors must comply. *See Bueno v. Mattner,* 829 F.2d 1380, 1382 (6th Cir.1987), *cert. denied,* 486 U.S. 1022, 108 S.Ct. 1994, 100 L.Ed.2d 226 (1988). AWPA also protects farmers by establishing a clear standard of acceptable conduct which minimizes the risk of "haphazard" and "burdensome" litigation. H.R. Rep. No. 885, 97th Cong., 2d Sess. 1 (1982), *reprinted in* 1982 U.S.C.C.A.N. 4547, 4547. As the legislative history explains, AWPA "[wa]s a consensus bill" enacted "only after extensive negotiation between representatives of the agricultural community, organized labor, migrant groups, the United States Department of Labor, and the committees of jurisdiction in both [houses of Congress]." *Id.*

Apparently believing that family farms pose little threat of worker exploitation, Congress has exempted such operations, under certain conditions, from AWPA's regulatory scope. 29 U.S.C. § 1803(a)(1).[1] AWPA's legislative history suggests that the family business exemption should "be construed narrowly in a manner that furthers the remedial purposes of this Act." H.R.REP. NO. 885, at 12, U.S.Code Cong. & Admin.News 1982 at 4558. *See Caro-Galvan v. Curtis Richardson, Inc.,* 993 F.2d 1500, 1505 (11th Cir.1993) ("AWPA is a remedial statute and should be construed broadly to effect its humanitarian purpose."); *Martinez v. Shinn,* 1991 WL 84473, at *16 (E.D.Wash.1991), *aff'd,* 992 F.2d 997 (9th Cir.1993). Courts applying the family business exemption must take great care to avoid exposing workers to any serious threat of abuse.

At the same time, any proper interpretation of section 1803(a)(1) must not frustrate Congress' deliberate exemption of family farms from AWPA regulation. As the legislative history notes, AWPA was a consensus bill, designed at least in part to protect farmers from haphazard and burdensome litigation which does not further the act's remedial purposes. This is not, of course, the first time that Congress has embraced a federal policy designed to benefit the oft-beleaguered family farmer. *See* 11 U.S.C. §§ 1201–1231 (providing special bankruptcy protection to family farmers). Because Congress has deliberately chosen to exclude these farmers from AWPA's regulatory scope, we must avoid any interpretation which "obliterate[s]" or "eviscerates" the exemption. *Calderon v. Witvoet,* 999 F.2d 1101, 1103 (7th Cir.1993).

The text of 1803(a)(1), *supra* note 1, indicates that the family business exemption applies to family-owned farms as long as all "farm labor contracting activity on behalf of [the] farm" is performed "exclusively" by family members. Thus, a court evaluating a farmer's claim to the family business exemption must conduct a two-step analysis. First, the court must identify the labor contracting activities involved in the farm's operation. Second,

---

1. 29 U.S.C. § 1803(a)(1) provides in pertinent part:
   The following persons are not subject to this chapter:
   Any individual who engages in a farm labor contracting activity on behalf of a farm … which is owned or operated exclusively by such individual or an immediate family member…, if such activities are performed only for such operation and exclusively by such individual or an immediate family member.…

the court must ascertain whether these farm labor contracting activities were performed exclusively by members of the farmer's family. The performance of any farm labor contracting activity by a non-family member "spoils" an agricultural employer's claim to the family business exemption.

To identify GCC's "farm labor contracting activities," and ultimately to determine whether all of these activities were performed exclusively by John and Jerry Schuett, we must first divine from the statute which practices Congress wished to treat as farm labor contracting activities. In 29 U.S.C § 1802(6), we find six relatively distinct contractual endeavors listed as examples of farm labor contracting activity: "recruiting, soliciting, hiring, employing, furnishing, or transporting" of migrant farm workers.

To qualify for AWPA's family business exemption, family members must perform all farm labor contracting activity necessary to operate the farm. Flores identifies three distinct sources of farm labor relied upon by GCC which he considers farm labor contracting activities not performed exclusively by the Schuetts. First, GCC borrowed surplus laborers from neighboring farms. Second, GCC hired workers referred by the Ohio Bureau of Employment Services, a state job placement agency. Third, GCC used its old workers to convey offers of employment to new workers. GCC admits to reliance upon these labor sources, but disputes whether such recruiting techniques constitute farm labor contracting activities performed by non-family members.

II. Borrowing of Workers

In their joint stipulations of fact, both parties agreed that GCC occasionally borrows workers from nearby farms:

> Sometimes, when [GCC] [is] in need of additional workers for an unusually busy day, [the Schuetts] will call a neighboring farm and ask the farmer or the farmer's crewleader if they have any people who are not busy that day that can work for [GCC] that particular day, and to make sure that the other farmer does not need the workers that day. If there are workers available, [the Schuetts] will go to the farmer's labor camp and ask the workers to come work for [GCC] for the day.

Joint Stipulation No. 11.

Flores argues that borrowing of workers defeats GCC's family business exemption because these laborers are supplied through a non-family member's contracting activity. Insisting that these workers are only in Ohio—and thus available to be borrowed—as a result of labor contracting activity performed by GCC's neighbors, Flores contends that such preliminary contracting activity should be attributed to GCC when it hires idle workers from nearby farms.

The district court disagreed with Flores, explaining that other farmers may have brought the workers to Ohio, but that the Schuetts brought these workers to GCC:

> [Flores] argue[s] that the workers are in Ohio and available for [GCC's] operations through someone else's farm labor activities. The Court disagrees. While someone else's labor contracting activities may indeed have brought the workers to Ohio, there is no nexus between the other person's contracting activity and [GCC's] solicitation of workers. The only farm labor contracting activity with some nexus to [GCC] takes place when the Schuetts personally go to the neighboring labor camp, and there is no basis to support [Flores'] contention that this should remove [GCC] from the family business exemption.

We agree with the district court that the labor contracting activities of other farmers cannot be attributed to GCC merely because GCC occasionally hires idle workers from nearby farms. The text of the family business exemption, 29 U.S.C. §1803(a)(1), *supra* note 1, specifically instructs us to examine the labor contracting activities performed "on behalf of" the family-owned farm. The labor contracting activities that brought the borrowed workers to Ohio, however, were not performed "on behalf of" the Schuetts' farm, and therefore cannot affect GCC's eligibility for the family business exemption. When a neighboring farmer spends time and money bringing workers to Ohio, such activities are clearly performed on the recruiting farmer's behalf, not GCC's.

Unlike Flores, we do not think this case is governed by *De La Fuente v. Stokely-Van Camp, Inc.,* 713 F.2d 225, 234–36 (7th Cir.1983), where a farming corporation was deemed a farm labor contractor because it lent out idle workers for a fee. *De La Fuente* dealt with the *lending* farmer's AWPA liability, whereas the defendant in today's case is the *borrowing* farmer. Furthermore, as the district court in *De La Fuente* noted, the lending farmer in that case actively sought to place the workers at other farms. *De La Fuente v. Stokely-Van Camp, Inc.,* 514 F.Supp. 68, 72 (C.D.Ill.1981). In stark contrast, the neighboring farmers in this case took no active role in the placement of their idle workers. As the parties stipulated, the Schuetts initiated all contact with the lending farmers. Once the Schuetts "ma[de] sure that the other farmer [did] not need the workers that day," they went "to the farmer's labor camp and ask[ed] the workers to come work for [GCC] for the day." Joint Stipulation No. 11, *supra.* By negotiating directly with the workers, the Schuetts exclusively performed all of their own farm labor contracting activities, as the family business exemption requires.

Allowing GCC to hire idle workers from other farms without losing its family business exemption comports not only with the text, but also with the spirit, of AWPA. Flores suggests no way in which the challenged practice of borrowing threatens workers. We perceive little risk of abuse resulting from the hiring of surplus laborers from other farms because the Schuetts directly negotiate a contract of employment with each worker. In fact, rather than posing some threat of harm, the practice of borrowing actually benefits idle workers by providing them with income at times when they would otherwise earn nothing. From this perspective, it is clear that the Schuetts' borrowing of workers poses none of the risk of exploitation that AWPA seeks to prevent.

III. The Ohio Bureau of Employment Services

Congress passed the Wagner-Peyser Act of 1933 "[i]n order to promote the establishment and maintenance of a national system of public employment offices." 29 U.S.C. §49. To encourage the creation of employment agencies at the state level, the Wagner-Peyser Act provides federal funding to any state submitting an acceptable organizational plan to the Department of Labor. 29 U.S.C. §49g. The Ohio Bureau of Employment Services ("OBES") was established pursuant to the Wagner-Peyser Act.

By providing job-seekers with access to a nationwide database of job listings, the Wagner-Peyser Act's employment service "improve[s] the functioning of the nation's labor markets by bringing together individuals who are seeking employment and employers who are seeking workers." 20 C.F.R. §652.2. As one court has explained, "[t]he objective of the Act [i]s to develop a national system of employment offices" which "connect the unemployed worker with a job." *Frederick Cty. Fruit Growers' Ass'n v. Marshall,* 436 F.Supp. 218, 220 (W.D.Va.1977).

GCC admits to hiring farm workers referred by OBES. As the parties have stipulated, GCC's "interactions with OBES are a two-way street." On some occasions, administrators from OBES will contact GCC in an effort to place particular workers. On other occasions, GCC will contact OBES to post job listings.

The proper treatment of state employment services under AWPA has not been addressed by any court of appeals.[2] Reasoning that OBES is merely "a state employment agency" which "bring[s] employers and applicants together," the district court determined that GCC did not lose its family business exemption by accepting OBES referrals. Perceiving little risk that exploitation would result from OBES' job placement efforts, the court suggested that "its ruling on this point is faithful to" AWPA's goal of protecting both workers and farmers.

In order to construe OBES referrals as a contracting activity, Flores recites the dictionary definitions for the verbs "to recruit," "to solicit," and "to furnish," which are three of the examples of farm labor contracting activity listed in 29 U.S.C. § 1802(6), *supra*. According to the definitions he has selected from the dictionary he prefers, Flores explains that "to recruit" means "to secure the services of," "to solicit" means "to move to action," and "to furnish" means "to provide with what is needed." Without suggesting that the relationship between OBES and GCC was *contractual* in any way, Flores nevertheless insists that OBES referrals must be considered non-family farm labor contracting activity because these referrals fit his dictionary definition of recruiting, soliciting, or furnishing farm labor.

We find Flores' dictionary-dependent argument unpersuasive for two reasons. First, the only authority justifying such inordinate reliance on the dictionary is a regulation promulgated under AWPA's predecessor, the Farm Labor Contractor Registration Act of 1963 ("FLCRA"). *See* 29 C.F.R. § 41.7 (1966) (using a dictionary to aid interpretation of FLCRA). However, FLCRA has been repealed, Pub.L. No. 97-470, § 523, 96 Stat. 2583, 2600 (1983), and its regulations have been replaced. 56 Fed.Reg. 54,786 (1991) ("remov[ing] the regulations found at 29 CFR parts 40 and 41," because they "do not affect the current operation of any program"). We see no reason to use withdrawn regulations from a repealed statute as a guide to interpret a new statute which expressly provides for its own regulations. *See* 29 U.S.C. § 1861 (authorizing AWPA regulations). The current regulation expressing the Secretary's interpretation of "farm labor contracting activity" merely recites the definition found in the statute. 29 C.F.R. § 500.20(i).

Our second reason for refusing to "make a fortress out of the dictionary," *Cabell v. Markham*, 148 F.2d 737, 739 (2d Cir.1945) (Hand, J.), *aff'd*, 326 U.S. 404, 66 S.Ct. 193, 90 L.Ed. 165 (1945), is our fundamental disagreement with Flores' a contextual approach to statutory interpretation. Laws cannot be interpreted by snatching single words out of statutory sentences and matching these words—without regard for context—up against one of the many definitions of that word found in the advocate's dictionary of choice. By splintering the text for purposes of statutory construction, Flores "overlooks, we think, th[e] fundamental principle of statutory construction (and indeed, of language itself) that the meaning of a word cannot be determined in isolation, but must be drawn from the context in which it is used." *Deal v. United States*, 508 U.S 129, ___, 113 S.Ct. 1993, 1996, 124 L.Ed.2d 44 (1993).

---

2. The use of state employment services has arisen in two "family business exemption" cases at the district court level, and these two opinions appear to reach conflicting results. In *Coronado v. Selkirk*, 113 Lab.Cas. (CCH) ¶ 35,283, 1989 WL 161165 (W.D.Mich.1989), the district court did not consider the farmer's use of the Michigan Employment Security Commission's Job Service to be an impediment to claiming the family business exemption. In contrast, the district court in *Martinez v. Hauch*, 838 F.Supp. 1209 (W.D.Mich.1993), ruled that a farmer could not claim the family business exemption after hiring workers referred by the very same agency.

Flores looks to the definitions of recruiting, soliciting, and furnishing, as those words might be used in casual conversation, without regard for the contractual context in which the exemption applies. But the words recruiting, soliciting, and furnishing are only relevant to our analysis as examples of labor contracting activity which the farm family must exclusively perform to be exempt. As the court in *Calderon* noted, all six practices listed by Congress as examples of farm labor contracting activity are distinctly *contractual* in nature:

> This definition collects a number of contractual endeavors: making a contract of employment ("hiring"), maintaining a worker in the labor force ("employing"), preparing to do these things ("recruiting" and "soliciting"), and doing them for others ("furnishing"). The final term in this sequence, "transporting," can be understood as still another contractual activity: obtaining and paying for a ticket that brings the worker to the farm or sends him to the next one. So understood, "farm labor contracting activity" covers the hiring and management of workers, the subject collectively called labor relations.

999 F.2d at 1103–04.

Interpreting these words within their proper context—the hiring and management of workers—we agree with the district court that OBES referrals do not "recruit, solicit, or furnish" farms with labor in any contractual sense. The OBES is a state agency that simply helps job-seekers locate prospective employers. The agency charges no fee for its services, and does not purport to represent either the employee or the employer. Both the farmer and the worker remain free at all times to accept or reject any of the agency's recommendations. An agency referral provides the worker with absolutely no assurance of employment—it merely provides the worker with a chance to find a job at a farm in need of labor. Within this framework, OBES job referrals plainly do not constitute non-family farm labor contracting activities.

Mindful of AWPA's protective goals, we see no reason to deter family farmers from using the public employment service when the challenged practice poses no threat to workers. Neither Flores nor his *amici* have suggested a single way in which the activities of the OBES expose the workers to any risk of abuse. In fact, the government's presence in the labor market can only serve to protect workers like Flores. The effectiveness of the public employment service directly reduces the workers' need to rely on potentially-abusive crew leaders to find agricultural employment. Furthermore, federal regulations require employers who wish to use a public employment service to comply with all relevant labor laws:

> The facilities … of the U.S. Employment Service, including the State agencies, authorized by the Wagner-Peyser Act may be denied to any person found … to have violated any employment-related laws.…

29 C.F.R. 500.1(f).

Flores contends that the Secretary of Labor agrees with his stance regarding the proper treatment of state employment agencies under AWPA. Citing our recent decision in *Smith v. Babcock,* 19 F.3d 257, 260–61 (6th Cir.1994), he suggests that the strong federal policy of deference to agency interpretations requires us to adopt what he calls the Secretary's view of the statute. Yet even the broadest policy of deference must have limits, and certainly no version of that doctrine permits an agency to revise the text of a statute. As Justice White has explained:

> The interpretation put on the statute by the agency charged with administering it is entitled to deference, but the courts are the final authorities on issues of

statutory construction. They must reject administrative constructions of the statute, whether reached by adjudication or by rulemaking, that are inconsistent with the statutory mandate or that frustrate the policy that Congress sought to implement.

Federal Election Comm'n v. Democratic Senatorial Campaign Committee, 454 U.S. 27, 32, 102 S.Ct. 38, 42, 70 L.Ed.2d 23 (1981).

Over a decade later, Justice Kennedy once again confirmed that "the clear meaning of statutes as written" ultimately trumps the policy of "judicial deference to a reasonable statutory interpretation by an administering agency." *Estate of Cowart v. Nicklos Drilling Co.,* 505 U.S. 469, ___, 112 S.Ct. 2589, 2594, 120 L.Ed.2d 379 (1992). Because Congress has spoken to the issue at hand with sufficient clarity to dictate the result we reach today, we cannot defer to an administrator who would contradict that legislative will. Accordingly, we agree with the district court that GCC's acceptance of OBES referrals does not affect the farm's eligibility for the family business exemption.

IV. Word of Mouth Referrals

Although GCC, unlike many farms, does not require its employees to assist in recruiting, GCC's farm workers have often taken the initiative in referring job-seekers to John and Jerry Schuett. Flores argues that these referrals constitute farm labor contracting activity not exclusively performed by members of the Schuett family. The parties stipulated to the following description of the impact "word of mouth" referrals have on GCC's operations:

> At times, some of [GCC's] current workers call [the Schuetts] to say that they know a good family of migrant farmworkers that is interested in working for [GCC] and ask if there is work available for the family. If [GCC] need[s] additional workers and ha[s] housing available for a new family, [the Schuetts] tell the caller that the family can come. If [the Schuetts] don't know whether they will need additional workers, [the Schuetts] tell the caller to have the family contact [them] before the season begins to see if [GCC] may need workers at that time. None of [GCC's] workers have the authority to hire any workers for [GCC].

Joint Stipulation No. 10.

Jose Flores was referred to GCC by Reyes Rios. According to the stipulations, Flores went to Rios' house in April of 1989 "to discus[s] working for Gibsonburg Canning." Joint Stipulation No. 23. During this meeting, "Flores said that his family wanted to work for Gibsonburg Canning and asked Rios to call the Schuetts to see if the Flores family could work for defendants." *Id.* Rios then called Jerry Schuett:

> Within the next few days, Reyes Rios called Jerry Schuett to ask if there was work and housing available for the Flores family. Jerry asked Rios how many workers there were in the Flores family and Rios told him that the Flores family had five workers. Jerry then told Rios that there was work and housing available.

Joint Stipulation No. 24.

Flores argues that Rios' job placement efforts should be considered a non-family farm labor contracting activity which defeats GCC's family business exemption. In contrast, the district court believed that word of mouth referrals do not constitute non-family labor contracting activity because the Schuetts never authorized Rios to hire workers:

The stipulated facts do not set forth that Reyes Rios or any other employee ever had the actual or apparent authority to hire anyone, but rather, that current employees might inquire as to whether work was available for another family. [The Schuetts] would give the current employee an answer, which would then be relayed to the prospective workers.

This court has analyzed the relationship between word of mouth referrals and the family business exemption once previously. In *Bueno v. Mattner, supra,* we recognized that farm employees impact the recruiting process in a variety of ways, some of which affect eligibility for the exemption, and others of which do not. On one hand, the court in *Bueno* determined that a farmer's specific delegation of recruiting authority to an employee wrecked the farmer's eligibility for the exemption. *Id.* at 1383–84. Delegation of such authority often eliminates all direct contact between the agricultural employer and the farm worker, and thus creates an untenable potential for abuse. On the other hand, the court in *Bueno* also determined that an employee's "gratuitous recommendation" that the farmer consider hiring a friend had no affect on the farmer's eligibility for the exemption. Such recommendations are beyond the farmer's control, and therefore cannot affect the farmer's exempt status. *Bueno,* 829 F.2d at 1384 n. 3.

The only other court of appeals to address this issue, the Seventh Circuit, also analyzed eligibility for the exemption in terms of the employee's role in the recruiting process. *See Calderon v. Witvoet, supra,* 999 F.2d at 1105. Like the court in *Bueno,* the court in *Calderon* determined that a purposeful delegation of recruiting authority would defeat the exemption, while a worker's unprompted referrals would not:

> What workers tell their friends is beyond the owners' control, and treating such activities as "farm labor contracting activities" would gut the exemption—for it is impossible to suppress word-of-mouth reports about the job.... The ensuing trial must focus on the [farmers'] own decisions and actions—including the choice, if they made one, to delegate recruitment and hiring to the foremen. Events beyond the owners' control do not affect the availability of the family farm exemption.

999 F.2d at 1105.

The case at bar is more difficult than *Bueno* because the recruiting practice Flores challenges was neither a sweeping delegation of authority, nor a mere gratuitous recommendation. As the parties have stipulated, no GCC employees have general hiring authority. Joint Stipulation No. 10, *supra.* But the circumstances surrounding the hiring of Flores placed Reyes Rios in a much more significant role than the hypothetical gratuitous recommender. Looking back to the parties' stipulated facts, we see that Rios not only recommended Flores for employment, but was also *solely responsible* for conveying the resulting offer of employment to Flores and his family:

> At Rios' house, Jose Flores ... asked Rios to call the Schuetts to see if the Flores family could work for [GCC]....
>
> Within the next few days, Reyes Rios called Jerry Schuett to ask if there was work and housing available for the Flores family.... Jerry then told Rios that there was work and housing available....
>
> Rios later told Jose Flores that he had called [GCC] and that there was work available.... Rios also told Flores the date that the Rios family was leaving Texas to go to Ohio....
>
> *[The Schuetts] did not have any conversations or contact with [the Flores family] prior to arriving at [GCC]. It was understood, however, that if the [Flores family]*

arrived at the cannery in Ohio in time to transplant tomatoes, [GCC] would give them a job and provide them housing in [GCC's] labor camp....

[The Flores family] drove to Ohio ... and began working for [GCC]....

Joint Stipulations Nos. 23–25, 27–28 (emphasis added).

The district court below properly understood that courts analyzing a farmer's eligibility for the exemption must focus upon the delegation of authority. But the court failed to appreciate that Rios must have wielded authority if GCC was able to hire the Flores family *without ever speaking to them.* In the district court's view, the fact that Rios merely "relayed" messages between the contracting parties undercut any suggestion of delegated authority. In contrast, we believe that the formation of a binding employment contract — in the absence of *any* direct contact between Schuett and Flores — *necessitates* the delegation of some authority. An absent principal simply cannot contract with a third party without delegating authority. The conclusory language of Joint Stipulation No. 10, *supra*, which opines that "[n]one of [GCC's] workers have the authority to hire," simply cannot contradict the more specific factual concessions GCC has made in other stipulations. Taken as a whole, these stipulations reveal that Rios, like the employee in *Martinez v. Shinn*, "informed" the farmer "that [he] had ... people wanting to work," and was told in return "to bring them and that they would be hired." *Id.*, 1991 WL 84473, at *16. By submitting Flores' job application, by vouching for Flores as a good farm worker, and by relaying the ensuing offer of employment, Rios played a far more influential role in the recruiting process than some disinterested maker of gratuitous recommendations. We cannot avoid concluding that Rios performed farm labor contracting activity on GCC's behalf, as the exemption forbids.

Our ruling in this case not only finds support in *Bueno, Calderon,* and *Martinez,* but also delicately reconciles the oft-conflicting goals of protecting farm workers from abuse and protecting farmers from needless litigation. The Schuetts must lose their exemption in this case because they have induced Flores to move his family across the country without ever speaking to him. Upon their arrival in Ohio, Flores and his family stood utterly at the Schuetts' mercy, and the Schuetts could have inflicted unacceptable hardship by reneging on the offer of employment, or by varying the terms or conditions of that offer. That is why the family business exemption only applies to farmers who personally conduct their own farm labor contracting activity. If the Schuetts wish to remain exempt, they are fully empowered to do so — by speaking directly to the employee they are hiring. It is not Rios' recommendation, but rather the lack of *any* direct contact between the employer and the migrant worker, that cost GCC its exemption. Only by interpreting the exemption in this way can *both* the worker and the farmer avail themselves of the protections Congress intended. Accordingly, we conclude that the Schuetts' use of Rios to hire Flores, and to instruct Flores to move his family from Texas to Ohio, must be considered a non-family farm labor contracting activity which defeats GCC's family business exemption.

For the foregoing reasons, the judgment below is REVERSED and REMANDED for further proceedings in the district court consistent with this opinion.

RYAN, Circuit Judge, concurring in the judgment.

Although I agree that the Gibsonburg Canning Company (GCC) has lost its family business exemption, I reach this conclusion on grounds that differ from the majority's. I therefore write separately to register my respectful disagreement with my colleagues' reasoning.

Rios's actions, from the stipulated facts, do not constitute "a farm labor contracting activity on behalf of" the GCC. 29 U.S.C. §1803(a)(1). The majority opinion recognizes "that a purposeful delegation of recruiting authority would defeat the exemption, while a worker's unprompted referrals would not," and that the inquiry "'must focus on the [farmers'] own decisions and actions,'" maj. op. at 515 (quoting *Calderon v. Witvoet,* 999 F.2d 1101, 1105 (7th Cir.1993)).

Here, the plaintiffs inquired, on their own initiative, about the availability of Ohio farm jobs. The plaintiffs, again on their own initiative, asked Rios to call the Schuetts. Rios then called and asked Jerry Schuett whether jobs and housing were available for the Flores family. These facts do not in any way suggest that the GCC delegated, expressly or impliedly, any authority to Rios. The stipulated facts do not indicate that the GCC had ever hired workers whom Rios mentioned or that the GCC prompted Rios to disseminate information about the farm. In short, Jerry Schuett merely answered Rios's questions; this civil gesture did not authorize Rios to recruit, solicit, hire, employ, furnish, or transport Flores. I would hold that Rios did not engage in "a farm labor contracting activity on behalf of" the GCC because it neither authorized nor could prevent Rios's discussions with the plaintiffs.

However, the GCC did lose the family business exemption when the Ohio Bureau of Employment Services (OBES) "furnished" migrant workers to the farm. According to the stipulated facts, when the farm's operation requires additional workers, the Schuetts occasionally call the OBES to see if the OBES has any available farm workers. Presumably, the OBES creates a pool of unemployed workers specifically qualified for farm work by sorting through the universe of unemployed workers who have come to the bureau's attention. The OBES then matches the unemployed farm worker to the Schuetts' request. This is "furnishing" workers to the GCC in the plain and common understanding of the word.

My colleague asserts that the OBES does not furnish the GCC with workers "in any contractual sense." He points out that the OBES does not charge a fee, does not purport to represent either the GCC or the worker, and does not guarantee employment upon referral. It is, of course, evident under the statute that the OBES has no "contractual" relationship with the Schuetts or with the migrant workers it refers to the Schuetts. In all events, those activities are inessential to concluding that the OBES furnished workers in a "contractual" sense: the OBES screens workers and supplies them to the farm in order for the farm and the worker to then enter into an employment contract. The majority opinion's critique of the plaintiffs' reliance on dictionary definitions misses the mark. In most cases, the dictionary provides helpful guidance as to the undisputed plain meaning of words—in this case, "furnish."

Finally, contrary to the majority's suggestion, it is irrelevant that the OBES may in fact behave as the most conscientious labor contractor ever to serve a migrant worker. The statute's language prohibits *any* nonfamily member from engaging in "a farm labor contracting activity on behalf of" the GCC. Once the actor is identified as a nonfamily member, the actor's benevolent nature is immaterial. Rather, the statute directs our attention to the nature of the "activity." That Congress chose sweeping language to define the activities that must be performed by family members is not the concern of this court. Indeed, Congress may have purposefully raised an overprotective shield so that cases at the margins would result in triggering the disclosure and record keeping requirements—even at the expense of including well-meaning labor contractors. It is such guessing at unwritten and obscure purposes that counsels us to remain faithful to the statutory text.

I would hold that the OBES's furnishing of migrant workers to the GCC destroyed the GCC's family business exemption.

―――――――

Notes

1. A recent report issued by the Farmworker Justice and Oxfam America charges that a lack of enforcement of labor laws on farms has led to increased abuses. Farmers who follow the law are penalized when their cost of production is higher than those who violate the labor provisions. A shortage of wage-hour investigators at the Department of Labor, the difficulty in enforcing labor laws in the dispersed farming community, and a low priority accorded farmworkers are all blamed.

> The huge decline in enforcement activities under the Migrant and Seasonal Agricultural Worker Protection Act (AWPA) and the Fair Labor Standards Act (FLSA)—about a 50 percent reduction from 20 years ago—has invited abuses. To give employers the realistic impression that they are likely to be investigated and punished for violations of employment laws, DOL must send the message that violations will be costly.

> The report calls the Obama administration's "announcement of the hiring of more wage-hour investigators in 2009 was a welcomed first step" and asks the Department of Labor to be "strategic in the use of its limited resources and address systemic problems that affect large numbers of farmworkers."

Farmworker Justice and Oxfam America, *Weeding Out Abuses: Recommendations for a Law-abiding Farm Labor System* (2010).

A Department of Labor Press Release:

> U.S. Secretary of Labor Hilda L. Solis today issued the following statement in response to the report "Weeding out Abuses: Recommendations for a Law-abiding Farm Labor System" co-authored by Farmworker Justice and Oxfam America:

> "This report makes clear that farmworkers face a number of challenges and that for too long the federal government has not taken the steps necessary to empower and protect these workers.

> "When I came into office, I immediately began to change the way the Department of Labor approaches farmworker issues.

> "As secretary of labor, I have made a priority of ensuring farmworkers are paid a fair wage, provided safe and healthy working conditions and given the opportunity to update their job skills. We've changed regulations, put more investigators in the field, made clear we won't stand for the exploitation of children in the fields and refocused our efforts on behalf of this important community.

> "While I'm very proud of what the Obama administration has accomplished on behalf of farmworkers in the last year, I look forward to continuing to work with the farmworker community on ways to protect the wages, safety and health of this important part of America's labor force."

The Department also issued a list of action steps taken by the DOL "to improve working conditions for farm labor."

- The U.S. Department of Labor has: Published new H-2A regulations that significantly strengthen worker protections for H-2A workers and domestic workers performing the same work alongside H-2A workers. The new regulations provide enhanced enforcement tools for the department, including revocation and debarment authority for the Wage and Hour Division, and an increased bonding requirement for labor contractors.

- The Wage and Hour Division is focusing on protecting youth working in agriculture through a variety of strategies. It has and will continue to increase investigations and outreach to farmers, farm labor contractors, workers, parents, teachers, others who provide services to farmworkers and other federal agencies. Ending illegal child labor is a top departmental priority, and Wage and Hour Division investigators are using every tool available—from imposing civil money penalties to using the "hot goods" provision—to end these violations.

- The department has explored additional regulatory changes to further bolster protections for children in the fields. The secretary is seeking to collaborate with Congress to address the protection gap in U.S. law for child farmworkers.

- More than 250 new Wage and Hour Division field investigators have been added in the last year.

- The department has worked with Congress, which recently appropriated additional funds to the department for enforcement activities in industries that are likely to employ foreign workers temporarily working in the United States under a work visa. The Wage and Hour Division and the department's Office of the Solicitor plan to use some of these funds to ensure that labor conditions for agricultural workers meet all the department's requirements.

- The department's Occupational Health and Safety Administration brought together nearly 1,000 participants to the National Action Summit for Latino Worker Health and Safety in Houston, Texas. The goal of the summit was to reduce injuries and illnesses among Latino workers by enhancing knowledge of their workplace rights and improving their ability to exercise those rights.

- The department's fiscal year 2011 budget request requested for its Employment and Training Administration the first funding increase in more than 20 years for the National Farmworker Jobs Program, which is authorized by the Workforce Investment Act. This increase would restore funding to the levels originally envisioned under the Workforce Investment Act while supporting services for 1,027 additional migrant and seasonal farmworkers and their families through the National Farmworker Jobs Program grantee community.

- The department's Employment and Training Administration's National Farmworker Jobs Program facilitates coordination of services through the public workforce system's One-Stop Career Centers for migrant and seasonal farmworkers. This coordination enables these workers to gain access to all available services, including education and career pathways, occupational skills training and other employment assistance leading to jobs that provide stable, year round employment both within and outside agriculture. Grantees, which include public agencies, private, nonprofit organizations and community-based organizations, are present in nearly every state. Between July 1, 2008, and June 30, 2009, these grantees provided services to 18,501 migrant and seasonal farmworkers.

- National and regional monitor advocates monitor and review state workforce agencies for compliance with Wagner-Peyser regulations affecting migrant and seasonal farmworkers on a continuing basis. Regulations require the provision of employment and training services to migrant and seasonal farmworkers that is qualitatively equivalent and quantitatively proportionate to services provided to non-migrant and seasonal farmworkers. The national monitor advocate ensures that state workforce agencies operate and maintain the nationwide Job Service Complaint System for filing and processing customer complaints related to alleged violations of state and/or federal employment laws, with special emphasis and follow-up on complaints filed by migrant and seasonal farmworkers.

• The Wage and Hour Division has enforced temporary farm labor camp requirements regarding the field sanitation provisions of potable drinking water, toilet and hand-washing facilities in those states in which it has enforcement authority under the Occupational Safety and Health Act. Fourteen states operate their own Occupational Safety and Health Authority-approved and -funded plans that further bolster enforcement of these standards.

• The department has announced the inclusion of the H-2B Temporary Nonagricultural Worker Program in its semiannual agenda, which lists all of the regulations the department expects to have under active consideration for promulgation, proposal or review during the coming one-year period. The department believes there are insufficient worker protections in the current attestation-based labor certification model. The proposed rule will address the critical issue of U.S. worker access to the jobs for which employers seek H-2B workers through a re-engineered program design, which focuses on enhanced U.S. worker recruitment and strengthened worker protections.

• The Wage and Hour Division today is implementing higher penalties for the illegal employment of children in agriculture.

• These increased penalties and reinvigorated enforcement by the Wage and Hour Division will help ensure children are safe and are given a chance to live long and productive lives.

2. Advocates for farmworkers are increasingly looking to the food processors and related corporate interests in their efforts to obtain better wages and working conditions for the workers. Farmers argue that the wages they pay are limited by the prices that the processors pay them.

A prominent example was the nationwide boycott of Taco Bell organized by the Coalition of Immokalee Workers, an advocacy group working on behalf of workers who pick tomatoes in southwest Florida. The boycott ended when Yum Brands, Inc., the corporate owner of Taco Bell, agreed to pay an additional penny per pound for the tomatoes it purchased, with the extra cent going directly to workers. *See,* Evelyn Nieves, *Accord with Tomato Pickers Ends Boycott of Taco Bel,* WASH. POST, A-6 (Mar. 9, 2005). Settlements were subsequently reached with other buyers, including McDonald's, Burger King, and Whole Foods.

However, the Florida Tomato Growers' Exchange, the Florida tomato industry cooperative threatened to fine any member-farmer that participated and called the agreements between the farmers and the companies illegal and unenforceable. It only reversed its position in February 2010 when it issued its first "social responsibility program." *See* http://floridatomatogrowers.org/news/newsdetails.aspx?id=41.

3. Success in holding a corporate processor liable under the labor laws remains difficult. In *Luna v. Del Monte Fresh Produce (Southeast), Inc.,* 2008 WL 754452 (N.D. Ga, May 19,

2008), the court held that the defendant was not a joint employer of the farmworkers even though its wholly-owned subsidiary was found to be an employer.

C. Current Issues

1. Slavery

In recent years, there have been a number of successful prosecutions that involved the shocking enslavement of farmworkers by farm labor contractors that supplied workers to farmers. The farm labor contractor is paid by the farmer and manages a work crew to perform agricultural labor. The workers, however, may be forced to work, held against their will, with their wages retained by the contractor. The contractor justifies retaining the wages by charging them for housing, meals, and other costs at rates that often add up to more than their wages.

> Since 1997, there have been seven cases of slavery prosecutions in Florida, six as a result of investigations by the Coalition of Immokalee Workers. The prosecution of these cases has resulted in the freedom of more than 1,000 people working in the vegetable fields and citrus groves of Florida, Georgia, and the Carolinas under slavery conditions. In the most recent case, the employers were charged with beating tomato pickers, holding them in debt, and chaining and locking them inside U-Haul trucks for punishment over a period of two years.

Farmworker Justice and Oxfam America, *Weeding Out Abuses: Recommendations for a Law-abiding Farm Labor System* (2010).

In May 2010, The St. Petersburg Times reported on a migrant farmworker, Jewel Goodman, freed after 8 years of bondage. John Pendygraft, *Slavery of Migrant Farmworkers Continues in the U.S. to This Day* (May 30, 2010) available at http://www.tampabay.com/features/humaninterest/slavery-of-migrant-farmworkers-continues-in-the-us-to-this-day/1098420. The contractor was eventually prosecuted and the workers freed. "In 2007, Ronald Evans was sentenced to 30 years in federal prison after holding Goodman and other farm workers "perpetually indebted" in what the U.S. Department of Justice called a 'form of servitude morally and legally reprehensible.'"

In Colorado, a farm labor contractor was found to have forged immigration papers for undocumented workers, then withheld wages from them and held them in debt bondage, forcing them to work and to live in a squalid labor camp. *See*, Felisa Cardona and Kevin Vaughan, *Fields of Fear for Colorado Illegal Farm Laborers*, The Denver Post (May 18, 2009), available at http://www.denverpost.com/ci_12387869.

The U.S. Department of Justice, Civil Rights Division reports as follows:

> It is profoundly troubling that the problem of slavery continues into the new millennium. While we discuss this problem using such terms as trafficking and worker exploitation, we should make no mistake about it—we are talking about slavery in its modern manifestations. While some of the schemes and practices employed by traffickers reflect the sophistication of the modern world, others are basic and barbaric. Regardless of how sophisticated or simple trafficking enterprises may be, at bottom they all deny the essential humanity of the victims and turn them into objects for profit.

The federal government is working to combat this tragic problem. In 1998, the Attorney General ordered the creation of an interagency task force to focus on the problem of worker exploitation. The Trafficking in Persons and Worker Exploitation Task Force (TPWETF) is co-chaired by the Assistant Attorney General for Civil Rights and the Solicitor of Labor. This effort has brought a range of investigative and prosecutorial agencies to the table. U.S. Department of Justice components include the Civil Rights and Criminal Divisions, the Federal Bureau of Investigation (FBI), the Immigration and Naturalization Service (INS), U.S. Attorneys' offices, the Office of Policy Development, the Office for Victims of Crime, and the Violence Against Women Office. U.S. Department of Labor components include the Office of the Solicitor, the Wage and Hour Division, and the Women's Bureau. Outside partners include the U.S. Departments of State and Agriculture, and the Equal Employment Opportunity Commission (EEOC). In addition, the TPWETF has created fifteen regional task forces, each of which has points of contacts from local U.S. Attorneys' offices, INS, the FBI, the Department of Labor, EEOC, and state and local law enforcement. The regional task force approach has allowed investigators and prosecutors to share information and coordinate their efforts. We believe that by pooling information, expertise, and resources and by using all of the legal authority available to these agencies, we can make a difference.

New Legislation, New Opportunities

The recently enacted Victims of Trafficking and Violence Protection Act of 2000 established important new tools and resources to combat trafficking and to provide vital assistance to its victims. An Internet link to the new legislation can be found at www.usdoj.gov/crt/crim/tpwetf.htm. The law creates new felony criminal offenses to address slavery and peonage; sex trafficking in children; and the unlawful confiscation of a victim's passport or other identification documents. It creates a new "forced labor" felony that will provide federal law enforcement with the ability to prosecute the sophisticated forms of nonphysical coercion that traffickers use today to exploit their victims. And it requires traffickers to pay full restitution to victims and to forfeit their assets if convicted.

The new law also provides essential services and protections for trafficking victims. The law makes victims eligible for a broad array of federal benefits, requires procedures to ensure victims' safety and assistance while in the government's custody, and creates grants to develop programs to assist trafficking victims. Moreover, the new law makes such victims eligible for temporary nonimmigrant visas so that they can remain in the United States to help law enforcement in the prosecution of traffickers. The new law also requires that several federal agencies establish public awareness and information programs about trafficking and the protections that are available to victims. Traffickers who prey on vulnerable individuals shall be brought to justice, and victims of trafficking must be treated with dignity and afforded vital assistance and protection.

The U.S. Departments of Justice and Labor, co-chairs of the Trafficking in Persons and Worker Exploitation Task Force, have taken the lead in prosecuting trafficking and worker abuse cases, balancing the special needs of trafficking victims with swift punishment for traffickers.

http://www.justice.gov/crt/crim/wetf/wetfpolicy.php

Included in the highlights of DOJ prosecutions was an agricultural farmworker case.

In the spring of 1999, three defendants were convicted of slavery and immigration violations arising from their enslavement of Mexican and Guatemalan farmworkers in the agricultural fields of southern Florida through threats of force. The lead defendant received a sentence of three years incarceration. The victims received legal status and are working in Florida, where they participate in a farmworker advocacy group.

Id.

For an analysis of this issue and a description of the work done by the Coalition of Immokalee Workers, see Kevin Bales and Ron Soodalter, The Slave Next Door: Human Trafficking and Slavery in America Today (2009) (highlighting farmworker labor camps and the successful prosecution of a slavery ring in South Carolina). *See also*, Barry Estabrook, *Politics of the Plate: The Price Of Tomatoes*, Gourmet (March 2009).

2. The "Fair Food" Movement

Many in the food and agriculture communities have taken a stand for the equitable treatment of farmworkers..

In April 2009, the Washington Post reported:

> Appalled by instances of what federal prosecutors have described as slavery, executives of one of the nation's largest food service companies promise to boycott Florida tomatoes if growers do not agree to improve conditions and increase pay for farmworkers.
>
> Bon Appetit Management today will issue a strict set of standards that farm worker advocates call a "rough draft" of the future of fairly produced food. If no grower agrees, the company is set to stop serving tomatoes on salad bars and sandwiches at its more than 400 college and corporate cafes across the country.
>
> The growers can do the right thing and our five million pounds of business can do to them, said Fedele Bauccio, Bon Appetit's chief executive. Or, they can let the tomatoes rot in the fields.
>
> Bon Appetit's decision is the latest salvo on a new front of the sustainable-food wars: social justice.

Jane Black, *A Squeeze for Tomato Growers, Boycott vs. Higher Wages*, Wash. Post (April 29, 2009).

Bon Appetit took its campaign to the college campuses that it serves, with educational messages such as the following, taken from their blog.

> *Farmworkers in Florida's tomato fields spend the day filling 32 lb buckets . . .*

March 23–24, 2010

Boston, MA

Do you know how many tomatoes a Florida farmworker has to pick in order to fill one 32-lb bucket? Do you know how many buckets Florida farmworkers have to fill in an hour in order to make the FL minimum wage?

These were the questions I asked students at Emmanuel College (Boston, MA) and Lesley University (Cambridge, MA) to answer during a recent visit. As students poured through the doors of the café, pushing past each other and trying to beat the lunch lines, I stood by the entrance shouting "Answer two quick questions and win a free pizza party!" And I was happy to learn that even though I'm almost a full year out of college, some things haven't changed: students still love pizza, (especially when it's free).

The purpose of this whole endeavor was to raise awareness among college students about the challenges faced by the farmworkers who provide us with the very produce we eat. So, "spoiler alert": In order to fill one 32-lb bucket of average sized tomatoes, a farmworker has to pick about 170 tomatoes. And in order to make the FL minimum wage ($7.25/hr), farmworkers have to fill about 16 buckets per hour. If you break that down, that means they have to fill one bucket every 3–4 minutes; that's about 45 tomatoes per minute, 1 tomato every 1.2 seconds.

And that doesn't include the amount of time it takes them to run—carrying the 32 lb bucket on their shoulder—to the truck, empty their buckets, and run back to their spot to continue picking. So, here's my next question:

How many Florida tomato farmworkers do you think actually make the minimum wage?

Post written by Carolina Fojo, Bon Appétit East Coast Fellow

http://bonappetit.typepad.com/bon_appetit/2010/04/farmworkers-in-floridas-tomato-fields-spend-the-day-filling-32-lb-buckets-.html.

The Fair Food Project website presents "Fair Food: Field to Table," a multimedia presentation "promoting a more socially just food system in the U.S." on its website at http://www.fairfoodproject.org/main/.

Through the stories and voices of farmworkers, growers, businesses and fair food advocates, viewers learn about the harsh realities of farmworker conditions and, more importantly, the promise of improved farm labor practices in American agriculture. The growing movement for "fair food" is tapping into rising consumer demand for food produced in accordance with their values.

The presentation consists of three parts:

Part 1: The Farmworkers

Part 2: The Farmers

Part 3: The Advocates

It was created by California Institute for Rural Studies and Rick Nahmias Photography.

VII

The Regulation of Livestock Sales

The stockyards are not a place of rest or final destination. Thousands of head of live stock arrive daily by carload and trainload lots, and must be promptly sold and disposed of and moved out, to give place to the constantly flowing traffic that presses behind. The stockyards are but a throat through which the current flows, and the transactions which occur therein are only incident to this current from the West to the East, and from one state to another.

Stafford v. Wallace, 258 U.S. 495, 499 (1922).

A. Introduction to the Packers and Stockyards Act

Christopher R. Kelley
An Overview of the Packers and Stockyards Act
2003 Ark. L. Notes 35 (2003)

Introduction

The Packers and Stockyards Act, 1921,[1] is intended to ensure fair competition and fair trade practices in the marketing of livestock, meat, and poultry.[2] It fulfills a need for specialized regulation of these industries in recognition of their unique marketing and distribution practices.[3]

---

1. 7 U.S.C. §§ 181–229 (2000). Hereinafter, all citations to the United States Code are to the 2000 edition except where, as noted in the text, a section was added by the 2002 Farm Bill, formally known as the Farm Security and Rural Investment Act of 2002.

2. For recent commentary on the effectiveness of the Act in achieving this goal, see Michael C. Stumo & Douglas J. O'Brien, *Antitrust Unfairness vs. Equitable Unfairness in Farmer/Meat Packer Relationships*, 8 DRAKE J. AGRIC. L. 91 (2003); Terence Stewart et al., *Trade and Cattle: How the System Is Failing an Industry in Crisis*, 9 MINN. J. GLOBAL TRADE 449, 509–11 (2000); Jon Lauck, *Toward an Agrarian Antitrust: A New Direction for Agricultural Law*, 75 N.D. L. REV. 449, 490–91 (1999); Edward P. Lord, *Fairness for Modern Farmers: Reconsidering the Need for Legislation Governing Production Contracts*, 33 WAKE FOREST L. REV. 1125, 1136–40 (1998); Douglas J. O'Brien, *The Packers and Stockyards Act of 1921 Applied to the Hog Industry of 1995*, 20 J. CORP. L. 651 (1995).

3. *See* Armour & Co. v. United States, 402 F.2d 712, 722 (7th Cir. 1968).

The Act also "is one of the most comprehensive regulatory measures ever enacted."[4] In broadly prohibiting monopolistic, unfair, deceptive, and unjustly discriminatory practices, the Act gives the Secretary of Agriculture "complete inquisitorial, visitorial, supervisory, and regulatory power over the packers, stockyards, and all activities connected therewith."[5]

As remedial legislation, the Act is liberally construed.[6] Under the Act, the Secretary has "jurisdiction to deal with *every* unjust, unreasonable, or discriminatory regulation or practice' involved in the marketing of livestock."[7] This authority, which extends to preventing "potential injury by stopping unlawful practices in their incipiency,"[8] is broader than the authority conferred under the Sherman, Clayton, and Federal Trade Commission Acts.[9]

The Act's regulatory regime has two basic purposes. First, it is intended to protect the immediate financial interests of livestock and poultry producers by, among other things, ensuring that they are paid promptly based on accurate animal weights. In this respect, the Act serves to ensure the integrity of livestock and poultry marketing transactions.[10]

Second, the Act is intended to protect producers and consumers by prohibiting monopolistic or predatory practices.[11] For example, it prohibits packers, swine contractors, and live poultry dealers from colluding to manipulate prices or to apportion territory to force sellers to accept lower prices than would exist under free competition.[12]

The Secretary has delegated responsibility for administering the Act to the Assistant Secretary for Marketing and Regulatory Programs who, in turn, has subdelegated that authority to the Administrator of the Grain Inspection, Packers and Stockyards Administration (GIPSA).[13] Prior to the enactment of the Federal Crop Insurance Reform and Department of Agriculture Reorganization Act of 1994,[14] the responsible agency was the Packers and Stockyards Administration (PSA). GIPSA assumed the responsibilities of the PSA under the USDA's reorganization.[15] GIPSA's regulations implementing the Act are codified at 9 C.F.R. Parts 201–203.[16]

---

4. Donald A. Campbell, *The Packers and Stockyards Act Regulatory Program, in* 1 AGRICULTURAL LAW § 3.01(John Davidson ed., 1981) [hereinafter Campbell].

5. 10 NEIL E. HARL, AGRICULTURAL LAW § 71.01 (1992) [hereinafter HARL] (footnote omitted); *see also* 1 JULIAN CONRAD JUERGENSMEYER & JAMES BRYCE WADLEY, AGRICULTURAL LAW § 16.1 (1982) (discussing the Act's scope).

6. *See, e.g.*, Bowman v. United States Dep't of Agric., 363 F.2d 81, 85 (5th Cir. 1966).

7. Rice v. Wilcox, 630 F.2d 586, 590 (8th Cir. 1980) (quoting 7 U.S.C. § 208(a)).

8. Daniels v. United States, 242 F.2d 39, 42 (7th Cir. 1957).

9. *See* Swift & Co. v. United States, 393 F.2d 247, 253 (7th Cir. 1968); Wilson v. Benson, 286 F.2d 891, 894 (7th Cir. 1961).

10. *See, e.g.*, Stafford v. Wallace, 258 U.S. 495, 514–15 (1922); Van Wyk v. Bergland, 570 F.2d 701, 704 (8th Cir. 1978); Bruhn's Freezer Meats of Chicago, Inc. v. United States Dep't of Agric., 438 F.2d 1332, 1337 (8th Cir. 1971).

11. *See, e.g.*, Mahon v. Stowers, 416 U.S. 100, 106 (1974).

12. *See* 7 U.S.C. § 192(c), (f).

13. *See* 7 C.F.R. §§ 2.22(3)(iii), 2.81 (2003). Hereinafter, all citations to federal regulations in this article are to the 2003 edition of the Code of Federal Regulations.

14. Pub. L. No. 103-354, 108 Stat. 3178–3242.

15. *See* 59 Fed. Reg. 66,517–19 (Dec. 27, 1994). GIPSA's current organizational structure and the functions of its various units are described at 9 C.F.R. Part 204.

16. GIPSA's enforcement activities on behalf of the Secretary often result in formal administrative adjudications. Hearings are conducted by administrative law judges (ALJs), and the ALJ's decision may be appealed by either party to the USDA's Judicial Officer. *See* 7 C.F.R. §§ 1.130–.151 (containing the USDA formal adjudication rules of practice). Final decisions of the Judicial Officer are published in *Agricultural Decisions* and are available in print and on database services such as Westlaw. Decisions issued after January 1, 2003, are also available at www.NationalAgLawCenter.org. The current Judicial Officer, William Jensen, was appointed in January, 1996, to succeed Donald A. Campbell, who

This article offers an overview of the structure and basic provisions of the Packers and Stockyards Act. It begins with brief accounts of the Act's history and of the industries the Act regulates. It then describes the manner in which the Act regulates those subject to it_packers, swine contractors, stockyard owners, market agencies, dealers, and live poultry dealers. It concludes with a description of a recently enacted statute that, while not a part of the Packers and Stockyards Act, will apply to some within the sectors that the Act regulates.

A. The Packers and Stockyards Act and Market Concentration

The Packers and Stockyards Act has been amended several times, but its core provisions were enacted in response to market concentration and anticompetitive practices in the livestock industry in the early 1900s. A major impetus for the Act was a 1919 Federal Trade Commission (FTC) report concluding that the five largest meat packers, the "Big Five," had engaged in anticompetitive practices:

> It appears that five great packing concerns of the country—Swift, Armour, Morris, Cudahy, and Wilson—have attained such a dominant position that they control at will the market in which they buy their supplies, the market in which they sell their products, and hold the fortunes of their competitors in their hands....

> The producer of live stock is at the mercy of these five companies because they control the market and the marketing facilities and, to some extent, the rolling stock which transports the product to the market....

> The power of the Big Five in the United States has been and is being unfairly and illegally used to—

> Manipulate live-stock markets;

> Restrict interstate and international supplies of foods;

> Control the prices of dressed meats and other foods;

> Defraud both the producers of food and consumers;

> Crush effective competition;

> Secure special privileges from railroads, stockyard companies, and municipalities; and

> Profiteer....

> The rapid rise of the packers to power and immense wealth and their present strangle hold on food supplies were not based necessarily on their ownership of packing houses, but upon their control of the channels of distribution, particularly the stockyards, private car lines, cold storage plants, and branch houses. Similarly the great profits which they have secured and are now securing are not primarily due to exceptional efficiency in operating packing houses and manufacturing plants, but are secured through their monopolistic control of the distributive machinery.[17]

---

had served since 1971. The circumstances of the creation of the Judicial Officer position and its functions are described in Thomas J. Flavin, *The Functions of the Judicial Officer, United States Department of Agriculture*, 26 Geo. Wash. L. Rev. 277 (1958). *See also* Russell L. Weaver, *Appellate Review in Executive Departments and Agencies*, 48 Admin. L. Rev. 251, 254 (1966) (discussing the function of the USDA Judicial Officer).

17. Campbell, *supra* note 4, § 3.02 (quoting FTC, *Report of the Federal Trade Commission on the Meat Packing Industry* 392 (1919)).

The FTC recommended governmental ownership of the stockyards and their related facilities. Congress, however, chose a less drastic alternative and enacted the Packers and Stockyards Act in 1921, a year after the "Big Five" packers and others entered into a consent decree under the Sherman Act.[18]

Ironically, nearly seventy-five years after the enactment of the Packers and Stockyards Act, the meat packing industry "is now more concentrated than it was in 1921."[19] In a 2002 report regarding the cattle and hog industries, GIPSA, in noting that "[c]oncentration in beef packing has increased over the years," found that "[t]he four largest firms' share of total commercial steer and heifer slaughter rose from 35 percent in 1980 to 72 percent in 1990 and 81 percent in 1993, but has remained relatively stable since then."[20]

As to hogs, the report concluded that "[c]oncentration has increased in the pork packing industry. The share of U.S. hog slaughter accounted for by the four largest hog packers rose from 34 percent in 1980 to 46 percent in 1995 and 55 percent in 1996, and has remained about the same since then."[21]

Although the Act is generally credited as having been effective in ensuring prompt and accurate payment to livestock sellers, the increased concentration in the livestock industry in the last two decades has called into question the Secretary's oversight of market competitiveness.[22] For example, the United States General Accounting Office (GAO) has repeatedly criticized the Secretary's oversight of the industry.[23]

One measure of the concern over concentration in the livestock industry was offered by former Secretary Glickman, who, in 1994, stated:

> Perhaps the single biggest issue I have heard about while traveling the country the last several months has been concern about concentration in the meat processing industry. Today, four companies control nearly 95% of the industry. Four companies control this country's supply of meat. . . .[24]

---

18. *Id.; see generally* HARL, *supra* note 5, at § 71.03 (discussing the consent decree).

19. U.S. Gen. Accounting Office, *Packers and Stockyards Administration: Oversight of Livestock Market Competitiveness Needs To Be Enhanced* (Pub. No. RCED-92-36, Oct. 1991) at 3 [hereinafter *Oversight of Livestock Market*]. Most of this concentration has occurred in the last twenty-five years:
Following the antitrust activity in the 1920s, market concentration by the larger beef-packing firms declined over the next 50 years. By 1975 the four largest firms slaughtered only 28 percent of the steer and heifer market. However, this situation reversed itself after 1975, culminating in mergers and acquisitions by two of the largest packers between 1986 and 1987. USDA reported that in 1988 the top four beef-packing firms slaughtered about 70 percent of steers and heifers, and they fabricated about 70 percent of the boxed beef on the market.
U.S. Gen. Accounting Office, *Beef Industry: Packer Market Concentration and Cattle Prices* (Pub. No. RCED-91-28, Dec. 1990) at 3 [hereinafter *Packer Market Concentration*].

20. USDA, GIPSA, *Assessment of the Cattle and Hog Industries: Calendar Year 2001* vii (2002) [hereinafter *Assessment of the Cattle and Hog Industries*].

21. *Id.* at ix.

22. *See generally* James M. MacDonald et al., *Consolidation in U.S. Meatpacking* (USDA, Econ. Research Serv., Agric. Econ. Rep. No. 785, Feb. 2000) (describing consolidation in the U.S. meatpacking industry); Kenneth H. Mathews, Jr., et al., *U.S. Beef Industry: Cattle Cycles, Price Spreads, and Packer Concentration* (USDA, Econ. Research Serv., Tech. Bul. No. 1874, Apr. 1999) (describing concentration in the cattle industry).

23. *See* U. S. Gen. Accounting Office, *Packers and Stockyards Programs: Actions Needed to Improve Investigations of Competitive Practices* (Pub. No. RCED-00-242, Sept. 2000); *Oversight of Livestock Market, supra* note 19.

24. Dan Glickman, *Address Before the National Press Club (Oct. 18, 1994)*, FEEDSTUFFS, Nov. 6, 1995, at 10.

Views differ over the effect of this concentration on livestock producers, especially with respect to the impact of the procurement of cattle by packers under forward contracts.[25] For example, those opposed to the use of forward contracts and the resulting "captive supply" of livestock in the hands of packers have urged GIPSA to adopt rules under the Packers and Stockyards Act to restrict the use of forward contracts.[26] In broad terms, those who hold this view advance two basic concerns. "First, the more packers control production, the less they will be aggressive in the marketplace, and second, the more this trend continues, the more packers will control production and the fewer cattle will be sold in open markets on negotiated terms."[27]

On the other hand, packers have vigorously opposed restrictions on the use of forward contracts. In administrative disciplinary proceedings brought by GIPSA under the Packers and Stockyards Act, for example, IBP successfully established that its use of an exclusive marketing agreement neither gave an undue or unreasonable preference to the cattle producers who were parties to the arrangement nor unduly or unreasonably prejudiced or disadvantaged similarly situated producers who were not parties to the agreement.[28]

An unsuccessful attempt was made to amend the Packers and Stockyards Act in the 2002 Farm Bill to more specifically address concentration in the livestock sector by restricting packer ownership of livestock.[29] Although unsuccessful, this attempt indicates that the Packers and Stockyards Act's prohibitions against anticompetitive practices will continue to receive attention. As noted by GIPSA in a May 30, 2003, announcement that it will conduct a congressionally mandated study of "marketing methods used in the livestock and red meat industries," "[t]he issue of packer ownership of livestock is highly contentious among livestock industry members."[30]

B. Livestock and Poultry Production

The Packers and Stockyards Act defines "livestock" to include "cattle, sheep, swine, horses, mules, or goats–whether live or dead."[31] The Act also applies to "poultry," which is defined to mean "chickens, turkeys, ducks, geese, and other domestic fowl."[32]

---

25. In general, a "forward contract" is an agreement to sell at a set price or pursuant to an established pricing formula with delivery to occur at a later date. *See, e.g.*, Christopher R. Kelley, *Agricultural Production Contracts: Drafting Considerations*, 18 Hamline L. Rev. 397, 398 (1995).

26. *See* 62 Fed. Reg. 1845 (Jan. 14, 1997) (notice of the filing of a petition for rulemaking by the Western Organization of Resource Councils (WORC) relating to packer livestock procurement practices). For GIPSA's response to the WORC petition, see USDA, GIPSA, *Review of Western Organization of Resource Councils (WORC) Petition for Rulemaking* (Aug. 29, 1997). *See also* USDA, GIPSA, *Captive Supply of Cattle and GIPSA's Reporting of Captive Supply* (Jan. 11, 2002) (discussing "captive supplies" of cattle).

27. Rod Smith, *Cattle Industry May Need To 'Leap' to New But Rewarding Industry Structure*, Feedstuffs, Nov. 20, 1995, at 9 (reporting on remarks made by Topper Thorpe, Executive Vice-President of Cattle Fax). *See also* Peter C. Carstensen, *Concentration and the Destruction of Competition in Agricultural Markets: The Case for Change in Public Policy*, 2000 Wis. L. Rev. 531 (discussing concentration in agricultural markets generally).

28. *See In re: IBP, Inc.*, 57 Agric. Dec. 1353 (1998); *see also IBP, Inc. v. Glickman*, 187 F.3d 974, 977–78 (8th Cir. 1999) (holding that a right of first refusal held by IBP under the marketing agreement did not violate the Packers and Stockyards Act).

29. For a description of this proposed amendment and an account of its failure to be enacted, see Roger A. McEowen et al., *The 2002 Senate Farm Bill: The Ban on Packer Ownership of Livestock*, 7 Drake J. Agric. L. 267 (2002).

30. 68 Fed. Reg. 32,455, 32,456 (May 30, 2003).

31. 7 U.S.C. § 182(4).

32. *Id.* at 182(6).

Poultry production is almost totally vertically integrated, with individual firms handling all stages of production from breeding to processing.[33] Feeding is typically done under contract with putatively independent growers.[34]

Hog production is becoming more vertically integrated, with increasing numbers of hogs being raised by producers who hold a production contract with a processor.[35] "About 19 percent of feeder pig producers and 34 percent of finished hog operations produced under contract in 1998, but these operations accounted for 82 percent of feeder pigs and 63 percent of finished hogs."[36]

Consolidation is also occurring in the hog industry. "Since 1994, the percent of hog and pig inventory on farms with 2,000 head or more increased from 37 percent to nearly 75 percent. Also, just over half of hogs and pigs were on farms with 5,000 head or more in 2001, compared with about a third in 1996."[37] "[B]etween 1994 and 1999, the number of hog farms fell by more than 50 percent, from over 200,000 to less than 100,000, and fell to just over 80,000 by 2001."[38]

Cattle production has three phases — breeding, feeding, and slaughter. Breeding is typically done by "cow-calf" operations that breed cows for the production and sale of young steers and heifers.[39] The number of these operations has been declining.[40] "There are about 900,000 cow-calf operations in the U.S., with about one-third of the beef cows on family-owned operations of less than 50 cows."[41]

---

33. *See generally* Steve W. Martinez, *Vertical Coordination of Marketing Systems: Lessons From the Poultry, Egg, and Pork Industries* (USDA, Econ. Research Serv., Agric. Econ. Rep. No. 807, Apr. 2002); Michael Ollinger et al., *Structural Change in U.S. Chicken and Turkey Slaughter* (USDA, Econ. Research Serv., Agric. Econ. Rep. No. 787, Sept. 2000).

34. *See generally* Neil D. Hamilton, *Broiler Contracting in the United States–A Current Contract Analysis Addressing Legal Issues and Grower Concerns*, 7 Drake J. Agric. L. 43 (2002); Randi Ilyse Roth, *Redressing Unfairness in the New Agricultural Labor Arrangements: An Overview of Litigation Seeking Remedies for Contract Poultry Growers*, 25 U. Memphis L. Rev. 1207, 1208–10 (1995) (discussing poultry production contracts) [hereinafter Roth]; Clay Fulcher, *Vertical Integration in the Poultry Industry: The Contract Relationship*, Agric. L. Update, Jan. 1992, at 4 (same); Janet Perry et al., *Broiler Farms' Organization, Management, and Performance* (USDA, Agric. Econ. Serv., Agric. Info. Bull. No. 748, Mar. 1999) (discussing the business and economic structure of broiler farms using production contracts).

35. *See, e.g.,* Steve W. Martinez et al., *Vertical Coordination and Consumer Welfare: The Case of the Pork Industry* (USDA, Econ. Research Serv., Agric. Econ. Rep. No. 753, Aug. 1997) at 1–2.

36. William D. McBride & Nigel Key, *Economic and Structural Relationships in U.S. Hog Production* (USDA, Econ. Research Serv., Agric. Econ. Rep. No. 818, Feb. 2003) at 25 [hereinafter McBride & Key]. *See also* Neil D. Hamilton, *State Regulation of Agricultural Production Contracts,* 25 U. Memphis L. Rev. 1051, 1056 (1995) (noting that, by the mid-1990s, "over 20% of swine [were] produced under contract, up from only 2% in 1980").

37. McBride & Key, *supra* note 37, at 5. *Compare with* Leland Southard & Steve Reed, *Rapid Changes in the U.S. Pork Industry*, Agric. Outlook, Mar. 1995, at 11, 12–13 (noting that, in 1995, "about 70 percent [of hog operations] are farrow-to-finish operations, and "hog operations with less than 100 head still account for 60 percent of all U.S. hog operations"). For additional information on economic conditions and business practices in the hog industry, see *Assessment of the Cattle and Hog Industries, supra* note 20, at 33–48.

38. McBride & Key, *supra* note 37, at 5. *See also* Chris Hurt, *Industrialization in the Pork Industry,* Choices, 4th Quarter 1994, at 9.

39. *See Packer Market Concentration, supra* note 19, at 2.

40. *See id.* at 5.

41. Teresa Glover & Leland Southard, *Cattle Industry Continues Restructuring,* Agric. Outlook, Dec. 1995, at 13, 15 [hereinafter Glover & Southard]. For additional information on economic conditions and business practices in the hog industry, see *Assessment of the Cattle and Hog Industries, supra* note 20, at 12–32.

Most cattle from cow-calf operations are fed at cattle-feeding operations before slaughter. Feedlot operators either purchase the cattle they feed or custom feed cattle owned by cow-calf operations or others, including beef-packing firms.[42] Economies of scale and technological advances, such as feed additives, computerized feed mills, and improved transportation, have encouraged the development of large-capacity feedlots.[43] This trend will probably continue.[44]

Fed cattle are sold either to a beef-packing firm or a packing firm's agent, and about 80 percent of all cattle slaughtered are fed cattle. Packing firm operations differ. Most slaughter the cattle and fabricate the carcasses into boxed beef. Others purchase the carcasses and fabricate them into box beef. Some only slaughter the cattle and sell the carcasses.[45]

C. The Packers and Stockyard Act's Provisions

The Packers and Stockyards Act contains four titles:

- Title I (7 U.S.C. §§ 181–183) provides general definitions;
- Title II (7 U.S.C. §§ 191–197) specifically addresses the practices of "packers," "swine contractors," and "live poultry dealers";
- Title III (7 U.S.C. §§ 201–217a) specifically addresses the practices of "stockyards," "dealers," and "market agencies"; and
- Title IV (7 U.S.C. §§ 221–229) contains administrative and other requirements.

As suggested by the subjects of the Act's four titles, the Act regulates four segments of the livestock, meat, and poultry industry. First, it imposes comprehensive restrictions on the practices of "packers." Packers include buyers of livestock for slaughter, meat processors, and wholesale distributors of meats, meat food products, or livestock products in an unmanufactured form.[46]

Second, by virtue of an amendment to the Act by the 2002 Farm Bill,[47] the Act now regulates "swine contractors." A "swine contractor" is a person "engaged in the business of obtaining swine under a swine production contract for the purpose of slaughtering the swine or for selling the swine for slaughter…."[48]

Third, the Act regulates certain activities of "live poultry dealers," defined as persons who purchase live poultry or who obtain live poultry under a poultry growing arrangement.[49] As discussed later in this article, live poultry dealers are subject to the major prohibitions codified in § 192 of the Act that also apply to packers and swine contractors, but the Secretary's enforcement authority is more limited relative to live poultry dealers.[50]

---

42. *See Packer Market Concentration, supra* note 19, at 2.

43. *See* Glover & Southard, *supra* note 41, at 14–15.

44. *See* Mark Drabenstott, *Industrialization: Steady Current or Tidal Wave*, CHOICES, Fourth Quarter 1994, at 4, 6 (predicting that cattle feeding will follow swine and poultry as the next livestock segment to become "industrialized").

45. *See Packer Market Concentration, supra* note 19, at 2–3.

46. *See* 7 U.S.C. § 191.

47. Farm Security and Rural Investment Act of 2002, Pub. L. No. 107-171, tit. X, § 10502, 116 Stat. 142, 509–10 (codified at 7 U.S.C. §§ 182(a), 192, 193, 194, 195, 209(a), 221, 223).

48. 7 U.S.C. § 182(12).

49. *See id.* §§ 182(10) (defining "live poultry dealer"), 182(9) (defining "poultry growing arrangement"), 182(8) (defining "poultry grower").

50. *See infra* notes 191–96 and the accompanying text.

Finally, the Act regulates various activities of "stockyard owners," "market agencies," and "dealers." "Stockyard" is broadly defined to include public markets for livestock producers and other facilities where livestock is received or held for sale or shipment in interstate commerce.[51] A "stockyard owner" is a person "engaged in the business of conducting or operating a stockyard."[52] A "market agency" is any person who buys or sells livestock on a commission basis or who furnishes stockyard services.[53] A "dealer" is a person who buys or sells livestock on his own behalf or as the employee or agent of a buyer or seller.[54]

As generally applicable matters, the term "person" includes individuals, partnerships, corporations, and associations.[55] The acts, omission, and failures of an agent are attributed to the principal.[56] Courts and the Secretary have used the *alter ego* doctrine to pierce the corporate veil to hold owners of corporations liable under the Act.[57]

The Act also expressly defines when a transaction is deemed "in commerce."[58] It expressly preempts certain state authority but permits some state regulation.[59]

1. Packers

a. "Packer" Defined

The Packers and Stockyards Act defines a "packer" as any person

> engaged in the business (a) of buying livestock in commerce for purposes of slaughter, or (b) of manufacturing or preparing meats or meat food products for sale or shipment in commerce, or (c) of marketing meats, meat food products, or livestock products in an unmanufactured form acting as a wholesale broker, dealer, or distributor in commerce."[60]

Under clause (c), which was added in 1976 amendments to the Act,[61] a person who purchases and then resells in the same form processed and packed meat in "sizes and quantities suitable for re-sale to institutions such as hospitals and schools and some restaurants and hotels" can be a "packer."[62] Likewise, large supermarket chains that cut, grind, and wrap meat can be "packers."[63] A freezer plant that cuts meat and wraps it in portions for sale to consumers can also be a "packer."[64] The retail sale of meat, however, is the primary responsibility of the FTC, even if a "packer" is involved.[65]

---

51. *See* 7 U.S.C. § 202(a).

52. *Id.* § 201(a).

53. *See id.* § 201(c); *see also id.* 201(b) (defining "stockyard services").

54. *See id.* § 201(d).

55. *Id.* § 182(1).

56. *See id.* § 223.

57. *See Bruhn's Freezer Meats*, 438 F.2d at 1343; In re Sebastopol Meat Co., Inc., 28 Agric. Dec. 435, 441 (1969).

58. *See* 7 U.S.C. § 183.

59. *See id.* § 228c.

60. *Id.* § 191.

61. *See* United States v. Jay Freeman Co., Inc., 473 F. Supp. 1265, 1267–68 (E.D. Ark. 1979).

62. *Id.* (also ruling that the phrase "in an unmanufactured form" only modifies "livestock products").

63. *See* Safeway Stores, Inc. v. Freeman, 369 F.2d 952, 954–55 (D.C. Cir. 1966).

64. *See Bruhn's Freezer Meats*, 438 F.2d at 1336–39.

65. 7 U.S.C. § 227(b)(3); *see also* Giant Foods, Inc. v. FTC, 307 F.2d 184, 187 (D.C. Cir. 1962), *cert. denied*, 372 U.S. 910 (1963).

b. Packer Bonds

Packers must be bonded unless their average annual purchases do not exceed $500,000.[66] The Secretary may seek a cease and desist order prohibiting or limiting the packer from purchasing livestock If the Secretary determines that a packer is insolvent.[67] Because of the statutory trust provisions discussed below, "claims against packers' bonds have been less than 1 percent of the average yearly bond coverage for packers ... because trust inventories and receivables are exhausted before claims on bonds are made, which ultimately reduces such claims."[68]

c. Prohibited Trade Practices

Packer practices are comprehensively regulated. Specifically, with respect to livestock, meats, meat food products, or livestock products in unmanufactured form, packers may not do the following:

(a) Engage in or use any unfair, unjustly discriminatory, or deceptive practice or device; or

(b) Make or give any undue or unreasonable preference or advantage to any particular person or locality in any respect whatsoever, or subject any particular person or locality to any undue or unreasonable prejudice or disadvantage in any respect whatsoever; or

(c) Sell or otherwise transfer to or for any other packer, swine contractor, or any live poultry dealer, or buy or otherwise receive from any other packer, swine contractor, or any live poultry dealer, any article for the purpose or with the effect of apportioning the supply between any such persons, if such apportionment has the tendency or effect of restraining commerce or of creating a monopoly; or

(d) Sell or otherwise transfer to or for any other person, or buy or otherwise receive from or for any other person, any article for the purpose of or with the effect of manipulating or controlling prices, or of creating a monopoly in the acquisition of, buying, selling, or dealing in, any article, or of restraining commerce; or

(e) Engage in any course of business or do any act for the purpose or with the effect of manipulating or controlling prices, or of creating a monopoly in the acquisition of, buying, selling, or dealing in, any article, or of restraining commerce; or

(f) Conspire, combine, agree, or arrange with any other person (1) to apportion territory for carrying on business, or (2) to apportion purchases or sales of any article, or (3) to manipulate or control prices; or

(g) Conspire, combine, agree, or arrange with any other person to do, or aid or abet the doing of, any act made unlawful by subdivisions (a), (b), (c), (d), or (e) of this section.[69]

---

66. 7 U.S.C. § 204; *see also* 9 C.F.R. §§ 201.29–.34 (prescribing the terms and conditions of packer bonds).

67. 7 U.S.C. § 204; *see also* 9 C.F.R. § 203.10 (statement of policy defining insolvency).

68. *Oversight of Livestock Market, supra* note 19, at 29.

69. 7 U.S.C. § 192 (also regulating "swine contractor[s] with respect to livestock, meats, meat food products, or livestock products in unmanufactured form" and "live poultry dealer[s] with respect to live poultry").

GIPSA's regulations add specificity to some of these prohibitions. For example, packers may not circulate misleading reports about market conditions or prices.[70] Purchases and sales on a weight basis must be based on actual weights.[71] Packers may not, in connection with the purchase of livestock, "charge, demand, or collect from the seller of the livestock any compensation in the form of commission, yardage, or other service charge."[72] Packers may not own, finance, or participate in the management or operation of a market agency selling livestock on a commission basis.[73] "[P]ackers and dealers engaged in purchasing livestock, in person or through employed buyers, … [must] conduct … [their] buying operations in competition with, and independently of, other packers and dealers similarly engaged."[74] Packers also must use reasonable care and promptness in the handling of livestock.[75] In addition, as a matter of policy, advertising allowances and other merchandising payments and services are subject to restrictions.[76] Finally, GIPSA has adopted policies concerning meat packer sales and purchase contracts, the giving of gifts to government employees, and the disposition of records.[77]

The phrase "unfair, unjustly discriminatory, or deceptive practice or device" is not defined in the Act. Accordingly, the meaning of the words in the phrase "must be determined by the facts of each case within the purposes of the Packers and Stockyards Act."[78] Conduct that has been held to be "unfair, unjustly discriminatory, or deceptive" has included discriminatory pricing,[79] predatory pricing,[80] and deceptive advertising.[81] A conspiracy to force auction stockyards to alter sale terms[82] and false weighing[83] have also been held to violate the Act.[84]

On the other hand, recent decisions have rejected claims that the Act was violated by the refusal to provide a producer with a contract that may have been offered to other producers,[85] by a right of first refusal,[86] and by a packer's direct ownership and contractual acquisition of hogs.[87] These and other decisions suggest that whether conduct violates the Act is a question of law, although one court has expressed doubt over "who should determine whether a particular act is unfair, discriminatory or deceptive under the [Packers and Stockyards Act]."[88]

---

70. See 9 C.F.R. § 201.53.

71. See id. § 201.55; see also id. §§ 201.71–.76 (pertaining to scales, weighing, and reweighing)

72. Id. § 201.98.

73. See id. § 201.67; see also id. §§ 203.19 (statement of policy with respect to packers engaging in the business of livestock dealers and buying agencies), 203.18 (statement of policy with respect to packers engaging in the business of custom feeding livestock).

74. Id. § 201.70.

75. See id. § 201.82.

76. See id. § 203.14 (statement of policy with respect to advertising allowances and other merchandising payments and services).

77. See id. §§ 203.7, 203.2, 203.4.

78. Capital Packing Co. v. United States, 350 F.2d 67, 76 (10th Cir. 1965) (citations omitted).

79. See Swift & Co. v. United States, 347 F.2d 53, 55 (7th Cir. 1963).

80. See Wilson & Co. v. Benson, 286 F.2d 891, 895 (7th Cir. 1961).

81. See Bruhn's Freezer Meats, 438 F.2d at 1342.

82. See DeJong Packing Co. v. United States Dep't of Agric., 618 F.2d 1329 (9th Cir.), cert. denied, 449 U.S. 1061 (1980).

83. See Burruss v. United States Dept. of Agric., 575 F.2d 1258, 1958 (8th Cir. 1978) (per curiam).

84. See generally Campbell, supra note 4, at §§ 3.45–.58 (discussing judicial applications of § 192); HARL, supra note 5, at § 71.08 (same).

85. See Jackson v. Swift Eckrich, Inc., 53 F.3d 1452, 1458 (8th Cir. 1995).

86. See IBP, Inc., 187 F.2d at 977–78.

87. See Griffin v. Smithfield Foods, Inc., 183 F. Supp.2d 824, 827–29 (E.D. Va. 2002).

88. Philson v. Cold Creek Farms, Inc., 947 F. Supp. 197, 201 n.5 (E.D.N.C. 1996).

d. Prompt Payment

The Act imposes a prompt payment requirement on packers. As a general rule, full payment of the livestock's purchase price must be made "before the close of the next business day following the purchase of livestock and transfer of possession thereof...."[89]

This rule is qualified in two respects. First, when livestock is purchased for slaughter, payment must be made to the seller or the seller's representative at the point of transfer or the funds must be wired to the seller's account by the close of the next business day.[90] If the sale is on a carcass weight basis, payment must be made at the point of transfer or the funds must be wired to the seller's account by the close of the next business day following the determination of the purchase amount.[91]

Second, "if the seller or his duly authorized representative is not present to receive payment at the point of transfer of possession ... the packer ... shall wire transfer funds or place a check in the United States mail for the full amount of the purchase price, properly addressed to the seller, within the time limits specified in this subsection, such action being deemed compliance with the requirement for prompt payment."[92]

The prompt payment requirement may be waived by written agreement.[93] However, if the seller agrees to extend credit to a packer, the seller loses his, her, or its interest in the statutory trust discussed below.[94] Any delay or attempt to delay the collection of funds by a packer is deemed to be an "unfair practice."[95]

Packers must maintain prescribed records of their business transactions and other matters.[96] Failure to do so is a criminal offense.[97] The records are subject to the Secretary's inspection.[98] Annual reports are required.[99] Written information, under oath or affirmation, may also be demanded by the Secretary.[100]

e. Statutory Trust

The Act establishes a statutory trust for livestock purchased by a packer whose average annual purchases exceed $500,000. The trust is for the benefit of unpaid cash sellers, and it extends to "all inventories of, or receivables or proceeds from meat, meat food products, or livestock products derived therefrom...."[101] "[A] cash sale means a sale in

---

89. 7 U.S.C. § 228b(a).

90. *See id.*

91. *See id.*

92. *Id.; see also* 9 C.F.R. § 201.43 (implementing the statutory prompt payment rule).

93. 7 U.S.C. § 228b(b); *see also* 9 C.F.R. §§ 201.200 (providing for the terms of credit sales agreements with respect to packers whose average annual purchases of livestock exceed $500,000), 203.16 (statement of policy regarding the mailing of checks in cash purchases of livestock for slaughter).

94. *See* 7 U.S.C. § 196(c); 9 C.F.R. § 201.200(a).

95. 7 U.S.C. § 228b(c).

96. *See id.* at § 221; 9 C.F.R. § 201.43.

97. *See* 7 U.S.C. § 221.

98. *See* 9 C.F.R. § 201.95; Western States Cattle Co., Inc. v. Edwards, 895 F.2d 438, 441–43 (8th Cir. 1990) (upholding warrantless search of records required to be maintained under the Act); *see also* 9 C.F.R. § 201.96 (prohibiting the unauthorized disclosure of business information).

99. *See* 9 C.F.R. § 201.97.

100. *See id.* § 201.94.

101. *See* 7 U.S.C. § 196(b).

which the seller does not expressly extend credit to the buyer."[102] "Even if there is a delay in payment, the transaction is a 'cash sale' unless there is an express agreement extending credit from the seller to the buyer."[103]

Because the trust assets do not become part of the bankruptcy estate if a packer files bankruptcy, unpaid cash sellers do not compete with secured creditors for the trust's assets.[104] To make a claim against the trust, the unpaid cash seller must give notice to the Secretary within thirty days of the final date for making prompt payment under § 228b or within fifteen business day of being notified that the payment of a promptly presented check was dishonored.[105] A trust modeled on the Act also is created under the Perishable Agricultural Commodities Act (PACA).[106]

f. Enforcement

When the Secretary has reason to believe that a packer has violated the Act, the Secretary may commence formal administrative adjudicatory proceedings against the packer.[107] The proceedings are conducted under the procedures prescribed in 7 C.F.R. §§ 1.130–.151.[108] A cease and desist order may be issued, and civil penalties of up to $10,000 may be assessed for each violation.[109]

Under the Hobbs Administrative Orders Review Act,[110] judicial review is available in the federal court of appeals for the circuit where the packer resides, has its principal place of business, or in the United States Court of Appeals for the District of Columbia Circuit.[111] The sixty-day time limit for filing the petition of review specified in § 2344 of the Hobbs Administrative Orders Review Act overrides the thirty-day limit found in § 194(a) of the Packers and Stockyards Act.[112]

Violation of a final cease and desist order is punishable by a fine and imprisonment.[113] The Secretary also has the authority to request a temporary injunction or a restraining order in certain circumstances.[114]

---

102. *Id.* § 196(c).

103. Kunkel v. Sprague Nat'l Bank, 128 F.3d 636, 646 (8th Cir. 1997) (citation omitted).

104. *See* Randy Rogers & Lawrence P. King, Collier Farm Bankruptcy Guide § 105[1] (1997) (discussing the livestock trust fund provisions of the Packers and Stockyards Act).

105. *See* 7 U.S.C. § 196(b); *see also* 9 C.F.R. § 203.15 (statement of policy regarding the preservation of trust benefits).

106. 7 U.S.C. §§ 499a–499t. *See generally* J.W. Looney, *Protection for Sellers of Perishable Agricultural Commodities: Reparation Proceedings and the Statutory Trust under the Perishable Agricultural Commodities Act,* 23 U.C. Davis L. Rev. 675, 689–94 (1990) (discussing the PACA statutory trust).

107. *See* 7 U.S.C. § 193(a).

108. *See* Campbell, *supra* note 4, at 203–23 (discussing administrative disciplinary proceedings under the Act); *see generally* Gary J. Edles & Jerome Nelson, Federal Regulatory Process: Agency Practices and Procedures 135–77 (2d ed. 1994) (generally discussing formal administrative adjudication procedures).

109. *See* 7 U.S.C. § 193(b). *See also* United States v. Great American Veal, Inc., 998 F. Supp. 416, 424 (D.N.J. 1998) (ruling that § 193(b) "mandates that an action to enforce a civil penalty in the district courts must await the imposition of a civil penalty in an administrative proceeding and the failure on the part of a violator to pay such a penalty").

110. 28 U.S.C. §§ 2342–2350.

111. *See id.* § 2343.

112. *See* Capitol Packing Co. v. United States, 350 F.2d 67, 72 (10th Cir. 1965).

113. *See* 7 U.S.C. § 195(3).

114. *See id.* § 228(a).

Private parties may seek damages for any violation of the Act or of an order of the Secretary by commencing an action in federal district court.[115] Other statutory and common law claims may be asserted.[116]

g. Swine Packer Marketing Contracts

Packers who offer to purchase swine under contracts with swine producers must provide to the Secretary certain information related to their contracts, including the types of contracts offered.[117] In turn, subject to the availability of appropriations, "the Secretary shall establish and maintain a library of each type of contract offered by packers to swine producers for the purchase of all or part of the producers' production of swine (including swine that are purchased or committed for delivery), including all available noncarcass merit premiums.[118] The Secretary is directed to make information on the types of contracts being offered available to "producers and other interested parties...."[119] Inaccurate or incomplete reporting by a packer is a violation of the Act.[120]

2. Swine Contractors

a. "Swine Contractor" Defined

A "swine contractor" is defined as

any person engaged in the business of obtaining swine under a swine production contract for the purpose of slaughtering the swine or selling swine for slaughter, if—

(A) the swine is obtained by the person in commerce;

or

(B) the swine (including products from the swine) obtained by the person is sold or shipped in commerce.[121]

A "swine production contract" is "any growout contract or other arrangement under which a swine production contract grower raises and cares for the swine in accordance with the instructions of another person."[122] A "swine production contract grower" is "any person engaged in the business of raising and caring for swine in accordance with the instructions of another person."[123]

In general, swine contractors are regulated in a manner similar to the regulation of packers. Notable exceptions, however, include the absence of bond requirement, the absence of a prompt payment requirement, and the absence of a statutory trust protecting the rights of unpaid sellers or growers.

---

115. *See id.* § 209.
116. *See id.* § 409(b).
117. *See* 7 U.S.C. § 198a(d).
118. *Id.* § 198a(a); *see also id.* § 198(7) (defining the term "type of contract").
119. *Id.* § 198a(b). The Secretary must also report on other information derived from these contracts. *See id.* § 198a(d).
120. *See id.* § 198a(e).
121. *Id.* § 182(12).
122. *Id.* § 182(13).
123. *Id.* § 182(14).

b. Prohibited Trade Practices

Swine contractors are subject to the same broad prohibitions under § 192 of the Act that apply to packers and live poultry dealers.[124] As they do for packers, these prohibitions apply to swine contractors "with respect to livestock, meats, meat food products, or livestock products in unmanufactured form...."[125]

c. Enforcement

The Secretary has co-extensive enforcement authority against swine contractors and packers.[126] In addition, persons injured by a violation of the Act or an order of the Secretary "relating to the purchase, sale, or handling of livestock" or a swine production contract are entitled to recover damages in federal district court.[127]

3. Stockyards, Market Agencies, and Dealers

a. "Stockyard" Defined

A "stockyard" is defined in the Act as

> any place, establishment, or facility commonly known as stockyards, conducted, operated, or managed for profit or nonprofit as a public market for livestock producers, feeders, market agencies, and buyers, consisting of pens, or other inclosures, and their appurtenances, in which live cattle, sheep, swine, horses, mules, or goats are received, held or kept for sale or shipment in commerce.[128]

A "stockyard owner" is any person "engaged in the business of conducting or operating a stockyard...."[129] "Stockyard services" are "services or facilities furnished at a stockyard in connection with the receiving, buying, or selling on a commission basis or otherwise, marketing, feeding, watering, holding, delivery, shipment, weighing, or handling in commerce, of livestock...."[130]

A feedlot is not a "stockyard," at least when its owner receives no fees for assisting the cattle's owners in making sales directly to packers.[131] The USDA, however, has taken a contrary view.[132]

b. "Market Agency" Defined

A "market agency" is any person "engaged in the business of (1) buying or selling in commerce livestock on a commission basis or (2) furnishing stockyard services."[133] The mere notation of "commission" on an invoice does not necessarily signify the existence of

---

124. *See id.* § 192.
125. *Id.*
126. *See id.* §§ 193, 194, 195.
127. *See id.* § 209.
128. *Id.* § 202(a).
129. *Id.* § 201(a).
130. *Id.* § 201(b).
131. *See* Soloman Valley Feedlot, Inc. v. Butz, 557 F.2d 717, 719–20 (10th Cir. 1977).
132. *See* In re Sterling Colorado Beef Co., 39 Agric. Dec. 184, 220–35 (1980) (holding that a custom feedlot that buys or sells livestock for its customers is subject to the Act); *see generally* Campbell, *supra* note 4, § 3.41 (discussing *Soloman Valley Feedlot* and *Sterling Colorado Beef Co.*); HARL, *supra* note 5, at § 71.07[11] (same).
133. 7 U.S.C. § 201(c).

a sale on a commission basis, for the proper inquiry is a fact-based inquiry into "the na-ture of the business relationship."[134]

c. "Dealer" Defined

A "dealer" is "any person, not a market agency, engaged in the business of buying or selling in commerce livestock, either on his own account or as the employee or agent of the vendor or purchaser."[135] A person may be a "dealer" even if buying and selling livestock is not his or her only business.[136]

d. Stockyard Postings

When the Secretary determines that a stockyard meets the statutory definition of a "stockyard," the stockyard is posted as such.[137] Within thirty days of a stockyard's post-ing, market agencies and dealers must obtain written authorization from the stockyard owner to do business at the stockyard and must register with the Secretary. Otherwise, after the thirty-day period has expired, they must cease doing business at the stockyard.[138]

e. Bonds

As a prerequisite to registration, market agencies and dealers must obtain a bond.[139] Registrants are prohibited from operating while insolvent.[140]

f. Prohibited Trade Practices

(i) Reasonable and Nondiscriminatory Services and Charges

Stockyard services furnished by a stockyard or market agency must be "reasonable and nondiscriminatory," and such services may not be refused "on any basis that is unrea-sonable or unjustly discriminatory."[141]

Rates or charges for stockyard services furnished at a stockyard by a stockyard owner or market agency must be "just, reasonable, and nondiscriminatory...."[142] Rates and charges must be filed with the Secretary and be open for public inspection.[143] Changes in rates and charges also must be filed, and the Secretary may hold a hearing on the lawfulness of a rate or charge or any regulation or practice affecting a rate or charge.[144] If the Secre-tary determines that a rate, charge, regulation, or practice violates the Act, the Secretary may prescribe the appropriate rate or charge.[145] The same authority applies to rates,

---

134. Ferguson v. United States Dept. of Agric., 911 F.2d 1273, 1278–79 (8th Cir. 1990).
135. 7 U.S.C. § 201(d).
136. Kelly v. United States, 202 F.2d 838, 841 (10th Cir. 1953); *see also* United States v. Rauch, 717 F.2d 448, 450 (8th Cir. 1983) (distinguishing a "dealer" from a "rancher").
137. *See id.* § 202(b).
138. *See id.* § 203; *see also* 9 C.F.R. §§ 201.10–.11 (specifying the registration requirements).
139. *See* 7 U.S.C. § 204; *see also* 9 C.F.R. §§ 201.29–.34 (specifying the bond requirements); United States v. Wehrein, 332 F.2d 469, 472 (8th Cir. 1964).
140. *See* 7 U.S.C. § 204.
141. *See id.* § 205; *see also* 9 C.F.R. § 203.12 (statement of policy with respect to providing services and facilities at stockyards on a reasonable and nondiscriminatory basis).
142. *Id.* § 206.
143. *Id.* § 207(a); *see also* 9 C.F.R. § 201.17 (specifying requirements for filing tariffs).
144. 7 U.S.C. § 207(e); *see also* 9 C.F.R. §§ 202.1–.7 (establishing the rules of practice applicable to rate proceedings), 203.17 (statement of policy with respect to rates and charges at posted stockyards).
145. 7 U.S.C. § 211.

charges, regulations, or practices that discriminate between intrastate and interstate commerce.[146]

Stockyard owners and market agencies have the duty "to establish, observe, and enforce just, reasonable, and nondiscriminatory regulations and practices in respect to the furnishing or stockyard services," and regulations and practices that are not just, reasonable, and nondiscriminatory are unlawful.[147] Stockyard owners must manage and regulate their stockyards so that persons buying and selling livestock at their stockyards "conduct their operations in a manner which will foster, preserve, or insure an efficient, competitive market."[148]

(ii) Unfair, Unjustly Discriminatory, or Deceptive Practices

Stockyard owners, market agencies, and dealers may not

> engage in or use any unfair, unjustly discriminatory, or deceptive practice or device in connection with determining whether persons should be authorized to operate at the stockyards, or with the receiving, marketing, buying, or selling on commission basis or otherwise, feeding, watering, holding, delivery, shipment, weighing, or handling of livestock.[149]

GIPSA's regulations elaborate on the statute's prohibitions. For example, stockyard owners, market agencies, and dealers may not circulate misleading reports about market conditions or prices.[150] Purchases and sales must be based on actual weights when livestock are bought or sold on a weight basis.[151] Market agencies must sell livestock "openly, at the highest available bid...."[152] and are restricted from purchasing livestock from consignments.[153] Market agencies' relationships with dealers and other buyers also are restricted.[154] Dealers and market agencies are restricted in the information they furnish to competitors.[155] Dealers must act independently of other dealers.[156] Dealers may not "charge, demand, or collect from the seller of ... livestock any compensation in the form of commission, yardage, or other service charge."[157] Scales, weighing, and livestock handling are also regulated.[158]

Violations of the prohibition against unfair, unjustly discriminatory, or deceptive practices may result in a cease and desist order and the assessment of a civil penalty up to $10,000 for each violation.[159] Market agencies and dealers may also have their registration suspended "for a reasonable specified period."[160] Any person who is responsible for or participated in the violation on which an order of suspension was based may not register under the Act during the suspension period.[161]

---

146. *See id.* § 212.
147. *Id.* § 208(a).
148. *Id.* § 208(b).
149. *Id.* § 213(a).
150. *See* 9 C.F.R. § 201.53.
151. *See id.* § 201.55.
152. *Id.* § 201.56(a).
153. *See id.* § 201.56(b)-(d).
154. *See id.* § 201.61.
155. *See id.* § 201.69.
156. *See id.* § 201.70.
157. *Id.* § 201.98.
158. *See id.* §§ 201.71–.82.
159. *See* 7 U.S.C. § 213.
160. *Id.* § 204.
161. *See* 9 C.F.R. § 201.11.

"In determining the amount of the civil penalty to be assessed…, the Secretary shall consider the gravity of the offense, the size of the business involved, and the effect of the penalty on the person's ability to continue in business."[162] The USDA Judicial Officer's current sanction policy is as follows:

> the sanction in each case will be determined by examining the nature of the violations in relation to the remedial purposes of the regulatory statute involved, along with all relevant circumstances, always giving appropriate weight to the recommendations of the administrative officials charged with the responsibility for achieving the congressional purpose.[163]

The Judicial Officer's sanctions are judicially reviewable.[164] A violation is wilful if a person carelessly disregards the Act's requirements.[165] A stricter standard may apply in some circuits.[166]

(iii) Prompt Payment

Like packers, market agencies and dealers are subject to the prompt payment provisions of § 228b. The failure to make prompt payment is deemed to be an "unfair practice."[167]

Financial irregularities may result in violations of § 213(a) and § 228b. For example, the issuance of insufficient funds checks is considered to be an unfair and deceptive practice in violation of § 213(a), and the resulting failure to pay when due and the failure to pay are considered violations of § 228b.[168]

(iv) Accounts and Records

Like packers and swine contractors, stockyard owners, market agencies, and dealers must "keep such accounts, records, and memoranda as fully and correctly disclose all transactions involved in … [their] business, including the true ownership of such business by stockholding or otherwise."[169] The failure to make and maintain correct accounts, records, and memoranda is punishable by fine or imprisonment.[170] Annual reports regarding compliance with the Act may be required.[171]

g. Compliance with the Secretary's Orders

Stockyard owners, market agencies, and dealers must obey orders rendered by the Secretary under § 211 (relating to rates, charges, regulations, or practices), § 212 (relating to discrimination between intrastate and interstate commerce), and § 213 (relating to unfair,

---

162. 7 U.S.C. § 213(b).

163. *In re* S.S. Farms Linn County, Inc., 50 Agric. Dec. 476, 497 (1991), *aff'd,* 991 F.2d 803 (9th Cir. 1993) (not to be cited as precedent under 9th Circuit Rule 36-3).

164. *Ferguson,* 911 F.2d at 1275–78.

165. *See, e.g.,* Butz v. Glover Livestock Comm'n Co., 411 U.S. 182, 186–88 (1973).

166. See Capital Produce Co. v. United States, 930 F.2d 1077, 1079–81 (4th Cir. 1991); Capital Produce Co. v. United States, 350 F.2d 67, 78–79 (10th Cir. 1965).

167. 7 U.S.C. § 228b(c).

168. *See* In re Jeff Palmer, 50 Agric. Dec. 1762, 1773 (1991); In re Richard N. Garver, 45 Agric. Dec. 1090, 1095 (1986), *aff'd sub nom.* Garver v. United States, 846 F.2d 1029 (6th Cir.), *cert. denied,* 488 U.S. 820 (1988).

169. 7 U.S.C. § 221; *see also* 9 C.F.R. §§ 201.43–.49 (specifying requirements for accounts and records).

170. *See* 7 U.S.C. § 221.

171. *See* 9 C.F.R. § 201.97.

unjustly discriminatory, or deceptive practices).[172] Civil penalties of $500 may be assessed for each offense, and, in the case of a continuing violation, each day is deemed a separate offense.[173]

The Secretary or any injured party is authorized to seek an injunction against any stockyard owner, market agency, or dealer who fails to obey "any order of the Secretary other than for the payment of money while the same is in effect...."[174] Orders of the Secretary, other than orders for the payment of money, take effect in not less than five days and remain in effect for the time specified in the order, unless suspended, modified, or set aside by the Secretary or set aside by a court.[175]

h. Custodial Accounts

The statutory trust provisions applicable to livestock purchases by packers do not apply to market agencies and dealers. Nonetheless, by regulation, payments made by a livestock buyer to a market agency selling on commission are deemed trust funds and must be deposited in a custodial account.[176] Deposits and withdrawals from custodial accounts are regulated.[177]

i. Reparation Proceedings

A person injured by a stockyard owner's, market agency's, or dealer's violation of the Act or order of the Secretary relating to the purchase sale, or handling of livestock or the purchase or sale of poultry may commence an action in federal district court "for the full amount of damages sustained in consequence of such violation."[178] The action may be subject to the doctrine of primary jurisdiction.[179]

Alternatively, persons complaining of a violation of the Act or an order of the Secretary by a stockyard owner, market agency, or dealer may commence a reparation proceeding for money damages.[180] By the Act's terms, reparation proceedings are not available against packers, swine contractors, and live poultry dealers.[181]

To initiate a reparation proceeding, the complaint must be filed within ninety days after the cause of action accrues.[182] The Secretary has adopted rules of practice for reparation proceedings.[183]

If the Secretary concludes that the complainant is entitled to an award of damages, the Secretary is required to order "the defendant to pay to the complainant the sum to which

---

172. *See* 7 U.S.C. §215.

173. *See id.*

174. *Id.* §216.

175. *See id.* §214.

176. *See* 9 C.F.R. §201.42(a), (b).

177. *See id.* §201.42(c), (d).

178. 7 U.S.C. §209(a), (b).

179. *See, e.g.,* McClenaghan v. Union Stockyards Co., 298 F.2d 659, 663–69 (8th Cir. 1962); *see generally* 2 RICHARD J. PIERCE, JR., ADMINISTRATIVE LAW TREATISE ch. 14 (4th ed. 2002) (discussing primary jurisdiction); BERNARD SCHWARTZ, ADMINISTRATIVE LAW §§8.26–.32 (3d ed. 1991) (same).

180. *See* 7 U.S.C. §§209(b), 210.

181. *See* Jackson v. Swift Eckrich, Inc. 53 F.3d 1452, 1457 (8th Cir. 1995) (noting that "[u]nder the plain language of the PSA, the administrative complaint procedure under §309 of the PSA is simply not available for claims against a live poultry dealer" (footnote omitted)).

182. *See* 7 U.S.C. §210(a).

183. *See* 9 C.F.R. §§202.101–.123. *See generally* Campbell, *supra* note 4, at §3.83 (discussing reparation proceedings); J.W. LOONEY ET AL., AGRICULTURAL LAW: A LAWYER'S GUIDE TO REPRESENTING FARM CLIENTS 374–92 (1990) (same); Jake Looney, *Reparations: An Alternative to Litigation under Federal Statutes,* 1987 ARK. L. NOTES 46, 46–48 (same).

he is entitled on or before a day named."[184] Such an order may be enforced in federal district court in an action brought within one year of the date of the order, and the order is prima facie evidence of the facts stated in it.[185] A prevailing petitioner is entitled to reasonable attorney's fees.[186]

4. Live Poultry Dealers

a. "Live Poultry Dealer" Defined

A "live poultry dealer" is a person

> engaged in the business of obtaining live poultry by purchase or under a poultry growing arrangement for the purpose of either slaughtering it or selling it for slaughter by another, if poultry is obtained by such person in commerce, or if poultry obtained by such person is sold or shipped in commerce, or if poultry products from poultry obtained by such person are sold or shipped in commerce....[187]

A "poultry growing arrangement" is "any growout contract, marketing agreement, or other arrangement under which a poultry grower raises and cares for live poultry for delivery, in accord with another's instructions, for slaughter...."[188] A "poultry grower" is "any person engaged in the business of raising and caring for live poultry for slaughter by another, whether the poultry is owned by such person or another, but not an employee of the owner of such poultry."[189]

b. Prohibited Trade Practices

With respect to live poultry, live poultry dealers are subject to the same prohibitions against unlawful practices as apply to packers under § 192. GIPSA has adopted regulations pertaining to these prohibitions.[190]

The enforcement authority provided to the Secretary in § 193 through § 195 does not apply, however, to live poultry dealers. By their terms, these provisions apply only to enforcement actions against packers and swine contractors.[191]

Under the Act, the Secretary's enforcement authority against live poultry dealers is limited to seeking injunctive relief under § 228a. Under § 228a, the Secretary may seek injunctive relief if he has reason to believe that

> (a) with respect to any transactions covered by this chapter, [a live poultry dealer] has failed to pay or is unable to pay for ... live poultry, or has failed to pay any poultry grower what is due on account of poultry obtained under a poultry

---

184. 7 U.S.C. § 210(b).
185. *See id.*
186. *See id.*
187. *Id.* § 182(10).
188. *Id.* § 182(9).
189. *Id.* § 182(8).
190. *See, e.g.,* 9 C.F.R. §§ 200.49 (specifying requirements regarding scale tickets evidencing weighing of live poultry), 201.53 (prohibiting false reports about market conditions), 201.71–.73 (specifying requirements for weighing live poultry), 201.76 (specifying requirements for reweighing live poultry), 201.82 (requiring care and promptness in the weighing and handling of live poultry), 201.100–.108-1 (specifying records to be furnished to poultry growers and sellers and instructions for weighing live poultry).
191. *But see* Roth, *supra* note 34, at 1216–23 (arguing that certain unfair practices might be enforceable under the "full and prompt payment" requirements of the Act, 7 U.S.C. § 228b-1).

growing arrangement ... ; or (b) has operated while insolvent, or otherwise in violation of this chapter in a manner which may reasonably be expected to cause irreparable damage to another person; ... and that it would be in the public interest to enjoin such person from operating subject to this chapter or enjoin him from operating subject to this chapter except under such conditions as would protect vendors or consignors of such commodities or other affected persons.... [192]

The Secretary, however, may report violations to the Attorney General, "who shall cause appropriate proceedings to be commenced and prosecuted in the proper courts of the United States without delay." [193] Because live poultry dealers are not required to register under the Act, the Secretary cannot use suspension of registration as a means of enforcement. [194]

Otherwise, the injured party may commence an action for damages in a federal district court. [195] Reparation proceedings are unavailable. [196]

c. Statutory Trust

The Act establishes a statutory trust for the benefit of unpaid cash sellers and poultry growers applying to all poultry obtained by a live poultry dealer, "unless such live poultry dealer does not have average annual sales of live poultry, or average annual value of live poultry obtained by purchase or by poultry growing arrangement, in excess of $100,000." [197] The trust and the procedures for preserving it are similar to that for the benefit of unpaid cash sellers to packers. [198] The Secretary may enforce the statutory trust requirement through administrative proceedings. [199]

d. Prompt Payment

Like packers, market agencies, and dealers who are subject to a prompt payment requirement under §228b, live poultry dealers are required to make prompt payment under a similar provision contained in §228b-1. Under §228b-1,

[e]ach live poultry dealer obtaining live poultry by purchase in a cash sale shall, before the close of the next business day following the purchase of poultry, and each live poultry dealer obtaining live poultry under a poultry growing arrangement shall, before the close of the fifteenth day following the week in which the poultry is slaughtered, deliver, to the cash seller or poultry grower from whom such live poultry dealer obtains the poultry, the full amount due to such cash seller or poultry grower on account of such poultry. [200]

For purposes of this provision, "a cash sale means a sale in which the seller does not expressly extend credit to the buyer." [201]

---

192. 7 U.S.C. §228a.

193. *Id.* §224.

194. *See id.* §§203 (requiring market agencies and dealers to register), 204 (authorizing the Secretary to suspend registrations).

195. *Id.* §209; *see generally* Roth, *supra* note 34, at 1216–23 (discussing damages claims against live poultry dealers under the Act).

196. *See* 7 U.S.C. §210; *Jackson v. Swift Eckrich, Inc.,* 53 F.3d at 1457.

197. 7 U.S.C. §197(b).

198. *Compare id.* §197 *with id.* §196; *see also* 9 C.F.R. §203.15 (providing the procedures for preserving trust benefits).

199. 7 U.S.C. §228b-2(a), (b).

200. *Id.* §228b-1.

201. *Id.* §228b-1(c).

Delaying or attempting to delay the collection of funds is deemed an "unfair practice" in violation of the Act.[202] GIPSA has adopted regulations pertaining to the prompt payment requirement.[203]

As with the statutory trust requirements, the Secretary may enforce the prompt payment requirements by initiating administrative proceedings.[204] Live poultry dealers may seek judicial review of the Secretary's final enforcement order.[205] Violation of a final order is a criminal offense.[206] Injunctive relief may also be available.[207]

e. Records

Like packers, swine contractors, stockyard owners, market agencies, and dealers, live poultry dealers must maintain complete and accurate records of their transactions and their ownership.[208] Failure to do so is a criminal offense.[209] GIPSA's regulations impose specific requirements for growout contracts, including their contents; condemnation and grading certificates; grouping or ranking sheets; and purchase invoices.[210]

D. Right To Discuss Contract Terms

Although not enacted as an amendment to the Packers and Stockyards Act, Congress, in the 2002 Farm Bill,[211] limited the use of confidentiality clauses in contracts between livestock and poultry producers and processors who obtain livestock and poultry for slaughter.[212]

The statute defines a "producer" as "any person engaged in the raising and caring for livestock or poultry for slaughter."[213] A "processor" is "any person engaged in the business of obtaining livestock or poultry for the purpose of slaughtering the livestock or poultry."[214]

The statute provides as follows:

Notwithstanding a provision in any contract between a producer and a processor for the production of livestock or poultry, or in any marketing agreement between a producer and a processor for the sale of livestock or poultry for a term of 1 year or more, that provides that information contained in the contract is confidential, a party to the contract shall not be prohibited from discussing any terms or details of the contract with—

(1) a Federal or State agency;

(2) a legal adviser to the party;

(3) a lender to the party;

(4) an accountant hired by the party;

(5) an executive or manager of the party;

---

202. *Id.* § 228b-1(b).
203. *See* 9 C.F.R. § 201.43.
204. *See* 7 U.S.C. § 228b-2.
205. *See id.* § 228b-3.
206. *See id.* § 228b-4.
207. *See id.* § 228a.
208. *See id.* § 221.
209. *See id.*
210. *See* 9 C.F.R. § 201.100.
211. Farm Security and Rural Investment Act of 2002, Pub. L. No. 107–171, tit. X, § 10503, 116 Stat. 142, 510 (codified at 7 U.S.C. § 229b).
212. *See* 7 U.S.C. § 229b.
213. *Id.* § 229b(a)(1).
214. *Id.* § 229b(a)(2).

(6) a landlord of the party; or

(7) a member of the immediate family of the party.[215]

This prohibition, however, is qualified as follows:

Subsection (b) of this section does not—

(1) preempt any State law that addresses confidentiality provisions in contracts for the sale or production of livestock or poultry, except any provision of State law that makes lawful a contract provision that prohibits a party from, or limits a party in, engaging in discussion that subsection (b) of this section requires to be permitted; or

(2) deprive any State court of jurisdiction under any such State law.[216]

This prohibition applies to contracts "entered into, amended, renewed, or extended after May 13, 2002.[217] It is apparently intended to address the "major problem in poultry contracts over the years, which is increasingly becoming a problem in livestock and grain contracts, … [of] confidentiality clauses which prohibit the producer from discussing the contract with anyone."[218]

Conclusion

For over eight decades, the Packers and Stockyards Act has regulated livestock marketing. In the years that have followed its enactment it has undergone changes that may well have been outpaced by the structural changes in the industries it regulates. Nevertheless, that its key provisions have survived largely intact since their original enactment suggests that its original comprehensive breadth was a sound decision by those who enacted it. Whether it should become more comprehensive is a question that will undoubtedly continue to be debated.

———

B. Structural Trends in the Livestock Industry

The Congressional Research Service provides an updated look at concentration and competition in the livestock industry.

Renee Johnson and Geoffrey S. Becker
Livestock Marketing and Competition Issues
Congressional Research Service, CRS Report No. RL33325, 2–8
(January 30, 2009)

Structural Trends

Market concentration in the cattle and hog sectors has increased sharply in the last two decades, with a few firms now dominating each sector. The "four-firm concentra-

---

215. *Id.* § 229b(b).
216. *Id.* § 229b(c).
217. *Id.* § 229b(d).
218. Joseph A. Miller, *Contracting in Agriculture: Potential Problems*, 8 DRAKE J. AGRIC. L. 57, 63 (2003).

tion ratio," which measures the four largest firms' share of total shipment values, is commonly cited as a summary indicator of concentration and overall structural change in the industry. As shown Figure 1, the four-firm concentration ratio for cattle and hog slaughter indicates that, over time, the top four firms are accounting for a growing share of the overall market (based on slaughter volumes). Four-firm concentration ratios from 1963 to 2004 rose from 26% to 72% of the cattle slaughtered, and from 33% to 66% of all hogs slaughtered. Continued consolidation and recent mergers could raise these concentration ratios even more, particularly in the beef sector.

Although observations about concentration and vertical integration are often ascribed to the meat and poultry sectors as a whole, individual production and marketing segments within these sectors do differ in how they are structured and function. The following discussion focuses primarily on the beef and pork industries, with some limited information for poultry production focused mostly on broiler meat.[1]

Beef Production

Most U.S. beef cattle are born, bred, and pastured on a large number of widely dispersed, often small-sized farms and ranches, called cow-calf operators. These operators keep some heifer calves from each year's crop for breeding herd replacement; the rest generally are sold at from 6 to 12 months of age to feedlots (or sometimes to an intermediary known as a backgrounder who readies them for feedlots). These lots fatten them to slaughter weight and sell them to the packing houses. Overall, the trend in U.S. agriculture is toward fewer, larger farms. This is also true in the beef industry: the number of beef operations has declined dramatically over the past few decades, and the largest operations now account for a growing share of total marketings. Still, operations with small herd sizes continue to provide calves to feedlots and backgrounding operations, and despite concentration in larger operations, the cattle sector remains structurally diverse.

Cattle feeding has also become more concentrated into larger feedlots, fewer facilities, and fewer states. A relatively small number of feedlots now fatten and market a significant portion of fed cattle (those ready for slaughter). In 2008, the top 10 companies had the capacity to feed more than 3.2 million cattle in 58 feedlots, representing about one-fourth of all cattle on feed on January 1, 2008 (at facilities with 1,000+ capacity feedlots). At these larger facilities, the top 30 operations account for nearly one-half of all cattle on feed.[2] There were 2,170 feedlots with 1,000+ capacity in 2006. Feedlots with a one-time capacity of less than 1,000 head still account for a large share (about 95%) of all U.S. feedlots, but these facilities account for a small share (less that 10%) of annual marketings.[3]

---

1. Information from A. Barkema et al., "*The New U.S. Meat Industry*," Economic Review of the Federal Reserve Bank of Kansas City, 2nd quarter 2001; Doug O'Brien, *Developments in Horizontal Consolidation and Vertical Integration*, National Agricultural Law Center and The Drake Agricultural Law Center, January 2005; American Farm Bureau Federation, *Making American Agriculture Productive and Profitable*, December 2005; and various reports from USDA's Economic Research Service (ERS), including *Structural Change in the Meat, Poultry, Dairy, and Grain Processing Industries*, ERR-3, March 2005; and *The Transformation of U.S. Livestock Agriculture: Scale, Efficiency, and Risks*, EIB-43, January 2009.

2. USDA/National Agricultural Statistics Service (NASS), "*Cattle on Feed*," at http://www.nass.usda.gov/Statistics_by_Subject/index.asp. Another statistical illustrator of recent change: feedlots that could hold more than 32,000 cattle each accounted for less than a third of all cattle marketed in the leading cattle feeding states in 1980; by 2006 these large feedlots were marketing approximately half of all U.S. fed cattle (USDA data).

3. C. E. Ward and T. C. Schroeder, "*Structural Changes in Cattle Feeding and Meat Packing*." Data are for 1995.

Cattle feeding is now concentrated in the middle part of the country, where five states marketed 80% of all fed cattle: Texas, Kansas, Nebraska, Colorado, and California. [4] Beef cow facilities are more widely dispersed, but also tend to be located in the central states.

Meatpacking is more concentrated than the production phase. Since the 1970s, the number of meatpacking plants has decreased from nearly 2,500 plant to 1,400 plants in 1992. In meat processing, the number of facilities remained more or less unchanged.[5] Concentration in meatpacking has increased: In 1985, the then-top four firms claimed 50% of all steer/heifer slaughter and 39% of all cattle slaughter; by 2007, four firms slaughtered 84% of all young cattle (steers and heifers), and 72% of U.S. cattle of all types.[6] Recent concentration numbers approach those of the early 1900s, when 50% to 75% of the market was dominated by five firms that slaughtered several species.[7]

Another way the federal government weighs concentration is the so-called Herfindahl-Hirschman Index (HHI), which is considered to be a more comprehensive measurement than the four-firm percentage cited above. An industry with an HHI below 1,000 is considered to be unconcentrated. An industry with an HHI between 1,000 and 1,800 is considered to be moderately concentrated; an HHI above 1,800 is highly concentrated. The beef packing industry reached the highly concentrated level by the mid 1990s; its 2004 HHI was 1,900.[8]

Market concentration in the U.S. beef sector could increase considerably following a series of mergers and acquisitions starting in 2007. In July 2007, JBS—a Brazilian company regarded as the world's largest meat processor—purchased the U.S. beef processor Swift & Co., then the third-largest U.S. beef processing company. In February and March 2008, JBS signed agreements to acquire the fourth- and fifth-largest U.S. beef packers, National Beef Packing Company and the Smithfield Beef Group, respectively. These planned acquisitions have undergone customary regulatory review by the U.S. Department of Justice's (DOJ's) Antitrust Division. In October 2008, DOJ and 13 states filed a complaint in U.S. District Court to block the JBS buyout of National Beef Packing Company, citing concerns that it could contribute to higher consumer prices and also to lower producer prices. That same day DOJ announced it would not challenge the JBS acquisition of Smithfield Beef Group, which was later purchased by JBS.

Some in Congress publicly applauded DOJ's lawsuit; opinion within the U.S. meat industry is mixed. If the DOJ lawsuit is not successful and JBS acquires National Beef in addition to Smithfield, this could raise the JBS combined share of the U.S. commercial cattle slaughter market to about 30%, assuming it does not divest some facilities.[9] JBS's acquisition of Five Rivers Ranch Cattle Feeding, which was part of the Smithfield deal, made JBS the largest cattle feeder in the United States. For more information on the JBS merger, see CRS Report RS22980, *Recent Acquisitions of U.S. Meat Companies.*

---

4. USDA/NASS, Commercial Slaughter, Cattle on Feed (Feedlots, Inventory and Marketings, U.S. and by State), http://www.nass.usda.gov/Publications/Statistical_Highlights/2007/tables/livestock.html #catslaugh (2006 marketings). Data are based on facilities with 1,000+ capacity feedlots.

5. USDA/ERS, Structural Change in the Meat, Poultry, Dairy, and Grain Processing Industries, ERR-3, March 2005.

6. Cattle Buyers Weekly, as of January 2008. The 1985 figures are from various USDA data sources.

7. USDA/ERS, U.S. Beef Industry: Cattle Cycles, Price Spreads, and Packer Concentration, Technical Bulletin No. 1874, April 1999.

8. Barkema; and USDA, Grain Inspection, Packers and Stockyards Administration (GIPSA), Assessment of the Cattle, Hog, and Poultry Industries, 2005 Report, March 2006.

9. Some media reports indicated the likelihood that JBS may be required to shed some plants under the acquisition (mostly located in the Southwest) to avoid antitrust concerns. *See, e.g.,* "JBS Is Closer to Completing Acquisitions," Cattle Buyers Weekly, Sept. 22, 2008.

[Note: The J.B.S./National Beef merger was withdrawn. *See, U.S. Dept. Just., Department of Justice Statement on the Abandonment of the JBS/National Beef Transaction*, available at http://www.justice.gov/atr/public/press_releases/2009/242857.htm (February 20. 2009).]

Pork Production

Hog production has experienced perhaps the most sweeping changes over the past 25 years. The number of U.S. farms with hogs declined from 667,000 in 1980 to 67,000 in 2005; those remaining have become much larger and less diversified. The average 1980 farm with hogs had less than 100 head and likely raised them from birth to slaughter weight as part of a more diversified crop-livestock operation. In 2005, the average hog farm had more than 900 head and might typically specialize in a single stage of hog production, such as finishing, according to USDA. Operations with at least 10,000 head now represent less than 1% of all producers but more than half of total U.S. production, USDA reports.

In fact, the hog production segment of the industry now has about 30 key firms, plus several hundred additional "significant" operators.[10] Rapid adoption of vertical coordination methods (see below) drove much of the consolidation in the hog industry, particularly during the 1990s, when farm prices declined to historic lows, causing tens of thousands of small operators to cease raising hogs. From 1993 to 1998 alone, U.S. farms with one or more hogs declined by nearly half, from 218,060 to 114,380, according to USDA. Six large producers—Smithfield, Premium Standard Farms, Seaboard, Prestage, Cargill, and Iowa Select—together accounted for nearly 30% of U.S. hog production in 2003.[11]

In hog packing in 2007, four firms slaughtered 64% of all U.S. hogs, compared with 32% in 1985. The HHI for the hog slaughter industry climbed above 1,000, the numerical threshold for moderately concentrated (see above) during the 1990s.[12]

Poultry Production

The poultry meat sectors have long been highly concentrated, owing in part to vertically integrated production, processing, and distribution systems, where a large share of production is organized and grown under contract between farmers and their poultry processors and handlers. In the U.S. broiler industry, processing firms called "integrators" own hatcheries, processing plants, and feed mills. These integrators contract with independent farmers to "grow out" broiler chicks to market weight, and to produce replacement breeder hens for hatcheries. This relationship is formalized under a production contract, whereby the integrator provides the farmer/grower with chicks, feed, and veterinary and transportation services, while the farmer provides labor, capital in the form of housing and equipment, and utilities. Typically, the birds are sent to slaughter after five to nine weeks on the farm, and the farmer is paid for its growing services.[13]

---

10. Informa Economics, Special Report: *The Changing U.S. Pork Industry*, November 1, 2004, at http://www.informaecon.com/LVNov1.pdf.

11. Informa.

12. *Cattle Buyers Weekly*; Barkema; and GIPSA.

13. J. M. MacDonald, *The Economic Organization of U.S. Broiler Production*, EIB-38, June 2008, http://www.ers.usda.gov/Publications/EIB38/EIB38.pdf; J. M. MacDonald and W. D. McBride, *The Transformation of U.S. Livestock Agriculture: Scale, Efficiency, and Risks*, EIB-43, January 2009, http://www.ers.usda.gov/Publications/ EIB43/EIB43a.pdf. *Also see* USDA/ERS, *Structural Change in U.S. Chicken and Turkey Slaughter*, AER-787, September 2000, http://www.ers.usda.gov/publications/ aer787/aer787.pdf.

Among broiler processors, market shares for the top four U.S. companies accounted for nearly three-fourths of all broiler meat processed in 2007. Broiler production is more highly concentrated within the area between Delaware, Georgia, and Alabama, Mississippi and Arkansas. The top producing states include Georgia, Arkansas, Alabama, Mississippi, North Carolina, Texas, Kentucky, and Maryland. In the turkey meat sector, a few of the larger companies also account for a large share of the industry.

Vertical Coordination and Contracting

Also apparent in the red meat industry in recent decades is the trend toward vertical coordination of production with processing and marketing. The Barkema article has characterized this trend as "supply chains — tightly orchestrated production, processing, and marketing arrangements stretching from genetics to grocery. Supply chains bypass traditional commodity markets and rely on contractual arrangements among the chain participants to manage the transformation of livestock on the farm to meat in the cooler."

This business model was pioneered in agriculture by the poultry industry, which began to integrate shortly after World War II.[14] Poultry producers were "the clear leader" in delivering nutritional and convenient products to consumers while at the same time sharply controlling costs, according to Barkema. The hog industry has been closely following in poultry's footsteps. Now typical are contract production arrangements with large integrators who may provide the genetics, pigs and other inputs, and a contracting producer (farmer) who provides facilities and labor. These arrangements take the form of agricultural contracts or agreements between farmers and their commodity buyers that are reached before harvest or the completion of a livestock production stage. Other alternative marketing arrangements also are used.

Contracts

Contracts can govern the terms for a promised transaction such as date of delivery, the expected price, and other specifications. Contracts enable a farmer to shift some financial risk to the buyer, cushion widely fluctuating price swings, and guarantee an outlet for production. In return, buyers gain a reliable and uniform supply of raw material. Consumers also benefit through lower prices, consistently higher quality, and a wider array of convenient products, it is argued. "The growth in contracting has come largely at the expense of spot (or cash) markets, where farmers retain full autonomy and receive prices based on prevailing market conditions and product attributes at the time of sale," USDA observes.[15] It distinguishes two types:

- Production contracts are when the farmer provides a service to the contractor who usually owns the commodity. The farmer's payment may resemble a fee for service rather than a payment for the commodity's value. For example, in poultry production, processing companies provide the chicks, feed, veterinary services, transportation and production specifications to farmers who raise the chicks for the companies, usually in facilities the farmers own.

- Marketing contracts emphasize the value of the commodity rather the farmer's services. They can specify in advance the basis for the price that will be paid, the

---

14. Although this CRS report focuses primarily on beef and pork, references are made to the poultry sector when pertinent, particularly since this sector competes with beef and pork for the consumer dollar.

15. USDA/ERS. *"Agricultural Contracting: Trading Autonomy for Risk Reduction,"* Amber Waves, February 2006.

quantity to be delivered and where, and product attributes, but the farmer retains major management control and ownership of the commodity until delivery.

In 2005, contracts (production or marketing) covered 50% of all livestock production value, up from 33% in 1991–1993. This compares with 30% of all crop production in 2005 and 25% in 1991–1993, according to USDA (see Table 3 for breakout by selected commodity).

Use of production (as opposed to marketing) contracts in the hog industry grew sharply from 34% of production value in 1996–1997 (1991–1993 data not available) to 76% in 2005, according to USDA. Use of contracts in cattle production has been more or less constant at about 20%. Poultry and eggs have long been raised by farmers under contract with a processing firm; today the value of production under contract is approximately 95% under contract. Marketing contracts are the prevalent type in dairy, with more than 50% produced under contract in 2005. Regardless of commodity type, larger farms tend to use contracts much more than smaller farms, studies have found.

Other Livestock Marketing Arrangements

A comprehensive study of livestock transaction methods by USDA's Grain Inspection, Packers and Stockyards Administration (GIPSA) describes a number of other "alternative marketing arrangements" (AMAs). The study defines AMAs as all alternatives to the cash market, including forward contracts, marketing agreements, procurement or marketing contracts, production contracts, packer ownership, custom feeding, and custom slaughter. (Cash transactions are those that occur immediately or "on the spot.")

The study, conducted by a private contracting firm, determined that all types of AMAs accounted for an estimated 38% of fed (slaughter-ready) beef cattle volume, 89% of finished hog volume, and 44% of lamb volume sold to packers between October 2002 and March 2005, the period studied. Within the beef sector, the 29 largest beef packing plants had obtained 62% of their cattle on the cash or spot market; 29% through marketing agreements; 4.5% through forward contracts; and 5% through packer ownership or other unknown methods. The use of one type of AMA—that is, packer ownership of the livestock they intend to slaughter—accounted for 5% or less of all beef and lamb transactions, but 20% to 30% of all pork transactions, the study found.[16] ...

Notes

1. It is instructive to examine marketing and production contracts that are used in the industry. Companies often prefer to keep their contract terms private, but in order to promote transparency, the Iowa State Attorney General's Office began posting contracts that were submitted by farmers. These contracts are available at http://www.state.ia.us/government/ag/working_for_farmers/contracts/index.html.

2. For an excellent comparison of production contracts used in the poultry industry, see Neil H. Hamilton, *Broiler Contracting in the United States—a Current Contract Analysis Addressing Legal Issues and Grower Concerns*, 7 DRAKE J. AGRIC. L. 43 (2002).

---

16. GIPSA, "*Livestock and Meat Marketing Study*," February 2007, at http://www.gipsa.usda.gov/GIPSA/webapp?area=home&subject=lmp&topic=ir-mms.

3. The Economic Research Service often portrays production and marketing contracts as part of a risk management strategy. With regard to marketing contracts, this approach focuses on the farmer's chance to lock in a sale price through a forward contract. With regard to production contracts, the focus is on the farmer's reduced input cost. *See* Nigel Key and James MacDonald, *Agricultural Contracting: Trading Autonomy for Risk Reduction*, 4 AMBER WAVES 26, USDA Economic Research Service (Feb. 2006). Production contracts, however, most often require the farmer to construct expensive facilities on their land —facilities that can only be used for the specific animal produced under the contract. These costs and the risk associated therewith far overshadow the input costs. Indeed, the risks are so high under poultry production contracts that lenders may not be willing to finance a new grower without a government backed loan guarantee. *See* Chapter IV, *Financing the Farm: Agriculture and Commercial Law*.

C. Unfair, Unjustly Discriminatory, or Deceptive Practices Under the Packers and Stockyards Act

There is a sharp split in opinion regarding the application of the Packers & Stockyards Act's prohibition against "unfair, unjustly discriminatory, or deceptive practice[s]." In *London v. Fieldale Farms Corporation*, the Eleventh Circuit held that a plaintiff needed to show that the unfair practices caused harm to competition or likely harm to competition in order to fall within the protection of the Packers and Stockyards Act. That case concerned poultry growers who alleged alleging retaliation, wrongful termination, and improper weighing claims. The court held that "in order to prevail under the PSA, a plaintiff must show that the defendant's 'unfair, unjustly discriminatory, or deceptive practices' either had an adverse economic impact or were likely to produce an adverse economic impact. To hold otherwise would subvert the purpose of the PSA." *London v. Fieldale Farms Corporation*, 410 F.3d 1295, 1307 (11th Cir. 2005).

The court applied the same reasoning to captive supply contracts in the cattle industry.

Picket v. Tyson Fresh Meats, Inc.
420 F.3d 1272 (11th Cir. 2005)

Before CARNES and COX, Circuit Judges, and MILLS, District Judge.

CARNES, Circuit Judge:

Henry Lee Pickett is the owner of a cattle-producing farm located thirty-five miles south of Montgomery, Alabama. In this class action lawsuit he is the lead plaintiff representing a national class of cattle producers who sell their fed cattle-cows raised specifically for slaughter-to meat-packing plants exclusively on the cash market.

Tyson Fresh Meats, Inc., formerly Iowa Beef Processors, Inc. (IBP), is the largest meat-packing company in the United States. It processes thirty-five to forty percent of the steaks, hamburgers, and other consumer beef products sold in restaurants and supermarkets nationwide. Tyson purchases some cattle on the cash market from producers like Pickett. Since 1994 Tyson has also purchased a significant portion of its cattle through marketing agreements with cattle producers instead of from the cash market.

Pickett contends that Tyson has used marketing agreements to deflate the price of fed cattle on the cash market and the market as a whole in order to reap the benefits of lower prices. To stop Tyson from using marketing agreements and to recover for losses incurred from the lower prices that resulted on the cash market, Pickett sued Tyson. He brought the lawsuit on behalf of all cash market sellers claiming that Tyson had engaged in unfair practices and manipulated prices in violation of the Packers and Stockyards Act of 1921, 7 U.S.C. § 181 *et seq.* The issues this case raises, and its procedural history, are best understood after a discussion of the cattle and meat-packing industries and the market where they meet.

I.

"Fed cattle" are born, raised, and marketed exclusively for slaughter. The process begins with the birth of a calf on a cattle-producing farm which exists solely to breed and raise cattle, feed them, and then sell them to meat-packing plants for processing into beef products. The first 200 days of a calf's life are spent feeding from her mother. After that, the calf is weaned and spends the next 200 days eating feed, grass, or wheat.

After the calf has been fed for 400 days, the producer sends it along with all the other calves being raised at the same time to a feed yard. The feed yard is a farm specifically designed to feed the calves intensively so they are in peak condition when sold to the meat packers. Some producers have feed yards on their farms, while others send their calves to third party feed yards which not only finish feeding them but also broker the cattle to the meat packers on the producer's behalf.

At the feed yards, each calf is put into a pen with fifty to 200 other calves for the intensive feeding program, which usually lasts 120 days. When the feeding program is finished, each animal ideally weighs 1250 pounds, the industry's target weight.

Once the cattle in a pen have been fed intensively for 120 days, and have hopefully reached the target weight, they must be sold to a meat-packing plant within two weeks. If the fed cattle are not sold within that time period, they become too expensive for the feed yard to maintain and also become less desirable to the meat packers. They become too expensive because cattle gain usable weight more slowly after reaching 1250 pounds and eventually stop gaining it at all, but they still must be fed. They become less desirable to meat packers because the cattle start to gain more fat and the market is for meat not fat. The point is that the two-week window for selling fed cattle after they have been at a feed yard for 120 days is critical to the producers, the feed yards, and the meat packers. (For ease of reference, from this point on we will refer to fed cattle as simply "cattle," except where quoting.)

Once a meat packer purchases a pen of cattle, it has those cattle hauled to its factory and slaughters them. The packer then processes the carcasses into different cuts of meat (e.g., hamburger, New York strip, and filet mignon), packages the different cuts, and sells them to meat wholesalers, restaurants, and grocery stores.

The process we have described has been used to prepare cattle for the market since packers began buying pens of cattle directly from producers on the cash market about sixty years ago. (Before that, the buying and selling of cattle was done through agents at stockyards in major cities in the Midwest with Chicago being the largest.) During all but the last decade or so, packers purchased cattle almost exclusively through the cash market.

This is how the cash market works. Buyers from the meat-packing companies spread out around the country to the different feed yards and inspect the pens of cattle that are ready to be sold. If the buyer likes the cattle in a pen, he makes an offer to the producer or feed yard operator. The producer or operator is free to accept or reject the packer's offer; in deciding whether to do so, he often considers offers being made for other pens of cattle around the country. (Much of this information is relayed over the telephone from one producer or operator to another.) Often, the producer or feed yard operator and the buyer from the packing plant haggle over the price. If they eventually agree on a price, the cattle in the pen are delivered to the packing plant seven days from the date of the agreement on price. The price the packer paid for the pen of cattle is reported to a central office and average prices are published each week.

In the mid-1980s a number of cattle producers began looking for a new method of marketing their cattle to packers, one that did not require as much time and hassle as negotiating every pen of cattle on the cash market. They came up with marketing agreements and eventually persuaded the packers, including Tyson, to begin using those agreements for some of their purchases. The use of marketing agreements spread slowly throughout the industry at first but began to pick up steam in the 1990s. By 1994 Tyson, among others, was using marketing agreements to procure a substantial part of the cattle it needed.[1]

Under the typical marketing agreement, a feed yard operator will call and tell the meat packer's buyer that he has a pen of cattle at its peak and ready to be sold. The feed yard operator promises to have the cattle delivered to the factory for slaughter within two weeks, with the packer getting to pick the exact date of delivery within that two-week period. The price paid for the cattle under the marketing agreement is pegged at the publicly released average cash-market price for the week prior to when the agreement is made. The agreement commonly provides that after the cattle are processed the price will be adjusted up or down based on the quality or the yield of the carcasses. The adjustment is quickly and easily calculated by Tyson as a matter of course in processing the cattle.

To summarize, the difference is that with marketing agreements, unlike cash-market purchases, the price is set not through bidding but automatically at the cash-market price the week before the agreement is made, the price is usually adjusted based on post-slaughter quality or yield, and the packer picks the actual delivery date within the two-week period that begins when the agreement is made.

II.

Pickett, and the class members he represents, sell their cattle exclusively on the cash market.[2] They claim that through marketing agreements Tyson has been able to manipulate the price of cattle on the cash market.[3] Tyson is the largest meat packer in the coun-

---

1. The record reflects that from 1994 to 2002 Tyson had purchased anywhere from twenty to fifty percent of its cattle supply through marketing agreements.

2. The class Pickett represents was initially certified as all cattle producers who sold cattle on the cash market to Tyson, including those who also sold cattle to Tyson through marketing agreements. We reversed this initial class certification after deciding that Pickett, who sold cattle to Tyson exclusively on the cash market and was challenging the legality of the marketing agreements, could not adequately and fairly represent the interests of producers who had sold cattle to Tyson through both the cash market and marketing agreements. *Pickett v. Iowa Beef Processors,* 209 F.3d 1276, 1280–81 (11th Cir.2000). On remand, the class definition was restricted to cattle producers who sold cattle to Tyson exclusively on the cash market. We denied Tyson permission to appeal this second class certification. *Iowa Beef Processors, Inc. v. Pickett,* No. 02-90002 (11th Cir. Mar. 5, 2002). It is this narrower class that Pickett represents.

3. In his complaint, Pickett claims that Tyson violated the Packers and Stockyards Act through the use of captive supply arrangements. "Captive supply" is Pickett's pejorative term for Tyson's procurement of cattle through either of two methods for purchasing cattle outside the cash market: mar-

try. It processes forty percent of all hamburgers and steaks on American dinner tables. Tyson slaughters 10 million cattle each year, nearly one-half of the 25 million cattle that are purchased and slaughtered by meat-packing plants in this country.

Pickett's theory is that Tyson has used marketing agreements and its large market share to artificially reduce prices on the cash market. Prices for cattle on the cash market are responsive to supply and demand. Pickett claims that by using marketing agreements Tyson has withdrawn a large amount of demand from the cash market, thereby substantially decreasing price pressure there. The result, in Pickett's view, is that producers selling on the cash market have gotten a lower price for their cattle. A reduced cash-market price benefits Tyson in two ways. First, Tyson is able to obtain the cattle that it still purchases on the cash market (millions of head each year) at a lower price. Second, because the price Tyson pays for marketing-agreement cattle is pegged to the average cash-market price, it pays less for those cattle too.

According to Pickett, the lower prices that Tyson pays for cattle are not an unintended consequence of its heavy use of marketing agreements to purchase much of its needs. To the contrary, Pickett alleges that those lower prices are the primary, intended consequence of marketing agreements. He claims that achieving lower prices in that manner constitutes an unfair practice and the manipulation of prices in violation of the Packers and Stockyards Act.

The case was tried for four weeks. Before the case was submitted to the jury, Tyson moved the district court for judgment as a matter of law under Fed.R.Civ.P. 50(a). The motion asserted, among other grounds, that Tyson had proven a number of competitive justifications for using marketing agreements, the factual existence of which were not disputed by any evidence. The district court almost granted Tyson's Rule 50(a) motion, observing that Pickett had presented "a very thin case," but it decided to reserve ruling on the motion to see what the jury would do. The district court explained that granting the motion before the jury verdict risked having to re-do the whole trial if the appellate court disagreed, and a retrial would be long and costly.

The jury's "verdict" consisted of answers to a number of interrogatories. Specifically, the jury was asked—"yes" or "no"—whether it found, by a preponderance of the evidence:

1. That there is a nationwide market for fed cattle?

2. That the defendant's use of [marketing agreements] had an anti-competitive effect on the cash market for fed cattle?

3. That the defendant lacked a legitimate business reason or competitive justification for using [marketing agreements]?

4. That the defendant's use of [marketing agreements] proximately caused the cash market price to be lower than it otherwise would have been?

---

keting agreements and forward contracts. The parties agree that Tyson buys only about three percent of its cattle through forward contracts, which is too little to have any effect on the cash market price. For that reason, the briefs essentially ignore forward contracts, and we will too. Marketing agreements account for a significant amount of Tyson's cattle purchases, enough to affect price, and for that reason they are the focus of the briefs and this opinion. We will not be referring to marketing agreements as "captive supply" arrangements because, as the district court pointed out, the term is a misnomer. Under marketing agreements, a producer's cattle is captive for no more than two weeks. *Pickett v. Tyson Fresh Meats, Inc.,* 315 F.Supp.2d 1172, 1175 n. 1 (M.D.Ala.2004). Moreover, "captive" means nothing more in this context than that Tyson has a contractual right to delivery of the cattle in exchange for which it must pay the purchase price. It would be as descriptive to refer to these cattle as "contractual supply."

5. That the defendant's use of [marketing agreements] injured each and every member of the plaintiffs' class?[4]

The jury answered "yes" to each of those five questions.

The verdict form instructed the jury that, if it did answer "yes" to all of those questions, it should answer these additional questions:

6. What amount, if any, do you find that defendant's use of [marketing agreements] damaged the cash market price of fed cattle sold to [the defendant] during the period from February 1, 1994, through October 31, 2002?

7. Did the defendant's use of [marketing agreements] depress the cash market price for fed cattle purchased by [the defendant] by an equal percentage for each year of the class period? If your answer is yes, by what percent?

The jury wrote "$1,281,690,000.00" in the question number 6 blank.[5] It answered question number 7 "no."

Following the verdict the district court granted Tyson's Rule 50(b) renewed motion for judgment as a matter of law, ruling "that [Pickett's] evidence is insufficient to support a finding that [Tyson] lacked a legitimate business justification for its use of [marketing agreements]." *Pickett v. Tyson Fresh Meats, Inc.*, 315 F.Supp.2d 1172, 1175 (M.D.Ala.2004). It entered final judgment for Tyson. This is Pickett's appeal from that judgment.[6]

III.

We review *de novo* a district court's grant of judgment as a matter of law, applying the same standard as the district court. A district court should grant judgment as a matter of law when the plaintiff presents no legally sufficient evidentiary basis for a reasonable jury to find for him on a material element of his cause of action. The court should deny it if

---

4. We have substituted "marketing agreement" for the term "captive supply" in the verdict form. *See ante,* at 1276 n. 3.

5. Before submitting the questions to the jury, the district court had made clear to the parties that even if it entered a judgment for Pickett and the class, it had no intention of using as the amount of damages the jury's answer to question number 6: "I'm not—and no matter what verdict this jury comes back with, I'm not going to enter a judgment on that number if they bring one in because what we're talking about here includes people who are not members of the class." The court's point was that the amount of reduction in the cash market price of cattle was too broad a measure of damages, because it included those who sold some cattle outside the cash market, and those producers were not in the class.

6. Before we get into the merits of the issues raised in this appeal, there is a procedural issue arising from the jury verdict form that we need to address. The form is unusual because it did not ask the jury to return a general verdict and the jury did not return one, even though it answered all of the interrogatories in favor of Pickett. A question arose at oral argument about whether an order granting Rule 50(b) relief properly may be entered where there has been no general verdict for either party. *Cf.* Fed.R.Civ.P. 49(a); *Mason v. Ford Motor Co.*, 307 F.3d 1271, 1274 (11th Cir.2002) ("When Rule 49(a) is employed, the jury makes specific factual findings; and the judge makes the ultimate legal conclusions based on those facts.").

The answer is found in Rule 50(b)(2)(B), which provides that "if no verdict was returned" by the jury, the district court is authorized to "direct entry of judgment as a matter of law" on a renewed motion for it. Fed.R.Civ.P. 50(b)(2)(B). This result makes sense. If the evidence that the plaintiff presented at trial is insufficient for the jury reasonably to return a verdict for the plaintiff, the defendant is entitled to judgment regardless of whether the jury did return a verdict. The absence of a verdict in these circumstances is not materially different from the situation where the district court grants a defendant's motion for judgment as a matter of law before the case is submitted to the jury, which is authorized under Rule 50(a).

the plaintiff presents enough evidence to create a substantial conflict in the evidence on an essential element of the plaintiff's case....

A.

Pickett and his fellow class members contend that Tyson's marketing agreements violated the Packers and Stockyards Act. The relevant sections of the PSA make it:

> unlawful for any packer or swine contractor with respect to livestock, meats, meat food products, or livestock products in unmanufactured form, or for any live poultry dealer with respect to live poultry, to:
>
> (a) Engage in or use any unfair, unjustly discriminatory, or deceptive practice or device; or ...
>
> (e) Engage in any course of business or do any act for the purpose or with the effect of manipulating or controlling prices, or of creating a monopoly in the acquisition of, buying, selling, or dealing in, any article, or of restraining commerce....

Packers and Stockyards Act § 202(a), (e), 7 U.S.C. § 192(a), (e).

It is undisputed that Tyson is a meat packer and that the PSA applies to its business. The dispute is over what is an "unfair" practice and what constitutes "any act for the purpose or with the effect of manipulating or controlling prices." Pickett contends he has established unfairness and price control or manipulation under the PSA by proving that Tyson's marketing agreements caused the cash-market price, and the overall market price, for cattle to be lower than it otherwise would be. If that were all Pickett were required to prove he might win, because there was evidence at trial to support the jury's finding that the use of marketing agreements has resulted in lower prices for cattle both on the cash market and the market as a whole.[7]

Tyson, of course, urges a contrary reading of the PSA. It takes the position that because the PSA was meant as a protection against anti-competitive practices by meat packers, Pickett must establish more than that the use of marketing agreements have decreased the price for cattle. He must establish that their use has adversely affected competition, which requires showing that marketing agreements have no pro-competitive justifications.

The district court resolved this issue in Tyson's favor. After it did so, this Court resolved the meaning of "unfair" practice in PSA § 202(a) in the same way. In *London v. Fieldale Farms Corp.,* 410 F.3d 1295 (11th Cir.2005), we held that "in order to succeed on a claim under the PSA, a plaintiff must show that the defendant's unfair, discriminatory or deceptive practice adversely affects or is likely to adversely affect competition." *Id.* at 1303. This, we explained, is consistent with the purpose and intent behind the PSA. "At the time of enactment, the chief evil Congress feared was the monopoly of the packers." *Id.* at 1302 (citing *Stafford v. Wallace,* 258 U.S. 495, 514–15, 42 S.Ct.

---

7. We say that Pickett "might win" because the critical evidence that the use of marketing agreements caused lower prices in the markets was the testimony of Professor Taylor, an expert witness for Pickett, and there are *Daubert* issues involving his testimony. *See Daubert v. Merrell Dow Pharms., Inc.,* 509 U.S. 579, 113 S.Ct. 2786, 125 L.Ed.2d 469 (1993). The existence and seriousness of those issues are partly reflected in the district court judge's comment that if he were the factfinder, "I'd say, Dr. Taylor, you're nuts." Given the basis of our decision to affirm the district court's judgment on grounds independent of any *Daubert* issues, we can assume for present purposes that Tyson's use of marketing agreements did lead to lower prices in the cattle markets.

397, 401, 66 L.Ed. 735 (1922)). "The primary purpose of the PSA was 'to assure fair competition and fair trade practices in livestock marketing and in the meatpacking industry.'" *Id.* (quoting H.R.Rep. No. 85-1048, at 1 (1958), U.S.Code Cong. & Admin.News 5212, 5213). It was aimed at halting practices whose purpose was to destroy competition. *Id.* The *London* decision settles in this circuit that by "unfair" practice, PSA § 202(a) means a practice that does or is likely to adversely affect competition. *Id.* at 1303 ...

In the *London* case there was no PSA § 202(e) price manipulation or control claim, as there is in this case, but the principles and purposes behind these two closely related provisions of the Act are the same. Section 202(e) is aimed at preventing a particular type of unfairness in the meat-packing industry, namely, price manipulation and control and the creation of monopolies. With section 202(e), as with section 202(a), "the chief evil Congress feared was the monopoly of the packers," and the primary purpose "was to assure fair competition and fair trade practices." *London,* 410 F.3d at 1302. For the same reasons a section 202(a) unfairness claim requires a plaintiff to show an adverse effect on competition, so does a section 202(e) price manipulation or control claim.

It was not Congress' intent in enacting the PSA to interfere with a meat packer's business practices where those practices did not interfere with competition. *See IBP, Inc. v. Glickman,* 187 F.3d 974, 978 (8th Cir.1999) ("[W]e are ... mindful that the purpose behind the Act was not to so upset the traditional principles of freedom of contract, as to require an entirely level playing field for all." (quotation omitted)). If a packer's course of business promotes efficiency and aids competition in the cattle market, the challenged practice cannot, by definition, adversely affect competition. *See London,* 410 F.3d at 1304 ("We note that elimination of a competitive impact requirement would subvert the policy justifications for the PSA's adoption."); *see also Jackson v. Swift Eckrich, Inc.,* 53 F.3d 1452, 1458 (8th Cir.1995) ("We are convinced that the purpose behind § 202 of the PSA, 7 U.S.C. § 192, was not to so upset the traditional principles of freedom of contract. The PSA was designed to promote efficiency, not frustrate it."); *Glickman,* 187 F.3d at 978 (same); *Griffin v. Smithfield Foods, Inc.,* 183 F.Supp.2d 824, 828 (E.D.Va.2002) (same).

In this case, the jury found that Tyson's use of marketing agreements "had an anticompetitive effect on the cash market for fed cattle" and that Tyson "lacked a legitimate business reason or competitive justification for using" marketing agreements. The district court, in granting Tyson's Rule 50(b) motion for judgment as a matter of law, concluded that Pickett had failed to present any evidence to call into question Tyson's evidence establishing that marketing agreements: (1) allow the company to keep up with competitors in the meat-packing industry who also were reaping the cost benefits of marketing agreements; (2) provide the company with a reliable and consistent supply of cattle to keep its factories at full capacity; (3) reduce the transaction costs of having to negotiate individually for 200,000 pens of cattle a year to meet its needs; and (4) permit the company to match its cattle purchases with the needs of its customers. *See Pickett,* 315 F.Supp.2d at 1175–77. In the district court's view, "the trial record is barren of any evidence which would permit the jury to conclude that [Tyson] lacked a legitimate business justification for its use of [marketing agreements]." *Id.* at 1176.

Pickett contends that the district court got it wrong. He argues that there was evidence to support a finding that all of Tyson's competitive justifications for using marketing agreements were pretextual, thus rendering reasonable the jury's finding that Tyson had no competitive justification for doing so. The pretext issue applied to the justifications Tyson asserted is what this case turns on. If there is evidence from which a jury reasonably could find that none of Tyson's asserted justifications are real, that each one is pretextual, Pickett wins. Otherwise, Tyson wins.

B.

We mentioned earlier in this opinion that marketing agreements were originated by cattle producers, not meat packers. Some cattle producers insist on selling their cattle through those agreements and will not use the cash market. Others prefer to use marketing agreements for some or all of their cattle. Tyson's first competitive justification for using the marketing agreements is that it must use them in order to have access to the cattle of those producers. Otherwise, it will lose all of that supply, which constitutes a significant share of the market, to its competitors who do use the agreements. As the district court found, restricting its own use of marketing agreements "would pose problems for [Tyson], as it would have fewer cattle to choose from, and the quality and reliability of its cattle supply would likely suffer." *Id.* at 1176. In other words, Tyson needs to use marketing agreements to meet the competition.

Tyson presented a number of witnesses who testified to the factual premise of this justification: Tyson's competitors use marketing agreements and Tyson would suffer a serious competitive disadvantage if it did not use them. Some of Pickett's own witnesses testified to the same thing. No one disputed this justification as a factual matter. Instead, Pickett's position is that this justification is legally insufficient. He insists that a practice of purchasers that is unfair to sellers should not be allowed on the ground that all purchasers do it. In other words, there ought not be a "meet the competition" defense to conduct that the PSA otherwise prohibits.

The law does recognize a meet the competition defense in another context. The Robinson-Patman Act, which amended the Clayton Antitrust Act, generally proscribes price discrimination between different purchasers of commodities of like grade and quality. Robinson-Patman Act § 2(a), 15 U.S.C. § 13(a). That is, a commodities dealer cannot charge its favored purchasers a lower price while selling at a higher price to others. The Robinson-Patman Act, however, recognizes an exception and provides for an absolute defense if a merchant's lower price to a purchaser "was made in good faith to meet an equally low price of a competitor." *Id.* § 13(b). That defense has been roundly criticized. *See Hoover Color Corp. v. Bayer Corp.,* 199 F.3d 160, 163 (4th Cir.1999) (collecting critiques of the Robinson-Patman Act by Justice Frankfurter and Judges Bork and Posner).

In any event, the PSA is not the Robinson-Patman Act. Unlike the latter, the PSA does not expressly provide a meet the competition defense. Congress could have written that defense into the PSA just as it did in the Robinson-Patman Act. We would be most reluctant to do Congress' writing for it, especially when the wisdom of the provision we are asked to write into the statute is debatable. But we need not go so far as to reject the meet the competition defense in PSA cases, because in this case that defense would not matter. It would not matter because Tyson has offered other justifications for its use of marketing agreements, and those justifications are legally permissible and factually uncontradicted in the record.

C.

Tyson's second proffered competitive justification for marketing agreements is that their use provides the company with a reliable and stable supply of cattle for its packing plants. This is an unquestionably legitimate justification. *See Glickman,* 187 F.3d at 978 ("The record demonstrates that the [business practice] is an effort by IBP to have a more reliable and efficient method of obtaining a supply of cattle. The [PSA] was designed to promote efficiency, not frustrate it." (quotation omitted)).

Tyson contends that, because there are not enough cattle in the market to meet the demands of the entire packing industry from week to week, and because it must purchase 200,000 head of cattle each week to keep its processing plants running at full productive capacity, the company has to struggle to keep a constant supply of cattle coming into its plants. Before 1994 Tyson had to negotiate individually for each pen of cattle it purchased. Its competitors were also negotiating on the same pens of cattle, and the producers were free to accept or reject Tyson's offered price for a pen. If Tyson's offers were rejected for enough pens, the company could not fill its factory for the next week and it would not have enough product to meet its customers' demands.

Marketing agreements make the inventory crunch much less crunchy for Tyson. They are negotiated two weeks in advance of delivery of the cattle, and Tyson picks the exact date of delivery within that two-week period. These features provide Tyson with greater ability to plan its purchases and to keep a steady flow of cattle coming into its plants. By contrast, the cash market provides Tyson with no leeway about the delivery date, because cattle purchased on it are always delivered seven days after purchase. On the cash market there is a greater risk that Tyson's buyers will purchase too little cattle for its needs, or too much for its plants to process within the constrictions of the delivery dates. The economic effect of these differences between the two procurement methods is critically important for a large meat packer whose profit depends on keeping its plants operating at full capacity without interruptions.

The underlying facts relating to this justification were not disputed at trial. Both Tyson's and Pickett's witnesses testified to them. James Herring, president of Friona Industries, a collection of feed yards in the Texas panhandle, testified that buying cattle through marketing agreements guarantees for Tyson a certain number of cattle per week. Lee Borck, the president and principal negotiator for the Beef Marketing Group, a consortium of thirteen feed yards in the Midwest, testified that marketing agreements ensure that Tyson will "have a percentage of their cattle that are going to be procured for a plant that's difficult to procure cattle for." Jerry Hausman, an economics professor from the Massachusetts Institute of Technology, testified that "what marketing agreements do is it helps [Tyson] to better schedule its plants. And by cutting down the variability, they're going to get greater capacity utilization and higher profits." And Bruce Bass, Tyson's head buyer, stated that marketing agreements ensure a consistent supply of cattle for the company's processing plants.

Professor Catherine Durham, one of Pickett's expert economists, agreed with this assessment when she was asked about the use of marketing agreements on cross-examination:

> Q. You would agree with me, Professor Durham, that marketing agreements also help [Tyson] guarantee a minimum supply of cattle at the plants that get marketing agreement cattle, right?
>
> A. Yes.
>
> Q. And [Tyson] has a valid business interest in having a steady supply of cattle at its packing plants, right?
>
> A. Yes.

The economics of this are simple. As Professor Hausman explained, being able to keep its processing plants operating at capacity has increased Tyson's efficiency. Keeping the doors to its plants open and the machinery running is a fixed cost for Tyson. No matter how many cattle the plant processes on a given day, Tyson has fixed costs for the facility and equipment, the electricity used to run the plant, and the salaries of a minimum number of employees needed to run the plant. Whether the plant slaughters 2,000 head or 20,000 head of cattle on a given day, the fixed cost will be the same.

If Tyson slaughters 20,000 head of cattle, the fixed costs of operating the plant are divided by a factor that is ten times larger than when it slaughters only 2,000 head. The more cattle Tyson processes on a given day, the less the fixed cost per head. By ensuring that the processing plants are consistently filled and operate at or near capacity, the use of marketing agreements provides Tyson with a more cost-effective operation. This result, which is entirely in harmony with the goals of the PSA, *see Jackson*, 53 F.3d at 1458 ("The PSA was designed to promote efficiency, not frustrate it."), is a legitimate, pro-competitive justification.

Pickett offered no evidence to dispute the existence of this justification. Instead, through examination of Tyson's witnesses, Pickett simply brought out the unremarkable fact that if Tyson were willing to pay "a high enough price" or "throw our billfold out the window" it could get from the cash market as many cattle as it wanted for its processing plants (and even then it would be difficult). Of course, in hypotheticals where economic constraints are assumed away, economic problems are not problems. But this is not a hypothetical case. Tyson is an actual business that operates in the real world through real markets where there are real economic limits. Tyson has competitors who stand ready, willing, and able to undercut the price of its product if it pays too much for the raw materials used to produce that product.

D.

Tyson's third proffered competitive justification for purchasing some of its cattle through marketing agreements is that doing so reduces its transaction costs by eliminating the need to negotiate for each individual pen of cattle, as it must on the cash market. With the cash market, buyers for Tyson are constantly on the road inspecting pens of cattle in a never-ending effort to see if the cattle in each pen match the quality the company needs to fill its customers' orders. Once the buyer finds a pen that appears to fit the needs, he places a bid with the producer. The producer usually is conducting simultaneous negotiations with one or more of Tyson's competitors for the same pen. After days of going back and forth, the producer chooses the highest bid, which may or may not be Tyson's. This process is costly for both the producers and Tyson because it takes so much time. Tyson has to successfully outbid other packers for more than 1,000 pens every week (the pens each consisting of between fifty and 200 cattle) in order to meet its need for 200,000 head per week.

As a number of Tyson's witnesses testified, marketing agreements eliminate the time and energy spent by packers and producers negotiating for individual pens. Under the agreements the price of the cattle is set at the average cash-market price (plus a yield adjustment that is determined after processing). Mr. Borck, the principal negotiator for BMG feed yards, testified that when using the cash market he was spending three or four days a week on the phone with meat packers negotiating the price for his peak cattle. This was "not very productive time." With the marketing agreement system, Mr. Borck estimated that it now takes "half a day a week" to sell the peak cattle to the packer. He spends the rest of this "high-priced management time to try and be more efficient in our operations and in the caretaking of the cattle."

Other cattle producers and feed yard operators agreed with Mr. Borck. Jim Keller, a feed yard operator in Kansas, testified that he preferred marketing agreements because he "didn't have to waste time talking about prices. Some people like that. They like haggling over price. I don't. I don't. I always think I could probably be doing something different." Professor Hausman testified that because the price in marketing agreements is set, "marketing agreements are going to decrease transactions costs and therefore decrease the costs for [Tyson] and also likewise for the feedlot operator as well." This was a valid business justification, he continued, "because it's economically efficient to decrease your transactions costs. Anything that decreases costs like that increases economic efficiency, both for [Tyson], for the feedlot operator, and also for the U.S. economy." Mr. Bass, Tyson's head buyer, confirmed this. He said that from 1994 to 2002, Tyson has been able to decrease the number of buyers it employs by about fifteen percent, partly because of the increasing popularity of marketing agreements among cattle producers and feed yards.

Pickett did not dispute any of this. In fact, many of his witnesses agreed with Tyson's witnesses that marketing agreements relieve producers and packers from the burden of spending their time on negotiating prices, instead of on raising and processing cattle. Brett Gottsch, a cattle producer from Nebraska who testified for Pickett, conceded that with marketing agreements buyers and feed yard operators do not need to "go through the process of bidding and negotiating prices." Robert Rothwell, a cattle producer and feed yard operator in Nebraska, testified that purchasing cattle through marketing agreements requires less time and energy than purchasing cattle through the cash-market system. And Jeff Biegert, another producer from the Midwest, joked that with marketing agreements, the buyers for packing companies "could be playing golf if [they] wanted to, and the cattle will still get marketed."

In sum, it was undisputed at the trial that marketing agreements are a more efficient means for both meat packers and cattle producers to operate in the market. It was undisputed that use of the agreements has lowered the transaction costs of producers and meat packers, including Tyson. Witnesses for both parties recognized that these are pro-competitive benefits for the industry. Those benefits are entirely consistent with the goals of the PSA. *See Glickman,* 187 F.3d at 978.

E.

Tyson's final competitive justification for using marketing agreements is that they allow the company to pay for each head of cattle in a pen individually based on the quality of the meat, rather than paying for the entire pen "on the average." Among other benefits, this gives producers an incentive to provide packers with the quality and yield of meat they need to satisfy their customers' demands.

In the cash-market system, buyers for the packing companies pay a single price for an entire pen of cattle which results in an average price per head in the pen. With this "on the average" system, producers can put some of their less desirable cattle-those with less quality meat or lower usable meat yields-in the same pen as high-quality, high-yield cattle. The packer who buys that pen gets some cattle that match its customers' needs and some that do not. The other side of the problem is that producers with a large share of high-quality or high-yield cattle do not always get rewarded for it. This disparity between the quality and yield of the cattle and the price paid for them on the cash market, which is a disparity that can go either way, is the result of buyers not being able to closely inspect and assess the quality and yield of fifty to 200 head of cattle in each of the many pens that they must haggle over in the cash market.

With marketing agreements, meat packers also buy an entire pen of cattle but with an important difference: the price paid for the cattle is adjusted up or down after slaughter to reflect the actual quality and yield of the meat. The final price depends not on the buyer's in-the-field estimate of the meat that a pen of cattle will produce, but on the actual meat that does result after slaughter. This feature of marketing agreements takes away the incentive for producers to mix low-quality and low-yield cattle in with better ones, and it gives them an incentive to increase the overall quality and yield of their cattle. Both results are good for the industry and for competition.

The factual premise for this justification was not disputed at trial. A number of witnesses, both for Tyson and for Pickett, testified to it. Mr. Gottsch, who testified for Pickett, stated that one advantage of marketing agreements is that the packer pays the producer for each cow in the pen based on the quality. Mr. Rothwell, another of Pickett's witnesses, agreed that individual pricing was a "valid business justification" for buying and selling cattle through marketing agreements. And, Mr. Biegert, one of the Nebraska producers testifying for Pickett, conceded that "paying a feedyard a premium for really high quality cattle will create economic incentives that go all the way back to the [producer] and can cause the [producer] to strengthen his cowherd."

Professor Hausman, Tyson's expert, agreed with the three producers who testified for Pickett. He said that by paying for each head of cattle, rather than paying for the pen on the average, the packer creates an economic incentive for the producers to grow better cattle. He went on to explain that "if you get paid the average, you don't have an economic incentive nearly as much; because if you have some bad cattle and some good cattle, they sort of average out." Mr. Keller, the feed yard manager from Kansas, concurred with the professor. He testified that one thing that "really bothered" him about the cash market was that "all the cattle were getting sold for the very same price. All cattle, no matter what they were, what quality, everything getting sold on the same price."

Because price is adjusted to fit actual quality and yield, marketing agreements provide Tyson with another, related competitive benefit. Like most other companies in our complex economy, Tyson has a specific niche market for its products—in its case, steaks and hamburgers. It is a volume meat dealer; its largest customers are supermarket chains. To provide for its customers in the most inexpensive and efficient way, Tyson prefers large, high-yielding cattle to leaner, high-quality cattle. High-yield cattle tend to have middle-grade meat, and that is fine with Tyson. By focusing its procurement on high-yield instead of high-quality cattle, Tyson is better able to meet the needs of its customers at lower costs.

Through marketing agreements, Tyson provides an incentive for producers to raise and sell more high-yield cattle. On the cash market, the best Tyson can do is have its buyers attempt to purchase pens that appear to have the highest number of high-yield cattle. But that is an inexact science. With marketing agreements, the post-slaughter price more closely matches the actual yield, which provides an incentive for producers to supply Tyson with the high-yield cattle it needs. *See Griffin*, 183 F.Supp.2d at 828–29 (rejecting pork producers' PSA claim in part because "[t]he Defendants decided that the guess work required to fulfill their needs at cash markets was inefficient for themselves and the consumer").

The factual existence of this pro-competitive benefit was not disputed at trial. Counsel for Tyson asked Professor Hausman: "[I]f a packer is buying cattle under a marketing agreement, can it do anything to try to influence the type of animals that the participating feedyards produce?" Professor Hausman responded:

> Yes. It has—it offers money. That's what it does. So it has this grid and it says, you know, if we want higher yield, we'll pay you more money for higher

yield. If it pays more money, the feedyard operator is going to say, you know, more money is good for me and my cattle owners, so I'm going to try to increase yield.

And, the incentive works. Since 1994, when it began to significantly increase its use of marketing agreements, the cattle that Tyson has purchased from marketing agreements has had a higher yield than the cattle it has purchased on the cash market.

Instead of producing evidence to dispute the existence of this advantage of marketing agreements, Pickett argues that the benefit could be obtained through the cash market if it were changed. One of Pickett's two experts, Professor Durham, testified that the cash market, like marketing agreements, can also provide incentives for quality by making the same sort of offers and discounts and premiums. She did not, however, contradict the fact that, as Pickett's witnesses described its current operation, the cash market does not provide incentives for quality and yield. We deal with real markets the way they are, not with how they might be redrawn on the blackboard in a classroom.

Pickett also argues that cattle sold on the cash market is of higher quality than cattle sold through marketing agreements. Professor Hausman, Tyson's expert, agreed that "those feedlots that sell cash-only cattle have a significantly higher percentage of prime and choice grades than the feedlots that sell marketing agreement cattle." That is, however, beside the point because Tyson is not looking for high-quality meat. As we have already explained, Tyson wants high-yield meat, which tends to be middle-quality. Tyson structures its marketing agreements to encourage producers to raise high-yielding cattle, not high-quality cattle. It uses marketing agreements to obtain the kind of meat that it needs to supply its customers at a competitive price. Tyson and its customers, not Pickett, get to decide what kind of meat it needs.

F.

In sum, while Pickett presented evidence at trial that Tyson's marketing agreements have decreased the price of cattle on the cash market and on the market as a whole, he did not present any evidence from which a reasonable jury could conclude that Tyson lacked pro-competitive justifications for using the agreements. The evidence is undisputed that marketing agreements provide a more reliable and stable supply of cattle for meat packers, reduce their transaction costs for purchasing cattle, and allow them to better match price to actual quality and yield. A jury could not reasonably find, as the one in this case did, that Tyson had no competitive justification for using marketing agreements.

The jury may have been swayed by more than the evidence relating to competition and markets. In his opening statement, Pickett's counsel sounded this theme:

> I want to pause to mention to you that we're talking here about a part of America's economy that is perhaps in some ways the most romanticized part. We celebrate the cattle business in our books and in our music and in our literature and in our movies, and have for years. And over the years, the one thing that the cattle business has stood for during the growth and the development of our country has been independence, fierce independence, meaningful and forceful independence.

While talk about the independence of cattle farmers has emotional appeal, the PSA was not enacted to protect the independence of producers from market forces. It was enacted to prevent unfair practices, price fixing and manipulation, and monopolization.

See London, 410 F.3d at 1301 ("At the time Congress enacted the PSA, the chief evil feared was the monopoly of the packers, enabling them unduly and arbitrarily to lower prices to the shipper, who sells, and unduly and arbitrarily to increase the price to the consumer, who buys." (quotations and alternations omitted)). The PSA was enacted to ensure that the market worked, and markets are notoriously unromantic.

The district court in *Griffin v. Smithfield Foods, Inc.* was faced with a similar argument by pork producers against the procurement methods of pork packers. In that case, Smithfield, the largest pork packer, had switched from buying its hogs on the cash market to buying them through marketing agreements or obtaining them from farms that Smithfield itself owned. The producers who did not want to sell their hogs through marketing agreements sued under the PSA, contending, as Pickett contends here, that the packer's conduct was unfair and had the effect of manipulating or controlling prices. *Griffin,* 183 F.Supp.2d at 825.

In rejecting the pork producers' claim, the court in that case explained that the lawsuit was premised not on Smithfield's unwillingness to do business with the producers. *Id.* at 828. Instead, the core of the producers' complaint was that Smithfield had "timing and quality control standards that the [producers] find an affront to their independence." *Id.* This, the court explained, was not enough to prohibit a more efficient, consistent, and consumer-friendly purchasing method:

> While such independence may be a virtue in many respects, the family farm, the corner grocer and the main street specialty store have all fallen victim to the direction in which the country's economy has developed. No degree of sympathy for the [producers'] difficulty in maintaining their traditional way of doing business translates to wrongdoing on the part of [Smithfield]....
>
> The [producers'] evidence demonstrates that economic developments in their industry have overtaken them; their evidence does not demonstrate that their economic woes were caused by any actionable wrongdoing of Smithfield under the PSA or any other theory.

Id. at 828, 830.

Exactly the same is true here. Pickett and his fellow class members could have entered into marketing agreements with Tyson. Many of the producers who testified on Pickett's behalf had themselves sold cattle through them. With marketing agreements, producers do lose some of their independence because meat packers get to dictate the date of delivery and adjust the price to the actual yield of the cattle. Some producers find the advantages of marketing agreements worth any loss of independence; it was, after all, producers who came up with the idea of marketing agreements. Other producers, like Pickett, place a higher premium on independence and prefer the cash market. They are entitled to their preferences, but they are not entitled to force those preferences on other producers and on the packers. *See Glickman,* 187 F.3d at 977 ("[W]e are ... mindful that the purpose behind the Act 'was not to so upset the traditional principles of freedom of contract....'" (quoting *Jackson,* 53 F.3d at 1458)).

AFFIRMED.

———————

The court's ruling in *Picket* did not deter those who allege that market concentration and abusive practices in the livestock industry present serious problems for both farmers and consumers. Livestock issues were a major area of debate when Congress considered the 2008 Farm Bill.

Renee Johnson and Geoffrey S. Becker
Livestock Marketing and Competition Issues
Congressional Research Service, CRS Report No. RL33325, 21–23
(January 30, 2009)

The enacted 2008 farm bill amends the P&S Act as follows. The enacted bill requires an annual report from USDA on detailed investigations into possible violations of the P&S Act (Sec. 11004); permits poultry and swine producers to cancel their contracts up to three business days after signing, unless a later date is specified in the contract; requires clear disclosure in contracts of cancellation terms; requires poultry/swine contracts to contain a conspicuous statement that additional large capital investments may be required during the term of the contract; contains provisions intended to assist producers deal with contract disputes, including arbitration terms and venue for any litigation (Sec. 11005); and requires USDA to issue rules on such criteria as, for example, the reasonable period of time a producer should be given to remedy a breach of contract before it is cancelled (Sec. 11006).

One issue that is likely to be of interest to some during the 111th Congress is the provision requiring USDA rulemaking under the P&S Act (Sec. 11006) related to alleged practices in the poultry and hog sectors. Per the 2008 farm bill provision, USDA must publish regulations within two years to establish criteria in determining (1) whether an "undue or unreasonable preference or advantage" has occurred in violation of the act; (2) whether a live poultry dealer has provided "reasonable notice" to poultry growers of any suspension of the delivery of birds under a poultry growing arrangement; (3) when a requirement of additional capital investments over the life of a poultry growing arrangement or swine production contract constitutes a violation of such act; and (4) if a live poultry dealer or swine contractor has provided a reasonable period of time for a poultry grower or a swine production contract grower to remedy a breach of contract that could lead to termination of the poultry growing arrangement or swine production contract. Sponsors of this provision claim USDA's rulemaking is relevant because they claim that many poultry growers have had their deliveries suspended for reasons that might constitute an undue or unreasonable preference, if other growers are not experiencing the same suspension.... The enacted 2008 farm bill requires USDA to conduct a study of the economic impacts of requiring plants to report pork product sales, focusing on wholesale pork cuts. It also directs USDA to improve electronic reporting and publishing under the program (Sec. 11001).

Following Congressional direction, the USDA's Grain Inspection, Packers and Stockyards Administration (GIPSA) conducted a series of public hearings and then issued a sweeping proposed rule strengthening the protections provided to producers. In its prefatory comments to the proposed rule, GIPSA noted that there were "multiple 'evils'" that Congress sought to remedy under the protections of the Packers and Stockyards Act. While "[t]he chief evil feared is the monopoly of the packers ... [a]nother evil, which it sought to provide against by the act, was exorbitant charges, duplication of commissions, deceptive practices in respect of prices, in the passage of the livestock through the stockyards, all made possible by collusion between the stockyards management and the commission men, on the one hand, and the packers and dealers, on the other." 75 Fed. Reg. 35,338, 35,340 (proposed June 22, 2010) (to be codified at 9 C.F.R. pt. 201) (citing *Stafford v. Wallace*, 258 U.S. 495, 514–15 (1922)). The proposed rule argues for the "long standing agency position" that a competitive injury is not essential to an unfair practice claim. 75 Fed. Reg. at 35,340.

Implementation of Regulations Required Under Title XI of the Food, Conservation and Energy Act of 2008; Conduct in Violation of the Act

75 Fed. Reg. 35,338, 35,338–45 (proposed June 22, 2010)
(to be codified at 9 C.F.R. pt. 201)

Background

The P&S Act sets forth broad prohibitions on the conduct of entities operating subject to its jurisdiction. These broad provisions make enforcement difficult and create uncertainty among industry participants regarding compliance. In enacting Title XI of the Food, Conservation and Energy Act of 2008 (Farm Bill) (Pub. L. 110-246), Congress recognized the nature of problems encountered in the livestock and poultry industries and amended the P&S Act. These amendments established new requirements for participants in the livestock and poultry industries and required the Secretary of Agriculture (Secretary) to establish criteria to consider when determining whether the P&S Act has been violated.

In accordance with the Farm Bill, GIPSA is proposing regulations under the P&S Act that would clarify when certain conduct in the livestock and poultry industries represents the making or giving of an undue or unreasonable preference or advantage or subjects a person or locality to an undue or unreasonable prejudice or disadvantage. These proposed regulations also establish criteria that GIPSA would consider in determining whether a live poultry dealer has provided reasonable notice to poultry growers of a suspension of the delivery of birds under a poultry growing arrangement; when a requirement of additional capital investments over the life of a poultry growing arrangement or swine production contract constitutes a violation of the P&S Act; and whether a packer, swine contractor or live poultry dealer has provided a reasonable period of time for a grower or a swine producer to remedy a breach of contract that could lead to termination of the growing arrangement or production contract.

The Farm Bill also instructed the Secretary to promulgate regulations to ensure that poultry growers, swine production contract growers and livestock producers are afforded the opportunity to fully participate in the arbitration process, if they so choose. We are proposing a required format for providing poultry growers, swine production contract growers and livestock producers the opportunity to decline the use of arbitration in those contracts that have an arbitration provision. We are also proposing criteria that we would consider in finding that poultry growers, swine production contract growers and livestock producers have a meaningful opportunity to participate fully in the arbitration process if they voluntarily agree to do so. We would use these criteria to assess the overall fairness of the arbitration process.

In addition to proposing regulations in accordance with the Farm Bill, GIPSA is proposing regulations that would prohibit certain conduct because it is unfair, unjustly discriminatory or deceptive, in violation of the P&S Act. These additional proposed regulations are promulgated under the authority of section 407 of the P&S Act, and complement those required by the Farm Bill to help ensure fair trade and competition in the livestock and poultry industries.

In recent years, there has been an increased use of contracting in the marketing and production of livestock and poultry by entities under the jurisdiction of the P&S Act. This increased contracting coupled with the market concentration has significantly changed the industry and the rural economy as a whole, making proposed regulations necessary, especially in those situations in which packers, live poultry dealers or swine contractors use their market power to harm producers or impair private property rights of growers and producers. Transparency, competition and financial integrity of the marketplace have also diminished.

Section 407 of the P&S Act (7 U.S.C. 228) provides that the Secretary "may make such rules, regulations, and orders as may be necessary to carry out the provisions of this Act." Pursuant to this authority, the Secretary has issued regulations, published as Part 201 of Title 9 of the Code of Federal Regulations (CFR). Sections 11005 and 11006 of the Farm Bill became effective June 18, 2008, and instruct the Secretary to promulgate additional regulations as described in this notice of proposed rulemaking. These regulations, if finalized, are also proposed to be published in Part 201 of Title 9 of the CFR.

Section 202 of the P&S Act (7 U.S.C. 192) prohibits packers, swine contractors and live poultry dealers from engaging in unfair and deceptive practices, giving undue preferences to persons or localities, apportioning supply among packers, swine contractors and live poultry dealers in restraint of commerce, manipulating prices, creating a monopoly, or conspiring to aid in unlawful acts. The Farm Bill requires promulgation of regulations under the P&S Act dealing with various industry behaviors. In addition, GIPSA has identified 11 terms requiring definition and three areas of concern in which regulations will be developed to address each of these behaviors. Definitions of the terms, *tournament system, principal part of performance, capital investment, additional capital investment, suspension of delivery of birds, forward contract, marketing agreement, production contract, competitive injury, and likelihood of competitive injury* would be added to § 201.2 of the regulations. The proposed regulations are grouped under the general headings of (1) undue or unreasonable preference or advantage, (2) unfair, unjustly discriminatory and deceptive practices, and (3) arbitration.

In preparing to issue these proposed regulations, GIPSA held three public meetings in October 2008, in Arkansas, Iowa, and Georgia to gather comments, information, and recommendations from interested parties. Attendees at these meetings were asked to give input on the Farm Bill requirements for production contracts, arbitration, and the four following topics included in Farm Bill section 11006: (1) Undue or unreasonable preferences or advantages, (2) adequate notice to poultry growers of suspension of delivery of birds, (3) criteria for determining when requiring additional capital investment over the life of a contract constitutes a violation, and (4) criteria for determining when packers, swine contractors and live poultry dealers have provided a reasonable period of time to remedy a breach of contract that could lead to contract termination. Attendees provided comments on these topics as well as other issues of concern under the P&S Act, including packer livestock procurement practices believed to unjustly discriminate against producers based on the volume of livestock they sell.

GIPSA also gathered data concerning market participants. There are roughly 30,000 swine producers and poultry growers operating under production contracts. More than 85 percent of these producers and growers will be contracted to one of the five largest slaughtering firms. The average gross sales revenue of the three largest of these slaughtering firms is 23,000 times that of a small grower or producer.

The proposed regulations are based on comments, information, and recommendations received in those meetings along with GIPSA's expertise, experience, and interactions in the livestock and poultry industries....

Sections 202(a) and (b) of the P&S Act

Section 202(a) of the P&S Act prohibits "any unfair, unjustly discriminatory, or deceptive practice." Section 202(b) prohibits "any undue or unreasonable preference or advantage [or] prejudice or disadvantage." USDA has consistently taken the position that, in some cases, a violation of section 202(a) or (b) can be proven without proof of predatory intent, competitive injury, or likelihood of injury.[19] At the same time, USDA has always understood that an act or practice's effect on competition can be relevant[20] and, in certain circumstances, even dispositive[21] with respect to whether that act or practice violates section 202(a) and/or (b).

The longstanding agency position that, in some cases, a violation of section 202(a) or (b) can be proven without proof of likelihood of competitive injury is consistent with the language and structure of the P&S Act, as well as its legislative history and purposes. Neither section 202(a) nor section 202(b) contains any language limiting its application to acts or practices that have an adverse effect on competition, such as acts "restraining commerce." Instead, these provisions use terms including "deceptive," "unfair," "unjust," "undue," and "unreasonable" — which are commonly understood to encompass more than anticompetitive conduct.[22] This is in direct contrast to sections (c)–(e), which expressly prohibit only those acts that have the effect of "restraining commerce," "creating a monopoly," or producing another type of antitrust injury. The fact that Congress expressly included these limitations in sections (c)–(e) but not in sections (a) and (b) is a strong indication that Congress did not intend sections (a) and (b) to be limited to harm to competition. And Congress confirmed the agency's position by amending the P&S Act to specify specific instances of conduct prohibited as unfair that do not involve any inherent likelihood of competitive injury.[23]

USDA's interpretation of sections 202(a) and (b) is also consistent with the interpretation of other sections of the P&S Act using similar language — sections 307 and 312. Courts have recognized that the proper analysis under these provisions depends on "the facts of each case,"[24] and that these sections may apply in the absence of harm to competition or competitors.[25]

---

19. *In re* Ozark county Cattle Co., 49 Agric. Dec. 336, 365 (1990); 1 John H. Davidson et al., Agricultural Law section 3.47, at 244 (1981).

20. *See In re* Sterling Colo. Beef Co., 39 Agric. Dec. 184, 235 (1980) (considering and rejecting respondent packer's business justification for challenged conduct).

21. *See* Armour & Co. v. United States, 402 F.2d 712, 717 (7th Cir. 1968) (a coupon promotion plan (here coupons for fifty cents off specified packages of bacon) is not per se unfair and violates section 202(a) if it is implemented with some predatory intent or carries some likelihood of competitive injury); *In re* IBP, Inc., 57 Agric. Dec. 1353, 1356 (1998) (contractual right of first refusal at issue violated section 202 "because it has the effect or potential of reducing competition").

22. International Dictionary defined "deceptive" as "[t]ending to deceive; having power to mislead, or impress with false opinions"; "unfair" as "[n]ot fair in act or character; disingenuous; using or involving trick or artifice; dishonest; unjust; inequitable" (2d. definition); "unjust" as "[c]haracterized by injustice; contrary to justice and right; wrongful"; "undue" as "[n]ot right; not lawful or legal; violating legal or equitable rights; improper" (2d. definition); and "unreasonable" as "[n]ot conformable to reason; irrational" or "immoderate; exorbitant." Webster's New International Dictionary 578, 2237, 2238, 2245, 2248 (1st ed. 1917). This is the same understanding of the terms today.

23. *See* sections 409, 410.

24. Capitol Packing Company v. United States, 350 F.2d 67, 76 (10th Cir. 1965); *see also* Spencer Livestock Comm'n Co. v USDA, 841 F.2d 1451, 1454 (9th Cir. 1988).

25. *See, e.g.*, Spencer, 841 F.2d at 1455 (Section 312 covers "a deceptive practice, whether or not it harmed consumers or competitors.").

Although proof of harm to competition is not necessary to satisfy the statutory language, it is sufficient to do so. Any act that harms competition is necessarily also "unfair" and therefore violates section 202(a).

The legislative history and purposes of the P&S Act also support USDA's position. The Act "is a most comprehensive measure and extends farther than any previous law in the regulation of private business, in time of peace, except possibly the interstate commerce act."[26]

In amending the P&S Act, Congress made clear that its goals for the statute extended beyond the protection of competition. In 1935, for instance, when Congress first subjected live poultry dealers to sections 202(a) and (b), Congress explained in the statute itself that "[t]he handling of the great volume of live poultry ... is attendant with various unfair, deceptive, and fraudulent practices and devices, resulting in the producers sustaining sundry losses and receiving prices far below the reasonable value of their live poultry ..."[27] Similarly, the House Committee Report regarding 1958 amendments stated that "[t]he primary purpose of [the P&S Act] is to assure fair competition *and fair trade practices*" and "to safeguard farmers ... against receiving less than the true market value of their livestock."[28] The Report further observed that protection extends to "unfair, deceptive, unjustly discriminatory" practices by "small" companies in addition to "monopolistic practices."[29] In accordance with this legislative history, courts and commentators have, over a span exceeding 70 years, recognized that the purposes of the P&S Act are not limited to protecting competition.[30]

Recently, three courts of appeals have disagreed with the USDA's interpretation of the P&S Act and have concluded (in cases to which the United States was not a party) that plaintiffs could not prove their claims under section 202(a) and/or (b) without proving harm to competition or likely harm to competition.[31] After carefully considering the analysis in these opinions, USDA continues to believe that its longstanding interpretation of the P&S Act is correct. These court of appeals opinions (two of which were issued over vigorous dissents)[32] are inconsistent with the plain language of the statute; they incorrectly assume that harm to competition was the only evil Congress sought to prevent by enacting the P&S Act; and they fail to defer to the Secretary of Agriculture's longstanding and consistent interpretation of a statute administered by the Secretary. To the ex-

---

26. H.R. Rep. 67–77, at 2 (1921); *see also* Swift & Co. v. United States, 308 F.2d 849, 853 (7th Cir. 1962) ("The legislative history showed Congress understood the sections of the [P&S Act] under consideration were broader in scope than antecedent legislation such as the Sherman Antitrust Act, sec. 2 of the Clayton Act, 15 U.S.C. 13, sec. 5 of the Federal Trade Commission Act, 15 U.S.C. 45 and sec. 3 of the Interstate Commerce Act, 49 U.S.C. 3.").

27. Pub. L. 74–272, 49 Stat. 648, 648 (1935).

28. H.R. Rep. No. 85–1048 (1957), *reprinted in* 1958 U.S.C.C.A.N. 5212, 5213 (emphasis added).

29. *Id.* at 5213.

30. *See, e.g., Stafford,* 258 U.S. at 513–14; Spencer Livestock Comm'n Co. v. USDA, 841 F.2d 1451, 1455 (9th Cir. 1988); United States v. Perdue Farms, Inc., 680 F.2d 277, 280 (2d Cir. 1982); Bruhn's Freezer Meats, 438 F.2d at 1336–37; Bowman v. USDA, 363 F.2d 81, 85 (5th Cir. 1966); United States v. Donahue Bros., 59 F.2d 1019, 1023 (8th Cir. 1932).

31. Wheeler, ___ F.3d ___, 2009 WL 4823002, No. 07–40651 (5th Cir. 2009) (en banc) (no violation of section 202(a) or (b) without a likely effect on competition); Been v. O.K. Indus., Inc., 495 F.3d 1217 (10th Cir. 2007) ("unfair practice" is one that injures or is likely to injure competition); London v. Fieldale Farms Corp., 410 F.3d 1295 (11th Cir. 2005) (P&S Act prohibits only those unfair, discriminatory, or deceptive practices that adversely affect or are likely to adversely affect competition). The issue is currently pending before one other court of appeals. Terry v. Tyson Farms, Inc., No. 08–5577 (6th Cir., argued March 3, 2009).

32. Wheeler, 2009 WL 4823002, at 14–28 (Garza, J., dissenting); Been, 495 F.3d at 1238–43 (Hartz, J., concurring in part and dissenting in part).

tent that these courts failed to defer to the USDA's interpretation of the statute because that interpretation had not previously been enshrined in a regulation,[33] the new regulations constitute a material change in circumstances that warrants judicial reexamination of the issue.[34]

Competitive Injury

Although it is not necessary in every case to demonstrate competitive injury in order to show a violation of section 202(a) and/or (b), any act that harms competition or is likely to harm competition necessarily violates the statute. Accordingly, proposed new § 201.2(t) defines competitive injury and proposed new § 201.2(u) defines likelihood of competitive injury. Competitive injury occurs when an act or practice distorts competition in the market channel or marketplace. How a competitive injury manifests itself depends critically on whether the target of the act or practice is a competitor (e.g., a packer harms other packers), or operates at a different level of the livestock or poultry production process (e.g., a packer harms a producer). The likelihood of competitive injury occurs when an act or practice raises rivals' costs, improperly forecloses competition in a large share of the market through exclusive dealing, restrains competition among packers, live poultry dealers or swine contractors or otherwise represents a misuse of market power to distort competition.[35] The likelihood of competitive injury also occurs when a packer, swine contractor, or live poultry dealer wrongfully depresses prices paid to a producer or grower below market value or impairs the producer or grower's ability to compete with other producers or growers or to impair a producer's or grower's ability to receive the reasonable expected full economic value from a transaction in the market channel or marketplace.

To establish an actual or likely competitive injury, it is not necessary to show that a challenged act or practice had a likely effect on resale price levels. Even the antitrust laws do not require such a showing. Because the P&S Act is broader than the antitrust laws, such a requirement of showing effect on resale price levels is not necessary to establish competitive injury under section 202 of the P&S Act either (though such a showing would suffice).

Unfair, Unjustly Discriminatory and Deceptive Practices

GIPSA is proposing to add to the regulations a new § 201.210(c) that reiterates the Secretary's position that the appropriate analysis under section 202(a) depends on the nature and circumstances of the challenged conduct. A finding of harm or likely harm to competition is always sufficient, but not always necessary, to establish a violation of sections 202(a) and/or (b) of the P&S Act.

In the Farm Bill, Congress required criteria to be established to determine: (1) Whether a live poultry dealer has provided reasonable notice to poultry growers of any suspension of the delivery of birds under a poultry growing arrangement; (2) when a requirement of additional capital investments over the life of a poultry growing arrangement or swine production contract constitutes a violation of the P&S Act; and (3) if a packer,

---

33. *See London*, 410 F.3d at 1226–27.

34. *See* National Cable & Telecomm. Ass'n v. Brand X Internet Servs., 545 U.S. 967, 982–84 (2005).

35. *See, e.g.*, Thomas G. Krattenmaker & Steven C. Salop, *Anticompetitive Exclusion: Raising Rivals' Costs to Achieve Power over Price*, 96 Yale L.J. 209 (1986); 11 Philip E. Areeda & Herbert Hovenkamp, Antitrust Law 1821 (2d ed. 2005).

swine contractor, or live poultry dealer has provided a reasonable period of time for a poultry grower or swine production contract grower to remedy a breach of contract that could lead to termination of the growing arrangement or production contract. Regulation in these areas (and other areas in which GIPSA is proposing regulation) is important to preserve the rights of poultry growers, swine production contract growers and livestock producers and maintain trust and integrity in the marketplace. GIPSA has been informed by growers and producers, particularly where contracts for the production or sale of livestock or poultry are involved, that poultry growers, swine production contract growers and livestock producers are sometimes at a distinct disadvantage in negotiating the terms of an agreement. These reports indicate that packers, swine contractors and live poultry dealers have exhibited a tendency to exert their disproportionate positions of power by misleading or retaliating against poultry growers, swine production contract growers or livestock producers, and that some growers or producers may have no choice but to acquiesce to the packer's, swine contractor's, or live poultry dealer's terms for entering into a contract or growing arrangement, or acquiesce to unfair conduct in order to continue in business.

Proposed new § 201.210(a) would first provide a statement of the broad coverage of section 202(a). It would then provide the following eight specific examples of conduct deemed unfair:

- An unjustified material breach of a contractual duty, express or implied, or an action or omission that a reasonable person would consider unscrupulous, deceitful or in bad faith in connection with any transaction in or contract involving the production, maintenance, marketing or sale of livestock or poultry.

- A retaliatory action or omission by a packer, swine contractor, or live poultry dealer in response to the lawful expression, spoken or written, association, or action of a poultry grower, livestock producer or swine production contract grower; a retaliatory action includes but is not limited to coercion, intimidation, or disadvantage to any producer or grower in an execution, termination, extension or renewal of a contract involving livestock or poultry;

- A refusal to provide to a contract poultry grower or swine production contract grower, upon request, the statistical information and data used to determine compensation paid to the contract grower or producer under a production contract, including, but not limited to, feed conversion rates, feed analysis, origination and breeder history;

An action or attempt to limit by contract a poultry grower's, swine production contract grower's, or livestock producer's legal rights and remedies afforded by law, including, but not limited to the following:

i. The right of a trial by jury (except when arbitration has been voluntarily agreed to);

ii. The right to all damages available under the law;

iii. Rights available under bankruptcy law;

iv. The authority of the judge or jury to award attorney fees to the appropriate party; or

v. A requirement that a trial or arbitration be held in a location other than the location where the principal part of the performance of the arrangement or contract occurs;

- Paying a premium or applying a discount on the swine production contract grower's payment or the purchase price received by the livestock producer from the sale of livestock without documenting the reason(s) and substantiating the revenue and cost justification associated with the premium or discount;

- Termination of a poultry growing arrangement or swine production contract with no basis other than the allegation by the packer, swine contractor, live poultry dealer or other person that the poultry grower or swine production contract grower failed to comply with an applicable law, rule or regulation. If the live poultry dealer or swine contractor believes that a poultry grower or swine producer is in violation, the live poultry dealer or swine contractor must immediately report the alleged violation to the relevant law enforcement authorities if they wish to use this alleged violation as grounds for termination.

- A representation, omission, or practice that is fraudulent or likely to mislead a reasonable poultry grower, swine production contract grower, swine contract producer or livestock producer regarding a material condition or a term in a contract or business transaction. Any act that causes competitive injury or creates a likelihood of competitive injury.

Proposed new § 201.212 would not be part of the definition of "unfair," but rather a separate and distinct regulation. It proposes to address various situations where a packer (or group of packers) is able to manipulate prices paid for livestock, such as where a packer-to-packer sale signals the price that packers will pay producers or where a packer purchases cattle through exclusive arrangements with dealers and is able to depress the price paid to producers through that conduct.[36] Proposed new § 201.212(c) would prohibit bonded packers from purchasing livestock from other packers or other packer-affiliated companies, but allows waivers in emergency situations such as a catastrophe or natural disaster that may severely impact operations at a particular packing company or plant. The proposed regulation is intended to limit the ability of packers to manipulate prices.

Congress recognized, and GIPSA has been informed by poultry growers and industry organizations, that the disproportionate negotiating power of a live poultry dealer may sometimes infringe on poultry grower's rights. Under a poultry growing arrangement, a live poultry dealer has discretion on whether it will perform under the agreement; i.e., whether it will place poultry on a poultry grower's farm. The poultry grower does not have the same discretion and must raise and care for poultry placed on his or her farm by the live poultry dealer. There have been instances in which a live poultry dealer has failed to place poultry on a poultry grower's farm for an extended period of time without notifying the poultry grower of the reasons for or the anticipated length of delay in placing additional poultry. Without sufficient information, a poultry grower is unable to protect his or her financial interests and make informed business decisions. GIPSA is proposing to add a new § 201.215 that would require a live poultry dealer to give adequate notice of any suspension of delivery of poultry. In proposed new § 201.215, live poultry dealers would be required to provide notice of any suspension of delivery of birds at least 90 days prior to the suspension taking effect. This 90-day period would allow the poultry grower time to consider options for utilizing his or her poultry houses and for keeping up with any loan payments, some of which are government guaranteed loans. Live poultry dealers may request a waiver from the GIPSA Administrator of the 90-day notice requirement in emergency situations such as a catastrophic or natural disaster where the dealer could not have foreseen the reduction in delivery of poultry.

---

36. Chapter 6 "Dynamic Price Competition and Tacit Collusion" in Jean Tirole's THE THEORY OF INDUSTRIAL ORGANIZATION (1988) provides a general discussion of price signaling and competition.

Capital investments required by a packer, swine contractor, or live poultry dealer during the life of a growing arrangement or production contract may violate the P&S Act. Congress required the Secretary to develop criteria to consider when determining if such a requirement is a violation of the P&S Act. Proposed new §§ 201.216 and 201.217 would provide several requirements designed to preserve trust between the parties and limit the risk incurred by poultry growers or swine production contract growers. Some contracts are multiyear and provide long-term security while others are short term and could terminate at the end of a single growing period. Among the proposed requirements is that a contract be of sufficient length to allow the poultry growers or swine production contract growers to recoup 80 percent of investment costs related to the capital investment. For example, in situations where a poultry grower or swine production contract grower is required to make capital investments as a condition to enter into or continue a contract, that requirement may be considered unfair if the packer, swine contractor, or live poultry dealer did not offer a contract duration that would allow the poultry grower or swine production contract grower to recover 80 percent of its investment cost, at a repayment rate based on a percentage of the grower's yearly compensation. The term "investment cost" includes any balance due on the initial capital investment and any additional capital investments, plus accrued loan interest, if any, at the legal rate of interest where the principal part of the performance takes place under the contract. We are proposing that 80 percent of the investment costs represent the portion of the overall value of the poultry grower's or swine production contract grower's property that the growing or raising facilities represent with a poultry growing arrangement or swine production contract in place.

Proposed new § 201.216 that would establish criteria the Secretary may consider when determining whether a requirement that a poultry grower or swine production contract grower make additional capital investments over the life of a swine production contract or poultry growing arrangement constitutes an unfair practice in violation of the P&S Act. Establishing these criteria is expected to deter or reduce unfair conduct and help preserve the value of the poultry grower's or swine production contract grower's property rights and protect against financial loss by the grower. Allowing for grower discretion to accept or reject proposed capital investments made by the live poultry dealer provides for increased flexibility to accommodate mutually advantageous investment opportunities.

Congress recognized the need for poultry growers or swine production contract growers to have reasonable time to remedy a breach of contract that could lead to termination of that contract. GIPSA's proposed new § 201.218 would include criteria that the Secretary will consider when determining whether a poultry grower or swine production contract grower has been given sufficient time to remedy a breach of contract. Proposed new § 201.218 would set forth procedures that a packer, swine contractor, or live poultry dealer must follow before it can terminate a contract or poultry growing arrangement based on a breach by the poultry grower or swine production contract grower.

Undue or Unreasonable Preference or Advantage

In enacting the 2008 Farm Bill, Congress required the Secretary to establish criteria to be considered in determining whether conduct constitutes an undue or unreasonable preference or advantage in violation of the P&S Act. Through telephone calls received from producers and poultry growers, complaints received by its field agents, and comments made at meetings, conferences and conventions, GIPSA has learned that packers, swine contractors and live poultry dealers sometimes treat similarly situated poultry growers and livestock producers differently. Disparate treatment of similarly situated growers and producers can be a violation of the P&S Act when that disparate treatment is undue or unreasonable. According to producer comments made at public meetings, as well as comments and complaints from individual producers, a packer may offer better price terms to producers that can provide larger volumes of livestock than the packer offers to a group of producers that collectively can provide the same volume of livestock of equal quality, without a legitimate justification for the disparity. In one case, a Midwestern packer was offering a higher price to an individual producer who could deliver full truck loads of cattle. A group of producers approached the same packer and offered collectively to provide a full truck load of like cattle, but the packer refused to offer the same price terms to the group of producers. GIPSA is therefore proposing a new § 201.211 to address undue or unreasonably preferential treatment of poultry growers, swine production contract growers or livestock producers.

New proposed § 201.211 establishes criteria that the Secretary may consider in determining if differential treatment constitutes an undue or unreasonable preference or advantage, or an undue or unreasonable prejudice or disadvantage, under the P&S Act. The criteria include whether contract terms are offered to all producers that can provide the required volume, kind and quality of livestock, either individually or collectively. Other considerations include whether any price premium based on a producer's or a group of producers' ability to deliver livestock meeting specified conditions is offered to other producers or groups of producers that can meet that condition. (For example, producers have reported to GIPSA that some packers will offer price premiums for early delivery to one producer that it does not offer to other producers or groups of producers that are willing and able to meet the same early morning delivery conditions at equal convenience to the packer). Finally, the Secretary may consider whether differences in price paid for livestock, based on the cost of acquiring or handling the livestock, are disclosed equally to all producers. GIPSA would consider the particular circumstances of any pricing disparity in determining whether to initiate an enforcement action alleging a violation of the P&S Act, including whether there is a legitimate justification for the disparity. This provision would not require packers to purchase livestock if their needs are already satisfied or impose a public utility duty to deal with all sellers.

In the course of its enforcement of the P&S Act, GIPSA has reviewed the records of many live poultry dealers and numerous poultry growing settlement documents. GIPSA has also received complaints from poultry growers regarding how settlements occur. These complaints indicate that some live likelihood of competitive injury. GIPSA is proposing a new § 201.214 that would require live poultry dealers that pay poultry growers on a tournament system to pay all poultry growers raising and caring for the same type of poultry the same base pay, and that would prohibit paying poultry growers less than the base pay amount. New proposed § 201.214 would also require that poultry growers be ranked in settlement groups with other poultry growers that raise and care for poultry in the same type of houses.

If a packer, swine contractor, or live poultry dealer believes it can justify disparate treatment of poultry growers, swine production contract growers or livestock producers, it must have a legitimate business reason for that differential treatment. GIPSA is proposing to add a new paragraph (b) to § 201.94 that would require packers, swine contractors or live poultry dealers to maintain records that justify their treatment of poultry growers, swine production contract growers, or livestock producers. This justification need not be extensive but should be enough to identify the benefit-cost basis of any pricing differentials received or paid, and may include increased or lower trucking costs; market price for meat; volume; labor, energy, or maintenance costs, etc. For example, a packer's participation in a branded program for a particular type of beef that returns a premium to the packer could be used to justify a higher price paid to producers that sell the type of cattle that meets the specifications of the branded program. In general, the data needed to justify a different treatment would identify those pecuniary costs and benefits associated with the treatment that demonstrate its decreased costs or increased revenues from a standard business practice. Therefore, GIPSA would consider the particular circumstances of any pricing disparity in determining whether a violation of the P&S Act occurred, including whether there is a legitimate justification for the disparity.

One of the common complaints that GIPSA has received regarding undue and unreasonable preferences or advantages is that packers, swine contractors and live poultry dealers offer considerably better contract terms to select sellers/growers, which impedes other sellers/growers' ability to compete. GIPSA is proposing to add a new § 201.212(a) that would prohibit dealers operating as packer buyers from purchasing livestock for any packer other than the packer identifying that dealer as its packer buyer. A dealer is defined in the P&S Act as "any person, not a market agency, engaged in the business of buying or selling in commerce livestock, either on his own account or as the employee or agent of the vendor or purchaser."[37] This section is proposed under the authority of section 303 of the P&S Act, requiring market agencies and dealers to register in such manner as the Secretary may prescribe. A packer buyer is any person regularly employed on salary, or other comparable method of compensation, by a packer to buy livestock for such packer. Proposed new § 201.212(b) would also prohibit packers from entering into exclusive purchase agreements with any dealer except those dealers the packer has identified as its packer buyers. This provision does not eliminate exclusive arrangements, but provides transparency by identifying the dealer as a packer buyer for a specific packer. Proposed new § 201.212(a) and (b) would work in conjunction to prevent apportioning territory by independent dealers and packers. This would open the market to other buyers, increasing participation in the cow and bull slaughter market and prevent collusion between multiple packers using one dealer as an exclusive agent to manipulate prices.

GIPSA has also been informed through discussion with livestock producers that most livestock sellers lack sufficient information on available contract terms. To increase the amount of information available that would allow sellers to make informed business decisions, GIPSA is proposing to add a new § 201.213, which would require packers, swine contractors, and live poultry dealers to submit copies of sample types of contracts to GIPSA and GIPSA to make those samples available for public viewing on its Web site.

Arbitration

With the Farm Bill, Congress amended the P&S Act to add section 210, which addresses arbitration. The Farm Bill requires that livestock contracts and poultry growing arrangements contain an option for poultry growers and livestock producers to accept or reject arbitration to settle disputes. Many of these contracts unilaterally drafted by packers, swine contractors, or live poultry dealers contain provisions limiting the legal rights and remedies afforded by law to poultry growers, swine production contract growers, or livestock producers. Section 210 of the P&S Act requires that poultry growers, swine production contract growers, or livestock producers have the opportunity, prior to entering a contract or poultry growing arrangement, to decline to use arbitration to resolve disputes arising out of the contract or growing arrangement. In accordance with section 210 of the P&S Act, under the proposed regulation, the poultry grower, swine production

---

37. Section 301(d).

contract grower, or livestock producer may decide later, after a dispute arises, to resolve the dispute using arbitration only if both parties voluntarily agree to the use of arbitration at that later time. Congress directed the Secretary to promulgate regulations to carry out section 210 of the P&S Act, and to establish criteria to consider when determining if the arbitration process provided in a contract provides a meaningful opportunity for the poultry growers, swine production contract growers, or livestock producers to participate fully in the arbitration process.

GIPSA has been informed by poultry growers, swine production contract growers, and livestock producers that often the cost of the arbitration process is prohibitive to resolving disputes between a packer, swine contractor, or live poultry dealer and a producer or grower. For example, fees for arbitration may need to be paid up front and can be substantial. A poultry grower, swine production contract grower, or livestock producer may not have sufficient resources available to pay the fees for arbitration. Prior to enactment of the Farm Bill, producers and growers with contracts that required mandatory and binding arbitration were often left with no means available to resolve disputes if they lacked sufficient resources to pay arbitration fees. In proposing this new rule, GIPSA relied on established fee structures in employment arbitration rules to determine appropriate fees to be assessed to a producer or grower.

GIPSA also examined numerous contracts offered, modified, amended, renewed or extended after the effective date of the Farm Bill to see how the requirements of new section 210 of the P&S Act were being implemented by packers, swine contractors, or live poultry dealers. GIPSA found little consistency among the contracts. Some contracts were very clear and allowed the poultry growers, swine production contract growers, or livestock producers to easily recognize the choice regarding arbitration. Other contracts created a burdensome procedure for poultry growers, swine production contract growers, or livestock producers to make the choice.

GIPSA is proposing to add a new §201.219(b) to the regulations under the P&S Act that would establish a uniform means by which poultry growers, swine poultry dealers have established pay schedules under which poultry growers that raise and care for the same type and kind of poultry receive different rates of pay; improperly grouped together those poultry growers who raise and care for live poultry in different types of poultry housing for settlement purposes; and, under a tournament system, paid some poultry growers less than the base pay amount in the poultry growing arrangement. These complaints also indicate that some poultry growers are not given the production information that is used in the compensation formula to determine their ranking in the tournament system. These practices, if not corrected, create a reasonable production contract growers, or livestock producers are offered the option to decline use of arbitration to resolve disputes arising out of a contract. Proposed new §201.219(a) would ensure that the poultry grower, swine production contract grower, or livestock producer has a meaningful opportunity to participate in the arbitration process. Proposed new §201.219(a) would also provide criteria the Secretary may consider in evaluating the fairness of the arbitration process. Among these criteria are: Overall fairness in the procedures, limits on costs to poultry growers, swine production contract growers, or livestock producers, reasonable time limits for completion of the process, reasonable access to discovery of information by the growers or producers, and a requirement that a reasoned written opinion be issued by the arbitrator.

———————

The proposed rule announced that USDA GIPSA will accept and consider comments received by August 23, 2010 and will issue a final rule after consideration.

Reaction to the proposal was mixed, with some heralding it as a victory for smaller farming operations and smaller feedlot operations. The Director of the Independent Cattlemen of Nebraska was quoted as saying that "[finally, the Packers and Stockyards Act will have teeth." See http://www.foodsysteminsider.com. In contrast, the National Cattlemen's Beef Association requested an extension on the comment period and warned that the proposal threatened to jeopardize the marketing alliances and arrangements that "compensate producers for providing higher quality cattle." *See*, http://www.northernag.net/AG NEWS/tabid/1

Notes

1. The Attorneys General of the states of Montana, Arizona, Delaware, Iowa, Louisiana, Maine, Maryland, Mississippi, New Hampshire, New Mexico, Ohio, Oklahoma, Oregon, South Dakota, Tennessee, Vermont, and West Virginia submitted joint *Comments Regarding Competition in the Agriculture Industry* as part of the hearing process prior to the issuance of the proposed rules.

> Concern over the economic welfare of U.S. farmers and ranchers, and their susceptibility to the harmful exercise of market power, helped lead to the passage of the nation's major antitrust legislation. And while much has changed in agriculture over the past century, one thing that has not changed is the vulnerability of our producers to anti-competitive conduct.

> For the most part, our farms and ranches remain relatively small businesses that are relied upon to produce a high quality product, with little regard to the cost of the inputs to produce and transport their products, or the prices they will receive upon completion of their labor.

> Hence, our farmers and ranchers are twice disadvantaged: Anti-competitive conduct injures farmers and ranchers as *consumers* in various input markets where monopoly or seller power is abused through lower output and higher prices. This conduct also injures them as *producers*, where monopsony or buyer power among processors is abused through lower demand and lower prices.

> The impacts do not end at the borders of the farm or ranch, either. The abuse of buyer power can also harm the consumer at the supermarket, as the lower demand at the agricultural processor level translates into lower output at the food consumer level.

> The States' agricultural sectors vary widely, from the dairy farms of New England to the corn and soybean farms of the Midwest to the ranches of the High Plains. We find common ground, however, in recognizing that our rural communities and our consumers alike depend on an efficient and vibrant agricultural marketplace. This, in turn, requires an integrated approach that includes increased cooperation among state and federal competition law enforcers as well as reconsideration of laws and regulations that may no longer serve their original pro-competitive purposes. The States therefore share the objectives of the USDA and USDOJ in these workshops: understand the state of competition in agricultural markets and explore appropriate advocacy, enforcement, and other solutions to meet the needs of agricultural producers and consumers alike.

The Attorneys General *Comments* included the following recommendation:

Increase federal, state, and interagency coordination in enforcement of the antitrust laws and the Packers and Stockyard Act. Collaborative efforts combine the practical experience and relationships that are strengths of the States with the expertise and enforcement resources of our federal counterparts. The States' involvement in PSA enforcement could help ease the burden on DOJ and Grain Inspection, Packers and Stockyards Administration (GIPSA).

Historically, the States have not brought PSA cases; however, exploration into methods of state enforcement of PSA should be supported by federal counterparts. USDA also should consider legislative and regulatory revisions to the PSA to ensure compliance with the Act. Under PSA, GIPSA should consider whether to adopt rules that regulate captive supply livestock procurement methods.

2. Anti-trust issues are also important in the dairy industry. The Attorneys General *Comments Regarding Competition in the Agriculture Industry* included the following:

Dairy farming is a quintessential part of many States' landscape and history. Dairy farming operations stretch from California and Oregon to the Midwest — from the southeast to New England. The dairy industry has been called "the paramount agricultural activity of the northeast," critical to the region's economy and rural character. Presently, however, the dairy industry is in crisis. The price of milk paid to farmers reached a thirty-year low in 2009. As prices have dropped below costs, family dairy farms around the country have closed. The peril facing dairy farmers across the country has received significant media attention, as well as recent congressional action in the form of increased subsidies. There has been renewed interest in antitrust review of the dairy industry over the past year.

The dairy industry's concentration is as pronounced as its current economic upheaval. Two players dominate the national dairy market: Dean Foods Company and Dairy Farmers of America, Inc., (DFA), the largest and most powerful dairy cooperative in the country. Private antitrust plaintiffs allege that DFA's agreements with Dean Foods and National Dairy Holdings, the two largest milk bottlers in the United States, have vested DFA with control of access to 70 to 77% of the fluid Grade A milk bottling capacity in parts of the country.

Both DOJ and state Attorneys General have challenged certain mergers and acquisitions by DFA and the entity that is now Dean Foods. DOJ and Attorneys General from Wisconsin, Illinois and Michigan recently filed a complaint alleging that Dean Foods, the largest milk processor in the area, unlawfully acquired two processing plants in Wisconsin from Foremost Farms, the fourth largest processor in the area. The complaint alleges that the acquisition would increase market concentration and eliminate an aggressive competitor of Dean Foods, which has approximately 57 percent of the market for processed milk in northeastern Illinois, the Upper Peninsula of Michigan, and Wisconsin.

Outside the merger context, the most recent antitrust litigation involving dairy cooperatives and processors has been in the form of private class actions. There is ongoing antitrust litigation entitled In re Southeastern Milk Antitrust Litigation, which involves multiple class actions against Dean Foods, National Dairy Holdings, and DFA, among others, alleging conspiracies to reduce prices paid to farmers and to raise prices charged to direct purchasers of processed milk. The plaintiffs' claims have survived initial Capper-Volstead Act defenses and the case is in discovery. In addition, on October 8, 2009, a private class action was filed in Vermont alleging unlawful monopsony and monopoly by Dean Foods, DFA,

Hood, and Dairy Marketing Services. The plaintiffs' allegations include claims that the defendants coerced farmers into joining DFA in order to get access to bottling plants owned by Dean Foods, and that all of the defendants conspired to artificially lower the price of milk paid to farmers.

Finally, during the last century a number of States promulgated pricing-related laws affecting milk that were aimed at preventing pricing discrimination against producers. These regulations may offer significant competitive pricing information. For example, Wisconsin State Statute 100.201(2)(a)(1), allows wholesalers and retailers to request copies of published price lists from any wholesaler. While this particular statute provides a mechanism to discourage price discrimination, published price lists could be used to encourage tacit collusion between competing wholesalers. It may be prudent to evaluate how such laws can discourage discrimination while also reducing the amount of competitive pricing information they make available to the industry.

Recommendation:

Review Capper-Volstead and milk marketing laws: At least two statutory schemes are integral to any anti-competitive review of this industry. The first is the antitrust immunity afforded to certain actions of agricultural cooperatives under the Capper-Volstead Act, 7 U.S.C. §§ 291, 292. The second is the "labyrinth" of federal milk-marketing regulation. The States recommend that the Capper-Volstead Act and particularly the current milk pricing scheme promulgated pursuant to the Agricultural Marketing Agreement Act, 7 U.S.C. §§ 601–14, 671–74; 7 C.F.R. §§ 1000–1199, be reviewed to ensure that they continue to protect and benefit farmers as originally intended. The AMAA and accompanying rules and regulations must not serve as a vehicle for large competitors to exclude smaller, independent entities from the market.

———————

Beginning in May 2010, the USDA and the Department of Justice (DOJ) began holding a series of joint public workshops "to explore competition issues affecting the agriculture industry in the 21st century and the appropriate role for antitrust and regulatory enforcement in that industry." The workshops have exposed major divisions within the livestock industry, with emotional rhetoric, calculated political strategies, and threats of lawsuits. Information about the workshops including some video and audio recordings as well as online links to the public comments are available at the DOJ website at http://www.justice.gov/atr/public/workshops/ag2010/index.html.

The comment period for the proposed regulations was extended until November 22, 2010.

VIII

Animal Welfare and Farm Animals Raised for Food

[R]espect for life, all life, and for humane treatment of all creatures is something that must never be lost.

Statement by Senator Robert C. Byrd on Cruelty to Animals, Congressional Record—Senate, July 9, 2001.

Animal law is one of the fastest growing areas of American legal study. It incorporates a variety of elements ranging from a discussion of whether traditional property law concepts apply to animals to a discussion of what inherent rights an animal may have in our society.[1] Animal welfare laws, i.e., those that impose a standard of care for animals, are in place at both the federal level and in all fifty states. Two factors indicate that interest in animal welfare issues may continue to rise.

1) Pets play an increasingly important role in American society.

There are approximately 77.5 million dogs owned as pets in the United States; thirty-nine percent of U.S. households own at least one dog. There are approximately 93.6 million cats owned as pets in the United States; thirty-three percent of U.S. households own at least one cat. Nearly half of pet owners, or 49.7%, considered their pets to be family members.

See, 2009–2010 National Pet Owners Survey, American Pet Products Manufacturers Association, http://www.appma.org. 2007 U.S. Pet Ownership & Demographics Sourcebook, American Veterinary Medical Association available at http://www.avma.org/reference/marketstats/sourcebook.asp

Legal issues involving pets arise in almost every area of law including criminal law, contract law, family law, estate planning, and tort law, and people take these issues very seriously.

2) There is increasing scientific evidence of animal sentience and intelligence.

It is now well-established that mammals and birds experience fear, pain and suffering; they make choices and seek comfort; they communicate with one another and sometimes with us; they are aware of their surroundings—they are "sentient beings."

Similarly, scientific views of animal intelligence have changed markedly in the past 30–40 years.

Certain skills are considered key signs of higher mental abilities: good memory, a grasp of grammar and symbols, self-awareness, understanding others' motives,

---

1. For ease, the term "animal" references non-human animals.

489

imitating others, and being creative. Bit by bit, in ingenious experiments, researchers have documented these talents in other species, gradually chipping away at what we thought made human beings distinctive while offering a glimpse of where our own abilities came from. Scrub jays know that other jays are thieves and that stashed food can spoil; sheep can recognize faces; chimpanzees use a variety of tools to probe termite mounds and even use weapons to hunt small mammals; dolphins can imitate human postures; the archerfish, which stuns insects with a sudden blast of water, can learn how to aim its squirt simply by watching an experienced fish perform the task.

Animal Minds: Minds Of Their Own—Animals Are Smarter Than You Think, NATIONAL GEOGRAPHIC MAGAZINE (March 2008) available at http://ngm.nationalgeographic.com/ 2008/03/animal-minds/virginia-morell-text.

Sentience and intelligence studies on farm animals have produced similar, sometimes surprising results. Cows, pigs, sheep, and chickens all learn to recognize people and tests show that they can tell different people apart. Scientific testing has revealed that pigs' problem solving skills are at least as good as those of dogs. They can remember where to find hidden food, learn to manipulate tools to obtain rewards, and have been observed using deception to prevent other pigs from eating their food. A study published in 2005 reported that chickens were prepared to wait longer before trying to get a reward when they knew that waiting would get them a larger reward. Chickens learn behaviors from watching other chickens and successfully remember what they have learned. Cows form "life-long friendships" and show excitement when they learn something new.

See, Compassion in World Farming Trust, *Stop—Look—Listen: Recognising the Sentience of Farm Animals* (citations to published studies provided as references)(2006), available at http://ciwf.org.uk/includes/documents/cm_docs/2008/s/stop_look_listen_2006.pdf.

See also, http://news.nationalgeographic.com/news/2001/11/1107_TVsheep.html (reporting on a study that found that sheep can recognize hundreds of faces, can distinguish between happy and sad expressions, and show a preference for happy expressions).

Once again, however, the agricultural setting raises distinct and sometimes unique issues, and special laws and exceptions have been carved out for the agricultural industry. How should we treat an animal that is raised in order to be slaughtered for food?

The increased interest and concern about animal welfare frequently collides with the historical view of animals as the property of their human owners. What an owner can or cannot do with his/her property has generally been guarded under the broad rubric of "property rights." This collision is particularly apparent in a study of animal law as applied to farm animals. The "property" is a living thing capable of experiencing fear and pain. Nevertheless, this living property is what is bought and sold for profit.

Many animal welfare laws have specific exemptions that apply to agriculture, taking all farm animals out of the reach of the statute. For example, the federal Animal Welfare Act, 7 U.S.C. 2131 *et seq.*, specifically excludes farm animals from its coverage. Many state animal cruelty statutes exempt farm animals from protection.

Other laws exempt farmers if they follow usual or "customary practices" or use practices accepted by colleges of agriculture or veterinary medicine.

These exemptions are generally based on the assumption that farmers would not do anything to harm their animals *because* the animals are their property and because the farmer is dependent on the animal's well-being for eventual profit. Farmers have historically taken good care of their animals in order to assure the health of the animals up to the point of slaughter.

This assumption, however, is subject to challenge. While farmers clearly want their animals to be alive and productive, animal science has developed agricultural production systems in which an animal can experience pain, discomfort, even great suffering without diminishing its economic value. In fact, sometimes a condition that increases suffering can increase profit. It is in this circumstance that the morale dilemma is most evident. Consider the following common agricultural practices, all of which are defended as economically efficient yet raise animal welfare concerns.

- [R]earing large numbers of livestock or poultry in close confinement with little or no room for natural movement and activity (e.g., housing sows in small gestation crates, chickens in battery cages);

- isolating veal calves in small crates;

- performing surgery such as docking hog tails, dehorning cattle, and trimming poultry beaks (so that confined animals do not hurt each other or their handlers);

- permitting commercial movement of nonambulatory livestock ("downers") that are disabled due to sickness or injury; and

- not fully stunning poultry (which are not covered by the humane slaughter act) and, sometimes, livestock (most of which are covered) before slaughter.

Geoffrey S. Becker, *Humane Treatment of Farm Animals: Overview and Issues*, Congressional Research Service, Report No.RS21978, 2–3 (March 9, 2010). Documented white-paper reports on the animal welfare problems associated with agricultural practices customary in the U.S. can be found on the Humane Society website at http://www.humane society.org/news/publications/whitepapers/farm_animal_welfare.html.

Thus, while Americans' general concern for the treatment of animals has increased, concentrated agricultural production systems have enabled the production of vast numbers of animals for meat production using methods that raise animal welfare concerns. Some commonly accepted agricultural practices in the United States would be considered animal cruelty under statutes applicable to pets. What ethical issues guide the treatment of sentient animals raised for economic profit?

This chapter selects two issues for introduction and analysis: efforts to impose animal welfare standards on livestock production and humane slaughter standards.

A. Efforts to Impose Welfare Standards on Livestock Production

American farmers have traditionally been allowed to raise livestock without government regulation. Aside from state laws that may criminalize extreme animal abuse, there are few laws that regulate how farm animals are treated. No federal law applies to animal welfare in farm production. The *Twenty-Eight Hour Law* applies to provide minimal guidelines for the transportation of livestock, although it does not apply to poultry. Only the Humane Methods of Slaughter Act, discussed *infra*, provides any federal guidance for the animal welfare of animals raised for food.

Consumers and animal welfare advocacy groups have engaged in a variety of initiatives to increase animal welfare standards for farm animals, often with the firm opposition of many in agriculture and the meat industry.

1. Citizen Initiatives

In a number of states, animal welfare standards have been presented for a vote as an initiative. These initiatives have generally been advanced by animal welfare advocacy groups, and in many cases opposed by major agricultural groups. In Florida, voters approved a 2002 ballot measure outlawing gestation crates for pigs. In 2006 in Arizona, voters outlawed gestation crates and veal crates. And, with much publicity, in 2008 California voters approved "Proposition 2," which will require that veal calves, egg-laying hens, and pregnant pigs be raised in conditions that allow them sufficient space to lie down, stand up, fully extend their limbs and turn around freely.

Proposition 2
Proposition–Animals–Prevention of Farm Animal Cruelty Act

[Approved by Voters on November 4, 2008.]

This initiative measure is submitted to the people in accordance with the provisions of Article II, Section 8, of the California Constitution.

PROPOSED LAW

SECTION 1. SHORT TITLE

This act shall be known and may be cited as the Prevention of Farm Animal Cruelty Act.

SECTION 2. PURPOSE

The purpose of this act is to prohibit the cruel confinement of farm animals in a manner that does not allow them to turn around freely, lie down, stand up, and fully extend their limbs.

SECTION 3. FARM ANIMAL CRUELTY PROVISIONS

Chapter 13.8 (commencing with Section 25990) is added to Division 20 of the Health and Safety Code, to read:

Chapter 13.8. Farm Animal Cruelty

25990. PROHIBITIONS. In addition to other applicable provisions of law, a person shall not tether or confine any covered animal, on a farm, for all or the majority of any day, in a manner that prevents such animal from:

(a) Lying down, standing up, and fully extending his or her limbs; and

(b) Turning around freely.

25991. DEFINITIONS. For the purposes of this chapter, the following terms have the following meanings:

(a) "Calf raised for veal" means any calf of the bovine species kept for the purpose of producing the food product described as veal.

(b) "Covered animal" means any pig during pregnancy, calf raised for veal, or egg-laying hen who is kept on a farm.

(c) "Egg-laying hen" means any female domesticated chicken, turkey, duck, goose, or guinea fowl kept for the purpose of egg production.

(d) "Enclosure" means any cage, crate, or other structure (including what is commonly described as a "gestation crate" for pigs; a "veal crate" for calves; or a "battery cage" for egg-laying hens) used to confine a covered animal.

(e) "Farm" means the land, building, support facilities, and other equipment that are wholly or partially used for the commercial production of animals or animal products used for food or fiber; and does not include live animal markets.

(f) "Fully extending his or her limbs" means fully extending all limbs without touching the side of an enclosure, including, in the case of egg-laying hens, fully spreading both wings without touching the side of an enclosure or other egg-laying hens.

(g) "Person" means any individual, firm, partnership, joint venture, association, limited liability company, corporation, estate, trust, receiver, or syndicate.

(h) "Pig during pregnancy" means any pregnant pig of the porcine species kept for the primary purpose of breeding.

(i) "Turning around freely" means turning in a complete circle without any impediment, including a tether, and without touching the side of an enclosure.

25992. EXCEPTIONS. This chapter shall not apply:

(a) During scientific or agricultural research.

(b) During examination, testing, individual treatment or operation for veterinary purposes.

(c) During transportation.

(d) During rodeo exhibitions, state or county fair exhibitions, 4-H programs, and similar exhibitions.

(e) During the slaughter of a covered animal in accordance with the provisions of Chapter 6 (commencing with Section 19501) of Part 3 of Division 9 of the Food and Agricultural Code, relating to humane methods of slaughter, and other applicable law and regulations.

(f) To a pig during the seven-day period prior to the pig's expected date of giving birth.

25993. ENFORCEMENT. Any person who violates any of the provisions of this chapter is guilty of a misdemeanor, and upon conviction thereof shall be punished by a fine not to exceed one thousand dollars ($1,000) or by imprisonment in the county jail for a period not to exceed 180 days or by both such fine and imprisonment.

25994. CONSTRUCTION OF CHAPTER.

The provisions of this chapter are in addition to, and not in lieu of, any other laws protecting animal welfare, including the California Penal Code. This chapter shall not be construed to limit any state law or regulations protecting the welfare of animals, nor shall anything in this chapter prevent a local governing body from adopting and enforcing its own animal welfare laws and regulations.

SECTION 4. SEVERABILITY

If any provision of this act, or the application thereof to any person or circumstances, is held invalid or unconstitutional, that invalidity or unconstitutionality shall not affect other provisions or applications of this act that can be given effect without the invalid or unconstitutional provision or application, and to this end the provisions of this act are severable.

SECTION 5. EFFECTIVE DATES

The provisions of Sections 25990, 25991, 25992, 25993, and 25994 shall become operative on January 1, 2015.

———————

During the Proposition 2 campaign period and after its enactment, opponents raised concerns about California's egg industry. It was predicted that California producers, burdened by the new cage requirements, would not be able to compete with eggs produced elsewhere. Largely in response to this concern, the California legislature passed a bill prohibiting the sale of shelled eggs for human consumption unless the egg-laying hen has been kept in compliance with the animal care standards adopted in Proposition 2. The new law also takes effect January 1, 2015.

The people of the State of California do enact as follows:

SECTION 1. Chapter 14 (commencing with Section 25995)
is added to Division 20 of the Health and Safety Code, to read:

Chapter 14. Shelled Eggs

25995. The Legislature finds and declares all of the following:

(a) According to the Pew Commission on Industrial Farm Production, food animals that are treated well and provided with at least minimum accommodation of their natural behaviors and physical needs are healthier and safer for human consumption.

(b) A key finding from the World Health Organization and Food and Agricultural Organization of the United Nations Salmonella Risk Assessment was that reducing flock prevalence results in a directly proportional reduction in human health risk.

(c) Egg-laying hens subjected to stress are more likely to have higher levels of pathogens in their intestines and the conditions increase the likelihood that consumers will be exposed to higher levels of food-borne pathogens.

(d) Salmonella is the most commonly diagnosed food-borne illness in the United States.

(e) It is the intent of the Legislature to protect California consumers from the deleterious, health, safety, and welfare effects of the sale and consumption of eggs derived from egg-laying hens that are exposed to significant stress and may result in increased exposure to disease pathogens including salmonella.

25996. (a) Commencing January 1, 2015, a shelled egg may not be sold or contracted for sale for human consumption in California if it is the product of an egg-laying hen that was confined on a farm or place that is not in compliance with animal care standards set forth in Chapter 13.8 (commencing with Section 25990).

(b) Any person who violates this chapter is guilty of a misdemeanor, and upon conviction thereof shall be punished by a fine not to exceed one thousand dollars ($1,000) or by imprisonment in the county jail for a period not to exceed 180 days or by both that fine and imprisonment.

(c) The provisions of this chapter are in addition to, and not in lieu of, any other laws protecting animal welfare, including the Penal Code. This chapter shall not be construed to limit any state law or regulation protecting the welfare of animals, nor shall anything in this chapter prevent a local governing body from adopting and enforcing its own animal welfare laws and regulations ...

———————

Notes

1. Arizona and Florida passed animal welfare initiatives regarding confined animals; Michigan, Maine, Colorado, and Oregon have passed related laws through the legislative process. A number of organizations monitor developments in this area. See, e.g, the Animal Welfare Reading Room at the National Agricultural Law Center's website nationalaglawcenter.org; the Animal Legal Defense Fund's Animal Protections Laws of the United States and Canada, on their website at http://www.aldf.org; Michigan State University's Animal Legal & Historical Web Center at http://www/animallaw.info/; and the Humane Society's Farm Animals webpage at http://hsus.org/farm_animals/index.html.

2. Defining "Humane" by Regulation

New Jersey Society for the Prevention of Cruelty to Animals v. New Jersey Department of Agriculture
955 A.2d 886 (N.J. 2008)

Justice HOENS delivered the opinion of the Court.

In 1996, with little discernable fanfare, the Legislature enacted a new section of the existing statute regulating animal cruelty. Although that statute, since at least 1898, had essentially left animal welfare and the protection of animals to the New Jersey Society for the Prevention of Cruelty to Animals ("NJSPCA") and its related county organizations, the Legislature decreed that the Department of Agriculture ("the Department") would be vested with certain authority relating to the care and welfare of domestic livestock, commonly referred to as farm animals.

In doing so, the Legislature directed the Department to create and promulgate regulations that would set standards governing the raising, keeping, and marketing of domestic livestock, but it specified that the guiding principle to be utilized in establishing those standards was to be whether the treatment of these animals was "humane." The statute required the Department to consult with the New Jersey Agricultural Experiment Station in developing and promulgating the regulations and established a presumption that compliance with those regulations would satisfy the other statutory standards defining animal cruelty. Although vesting the Department with this rulemaking function, the Legislature left the preexisting enforcement mechanisms, which have long relied on the NJSPCA, largely undisturbed.

This matter presents us with a broad challenge to the regulations promulgated by the Department pursuant to this legislative directive. More particularly, we are called upon to consider whether the Department, in promulgating the regulations relating to the care of domestic livestock: (1) failed in general to comply with the mandate of the Legislature that it create standards that are "humane," either objectively or as tested against the definition that the Department itself adopted; (2) created an impermissibly broad and vague category of permitted practices by referring to "routine husbandry practices" as generally acceptable; (3) failed to create an adequate regulatory scheme by utilizing undefined or ill-defined terms that cannot serve as objectively enforceable standards; and (4) embraced a variety of specific practices that are either objectively inhumane or supported by inadequate scientific evidence as to their usefulness, or that fail to meet any accepted definition of the term humane.

In part, the issues before this Court require us to evaluate the very methodology utilized by the Department in its creation of the challenged regulations; in part, the issues before us raise questions and debates arising from deeply held notions concerning the welfare of animals generally. Nonetheless, the dispute before this Court has nothing to do with anyone's love for animals, or with the way in which any of us treats our pets; rather, it requires a balancing of the interests of people and organizations who would zealously safeguard the well-being of all animals, including those born and bred for eventual slaughter, with the equally significant interests of those who make their living in animal husbandry and who contribute, through their effort, to our food supply.

In the end, our focus is not upon, nor would it be appropriate for us to address, whether we deem any of the specifically challenged practices to be, objectively, humane. To engage in that debate would suggest that we have some better understanding of the complex scientific and technical issues than we possibly could have, or that we are in some sense better able to evaluate the extensive record compiled by the Department than is that body itself. To engage in that discussion would also suggest that in a realm in which the Legislature has expressed its intention that an administrative agency bring its expertise to bear upon the issues, this Court is better equipped to do so. More to the point, it would suggest that we, rather than the Legislature or the Department, know which farming and livestock practices are objectively humane and which are not.

To accept such a challenge would be to overstep our role in our constitutional system, for it would be little more than our effort to substitute our view for that of the bodies authorized to act. It is, simply put, an invitation that we decline to accept. Rather, we confine our analysis, as we must, to a consideration about whether the agency in question did or did not carry out the function assigned to it by the Legislature, as tested in accordance with our ordinary standard of review of final agency actions and with due deference to the considerable expertise of that agency.

Notwithstanding all of the foregoing, our review of the record compels us to conclude that in its wholesale embrace of the regulations adopted by the Department, the Appellate Division erred. Because we find in those regulations both unworkable standards and an unacceptable delegation of authority to an ill-defined category of presumed experts, we conclude that the Department failed, in part, to carry out its mandate. We therefore conclude that some, but not all, of the regulations are invalid and we reverse only those aspects of the Appellate Division's judgment that concluded otherwise....

As enacted, the bill had two sections, the first of which was codified as *N.J.S.A.* 4:22-16.1. That section provides, in relevant part, as follows:

a. The State Board of Agriculture and the Department of Agriculture, in consultation with the New Jersey Agricultural Experiment Station and within six months of the date of enactment of this act, shall develop and adopt, pursuant to the "Administrative Procedure Act," P.L. 1968, c. 410 (*C. 52:14B-1* et seq.): (1) standards for the humane raising, keeping, care, treatment, marketing, and sale of domestic livestock; and (2) rules and regulations governing the enforcement of those standards.

b. Notwithstanding any provision in this title to the contrary:

(1) there shall exist a presumption that the raising, keeping, care, treatment, marketing, and sale of domestic livestock in accordance with the standards developed and adopted therefor pursuant to subsection a. of this section shall not constitute a violation of any provision of this title involving alleged cruelty to, or inhumane care or treatment of, domestic livestock....

[*N.J.S.A.* 4:22-16.1.]

The bill also amended *N.J.S.A.* 4:22-16, which more generally defines the manner in which the animal cruelty statutes are to be construed. The bill added a new section that created an exception to the animal cruelty statutes for any activity or practice performed in accordance with the regulations that the Department was directed to promulgate. *See N.J.S.A.* 4:22-16(e). In addition, the bill extended the exemption granted in *N.J.S.A.* 4:22-16(a) for "[p]roperly conducted scientific experiments" performed under the authority of certain entities, by adding an exemption for such activities as were authorized by the United States Department of Agriculture.

A.

Notwithstanding the six month time frame within which the Department was directed to act, regulations designed to implement this statutory mandate were not drafted and published as proposed regulations for public comment until 2003. In response to the proposed regulations, the Department received over 6,500 written comments, and heard testimony from numerous witnesses who appeared at a public hearing on the proposals. After considering the comments and the testimony, the Department amended certain of the proposed regulations and formally adopted the regulations, to be codified at *N.J.A.C.* 2:8-1.1 to -8.7, on June 7, 2004. In doing so, the Department stated that it intended to "establish the minimum level of care that can be considered to be humane." Moreover, the Department noted that the regulations were developed after extensive "consultations with the New Jersey Agricultural Experiment Station, as well as with other academicians, the New Jersey Society for the Prevention of Cruelty to Animals, veterinarians, Department staff, extension agents, producers, and allied industries." As explained by the Department:

[t]he rules were also developed with consideration of the Department's overarching mission as reflected in Governor James McGreevey's statement to Charles M. Kuperus, Secretary of Agriculture: "My charge to Charlie is clear-preserve our farms, fight for our farmers, and ensure that our agricultural industry is profitable and strong, innovative and poised for a bright future."

As the Department understood its legislative mandate, and as it expressed that understanding as part of its adoption of these regulations in 2004, "[t]he rule proposal was designed to meet the complementary objectives of developing standards to protect animals from inhumane treatment and … fostering industry sustainability and growth." … As adopted, the regulations are substantially similar to those that were originally proposed, but the notice and comment period had alerted the Department to a number of aspects of the regulations that were in need of amendment....

Following its consideration and its further response to the comments that were relevant to the new proposals, the Department, on June 1, 2005, formally adopted the amendments to the earlier version of the regulations.

Finally, on April 3, 2006, the Department, responding to continued criticism of one part of the previously promulgated regulations, proposed a further amendment that would alter the definitions and the regulations relating to a specific practice used in the management of poultry. In particular, the newly proposed regulations were designed to limit induced molting procedures and to ban full feed-removal forced molting[4] techniques....

B.

Petitioners are a variety of entities, including the NJSPCA, and individuals which describe themselves collectively as "a wide coalition of animal protection organizations, consumers, farmers, and concerned citizens." Petitioners, many of whom had participated in the notice and comment process that led to the adoption of the regulations, raised this challenge to the final agency action adopting the regulations through an appeal in the Appellate Division, ...

First, petitioners argued that several subsections of the regulations include a broadly-worded exemption for any practice that meets the definition of a "routine husbandry practice" and that the definition as adopted is both impermissibly vague and not grounded on any evidence in the record. Second, petitioners asserted that some of the subsections included vague or undefined terms and failed to create enforceable standards. Third, petitioners asserted that the regulations authorized a variety of specific practices that do not meet the Department's definition of "humane" and are not in fact humane.

In defending the regulations before the Appellate Division, the Department argued that they were consistent with both the intent and the spirit of the statute and supported by ample scientific evidence. In part, the Department argued that its statutory mandate required it to meet two public policy objectives, namely, preventing cruelty to animals and promoting the continuation of sustainable agriculture in New Jersey. The Department defended its election of "routine husbandry practices" as an appropriate criterion for its safe harbor exemption, explained how the regulations established objectively enforceable standards, and argued that none of the specific practices that petitioners challenged is in fact inhumane.

C.

The Appellate Division, in an unpublished opinion, rejected each of petitioners' challenges and sustained all of the challenged regulations. Relying in large part on the presumption of reasonableness afforded to acts of administrative agencies and the deferential standard of review that courts employ when reviewing matters involving an agency's scientific or technical expertise, the Appellate Division found no basis on which to invalidate any part of these regulations....

---

4. Any forced molting procedure is designed to increase egg production. These procedures do so by essentially forcing the hen to molt and to lay eggs on an unnatural schedule. As adopted, the regulations do not ban such procedures in general. However, full feed-removal forced molting, which involves starving fowl or poultry for fourteen days, has been deemed to be inhumane and it has now been banned.

Petitioners sought certification from this Court, asserting a number of the challenges that they had raised before the Appellate Division. We granted that petition for certification, and we thereafter granted leave to several entities and individuals to participate as amicus curiae.

II.

Petitioners argue before this Court that the Appellate Division erred in its analysis and failed to recognize that the regulations authorize the continuation, as humane, of practices that are not. Asserting that the statute itself is remedial legislation entitled to be broadly read, petitioners argue that the Appellate Division failed to recognize the particular legislative purpose in utilizing the "humane" standard. According to petitioners, that standard was used by the Legislature to avoid simply allowing the continuation of practices that are merely routine or common. They assert that the Legislature intended instead to require the Department to consider separately whether any particular practice, even if commonly or routinely utilized, is in fact humane. Petitioners urge us to conclude that although the Department recognized this mandate, as evidenced by the definition of humane that it adopted, its regulations fall short by ignoring that definition and by effectively doing precisely what the Legislature sought to avoid.

Reiterating the specific arguments they expressed before the appellate panel, petitioners urge this Court to invalidate the regulations in their entirety. They argue that the regulations, by relying on the "routine husbandry practices" definition, created a safe harbor that cannot be sustained. Petitioners point out that because the definition of this phrase permits any practice, and equates it with a humane practice, if it is "commonly taught" at a wide variety of educational institutions, it amounts to an impermissible delegation of the Department's authority and permits as humane those practices that are not. Before this Court, petitioners have expanded this argument to include an assertion that the Department, in including this wide assortment of educational and other institutions within its definition, failed to review or analyze their curricula or their programs to ensure that any of them actually teaches practices that are humane. They assert that because of this shortcoming, the Department acted without an essential basis in the record, resulting in the adoption of regulations not entitled to the Court's deference.

Petitioners also reiterate the other arguments that they pressed before the Appellate Division, They urge the Court to conclude that the regulations fail to set an enforceable standard by utilizing language, such as "minimize pain," without further definition, so as to provide insufficient guidance to those charged with enforcement and that the regulations therefore fail to establish any standard. Finally, they point to a large number of particular practices that are permitted to be performed by the regulations but that, they assert, are not humane in accordance with the Department's definition or which are of dubious benefit according to the scientific evidence. In short, because the regulations have both specific shortcomings and general ones, petitioners urge this Court to invalidate the regulations in their entirety.

The Department urges this Court to affirm the Appellate Division's carefully analyzed and lengthy opinion and to uphold the regulations both in general and in all of their particulars. More specifically, the Department argues that its regulations should be afforded great deference and that the Appellate Division correctly determined that petitioners did not meet their heavy burden to overcome the agency's expertise in setting up appropriate standards. It stresses that its regulations are supported by an extensive record and represent its considered judgment in carrying out its role of both promoting viable agriculture and ensuring animal and public health.

The Department argues in particular that its "routine husbandry practices" exemption is consistent with the statutory mandate and is an appropriate means to permit the continuation of practices that should be permitted. It points out that in response to criticism that its original definition of "routine husbandry practices" was too broad, it introduced and adopted the amended definition, limiting such practices only to those that are "commonly taught" at veterinary schools, land grant colleges, and universities or by agricultural extension agents. At the same time, the Department urges the Court to reject petitioners' assertion that it did not review the curricula of these institutions before relying on them as part of its safe harbor. The Department notes instead that it consulted with educators and experts, reviewed various curricula, texts, federal and state statutes, as well as state and national standards, and asserts that it therefore fully discharged its statutory obligations.

The Department also urges this Court to reject petitioners' other arguments that the regulations fail to establish enforceable standards, as well as the challenges to each of the specific practices that the agency elected to include within the subsections identifying techniques that are permissible. It asserts that it has faithfully carried out its mandate to ensure that the practices used in animal husbandry are humane, and has exercised its expertise in order to do so. In support of this argument, the Department explains that in those cases in which it identified practices that are not humane, it has acted to eradicate them, pointing to its decision to ban full feed-removal forced molting.

The Department argues that the regulations set forth a baseline of behavior that farmers are free to exceed if they so desire and explains that underlying the regulations it adopted is the belief that farmers genuinely care for their animals and are aware of the basics of animal biology and behavior. As such, the Department urges us to reject the arguments raised by petitioners and to agree with the Appellate Division that there is no ground on which to invalidate any aspect of the regulations.

In addition to the arguments made by petitioners and by the Department, we granted leave to a number of other interested individuals and entities to file briefs as amicus curiae. In particular, the Monmouth County Society for the Prevention of Cruelty to Animals and the Cumberland County Society for the Prevention of Cruelty to Animals filed a joint brief in which they supported the arguments advanced by petitioners. They argue that the exemption in the regulation for "routine husbandry practices" fails to create an enforceable standard, that in adopting it the Department failed to review the curricula of the institutions that will serve as the arbiter of what is either routine or commonly taught, and that the exemption therefore is an impermissible delegation of the Department's statutory mandate. Moreover, they assert that this exemption impairs the ability of any of the SPCAs to carry out their obligation to enforce the anti-cruelty laws. In addition, they argue that the Department, in adopting the safe harbor based on "routine husbandry practices," impermissibly embraced and permitted numerous practices that have not been demonstrated to be humane, and thus failed to adhere to the statutory mandate that it only authorize those practices that it has concluded have been shown affirmatively to be humane. Finally, they argue that the Department failed to apply the very standard of "humane" that its own regulations adopted.

Bernard E. Rollin, Ph.D., who identified himself as an animal welfare expert, also filed a brief, as amicus curiae, in which he raised other concerns about the challenged regulations. The gravamen of his argument is that many practices and procedures used in veterinary medicine, including many that are commonly used and taught in veterinary schools, are not humane, with the result that many practices that would meet the regulation's safe harbor definition of being "routine husbandry practices" cannot also be defined as humane. He further argues that the Department failed to discharge its statutory mandate because it relied on entities whose focus is on economic productivity rather than on animal welfare. He urges this Court to recognize that our Legislature chose instead a loftier standard, one that the Department was directed, but failed, to enforce, thus requiring that the regulations be invalidated....

IV.

Petitioners attack the regulations both generally and specifically, as a result of which our analysis must proceed in like fashion. We therefore begin with a consideration of whether the regulations in general are invalid.

A.

The regulations themselves are divided into several subchapters, each of which addresses a different aspect of the statutory mandate in the context of the care and treatment of domestic livestock. The first part of the regulations sets forth the agency's statement of purpose, its presumption that acts in accordance with the regulations will "not constitute cruelty ... or inhumane care and treatment" in violation of the statute and lists the definitions that shall apply to the terms used in the regulations.

The next six subchapters of the regulations set forth standards that relate to particular types of domestic livestock, including cattle, horses, poultry, rabbits, small ruminants,[9] and swine, *N.J.A.C.* 2:8-7.1 to -7.7. Although each of these subchapters includes subsections about similar areas of raising, keeping, or caring for domestic livestock that are being regulated and although each includes certain standards that apply generally to all domestic livestock, the majority of each subchapter is devoted to individualized practices and management techniques for each animal or group of animals.

For example, each includes subsections setting forth general provisions, as well as standards relating to "feeding," "watering," "keeping," "marketing and sale," and "care and treatment" of the particular group of animals in question. Each subchapter, however, also includes a subsection entitled "exceptions," that creates a so-called "safe harbor" provision. As to each type of farm animal, this provision identifies a number of particular practices that are explicitly permitted if they are performed by "knowledgeable individuals in a sanitary manner in a way to minimize pain," and authorizes other techniques by reference to "routine husbandry practices" as defined in *N.J.A.C.* 2:8-1.2.

The final subchapter of the regulations, *N.J.A.C.* 2:8-8.1 to -8.7, provides standards governing "the investigation and enforcement of alleged violations of humane standards" applicable to domestic livestock....

B.

The statutory provisions relating to the prevention of cruelty to animals are found in Chapter 22 of Title 4, which is devoted to Agriculture....

As an integral part of the enforcement scheme, Chapter 22 includes several sections that define the meaning and scope of animal cruelty and its prevention. It does so in part by defining both in general and in very specific terms the acts that will constitute cruelty and by identifying the penalties, both civil and criminal, that will be imposed for particular violations....

---

9. The regulations define small ruminants as follows: "'Small ruminants' include sheep, goats, llama, alpaca, and farm-raised Cervidae." *N.J.A.C.* 2:8-1.2.

In addition, however, the statute specifies a large variety of acts and practices that shall not be "prohibit[ed] or interfere[d] with," that is, acts and practices that shall not, by definition, constitute cruelty. These acts and practices include, for example, certain rather broadly defined scientific experiments, training of dogs for various purposes, and hunting and fishing in accordance with relevant regulations as to time and manner. It is in this section of the statute that the Legislature added, as part of the 1996 statutory amendment, a general exception from the acts comprising cruelty for "raising, keeping, care, treatment, marketing, and sale of domestic livestock" if performed in accordance with the regulations that were to be adopted ...

The statute therefore, although it generally prohibits acts and practices that constitute cruelty, also explicitly permits other acts that fall within one of its exceptions. For purposes of this appeal, the result is that any act that meets the standards embodied in the Department's regulations as a permitted act, practice or technique, is, by definition, not an act of cruelty. As a result, all of the acts included in the several "safe harbor" provisions of these regulations, as long as they are performed in accordance with the standards that those provisions impose, are permitted by the statute because, by definition, they are not acts of cruelty.

By extension, however, if the safe harbor provisions themselves cannot be sustained, or if one or more of the acts now included in the safe harbor provisions lacks sufficient support in the record for it to withstand our review, the effect would not be that any of these procedures is banned. Rather, the effect would be that any of them could still be performed if otherwise consistent with the statutory definition of what is cruel and what is not. That is to say, even if this Court were to strike the safe harbor subsections in their entirety or strike the inclusion of specific practices that are now there permitted, it would not constitute a ban on those practices. Instead, the ordinary statutory provisions regarding what acts constitute cruelty, as well as those that govern the detection, investigation, and prosecution of violations, would operate as the appropriate regulatory mechanism pending promulgation of new regulations by the Department....

C.

In its lengthy consideration of the questions about animal cruelty in the context of domestic livestock, the Department compiled an extensive record. That record includes a wide variety of materials, representing input from numerous organizations (e.g., Animal Welfare Institution, National Pork Board, United Egg Producers), individuals and interest groups from New Jersey and nationally (e.g., Temple Grandin, Bernard Rollin, People for the Ethical Treatment of Animals, Farm Sanctuary, Professional Rodeo Cowboys Association), as well as materials from other states (e.g., Pennsylvania, New York, Maine, Texas, West Virginia, Montana, New Mexico), and even from other countries (e.g., England, Australia, New Zealand).

The record before this Court is not only extensive, but it is broad in its scope. On its face, the record demonstrates that the Department took seriously its charge to consider all aspects of the questions about the welfare of domestic livestock. In doing so, the Department did not simply consider the views and the input of farmers, agriculture professionals and their trade organizations, but it also received and took into account the views of animal rights activists and animal welfare organizations.

At the same time, the Department received input into its decisions from a wide variety of professionals, scholars, veterinarians, and other experts in all phases of animal welfare, animal health, and farming practices. The record includes a large number of scientific studies and scholarly publications reflecting both existing practices and trends, in this country and abroad, and representing current thinking about humane practices in the fields of animal husbandry, veterinary sciences, and agriculture. In addition, during the rulemaking process, the Department received and responded to thousands of comments, including many objections to its proposed regulations, in its effort to adopt regulations that more accurately carried out the legislative goal of ensuring that farm animals are treated humanely....

V.

Petitioners first assert that the regulations, in their entirety, fail to carry out the fundamental goal of the Legislature to have the Department create regulations that embody standards that are humane. They assert that the regulations neither comply with the meaning of humane as it is contemplated by the statute, nor do they even accord with the definition of humane that the agency itself adopted.

Petitioners first point out that, in enacting the statute, the Legislature referred explicitly to "humane" practices relating to livestock rather than, as other states have done, referring to a lesser standard, such as "routine" or "commonly practiced" management techniques. In order to give full meaning and effect to the intent of the Legislature, therefore, petitioners argue that the agency was required to look beyond the practices currently utilized and to identify and permit only those practices that meet this higher standard, but that it failed in this mission.

More to the point, petitioners point out that the Department itself adopted a definition of humane that many of the practices that are explicitly permitted or that fall within the safe harbor cannot meet. Although they point to several particular practices that they argue are examples of the way in which the regulations fall short, petitioners insist that this defect is so pervasive that the regulations cannot be sustained at all.

The Department argues that its regulations do not violate the requirements of the statute. The Department rejects the suggestion that the statute required an elevated standard and asserts that nothing in the regulations in fact violates the definition of humane that it adopted.

Our review of this record compels us to reject both aspects of petitioners' broad attack on these regulations....

Plainly, the Department recognized that part of its charge was to adopt regulations that would ensure that the treatment of farm animals was humane, as opposed to merely reciting those practices that were accepted, routine, common, or prevalent. Just as plainly, the Department understood that the effectuation of its legislative mandate required that it adopt a definition of humane, because this is the critical term in the statute. As a result, the Department included in its regulations, both as originally proposed and as finally adopted, the following definition: "'Humane' means marked by compassion, sympathy, and consideration for the welfare of animals."

In addition, although not part of the definition of "humane," the Department also proposed and adopted definitions of two related terms. As such, it defined both "Animal welfare" and "Well-being." The former, which is included in the list of defined terms, "means a state or condition of physical and psychological harmony between the animal and its surroundings characterized by an absence of deprivation, aversive stimulation, over stimulation or any other imposed condition that adversely affects health and productivity of the animal." The latter, found in the same part of the regulations, is defined as follows: "'Well-being' means good health and welfare."

We do not read in this statute or in these definitions any standard that requires that the regulations be invalidated in their entirety. In order to do so we would need to conclude either that the agency failed to consider the requirement of the statute that "humane" treatment be the touchstone or that, in light of the statutory standard and the definition adopted by the Department itself, its regulations as a whole are arbitrary, capricious or unreasonable. Indeed, because these regulations are the expression of the agency's determinations in an area within its technical expertise, in order to invalidate them in their entirety, we would need to discern an inherent flaw in the very process by which they were drafted and adopted or in the record that supports them.

The extensive record and careful response of the Department to the overwhelming number of comments does not permit us to so conclude. Even though there may be particular practices that the regulations specifically embrace and that might fall short of this lofty language, we cannot say that this is true as to each and every aspect of the regulations, or as to all of the practices that they permit....

In so concluding, we are guided by two considerations. First, petitioners suggest that they have merely pointed to specific examples of treatment that they have identified as falling short of the definition of "humane," in an effort to illustrate a larger defect in the regulations. They argue that these examples alone should suffice to prove the bankruptcy of the process used by the Department in adopting the regulations and should therefore support a decision to invalidate the regulations in their entirety.

We, however, do not agree. Rather, we interpret petitioners' failure to suggest that the great majority of the practices permitted in these apparently uncontroversial requirements are not humane, as significant....

Second, the record reflects that the Department has considered objections to some of the originally proposed and adopted regulations and then concluded, on further review, that the objections were meritorious. In particular, as it relates to the challenged practice of full feed-removal during induced molting, the Department has not only been responsive to the continued objections to that particular technique, but has concluded that it should be banned. Far from the picture of an agency held hostage by the interests of agribusiness that petitioners would paint, the Department has not been unresponsive to arguments about specific practices that do not meet its definition of those that are humane....

VI.

Petitioners next challenge the inclusion in the regulations of language creating a safe harbor for any act or technique that meets the definition of "routine husbandry practices." This exception ... essentially authorizes the use of any and all techniques that meet this definition because it identifies this class of practices as not being prohibited.[12]

The phrase "routine husbandry practices" is among the terms that the Department included in its section on definitions as follows:

> "Routine husbandry practices" means those techniques commonly taught by veterinary schools, land grant colleges, and agricultural extension agents for the benefit of animals, the livestock industry, animal handlers and the public health and which are employed to raise, keep, care, treat, market and transport livestock, including, but not limited to, techniques involved with physical restraint;

---

12. In actuality, the regulations also require that, in order to be included in the safe harbor, any such practice must also be "performed in a sanitary manner by a knowledgeable individual and in such a way as to minimize pain." ...

animal handling; animal identification; animal training; manure management; restricted feeding; restricted watering; restricted exercising; animal housing techniques; reproductive techniques; implantation; vaccination; and use of fencing materials, as long as all other State and Federal laws governing these practices are followed.

Petitioners assert that the definition of "routine husbandry practices" is so broad and all-encompassing that it amounts to an improper delegation of the agency's authority, contrary to its legislative mandate. Moreover, they argue that the record reveals that the Department, in adopting this definition and this standard for what constitutes "humane," failed to even review or evaluate the practices that it would permit. In particular, they assert that the definition includes a wide variety of institutions, each of which has become the arbiter of which practices are humane, but that the Department did not undertake any analysis of these institutions. In part, they point out that the record includes no evaluation of any of the texts used or the curricula that they follow, and no investigation of their course catalogs or instructional personnel. In short, petitioners argue that there is nothing in the record that would suggest that any of these institutions teaches practices that would meet the Department's own definition of "humane."

Amicus Rollin concurs, arguing that merely because a practice is routinely employed or taught, even if taught at a veterinary school, does not mean that it is humane. Rather, he argues that many practices taught at these institutions are motivated by concerns about the economics of agriculture, focusing on productivity alone, and ignoring any concerns about the welfare of the animals involved. As such, he argues that these practices, even if commonly taught, simply cannot be equated with practices or techniques that are also humane.

The Department argues that there is nothing in its definition of "routine husbandry practices" that fails to meet its mandate. It argues that the record fully supports its decision to rely on a variety of educational institutions as a mechanism to define and to identify permissible practices, contending that this choice was in keeping with its charge to create regulations that are "humane." In particular, the Department asserts that it undertook to review a variety of texts and curricula from many educational institutions as part of its consideration of this part of the regulations.

In support of its decision, the Department also points out that the statute itself directed the agency to cooperate with the New Jersey Agricultural Experiment Station, suggesting that this is evidence that the Legislature intended that the agency would rely on similar institutions, even to the point of including them within the safe harbor exception. Finally, the Department asserts that its mandate was not to create a complex series of detailed regulations about particular practices, but to implement general standards that would permit individual farmers to utilize their judgment in the same way that regulations governing doctors or accountants operate. In light of these considerations, the Department urges us to reject the challenge to the "routine husbandry practices" exception.

[N]otwithstanding its insistence that its review was careful prior to its decision to effectively place into the hands of this wide-ranging and ill-defined group of presumed experts the power to determine what is humane, there is no evidence in the record that the Department undertook any review, organized or passing, of what these institutions actually teach. On the contrary, there is clear evidence in the record that the Department only attempted to collect and review the curricula of any of these institutions during the pendency of the appeal to this Court. Although one might well debate whether review of curricula or course guides alone would be sufficient, failing to do so at all leaves the agency's decision to rely on these institutions without any basis in the record.

Nor is there any evidence that the Department considered whether the techniques taught in these institutions, whatever those techniques might be, rest in any way on a concern about what practices are humane or have any focus other than expedience or maximization of productivity. Contrary to the Department's assertion, there is no evidence that it considered the intersection between the interests of those who attend these institutions or are taught by them and those who are concerned with the welfare of the animals.

Our review of this aspect of the appeal leads us to conclude that this part of the safe harbor exemption demonstrates two separate flaws. First, it cannot be denied that in enacting this statute, the Legislature directed the Department to achieve a specific goal and that it chose to do so in language that differed from similar statutes in other states. It is significant that the Legislature sought to exempt only "humane" practices from prosecution under the cruelty code. Whereas other states have exempted routine, common, or accepted practices from their cruelty codes, *see, e.g.,* 18 Pa. Cons.Stat. Ann. 5511(c)(3) (exempting activities in "normal" agricultural operation from prosecution in Pennsylvania); Colo.Rev.Stat. 18-9-201.5(1) (authorizing "accepted" animal husbandry practices in Colorado), our Legislature chose not to use that language, selecting a different course.

To suggest, as the Department's "routine husbandry practices" definition implies, that the Legislature meant "routine" when it said "humane" would "abuse the interpretive process and ... frustrate the announced will of the people." ... The wholesale adoption, as the equivalent of "humane," of "routine husbandry practices," however, does precisely that.

Second, in light of the direct mandate to the Department to adopt regulations that establish practices that are humane, the decision by that agency to authorize an exemption, and therefore to embrace wholesale any technique as long as it is "commonly taught" at any of these institutions, under the circumstances, is an impermissible subdelegation. As our Appellate Division has recognized, the "power ... delegated by statute to an administrative agency cannot be subdelegated in the absence of any indication the Legislature so intends." In fact, because of the nature of the entities included within the safe harbor exemption, the Department did not simply engage in a subdelegation, but did so in favor of some entities that also might be described as private interests.

We are not persuaded, in these circumstances, that the direction from the Legislature to the Department to work with the New Jersey Agricultural Experiment Station is an indication that the Legislature intended that the agency would thereafter subdelegate its authority in so thorough a fashion. Although it might suggest that a limited subdelegation to that specific entity would be permitted, the Department went far beyond that narrow reading of the statute.

As an example, the Department could have reviewed the curriculum and faculty at a number of land grant colleges, universities, and veterinary schools and identified some where animal welfare concerns resulted in teaching of practices that meet the Department's definition of humane. Had it done so and had it then used those institutions as its safe harbor yardstick, there would be no basis for a challenge. Indeed, had the Department reviewed and relied on practices taught at Rutgers School of Environmental and Biological Sciences, formerly known as Cook College, and, perhaps, a veterinary school in New York or Pennsylvania, there would likely be no warrant for our interference. Instead, it accepted, without analysis, the practices that are taught in every veterinary school, land grant college, and agricultural extension agent not only in this state, but in the rest of the country and, it would appear, wherever they might be found around the globe. Although some of those institutions might teach or require practices that are far more humane than do our own, nothing in the record suggests that all of them will meet the standard set by our Legislature.

Our analysis of petitioners' objections to the several subsections of the regulations that create a safe harbor by reliance on "routine husbandry practices" compels us to conclude that these objections have merit. By adopting a definition of exceptional breadth, by failing to create an adequate record in support of this decision, and by implicitly permitting techniques that cannot meet the statutory mandate to base its regulations on a determination about what is humane, the Department has adopted regulations that are arbitrary and capricious. We therefore strike as invalid the definition of "routine husbandry practices …"

VII.

Petitioners also challenged individually a number of practices that are specifically permitted by the regulations, asserting that they are demonstrably inhumane and that the Department's authorization thereof is unsupported by sound science. In particular, petitioners point to several procedures utilized by some farming operations that are physically painful and, they contend, are emotionally distressing to the animals. At the same time, they argue, these same practices cannot be justified because they are often of little or no value. In response, the Department counters that there is ample scientific evidence in the record that supports the continued use of each of these procedures. Moreover, the Department asserts that because the regulations include limits on the manner and circumstances in which any of these disputed practices is permitted, the practical result is that each of them is only performed in a humane manner....

This part of the challenge focuses on several practices that are identified in the regulations, as part of the safe harbor provisions or as otherwise permissible, and that therefore are presumptively humane. The challenged practices are: tail docking of cattle; use of crates or tethering of swine, cattle, and veal calves; castration (without required anesthesia) of cattle, horses, and swine; de-beaking of poultry; toe-trimming of turkeys (without required anesthesia); and transporting sick and downed cattle to slaughter.

A.

The first specific practice that petitioners attack relates only to dairy cattle. This practice, known as "tail docking," is a procedure that involves "the amputation of the lower portion of a dairy cow's tail." Petitioners contend that tail docking cannot meet the Department's definition of humane, and they point to evidence of a consensus among scientists that tail docking is without any "apparent animal health, welfare, or human health justification." *See* C.L. Stull et al., *Evaluation of the scientific justification for tail docking in dairy cattle*, 220 *J. Veterinary Med. Assoc.* 1298, 1302 (May 1, 2002).

They further assert that tail docking causes acute pain and interferes with the ability of the affected animals to perform natural behaviors, including flicking their tails to chase away flies in the summer. *See* S.D. Eicher & J.W. Dalley, *Indicators of Acute Pain and Fly Avoidance Behaviors in Holstein Calves Following Tail-docking*, 85 *J. Dairy Sci.* 2850 (2002). Moreover, petitioners note that both the American (AVMA) and Canadian (CVMA) Veterinary Medical Associations oppose tail docking of dairy cattle, and they point to the AVMA's position paper that states: "[c]urrent scientific literature indicates that routine tail docking provides no benefit to the animal, and that tail docking can lead to distress during fly seasons." *See* AVMA, *Animal Welfare Position Statements: Tail Docking of Cattle* (2005), *see also* CVMA, *Animal Welfare Position Statements: Tail Docking of Dairy Cattle* (2003). Petitioners argue that a practice from which the animal derives no benefit, and that will cause it to suffer distress, cannot be humane.

The Department contends that, despite the AVMA's position paper, its decision to permit tail docking to continue to be performed complied with its statutory mandate to create humane standards. The agency points out that it responded to comments objecting to the practice, and that it reasoned that the practice should be permitted because it may lead to better milk quality and udder health, and it may also reduce the spread of diseases.

Nonetheless, the agency also commented that because the science is inconclusive concerning whether these benefits will be achieved, the Department "discourages" routine tail docking, leaving it to each producer to decide whether to engage in the practice. In doing so, the agency points out that its position is consistent with that espoused by the American Association of Bovine Practitioners, and it assures this Court that it intends to monitor the effects of this procedure and that it will ban the practice in the future if it concludes that the procedure is cruel or inhumane.

Although we recognize the considerable expertise that the Department brought to bear in reaching its decision to include tail docking within its list of permitted practices, it is difficult to find in this record any support for this particular practice, and none that meets the requisite standard of our review. The record amply demonstrates that, far from being humane, this practice is specifically disparaged by both the AVMA and the CVMA as having no benefit and as leading to distress. The only scientific evidence that even suggests that the practice might have some possible benefit is inconclusive at best.

More to the point, the record in support of the practice is so weak that even the industry trade group, like the Department, "discourages" it, leaving it apparently to the individual conscience of each dairy farmer. In light of the regulatory scheme, however, the practice was listed among those that are permitted and presumptively humane. The result is, therefore, to generally permit a practice for no apparent reason, and to permit it to be performed in accordance with no particular safeguards or standards, save for the Department's promise that it will ban tail docking in the future if it concludes that the practice is inhumane.

Apart from failing to adhere to the Legislative mandate that the agency permit only those practices that it finds to be humane (as opposed to not inhumane), because this practice finds no support at all in the record, to the extent that the regulation permits it, that aspect of the regulation is both arbitrary and capricious. In the absence of evidence in the record to support the practice or to confine it to circumstances in which it has a benefit and is performed in a manner that meets an objective definition of humane, this aspect of the regulation cannot stand.

B.

For purposes of our analysis, we have identified several of the challenged practices that we find it appropriate to consider together. This group comprises three specific practices that are similar in terms of petitioners' focus and our evaluation of the record: (1) castration of swine, horses, and calves; (2) de-beaking of chickens and turkeys; and (3) toe-trimming of turkeys. Each is a procedure that petitioners assert is, by and large, unnecessary, because each seeks to prevent behaviors, or the effects thereof, in which animals would likely not engage were they not raised in close quarters. In addition, petitioners challenge these practices because each is performed without anesthetics, thus causing the animals significant, if not severe, pain.

As to each of these practices, the Department implicitly recognizes that there are sound animal husbandry and management reasons for raising livestock in relatively close quarters that it elects not to prohibit. In light of that largely philosophical viewpoint, the Department asserts that its review of the scientific and professional literature supports its conclusion that the specific practices provide benefits to the health and safety of livestock. Moreover, the Department points out that its regulations address the question of pain and do so by adding the limitation on use of each of these procedures, requiring that they be performed by "knowledgeable persons" who are required to "minimize pain." In this manner, the agency asserts that it has ensured that each procedure will be performed in a manner that is in fact humane.

It is apparent from the record that each of these specific practices is rather controversial. Part of that controversy, however, stems from the larger question of whether farm animals are to be raised in close quarters or in spacious and relatively unconfined surroundings. That philosophical debate about how farm animals are raised and kept in general cannot help but affect one's views about whether some of these procedures are, on the one hand, pointless and cruel, or on the other hand, necessary techniques for managing the livestock in one's care.

That debate about whether domestic livestock should be kept in close quarters or left relatively unconfined, however, is not addressed in the statute. Nothing in the statute suggests that the Legislature intended to embrace the latter and reject the former; the record instead reflects that the agency was charged with finding an appropriate balance between the interests of animal welfare advocates and the need to foster and encourage agriculture in this state. Notwithstanding the ardent views of some of the individuals who have voiced opinions throughout the regulatory process, we do not view our role as including the right or the obligation to weigh in on that debate; we consider instead that it remains within the scope of the agency's expertise to strike a balance between the competing positions of the parties, guided only by the standards of review to which we have adverted.

The record reflects that there is evidence that demonstrates these practices confer a benefit on the animals in light of their living conditions. For example, castration is generally employed to reduce aggression between male animals, including horses and cattle, when they are kept together in a herd. *See, e.g.,* The European Commission, Scientific Committee on Animal Health and Animal Welfare, *The Welfare of Cattle Kept for Beef Production* 75 (April 25, 2001). Similarly, beak trimming is used to reduce such behaviors as cannibalism and pecking within a flock. *See, e.g.,* K. Keshavarz, *The Impact of Genetic Engineering on Plant Breeding,* 50 *Cornell Poultry Pointers* 9 (July 2000); Donald Bell et al., *Animal Care Series: Egg-Type Layer Flock Care Practices* 4 (1998). In a like manner, toe-trimming is performed to prevent turkeys from climbing on one another and causing injury and to prevent them from inflicting injury on their caregivers or handlers. *See, e.g.,* National Turkey Federation, *Animal Care Best Management Practices For the Production of Turkeys* (July 2004). Although there are other management techniques that might achieve the desired results without employing these particular methods, there is sufficient credible evidence in the record to support the agency's conclusion that these techniques can be performed in a humane manner and should be permitted.

Were the issue before this Court merely a matter of deciding whether the scientific evidence supports the use of the procedures at all, our task would be a simple one; were that our task, we would be constrained to conclude that there is sufficient evidence in the record to support the Department's decision that they be permitted. That, however, is not the only question before this Court. Instead, the question is whether there is sufficient support in the record for the Department's decision to specifically permit these practices in the context of its mandate that it adopt regulations that will ensure that the treatment of animals is humane.

As to that more specific question, petitioners argue that the particular procedures cannot be humane if they are performed without the use of anesthetics or other pain management techniques. They point to literature suggesting that all of these procedures are painful, often greatly or severely so. *See, e.g.,* Tina Widowski & Stephanie Torrey, *Neonatal Management Practices* (2002) (explaining that castration is a painful procedure for piglets); *The Welfare of Cattle Kept for Beef Production, supra,* at 80 (concluding that "castration [of cattle] causes severe pain and distress"); AVMA Animal Welfare Committee, *Bird Welfare Positions Modified,* 220 J. Am. Veterinary Med. Assoc. 151 (Jan. 15, 2002) (reporting that removing a bird's beak with a metal blade causes "short-term" and "chronic" pain, as well as "acute stress"); I.J.H. Duncan, *Pain, fear and distress,* Global Conf. Animal Welfare Proc., Feb. 23–25, 2004, at 164–65 (concluding that performing toe-trimming on turkeys without anesthesia causes acute pain).

The Department responds by pointing out that there is scientific evidence that supports the conclusion that use of anesthesia in animals is often not recommended. Moreover, the agency notes that both de-beaking and toe-trimming are specifically limited by reference to the maximum age of the poultry on which these procedures may be performed, itself an effort to limit the consequential pain and distress that these procedures cause.

In addition, the Department asserts that the key to ensuring humane treatment of the animals rests on the requirement that all of these procedures be performed by an "appropriately trained person." For this reason, the agency notes that its regulations do not give broad permission for the use of any of these procedures, but instead limit the practices in a significant way. Each such practice is permitted only if it is "performed in a sanitary manner by a knowledgeable individual and in such a way as to minimize pain." Because of this limitation, the Department asserts that in practice the procedures will only be performed in a humane manner.

Our review of the record certainly supports the conclusion that the agency's determination, in general, that these procedures should be permitted is neither arbitrary nor capricious. We are, as part of this analysis, mindful of the significant limitations imposed relating to the age of the particular livestock on which some of these procedures may be performed, which we see as evidence of the agency's care in the decision-making process. Notwithstanding the foregoing, however, the limitation that the agency asserts is the lynchpin of ensuring that these procedures are performed in a humane manner cannot pass muster. The regulations do not define the terms "sanitary manner," "knowledgeable individual," or "minimize pain," nor is there any objective criteria against which to determine whether any particular individual performing the procedure measures up to these standards. As a result, the regulations that the Department suggests will ensure that the procedures will be accomplished in a humane manner provide no standard against which to test that they are in fact so performed. Although one farm may conclude that a knowledgeable individual, for example, means someone with either veterinary training or some similar level of expertise, another might conclude that merely having performed the procedure in the past, humanely or not, or merely having observed it being performed by others, humanely or not, meets the standard set forth in the regulations.

The lack of specificity in the regulations is illustrated by the Department's argument as set forth in its brief. There, notwithstanding the actual language of the regulations, the agency describes the intent of the regulation to be that an "experienced handler with skill and knowledge" must perform the various procedures, rather than merely a knowledgeable one. Moreover, in the agency's brief, it asserts that because the person performing the procedure will be "experienced" and will have "skill and knowledge," he or she will be able to individually assess and evaluate each animal so as to perform the procedure humanely. In that context, the agency argues that the phrase "minimize pain" provides an objective standard that can be followed and enforced.

Our review compels a contrary conclusion. The agency's subtle rephrasing suggests that the language used in the regulation is insufficient and that only a different, and perhaps a significantly higher standard, would suffice. Perhaps that subtle rephrasing suggests the standard that the Department intended to include in the regulation. Had the Department, for example, defined "knowledgeable individual" in terms of having been taught at a course given by a particular institution, or having had the technique demonstrated by a veterinarian or an agricultural extension agent, or by use of similarly objective criteria, it would likely withstand our scrutiny. Indeed, in the context of the kinds of farming operations prevalent in this State, were the Department to conclude, based on an appropriate record, that there is sufficient support to include within the definition a set of objective criteria that would apply to individuals who have learned practices through others in their farming family, it might also be permissible. It is the failure to give meaning to the term that makes it fall short, rather than the sufficiency of a basis on which to choose to rely on such individuals.

Similarly, without any standard as to what the regulation means in terms of minimizing pain, there is no standard at all. One could, of course, conclude that each of these practices causes pain for a period of time, but that the benefits outweigh that adverse consequence. At the same time, one might conclude that, in light of the mandate of the Legislature that all of these practices be performed only consistent with being humane, they can only be performed if sufficient pain medication or anesthesia is utilized. Alternatively, one might conclude that a particular practice is only humane if it is performed on an animal of a particular age or if a particular instrument is utilized. As it is, the Department adopted none of these standards.

The record reflects that the Department chose not to define the terms that form the basis for the inclusion of these practices as permissible and chose as well not to include specific requirements about the methods to use in performing these procedures. As such, however, this aspect of petitioners' challenge illustrates a significant flaw in this aspect of the regulations. Rather than creating a series of regulations that permit or disallow practices in accordance with whether they are humane, and rather than permitting practices only if performed in a specified manner, the agency instead authorized the practices in general and defined them as being humane by implicitly redefining humane itself. That is, the agency authorized the practices if performed by a knowledgeable person so as to minimize pain and equated that otherwise undefined person's choices with humane. This, however, has resulted in a regulation that is entirely circular in its logic, for it bases the definition of humane solely on the identity of the person performing the task, while creating the definition of that identity by using an undefined category of individuals of no discernable skill or experience.

Although it might be difficult to create a list of permitted practices with sufficient definition to ensure that they are in fact being performed humanely, the Legislature did not direct the Department to only do as much as it believed was expedient. We do not fault the Department for its decision not to attempt to create an exhaustive list of what is permitted and the precise circumstances that pertain. Nor do we dispute the Department's conclusion, as it is one that the Department is well-qualified to make, that these practices are beneficial to the animals or to the farmers. We do not suggest that these procedures cannot be carried out in a manner that is, objectively, humane. In the absence of sufficient guidance in the regulations to ensure that the practices are being performed in a manner that is humane, however, they should not be included within the blanket permission granted in these subsections.

Moreover, by including these practices in the subsections of the regulations that authorize them to be performed, the Department has created an unworkable enforcement scheme. That is to say, there is no standard against which to judge whether a particular individual is "knowledgeable" or whether a method is "sanitary" in the context of an agricultural setting or whether the manner in which the procedure is being performed constitutes a "way as to minimize pain." That being the case, we are constrained to conclude that these aspects of the regulations fail to fix a standard that will ensure that the practices are in fact humane and, at the same time, are too vague to establish a standard that is enforceable.

C.

Petitioners next attack the regulations relating to the use of crates and tethering for swine (sow gestation techniques) and for veal calves (cattle intended to be raised as "Special-Fed veal"), each of which they assert fails to meet the statutory standard of humane. In short, petitioners contend that these techniques do not permit the animals to move freely and to turn around and that they therefore cause significant distress in the animals not consistent with humane treatment. They rely on a number of publications relating to the use of crates for swine gestation that so conclude. *See, e.g.,* European Union, *Report of the Scientific Veterinary Committee, The Welfare of Intensively Kept Pigs,* ¶ 5.2.2, EU Doc XXIV/B3/ScVC/0005/1997, (Sept. 30, 1997) (*"The Welfare of Intensively Kept Pigs"*); J.L. Barnett, et al., *A review of the welfare issues for sows and piglets in relation to housing,* 52 *Austl. J. Agric. Res.* 1–28 (2001); J.N. Marchant et al., *The effects of housing on heart rate of gestating sows during specific behaviours,* 55 *Applied Animal Behav. Sci.* 67, 75 (1997) (concluding that use of sow gestation crates likely causes cardiovascular disease). Petitioners further point out that this practice is banned in Florida, *see* Fla. Const. Art. X, §21 (2005), and is currently being phased out and scheduled to be banned in member states of the European Union by 2013, *see European Union Council Directive 2000/88/EC of 23 October 2001.*

Petitioners refer to similar literature in support of their objections to the use of crates and tethering techniques for raising veal calves. They argue that this scientific evidence demonstrates that close confinement creates stress and causes the animals to engage in behaviors that demonstrate that they are in distress. *See, e.g.,* A.F. Fraser & D.M. Broom, *Farm Animal Behaviour and Welfare* (1997) (finding that confined calves often excessively groom and lick those portions of the body that are within reach and tongue-roll to excess); Ted H. Friend & Gisela R. Dellmeier, *Common Practices and Problems Related to Artificially Rearing Calves: An Ethological Analysis,* 20 *Applied Animal Behav. Sci.* 47–62 (1988) (concluding that confined calves exhibit increased motivation for locomotion and greater incidence of impaired locomotion ability, which can be accompanied by physiological changes indicative of stress); K.A. Cummins & C.J. Brunner, Alabama Agriculture Experiment Station, *Effect of Calf Housing on Plasma Ascorbate and Endocrine and Immune Function,* 74 *J. Dairy Sci.* 1582 (1991) (concluding that confined calves experience stress that weakens immune systems).

In response, the Department also points to an impressive array of scientific studies that, it asserts, support the regulations that permit the use of crating and tethering techniques, particularly as they relate to sows. *See, e.g., The Welfare of Intensively Kept Pigs, supra;* J.J. McGlone et al., *Review: Compilation of the Scientific Literature Comparing Housing Systems for Gestating Sows and Gilts Using Measures of Physiology, Behavior, Performance, and Health,* 20 *Prof. Animal Sci.* 105–06 (2004) (concluding that "gestation stalls (non-tethered) or well managed pens generally (but not in all cases) produced similar states of welfare for pregnant gilts or sows in terms of physiology, behavior, performance and health"); J.L. Barnett et al., *A Review of the Welfare Issues for Sows and Piglets in Relation to Housing,* 52 *Austl. J. Agric. Res.* 1 (2001).

Although there are no veal farms in the State of New Jersey, as a result of which the challenge to the aspect of the regulation that would permit tethering or crates for their management is, perhaps, only theoretical, the Department also defends its decision to include permission for this technique in the regulations as well. In part, it does so by pointing out that the Legislature has twice declined to act on bills that would specifically require that veal calves be maintained in quarters that permit them to turn around completely, *see, e.g.,* Assembly Bill No. 1948 (introduced Feb. 28, 2002); Assembly Bill No. 329 (introduced Jan. 13, 2004), thus suggesting that the Legislature itself has considered this issue and spoken in a voice in full accord with the regulations.

In part, the agency relies on guidelines prepared and distributed by the American Veal Association (AVA). Those guidelines set forth four potential alternatives for housing veal calves, including the individual stall system that the regulations permit. The Department points out that the AVA Guide describes a number of sound reasons that support its decision to permit housing calves in individual stalls, including the reduced likelihood of disease passing among calves, a lessened possibility of fecal contamination, and greater ease in performing health examinations on the calves that result in less stress for the animals.

Our review of the literature relied on by the Department as compared with that cited by petitioners compels us to conclude that the agency's decision to permit these crating and tethering techniques, although controversial, falls well within its area of expertise. Moreover, the record demonstrates that the agency considered a wide variety of scientific and other studies before reaching its decision to include these particular management techniques within the regulations as permitted practices.

Far from simply adopting techniques already in place or embracing practices that serve only the economic ends of the agricultural community as petitioners suggest, these regulations reflect that the Department took seriously its mandate to identify humane practices, but did so in recognition of the need to balance those concerns with the interests of the farmers whose livelihood depends on such techniques and whose existence would be threatened were they to be banned. More to the point, because those aspects of the regulations are supported by sufficient credible evidence in the record, and because they are neither arbitrary nor capricious, we find no basis on which to interfere with them.

D.

Finally, petitioners argue that the regulations permit the transport of sick and downed animals to slaughter, a practice that is not humane. They assert that because the regulations permit cattle with an extremely low BCS to be accepted for slaughter, by implication, their transport is also permitted. *See N.J.A.C.* 2:8-2.2(b)(4)(iv) (cattle with body condition score of 1.0 (emaciated) is permitted at slaughter). They contrast this with the prohibition on the transport of such animals to market, arguing that this makes the regulation arbitrary and capricious. Petitioners argue that because "downed" animals are unable to stand or walk on their own, the process of loading them onto transport trucks is inherently painful. *See, e.g.,* Temple Grandin, *Farm animal welfare during handling, transport, and slaughter,* 204 *J. Am. Veterinary Med. Assoc.* 372 (Feb. 1, 1994) (reporting that "[l]ess than 1% of the cattle handled and transported are downers, but these animals may suffer greatly").

In response, the Department suggests that petitioners have misinterpreted the regulation and have failed to consider the implication of federal law, *see* Federal Meat Inspection Act, 21 *U.S.C.A.* §§ 601–605; Federal Food, Drug, and Cosmetic Act, 21 *U.S.C.A.* §§ 301–399, that bears upon the slaughter of disabled cattle for use in the food chain. In light of those significant limitations, the Department argues that a downed animal simply will not be transported for slaughter and that the only instance of a sick or downed animal being transported at all would, in all likelihood, involve taking it to a veterinarian for treatment.

Our review of the record reveals that the Department's reliance on the federal authorities does not completely address petitioners' concerns. As we understand it, the federal authorities on which the Department has relied are only designed to prevent downed animals from entering the food supply but do not otherwise prohibit them from being transported. The question thus remains whether the regulations, adopted by the Department, that permit their transport for slaughter can be sustained. This aspect of the regulations must be understood in its appropriate context.

The relevant regulations begin with a general requirement that sick or injured cattle must be treated or euthanized. In fact, the regulation requires that treatment be "prompt" and that euthanasia be "humane." The regulations specifically limit acceptable methods of euthanasia, incorporating by reference standards adopted by the AVMA. Those standards include detailed information about acceptable methods as to each type of animal and about how each is performed. As a result, the options available to a farmer who needs to euthanize an animal are limited.

The regulations also include a subsection that governs downed cattle. These regulations, like their federal counterparts, prohibit transport to a livestock market, but do not prohibit transport for other purposes. However, the regulations specifically prohibit dragging such an animal while it is conscious and require that it be treated humanely, even if it is going to be slaughtered or euthanized,

During the notice and comment period, one commenter urged the Department to extend the prohibition on transport of downed cattle to livestock markets so that transport for slaughter would also be banned. 37 *N.J.R.* 2472 (July 5, 2005). The Department declined to do so, explaining that "[w]hile owners of downed animals may have the animal euthanized on the farm, the Department believes it is appropriate to provide some flexibility to owners on where and when slaughter may take place." *Ibid.* Although there is evidence in the record that a downed animal "may suffer greatly," in light of the strict limits on permitted euthanasia methods, we cannot conclude that the Department's decision to permit farmers the option of choosing transport for slaughter is arbitrary or capricious. We therefore perceive of no failure on the part of the agency in its decision to adopt this regulation that requires our intervention.

VIII.

Our consideration of the issues raised in this appeal and our review of the record have led us to conclude that certain aspects of these regulations cannot be sustained. We do not intend, however, to suggest that the defects in the regulations are pervasive or that all of the many practices that the Department specifically considered and permitted cannot be performed in a humane manner. To be sure, we have concluded that the "routine husbandry practices" and the "knowledgeable individual and in such a way as to minimize pain" safe harbors cannot be sustained as written, but neither of these determinations effects a ban on any of the particular practices. Rather, any practice, technique, or procedure not otherwise prohibited by the regulations may be utilized by any farmer, risking only that the practice, technique, or procedure will be challenged by an appropriate enforcement authority as inhumane....

Our decision, therefore, should not be understood to be a ban on the continuation of any specific practice, but merely a recognition that some of the standards that purport to define them so as to ensure that they are actually performed in a manner that meets the statute's command that all such practices be humane have fallen short.

IX.

The facial challenge to the regulations in their entirety is rejected. The specific challenges to the reliance on "routine husbandry practices" as defined in the regulations, and to the reliance on "knowledgeable individual and in such a way as to minimize pain" are sustained. The specific challenges to the practices, with the exception of the practice of tail docking, are otherwise rejected.

The judgment of the Appellate Division is affirmed in part and reversed in part and the matter is remanded to the Department for further proceedings consistent with this opinion.

Notes

1. A variety of voluntary efforts address consumer concern about animal welfare.

An increasing number of producers advertise practices that provide significantly higher standards of animal welfare. For example, Niman Ranch is a network of over 650 independent farmers and ranchers who adhere to a strict protocol of animal welfare and sustainability standards. See the Niman Ranch website, available at http://www.nimanranch.com. *See also*, White Oak Pastures, a grass-fed beef operation that stresses the animal welfare advantages. Information including a video on the operation, *Cud,* is available at http://www.whiteoakpastures.com.

Joel Salatin's Polyface Farm is featured in Michael Pollan's book OMNIVORE'S DILEMMA, A NATURAL HISTORY OF FOUR MEALS, and in the documentary film, FOOD INC. Saltin is not only a successful producer of "pasture-based, beyond-organic, local-market" meat, he is an outspoken advocate for "healing the land, healing the food, healing the economy, and healing the culture" through more natural production methods. *See*, http://www.polyfacefarms.com.

Some major food retailers have developed humane animal care standards that their suppliers must follow. Chipotle Restaurants advertises "food with integrity" and claims that 100% of the pork used in their products comes from "ranchers whose pigs are raised outside or in deeply bedded pens, are never given antibiotics and are fed a vegetarian diet"; eighty-five percent of their beef comes from ranches that "meet or exceed naturally raised standards"; and, thirty-five percent of the dairy products served come from pasture-raised cows, with none from cows treated with rBGH. http://www.chipotle.com The Humane Society lists Subway, Denny's Burger King, Wendy's, Quiznos, Sonic, IHOP, Carl's Jr., Hardee's, and Red Robin as all having adopted animal welfare standards of some kind.

Industry groups have published voluntary standards for care that they encourage members to meet, including the American Meat Institute, American Sheep Industry Association, National Cattlemen's Beef Association, National Chicken Council, Pork Board, and United Egg Producers. Geoffrey S. Becker, *Humane Treatment of Farm Animals: Overview and Issues*, Congressional Research Service, Report No.RS21978, 2–3 (March 9, 2010). These standards generally support most of the customary industrialized practices.

Third party private certifications are available, including Certified Humane Raised and Handled (http://www.certifiedhumane.org), and American Humane Certified (http://www.americanhumane.org).

For a discussion of the difficulties associated with meat production claims and food labeling, see Susan A. Schneider, *Reconnecting Consumers and Producers: On a Path Toward a Sustainable Food & Agriculture Policy*, Drake J. Agric. L. 92–94 (2009) (discussing production claims in meat production, focusing on "antibiotic-free chicken").

2. Federal farm animal welfare legislation has been proposed, but has not been enacted. The Congressional Research Service reports:

> In the 110th Congress, a key provision in the potentially sweeping *Farm Animals Anti-Cruelty Act* (H.R. 6202) stated, "[w]hoever, without justification, kills, mutilates, disfigures, tortures, or intentionally causes an animal held for commercial use pain or suffering, or has responsibility for an animal held for commercial use and fails to provide food, water, shelter, and health care as is necessary to assure the animal's health and well-being appropriate to the animal's age and species," is subject to penalties of up to one year in jail and/or $100,000 in fines. "Commercial use" would mean "use, or intended for use, as food or fiber or for food or fiber production." A separate bill, H.R. 1726, would have required the federal government to purchase products derived from animals only if they were raised according to humane standards (i.e., had adequate shelter with sufficient space to walk and move around with limbs fully extended, had adequate food and water with no starvation or force-feeding, and had adequate veterinary care).
>
> A differing version of H.R. 1726 is pending in the 111th Congress. *The Prevention of Farm Animal Cruelty Act* (H.R. 4733), introduced on March 2, 2010, would prohibit a federal agency from purchasing any food product derived from a "covered animal"—a pregnant pig, a veal calf, or egg-laying hen—unless the animal was raised with adequate space to "stand up, lie down, and turn around freely" and to "fully extend all limbs." (These phrases are defined more specifically in the bill.) The measure also exempts covered animals from this compliance requirement during lawful transport; during slaughter, in compliance with the Humane Methods of Slaughter Act; in lawful rodeo, state or county, or other exhibitions; in lawful scientific or agricultural research; while undergoing veterinary procedures; and, in the case of a pregnant pig, during the seven-day period immediately before the expected birth date.

Geoffrey S. Becker, *Humane Treatment of Farm Animals: Overview and Issues*, Congressional Research Service, Report No.RS21978, 2–3 (March 9, 2010).

3. The European Union adopted "The Five Freedoms" as policy guidance for setting minimum animal welfare guidelines. These are:

- Freedom from hunger and thirst: by ready access to fresh water and a diet to maintain full health and vigour;

- Freedom from discomfort: by providing an appropriate environment including shelter and a comfortable resting area;

- Freedom from pain, injury and disease: by prevention or rapid diagnosis and treatment;

- Freedom to express normal behaviour: by providing sufficient space, proper facilities and company of the animal's own kind;

- Freedom from fear and distress: by ensuring conditions and treatment which avoid mental suffering.

See http://ec.europa.eu/food/animal/welfare/actionplan/actionplan_en.htm.

Many practices associated with U.S industrialized animal production have been severely restricted or banned under EU regulations. *See* http://ec.europa.eu/food/animal/welfare/farm/index_en.htm.

B. Humane Slaughter Standards

As Dr. Temple Grandin states succinctly on her animal welfare website, "[t]reating animals in a humane manner is the right thing to do." (http://www.grandin.com/welfare/public.welfare.html.) Dr. Grandin, a Doctor of Animal Science and professor at Colorado State University, is renowned for her work in animal behavior studies and her design of humane slaughter facilities. While basic animal welfare is clearly a sufficient reason to support humane slaughter standards, Dr. Grandin notes that there are also economic reasons that support the humane treatment of animals at the time that they are slaughtered. The use of electric prods can bruise meat and in pigs can result in a pale, soft texture. Excitement and fear also negatively impacts meat, with research studies finding that agitated cattle produce tougher meat. Labor costs, worker injury rates, and equipment repair costs are lowered if animal stress is lessened. *See,* Temple Grandin, *The Effect of Economics on the Welfare of Cattle, Pigs, Sheep, and Poultry,* available at http://www.grandin.com/welfare/ economic.effects.welfare.html.

Nevertheless, maintaining humane slaughter conditions remains a challenging goal for the meat industry. In 2001, the Washington Post published a disturbing investigative report on modern slaughterhouses. Joby Warrick, *They Die Piece by Piece: In Overtaxed Plants, Humane Treatment of Cattle is Often a Battle Lost,* WASH. POST (April 10, 2001), available at https://hfa.org/hot_topic/wash_post.html. The report detailed animals that were still alive and conscious as they were processed. One experienced worker, a "second-legger" whose job was "cutting the hocks off carcasses as they whirl past at a rate of 309 per hour" reported animals alive when they reached his station, some surviving as far as "the tail cutter, the belly ripper, or the hide puller."

In 2008, an alarming undercover video from the Westland/Hallmark Meat Co. in Chino, California showed workers using fork lifts and electric prods in an attempt to force "downer" cows, i.e., those too ill or weak to stand without assistance, onto their feet so that they could be slaughtered. *See, Rampant Animal Cruelty at California Slaughter Plant* (with video posted) on the Humane Society website at http:www.humanesociety.org/news/news/2008/01/undercover_investigation_013008.html.

In 2009, the Humane Society released another undercover video showing highly disturbing abuse of calves at a Vermont slaughterhouse. *Abused Calves at Vermont Slaugh-*

ter Plant (with video posted) on the Humane Society website at http:www.humane soci-ety.org/news/news/2009/10/calf_investigation_103009.html. USDA Secretary Vilsack and Vermont Agriculture Secretary Roger Allbee were credited with taking immediate action to close the plant and bring criminal charges, as the actions violated the Humane Methods of Slaughter Act.

United States Code
Title 7. Agriculture
Chapter 48. Humane Methods of Livestock Slaughter

§ 1902. Humane methods

No method of slaughtering or handling in connection with slaughtering shall be deemed to comply with the public policy of the United States unless it is humane. Either of the following two methods of slaughtering and handling are hereby found to be humane:

(a) in the case of cattle, calves, horses, mules, sheep, swine, and other livestock, all animals are rendered insensible to pain by a single blow or gunshot or an electrical, chemical or other means that is rapid and effective, before being shack-led, hoisted, thrown, cast, or cut; or

(b) by slaughtering in accordance with the ritual requirements of the Jewish faith or any other religious faith that prescribes a method of slaughter whereby the animal suffers loss of consciousness by anemia of the brain caused by the si-multaneous and instantaneous severance of the carotid arteries with a sharp in-strument and handling in connection with such slaughtering.

The USDA Food Safety & Inspection Service (FSIS) is charged with enforcing the Humane Methods of Slaughter Act (HMSA). Regulations promulgated by the FSIS are found at 9 C.F.R. parts 313 and 500, and a directive (6900.2) for inspection personnel is also available. The directive covers the proper maintenance of pens and rampways; how to handle livestock during unloading and during movement to the stunning area; the proper use of electric prods and other instruments; and the approved methods of stunning the animals prior to killing and processing.

The USDA reports that there are approximately 6,200 federally inspected meat and poultry slaughtering and processing establishments. More than 900 of them slaughter livestock and are subject to the HMSA. Poultry are not considered livestock and are not protected under the HMSA. No federal law provides any regulation of poultry slaughter. For a discussion of the history of this exclusion, see *Levine v. Vilsack*, 540 F.Supp.2d 1113 (N.D. Cal. 2008) (rejecting a challenge to the definition of livestock), *vacated and remanded*, 587 F.3d 986 (9th Cir. 2009) (rejecting the challenge on standing grounds).

Lisa Shames
Humane Methods of Slaughter Act: Actions Are Needed to Strengthen Enforcement
U.S. Government Accountability Office, GAO-10-203 (February 2010)

Concerns about the humane handling and slaughter of livestock have increased in recent years, particularly after a widely publicized video in 2008 of actions at a slaughter plant in California. The 2008 video showed employees at the plant delivering electric shocks to nonambulatory cows, spraying them with high-pressure water hoses, and ramming them with a forklift to force them to rise for slaughter. The U.S. Department of Agriculture (USDA) suspended operations at the California plant, citing the egregious nature of its actions and its failure to maintain and implement controls to prevent the inhumane handling and slaughter of nonambulatory cows at the facility. More recently, in October 2009, USDA received a video recording of employees at a Vermont slaughter plant that shows employees skinning and decapitating conscious veal calves, which are about 1-week old. USDA and the state of Vermont suspended the operating licenses for this plant, effectively shutting down operations, pending the results of an ongoing investigation. Such actions may violate the Humane Methods of Slaughter Act of 1978, as amended (HMSA). HMSA prohibits the inhumane treatment of livestock in slaughter plants and generally requires that animals be rendered insensible—typically referred to as stunning—before proceeding with slaughter.

USDA's Food Safety and Inspection Service (FSIS) is responsible for ensuring the safety of meat and other products in the United States, as well as for enforcing HMSA. Since 2002, Congress has urged USDA to fully enforce HMSA, directed it to enhance staffing for HMSA-related inspections and enforcement, and designated funding to develop and maintain a system for tracking the amount of time that inspectors spend on HMSA enforcement.

We have previously reported on weaknesses in FSIS's management of HMSA, particularly its reporting of violations and use of inconsistent criteria for enforcement.[1] In 2004, we recommended that FSIS take several actions to improve HMSA oversight, including providing informative data on HMSA violations and assessing whether FSIS resources are sufficient to effectively enforce the act. In 2008, USDA's Office of Inspector General reported that FSIS management controls over preslaughter activities could be strengthened to minimize the possibility of egregious humane handling events.[2]

In this context, you asked us to (1) evaluate FSIS's efforts to enforce HMSA, (2) identify the extent to which FSIS tracks recent trends in FSIS inspection resources for enforcing HMSA, and (3) evaluate FSIS's efforts to develop a strategy to guide HMSA enforcement.

To evaluate FSIS's efforts to enforce HMSA, we examined a sample of FSIS noncompliance reports, suspension data, and district veterinary medical specialist reports in all 15 of FSIS's district offices for fiscal years 2005 through 2009. To assess the reliability of these data, we examined the data for obvious errors in completeness and accuracy, reviewed existing documentation about the systems that produced the data, and questioned knowledgeable officials about the data and systems. We determined that the data were sufficiently reliable for the purposes of this report, with any limitations noted in the text. From May 2009 through July 2009, we also surveyed inspectors-in-charge—those responsible for reporting on humane handling enforcement in the plants—from a random sample of inspectors-in-charge at 257 livestock slaughter plants. We selected the

1. GAO, *Humane Methods of Slaughter Act: USDA Has Addressed Some Problems but Still Faces Enforcement Challenges*, GAO-04-247 (Washington, D.C.: Jan. 30, 2004). Also, see GAO, *Humane Methods of Handling and Slaughter: Public Reporting on Violations Can Identify Enforcement Challenges and Enhance Transparency*, GAO-08-686T (Washington, D.C.: Apr. 17, 2008).

2. U.S. Department of Agriculture, Office of Inspector General, Great Plains Region, Audit Report: *Evaluation of FSIS Management Controls Over Pre-Slaughter Activities*, Report No. 24601-0007KC (November 2008).

sample of 257 plants, stratified by size, from a universe of 782 plants, and then surveyed inspectors-in-charge at the sample plants. Our sample allows us to make estimates about the observations and opinions of all inspectors-in-charge at U.S. slaughter plants. We obtained an overall survey response rate of 93 percent.[3] This report does not contain all of the results from our survey. The survey can be viewed at GAO-10-244SP. We also met with key officials from FSIS's Office of Field Operations who are responsible for implementing HMSA at the headquarters level. To understand district officials' perspectives on HMSA enforcement, we conducted semi-structured interviews with each of FSIS's 15 district veterinary medical specialists (DVMS) and 15 district managers. We also obtained the views of experts in humane handling to understand key principles of humane handling techniques and enforcement. In particular, we consulted with Dr. Temple Grandin, a world-renowned expert on animal welfare, who provided her expert opinion on particular humane handling incidents we identified as possible HMSA violations.[4] To identify the extent to which FSIS tracks recent trends in inspection resources for enforcing HMSA, we reviewed FSIS funding and staffing data for each district. We also conducted semi-structured interviews with resource management analysts in each of FSIS's 15 district offices and interviewed key officials in the Resource Management and Planning Office within the Office of Field Operations. To assess FSIS's efforts to develop a strategy to enforce HMSA, we reviewed relevant FSIS strategies, including the most recent FSIS Strategic Plan FY 2008 through FY 2013, the Office of Field Operations' Workforce Plan, and other relevant planning documents....

Background

In 2008, the most recently available data, more than 153 million cattle, sheep, hogs, and other animals ultimately destined to provide meat for human consumption were slaughtered at about 800 slaughter plants throughout the United States that engage in interstate commerce. Under federal law, meat-processing facilities that engage in interstate commerce must have federal inspectors on site. FSIS classifies plants according to size and the number of employees. Specifically, large plants have 500 or more employees; small plants have from 10 to 499 employees; and very small plants have fewer than 10 employees, or annual sales of less than $2.5 million. Under HMSA, FSIS inspectors are to ensure that animals are humanely treated from the moment they arrive at a plant until they are slaughtered. FSIS deploys these inspectors from 15 district offices nationwide....

After livestock arrive at a slaughter plant, plant employees monitor their movements as they are unloaded from trucks to holding pens and eventually led into the stunning chute. Plant employees typically restrain an animal in the chute and stun it by using one of several devices—carbon dioxide gas, an electrical current, a captive bolt gun,[5] or a gunshot—that, as required by HMSA regulations, is rapid and effective in rendering the animal insensible. Under HMSA, animals must be rendered insensible—that is, unable to feel pain—on the first stun before being shackled, hoisted on the bleed rail, thrown,

3. All full sample percentage estimates from the survey have margins of error at the 95 percent confidence level of plus or minus 7 percentage points or less, unless otherwise noted. Percentage estimates by plant size have margins of error at the 95 percent confidence level of plus or minus 10 percentage points or less, unless otherwise noted.

4. Dr. Grandin has served as a consultant to industry and FSIS, written extensively on modern methods of livestock handling, and has designed slaughter facilities that have helped improve animal welfare in the United States.

5. A captive bolt gun contains a steel bolt—powered by either compressed air or a blank cartridge—that is driven into an animal's brain and then retracted into the gun, which resets the bolt for the next animal. This gun has the same effect as a gun with live bullets but is safer than a firearm.

cast, or cut. According to the expert we consulted, animals on the bleed rail that exhibit any of the following signs are considered sensible and would therefore need to be restunned:

- natural blinking,
- lifting head straight up and keeping it up (righting reflex),
- rhythmic breathing, and
- vocalizing.

Once the animals are considered stunned, they are shackled and hoisted onto a processing line, where their throats are cut, and they are fully bled before processing continues. HMSA exempts only ritual slaughter, such as kosher and halal slaughter, from the HMSA requirement that animals be rendered insensible on the first blow.... FSIS has issued a variety of regulations and directives instructing FSIS inspectors on how to enforce HMSA. Overall, the regulations emphasize the minimization of "excitement and discomfort" to the animals and require that they are effectively stunned before being slaughtered. In 2003, FSIS guidance on humane handling enforcement stated that inspectors were to determine whether a humane handling incident does, or will immediately lead to, an injured animal or inhumane treatment. The guidance also specified the types of actions inspectors should take when these situations occur. Also in 2003, FSIS began providing "humane interactive knowledge exchange" scenarios as an educational tool to enhance inspectors' understanding of appropriate enforcement actions. These eight written scenarios, available on FSIS's Web site, provide examples of inhumane incidents and suggest enforcement actions. In 2005, the agency issued additional guidance specifying egregious humane handling situations.[6] This guidance defines egregious as any act that is cruel to animals or a condition that is ignored and leads to the harming of animals. The guidance provided the following examples of egregious acts:

- making cuts on or skinning conscious animals,
- excessively beating or prodding ambulatory or nonambulatory disabled animals,
- dragging conscious animals,
- driving animals off semitrailers over a drop-off without providing adequate unloading facilities so that animals fall to the ground,
- running equipment over animals,
- stunning animals and then allowing them to regain consciousness,
- leaving disabled livestock exposed to adverse climate conditions while awaiting disposition, or
- otherwise intentionally causing unnecessary pain and suffering to animals.

If inspectors determine that an egregious humane handling incident has occurred, they may suspend inspection at the plant immediately, effectively shutting down the plant's entire operation, and determine corrective actions with plant management and the district office.

In 2008, after the reported inhumane handling incident in California, which was at the Westland/Hallmark plant, FSIS expanded its guidance to include two more examples of egregious actions for which inspectors may suspend a plant: (1) multiple failed stuns, especially in the absence of corrective actions, and (2) dismemberment of live animals.

---

6. U.S. Department of Agriculture, Food Safety and Inspection Service, FSIS Notice 12-05, Documentation of Humane Handling Activities (Feb. 18, 2005).

According to FSIS guidance, when FSIS inspectors observe a violation of HMSA or its implementing regulations and determine that animals are being injured or treated inhumanely, they are to take both of the following enforcement actions, which may restrict a facility's ability to operate:

- *Issue a noncompliance report.* This report documents the humane handling violation and the actions needed to correct the deficiency in cases where the animal may be injured or harmed. Inspectors are also directed to notify plant management when issuing a noncompliance report.

- *Issue a regulatory control action.* Inspectors place a regulatory control action or a reject tag on a piece of equipment or an area of the plant that was involved in harming or inhumanely treating an animal. This tag is used to alert plant management to the need to quickly respond to violations that they can readily address. The tag prohibits the use of a particular piece of equipment or area of the facility until the equipment is made acceptable to the inspector.

When inspectors determine that an egregious humane handling incident has occurred, in addition to issuing a noncompliance report and regulatory control action, FSIS may also take the following actions:

- *Suspend plant operations.* An on-site FSIS supervisor—known as an inspector-in-charge—can initiate an action to suspend plant operations when an inspector observes egregious abuse to the animals. The inspector must document the facts that serve as the basis of the suspension action in a written memorandum of interview and promptly provide that information electronically to district officials. Ultimately, district officials assess the facts supporting the suspension, take any final action, and notify officials in headquarters.

- *Withdraw the plant's grant of inspection.* If the plant fails to respond to FSIS's concerns about repeated and/or serious violations, the district offices may decide to withdraw all inspectors. Without FSIS inspectors on site, the plant's products cannot enter interstate or foreign commerce. The FSIS Administrator may file a complaint to withdraw the plant's grant of inspection and if the grant of inspection is withdrawn, the plant must then reapply for and be awarded a grant of inspection before it may resume operations.

FSIS employs inspectors at plants and in FSIS districts to help enforce HMSA and its food safety inspections. In the plant, FSIS employs inspectors-in-charge, online and offline inspectors, and relief inspectors. Inspectors-in-charge are the chief inspectors in the plant and may or may not be veterinarians. These inspectors are responsible for reporting humane handling activities for each shift, as well as carrying out food safety responsibilities, and making enforcement decisions in consultation with district officials when necessary. Online inspectors are typically assigned specific duties on the slaughter line, such as inspecting carcasses and animal heads; however, they may also perform some humane handling inspection duties as well. Offline inspectors conduct a variety of inspection activities throughout the plant and may also perform some humane handling inspection activities. FSIS also employs permanent relief inspectors, who step in for plant inspectors who are absent for a period of time, and may also observe humane handling. The plant inspectors and the inspectors-in-charge are supervised by frontline supervisors, who oversee multiple plants. Each plant has at least one FSIS veterinarian who is responsible for examining livestock prior to slaughter and performing humane handling activities. Some plants may require two veterinarians, depending on the volume of animals slaughtered at the plant and the number of operating shifts....

Although FSIS does not require inspectors to observe the entire handling and slaughter process during a shift, it requires inspectors-in-charge to record the amount of time that the FSIS inspectors collectively devoted to observing humane handling during one shift. The inspectors-in-charge enter this information into a data tracking system known as the Humane Activities Tracking System.

At the district level, the DVMS in each of FSIS's 15 districts serves as the liaison between the district office and headquarters on all humane handling matters. These employees are directed to visit each plant within their district over a 12- to 18-month period and review the humane handling practices at each plant. DVMSs may also coordinate the verification of humane handling activities and educate plant inspectors on relevant humane handling information in directives, notices, and other information from headquarters through the district office to inspectors in the field.

Industry groups and animal welfare organizations have recently recommended actions to improve HMSA enforcement. As an expert witness, in 2008 testimony, Dr. Grandin proposed that FSIS guidance on humane handling be clearer — especially in determining when humane handling incidents at slaughter plants should be considered egregious violations of the HMSA.[7] She has also suggested that FSIS adopt a numerical scoring system — which has been adopted by the American Meat Institute — to determine how well animals were being stunned and handled at the plants. The system has different standards for different species of animal and can be adjusted to fit plants that slaughter fewer animals. Overall, the system seeks to reduce the subjective nature of inspections by using objective measures to help slaughter plants improve their humane handling performance. In addition, the Humane Society of the United States has proposed a variety of reforms to strengthen HMSA enforcement, including requiring FSIS inspectors to observe the entire humane handling and slaughter process during a shift.

Weaknesses Persist in FSIS's Enforcement, Training and Guidance, and Data Management

According to our survey results and analysis of FSIS data, inspectors have not taken consistent actions to enforce HMSA once they have identified a violation. These inconsistencies may be due, in part, to weaknesses in FSIS's guidance and training for key inspection staff. While FSIS expects its inspectors to use their professional judgment based on the guidance in deciding enforcement actions, industry and others are using other tools to assist their efforts to improve humane handling performance. Furthermore, although FSIS has taken steps to correct data weaknesses in HMSA reporting that we noted in 2004, it has not used these data to analyze HMSA enforcement across districts and plants to identify inconsistent enforcement. For these reasons, FSIS cannot ensure that it is preventing the abuse of livestock at slaughter plants or that it is meeting its responsibility to fully enforce HMSA.

GAO Survey Results and FSIS Data Indicate Inconsistent Enforcement

According to FSIS officials, inspectors are to use their judgment in deciding whether to suspend a plant's operations or take the less stringent enforcement action (that is, issue a noncompliance report and a regulatory control action) when a humane handling violation occurs. For example, FSIS guidance is unclear on what constitutes excessive elec-

---

7. Dr. Temple Grandin, testimony before the Domestic Policy Subcommittee, House Committee on Oversight and Government Reform, "After the Beef Recall: Exploring Greater Transparency in the Meat Industry" (Washington, D.C.: Apr. 17, 2008).

trical prodding, such as the number of times an animal can be prodded before the inspector should consider the prodding to be excessive and therefore egregious. According to FSIS's guidance, if the inspector determines that the action was egregious, the inspector may also choose to suspend plant operations but is not required to do so.

U.S. meat industry representatives have expressed concerns in interviews about the inconsistency of HMSA enforcement across districts. For example, according to American Meat Institute officials, the inconsistency in HMSA enforcement is the single most critical issue for the industry; furthermore, one official noted that a number of the differences in interpretation of HMSA compliance are related to determining whether or not an animal is sensible after stunning. In addition, the expert we consulted testified in April 2008 that FSIS inspectors need better training and clear directives to improve consistency of HMSA enforcement.[8]

Our survey results indicate differences in the enforcement actions that inspectors reported they would take when faced with a humane handling violation. In our survey, we asked inspectors their views on electrically prodding over 50 out of 100 animals.... Under FSIS's guidance, inspectors are directed to issue a noncompliance report and take a regulatory control action in cases of excessive electrical prodding, but suspension is not required. However, the expert we consulted told us that she considers these cases to be egregious humane handling violations that should result in suspensions. In addition, according to an FSIS training scenario, electrical prods are never to be used on the anus, eyes, or other sensitive parts of the animal.

[Forty-nine] percent of the inspectors surveyed reported that they would either take a regulatory control action, such as placing a reject tag on a piece of equipment or suspending a plant's operations for electrical prodding of most animals, and 29 percent reported that they would take none of these actions or did not know what action to take for electrical prodding most animals. Furthermore, 67 percent of the inspectors surveyed reported that they would either take a regulatory control action or suspend operations for electrical prodding in the rectal area, and 10 percent reported that they would take none of these actions or did not know what action to take for electrical prodding in the rectal area. FSIS regulations prohibit electrical prodding that the inspector considers to be excessive.[9] FSIS guidance also states that excessive beating or prodding of ambulatory or nonambulatory disabled animals is egregious abuse—and may therefore warrant suspension of plant operations. From inspectors' compliance reports, we identified several specific incidents in which inspectors did not either take a regulatory control action or suspend plant operations. For example:

- In 2008, in the Denver district, the FSIS inspector reported observing a plant employee excessively using an electrical prod as his primary method to move the cattle—using the prod approximately 55 times to move about 46 head of cattle into the stun box. Cattle vocalized at least 15 times, which the inspector believed indicated a high level of stress. The FSIS inspector stated that this incident constituted excessive use of the electrical prod. As stated in FSIS guidance, excessive use of an electrical prod is an egregious violation that calls for the issuance of both a noncompliance report and a regulatory control action and for which an inspector may suspend plant operations. In this instance, the inspector stated that he

---

8. Dr. Temple Grandin, testimony before the Domestic Policy Subcommittee, House Committee on Oversight and Government Reform, "After the Beef Recall: Exploring Greater Transparency in the Meat Industry" (Washington, D.C. Apr. 17, 2008).

9. 9 C.F.R. § 313.2(b).

had issued a noncompliance report. The inspector did not state that he took a regulatory control action and did not suspend operations at the plant, as the guidance allows. In the opinion of the expert we consulted, this was an egregious instance that should have resulted in a suspension.

- In 2007, in the Minneapolis district, an FSIS inspector reported observing plant employees using the electrical prods excessively to move hogs into the stunning chute. The animals became excited, jumping on top of one another, and vocalizing excessively. From the noncompliance report, it is unclear what, if any, regulatory actions were taken. According to FSIS regulations, electrical prods are to be used as little as possible in order to minimize excitement and injury; any use of such implements that an inspector considers excessive is prohibited.

- In 2008, in the Dallas district, the FSIS inspector reported that a plant employee used an electrical prod to repeatedly shock cows in the face and neck in an effort to turn them around in an overcrowded area. The inspector deemed the use of the electrical prod excessive, but the report does not indicate whether any regulatory control action was taken.

With regard to stunning, our survey results and review of noncompliance records also show inconsistent enforcement actions when humane handling violations occurred. [Twenty-three] percent of inspectors reported they would suspend operations, while 38 percent would issue a regulatory control action for multiple unsuccessful captive bolt gun stuns. Similarly, 17 percent reported they would suspend operations for multiple misplaced electrical stuns, and 37 percent would issue a regulatory control action. According to FSIS guidance, egregious abuses that could result in a plant suspension include stunning animals and allowing them to regain consciousness and multiple attempts to stun an animal, especially in the absence of immediate corrective measures. However, it is unclear when a suspension is warranted, even if the acts are deemed to be egregious. FSIS's guidance simply states that an inspector-in-charge may immediately suspend the plant if there is an egregious humane handling violation—however, there is no clear directive to do so in guidance. In the opinion of the expert we consulted, if over 10 percent of the animals require a second shot or if over 5 percent of pigs had experienced an improperly placed electrical stun,[10] plant operations should be suspended. FSIS agreed that these incidents are troubling, and possibly egregious, but did not comment further.

We also identified several incidents in FSIS's noncompliance reports in which inspectors did not suspend plant operations or take a regulatory control action. For example,

- In 2009, in the Raleigh district, a plant employee stunned a bull twice in the head with a captive bolt, but the bull remained sensible. Instead of restunning the animal with the captive bolt gun, the employee then drove a steel instrument used to sharpen knives into the open hole in the bull's head in an attempt to make the animal insensible. The bull rose to its feet and vocalized in apparent pain until it was eventually rendered insensible with a bullet to the head. FSIS regulations do not recognize this steel instrument as an acceptable stunning method.[11] However the inspector placed a reject tag on the stun box and cited the incident as egregious in the noncompliance report but did not suspend operations. In the opinion of

---

10. Electrical stuns must be properly placed on the animal to ensure effective stunning; that is, the current must go through the brain.

11. *See* 9 C.F.R. §§ 313.5, 313.15, 313.16, 313.30.

the expert we consulted, this incident was an example of an egregious HMSA violation that should have resulted in a suspension.

- In 2008, in the Denver district, the inspector reported that the first attempt to stun a bull with a captive bolt stunner appeared to misfire, resulting in smoke and the smell of powder and no response by the bull.[12] A second stunning attempt appeared to render the bull unconscious in the stun box. However, it was followed by a third stunning attempt while the bull was still in the stun box. The employee then allowed the bull to roll out into the pit for shackling. The bull appeared unconscious but still was breathing rhythmically, indicating that the animal was still sensible. The employee then entered the pit and stunned the bull again and started conversing with another employee. The bull once again started breathing rhythmically while being shackled, a sign that the bull still had not been rendered insensible to pain as the law requires. In response, the DVMS asked the employee to stun the bull again, and this stun rendered the bull unconscious and no longer breathing rhythmically. According to the report, the plant received a noncompliance report, but no regulatory control action was taken, as called for by guidance. In the opinion of our expert consultant, a regulatory control action should have been taken in this case because of multiple stuns that left the animal breathing rhythmically.

We also identified several other types of humane handling violations for which inspectors took inconsistent enforcement actions. For example, according to FSIS's regulations, animals are not to be moved from one area to another faster than a normal walking speed, with minimum excitement and discomfort. A faster speed could result in animals being driven over each other. Furthermore, animals in a holding pen are to have access to water and, if held longer than 24 hours, access to food. According to the expert we consulted, deliberately driving animals over the top of others and failing to provide water for animals held over a weekend are egregious humane handling violations and, in her opinion, these actions should result in plant suspensions. However, ... although most inspectors would take an enforcement action, including a regulatory control action, for these violations, 40 percent of inspectors surveyed would suspend plant operations for driving animals over each other, and 55 percent would suspend plant operations for failing to provide water over the weekend.

The lack of consistency in enforcement actions is highlighted by inspectors' responses to our question about when they would suspend plant operations. According to our survey results, less than one-third of the inspectors-in-charge in the very small and small plants reported that they would be likely to suspend plant operations for multiple incorrect placements of electrical stunners and electrical prodding of most animals. Inspectors-in-charge at large plants with more frequently reported plant suspensions had more stringent views on enforcement actions than those at very small plants. For example, inspectors-in-charge at large plants more frequently reported suspensions as the enforcement actions that should be taken compared with inspectors-in-charge at very small plants.... For example, large plants were more likely than very small plants to suspend plant operations for multiple incorrect electrical stuns, driving animals over the top of others, and electrically prodding most animals.

We found similar indications of inconsistent enforcement across districts. According to our analysis of FSIS data, from calendar years 2005 through 2007, 10 districts of 15 FSIS

---

12. The inspector's report did not indicate whether the original captive bolt stun gun was functioning properly.

districts — responsible for overseeing 44 percent of all animals slaughtered nationwide — suspended 35 plants for HMSA violations. The remaining 5 districts — responsible for overseeing 56 percent of all livestock slaughtered nationwide — did not suspend any plants.[13] For example, the Des Moines and the Chicago districts, which oversee the first and second highest volume of livestock slaughtered nationwide, respectively, were among the 5 districts that had never issued a suspension until February 2008, according to our analysis.

Before 2008, these five districts issued noncompliance reports, sometimes with regulatory control actions, such as a reject tag on a piece of equipment, rather than suspending an entire plant's operations. For example, in 2007, in the Lawrence district, a hog was observed walking around the stunning chute grunting and bleeding from the mouth and forehead. The animal had been stunned improperly, and plant personnel stated that both stun guns were not working and were being repaired. Because the plant did not have an operable stun device, the animal suffered for at least 10 minutes while the plant repaired the gun. The FSIS inspector applied a reject tag to the stunning box; stunning operations in the area were halted until the plant had taken corrective actions, but the record did not state the amount of time that stunning was stopped. According to FSIS's guidance, however, stunning animals and then allowing them to regain consciousness is considered egregious.

Suspensions increased overall following the February 2008 Westland/Hallmark incident in California. For calendar years 2007 and 2008, more than three-quarters of all suspensions were for stun-related violations for all districts. In the 10 districts that suspended operations for calendar years 2005 and 2006, over 40 percent of those suspensions were for stunning violations.... Furthermore, following that incident, FSIS directed the inspectors to increase the amount of time they devoted to humane handling by 50 to 100 percent for March through May 2008. FSIS found that, when the amount of time spent on humane handling was increased, the number of noncompliance reports increased as well.

The Westland/Hallmark incident highlighted the problems that could occur when inspection staff inconsistently apply their discretion in determining which enforcement actions to take for humane handling violations. According to the USDA Inspector General's 2008 report that followed the Westland/Hallmark incident, between December 2004 and February 2008, FSIS inspectors did not write any noncompliance reports or suspend operations for humane handling violations at the Westland/Hallmark plant. Nevertheless, FSIS personnel acknowledged that at least two incidents of humane handling violations had occurred at the Westland/Hallmark plant during this period, both of which involved active abuse of animals. Instead of taking an enforcement action, the inspectors verbally instructed plant personnel to discontinue the action or practice in question. The report also stated that Westland/Hallmark had an unusual lack of noncompliance reports and that inspectors did not believe they should write a noncompliance report if an observed violation was immediately resolved.

Finally, our analysis of FSIS enforcement data for calendar years 2005 through August 2009 shows that suspensions were not consistently used to enforce HMSA.... [S]uspensions spiked from a low of 9 in calendar year 2005 to a high of 98 in 2008 — a nearly 11-fold increase overall — and, as of August 2009, FSIS had suspended operations at 50 plants. Based on our review of the suspension records, it appears that this spike followed the

---

13. These five FSIS districts are Albany, Beltsville, Chicago, Des Moines, and Lawrence.

February 2008 Westland/Hallmark incident. Also, more than three quarters of these suspensions resulted from failure to render at least one animal insensible on the first stun. From calendar year 2005 through 2008, the number of noncompliance reports issued for humane handling decreased overall, while the number of animals slaughtered increased from about 128 million in 2004 to about 153 million in 2008....

Weakness in Guidance and Training May Contribute to Inconsistent Enforcement

We found that incomplete guidance and inadequate training may contribute to the inconsistent enforcement of HMSA....

With respect to guidance, in 2004, we had recommended that FSIS establish additional clear, specific, and consistent criteria for district offices to use when considering whether to take enforcement actions because of repeat violations.[14] FSIS agreed with this recommendation and delegated to the districts the responsibility for determining how many repeat violations should result in a suspension. However, incidents such as those at the Bushway Packing plant in Vermont suggest that this delegation was not successful. To date, FSIS has not issued additional guidance.

Operations at this Vermont plant were suspended three times in May, June, and July 2009 for egregious humane handling violations. Two of the suspensions were for dragging nonambulatory conscious veal calves that were about 1-week old. According to a document describing the third incident, an employee threw a calf from the second tier of a truck to the first so that the calf landed on its head and side. FSIS has not issued any guidance to the district offices on how many suspensions should result in a request for a withdrawal of a grant of inspection. If specific guidance had been available on when to request a withdrawal of grant of inspection, the district office might have decided to request such a withdrawal before the October 2009 incident. If FSIS ultimately withdrew the grant, it would have required the plant to reapply for, and be awarded, a grant of inspection license before it could resume operations.

Regarding training, FSIS relies primarily on "on-the-job" training by DVMSs—who are directed to visit each plant within their district over a 12- to 18-month period. In addition, supervisory veterinarians and inspectors in-charge provide on-the-job training. FSIS officials we spoke with said that the on-the-job training needs to be integrated into a formal training program and that efforts are under way to do so. FSIS also provides some humane handling training electronically. For example, in February 2009, all inspectors assigned to slaughter plants were required to complete a mandatory 1-hour basic humane handling course online, which the agency can track centrally.

FSIS officials also stated that, since 2005, incoming inspectors have been required to complete some humane handling training during orientation. According to FSIS officials we spoke with, the agency has asked the districts to begin entering data on the completion of other humane handling courses so that this information can also be tracked centrally. Our survey results suggest, however, that even inspectors-in-charge who had to complete mandatory humane handling training in February 2009 may not have been sufficiently trained. For example, an estimated 449, or 57 percent, of the inspectors-in-charge at the plants we surveyed from May through July 2009, reported incorrect answers on at least one of six possible signs of sensibility.[15] Specifically, an estimated 133, or 18

---

14. GAO-04-247.

15. Our survey presented the four signs of sensibility—natural blinking, lifting head straight up and keeping it up (righting reflex), rhythmic breathing, and vocalizing—and added two that, alone, do not generally indicate sensibility—rear leg(s) kicking and tail moving. In our assessment, if the

percent, of the inspectors–in-charge, failed to identify rhythmic breathing as a sign of sensibility. In addition, in 2004, we had reported that inspectors did not have the knowledge they needed to take enforcement actions when appropriate.[16] At that time, most of the deputy district managers, and about one-half of the DVMSs, noted that an overall lack of knowledge among inspectors about how they should respond to an observed noncompliance had been a problem in enforcing the HMSA. Several outside observers have also commented on the need for better FSIS training.[17] Specifically:

- In November 2008, USDA's Office of Inspector General found that FSIS does not have a formal, structured developmental program and system in place to ensure that all of its inspection and supervisory staff receive both formal and on-the-job training to demonstrate that they possess the competencies essential for FSIS's mission-critical functions. The Inspector General recommended a structured training and development program that includes continuing education to provide the organizational control needed to demonstrate the competency of the inspection workforce. The Inspector General also stated that the workforce needs to be certified annually.

- In 2009, the National Academies' Institute of Medicine recommended testing and improved training, with special emphasis on the quality and consistency of noncompliance reports for food safety issues.[18] The institute noted that the decision to issue a noncompliance report is subjective and inspectors' experience levels and training differ. Supervisory review by inspectors-in-charge may likewise be variable or subject to bias and, therefore, unreliable.

- In 2009, representatives of the three major industry associations—the American Meat Institute, the American Association of Meat Processors, and the National Meat Association—told us that more training on humane handling is needed for FSIS inspectors. Specifically, the American Meat Institute identified insensibility as a critical issue in enforcement and noted that additional training on the signs of insensibility, such as blinking and the righting reflex, would be helpful.

- In 2009, the Humane Society of the United States recommended that FSIS inspectors receive adequate in-person, on-the-ground training so they can properly assess the conditions and treatment of animals.

FSIS officials stated that it launched a voluntary HMSA training program for plant employees at small slaughter plants in 2009. These plants represent the highest humane handling risk, according to FSIS officials, because plant management may not have sufficient resources to fully train plant employees on HMSA practices.

FSIS Has Only Recently Begun to Consider Using Additional Tools to Evaluate HMSA Performance

In recent years, the meat industry has adopted numerical scoring and video surveillance to improve plants' humane handling performance overall. According to FSIS offi-

---

respondent selected at least one of the two signs that do not indicate sensibility or if he or she indicated that they did not know the answer, the respondent's answer was considered to be incorrect in our calculation.

16. GAO-04-247.

17. In addition, we identified a set of principles to help federal agencies improve the effectiveness of their training efforts. *See* GAO, *Human Capital: A Guide for Assessing Strategic Training and Development Efforts in the Federal Government*, GAO-04-546G (Washington, D.C.: Mar. 1, 2004).

18. Institute of Medicine of the National Academies, Review of the Use of Process Control Indicators in the FSIS Public Health Risk-Based Inspection System (Washington, D.C.: Mar. 3, 2009).

cials, the agency does not require the use of such objective measures or scoring to aid judgment for enforcement purposes because situations are highly variable, and inspectors and higher-level officials are to use their judgment in conjunction with FSIS guidance. However, in December 2009, FSIS provided DVMSs with guidance on what it characterized as, an objective system to facilitate determinations of the problems that plants in their districts need to address.[19] Several of the DVMSs we interviewed acknowledged that they have been using a form of numerical scoring on their own to assist their efforts in evaluating HSMA enforcement at the plants.

The numerical scoring system was developed in 1996 by Dr. Grandin to determine how well animals were being stunned and handled at the plants. The system has different standards for different species of animal and can be adjusted to fit plants that slaughter fewer animals. This system seeks to reduce the subjective nature of inspections and uses the scoring system to help identify areas in need of improvement. For example, in a large plant, if more than 5 out of 100 animals were not rendered insensible on the first stun, the plant would fail the evaluation. Other standards include the percentage rates for slips and falls and the number of animals moved by an electrical prod. Once the plant is aware of the weaknesses, it can consider its options to improve its humane handling performance, such as repairing equipment and floors to provide better footing for the animals and targeting employee training in those specific areas.

The numerical scoring system has been adopted by industry and animal welfare organizations, as well as one federal agency. At the federal level, according to agency officials, USDA's Agricultural Marketing Service uses this system to rate slaughter plants to determine whether to approve or deny them to provide meat to the National School Lunch Program. In addition, the American Meat Institute and independent audit firms employed by restaurant chains, such as Burger King and McDonald's, have adopted this numerical scoring system to evaluate humane handling at their associated slaughter plants. According to industry experts, a publicized humane handling incident at their plants would potentially damage their business interests. Recently, the Canadian Food Inspection Agency proposed adoption of numerical scoring for federally inspected plants in Canada.

FSIS officials have stated that while the numerical scoring system may be useful in helping plants determine their humane handling performance; it should not be used to assess compliance with HMSA. Because the numerical scoring system allows for a certain percentage of stunning failures, using it would be inconsistent with the HMSA requirement that all animals must be rendered insensible on the first blow. However, as we noted earlier, this requirement has not been met consistently by slaughter plants because of human error, equipment failures, and animal movement, leaving FSIS to exercise its discretion in determining which violations require enforcement action.

Video surveillance is another tool being increasingly used by slaughter plants. Specifically, slaughter plants can hire specialized video technology companies to record plant operations and audit plant performance through remote video surveillance and the use of the American Meat Institute numerical scoring system to assess humane handling performance at the plant. These video technology companies can also provide slaughter plant management with continuous feedback and customized progress reports documenting humane handling performance at their plants. According to the testimony of one video surveillance company, this technology helps plant management provide positive rein-

---

19. U.S. Department of Agriculture, Food Safety and Inspection Service, FSIS Directive 6910.1, Rev. 1, District Veterinary Medical Specialist Work Methods (Dec. 7, 2009).

forcement to the workers who are performing well and helps identify workers who may need further training.

In November 2008, the Office of the Inspector General recommended that FSIS determine whether FSIS-controlled, in-plant video monitoring would be beneficial in preventing and detecting animal abuses. However, FSIS officials responded that FSIS-controlled video cameras would not provide the definitive data needed to support enforcement of humane handling requirements, as compared with the direct, ongoing and random verification of humane handling practices at the plants.[20] According to the Humane Society of the United States, while video surveillance might serve as a supplemental tool, it does not negate the need for real-time inspectors' observations. According to our survey results, between 52 to 66 percent of inspectors-in-charge at large plants reported that video surveillance would be moderately or very useful in each of the five plant areas. Figure 10 illustrates our survey results on the usefulness of video surveillance for all plants. FSIS officials recently told us that they are exploring potential uses of video surveillance, but the agency had not released any official policy change, as of November 2009.

In addition, of 96 inspectors who provided written comments on the usefulness of video surveillance in our survey, most frequently reported that video surveillance would facilitate more inspections in different plant locations and provide a true picture of animal handling while plant staff do not know that the inspector is watching. Since video surveillance can provide continuous footage of ongoing activities in the plant, it may provide evidence regarding alleged violations when inspectors do not directly observe humane handling. For example, according to 39 percent of inspectors-in-charge at large plants, plant staff improved their handling behavior upon the inspectors' arrival. Furthermore, 25 percent of inspectors-in-charge at the large plants in our survey reported that plant staff often, or always, alert each other about inspectors' movements between areas by radio or whistle, for example.

FSIS Has Not Fully Analyzed Humane Handling Data to Consistently Enforce HMSA

Although FSIS collects humane handling data, we found that it is not fully analyzing and using these data to help ensure more consistent HMSA enforcement. For example, we found substantial differences in the range of time devoted to humane handling for large plants that slaughter market swine when we compared the amount of time devoted to humane handling activities for plants of similar size and species in an effort to determine if there were any inconsistencies among districts. Specifically, out of the six slaughter plants that kill between 700,000 to 900,000 market swine, the average time that a plant would devote to humane handling ranged from 1.8 to 9.7 hours per shift in 2008. For the nine plants that slaughter between 2 and 3 million market swine, we found that the average amount of time per shift ranged from 2.7 to 5.2 hours per shift in 2008….

FSIS Cannot Fully Identify and Plan Resource Needs for HMSA Enforcement

FSIS cannot fully identify trends in its inspection resources—specifically, funding and staffing—for HMSA enforcement, in part because it cannot track humane handling inspection funds separately from the inspection funds spent on other food safety activities. Furthermore, FSIS does not have a current workforce planning strategy to guide its efforts to allocate staff to inspection activities, including humane handling….

---

20. U.S. Department of Agriculture, Office of Inspector General, Great Plains Region, Evaluation of FSIS Management Controls Over Pre-Slaughter Activities, Report No. 24601-0007KC (November 2008).

Conclusion

It is difficult to know whether the reported incidents of egregious animal handling at the slaughter plants in California and Vermont are isolated cases or indicative of a more widespread problem. Either way, it is evident from our survey results and our analysis of HMSA enforcement data that inspectors did not consistently identify and take enforcement action for humane handling violations for the period we reviewed. Furthermore, our survey results suggest that inspectors are not consistently applying their discretion as to which actions to take when egregious humane handling incidents occur, or when they are repeated, in part because the guidance is unclear. That is, the guidance states that inspectors-in-charge "may" suspend plant operations. Consequently, plants cited for the same type of humane handling incident may be subject to different enforcement actions. In January 2004, we recommended that FSIS establish additional clear, specific, and consistent criteria for enforcement actions to take when faced with repeat violations. FSIS responded by delegating this responsibility to the districts. However, incidents such as those at the Vermont plant suggest that this delegation has not been effective. While FSIS has stated that inspectors require discretion in enforcement, that discretion needs to be informed by an agency policy that ensures a consistent level of enforcement within plants and across districts. Without consistent enforcement actions, FSIS does not clearly signal its commitment to fully enforce HMSA. In addition, to improve plants' humane handling performance, the Agricultural Marketing Service, DVMSs, and others have adopted objective industry tools, such as numerical scoring, to help identify weaknesses. However, inspectors-incharge, who are responsible for assessing daily HMSA performance at the plants, are not directed to use such scoring tools.

Effective oversight of HMSA enforcement also requires FSIS to use available data to effectively manage the program, including allocating resources. FSIS has only recently begun to do so. Until 2009, FSIS did not routinely track and evaluate HMSA enforcement data — by geographic location, species, plant size, and history of compliance across districts. Although these analyses will be useful, FSIS has yet to analyze the narratives of humane handling incidents found in noncompliance reports, which would also help the agency identify weaknesses and trends in enforcement and develop appropriate strategies. Furthermore, we reiterate our January 2004 recommendation, which FSIS has not yet acted on, to periodically reassess whether its estimates still accurately reflect the resources necessary to effectively enforce the act. Finally, because FSIS does not have a comprehensive strategy for enforcing HMSA that aligns the agency's available resources with its mission and goals, and that identifies time frames for achieving these goals and performance metrics for meeting its goals, it is not well positioned to improve its ability to enforce HMSA.

We are making the following four recommendations to the Secretary of Agriculture to strengthen the agency's oversight of humane handling and slaughter methods at federally inspected facilities.

Recommendations for Executive Action

To ensure that FSIS strengthens its enforcement of the Humane Methods of Slaughter Act of 1978, as amended, we recommend that the Secretary of Agriculture direct the Administrator of FSIS to take the following three actions:

- establish clear and specific criteria for when inspectors-in-charge should suspend plant operations for an egregious HMSA violation and when they should take enforcement actions because of repeat violations;

- identify some type of objective tool, such as a numerical scoring mechanism, and instruct all inspectors-in-charge at plants to use this measure to assist them in evaluating the plants' HMSA performance and determining what, if any, enforcement actions are warranted; and

- strengthen the analysis of humane handling data by analyzing the narrative in noncompliance reports to identify areas that need improvement. To ensure that FSIS can demonstrate how efficiently and effectively it is enforcing HMSA, we recommend that the Secretary of Agriculture direct the Administrator of FSIS to develop an integrated strategy that clearly defines goals, identifies resources needed, and establishes time frames and performance metrics specifically for enforcing HMSA....

Notes

1. The condition of animals at the time of slaughter raises important food safety issues as well as animal welfare issues. The Weston/Hallmark incident involving downer cows was recognized as presenting a food safety risk as much as an animal welfare violation. In general, cows that cannot stand are supposed to be kept out of the food supply because they may be infected with Bovine Spongiform Encephalopathy (BSE) or mad cow disease. However, the regulations at that time permitted "downer" cows from being slaughtered if they passed initial inspection and became non-ambulatory. This was supposed to permit the slaughtering of animals that would become injured during the process, while still preventing diseased animals from entering the food supply. However, lax initial inspection, such as was evident at Weston/Hallmark, allowed abuse of the regulation. The USDA under the Bush administration defended the regulation. *See, USDA Rejects "Downer" Cow Ban: Agriculture Secretary Finds Existing Meat-Processing Rules Adequate*, WASH. POST. (Feb. 29, 2008). USDA Secretary Vilsack, however, eliminated the exception, declaring that no "downer" cow should enter the food supply under any circumstances. 74 Fed. Reg. 11,463 (codified at 9 C.F.R. pt. 309) (2009).

2. Some in the meat production and food industries have taken aim at the Humane Society for its advocacy for farm animal welfare and in particular, its undercover videos. Most vocal has been the Center for Consumer Freedom, a lobbying group funded largely by restaurant and food companies.

3. Horse Slaughter continues to raise concern and a variety of legal issues.

> For many years, horse protection groups have sought to end the slaughter of horses for human food. Policy issues focus on the acceptability of the practice and on how to dispose of or care for unwanted horses no longer being slaughtered. Until 2007, two foreign-owned plants in Texas and one in Illinois slaughtered horses for human food (105,000 in 2006), all for export. On January 19, 2007, however, a federal appeals court panel declared a Texas law banning commerce in horsemeat to be enforceable, effectively closing the two plants there. The remaining foreign plant in Illinois closed later in 2007 after a federal appeals court ruled that a new state law banning the practice was constitutional. The U.S. Supreme Court declined to hear the case in June 2008.

> These developments had occurred as Congress considered a succession of measures to ban or otherwise limit equine slaughter. During respective floor debates on USDA's FY2006 appropriation (P.L. 109-97), the House and Senate approved

amendments to ban use of appropriated funds to pay for the inspection of these horses. The presumption was that since inspection is required for any meat to enter the human food supply, a ban on inspection funding would halt the practice. However, the three plants petitioned USDA for voluntary ante-mortem inspection services, as authorized by the Agricultural Marketing Act of 1946, with the ante-mortem portion funded by user fees. USDA agreed to this plan, which took effect in early 2006. Subsequently, the FY2008 USDA appropriation (§ 741, Division A, of the Consolidated Appropriations Act, 2008, P.L. 110-161) both prohibited the use of appropriated funds to inspect horses prior to slaughter for human food, and also the USDA rule ... that provided for the collection of user fees.

Animal welfare groups have continued to seek new federal legislation, such as companion bills H.R. 503/S. 311, and H.R. 6598 in the 110th Congress, permanently ending horse slaughter for human food. The American Veterinary Medical Association (AVMA), which has opposed the bills, has asserted that horses that otherwise would have been transported and slaughtered in the United States—under more humane conditions—are now going to Mexico and Canada for processing. In 2007, more than 44,000 horses were shipped for slaughter to Mexico and 35,000 to Canada, respectively a 312% and 41% increase from 2006, according to AVMA. Bill supporters argued that one of the intents of H.R. 503/S. 311 and of H.R. 6598 was to prevent such exports; bill critics countered that once horses leave the country, enforcement and oversight would be problematic at best. A separately pending bill (H.R. 6278) would have prohibited the interstate transportation of horses in double-decked trailers. (See also CRS Report RS21842, Horse Slaughter Prevention Bills and Issues, by Geoffrey S. Becker.)

Both H.R. 503 and H.R. 6278 have been reintroduced into the 111th Congress, as H.R. 503 (Conyers)/S. 727 (Landrieu), respectively. The ban on transporting horses in double-decked trailers has been reintroduced as H.R. 305 (Kirk).

Geoffrey S. Becker, *Humane Treatment of Farm Animals: Overview and Issues*, Congressional Research Service, Report No.RS21978, 4–5 (March 9, 2010).

IX

Biotechnology and Agricultural Law

To some, agricultural biotechnology represents the future of agricultural production—producing more food, with less environmental damage; producing better food with enhanced nutrition; and producing pharmaceuticals through "bio-pharming." Monsanto boasts on its website that "[a]fter a decade of use on more than one billion acres worldwide, plant biotechnology delivers proven economic and environmental benefits, a solid record of safe use and promising products for our future."[1] To others, agricultural biotechnology is moving too fast, too little is known about the long term effects, and too much is driven by corporations who profit from its development. Concerns about the loss of genetic diversity, unintended consequences, inadequate testing, and consolidation of control over seeds are voiced.[2]

This chapter introduces the subject of agricultural biotechnology and its regulation in the United States. It then considers three issues that reflect four different areas of the legal landscape: 1) the patenting of genetically engineered seeds; 2) challenges to the approval process for new genetically engineered seeds; 3) the decision not to require the labeling of genetically engineered products; and 4) international trade issues regarding genetically engineered products.

A. An Introduction to Agricultural Biotechnology and its Regulation

Tadlock Cowan & Geoffrey S. Becker
Agricultural Biotechnology: Background and Recent Issues
Congressional Research Report RL-32809
Feb. 13, 2009

Adoption of Biotechnology in Agriculture[3]

Farmers have always modified plants and animals to improve growth rates and yields, create varieties resistant to pests and diseases, and infuse special nutritional or handling

---

1. Available at http://www.monsanto.com/products/benefits/biotechnology.asp.
2. *See e.g.*, Union of Concerned Scientists website at http://www.ucsusa.org; Center for Food Safety, http://centerforfoodsafety.org.
3. Among the sources for this report are various materials by USDA's Economic Research Service (ERS) and Animal and Plant Health Inspection Service (APHIS), the Pew Initiative on Food and

characteristics. Such modifications have been achieved by crossbreeding plants and animals with desirable traits, through hybridization, and other methods. Now, using recombinant DNA techniques, scientists also genetically modify plants and animals by selecting individual genes that carry desirable traits (e.g., resistance to a pest or disease) from one organism, and inserting them into another, sometimes very different, organism, that can be raised for food, fiber, pharmaceutical, or industrial uses.

Karl Ereky, a Hungarian engineer, coined the term "biotechnology" in 1919 to refer to the science and the methods that permit products to be produced from raw materials with the aid of living organisms.[4] According to the Convention of Biological Diversity, biotechnology is "any technological application that uses biological systems, living organisms, or derivatives thereof, to make or modify products or processes for specific use" (Article 2). According to the FAO's statement on biotechnology, "interpreted in a narrow sense, … [biotechnology] covers a range of different technologies such as gene manipulation and gene transfer, DNA typing and cloning of plants and animals."[5]

Since genetically engineered (GE, sometimes called genetically modified organism or GMO) crop varieties first became commercially available in the mid-1990s, U.S. soybean, cotton, and corn farmers have rapidly adopted them in order to lower production costs and increase crop yields. Proponents point to the emergence of "second generation" GE commodities that could shift the focus of biotechnology from the "input" side (creating traits that benefit crop production, such as pest resistance) to the "output" side (creating traits that benefit consumers, such as lowerfat oils). These second generation products could offer enhanced nutritional and processing qualities and also industrial and pharmaceutical uses. Future products are expected to be livestock—as well as crop-based. Critics, meanwhile, complain that biotechnology companies generally have not yet delivered the consumer benefits they have been promising for years.

Incidents of regulatory noncompliance have continued to spike concern about the adequacy of regulatory structures. In December 2008, a small amount of unapproved GE cotton was harvested along with commercially available GE cotton. The unapproved GE cotton variety produces a pesticide that is a plant-incorporated protectant (PIP). In August 2006, traces of an unapproved variety of GE rice were reported in commercial rice samples from parts of the southern United States. These incidents have added to the ongoing interest in a number of public policy questions. What are the environmental and food safety impacts of GE crops and animals? What obstacles and opportunities are exporters of GE crops encountering in the global marketplace? Is the current U.S. regulatory framework, which is based primarily upon statutory authorities enacted before the rise of agricultural biotechnology, adequate for these new technologies and products?

Current Applications

Crops

In 2008, GE crops were planted on an estimated 308.8 million acres worldwide, a year-over-year increase of 26.4 million acres … The total number of countries growing such crops reached 25 in 2008. Most of the acreage was highly concentrated among four crops—

Biotechnology, various issues of *Food Chemical News*, a weekly trade publication, and the Biotechnology Industry Organization (BIO).

4. OECD. Policy Brief, Modern Biotechnology and the OECD, June 1999. [http://www.oecd.org/dataoecd/29/40/1890904.pdf].

5. FAO. FAO Biotechnology Glossary, [http://www.fao.org/biotech/index_glossary.asp].

soybeans, corn, cotton, and canola—and six countries. The United States has approximately 50% of global acreage (154.4 million acres), and Argentina had 16.8% (51.9 million acres). Brazil (12.6%, 39.0 million acres), Canada (6.1%, 18.8 million acres), India (6.1%, 18.8 million acres), and China (3.0%, 9.4 million acres) have the largest shares of the remaining planted acres.[6]

In the United States, over 60 GE plant varieties were approved by APHIS for commercial use through early 2005.[7] Ninety-two percent of all U.S. soybean, 86% of all upland cotton, and 80% of all corn acres were planted with GE seed varieties in 2007, according to USDA's National Agricultural Statistics Service ... Virtually all current commercial applications benefit the production side of agriculture, with weed and insect control by far the most widespread uses of GE crops in the United States and abroad.

Herbicide-tolerant (HT) crops are engineered to tolerate herbicides that would otherwise kill them along with the targeted weeds. These include HT soybeans, HT upland cotton, and to a lesser extent, HT corn. Many of these are referred to as "Roundup Ready" because they are engineered to resist Monsanto's glyphosate herbicide, marketed under the brand name "Roundup." More recently, Monsanto has announced various "stacked trait" varieties—varieties that combine resistance not only to glyphosate/Roundup, but also to the herbicides dicamba and glufosinate.

Insect-resistant crops effectively have the pesticide inserted into the plants themselves to control insect pests for the life of the crop. These varieties are often referred to as having a plantincorporatedprotectant (PIP). Many of these crops have been genetically engineered with Bt (Bacillus thuringiensis, a soil bacterium), which produces a naturally occurring pesticide.[8] These insect-resistant varieties are most prevalent in upland cotton to control tobacco budworm, bollworm, and pink bollworm; and in corn to control earworm and several types of corn borers. Monsanto is also developing "stacked trait" varieties of soybeans and sugar cane that are resistant to insects as well as glyphosate/Roundup.

Table 1. U.S. Acreage in Major GE Crops, 1996 and 2008
(acres in millions)

	Soybeans		Upland Cotton (UC)		Corn	
	Acres	% of all soy acres	Acres	% of all UC acres	Acres	% of all corn acres
1996	4.2	7%	2.2	17%	2.9	4%
2008	68.6	92%	7.7	86%	69.9	80%

Source: USDA-NASS. *Acreage Report*, June 2008.

---

6. International Service for the Acquisition of Agri-biotech Applications (ISAAA), ISAAA Brief 39-2008, *Executive Summary: The First Thirteen Years, 1996 to 2008 Report on the Global Status of Biotech/GM Crops.* Accessed January 2008 at [http://www.isaaa.org/resources/publications/briefs/39/executivesummary/default.html]

7. Sources: Information Systems for Biotechnology at Virginia Tech; also, USDA, ERS, *The First Decade of Genetically Engineered Crops in the United States*, April 2006, which can be accessed at http://www.ers.usda.gov/Publications/eib11/.

8. Because Bt is a natural occurring pesticide, it can be used under certain conditions on organically produced plants. Its incorporation into GE commodities concerns some organic producers because of the risk of creating Bt tolerant pests thereby decreasing the utility of Bt to organic farming operations.

Other crops approved for commercialization have included varieties of flax, papaya, potatoes, radicchio, rapeseed, rice, squash, sugar beets, tobacco, and tomatoes. However, these are either not commercialized or not widely planted. For example, the biotechnology firm Calgene's FlavrSavr tomato, first marketed to consumers from 1995 to 1997, was withdrawn after Calgene determined that the varieties being grown were not of consistently high quality. GE potato varieties peaked several years ago at 2%–3% of the market; they were discontinued by the seed developer in 2001, mainly after several fast food and snack food companies declined to buy them.

Varieties of GE wheat and rice, as well as flax and radicchio, have received regulatory approval but have not been commercially marketed (and/or research has been discontinued), presumably due largely to perceived producer or consumer unease with them. In contrast to abandoning certain approved GE products, a variety of white GE corn has recently begun to be used in tortilla making after initial resistance by food processors. Herbicide resistant GE sugar beets were only planted in large acreage in the 2008 crop year. While commercially available since 2000, Western beet growers did not plant them because sugar-using food companies (e.g., Hershey, Mars) and beet sugar industry groups (e.g., American Crystal Sugar) balked at the idea of GE beets thinking that consumers would be opposed. That opposition—real or potential—has apparently subsided to the point that processors have cleared their growers to plant the GE variety.[9] Nonetheless, the Center for Food Safety filed suit in January 2008 challenging APHIS's deregulation of GE sugar beets arguing that wind-pollinated GE sugar beets will inevitably cross-pollinate with related crops being grown in proximity, contaminating conventional sugar beets and organic chard and table beet crops.[10]

Nonetheless, USDA reported that between 1987 and early 2005, APHIS had approved more than 10,700 applications to conduct field tests of various GE crop varieties (out of 11,600 received from companies and other researchers), which the USDA characterized as "a useful indicator of R&D efforts on crop biotechnology." Nearly 5,000 applications were approved for corn alone, followed by soybeans, potatoes, cotton, tomatoes, and wheat. More than 6,700 applications were for HT and insect resistant varieties; the others were to test product quality, virus or fungal resistance, or agronomic (e.g., drought resistance) properties.[11] By October 2008, APHIS had approved more than 13,000 field trials of GE plants, most of which continued to be crop plants bearing genes conferring resistance to certain insects or tolerance to certain herbicides.

Animal Products

Fewer animal-based GE products are commercially available, notably excepting dairy production. Chymosin, a biotechnology-produced enzyme, is used widely in cheese production. Bovine somatotropin (BST, also known as "bovine growth hormone") is a naturally occurring protein that can be produced in greater quantities through genetic engineering. The GE version of BST (rBST) was first approved by the

---

9. Some of the reduced public opposition to the GE beets may be based on the fact that sugar crystals do not contain any remnants of the GE modified protein and, thus, could pose no dietary risk.

10. The legal challenge seeking an injunction against was filed in the U.S. District Court for the Northern District of California and also includes the Sierra Club and the Organic Seed Alliance as plaintiffs. The court filing may be accessed at [http://www.centerforfoodsafety.org/pubs/Final%20 Complaint.pdf].

11. ERS, *The First Decade of Genetically Engineered Crops in the United States.* April, 2006. [http://www.ers.usda.gov/publications/eib11/eib11.pdf].

U.S. Food and Drug Administration (FDA) in 1993. Reports suggest that more than 30% of all U.S. dairy cows are administered BST to boost milk production (by an estimated 10%–15%).[12] Several other emerging animal biotechnologies, while not yet commercialized, are believed by researchers to hold great promise (see "Future GE Applications," below).[13] In February 2009, FDA approved the first product from a transgenic animal, an anti-clotting protein derived from the milk of transgenic goats.[14] The animals are genetically engineered to produce a recombinant human antithrombin III protein in their milk.[15] A Netherlands-based biotechnology firm also announced plans to seek U.S. and European approval in 2009 for Rhucin, made from a human protein purified from the milk of genetically engineered rabbits. The protein, C1 esterase inhibitor, helps control inflammation.

U.S. Food Crops Containing GE Materials[16]

An estimated 70% of all processed U.S. foods likely contain some GE material. That is largely because two such plants (corn and soybeans, where farmers have widely adopted GE varieties) are used in many different processed foods. U.S. biotechnology rules do not require segregation and labeling of GE crops and foods, as long as they are substantially equivalent to those produced by more conventional methods (see "Regulation and Oversight," below).

Soy-based ingredients include oil, flour, lecithin, and protein extracts. Corn-based ingredients include corn meal and corn syrups, used in many processed products. Canola oil (mostly imported from Canada, where GE-canola is grown) and cottonseed oil are used in cooking oils, salad dressings, snack foods, and other supermarket items. No GE-produced animals are yet approved for human consumption, although cheeses may contain chymosin, and dairy products may have been produced from milk containing GE-BST.

As noted earlier, because most other government-approved GE crops are not being grown commercially, few other GE-derived foods are reaching consumers.

Analysts say some farmers are wary of planting GE crop varieties because their customers may be worried about their safety, although as the case of sugar beets noted above suggests, public opposition to GE products in processed food may be declining. Biotechnology supporters contend that safety concerns are unfounded because scientific reviews have found approved GE crop varieties to be safe, and that foreign governments are simply using such concerns to maintain barriers to imports.

---

12. Milk containing rBST may be falling out of favor in some places. Wal-Mart, the largest grocery retail outlet in the United States, has a private label milk (Great Value Milk) that will be rBST free. Kroger completed a phase-out of rBST milk in February 2008. Safeway switched to rBST free milk in its private line, although it continues to sell other rBST milk. Starbucks began using only rBST free milk in January 2008.

13. Also see CRS Report RL33334, *Biotechnology in Animal Agriculture: Status and Current Issues*, by Geoffrey S. Becker and Tadlock Cowan.

14. "FDA approves drug product from transgenic goats." Food Chemical News, February 9, 2009.

15. In September 2008, APHIS announced a request for public comment and technical empirical data concerning ongoing and future research on genetically engineered animals.

16. Sources include Cornell University, Genetically Engineered Organisms Public Issues Education Project (GEO-PIE), at http://www.geo-pie.cornell.edu/crops/eating.html, accessed on February 3, 2009; USDA, APHIS, Petitions of Nonregulated Status Granted or Pending by APHIS, at [http://www.aphis.usda.gov/brs/not_reg.html] and Colorado State University, *Transgenic Crops: An Introduction and Resource Guide*. The latter report is available at [http://www.colostate.edu/programs/lifesciences/TransgenicCrops/index.html]. The site is not regularly maintained but archived materials are available through 2004.

Future GE Applications[17]

For farmers, new insect-resistant and herbicide-tolerant GE varieties are under development or have been developed for other crops besides corn, cotton, and soybeans. These include wheat and rice (see below), alfalfa, peanuts, sunflowers, forestry products, sugarcane, apples, bananas, lettuce, strawberries, and eventually other fruits and vegetables. Other traits being developed through genetic engineering include drought and frost tolerance, enhanced photosynthesis, and more efficient use of nitrogen. Tomatoes that can be grown in salty soils, and recreational turf grasses that are herbicide tolerant, pest resistant, and/or more heat and drought tolerant, also are under development. In animal agriculture, pigs have been engineered for increased sow milk output to produce faster-growing piglets. Cloned cattle also have been developed to resist mastitis. APHIS approved field trials in June 2007 for a transgenic sunflower with a carp growth hormone inserted. The GE sunflower would be used in aquaculture feed for farm raised shrimp. Currently awaiting government approval for food use are GE salmon that require as little as half the usual time to grow to market size. Other such fish could follow later.[18]

For processors and consumers, research on a range of GE products is continuing: oilseeds low in saturated and transfats; tomatoes with anti-cancer agents; grains with optimal levels of amino acids; rice with elevated iron levels; and rice with beta-carotene, a precursor of Vitamin A ("golden" rice). Other future products could include "low-calorie" sugar beets; strawberries and corn with higher sugar content to improve flavor; colored cotton; improved cotton fiber; delayed-ripening melons, bananas, strawberries, raspberries, and other produce (delayed-ripening tomatoes already are approved); and naturally decaffeinated coffee. Critics, however, point out that, although biotechnology advocates have been forecasting the adoption of various "output" traits for some time, few have actually reached the marketplace.

Other plants being developed could become "factories" for pharmaceutical compounds. The compounds would be extracted and purified for human and animal health uses (among concerns are whether they could "contaminate" food crops; see "Plant-Based Pharmaceuticals from Biotechnology," below). Some varieties of plants under development could also produce "bioindustrials," including plastics and polyurethane. Future transgenic livestock also might yield pharmaceuticals and/or human organ and tissue replacements. To date, none of these innovations have been commercialized, although some have begun field trials....

The regulation of agricultural biotechnology and the entrance of new genetically engineered products onto the market in the United States is guided by two key principles. First, genetically engineered products should be regulated according to their specific characteristics and not treated differently or subject to additional scrutiny because of the process by which they are created. Second, related to this, because genetically engineered

---

17. Sources include "Review of Agricultural Biotechnology," hearing before the Subcommittee on Conservation, Credit, Rural Development, and Research of the U.S. House Committee on Agriculture, June 23, 2004 (Serial No. 108-34); BIO; Colorado State University; and ERS, *Economic Issues in Agricultural Biotechnology* (AIB-762), February 2001 (table, p. 19), at http://www.ers.usda.gov/publications/aib762/; and *The First Decade of Genetically Engineered Crops in the United States.*

18. So far one GE fish, the "Glofish," has been marketed in the United States. It is an aquarium fish that is not approved for consumption. For more on genetically engineered fish, see CRS Report RL32974, Genetically Engineered Fish and Seafood, by Rachel Borgatti and Eugene H. Buck.

products should not be treated differently, new laws and/or an integrated framework for their regulation is unnecessary. The existing legal framework is sufficient.

Three different agencies are involved in regulating genetically engineered products. The USDA, through the Animal & Plant Health Inspection Service (APHIS) is responsible for regulating "plant pests" under the Plant Protection Act and animal biologics under the Virus, Serum, and Toxins Act. The Food & Drug Administration (FDA) at the Department of Health and Human Services regulates food and animal feed under the Federal Food, Drug & Cosmetic Act. And, the Environmental Protection Agency (EPA) regulates the use of pesticides, including those that are genetically engineered into plants under the Federal Insecticide, Fungicide, and Rodenticide Act (FIFRA). The excerpt from following article explains the workings of this trifurcated regulatory scheme, while criticizing some of the weakness inherent in the system.

Rebecca Bratspies
Some Thoughts on the American Approach to Regulating Genetically Modified Organisms
16 Kan. J.L. & Pub. Pol'y 393, 405–414 (2007)

III. The Regulatory Matrix

In theory, no genetically engineered organism is approved for commercial use until its proponent has demonstrated that the organism conforms with the standards set by federal law. These standards are intended to protect human health and the environment, while encouraging the development of new, potentially lucrative technologies. Unfortunately, the gap between theory and reality is significant. Part of the problem is that no regulatory agency has a clear statutory mandate to regulate agricultural biotechnology. As a result, there are no coherent overarching government policies capable of ensuring that this new technology is safely explored and exploited.

A. Birth of a regulatory regime — OSTP during the Reagan Years

In response to the successful Foundation on Economics Trend lawsuit [challenging the approval of a genetically engineered bacterium] the Reagan administration convened an interagency working group to consider how to regulate biotechnology. The working group was explicitly tasked with achieving a "balance between regulation adequate to ensure health and environmental safety while maintaining sufficient regulatory flexibility to avoid impeding the growth of an infant industry."[57] In its 1984 proposal for the Coordinated Framework for Regulation of Biotechnology, the Office of Science and Technology Policy (OSTP) made the goals of the Coordinated Framework clear. Although it began with a clear statement that "(t)he fundamental purpose of the Working Group is to insure that the regulatory process adequately considers health and environmental safety consequences of the products and processes of the new biotechnology as they move from the research laboratory to the marketplace,"[58] the proposal focused far more on the needs of industry for "sensible" regulation that would not stifle inno-

---

57. Coordinated Framework for the Regulation of Biotechnology, 51 Fed. Reg. 23,302-01, 23,303 (June 26, 1986).
58. Proposal for a Coordinated Framework for Biotechnology, 49 Fed. Reg. 50,856, 50,857 (Dec. 31, 1984).

vation than on the needs of the public for rigorous regulation to protect public safety.[59] The proposal similarly emphasized the United States' commitment to reducing barriers to trade in biotechnology.[60] A comparable degree of commitment to preserving environmental safety is less evident in either the proposal or the ultimately adopted Coordinated Framework.

The Coordinated Framework purported to describe the comprehensive federal regulatory policy for ensuring the safety of biotechnology research and products. It announced that no new laws would be needed to respond to challenges posed by this new technology. Instead, products of biotechnology would be regulated under "a mosaic" of existing laws based upon the products' intended use. Thus, food would be regulated under the Federal Food Drug and Cosmetic Act, pesticides under the Federal Insecticide Fungicide Pesticide and Rodenticide Act, agricultural plants under the Plant Protection Act, and so on.[61] EPA and the United States Department of Agriculture (USDA) are involved before GM crops can be produced commercially and thus regulate the environmental release of plants derived from agro-biotechnology. The United States Food and Drug Administration (FDA), on the other hand, has regulatory authority only over the marketing of GM crops as food for humans and animals.[62] Each agency regulates under the authority of a handful of federal statutes, each with its own mission and regulatory structure, none of which were enacted to address biotechnology.[63]

The Coordinated Framework offered some framing principles for U.S. regulation: biotechnology poses no unique risks; the products of biotechnology should be regulated, not the process; existing laws should be used to regulate the products of biotechnology (no new legislation is needed); and any gaps should be addressed through coordination among agencies and designation of lead agencies as appropriate.

The central principle behind the Coordinated Framework is the idea of "substantial equivalence"[64]—that GMOs are functionally equivalent to their unmodified counterparts and should be treated accordingly. A major problem with "substantial equivalence" is that it permits agencies to act simultaneously as regulators and promoters for this new tech-

---

59. *Id.* The proposal provided in relevant part:

The Working Group recognizes the need for a coordinated and sensible regulatory review process that will minimize the uncertainties and inefficiencies that can stifle innovation and impair the competitiveness of U.S. industry.... The importance of addressing the emerging commercial aspects of biotechnology in a coordinated and timely fashion is captured in the recent report by the Congressional Office of Technology Assessment which warned: 'Although the United States is currently the world leader in both basic science and commercial development of new biotechnology, continuation of the initial preeminence of American companies in the commercialization of new biotechnology is not assured.'

This focus on competitiveness reflected a contemporaneous sense that the United States had lost its competitive edge in the electronics industry. Determined to ensure that the nascent biotechnology industry did not suffer the same fate, the government sent a clear message that "regulatory agencies were not to stand in the way of biotechnology." *See*, Mary Jane Angelo, *Embracing Uncertainty, Complexity and Change: An Eco-Pragmatic Reinvention of First Generation Environmental Law*, 33 ECOLOGY L. Q. 105, 171 n. 328 (2006). As a result, there was no new legislation directly responsive to the challenges posed by biotechnology, and agencies instead adapted existing regulatory programs.

60. Coordinated Framework, *supra* note 57, at 23,303.

61. *Id.*

62. *See* Rebecca Bratspies, *Myths of Voluntary Compliance: Lessons from the StarLink Corn Fiasco*, 27 WM. & MARY ENVTL. L. & POL'Y REV. 593, 605 (Spring 2003).

63. Rebecca Bratspies, *The Illusion of Care: Regulation, Uncertainty, and Genetically Modified Food Crops*, 10 N.Y.U. ENVTL. L.J. 297, 312 (2002).

64. *See, e.g.*, Jan-Peter Nap et al., *The Release of Genetically Modified Crops into the Environment*, 33 PLANT J. 1, 10 (2003); Rebecca M. Bratspies, *Consuming (F)ears of Corn: Public Health and Biopharming*, 30 AM. J. L. & MED. 371, 390 (2004).

nology. The conflict is particularly acute at USDA, which has a statutory mission of developing new markets for the United States' agriculture.

The Coordinated Framework assumes that "(b)y the time a genetically engineered product is ready for commercialization, it will have undergone substantial review and testing during the research phase, and thus, information regarding its safety should be available."[65] However, the limited nature of regulatory review shapes the development of safety information in a fashion that does not promote a full consideration of all risks associated with these novel organisms. Because of the assumption of substantial equivalence, the onus and burden of proof is on the authorities to prove that a GMO is unsafe before they may impose use restrictions. This is directly contrary to the European approach and has led to jockeying in the international trade context.[66]

B. Current United States Regulatory Practices

The Coordinated Framework remains the United States' basic organizing principle for regulating GMOs. The Coordinated Framework fits the products of genetic engineering into an already-existing set of laws and regulations. Because these laws were drafted before the development of this technology, they are not always well suited to their new tasks. With no single agency considering the full range of problems posed by GM crops, regulatory gaps are inevitable. Each agency concentrates on its own narrow piece of the GM universe while overarching questions of safety often go unexplored.

At its most superficial, the regulatory regime established by the Coordinated Framework is very easy to describe: the FDA is responsible for food safety, the EPA is responsible for microbes and pesticides, and USDA's Animal and Plant Health Inspection Service (APHIS) is responsible for all plants. In practice, however, the regulatory interactions are far more complex than this deceptively simple division of authority. Many GM products fall into multiple categories. For example, a corn plant that has been engineered to produce its own pesticide is a plant, a pesticide, and a food, so it falls under the purview of all three agencies. Each of the three agencies uses different laws to govern the products of biotechnology, and most of these laws were passed well before the advent of biotechnology. What follows is a brief overview of the relevant regulatory regimes.

1. FDA

FDA is responsible for food safety under the authority of the Federal Food, Drug and Cosmetics Act (FDCA).[67] This Act empowers FDA to, inter alia: identify and remove adulterated foods from the human food supply, regulate food labeling, and approve all food additives. The FDCA applies to all food, including GM foods. However, no statutory provisions of the FDCA expressly regulate GMOs, nor do any FDA regulations specifically apply to these novel foods. Instead, FDA treats GM foods, again, as the "substantial equivalent" of conventional foods. As a result, foods produced from plants modified through genetic engineering are not treated any differently from conventional foods.

The FDCA authorizes FDA to protect the food supply from becoming "adulterated," meaning from foods that "bear[] or contain[] any poisonous or deleterious substance

---

65. *See generally*, Coordinated Framework, *supra* note 57.

66. For a discussion of these differences, see Rebecca Bratspies, *Trail Smelter's (semi)Precautionary Legacy,* in Transboundary Harm In International Law: Lessons From the Trail Smelter Arbitration (R. Bratspies and R. Miller, eds, 2006).

67. 21 U.S.C. § 301, *et seq.*

which may render it injurious to health."[68] FDA also has authority to regulate food additives, defined as substances that are intended for use in food, that may reasonably be expected to become a component of food, or that otherwise may affect the characteristics of food.[69] A food additive must receive FDA approval prior to its use in a food product. Both the gene inserted into a transgenic food plant and the protein produced by that gene clearly fall within the definition of food additives.

In theory, this regulatory framework should give FDA all the regulatory authority it needs to effectively oversee GM food crops.[70] In practice it does not work that way. FDA treats GM foods as the substantial equivalent of conventional crops, a crucial regulatory decision that drastically limits the scope of FDA's review. Under this "substantial equivalence" analysis, GM crops are treated as mere variants of existing, well-accepted foods with no different or greater safety concerns.

The FDCA contains a provision exempting food additives that are "generally regarded as safe" (GRAS) from the requirement of pre-market approval and/or labeling. Relying upon the principle of substantial equivalence, FDA determined that "(i)n most cases, the substances expected to become components of food as a result of genetic modification of a plant will be the same as or substantially similar to substances commonly found in food, such as proteins, fats and oils, and carbohydrates." In light of this determination, FDA presumes that most GMOs will be GRAS.[71] In fact, FDA justified its decision not to mandate specific labeling for foods derived from GM plants based upon this GRAS presumption.

It is the food additive manufacturer, not the FDA that determines whether a GMO is GRAS in the first instance. A manufacturer need not report a GRAS determination to FDA, but the agency does offer a voluntary consultation process.[72] Thus, at most, the vaunted FDA pre-market "approval" of GMOs amounts to FDA reviewing GRAS determinations that manufacturers voluntarily submit for review.[73]

Critics label this reliance on "substantial equivalence" as misguided because it relies wholly on chemical similarity, with no biological, toxicological, or immunological data to back up the assumption of safety. This regulatory policy does not seem to contemplate the possibility that a company might perpetuate a fraud by concealing important information about a GM food. Most of the time, food manufacturers have a fairly clear incentive not to expose the public to known risks, but known risks are not the main concern. This policy creates little incentive for manufacturers to explore possible risks and to develop the kind of information that would enable a full assessment of food safety.

---

68. Federal Food, Drug and Cosmetics Act, 21 U.S.C. §342(a)(1) (2000).

69. 21 U.S.C. §348(a) (2000).

70. FDA has no authority over "biopharmed" or industrial crops as they are not intended to produce foods. However, the possibility of cross-contamination is significant. FDA, of course, has regulatory authority over any drugs produced from biopharming, under its normal drug approval process. However, that drug approval process will not consider the potential health effects of cross-contamination from biopharm crops.

71. *See* Thomas O. McGarity, *Seeds of Distrust: Federal Regulation of Genetically Modified Foods*, 35 U. Mich. J. L. Reform 403, 408 (2002); *see also* Jeffrey K. Francer, *Frankenstein Foods or Flavor Savers?: Regulating Agricultural Biotechnology in the United States and European Union*, 7 Va. J. Soc. Pol'y & L. 257, 270 (2000). This GRAS presumption was challenged in court, and upheld, in *Alliance for Bio-Integrity v. Shalala*, 116 F.Supp.2d 166 (D.D.C. 2000).

72. Statement of Policy: Foods Derived from New Plant Varieties, 57 Fed. Reg. 22984, (May 29, 1992); Guidance on Consultation Procedures: Foods Derived From New Plant Varieties (October 1997) available at http:// www.cfsan.fda.gov/~lrd/consulpr.html.

73. U.S. Food and Drug Administration, List of Completed Consultations on Bioengineered Foods, available at http://www.fda.gov/food/biotechnology/submissions/default.htm.

In January 2001, the FDA proposed regulations that would have required manufacturers to submit data and information about plant-derived bioengineered foods or animal feeds at least 120 days prior to commercial distribution.[74] This mandatory process would have replaced the voluntary consultation process. It would also have required companies to provide FDA with data and information on plant-derived bioengineered foods to be consumed by humans or animals.[75] One of the first acts of the incoming Bush administration was to suspend and withdraw these rules for further consideration.[76] They have never been reissued.

In June 2006, FDA issued new guidance encouraging manufacturers to contact the agency early in their product development process in order to address safety issues.[77] The recommendation focused on avoiding "possible intermittent, inadvertent introductions into the food supply of proteins from biotech crops under development."[78] This recommendation has not been applied to plants engineered to endogenously produce pesticides, or to be resistant to herbicide application—the overwhelming majority of GMOs currently on the market.

Although FDA is tasked with both enforcing EPA tolerances for pesticides in food and removing food contaminated with unapproved pesticides or the unintended, unauthorized presence of unapproved transgenic material,[79] it neither engages in any systematic compliance-monitoring of GM foods nor monitoring of the same for contamination. This point of concern will become even more pressing once GMOs developed elsewhere in the world begin to reach the international commodities market. Such GMOs may be imported into the United States without pre-market FDA approval or subsequent FDA monitoring. A number of recent legislative proposals would have statutorily expanded FDA's oversight of GMOs,[80] but, to date, none of these proposals have made it out of committee.

---

74. *See* Premarket Notice Concerning Bioengineered Foods, 66 Fed. Reg. 4706, 4706–38 (proposed Jan. 19, 2001) (to be codified at 21 C.F.R. pts. 192, 592).

75. Press Release, U.S. Department of Health & Human Services, *FDA Announces Proposal and Draft Guidance for Food Developed Through Biotechnology* (Jan. 17, 2001), available at http://www.cfsan.fda.gov/~lrd/hhbioen3.html.

76. Memorandum from the Assistant to the President and Chief of Staff, White House Office, to the Heads and Acting Heads of Executive Departments and Agencies, 66 Fed. Reg. 7702 (Jan. 24, 2001) (directing that regulations sent to the Office of the Federal Register, but not yet published, be withdrawn, and that regulations already published but not yet in effect be postponed).

77. FDA, Guidance for Industry: Recommendations for Early Food Safety Evaluation of New Non-Pesticidal Proteins Produced by New Plant Varieties Intended for Food Use, available at http://www.fda.gov/OHRMS/DOCKETS/98fr/04d-0369-gdl0002.pdf.

78. *Id*. at 3–4.

79. The unintended contamination of food crops with unauthorized and unapproved genetic material is a growing problem. *See* Bratspies, *Myths of Voluntary Compliance*, *supra* note 62; Bratspies, *Consuming (F)ears of Corn*, *supra* note 64, at 386–90.

80. Among the many introduced bills, H.R. 4813, the Genetically Engineered Food Safety Act, would have 'amend[ed] the Federal Food, Drug, and Cosmetic Act with respect to the safety' of biotech foods. Genetically Engineered Food Safety Act of 2002, H.R. 4813, 107th Cong. (2002). This bill would have required a pre-market agency determination that a GMO is safe for human consumption, and it would have given the FDA a right to impose independent testing and to seek input from the National Academy's Institute of Medicine. Id. Similarly, S. 3095, the Genetically Engineered Foods Act, would have required that FDA to review and approve all genetically engineered foods prior to introduction into interstate commerce. Genetically Engineered Foods Act, S. 3095, 107th Cong. (2002). State legislatures are quite active in this area as well. For further information, see Pew Initiative on Biotechnology, Factsheet: State Legislative Activity Related to Agricultural Biotechnology in 2005–2006, http://pewagbiotech.org/resources/factsheets/legislation/factsheet.php.

2. EPA

EPA's authority over GM crops stems largely from its regulatory oversight over the human health and environmental consequences of pesticides, arising under both the Federal Insecticide, Fungicide and Rodenticide Act (FIFRA)[81] and the FDCA.[82] This responsibility includes the duty to determine acceptable tolerances for pesticide residues in food. Because most of the GM crops currently on the market have been genetically modified to produce endogenous pesticides, EPA plays a critical regulatory role.

EPA has interpreted FIFRA's pesticide registration provisions to encompass plant produced pesticides (so-called "plant incorporated protectants" or "PIPs"). No plant that has been modified to endogenously produce a pesticide can be sold unless registered under FIFRA. Registration requires a demonstration that there will be no unsafe environmental or human dietary effects. As part of this analysis, no such GM food crop can lawfully be sold for planting until EPA has either established a tolerance level for the endogenously produced pesticide or has exempted the GMO from the tolerance requirement.[83] In the absence of a duly promulgated tolerance or exemption, or if the residue level detected in food exceeds the tolerance, the food is deemed adulterated under the FDCA and is subject to enforcement by FDA.[84] To date, EPA has registered only a few endogenously produced pesticides, and with one exception, all have been crops with genes that encode Bt proteins.[85] EPA has granted many of these Bt crops exemptions from the requirement for a tolerance level.[86]

Under FIFRA, EPA has no regulatory authority over plants that do not produce pesticides. Thus, EPA's regulatory authority is narrow, and notably, it does not cover bio-pharmed crops, or crops modified to be resistant to herbicides.

3. USDA

USDA's primary duty with regard to genetically engineered crops is to evaluate whether there is risk that a novel organism will pose a plant pest risk when introduced into the environment or interstate commerce. USDA interprets this authority narrowly, treating GM crops exactly like their conventional counterparts and evaluating them for the same risks.

---

81. 7 U.S.C. § 136a(a)(2000). EPA's pesticide regulations are set out in 40 C.F.R. pts. 150–189.

82. See FIFRA and FDCA, as clarified by the Food Quality Protection Act of 1996, Pub. L. No. 104-170, 110 Stat. 1489 (1996).

83. EPA may, by regulation, exempt any pesticide from some or all of the requirements of FIFRA, if the pesticide is "of a character which is unnecessary to be subject to" FIFRA in order to carry out the purposes of the Act. 7 U.S.C. § 136w(b)(2) (2000). EPA generally exempts pesticides that pose low probabilities of risk to the environment in the absence of regulatory oversight. See Regulations Under the Federal Insecticide, Fungicide, and Rodenticide Act for Plant Incorporated Protectants (Formerly Plant-Pesticides), 66 Fed. Reg. 37,772 (July 19 2001) (Pesticides that do not qualify for exemption can still be approved for specific uses, but only if they do not "cause unreasonable adverse effects.").

84. FDCA, 21 U.S.C. § 408(1) defines any pesticide chemical residue contained in food as adulterated unless EPA has exempted the pesticide from the tolerance requirement, or EPA has issued a tolerance level and the residue in question complies with that tolerance level.

85. See Donna U. Vogt, U.S. Congressional Research Service, Food Biotechnology in the United States: Science, Regulation, and Issues, RL30198 tbl. 2, 15 (Jan. 19, 2001).

86. Many Bt genes, and their proteins, have not shown toxicity to humans. EPA has therefore typically granted the Bt crops exemptions from the requirement for a tolerance level. See, e.g., 40 C.F.R. § 180.1155 (2002) (exempting CryIA(c)), 40 C.F.R. § 180.1173 (2002) (exempting CryIA(b)). For an explanation of these decisions to exempt certain Bt genes and proteins, see 40 C.F.R. § 180.1173 (1996); see also 40 C.F.R. § 180.1155 (1995).

Under the Plant Protection Act, USDA has the authority to adopt regulations preventing the introduction and dissemination of plant pests.[87] Pursuant to this authority, USDA, through APHIS, regulates "organisms and products altered or produced through genetic engineering that are plant pests or are believed to be plant pests."[88] The statute's implementing regulations define a plant pest as "(a)ny living ... [organism] ... which can directly or indirectly injure[] or cause[] disease or damage in or to any plant."[89]

APHIS's regulatory oversight of products of modern biotechnology is narrowly focused on whether these novel organisms might pose such a risk.[90] APHIS thus permits GM plants to be deregulated if field tests show that the GMO will not pose a plant pest risk.[91] In conducting this regulatory review, APHIS treats GM crops exactly like their conventional counterparts and evaluates them for exactly the same risks. APHIS does not consider whether planting a GM crop modified to be resistant to a herbicide is likely to spread the trait of resistance more generally, nor does the agency consider the possible contamination that might result from pollen drift from GM plants to unmodified plants.

Like its sister agencies, APHIS starts from the assumption that products developed through biotechnology are "substantially equivalent" to their conventional counterparts. Indeed, the Coordinated Framework expects that in most cases, genetically engineered crops "will be improved, and would therefore not pose any new threat to humans, other animal species, or to the environment."[92] A 1988 analysis by the General Accounting Office (now the Government Accountability Office) (GAO) roundly criticized shortcomings in USDA's oversight, echoing calls by the scientific community that certain regulatory decisions were "scientifically indefensible."[93] In particular, GAO criticized the decision to exempt certain categories of GMOs from regulatory scrutiny "prior to developing scientific information on the behavior of these organisms in the environment."[94]

Moreover, APHIS typically does not require permits for field testing of GM food crops but instead permits purveyors to proceed under a notification procedure.[95] Since 1987, APHIS

---

87. PPA, 7 U.S.C. § 7711(a).

88. 7 C.F.R. § 340.0(a)(2) n.1; *see generally*, Introduction of Organisms and Products Altered or Produced Through Genetic Engineering Which are Plant Pests or Which There is Reason to Believe are Plant Pests, 7 C.F.R. § 340 et seq. This definition may exclude the growing number of plants that are transformed using "gene gun" technology rather than through agrobacterium transformation. For an explanation of these techniques and their differences, *see* [Rebecca M. Bratspies, American Law Institute-American Bar Association, Biotechnology Primer for Lawyers 1, 9 (2003) (offering a more detailed explanation of the technology behind genetic engineering)].

89. 7 C.F.R. § 340.1.

90. For a detailed discussion, *see generally*, Bratspies, *Illusions of Care, supra* note 63.

91. For a description of this process, see Petition for Determination of Nonregulated Status, 7 C.F.R. § 340.6(a) (2003). After receiving a petition, USDA publishes a notice in the Federal Register and accepts comments for sixty days. 7 C.F.R. § 340.6(d)(2) (2003). USDA has one hundred and eighty days to deny or approve the petition. 7 C.F.R. § 340.6(d)(3) (2003).

92. Coordinated Framework, *supra* note 48, at 23,339.

93. U.S. Gen. Accounting Office, *Biotechnology: Managing the Risks of Field Testing Genetically Engineered Organisms*, GAO/RCED-88-27, at 48 (June 1988).

94. *Id.* at 3.

95. Notification for the Introduction of Certain Regulated Articles, 7 C.F.R. § 340.3(a) (2003). This position contrasts sharply with the European Union's regulatory approach.

has authorized more than 10,000 field tests of GM crops.[96] Once a GM crop has been field tested, its developer can petition for non-regulated status and approval for commercial sales.[97] After a deregulation petition is granted, the subject plant is no longer considered a regulated article and is no longer subject to APHIS's oversight. More than 60 genetically engineered plants have been deregulated under this process. Most of these deregulated plants endogenously produce the pesticide Bt or are engineered to be tolerant to herbicide exposure (or both traits in combination).[98]

The second generation of GM plants pose an even greater challenge to adequate USDA regulation, particularly "biopharm"[99] crops that produce industrial or pharmaceutical compounds. Because the biopharm crops are not intended for food, they fall entirely outside FDA's regulatory authority. Because they do not produce pesticides, they similarly are not within EPA's purview. By elimination, USDA stands as the sole regulatory agency. Unfortunately, USDA has little experience or familiarity with the non-food compounds involved in biopharming,[100] some of which are known to have deleterious effects on human health.[101] A limited "plant pest" analysis will not begin to cover the myriad risks that accompany the exciting new possibilities offered by these crops.

C. Gaps and Overlaps

The United States regulatory system for GMOs is a complex net woven from pre-existing regulatory strands. The problem is that, like all nets, this regulatory net has holes. Among the holes or gaps associated with biotechnology, some of the most pressing include: the risk of transferring herbicide resistance from crops to weeds; the prospect of biopharm industrial or pharmaceutical compounds entering the food chain; the lack of consumer choice because bio-engineered food is not labeled as such; the introduction new allergens and toxins into the food chain; and the certainty of unexpected consequences. Indeed, even USDA's Advisory Committee on Biotechnology and 21st Century Agriculture concedes that statutes written before the development of modern biotechnology "may not be optimal to meet the needs of producers and consumers."[102] These statutes simply fail to cover the range of problems posed by GM crops. In particular, the advisory committee pointed to a few notable gaps in the United States regulatory scheme —transgenic animals, biopharming, adventitious presence, and the need to address imports of GMOs developed in other countries.[103]

---

96. BRS Factsheet: Biotechnology Regulatory Services, U.S. Department of Agriculture, http://www.aphis.usda.gov/publications/biotechnology/content/printable_version/BRS_FS_ FedReg_02-06.pdf (February 2006).

97. Restriction on the Introduction of Regulated Articles, 7 C.F.R. § 340.0(a)(1) (2002).

98. *Id.*

99. *See infra* note 100 (discussing "biopharming").

100. Industry's preferred term for this process is "plant made pharmaceuticals" or PMPs. Because I believe this term obscures the GM nature of these plants in an attempt to deflect conversation about the troubling issues their production raises, I deliberately choose to use the term biopharming.

101. *See* Bratspies, *Consuming (F)ears of Corn*, *supra* note 64, at 382–386.

102. USDA Advisory Committee on Biotechnology and 21st Century Agriculture, Opportunities and Challenges in Agricultural Biotechnology: The Decade Ahead 5 (July 13, 2006) available at http://www.usda.gov/documents/final_main_report-v6.pdf. Despite this caveat, the overall tenor of this report was optimistic.

103. *Id.*

For example, the primary strategy for preventing cross-contamination between GM crops and conventional or organic crops are physical containment measures. Physical containment measures involve using planting distances or timing to prevent contamination of conventional crops with GM crops. Unfortunately, for existing GM crops, physical contamination measures have largely been ineffectual, either because the requirements are too lenient or because they are not being implemented. Indeed, a 2003 USDA survey found that approximately 20% of farms growing GM crops failed to comply with planting regulations intended to ensure physical containment.[104]

Industry trade groups acknowledge that cross-pollination, adventitious commingling and other "causes" make it virtually impossible to assure that any U.S.-origin corn shipment is 100% non-GMO.[105] The same holds true for soybeans. There is no comprehensive domestic policy regarding adventitious presence of transgenic events in seed, grain, or food. This problem will only become more significant as other countries begin to develop and approve GMOs and thereafter seek approval to import these new organisms into the United States. There are real questions about whether the United States regulatory system will be able to cope with the possibilities that arise from considering the problem of contamination and adventitious presence of novel organisms that have not been through the United States regulatory procedures....

Notes

1. On October 9, 2008, APHIS published a proposed rule that sought to revise the regulations regarding the importation, interstate movement, and environmental release of genetically engineered organisms "in order to bring the regulations into alignment with provisions of the Plant Protection Act" and to "update the regulations in response to advances in genetic science and technology and our accumulated experience in implementing the current regulations." The proposed rule noted that this was "the first comprehensive review and revision of the regulations since they were established in 1987." 73 Fed. Reg. 60,008 (proposed Oct. 9, 2008) (to be codified at 7 C.F.R. pt. 340). The public comment period for the proposed rule ended November 24, 2008.

The Congressional Research Service reported that

---

104. Emily Gerseney, *USDA Survey Shows Biotech Rules Breaches*, WASHINGTON POST, Sept. 10, 2003. The survey itself can be found at http://www.nass.usda.gov/Publications/Corn_and_Biotechnology_Special_ Analysis/bioc0703.pdf. An in-depth analysis of the prior year's data, conducted by the Center for Science in the Public Interest, reached similar conclusions. *See,* Gregory Jaffe, *Planting Trouble: Are Farmers Squandering Bt Corn Technology?*, at http://cspinet.org/new/pdf/bt_corn_report.pdf (June 19, 2003) (analyzing USDA data).

105. See Organic Trade Association, Comments on Proposed Free Trade Agreement With the Republic of Korea (March 23, 2006) available at http://www.ota.com/pp/otaposition/frc/USTR/03-23-06.html; Drew L. Kershen and Alan McHughen, *CAST Commentary: Adventitious Presence: Inadvertent Commingling and Coexistence Among Farming Methods*, (July 2005) available at http://www.cast-science.org/websiteUploads/publicationPDFs/advenpresence%20rev.pdf; Pew Initiative on Biotechnology, *Detecting Genetically Modified Organisms: Confronting the Limits of Testing to Resolve a Biotech Food Fight*, available at http://pewagbiotech.org/events/0225/proceedings.pdf. (discussing the problem); CropChoice, *Is GMO-free Production Possible? Costs and Methods of Crop Segregation*, (November 23, 2001) available at http://www.cropchoice.com/leadstryd5d6-2.html?recid=517.

Reactions to the proposed revisions were mixed. The Biotechnology Industry Organization and the Grocery Manufacturers Association generally supported the revisions. The Center for Food Safety (CFS) denounced the proposal stating that, '... these proposed regulations may set in motion a process that would put many GE crops completely beyond the bounds of regulation ...' CFS said that its biggest concern is that the proposed rules remove established criteria in determining the very scope of regulation. In a similar response, the Union of Concerned Scientists denounced the proposed rules for failing to adequately protect the U.S. food supply from potential contamination from biopharm crops through cross-pollination or seed mixing between biopharm food crops and those food crops intended for consumption."

Tadlock Cowan & Geoffrey S. Becker, *Agricultural Biotechnology: Background and Recent Issues,* Congressional Research Report RL-32809 (Feb. 13, 2009).

On January 16, 2009 APHIS reopened the comment period, which ran until the end of June 2009. APHIS received over 60,000 comments, and as of this writing, the analysis of these comments continues.

2. Genetically-engineered animals also present an emerging area of production and a developing area of regulation. On January 15, 2009, the FDA issued a Final Guidance for the industry on the regulation of genetically engineered animals. The Food, Drug & Cosmetic Act gives the FDA the authority to regulate both food and drugs, and defines a "drug" as including "articles (other than food) intended to affect the structure or any function of the body of man or other animals." 21 U.S.C. § 321(1). Under this definition, the FDA considers the rDNA construct that is in a genetically engineered animal to be an animal drug, subject to its regulatory authority. If the animal or products from the animal are used as food, FDA also has regulatory authority over the food product under the Food, Drug & Cosmetic Act. 21 U.S.C. § 301 *et seq.* Meat, poultry, and egg products, however, are regulated by the USDA under the Federal Meat Inspection Act, 21 U.S.C. § 601 *et seq.*, the Poultry Products Inspections act, 21 U.S.C. § 451 *et seq.*, and the Eggs Products Inspection Act, 21 U.S.C. § 1031 *et seq.* Under the Guidance, the FDA requires pre-market approval for new animals and products. The FDA is clearly supportive of this new technology, however, and much of the information provided on the FDA website focuses on the benefits possible through the genetic engineering of animals and seeks to allay consumer concern. For an overview of the regulation of genetic engineering and animal production, see Geoffrey S. Becker and Tadlock Cowan, *Biotechnology in Animal Agriculture: Status and Current Issues,* CRS Report RL-33334 (Feb. 11, 2009).

B. The Patenting of Genetically-Engineered Seeds

Two U.S. Supreme Court cases helped to set the stage for the successful advancement of the agricultural biotechnology industry. In 1980, in the case of *Diamond v. Chakabarty,* the Court ruled that live, human-made microorganisms could be patented; and, in 2001, in the case of *J.E.M. Ag Supply, Inc. v. Pioneer Hi-bred International, Inc.,* the Court held that newly developed plant breeds are patentable subject matter, despite the alternative framework established by the Plant Variety Protection Act. Together, these cases have rendered the historic tradition of farmers saving seeds from one year to the next illegal in most instances.

1. Patenting Live, Human-made Organisms

Diamond v. Chakrabarty
447 U.S. 303 (1980)
Supreme Court of the United States

Mr. Chief Justice BURGER delivered the opinion of the Court. Mr. Justice Brennan dissented and filed opinion in which Mr. Justice White, Mr. Justice Marshall and Mr. Justice Powell joined.

We granted certiorari to determine whether a live, human-made micro-organism is patentable subject matter under 35 U.S.C. § 101.

I

In 1972, respondent Chakrabarty, a microbiologist, filed a patent application, assigned to the General Electric Co. The application asserted 36 claims related to Chakrabarty's invention of "a bacterium from the genus Pseudomonas containing therein at least two stable energy-generating plasmids, each of said plasmids providing a separate hydrocarbon degradative pathway."[1] This human-made, genetically engineered bacterium is capable of breaking down multiple components of crude oil. Because of this property, which is possessed by no naturally occurring bacteria, Chakrabarty's invention is believed to have significant value for the treatment of oil spills.[2]

Chakrabarty's patent claims were of three types: first, process claims for the method of producing the bacteria; second, claims for an inoculum comprised of a carrier material floating on water, such as straw, and the new bacteria; and third, claims to the bacteria themselves. The patent examiner allowed the claims falling into the first two categories, but rejected claims for the bacteria. His decision rested on two grounds: (1) that micro-organisms are "products of nature," and (2) that as living things they are not patentable subject matter under 35 U.S.C. § 101.

Chakrabarty appealed the rejection of these claims to the Patent Office Board of Appeals, and the Board affirmed the Examiner on the second ground.[3] Relying on the legislative history of the 1930 Plant Patent Act, in which Congress extended patent protection to certain asexually reproduced plants, the Board concluded that § 101 was not intended to cover living things such as these laboratory created micro-organisms.

---

1. Plasmids are hereditary units physically separate from the chromosomes of the cell. In prior research, Chakrabarty and an associate discovered that plasmids control the oil degradation abilities of certain bacteria. In particular, the two researchers discovered plasmids capable of degrading camphor and octane, two components of crude oil. In the work represented by the patent application at issue here, Chakrabarty discovered a process by which four different plasmids, capable of degrading four different oil components, could be transferred to and maintained stably in a single Pseudomonas bacterium, which itself has no capacity for degrading oil.

2. At present, biological control of oil spills requires the use of a mixture of naturally occurring bacteria, each capable of degrading one component of the oil complex. In this way, oil is decomposed into simpler substances which can serve as food for aquatic life. However, for various reasons, only a portion of any such mixed culture survives to attack the oil spill. By breaking down multiple components of oil, Chakrabarty's micro-organism promises more efficient and rapid oil-spill control.

3. The Board concluded that the new bacteria were not "products of nature," because Pseudomonas bacteria containing two or more different energy-generating plasmids are not naturally occurring.

The Court of Customs and Patent Appeals, by a divided vote, reversed on the authority of its prior decision in *In re Bergy*, which held that "the fact that microorganisms ... are alive ... [is] without legal significance" for purposes of the patent law.[4] ...

II

The Constitution grants Congress broad power to legislate to "promote the Progress of Science and useful Arts, by securing for limited Times to Authors and Inventors the exclusive Right to their respective Writings and Discoveries." Art. I, § 8, cl. 8. The patent laws promote this progress by offering inventors exclusive rights for a limited period as an incentive for their inventiveness and research efforts. The authority of Congress is exercised in the hope that "[t]he productive effort thereby fostered will have a positive effect on society through the introduction of new products and processes of manufacture into the economy, and the emanations by way of increased employment and better lives for our citizens."

The question before us in this case is a narrow one of statutory interpretation requiring us to construe 35 U.S.C. § 101, which provides:

> Whoever invents or discovers any new and useful process, machine, manufacture, or composition of matter, or any new and useful improvement thereof, may obtain a patent therefor, subject to the conditions and requirements of this title.

Specifically, we must determine whether respondent's micro-organism constitutes a "manufacture" or "composition of matter" within the meaning of the statute.[5]

III

In cases of statutory construction we begin, of course, with the language of the statute. And "unless otherwise defined, words will be interpreted as taking their ordinary, contemporary common meaning." We have also cautioned that courts "should not read into the patent laws limitations and conditions which the legislature has not expressed."

Guided by these canons of construction, this Court has read the term "manufacture" in § 101 in accordance with its dictionary definition to mean "the production of articles for use from raw or prepared materials by giving to these materials new forms, qualities, properties, or combinations, whether by hand-labor or by machinery." Similarly, "composition of matter" has been construed consistent with its common usage to include "all compositions of two or more substances and ... all composite articles, whether they be the results of chemical union, or of mechanical mixture, or whether they be gases, fluids, powders or solids." In choosing such expansive terms as "manufacture" and "composition of matter," modified by the comprehensive "any," Congress plainly contemplated that the patent laws would be given wide scope.

The relevant legislative history also supports a broad construction. The Patent Act of 1793, authored by Thomas Jefferson, defined statutory subject matter as "any new and useful art, machine, manufacture, or composition of matter, or any new or useful improvement [thereof]." The Act embodied Jefferson's philosophy that "ingenuity should receive a liberal encouragement." Subsequent patent statutes in 1836, 1870, and 1874 employed

---

4. *Bergy* involved a patent application for a pure culture of the micro-organism Streptomyces vellosus found to be useful in the production of lincomycin, an antibiotic.

5. This case does not involve the other "conditions and requirements" of the patent laws, such as novelty and nonobviousness. 35 U.S.C. §§ 102, 103.

this same broad language. In 1952, when the patent laws were recodified, Congress replaced the word "art" with "process," but otherwise left Jefferson's language intact. The Committee Reports accompanying the 1952 Act inform us that Congress intended statutory subject matter to "include anything under the sun that is made by man."[6]

This is not to suggest that § 101 has no limits or that it embraces every discovery. The laws of nature, physical phenomena, and abstract ideas have been held not patentable. Thus, a new mineral discovered in the earth or a new plant found in the wild is not patentable subject matter. Likewise, Einstein could not patent his celebrated law that $E=mc2$; nor could Newton have patented the law of gravity. Such discoveries are "manifestations of ... nature, free to all men and reserved exclusively to none."

Judged in this light, respondent's micro-organism plainly qualifies as patentable subject matter. His claim is not to a hitherto unknown natural phenomenon, but to a non-naturally occurring manufacture or composition of matter—a product of human ingenuity "having a distinctive name, character [and] use." The point is underscored dramatically by comparison of the invention here with that in [*Funk Brothers Seed Co. v. Kalo Inoculant Co.*] There, the patentee had discovered that there existed in nature certain species of root-nodule bacteria which did not exert a mutually inhibitive effect on each other. He used that discovery to produce a mixed culture capable of inoculating the seeds of leguminous plants. Concluding that the patentee had discovered "only some of the handiwork of nature," the Court ruled the product nonpatentable:

> Each of the species of root-nodule bacteria contained in the package infects the same group of leguminous plants which it always infected. No species acquires a different use. The combination of species produces no new bacteria, no change in the six species of bacteria, and no enlargement of the range of their utility. Each species has the same effect it always had. The bacteria perform in their natural way. Their use in combination does not improve in any way their natural functioning. They serve the ends nature originally provided and act quite independently of any effort of the patentee.

333 U.S., at 131, 68 S.Ct., at 442.

Here, by contrast, the patentee has produced a new bacterium with markedly different characteristics from any found in nature and one having the potential for significant utility. His discovery is not nature's handiwork, but his own; accordingly it is patentable subject matter under § 101.

IV

Two contrary arguments are advanced, neither of which we find persuasive.

(A)

The petitioner's first argument rests on the enactment of the 1930 Plant Patent Act, which afforded patent protection to certain asexually reproduced plants, and the 1970 Plant Variety Protection Act, which authorized protection for certain sexually reproduced plants

---

6. This same language was employed by P. J. Federico, a principal draftsman of the 1952 recodification, in his testimony regarding that legislation: "[U]nder section 101 a person may have invented a machine or a manufacture, which may include anything under the sun that is made by man...." Hearings on H.R. 3760 before Subcommittee No. 3 of the House Committee on the Judiciary, 82d Cong., 1st Sess., 37 (1951).

but excluded bacteria from its protection.[7] In the petitioner's view, the passage of these Acts evidences congressional understanding that the terms "manufacture" or "composition of matter" do not include living things; if they did, the petitioner argues, neither Act would have been necessary.

We reject this argument. Prior to 1930, two factors were thought to remove plants from patent protection. The first was the belief that plants, even those artificially bred, were products of nature for purposes of the patent law. This position appears to have derived from the decision of the patent office in *Ex parte Latimer*, 1889 Dec.Com.Pat. 123, in which a patent claim for fiber found in the needle of the Pinus australis was rejected. The Commissioner reasoned that a contrary result would permit "patents [to] be obtained upon the trees of the forest and the plants of the earth, which of course would be unreasonable and impossible." The Latimer case, it seems, came to "se[t] forth the general stand taken in these matters" that plants were natural products not subject to patent protection.[8] The second obstacle to patent protection for plants was the fact that plants were thought not amenable to the "written description" requirement of the patent law. Because new plants may differ from old only in color or perfume, differentiation by written description was often impossible.

In enacting the Plant Patent Act, Congress addressed both of these concerns. It explained at length its belief that the work of the plant breeder "in aid of nature" was patentable invention.

And it relaxed the written description requirement in favor of "a description ... as complete as is reasonably possible." No Committee or Member of Congress, however, expressed the broader view, now urged by the petitioner, that the terms "manufacture" or "composition of matter" exclude living things. The sole support for that position in the legislative history of the 1930 Act is found in the conclusory statement of Secretary of Agriculture Hyde, in a letter to the Chairmen of the House and Senate Committees considering the 1930 Act, that "the patent laws ... at the present time are understood to cover only inventions or discoveries in the field of inanimate nature." Secretary Hyde's opinion, however, is not entitled to controlling weight. His views were solicited on the administration of the new law and not on the scope of patentable subject matter — an area beyond his competence. Moreover, there is language in the House and Senate Committee Reports suggesting that to the extent Congress considered the matter it found the Secretary's dichotomy unpersuasive. The Reports observe:

> There is a clear and logical distinction *between the discovery of a new variety of plant and of certain inanimate things*, such, for example, as a new and useful natural mineral. The mineral is created wholly by nature unassisted by man.... On

---

7. The Plant Patent Act of 1930, 35 U.S.C. § 161, provides in relevant part: "Whoever invents or discovers and asexually reproduces any distinct and new variety of plant, including cultivated sports, mutants, hybrids, and newly found seedlings, other than a tuber propagated plant or a plant found in an uncultivated state, may obtain a patent therefor...."

The Plant Variety Protection Act of 1970, provides in relevant part: "The breeder of any novel variety of sexually reproduced plant (other than fungi, bacteria, or first generation hybrids) who has so reproduced the variety, or his successor in interest, shall be entitled to plant variety protection therefor...." 84 Stat. 1547, 7 U.S.C. § 2402(a).

8. Writing three years after the passage of the 1930 Act, R. Cook, Editor of the Journal of Heredity, commented: "It is a little hard for plant men to understand why [Art. I, § 8] of the Constitution should not have been earlier construed to include the promotion of the art of plant breeding. The reason for this is probably to be found in the principle that natural products are not patentable." Florists Exchange and Horticultural Trade World, July 15, 1933, p. 9.

the other hand, a plant discovery resulting from cultivation is unique, isolated, and is not repeated by nature, nor can it be reproduced by nature unaided by man....

S.Rep.No.315; H.R.Rep.No.1129 (emphasis added).

Congress thus recognized that the relevant distinction was not between living and inanimate things, but between products of nature, whether living or not, and human-made inventions. Here, respondent's micro-organism is the result of human ingenuity and research. Hence, the passage of the Plant Patent Act affords the Government no support.

Nor does the passage of the 1970 Plant Variety Protection Act support the Government's position. As the Government acknowledges, sexually reproduced plants were not included under the 1930 Act because new varieties could not be reproduced true-to-type through seedlings. By 1970, however, it was generally recognized that true-to-type reproduction was possible and that plant patent protection was therefore appropriate. The 1970 Act extended that protection. There is nothing in its language or history to suggest that it was enacted because § 101 did not include living things.

In particular, we find nothing in the exclusion of bacteria from plant variety protection to support the petitioner's position. The legislative history gives no reason for this exclusion. As the Court of Customs and Patent Appeals suggested, it may simply reflect congressional agreement with the result reached by that court in deciding In re Arzberger which held that bacteria were not plants for the purposes of the 1930 Act. Or it may reflect the fact that prior to 1970 the Patent Office had issued patents for bacteria under § 101.[9] In any event, absent some clear indication that Congress "focused on [the] issues ... directly related to the one presently before the Court," there is no basis for reading into its actions an intent to modify the plain meaning of the words found in § 101.

(B)

The petitioner's second argument is that micro-organisms cannot qualify as patentable subject matter until Congress expressly authorizes such protection. His position rests on the fact that genetic technology was unforeseen when Congress enacted § 101. From this it is argued that resolution of the patentability of inventions such as respondent's should be left to Congress. The legislative process, the petitioner argues, is best equipped to weigh the competing economic, social, and scientific considerations involved, and to determine whether living organisms produced by genetic engineering should receive patent protection. In support of this position, the petitioner relies on our recent holding in *Parker v. Flook* and the statement that the judiciary "must proceed cautiously when ... asked to extend patent rights into areas wholly unforeseen by Congress."

It is, of course, correct that Congress, not the courts, must define the limits of patentability; but it is equally true that once Congress has spoken it is "the province and duty of the judicial department to say what the law is." Congress has performed its constitutional role in defining patentable subject matter in § 101; we perform ours in construing the language Congress has employed. In so doing, our obligation is to take statutes as we find them, guided, if ambiguity appears, by the legislative history and statutory purpose. Here, we perceive no ambiguity. The subject-matter provisions of the patent law have been cast

---

9. In 1873, the Patent Office granted Louis Pasteur a patent on "yeast, free from organic germs of disease, as an article of manufacture." And in 1967 and 1968, immediately prior to the passage of the Plant Variety Protection Act, that Office granted two patents which, as the petitioner concedes, state claims for living micro-organisms.

in broad terms to fulfill the constitutional and statutory goal of promoting "the Progress of Science and the useful Arts" with all that means for the social and economic benefits envisioned by Jefferson. Broad general language is not necessarily ambiguous when congressional objectives require broad terms.

Nothing in *Flook* is to the contrary. That case applied our prior precedents to determine that a "claim for an improved method of calculation, even when tied to a specific end use, is unpatentable subject matter under § 101." The Court carefully scrutinized the claim at issue to determine whether it was precluded from patent protection under "the principles underlying the prohibition against patents for 'ideas' or phenomena of nature." We have done that here. *Flook* did not announce a new principle that inventions in areas not contemplated by Congress when the patent laws were enacted are unpatentable per se.

To read that concept into *Flook* would frustrate the purposes of the patent law. This Court frequently has observed that a statute is not to be confined to the "particular application[s] ... contemplated by the legislators." This is especially true in the field of patent law. A rule that unanticipated inventions are without protection would conflict with the core concept of the patent law that anticipation undermines patentability. Mr. Justice Douglas reminded that the inventions most benefiting mankind are those that "push back the frontiers of chemistry, physics, and the like." Congress employed broad general language in drafting § 101 precisely because such inventions are often unforeseeable.[10]

To buttress his argument, the petitioner, with the support of amicus, points to grave risks that may be generated by research endeavors such as respondent's. The briefs present a gruesome parade of horribles. Scientists, among them Nobel laureates, are quoted suggesting that genetic research may pose a serious threat to the human race, or, at the very least, that the dangers are far too substantial to permit such research to proceed apace at this time. We are told that genetic research and related technological developments may spread pollution and disease, that it may result in a loss of genetic diversity, and that its practice may tend to depreciate the value of human life. These arguments are forcefully, even passionately, presented; they remind us that, at times, human ingenuity seems unable to control fully the forces it creates—that with Hamlet, it is sometimes better "to bear those ills we have than fly to others that we know not of."

It is argued that this Court should weigh these potential hazards in considering whether respondent's invention is patentable subject matter under § 101. We disagree. The grant or denial of patents on micro-organisms is not likely to put an end to genetic research or to its attendant risks. The large amount of research that has already occurred when no researcher had sure knowledge that patent protection would be available suggests that legislative or judicial fiat as to patentability will not deter the scientific mind from probing into the unknown any more than Canute could command the tides. Whether respondent's claims are patentable may determine whether research efforts are accelerated by the hope of reward or slowed by want of incentives, but that is all.

---

10. Even an abbreviated list of patented inventions underscores the point: telegraph (Morse, No. 1,647); telephone (Bell, No. 174,465); electric lamp (Edison, No. 223,898); airplane (the Wrights, No. 821,393); transistor (Bardeen & Brattain, No. 2,524,035); neutronic reactor (Fermi & Szilard, No. 2,708,656); laser (Schawlow & Townes, No. 2,929,922). *See generally* Revolutionary Ideas, Patents & Progress in America, United States Patent and Trademark Office (1976).

What is more important is that we are without competence to entertain these arguments–either to brush them aside as fantasies generated by fear of the unknown, or to act on them. The choice we are urged to make is a matter of high policy for resolution within the legislative process after the kind of investigation, examination, and study that legislative bodies can provide and courts cannot. That process involves the balancing of competing values and interests, which in our democratic system is the business of elected representatives. Whatever their validity, the contentions now pressed on us should be addressed to the political branches of the Government, the Congress and the Executive, and not to the courts.[11]

We have emphasized in the recent past that "[o]ur individual appraisal of the wisdom or unwisdom of a particular [legislative] course … is to be put aside in the process of interpreting a statute." Our task, rather, is the narrow one of determining what Congress meant by the words it used in the statute; once that is done our powers are exhausted. Congress is free to amend § 101 so as to exclude from patent protection organisms produced by genetic engineering.… Or it may chose to craft a statute specifically designed for such living things. But, until Congress takes such action, this Court must construe the language of § 101 as it is. The language of that section fairly embraces respondent's invention.

Accordingly, the judgment of the Court of Customs and Patent Appeals is

Affirmed.

Mr. Justice BRENNAN, with whom Mr. Justice WHITE, Mr. Justice MARSHALL, and Mr. Justice POWELL join, dissenting.

I agree with the Court that the question before us is a narrow one. Neither the future of scientific research, nor even, the ability of respondent Chakrabarty to reap some monopoly profits from his pioneering work, is at stake. Patents on the processes by which he has produced and employed the new living organism are not contested. The only question we need decide is whether Congress, exercising its authority under Art. I, § 8, of the Constitution, intended that he be able to secure a monopoly on the living organism itself, no matter how produced or how used. Because I believe the Court has misread the applicable legislation, I dissent.

The patent laws attempt to reconcile this Nation's deep seated antipathy to monopolies with the need to encourage progress. Given the complexity and legislative nature of this delicate task, we must be careful to extend patent protection no further than Congress has provided. In particular, were there an absence of legislative direction, the courts should leave to Congress the decisions whether and how far to extend the patent privilege into areas where the common understanding has been that patents are not available.[1]

In this case, however, we do not confront a complete legislative vacuum. The sweeping language of the Patent Act of 1793, as re-enacted in 1952, is not the last pronouncement Congress has made in this area. In 1930 Congress enacted the Plant Patent Act affording patent protection to developers of certain asexually reproduced plants. In 1970

---

11. We are not to be understood as suggesting that the political branches have been laggard in the consideration of the problems related to genetic research and technology. They have already taken action. In 1976, for example, the National Institutes of Health released guidelines for NIH-sponsored genetic research which established conditions under which such research could be performed. In 1978 those guidelines were revised and relaxed. And Committees of the Congress have held extensive hearings on these matters.…

1. I read the Court to admit that the popular conception, even among advocates of agricultural patents, was that living organisms were unpatentable.

Congress enacted the Plant Variety Protection Act to extend protection to certain new plant varieties capable of sexual reproduction. Thus, we are not dealing—as the Court would have it—with the routine problem of "unanticipated inventions." In these two Acts Congress has addressed the general problem of patenting animate inventions and has chosen carefully limited language granting protection to some kinds of discoveries, but specifically excluding others. These Acts strongly evidence a congressional limitation that excludes bacteria from patentability.[2]

First, the Acts evidence Congress' understanding, at least since 1930, that § 101 does not include living organisms. If newly developed living organisms not naturally occurring had been patentable under § 101, the plants included in the scope of the 1930 and 1970 Acts could have been patented without new legislation. Those plants, like the bacteria involved in this case, were new varieties not naturally occurring.[3] Although the Court rejects this line of argument, it does not explain why the Acts were necessary unless to correct a pre-existing situation.[4] I cannot share the Court's implicit assumption that Congress was engaged in either idle exercises or mere correction of the public record when it enacted the 1930 and 1970 Acts. And Congress certainly thought it was doing something significant. The Committee Reports contain expansive prose about the previously unavailable benefits to be derived from extending patent protection to plants.[5] Because Congress thought it had to legislate in order to make agricultural "human-made inventions" patentable and because the legislation Congress enacted is limited, it follows that Congress never meant to make items outside the scope of the legislation patentable.

Similarly, Representative Poage, speaking for the 1970 Act, after noting the protection accorded asexually developed plants, stated that "for plants produced from seed, there has been no such protection."

Second, the 1970 Act clearly indicates that Congress has included bacteria within the focus of its legislative concern, but not within the scope of patent protection. Congress specifically excluded bacteria from the coverage of the 1970 Act. The Court's attempts to supply explanations for this explicit exclusion ring hollow. It is true that there is no men-

---

2. But even if I agreed with the Court that the 1930 and 1970 Acts were not dispositive, I would dissent. This case presents even more cogent reasons ... not to extend the patent monopoly in the face of uncertainty. At the very least, these Acts are signs of legislative attention to the problems of patenting living organisms, but they give no affirmative indication of congressional intent that bacteria be patentable. The caveat of *Parker v. Flook*, an admonition to "proceed cautiously when we are asked to extend patent rights into areas wholly unforeseen by Congress," therefore becomes pertinent. I should think the necessity for caution is that much greater when we are asked to extend patent rights into areas Congress has foreseen and considered but has not resolved.

3. The Court refers to the logic employed by Congress in choosing not to perpetuate the "dichotomy" suggested by Secretary Hyde. But by this logic the bacteria at issue here are distinguishable from a "mineral ... created wholly by nature" in exactly the same way as were the new varieties of plants. If a new Act was needed to provide patent protection for the plants, it was equally necessary for bacteria. Yet Congress provided for patents on plants but not on these bacteria. In short, Congress decided to make only a subset of animate "human-made inventions," patentable.

4. If the 1930 Act's only purpose were to solve the technical problem of description referred to by the Court, ante, at 2209, most of the Act, and in particular its limitation to asexually reproduced plants, would have been totally unnecessary.

5. Secretary Hyde's letter was not the only explicit indication in the legislative history of these Acts that Congress was acting on the assumption that legislation was necessary to make living organisms patentable. The Senate Judiciary Committee Report on the 1970 Act states the Committee's understanding that patent protection extended no further than the explicit provisions of these Acts: "Under the patent law, patent protection is limited to those varieties of plants which reproduce asexually, that is, by such methods as grafting or budding. No protection is available to those varieties of plants which reproduce sexually, that is, generally by seeds." S.Rep.No.91-1246, p. 3 (1970)

tion in the legislative history of the exclusion, but that does not give us license to invent reasons. The fact is that Congress, assuming that animate objects as to which it had not specifically legislated could not be patented, excluded bacteria from the set of patentable organisms.

The Court protests that its holding today is dictated by the broad language of §101, which cannot "be confined to the 'particular application[s] … contemplated by the legislators.'" But as I have shown, the Court's decision does not follow the unavoidable implications of the statute. Rather, it extends the patent system to cover living material even though Congress plainly has legislated in the belief that §101 does not encompass living organisms. It is the role of Congress, not this Court, to broaden or narrow the reach of the patent laws. This is especially true where, as here, the composition sought to be patented uniquely implicates matters of public concern.

---

2. Utility Patent Rights, the Plant Variety Protection Act, and the Plant Patent Act

J.E.M. Ag Supply, Inc. v. Pioneer Hi-bred International, Inc.
534 U.S. 124 (2001)

THOMAS, J., delivered the opinion of the Court, in which REHNQUIST, C.J., and SCALIA, KENNEDY, SOUTER, and GINSBURG, JJ., joined. SCALIA, J., filed a concurring opinion, BREYER, J., filed a dissenting opinion, in which STEVENS, J., joined. O'CONNOR, J., took no part in the consideration or decision of the case.

This case presents the question whether utility patents may be issued for plants under 35 U.S.C. §101, or whether the Plant Variety Protection Act, as amended, 7 U.S.C. §2321 *et seq.*, and the Plant Patent Act of 1930, 35 U.S.C. §§161–164, are the exclusive means of obtaining a federal statutory right to exclude others from reproducing, selling, or using plants or plant varieties. We hold that utility patents may be issued for plants.

I

The United States Patent and Trademark Office (PTO) has issued some 1,800 utility patents for plants, plant parts, and seeds pursuant to 35 U.S.C. §101. Seventeen of these patents are held by respondent Pioneer Hi-Bred International, Inc. (Pioneer). Pioneer's patents cover the manufacture, use, sale, and offer for sale of the company's inbred and hybrid corn seed products. A patent for an inbred corn line protects both the seeds and plants of the inbred line and the hybrids produced by crossing the protected inbred line with another corn line. A hybrid plant patent protects the plant, its seeds, variants, mutants, and trivial modifications of the hybrid. Pedigree inbred corn plants are developed by crossing corn plants with desirable characteristics and then inbreeding the resulting plants for several generations until the resulting plant line is homogenous. Inbreds are often weak and have a low yield; their value lies primarily in their use for making hybrids.

Hybrid seeds are produced by crossing two inbred corn plants and are especially valuable because they produce strong and vibrant hybrid plants with selected highly desirable characteristics. For instance, Pioneer's hybrid corn plant 3394 is "characterized by superior yield for maturity, excellent seedling vigor, very good roots and stalks, and exceptional stay green." Hybrid plants, however, generally do not reproduce true-to-type, *i.e.*, seeds produced by a hybrid plant do not reliably yield plants with the same hybrid characteristics. Thus, a farmer who wishes to continue growing hybrid plants generally needs to buy more hybrid seed.

Pioneer sells its patented hybrid seeds under a limited label license that provides: "License is granted solely to produce grain and/or forage." The license "does not extend to the use of seed from such crop or the progeny thereof for propagation or seed multiplication." It strictly prohibits "the use of such seed or the progeny thereof for propagation or seed multiplication or for production or development of a hybrid or different variety of seed."

Petitioner J.E.M. Ag Supply, Inc., doing business as Farm Advantage, Inc., purchased patented hybrid seeds from Pioneer in bags bearing this license agreement. Although not a licensed sales representative of Pioneer, Farm Advantage resold these bags. Pioneer subsequently brought a complaint for patent infringement against Farm Advantage and several other corporations and residents of the State of Iowa who are distributors and customers for Farm Advantage (referred to collectively as Farm Advantage or petitioners). Pioneer alleged that Farm Advantage has "for a long-time past been and still [is] infringing one or more [Pioneer patents] by making, using, selling, or offering for sale corn seed of the … hybrids in infringement of these patents-in-suit."

Farm Advantage answered with a general denial of patent infringement and entered a counterclaim of patent invalidity, arguing that patents that purport to confer protection for corn plants are invalid because sexually reproducing plants are not patentable subject matter within the scope of 35 U.S.C. § 101. Farm Advantage maintained that the Plant Patent Act of 1930 (PPA) and the Plant Variety Protection Act (PVPA) set forth the exclusive statutory means for the protection of plant life because these statutes are more specific than § 101, and thus each carves out subject matter from § 101 for special treatment.[1]

The District Court granted summary judgment to Pioneer. Relying on this Court's broad construction of § 101 in *Diamond v. Chakrabarty*, the District Court held that the subject matter covered by § 101 clearly includes plant life. It further concluded that in enacting the PPA and the PVPA Congress neither expressly nor implicitly removed plants from § 101's subject matter. In particular, the District Court noted that Congress did not implicitly repeal § 101 by passing the more specific PVPA because there was no irreconcilable conflict between the PVPA and § 101. The United States Court of Appeals for the Federal Circuit affirmed the judgment and reasoning of the District Court. We granted certiorari and now affirm.

II

The question before us is whether utility patents may be issued for plants pursuant to 35 U.S.C. § 101. The text of § 101 provides:

> Whoever invents or discovers any new and useful process, machine, manufacture, or composition of matter, or any new and useful improvement thereof, may obtain a patent therefor, subject to the conditions and requirements of this title.

---

1. Petitioners favor a holding that the PVPA is the only means of protecting these corn plants primarily because the PVPA's coverage is generally less extensive and the hybrid seeds at issue do not have PVPA protection. Most notably, the PVPA provides exemptions for research and for farmers to save seed from their crops for replanting. Utility patents issued for plants do not contain such exemptions.

As this Court recognized over 20 years ago in *Chakrabarty*, the language of § 101 is extremely broad. "In choosing such expansive terms as 'manufacture' and 'composition of matter,' modified by the comprehensive 'any,' Congress plainly contemplated that the patent laws would be given wide scope." This Court thus concluded in *Chakrabarty* that living things were patentable under § 101, and held that a manmade micro-organism fell within the scope of the statute. As Congress recognized, "the relevant distinction was not between living and inanimate things, but between products of nature, whether living or not, and human-made inventions."

In *Chakrabarty*, the Court also rejected the argument that Congress must expressly authorize protection for new patentable subject matter:

> It is, of course, correct that Congress, not the courts, must define the limits of patentability; but it is equally true that once Congress has spoken it is 'the province and duty of the judicial department to say what the law is.' *Marbury v. Madison*, 1 Cranch 137 (1803). Congress has performed its constitutional role in defining patentable subject matter in § 101; we perform ours in construing the language Congress has employed.... The subject-matter provisions of the patent law have been cast in broad terms to fulfill the constitutional and statutory goal of promoting 'the Progress of Science and the useful Arts' with all that means for the social and economic benefits envisioned by Jefferson.

Thus, in approaching the question presented by this case, we are mindful that this Court has already spoken clearly concerning the broad scope and applicability of § 101.

Several years after *Chakrabarty*, the PTO Board of Patent Appeals and Interferences held that plants were within the understood meaning of "manufacture" or "composition of matter" and therefore were within the subject matter of § 101. It has been the unbroken practice of the PTO since that time to confer utility patents for plants. To obtain utility patent protection, a plant breeder must show that the plant he has developed is new, useful, and non-obvious. In addition, the plant must meet the specifications of § 112, which require a written description of the plant and a deposit of seed that is publicly accessible.

Petitioners do not allege that Pioneer's patents are invalid for failure to meet the requirements for a utility patent. Nor do they dispute that plants otherwise fall within the terms of § 101's broad language that includes "manufacture" or "composition of matter." Rather, petitioners argue that the PPA and the PVPA provide the exclusive means of protecting new varieties of plants, and so awarding utility patents for plants upsets the scheme contemplated by Congress. We disagree. Considering the two plant specific statutes in turn, we find that neither forecloses utility patent coverage for plants.

A.

The 1930 PPA conferred patent protection to asexually reproduced plants. Significantly, nothing within either the original 1930 text of the statute or its recodified version in 1952 indicates that the PPA's protection for asexually reproduced plants was intended to be exclusive.

Plants were first explicitly brought within the scope of patent protection in 1930 when the PPA included "plants" among the useful things subject to patents. Thus the 1930 PPA amended the general utility patent provision, Rev. Stat. § 4886, to provide:

> Any person who has invented or discovered any new and useful art, machine, manufacture, or composition of matter, or any new and useful improvements

thereof, or who has invented or discovered and asexually reproduced any distinct and new variety of plant, other than a tuber-propagated plant, not known or used by others in this country, before his invention or discovery thereof, … may … obtain a patent therefor.

Act of May 23, 1930, § 1, 46 Stat. 376.

This provision limited protection to the asexual reproduction of the plant. Asexual reproduction occurs by grafting, budding, or the like, and produces an offspring with a genetic combination identical to that of the single parent-essentially a clone.[3] The PPA also amended Revised Statutes § 4888 by adding: "No plant patent shall be declared invalid on the ground of noncompliance with this section if the description is made as complete as is reasonably possible."

In 1952, Congress revised the patent statute and placed the plant patents into a separate chapter 15 of Title 35 entitled, "Patents for plants." 35 U.S.C. §§ 161–164.[4] This was merely a housekeeping measure that did nothing to change the substantive rights or requirements for a plant patent. A "plant patent"[5] continued to provide only the exclusive right to asexually reproduce a protected plant, § 163, and the description requirement remained relaxed, § 162.[6] Plant patents under the PPA thus have very limited coverage and less stringent requirements than § 101 utility patents.

Importantly, chapter 15 nowhere states that plant patents are the exclusive means of granting intellectual property protection to plants. Although unable to point to any language that requires, or even suggests, that Congress intended the PPA's protections to be exclusive, petitioners advance three reasons why the PPA should preclude assigning utility patents for plants. We find none of these arguments to be persuasive.

First, petitioners argue that plants were not covered by the general utility patent statute prior to 1930. ("If the patent laws before 1930 allowed patents on 'plants' then there would have been no reason for Congress to have passed the 1930 PPA …"). In advancing this argument, petitioners overlook the state of patent law and plant breeding at the time of the PPA's enactment.

The Court in *Chakrabarty* explained the realities of patent law and plant breeding at the time the PPA was enacted: "Prior to 1930, two factors were thought to remove plants from patent protection. The first was the belief that plants, even those artificially bred, were products of nature for purposes of the patent law.… The second obstacle to patent protection for plants was the fact that plants were thought not amenable to the 'written description' requirement of the patent law." Congress addressed these concerns with the 1930 PPA, which recognized that the work of a plant breeder was a patentable invention and relaxed the written description requirement. The PPA thus gave patent protection to breeders who were previously unable to overcome the obstacles described in *Chakrabarty*.

---

3. By contrast, sexual reproduction occurs by seed and sometimes involves two different plants.

4. The PPA, as amended, provides: "Whoever invents or discovers and asexually reproduces any distinct and new variety of plant, including cultivated sports, mutants, hybrids, and newly found seedlings, other than a tuber propagated plant or a plant found in an uncultivated state, may obtain a patent therefor, subject to the conditions and requirements of this title." 35 U.S.C. § 161 (1994 ed.).

5. Patents issued under § 161 are referred to as "plant patents," which are distinguished from § 101 utility patents and § 171 design patents.

6. To obtain a plant patent under § 161 a breeder must meet all of the requirements for § 101, except for the description requirement. See § 162 ("No plant patent shall be declared invalid for noncompliance with section 112 [providing for written description] of this title if the description is as complete as is reasonably possible").

This does not mean, however, that prior to 1930 plants could not have fallen within the subject matter of § 101. Rather, it illustrates only that in 1930 Congress *believed* that plants were not patentable under § 101, both because they were living things and because in practice they could not meet the stringent description requirement. Yet these premises were disproved over time. As this Court held in *Chakrabarty,* "the relevant distinction" for purposes of § 101 is not "between living and inanimate things, but between products of nature, whether living or not, and human-made inventions." In addition, advances in biological knowledge and breeding expertise have allowed plant breeders to satisfy § 101's demanding description requirement.

Whatever Congress may have believed about the state of patent law and the science of plant breeding in 1930, plants have always had the *potential* to fall within the general subject matter of § 101, which is a dynamic provision designed to encompass new and unforeseen inventions. "A rule that unanticipated inventions are without protection would conflict with the core concept of the patent law that anticipation undermines patentability."

Petitioners essentially ask us to deny utility patent protection for sexually reproduced plants because it was unforeseen in 1930 that such plants could receive protection under § 101. Denying patent protection under § 101 simply because such coverage was thought technologically infeasible in 1930, however, would be inconsistent with the forward-looking perspective of the utility patent statute. As we noted in *Chakrabarty,* "Congress employed broad general language in drafting § 101 precisely because [new types of] inventions are often unforeseeable."

Second, petitioners maintain that the PPA's limitation to asexually reproduced plants would make no sense if Congress intended § 101 to authorize patents on plant varieties that were sexually reproduced. But this limitation once again merely reflects the reality of plant breeding in 1930. At that time, the primary means of reproducing bred plants true-to-type was through asexual reproduction. Congress thought that sexual reproduction through seeds was not a stable way to maintain desirable bred characteristics.[7] Thus, it is hardly surprising that plant patents would protect only asexual reproduction, since this was the most reliable type of reproduction for preserving the desirable characteristics of breeding.

Furthermore, like other laws protecting intellectual property, the plant patent provision must be understood in its proper context. Until 1924, farmers received seed from the Government's extensive free seed program that distributed millions of packages of seed annually ...[8] In 1930, seed companies were not primarily concerned with varietal

---

7. The Senate Report accompanying the bill notes: "All such plants must be asexually reproduced in order to have their identity preserved. This is necessary since seedlings either of chance or self-pollenization from any of these would not preserve the character of the individual." S.Rep. No. 315, 71st Cong., 2d Sess., 3 (1930). This Report, like the text, indicates Congress' intent to limit plant patent coverage to asexual reproduction, but explains that this limitation "recognizes a practical situation" —i.e., that propagation by seeds does not preserve the character of the original. ("[T]he patent right granted is a right to propagate the new variety by asexual reproduction. It does not include the right to propagate by seeds. This limitation in the right granted recognizes a practical situation and greatly narrows the scope of the bill"). The limitation to asexual reproduction was a recognition of the "practical situation" that seedlings did not reproduce true-to-type. An exclusive right to asexual reproduction was the only type of coverage needed and thought possible given the state of plant breeding at the time.

8. At its high point in 1897, over 20 million packages of seed were distributed to farmers. Even at the time the program was eliminated in 1924, it was the third largest line item in the Department of Agriculture's budget.

protection, but were still trying to successfully commodify seeds. There was no need to protect seed breeding because there were few markets for seeds ... "Seed companies' first priority was simply to establish a market, and they continued to view the congressional distribution as a principal constraint."

By contrast, nurseries at the time had successfully commercialized asexually reproduced fruit trees and flowers. These plants were regularly copied, draining profits from those who discovered or bred new varieties. Nurseries were the primary subjects of agricultural marketing and so it is not surprising that they were the specific focus of the PPA.

Moreover, seed companies at the time could not point to genuinely new varieties and lacked the scientific knowledge to engage in formal breeding that would increase agricultural productivity.... In short, there is simply no evidence, let alone the overwhelming evidence needed to establish repeal by implication, that Congress, by specifically protecting asexually reproduced plants through the PPA, intended to preclude utility patent protection for sexually reproduced plants.

Third, petitioners argue that in 1952 Congress would not have moved plants out of the utility patent provision and into § 161 if it had intended § 101 to allow for protection of plants. Brief for Petitioners 20. Petitioners again rely on negative inference because they cannot point to any express indication that Congress intended § 161 to be the exclusive means of patenting plants. But this negative inference simply does not support carving out subject matter that otherwise fits comfortably within the expansive language of § 101, especially when § 101 can protect different attributes and has more stringent requirements than does § 161.

This is especially true given that Congress in 1952 did nothing to change the substantive rights or requirements for obtaining a plant patent. Absent a clear intent to the contrary, we are loath to interpret what was essentially a housekeeping measure as an affirmative decision by Congress to deny sexually reproduced plants patent protection under § 101.

B

By passing the PVPA in 1970, Congress specifically authorized limited patent-like protection for certain sexually reproduced plants. Petitioners therefore argue that this legislation evidences Congress' intent to deny broader § 101 utility patent protection for such plants. Petitioners' argument, however, is unavailing for two reasons. First, nowhere does the PVPA purport to provide the exclusive statutory means of protecting sexually reproduced plants. Second, the PVPA and § 101 can easily be reconciled. Because it is harder to qualify for a utility patent than for a Plant Variety Protection (PVP) certificate, it only makes sense that utility patents would confer a greater scope of protection.

1

The PVPA provides plant variety protection for:

> The breeder of any sexually reproduced or tuber propagated plant variety (other than fungi or bacteria) who has so reproduced the variety....

7 U.S.C. § 2402(a).

Infringement of plant variety protection occurs, *inter alia*, if someone sells or markets the protected variety, sexually multiplies the variety as a step in marketing, uses the variety in producing a hybrid, or dispenses the variety without notice that the variety is protected.[10]

Since the 1994 amendments, the PVPA also protects "any variety that is essentially derived from a protected variety," and "any variety whose production requires the repeated use of a protected variety." Practically, this means that hybrids created from protected plant varieties are also protected; however, it is not infringement to use a protected variety for the development of a hybrid.[11]

The PVPA also contains exemptions for saving seed and for research. A farmer who legally purchases and plants a protected variety can save the seed from these plants for replanting on his own farm. ("[I]t shall not infringe any right hereunder for a person to save seed produced by the person from seed obtained, or descended from seed obtained, by authority of the owner of the variety for seeding purposes and use such saved seed in the production of a crop for use on the farm of the person …") In addition, a protected variety may be used for research. ("The use and reproduction of a protected variety for plant breeding or other bona fide research shall not constitute an infringement of the protection provided under this chapter.") The utility patent statute does not contain similar exemptions.[12]

Thus, while the PVPA creates a statutory scheme that is comprehensive with respect to its particular protections and subject matter, giving limited protection to plant varieties that are new, distinct, uniform, and stable, § 2402(a), nowhere does it restrict the scope of patentable subject matter under § 101. With nothing in the statute to bolster their view that the PVPA provides the exclusive means for protecting sexually reproduc-

---

10. Title 7 U.S.C. § 2541(a) provides in full:

(a) Acts constituting infringement

Except as otherwise provided in this subchapter, it shall be an infringement of the rights of the owner of a protected variety to perform without authority, any of the following acts in the United States, or in commerce which can be regulated by Congress or affecting such commerce, prior to expiration of the right to plant variety protection but after either the issue of the certificate or the distribution of a protected plant variety with the notice under section 2567 of this title:

(1) sell or market the protected variety, or offer it or expose it for sale, deliver it, ship it, consign it, exchange it, or solicit an offer to buy it, or any other transfer of title or possession of it;

(2) import the variety into, or export it from, the United States;

(3) sexually multiply, or propagate by a tuber or part of a tuber, the variety as a step in marketing (for growing purposes) the variety;

(4) use the variety in producing (as distinguished from developing) a hybrid or different variety therefrom;

(5) use seed which had been marked 'Unauthorized Propagation Prohibited' or 'Unauthorized Seed Multiplication Prohibited' or progeny thereof to propagate the variety;

(6) dispense the variety to another, in a form which can be propagated, without notice as to being a protected variety under which it was received;

(7) condition the variety for the purpose of propagation, except to the extent that the conditioning is related to the activities permitted under section 2543 of this title;

(8) stock the variety for any of the purposes referred to in paragraphs (1) through (7);

(9) perform any of the foregoing acts even in instances in which the variety is multiplied other than sexually, except in pursuance of a valid United States plant patent; or

(10) instigate or actively induce performance of any of the foregoing acts.

11. It is, however, infringement of a utility patent to use a protected plant in the development of another variety.

12. The dissent argues that our "reading would destroy" the PVPA's exemptions. Post, at 611. Yet such bold predictions are belied by the facts. According to the Government, over 5,000 PVP certificates have been issued, as compared to about 1,800 utility patents for plants. Since 1985 the PTO has interpreted § 101 to include utility patents for plants, and there is no evidence that the availability of such patents has rendered the PVPA and its specific exemptions obsolete.

ing plants, petitioners rely on the legislative history of the PVPA. They argue that this history shows the PVPA was enacted because sexually reproducing plant varieties and their seeds were not and had never been intended by Congress to be included within the classes of things patentable under Title 35.[13]

The PVPA itself, however, contains no statement that PVP certificates were to be the exclusive means of protecting sexually reproducing plants. The relevant statements in the legislative history reveal nothing more than the limited view of plant breeding taken by some Members of Congress who believed that patent protection was unavailable for sexually reproduced plants. This view stems from a lack of awareness concerning scientific possibilities.

Furthermore, at the time the PVPA was enacted, the PTO had already issued numerous utility patents for hybrid plant processes. Many of these patents, especially since the 1950's, included claims on the products of the patented process, *i.e.*, the hybrid plant itself. Such plants were protected as part of a hybrid process and not on their own. Nonetheless, these hybrids still enjoyed protection under § 101, which reaffirms that such material was within the scope of § 101.

2

Petitioners next argue that the PVPA altered the subject-matter coverage of § 101 by implication. Yet "the only permissible justification for a repeal by implication is when the earlier and later statutes are irreconcilable." *Morton v. Mancari,* 417 U.S. 535, 550 (1974). "The rarity with which [the Court has] discovered implied repeals is due to the relatively stringent standard for such findings, namely, that there be an irreconcilable conflict between the two federal statutes at issue."

To be sure, there are differences in the requirements for, and coverage of, utility patents and PVP certificates issued pursuant to the PVPA. These differences, however, do not present irreconcilable conflicts because the requirements for obtaining a utility patent under § 101 are more stringent than those for obtaining a PVP certificate, and the protections afforded by a utility patent are greater than those afforded by a PVP certificate. Thus, there is a parallel relationship between the obligations and the level of protection under each statute.

It is much more difficult to obtain a utility patent for a plant than to obtain a PVP certificate because a utility patentable plant must be new, useful, and nonobvious, 35 U.S.C. §§ 101–103. In addition, to obtain a utility patent, a breeder must describe the plant with sufficient specificity to enable others to "make and use" the invention after the patent term expires. § 112. The disclosure required by the Patent Act is "the *quid pro quo* of the right to exclude." The description requirement for plants includes a deposit of biological material, for example, seeds, and mandates that such material be accessible to the public.

By contrast, a plant variety may receive a PVP certificate without a showing of usefulness or nonobviousness. See 7 U.S.C. § 2402(a) (requiring that the variety be only new, distinct, uniform, and stable). Nor does the PVPA require a description and disclosure as extensive as those required under § 101. The PVPA requires a "description of the variety

---

13. Petitioners point to a House Report that concluded: "Under patent law, protection is presently limited to those varieties of plants which reproduce asexually, that is, by such methods as grafting or budding. No protection is available to those varieties of plants which reproduce sexually, that is, generally by seeds." H.R.Rep. No. 91-1605, p. 1 (1970).

setting forth its distinctiveness, uniformity and stability and a description of the geneal-
ogy and breeding procedure, when known." 7 U.S.C. § 2422(2). It also requires a deposit
of seed in a public depository, but neither the statute nor the applicable regulation mandates that such material be accessible to the general public during the term of the PVP certificate.

Because of the more stringent requirements, utility patent holders receive greater rights
of exclusion than holders of a PVP certificate. Most notably, there are no exemptions for
research or saving seed under a utility patent. Additionally, although Congress increased
the level of protection under the PVPA in 1994, a PVP certificate still does not grant the
full range of protections afforded by a utility patent. For instance, a utility patent on an
inbred plant line protects that line as well as all hybrids produced by crossing that inbred
with another plant line. Similarly, the PVPA now protects "any variety whose production
requires the repeated use of a protected variety." 7 U.S.C. § 2541(c)(3). Thus, one cannot
use a protected plant variety to produce a hybrid for commercial sale. PVPA protection
still falls short of a utility patent, however, because a breeder can use a plant that is protected by a PVP certificate to "develop" a new inbred line while he cannot use a plant
patented under § 101 for such a purpose. *See* 7 U.S.C. § 2541(a)(4) (infringement includes
"use [of] the variety in producing (as distinguished from developing) a hybrid or different variety therefrom").

For all of these reasons, it is clear that there is no "positive repugnancy" between the
issuance of utility patents for plants and PVP coverage for plants. Nor can it be said that
the two statutes "cannot mutually coexist." Indeed, "when two statutes are capable of coexistence, it is the duty of the courts, absent a clearly expressed congressional intention
to the contrary, to regard each as effective." Here we can plainly regard each statute as effective because of its different requirements and protections. The plain meaning of § 101,
as interpreted by this Court in *Chakrabarty,* clearly includes plants within its subject matter. The PPA and the PVPA are not to the contrary and can be read alongside § 101 in
protecting plants.

3

Petitioners also suggest that even when statutes overlap and purport to protect the
same commercially valuable attribute of a thing, such "dual protection" cannot exist. Yet
this Court has not hesitated to give effect to two statutes that overlap, so long as each
reaches some distinct cases. Here, while utility patents and PVP certificates do contain some
similar protections, as discussed above, the overlap is only partial.

Moreover, this Court has allowed dual protection in other intellectual property cases.
"Certainly the patent policy of encouraging invention is not disturbed by the existence of
another form of incentive to invention. In this respect the two systems [trade secret protection and patents] are not and never would be in conflict." *Kewanee Oil* at 484; see also
Mazer v. Stein, 347 U.S. 201 (1954) (the patentability of an object does not preclude the
copyright of that object as a work of art). In this case, many plant varieties that are unable to satisfy the stringent requirements of § 101 might still qualify for the lesser protections afforded by the PVPA.

III

We also note that the PTO has assigned utility patents for plants for at least 16 years
and there has been no indication from either Congress or agencies with expertise that
such coverage is inconsistent with the PVPA or the PPA. The Board of Patent Appeals

and Interferences, which has specific expertise in issues of patent law, relied heavily on this Court's decision in *Chakrabarty* when it interpreted the subject matter of § 101 to include plants. This highly visible decision has led to the issuance of some 1,800 utility patents for plants. Moreover, the PTO, which administers § 101 as well as the PPA, recognizes and regularly issues utility patents for plants. In addition, the Department of Agriculture's Plant Variety Protection Office acknowledges the existence of utility patents for plants.

In the face of these developments, Congress has not only failed to pass legislation indicating that it disagrees with the PTO's interpretation of § 101; it has even recognized the availability of utility patents for plants. In a 1999 amendment to 35 U.S.C. § 119, which concerns the right of priority for patent rights, Congress provided: "Applications for plant breeder's rights filed in a WTO [World Trade Organization] member country … shall have the same effect for the purpose of the right of priority … as applications for patents, subject to the same conditions and requirements of this section as apply to applications for patents." 35 U.S.C. § 119(f). Crucially, § 119(f) is part of the general provisions of Title 35, not the specific chapter of the PPA, which suggests a recognition on the part of Congress that plants are patentable under § 101.

IV

For these reasons, we hold that newly developed plant breeds fall within the terms of § 101, and that neither the PPA nor the PVPA limits the scope of § 101's coverage. As in *Chakrabarty*, we decline to narrow the reach of § 101 where Congress has given us no indication that it intends this result. Accordingly, we affirm the judgment of the Court of Appeals.

It is so ordered.

Justice O'CONNOR took no part in the consideration or decision of this case.

Justice SCALIA, concurring.

This case presents an interesting and difficult point of statutory construction, seemingly pitting against each other two perfectly valid canons of interpretation: (1) that statutes must be construed in their entirety, so that the meaning of one provision sheds light upon the meaning of another; and (2) that repeals by implication are not favored. I think these sensible canons are reconcilable only if the first of them is limited by the second. That is to say, the power of a provision of law to give meaning to a previously enacted ambiguity comes to an end once the ambiguity has been authoritatively resolved. At that point, use of the later enactment produces not clarification (governed by the first canon) but amendment (governed by the second).

In the present case, the only ambiguity that could have been clarified by the words added to the utility patent statute by the Plant Patent Act of 1930 (PPA) is whether the term "composition of matter" included living things. The newly enacted provision for plants invited the conclusion that this term which preceded it did not include living things. (The term "matter," after all, is sometimes used in a sense that excludes living things. See Webster's New International Dictionary 1515 (2d ed. 1950): "Physical substance as made up of chemical elements and distinguished from incorporeal substance, action, qualities, etc.… 'Matter is inert, senseless, and lifeless.' Johnson.") It is important to note that this is the only way in which the new PPA language could have clarified the ambiguity: There was no way in which "composition of matter" could be regarded as a category separate from plants, but not separate from other living things.

Stare decisis, however, prevents us from any longer regarding as an open question—as ambiguous—whether "composition of matter" includes living things. *Diamond v. Chakrabarty* holds that it does. As the case comes before us, therefore, the language of the PPA—if it is to have any effect on the outcome—must do so by way of amending what we have held to be a statute that covers living things (and hence covers plants). At this point the canon against repeal by implication comes into play, and I agree with the Court that it determines the outcome. I therefore join the opinion of the Court.

Justice BREYER, with whom Justice STEVENS joins, dissenting.

The question before us is whether the words "manufacture" or "composition of matter" contained in the utility patent statute cover plants that also fall within the scope of two more specific statutes, the Plant Patent Act of 1930 (PPA), and the Plant Variety Protection Act (PVPA). I believe that the words "manufacture" or "composition of matter" do not cover these plants. That is because Congress intended the two more specific statutes to exclude patent protection under the Utility Patent Statute for the plants to which the more specific Acts directly refer. And, as the Court implicitly recognizes, this Court neither considered nor decided this question in *Diamond v. Chakrabarty*. Consequently, I dissent.

I

Respondent and the Government claim that *Chakrabarty* controls the outcome in this case. This is incorrect, for *Chakrabarty* said nothing about the specific issue before us. *Chakrabarty* in considering the scope of the Utility Patent Statute's language "manufacture, or composition of matter," asked whether those words included such living things as bacteria—a substance to which neither of the two specific plant Acts refers. The Court held that the Utility Patent Statute language included a "new" bacterium because it was "a nonnaturally occurring manufacture or composition of matter" that was "not nature's handiwork." It quoted language from a congressional Committee Report indicating that "Congress intended statutory subject matter to 'include anything under the sun that is made by man.'" But it nowhere said or implied that this Utility Patent Statute language also includes the very subject matter with which the two specific statutes deal, namely, plants. Whether a bacterium technically speaking is, or is not, a plant, the Court considered it a "life form," and not the kind of "plant" that the two specific statutes had in mind (noting that the PVPA specifically excluded bacteria, and that the Court of Customs and Patent Appeals had held that bacteria were not plants for purposes of the PPA).

The Court did consider a complicated argument that sought indirectly to relate the two specific plant statutes to the issue before it. That argument went roughly as follows: (1) Congress enacted two special statutes related to plants. (2) Even though those two statutes do not cover bacteria, the fact that Congress enacted them shows that Congress thought the Utility Patent Statute's language ("manufacture, or composition of matter") did not cover any living thing, including bacteria. (3) Congress consequently must have intended the two special Acts to provide exclusive protection for all forms of "life" whether they do, or do not, count as the kinds of "plants" to which the specific statutes refer.

The Court, in reply, wrote that Congress, when enacting the specific statutes, might have (wrongly) believed that the Utility Patent Statute did not apply to plants, probably because Congress thought that plants were "natural products," not human products. It added that Congress also might have believed that it was too difficult for plant inventors to meet patent law's ordinary "written description" requirement. In addition, the Court pointed out that the relevant distinction between unpatentable and patentable subject matter was not between living and inanimate things, but rather between products of nature and human-made inventions. As such, the bacteria at issue were patentable because they were products of human invention. And the Court concluded that "nothing" in Congress' decision to *exclude* bacteria from the PVPA supported "petitioner's position," namely, that Congress intended no utility patent protection for any living thing.

Neither this refutation nor the argument itself decides the question here. That question is not about general coverage for matters that the special statutes *do not* mention (namely, nonplant life forms such as bacteria). It is about general coverage for matters to which the special plant statutes do refer (namely, plants). *Chakrabarty* neither asked, nor answered, this latter question, the question now before us. And nothing in the Court's opinion indicates the contrary.

II

The critical question, as I have said, is whether the two specific plant statutes embody a legislative intent to deny coverage under the Utility Patent Statute *to those plants to which the specific plant statutes refer*. In my view, the first of these statutes, the PPA, reveals precisely that intent. And nothing in the later history of either the Utility Patent Statute or the PVPA suggests the contrary.

As initially enacted in 1930, the PPA began by amending the Utility Patent Statute to read as follows:

> "Any person who has invented or discovered any new and useful art, machine, manufacture, or composition of matter, or any new and useful improvements thereof, *or who has invented or discovered and asexually reproduced any distinct and new variety of plant, other than a tuber-propagated plant* ... may ... obtain a patent therefor[e]." (language added by the PPA italicized).

This language refers to *all* plants. It says that an inventor—in principle—can obtain a patent on any plant (the subject matter of the patent) that meets three requirements. It must be distinct; it must be new; and on one or more occasions it must have been "asexually reproduced," *e.g.*, reproduced by means of a graft.

This last-mentioned "graft" requirement does not separate (1) those plants that can reproduce through grafting from (2) those plants that can reproduce by seed. The two categories are not mutually exclusive. Many plants—perhaps virtually any plant—can be reproduced "asexually" as well as by seed. Rather, the "asexual reproduction" requirement sought to ensure that the inventor was capable of reproducing the new variety "asexually" (through a graft) because that fact would guarantee that the variety's new characteristics had genetic (rather than, say, environmental) causes and would prove genetically stable over time. ("A plant patent covers only the exclusive right of asexual reproduction, and obviously it would be futile to grant a patent for a new and distinct variety unless the variety had been demonstrated to be susceptible to asexual reproduction"); cf. *Dunn v. Ragin*, noting that asexual reproduction "determine[s] that the progeny in fact possess the characteristic or characteristics which distinguish it as a new variety."

Although the section defining the PPA's coverage does not limit its scope to plants that reproduce primarily through grafting, a later section does so limit the protection that it offers. That section specifies that the patent holder will receive "the exclusive right to asexually reproduce the plant," *e.g.*, the right to reproduce it through grafting, but he will not receive an exclusive right to reproduce the plant sexually, *i.e.*, the right to reproduce it through seeds. And this is true *regardless* of whether the patent holder could reproduce true to type offspring through seeds. See S.Rep. No. 315, at 4 ("On the other hand, [the

PPA] does not give any patent protection to the right of propagation of the new variety by seed, irrespective of the degree to which the seedlings come true to type"). This was a significant limitation because, the Court's contrary claim notwithstanding, it was readily apparent in 1930 that a plant's desirable characteristics *could* be preserved through reproduction by seed.

In sum, the PPA permits patenting of new and distinct varieties of (1) plants that breeders primarily reproduce through grafts (say, apple trees), (2) plants that breeders primarily reproduce through seeds (say, corn), and (3) plants that reproduce both ways (say, violets). But, because that statute left plant buyers free to keep, to reproduce, and to sell seeds, the statute likely proved helpful only to those in the first category. Both the PPA's legislative history and the earliest patents granted under the Act fully support this interpretation. See S.Rep. No. 315, at 3 explaining that varieties that "resul[t] from seedlings of cross pollenization [sic] of two species" were patentable under the Act).

Given these characteristics, the PPA is incompatible with the claim that the Utility Patent Statute's language ("manufacture, or composition of matter") also covers plants. To see why that is so, simply imagine a plant breeder who, in 1931, sought to patent a new, distinct variety of plant that he invented but which he has *never been able to reproduce through grafting, i.e., asexually*. Because he could not reproduce it through grafting, he could not patent it under the more specific terms of the PPA. Could he nonetheless patent it under the more general Utility Patent Statute language "manufacture, or composition of matter?"

Assume the court that tried to answer that question was prescient, i.e., that it knew that this Court, in *Chakrabarty* would say that the Utility Patent Statute language ("manufacture," or "composition of matter") in principle might cover "anything under the sun," including bacteria. Such a prescient court would have said that the Utility Patent Statute did cover plants had the case reached it in 1929, before Congress enacted the more specific 1930 law. But how could any court decide the case similarly in 1931 after enactment of the 1930 amendment? To do so would virtually nullify the PPA's primary condition—that the breeder have reproduced the new characteristic through a graft—reading it out of the Act. Moreover, since the Utility Patent Statute would cover, and thereby forbid, reproduction by seed, such a holding would also have read out of the statute the PPA's more limited list of exclusive rights. Consequently, even a prescient court would have had to say, as of 1931, that the 1930 Plant Patent Act had, in amending the Utility Patent Statute, placed the subject matter of the PPA—namely, plants—outside the scope of the words "manufacture, or composition of matter."

Nothing that occurred after 1930 changes this conclusion. In 1952, the Utility Patent Statute was recodified, and the PPA language I have quoted was given its own separate place in the Code. As Pioneer itself concedes, that change was not "substantive." Indeed, as recodified the PPA still allows a breeder to obtain a patent when he "invents or discovers and asexually reproduces *any* distinct and new variety of plant," 35 U.S.C. § 161(emphasis added), but it only allows the patent holder to "exclude others from *asexually* reproducing the plant or selling or using the plant so reproduced," § 163 (emphasis added).

Nor does the enactment of the Plant Variety Protection Act of 1970 change the conclusion. The PVPA proved necessary because plant breeders became capable of creating new and distinct varieties of certain crops, corn, for example, that were valuable only when reproduced through seeds—a form of reproduction that the earlier Act freely permitted. Just prior to its enactment a special Presidential Commission, noting the special problems that plant protection raised and favoring the development of a totally new plant protection scheme, had recommended that "[a]ll provisions in the patent statute for plant patents be deleted. . . ." Instead Congress kept the PPA while adding the PVPA. The PVPA gave patent-like protection (for 20 years) to plants reproduced by seed, and it excluded the PPA's requirement that a breeder have "asexually reproduced" the plant. It imposed certain specific requirements. [The] variety must be new, distinct, uniform, and stable. And it provided the breeder with an exclusive right to sell, offer to sell, reproduce, import, or export the variety, including the seeds.

At the same time, the PVPA created two important exceptions. The first provided that a farmer who plants his fields with a protected plant "shall not infringe any right hereunder" by saving the seeds and planting them in future years. § 2543. The second permitted "use and reproduction of a protected variety for plant breeding or other bona fide research." § 2544.

Nothing in the history, language, or purpose of the 1970 statute suggests an intent to reintroduce into the scope of the general words "manufacture, or composition of matter" the subject matter that the PPA had removed, namely, plants. To the contrary, any such reintroduction would make meaningless the two exceptions—for planting and for research—that Congress wrote into that Act. It is not surprising that no party argues that passage of the PVPA somehow enlarged the scope of the Utility Patent Statute.

III

The Court replies as follows to the claim that its reading of the Utility Patent Statute nullifies the PPA's limitation of protection to plants produced by graft and the PVPA's exemptions for seeds and research: (1) The Utility Patent Statute applies only to plants that are useful, novel, nonobvious, and for which the inventor provides an enabling written description of the invention. (2) The PVPA applies to plants that are novel, distinct, uniform, and stable. (3) The second set of criteria seem slightly easier to meet, as they do not include nonobviousness and a written description (Pioneer does not argue that the "useful" requirement is significant). (4) And Congress could reasonably have intended the planting and research exceptions to apply only to the set of plants that can meet the easier, but not the tougher, criteria.

I do not find this argument convincing. For one thing, it is not clear that the general patent law requirements are significantly tougher. Counsel for Pioneer stated at oral argument that there are many more PVP certificates than there are plant patents. But he added that the major difference in criteria is the difference between the utility patent law's "nonobviousness" requirement and the specific Acts' requirement of "newness"—a difference that may reflect the Patent Office's more "rigorous" examination process. But see S. Doc., at 20–21 (suggesting little difference because patent office tends to find "nonobviousness" as long as the plant is deemed "new" by the Department of Agriculture).

In any case, there is no relationship between the criteria differences and the exemptions. Why would anyone want to limit the exemptions—related to seedplanting and research—only to those new plant varieties that are slightly less original? Indeed, the research exemption would seem more useful in respect to more original, not less original, innovation. The Court has advanced no sound reason why Congress would want to destroy the exemptions in the PVPA that Congress created. And the Court's reading would destroy those exemptions.

The Court and Justice SCALIA's concurrence also rely upon the interpretive canon that disfavors repeal by implication. The Court says that "there is simply no evidence" that the PPA was meant to preclude § 101 protection for sexually reproduced plants. But reliance on the canon of "implied repeal" is misplaced. The canon has traditionally been embraced when a party claims that a later statute—that does not actually modify an earlier statute—implicitly repeals the earlier legislation. That canon has no relevance to the PPA—which explicitly amended the Utility Patent Statute by limiting protection to plants produced by graft. Even were that not so, the Court has noted that a later, more specific statute will ordinarily trump the earlier, more general one.

Regardless, canons are not mandatory rules. They are guides to help courts determine likely legislative intent. And that intent is critical. Those who write statutes seek to solve human problems. Fidelity to their aims requires us to approach an interpretive problem not as if it were a purely logical game, like a Rubik's Cube, but as an effort to divine the human intent that underlies the statute. Here that effort calls not for an appeal to canons, but for an analysis of language, structure, history, and purpose. Those factors make clear that the Utility Patent Statute does not apply to plants. Nothing in *Chakrabarty* holds to the contrary.

For these reasons, I dissent.

———————

3. Enforcing Patent Rights in Seed

Farmers Legal Action Group, Inc. (FLAG) advises in its FARMERS GUIDE TO GMOs:[1]

> As a result of U.S. law, as interpreted by the courts, "Agribusiness or biotech companies maintain control of—and secure the greatest financial return on.— their GM seeds by patenting either the seeds or the genetic traits used to modify the seeds. Once a GM seed contains a patented genetic trait, no one may lawfully plant, sell, or use it in any manner without first obtaining the permission of the company holding the patent .This permission is often referred to as a "license." Licenses to use GM seed containing patented material severely restrict the manner in which the seeds may be used, including prohibiting farmers from saving seed from GM crops for planting another crop. Farmers are granted licenses to use GM seed for limited purposes through a contract usually called a *Technology Agreement*. Patent infringement may occur when a person uses seeds or sells crops containing patented GM technologies in a manner not covered by a valid license from the patent holder. The financial penalties for patent infringement can be quite severe....
>
> In exchange for receiving a limited license to use the GM seed, a farmer who enters into a GM seed contract generally agrees to: (1) pay the technology fees included with the seed purchase; and (2) comply with all of the company's production, management, and marketing requirements and restrictions. Biotech companies also generally use these contracts to get the farmer's agreement to a number of protections for the companies' interests. Under a GM seed contract,

———————

1. Farmers' Legal Action Group, Inc. (FLAG) is "a nonprofit law center dedicated to providing legal services to family farmers and their rural communities in order to help keep family farmers on the land. Since its inception, FLAG has provided an extensive array of legal services to financially distressed farmers and their advocates and attorneys nationwide." The Farmers Guide to GMOs is available for download on the FLAG website http://www.flaginc.org/topics/pubs/biotech.php# FGtoGMOs2009.

farmers typically agree to the following practices. Follow specific farming practices required by the company. Save no seed from the crop produced from the purchased GM seed. Take specified measures to protect the company's intellectual property rights in the GM seed. Sell the crop produced from the GM seed in specifically approved markets. Allow company representatives access to fields to inspect crops. Resolve any disputes under the contract either through binding arbitration or in a court convenient to the company. Monsanto uses a single contract, called a Technology/Stewardship Agreement ... to grant farmers the limited license to use many of its GM corn, cotton, soybean, sugar beet, and alfalfa seeds.... GMO contracts are almost always standard form contracts written by the biotech company. Farmers will not have an opportunity to negotiate the terms of the contract. The biotech companies offer these contracts on a take it or leave it basis as part of the seed purchase....

Monsanto v. David
516 F.3d 1009 (Fed. Cir. 2008)

LOURIE, Circuit Judge.

Loren David appeals from the final judgment of the United States District Court for the Eastern District of Missouri. On April 20, 2006, the court held that David knowingly infringed U.S. Patent 5,352,605 (the "'605 patent"), and awarded Monsanto Company and Monsanto Technology LLC (collectively "Monsanto") compensatory damages in the amount of $226,214.00. On July 25, 2006, the court awarded Monsanto attorney fees, prejudgment interest, and costs, bringing the total damages award to $786,989.43. Because we hold that the district court correctly held that the '605 patent was infringed, but find that portions of the damages award were clearly erroneous, we affirm in part, vacate in part, and remand.

BACKGROUND

One of the many products that Monsanto sells is Roundup® brand herbicide. Glyphosate-based herbicides, such as Roundup®, kill vegetation by inhibiting the metabolic activity of a particular enzyme, common in plants, that is necessary for the conversion of sugars into amino acids. Herbicides that have glyphosate as the active ingredient are non-selective; that is, they kill all types of plants whether the plant is a weed or a crop.

In addition to developing and selling herbicides, Monsanto sells other products made using biotechnology. Monsanto has developed Roundup Ready® Technology, which involves inserting a chimeric gene into a seed that allows the plant to advantageously continue to break down sugars in the presence of glyphosate. Crops grown from such seeds are resistant to Roundup® and other glyphosate-based herbicides. When Roundup Ready® seeds are planted and used in conjunction with a glyphosate-based herbicide, Roundup Ready® plants will survive, while weeds and other plants lacking the Roundup Ready® gene will be killed. Monsanto has claimed this technology in the '605 patent.

Roundup Ready® genes have been introduced into numerous agricultural products, including soybeans, the subject of the present case. Monsanto licenses seed companies to incorporate the Roundup Ready® genes into their plants and to sell soybean seeds containing the Roundup Ready® gene. All purchasers of such seeds are required to enter into a Technology Agreement that grants them the right to use the seeds. The Technology Agreement stipulates that buyers may use the seeds for the planting of only a single commercial crop, but that no seeds from that crop may be saved for future harvests. The Technology Agreement assures Monsanto that farmers must purchase new Roundup Ready® seeds each harvesting season, rather than simply saving seeds from the prior year's harvest, as they normally would with conventional soybean seeds. Monsanto also charges a Technology Fee for each unit of Roundup Ready® soybean seeds sold.[2] The Technology Agreement also contains a clause granting Monsanto the full amount of its legal fees and other costs that may have to be expended in enforcing the agreement.

David is a commercial farmer who owns soybean fields in North and South Dakota. On May 3, 1999, David executed a Monsanto Technology Agreement. In 2003, David planted the contested soybeans at issue in this case.[3] Monsanto claims that the seeds that David planted were Roundup Ready® soybeans improperly saved from the previous year's harvest, but David claims he did not save any Roundup Ready® seed. It is undisputed that, prior to planting his soybean fields in 2003, David purchased 645 units[4] of Roundup Ready® soybean seeds and it is also undisputed that that amount of seeds alone would have been insufficient to completely plant David's soybean fields in 2003. Also undisputed is the fact that David purchased over 1,000 gallons of glyphosate-based herbicides in 2003, herbicide that would destroy any plants that did not contain the Roundup Ready® gene, and would therefore have destroyed any conventional soybean seeds David planted.

At some time in 2003, Monsanto began to suspect that David had saved soybean seed from his previous year's harvest in violation of the Technology Agreement. In April 2004, after David's 2003 crop had already been harvested and sold, Monsanto obtained samples of the soybean plant material remaining from some of David's fields. On the basis of those tests, on April 12, 2004, Monsanto filed suit for patent infringement, breach of contract, unjust enrichment, and conversion, alleging that David had illicitly saved and planted Roundup Ready® seeds.

A bench trial was held in February 2006 during which Monsanto presented crop insurance records with planting dates provided by David. In those records, David claimed to have planted nearly all of his soybean fields as of May 6, 2003. Monsanto also presented an invoice from Red River Grain for David's purchase of 993 units of Roundup Ready® soybean seed on May 31, 2003, nearly a month after David claimed to have planted the vast majority of his soybean crop for the year. Monsanto argued that that purchase was merely David's attempt to convince Monsanto that he had purchased enough Roundup Ready® seed to plant his crops and that he had not saved any seed.

On April 20, 2006, the district court entered judgment against David. The court found David's claim that he purchased and planted the seeds from Red River Grain more than a month before the date of the invoice to be "unreliable." Furthermore, the court found David's testimony regarding his claimed purchase of conventional herbicides "not believable." The court found David to be unreliable as a witness, and also found that he had failed to overcome the scientific evidence showing that he had planted his soybean fields

---

2. The Technology Fee for soybean seeds in 2003 was $7.75 per unit.

3. The 1999 Monsanto Technology Agreement states "this agreement remains in effect until you or Monsanto choose to terminate the Agreement." Neither party in this appeal contends that the 1999 Agreement was not in effect when David planted his fields in 2003.

4. Roundup Ready® soybeans are typically sold in fifty-pound units, while conventional seeds typically are sold in sixty-pound bushels.

exclusively with Roundup Ready® seeds, yet he had not purchased sufficient quantities of such seed in 2003 to do so. The court, therefore, held that David had willfully infringed the '605 patent and breached the Technology Agreement by planting saved seed from a prior year's crop. A damages award of $226,214.40 was entered in favor of Monsanto.

After the ruling, Monsanto filed four motions: for attorney fees, prejudgment interest, costs, and treble damages. On July 25, 2006, the court awarded Monsanto an additional $10,000 in enhanced damages in lieu of treble damages, and found that Monsanto was entitled to recover attorney fees in the amount of $323,140.05. The court awarded Monsanto costs in the amount of $164,608.03 pursuant to the Technology Agreement, and, alternatively, costs in the amount of $30,542.99 pursuant to 28 U.S.C. § 1920. Lastly, the court awarded Monsanto prejudgment interest in the amount of $63,026.95. In sum, David was found liable to Monsanto for $786,989.43. David filed two motions to amend the April 20, 2006 judgment, both of which were denied by the court on October 27, 2006.

David timely appealed the district court's judgment. We have jurisdiction pursuant to 28 U.S.C. § 1295(a)(1).

DISCUSSION

A. Infringement

The '605 patent claims a gene sequence, not a plant variety or a seed. U.S. Patent No. 5,352,605 (filed Oct. 28, 1993). Therefore, David argues that the '605 patent cannot be infringed merely by saving seeds from plants containing the patented gene sequence. David argues that the written description of the '605 patent lacks the specificity that would be required of a patented plant variety under the utility patent statute; thus, the '605 patent is limited to the gene sequence and does not cover the plant containing such a gene. David argues that *J.E.M. Ag Supply, Inc. v. Pioneer Hi-Bred International, Inc.* stands for the proposition that plants can only receive patent protection under the Plant Patent Act of 1930, (the "P.P.A."), the Plant Variety Protection Act of 1970,(the "P.V.P.A."), or under a utility patent on a plant variety. A utility patent on a gene sequence, David claims, does not entitle the holder of that patent to enforce its grant of exclusivity against growers of plant varieties that contain the gene sequence.

Monsanto responds by arguing that the holding of *J.E.M.* is the opposite of what David claims it to be; the broad language of 35 U.S.C. § 101 relating to patentable subject matter remains unmodified by the existence of the P.V.P.A. and the P.P.A. Moreover, Monsanto points to various decisions of this court that have read the '605 patent onto plants and seeds containing the patented gene and holding those who save such seeds liable for infringement.

David's brief makes much of the Supreme Court's decision in *J.E.M.* *J.E.M.* involved utility patents issued for corn seed products that were held by Pioneer Hi-Bred International, Inc. The petitioner in *J.E.M.* argued that Pioneer's patents were invalid because plant varieties were only patentable under the P.P.A. or the P.V.P.A. The Supreme Court disagreed, holding that the existence of statutes specifically authorizing the patenting of plants (the P.P.A. and the P.V.P.A.) did not eliminate the availability of utility patent protection covering plants. We disagree also. Contrary to David's arguments on appeal, nothing in *J.E.M.* invalidates or limits the '605 patent or any utility patent on a gene sequence in a seed or a plant. In fact, in J.E.M., the Supreme Court explicitly refused to limit the extent of patentable subject matter: "we decline to narrow the reach of § 101 where Congress has given us no indication that it intends this result." The '605 patent covering the gene sequence is infringed by planting a seed containing the gene sequence because the seed contains the gene. The gene itself is being used in the planting, an infringing act.

David's real complaint seems to be that he should be able to save seed from his harvest, regardless of Monsanto's patent. We have dealt with this complaint before. *See e.g. Monsanto Co. v. McFarling*, 302 F.3d 1291 (Fed.Cir.2002). In *McFarling*, we held that a farmer who saved seed containing a patented gene was liable for patent infringement. *McFarling* further established that "the right to save seed of plants registered under the PVPA does not impart the right to save seed of plants patented under the Patent Act." We note that *McFarling* dealt with the very patent at issue in this case—the '605 patent. We may not disregard a prior decision of this court regarding the same matter.

David next argues that the district court's finding of infringement was clearly erroneous and that there was no evidence from which to infer that he saved Roundup Ready® soybeans from his 2002 harvest for planting in 2003. Additionally, he argues that the district court's admission of expert testimony and exhibits was an abuse of discretion.

Monsanto urges this court to uphold the factual findings of the district court. Monsanto also argues that David ignores Federal Rule of Evidence 703, which allows an expert witness to base his opinion on evidence that itself may be inadmissible.

We agree with Monsanto that the factual findings of the district court were not clearly erroneous. David does not dispute that he planted Roundup Ready® soybean seeds in 2003; rather, he claims that the Roundup Ready® seeds that he planted were acquired from authorized dealers. To dispute this claim, Monsanto presented scientific field tests demonstrating that David's soybean fields had been planted exclusively with Roundup Ready® soybeans, invoices proving that David had purchased large quantities of glyphosate-based herbicides, government documents of David's planting dates, and evidence that David had not purchased enough Roundup Ready® seeds to fully plant his fields by those dates. In response, David offered inconsistent testimony regarding what he actually planted in 2003. David changed his version of events at least three times, including claiming that he planted only the perimeters of his fields with Roundup Ready® seed, while planting the interior of his fields with conventional seed. David's testimony, and that of his daughter, was the only evidence offered to refute Monsanto's case. Due to his continually changing testimony, the court disregarded much of David's testimony. Given David's unreliability as a witness, and a complete lack of other evidence supporting his claims, we conclude that the district court did not clearly err in determining that David planted saved seed.

David also argues that the seed report tests conducted by Monsanto and the testimony of Monsanto's expert Koppatschek, which relied on those seed report tests, were improperly admitted at trial. David further argues that had those pieces of evidence been excluded, the court would not have had sufficient evidence from which to find that David saved seed.

David's arguments to exclude Koppatschek's testimony are unpersuasive. Rule 702 of the Federal Rules of Evidence allows expert testimony if "(1) the testimony is based upon sufficient facts or data, (2) the testimony is the product of reliable principles and methods, and (3) the witness has applied the principles and methods reliably to the facts of the case." David does not suggest that Koppatschek's testimony is unreliably applied or based on unreliable methods or insufficient data; rather, he challenges Koppatschek's reliance on the seed report tests that were produced by Monsanto's scientific team, but not by Koppatschek personally.

David's challenge fails, however, because the Federal Rules of Evidence establish that an expert need not have obtained the basis for his opinion from personal perception. Likewise, numerous courts have held that reliance on scientific test results prepared by others may constitute the type of evidence that is reasonably relied upon by experts for purposes of Rule of Evidence 703. "Unlike an ordinary witness, see Rule 701, an expert is permitted wide latitude to offer opinions, including those that are not based on first hand knowledge." Koppatschek's reliance on the scientific reports prepared by his team is therefore the type of reliance that is reasonable for expert witnesses. Furthermore, Koppatschek's testimony is admissible, regardless of the admissibility of the seed report.[5] Rule 703 expressly authorizes the admission of expert opinion that is based on "facts or data" that themselves are inadmissible, as long as the evidence relied upon is "of a type reasonably relied upon by experts in the particular field in forming opinions." The tests conducted in this case are certainly of the type relied upon by experts, and Koppatschek's testimony was therefore admissible.

B. Damages

David also appeals the district court's damages calculation. The district court awarded Monsanto a reasonable royalty for David's infringing use of the '605 patent, enhanced damages, attorney fees, costs, and prejudgment interest. David challenges the attorney fees and cost awards, as well as the reasonable royalty, but does not challenge the enhanced damages or prejudgment interest. We review the district court's damages decision for an "erroneous conclusion of law, clearly erroneous factual findings, or a clear error of judgment amounting to an abuse of discretion."

1. Attorney Fees and Costs

On appeal, David makes four arguments for reducing or eliminating the district court's award of attorney fees and costs. First, he argues that this is not an exceptional case as required for the award of attorney fees under 35 U.S.C. § 285. Second, he argues that the attorney fee provision in the Technology Agreement is unenforceable because that provision appears on the reverse side of the agreement, while the signature page is on the front. Third, David claims that the amount of the attorney fee award ($323,140.05) does not bear a reasonable relation to the result achieved as required under *Perricone v. Medicis Pharmaceutical Corp.* And fourth, David urges this court to limit the amount of attorney fees awarded under the Technology Agreement to an amount that would be recoverable under 35 U.S.C. § 285 and 28 U.S.C. §§ 1920, 1821(b).

In reply, Monsanto maintains that the district court had ample reason to conclude that David's case was "exceptional." According to Monsanto, David's "deceitful" litigation tactics prolonged Monsanto's case and increased its fees and costs, and the district court was within its discretion to award additional fees to Monsanto. Furthermore, Monsanto argues that David's legal arguments limiting the attorney fees and costs are without merit.

We review a finding that a case is "exceptional" for clear error. *Perricone*, 432 F.3d at 1380. We review an award of attorney fees in an exceptional case for abuse of discretion. Id.

---

5. We need not decide whether the seed report itself was admissible, nor does it appear that David makes this argument on appeal. Even assuming, arguendo, that it was improperly admitted, in this case it is cumulative and does not appear to have had any prejudicial effect; it was therefore harmless error.

We agree with Monsanto that the district court's decision to award attorney fees was not an abuse of discretion. David knew that saving seed was a violation of the Technology Agreement, yet he did so anyway. He attempted to cover up his infringement and deceive Monsanto. This is not a case of a farmer unknowingly infringing a patent. It is a case of a farmer with apparent disregard for patent rights, license agreements, and the judicial process. With that in mind, as well as the record evidence of David's inconsistent testimony, we agree with the district court that this is an "exceptional" case under *Perricone*, and we find that the awarding of attorney fees was within the discretion of the district court.

David's argument that the contractual provision is invalid also fails. We have decided this same issue — whether contractual provisions appearing on the back of a contract are enforceable — in a case involving a nearly identical Technology Agreement. In *McFarling*, we held that, absent a showing of fraud, a "party who signs an agreement is bound by its terms." We see no reason to deviate from that ruling here, and David has not claimed that his signing of the Technology Agreement was fraudulently procured.

Lastly, we reject David's argument that the attorney fees and costs stipulated to in the Technology Agreement are limited by statute. David urges this court to limit attorney fees to those recoverable under 35 U.S.C. §285. He also urges us to limit the award of costs to the amount available under 28 U.S.C. §1920. David's use of 35 U.S.C. §285 in this case, however, is inapposite. That statute awards attorney fees to patent holders like Monsanto, but the Technology Agreement here also does. Having violated the Technology Agreement, there is no reason why its attorney fee provision cannot be enforced.

Similarly, 28 U.S.C. §1920 does not set maximum costs around which private parties may not contract. That statute limits the amount that federal courts may tax as costs in the absence of "explicit statutory or contractual authorization to the contrary." Having held that David breached the Technology Agreement, there is no reason that the amount of contractual costs authorized therein should be limited by §1920. Thus, the costs agreed to in the Technology Agreement are enforceable, even though those costs exceed the costs recoverable under §1920.

The district court awarded Monsanto the full amount of its requested costs pursuant to the Technology Agreement; $164,608.03. The district court alternatively awarded Monsanto costs of $30,542.99, the amount requested under 28 U.S.C. §1920. Those costs appear to be duplicative of the Technology Agreement costs award granted to Monsanto and therefore are not recoverable in light of our affirmance of the Technology Agreement costs award. There is no basis for a double assessment of costs.

We therefore affirm the district court's award to Monsanto of $10,000 in enhanced damages, $164,608.03 in costs, and $323,140.05 in attorney fees.

2. Reasonable Royalty

David next argues for a reduction of the district court's infringement damages award. David argues that the number of infringing units of seed that the district court found he had planted (4,110 units) was not supported by the evidence. He also claims that the reasonable royalty awarded for each unit ($55.04) was not supported by the evidence, that the court's adoption of that figure was a violation of the doctrine of collateral estoppel, and that the court should have used the $7.75 Technology Fee as the reasonable royalty figure.

Monsanto counters that the number of infringing seed units planted by David was correctly calculated by the district court, and that the district court properly relied on expert testimony in arriving at the 4,110 unit figure. Monsanto also notes that the royalty for each unit of seed is the same as that upheld in *Monsanto Co. v. McFarling*, and *Monsanto Co. v. Ralph* and should thus be upheld here as well.

At trial, Monsanto's expert testified that after applying the multi-factor *Georgia Pacific* test he calculated a reasonable royalty for David's infringement at $66 per bag. The district court, however, relying on this court's decision in *Ralph*, awarded a $55.04 royalty instead. David's argument that the court should have adopted the technology fee paid on each purchase of Roundup Ready® soybean has come before this court previously in both *Ralph* and *McFarling*. As in those cases, we reject the argument here. *Ralph* held that the Technology Fee is "not an established royalty for planting ... saved seed." David argues that his case is distinguishable from *Ralph* due to the fact that there is no evidence that David, unlike *Ralph*, transferred seed to others. Regardless of any perceived difference in the relative levels of culpability between David and Ralph, our decision in *Ralph* stands for the fact that the Technology Fee is not an established royalty for the infringing act of saving seed. As for the specifics of this case, the district court was within its discretion to rely on the only reasonable testimony presented to it, that of Monsanto's expert. Furthermore, we do not see how the court's reduction of the royalty from $66.00 to $55.04 implicates the doctrine of collateral estoppel. We therefore uphold the district court's finding of a royalty of $55.04 per unit.

In calculating the number of infringing seed units planted by David, the district court had the difficult task of determining the total soybean acreage planted by David in 2003 and the density of seed used in those fields.[6] David does not challenge the district court's finding that he planted a total of 2,222 acres in 2003. He does, however, challenge the district court's finding of an average planting density of 107.5 pounds per acre. To arrive at that figure, the district court averaged two density figures offered at trial; Monsanto's expert Koppatschek established a planting rate of 95 pounds per acre, based on samples taken from David's fields, and David offered a high estimate of 120 pounds per acre during a deposition taken on November 9, 2004. David argues that the density calculated by the district court was not supported by the evidence and furthermore that the evidence supports a much lower figure.

Monsanto counters that the density calculation is supported both by expert testimony and David's own testimony at deposition. Monsanto claims that the testimony David cites as supporting a lower density figure was based on merely hypothetical discussions of soybean farming generally, and not related to the specifics of David's actions in 2003.

On this point, we agree with David that the density calculation was clearly erroneous. In so concluding, we appreciate the difficulty faced by the district court in arriving at a density figure in this case. In arguing for reduction of the density calculation, David's appellate brief lists at least four different rates at which he claimed to have planted soybeans, ranging from three-quarters of a unit (37.5 pounds) to one and one-half units (75 pounds). The record demonstrates that much of this confusion stemmed from the different planting rates used for conventional soybean seeds and Roundup Ready® seeds, due both to the better yield and the higher price of the Roundup products. The confusion, certainly, also stemmed from David's unreliability, as noted by the district court and as evidenced throughout the record.

---

6. The district court multiplied David's soybean acreage by the planting density to obtain the total weight of soybean seeds planted. The court then divided that total by fifty pounds to obtain the total number of soybean units planted. Subtracting the 645 units legitimately purchased before planting, the court obtained the total infringing units. Multiplying that number by the reasonable royalty ($55.04/bag), the court obtained the final damage figure.

However, David's estimate of 120 pounds per acre, when properly read in context, did not refer to the density of his Roundup Ready® planting. In the testimony at issue, there was some confusion between David and the questioning attorney as to the type of seed being referred to. In fact, immediately following David's response there was a discussion between Monsanto's attorney and David's attorney as to which type of seed was being referenced. Directly following this exchange, Monsanto's attorney rephrased his question and directly referenced Roundup Ready® seed. David answered that the density "could be like a unit," or fifty pounds. In all of David's extensive previous testimony, he testified that the upper limit for his planting of Roundup Ready® seed never exceeded one and one-half units (seventy-five pounds). The 120 pound density figure David offered clearly was not based on Roundup Ready seed, but rather conventional seed. The use of this anomalous 120 pound figure, in a confused context, amounted to clear error.

We thus remand to the district court for additional fact finding concerning the Roundup Ready® soybean density in David's fields in 2003. We note that there was testimony on the record in which David directly addressed his Roundup Ready® soybean planting rate; this testimony varied widely, but seems to have ranged from three-quarters of a unit (37.5 pounds) to one and one-half units (75 pounds). Use of any of those figures, which are explicitly directed to the density of Roundup Ready® soybeans, would be appropriate. Additionally, we find that, although the court's use of David's estimate of 120 pounds per acre was clearly erroneous, the court's use of the 95 pounds per acre figure arrived at by Monsanto's expert, Koppatschek, was not. Should the court decide that David's testimony on this issue was so unreliable as to be without value, the court would be well within its discretion to adopt the figure obtained by Koppatschek. The district court should make this determination, however, not this court, following which the reasonable royalty calculation outlined in footnote 5 should be followed.[7]

CONCLUSION

Accordingly, we affirm the district court's finding of infringement of the '605 patent, the court's award of attorney fees, costs, enhanced damages, and prejudgment interest, and the court's reasonable royalty calculation of $55.04 per unit. We vacate the district court's calculation of seed density of 107.5 pounds per acre. The case is remanded to the district court for further proceedings consistent with this opinion.

AFFIRMED IN PART, VACATED IN PART, and REMANDED

Notes

1. Farmers who have not signed a contract but use the patented seed can also be found liable for violating the patent. *See, Monsanto v. Dawson*, 2000 U.S. Dist. LEXIS 22392 (E.D. Mo. 2000).

The FARMERS GUIDE TO GMOs: reports that

> When farmers are found to have infringed a biotech company's patent on GM seed by saving seed and planting another crop, they are often ordered to pay tens and even hundreds of thousands of dollars in damages to the company.... [S]uch

---

7. In light of our adjustment of the total damages awarded, the district court should adjust the amount of prejudgment interest accordingly.

money damages are likely to include a "reasonable royalty" for each bag of seed found to have been saved and replanted, attorneys' fees, and court costs, and may include "enhanced damages" if the court finds that the infringement was willful. The "reasonable royalty" farmers have been required to pay has ranged from $40 to $55 per bag for GM soybean seed to $556 per bag for GM cotton-seed, to $1,113 per bag for GM cottonseed that was saved and transferred to an-other person. Monsanto is very aggressive in pursuing patent infringement lawsuits against farmers for saving and misuse of GM seed and crops contain-ing Monsanto's patented technologies, investigating roughly 500 U.S. farmers each year. Reports indicate that Monsanto is collecting more than $85 million an-nually from U.S. farmers in out-of-court settlements, while courts have awarded Monsanto more than $21,500,000 in recorded judgments against U.S. farmers.

FARMERS GUIDE TO GMOs (FLAG, Inc. 2009) available at http://www.flaginc.org/topics/pubs/biotech.php#FGtoGMOs2009

In at least one case, the damages awarded to Monsanto were found to be non-dis-chargeable in the farmer's Chapter 7 bankruptcy. The court held that the unlicensed use of patented seeds fell within the exception from discharge for debts "for willful and ma-licious injury by the debtor to another entity or to the property of another entity" from discharge in bankruptcy. 11 U.S.C. § 523(a)(6). *In re Trantham*, 304 B.R. 298 (B.A.P. 6th Cir. 2004).

2. In a much publicized case, Maurice Parr, a seed cleaner from Indiana was sued by Monsanto for encouraging farmers to save seeds in violation of Monsanto's patent rights. Mr. Parr was featured in the documentary, *Food Inc.* The case was settled and an injunc-tion entered requiring Parr to obtain certification from his clients that their seeds were not Monsanto patented seeds and to advise clients that seed-saving of patented seeds is illegal. *Monsanto v. Parr*, No. 4:07CV0008AS (N.D. Ind. Apr. 22, 2008).

Monsanto's aggressive pursuit of those it believes have violated its patents has been widely reported in the media. VANITY FAIR magazine is one of several publications that have critically described the tactics used by the corporation. The use of private investi-gators, surveillance videos, and the threat of lawsuits are all techniques employed in the protection of Monsanto's patent rights.

Donald L. Barlett and James B. Steele
Investigation: Monsanto's Harvest of Fear

VANITY FAIR MAGAZINE (May 2008) available at
http://www.vanityfair.com/politics/features/2008/05/monsanto200805

Gary Rinehart clearly remembers the summer day in 2002 when the stranger walked in and issued his threat. Rinehart was behind the counter of the Square Deal, his "old-time country store," as he calls it, on the fading town square of Eagleville, Missouri, a tiny farm community 100 miles north of Kansas City....

As Rinehart would recall, the man began verbally attacking him, saying he had proof that Rinehart had planted Monsanto's genetically modified (G.M.) soy-beans in violation of the company's patent. Better come clean and settle with Monsanto, Rinehart says the man told him—or face the consequences.

Rinehart was incredulous, listening to the words as puzzled customers and em-ployees looked on. Like many others in rural America, Rinehart knew of Mon-santo's fierce reputation for enforcing its patents and suing anyone who allegedly violated them. But Rinehart wasn't a farmer. He wasn't a seed dealer. He hadn't planted any seeds or sold any seeds. He owned a small—a really small—country store in a town of 350 people. He was angry that somebody could just barge into the store and embarrass him in front of everyone. "It made me and my business look bad," he says. Rinehart says he told the intruder, "You got the wrong guy."

When the stranger persisted, Rinehart showed him the door. On the way out the man kept making threats. Rinehart says he can't remember the exact words, but they were to the effect of: "Monsanto is big. You can't win. We will get you. You will pay."

The article reports that Monsanto went on to file a federal law suit against Mr. Rinehart, alleging that he "knowingly, intentionally, and willfully" planted seeds "in violation of Monsanto's patent rights." Mr. Rinehart retained a lawyer for his defense, and Monsanto eventually realized it had brought charges against the wrong person. The article continues, "Rinehart later learned that the company had been secretly investigating farmers in his area. Rinehart never heard from Monsanto again: no letter of apology, no public concession that the company had made a terrible mistake, no offer to pay his attorney's fees. "I don't know how they get away with it," he says. "If I tried to do something like that it would be bad news. I felt like I was in another country." …

3. Monsanto defends its aggressive stance on its website page, *Why Does Monsanto Sue Farmers Who Save Seeds?*[8]

Monsanto patents many of the seed varieties we develop. Patents are necessary to ensure that we are paid for our products and for all the investments we put into developing these products. This is one of the basic reasons for patents. A more important reason is to help foster innovation. Without the protection of patents there would be little incentive for privately-owned companies to pursue and reinvest in innovation. Monsanto invests more than $2.6 million per day in research and development that ultimately benefits farmers and consumers. Without the protection of patents, this would not be possible.

When farmers purchase a patented seed variety, they sign an agreement that they will not save and replant seeds produced from the seed they buy from us. More than 275,000 farmers a year buy seed under these agreements in the United States. Other seed companies sell their seed under similar provisions. They understand the basic simplicity of the agreement, which is that a business must be paid for its product. The vast majority of farmers understand and appreciate our research and are willing to pay for our inventions and the value they provide. They don't think it's fair that some farmers don't pay.

A very small percentage of farmers do not honor this agreement. Monsanto does become aware, through our own actions or through third-parties, of individuals who are suspected of violating our patents and agreements. Where we do find violations, we are able to settle most of these cases without ever going to trial. In many cases, these farmers remain our customers. Sometimes however, we are forced to resort to lawsuits. This is a relatively rare circumstance, with 144 lawsuits filed since 1997 in the United States, as of April 2010. This averages

---

8. This article is available at http://www.monsanto.com/monsanto_today/for_the_record/monsanto_saved_seed_lawsuits.asp

about 11 per year for the past 13 years. To date, only 9 cases have gone through full trial. In every one of these instances, the jury or court decided in our favor.

Whether the farmer settles right away, or the case settles during or through trial, the proceeds are donated to youth leadership initiatives including scholarship programs....

4. Consolidation in the Seed Industry

On August 5, 2009 — USDA Secretary Tom Vilsack and Attorney General Eric Holder announced that the USDA and the Department of Justice would hold joint public workshops "to explore competition issues affecting the agriculture industry in the 21st century and the appropriate role for antitrust and regulatory enforcement in that industry."

"For the first time ever, farmers, ranchers, consumers groups, agribusinesses and the federal government will openly discuss legal and economic issues associated with competition in the agriculture industry," said Christine A. Varney, Assistant Attorney General in charge of the Department of Justice's Antitrust Division. "This is an important step forward in determining the best course of action to address the unique competition issues in agriculture."

The USDA and Department of Justice requested the submission of comments on the application of antitrust laws to monopsony and vertical integration in the agricultural sector including, the scope, functionality, and limits of current or potential rules. They also requested input on "additional topics that might be discussed at the workshops, including the impact of agriculture concentration on food costs, the effect of agricultural regulatory statutes or other applicable laws and programs on competition, issues relating to patent and intellectual property affecting agricultural marketing or production, and market practices such as price spreads, forward contracts, packer ownership of livestock before slaughter, market transparency, and increasing retailer concentration." The comments received are available for review at http://www.justice.gov/atr/public/workshops/ag2010/ index.htm#publiccomments.

The Attorney Generals representing the states of Montana, Iowa, Maine, Maryland, Mississippi, New Hampshire, New Mexico, Ohio, Oklahoma, Oregon, South Dakota, Tennessee, Vermont, and West Virginia submitted joint comments. The section of their comments that addresses consolidation in the seed industry is as follows:

Comments Regarding Competition in the Agriculture Industry

Introduction

The Attorneys General of the undersigned states[9] (the "States") submit these comments in response to the request by the Department of Agriculture and the Department of Justice.[10]

Concern over the economic welfare of U.S. farmers and ranchers, and their susceptibility to the harmful exercise of market power, helped lead to the passage of the nation's major antitrust legislation.[11] And while much has changed in agriculture over the past

---

9. Montana, Iowa, Maine, Maryland, Mississippi, New Hampshire, New Mexico, Ohio, Oklahoma, Oregon, South Dakota, Tennessee, Vermont, and West Virginia.

10. 74 Fed. Reg. 43725-6 (08/27/09).

11. ABA Section of Antitrust Law, *Antitrust Law Developments (Sixth), Volume II,* at 1305.

century, one thing that has not changed is the vulnerability of our producers to anti-competitive conduct.

For the most part, our farms and ranches remain relatively small businesses that are relied upon to produce a high quality product, with little regard to the cost of the inputs to produce and transport their products, or the prices they will receive upon completion of their labor. Hence, our farmers and ranchers are twice disadvantaged: Anti-competitive conduct injures farmers and ranchers as *consumers* in various input markets where monopoly or seller power is abused through lower output and higher prices. This conduct also injures them as *producers*, where monopsony or buyer power among processors is abused through lower demand and lower prices.

The impacts do not end at the borders of the farm or ranch, either. The abuse of buyer power can also harm the consumer at the supermarket, as the lower demand at the agricultural processor level translates into lower output at the food consumer level.

The States' agricultural sectors vary widely, from the dairy farms of New England to the corn and soybean farms of the Midwest to the ranches of the High Plains. We find common ground, however, in recognizing that our rural communities and our consumers alike depend on an efficient and vibrant agricultural marketplace. This, in turn, requires an integrated approach that includes increased cooperation among state and federal competition law enforcers as well as reconsideration of laws and regulations that may no longer serve their original pro-competitive purposes. The States therefore share the objectives of the USDA and USDOJ in these workshops: understand the state of competition in agricultural markets and explore appropriate advocacy, enforcement, and other solutions to meet the needs of agricultural producers and consumers alike.

I. Crop Markets

A. Seeds

Historically, most commercial seed suppliers were small, often family-owned businesses that multiplied seed varieties developed in the public domain by, for example, state agricultural experiment stations.[12] With the development of hybrids and greater intellectual property right protections, the number of private firms engaged in plant breeding grew rapidly for some time. However, consolidation has prevailed since the early 1990s.[13] By 1998, Pioneer Hi-Bred International, the then-largest hybrid seed company, had a 41% market share in hybrid corn.

The trend towards consolidation came along with increasingly sophisticated development of hybrid germplasm and the introduction of transgenic technology into plant germplasm. The new transgenic traits were licensed to seed developers which bred them into the germplasm. These traited seeds provided resistance to herbicides or insect protection. For example, in 1996 Monsanto introduced the "Roundup Ready" trait in soy. By virtue of its market acceptance and broad licensing to third party seed developers, Monsanto increased its market share from *less than 2% of total planted major field crops in the U.S. in 1996, to 68% of major field crops—and 91% of the U.S. soy crop—in 2007.*[14]

---

12. Jorge Fernandez-Cornejo and Richard E. Just, *Researchability of Modern Agricultural Input Markets and Growing Concentration*, Amer. J. Agr. Econ. 89 (Number 5, 2007), 1269.

13. *Id.*

14. See, "Adoption of Genetically Engineered Crops in the U.S.: Extent of Adoption" at http://www.ers.usda.gov/Data/BiotechCrops/adoption.htm (Visited 2-23-10).

The rapid acceptance of transgenic traits coincided with a trend towards concentration within the industry, so that today five multi-national companies own the most commercially successful trait technologies for crops. Transgenic seeds now account for 80% of planted corn, 92% of planted soybeans, and 86% of planted cotton.[15] Monsanto's Roundup Ready trait has been bred into most seeds offered by third party seed developers, including Pioneer.

These developments in transgenic traits and improved germplasm have coincided with increased crop yields: since the mid-1990s, overall corn yields have increased 36%, soy yields have increased 12%, and cotton yields have increased 31%.[16] The introduction of genetic traits has also been credited with reducing input costs for herbicides and pesticides, saving farmers more than $1 billion a year in such chemical and labor costs, in addition to less tangible savings in time, effort and known environmental impacts.[17] Yet the prices charged for the transgenic traits, as well as for the underlying germplasm, have increased dramatically: corn seed in 2009 is reported to be 30% more expensive than it was in 2008, while soybean seed was 25% more expensive in 2009 than in 2008.[18]

These prices are a factor of both the germplasm price and the so-called "technology fee," which functions as a royalty fee for the transgenic trait.[19] The royalties are a consequence of patent protection for the specific event causing the mutation or modification in the genetic material which creates the herbicide tolerance, insect resistance or other beneficial trait. Patents provide an inventor nearly unfettered control over access to an invention during the life of the patent, including the ability to charge for that access.[20] However, if an inventor licenses its invention to others and, through that process, restrains com-

---

15. *See* Diana L. Moss, *Transgenic Seed Platforms: Competition Between a Rock and a Hard Place?*, American Antitrust Institute at 10. http://www.antitrustinstitute.org/archives/files/AAI_Platforms%20 and%20Transgenic%20Seed_102320091053.pdf.

16. Council for Biotechnology Information; Factsheet: "Helping Increase Crop Yields for America's Farmers," available at http://www.whybiotech.com/resources/CBIAgriculture2009.pdf.

17. Sankula, Sujatha. 2006. *Quantification of the Impacts on U.S. Agriculture of Biotechnology-derived Crops Planted in 2005* (Executive Summary), National Center for Food and Agricultural Policy.

18. *See,* Kristina Hubbard, *Out of Hand: Farmers Face the Consequences of a Consolidated Seed Industry,* Farmer to Farmer Campaign Report, Dec. 2009 at 21. http://farmertofarmercampaign.com/Out %20of%20Hand.FullReport.pdf.

19. *Id.*

20. United States patent law is generally intended to protect an inventor's right to fully control and benefit from an invention for a term of years—until that patent expires, the inventor holds exclusive control, within the scope of its patent, and may limit any rights to use that invention. *Monsanto v. Scruggs,* 459 F. 3d 1328, 1338 (Fed. Cir 2006); see also, *Miller Insituform, Inc. v. Insituform of N. Am. , Inc.,* 830 F.2d 606, 609 (6th Cir. 1987) ("A patent holder who lawfully acquires a patent cannot be held liable under Section 2 of the Sherman Act for maintaining the monopoly power he lawfully acquired by refusing to license the patent to others.") Antitrust laws do not prevent a monopolist from charging a high royalty for use of an invention. *Verizon Communications v. Law Offices of Curtis V. Trinko, LLP,* 540 U.S. 398, 407 (2004) ("The mere possession of monopoly power, and the concomitant charging of monopoly prices, is not only not unlawful; it is an important element of the free-market system. The opportunity to charge monopoly prices—at least for a short period—is what attracts 'business acumen' in the first place; it induces risk taking that produces innovation and economic growth."). Evidencing the right of control over its intellectual property, the patent owner may charge different licensees different royalties. *E.g., Akzo, N.V. v. International Trade Comm'n,* 808 F.2d 1471, 1488–89 (Fed. Cir. 1986) (Patentee was free to charge higher prices for those uses of its patented process that have greater value). Case law has also recognized the ability of a patent holder to impose restrictions that might carry over to subsequent purchasers. *Mallinckrodt, Inc. v. Medipart, Inc.,* 976 F.2d 700 (Fed. Cir. 1992); see also *Monsanto Co. v. McFarling,* 363 F.3d 1336, 1340 (Fed. Cir. 2004) (Not an antitrust violation or misuse of Monsanto's licenses to prevent farmers from replanting the progeny of its patented seed because the progeny also contain the patented invention.).

petition that would have occurred absent the license, antitrust liability could arise.[21] In a concentrated industry, law enforcers must carefully analyze whether any holder of intellectual property is acting within the scope of its patent in imposing any restrictions on the use of the claimed invention.

While the increase in seed and trait prices may be offset by savings in other inputs or other additives, it is unclear to what extent rising transgenic seed prices have led to sufficient corresponding benefits to agricultural producers. There is additional concern that increased vertical integration and acquisitions may have raised the bar for entry so high that entry into the trait market is difficult, or nearly impossible.

Recommendation:

Continue awareness and scrutiny. To the extent there is consensus as to the existence of any problem, there is no simple solution due to both the interplay of long-standing policies of protecting property rights governed by patent laws and the economic efficiencies claimed by the multi-national companies that now dominate the industry.

The complexity of the seed industry requires a thorough understanding of the industry, current antitrust jurisprudence, and intellectual property laws. State Attorneys General, the DOJ and USDA should explore the concerns which have been raised and consider whether there are bases for changes in policy and existing laws....

———————

Notes

1. Many farmers and their advocates take a much stronger position against consolidation in the seed industry. *See, e.g.*, Kristina Hubbard, *Out of Hand, Farmers Face the Consequences of a Consolidated Seed Industry*, National Family Farm Coalition (Dec. 2009). *Out of Hand* is a publication resulting from the Farmer to Farmer Campaign on Genetic Engineering, a network of 34 farm organizations that seek to build a farmer driven campaign focused on their concerns about the agricultural biotechnology industry. According to this report, ten companies account for 65% of the world's proprietary seed; four of those firms own rights to 50% of that market and 43% of the overall commercial seed market. The report blames U.S. intellectual property law and lax enforcement of antitrust laws by the Department of Justice as consolidations and mergers limited competition. Another factor discussed is the privatization of public research funding at Universities, where private companies fund research and results are patented rather than being publicly available. Morever, farmers complain that access to conventional (non-genetically engineered) seeds is increasingly limited. *Out of Hand* is available for download at http://farmerto farmercampaign.org.

2. Professor Philip H. Howard at Michigan State University has developed a series of graphical representations of consolidation and cross-licensing agreements involving seed genetics, including a network animation of changes in the seed industry 1996–2008. These are available at https://msu.edu/~howardp/seedindustry.html.

3. The comments from the Attorneys General reference the reduced use of pesticides resulting from the use of genetically engineered crops. As the USDA noted in its draft Environmental Impact Statement for genetically engineered alfalfa, a controversy exists over

———————

21. *See* Antitrust Guidelines for the Licensing of Intellectual Property, § 3.1 at http://www.justice.gov/ atr/public/guidelines/0558.htm#t3.

whether herbicide use overall has increased or decreased as a result of GT [glyphospho-sate-tolerant] crops.

C. Challenge to the Approval Process for New Genetically Engineered Seeds

Geertson Seed Farms v. Johanns
No. C 06-01075 CRB
United States District Court for the Northern District of California
Feb. 13, 2007

MEMORANDUM AND ORDER

In this lawsuit plaintiff alfalfa growers along with the Sierra Club and other farmer and consumer associations challenge the Department of Agriculture's decision to deregulate alfalfa genetically engineered to resist the herbicide glyphosate, the active ingredient in RoundUp ("Roundup Ready alfalfa"). Plaintiffs bring their claims pursuant to the National Environmental Policy Act ("NEPA"), the Endangered Species Act ("ESA"), and the Plant Protection Act ("PPA"). Now pending before the Court are the parties' cross-motions for summary judgment. The motions raise a close question of first impression: whether the introduction of a genetically engineered crop that might significantly decrease the availability or even eliminate all non-genetically engineered varieties is a "significant environmental impact" requiring the preparation of an environmental impact statement, at least when it involves the fourth largest crop in the United States.

BACKGROUND

The federal Plant Protection Act gives the Secretary of the United States Department of Agriculture ("USDA") the authority to adopt regulations preventing the introduction and dissemination of plant pests. Pursuant to this authority, the USDA, through the Animal and Plant Health Inspection Service ("APHIS"), regulates "organisms and products altered or produced through genetic engineering that are plant pests or are believed to be plant pests." Such products/organisms are known as "regulated articles." APHIS originally considered Roundup Ready alfalfa a regulated article; as such, it was unlawful for any person to introduce the alfalfa without first obtaining permission from APHIS.

Any person may submit a petition seeking a determination that a regulated article does not present a plant pest risk and therefore should not be regulated. In May 2003, Monsanto, the manufacturer of Roundup, submitted a petition requesting nonregulated status for Roundup Ready alfalfa, designated as event J101 and J163. Roundup Ready alfalfa is engineered to be glyphosate-tolerant by inserting a gene that codes for the enzyme 5-enolpyruvylshikimate-3-phosphate synthase into the alfalfa genome.

APHIS had several possible responses: it could approve the petition in whole, approve the petition in part, or deny the petition. If it denied the petition, commercial scale production of Roundup Ready alfalfa would continue to be precluded, although the plant could still be grown in field trials, as it has since 1998. APHIS could also determine that Roundup Ready alfalfa poses no significant risk in certain geographic areas, but a significant risk in others, and therefore approve the petition in part; that is, approve the petition with a geographic limitation on where the genetically engineered alfalfa could be grown. Finally, APHIS could approve the petition in whole, which means that Roundup Ready alfalfa would no longer be subject to USDA regulation.

Before deciding Monsanto's petition, APHIS prepared an Environmental Assessment ("EA") and took public comments on the EA and the petition for deregulation. Of the 663 comments received by the agency, 520 opposed deregulation.

One of the primary objections raised is that gene transmission may occur between glyphosate tolerant alfalfa and conventional and organic alfalfa, that is, that conventional and organic alfalfa will become "contaminated" with the engineered gene that makes Roundup Ready alfalfa tolerant to glyphosate. Such gene transmission is possible because alfalfa is pollinated by bees "and so the potential exists to move pollen from the glyphosate tolerant crop to hay and seed fields, as well as wild populations of alfalfa." Indeed, it is undisputed that insect pollination for alfalfa can occur up to at least two miles from the pollen source. Farmers complained to APHIS that if Roundup Ready alfalfa is deregulated they will no longer be able to market their products as "organic," or at least as non-genetically engineered, and that this "contamination" will also impact those who sell organic livestock or livestock that is not fed any genetically engineered foods. In addition, 75 percent of the alfalfa exported from the United States (five percent of the alfalfa market) is exported to Japan and Japan does not permit the import of glyphosate tolerant alfalfa; thus, the introduction of Roundup Ready alfalfa might also impact the export market.

Commentators also expressed concern that the deregulation of Roundup Ready alfalfa, and the concomitant increase in the use of Roundup, will cause the development of additional glyphosate-resistant weeds, as well as a dramatic increase in the amount of Roundup used in the environment. Nonetheless, in June 2005, APHIS issued a Finding of No Significant Impact ("FONSI") and approved Monsanto's deregulation petition in whole; that is, the agency concluded that Roundup Ready alfalfa should be deregulated and sold without direct regulation by the USDA. The FONSI acknowledges that once Roundup Ready alfalfa is deregulated, it will not be subject to any "isolation distances"; that is, it will not be required to be grown more than two miles from conventional or organic alfalfa crops. ("If APHIS grants non-regulated status to a transgenic events, APHIS does not have any further regulatory authority over this particular transgenic event.") APHIS nevertheless concluded that the risk of gene transmission is not significant because "organic production operations must develop and maintain an organic production system plan that outlines the steps it will take to avoid cross pollination from neighboring operations." In other words, it would be "up to the individual organic seed or hay grower to institute those procedures that will assure" that their crops will not include any genetically engineered alfalfa. APHIS also noted that the states would still have the authority to establish some type of production zone. As for exports to Japan, APHIS concluded, without elaboration, that "[b]y employing reasonable quality control, it is highly unlikely that the level of glyphosate tolerant alfalfa will exceed 1% in conventional alfalfa hay" and that since Japan allows one percent of exports of a crop to contain genetically modified product, exports to Japan would not be affected.

In the EA, APHIS concluded that organic farmers and farmers who otherwise do not want to grow genetically engineered alfalfa will not be significantly impacted by the commercial use of Roundup Ready alfalfa because (1) non-genetically engineered alfalfa will "likely still be sold and available to those who wish to plant it"; and (2) farmers purchasing seed will know what they are purchasing because the seed will be labeled as glyphosate tolerant.

APHIS agreed with the objectors that the deregulation of Roundup Ready alfalfa could lead to the development of additional glyphosate-resistant weeds, but reasoned that this impact was not significant because weed species have developed resistance to every widely used herbicide; alternative herbicides are available to minimize the problem; and, in any event, "good stewardship may be the only defense against this potential problem." Plaintiffs now challenge APHIS's decision to deregulate Roundup Ready alfalfa.

DISCUSSION

I. NEPA

NEPA "requires a federal agency such as [APHIS] to prepare a detailed EIS for all 'major Federal actions significantly affecting the quality of the human environment.'" *Blue Mountains Biodiversity Project v. Blackwood*, 161 F.3d 1208, 1211–12 (9th Cir. 1998) (quoting 42 U.S.C. §4332(2)(C)). "NEPA ensures that the agency ... will have available, and will carefully consider, detailed information concerning significant environmental impacts; it also guarantees that the relevant information will be made available to the larger [public] audience."

Accordingly, "[a] threshold question in a NEPA case is whether a proposed project will 'significantly affect' the environment, thereby triggering the requirement for an EIS." "Where an EIS is not categorically required, the agency must prepare an Environmental Assessment to determine whether the environmental impact is significant enough to warrant an EIS." *Ocean Advocates v. U.S. Army Corps of Engineers*, 402 F.3d 846, 863 (9th Cir. 2005). "An EA is a concise public document that briefly provide[s] sufficient evidence and analysis for determining whether to prepare an EIS or a finding of no significant impact." *Blue Mountains Biodiversity Project*, 161 F.3d at 1212.

Here, APHIS prepared an EA and, after receiving public comment, issued a finding of no significant impact and approved the deregulation of Roundup Ready alfalfa. *See Anderson v. Evans*, 371 F.3d 475, 488 (9th Cir. 2004) (if an EA results in a "finding of no significant impact"—known as a FONSI—the agency need not prepare an environmental impact statement). Plaintiffs contend that APHIS is required to prepare an EIS.

A. Standard of Review

The Court must determine whether APHIS's "decision was based on consideration of the relevant factors, or whether its actions were arbitrary, capricious, an abuse of discretion or otherwise not in accordance with the law." *Blue Mountains Biodiversity Project*, 161 F.3d at 1211. "In short, [the Court] must ensure that the agency has taken a 'hard look' at the environmental consequences of its proposed action." *Id.* "A hard look includes considering all foreseeable direct and indirect impacts.'" *Earth Island Inst. v. U.S. Forest Serv.*, 442 F.3d 1147, 1159 (9th Cir. 2006). "An agency's decision not to prepare an EIS will be considered unreasonable if the agency fails to supply a convincing statement of reasons why potential effects are insignificant." *Blue Mountains Biodiversity Project*, 161 F.3d at 1211; *see also Ocean Advocates*, 402 F.3d at 865 ("[T]he agency must put forth a 'convincing statement' of reasons that explain why the [agency action] will impact the environment no more than insignificantly"). "The statement of reasons is crucial to determining whether the agency took a 'hard look' at the potential environmental impact of a project." *Blue Mountains Biodiversity Project*, 161 F.3d at 1212.

B. Analysis

"[A]n EIS must be prepared if 'substantial questions are raised as to whether a project may cause significant degradation of some human environmental factor.'" *Idaho Sporting Cong. v. Thomas*, 137 F.3d 1146, 1149 (9th Cir. 1998) …"Thus to prevail on a claim that [APHIS] violated its statutory duty to prepare an EIS, a plaintiff need not show that significant effects will in fact occur. It is enough for the plaintiff to raise substantial questions whether a project may have a significant effect on the environment." *Blue Mountains Biodiversity Project*, 161 F.3d at 1212. "Put another way, a proposal can be considered controversial if substantial questions are raised as to whether a project may cause significant degradation of some human environmental factor." *Anderson,* 371 F.3d at 489.

"In determining whether a federal action requires an EIS because it significantly affects the quality of the human environment, an agency must consider what 'significantly' means." *Ocean Advocates*, 402 F.3d at 865. "Significantly," has two components: context and intensity. *Id.* (citing 40 C.F.R. §1508.27). "Context refers to the setting in which the proposed action take place." *Id.* (citing 40 C.F.R. §1508.27(a)). "Intensity means 'the severity of the impact.'" *Id.* (citing 40 C.F.R. §1508.27(b)).

Several factors must be considered in evaluating intensity, including the "degree to which the effects on the quality of the human environment are likely to be highly controversial"; "[t]he degree to which the possible effects on the human environment are highly uncertain or involve unique or unknown risks"; and "[t]he degree to which the proposed action affects public health and safety." 40 C.F.R. §1508.27(b)(2), (4), (6).

The context of the inquiry in this case is undisputed. Alfalfa is the fourth most widely grown crop in the United States. The bulk of alfalfa seed (as opposed to alfalfa forage) is grown in limited geographic areas within a few states. California is the largest producer of alfalfa seed, and California, Idaho, Washington and Nevada together produce 85 percent of all domestic alfalfa seed. In this context, plaintiffs identify what they believe are several significant environmental impacts that will be caused by Roundup Ready alfalfa, or that at least may be caused by the deregulation of the genetically engineered alfalfa.

1. Gene transmission to non-genetically engineered alfalfa

Plaintiffs contend that one significant environmental impact resulting from the introduction of Roundup Ready alfalfa is that genetically engineered alfalfa will modify nongenetically engineered alfalfa such that it, too, will contain the gene that confers tolerance to the herbicide glyphosate. Plaintiffs label such effect "biological contamination." Biological contamination can occur through pollination of non-genetically engineered plants by genetically engineered plants or by the mixing of genetically engineered seed with natural, or non-genetically engineered seed. Alfalfa seeds are pollinated by bees and, as a result, there is a realistic potential for contamination from seed fields to nearby seed fields; indeed, APHIS admits that insects pollinate alfalfa up to two miles from the pollen source. Such gene transmission is especially likely in this context given the geographic concentration of alfalfa seed production. Once the gene transmission occurs and a farmer's seed crop is contaminated with the Roundup Ready gene, there is no way for the farmer to remove the gene from the crop or control its further spread. And alfalfa is a perennial crop; the crop is only replanted every three to four years.

Plaintiffs complain that the "contamination" of organic and conventional crops with the genetically engineered gene will have negative economic and socioeconomic effects on farmers. Organic farmers will no longer be able to market their seed as non-genetically engineered, rendering their crops less valuable; consumers pay a premium for organic and non-genetically engineered food. Similarly, organic livestock farmers will have a more difficult time purchasing non-genetically engineered alfalfa as food for livestock and thus will be unable to market their livestock as organic or at least fed with non-genetically engineered food. All of these farmers may be required to test their crops and livestock for traces of the genetically-engineered alfalfa. Even non-organic farmers who want to raise genetically-engineered free plants and livestock will be impacted.

APHIS acknowledges that once Roundup Ready alfalfa is deregulated the government will not be able to impose isolation distances on the growers of genetically engineered alfalfa; in other words, it cannot ensure that farmers using the genetically engineered seed will be more than two miles away from seed farmers who do not wish to grow engineered alfalfa. APHIS nonetheless concluded that the introduction of Roundup Ready alfalfa will have no significant environmental impact, reasoning as follows:

> [T]he National Organic Program, which is administered by USDA's Agricultural Marketing Service, requires organic production operations to have distinct, defined boundaries and buffer zones to prevent unintended contact with prohibited substances, such as modified genes, from adjoining land that is not under organic management. However, the determination of the size of the buffer zones is left up to the organic producer and the certifying agent on a case-by-case basis. Furthermore, organic production operations must develop and maintain an organic production system plan that outlines the steps it will take to avoid cross pollination from neighboring operations.

It also reasoned that federal organic standards do not require the testing of inputs or products for genetically engineered genes and that the unintentional presence of the engineered genes will not "necessarily" constitute a violation of national organic standards.

In the EA, APHIS concluded, without further elaboration, that non-genetically engineered alfalfa seed "will likely still be sold and will be available to those who wish to plant it," and that genetically engineered seed will be marketed and labeled as glyphosate tolerant so farmers will know when they are purchasing Roundup Ready alfalfa seed. APHIS also found that gene transmission is not likely to occur with forage as opposed to seed crops because forage fields are typically harvested before the seed is set and allowed to mature. *Id.*

APHIS's reasons for concluding that the potential for the transmission of the genetically engineered gene is not significant are not "convincing" and do not demonstrate the "hard look" that NEPA requires. *See Blue Mountains Biodiversity Project*, 161 F.3d at 1211. APHIS did not conclude that gene transmission would not occur; indeed, an internal APHIS email acknowledges that "[i]t may be hard to guarantee that seeds or sprouts are GE free." Instead, it in effect concluded that whatever the likelihood of gene transmission, such impact is not significant because it is the organic and conventional farmers' responsibility to ensure that such contamination does not occur. It rested its "no significant impact" decision on this conclusion even though it made no inquiry into whether those farmers who do not want to grow genetically engineered alfalfa can, in fact, protect their crops from contamination, especially given the high geographic concentration of seed farms and the fact that alfalfa is pollinated by bees that can travel more than two miles. Neither the EA nor the FONSI identify a single method that an organic farmer can employ to protect his crop from being pollinated by a bee that travels from a nearby genetically engineered seed farm, even assuming the farmer maintains a "buffer zone."

"Preparation of an EIS is mandatory where uncertainty may be resolved by further collection of data, or where the collection of data may prevent speculation on potential ... effects. The purpose of an EIS is to obviate the need for speculation by insuring that available data are gathered and implemented prior to the proposed action." *National Parks Conservation Ass'n v. Babbitt*, 241 F.3d 722, 732 (9th Cir. 2001). The further collection of data can inform APHIS as to the likely extent of any gene transmission and the realistic measures, if any, that may be taken to prevent or at least reduce such contamination. Such data is especially important given that one option APHIS has is to approve Monsanto's "petition with a geographic limitation stipulating that the Roundup Ready could only be grown without APHIS authorization in certain geographic areas." APHIS's rejection of this option without making any inquiry into the extent of likely gene transmission from genetically engineered seed crops to non-engineered seed crops is arbitrary and capricious; it did not obtain the very information it needs to determine if such an option is warranted. *See Earth Island Institute*, 442 F.3d at 1160 ("If an agency has failed to make a reasoned decision based on an evaluation of the evidence, [a court] may properly conclude that the agency has acted arbitrarily and capriciously."); *Foundation for N. Am. Wild Sheep v. U.S. Dep't of Agr.*, 681 F.2d 1172, 1178 (9th Cir. 1982) (holding that agency violated NEPA when its EA "failed to address certain crucial factors, consideration of which was essential to a truly informed decision whether or not to prepare an EIS").

APHIS's conclusion that forage alfalfa will not be contaminated is also arbitrary and capricious. APHIS baldly concluded that such gene transmission is not likely because farmers typically harvest alfalfa forage fields before the seed matures. APHIS failed to consider, however, that because of weather—which is beyond a farmer's control—a farmer cannot always harvest his field at the most optimal time. APHIS made no inquiry into how often farmers are actually able to harvest their forage crop before seeds mature and no inquiry into the likelihood of gene transmission when they cannot. Without such data, APHIS's conclusion is arbitrary. *See Earth Island Institute*, 442 F.3d at 1159 ("A hard look should involve a discussion of adverse impacts that does not improperly minimize negative side effects").

APHIS's reasoning that farmers will not "necessarily" be prohibited from labeling their products as organic is wholly inadequate. First, the statement itself is equivocal; even APHIS is uncertain whether farmers can still label their products organic under the federal government's organic standards. Second, many farmers and consumers have higher standards than what the federal government currently permits; to these farmers and consumers organic means not genetically engineered, even if the farmer did not intend for his crop to be so engineered. And, as APHIS acknowledges, many countries, including Japan, do not allow for the importation of genetically engineered alfalfa regardless of what the United States government permits. Third, and most importantly, APHIS's comment simply ignores that these farmers do not want to grow or feed to their livestock genetically engineered alfalfa, regardless of how such alfalfa can be marketed.

APHIS's assertion that exports to Japan will not be harmed because Japan allows one percent of its imported alfalfa to be transgenic and "[b]y employing reasonable quality control, it is highly unlikely that the level of glyphosate tolerant alfalfa will exceed 1% in conventional alfalfa hay," is also not convincing. Neither the EA nor the FONSI contain any reference to any material in support of APHIS's conclusion that gene transmission is "highly unlikely" to occur with "reasonable quality control." APHIS does not identify any "quality control" that will prevent gene transmission between neighboring seed farms. It similarly does not identify any material to support its EA statement that nongenetically engineered alfalfa will "likely still be sold and available to those who wish to plant it." *See Blue Mountains Biodiversity Project*, 1161 F.3d at 1214 ("The EA contains virtually no reference to any material in support of or in opposition to its conclusions. That is where the Forest Service's defense of its position must be found").

APHIS argues in its brief that the extent of any gene transmission is, in any event, irrelevant because NEPA requires an agency to consider physical environmental impacts, not economic or financial impacts. APHIS overstates the law. To determine whether NEPA requires an agency to consider a particular effect, courts must "look at the relationship between that effect and the change in the physical environment caused by the major federal action at issue." *Metropolitan Edison Co. v. People Against Nuclear Energy*, 460 U.S. 766, 773 (1983); *see also San Luis Obispo Mothers for Peace v. Nuclear Regulatory Comm'n*, 449 F.3d 1016, 1029 (9th Cir. 2006) ("[T]he essential analysis must focus on the closeness of the relationship between the change in the environment and the 'effect' at issue"); *Ashley Creek Phosphate Co. v. Norton*, 420 F.3d 934, 943 (9th Cir. 2005) ("NEPA does not require an agency to assess all impacts of a project, only those that have a 'reasonably close causal relationship' with 'a change in the physical environment'"). Economic effects are relevant "when they are 'interrelated' with 'natural or physical environmental effects.'" *Ashley Creek Phosphate Co.*, 420 F.3d at 944 (quoting 40 C.F.R. § 1508.14 ("[E]conomic or social effects are not intended by themselves to require preparation of an environmental impact statement. When an environmental impact statement is prepared and economic or social and natural or physical environmental effects are interrelated, then the environmental impact statement will discuss all of these effects on the human environment")).

Here, the economic effects on the organic and conventional farmers of the government's deregulation decision are interrelated with, and, indeed, a direct result of, the effect on the physical environment; namely, the alteration of a plant specie's DNA through the transmission of the genetically engineered gene to organic and conventional alfalfa. APHIS was required to consider those effects in assessing whether the impact of its proposed action is "significant." And, in fact, APHIS did mention those effects in the FONSI and EA, but, as explained above, its reasons for concluding that the effect on organic and conventional farmers is not significant are not "convincing."

Finally, the government argues that even if the deregulation of Roundup Ready alfalfa could result in the elimination of all non-genetically engineered alfalfa—in other words, there would be no alfalfa grown in the United States that does not contain the engineered gene that confers tolerance to glyphosate—such a result would still not constitute a significant environmental impact because APHIS has determined that the introduction of that gene to alfalfa is harmless to humans and livestock, that is, it is not toxic or pathogenic. APHIS's position is based on its finding that the engineered gene is similar to another gene already present in non-engineered alfalfa and is the equivalent to a natural enzyme found in both green plants and microorganims that are common in nature. In sum, APHIS concluded that the engineered enzyme is equivalent in all biological respects to those that are common and harmless in nature and therefore the introduction of that engineered gene into conventional or organic alfalfa is not a significant environmental impact as a matter of law.

The Court accepts, as it must, the agency's determination that Roundup Ready alfalfa does not have any harmful health effects on humans or lifestock. *See Natural Res. Defense Council, Inc. v. EPA*, 863 F.2d 1420, 1430 (9th Cir. 1988) ("A reviewing court should be at its most deferential in reviewing an agency's scientific determinations in an area within the agency's expertise"). Public health and safety, however, is only *one* of factors that an agency should consider when determining whether a major federal action may have a significant environmental impact. 40 C.F.R. § 1508.27(b). The government does not cite any case, and the Court is aware of none, which holds that an impact is not significant simply because a federal agency determines that the major federal action does not jeopardize the public's health and safety. The paucity of caselaw is unsurprising given that one of Congress's express goals in adopting NEPA was to "attain the widest range of beneficial uses of the environment without degradation, risk to health and safety, *or other undesirable and unintended consequences.*" 42 U.S.C. § 4331(b)(3) (emphasis added). A federal action that eliminates a farmer's choice to grow non-genetically engineered crops, or a consumer's choice to eat non-genetically engineered food, is an undesirable consequence: another NEPA goal is to "maintain, wherever possible, an environment which supports diversity and variety of individual choice." 42 U.S.C. § 4331(b)(4).

To put it another way, if the government's action could eliminate all alfalfa, there would be no dispute that such action has a significant environmental impact, even though the primary impact is the economic effect on alfalfa and livestock farmers. For those farmers who choose to grow non-genetically engineered alfalfa, the possibility that their crops will be infected with the engineered gene is tantamount to the elimination of all alfalfa; they cannot grow their chosen crop. The government's apparent belief that the farmers' and consumers' choice is irrational because the engineered gene is similar in all biological respects to a gene found in nature (although never in alfalfa) is beside the point. An action which potentially eliminates or least greatly reduces the availability of a particular plant—here, non-engineered alfalfa—has a significant effect on the human environment. *See* 40 C.F.R. § 1508.27(b) ("A significant effect may exist even if the Federal agency believes that on balance the effect will be beneficial").

One other point bears mention. At oral argument the Court asked the government why APHIS addressed (albeit inadequately) the economic impact on farmers if it is the agency's position that, regardless of how much gene transmission occurs, such transmission is insignificant because it is harmless. The government candidly explained that it addressed these possible effects because Roundup Ready alfalfa is the first crop that has been engineered to resist a herbicide "and in which the record suggests that there's at least a chance that the [genetically engineered] gene could be transmitted." The government's response highlights that APHIS is operating in uncharted territory. In light of the Court's conclusion that the permanent modification of a plant's genetic makeup through genetic engineering is an effect on the human environment, and the evidence that such transmission can and will occur, and that APHIS did not adequately analyze the extent of such transmission, the possible effects of APHIS's deregulation decision are "highly uncertain or involve unique or unknown risks." 40 C.F.R. § 1508.27(5).

The Court cautions that it is not ruling that Roundup Ready alfalfa is harmful to consumers or livestock. Rather, the significant impact that requires the preparation of an EIS is the possibility that the deregulation of Roundup Ready alfalfa will degrade the human environment by eliminating a farmer's choice to grow non-genetically engineered alfalfa and a consumer's choice to consume such food.

2. The development of alfalfa weeds resistant to herbicides

Plaintiffs also complain that the deregulation of Roundup Ready alfalfa will cause Roundup-resistant weeds, and that such an effect is sufficiently significant to require the preparation of an EIS. APHIS acknowledges that the use of Roundup Ready alfalfa may result in the development of Roundup-tolerant weeds. The resistance develops because of the increased use of Roundup on the crops. APHIS found that such a possible impact nevertheless does not warrant the preparation of an EIS because weed species often develop resistance to herbicides and the agricultural community is addressing the issue. "Alternative herbicides and strategies are available that may minimize the problem. Based on the comments, the alfalfa growers and weed scientists understand that good stewardship may be the only defense against this potential problem."

APHIS's reasons for finding the development of glyphosate resistant weeds not to be significant are not convincing. Reasoning that weed species often develop resistance to herbicides is tantamount to concluding that because this environmental impact has occurred in other contexts it cannot be significant. Nothing in NEPA, the relevant regulations, or the caselaw support such a cavalier response.

The assertion that "good stewardship" may be the only defense against such weeds is equally unconvincing. Such a conclusion is not the same as a finding that the development of the weeds is not a significant environmental impact. This is especially so given that neither the FONSI nor the EA contain any analysis as to what exactly constitutes good stewardship and how likely it is to be practiced successfully. *See Blue Mountains Biodiversity Project*, 161 F.3d at 1214. There may be ways to reduce the proliferation of weeds, but if farmers are not engaging (or cannot engage) in those practices, then the availability of those practices does not ameliorate the potential environmental impact.

Finally, APHIS failed to evaluate the cumulative impact of the deregulation of Roundup Ready alfalfa. 40 C.F.R. § 1508.7 ("'Cumulative impact' is the impact on the environment which results from the incremental impact of the action when added to other past, present, and reasonably foreseeable future actions regardless of what agency (Federal or non-federal) or person undertakes such other actions. Cumulative impacts can result from individually minor but collectively significant actions taking place over a period of time."). While alfalfa is the first large scale perennial Roundup Ready crop, APHIS has deregulated other Roundup Ready crops, including corn and soybeans, and other deregulation petitions are pending. While the deregulation of one crop in and of itself might not pose a significant risk for the development of glyphosate resistant weeds, when all the crops are considered cumulatively such a risk may become apparent. There is nothing in the FONSI or EA that suggests APHIS even considered how much Roundup use will increase, or even how much such use has increased since the introduction of the other Roundup Ready crops; to the contrary, the EA specifically states that it "does not address the separate issue of the potential use of the herbicide glyphosate in conjunction with these plants." APHIS's failure to consider in the context of the development of Roundup resistant weeds that there are already other Roundup Ready crops on the market, and more crops seeking to enter the market, means that it did not take the "hard look" NEPA requires.

3. Increased use of glyphosate

In a related argument, plaintiffs assert that — even apart from the development of glyphosate-resistant weeds — APHIS failed to consider that the deregulation of Roundup Ready alfalfa will result in the increased use of Roundup, and likewise failed to consider how that increased use of Roundup, perhaps doubling its use on alfalfa fields in California alone, will impact the environment. And, argue plaintiffs, APHIS should have considered this increased use in the context of its deregulation of other Roundup Ready crops; in other words, APHIS must inquire whether the introduction of the many Roundup Ready crops will together increase the use of Roundup and impact the environment.

APHIS responds that there are other federal agencies, primarily the Environmental Protection Agency ("EPA"), that are responsible for regulating herbicides and tolerance levels in crops for such chemicals. It also contends that there is no evidence that farmers will misuse Roundup, that is, use it contrary to the manufacturer's instructions and it notes that Roundup use will replace more toxic herbicides. Since the Court has concluded that APHIS must consider the cumulative impact of increased glyphosate use with respect to the development of glyphosate-resistant weeds, APHIS will have to examine the increased use of glyphosate; thus, the Court declines to specifically rule on this claim. The Court notes, however, that it is unclear from the record whether any federal agency is considering the cumulative impact of the introduction of so many glyphosate resistant crops; one would expect that some federal agency is considering whether there is some risk to engineering all of America's crops to include the gene that confers resistance to glyphosate....

CONCLUSION

NEPA "is our basic national charter for protection of the environment." 40 C.F.R. § 1500.1(a). "NEPA emphasizes the importance of coherent and comprehensive up-front environmental analysis to ensure informed decision making to the end that 'the agency will not act on incomplete information, only to regret its decision after it is too late to correct.'" *Blue Mountains Biodiversity Project*, 161 F.3d at 1216 (quoting *Marsh v. Oregon Natural Resources Council*, 490 U.S. 360, 371 (1989)). "An EIS is required of an agency in order that it explore, more thoroughly than an EA, the environmental consequences of a proposed action whenever 'substantial questions are raised as to whether a project may cause significant [environmental] degradation.'"

"That is exactly the circumstances of this case." Substantial questions are raised as to whether (1) the deregulation of Roundup Ready alfalfa without any geographic restrictions will lead to the transmission of the engineered gene to organic and conventional alfalfa; (2) the possible extent of such transmission; and (3) farmers' ability to protect their crops from acquiring the genetically engineered gene. Substantial questions are also raised as to the extent to which Roundup Ready alfalfa will contribute to the development of Roundup-resistant weeds, especially when considered in conjunction with the already deregulated and soon-to-be deregulated Roundup Ready crops, and as to how farmers will address such weeds. APHIS failed to answer these substantial questions, concluding instead that any environmental impact is insignificant because gene transmission is the problem of the organic and conventional farmers and weeds always develop resistance to herbicides. As such reasons are not "convincing" and do not demonstrate that the agency took a "hard look" at the potential environmental impacts of its deregulation decision, plaintiffs' motion for summary judgment on its NEPA claim that APHIS is required to prepare an EIS is GRANTED. Defendants' cross motion on the NEPA claim is DENIED, and the parties' cross-motions on the other claims are dismissed as moot in light of the Court's dismissal of those claims without prejudice....

IT IS SO ORDERED.

———————

Notes

1. Following the issuance of the order granting summary judgment, the court in *Geertson v. Johanns* turned to the question of an appropriate remedy for the NEPA violation. APHIS agreed to conduct the EIS and proposed to cure the violation by imposing restrictions on the planting and handling of RRA until the EIS could be completed. The district court rejected this suggestion and instead ordered a permanent nationwide injunction against the planting of RRA. *Geertson v. Johanns*, 2007 WL 776146 (N.D. Cal. Mar. 12, 2007).

APHIS and Monsanto appealed to the Ninth Circuit, but the injunction was affirmed. The court held that Geertson had met the traditional four-part test for the issuance of a permanent injunction—including the showing of a likelihood of irreparable harm in the absence of an injunction.

Monsanto filed a petition for certiorari focusing its challenge on the court finding of irreparable harm. The Court granted certiorari and oral arguments were heard on April 29, 2010. At least ten amicus briefs were filed, representing a wide range of agricultural, environmental, food policy and consumer groups. *See* the SCOTUS wiki for the case, available at http://www.scotuswiki.com/index.php?title=Monsanto_Company_v._Geertson_Seed_Farms. On June 21, 2010, the Supreme Court reversed the order of the preliminary injunction.

APHIS prepared a Draft Environmental Impact Statement and on December 18, 2009, published a notice in the Federal Register announcing its availability. The comment period was initially opened for 60-days, but was extended for 15 days, closing on March 3, 2010. APHIS also held four public meetings throughout the U.S. during the open comment period. A copy of the Draft EIS is available on the USDA APHIS website at http://www.aphis.usda.gov/biotechnology/alfalfa_eis.shtml. The Draft EIS reaffirms the decision to grant non-regulated status to the genetically engineered alfalfa, finding no significant impacts. APHIS has indicated that it will prepare a final EIS after considering the comments received.

Japan and South Korea, America's most significant alfalfa customers, have warned that they will discontinue imports of U.S. alfalfa if a GE variety were grown in this country. U.S. alfalfa exports total nearly $480 million per year, with about 75% going to Japan. *See* Tadlock Cowan & Geoffrey S. Becker, *Agricultural Biotechnology: Background and Recent Issues*, Congressional Research Report RL-32809, 16 (Feb. 13, 2009).

2. In the case of *Center for Food Safety v. Vilsack*, No. C 08-00484, 2009 WL 3047227 (N.D.Cal., Sept. 21, 2009), the District Court for the Northern District of California also found that APHIS should have conducted an EIS prior to de-regulating genetically engineered sugar beets. However, in a subsequent ruling, the court held that a preliminary injunction was not appropriate, largely due to the amount of time that had transpired since the deregulation and the filing of the lawsuit. The court noted that 95% of the sugar beets planted in the United States are now genetically engineered. *Center for Food Safety v. Vilsack*, No. C 08-00484, 2009 WL 964017 (N.D.Cal., Mar. 16, 2010). Nevertheless, pursuant to the court's order, the USDA is now undertaking the development of an Environmental Impact Statement for the de-regulation of genetically engineered sugar beets.

3. Environmental and consumers groups have also brought successful cases on a regional level to protect National Wildlife Refuges from the use of genetically engineered crops. *See, DE Audubon v. Sec. of US Dept of the Interior*, 612 F.Supp. 2d 442 (D. Del. 2009) (order enjoining U.S. Fish and Wildlife Service from planting Roundup Ready soybeans and corn at the Prime Hook National Wildlife Refuge without first preparing either an Environmental Impact Statement or an Environmental Assessment).

4. The development of weeds that are resistant to glyphosate remains a serious concern. Recent reports confirm the development of "super weeds" resistant to Roundup. *See, William Neuman and Andrew Pollack, Rise of the Superweeds: Herbicide's Wide Use Fosters the Spread of Resistant Pests*, NY TIMES, Tues., May 4, 2010, p. B1. This article reports that ten resistant species in at least 22 states now present significant problems, particularly with respect to corn, soybeans and cotton production. "It is the single largest threat to production agriculture that we have ever seen," said Andrew Wargo III, the president of the Arkansas Association of Conservation Districts. While chemical and seed

companies are seeking to develop new biotech crops resistant to other kinds of pesticides, Roundup is referred to as "a once-in-a-century discovery." Farmers in Georgia and Arkansas are particularly concerned about a resistant variety of a giant pigweed so large it damages harvesting equipment and are "plowing their fields and mixing herbicides into the soil" to control the weeds.

5. While some attempt to slow the release of additional genetically engineered crops, others are frustrated that the approval time for new seeds is too slow. Industry representatives complain that approval time has almost doubled under the Obama administration, and they are pressuring Washington to clear inventions more quickly. The Wall Street Journal reported:

> The logjam at the U.S. Department of Agriculture, which must clear genetically modified seeds, is slowing the launch of products that could give farmers more alternatives to seeds from crop biotech giant Monsanto Co.

> Also, some biotech-industry executives worry the delays signal that the Obama administration, which has painted itself as pro-biotech, is gearing up for a far tougher analysis of the potential environmental impact of these crops, which could make it harder for inventions to reach the marketplace.... The agency, long a cheerleader for U.S. crop biotechnology, has never turned down a genetically modified crop, although inventors have withdrawn some candidates. Caleb Weaver, USDA press secretary, said the department is "looking into both immediate and long-term solutions to increase the efficiency and effectiveness of the review process." Among other things, the USDA is asking Congress to increase its annual biotechnology oversight budget by 46% to $19 million. Scott Kilman, *Biotech Firms Seek Speedier Reviews of Seeds*, Wall Street Journal, Apr. 28, 2010.

6. In April 2010, the National Research Council released a report detailing its recent study of Roundup Ready crops, *Genetically Engineered Crops Benefit Many Farmers, But The Technology Needs Proper Management to Remain Effective* (National Academies Press 2010) available at http://www8.nationalacademies.org/onpinews/newsitem.aspx?RecordID=12804. The National Academy of Sciences summarizes the conclusions contained in the report as follows:

> Many U.S. farmers who grow genetically engineered (GE) crops are realizing substantial economic and environmental benefits—such as lower production costs, fewer pest problems, reduced use of pesticides, and better yields—compared with conventional crops, says a new report from the National Research Council. However, GE crops resistant to the herbicide glyphosate—a main component in Roundup and other commercial weed killers—could develop more weed problems as weeds evolve their own resistance to glyphosate. GE crops could lose their effectiveness unless farmers also use other proven weed and insect management practices.

> The report provides the first comprehensive assessment of how GE crops are affecting all U.S. farmers, including those who grow conventional or organic crops. The new report follows several previous Research Council reports that examined the potential human health and environmental effects of GE crops.

> "Many American farmers are enjoying higher profits due to the widespread use of certain genetically engineered crops and are reducing environmental impacts on and off the farm," said David Ervin, professor of environmental management and economics, Portland State University, Portland, Ore., and chair of the committee that wrote the report. "However, these benefits are not universal for all farm-

ers. And as more GE traits are developed and incorporated into a larger variety of crops, it's increasingly essential that we gain a better understanding of how genetic engineering technology will affect U.S. agriculture and the environment now and in the future. Such gaps in our knowledge are preventing a full assessment of the environmental, economic, and other impacts of GE crops on farm sustainability."

First introduced in 1996, genetically engineered crops now constitute more than 80 percent of soybeans, corn, and cotton grown in the United States. GE soybeans, corn, and cotton are designed to be resistant to the herbicide glyphosate, which has fewer adverse environmental effects compared with most other herbicides used to control weeds. In addition to glyphosate resistance, GE corn and cotton plants also are designed to produce Bacillus thuringiensis (Bt), a bacterium that is deadly when ingested by susceptible insect pests.

Farmers need to adopt better management practices to ensure that beneficial environmental effects of GE crops continue, the report says. In particular, farmers who grow GE herbicide-resistant crops should not rely exclusively on glyphosate and need to incorporate a range of weed management practices, including using other herbicide mixes. To date, at least nine species of weeds in the United States have evolved resistance to glyphosate since GE crops were introduced, largely because of repeated exposure. Federal and state government agencies, technology developers, universities, and other stakeholders should collaborate to document weed resistance problems and develop cost-effective ways to control weeds in current GE crops and new types of GE herbicide-resistant plants now under development.

Environmental Benefits

Improvements in water quality could prove to be the largest single benefit of GE crops, the report says. Insecticide use has declined since GE crops were introduced, and farmers who grow GE crops use fewer insecticides and herbicides that linger in soil and waterways. In addition, farmers who grow herbicide-resistant crops till less often to control weeds and are more likely to practice conservation tillage, which improves soil quality and water filtration and reduces erosion.

However, no infrastructure exists to track and analyze the effects that GE crops may have on water quality. The U.S. Geological Survey, along with other federal and state environmental agencies, should be provided with financial resources to document effects of GE crops on U.S. watersheds.

The report notes that although two types of insects have developed resistance to Bt, there have been few economic or agronomic consequences from resistance. Practices to prevent insects from developing resistance should continue, such as an EPA-mandated strategy that requires farmers to plant a certain amount of conventional plants alongside Bt plants in "refuge" areas.

Economic and Social Effects

In many cases, farmers who have adopted the use of GE crops have either lower production costs or higher yields, or sometimes both, due to more cost-effective weed and insect control and fewer losses from insect damage, the report says. Although these farmers have gained such economic benefits, more research is needed on the extent to which these advantages will change as pests adapt to GE crops, other countries adopt genetic engineering technology, and more GE traits are incorporated into existing and new crops.

The higher costs associated with GE seeds are not always offset financially by lower production costs or higher yields, the report notes. For example, farmers in areas with fewer weed and pest problems may not have as much improvement in terms of reducing crop losses. Even so, studies show that farmers value the greater flexibility in pesticide spraying that GE crops provide and the increased safety for workers from less exposure to harmful pesticides.

The economic effects of GE crops on farmers who grow organic and conventional crops also need further study, the report says. For instance, organic farmers are profiting by marketing their crops as free of GE traits, but their crops' value could be jeopardized if genes from GE crops flow to non-GE varieties through cross-pollination or seed mingling.

Farmers have not been adversely affected by the proprietary terms involved in patent-protected GE seeds, the report says. However, some farmers have expressed concern that consolidation of the U.S. seed market will make it harder to purchase conventional seeds or those that have only specific GE traits. With the exception of the issue of seed industry consolidation, the effects of GE crops on other social factors of farming—such as labor dynamics, farm structure, or community viability—have largely been overlooked, the report says. More research is needed on the range of effects GE crops have on all farmers, including those who don't grow GE crops or farmers with less access to credit. Studies also should examine impacts on industries that rely on GE products, such as the livestock industry.

Research institutions should receive government support to develop GE traits that could deliver valuable public benefits but provide little market incentive for the private sector to develop. Examples include plants that decrease the likelihood of off-farm water pollution or plants that are resilient to changing climate conditions. Intellectual property that has been patented in developing major crops should be made available for these purposes whenever possible.

D. The Labeling of Genetically Engineered Food Products

1. General Principles

The FDA has consistently affirmed its adherence to the principle that genetically engineered products should be regulated only according to the specific features of the product and not the process by which the product was created. Under this principle, many genetically engineered products have been approved as food products. Indeed, it is estimated that 70% of all processed U.S. foods are likely to contain some genetically engineered ingredients, due primarily to the high incidence of genetically modified corn and soybeans.

However, the widespread consumption of genetically engineered products does not necessarily mean that there the same widespread level of consumer support for genetic engineering. The FDA has long expressed the concern that consumers have unfounded fears about genetic engineering, despite FDA's approval of them.

These two factors support FDA's opposition to any special labeling of food containing genetically engineered ingredients or produced with the aid of genetically engineered products. FDA's concern about consumer fear also explains FDA's hesitancy to allow the voluntary labeling of products as not containing genetically engineered ingredients. FDA has often stated that labeling a food as developed without genetic engineering implies that such food is superior, and as such is misleading to the consumer. Restricting the labeling of foods in this way has proven more controversial than FDA's decision to not requiring the labeling of genetically engineered foods.

FDA's policy is explained in the following Industry Guidance. This document was released in January 2001 and noticed in the Federal Register at 66 Fed. Reg. 4839 (Jan. 18, 2001). It has never been made final nor withdrawn. It represents current FDA labeling policy.

Guidance for Industry: Voluntary Labeling Indicating Whether Foods Have or Have Not Been Developed Using Bioengineering; Draft Guidance

January 2001

U.S. Department of Health and Human Services
Food and Drug Administration
Center for Food Safety and Applied Nutrition

This draft guidance represents FDA's current thinking on voluntary labeling of foods indicating whether foods have or have not been developed using bioengineering. It does not create or confer any rights for or on any person and does not operate to bind FDA or the public. An alternative approach may be used if such an approach satisfies the requirements of applicable statutes and regulations. The draft guidance is being distributed for comment purposes in accordance with FDA's Good Guidance Practices (65 FR 56468, September 19, 2000).

BACKGROUND

In the Federal Register of May 29, 1992 (57 FR 22984), FDA published its "Statement of Policy: Foods Derived from New Plant Varieties" (the 1992 policy). The 1992 policy applies to foods developed from new plant varieties, including varieties that are developed using recombinant deoxyribonucleic acid (rDNA) technology (which is often referred to as "genetic engineering" or "biotechnology"). This guidance document refers to foods derived from plant varieties that are developed using rDNA technology as "bioengineered foods." In addition, because the Federal Food Drug, and Cosmetic Act (the act) defines food as articles used for food or drink for man or other animals, this guidance document applies to animal feeds as well as to human foods. The 1992 policy provides guidance to industry on scientific and regulatory issues related to bioengineered foods and solicited written comments from interested persons. The policy includes guidance on questions to be answered by developers of foods from new plant varieties, to ensure that the new products are safe and comply with applicable legal requirements. It also encourages continuation of the general practice of the food industry to consult with the agency about the safety of new foods, e.g., bioengineered foods.

In the 1992 policy, FDA also addresses the labeling of foods derived from new plant varieties, including plants developed by bioengineering. The 1992 policy does not establish special labeling requirements for bioengineered foods as a class of foods. The policy states that FDA has no basis for concluding that bioengineered foods differ from other foods in any meaningful or uniform way, or that, as a class, foods developed by the new techniques present any different or greater safety concern than foods developed by traditional plant breeding.

To fully understand the agency's mandate and authority in requiring labeling of foods, one must refer to the Federal Food, Drug, and Cosmetic Act (the act) to determine the extent to which the agency is charged with governing labeling of foods. Section 403 governs the labeling of foods. Under section 403(a)(1), a food is misbranded if its labeling is false or misleading in any particular. Section 201(n) of the act provides additional guidance on how labeling may be misleading. It states that labeling is misleading if it fails to reveal facts that are material in light of representations made or suggested in the labeling, or material with respect to consequences that may result from the use of the food to which the labeling relates under the conditions of use prescribed in the labeling, or under such conditions of use as are customary or usual. While the legislative history of section 201(n) contains little discussion of the word "material," there is precedent to guide the agency in its decision regarding whether information on a food is in fact material. Historically, the agency has generally interpreted the scope of the materiality concept to mean information about the attributes of the food itself. FDA has required special labeling on the basis of it being "material" information in cases where the absence of such information may: 1) pose special health or environmental risks (e.g., warning statement on protein products used in very low calorie diets); 2) mislead the consumer in light of other statements made on the label (e.g., requirement for quantitative nutrient information when certain nutrient content claims are made about a product); or 3) in cases where a consumer may assume that a food, because of its similarity to another food, has nutritional, organoleptic, or functional characteristics of the food it resembles when in fact it does not (e.g., reduced fat margarine not suitable for frying).

Although the 1992 policy does not require special labeling for bioengineered foods, the agency advised in that policy that labeling requirements that apply to foods in general also apply to foods produced using biotechnology. Section 403(i) of the act requires that each food bear a common or usual name or, in the absence of such a name, an appropriately descriptive term. In addition, under section 201(n), the label of the food must reveal all material facts about the food. Thus:

- If a bioengineered food is significantly different from its traditional counterpart such that the common or usual name no longer adequately describes the new food, the name must be changed to describe the difference.

- If an issue exists for the food or a constituent of the food regarding how the food is used or consequences of its use, a statement must be made on the label to describe the issue.

- If a bioengineered food has a significantly different nutritional property, its label must reflect the difference.

- If a new food includes an allergen that consumers would not expect to be present based on the name of the food, the presence of that allergen must be disclosed on the label.

In the Federal Register of April 28, 1993 (58 FR 25837), the agency requested data and information on certain labeling issues that had arisen from the labeling guidance in the 1992 policy. In 1999, the agency announced that it would hold three public meetings (64 FR 57470; October 25, 1999). The purpose of those meetings was for the agency to share its current approach and experience over the previous five years regarding bioengineered foods, to solicit views on whether FDA's policies should be modified, and to gather information to be used to assess the most appropriate means of providing information to the public about bioengineered products in the food supply. The agency received more than 50,000 written comments about its policy regarding safety and labeling of bioengineered foods. The theme related to labeling in those comments and the testimony at the meetings was that there are very strongly held but divergent views as to whether bioengineered foods should be required to bear special labeling. However, there was general agreement that providing more information to consumers about bioengineered foods would be useful. A number of comments supported the need for guidance from FDA regarding appropriate ways that industry could voluntarily provide information on a food label about bioengineering.

FDA has reviewed information in the comments received in response to the 1992 policy and the 1993 information request as well as the comments from the 1999 meetings. Most of the comments that addressed labeling requested mandatory disclosure of the fact that the food or its ingredients was bioengineered or was produced from bioengineered food. However, these comments did not provide data or other information regarding consequences to consumers from eating the foods or any other basis for FDA to find under section 201(n) of the act that such a disclosure was a material fact. Many of the comments expressed concern about possible long term consequences from consuming bioengineered foods, but they did not contend that any of the bioengineered foods already on the market have adverse health effects. The comments were mainly expressions of concern about the unknown. The agency is still not aware of any data or other information that would form a basis for concluding that the fact that a food or its ingredients was produced using bioengineering is a material fact that must be disclosed under sections 403(a) and 201(n) of the act. FDA is therefore reaffirming its decision to not require special labeling of all bioengineered foods.

The agency is providing the following guidance to assist manufacturers who wish to voluntarily label their foods as being made with or without the use of bioengineered ingredients. While the use of bioengineering is not a material fact, many consumers are interested in the information, and some manufacturers may want to respond to this consumer desire. The guidance was developed using information from the comments and from focus groups, as well as other resources, and is intended to help ensure that labeling is truthful and not misleading.

GUIDANCE

In determining whether a food is misbranded, FDA would review label statements about the use of bioengineering to develop a food or its ingredients under sections 403(a) and 201(n) of the act. Under section 403(a) of the act, a food is misbranded if statements on its label or in its labeling are false or misleading in any particular. Under section 201(n), both the presence and the absence of information are relevant to whether labeling is misleading. That is, labeling may be misleading if it fails to disclose facts that are material in light of representations made about a product or facts that are material with respect to the consequences that may result from use of the product. In determining whether a statement that a food is or is not genetically engineered is misleading under sections 201(n) and 403(a) of the act, the agency will take into account the entire label and labeling.

Statements about foods developed using bioengineering

FDA recognizes that some manufacturers may want to use informative statements on labels and in labeling of bioengineered foods or foods that contain ingredients produced from bioengineered foods. The following are examples of some statements that might be used. The discussion accompanying each example is intended to provide guidance as to how similar statements can be made without being misleading.

- "Genetically engineered" or "This product contains cornmeal that was produced using biotechnology."

The information that the food was bioengineered is optional and this kind of simple statement is not likely to be misleading. However, focus group data indicate that consumers would prefer label statements that disclose and explain the goal of the technology (why it was used or what it does for/to the food). Consumers also expressed some preference for the term "biotechnology" over such terms as "genetic modification" and "genetic engineering."

- "This product contains high oleic acid soybean oil from soybeans developed using biotechnology to decrease the amount of saturated fat."

This example includes both required and optional information. As discussed above in the background section, when a food differs from its traditional counterpart such that the common or usual name no longer adequately describes the new food, the name must be changed to describe the difference. Because this soybean oil contains more oleic acid than traditional soybean oil, the term "soybean oil" no longer adequately describes the nature of the food. Under section 403(i) of the act, a phrase like "high oleic acid" would be required to appear as part of the name of the food to describe its basic nature. The statement that the soybeans were developed using biotechnology is optional. So is the statement that the reason for the change in the soybeans was to reduce saturated fat.

- "These tomatoes were genetically engineered to improve texture."

In this example, the change in texture is a difference that may have to be described on the label. If the texture improvement makes a significant difference in the finished product, sections 201(n) and 403(a)(1) of the act would require disclosure of the difference for the consumer. However, the statement must not be misleading. The phrase "to improve texture" could be misleading if the texture difference is not noticeable to the consumer. For example, if a manufacturer wanted to describe a difference in a food that the consumer would not notice when purchasing or consuming the product, the manufacturer should phrase the statements so that the consumer can understand the significance of the difference. If the change in the tomatoes was intended to facilitate processing but did not make a noticeable difference in the processed consumer product, a phrase like "to improve texture for processing" rather than "to improve texture" should be used to ensure that the consumer is not misled. The statement that the tomatoes were genetically engineered is optional.

- "Some of our growers plant tomato seeds that were developed through biotechnology to increase crop yield."

The entire statement in this example is optional information. The fact that there was increased yield does not affect the characteristics of the food and is therefore not necessary on the label to adequately describe the food for the consumer. A phrase like "to increase yield" should only be included where there is substantiation that there is in fact the stated difference.

Where a benefit from a bioengineered ingredient in a multi-ingredient food is described, the statement should be worded so that it addresses the ingredient and not the food as a whole; for example, "This product contains high oleic acid soybean oil from soybeans produced through biotechnology to decrease the level of saturated fat." In addition, the amount of the bioengineered ingredient in the food may be relevant to whether the statement is misleading. This would apply especially where the bioengineered difference is a nutritional improvement. For example, it would likely be misleading to make a statement about a nutritionally improved ingredient on a food that contains only a small amount of the ingredient, such that the food's overall nutritional quality would not be significantly improved.

FDA reminds manufacturers that the optional terms that describe an ingredient of a multi-ingredient food as bioengineered should not be used in the ingredient list of the multi-ingredient food. Section 403(i)(2) of the act requires each ingredient to be declared in the ingredient statement by its common or usual name. Thus, any terms not part of the name of the ingredient are not permitted in the ingredient statement. In addition, 21 CFR 101.2(e) requires that the ingredient list and certain other mandatory information appear in one place without other intervening material. FDA has long interpreted any optional description of ingredients in the ingredient statement to be intervening material that violates this regulation.

Statements about foods that are not bioengineered or that do not contain ingredients produced from bioengineered foods

Terms that are frequently mentioned in discussions about labeling foods with respect to bioengineering include "GMO free" and "GM free." "GMO" is an acronym for "genetically modified organism" and "GM" means "genetically modified." Consumer focus group data indicate that consumers do not understand the acronyms "GMO" and " GM" and prefer label statements with spelled out words that mean bioengineering.

Terms like "not genetically modified" and "GMO free," that include the word "modified" are not technically accurate unless they are clearly in a context that refers to bioengineering technology. "Genetic modification" means the alteration of the genotype of a plant using any technique, new or traditional. "Modification" has a broad context that means the alteration in the composition of food that results from adding, deleting, or changing hereditary traits, irrespective of the method. Modifications may be minor, such as a single mutation that affects one gene, or major alterations of genetic material that affect many genes. Most, if not all, cultivated food crops have been genetically modified. Data indicate that consumers do not have a good understanding that essentially all food crops have been genetically modified and that bioengineering technology is only one of a number of technologies used to genetically modify crops. Thus, while it is accurate to say that a bioengineered food was "genetically modified," it likely would be inaccurate to state that a food that had not been produced using biotechnology was "not genetically modified" without clearly providing a context so that the consumer can understand that the statement applies to bioengineering.

The term "GMO free" may be misleading on most foods, because most foods do not contain organisms (seeds and foods like yogurt that contain microorganisms are exceptions). It would likely be misleading to suggest that a food that ordinarily would not contain entire "organisms" is "organism free."

There is potential for the term "free" in a claim for absence of bioengineering to be inaccurate. Consumers assume that "free" of bioengineered material means that "zero" bioengineered material is present. Because of the potential for adventitious presence of bioengineered material, it may be necessary to conclude that the accuracy of the term "free" can only be ensured when there is a definition or threshold above which the term could not be used. FDA does not have information with which to establish a threshold level of bioengineered constituents or ingredients in foods for the statement "free of bioengineered material." FDA recognizes that there are analytical methods capable of detecting low levels of some bioengineered materials in some foods, but a threshold would require methods to test for a wide range of genetic changes at very low levels in a wide variety of foods. Such test methods are not available at this time. The agency suggests that the term "free" either not be used in bioengineering label statements or that it be in a context that makes clear that a zero level of bioengineered material is not implied. However, statements that the food or its ingredients, as appropriate, was not developed using bioengineering would avoid or minimize such implications.

For example,

- "We do not use ingredients that were produced using biotechnology";
- "This oil is made from soybeans that were not genetically engineered"; or
- "Our tomato growers do not plant seeds developed using biotechnology."

A statement that a food was not bioengineered or does not contain bioengineered ingredients may be misleading if it implies that the labeled food is superior to foods that are not so labeled. FDA has concluded that the use or absence of use of bioengineering in the production of a food or ingredient does not, in and of itself, mean that there is a material difference in the food. Therefore, a label statement that expresses or implies that a food is superior (e.g., safer or of higher quality) because it is not bioengineered would be misleading. The agency will evaluate the entire label and labeling in determining whether a label statement is in a context that implies that the food is superior.

In addition, a statement that an ingredient was not bioengineered could be misleading if there is another ingredient in the food that was bioengineered. The claim must not misrepresent the absence of bioengineered material. For example, on a product made largely of bioengineered corn flour and a small amount of soybean oil, a claim that the product "does not include genetically engineered soybean oil" could be misleading. Even if the statement is true, it is likely to be misleading if consumers believe that the entire product or a larger portion of it than is actually the case is free of bioengineered material. It may be necessary to carefully qualify the statement in order to ensure that consumers understand its significance.

Further, a statement may be misleading if it suggests that a food or ingredient itself is not bioengineered, when there are no marketed bioengineered varieties of that category of foods or ingredients. For example, it would be misleading to state "not produced through biotechnology" on the label of green beans, when there are no marketed bioengineered green beans. To not be misleading, the claim should be in a context that applies to the food type instead of the individual manufacturer's product. For example, the statement "green beans are not produced using biotechnology" would not imply that this manufacturer's product is different from other green beans.

Substantiation of label statements

A manufacturer who claims that a food or its ingredients, including foods such as raw agricultural commodities, is not bioengineered should be able to substantiate that the claim is truthful and not misleading. Validated testing, if available, is the most reliable way to identify bioengineered foods or food ingredients. For many foods, however, particularly for highly processed foods such as oils, it may be difficult to differentiate by validated analytical methods between bioengineered foods and food ingredients and those obtained using traditional breeding methods. Where tests have been validated and shown to be reliable they may be used. However, if validated test methods are not available or reliable because of the way foods are produced or processed, it may be important to document the source of such foods differently. Also, special handling may be appropriate to maintain segregation of bioengineered and nonbioengineered foods. In addition, manufacturers should consider appropriate recordkeeping to document the segregation procedures to ensure that the food's labeling is not false or misleading. In some situations, certifications or affidavits from farmers, processors, and others in the food production and distribution chain may be adequate to document that foods are obtained from the use of traditional methods. A statement that a food is "free" of bioengineered material may be difficult to substantiate without testing. Because appropriately validated testing methods are not currently available for many foods, it is likely that it would be easier to document handling practices and procedures to substantiate a claim about how the food was processed than to substantiate a "free" claim.

FDA has been asked about the ability of organic foods to bear label statements to the effect that the food (or its ingredients) was not produced using biotechnology. On December 21, 2000, the Agriculture Marketing Service of the U.S. Department of Agriculture (USDA) published final regulations on procedures for organic food production (National Organic Program final rule; 65 FR 80548). That final rule requires that all but the smallest organic operations be certified by a USDA accredited agent and lays out the requirements for organic food production. Among those requirements is that products or ingredients identified as organic must not be produced using biotechnology methods. The national organic standards would provide for adequate segregation of the food throughout distribution to assure that non-organic foods do not become mixed with organic foods. The agency believes that the practices and record keeping that substantiate the "certified organic" statement would be sufficient to substantiate a claim that a food was not produced using bioengineering.

References

1. Levy, A.S., Derby, B.M., "Report on Consumer Focus Groups on Biotechnology", Consumer Studies Team, Center for Food Safety and Nutrition, Food and Drug Administration, Washington, D.C., 2000.

Notes

1. The United States and a number of its trading partners have long disagreed about the labeling of genetically engineered ingredients in food products. This issue was debated at the May 2010 meeting of the Codex Alimentarius Commission's Committee on Food Labeling. The Codex Alimentarius commission was established by the Food & Agriculture Organization (FAO) and the World Health Organization (WHO) of the United Nations. It is charged with developing international food standards to serve as a model for countries seeking to improve their food safety and quality standards and to serve as an export standard for trading nations. The Committee on Food Labeling proposed to allow different countries to adopt different positions for labeling genetically engineered foods, consistent with its current guidance. The U.S. through the USDA and the FDA, argued that allowing countries the option of mandatory labeling would suggest that genetically engineered foods were somehow different from other foods.

It was reported that the U.S. position was opposed by most countries, with only Mexico, Argentina, and Costa Rica supporting it. Moreover, 80 food, farm, and consumer organizations including the Consumers Union, the Organic Trade Association, the Union of Concerned Scientists, and the Center for Food Safety sent a letter to FDA and USDA officials objecting to the U.S. position, arguing that it "could potentially create problems for food producers in the U.S. who want to indicate that their products contain no GE ingredients, including organic food, where genetic engineering is a prohibited method." They argued that it was inconsistent to oppose mandatory labeling as misleading when voluntary labeling in the U.S. is allowed and not considered misleading.

An agreement was not reached at the meeting.

2. Case Study: Bovine Somatotropin

Bovine somatotropin (bST), sometimes called bovine growth hormone or BGH, is a naturally occurring hormone produced in cattle. In the early 1990s, Monsanto used recombinant DNA technology to synthesize bST in large quantities, and in 1994 gained approval to market it as Prosilac, a cattle drug to be used to increase milk production.

The use of rbST has been controversial for a variety of reasons. Given the importance of milk as a staple food, particularly for children, the notion that extra hormones were being given to dairy cows raised concerns about the human health consequences. While most studies have refuted these concerns, they persist in the minds of many consumers.

Animal welfare concerns have been persistent and documented. The extra productivity comes at a health cost to the dairy cow, with studies indicating an increased incidence of mastitis, increased lameness, diminished body condition, and a shortened production life. Animal welfare concerns led to a ban on the use of rbST in Canada, Australia, New Zealand, much of Europe.

Opponents of rbST also raise their support of small family farm operations as another reason to oppose the use of the hormone. They argue that its use, most common and most profitable in the largest dairies, has resulted in the displacement of many of the smaller dairy operations. Over-production of milk is often cited as a factor in the financial problems of the dairy industry, although consumers benefit from reduced milk prices.

From its initial approval of rbST, the FDA has been unwavering in its approval. It has been steadfast in asserting that there is no human health risk associated with its use and that any animal welfare issues are insignificant. The impact of rbST on the dairy industry is a factor that is clearly outside of FDA's jurisdiction or concern.

With respect to the labeling of milk produced from cows who received rbST, consistent with its policy with respect to genetically engineered products, the FDA required no special labeling. It found "no measurable compositional difference between milk from cows that receive rbST and those that do not."

At least one state saw the issue differently. In 1994, Vermont enacted a statute requiring that "[i]f rBST has been used in the production of milk or a milk product for retail sale in the state, the retail milk or milk product shall be labeled as such." The International Dairy Foods Association sued, arguing that the statute was unconstitutional. The Second Circuit Court of Appeals agreed, holding that the statute violated the plaintiff's First Amendment rights. *International Dairy Foods Association v. Amestoy*, 92 F.3d 67 (2nd Cir. 1996).

The more controversial issue, however, has been efforts to restrict the voluntary labeling of milk produced without the use of rbST. The right or lack thereof of dairies and food processors to voluntarily label their food as "rbST-free" has spawned a variety of legal issues on both the state and federal levels.

The FDA's position on rbST labeling is set forth in an Interim Guidance published in the Federal Register in 1994. 59 Fed. Reg. 6279 (Notice) (Feb. 10, 1994). The following excerpt explains FDA's guidance.

Interim Guidance on the Voluntary Labeling of Milk and Milk Products From Cows That Have Not Been Treated With Recombinant Bovine Somatotropin

Appropriate Labeling Statements

At the Federal level, statements about rbST in the labeling of food shipped in interstate commerce would be reviewed under sections 403(a) and 201(n) of the act. Under section 403(a) of the act, a food is misbranded if statements on its label or in its labeling are false or misleading in any particular. Under section 201(n), both the presence and the absence of information are relevant to whether labeling is misleading. That is, labeling may be misleading if it fails to disclose facts that are material in light of representations made about a product or facts that are material with respect to the consequences that may result from use of the product. Thus, certain labeling statements about the use of rbST may be misleading unless they are accompanied by additional information. This guidance is based on the use of the false or misleading standard in the Federal law, which is incorporated in many States' food and drug laws. States may also have additional authorities that are relevant in regulating such claims.

Because of the presence of natural bST in milk, no milk is "bST-free," and a "bST-free" labeling statement would be false. Also, FDA is concerned that the term "rbST free" may imply a compositional difference between milk from treated and untreated cows rather than a difference in the way the milk is produced. Instead, the concept would better be formulated as "from cows not treated with rbST" or in other similar ways. However, even such a statement, which asserts that rbST has not been used in the production of the subject milk, has the potential to be misunderstood by consumers. Without proper context, such statements could be misleading. Such unqualified statements may imply that milk from untreated cows is safer or of higher quality than milk from treated cows. Such an implication would be false and misleading.

FDA believes such misleading implications could best be avoided by the use of accompanying information that puts the statement in a proper context. Proper context could be achieved in a number of different ways. For example, accompanying the statement "from cows not treated with rbST" with the statement that "No significant difference has been shown between milk derived from rbST-treated and non-rbST-treated cows" would put the claim in proper context. Proper context could also be achieved by conveying the firm's reasons (other than safety or quality) for choosing not to use milk from cows treated with rbST, as long as the label is truthful and nonmisleading....

Notes

1. Oakhurst Dairy in Maine claims to be the first major U.S. dairy to reject the use of rbST in the production of its milk. Oakhurst included the following label on its milk cartons: "Farmers' Pledge: No Artificial Growth Hormone Used."

Monsanto sued Oakhurst in 2003, alleging that the label was misleading under the Food, Drug and Cosmetic Act and in violation of FDA standards. Oakhurst, capitalizing on its status as a family-owned independent dairy up against a multinational corporation, held firm. The case generated a good deal of publicity and eventually settled. Oakhurst retained the right to put its Farmers' Pledge on its milk label but added a disclaimer: "FDA states: No significant difference in milk from cows treated with artificial growth hormone."

2. As a result of consumer demand, milk produced without rbST and labeled in a similar fashion is widely available, with most major supermarkets offering at least one brand. Nevertheless, some in the industry still seek to restrict the ability of dairies to segregate and label their milk in this manner. Missouri, Pennsylvania, and Ohio have all had recent laws proposed that would prohibit milk producers and processors from using labels that state the milk was produced from cows not treated with rbST.

3. The National Organic Standards prohibit the use of rbST in the production of milk that is labeled organic, as all "animal drugs, including hormones, to promote growth" are prohibited. 7 C.F.R. § 205.237. Legal scholar Dean Jim Chen explores potential conflicts between the FDA's labeling policies and the National Organic Standards with respect to genetically modified foods in the article, *Beyond Food and Evil*, 56 Duke L.J. 1581 (2007).

4. Monsanto sold its POSILAC Brand Dairy Product and Related Business to Elanco Animal Health, a division of Eli Lilly and Company in August 2008.

E. International Trade and Genetically Engineered Products

Tadlock Cowan & Geoffrey S. Becker
Agricultural Biotechnology: Background and Recent Issues
Congressional Research Report RL-32809
Feb. 13, 2009

* * *

The U.S. approach to biotechnology regulation contrasts with that of many major trading partners. For example, the European Union (EU), Japan, South Korea, New Zealand, and Australia either have or are establishing separate mandatory labeling requirements for products containing genetically modified ingredients; in many of these countries, consumer and official attitudes toward GE foods are more skeptical. Differing regulatory approaches have arisen at least partly because widely accepted international standards continue to evolve. Incidents, such as those discussed below, have been disrupted U.S. exports and contributed to trade tensions.

GE Rice

Although several GE varieties of rice have been approved for commercial use ("deregulated," in regulatory parlance), none have been marketed, although they have been planted on test plots in the United States. In August 2006, the Secretary of Agriculture announced that "trace amounts" of an unapproved variety of GE rice had been found in samples of the 2005 crop of U.S. long grain rice. The Secretary and other USDA officials sought to reassure the rice trade and consumers that the findings posed no human health, food safety, or environmental concerns.

Owner Bayer CropScience had not asked APHIS to deregulate this particular line, called LLRICE601, which had been field tested between 1998 and 2001. Two other Bayer GE rice varieties, known as LLRICE62 and LLRICE06, had received commercial approval but have not been commercialized, USDA stated. Also, "[t]he protein in LLRICE601 is approved for use in other products" and "has been repeatedly and thoroughly scientifically reviewed and used safely in food and feed, cultivation, import and breeding in the United States, as well as nearly a dozen other countries around the world."

Nonetheless, the discovery unsettled rice markets and rekindled longtime criticisms of U.S. biotechnology regulatory policies. The U.S. rice crop is valued at nearly $2 billion annually. Exports represent approximately one-half or more of U.S. rice production annually on a volume basis, of which about 80% is long grain (the type in which GE material was detected), according to USDA statistics. Although the United States produces only about 1.5%–2% of the world rice crop, it was the fourth leading exporter (behind Thailand, Vietnam, and India), with more than 13% of world market share in 2005.

Of the 4.4 million metric tons (MMT) exported in 2005, Mexico was by far the leading buyer, at 753,000 MT. Japan was the second leading market at nearly 424,000 MT. Various Central American and Caribbean countries took a total of 1.4 MMT; Iraq, 310,000 MT; and European Union (EU) countries, a total of 306,000 MT, USDA data show. Much of the long grain crop is produced in southern U.S. states, which generally ship from Gulf ports to Latin America, the Caribbean, and Europe, for example. California grows mainly medium and short grain rice varieties, which are marketed in Asia, including Japan.

Following USDA's notification that U.S. rice supplies had traces of GE material, September 2006 closing rice futures dropped from $9.70 per cwt. (100 pounds) on August 18, closing at $8.99 per cwt. on August 25, 2005. (One year ago, the closing price was less than $7.00 per cwt.) The European Union (EU), which bought 279,300 MT of U.S. long grain rice in 2005, reacted by adopting a measure requiring all such shipments to be tested and certified as free of LLRICE601.

Japan has indicated that it was suspending shipments of U.S. long grain rice although, as noted, most U.S. rice exports there are short and medium grain. According to a statement by the producer cooperative Riceland Foods, Inc., of Stuttgart, Arkansas, the GE material was initially discovered by one of its export customers in January 2006. Riceland then sent a sample to a U.S. laboratory, which confirmed the Bayer GE trait, which is known to be present in (and approved for) corn, soybeans, canola, and cotton. Riceland said it collected samples from several storage locations in May 2006 and found positive results that were "geographically dispersed and random throughout the rice-growing area." Bayer was notified in early June, and its tests confirmed the presence of the GE trait in the equivalent of 6 per 10,000 kernels (0.06%).

In August 2006, USDA officials offered few additional details about the cause or extent of the problem. They indicated that they had not been informed by Bayer of the discovery until July 31, after which the Department began its own investigation, they stated. Among other actions, USDA said that APHIS was now moving to approve (i.e., deregulate) LLRICE601. Also, USDA's Grain Inspection, Packers, and Stockyards Administration (GIPSA) has verified the use of two standardized tests that can test for the GE protein in rice shipments.

Consumer and environmental advocacy groups were harshly critical of APHIS and USDA, noting that officials waited three weeks to make the discovery public—and still did not know where the samples were grown or how they entered the food supply. One group, the Center for Food Safety, subsequently called for a moratorium on all new field testing permits until oversight can be improved. In August 2006, rice farmers in Arkansas, Missouri, Mississippi, Louisiana, Texas and California filed a class action lawsuit against Bayer CropScience, accusing the company of negligence in allowing unapproved genetically engineered rice to find its way into the commercial supply chain. By November 2006, APHIS declared the rice variety LLRICE601 safe for human consumption and deregulated the variety. USDA essentially declared that the new variety was similar to two Bayer varieties that had already been approved.

GE Wheat

Trade concerns were apparent in the debate over whether to introduce (commercialize) GE herbicide-tolerant wheat. Monsanto had asked the U.S. and Canadian governments for their approval, and other GE wheat varieties had been under development. Some producers wanted to plant the wheat as soon as it became available; others feared rejection by foreign customers of not only GE wheat, but all U.S. and Canadian wheat, out of concern that even non-GE shipments might unintentionally contain some GE grain. The latter group wanted developers and regulators to wait for more market acceptance before releasing GE wheat varieties.

In early 2003, a group of U.S. wheat producers had petitioned the Administration to conduct a more thorough assessment of the environmental impacts of the Monsanto request; 27 farm, religious, and consumer advocacy organizations endorsed the petition in early 2004. Underlining these concerns, Japanese consumer groups in March 2004 reportedly told U.S. officials in wheat-dependent North Dakota that their country would not import any U.S. wheat products if the Monsanto application was approved.

This resistance likely contributed to a decision by Monsanto to discontinue its efforts to win regulatory approval of a genetically modified wheat variety. Monsanto announced its decision in May 2004. Although Monsanto withdrew its applications for regulatory approval from EPA and APHIS, it did not withdraw its FDA application. FDA subsequently approved the application in July 2004. However, FDA approval alone is not sufficient to bring the GM wheat to market. While opposition to GE wheat remains strong among many U.S. trading partners, a spokesman for the joint biotechnology committee of the National Association of Wheat Growers and U.S. Wheat Associates, indicated in 2007 that support for planting and exporting GE wheat was growing among some U.S wheat producers.

U.S.-EU Dispute

In May 2003, the United States, Canada, and Argentina initiated a complaint before the World Trade Organization (WTO) regarding the EU's de facto moratorium on approvals of new GE crops. U.S. agricultural interests contended that the moratorium not only blocked exports such as corn and other products to the EU, but also was fueling unwarranted concerns about the safety of agricultural biotechnology throughout the world. The United States and its allies further argued that the EU moratorium was violating WTO rules stating that a country's actions to protect health and the environment must be scientifically based, and approval procedures must be operated without undue delay.

The WTO named a panel in March 2004 to consider the case. Although the EU effectively lifted the moratorium in May 2004 by approving a genetically engineered corn variety, the three complainants pursued the case, in part because a number of EU member states have continued to block approved biotech products. In February 2006, the WTO dispute panel, in its interim confidential report, ruled that a moratorium existed, that bans on EU-approved GE crops in six EU member countries (Austria, France, Germany, Greece, Italy, and Luxembourg) violated WTO rules, and that the EU failed to ensure that its approval procedures were conducted without "undue delay." The final ruling was circulated to the parties in May 2006 and made public in September 2006.

The dispute panel's ruling dismissed several other U.S. and co-complainant claims, and did not address such sensitive issues as whether GE products are safe or whether an EU moratorium on GE approvals continued to exist. The final ruling, among other things, directed the EU to bring its practices in line with WTO rules. It concluded that the EU had breached its commitments with respect to 21 products, including types of oilseed rape, maize and cotton. It also said individual bans in Austria, France, Germany, Greece, Italy and Luxembourg were illegal.

The EU initially agreed on a November 2007 deadline for compliance with the WTO dispute ruling. The parties subsequently agreed to extend the time for EU compliance with the ruling to January 2008. The EU missed this deadline in large measure. Brussels has found it hard to implement the WTO ruling because some of the 27 EU member states operate their own bans on GE crops. Individual countries (e.g., Austria, France, Greece) have prohibited the sale or cultivation of certain EU-approved varieties of GE corn (e.g., MON810, a variety produced by Monsanto). In 2008, France also initiated a temporary national moratorium on GE crops. Spain continues to dominate the EU in GE crop cultivation.

Although positive action has been slow, the United States has temporarily suspended WTO sanctions. U.S. agricultural interests, however, remain concerned that the stricter EU rules for labeling and tracing GE products will continue to discriminate against U.S. exports. If progress is not made, the issue is likely to return to the WTO's dispute settlement body. The United States could retaliate against the EU to compensate for the annual value of lost U.S. exports, royalties and licensing fees to the EU from biotech crops. These could be levied by imposing extra tariffs on EU goods or lifting other WTO agreements regulating agriculture or health and safety.

The WTO case did not involve the EU's new "labeling and traceability" regulations, in effect as of April 2004, to require most food, feed, and processed products from GMOs to be labeled. GE-based products also must be segregated from non-GE products, with documentation. U.S. agricultural interests argue that, even if the EU regularly approves GMOs, the labeling and traceability rules are themselves unworkable and unnecessary, and can mislead consumers by wrongly implying that GM-derived products are inherently different than non-GM foods or pose safety concerns. The EU, however, continues to defend its mandatory labeling regime. At least one EU country, Germany, has addressed the issue of potential liability from GM crops—passing a law in November 2004 that holds farmers who plant GM crops liable for damages to nearby non-GM fields (even if the GM farmers adhered to planting instructions and regulations). Some U.S. interests countered that the moratorium will not effectively end until the EU clears more of some two dozen or more GE food and agricultural products still awaiting regulatory approval—and EU member states actually implement the approvals.

The Biosafety Protocol

The Cartagena Biosafety Protocol, an outgrowth of the 1992 Convention on Biological Diversity (CBD), was adopted in January 2000 and took effect in 2003. The United States is not a party to the 1992 CBD, and therefore cannot be a party to the protocol. However, because its shipments to ratifying countries are affected, it has actively participated in the negotiations over the protocol text and in countries' preparations for implementation.

The protocol, which 134 other nations had ratified as of August 2006, permits a country to require formal prior notifications from countries exporting biotech seeds and living modified organisms (LMOs) intended for introduction into the environment. The protocol requires that shipments of products that may contain LMOs, such as bulk grains, be appropriately labeled and documented, and provides for an international clearinghouse for the exchange of LMO information, among other provisions. The Protocol further establishes a process for considering more detailed identification and documentation of LMO commodities in international trade.

The United States objected to implementing measures approved during an international conference in Kuala Lumpur in February 2004. According to the United States, the measures would mandate overly detailed documentation requirements and potentially expose exporters to unwarranted liability damages if imported GMOs harm the environment or human health. U.S. government and industry officials believe that these and other rules could disrupt U.S. exports.

GMOs in the Developing World

In Asia, particularly China and India, governments view GMOs as a way to produce more food for burgeoning populations, despite some in-country opposition and support for labeling GE products. China has been researching GE corn, cotton, wheat, soy, tomatoes, and peppers since 1986. It has, however, been reluctant to approve commercial varieties of GE, which have been under development there. If so, it would be the first time a GE plant was used widely as a staple food, and may influence the decisions of other Asian countries with regard to accepting GE foods.

In the debate over the potential contribution of biotechnology to food security in developing countries, critics argue that the benefits of biotechnology in such countries have not been established and that the technology poses unacceptable risks. They also suggest that intellectual property rights (IPR) protection gives multinational companies control over developing country farmers. Proponents say that the development of GE technology appears to hold great promise, with the potential to complement other, more traditional research methods, as the new driving force for sustained agricultural productivity in the 21st century. They maintain that IPR difficulties have been exaggerated.

According to a recent report published by the International Service for the Acquisition of Agribiotech Applications, 12 developing nations planted GE crops in 2007. Of the total 114.3 million hectares of GE crops cultivated worldwide, 43% of the global GE crop area is in developing countries. Differences on this issue were featured in 2002, when the United Nations (UN) World Food Program (WFP) announced an appeal for food aid to meet the needs of some 14 million food-short people in six southern African countries: Lesotho, Malawi, Mozambique, Swaziland, Zambia, and Zimbabwe. However, a debate over the presence of genetically modified corn in U.S. food aid shipments made the provision of food aid more difficult and costly. Some of the countries expressed reluctance to accept unmilled GE corn on account of perceived environmental and commercial risks associated with potential introduction of GE seeds into southern African agriculture. Zambia refused all shipments of food aid with GE corn out of health concerns as well. In March 2004, Angola said it too would ban imports of GE food aid, including thousands of tons of U.S. corn, despite a need to feed approximately 2 million Angolans. The United States has blamed EU policies for southern African countries' views on food aid containing GE products. The United States maintains that genetically modified crops are safe to eat and that there is little likelihood of GE corn entering the food supply of African countries for several reasons, including the fact that current bioengineered varieties of corn are not well adapted to African growing conditions. South Africa is the only African country to commercialize biotech crops.

The Food and Agriculture Organization (FAO) of the United Nations has also offered a qualified endorsement of agricultural biotechnology, stating that it "can benefit the poor when appropriate innovations are developed and when poor farmers in poor countries have access to them ... Thus far, these conditions are only being met in a handful of developing countries." Biotechnology research and development should complement other agricultural improvements that give priority to the problems of the poor, FAO said, adding: "Regulatory procedures should be strengthened and rationalized to ensure that the environment and public health are protected and that the process is transparent, predictable and science-based." Other groups have been more pointed in criticizing GE crops, arguing that they can have hidden costs that are inadequately examined by biotechnology advocates.

———————

X

Food and Agriculture

One way to think about America's national eating disorder is as the return, with an almost atavistic vengeance, of the omnivore's dilemma. The cornucopia of the American supermarket has thrown us back on a bewildering food landscape where we once again have to worry that some of those tasty-looking morsels might kill us. (Perhaps not as quickly as a poisonous mushroom, but just as surely.) Certainly, the extraordinary abundance of food in America complicates the whole problem of choice....

MICHAEL POLLAN, THE OMNIVORE'S DILEMMA: A NATURAL HISTORY OF FOUR MEALS (2006).

This chapter presents a variety of topics focused on the intersection of agricultural law and food law, areas where the interests of the farmer and the consumer interact. The issues selected for discussion are food safety, the regulation of organic production, and the local food movement. The book concludes with thoughts on future issues to be resolved.

A. Food Safety

1. The Structure of Government Regulation

Geoffrey S. Becker
The Federal Food Safety System: A Primer
Congressional Research Service Report, Rept. No. RS22600, 1–5
(April 20, 2010)

Background

Americans spend more than $1 trillion on food each year, nearly half of it in restaurants, schools, and other places outside the home.[2] Federal laws give food manufacturers, distributors, and retailers the basic responsibility for assuring that foods are wholesome, safe, and handled under sanitary conditions. A number of federal agencies, cooperating with state, local, and international entities, play a major role in regulating food quality and safety under these laws.

---

2. Roughly two-thirds of the $1 trillion is for domestically produced farm foods; imports and seafood account for the balance. Source: USDA, Economic Research Service, data accessed January 2008 at the "Food Sector" Web page at http://www.ers.usda.gov/Browse/FoodSector/.

The combined efforts of the food industry and the regulatory agencies often are credited with making the U.S. food supply among the safest in the world. Nonetheless, public health officials estimate that each year 76 million people become sick, 325,000 are hospitalized, and 5,000 die from foodborne illnesses caused by contamination from any one of a number of microbial pathogens.[3] In addition, experts have cited numerous other hazards to health, including the use of unapproved veterinary drugs, pesticides, and other dangerous substances in food commodities, of particular concern at a time when an growing share of the U.S. food supply is from overseas sources.

At issue is whether the current U.S. regulatory system has the resources and structural organization to protect consumers from these dangers. Also at issue is whether the federal food safety laws themselves, first enacted in the early 1900s, have kept pace with the significant changes that have occurred in the food production, processing, and marketing sectors since then.

The Agencies and Their Roles

The Government Accountability Office (GAO) has identified as many as 15 federal agencies collectively administering at least 30 laws related to food safety. The Food and Drug Administration (FDA), which is part of the U.S. Department of Health and Human Services (HHS), and the Food Safety and Inspection Service (FSIS), which is part of the U.S. Department of Agriculture (USDA), together comprise the majority of both the total funding and the total staffing of the government's food regulatory system.[4]

FSIS's FY2009 budget was approximately $972 million in appropriated funds plus another estimated $140 million in industry-paid user fees. FDA's budget for foods was $649 million in FY2009, virtually all of it appropriated (plus an additional $137 million for regulation of animal drugs and feeds, which includes $20 million in user fees). Thus, FSIS had approximately 65% of the two agencies' combined food safety budget, and FDA had the other approximately 35%.[5] Conversely, FSIS is responsible for approximately 20% of the U.S. food supply, but FDA is responsible for 80%.[6]

Among other agencies with smaller but still significant shares of the food safety portfolio are the National Marine Fisheries Service (NMFS), which is part of the U.S. Department of Commerce (DOC), the Environmental Protection Agency (EPA), and the Centers for Disease Control and Prevention (CDC) in HHS.

---

3. U.S. Department of Health and Human Services, Centers for Disease Control and Prevention, "Foodborne Illness: Frequently Asked Questions," accessed at http://www.cdc.gov/foodsafety/. However, this estimate appears to be based primarily on 1997 and earlier data in a report by Paul S. Mead et al., "Food-related Illness and Death in the United States," Emerging Infectious Diseases, vol. 5, pp. 607–625, 1999.

4. *High Risk Series: An Update* (GAO-07-310), January 2007.

5. Data source: various documents of the Agriculture, Rural Development, Food and Drug Administration, and Related Agencies Subcommittee of the House Committee on Appropriations.

6. Source for the food supply proportions is GAO, "*Revamping Oversight of Food Safety*," urgent issues prepared for the 2009 Congressional and Presidential Transition, accessed December 2008 at http://www.gao.gov/transition_2009/urgent/food-safety.php. GAO here does not provide a basis for its calculations, although they appear to represent proportions of total spending for food consumed at home. Examined another way, meat and poultry could account for as little as 10% of U.S. per capita food consumption, according to data maintained by USDA's Economic Research Service (ERS); these per capita data adjust food availability for spoilage, plate waste, and other losses. Source: ERS Food Availability (Per Capita) Data System, accessed December 29, 2008, at http://www.ers.usda.gov/data/foodconsumption/.

Food and Drug Administration

The FDA is responsible for ensuring that all domestic and imported food products—except for most meats and poultry—are safe, nutritious, wholesome, and accurately labeled. Examples of FDA-regulated foods are produce, dairy products, seafood, and processed foods. FDA has jurisdiction over meats from animals or birds that are not under the regulatory jurisdiction of FSIS. FDA shares responsibility for the safety of eggs with FSIS. FDA has jurisdiction over establishments that sell or serve eggs or use them as an ingredient in their products. FDA is also responsible for ensuring that most seafood products do not endanger public health (FSIS is to begin inspecting farmed catfish products under a 2008 farm bill provision). The primary statutes governing FDA's activities are the Federal Food, Drug, and Cosmetic Act, as amended (21 U.S.C. 301 et seq.); the Public Health Service Act, as amended (42 U.S.C. 201 et seq.); and the Egg Products Inspection Act, as amended (21 U.S.C. 1031 et seq.).

FDA's food inspection force numbers more than 1,900 in field offices throughout the United States, plus nearly 900 in the Washington, DC, area. FDA regulates food manufacturers' safety practices by relying on companies' self-interest in producing safe products, and by working with the industry to improve production practices. Overall, FDA has oversight of more than 44,000 U.S. food manufacturers, plus well over 100,000 additional registered food facilities such as warehouses and grain elevators. In addition, some 200,000 foreign food facilities are registered with the agency. Various estimates of unannounced compliance inspections of domestic establishments by FDA officials range from once every five years to once every 10 years, on average, although the agency claims to visit about 6,000 so-called high-risk facilities on an annual basis. FDA relies on notifications from within the industry or from other federal or state inspection personnel, as well as other sources, to alert it to situations calling for increased inspection.

A report by HHS's Office of Inspector General (OIG) provided additional insights into the FDA's inspections of domestic facilities. The OIG reported that the number of facilities subject to such inspections has risen from about 59,000 in 2004 to nearly 68,000 in 2008. However, the number of inspections conducted declined from about 17,000 in 2004 (29% of the total) to about 15,000 in 2008 (22%). During the five-year period examined by the OIG, 56% of food facilities were not inspected at all.[7]

In the Washington, DC, area, two FDA offices are the focal point for food safety-related activities. The Center for Food Safety and Applied Nutrition (CFSAN) is responsible for (1) conducting and supporting food safety research; (2) developing and overseeing enforcement of food safety and quality regulations; (3) coordinating and evaluating FDA's food surveillance and compliance programs; (4) coordinating and evaluating cooperating states' food safety activities; and (5) developing and disseminating food safety and regulatory information to consumers and industry. FDA's Center for Veterinary Medicine (CVM) is responsible for ensuring that all animal drugs, feeds (including pet foods), and veterinary devices are safe for animals, are properly labeled, and produce no human health hazards when used in food-producing animals.

The FDA also cooperates with over 400 state agencies across the nation that carry out a wide range of food safety regulatory activities. However, the state agencies are primarily responsible for actual inspection. FDA works with the states to set the safety standards for food establishments and commodities and evaluates the states' performance in upholding such standards as well as any federal standards that may apply. FDA also con-

---

7. HHS OIG, FDA Inspections of Domestic Food Facilities (OEI-02-08-00080), April 2010.

tracts with states to use their food safety agency personnel to carry out certain field inspections in support of FDA's own statutory responsibilities.

Food Safety and Inspection Service

FSIS regulates the safety, wholesomeness, and proper labeling of most domestic and imported meat and poultry and their products sold for human consumption. Under the Federal Meat Inspection Act of 1906, as amended (21 U.S.C. 601 et seq.), FSIS is required to inspect all cattle, sheep, swine, goats, and equines during slaughtering and processing. Under the Poultry Products Inspection Act of 1957, as amended (21 U.S.C. 451 et seq.), FSIS is required to inspect "any domesticated bird" being processed for human consumption; however, USDA regulations implementing this law limit the definition of domesticated birds to chickens, turkeys, ducks, geese, ratites (emus, ostriches, and rheas), and guineas. FDA has jurisdiction over exotic and alternative meats not inspected by FSIS, and shares the responsibility for egg safety with FSIS. The latter is responsible for the safety of liquid, frozen, and dried egg products, domestic and imported, and for the safe use or disposition of damaged and dirty eggs under the Egg Products Inspection Act, as amended (21 U.S.C. 1031 et seq.).

FSIS staff numbers around 9,400; roughly 8,000 of them, including about 1,000 veterinarians, are in about 6,300 meat slaughtering and/or processing plants nationwide. FSIS personnel inspect all meat and poultry animals at slaughter on a continuous basis, and at least one federal inspector is on the line during all hours the plant is operating. Processing inspection does not require an FSIS inspector to remain constantly on the production line or to inspect every item. Instead, inspectors are on site daily to monitor the plant's adherence to the standards for sanitary conditions, ingredient levels, and packaging, and to conduct statistical sampling and testing of products. Because all plants are visited daily, processing inspection also is considered to be continuous.

FSIS also is responsible for certifying that foreign meat and poultry plants are operating under an inspection system equivalent to the U.S. system before they can export their product to the United States. FSIS inspectors located at U.S. ports of entry carry out a statistical sampling program to verify the safety of imported meats from cattle, sheep, swine, goats, and equines and imported poultry meat from chickens, turkeys, ducks, geese, quail, ratites, and guineas before they are released into domestic commerce. FDA is responsible for ensuring the safety of imported meat from any other species.

Twenty-seven states operate their own meat and/or poultry inspection programs. FSIS is statutorily responsible for ensuring that the states' programs are at least equal to the federal program. Plants processing meat and poultry under state inspection can market their products only within the state. If a state chooses to discontinue its own inspection program, or if FSIS determines that it does not meet the agency's equivalency standards, FSIS must assume the responsibility for inspection if the formerly state-inspected plants are to remain in operation. FSIS also has cooperative agreements with more than two dozen states under which state inspection personnel are authorized to carry out federal inspection in meat and/or poultry plants. Products from these plants may travel in interstate commerce.[8]

Centers for Disease Control and Prevention (HHS)

CDC is responsible for (1) monitoring, identifying, and investigating foodborne disease problems to determine the contributing factors; (2) working with FDA, FSIS, NMFS,

---

8. The 2008 farm bill (P.L. 110-246) contains new provisions intended to enable more interstate shipment of state inspected products; USDA published proposed regulations to implement these provisions in the September 16, 2009, *Federal Register*.

state and local public health departments, universities, and industry to develop control methods; and (3) evaluating the effect of control methods. In 1995, CDC launched "Food-Net," a collaborative project with the FDA and USDA to improve data collection on food-borne illness outbreaks. FoodNet includes active surveillance of clinical microbiology laboratories to obtain a more accurate accounting of positive test results for foodborne illness; a physician survey to determine testing and laboratory practices; population surveys to identify illnesses not reported to doctors; and research studies to obtain new and more precise information about which food items or other exposures may cause diseases. FoodNet data allows CDC to have a clearer picture of the incidence and causes of foodborne illness and to establish baseline data against which to measure the success of changes in food safety programs. The Public Health Service Act provides legislative authority for CDC's food safety-related activities.

National Marine Fisheries Service (DOC)

Although the FDA is the primary agency responsible for ensuring the safety, wholesomeness and proper labeling of domestic and imported seafood products, NMFS conducts, on a fee-for-service basis, a voluntary seafood inspection and grading program that focuses on marketing and quality attributes of U.S. fish and shellfish. The primary legislative authority for NMFS's inspection program is the Agricultural Marketing Act of 1946, as amended (7 U.S.C. 1621 et seq.). NMFS has approximately 160 seafood safety and quality inspectors, and inspection services are funded with user fees.

Environmental Protection Agency

EPA has the statutory responsibility for ensuring that the chemicals used on food crops do not endanger public health. EPA's Office of Pesticide Programs is the part of the agency that (1) registers new pesticides and determines residue levels for regulatory purposes; (2) performs special reviews of pesticides of concern; (3) reviews and evaluates all the health data on pesticides; (4) reviews data on pesticides' effects on the environment and on other species; (5) analyzes the costs and benefits of pesticide use; and (6) interacts with EPA regional offices, state regulatory counterparts, other federal agencies involved in food safety, the public, and others to keep them informed of EPA regulatory actions. The Federal Insecticide, Fungicide, and Rodenticide Act, as amended (7 U.S.C. 136 et seq.), and the Federal Food, Drug, and Cosmetic Act, as amended (21 U.S.C. 301 et seq.), are the primary authorities for EPA's activities in this area.

Other Federal Agencies with Food Safety Responsibilities

Among the other agencies that play a role in food safety, USDA's Agricultural Research Service (ARS) performs food safety research in support of FSIS's inspection program. It has scientists working in animal disease bio-containment laboratories in Plum Island, NY, and Ames, IA. USDA's Animal and Plant Health Inspection Service (APHIS) indirectly protects the nation's food supply through programs to protect plant and animal resources from domestic and foreign pests and diseases, such as brucellosis and bovine spongiform encephalopathy (BSE, or "mad cow" disease). The Department of Homeland Security (DHS) is to coordinate many food security activities, including at U.S. borders.

Congressional Committees

In the Senate, food safety issues are considered by the Committees on Agriculture, Nutrition, and Forestry; Homeland Security and Governmental Affairs; and Health, Education, Labor, and Pensions. In the House, various food safety activities fall under the jurisdiction of the Committees on Agriculture; Energy and Commerce; Oversight and Government Reform; and Science. Agriculture subcommittees of the House and Senate Appropriations Committees also serve oversight and funding roles in how the major agencies carry out food safety policies.

Selected Issues

Food safety-related incidents have tended to heighten congressional scrutiny of the issue and to fuel interest in food safety reform, as a number of developments in recent years have illustrated. Recent incidents have included a major outbreak of Salmonella Typhimurium infections linked to the consumption of products containing peanut ingredients from a single firm, the Peanut Corporation of America. Between September 1, 2008, and mid-March, 2009, the CDC identified nearly 700 cases in 46 states; the infection may have contributed to the deaths of nine people, according to the CDC. A series of expanding recalls has been announced by FDA in early 2009, involving thousands of products from more than 200 companies (though none have been the major peanut butter brands). These developments are unfolding two years after a different nationwide recall of peanut butter, in February 2007, due to Salmonella contamination, when hundreds of illnesses, dating back to August 2006, were linked to the bacterium.

In April–July 2008, more than 1,300 persons in 43 states, the District of Columbia, and Canada were found to be infected with the same unusual strain of bacteria (Salmonella Saintpaul). Officials first suspected fresh tomatoes as the vehicle, but later genetic tests confirmed the pathogen on samples of a serrano pepper and irrigation water from a farm in Mexico. Throughout 2007 and 2008, USDA announced numerous recalls totaling many million pounds of ground beef products due to concerns about E. coli O157:H7 contamination.

Attention also expanded to the safety of food imports in early 2007, when adulterated pet food ingredients imported from China sickened or killed numerous dogs and cats and subsequently were found in some hog, chicken, and fish feed.10 In June 2007, FDA announced that it was detaining imports of certain types of farm-raised seafood from China (specifically, shrimp, catfish, basa, dace, and eel) until their shippers could confirm that they are free of unapproved drug residues. In late 2008, FDA announced that all Chinese dairy products and dairy ingredients were being detained until importers could prove they were free of melamine (the same adulterant found earlier in the pet food ingredients). The toxic chemical was being added to milk in China to boost protein readings; seven infants reportedly were killed and approximately 300,000 sickened there after consuming tainted infant formula.

These types of incidents have been cited repeatedly in a series of congressional and non-congressional hearings, reports, and studies, issued throughout the 110th Congress, as evidence of significant shortcomings in the federal food safety system. In the last Congress, a subcommittee of the House Energy and Commerce Committee alone held eight hearings on food safety problems, and various other Senate and House panels held similarly focused hearings....

Food safety provisions in the 2008 farm bill (P.L. 110-234) include subjecting farmed catfish products to FSIS mandatory inspections similar to those for red meat and poultry; creating an option for state-inspected meat and poultry plants to ship products across state lines; and requiring meat and poultry establishments to notify USDA about potentially adulterated or misbranded products. Congressional appropriators also increased funding for food safety activities for FY2008 and FY2009.

However, a number of more comprehensive food safety proposals were not enacted by the 110th Congress, and similar measures have emerged in the 111th Congress, where major new legislation is possible although by no means certain....

———————

David M. Walker
Federal Oversight of Food Safety: High-Risk Designation Can Bring Needed Attention to Fragmented System

Testimony Before the Subcommittee on Agriculture, Rural Development, FDA, and Related Agencies, Committee on Appropriations, House of Representatives Government Accountability Office, GAO Report No. GAO-07-449T (February 8, 2007)

Fragmented Federal Oversight of Food Safety Led to High-Risk Designation

For several years, we have reported on issues that suggest that food safety could be designated as a high-risk area because of the need to transform the federal oversight framework to reduce risks to public health as well as the economy. Specifically, the patchwork nature of the federal food oversight system calls into question whether the government can plan more strategically to inspect food production processes, identify and react more quickly to outbreaks of contaminated food, and focus on promoting the safety and the integrity of the nation's food supply. This challenge is even more urgent since the terrorist attacks of September 11, 2001, heightened awareness of agriculture's vulnerabilities to terrorism, such as the deliberate contamination of food or the introduction of disease to livestock, poultry, and crops.

An accidental or deliberate contamination of food or the introduction of disease to livestock, poultry, and crops could undermine consumer confidence in the government's ability to ensure the safety of the U.S. food supply and have severe economic consequences. Agriculture, as the largest industry and employer in the United States, generates more than $1 trillion in economic activity annually, or about 13 percent of the gross domestic product. The value of U.S. agricultural exports exceeded $68 billion in fiscal year 2006. An introduction of a highly infectious foreign animal disease, such as avian influenza or foot-and-mouth disease, would cause severe economic disruption, including substantial losses from halted exports. Similarly, food contamination, such as the recent E. coli outbreaks, can harm local economies. For example, industry representatives estimate losses from the recent California spinach E. coli outbreak to range from $37 million to $74 million.

While 15 agencies collectively administer at least 30 laws related to food safety, the two primary agencies are the U.S. Department of Agriculture (USDA), which is responsible for the safety of meat, poultry, and processed egg products, and the Food and Drug Administration (FDA), which is responsible for virtually all other foods. Among other agencies with responsibilities related to food safety, the National Marine Fisheries Service (NMFS) in the Department of Commerce conducts voluntary, fee-for-service inspections of seafood safety and quality; the Environmental Protection Agency (EPA) regulates the use of pesticides and maximum allowable residue levels on food commodities and animal feed; and the Department of Homeland Security (DHS) is responsible for coordinating agencies' food security activities. The food safety system is further complicated by the subtle differences in food products that dictate which agency regulates a product as well as the frequency with which inspections occur. For example, how a packaged ham and cheese sandwich is regulated depends on how the sandwich is presented. USDA inspects manufacturers of packaged open-face meat or poultry sandwiches (e.g., those with one slice of bread), but FDA inspects manufacturers of packaged closed-face meat or poultry sandwiches (e.g., those with two slices of bread). Although there are no differences in the risks posed by these products, USDA inspects wholesale manufacturers of open-face sandwiches sold in interstate commerce daily, while FDA inspects manufacturers of closed-face sandwiches an average of once every 5 years.

This federal regulatory system for food safety, like many other federal programs and policies, evolved piecemeal, typically in response to particular health threats or economic crises. During the past 30 years, we have detailed problems with the current fragmented federal food safety system and reported that the system has caused inconsistent oversight, ineffective coordination, and inefficient use of resources. Our most recent work demonstrates that these challenges persist. Specifically:

- Existing statutes give agencies different regulatory and enforcement authorities. For example, food products under FDA's jurisdiction may be marketed without the agency's prior approval. On the other hand, food products under USDA's jurisdiction must generally be inspected and approved as meeting federal standards before being sold to the public. Under current law, thousands of USDA inspectors maintain continuous inspection at slaughter facilities and examine all slaughtered meat and poultry carcasses. They also visit each processing facility at least once during each operating day. For foods under FDA's jurisdiction, however, federal law does not mandate the frequency of inspections.

- Federal agencies are spending resources on overlapping food safety activities. USDA and FDA both inspect shipments of imported food at 18 U.S. ports of entry. However, these two agencies do not share inspection resources at these ports. For example, USDA officials told us that all USDA-import inspectors are assigned to, and located at,USDA-approved import inspection facilities and some of these facilities handle and store FDA-regulated products. USDA has no jurisdiction over these FDA-regulated products. Although USDA maintains a daily presence at these facilities, the FDA-regulated products may remain at the facilities for some time awaiting FDA inspection. In fiscal year 2003, USDA spent almost $16 million on imported food inspections, and FDA spent more than $115 million.

- Food recalls are voluntary, and federal agencies responsible for food safety have no authority to compel companies to carry out recalls—with the exception of FDA's authority to require a recall for infant formula. USDA and FDA provide guidance to companies for carrying out voluntary recalls. We reported that USDA and FDA can do a better job in carrying out their food recall programs so they can quickly remove potentially unsafe food from the marketplace. These agencies do not know how promptly and completely companies are carrying out recalls, do not promptly verify that recalls have reached all segments of the distribution chain, and use procedures that may not be effective to alert consumers to a recall.

- The terrorist attacks of September 11, 2001, have heightened concerns about agriculture's vulnerability to terrorism. The Homeland Security Act of 2002 assigned DHS the lead coordination responsibility for protecting the nation against terrorist attacks, including agroterrorism. Subsequent presidential directives further define agencies' specific roles in protecting agriculture and the food system against terrorist attacks. We reported that in carrying out these new responsibilities, agencies have taken steps to better manage the risks of agroterrorism, including developing national plans and adopting standard protocols. However, we also found several management problems that can reduce the effectiveness of the agencies' routine efforts to protect against agroterrorism. For example, there are weaknesses in the flow of critical information among key stakeholders and shortcomings in DHS's coordination of federal working groups and research efforts.

- More than 80 percent of the seafood that Americans consume is imported. We reported in 2001 that FDA's seafood inspection program did not sufficiently protect consumers. For example, FDA tested about 1 percent of imported seafood products. We subsequently found that FDA's program has improved: More foreign firms are inspected, and inspections show that more U.S. seafood importers are complying with its requirements. Given FDA officials' concerns about limited inspection resources, we also identified options, such as using personnel in the National Oceanic and Atmospheric Administration's (NOAA) Seafood Inspection Program to augment FDA's inspection capacity or state regulatory laboratories for analyzing imported seafood. FDA agreed with these options....

––––––––––

Although there have been many calls for restructuring, with the goal of creating one agency responsible for food safety, political pressures, industry lobbying, and vested interests in the existing agencies and associated congressional committees make that result unlikely. Acknowledging the problems associated with the fragmented system of food safety regulation, President Obama created a "Food Safety Working Group" chaired by USDA Secretary Vilsack and HHS Secretary Sebellius. This group was charged with advising the President on how to upgrade the U.S. food safety system and coordinating work of the USDA and FDA. The group recommended a public health-focused approach to food safety based on three core principles: prioritizing prevention; strengthening inspection and enforcement; and improving response and recovery. In a July 2010 press release, the working group issued the following list of accomplishments:

Prioritizing Prevention

- Salmonella in poultry and eggs: USDA issued revised draft standards for the presence of Salmonella to reduce consumers' exposure to this pathogen in raw poultry products. HHS issued a rule to control Salmonella contamination of eggs during production, storage, and transportation, and by July 9, 2010, approximately 82 percent of shell eggs will be covered under the new requirements.

- Produce safety: On July 31, 2009, HHS issued commodity-specific draft guidance documents to industry on agricultural practices to reduce the risk of microbial contamination in the production and distribution of tomatoes, melons and leafy greens and is developing a proposed produce safety rule.

- E. coli O157:H7 in beef products: USDA began a new verification testing program for beef bench trim and issued draft guidelines on methods for controlling E. coli O157:H7 on the farm, before cattle come to slaughter.

- Laboratory diagnosis of E. coli: In October 2009, HHS published new guidance for clinical laboratories to improve diagnosis and surveillance for Shiga toxin-producing E. coli infections.

- Campylobacter: USDA proposed the first ever standards for Campylobacter in poultry.

- Measuring progress on food safety: Knowing what food safety interventions are working helps in designing future preventive efforts. HHS and USDA are collaborating to address the methodological and data challenges involved in the development of feasible and effective food safety metrics, with a joint meeting scheduled for July 21 in Chicago.

Strengthening Inspection and Enforcement

- Reportable Food Registry: HHS launched the Reportable Food Registry (RFR), an electronic portal for industry and public health officials to report when there is reasonable probability that a food item will cause serious adverse health consequences.

- Environmental assessments: USDA and HHS are developing a training program for environmental health specialists on how to properly conduct an environmental assessment during a foodborne outbreak investigation, leading to quicker and more definitive results.

- Data analysis: USDA is preparing to launch a dramatically improved surveillance and data collection and analysis system in the fall. The Public Health Information System (PHIS) will help USDA/FSIS respond more rapidly to current and potential threats in the food safety system, which is crucial to preventing contamination, recalls and, ultimately, foodborne illnesses.

Improving Response and Recovery

- Improving disease surveillance: HHS launched a new web-based surveillance platform to enhance the speed and completeness of foodborne outbreak reports, and developed an online database to make the data more easily accessible by the public. HHS and USDA published the first joint executive report on antimicrobial resistance among pathogens from food animals, retail meats and human clinical cases based on this data up to 2007; this was the first time all the data was available in one report.

- Product tracing systems: HHS and USDA held a public meeting on steps the food industry can take to establish product tracing systems and are seeking public comment. HHS/FDA completed a pilot study on tracing with the tomato industry and is planning several other pilot studies to assess the feasibility of different tracing systems and technology/commodity combinations.

- Collaborative investigation or identification of outbreaks: Since July 2009, HHS has coordinated or led more than 15 major multistate outbreak food-related investigations. These investigations have identified new food vehicles, including peppered Italian-style deli meat, and a new foodborne pathogen (Shiga-toxin producing E. coli O145), and have led to major product recalls. All involved close collaboration among federal agencies.

- New efforts to strengthen investigation and response: USDA and HHS have begun piloting the use of dedicated local or state interview teams to increase the completeness of routine case interviews and have announced funding of expanded programs in sentinel sites for FY2010, leading to best practices for rapid outbreak investigation and response in a variety of local settings. In July 2009, the Council to Improve Foodborne Outbreak Response (CIFOR) published the Guidelines for Foodborne Outbreak Disease Response, which was endorsed by the Secretaries of HHS and USDA, and distributed to all county and state health and food safety agencies.

- Supporting State and Local Health Agencies: HHS supported eight domestic training courses on epidemiological and laboratory methods related to food safety, and trained 20 state public health laboratories in the new molecular Salmonella serotyping method, which will make laboratory surveillance to detect outbreaks faster and more complete.

- Rapid response to contamination incidents: Federal agencies are responding more aggressively to reports of contamination in an effort to remove potentially contaminated product from the market before it can cause illness. HHS and USDA formed an "Improving Foodborne Outbreak Investigations" working group to determine and implement best practices, including training, early detection, communications and response. In addition, USDA/FSIS and HHS/FDA have established Chief Medical Officer (CMO) positions, with each CMO leading and overseeing all phases of foodborne outbreak investigations including planning, training, early detection, improved communication, response and incorporating lessons learned into prevention based efforts within our programs.

- New consumer communication technologies: HHS and USDA rolled out an enhanced and updated www.foodsafety.gov site in September 2009. As part of that release, a new food safety widget was created to provide customers rapid access to information on food recalls. HHS and USDA also collaborated on a new mobile application for smartphones that provides consumers with easy access to recent food recalls and alerts.

- Incident Command System: Federal agencies implemented a new incident command system that links all relevant agencies to address outbreaks of foodborne illness. This approach facilitates communication and decision-making in an emergency, including with state and local governments.

———————

No amount of agency coordination or cooperation, however, changes the bifurcated system of regulating most meat products according to one system and all other food products according to another. The following report introduces the system of regulating meat and poultry products.

Geoffrey S. Becker
Meat and Poultry Inspection: Background and Selected Issues
Congressional Research Service, Report No. RL32922 (March 22, 2010)

Statutory Authorities

Federal Meat Inspection Act of 1906

This law as amended (21 U.S.C. 601 *et seq.*) has long required USDA to inspect all cattle, sheep, swine, goats, horses, mules, and other equines brought into any plant to be slaughtered and processed into products for human consumption. Since passage of the FY2006 USDA appropriation (P.L. 109-97, Section 798), these types of animals are now called "amenable species." P.L. 109-97 also gave the Secretary of Agriculture the discretion to add additional species to the list. As noted, the 2008 farm bill makes catfish an amenable species.

Poultry Products Inspection Act of 1957

This law as amended (21 U.S.C. 451 *et seq.*) makes poultry inspection mandatory for any domesticated birds intended for use as human food. The current list of included species is chickens, turkeys, ducks, geese, guineas, ratites (ostrich, emu, and rhea), and squabs (pigeons up to one month old).

Agricultural Marketing Act of 1946

Under this law as amended (7 U.S.C. 1621), FSIS also provides voluntary inspection for buffalo, antelope, reindeer, elk, migratory waterfowl, game birds, and rabbits, which the industry can request on a fee-for-service basis. These meat and poultry species (which are not specifically covered by the mandatory inspection statutes) are still within the purview of FDA under the Federal Food, Drug, and Cosmetic Act (FFDCA, 21 U.S.C. 301 et seq.), whether or not inspected under the voluntary FSIS program. FDA has jurisdiction over meat products from such species in interstate commerce, even if they bear the USDA inspection mark.

Egg Products Inspection Act

This law as amended (21 U.S.C. 1031 *et seq.*) is the authority under which FSIS assures the safety of liquid, frozen, and dried egg products, domestic and imported, and the safe disposition of damaged and dirty eggs. FDA holds regulatory authority over shell eggs in restaurants and stores.

System Basics

Coverage

FSIS's legal inspection responsibilities begin when animals arrive at slaughterhouses, and they generally end once products leave processing plants. Certain custom slaughter and most retail store and restaurant activities are exempt from federal inspection; however, they may be under state inspection.

Plant Sanitation

No meat or poultry establishment can slaughter or process products for human consumption until FSIS approves in advance its plans and specifications for the premises, equipment, and operating procedures. Once this approval is granted and operations begin, the plant must continue to follow a detailed set of rules that cover such things as proper lighting, ventilation, and water supply; cleanliness of equipment and structural features; and employee sanitation procedures.

USDA Meat Grading

USDA meat and poultry grading is distinct and separate from the FSIS safety inspection program. Upon request, firms may request that inspectors from a separate USDA agency, the Agricultural Marketing Service (AMS), grade their products for quality attributes, but only after it has been cleared by FSIS for safety and wholesomeness. Unlike safety inspection, which is mandatory and largely covered by appropriated funds, grading services are voluntary and funded by industry user fees. Nationally uniform quality grades are used to convey, to buyers and sellers, such traits as tenderness, flavor, and juiciness, and so forth. For example, AMS now grades beef carcasses as prime, choice, select, standard and commercial, utility, cutter, and canner; these grades are not usually visible on individual retail cuts but can appear on the packages. Grades are also available for veal, lamb, and poultry. Legislative authority for quality (and yield) grades comes through the Agricultural Marketing Act (7 U.S.C. 1621).

HACCP

Plants are required to have a Hazard Analysis and Critical Control Point (HACCP) plan for their slaughter and/or processing operations. Essentially, a plant must identify each point in the process where contamination could occur, called a "critical control point," have a plan to control it, and document and maintain records. Under HACCP regulations, all operations must have site-specific standard operating procedures (SOPs) for sanitation. USDA inspectors check records to verify a plant's compliance.

Slaughter Inspection

FSIS inspects all meat and poultry animals to look for signs of disease, contamination, and other abnormal conditions, both before and after slaughter ("antemortem" and "postmortem," respectively), on a continuous basis—meaning that no animal may be slaughtered and dressed unless an inspector has examined it. One or more federal inspectors are on the line during all hours the plant is operating.

Processing Inspection

The inspection statutes appear to be silent on how frequently USDA inspector must visit facilities that produce processed products like hot dogs, lunch meat, prepared dinners, and soups. Under current policies, processing plants visited once every day by an FSIS inspector are considered to be under continuous inspection in keeping with the laws. Inspectors monitor operations, check sanitary conditions, examine ingredient levels and packaging, review records, verify HACCP processes, and conduct statistical sampling and testing of products during their on-site visits.

Pathogen Testing

The HACCP rule also mandates two types of microbial testing: for generic E. coli and for Salmonella. Levels of these two organisms are indicators of conditions that either suppress or encourage the spread of such potentially dangerous bacteria as Campylobacter and E. coli O157:H7, as well as Salmonella itself. Test results (plants test for E. coli and FSIS for Salmonella) help FSIS inspectors verify that plant sanitation procedures are working, and to identify and assist plants whose process controls may be underperforming.

Enforcement

FSIS has a range of enforcement tools to prevent adulterated or mislabeled meat and poultry from reaching consumers. On a day-to-day basis, if plant conditions or procedures are found to be unsanitary, an FSIS inspector can, by refusing to perform inspection, temporarily halt the plant's operation until the problem is corrected. FSIS can condemn contaminated, adulterated, and misbranded products, or parts of them, and detain them so they cannot progress down the marketing chain. FSIS does not have mandatory recall authority; if potentially dangerous or mislabeled products do enter commerce, the agency relies on establishments to voluntarily recall them.

Other tools include warning letters for minor violations; requests that companies voluntarily recall a potentially unsafe product; a court-ordered product seizure if such a request is denied; and referral to federal attorneys for criminal prosecution. Prosecutions under certain conditions may lead to the withdrawal of federal inspection from offending firms or individuals, which results in plant closure.

Funding

Federal appropriations pay for most, but not all, mandatory inspection. For FY2010, FSIS received an annual appropriation of approximately $1 billion. In addition, FSIS uses revenue from fees paid by the meat and poultry industries for FSIS inspection that occurs beyond regularly scheduled shifts and on holidays, and by private laboratories that apply for FSIS certification to perform official meat testing and sampling. In FY2010, revenue from the fees is expected to add approximately $150 million in additional program support.

Staffing

FSIS carries out its duties with about 9,400 total staff (full-time equivalent). Approximately 7,800 of FSIS's employees, roughly 1,000 of them veterinarians, are in approximately 6,200 establishments and import inspection facilities nationwide.

State Inspection

Twenty-seven states have their own meat and/or poultry inspection programs covering nearly 1,900 small or very small establishments. The states run the programs cooperatively with FSIS, which provides up to 50% of the funds for operating them, comprising about $65 million of the total FSIS budget annually. A state program operating under a cooperative agreement with FSIS must demonstrate that its system is equivalent to federal inspection. However, state-inspected meat and poultry products are limited to intrastate commerce only. In states that have discontinued their inspection systems for meat or poultry (or both), FSIS has assumed responsibility for inspection at the formerly state-inspected plants. However, actual inspection is performed by state personnel.[2]

Approximately 360 meat and poultry establishments in nine states are covered by a separate federal-state program, the so-called Talmadge-Aiken plants. Under this program, USDA has signed cooperative agreements with states whereby state employees are used to conduct federal inspections, and passed products carry the federal mark of inspection. Established by the Talmadge-Aiken Act of 1962 (7 U.S.C. 450), the arrangement was intended to achieve federal coverage in remote locations to offset the higher cost of assigning federal inspectors there.

Import Inspection

FSIS conducts evaluations of foreign meat safety programs and visits establishments to determine that they are providing a level of safety equivalent to that of U.S. safeguards. No foreign plant can ship meat or poultry to the United States unless its country has received such an FSIS determination. Once they reach U.S. ports of entry, meat and poultry import shipments must first clear Department of Homeland Security (DHS) inspection to assure that only shipments from countries free of certain animal and human disease hazards are allowed entry. This function was transferred to DHS from USDA's Animal and Plant Health Inspection Service (APHIS) when DHS was established by the Homeland Security Act of 2002 (P.L. 107-296). After DHS inspection, imported meat and poultry shipments go to one of approximately 150 nearby FSIS inspection facilities for final clearance into interstate commerce.[3]

Microbiological Contamination and HACCP

The U.S. Centers for Disease Control and Prevention (CDC) observed in April 2009:

---

3. As of December 2009, meat or poultry products from 33 countries were eligible for import. An August 2008 audit report by USDA's Office of Inspector General made a number of recommendations for improving oversight of imports, including on the methodology for selecting foreign establishments for review and on production reinspections at the border. Followup Review of Food and Safety Inspection Service's Controls Over Imported Meat and Poultry Products, at http://www.usda.gov/oig/webdocs/24601-08-Hy.pdf. See also CRS Report RL34198, U.S. Food and Agricultural Imports: Safeguards and Selected Issues, by Geoffrey S. Becker.

Despite numerous activities aimed at preventing foodborne human infections, including the initiation of new control measures after the identification of new vehicles of transmission (e.g., peanut butter-containing products), progress toward the national health objectives has plateaued, suggesting that fundamental problems with bacterial and parasitic contamination are not being resolved. Although significant declines in the incidence of certain pathogens have occurred since establishment of FoodNet, these all occurred before 2004. Of the four pathogens with current Healthy People 2010 targets, Salmonella, with an incidence rate of 16.2 cases per 100,000 in 2008, is farthest from its target for 2010 (6.8). The lack of recent progress toward the national health objective targets and the occurrence of large multistate outbreaks point to gaps in the current food safety system and the need to continue to develop and evaluate food safety practices as food moves from the farm to the table.[4]

Not all of these infections are from consumption of meat and poultry products. A more recent CDC article reported that, among 243 foodborne disease outbreaks attributed to a single commodity in 2006, the most outbreaks were attributed to fish (47), poultry (35), and beef (25). However, the most cases were attributed to poultry (1,355), leafy vegetables (1,081) and fruits/nuts (1,021). Pairing pathogens with commodities, the CDC found that the most outbreak related cases were Clostridium perfringens in poultry (902 cases), Salmonella in fruits nuts (776), norovirus in leafy vegetables (657), shiga-toxin E. coli in leafy vegetables (398), Salmonella in vine-stalk vegetables (331), and V. parahaemolyticus in mollusks (223).[5] Nonetheless, large recent recalls of meat and poultry products, often due to microbiological contamination, have brought closer attention to USDA's and industry's record in detecting harmful pathogens and preventing them from reaching consumers and making them sick. Although government officials had asserted that the number of both recalls and illnesses had declined over the long term, illness data from the past several years appear to indicate that this overall decline has not continued.

Development of HACCP

In the early 1990s, following years of debate over how to respond to mounting evidence that invisible, microbiological contamination on meat and poultry posed greater public health risks than visible defects (the focus of traditional inspection methods), FSIS began to add testing for pathogenic bacteria on various species and products to its inspection system. In 1995, under existing statutes, FSIS published a proposed rule to systematize these changes in a mandatory program called the Hazard Analysis and Critical Control Point (HACCP) system. In this system, firms must analyze risks in each phase of production, identifying and then monitoring "critical control points" for preventing such hazards, and taking corrective actions when necessary. Recordkeeping and verification ensure that the system is working. FSIS published the final rule on July 25, 1996, and since January 2000 all slaughter and processing operations are required to have HACCP plans in place. HACCP is intended to operate as an adjunct to the traditional methods of inspection, which still are mandatory under the original statutes.[7]

---

4. "Preliminary FoodNet Data on the Incidence of Infection with Pathogens Transmitted Commonly Through Food—10 States, 2008," *Morbidity and Mortality Weekly Report*, April 10, 2009.

5. "Surveillance for Foodborne Disease Outbreaks—United States, 2006," *Morbidity and Mortality Weekly Report*, June 12, 2009. A case is a single person; and outbreak is two or more cases.

7. The final rule appeared in 61 Federal Register 38805–38855.

Pathogen Performance Standards and *Salmonella*

The CDC has noted that poultry is an important source of human *Salmonella* infections. The pathogen also periodically has been found in beef, as well as non-animal foods such as fresh produce. According to CDC reports, the overall incidence of *Salmonella* infections through all types of food has not decreased significantly.[8] CDC also has reported that *Salmonella* has been the most common foodborne pathogen, although exposure to live animals also has been an important nonfood source.

In the initial years of HACCP implementation, plants that failed three consecutive *Salmonella* tests could have their USDA inspectors withdrawn. This would effectively shut down the plant until the problem could be remedied. However, a federal court ruled in 2000 that the meat and poultry inspection statutes do not give USDA the authority to use failure to meet *Salmonella* standards as the basis for withdrawing inspection. An appeals court upheld this decision in 2001. Subsequently, USDA has adopted the position that the court decision did not affect the agency's ability to use the standards as part of the verification of plants' sanitation and HACCP plans.

Nonetheless, the appeals court ruling supports arguments of those who say that pathogen testing results should not be a basis for enforcement actions until scientists can determine what constitutes an unsafe level of *Salmonella* in ground meat and a number of other meat and poultry products. Consumer groups and other supporters of mandatory testing and microbiological standards, as well as of increased enforcement powers, have used the case to bolster their argument for amending the meat and poultry inspection statutes to expressly require microbiological standards. [*See Supreme Beef Processors v. USDA*, 275 F.3d 432 (5th Cir. 2001), *infra.*]

FSIS had reported its concern about increases in *Salmonella* rates observed over a three-year period (2003–2005) among the three poultry product categories, broiler carcasses, ground chicken, and ground turkey. To address the problem, in early 2006 the agency launched an initiative to reduce the pathogen in raw meat and poultry products, including the concentration of more inspection resources at establishments with higher levels, and quarterly rather than annual reporting of *Salmonella* test results. Sampling frequency was to be based on a combination of factors such as a plant's regulatory history and its incidence of the pathogen.[9]

FSIS on January 28, 2008 issued a notice on new policies and procedures for *Salmonella* sampling and testing.[10] One change was to begin posting on its website sampling test results from establishments, with their names and locations—beginning with young chicken slaughter establishments—that have substandard or variable records in meeting *Salmonella* performance standards. The agency stated that it was taking this unprecedented action in part because at least 90% of such establishments were not testing consistently for low *Salmonella* rates. The FSIS performance standard for *Salmonella* in young chickens is 20% (i.e., 12 positive samples out of 51 taken). Tested plants are placed in one of three categories, as follows:

> **Category 1** establishments have results from their two most recent completed sample sets that are at or below half of the standard (i.e., at or below 10%);

---

8. CDC, "Preliminary FoodNet Data on the Incidence of Infection with Pathogens Transmitted Commonly Through Food— 10 States, 2006," Morbidity and Mortality Weekly Report, April 13, 2007; "…— 10 States, 2007," Morbidity and Mortality Weekly Report, April 11, 2008; and "…— 10 States, 2008," Morbidity and Mortality Weekly Report, April 10, 2009.

9. *Food Chemical News*, July 3, 2006. A notice and request for comments on this initiative were published in the February 27, 2006, *Federal Register*.

10. 73 *Federal Register* pp. 4767–4774.

Category 2 establishments have results from their most recent completed sample set that are higher than half of the standard but do not exceed the standard (i.e., above 10% but below 20%);

Category 3 establishments have results from their most recent completed sample set that exceed the standard (i.e., above 20%).

Twenty-one category 2 or category 3 plants, out of 195 tested, were named in the first report, accessed in April 2008. The December (fourth quarter) 2009 report showed 12 establishments in category 2 and four in category 3.[11]

The CDC in 2009 credited the industry's response to the FSIS Salmonella initiative with a decrease in the percent-positive rate for Salmonella in raw broiler chicken, from 11.4% in 2006 to 7.3% in 2008.[12] The rate was 8.6% in the fourth quarter of 2009....

Concerns regarding *Salmonella* contamination are not limited to poultry, as illustrated by recalls of 825,769 pounds of ground beef products in August 2009 and another 22,723 pounds of ground beef products in December 2009, both by a California establishment, Beef Packers Inc. The recalls were associated with investigations of *Salmonella* illness outbreaks, according to FSIS.[14] Media reports in late 2009 on these recalls by the company, a supplier of beef to the federal school lunch program, and on pathogens found in ground beef produced by another school lunch supplier, Beef Products Inc., raised questions about the safety of these USDA-purchased commodities ...

(FSIS's quarterly Salmonella reports also list performance standards and testing results for, in addition to broilers and turkeys, market hogs, steers and heifers, cows and bulls, and ground products—chicken, turkey and beef.)

In another recent incident, Danielle International of Rhode Island had, through February 2010, recalled approximately 30 Italian-style meat products totaling nearly 1.4 million pounds after reports of a multistate outbreak of *Salmonella* Montevideo infections in 252 persons in 44 states and the District of Columbia.[15] Samples of black pepper used on the products tested positive for *Salmonella*, indicating that outside ingredients can be a source of concern. FDA, which oversees pepper and other spices, has been coordinating with FSIS regarding the recall.

E. coli O157:H7

Illness outbreaks continue to be linked to the pathogen *E. coli* O157:H7 in beef products. This has led to calls from critics for improvements in testing for *E. coli* and for minimizing its presence. Some consumer groups have argued that more tests should be mandated; meat industry representatives counter that while an effective sampling and testing program is important to help determine whether a plant's pathogen control measures are working, testing itself cannot assure safety.

---

11. The testing results are posted monthly. A description of the testing and the most recent results can be accessed at http://www.fsis.usda.gov/science/Salmonella_Verification_Testing_Program/index.asp. Another description of, and more critical look at, the Salmonella testing program is in More Foul Fowl: An Updated Analysis of Salmonella Contamination in Broiler Chickens, March 2008, by the advocacy group Food and Water Watch. It was accessed in July 2008 at http://www.foodandwater watch.org/food/pubs/reports/more-foul-fowl.

12. *Morbidity and Mortality Weekly Report*, April 10, 2009.

14. FSIS, "Constituent Update," December 31, 2009.

15. U.S. Centers for Disease Control (CDC) and Prevention, "Investigation Update: Multistate Outbreak of Human Salmonella Montevideo Infections," update for March 17, 2010.

CDC noted that "*E. coli* O157:H7 is one of hundreds of strains of the bacterium Escherichia coli. Although most strains are considered harmless and live in the intestines of healthy humans and animals, this strain produces a powerful toxin and can cause severe illness. *E. coli* O157:H7 was first recognized as a cause of illness in 1982 during an outbreak of severe bloody diarrhea; the outbreak was traced to contaminated hamburgers. Since then, most infections have come from eating undercooked ground beef." CDC also noted that "people have also become ill from eating contaminated bean sprouts or fresh leafy vegetables such as lettuce and spinach. Person-to-person contact in families and child care centers is also a known mode of transmission. In addition, infection can occur after drinking raw milk and after swimming in or drinking sewage contaminated water."[16]

The CDC foodborne illness reports for 2006 and 2007 indicated that the incidence of all foodborne infections caused by *E. coli* O157:H7 had declined significantly from the 1996–1998 baseline through 2004, but not since then. The CDC reported that it did not know why reductions had not been maintained, but it did point out that the 2006 outbreaks caused by contaminated spinach and lettuce highlighted the need for more effective prevention. The earlier CDC report (on 2006) stated that the frequency of *E. coli* O157:H7 in ground beef samples taken in 2005 and 2006 had remained about the same as in 2004.[17]

The CDC report on 2007 concluded that "additional efforts are needed" to control the pathogen in cattle "and to prevent its spread to other food animals and food products, such as produce."[18] The CDC reported an increase in the percentage of ground beef samples yielding O157:H7 — from 0.24% in 2007 to 0.47% in 2008 — but said it was unknown whether this was related to focused sampling of higher-risk facilities, improved laboratory detection, or an actually higher microbial load.[19]

During calendar 2006, FSIS announced eight recalls due to *E. coli* O157:H7 contamination, mostly of ground beef products, and none were related to human illness.[20] In 2005, the agency announced five recalls. In 2007 FSIS announced 20 recalls, totaling more than 33 million pounds, mostly ground beef products, due to *E. coli* concerns. At least nine of the 2007 recalls were related to human illnesses (the rest came about after routine testing). Although many of the recalls were relatively small, a June recall involved nearly 6 million pounds of beef, and the Topps recall 21.7 million pounds … [21]

In 2008, 17 *E. coli*-related recalls were listed on the FSIS website. The largest was by Nebraska Beef, of Omaha, of approximately 5.3 million pounds of beef manufacturing trimmings and other products intended for use in raw ground beef produced between May 16 and June 26. Nebraska Beef was involved in another large recall, of 1.36 million pounds of primal cuts, subprimal cuts, and boxed beef, produced on June 24 and on July 8, 2008. Dozens of illnesses were linked to products in the two Nebraska Beef recalls. Nebraska-processed products sold under the Coleman Natural Beef brand were also recalled by the Whole Foods Market chain.[24]

---

16. Background information on this pathogen may be viewed at the following CDC website: http://www.cdc.gov/nczved/dfbmd/disease_listing/stec_gi.html.

17. *Morbidity and Mortality Weekly Report*, April 13, 2007.

18. *Morbidity and Mortality Weekly Report*, April 11, 2008.

19. *Morbidity and Mortality Weekly Report*, April 10, 2009.

20. Source: FSIS press releases on recalls posted at http://www.fsis.usda.gov/Fsis_Recalls/index.asp.

21. Recall updates are at the FSIS website, http://www.fsis.usda.gov/Fsis_Recalls/index.asp. Also, CRS has tallied recalls, by product type and reason, for 1994 through 2009; see the appendix in CRS Report RL34313, *The USDA's Authority to Recall Meat and Poultry Products*, by Cynthia Brougher and Geoffrey S. Becker.

24. "Nebraska Beef *E. coli* recall gets a sequel," *Food Chemical News*, August 18, 2008.

For 2009, a total of 15 *E. coli*-related recalls were announced by FSIS, four of which were linked to an illness outbreak investigation. The others generally were the result of routine testing. Two large recalls late in the year included 545,699 pounds of fresh ground beef products from a New York State establishment in October, following an investigation of 26 *E. coli*-related illnesses among 26 persons from eight states;[25] and 248,000 pounds of primarily whole beef cuts from an Oklahoma establishment in December, linked to 21 illnesses in 16 states.[26]

FSIS had begun testing samples of raw ground beef for *E. coli* O157:H7 in October 1994, declaring that any such product found with this pathogen would be considered adulterated—the first time a foodborne pathogen on raw product was declared an adulterant under the meat inspection law. Industry groups immediately asked a Texas federal court for a preliminary injunction to halt this effort, on the grounds that it was not promulgated through appropriate rulemaking procedures, was arbitrary and capricious, and exceeded USDA's regulatory authority under law. In December 1994, the court denied the groups' request, and no appeal was filed, leaving the program in place. FSIS has taken tens of thousands of samples since the program began; to date, hundreds of samples have tested positive.

In September 2002, FSIS issued a press release stating that "[t]he scientific data show that *E. coli* O157:H7 is more prevalent than previously estimated," and in October 2002 the agency published a notice requiring manufacturers of all raw beef products (not just ground beef) to reassess their HACCP plans and add control points for *E. coli* O157:H7 if the reassessment showed that the pathogen was a likely hazard in the facility's operations. FSIS inspectors are to verify that corrective steps have been taken and conduct random testing of all beef processing plants, including all grinders (some previously had been exempted). In addition, the agency announced guidelines for grinding plants advising them to increase the level of pathogen testing by plant employees, and to avoid mixing products from different suppliers.[27]

By June 2007, after FSIS had identified an increased number of positive *E. coli* O157:H7 beef samples, along with a larger number of recalls and illnesses linked to the pathogen than in recent years, it increased the number of tests on ground beef by more than 75%, the agency stated. It also began or accelerated implementation of several other *E. coli* prevention initiatives that had been under development. Among the actions it cited in October 2007 were the testing (starting in March 2007) of beef trim, which is used in ground beef; requiring beef plants to verify that they are effectively controlling *E. coli* O157:H7 during slaughter and processing; directing its inspectors to use a new checklist to review establishment control procedures; beginning testing other types of materials used in ground beef in addition to beef trim and requiring importing countries to conduct equivalent sampling; better targeting its routine *E. coli* testing; and working to speed up recalls.[28]

---

25. CDC, "Multistate Outbreak of *E. coli* O157:H7 Infections Associated with Beef from Fairbank Farms Final Update," November 24, 2009; at http://www.cdc.gov/ecoli/2009/.

26. The December recall was of products that had been mechanically tenderized. Consumer advocates argue that this process can transfer surface pathogens into the center of the meat, which, if not cooked thoroughly, can sicken those who eat it. FSIS also stated in its December 24, 2009, recall announcement "that there is an association between nonintact steaks (blade tenderized prior to further processing) and illnesses" in a number of states. *See also* "E. coli-Tainted Beef Infects 21 in 16 States," *Washington Post*, December 30, 2009.

27. 67 *Federal Register* 62325.

28. USDA, FSIS. "FSIS Takes Aggressive Actions To Combat *E. coli* O157:H7," October 23, 2007, at http://www.fsis.usda.gov/News_&_Events/NR_102307_01/index.asp. FSIS has published an August 2008 report on its findings in *Results of Checklist and Reassessment of Control for Escherichia coli O157:H7 in Beef Operations*, at http://www.fsis.usda.gov/PDF/Ecoli_Reassement_&_Checklist.pdf.

Additional FSIS *E. coli* initiatives were announced as one of the items on the FSWG list of actions on July 7, 2009. The working group stated that FSIS is increasing its sampling, focusing on the components that go into ground beef, and also improving its instructions to field staff on how to verify beef establishment controls over the pathogen. These beef components are typically are referred to as "bench trim" and are the trimmings from larger cuts of primal and sub-primal cuts of beef. A notice on sampling bench trim and a directive on *E. coli* verification activities were issued on July 31, 2009.[29] Meanwhile, FSIS reportedly was considering whether to define all cuts of beef as adulterated if they test positive for *E. coli* O157:H7, something a number of groups requested after a recent recall of 421,000 pounds of such "muscle cuts."[30]

The agency also is planning or contemplating a number of other efforts aimed at addressing *E. coli* O157:H7, including directing its enforcement investigators to gather more information within 48 hours of a presumed positive test for the pathogen (to improve ability to trace contaminated products back to their source); proposing rules requiring products to be held until testing results are completed; requiring labels on whole meat cuts that have been mechanically tenderized; and possibly instituting new record-keeping requirements aimed at enhancing traceback capabilities.[31]

FSIS reported that, of an average of nearly 10,000 ground beef samples tested annually in 2004, 2005, and 2006, a total of 43 (less than 0.2%) tested positive for *E. coli* O157:H7, part of a significant decline in the percentage of positive samples since 2000, when it was 0.86%. FSIS asserted that the reduction reflected the success of its HACCP-based and related regulatory policies. However, increases were recorded in 2007, when 29 or 0.24% of 12,200 ground beef samples tested positive, and in 2008, when 54 or 0.47% of 11,535 were positive. FSIS and other food safety experts were speculating as to whether the increase was due to a higher prevalence of the bacteria, or simply to the fact that the agency had changed its testing method in 2008. It is possible, for example, that the newer method is more sensitive to the presence of *E. coli*.[32] In 2009, through December 27, a total of 41 or 0.32% out of 12,685 ground beef samples tested positive. In 2009 testing of ground beef components, FSIS reported that 30 or 0.86% out of 3,496 samples tested positive.

Listeria monocytogenes

In February 2001, FSIS published a proposed rule to set performance standards that meat and poultry processing firms would have to meet to reduce the presence of *Listeria monocytogenes* (*Lm*), a pathogen in ready-to-eat foods (e.g., cold cuts and hot dogs). The proposal covered over 100 different types of dried, salt-cured, fermented, and cooked or processed meat and poultry products. Lm causes an estimated 2,500 illnesses and 499 deaths each year (from listeriosis), and has been a major reason for meat and poultry product recalls.

---

29. FSIS Notice 51-09 and FSIS Directive 10,010.1, Revision 2, respectively.

30. Source, "USDA Mulls E. coli As Adulterant on Cuts," Cattle Buyers Weekly, August 24, 2009.

31. The agency's "current thinking" on *E. coli* O157:H7 actions was discussed at a public meeting in Washington, D.C., on March 10, 2010. See for example: "FSIS surprises attendees with details on new E. coli policies," Food Chemical News, March 15, 2010; and "USDA to mandate test and hold, non-intact meat labels," Meatingplace.com, March 19, 2010.

32. "Explanation to higher number of E. coli positives may be in broth," Food Chemical News, October 20, 2008. A March 12, 2009, FSIS Notice (18-09) announced that the agency was "increasing sampling at high volume ground beef establishments because these establishments produce product that is most widely consumed. The increase in sampling will allow the Agency to estimate the amount of uncontaminated raw ground beef with a higher degree of certainty." A new sampling notice (44-09) dated June 1, 2009, modifies and clarifies some of the provisions in the March notice it replaced.

The proposed rule raised controversy among affected constituencies. The meat industry argued that the benefits to consumers would not outweigh the cost to packers of additional testing. Representatives of food manufacturers criticized the proposed regulations for covering some categories of foods too broadly and heavily, while not covering some other high-risk foods at all (such as milk, which is under FDA jurisdiction). Consumer groups said the proposed rule would not require enough testing in small processing plants and that products not tested for *Lm* should not be labeled "ready-to-eat" because they would still require cooking to be 100% safe.

Interest in the *Listeria* issue had grown in 1998 and 1999, following reports of foodborne illnesses and deaths linked to ready-to-eat meats produced by a Sara Lee subsidiary.[33] Interest increased significantly after October 2002, when Pilgrim's Pride Corporation recalled a recordbreaking 27.5 million pounds of poultry lunch meats for possible *Lm* contamination after a July 2002 outbreak of listeriosis in New England. CDC confirmed 46 cases of the disease, with seven deaths and three stillbirths or miscarriages. The recall covered products made as early as May 2002, and officials stated that very little of the meat was still available to be recovered.

In December 2002, FSIS issued a directive to inspection program personnel giving new and specific instructions for monitoring processing plants that produce hot dogs and deli meats.[34] In June 2003, FSIS announced the publication of an interim final rule to reduce *Listeria* in ready-to-eat meats. Rather than set performance standards, as the February 2001 proposed rule would have, the new regulation requires plants that process RTE foods to add control measures specific to Listeria to their HACCP and sanitation plans, and to verify their effectiveness by testing and disclosing the results to FSIS. The rule directs FSIS inspectors to conduct random tests to verify establishments' programs. Plants are subject to different degrees of FSIS verification testing depending upon what type of control steps they adopt in their HACCP and sanitation plans.[35]

On January 4, 2005, the Consumer Federation of America (CFA) issued a report sharply criticizing USDA's *Listeria* rulemaking. CFA asserted that the Department essentially adopted meat industry positions in weakening the final rule, such as by deleting proposed plant testing requirements and by not explicitly requiring that HACCP plans include *Listeria* controls. In 2003, *Listeria* illnesses increased by 22%, CFA contended, citing CDC data.[36]

USDA and meat industry officials countered that the number of product recalls related to Listeria had declined from 40 in 2002 to 14 in 2003, that the rise in Listeriosis cases was quite small in 2003 after four years of declines, and that the interim rule provides more incentives for plants to improve safety. The CDC's 2006 and 2007 FoodNet reports indicated that the incidence of foodborne illness caused by Listeria, which had reached its lowest level in 2002 compared with a 1996–1998 baseline, has not continued to decline significantly in more recent years.[37]

Recalls of FSIS-regulated products continue. In 2005, the largest was a December 2005 recall of 2.8 million pounds of various bologna, ham, and turkey lunchmeat products by ConAgra. Another 28 Listeria-related recalls were announced during 2005, involving approximately 649,000 pounds of processed meat and poultry products, according to the

33. Source: *Food Chemical News*, various issues.
34. The guidelines can be found on the FSIS website at http://www.fsis.usda.gov.
35. See the FSIS website for more details on the rule.
36. CFA website: http://www.consumerfed.org/.
37. *Morbidity and Mortality Weekly Report*, April 13, 2007, and April 11, 2008.

agency's website. The website had posted six *Listeria* recalls in 2006 and another 11 in 2007, including, in January and February 2007, 2.8 million pounds of Oscar Mayer/Louis Rich chicken breast cuts and strips.[38] Fifteen *Listeria*-related recalls were posted in 2008, and eight in 2009....

----

2. Limited Authority

Supreme Beef Processors, Inc. v. U.S. Dept. of Agriculture
275 F.3d 432 (5th Cir. 2001)

Certain meat inspection regulations promulgated by the Secretary of Agriculture, which deal with the levels of *Salmonella* in raw meat product, were challenged as beyond the statutory authority granted to the Secretary by the Federal Meat Inspection Act. The district court struck down the regulations. We hold that the regulations fall outside of the statutory grant of rulemaking authority and affirm.

I

The Federal Meat Inspection Act authorizes the Secretary of Agriculture to "prescribe the rules and regulations of sanitation" covering

> slaughtering, meat canning, salting, packing, rendering, or similar establishments in which cattle, sheep, swine, goats, horses, mules and other equines are slaughtered and the meat and meat food products thereof are prepared for commerce....[1]

Further, the Secretary is commanded to,

> where the sanitary conditions of any such establishment are such that the meat or meat food products are rendered adulterated, ... refuse to allow said meat or meat food products to be labeled, marked, stamped, or tagged as "inspected and passed."[2]

In sum, the FMIA instructs the Secretary to ensure that no adulterated meat products pass USDA inspection, which they must in order to be legally sold to consumers.[3]

The FMIA contains several definitions of "adulterated," including 21 U.S.C. §601(m)(4), which classifies a meat product as adulterated if "it has been prepared, packed, or held under insanitary conditions whereby it may have become contaminated with filth, or whereby it may have been rendered injurious to health."[4] Thus, the FMIA gives the Secretary the power to create sanitation regulations and commands him to withhold meat approval where the meat is processed under insanitary conditions. The Secretary has delegated the authority under the FMIA to the Food Safety and Inspection Service.

In 1996, FSIS, after informal notice and comment rulemaking, adopted regulations requiring all meat and poultry establishments to adopt preventative controls to assure

----

38. FSIS recall website: http://www.fsis.usda.gov/FSIS_Recalls/index.asp.

1. 21 U.S.C. §608.

2. *Id.*

3. The FMIA requires that adulterated meat products be stamped "inspected and condemned" and destroyed. 21 U.S.C. §606.

4. *Id.* §601(m)(4).

product safety. These are known as Pathogen Reduction, Hazard Analysis and Critical Control Point Systems or "HACCP."[5] HACCP requires, *inter alia,* that meat and poultry establishments institute a hazard control plan for reducing and controlling harmful bacteria on raw meat and poultry products. In order to enforce HACCP, FSIS performs tests for the presence of *Salmonella* in a plant's finished meat products.

The *Salmonella* performance standards set out a regime under which inspection services will be denied to an establishment if it fails to meet the standard on three consecutive series of tests.[6] The regulations declare that the third failure of the performance standard "constitutes failure to maintain sanitary conditions and failure to maintain an adequate HACCP plan ... for that product, and will cause FSIS to suspend inspection services."[7] The performance standard, or "passing mark," is determined based on FSIS's "calculation of the national prevalence of *Salmonella* on the indicated raw product."[8]

In June, 1998, plaintiff-appellee Supreme Beef Processors, Inc., a meat processor and grinder, implemented an HACCP pathogen control plan, and on November 2, 1998, FSIS began its evaluation of that plan by testing Supreme's finished product for *Salmonella.* After four weeks of testing, FSIS notified Supreme that it would likely fail the *Salmonella* tests. Pursuant to the final test results, which found 47 percent of the samples taken from Supreme contaminated with *Salmonella,*[9] FSIS issued a Noncompliance Report, advising Supreme that it had not met the performance standard. Included in the report was FSIS's warning to Supreme to take "immediate action to meet the performance standards." Supreme responded to FSIS's directive on March 5, 1999, summarizing the measures it had taken to meet the performance standard and requesting that the second round of testing be postponed until mid-April to afford the company sufficient time to evaluate its laboratory data. FSIS agreed to the request and began its second round of tests on April 12, 1999.

On June 2, 1999, FSIS again informed Supreme that it would likely fail the *Salmonella* tests and, on July 20, issued another Noncompliance Report—this time informing Supreme that 20.8 percent of its samples had tested positive for *Salmonella.* Supreme appealed the Noncompliance Report, citing differences between the results obtained by FSIS and Supreme's own tests conducted on "companion parallel samples." Those private tests, Supreme asserted, had produced only a 7.5 percent *Salmonella* infection level, satisfying the performance standard. FSIS denied the appeal; but based on Supreme's commitment to install 180 degree water source on all boning and trimming lines, granted the company's request to postpone the next round of *Salmonella* testing for 60 days. FSIS later withdrew the extension, however, after learning that Supreme was merely considering installation of the water source.

The third set of tests began on August 27, 1999, and after only five weeks, FSIS advised Supreme that it would again fall short of the ground beef performance standard. On October 19, 1999, FSIS issued a Notice of Intended Enforcement Action, which notified Supreme of the agency's intention to suspend inspection activities. The Notice gave Supreme Beef until October 25, 1999 to demonstrate that its HACCP pathogen controls were adequate or to show that it had achieved regulatory compliance. Although Supreme Beef promised to achieve the 7.5 percent performance standard in 180 days, it failed to

5. 9 C.F.R. Pt. 417.

6. *Id.* § 310.25(b).

7. *Id.* § 310.25(b)(3)(iii).

8. *Id.* § 310.25(b)(2) tbl. 2 n.a.

9. The performance standard for raw ground beef is 7.5 percent. *Id.*

provide any specific information explaining how it would accomplish that goal, and FSIS decided to suspend inspection of Supreme's plant.

On the day FSIS planned to withdraw its inspectors, Supreme brought this suit against FSIS's parent agency, the USDA, alleging that in creating the *Salmonella* tests, FSIS had overstepped the authority given to it by the FMIA. Along with its complaint, Supreme moved to temporarily restrain the USDA from withdrawing its inspectors. The district court granted Supreme's motion and, after a subsequent hearing, also granted Supreme's motion for a preliminary injunction.

The National Meat Association filed a motion to intervene as a plaintiff in the district court. The district court denied the motion on the grounds that NMA was adequately represented by Supreme in this litigation. The district court allowed NMA and other industry groups, as well as various consumer advocacy groups, to file briefs.

On cross-motions for summary judgment, the district court granted summary judgment in favor of Supreme, finding that the *Salmonella* performance standard exceeded the USDA's statutory authority and entering a permanent injunction against enforcement of that standard against Supreme. The USDA now appeals....

A

Following *Chevron*, we first repair to the text of the statute that the USDA relies upon for its authority to impose the *Salmonella* performance standard. The USDA directs us to 21 U.S.C. §601(m)(4), which provides that a meat product is adulterated

> if it has been prepared, packed or held under insanitary conditions whereby it may have become contaminated with filth, or whereby it may have been rendered injurious to health.

This statutory definition is broader than that provided in 21 U.S.C. §601(m)(1), which provides that a meat product is adulterated

> if it bears or contains any poisonous or deleterious substance which may render it injurious to health; but in case the substance is not an added substance, such article shall not be considered adulterated under this clause if the quantity of such substance in or on such article does not ordinarily render it injurious to health.

Thus if a meat product is "prepared, packed or held under insanitary conditions" such that it *may* be adulterated for purposes of §601(m)(1), then it is, by definition, adulterated for purposes of §601(m)(4). The USDA is then commanded to refuse to stamp the meat products "inspected and passed."[20]

The difficulty in this case arises, in part, because *Salmonella*, present in a substantial proportion of meat and poultry products, is not an adulterant *per se*,[21] meaning its presence does not require the USDA to refuse to stamp such meat "inspected and passed."[22] This is because normal cooking practices for meat and poultry destroy the *Salmonella* organism,[23] and therefore the presence of *Salmonella* in meat products does not render them

---

20. 21 U.S.C. §608.

21. *See American Pub. Health Ass'n v. Butz*, 511 F.2d 331, 334 (D.C.Cir.1974) ("[T]he presence of salmonellae on meat does not constitute adulteration within this definition [of 'adulterated,' provided in 21 U.S.C. §601(m)]."). The USDA agrees in this case that Salmonella is not an adulterant per se, meaning it is not a §601(m)(1) adulterant. Appellant's Brief at 11.

22. 21 U.S.C. §608.

23. *Butz*, 511 F.2d at 334 ("American housewives and cooks normally are not ignorant or stupid and their methods of preparing and cooking of food do not ordinarily result in salmonellosis.").

"injurious to health"[24] for purposes of § 601(m)(1). *Salmonella*-infected beef is thus routinely labeled "inspected and passed" by USDA inspectors and is legal to sell to the consumer.

Supreme maintains that since *Salmonella*-infected meat is not adulterated under § 601(m)(1), the presence or absence of *Salmonella* in a plant cannot, by definition, be "insanitary conditions" such that the product "may have been rendered injurious to health," as required by § 601(m)(4). The USDA, however, argues that *Salmonella*'s status as a non-adulterant is not relevant to its power to regulate *Salmonella* levels in end product. This is because the USDA believes that *Salmonella* levels can be a proxy for the presence or absence of means of pathogen[25] controls that are required for sanitary conditions under § 601(m)(4). However, as we discuss, and as the USDA admits, the *Salmonella* performance standard, whether or not it acts as a proxy, regulates more than just the presence of pathogen controls.

The district court agreed with Supreme and reasoned that "[b]ecause the USDA's performance standards and *Salmonella* tests do not necessarily evaluate the *conditions* of a meat processor's establishment, they cannot serve as the basis for finding a plant's meat adulterated under § 601(m)(4)."[26] The district court therefore held that the examination of a plant's end product is distinct from "conditions" within the plant for purposes of § 601(m)(4) because *Salmonella* may have come in with the raw material.

We must decide two issues in order to determine whether the *Salmonella* performance standard is authorized rulemaking under the FMIA: a) whether the statute allows the USDA to regulate characteristics of raw materials that are "prepared, packed or held" at the plant, such as *Salmonella* infection; and b) whether § 601(m)(4)'s "insanitary conditions" such that product "may have been rendered injurious to health" includes the presence of *Salmonella*-infected beef in a plant or the increased likelihood of cross-contamination with *Salmonella* that results from grinding such infected beef. Since we are persuaded that the *Salmonella* performance standard improperly regulates the *Salmonella* levels of incoming meat and that *Salmonella* cross-contamination cannot be an insanitary condition such that product may be rendered "injurious to health," we conclude that the *Salmonella* performance standard falls outside of the ambit of § 601(m)(4).

B

1

In order for a product to be adulterated under § 601(m)(4), as the USDA relies on it here,[27] it must be "prepared, packed or held under insanitary conditions ... whereby it may have been *rendered* injurious to health."[28] The use of the word "rendered" in the statute

---

24. *Cf. Continental Seafoods, Inc. v. Schweiker,* 674 F.2d 38, 41 (D.C.Cir.1982) (stating that *Salmonella* is a *per se* adulterant in shrimp).

25. The USDA uses the term "pathogen" to refer to both § 601(m)(1) adulterants, such as pathogenic *E.coli*, and non-adulterants, such as *Salmonella*. Thus, under the proxy theory, *Salmonella* control correlates with adulterant-pathogen control.

26. *Supreme Beef Processors, Inc. v. USDA,* 113 F.Supp.2d 1048, 1052–53 (N.D.Tex.2000) (emphasis in original).

27. The USDA does not contend that failure of the *Salmonella* performance standard serves as a proxy for contamination with filth, the other prong dealt with by § 601(m)(4). Even if the USDA made such an assertion, § 601(m)(4) speaks of insanitary conditions such that a product "becomes" contaminated with filth, which has a similar textual meaning as "rendered."

28. 21 U.S.C. § 601(m)(4) (emphasis added).

indicates that a deleterious change in the product must occur while it is being "prepared, packed or held" owing to insanitary conditions. Thus, a characteristic of the raw materials that exists before the product is "prepared, packed or held"[29] in the grinder's establishment cannot be regulated by the USDA under § 601(m)(4).[30] The USDA's interpretation ignores the plain language of the statute, which includes the word "rendered." Were we to adopt this interpretation, we would be ignoring the Court's repeated admonition that, when interpreting a statute, we are to "give effect, if possible, to every clause and word of a statute."[31]

The USDA claims, however, that the *Salmonella* performance standard serves as a proxy for the presence or absence of pathogen controls, such that a high level of *Salmonella* indicates § 601(m)(4) adulteration.[32] Supreme oversimplifies its argument by claiming, essentially, that the USDA can never use testing of final product for a non-adulterant, such as *Salmonella,* as a proxy for conditions within a plant.

We find a similar, but distinct, defect in the *Salmonella* performance standard. The USDA admits that the *Salmonella* performance standard provides evidence of: (1) whether or not the grinder has adequate pathogen controls; and (2) whether or not the grinder uses raw materials that are disproportionately infected with *Salmonella.* Supreme has, at all points in this litigation, argued that it failed the performance standard not because of any condition of its facility, but because it purchased beef "trimmings" that had higher levels of *Salmonella* than other cuts of meat. The USDA has not disputed this argument, and has merely argued that this explanation does not exonerate Supreme, because the *Salmonella* levels of incoming meat are fairly regulated under § 601(m)(4).[33] Our textual analysis of § 601(m)(4) shows that it cannot be used to regulate characteristics of the raw

---

29. This case does not require us to define precisely when a product begins the process of being "prepared, packed or held." We recognize only that this process cannot begin until the raw materials are brought to the plant. Thus, the condition of the raw materials may not be regulated by § 601(m)(4).

30. However, measures that would alter such a characteristic, such as heating fish to destroy the bacteria that causes botulism, are within the scope of § 601(m)(4). *See* Part III.B.2.

31. *Duncan v. Walker,* 533 U.S. 167, 121 S.Ct. 2120, 2125, 150 L.Ed.2d 251 (2001) (quoting *United States v. Menasche,* 348 U.S. 528, 538–39, 75 S.Ct. 513, 99 L.Ed. 615 (1955)).

32. We note that the USDA's assertions on this point are suspect. It is clear that the motivation behind the *Salmonella* performance standard was the regulation of *Salmonella* itself, and the FSIS has admitted as much in the Final Rule, though this admission is absent from the USDA's briefs in this case. *See* Pathogen Reduction; Hazard Analysis and Critical Control Point (HACCP) Systems; Final Rule, 61 Fed.Reg. 38806, 38850 ("Because testing for *E. coli* cannot serve as a surrogate for the presence of *Salmonella,* FSIS's *specific public health objective of reducing nationwide* Salmonella *levels on raw meat and poultry products, including raw ground products,* requires a standard and testing regime that are directed at *that* pathogen." (emphasis added)). The difficulty with this, of course, is that the USDA has no statutory authority to regulate the levels of non-adulterant pathogens.

While we do not question the agency's expertise, we also note that several equivocal statements about the effectiveness of *Salmonella* levels as a proxy for pathogen controls appear in the Final Rule. *See Id.* at 38835 ("And, interventions targeted at reducing *Salmonella may be beneficial* in reducing contamination by other enteric pathogens." (emphasis added)); *Id.* at 38846 ("[I]ntervention strategies aimed at reducing fecal contamination and other sources of *Salmonella* on raw product *should be* effective against other pathogens.").

33. The USDA repeatedly asserts that it has the power to regulate the *Salmonella* levels of incoming raw materials used in grinding establishments. *See, e.g.,* Appellant's Reply Brief at 12 ("To operate in a sanitary manner, a plant must match the level of its pathogen controls to the nature of the meat it purchases. The greater the risk of contamination in the incoming product, the greater the need for strategies to reduce microbial contamination."); 61 Fed.Reg. at 38846 ("Establishments producing raw ground product from raw meat or poultry supplied by other establishments cannot use technologies for reducing pathogens that are designed for use on the surfaces of whole carcasses at the time of slaughter. *Such establishments may require more control over incoming raw product, including*

materials that exist before the meat product is "prepared, packed or held." Thus, the regulation fails, but not because it measures *Salmonella* levels and *Salmonella* is a non-adulterant. The performance standard is invalid because it regulates the procurement of raw materials.

2

Our determination here is not in tension with the Second Circuit's decision interpreting identical language under the Food, Drug, and Cosmetic Act in *United States v. Nova Scotia Food Products Corp.*[34] In *Nova Scotia* the defendant challenged an FDA regulation requiring the heating of smoked fish to combat the toxin formation of *Clostridium botulinum* spores, which cause botulism. The defendant argued that "the prohibition against 'insanitary conditions' embraces conditions only in the plant itself, but does not include conditions which merely inhibit the growth of organisms already in the food when it enters the plant in its raw state."[35] The court gave "insanitary conditions" a broad reading and upheld the regulation.[36] Nevertheless, it conceded that "a plausible argument can, indeed, be made that the references are to insanitary conditions in the plant itself, such as the presence of rodents or insects...."[37]

While this may appear to conflict with our determination that pre-existing characteristics of raw materials before they are "prepared, packed or held" are not within the regulatory reach of §601(m)(4), the regulations at issue in *Nova Scotia* did not attempt to control the levels of *Clostridium botulinum* spores in incoming fish, as the performance standard does to *Salmonella* in incoming raw meat. Instead, the regulations in *Nova Scotia* required the use of certain heating and salination procedures to inhibit growth of the spores.[38]

Nova Scotia did not consider the argument before us today, which is that the statute does not authorize regulation of the levels of bacterial infection in incoming raw materials. The argument that *Nova Scotia* entertained was that "Congress did not mean to go so far as to require sterilization sufficient to kill bacteria that may be in the food itself rather than bacteria which accreted in the factory through the use of insanitary equipment."[39] The required sterilization under the regulations at issue in *Nova Scotia* obviously occurred within the plant and did not regulate the quality of incoming fish.

---

contractual specifications to ensure that they begin their process with product that meets the standard....") (emphasis added).

34. 568 F.2d 240 (2d Cir.1977).

35. *Id.* at 245.

36. *Id.* at 246 ("When agency rulemaking serves the purposes of the statute, courts should refuse to adopt a narrow construction of the enabling legislation which would undercut the agency's authority to promulgate such rules.").

37. *Id.* at 245

38. *Id.* at 243 (describing time-temperature-salinity regulations for hot-process smoked fish). This is consistent with the entirety of cases dealing with this statute, none of which concern "conditions" extrinsic to the place where the products are "prepared, packed or held." *See, e.g., United States v. Gel Spice Co., Inc.*, 773 F.2d 427, 430 (2d Cir.1985) (rodent infestation in plant); *United States v. King's Trading, Inc.*, 724 F.2d 631, 632 (8th Cir.1983) (rodent infestation in warehouse); *United States v. 1,638 Cases of Adulterated Alcoholic Beverages and Other Articles of Food*, 624 F.2d 900, 901–02 (9th Cir.1980) (flooding in storage area); *United States v. Certified Grocers Co-op.*, 546 F.2d 1308, 1310–11 (7th Cir.1976) (rodent infestation in warehouse). Even the USDA does not argue that §601(m)(4) reaches "conditions" external to the establishment, but rather that control of pathogen levels in incoming raw materials are necessary to maintain sanitary conditions *inside* of the establishment. *See* Appellant's Brief at 38–39.

39. *Id.* at 246.

3

The USDA and its amicus supporters argue that there is no real distinction between contamination that arrives in raw materials and contamination that arises from other conditions of the plant. This is because *Salmonella* can be transferred from infected meat to non-infected meat through the grinding process. The *Salmonella* performance standard, however, does not purport to measure the differential between incoming and outgoing meat products in terms of the *Salmonella* infection rate. Rather, it measures final meat product for *Salmonella* infection. Thus, the performance standard, of itself, cannot serve as a proxy for cross-contamination because there is no determination of the incoming *Salmonella* baseline.

Moreover, the USDA has not asserted that there is any correlation between the *presence* of *Salmonella* and the *presence* of §601(m)(1) adulterant pathogens. The rationale offered by the USDA for the *Salmonella* performance standard—that "intervention strategies aimed at reducing fecal contamination and other sources of *Salmonella* on raw product should be effective against other pathogens"[40]—does not imply that the presence of *Salmonella* indicates the presence of these other, presumably §601(m)(1) adulterant, pathogens.[41] Cross-contamination of *Salmonella* alone cannot form the basis of a determination that a plant's products are §601(m)(4) adulterated, because *Salmonella* itself does not render a product "injurious to health" for purposes of both §§601(m)(1) and 601(m)(4).

Not once does the USDA assert that *Salmonella* infection indicates infection with §601(m)(1) adulterant pathogens.[42] Instead, the USDA argues that the *Salmonella* infection rate of meat product correlates with the use of pathogen control mechanisms and the quality of the incoming raw materials. The former is within the reach of §601(m)(4), the latter is not.

IV

Because we find that the *Salmonella* performance standard conflicts with the plain language of 21 U.S.C. §601(m)(4), we need not reach Supreme's numerous alternative arguments for invalidating the standard, which were not addressed by the district court.

V

We AFFIRM and REMAND with instructions that the final judgment of the district court be amended to include the National Meat Association.

———————

Notes

1. Michael Pollan alleges that many food safety problems, in particular, E. coli 0157:H7, can be traced back to industrialized production. The microbe E. coli 0157:H7 has been

———————

40. 61 Fed.Reg. at 38846.

41. One might speculate that such a conclusion would create problems for the USDA, because a statement that *Salmonella* was a proxy for, for example, pathogenic *E. coli* could arguably require the determination that the presence of *Salmonella* rendered a product §601(m)(1) adulterated. This would prevent *Salmonella*-infected meat from being sold in the United States to consumers.

42. The *amicus curiae* consumer groups in their brief appear not to recognize the distinction between a correlation between *Salmonella* and other enteric pathogens in raw materials and a correlation between reductions in *Salmonella* and reductions in other enteric pathogens when the same control methods are used. *See* Brief of Amicus Curiae Consumer Groups at 10–11.

associated with cows that are fed rich diets of corn as opposed to their more natural grass diet, and when foods are combined into a centralized system, contamination is spread from one source to literally thousands of products. *See,* Michael Pollan, *The Vegetable-Industrial Complex* NEW YORK TIMES MAGAZINE (Oct. 15, 2006). He criticizes the industry and regulators for seeking new technologies to "fix" the food safety problem, rather than dealing with its root cause.

2. The use of antibiotics for growth promotion and preventative care (as opposed to the treatment of infection) in animal production has also raised public health and safety concerns. The Pew Commission reported:

> The use of antibiotics for growth promotion began with the poultry industry in the 1940s when it discovered that the use of tetracycline-fermentation byproducts resulted in improved growth (Stokstad, 1954; Stokstad and Jukes, 1958–1959). Since then, the practice of adding low levels of antibiotics and growth hormones to stimulate growth and improve production and performance parameters has been common among IFAP [Industrialized Farm Animal Production] operations for all species. Because any use of antibiotics results in resistance, this widespread use of low-level antibiotics in animals, along with use in treating humans, contributes to the growing pool of antimicrobial resistance in the environment.
>
> The threat from antimicrobial resistance became more apparent in the 1990s as the number of cases of drug resistant infections increased in humans. A World Health Organization (WHO) Report on Infectious Diseases published in 2000 expressed alarm at the spread of multi-drug—resistant infectious disease agents, and pointed to food as a major source of antimicrobial-resistant bacteria. Since the discovery of the growth-promoting and disease fighting capabilities of antibiotics, farmers, fish-farmers, and livestock producers have used antimicrobials. This ongoing and often low-level dosing for disease prevention and growth inevitably results in the development of resistance in bacteria in or near livestock because a selective pressure that does not kill fosters resistance (WHO, 2000).
>
> While it is difficult to measure what percent of resistant infections in humans are caused by antimicrobial use in agriculture as opposed to other settings, it can be assumed that the wider the use of antimicrobials, the greater the chance for the development of resistance. Reports on the amount of antibiotics used in animals range from 17.8 to 24.6 million pounds per year. The Union of Concerned Scientists estimates that 70% of the antibiotics used in the United States annually are used in farm animals (Mellon et al., 2001).

Putting Meat on the Table: Industrial Farm Animal Production, Pew Commission on Industrial Farm Animal Production in America, 5 (A Project of The Pew Charitable Trusts and Johns Hopkins Bloomberg School of Public Health) (2008), available at http://www.ncIFAP.org/ (citing environmental problems, public health problems, and the social and economic decline of rural areas as all unanticipated costs associated with large scale industrialized animal production).

The use of antibiotics is regulated by the FDA under the Food, Drug, & Cosmetic Act, 21 U.S.C. §321 *et seq.* On June 28, 2010, the FDA issued its new *Draft Guidance on the Judicious Use of Medically Important Antimicrobials in Food-Producing Animals.* The draft summarizes recent scientific reports on the development of antimicrobial resistance and recommends phasing in measures that would limit the use of medically important antibiotics in animal production. *See* 75 Fed. Reg. 37,450 (June 29, 2010). Congress has considered legislation restricting the nontherapeutic use of antibiotics in animal production. *See, e.g.*, *Preservation of Antibiotics for Medical Treatment Act of 2009*, S. 619, 111h Cong. (1st Sess., 2009) (amending the Federal Food, Drug, and Cosmetic Act to "preserve the effectiveness of medically important antibiotics").

3. The Marler Clark law firm, a firm recognized for its successful representation of victims of food borne illness, established an extensive online daily newspaper dedicated to reporting on issues involving food safety. It provides accurate, up-to-date reporting on a wide variety of food law issues and is an excellent resource. It is available at http://foodsafetynews.com.

In addition to representing clients in most of the major food borne illness outbreaks since the Jack-in-the-Box cases in 1993, Marler Clark founder, Bill Marler, has been a determined advocate for food safety reform. One area of concern relates to the additional deadly strains of E. coli that are not currently considered adulterants and for which the USDA does not test. Current regulations only recognize the E. coli 0157:H7 strain. Marler advocates for the regulation of the additional strains and petitioned the USDA. The USDA has granted an expedited review of Marler's petition. Lynne Terry, *Failure to Test for Six Strains of E. coli Leaves Gap in Nation's Food Safety Network*, OREGONIAN (May 3, 2010) (noting possible Congressional action in addition to Marler's petition). Updates on this issue can be found on Marler's blog at marlerblog.com.

4. The Public Broadcasting Service documentary, *Modern Meat,* part of the PBS *Frontline* series, presents information about the safety regulation of meat, highlighting problems associated with salmonella and E. coli contamination of hamburger. It is available online at http://www.pbs.org/wgbh/pages/frontline/shows/meat/. The documentary *Food Inc.*, also presents food safety issues, focusing on the death of a child from an E. Coli infection and the subsequent efforts of his family to strengthen the USDA's authority to close down plants and order recall of contaminated products. *See* http://www.foodincmovie.com.

5. In response to several deadly outbreaks of contaminated fresh produce, FDA has been working on a proposed rule for the safe production, harvesting and packing of fresh produce. As the regulation of produce at the farm level is a new area of focus, FDA states that it as been working "more closely than ever with the U.S. Department of Agriculture and its agencies, the Environmental Protection Agency, state departments of agriculture, advocacy groups, and growers." There have been "listening sessions" and comments requested, with a comment deadline of July 23, 2010 indicated. Updated information can be found on the FDA Produce Safety Activities page: http://www.fda.gov/Food/FoodSafety/Product-SpecificInformation/FruitsVegetablesJuices/FDAProduceSafetyActivities/default.htm.

B. The Regulation of Organic Food

1. Introduction

The Organic agriculture emerged in the1920s, first in England (via the work of Sir Robert McCarrison, Sir Albert Howard, and Richard St. Barbe Baker) and Germany (via Rudolf Steiner). Organic agriculture did not cross the ocean until years later, when a student of Steiner, Ehrenfried Pfieffer, moved to the U.S. in 1938. J.I. Rodale, along with others, facilitated further growth in the U.S. organic industry. In both regions, organic agriculture has made great strides since these early pioneers began farming organically.

Carolyn Dimitri and Lydia Oberholtzer, *Market-Led Versus Government-Facilitated Growth: Development of the U.S. and EU Organic Agricultural Sectors*, Economic Research Service, Report No. WRS-05-05 (August 2005).

Michael Pollan discussed the origins of organic agriculture in his book, THE OMNIVORE'S DILEMMA, 145 (2006).

> Perhaps more than any other single writer, Sir Albert Howard (1873–1947), an English agronomist knighted after his thirty years of research in India, provided the philosophical foundations for organic agriculture. Even those who never read his 1940 [AN AGRICULTURAL] TESTAMENT nevertheless absorbed his thinking through the pages of Rodale's ORGANIC GARDENING AND FARMING, where he was lionized, and in the essays of Wendell Berry, who wrote an influential piece about Howard in the THE LAST WHOLE EARTH CATALOG in 1971. Berry seized particularly on Howard's arresting—and prescient—idea that we needed to treat "the whole problem of health in soil, plant, animal and man as one great subject.

In a thoughtful essay, *The Road Also Taken: Lessons from Organic Agriculture for Market- and Risk-based Regulation* by Donald T. Hornstein, three different views of organic agriculture were presented.

> Organic agriculture can be understood on three levels, each one of which can be helpful to policy and legal analyses. At its broadest level, organic agriculture reflects a set of ethical positions—toward the environment, toward socioeconomic justice, and toward animal welfare—as well as a set of agricultural methods. The International Federation of Organic Agriculture Movements speaks of four overarching principles of organic agriculture—of health, ecology, fairness, and care—and stresses their applicability "to agriculture in the broadest sense, including the way people tend soils, water, plants and animals" and to the way people "relate to one another and shape the legacy of future generations." It is not hard to catch in such meta-principles the philosophical, as well as technical, aspects of the "other road" that Rachel Carson propounded. And, while still describing organic agriculture at this broadest level, it bears mention that organic agriculture also has social and organizational dimensionality; there are hundreds of regional and local organic industry trade groups, each often having slightly varying standards. Moreover, at the international level, in addition to the standards set by the private International Federation of Organic Agriculture Movements, there are also standards for organic food products set by the Codex Alimentarius Commission, an entity operating under the United Nations Food and Agriculture Organization and the World Health Organization. Thus, broadly speaking, organic agriculture has all the earmarks of a self-generating, self-policing private organization centered on core norms that might simultaneously deliver both private goods and public beneficial externalities.

> At a second, narrower level, organic agriculture can be understood as one of several "alternative" agricultural systems. All of these systems share the goal of reducing, if not eliminating, reliance on such chemical or artificial agricultural inputs as conventional pesticides and fertilizers. There are roughly four alternative methods most often suggested as substitutes. First, there are cultural methods of disease, weed, and pest control, such as crop rotations and staggered planting dates. Second, there are biological control methods, such as the release of "beneficial" predatory or parasitic insects that can attack pests. Third, there

are "biorational" pest control measures such as pheromone-baited traps. And fourth—although not an option embraced by organic agriculturalists—there is "integrated pest management," (IPM) a "decisionmaking system designed to use all 'suitable' pest control techniques, including chemical pesticides, to keep pest populations below economically injurious levels while satisfying environmental and production objectives." The National Academy of Sciences spoke of alternative agriculture generally when it concluded in 1989 that "[w]ider adoption of proven alternative systems would result in even greater economic benefits to farmers and environmental gains for the nation."

Finally, there is the legal regime governing organic agriculture developed under the Organic Foods Production Act. In the late 1980s, against the backdrop of legislation in over twenty states regulating organic food labeling in different ways, the organic food industry petitioned Congress for legislation that would create a set of national standards for organic products. The OFPA, from the point of view of regulatory design and administrative law, was strikingly innovative. At the same time that alternatives to traditional command-and-control regulation such as risk-based decisionmaking and market-like incentives were drawing so much attention, the OFPA created a system that could tie public environmental and ethical values into existing, real markets; that informed the development of governmental organic standards with input from a National Organic Standards Board composed of nongovernmental representatives from different facets of the organic industry; and that centered regulatory compliance on a system of approved private-sector certification rather than a large federal bureaucracy.

The OFPA is a marketing-oriented statute designed to regularize what was at the time a potentially confusing Babel of competing standards with an official federal "organic" label. Not only was a federal label thought useful in promoting consumer confidence in the growing organic industry within the United States, but it was also viewed as helpful in facilitating trade in "a potentially lucrative international organic market." For this reason, the OFPA's primary administrative delegation to develop the National Organic Program was to the USDA's Agricultural Marketing Service (AMS)....

Donald T. Hornstein, *The Road Also Taken: Lessons from Organic Agriculture for Market- and Risk-based Regulation*, 56 Duke L.J. 1541, 1547–50 (2007) (citations omitted).

Catherine Greene, Carolyn Dimitri, Biing-Hwan Lin, William McBride, Lydia Oberholtzer, and Travis Smith
Emerging Issues in the U.S. Organic Industry
Economic Research Service, Economic Information Bulletin No. 55, 2
(June 2009)

Private organizations, mostly nonprofit, began developing certification standards in the early 1970s as a way to support organic farming and prevent consumer fraud. Some States began offering organic certification services in the late 1980s for similar reasons. The resulting patchwork of standards in the various certification programs, however, caused a variety of market problems.

Congress passed the Organic Foods Production Act of 1990 to establish national standards for organically produced commodities, and USDA promulgated final rules for implementing this legislation in December 2000, with an 18-month transition period. As of

October 2002, all agricultural products sold, labeled, or represented as organic need to be in compliance with the regulations. They require that organic growers and handlers (including food processors and distributors) be certified by State or private agencies/organizations under the uniform standards developed by USDA, unless the farmers and handlers sell less than $5,000 a year in organic agricultural products. Retail food establishments that sell organically produced agricultural products, but do not process them, are also exempt from certification.

The national organic standards address the methods, practices, and substances used in producing and handling crops, livestock, and processed agricultural products. Although specific practices and materials used by organic operations may vary, the standards require every aspect of organic production and handling to comply with the provisions of the Organic Foods Production Act. Organically produced food cannot be produced using genetic engineering, sewage sludge, or ionizing radiation. These standards include a national list of approved synthetic, and prohibited nonsynthetic, substances for use in organic production and handling.

USDA organic standards for food handlers require that all nonagricultural ingredients, whether synthetic or nonsynthetic, be included on the national list. Handlers must prevent the commingling of organic with nonorganic products and protect organic products from contact with prohibited substances. In a processed product labeled as "organic," all agricultural ingredients must be organically produced unless the ingredient(s) is (are) not commercially available in organic form. National Organic Program regulation 7 CFR 205, Section 205.606, specifies which nonorganic agricultural products may be considered as commercially unavailable.

The labeling requirements under the national standards apply to raw, fresh, and processed products that contain organic ingredients and are based on the percentage of organic ingredients in a product. Agricultural products labeled "100-percent organic" must contain (excluding water and salt) only organically produced ingredients. Products labeled "organic" must consist of at least 95 percent organically produced ingredients. Products labeled "made with organic ingredients" must contain at least 70 percent organic ingredients. Products with less than 70 percent organic ingredients cannot use the term organic anywhere on the principal display panel but may identify the specific ingredients that are organically produced on the ingredients statement on the information panel. The USDA organic seal—the words "USDA organic" inside a circle—may be used on agricultural products that are "100-percent organic" or "organic." A civil penalty of up to $11,000 per violation can be levied on any person who knowingly sells or labels a product as organic that is not produced and handled in accordance with the regulations. For further information, visit USDA's Agricultural Marketing Service/National Organic Program website, at www.ams.usda.gov/nop/....

Since the late 1990s, U.S. organic production has more than doubled, but the consumer market has grown even faster. Organic products are now firmly established in the American food culture: once available only in natural product stores, organic foods are now found in mainstream venues like Wal-Mart, Target, and Costco. While organic food sales are rising from a small base and still account for only about 3 percent of total food sales, most Americans now purchase organic products at least occasionally. According to an annual industry survey, 69 percent of U.S. consumers purchased organic products in 2008 (Hartman Group, 2008).

Growing consumer interest in organic food has brought a number of changes to markets and supply chains. Long-time organic retailers, manufacturers, distributors, and farmers face new competition from their conventional food counterparts. For example, large conventional food manufacturers—such as General Mills, Kellogg's, and Dean Foods—initially gained access to organic markets by acquiring independent, successful organic companies. More recently, conventional food manufacturers have competed head-on with independent organic companies by introducing organic versions of their well-known products, such as Gerber baby food. Conventional supermarkets are introducing "private label" store-brand lines of organic food. And organic food supplies are increasingly being imported from farmers in dozens of other countries that are producing products to meet USDA's organic standards.

Organic Sales Have Quintupled Since 1997

Organic food sales increased from $3.6 billion in 1997 to $21.1 billion in 2008 (fig. 1). Sales of organic foods increased annually between 12 and 21 percent during this period (Nutrition Business Journal, 2008). Market penetration has also grown steadily; organic food products accounted for over 3 percent of total U.S. food sales in 2008. The top two categories—produce and dairy products—accounted for over half of organic food sales (fig. 2). These categories are followed by soymilk and other beverages, packaged foods, breads/grains, snack foods, condiments, and meat. Other organic products (herbal supplements, personal care products, pet food, flowers, linens, and clothing) are growing from a smaller base—$1.6 billion in sales in 2007—but are forecast to grow even faster than organic food sales through the end of the decade (Organic Trade Association, 2008). The fast-paced growth of organic food and other products has led to complaints of supply shortages throughout the organic supply chain.

---

1. The National Organic Standards are found at 7 C.F.R. pt. 205 (2010), and it is instructive to review not only the requirements but the certification process. Note that the regulations were modified by a final rule published in February 2010, *see infra, Maintaining the Integrity of the Organic Label.*

As noted, there was a ten year gap between the enactment of the Organic Foods Production Act in 1990 and promulgation of the final organic standards as regulations in 2000. The USDA's first attempt at standards produced an outcry from the organic community. As the USDA later reported, "your comments do matter. On December 16, 1997, the first proposed rule was published in the Federal Register, and 275,603 people wrote to us to explain why and how the rule should be rewritten, the largest public response to a proposed rule in USDA history." 65 Fed. Reg. 13,512 (March 13, 2000) (prefatory comments to the proposed rule, to be codified at 7 C.F.R. pt. 205). The rules were indeed re-written, and the final rules were much more strict than the original proposal.

2. The Organic Trade Association posts the following current statistics regarding organic customers on their website.

   • Organic usage remains strong, with three-fourths of U.S. consumers purchasing organic products, according to The Hartman Group's "Beyond Organic and Natural 2010" report. One-third of the consumers polled indicated they buy organic products monthly, up from 22 percent in 2000. The overview of the report, which looks at what consumers say about what they eat, is posted online (http://www.hartman-group.com/publications/reports/beyond-organic-and-natural).

   • According to the 2009 U.S. Families' Organic Attitudes and Belief Study, nearly three-quarters (73 percent) of U.S. families buy organic products at least occasionally, chiefly for health reasons. The study also shows that three in ten U.S. families (31 percent) in 2009 were actually buying more organic foods compared to a year earlier, with many parents preferring to reduce their spending in other areas before targeting organic product cuts. In fact, 17 percent of U.S. families said their largest increases in spending in the past year were for organic products. Source: 2009 U.S. Families' Organic Attitudes and Belief Study, http://ota.com/organic/www.ota.com/pics/documents/01b_FinalOTA-KiwiExecutiveSummary.pdf.

· According to Mintel's latest report on green living released in 2010, more than one-third (35 percent) of survey respondents said they would pay more for environmentally friendly products. Findings showed that only 21 percent of organic food buyers cut down or eliminated organic purchasing during the recession, while 20 percent have switched to less expensive organic options. Meanwhile, 48 percent are buying as much or more organic food than before the economic downturn.

Organic Trade Association, at http://www.ota.com/organic/mt/consumer.html.

3. Dr. Phillip Howard, a professor at Michigan State University, has developed a remarkable series of charts detailing the consolidation that has occurred in the organic foods industry since the first draft of the organic standards was issued in 1997. Each of the major food processors has been successful in acquiring at least one line of organic products, with a dramatically different and highly consolidated industry resulting. Professor Howard's charts and links to his research on our food system are available at https//www.msu.edu/~howardp/organicindustry.html.

4. The awkward interplay between the non-labeling of genetically-modified food products and the restriction against the use of genetically-modified ingredients in organic foods raises an interesting dichotomy. *See* Jim Chen, *Beyond Food and Evil*, 56 Duke L. Rev. 1581 (2007) (analyzing the tension between the Organic Foods Production Act and both the Food, Drug, & Cosmetic Act and the commercial speech doctrine).

2. Maintaining the Integrity of the Organic Label

As noted, the economic success of the organic market has led to a significant expansion of companies interested in organic production. There has been significant concern within the organic community that the standards do not adequately assure acceptable production practices. Similarly, consumers interested in purchasing organic food have sometimes assumed production systems that were not in fact mandated by the standards. The "access to pasture" and related provisions of the "livestock living conditions" regulations, particularly as applied to dairy cows producing organic milk provide one example.

Section 205.239 of the regulations provided that livestock must be maintained in "living conditions which accommodate the health and natural behavior of animals, including; (1) access to the outdoors, shade, shelter, exercise areas, fresh air, and direct sunlight suitable to the species." 7 C.F.R. § 205.239 (2010). Ruminants were specifically required to have "access to pasture." *Id.* The regulation further provided, however, that a producer could "provide temporary confinement for an animal because of … [t]he animal's stage of production"; or in "conditions under which the health, safety, or well being of an animal could be jeopardized." *Id.*

As consumer interest in purchasing organic milk increased, large industrialized dairies emerged. Their interest and focus in organic production was based on the market opportunity associated with the label and not a holistic approach that captured the spirit of the organic movement. Concentrated production systems were found to have inadequate pasture facilities for the size of the herds, and liberal advantage was taken of what were thought to be narrow exceptions to the "access to pasture" requirement for ruminants. The regulations as then drafted did not define how much time cattle should actually spend outdoors nor did it define how much of the cattle's feed should come from pasture grazing. Temporary confinement during a "stage of production," which some argued was intended to apply only to birthing was extended in to all of the cow's lactation periods.

Criticism of the lax standard came from other organic farmers, from organic advocacy groups, from the media, and from consumers. Complaints were filed with the USDA, and the USDA eventually proposed a revocation of the organic certification held by one of the offenders, Aurora Dairy. And, USDA began the process of amending the regulations. *See* A. Bryan Endres, *United States Food Law Update: Food Safety Planning, Attribute Labeling, and the Irradiation Debate*, 4 J. FOOD L. & POL'Y 129, 143–46 (2008) for a discussion of the criticism of Aurora and the efforts to develop a more stringent standard. See also, Faterna Merchant, *Got Organic Milk? "Pasture"-ize it! An Analysis of USDA's Pasture Regulations for Organic Dairy Farms*, 14 ANIMAL L. 237 (2008).

After a great deal of debate and over 80,000 comments, a new final rule was published in February 2010. Excerpts from the Federal Register publication are provided below.

75 Federal Register 7154 (Feb. 17, 2010) (to be codified at 7 C.F.R. pt. 205).

This final rule amends livestock and related provisions of the NOP regulations. Under the NOP, the Agricultural Marketing Service (AMS) oversees national standards for the production and handling of organically produced agricultural products. AMS has taken this action to ensure that NOP livestock production regulations have sufficient specificity and clarity to enable AMS and accredited certifying agents to efficiently administer the NOP and to facilitate and improve compliance and enforcement.

This action is also intended to satisfy consumer expectations that ruminant livestock animals graze on pastures during the grazing season. This action provides clarification and specificity to the livestock feed and living conditions provisions and establishes a pasture practice standard for ruminant animals. In doing so, producers are required to: provide year-round access for all animals to the outdoors, recognize pasture as a crop, establish a functioning management plan for pasture, incorporate the pasture management plan into their organic system plan (OSP), provide ruminants with pasture throughout the grazing season for their geographical location, and ensure ruminants derive not less than an average of 30 percent of their dry matter intake (DMI) requirement from pasture grazed over the course of the grazing season. The proposed requirements for fencing of water bodies and providing water at all times, indoors and outdoors, and the requirement for a sacrificial pasture have been deleted in this final rule. In addition, the proposed amendment to the origin of livestock section has been deleted in this final rule as issues pertaining to that topic will be reviewed and evaluated separately from this action.

This final rule requires that producers maintain ruminant slaughter stock on pasture for each day that the finishing period corresponds with the grazing season for the geographical location. However, this rule exempts ruminant slaughter stock from the 30 percent DMI from grazing requirement during the finishing period. Although we are issuing this as a final rule, we are requesting comments on the exceptions for finish feeding of ruminant slaughter stock, as discussed below under "Livestock living conditions—Changes based on comments." The agency is providing an additional 60 day period to receive comments on provision § 205.239(d).

DATES: Effective Date: This rule becomes effective June 17, 2010....

[The prefatory comments are omitted but provide an excellent source of information about the debate concerning this issue. *See* 75 Fed. Reg. 7194-7191 (2010).]

Part 205 — National Organic Program

1. The authority citation for 7 CFR Part 205 continues to read:

Authority: 7 U.S.C. 6501.6522.

2. Section 205.2 is amended by revising the definitions of "crop" and "livestock" and adding 15 new terms in alphabetical order to read as follows:

§ 205.2 Terms defined.

Class of animal. A group of livestock that shares a similar stage of life or production. The classes of animals are those that are commonly listed on feed labels....

Crop. Pastures, cover crops, green manure crops, catch crops, or any plant or part of a plant intended to be marketed as an agricultural product, fed to livestock, or used in the field to manage nutrients and soil fertility....

Dry lot. A fenced area that may be covered with concrete, but that has little or no vegetative cover. Dry matter. The amount of a feedstuff remaining after all the free moisture is evaporated out. Dry matter demand. The expected dry matter intake for a class of animal. Dry matter intake. Total pounds of all feed, devoid of all moisture, consumed by a class of animals over a given period of time....

Feedlot. A dry lot for the controlled feeding of livestock.

Graze. (1) The consumption of standing or residual forage by livestock. (2) To put livestock to feed on standing or residual forage. Grazing. To graze. Grazing season. The period of time when pasture is available for grazing, due to natural precipitation or irrigation. Grazing season dates may vary because of mid-summer heat/ humidity, significant precipitation events, floods, hurricanes, droughts or winter weather events. Grazing season may be extended by the grazing of residual forage as agreed in the operation's organic system plan. Due to weather, season, or climate, the grazing season may or may not be continuous. Grazing season may range from 120 days to 365 days, but not less than 120 days per year....

Inclement weather. Weather that is violent, or characterized by temperatures (high or low), or characterized by excessive precipitation that can cause physical harm to a given species of livestock. Production yields or growth rates of livestock lower than the maximum achievable do not qualify as physical harm....

Livestock. Any cattle, sheep, goats, swine, poultry, or equine animals used for food or in the production of food, fiber, feed, or other agricultural-based consumer products; wild or domesticated game; or other nonplant life, except such term shall not include aquatic animals for the production of food, fiber, feed, or other agricultural based consumer products....

Residual forage. Forage cut and left to lie, or windrowed and left to lie, in place in the pasture....

Shelter. Structures such as barns, sheds, or windbreaks; or natural areas such as woods, tree lines, large hedge rows, or geographic land features, that are designed or selected to provide physical protection or housing to all animals....

Stage of life. A discrete time period in an animal's life which requires specific management practices different than during other periods (e.g., poultry during feathering). Breeding, freshening, lactation and other recurring events are not a stage of life....

Temporary and Temporarily. Occurring for a limited time only (e.g., overnight, throughout a storm, during a period of illness, the period of time specified by the Administrator when granting a temporary variance), not permanent or lasting....

Yards/Feeding pad. An area for feeding, exercising, and outdoor access for livestock during the non-grazing season and a high traffic area where animals may receive supplemental feeding during the grazing season.

3. Section 205.102 is amended by revising paragraph (a) to read as follows:

§ 205.102 Use of the term, "organic."

(a) Produced in accordance with the requirements specified in § 205.101 or §§ 205.202 through 205.207 or §§ 205.236 through 205.240 and all other applicable requirements of part 205; and....

4. Section 205.237 is amended as follows:

A. Revising paragraphs (a), (b)(5), and (b)(6);

B. Adding new paragraphs (b)(7), (b)(8), (c) and (d) to read as follows:

§ 205.237 Livestock feed.

(a) The producer of an organic livestock operation must provide livestock with a total feed ration composed of agricultural products, including pasture and forage, that are organically produced and handled by operations certified to the NOP, except as provided in § 205.236(a)(2)(i), except, that, synthetic substances allowed under § 205.603 and nonsynthetic substances not prohibited under § 205.604 may be used as feed additives and feed supplements, Provided, That, all agricultural ingredients included in the ingredients list, for such additives and supplements, shall have been produced and handled organically.

(b)....

(5) Feed mammalian or poultry slaughter by-products to mammals or poultry; (6) Use feed, feed additives, and feed supplements in violation of the Federal Food, Drug, and Cosmetic Act; (7) Provide feed or forage to which any antibiotic including ionophores has been added; or (8) Prevent, withhold, restrain, or otherwise restrict ruminant animals from actively obtaining feed grazed from pasture during the grazing season, except for conditions as described under § 205.239(b) and (c).

(c) During the grazing season, producers shall:

(1) Provide not more than an average of 70 percent of a ruminant's dry matter demand from dry matter fed (dry matter fed does not include dry matter

grazed from residual forage or vegetation rooted in pasture). This shall be calculated as an average over the entire grazing season for each type and class of animal. Ruminant animals must be grazed throughout the entire grazing season for the geographical region, which shall be not less than 120 days per calendar year. Due to weather, season, and/or climate, the grazing season may or may not be continuous.

(2) Provide pasture of a sufficient quality and quantity to graze throughout the grazing season and to provide all ruminants under the organic system plan with an average of not less than 30 percent of their dry matter intake from grazing throughout the grazing season:

Except, *That,*

 (i) Ruminant animals denied pasture in accordance with § 205.239(b)(1) through (8), and § 205.239(c)(1) through (3), shall be provided with an average of not less than 30 percent of their dry matter intake from grazing throughout the periods that they are on pasture during the grazing season;

 (ii) Breeding bulls shall be exempt from the 30 percent dry matter intake from grazing requirement of this section and management on pasture requirement of § 205.239(c)(2);

Provided, *That, any animal maintained under this exemption shall not be sold, labeled, used, or represented as organic slaughter stock.*

(d) Ruminant livestock producers shall:

(1) Describe the total feed ration for each type and class of animal. The description must include:

 (i) All feed produced on-farm;

 (ii) All feed purchased from off-farm sources;

 (iii) The percentage of each feed type, including pasture, in the total ration; and

 (iv) A list of all feed supplements and additives.

(2) Document the amount of each type of feed actually fed to each type and class of animal.

(3) Document changes that are made to all rations throughout the year in response to seasonal grazing changes.

(4) Provide the method for calculating dry matter demand and dry matter intake.

5. Section 205.239 is amended as follows:

A. Revising paragraph (a), introductory text, and paragraphs (a)(1) through (3);

B. Revising paragraph (b), introductory text, and paragraphs (b)(2) through (b)(4);

C. Redesignating paragraph (c) as (e);

D. Revising newly designated paragraph (e); and

E. Adding new paragraphs (a)(5), (b)(5) through (b)(8), (c), and (d) to read as follows:

§ 205.239 Livestock living conditions.

(a) The producer of an organic livestock operation must establish and maintain year-round livestock living conditions which accommodate the health and natural behavior of animals, including:

(1) Year-round access for all animals to the outdoors, shade, shelter, exercise areas, fresh air, clean water for drinking, and direct sunlight, suitable to the species, its stage of life, the climate, and the environment: Except, that, animals may be temporarily denied access to the outdoors in accordance with §§ 205.239(b) and (c). Yards, feeding pads, and feedlots may be used to provide ruminants with access to the outdoors during the non-grazing season and supplemental feeding during the grazing season. Yards, feeding pads, and feedlots shall be large enough to allow all ruminant livestock occupying the yard, feeding pad, or feedlot to feed simultaneously without crowding and without competition for food. Continuous total confinement of any animal indoors is prohibited. Continuous total confinement of ruminants in yards, feeding pads, and feedlots is prohibited.

(2) For all ruminants, management on pasture and daily grazing throughout the grazing season(s) to meet the requirements of § 205.237, except as provided for in paragraphs (b), (c), and (d) of this section.

(3) Appropriate clean, dry bedding. When roughages are used as bedding, they shall have been organically produced in accordance with this part by an operation certified under this part, except as provided in § 205.236(a)(2)(i), and, if applicable, organically handled by operations certified to the NOP. . . .

(5) The use of yards, feeding pads, feedlots and laneways that shall be welldrained, kept in good condition (including frequent removal of wastes), and managed to prevent runoff of wastes and contaminated waters to adjoining or nearby surface water and across property boundaries.

(b) The producer of an organic livestock operation may provide temporary confinement or shelter for an animal because of: . . .

(2) The animal's stage of life: Except, that lactation is not a stage of life that would exempt ruminants from any of the mandates set forth in this regulation;

(3) Conditions under which the health, safety, or well-being of the animal could be jeopardized;

(4) Risk to soil or water quality;

(5) Preventive healthcare procedures or for the treatment of illness or injury (neither the various life stages nor lactation is an illness or injury);

(6) Sorting or shipping animals and livestock sales: Provided, that, the animals shall be maintained under continuous organic management, including organic feed, throughout the extent of their allowed confinement;

(7) Breeding: Except, that, bred animals shall not be denied access to the outdoors and, once bred, ruminants shall not be denied access to pasture during the grazing season; or

(8) 4.H, Future Farmers of America and other youth projects, for no more than one week prior to a fair or other demonstration, through the event and up to 24 hours after the animals have arrived home at the conclusion of the event.

These animals must have been maintained under continuous organic management, including organic feed, during the extent of their allowed confinement for the event.

(c) The producer of an organic livestock operation may, in addition to the times permitted under § 205.239(b), temporarily deny a ruminant animal pasture or outdoor access under the following conditions:

(1) One week at the end of a lactation for dry off (for denial of access to pasture only), three weeks prior to parturition (birthing), parturition, and up to one week after parturition;

(2) In the case of newborn dairy cattle for up to six months, after which they must be on pasture during the grazing season and may no longer be individually housed: Provided, That, an animal shall not be confined or tethered in a way that prevents the animal from lying down, standing up, fully extending its limbs, and moving about freely;

(3) In the case of fiber bearing animals, for short periods for shearing; and

(4) In the case of dairy animals, for short periods daily for milking. Milking must be scheduled in a manner to ensure sufficient grazing time to provide each animal with an average of at least 30 percent DMI from grazing throughout the grazing season. Milking frequencies or duration practices cannot be used to deny dairy animals pasture.

(d) Ruminant slaughter stock, typically grain finished, shall be maintained on pasture for each day that the finishing period corresponds with the grazing season for the geographical location: Except, that, yards, feeding pads, or feedlots may be used to provide finish feeding rations. During the finishing period, ruminant slaughter stock shall be exempt from the minimum 30 percent DMI requirement from grazing. Yards, feeding pads, or feedlots used to provide finish feeding rations shall be large enough to allow all ruminant slaughter stock occupying the yard, feeding pad, or feed lot to feed simultaneously without crowding and without competition for food. The finishing period shall not exceed one fifth (1/5) of the animal's total life or 120 days, whichever is shorter.

(e) The producer of an organic livestock operation must manage manure in a manner that does not contribute to contamination of crops, soil, or water by plant nutrients, heavy metals, or pathogenic organisms and optimizes recycling of nutrients and must manage pastures and other outdoor access areas in a manner that does not put soil or water quality at risk.

6. Section 205.240 is added to subpart C to read as follows:

§ 205.240 Pasture practice standard.

The producer of an organic livestock operation must, for all ruminant livestock on the operation, demonstrate through auditable records in the organic system plan, a functioning management plan for pasture.

(a) Pasture must be managed as a crop in full compliance with §§ 205.202, 205.203(d) and (e), 205.204, and 205.206(b) through (f). Land used for the production of annual crops for ruminant grazing must be managed in full compliance with §§ 205.202 through 205.206. Irrigation shall be used, as needed, to promote pasture growth when the operation has irrigation available for use on pasture.

(b) Producers must provide pasture in compliance with § 205.239(a)(2) and manage pasture to comply with the requirements of: § 205.237(c)(2), to annually provide a minimum of 30 percent of a ruminant's dry matter intake (DMI), on average, over the course of the grazing season(s); § 205.238(a)(3), to minimize the occurrence and spread of diseases and parasites; and § 205.239(e) to refrain from putting soil or water quality at risk.

(c) A pasture plan must be included in the producer's organic system plan, and be updated annually in accordance with § 205.406(a). The producer may resubmit the previous year's pasture plan when no change has occurred in the plan. The pasture plan may consist of a pasture/rangeland plan developed in cooperation with a Federal, State, or local conservation office: *Provided*, that, the submitted plan addresses all of the requirements of § 205.240(c)(1) through (8). When a change to an approved pasture plan is contemplated, which may affect the operation's compliance with the Act or the regulations in this part, the producer shall seek the certifying agent's agreement on the change prior to implementation. The pasture plan shall include a description of the:

(1) Types of pasture provided to ensure that the feed requirements of § 205.237 are being met.

(2) Cultural and management practices to be used to ensure pasture of a sufficient quality and quantity is available to graze throughout the grazing season and to provide all ruminants under the organic system plan, except exempted classes identified in § 205.239(c)(1) through (3), with an average of not less than 30 percent of their dry matter intake from grazing throughout the grazing season.

(3) Grazing season for the livestock operation's regional location.

(4) Location and size of pastures, including maps giving each pasture its own identification.

(5) The types of grazing methods to be used in the pasture system.

(6) Location and types of fences, except for temporary fences, and the location and source of shade and the location and source of water.

(7) Soil fertility and seeding systems.

(8) Erosion control and protection of natural wetlands and riparian areas practices.

7. Section 205.290 is amended by revising paragraph (a) introductory text to read as follows:

§ 205.290 Temporary variances.

(a) Temporary variances from the requirements in §§ 205.203 through 205.207, 205.236 through 205.240 and 205.270 through 205.272 may be established by the Administrator for the following reasons: …

Notes

1. The organic standards for meat should not be confused with the "grass fed" or "naturally raised" certification process. The USDA has voluntary certification standards for

marketing meat as USDA certified grass fed. *See, United States Standards for Livestock and Meat Marketing Claims, Grass (Forage) Fed Claim for Ruminant Livestock and Meat Products Derived from Such Livestock*, 72 Fed. Reg. 58,631 (Oct. 16, 2007). There is also a standard for "naturally raised." See *United States Standards for Livestock and Meat Marketing Claims, Naturally Raised Claim for Livestock and the Meat and Meat Products Derived from Such Livestock*, 74 Fed. Reg. 3541 (Jan. 21, 2009). Both standards address similar issues. For an excellent discussion of the USDA process in setting the grass fed certification standard, see A. Bryan Endres, *United States Food Law Update: Food Safety Planning, Attribute Labeling, and the Irradiation Debate*, 4 J. Food L. & Pol'y 129, 135–42 (2008).

2. Private standards are also available for meat producers. *See, e.g.*, American Grassfed certification at http://www.americangrassfed.com and Food Alliance grass fed certification at http://Food Alliance.org/grassfed. Private certification standards are generally more strict.

3. There are a number of well recognized efforts to promote production practices that exceed the standards established by the National Organic Standards Board. For example, Angelica Organics, featured in the documentary film, *The Real Dirt on Farmer John* (2005) offers organic biodynamic produce. *See* http://angelicaorganics.com Biodynamics is an enhanced system of organic production based on work done by Austrian social philosopher Rudolf Steiner. Specially prepared, natural soil applications are designed to enhance biological activity in the soil.

Joel Salatin advocates for a farming system that adheres to more rigorous principles than set forth in the organic standards, including an elaborate grass-based feeding system (termed the "salad bar"), a focus on soil health, and local sales only. *See* Polyfacefarms.com.

A. Bryan Endres referred to "organics as religion" in his article *An Awkward Adolescence in the Organics Industry: Coming to Terms with Big Organics and Other Legal Challenges for the Industry's Next Ten Years*, 12 Drake Journal of Agricultural Law 17, 19 (Spring 2007).

For a discussion of the organic standards and efforts to incorporate more stringent production standards, see also, Kate L. Harrison, *Organic Plus: Regulating Beyond the Current Organic Standards* 25 Pace Envtl. L. Rev. 211 (2008).

3. Changing Perspectives

In 2005, an Economic Research Service report described the U.S government's view of organic agriculture as primarily a marketing opportunity. This view was in sharp contrast with the European Union approach.

> The organic sector is rapidly growing in the European Union (EU) and the United States. Together, consumer purchases in these two regions made up 95 percent of the €19 billion (€= euro), or $25 billion, in estimated world retail sales of organic food products in 2003 Agricultural land under organic production has also increased rapidly in both regions. Government policy regarding organic agriculture differs markedly in the two regions, however. The EU actively promotes sector growth via conversion subsidies and direct payments to farmers, while the U.S. largely takes a free-market approach, with policies that focus on facilitating market development. As a result of the different policies, the EU-15 has more certified organic farmland than does the U.S. (4.4 million hectares versus 949,000 hectares in 2001), a greater share of farmland under organic man-

agement (2 percent versus 0.25 percent in 2001), and more organic farms (143,607 versus 6,949 in 2001).

The reasons for the different policy approaches may be that the EU and U.S. governments have inherently different ideas about agriculture, the environment, and by extension, organic agriculture. From the perspective of many EU countries, organic agriculture delivers environmental, social, and other benefits to society and is an infant industry that needs support until it is mature and able to compete in established markets. The U.S. Government, while acknowledging organic agriculture's positive impact on soil quality and erosion, considers the organic sector primarily an expanding market opportunity for producers and regards organic food as a differentiated product available to consumers. Despite policy differences, organic agriculture and sales are rapidly increasing in both regions. In comparison, other sectors of agriculture have been stagnating in developed countries.

Carolyn Dimitri and Lydia Oberholtzer, *Market-Led Versus Government-Facilitated Growth: Development of the U.S. and EU Organic Agricultural Sectors*, Economic Research Service, Report No. WRS-05-05 (August 2005).

A 2009 Economic Research Report reveals a very different U.S. attitude toward organic production. While it is still recognized as a market opportunity, its success in that regard has astounded many in conventional agricultural circles. And, as the environmental problems associated with conventional agriculture have come into greater focus, the environmental advantages of organic production have similarly been recognized. This report discusses the need for additional organic products to meet the market needs, the changed approach toward organic agriculture, and government's efforts to encourage organic production.

Catherine Greene, Carolyn Dimitri, Biing-Hwan Lin, William McBride, Lydia Oberholtzer, and Travis Smith
Emerging Issues in the U.S. Organic Industry
USDA Economic Research Service, Economic Information Bulletin No. 55, 2
(June 2009)

U.S. Organic Acreage Has Doubled Since 1997, But Producers Face Challenges

U.S. certified organic crop acreage more than doubled between 1997 and 2005, and organic production has spread to every State and commodity sector The structure of the U.S. organic production sector differs substantially from the conventional sector: fruits and vegetables account for a much larger percentage of total organic acreage, and organic farms tend to be smaller than conventional farms. Small-scale organic operations market directly to consumers, as well as to wholesalers, natural food stores, and supermarkets. Many organic production sectors, including fruits, vegetables, dairy, and poultry, are expanding rapidly in the United States. However, the pace of expansion has slowed in some sectors, and organic acreage for some crops—including cotton and soybeans—declined between 2000 and 2005.

The overall adoption level for organic agriculture is still low—only about 0.5 percent of all U.S. cropland and 0.5 percent of all U.S. pasture was certified organic in 2005. Although nearly 5 percent of U.S. vegetable acreage and 2.5 percent of fruit and nut acreage was under organic management in 2005, only 0.2 percent of U.S. corn and soybean crops were grown under certified organic farming systems (fig. 4). Conventional grain producers in the United States associate a wide variety of financial and other risks with organic production.

Organic Handlers Cope With Supply Shortfalls

During the early 1990s, organic farmers identified lack of consumer demand as a major marketing problem, and organic farmers frequently sold organic products into conventional markets. While limited demand can still be a problem at times for organic products, limited organic supply has become a bigger issue over the last decade. By the late 1990s, organic handlers—the intermediaries in organic supply chains—faced difficulty procuring large enough quantities of organic products to distribute to retailers, locating organic producers to buy from, and gaining access to shelf space in supermarkets.

More recently, long-time organic handlers have reported that the lack of reliable supplies for organic raw materials is a major factor that has constrained business growth. One of the most recurrent themes in a congressional public hearing on organic agriculture, held in April 2007, was the shortage of organic inputs, ingredients, and products. According to testimony from the Organic Trade Association (OTA), 52 percent of the organic companies responding to an OTA membership survey reported that "a lack of dependable supply of organic raw materials has restricted their company from generating more sales of organic products."

In particular, organic dairy producers and soy food processors face shortages of domestically produced organic feed grains and soybeans. Quarterly farm-level prices for organic grains and feedstuffs have risen steadily since USDA began tracking prices for these products in January 2007—in some cases more than tripling by third-quarter 2008—outpacing conventional grain price increases and reflecting tight organic supplies. In 2005, ERS surveyed all certified organic handlers in the United States (approximately 2,790 facilities) about their practices in 2004. Organic handlers (including brokers, distributors, wholesalers, and manufacturers) must maintain the organic integrity of a product as it moves along the supply chain, but can achieve compliance with the national standards quicker than farmers. Facilities were few in most States, with the Pacific States accounting for 41 percent of the total. In 2004, many organic handlers were small; 48 percent reported $1 million or less in total gross sales (both organic and conventional products). Just 3 percent of handlers reported over $100 million in sales. Most organic handling firms are mixed operations, handling both organic and conventional products; on average, 34 percent of the sales handled by these firms were organic.

According to the survey findings, 13 percent of all handlers were unable to meet market demand (that is, they experienced critical shortages for at least one of their organic products) during 2004. The share of handlers unable to meet market demand varied by the product sold and was highest for milk. These product shortages are mirrored by handlers' difficulties procuring ingredients: 44 percent of handlers found needed ingredients or products in short supply during 2004. The main products and ingredients handlers found in limited supply were coffee, soybeans, milk, seeds (includes seeds for planting), corn, and nuts.

Organic handlers are using a number of mechanisms to cope with shortfalls, such as developing relationships with new or less experienced suppliers, being flexible on shipment size, and providing technical advice. Handlers willing to work with suppliers new to the organic industry have access to a wider range of supply. Feedgrain handlers are the most willing to work with suppliers new to the sector and, along with soy handlers, are the most flexible about accepting smaller shipments of organic supplies.

The Search for Organic Supply Goes Global

The U.S. National Organic Program (NOP) streamlined the certification process for international as well as domestic trade when it was implemented in 2002. Organic farmers and handlers anywhere in the world are permitted to export organic products to the United States if they meet NOP standards, along with other regulatory standards, and are certified by a public or private organic certification body with USDA accreditation. In 2007, USDA accredited groups certified 27,000 producers and handlers worldwide to the U.S. organic standard, with approximately 16,000 in the United States and 11,000 in over 100 foreign countries (fig. 8). Farmers and handlers certified to NOP standards are most numerous in Canada, Italy, Turkey, China, and Mexico, which together accounted for half the total foreign organic farmers/handlers in 2007.

The United States does not have updated, consistent data on organic trade because organic product codes have not yet been added to the U.S. and international harmonized system of trade codes. A USDA report estimated that the value of U.S. organic imports in 2002 was $1.0–$1.5 billion and the value of U.S. organic exports was $125–$250 million. Organic imports have increased substantially since 2002, and include fresh fruits and vegetables, products not grown in the United States (such as coffee, tea, cocoa, and tropical produce), and raw ingredients, including soybeans.

Imports have increased as growth in organic demand has exceeded domestic supply. Organic farming is often labor intensive, and developing countries with lower farm labor costs may have a competitive advantage for some organic products. While USDA's survey of organic distributors, processors, and other handlers indicated that they relied primarily on domestic suppliers, 38 percent imported some or all of their organic products in 2004.

Despite the rapid growth of the organic sector and entry of larger organic farms over the last decade, the smallest U.S. organic farms have maintained a stable share of the organic sector (Grow and Greene, 2009). Small-scale farmers producing a wide variety of horticultural products—and increasingly livestock products—for sale in direct markets have likely seen the least impact from competition with more distant suppliers. Organic consumers at farmers' markets, independent restaurants, small food shops, and other direct markets are explicitly seeking locally grown organic products. However, some fruit and vegetable growers who marketed to natural foods grocery stores during the 1990s have reported losing some of their markets to imports and to larger domestic producers as these stores have expanded beyond their original markets.

U.S. organic grain and oilseed producers also face international market competition. U.S. organic cotton producers began losing market share in the 1990s to countries with lower labor, input, and technology costs (Greene and Kremen, 2003). U.S. organic soybean production started declining several years ago despite increasing demand for organic feed grains and consumer products such as soymilk. U.S. feed grain distributors and soy product manufacturers report sourcing organic soybeans from other countries....

Organic Agriculture Provides Ecosystem Services

USDA's national regulatory program explicitly defines organic agriculture as an ecological production system, established "to respond to site-specific conditions by integrating cultural, biological, and mechanical practices that foster cycling of resources, promote ecological balance, and conserve biodiversity" (USDA AMS, 2000). In setting soil fertility and crop nutrient management practice standards, USDA requires organic producers to use practices that maintain or improve the physical, chemical, and biological condition of soil and minimize soil erosion. In setting standards for organic livestock,

USDA specifies that producers must accommodate an animal's natural nutritional and behavioral requirements, ensuring that dairy cows and other ruminants, for example, have access to pasture. USDA's organic livestock standards also incorporate requirements for living conditions, feed rations, and health care practices suitable to the needs of the particular species.

Environmental benefits that can be attributed to organic production systems include the following:

- Reduced pesticide residues in water and food. Organic production systems virtually eliminate synthetic pesticide use, and reducing pesticide use has been an ongoing U.S. public health goal as scientists continue to document its unintentional effects on nontarget species, including humans.

- Reduced nutrient pollution; improved soil tilth, soil organic matter, and productivity; and lower energy use. A number of studies have documented these environmental improvements in comparing organic farming systems with conventional systems.

- Carbon sequestration. Soils in organic farming systems (which use cover crops, crop rotation, fallowing, and animal and green manures) may also sequester as much carbon as soils under other carbon sequestration strategies and could help reduce carbon levels in the atmosphere.

- Enhanced biodiversity. A number of studies have found that organic farming practices enhance the biodiversity found in organic fields compared with conventional fields and improve biodiversity in field margins.

Despite the potential for organic agriculture to improve the environmental performance of U.S. agriculture, the national standard is having only a modest impact on environmental externalities caused by conventional production methods because the organic adoption rate is so low....

New Directions in U.S. Organic Policy

Until recently, Federal organic policy was oriented toward using market support mechanisms to facilitate the growth in the U.S. organic sector. In the Food, Conservation, and Energy Act of 2008 (2008 Farm Act), U.S. Federal organic policy changed course with provisions that provide financial support to farmers to convert to organic production. Under the Organic Transition Support provision in the Environmental Quality Incentives Program, conservation practices related to organic production and the transition to organic production are eligible for payments, subject to a $20,000 annual limit and an $80,000 cap over a 6-year period to persons or legal entities.

The 2008 Farm Act also increased mandatory funds for a national certification cost-share program and a data initiative and boosted mandatory organic research funds five-fold from levels mandated in the 2002 Act, specifying two new research priorities. One is to study the conservation and environmental outcomes of organic practices. Although experimental trials have found enhanced soil fertility, higher biodiversity, lower energy use, and increased retention of carbon and nitrogen in organic plots compared with conventional plots, this funding will support more comprehensive research. The potential of organic farming to capture atmospheric carbon and store it in the soil was specifically mentioned in the conference report of the 2008 Farm Act as an example of organic research that needs support.

The other new priority of the organic research initiative is to develop new and improved seed varieties for use in organic production systems. Interest in organic seed variety development was heightened after USDA banned the use of seeds treated with fungicides and the use of genetically modified organism seeds, when national organic standards were implemented in October 2002.

The 2008 Farm Act includes a number of other provisions to facilitate growth in the U.S. organic sector, including technical assistance on organic conservation practices; the inclusion of organic commodities in a costshare funding program to expand export markets for U.S. agricultural products; a provision to give priority to qualified beginning and socially disadvantaged producers, owners, or tenants who use the loans to convert to sustainable or organic agricultural production systems; funding to expand data collection on organic production and marketing; support for USDA's regulatory program; and a provision to contract for studies of improvement in organic production insurance coverage.

Conclusions

The organic industry has experienced growing pains since publication of the "USDA organic" label and standards in 2000, which strengthened consumer demand for organic products. Adoption of organic production systems has been uneven across production sectors and regions in the United States, and supply shortages have emerged in some organic food sectors. New public investments in organic research, technical assistance, and support for organic farmers and handlers were included in the 2008 Farm Act. This public investment complements ongoing private efforts to expand organic supply and procure organic products closer to the point of sale. Technical assistance on organic production and financial incentives for organic transition are aimed at providing the tools to help expand the domestic organic grain supply—which in turn supports the fast-growing milk, meat, and poultry sectors—and facilitate organic production in U.S. regions where adoption has been slow. Most American consumers now buy organic products at least occasionally, and could benefit from wider accessibility and enhanced product selection.

Significant price premiums exist for fresh organic produce and organic milk, the two top organic food sales categories, compared with conventional products, reflecting short supply and higher organic production costs. Even if price premiums for organic products can be maintained, the public-goods nature of environmental services, such as biodiversity and water quality, implies that prices do not reflect the true social value of these services. Public investment in organic agriculture facilitates wider access to organic food for consumers and helps farmers capture high-value markets and boost farm income, as well as conserve nonrenewable natural resources and protect U.S. soil and water.

C. The Local Food Movement

Steve Martinez, Michael Hand, Michelle Da Pra, Susan Pollack, Katherine Ralston, Travis Smith, Stephen Vogel, Shellye Clark, Luanne Lohr, Sarah Low, and Constance Newman
Local Food Systems: Concepts, Impacts, and Issues
USDA Economic Research Service, Report No. 97 (May 2010)

Growing interest in local foods in the United States is the result of several movements. The environmental movement encourages people to consider geographic dimensions in their food choices. Long-distance transport of food is considered to contribute to greenhouse gas emissions. The community food-security movement seeks to enhance access to safe, healthy, and culturally appropriate food for all consumers. Challenges to the dominance of large corporations also have contributed to efforts to expand local food. The Slow Food movement, which originated in Italy, is a response to homogenous, mass-produced food production, and the "fast" nature of people's lives, by encouraging traditional ways of growing, producing, and preparing food. The local food movement also reflects an increasing interest by consumers in supporting local farmers, and in better understanding the origin of their food....

What is Local Food?

Unlike organic food, there is no legal or universally accepted definition of local food. In part, it is a geographical concept related to the distance between food producers and consumers. In addition to geographic proximity of producer and consumer, however, local food can also be defined in terms of social and supply chain characteristics. In this section, we first describe local foods as a geographic concept. Then, we examine other features that have been used to define "local" foods. Finally, we briefly describe a typology of local food markets, which adds a more tangible perspective to the local foods concept.

Geography

Terms such as "local food," "local food system," and "(re)localization" are often used interchangeably to refer to food produced near its point of consumption in relation to the modern or mainstream food system. The New Oxford American Dictionary (NOAD) defines a "locavore," which was NOAD's 2007 word of the year, as a local resident who tries to eat only food grown or produced within a 100-mile radius. This 100-mile radius measure is not, however, a standard for local markets. [M]any consumers disagree with the 100-mile designation for fresh produce.

In terms of defining distance, opinions are quite varied. Distances that are perceived to constitute local may vary by region. Population density is important because what is considered local in a sparsely populated area may be quite different from what constitutes local in a more heavily populated region. This is referred to as "flexible localism," with the definition of "local" changing depending on the ability to source supplies within a short distance or further away, such as within a State. For example, in King County, WA, a densely populated urban county, a survey of 54 producers found that 66 percent defined local market as their own or surrounding counties . On the other hand, in Grant County, a sparsely populated rural and agriculturally based county, only 20 percent of 61 producers surveyed considered their local market to be their own or surrounding counties.

Different definitions may also be appropriate, depending on the situation. For example, with regards to the Value-Added Agricultural Market Development program, run by USDA Rural Development, the 2008 Farm Act defines the total distance that a product can be transported and still be eligible for marketing as a "locally or regionally produced agricultural food product" as less than 400 miles from its origin, or the State in which it is produced.

Geographic proximity considerations have led to some controversy as to whether State-funded branding programs, which are aimed at promoting or identifying State-produced agricultural products, are part of the local food system. While some studies also include State-branded products as a type of local food product, other studies consider State labels not to be a good proxy for local food. This is because consumers generally define "local" in terms smaller than their State, and many State-branding programs target consumers in other States, or perhaps internationally. For example, the Florida Department of Agriculture recently partnered with a supermarket chain in Ireland to promote the State's strawberries as part of its "Fresh from Florida" marketing campaign. Foods that have a brand associated with a particular locality or region, but serve largely external markets, are sometimes referred to as "locality foods" to distinguish from local foods.

Other Characteristics That Consumers Attribute to "Local Food"

Geographic proximity is only one component of the local foods definition. There are a host of other characteristics that may be used by consumers to define local food systems. Some may associate production methods as part of what defines local food . For instance, sustainable production and distribution practices reduce use of synthetic chemicals and energy-based fertilizers, are environmentally friendly, and limit chemical and pesticide residue on food.[1] Some consumers also extend sustainable production to include fair farm labor practices and animal welfare.

The concept of local food may also extend to who produced the food: the personality and ethics of the grower; the attractiveness of the farm and surrounding landscape; and other factors that make up the "story behind the food." The term "provenance," which describes the method or tradition of production that is attributable to local influences, seems to capture the essence of this component of the local food definition.[2] Local food systems have also been synonymous with small farms that are committed to place through social and economic relationships. Social embeddedness in the sense of social connections, mutual exchange, and trust is viewed by some as an important feature of direct agricultural marketing.

Local food may be defined by the characteristics of intermediate stages of the supply chain, such as processing and retailing. [A] short food supply chain (SFSC) facilitates some form of connection between the food consumer and producer by providing clearer signals related to the origin of the food product. The most important feature of a SFSC is that the product reaches the consumer embedded with information, such as through package labeling or personal communication. This enables consumers to connect with the place of production and, perhaps, the people involved and methods used to produce the product. One type of SFSC is spatial proximity, where products are produced and retailed in a specific region of production, and consumers are made aware of the local nature of products.[3]

---

1. For some consumers, the importance of "environmentally sustainable" practices may exclude some products that are produced and consumed within "close" proximity from fitting a local definition. For example, a case study of a certified organic produce grower in southern Idaho found that when the grower sells to Albertsons, a mainstream grocery retailer, the food must be shipped from the farm to a distribution center located 235 miles away in Utah. It can then be shipped back to Idaho for sales in local stores.

2. The European concept of "terroir," or "sense of place," encompasses characteristics of both locality foods and provenance. It refers to a geographical area through the name of the product, brand, or signals of quality, and to the reputation of the place in terms of culture, history, and other features.

3. Two other types of SFSCs include face-to-face and spatially extended. In a face-to-face SFSC, the consumer purchases directly from the producer or processor, but it may not be considered a local food supply chain. A spatially extended SFSC communicates information about the place of production and those producing the food to consumers who are outside of the production region, and who may have had no experience with the region.

Local Food Market Typology

Because there is no universal definition of local food, defining types of local food markets facilitates our ability to evaluate these markets. Two basic types of local food markets include those where transactions are conducted directly between farmers and consumers (direct-to-consumer), and direct sales by farmers to restaurants, retail stores, and institutions such as government entities, hospitals, and schools (direct-to-retail/foodservice).[4] Venues for direct-to-consumer marketing of local foods include farmers' markets, community supported agriculture (CSAs), farm stands/on farm sales, and "pick your own" operations. Other less formal sources of local foods that are typically difficult to measure or are unmeasured include home gardening and sharing among neighbors, foraging and hunting, and gleaning programs.

Direct-to-Consumer Marketing

The Census of Agriculture, conducted by USDA's National Agricultural Statistics Service every 5 years, currently provides the only measurable indicator of the direct-to-consumer local food marketing channel. However, "direct-to-consumer marketing" and "direct sales to consumers" as defined by the most recent agricultural census (2007) are not equivalent concepts.[5] For example, catalog or Internet sales are included in the agricultural census's direct sales to consumers, but customers are typically not local (Hughes et al., 2007).[6]

Direct-to-consumer sales of agricultural products account for a small, but fast-growing segment of U.S. agriculture, increasing by $399 million (49 percent) from 2002 to 2007, and by $660 million (120 percent) from 1997 to 2007. According to the 2007 Census, 136,800 farms, or 6 percent of all farms in the United States, sold $1.2 billion worth of farm products directly to consumers, or 0.4 percent of all agricultural sales. If non-edible products are excluded from total agricultural sales, then direct-to-consumer sales as a percentage of agricultural sales increases to 0.8 percent in 2007 (Soto and Diamond, 2009). Direct-to-consumer marketing is also a small but growing share of U.S. at-home food consumption. In 2007, direct-to-consumer sales grew to 0.21 percent of total home consumption, compared to 0.15 percent in 1997. Nationally, direct-to-consumer sales per farm averaged $8,853.

Recent growth in direct-to-consumer marketing farms and sales has come from larger operations, and fruit, vegetable, and beef farms. For example, operations with $50,000 or more in annual sales increased direct-to-consumer sales by 64 percent, or $274 mil-

---

4. Local food products may also move through an intermediary, such as a wholesaler or the firm's distribution center, before reaching a retail outlet or consumer. For example, buying clubs are often operated out of someone's home or office. They are formed by groups of people that place large orders directly with a distributor, allowing them to order in bulk quantities at wholesale prices. The shipments are delivered directly to a drop-off destination where club members receive and sort the products.

5. Specifically, the ag census defines direct sales to consumers as the value of agricultural products sold directly to individuals for human consumption from roadside stands, farmers' markets, pick-your-own sites, etc. It excludes nonedible products, but includes livestock sales. Sales of agricultural products by vertically integrated operations through their own processing and marketing operations are also excluded.

6. There are websites that facilitate online local food transactions. For example, one new website offers consumers within a 30-mile radius of Farmington, ME, an opportunity to order local food online for pickup at specific times and locations. Consumers can learn about the producers, link to their websites, and place orders, which are paid through Internet payment sites, such as PayPal. Also, see http://www.farmersonlinemarket.net/index.cfm/.

lion, from 2002 to 2007, which exceeded all other size categories. The number of beef farms involved in direct-to-consumer marketing grew by 33 percent (or 8,851 farms) from 2002 to 2007, followed by farms marketing vegetables and melons, which grew by 24 percent (or 3,474 farms).

Farmers' Markets

A farmers' market is a common area where several farmers gather on a recurring basis to sell a variety of fresh fruits, vegetables, and other farm products directly to consumers. They were once the core focal point for selling fresh products in urban centers, but their significance gradually declined as cities grew larger and more mobile. Most established farmers' markets have hired individuals to oversee the organization, rules and regulations, and promotions for all growers. Most also charge vendor fees for selling privileges, including a flat fee as space is available, a membership fee for the entire season, or a fee based on a percentage of vendor sales.

The number of farmers' markets grew to 5,274 markets in 2009, a 92-percent increase from 1998. They are concentrated in densely populated areas of the Northeast, Midwest, and West Coast. According to the USDA Agricultural Marketing Service's 2006 National Farmers' Market Survey, the most popular product category sold at farmers' markets was fresh fruits and vegetables, which was sold by nearly 92 percent of farmers' market managers in 2005, followed by herbs and flowers, and honey, nuts, and preserves. However, not all products sold at farmers' markets are part of the local food system. For example, some vendors may come from outside the local region, and some local vendors may not sell products that are produced within the region.

A sample of nine farmers' markets in central Virginia illustrates the variation in local food definitions, monitoring procedures, and selling facilities across farmers' markets, even within the same region.[7] Four of the markets define "local" as goods grown or produced within a 100-mile radius and in Virginia. Two markets required food to be grown within a 75-mile radius, and one required food to be grown within the county. Two others have looser requirements, allowing some vendors to sell non-local produce.

For the seven markets with specific growing location requirements, site visits are conducted at five markets to verify compliance. One market also had restrictions on reselling goods. According to the USDA survey, 63 percent of farmers' market managers reported that vendors were required to sell only the products that they produced.

Community Supported Agriculture (CSA)

During the 1960s, the concept of community supported agriculture originated in Switzerland and Japan. A group of people buy shares for a portion of the expected harvest of a farm. CSAs traditionally required a one-time payment at the beginning of the season, but have since become more flexible, offering two- to four-installment payment plans or payments on a monthly basis. Consumers often take on added risk because they pay a fixed amount in advance, regardless of the realized quantity and quality of the harvest. Some CSAs offer members a price discount in exchange for providing farm labor. Members may be required to pick up their food at the farm, or it may be delivered to a centralized location, farmers' market, or directly to the home or office.

---

7. More than two-thirds of farmers' market managers surveyed by USDA reported that the market manager (36.6 percent) or vendor-operated board of directors (32 percent) was responsible for creating market rules and bylaws.

In 1986, there were 2 CSA operations in the United States. By 2005, there were 1,144 CSAs compared to 761 in 2001, an increase of 50 percent. In 2010, the Robyn Van En Center, provider of a national resource center about CSAs based at Wilson College in Chambersburg, PA, estimates that there are over 1,400 CSAs in operation, but a 2009 survey found 700 CSAs in 9 States, which suggests the number could be much greater. An online registry estimates that the number of CSAs exceed 2,500 and are concentrated in the Northeast, areas surrounding the Great Lakes, and coastal regions of the West.

Business organizations for CSA programs include sole proprietorships (single farm), partnerships and farm cooperatives (multiple farms), and limited liability corporations. The larger CSAs tend to have more complex business structures (Woods et al., 2009). One advantage of multifarm CSAs is that farms can specialize in production to provide more variety in the total share.

The typical CSA offers a mix of between 8 and 12 types of produce and herbs per week per shareholder throughout the growing season. The types of products offered have greatly expanded. According to a recent survey of 205 CSA producers in 9 States, 75 percent of survey respondents indicated that members could purchase nonproduce items, in addition to their CSA shares (Woods et. al., 2009). The most popular types of non-produce items were eggs, meat, and flowers. CSAs do not necessarily produce all of the products distributed in their CSA shares. Woods et al., (2009) found that 29 percent of CSAs surveyed did not produce all of their own products, with most reporting purchases from other local growers.

Other Types of Direct-to-Consumer Marketing

Other types of direct-to-consumer marketing include pick-your own, farm stands, community gardening, and on-farm stores. Pick-your-own (PYO), or U-pick, operations became popular in the 1930s and 1940s, during the Depression and after World War II, when produce prices were low and producers could not cover labor and material costs. Crops that are well-suited for PYO operations include those with high labor requirements per acre, yet require little expertise to harvest. Examples include berries, tomatoes, pumpkins and Christmas trees. Roadside farm stands and on-farm stores operate year round from a permanent structure, or only during harvest periods from a truck, trailer, or tent. In urban areas, mobile fruit and vegetable vending provides opportunities for local produce to be introduced as impulse purchases for consumers in public areas such as parks and on city sidewalks. Mobile venders offer opportunities to provide underserved communities with fresh produce in locations where brick-and-mortar stores are not feasible, and can be adept at providing culturally appropriate food items.

Community gardening, household gardening, and garden sharing are technically not market sources of local foods, but are important in providing households with local food access. According to the National Gardening Association's Impact of Home and Community Gardening in America Survey, 43 million U.S. households intended to grow their own fresh fruits, vegetables, berries, and herbs in 2009, up from 36 million, or 19 percent more than 2008. Food gardening in 2008 was valued at $2.5 billion. About $2.8 billion was spent on gardening inputs in 2008, or about $70 per gardening household. Vegetables, the most popular type of food gardening product, were grown by 23 percent of all households, fruit trees by 10 percent, berries by 6 percent, and herbs by 12 percent. The average garden size was 600 square feet in 2008, but the median size was 96 square feet. Most food gardeners were women (54 percent), 45 years of age and older (68 percent), residents of the South (29 percent) and Midwest (26 percent), in households with annual incomes of $50,000 and over (49 percent), in married households (64 percent), and in households with no children at home (67 percent).

Among gardening households, 23 percent stated that one reason for gardening is to share food with others. About 33 million households (91 percent of gardening households) had a food garden at home, and 2 million (5 percent) had one at the home of a friend, neighbor, or relative (known as garden sharing), while 1 million (3 percent) participated in a community garden. Not only do households consume and share their produce with neighbors, relatives, and friends, but food banks also benefit from and participate in community gardens. Through the Garden Writers Association program Plant a Row for the Hungry, gardeners have supplied more than 14 million pounds of herbs and vegetables to food banks and soup kitchens since 1995. Gardening is also correlated with increased awareness and consumption of fresh fruits and vegetables and greater physical activity among children, urban adults, and seniors.

Direct-to-Retail/Foodservice Marketing

Most local food may not be direct-to-consumer. According to [a] research firm, local food sales through all marketing channels in the United States were $5 billion in 2007, compared to $1.2 billion in direct-to-consumer sales for human consumption. [I]nterviews [were conducted] with seven owners and managers of different types of grocery stores in one New York county to assess their experiences with selling locally produced foods. Based on interview results, produce and, to a lesser extent, dairy and other perishables are the most important focus in promoting local food. In addition, local foods are consistently promoted as "special" or "premium" products. Geographic definitions of local included the local county and surrounding counties, or a 30-mile radius, which covers much of the same territory.

Based on site visits to 38 grocery stores in Wisconsin and neighboring areas, ... common marketing strategies [were found] among the stores. For example, many stores included the location of the produce source, such as Wisconsin-grown or photographs of farm suppliers. Fresh produce was the most popular local food item, followed by dairy and eggs. On average, 57 percent of their local food purchases were directly from farmers rather than wholesalers.

Small, independent grocery retailers, whose identity and store assortment practices have closer links to specific geographic locations, are better positioned to incorporate local food as part of their corporate identity. Dorothy Lane Market, a small independent supermarket with three gourmet stores in Dayton, OH, began as a fruit stand in 1948. Since that time, it has developed a strong relationship with local farmers and now carries products that traveled a short distance in all departments. However, just last year it adopted a definition of "local" as food locally grown or raised within a 250-mile radius of Dayton.

While the relationship is indirect, the results of a 2008 USDA survey about organic foods reveal the importance of niche retail marketing channels in distributing highly differentiated farm products to consumers. According to the survey, a surprisingly large percentage of organic farm products were sold by retail stores specializing in natural foods (6.7 percent), compared to conventional supermarkets (12.1 percent). Whole Foods, a natural and organic food retailer, has its own guidelines for using the term "local" in stores, which vary by store. To be considered for the local designation, products must have traveled less than a day (7 or fewer hours by car or truck) from farm to store. However, most of its stores have established even shorter maximum distances.

As food companies strive to grow or maintain market share in a slowly growing domestic food economy, mainstream distribution channels for marketing food products in the United States are changing. Over the past 10 years, the food industry has seen an influx of store types not traditionally involved in food sales, led by supercenters. This has created incentives for firms to differentiate from the competition by responding to consumer demand for new product offerings, including local foods. More supermarkets are installing local aisles in their stores, and more small specialty plants are being built to handle locally produced food for those stores (Smith, 2009).

Several leading retailers have recently announced local food initiatives. In a July 1, 2008, press release, Wal-Mart expressed its commitment to "source more local fruits and vegetables to keep produce prices down and provide affordable selections that are fresh and healthful." More recently, Safeway, the fifth-largest U.S. food retailer, announced that it is launching a campaign to significantly increase its focus on locally grown produce. Publix, the sixth-largest U.S. grocer, recently indicated that it will promote Redlands Raised produce in its Florida stores. The Redlands Raised produce is grown in southwest Miami-Dade County and uses the "Fresh from Florida" State brand in its other southeastern stores.[8] Grand Rapids, MI-based Meijer, the tenth-largest grocery retailer in the Nation, announced that it will expand its "Home Grown" initiative by working with more than 65 local growers to increase sourcing of local produce. Sudbury, PA-based Weis Markets, a large regional grocer in Pennsylvania, Maryland, New York, New Jersey, and West Virginia, launched its new "Local and Proud of It" campaign to highlight its commitment to offering locally grown produce, which accounts for 20 percent of its total in-season produce sales. Grand Rapids, MI-based Spartan Stores, a food wholesaler that owns 84 corporate grocery stores, promotes a relatively new "Michigan's Best" campaign and highlights fresh food produced in Michigan on its website.

A recent inspection of the top 10 U.S. food retailers' websites provides some insight into mainstream retailer ventures into local food marketing and prominence attained by the local food movement. Seven sites have some reference to local foods. Only Wal-Mart and Delhaize America (operator of Food Lion, Bloom, Bottom Dollar, and other supermarkets) have a specific definition of local food. Texas-based H.E. Butt and Ahold (a Netherlands based international grocery retailer who owns the Giant and Stop & Shop grocery chains in the United States) simply advertise State-grown produce without providing a specific definition of "local." Three of the retailers provide information about the quantity of produce they sell that is sourced locally within season, ranging from 20 percent for Wal-Mart to 30 percent for Safeway and Meijer. Kroger and Meijer also mention auditing practices as part of their quality and safety assurances.

Consumer-owned retail food cooperatives are another type of distribution channel for marketing local foods. These are organizations that are owned and operated by their members. They are similar to grocery stores that offer price discounts to members, stock many products in bulk, and are often committed to purchasing organic and locally grown foods. Membership is open to anyone who invests a small fee, which enables them to provide input into the operation of the co-op. Many co-ops offer discounted member fees to those who work at the store, often committing a few hours a week to help unload deliveries, shelve products, or work as cashiers.

In 2006, 87 percent of fine-dining establishments served local items, as did 75 percent of family dining and casual dining restaurants. Some restaurants exclusively offer locally grown foods and are willing to have a more limited menu in order to offer in-season

---

8. State-funded branding programs grew from 23 States in 1995 to 43 in 2006.

products that they believe their customers want. These types of restaurants typically open in places where consumers are highly supportive of the local foods movement.

Surveys conducted by the National Restaurant Association (NRA) suggest increasing interest in local foods by restaurants and their patrons. An annual survey of professional chef members of the American Culinary Federation found that locally grown produce ranked first in hot trends for 2010, and locally sourced meats and seafood ranked second (see more details at: http://www.restaurant.org/pdfs/research/whats_hot_2010.pdf/). Eighty-eight percent of chefs rated locally grown produce as a hot trend, 10 percent considered it a "perennial favorite," and 2 percent ranked it as "yesterday's news." The local-foods trend has become particularly popular at fine-dining establishments. According to NRA's 2008 operator survey, 89 percent of fine-dining operators served locally sourced items, and 90 percent believed it will become more popular.

Nearly 30 percent of quickservice operators served locally sourced items in 2008, and nearly half believe these items will grow more popular. Locally sourced items ranked third on the list of "hot/trendy" food items in the quickservice segment. Seventy percent of adults said they were more likely to visit a restaurant that offers locally produced food items. In 2008, Chipotle Mexican Grill, one of the fastest growing quick-service chains, began purchasing 25 percent of at least one produce item for each of its stores from farms located within 200 miles.

A survey of restaurant chefs and food buyers belonging to Chefs Collaborative, a national network of more than 1,000 members who support sustainable cuisine, found that many members have significant expertise in purchasing local food. Ninety percent of survey respondents indicated that their establishments have promoted the use of locally grown food on their menus or advertising material. Thirty-four percent reported that over half of their food purchases were locally grown, and 16 percent purchased at least 75 percent of their food from local sources. Eighty-one percent have purchased ingredients directly from farmers, 71 percent have shopped at farmers' markets, 54 percent have bought locally grown products from foodservice distributors, 46 percent from local processors, and 39 percent from farmers' co-operatives. More than half indicated a preference for purchasing directly from a farmer.

Farm to school programs represent an important component of the institutional market for locally grown produce. These are collaborative programs that connect schools to local farmers. For most of these programs, school food authorities buy fresh produce directly from local farmers for some or all of their produce needs. In other programs, schools sponsor school garden projects or field trips to nearby farms as part of an expanded nutrition education curriculum.

The overall goals of the programs are to provide children with access to fresh fruits and vegetables, and promote relationships between schools and farms that can strengthen over time. Many school foodservice directors are seeking approaches to increasing fruit and vegetable consumption in response to concerns about childhood obesity and school meal quality. Proponents believe that farm to school programs provide many benefits to students and small farmers. Students, it is argued, will be more interested in eating healthy fruits and vegetables because local produce is fresher and more flavorful. In addition, they will be more inclined to eat fruits and vegetables that they have seen growing in the fields or in their own gardens. Proponents also argue that schools can provide an environment that stimulates better eating habits from an early age by showcasing local produce and how to prepare it. For farmers, schools can provide a relatively larger and more dependable market for their produce. Farm to school programs have grown rapidly over the last decade.

The National Farm to School Network, a collaboration of groups supporting farm to school programs, estimated that there were 2,051 farm to school programs in the United States in 2009; twice as many as in 2005–06. As of August 2009, they estimated that 41 States had some kind of farm to school program, and 8,943 schools in 2,065 districts participated.

While data and analysis of farm to school programs are scarce, a recent survey about school nutrition issues included questions about the purchase of locally grown food and State farm to school programs. The nationally representative 2005 School Nutrition Dietary Study-III (SNDA III) asked: "Does your school district have guidelines on purchasing locally grown foods" and "Does your district purchase food from the 'State Farm to School' program?"

Participation in the State farm to school programs was reported to be fairly high given the newness of the programs. Fourteen percent of school districts reported participating. Even more school districts reported having guidelines for purchasing locally grown produce.

Another source of information about the growth of local markets in schools comes from the School Nutrition Association (SNA).[9] Each year, the group publishes results from a member survey on practices, trends, and policy issues. The 2009 SNA survey included a question about the extent to which school food authorities (SFAs) purchase local foods ("Does your foodservice program purchase food items from local growers?").[10] Thirty-four percent of the 1,207 SFA members sampled answered yes, and 22 percent said that they did not, but are considering doing so (table 6). They also found that the largest districts were most likely to purchase local foods; 44 percent compared to 27 percent for the smallest schools. Districts in the Northeast were the most likely to purchase local foods, with 57 percent saying "yes," while the Mideast was least likely.[11]

Hospital and foodservice administrators note that healthcare institutions can influence better eating habits through purchasing local foods for use in cafeteria or food-court service and patient meals. Local seasonal produce can be less expensive than nonlocal purchases, and featuring local foods has been found to increase sales at hospital cafeterias, and represents a potential strategy to attract employees and patients. Health Care Without Harm (http://www.noharm.org), an international coalition of 430 organizations in 52 countries, works with hospitals to develop and promote food-purchasing practices consistent with social, environmental, and healthy diet goals. As of 2009, 284 hospital facilities, including several private corporate hospitals, had signed the Health Care Without Harm Healthy Food Pledge to: increase offerings of fruits and vegetables, along with minimally processed foods; identify and adopt sustainable food procurement, including purchasing local foods; and promote and educate about healthy foods. (For more details, see: http://www.noharm.org/us_canada/issues/food/signers.php/)....

---

9. SNA is a national, nonprofit professional organization for school food authorities, representing more than 55,000 members.

10. The 2009 survey, called The School Nutrition Operations Report: The State of School Nutrition 2009, had a 34-percent response rate and a sample of 1,207 members.

11. The SNA results are at best representative of SNA members, but they are not designed to be representative of all school districts. Compared to the SNA survey, the question posed in SNDA-III is slightly different, since it only asks whether there are district guidelines or not. Therefore, the SNDA-III results could be failing to count schools or districts that purchase local foods, but do not have guidelines for doing so. In addition, some schools may have guidelines, but do not purchase local products.

Barriers to Market Entry and Expansion

Barriers to entry and expansion may hinder progress in local-food market development. Market barriers and solutions to these constraints follow:

Capacity Limitations Constrain Small, Local Growers

For producers of local foods, who often run small-scale farm operations, it can be difficult to meet intermediary demands for high volumes, consistent quality, timely deliveries, and out-of-season availability. It may be difficult for small local growers to scale up, as much time is spent off-farm, selling products to consumers. Findings from the USDA Agricultural Management Survey (ARMS) indicate that growers who work off-farm generally have fewer incentives to expand and become more efficient than do small growers who do not participate in alternative, off-farm marketing activities. In other words, the incentive of smaller farmers to expand and become more efficient is diminished as more time is spent off-farm performing additional entrepreneurial activities such as marketing at farmers' markets.

Significant costs of direct marketing and on-farm processing, especially those related to time and labor, can present obstacles to expansion of local food sales. Interviews with farmers in New York and California indicated that shortage of labor related specifically to marketing activities is consistently reported by farmers as being a barrier to direct marketing. Proximity to metro areas only somewhat alleviates labor constraints if farm wages and work availability are not competitive with urban labor conditions. Time involved in customer relations, travel and delivery, processing and packing, and scheduled harvesting to meet the needs of direct marketing varies across direct-marketing venues, but is particularly extensive for farmers' markets and u-pick operations.

From the farmers' perspective, marketing risks when selling in local markets include low sales volume, price competition from multiple sellers with the same product and local angle, rejection based on quality requirements, inability to meet specifications, inability to meet logistical requirements, and buyers backing out of contracts. These concerns are not easily managed by the smallest growers, particularly differences in specifications and packaging across outlets. Many farmers who successfully bridge multiple direct outlets invest in technologies and management strategies that permit the same harvesting, processing, and transportation systems to be used across outlets. For example, bagged lettuces can be sold to both school lunch programs and at farmers' markets, possibly in different sized bags but using the same postharvest supply and marketing chain. By having a single production process that appeals to multiple markets, risk of sales shocks in one outlet may be offset by availability of different outlets.

Obstacles to restaurant purchases include inconsistent availability and quality, difficulty identifying reliable local suppliers, difficulty in making purchases (due to farmers' ordering procedures), and dealing with multiple suppliers. These concerns are echoed in surveys of institutional buyers: year-round availability, local and State regulations, working with multiple vendors, obtaining adequate supply, reliable food quantity, and on-time delivery.

While foodservice directors in Minnesota have expressed interest in a wide variety of locally produced products, many felt that they had limited knowledge about what products were available locally and at what times of the year. Some of these obstacles can be reduced by training sessions that explain what is grown in the region, and teach foodservice staffs how and when to introduce these products into school menus. In addition, many directors noted problems finding farmers who have the needed product, price, and delivery capacity. In some cases where farmers lacked the delivery capacity to deliver to multiple schools, foodservice staff had to arrange transportation or deliver the food themselves. Time needed to negotiate terms and coordinate deliveries was cited by many directors as reasons for purchasing a limited number of local products. A significant number of foodservice directors also expressed displeasure with products not being delivered at the date and time expected, and with the quality dimensions specified. In most cases, the districts relied on a single farmer and had no contingency plan.

In addition to budget constraints, major challenges to local purchasing in hospitals include: large volumes needed; efficiencies required in ordering, delivery, and billing; contract requirements with existing vendors; lack of staff skills in preparing fresh foods; and lack of administrative support. School lunch programs face similar constraints.

Some Federal purchasing programs may have an uncertain effect on local food procurement. USDA purchases and processes food through several programs including The Emergency Food Assistance Program and the Commodity Supplemental Food Program.[17] Without a specific policy to encourage local purchases, these national programs may favor purchases from large suppliers who can offer discounts on pricing and can better facilitate bulk shipments.

Small local growers sometimes overcome scale limitations by pooling resources and diversifying tasks within the supply chain. Production pooling allows small local farmers to capture the advantages that come with larger scale production systems (economic and logistical efficiencies), and may work to meet the supply requirements of large institutional markets. [One study] found that recommendations made by farmers to increase direct farm sales to institutions included building a local customer base and partnering with other farmers. They also found that the most commonly cited factor to increase the likelihood of farm to school program success was farmer co-ops/regional brokers to allow "one-stop shopping." Interviews with small-scale farmers found cooperation between farmers in promoting or managing direct marketing ventures to be an important ingredient in their success. None of the farmers interviewed in the study expressed interest in expanding sales to local restaurants without working together in a joint effort.

Producers can move higher volumes of local food along the supply chain by using an intermediary to pack, distribute, or ship local products to consumers through traditional supermarket channels, restaurants, or institutions. Such intermediaries allow growers to spend more time managing the farm. However, … few cases [were found] where school districts were working through distributors to purchase local produce on a large scale.

Production Capacity Is Constrained by Lack of Infrastructure

Lack of infrastructure related to distribution of local and regional food has also been reported as a barrier to local food market development. The local food supply chain lacks mid-scale, aggregation and distribution systems that move local food into mainstream markets in a cost-effective manner. Lack of investment capital for supply chain infrastructure, such as vehicles, temperature-controlled storage facilities, and processing plants, can be a significant barrier to starting local aggregation and distribution businesses. Farmers have stated that regulatory and processing barriers to meat and value-added product sales present significant obstacles to increasing local sales. Small-scale meat processing

---

17. The 2008 Farm Act contains a provision authorizing $60 million of Commodity Credit Corporation funds over 4 years for a pilot project to assess local/regional purchases of food aid for emergency relief.

facilities often lack capacity, equipment, acceptable inspection status, and human/financial capital to meet demand requirements. In addition, both growers and buyers express a need for more midscale food processing to improve efficiencies in institutional food preparation.

[W]hile institutional food buyers may be interested in regional foods, it was seldom a priority because of few supporting programs and inadequate distribution channels. Commonly cited barriers included the convenience of current ordering method, complicated logistics for negotiations, unreliable supply and on-time delivery due to seasonality or small farm size that make planning difficult, and information about regional growers. Entrepreneurs that have access to funding or in-kind resources for infrastructure, professional marketing, and other services have clear advantages in the supply chain.

One of the biggest problems faced by school districts is their dependence on large, steady supplies of precooked food. Many school systems are not prepared to handle foods that come directly from farms. Further processing of products such as whole carrots, potatoes, and chickens present problems for small, understaffed school kitchens, and may discourage school districts from "scaling up" their purchases of local foods. This suggests a role for distributors in purchasing and processing farm products, and ensuring that foods meet sanitation standards.

The Food, Conservation and Energy Act of 2008 required that the Secretary of Agriculture encourage institutions operating all Child Nutrition Programs to purchase unprocessed locally grown and locally raised agricultural products. As of October 1, 2008, such institutions could apply an optional geographic preference when buying unprocessed locally grown or locally raised agricultural products; this could affect farm to school programs. This option also could be used by the Department of Defense Fresh Program when purchasing for Child Nutrition Programs. USDA published a proposed rule defining "unprocessed agricultural products" to be used for the purpose of applying the optional geographic preference.

The proposed rule is currently being implemented until a final rule is published. For purposes of applying the optional geographic preference provision, "unprocessed locally grown or locally raised agricultural products" means only those agricultural products that retain their inherent character. Agricultural products that undergo the following food handling and preservation techniques are considered to be unprocessed: cooling; refrigerating; freezing; size adjustment made by peeling, slicing, dicing, cutting, chopping, shucking or grinding; drying/dehydration; washing; applying high water pressure or "cold pasteurization;" packaging (such as placing eggs in cartons); vacuum packing and bagging (such as placing vegetables in bags); butchering livestock and poultry; cleaning fish; and the pasteurization of milk. However, the following processing activities disqualify a product from geographic preference: cooking, seasoning, canning, combining with other products, and processing meat into a hamburger patty.

Restrictions on handling may be a limitation to local food growers who have difficulty selling to schools without kitchens, or to growers or handlers looking to market locally produced, value-added products. Budget pressures have forced many school food authorities to switch to central kitchens and satellite heat-and-serve facilities, so many schools are unable to handle unprocessed fresh produce. Barriers that were consistently cited by food buyers included inadequate labor to process food, limited storage and processing facilities at schools, and extra preparation time required for unprocessed produce. Additionally, there is often confusion in schools over what is considered "de minimis [minimal] handling," and what is classified as "local," given that the individual institution is responsible for defining the area for any geographic preference (e.g., State, county, region, etc.).

Traceback Mechanisms

Because most small farmers must combine their products with other farmers' products to make processing and shipping more economical, challenges are posed for product quality, consistency, and traceability. With two or more suppliers, which is often the case in mainstream supply chains, traceback can be more difficult if not impossible. Once a product is combined (aggregated) with others, it is no longer identified with the origin and production processes of a particular farm. Many enterprises communicate this information using multiple strategies tailored to distinct market segments. In many cases, knowing how the food was produced supersede third-party certification to differentiate products.

Without traceability in place, buyers must assume higher levels of risk and liability in cases of foodborne illness. Because these buyers attempt to reduce risk, they often look for established recordkeeping processes before purchasing local food from their supplier. However, many small and local growers lack the knowledge or resources necessary to create product monitoring systems that would facilitate quick and easy product identification and traceback. Traceability requirements may be hindering the growth of local foods because they may be cost-prohibitive for small producers. Adoption of easy-to-use record-keeping devices and farm-level information labeling can facilitate identification of farm source during a foodborne illness outbreak and encourage local food purchases by large commercial buyers.

Limited Farmer Expertise and Training

The process of producing and selling fresh, local commodities includes inherent risks, such as exposure to bad weather, pest infestations, quality inconsistencies, food safety liability, and fluctuating input prices. Growers often need education and training at the local level to meet market requirements and expand access to local customers on issues related to risk management; appropriate postharvest practices; recordkeeping; good agricultural practices (GAP)[18] certification; and liability insurance requirements. [R]etailers in Virginia believed local producers were capable of producing fresh produce of retail quality, but lacked the commitment, expertise, and resources to cool, grade, and package the produce in a commercially acceptable manner. Lack of accounting skills for direct sales to retail food stores or foodservice outlets has impeded further increases in direct marketing. For producers who had never sold directly to local foodservice operations, ... some obstacles [were] more important including local and State regulations; knowledge of foodservice's purchasing practices; and ensuring a safe food supply. Leadership and training for young farmers and farmers' market participants has been reported to be a necessary element for local food systems growth. Encouraging volunteerism either on-farm or at marketing outlets, such as local farm stands, has been reported as one successful way to train a new generation of farmers interested in local marketing.

Regulatory Uncertainties

Uncertainties exist in regulatory scope and enforcement jurisdiction of local food requirements across State, County, and municipal lines, as well as between Federal agen-

---

18. These are U.S. Food and Drug Administration guidelines for reducing microbial contamination.

cies which may impede the flow of information between various regulators. For example, what may be a "voluntary" food safety requirement by the Federal Government may not be interpreted as such by enforcing authorities at the State level. Another example is the application process for participation in the WIC Farmers' Market Nutrition Program, which provides WIC participants with coupons that can be used at local food outlets. While the program is administered by USDA's Food and Nutrition Service, it is implemented by various States, regions, and local entities that sometimes apply different standards for vendor participation. Lack of clear rules and jurisdictional lines sometimes means that growers must determine which regulations apply to their situation and who is responsible for developing and enforcing regulations.

Costs and uncertainties related to food safety and processing regulations affect direct-to-consumer marketing activities across State, county, and municipal boundaries, especially on-farm production and post-harvest handling practices. For example, there may be costs related to complying with State rules on processing, and uncertainty about whether direct farm sales are exempt from existing food safety and processing regulations in certain locations. Clearly stated health and safety rules and licensing and inspection requirements can facilitate the successful operation of farmers' markets.

Characteristics of Local Food Demand

Consumer Preferences

Several studies, both national and smaller scale, have explored consumer preferences for locally produced food. While some studies have investigated characteristics and attitudes of those who purchase local food, others have asked respondents about their perceptions of local food. Also, some studies have measured the premium that consumers would be willing to pay for local food in a hypothetical context. In this section, we summarize the aforementioned studies that examined: (1) characteristics, perceptions, and attitudes of local food buyers, and (2) magnitude and determinants of willingness to pay.

Preferences Drive Local Food Purchases

The most recent national data suggest that while local food consumers are demographically diverse, they are very similar in their motivations for buying local. The majority of respondents to a national study cited freshness (82 percent), support for the local economy (75 percent), and knowing the source of the product (58 percent) as reasons for buying local food at direct markets or in conventional grocery stores. Two national studies found that consumers with varying educational and income levels were equally likely to purchase local food, while other studies have found local food patrons to be more educated and earning above-average income. Consumers who enjoy cooking, growing a food garden, frequenting health food stores, and purchasing organic food were more likely to buy local food. On the other hand, environmental and health-related attitudes and behaviors, while well received among local food consumers, were not important factors affecting actual food purchases. Those who frequented direct markets purchased local foods for their quality and freshness. Not surprisingly, those who placed a greater emphasis on supporting local businesses and producers, or who preferred to purchase fresh rather than processed produce, were more likely to shop at direct markets.

Differences in access to local food and relative prices across regions could lead to differences in buyer profiles. Since the 1980s, geographically limited studies of local food buyers found that buyers judged local produce to be fresher looking and tasting, of higher quality, and a better value for the price. Among shoppers in the southeastern United States, demographic characteristics were weak predictors of the decision to purchase locally produced dairy products. On the other hand, respondents who consider locally produced milk as a unique product, or of better quality, were more likely to express an interest in buying local dairy products. A survey of New Jersey farmers' markets patrons revealed that consumer decisions to purchase from farmers' markets were affected most by quality and freshness (63 percent and 59 percent, respectively), then by convenience (20 percent) and by price (16 percent). A survey of Tennessee farmers' markets patrons found that customers frequently visited a farmers' market to support local farmers; to find locally produced foods; for nutritional reasons; and for the freshness, value, and quality of the produce. Consumers were found to associate local food with enhancing the local economy and benefiting the environment. Farm background was also associated with those consumers that purchased local foods.

In other studies, the role of demographic characteristics was somewhat stronger. Consumers who were female, older, more educated, higher income earners, and members of environmental groups were more likely to buy local food. CSA membership was found to be positively linked to higher education, a preference for organic products, and finding out about the CSA via word-of-mouth. Whether the observed variation in the role of education and income reflects a trend or differences in availability and prices of local food is difficult to assess: separating the influence of location from time is difficult due to lack of comparability among the studies.

Local foods may be more difficult for consumers to find than mainstream food due to seasonal constraints, limited accessibility, or limited awareness of farmers' markets accessibility. These barriers may be considered as transaction costs, which include costs of finding local food markets, obtaining information on their product offerings, obtaining access to markets, and searching for the best prices. Surveys suggest that reasons for not shopping at a farmers' market include: absence of availability in the patron's vicinity; lack of knowledge about market existence; inconvenience (too far to drive); food of comparable quality at more convenient locations; and prices being too high (possibly due to timing of survey—beginning of the season). Consumers who never shop at direct markets placed an emphasis on convenience and aesthetics.

A lack of product choice and the amount of produce provided, as well as transportation and inconvenience of pickup place or time, has been found to deter CSA membership. Income does not seem to be an important factor in choice of where to purchase fresh produce, but time-constraining factors, such as presence of children under the age of 18, do appear to matter. As with other market choices, price, availability, and transaction costs associated with obtaining local foods can be a barrier to consumers, especially in low-income areas where access to supermarkets is limited (food deserts).

Quality, Nutrition, and Environmental Concerns Increase Willingness To Pay

While most consumers report buying local foods at least occasionally, knowing the amount that consumers would be willing to pay is useful for marketing local foods. Eight studies have measured the additional premium that consumers would be willing to pay for locally produced foods in 10 States: Colorado, Ohio, Tennessee, Louisiana, Michigan, South Carolina, Kentucky, Pennsylvania, Maine, and West Virginia, as well as New England. Products included produce (potatoes, strawberries, salad greens), animal products (beef and pork), and value-added products (syrup, salsa, blueberry products, and applesauce).

There are several approaches to eliciting a consumer's willingness to pay for a hypothetical item. First, some studies asked consumers to indicate the premium they would be willing to pay for a locally produced product. A second version asked consumers to indicate whether they would pay a given amount. If the consumer answers "yes," then a higher value is presented, and if the consumer answers "no," then a lower value is presented. Starting values are varied to adjust for some consumers' tendency to take the starting value as a norm. A third version asks consumers to rate several prices as "reasonable to pay" or "beginning to be too expensive" and "too expensive." A fourth approach asks respondents to choose between alternatives in pairs designed to contrast hypothetical prices and levels of other attributes of a product. This is useful for determining the relative importance of different attributes associated with local food.

[S]tudies ... measured the magnitude of willingness to pay ... Values range from about 9 percent for New England specialty products (syrup, salsa) and Colorado potatoes to 50 percent for fresh Florida-grown produce. Differences in methodology used by each study may account for some of the variation, but other factors are likely to contribute to differences in consumer willingness to pay, including product perishability, base price, and regional differences in attitudes toward local food and food in general.

[C]onsumers associate many attributes with "local," including freshness, support for the local economy, support for small farms, and environmental sustainability. To decompose the effects of multiple attributes on willingness to pay for strawberries, survey takers asked respondents to choose between alternatives in pairs designed to contrast levels of proximity, "corporateness," freshness, and price. The study also separated grocery-store shoppers from direct-market shoppers, and found that grocery-store shoppers were willing to pay more for a "freshness guarantee" marked as "harvested yesterday" than for food that was produced within closer proximity but not "guaranteed" fresh. On the other hand, direct-market shoppers were willing to pay more for both attributes, but placed a higher premium on information about production location (proximity) than on a marked freshness guarantee.

While measurements of mean willingness to pay give some indication of consumer interest in a product, the distribution and determinants of willingness to pay are more useful for identifying the potential market for local foods. That is, how many consumers will pay a given amount, and what characteristics do they share? All of the studies that measured willingness to pay examined demographic characteristics, and some also looked at attitudes and perceptions....

Taken together, available studies suggest that purchase of local food is widespread, and willingness to pay a premium is not limited to consumers with higher incomes. Consumers with higher willingness to pay placed higher importance on quality, nutrition, the environment , and helping farmers in their State.

Similar to studies discussed earlier, findings related to demographic characteristics were not consistent across studies. Gender was a significant determinant in three of nine studies, but with opposing results—female respondents were more likely to pay more in Missouri and South Carolina, while the likelihood of male respondents paying more was higher in Ohio. Income was statistically significant in five studies, but willingness to pay was not always higher at higher incomes. In a study of Knoxville, TN, consumers ... the second-lowest income group ($10,000–20,000) was more willing to pay a premium for local apples than the lowest income group (< $10,000), but willingness to pay was not higher for higher income groups. For locally produced broccoli and cabbage, higher income individuals were significantly less willing to pay a premium. College education was also associated with lower willingness to pay a premium for broccoli, cabbages, and peaches.

Differences in knowledge mattered. In a study of willingness to pay for applesauce from local apples, [one study] asked consumers to answer questions that tested their knowledge of agriculture, nutrition, and the environment. Respondents with higher knowledge scores had lower willingness to pay for locally produced food. On the other hand, studies in Missouri and South Carolina found that having been raised on a farm or having worked in agriculture increased willingness to pay for locally produced food.

Foodservice Demand

Among restaurateurs, chefs buy locally grown foods for perceived superior quality and freshness, to meet customer requests, to access unique products, and to support local businesses. From the restaurants' perspective, local products add consumer appeal and represent a way of differentiating from the competition.

[One study] interviewed chain restaurants, locally-owned restaurants, and institutions (schools, prisons, nursing homes). Those that purchased local food products were more likely than the others to report that supporting local business is important. For local restaurants, important factors in increasing the likelihood of buying local foods were minimizing environmental impact and being located in an agricultural region. For institutions, emphasis on buying food that is free of pesticides increased the likelihood. The authors surmise that this may be due to the presence of schools in the institution sample, and potential health threat to children. Factors not considered statistically important by local food buyers included price, dependability of supply, freshness, and size of operation.

Another survey of buyers for foodservice establishments found that they agreed, or strongly agreed, that purchasing local can be profitable. Reasons for purchasing locally grown food included:

- Locally grown foods have higher or better quality.
- Locally grown products are fresher.
- Positive relationships have developed with producers.
- Customer requests have been received for locally grown products, especially after carrying local foods for a period of time.
- The availability of unique or specialty products.

Five surveys conducted of foodservice directors in several States, some of whom already purchased locally,[19] identified several motives for local food purchases by institutional foodservice directors, including public K–12 schools, colleges, universities, and hospitals. Desire for fresher produce or increased consumption of fresh fruits and vegetables was important in all of the studies. Support for local farms, businesses, and community was the top motivation cited in three studies. Two studies ranked public relations as the first or second leading motive. Ability to purchase small quantities was a reported benefit in two studies.

Food Retailers

Despite recent interest by food retailers, there are few studies of retailer perspectives of local food procurement. [One study] interviewed seven grocery store owners and managers. Most stated that locally grown food is a growing trend that is important to consumers

---

19. Response rates for some of the surveys were low, so results are difficult to generalize.

and their organization. Most also perceived that consumer interest derives from their preference for high-quality fresh produce, and concerns about the local economy, food safety, chemical use, and genetic engineering.

[One study] surveyed both retailers and farmers and found that they believed great opportunities exist for selling more local foods if larger grocers were to source more local farm products. Retailers reported that local foods were valued and purchased for their social and food quality benefits. Social benefits included support for the local economy and perceived environmental benefits. Quality benefits included freshness, taste, and high quality. It was further revealed that consumers' perceived benefits of locally sourced food may provide a competitive advantage over mainstream food.

As part of the global emergence of the corporate social responsibility (CSR) movement and firms' efforts to differentiate from the competition, leading retailers Safeway, Ahold, and Delhaize included local food procurement activities in their CSR reports. These are voluntary reports of a company's social and environmental activities, and financial information.[20] In addition, Ahold and Delhaize include the global reporting initiative (GRI) index. The GRI is an independent institution whose goal is to develop guidelines for CSR reporting. The GRI index provides standardized guidelines for reporting progress on corporate economic, environmental, and social performance. Local food policy, practices, and share of expenditures were reported as part of Ahold's economic performance indicators related to sustainable trade that benefits communities and small local businesses. Belgium-based Delhaize Group, the parent company of Delhaize America, reported "local suppliers: practices and spending" as part of their economic performance under "management approach and performance" indicators.

Government Programs and Policies Supporting Local Foods

Government programs and policies that address barriers to local food production and directly support local food purchases can serve as a catalyst for growth of local food markets. Although the United States does not have a broad strategy of public procurement of local foods, there are policies and programs that support local food initiatives....

Federal Policies

In 1994, the U.S. Department of Defense (DoD) began a project that offers its food-buying services to local institutions, such as schools and hospitals, to take advantage of unused trucking capacity in DoD. In 1996, the program, referred to as the Fresh Program, partnered with USDA to procure produce for institutions that was grown within their State, with preferences increasingly given to small and medium-sized farms. By the 1997/98 school year, the program had expanded to 38 States. Although programs vary by State, DoD typically organizes a meeting with foodservice and State agriculture employees, assisting farmers in obtaining a fair price and necessary certification, and ensuring that standards and requirements are met.

---

20. Proponents of CSR argue that company objectives should broaden to include sustainable growth, equitable employment practices, and long-term social and environmental well-being. In addition, they believe that other groups should be included in corporate decisions, not only employees, but also residents affected by the decisions, governments, and organizations that are advocates for environmental and social causes. CSR shifts the emphasis from traditional government regulation of corporate conduct to the promotion of corporate disclosure of activities that address social and environmental issues.

Through congressional passage of the Community Food Security Act, as part of the 1996 Farm Act, the Community Food Project Grants Program (CFP) was established. It is a Federal grants program administered through USDA's National Institute of Food and Agriculture (formerly the Cooperative State Research, Extension, and Education Service (CSREES)). The CFP awards grants to projects that address food insecurity issues by supporting community-based food projects in low-income communities. Examples include training and technical assistance to increase the capacity of local food production and promote "buy local" campaigns, and support to better understand the opportunities and obstacles to local food production and consumption.

In 1999, USDA launched the Community Food Security Initiative. This nationwide initiative sought to forge partnerships between USDA and local communities to build local food systems, increase food access, and improve nutrition. These include farmers' markets and CSAs designed for low-income communities that lack the funding for investing upfront in future harvests.

The Child Nutrition and WIC Reauthorization Act of 2004 requires school districts participating in federally funded meal programs to implement local wellness policies. As wellness programs became established in elementary schools across the Nation, the combination of nutritional education and agricultural production has led proponents to tout local foods as part of a healthy eating solution. Over the past decade, a number of federally created programs have been developed and implemented in a variety of venues, from farm to school programs to local food as part of healthcare initiatives. The programs, administered at the State level, are described in the following sections:

Food and Nutrition Service Programs

USDA's Food and Nutrition Service administers two important programs that promote the use of farmers' markets, and are available in most States; the WIC Farmers' Market Nutrition Program (FMNP) and the Senior Farmers' Market Nutrition Program (SFMNP) (Hamilton, 2005). The FMNP was established by Congress in 1992 to provide Special Supplemental Nutrition Program for Women, Infants, and Children (WIC) participants with coupons, in addition to their regular WIC benefits, that can be exchanged for eligible foods from farmers, farmers' markets, and roadside stands. In 2006, the USDA issued final regulations for the seniors program, making it a permanent program rather than a competitive grant. Low-income seniors are provided SFMNP coupons that can be used at authorized farmers' markets, roadside stands, and CSA programs.

The FMNP is currently authorized in 45 States, territories, and Indian Tribal Organizations. State agencies, such as agriculture or health departments, apply for funds and administer the program. During fiscal year (FY) 2008, 2.3 million WIC participants received FMNP benefits (over 25 percent of all participants), and coupons redeemed resulted in over $20 million in revenue to farmers. Eligible food was available from 16,016 farmers, 3,367 farmers' markets (72 percent of all farmers' markets), and 2,398 roadside stands that were authorized to accept FMNP coupons. Congress provides funds for the program that supports all food costs and 70 percent of administrative costs. For FY 2009, $19.8 million was appropriated for FMNP, down from $23.8 million in 2006. From 2006 to 2008, five States and Puerto Rico accounted for over half of the program grant levels.

For the SFMNP, the 2008 Farm Act provides $20.6 million annually to operate the program through 2012. In FY 2008, the grant level was increased to $21.8 million, after ranging from $14.9 to $16.8 million between FY 2001 and FY 2007. Grants were awarded to 49 State agencies and federally recognized Indian tribal governments, and 963,685 people received SFMNP coupons. In 2008, products were available from over 17,156 farmers at 3,159 farmers' markets, 2,512 roadside stands, and 199 CSAs.

Agricultural Marketing Service Programs

USDA's Agricultural Marketing Service administers several grant programs supporting local food initiatives across the country. The Federal State Marketing Improvement Program (FSMIP) provides matching funds to State agencies to assist in exploring new market opportunities for food and agricultural products, and encourage research to improve the performance of the food marketing system. In 2009, 8 out of 23 grants awarded went to projects supporting local foods, such as funding to improve the effectiveness of Colorado MarketMaker;[21] develop a centralized State wholesale distribution system for locally grown foods; and develop an analytical model for more efficiently allocating State resources to promote locally grown food.

Introduced in the 2002 Farm Act, the National Farmers' Market Promotion Program (FMPP) was funded for the first time in 2006. FMPP is a competitive grants program for local governments, agricultural cooperatives, farmers' markets, and other eligible groups to improve and expand farmers' markets, CSAs, and other local food markets. Projects that were awarded grants in FY 2008 included training for farmers' market managers; promotion of farmers' markets through signage and local TV, newspaper, and radio advertisement; and educating produce growers about the profit potential of season-extending, high-tunnel production technology. Approximately $5 million is allocated for FMPP for FY 2009 and FY 2010, and $10 million for FY 2011 and FY 2012.

The Specialty Crop Block Grant Program (SCBGP) was authorized in 2004 to provide grants to States to enhance the competitiveness of specialty crops, which include fruits, vegetables, and floriculture. State agencies are eligible to apply for grant funds for uses that include "buy local" and State product marketing campaigns. For example, in FY 2008, grants were awarded to projects that promote local food through print materials, electronic media, and a specialty crop website; educate consumers about how to locate and purchase local specialty crops; and evaluate the development of a farm to school program.

Rural Development

USDA's Rural Development administers the Community Facilities Program that supports rural communities by providing loans and grants for construction, acquisition, or renovation of community facilities or the purchase of equipment for community projects. Projects must benefit the community as a whole rather than private, commercial entities. Examples include projects that support farmers' markets, community kitchens, and food processing centers. Loan amounts averaged $665,229 in FY 2008, but vary widely.

2008 Farm Act

Currently, the primary Federal policy that supports local and regional food systems is the 2008 Food, Conservation, and Energy Act, commonly referred to as the 2008 Farm Act. Provisions include funds under the Business and Industry Guarantee Loan Program

---

21. MarketMaker is a national partnership of land grant institutions and State departments of agriculture dedicated to building an electronic infrastructure that would more easily connect farmers with economically viable new markets. It provides an interactive mapping system that locates buyers (e.g., retailers, wholesalers, processors) and sources of agricultural products (e.g., farmers, farmers' markets).

(B&I) to aid rural food enterprise entrepreneurs and local food distribution, and funding for the Value-Added Agricultural Market Development (VAAMD) program emphasizing local food distribution. The 2008 Farm Act supports locally and regionally produced food through a set-aside within the B&I loan program for facilitating the storing, processing, and distribution of local and regional food products. Through FY 2012, at least 5 percent of the funds made available to the program will be reserved for local food initiatives, amounting to over $100 million in FY 2010.

The VAAMD program, formerly the Value-Added Producer Grant Program (VAPG), provides grant funding for agricultural producers who add value to their products through processing or marketing, thereby raising farm income. Under the 2008 Farm Act, producers of food that is marketed locally are eligible for the program, which supports activities such as business planning and website development, and additional marketing staff to increase the farmers' share of the food dollar. Through FY 2012, 10 percent of funds will be reserved for developing local and regional supply networks that connect small- and medium-sized farms to markets, thereby increasing competitiveness and profits.

The Rural Business and Industry Guaranteed Loan Program was modified to give priority for loan guarantees to those involved in local food distribution. The National School Lunch Act was amended to encourage institutions receiving funds to purchase locally grown unprocessed agricultural products. Funding was also increased for the Farmers' Market Promotion Program, Senior Farmers' Market Nutrition Program, and Specialty Crop Block Grants.

The 2008 Farm Act reauthorizes the Community Food Project Grants Program (CFP) as a permanent program with $5 million per year in mandatory funding. The 2008 Farm Act also created, within the CFP program, the Healthy Urban Food Enterprise Development Center to provide grants for promoting development of enterprises that distribute and market healthy and locally produced food to underserved communities. Mandatory funding was authorized for 3 years at $1 million annually.

The 2008 Farm Act created a new program, the Rural Microentrepeneur Assistance Program, to provide entrepreneurs in rural areas with skills to establish new businesses and continue operation of existing microenterprises. Although not directed specifically at agriculture-related businesses, examples include funding to initiate a marketing business to sell local food or provide working capital to renovate a small store. Funding was authorized at $15 million in mandatory funding from FY 2009 to FY 2012.

"Know Your Farmer, Know Your Food" Initiative

In 2009, USDA launched the "Know Your Farmer, Know Your Food" initiative, an agencywide effort to create new economic opportunities by better connecting consumers with local producers. As part of the initiative, several funding efforts and programs were announced to assist farmers, help consumers access nutritious foods, and support rural community development. Representatives from various USDA agencies have identified the following funding efforts and programs, which may be used to cultivate local capacity to strengthen local and regional food systems, including:

- $18 million for the Value-Added Agricultural Market Development Program (VAAMD).
- A new voluntary cooperative program created by the 2008 Farm Act will allow select State-inspected establishments to ship meat and poultry products in interstate commerce. The program supplements the existing Federal-State cooperative inspection program to allow State-inspected plants with 25 or fewer employees to

ship products across State lines. This will create new economic opportunities for small establishments with limited markets.[22]

- "Farm to School Tactical Teams" formed by AMS and FNS to assist school administrators as they transition to purchasing more locally grown foods.

- $8.6 million awarded by USDA's Risk Management Agency to provide producers with opportunities to learn more about managing risk in their businesses, and providing educational opportunities for underserved farmers with limited resources.

State and Local Policies

Most regulations that directly affect local food systems take place at the State or local level, such as those related to public safety and health, or application of sales taxes. At the State level, a range of policies help create the environment in which farmers' markets operate. These include programs to expand the number of farmers' markets and use the markets to accomplish other economic development goals, such as the marketing of State identified food. For States participating in the Farmers' Market Nutrition Programs, significant questions relate to who will administer the program and where the required matching funds for administration will come from.

State and local policies can have important impacts in areas such as farm to institution procurement policies and the use of electronic benefit transfer (EBT) cards at farmers' markets. Paper food stamp coupons were replaced with EBT cards in June 2009. EBT allows recipients to authorize transfer of their government benefits from a Federal account to a retailer account to pay for food products received. Although SNAP is federally funded, it is administered at the State and local levels, so policies on acceptance of EBT at farmers' markets vary. A USDA survey of farmers' market managers found that the use of EBT terminals to accept food stamps ranged from 0 percent of farmers' markets in the Southwest to 15.9 percent in the Far West. Some States have enacted laws to fund pilot programs that provide EBT access to farmers' markets, while other States have partnered with local businesses, farm groups, and banks to create pilot programs. USDA also provides free wired point-of-sale machines in some States for EBT transactions.[23]

Some States and localities offer incentives to low-income people to shop at farmers' markets. New York City's Health Bucks Incentive Program distributes free coupons to low-income consumers for purchasing fresh produce at farmers' markets. States and municipalities can also support farmers' markets by supporting land use policies that favor small farms and zoning policies that make space for markets.

Legislatures in a few States have funded efforts to promote farmers' markets and expand their availability. Several States have implemented programs to regulate the development and operation of farmers' markets, and specify the types of products that can be sold in order to develop consistent statewide standards. In recent years, a number of States have created State Food Policy Councils to stimulate statewide discussion of opportunities and potential impact of government policies.[24] At the local and regional levels, poli-

---

22. The U.S. Census Bureau provides information on animal slaughtering and processing plants with paid labor, and 19 or fewer employees. In 2007, States with the highest number of these plants included Texas (130), California (113), and Missouri (101) (U.S. Census Bureau, 2009).

23. Congress recently authorized AMS to set aside 10 percent of Farmers' Market Promotion funds to help farmers' markets acquire wireless EBT terminals.

24. Food Policy Councils are comprised of a broad range of individuals from farm and consumer groups, food processors and distributors, anti-hunger groups, academia, and State government.

cies relating to farmers' markets are among the most common activities undertaken by the councils.

There is also some policy movement at the State level on broader systemwide legislation. For example, the Illinois Food, Farms, and Jobs Act was signed into law in 2007 to create a task force to encourage and promote local food production.

The National Conference of State Legislatures has compiled a comprehensive, searchable database that lists all State policies and policy proposals related to local foods since 2004.[25] Most of these bills address development and promotion of farmers' markets and farm to school programs. Other local food topics include establishing commissions to provide advice on creating and sustaining local food markets; amending laws to permit farm operations to advertise with roadside signage; and strengthening distribution networks for local foods.

Most policy issues facing farmers' markets develop at the local level because farmers' markets are a local activity. The most commonly encountered local policy issues relating to farmers' markets are operational questions, such as where the market can operate, parking, security, and conflicts with adjacent businesses. These policies can be significant factors in determining the success and existence of a market. Cities also address issues related to regulation of farmers' markets, such as the need for permits, zoning exceptions, or approval of a market ordinance. Cities may be involved in promoting and developing markets as part of a local food policy initiative or may assume responsibility for operating and funding markets. For example, Berkshire Grown, originally the Berkshire Regional Food and Land Council, promotes food, flowers, and plants produced in the Berkshire region of Massachusetts and builds partnerships between farmers, chefs, and consumers (http://www.berkshiregrown.org).

Benefits of Local Food Markets: A Look at the Evidence

Recent expansion of public programs that support local food systems suggests that interest in local foods extends beyond the motivations of consumers and producers. The Federal, State, and local programs discussed in the previous section devote significant resources to support local foods, because growth in local foods is expected to generate public benefits that are currently lacking in the food marketing system. Examining the costs, benefits, and unintended consequences of local food markets can provide input into effective design of programs that involve local foods. It can also identify situations in which adopting local food characteristics is a cost-effective tool for accomplishing policy goals. In the aggregate or at a national level, however, impacts of local food systems may be difficult to discern because of the relatively small portion of food that is produced and consumed in local food markets.

In this section, we examine the conceptual framework for four potential impacts of local food systems compared to mainstream systems, and review the empirical evidence of their existence. These include economic development impacts, health and nutrition benefits, impacts on food security, and effects on energy use and greenhouse gas emissions. We selected these impacts because they are the focus of programs and policies that involve local foods or have been the focus of numerous empirical analyses. Programs and policies are commonly focused on economic and business development, health and nutrition, or a combination of these goals. For example, the Farmers' Market Nutrition Program is designed to work within the existing framework of the WIC program to provide

---

25. The status of the bills is categorized as active, inactive, adopted as law, vetoed, or carried over.

locally grown produce to participants. Farm to school programs may seek to increase the availability of healthy food options in schools, while also supporting farms and other businesses in the local economy. Studies of relationships between local foods, energy use, and greenhouse gas emissions have been the focus of much of the empirical literature on local food impacts. The U.S. food system accounts for about 16 percent of total U.S. energy consumption, and much of this energy is derived from burning fossil fuels that release carbon dioxide and other greenhouse gases (GHG).

It should be noted that local food systems have the potential to generate other public benefits. It has been suggested that local food systems could reduce food safety risks by decentralizing production. Eating locally has been viewed as a way to help preserve farmland by allowing new residential communities to be established on farms in urbanizing areas. Other public benefits include the development of social capital in a community, preservation of cultivar genetic diversity, and environmental quality. This is likely not an exhaustive list. Not all potential benefits of local food systems are discussed in this report because there is not adequate empirical research in 2010 on a particular topic, due to limited applicability to existing government programs, or a lack of a clear conceptual framework that relates local foods to these other potential impacts.

Economic Development

The expansion of local food markets implies that consumers in a particular area are purchasing more of their food from nearby sources, and that more of the money they spend remains in their local community. Hence, local food systems have the potential to positively impact the local economy. Claims of economic development impacts—in the form of income and employment growth—are common in local foods research. [F]armers [retain] a greater share of the food dollar by eliminating money going to the "middlemen" as a possible benefit. [L]ocal food systems may encourage growth in local labor markets.

The most direct way that expansion in local food systems could impact local economies is through import substitution. If consumers purchase food produced within a local area instead of imports from outside the area, sales are more likely to accrue to people and businesses within the area. This may then generate additional economic impacts as workers and businesses spend the additional income on production inputs and other products within the area.

Shifting the location of intermediate stages of food production and direct-to-consumer marketing can also be considered forms of import substitution. For example, shifting processing activities (e.g., beef slaughtering and processing) to the local area may result in a larger portion of the value of the finished product remaining in the local area. Part of this effect may be due to producers retaining a greater share of the retail price of their products as they assume responsibility for additional supply chain functions (e.g., distribution and marketing).

Empirical studies suggest that local foods can have a positive impact on local economic activity through import substitution and localization of processing activities. Using an input-output model … [it has been] predicted that locally produced fruits, vegetables, and meat products would increase output, employment, and labor incomes in Iowa. This was due, in part, to development of direct-marketing facilities and increases in local meat slaughtering and processing.

Farmers' markets have been found to have positive impacts on local economies. [It has been] estimated that each dollar spent at farmers' markets in Iowa generated 58 cents in indirect and induced sales, and that each dollar of personal income earned at farmers' markets generated an additional 47 cents in indirect and induced income (multipliers of 1.58 and 1.47, respectively). The multiplier effect for jobs was 1.45; that is, each full-time equivalent job created at farmers' markets supported almost half of a fulltime equivalent job in other sectors of the Iowa economy. Similarly, multipliers associated with farmers' markets in Oklahoma have been estimated to be between 1.41 and 1.78.

The magnitude of the economic impact from import substitution depends on the sources of inputs for local production and processing (i.e., whether money spent on inputs is retained locally or not), and the degree to which a local supply chain displaces local economic activity that supported nonlocal products. This could include reductions in traditional commodity marketing (e.g., grains) or industries that support distribution and marketing of nonlocal food products (e.g., supermarkets).

Accounting for displaced economic activity within the local community reduces the positive economic impacts of localization, although estimated overall benefits are still positive. [One study] assumed that an increase in acreage devoted to local fruit and vegetable production would replace corn and soybean acreage, which partially offsets some of the predicted economic benefits. [Another] account[s] for lost spending at mainstream retail stores due to spending at farmers' markets in West Virginia. The net economic impacts of farmers' markets in the State were found to be positive, but lost sales at retail stores offset some of this impact. Farmers' markets in West Virginia were estimated to generate $656,000 in annual labor income, $2.4 million in industry output, and 69.2 full-time equivalent jobs. While still positive, these impacts were offset by $463,000 in lost labor income, $1.3 million in lost industry output, and 26.4 lost full-time equivalent jobs generated by mainstream retail stores.

Local food markets may stimulate additional business activity within the local economy by improving business skills and opportunities. [One study] examined the role of farmers' markets in creating and sustaining new rural businesses. Farmers' markets helped medium ($10,000–$99,999 gross sales) and large-scale ($100,000 or more gross sales) enterprises to expand or complemented existing, well established businesses. For small vendors (less than $10,000 gross sales), farmers' markets appeared to operate as a relatively low-risk incubator for new businesses and a primary venue for part-time enterprises in a nurturing environment. These types of benefits are difficult to quantify because investments in business skills and development may take years to generate observable benefits. However, business skill development may be an attractive benefit in areas where few other options are available to acquire additional skills and market experience.

The presence of local food markets may also spur consumer spending at other businesses in a community. This spillover spending could support the retail sector in a community if, for example, a farmers' market draws consumers to an area where they would not have otherwise spent money. [It has been] found that many farmers' market shoppers traveled to downtown areas specifically to patronize the market, and also spent additional money at neighboring businesses.

These empirical examples suggest that the economic benefits of expanding local food systems can be unevenly distributed. Some sectors of the economy will lose sales, income, and jobs, while others will gain. Also, the geographic distribution of benefits and costs may not be uniform. By definition, economic benefits generated via import substitution in one location would result in reduced economic activity in areas from where the goods were previously exported. The location, distribution, and magnitude of these costs have not been studied for local food systems.

It is also not clear how estimates of net economic benefits would be affected if the costs of public investments in local food markets are accounted for.[26] Some programs have provided public financing to support local food systems for several years (e.g., the Farmers Market Promotion Program began in 1976), and local governments often either directly operate local markets or provide resources to support their operation (e.g., use of public space for markets). These costs have not been accounted for in existing research on the economic impacts of local food markets.

Health and Nutrition

The relationship between local foods and healthy food items, such as fresh fruits and vegetables, has led to claims that local food systems may provide health benefits from improved nutrition, obesity prevention, and a reduced risk of chronic diet-related disease. Potential health benefits have been cited as a justification for farm-to-institution marketing programs, including farm to school programs, and as a benefit of joining a community supported agriculture (CSA) program. Others have suggested that promoting locally grown food can improve community health outcomes.

Local foods may affect health and nutrition in one of two general ways. First, local food systems may offer food items that are fresher, less processed, and retain more nutrients (e.g., because of shorter travel distances) than items offered in nonlocal systems. For example, locally obtained food may be healthier because "freshly picked foods ... retain more nutrients than less fresh foods". Consumers may purchase the same amounts and types of fruits and vegetables, but since local foods are fresher, the nutrient content of diets is improved. Whether or not local food systems tend to improve health and nutrition in this way is largely an unresolved empirical question. Locality may be only one factor that determines product freshness or retention of nutrients, and a link between travel distance and nutrient content has not yet been established.

Second, local food systems may increase the availability of healthy food items in a community and encourage consumers to make healthier food choices. For this to be true, at least two conditions must be met: Local foods systems must increase the availability of healthy food items in a way that is infeasible or impractical for non-local systems, and consumers who purchase local food must make different dietary choices that they would not have made without the local option available.

[Studies] suggest that improved access to healthy foods is associated with healthier dietary choices. Also, anecdotal evidence indicates that CSA membership is associated with increased fruit and vegetable consumption. However, it is not clear that there is a relationship between improved access and health outcomes, or that local characteristics, as opposed to access in general, play a role in consumer and dietary choices.

Introducing healthy food options in schools may be an effective means of improving children's diets. Farm to school initiatives that increase availability, reduce prices, and provide point of purchase information have been found to be effective strategies to increase fruit and vegetable consumption in schools. What is still unclear is whether local characteristics are driving these results, or if innovative curricula and cafeteria menu changes are responsible. For example, found that children exposed to a garden-based education curriculum reported greater fruit and vegetable consumption, even though no effort was made to improve the availability of local foods at the schools.

---

26. Public investments are also made for reasons that may not be related to increases in sales, incomes, and employment, such as health and nutrition (discussed in this section).

Food Security

Local food characteristics have commonly been associated with efforts to improve food security, particularly at the community level. Food security means that all people at all times have access "to enough food for an active, healthy life," and is a necessary condition for a nourished and healthy population. Those who are food insecure have limited or uncertain availability of healthy and safe food or have uncertain ability to acquire food in normal ways. As of 2008, more than 6.7 million households in the United States had very low food security (i.e., multiple instances of reduced food intake and disrupted eating patterns).

Direct marketing has been a key component of community food security programs, with the goal of reducing community food insecurity and supporting rural communities by strengthening traditional ties between farmers and urban consumers. In particular, farmer's markets have been associated with food security programs because they are increasingly capable of accepting benefits from Federal and State food and nutrition programs (e.g., food stamps).

The potential for local food systems to improve food security is conceptually similar to claims related to health benefits. That is, expanding local food options may increase the availability of healthy food items, particularly in areas with limited access to fresh food. The prevalence of healthy food items may encourage increased intake of fruits and vegetables, and improved availability may reduce problems related to food access and uncertainty. An implicit assumption in this argument is that local food systems improve access and reduce uncertainty.

Despite the use of local foods as a strategy to reduce food insecurity, little research has been conducted to examine its efficacy in reducing insecurity. Evidence suggests that healthy eating habits are associated with participation in the Senior Farmers' Market Nutrition Program, and in the WIC Farmers' Market Nutrition Program when nutrition education accompanied coupon distribution. These programs have been cited as important components that impact food security. However, while these studies make the case that programs with local food characteristics impact healthy food choices, food security is influenced by other factors, such as economic conditions, income, and poverty status. To our knowledge, no study has attempted to demonstrate a clear relationship between these factors, observed food security, and local food characteristics.

The potential for local foods to affect food security may be limited by several factors. For example, farmers' markets may experience low-volume sales that are similar to those faced by other retailers in low-income neighborhoods. There is also no a priori expectation that local food systems will address the needs of low-income households who are subject to food insecurity. Prices depend on the market dynamics in a particular location. Prices for some products in local food markets may be comparable to or below prices in other markets in a community, but may be higher for other products or in other locations. For example, some farmers may use local food markets as a residual or supplemental revenue stream and be willing to accept lower retail prices than farmers who use local markets as their primary source of income.

Although the precise role of local food characteristics in affecting food security is ambiguous, it is possible that a relationship is difficult to detect due to the current size and scope of local food markets. Given that a relatively small portion of food is produced and consumed in local food markets, any observable impacts may be overwhelmed by other factors, such as the myriad programs and policies that impact food security.

Food Miles, Energy Use, and Greenhouse Gas Emissions[27]

[Food] is traveling further from farmers to consumers as the food system increasingly relies on long-distance transport and global distribution networks. Concerns about fossil fuel use and greenhouse gas (GHG) emissions have increased scrutiny of the environmental impacts of transportation in the food system and the distance food travels to consumers. Advocates of localization of the food system argue that reducing transport distances for food, or food miles, can reduce fossil fuel energy use, pollution, and GHG emissions. This claim has also been cited as a potential benefit of localization among local food system researchers.

Distance is clearly a factor that determines energy use and emissions resulting from food transport. Given two otherwise identical supply chains, the supply chain with greater food travel distance will use more energy and emit more pollution. But supply chains of different lengths (i.e., different number of production and marketing stages) are seldom identical; the mode of transport, load sizes, fuel type, and trip frequency all affect energy use and emissions.

[A 2007 report] reviewed studies that focused on transport elements of the food supply chain, with emphasis on the United Kingdom.[28] These studies highlight the importance of transportation mode in determining fuel use and carbon-dioxide (CO_2) emissions. For example, cherries imported from North America had the highest ratio of emissions to product transported, reflecting the use of air freight. On the other hand, apples imported from New Zealand traveled a greater distance, but had a lower emissions ratio because they traveled by sea, a highly energy-efficient means of moving goods.

[S]everal studies that compare energy use and emissions from locally sourced products, domestic products sourced from a mainstream retailer, and imported products [were also reviewed]. Transportation CO_2 emissions were found to be greater for imported produce than domestic produce. Comparisons of local food systems to food sourced from mainstream retailers found no significant differences in transportation energy use, except for those products transported by air. The shorter distance traveled in local markets was offset by the greater transportation efficiency of the mainstream system, which lowered energy use per unit transported.[29]

A complete assessment of food system energy use and GHG emissions requires the consideration of all stages of food production and distribution. Other contributions to energy use and emissions—particularly related to production, processing, storage, and preparation—may be as important as transportation in assessing the overall impact of

---

27. Other environmental impacts of alternative food systems are excluded. For example, the continued shift of production to larger dairy operations in the mainstream dairy system creates increased environmental risks associated with the concentration of manure-based nitrogen and phosphorus (MacDonald et al., 2007).

28. Many studies of energy use and GHG emissions focus on the food system in the United Kingdom or the rest of Europe. These studies are useful for providing a conceptual framework for how energy use and GHG emissions are generated in the U.S. food system, but empirical estimates may not be directly applicable. Production practices, transportation modes, the composition of the food basket, consumer preferences, and the origin of food imports may not be comparable to the U.S. food system.

29. Fuel use per unit of product hauled depends on distance traveled, the fuel efficiency of the transport mode (i.e., miles per gallon), and the total load size hauled. Transportation modes that move large loads of food from production to retail may reduce the effects of longer distances traveled. This suggests that local food systems can achieve reductions in per unit fuel use when short transport distances are coupled with larger load sizes.

local food systems. Life-cycle assessments (LCA) of inputs and outputs are one way to account for energy use and emissions in the food system. LCA generally considers both the direct emissions from activities, such as production and transport, and emissions generated during the manufacture of inputs, such as fertilizer, pesticides, and electricity.[30] A full life-cycle assessment would also extend beyond national boundaries and would not end with the consumption of final market goods.

Empirical studies of food transportation energy use and GHG emissions do not agree on whether local food systems are more energy and emissions efficient, reflecting great variation among local foods markets. In some cases, local and regional food systems are more efficient, and distance is an important factor in determining environmental impacts from transportation. Others have found that distance is neither an adequate measure of impact, nor particularly relevant, because transportation accounts for a relatively small share of energy use and emissions in the food system. In the United States, agricultural production, processing, and household storage and preparation each account for a larger share of food system energy use than transportation. Total energy use and emissions are affected by differences in inputs used in each segment in the food supply chain, production practices and natural endowments, and crop yields and fertilizer use. Finally, [it is] suggest[ed] that differences in types of food products and diet composition may have important implications for energy use and emissions in the food system.

Research Gaps in Understanding the Role of Local Foods

As interest in local food systems as a component of food and agriculture policy has increased in recent years, so has the desire to understand how expanding local food markets impact farmers, consumers, and communities. Consumer, distributor, and producer interest in local foods has increased rapidly as consumers demand unique product characteristics and producers seek additional viable revenue streams. Local food has also generated great enthusiasm for its potential benefits. Yet local foods still represent a small portion of U.S. agriculture, and much remains to be learned about the future role of local foods in the United States.

Assessing the future growth in local food systems will require detailed knowledge about how and why farms sell products in local markets. USDA's Census of Agriculture and Agricultural Resource Management Survey are useful tools for pinpointing certain local food marketing activities (e.g., sales direct to consumers) and the farms that engage in these activities. But future research will need to examine relationships between farm size and location, land and operator characteristics, mix of products and marketing outlets, and relative costs and returns associated with local food marketing. Understanding these relationships will help uncover the incentives and disincentives that exist for participating in local food markets, how they vary across the farm landscape, and how policies can encourage participation. Future research on farm participation in local food markets will require more detailed data about the different types of local food activities. Data currently available could be improved along two dimensions. First, more detailed information about the relative magnitude of local food sales, including types of products sold by market type, would provide a more complete picture of the size of local foods markets. Second, surveys that gather detailed farm business and operator characteristics, such as

---

30. LCAs attempt to capture a broader scope of energy use and emissions in the food system, but have limitations. Selection of the types of impacts to consider and how to model them, the spatial scope of the analysis, and the time horizon of the analysis can all affect LCA results and may limit their interpretability.

ARMS, are not designed to provide a detailed description of local food marketing activities.

Oversampling of direct-marketing farms or other operations that are likely to participate in local foods markets could increase the ability to answer research questions about farm-level decisions in local foods markets. A second gap in the research on local foods is an understanding of the potential public benefits of expanding local food systems, particularly as they relate to public policies and programs that support local foods. With increasing food insecurity, lack of food access (food deserts), and diet-related health problems, local food systems may be a way to circumvent these problems. But as the research in the previous section makes clear, definitive links between local foods and desirable public policy outcomes need to be studied to fill knowledge gaps.

Of particular interest is whether local food systems are capable of effectively improving access to healthy foods in underserved communities, and whether improved access can translate into improved health and diet-related outcomes. Further, farm to school programs that combine local food availability with innovative curricula and food-related education may be a desirable method for encouraging healthy eating habits at a young age. Many of these programs are currently in their infancy, which limits the ability of researchers to draw definitive conclusions about their efficacy. Future evaluation of these programs will help to determine situations when supporting local foods can support policy goals.

Notes

1. The ERS report on local foods excerpted above as well as the ERS report, *Emerging Issues in the U.S. Organic Industry*, excerpted previously can both be found on the USDA ERS website, http://www.ers.usda.gov. Both contain citations to the studies referenced as well as tables that graphically illustrate the study results.

2. Neil Hamilton has been a driving force for the local food movement and has written about, lectured on, and advocated for local food systems for many years. His book, THE LEGAL GUIDE TO DIRECT FARM MARKETING (1999) has been called the "bible" of direct farm marketing legal issues. His article, *Putting a Face on our Food: How State and Local Food Policies Can Promote the New Agriculture*, made persuasive arguments for the advantages of a local food system and is widely credited with the rise in Food Policy Councils at the state level. Neil D. Hamilton, *Putting a Face on our Food: How State and Local Food Policies Can Promote the New Agriculture*, 7 Drake J. Agric. L. 407 (2002).

3. The Leopold Center for Sustainable Agriculture at Iowa State University released a study that considered the potential impact of farmers in six Midwestern states (Illinois, Indiana, Iowa, Michigan, Minnesota, and Wisconsin) raising 28 edible fruit and vegetable crops in quantities large enough to meet local demand. The study predicted that this production would spur $882 million in sales, create more than 9,300 jobs, and result in about $395 million in labor income. As to the acreage diversion required, the study also noted that just one Iowa county could meet the demand for all six states. Dave Swenson, *Selected Measures of the Economic Values of Increased Fruit and Vegetable Production and Consumption in the Midwest*, Leopold Center for Sustainable Agriculture, Iowa State University (March 2010). For additional commentary on the impact of local food systems see, Marne Coit, *Jumping on the next Bandwagon: An Overview of the Policy and Legal Aspects of the Local Food Movement*, 4 J. Food L. & Pol'y 45 (2008).

4. Questions have been raised about whether locally grown food competes with or complements the organic label. The Economic Research Service addresses this question as follows:

A recent national survey of U.S. consumers who shop at "natural food" stores posed the following question: "If you were purchasing a particular ingredient for a recipe and you had a choice of either a local product or a non-local organic one, which would you choose, assuming equivalent price and quality?" In this head-to-head comparison, 35 percent of respondents chose local and 22 percent chose organic (41 percent chose both equally). Other researchers have reported similar findings on consumer preferences for local over organic food, and willingness to pay higher premiums for local

The ERS nationwide survey of U.S. organic handlers found that 24 percent of organic sales in 2004 were made locally — within an hour's drive of the handlers' facilities — 30 percent were made regionally, and 39 percent were made nationally. A small proportion of domestic organic sales (7 percent) was exported in 2004. Although most retail chains that initiate local programs usually purchase local products from a multi-state region, most consumers consider local products as being produced much closer to home — in their State, within 100 miles of their community. Consumers may also have other misperceptions, such as the belief that local production is environmentally responsible, even though local labels are not typically associated with production standards. According to recent census of agriculture results, approximately 136,000 farmers reported selling agricultural products directly to consumers, while only about 20,000 farmers reported producing organic products.

Organic and local labels are not necessarily competitive. Many long-time participants in the organic market perceive organic and local agriculture as "two sides of the same coin." Some organic certifying entities, both State and private, already certify producers and processors to a number of other standards — including food safety standards and international organic standards that incorporate a social justice component. A product might easily carry both an organic label, denoting the ecologically based production system used, and a locally grown logo, denoting the number of miles to deliver the product to the consumer.

As the number of farmers' markets in the United States continues to grow, many market managers report strong unmet demand for organic vendors. A variety of local-organic food initiatives are emerging in response to the unmet needs for local and organic products in farmers' markets, supermarkets, and institutional settings. Legislation to support local agriculture has been proposed in a number of States in recent years. For example, Illinois passed legislation in 2007 designed to make Illinois the Midwest leader in local and organic food and fiber production, creating a task force to develop strategies to increase local, organic buying programs for public institutions and supporting farmers in transition to organic production. A county in Iowa has enacted policies to rebate 100 percent of real property taxes to farmers who convert to organic production and to support local and organic food purchases in county institutional settings. At the Federal level, USDA's Agricultural Marketing Service administers several grant programs that have helped a number of local-organic initiatives in different parts of the country.

Catherine Greene, Carolyn Dimitri, Biing-Hwan Lin, William McBride, Lydia Oberholtzer, and Travis Smith, *Emerging Issues in the U.S. Organic Industry*, USDA Economic Research Service, Economic Information Bulletin No. 55, 16–17 (June 2009).

5. While the United States struggles to recreate its access to local foods, some developing countries struggle to develop mechanisms that allow for trade outside of local markets.

The PBS international current affairs broadcast, *Wide Angle* presented the fascinating story behind the creation of the Ethiopian commodities exchange.

> Eleni Gabre-Madhin is a woman with a dream. The charismatic Ethiopian economist wants to end hunger in her famine-plagued country. But, rather than relying on foreign aid of new agricultural technology, she has a truly radical plan. She has designed the nation's first commodities exchange, which she hopes will revolutionize an ancient market system whose inefficiencies have been partly responsible for the country's persistent food shortages.

The Market Maker, available at http://www.pbs.org/wnet/wideangle/episodes/the-market-maker/introduction/5000/.

6. *Urban agriculture*, i.e., the growing and distribution of food through intensive plant cultivation and animal husbandry in urban areas, is generating a great deal of interest. It is estimated that up to 30% of agricultural production originates from within a metropolitan area. While some of this is food produced in acreage surrounding cities, an increasing amount is produced in high density urban centers through the cultivation of vacant lots, roof top gardens, and both individual and community gardens.

Because of the intensity of production on small acreage, sustainable agricultural systems are critical. Perhaps the most well known urban agriculturalist is Will Allen, founder of Growing Power, a nonprofit urban farm organization based in Milwaukee. Growing Power's goal is "the development of Community Food Systems ... to provide high-quality, safe, healthy, affordable food for all residents in the community." On one two-acre lot in Milwaukee, Allen produces enough food to feed thousands in the community through an intense and completely sustainable system. Winner of a McCarthy Genius grant and listed as one of Time Magazine's 100 most influential people in 2010, *See,* http://www.growingpower.org/aout_us.htm.

7. The *Agile Agriculture* project of the Center for Applied Sustainability at the University of Arkansas School of Law, funded largely by Walmart, seeks to bring the full spectrum of those involved in agriculture and the U.S. food system together to develop ways to link small farm producers to large scale markets. *See* http://asc.uark.edu/323.asp. *See also,* Corby Kummer, *The Great Grocery Smackdown: Will Walmart, not Whole Foods, Save the Small Farm and Make America Healthy?* THE ATLANTIC MAGAZINE (March 2010) (describing Walmart's efforts to work with local producers). While prices paid for produce purchased from local farmers may be higher than that paid to larger growers or produce brokers, savings in transportation costs and the elimination of middlemen in the transaction may more than make up the difference. Ron McCormick, the senior director of local and sustainable sourcing for Walmart stated that while Walmart's local sourcing is now only 4–6 percent of produce spending, he hopes it will climb to 20 percent. *Id.*

D. Food for the Future

1. Food Security

The following report provides statistics from the USDA on food security and insecurity in the United States, relying on statistics that preceded the full impact of the current recession. It notes that 14.6 percent of households were food insecure at least at some point during 2008, up from 11.1 percent in 2007. This is the highest recorded prevalence rate of food insecurity since 1995 when the first national food security survey was conducted. *Food Security in the United States,* USDA, Economic Research Service, Briefing Room: Food Security, available at http://www.ers.usda.gov/Briefing/FoodSecurity/. Food insecurity rates are estimated to be higher in the current economy.

Mark Nord, Margaret Andrews, and Steven Carlson
Household Food Security in the United States, 2008
USDA Economic Research Service, Report No. ERR-83 (November 2009)
(Report Summary)

Most U.S. households have consistent, dependable access to enough food for active, healthy living—they are food secure. But a minority of American households experience food insecurity at times during the year, meaning that their access to adequate food is limited by a lack of money and other resources. The U.S. Department of Agriculture (USDA) monitors the extent and severity of food insecurity in U.S. households through an annual, nationally representative survey and has published statistical reports on household food security in the United States for each year since 1995. This report presents statistics on households' food security, food expenditures, and use of food and nutrition assistance programs in 2008.

In 2008, 85.4 percent of U.S. households were food secure throughout the year. Food-secure households had consistent access to enough food for active healthy lives for all household members at all times during the year. The remaining 14.6 percent (17 million households) were food insecure. These households, at some time during the year, had difficulty providing enough food for all their members due to a lack of resources. The prevalence of food insecurity was up from 11.1 percent (13 million households) in 2007 and was the highest observed since nationally representative food security surveys were initiated in 1995.

About one-third of food-insecure households (6.7 million households, or 5.7 percent of all U.S. households) had very low food security, up from 4.7 million households (4.1 percent) in 2007, and the highest level observed since nationally representative food security surveys were initiated in 1995. In households with very low food security, the food intake of some household members was reduced, and their normal eating patterns were disrupted because of the household's food insecurity. The other two-thirds of food-insecure households obtained enough food to avoid substantial disruptions in eating patterns and food intake, using a variety of coping strategies, such as eating less varied diets, participating in Federal food and nutrition assistance programs, or obtaining emergency food from community food pantries or emergency kitchens.

Even when resources are inadequate to provide food for the entire family, children are usually shielded from the disrupted eating patterns and reduced food intake that characterize very low food security. However, children as well as adults experienced instances of very low food security in 506,000 households (1.3 percent of households with children) in 2008, up from 323,000 households (0.8 percent of households with children) in 2007.

On a given day, the number of households with very low food security was a small fraction of the number that experienced this condition "at some time during the year." Typically, households classified as having very low food security experienced the condition in 7 or 8 months of the year, for a few days in each of those months. On an average day in late November or early December, 2008, for example, an estimated 1.1 million to 1.4 million households (0.9–1.2 percent of all U.S. households) had members who experienced very low food security, and children experienced these conditions in 86,000 to 111,000 households (0.22 to 0.28 percent of all U.S. households with children).

The prevalence of food insecurity varied considerably among different types of households. Rates of food insecurity were substantially higher than the national average for households with incomes near or below the Federal poverty line, households with children headed by single women or single men, and Black and Hispanic households. Food insecurity was more common in large cities and rural areas than in suburban areas and other outlying areas around large cities. Regionally, food insecurity was most prevalent in the South, intermediate in the Midwest and West, and least prevalent in the Northeast.

Food-secure households spent more for food than food-insecure households. In 2008, the median U.S. household spent $43.75 per person for food each week—about 14 percent more than the cost of USDA's Thrifty Food Plan (a low-cost food "market basket" that meets dietary standards, taking into account household size and the age and gender of household members). The median food-secure household spent 18 percent more than the cost of the Thrifty Food Plan, while the median food-insecure household spent 10 percent less than the cost of the Thrifty Food Plan.

Some food-insecure households turn to Federal food and nutrition assistance programs or emergency food providers in their communities when they are unable to obtain enough food. Fifty-five percent of the food-insecure households surveyed in 2008 said that in the previous month they had participated in one or more of the three largest Federal food and nutrition assistance programs—the National School Lunch Program, Supplemental Nutrition Assistance Program (SNAP, the new name for the Food Stamp Program), and Special Supplemental Nutrition Program for Women, Infants, and Children (WIC). About 20 percent of food-insecure households obtained emergency food from a food pantry at some time during the year, and 2.6 percent ate one or more meals at an emergency kitchen in their community.

Notes

1. The excerpt of the Household Food Security report provided above is a summary. The full report can be accessed on the USDA website at http://www.ers.usda.gov/Publications/Err83/.

2. The USDA Household Food Security report lists ten states with statistically higher household food insecurity rates than the national average for the years 2006–2008 of 12.2%.

1.	Mississippi	17.4%
2.	Texas	16.3%
3.	Arkansas	15.9%
4.	Georgia	14.2%
5.	New Mexico	14.1%
6.	Missouri	14.0%
7.	Oklahoma	14.0%
8.	Kansas	13.8%
9.	Maine	13.7%
10.	North Carolina	13.7%

It is ironic to note that most of the states included in this listing have a significant agricultural industry. Texas, Kansas, and North Carolina are considered to be among the top ten agricultural producing states in the nation. The states of Mississippi, Arkansas, Georgia, and Kansas each claim agriculture as its largest industry, with significant agricultural interests in each of the other states.

2. The Obesity Epidemic

> Results from the 2007–2008 National Health and Nutrition Examination Survey (NHANES), using measured heights and weights, indicate that an estimated 34.2% of U.S. adults aged 20 years and over are overweight, 33.8% are obese, and 5.7% are extremely obese ... Body mass index (BMI), expressed as weight in kilograms divided by height in meters squared (kg/m2), is commonly used to classify overweight (BMI 25.0–29.9), obesity (BMI greater than or equal to 30.0), and extreme obesity (BMI greater than or equal to 40.0).

Cynthia L. Ogden, Ph.D., and Margaret D. Carroll, *Prevalence of Overweight, Obesity, and Extreme Obesity Among Adults: United States, Trends 1976–1980 Through 2007–2008*, National Center for Health Statistics, Center for Disease Control and Prevention (June 2010).

> Over the past three decades, childhood obesity rates in America have tripled, and today, nearly one in three children in America are overweight or obese. One third of all children born in 2000 or later will suffer from diabetes at some point in their lives; many others will face chronic obesity related health problems like heart disease, high blood pressure, cancer, and asthma ... This epidemic also impacts the nation's security, as obesity is now one of the most common disqualifiers for military service.

First Lady Michele Obama Launches Let's Move: America's Move to Raise a Healthier Generation of Kids, The White House Office of the First Lady (February 9, 2010).

A 2009 study by the Center for Disease Control and Prevention along with a nonprofit research group estimated that the direct and indirect cost of obesity was as high as $147 billion annually, over 9 % of total medical spending per year. Obese patients spend $1,429 more for their medical care than did people within a normal weigh range. Child hood obesity rates are predicted to increase these medical costs as children develop serious medical conditions as a result of their weight.

Dietary Guidelines for Americans
A Report of the Dietary Guidelines Advisory Committee, (2010)

The 2010 Dietary Guidelines Advisory Committee (DGAC) was established jointly by the Secretaries of US Department of Agriculture (USDA) and the US Department of Health and Human Services (HHS). The Committee's task was to advise the Secretaries of USDA and HHS on whether revisions to the 2005 Dietary Guidelines were warranted, and if so, to recommend updates to the Guidelines. The DGAC immediately recognized that, on the basis of the vast amount of published research and emerging science on numerous relevant topics, an updated report was indeed needed.

The 2010 DGAC Report is distinctly different from previous reports in several ways. First, it addresses an American public of whom the majority are overweight or obese and yet under-nourished in several key nutrients. Second, the Committee used a newly developed, state-of-the-art, web-based electronic system and methodology, known as the Nutrition Evidence Library (NEL), to answer the majority of the scientific questions it posed. The remaining questions were answered by data analyses, food pattern modeling analyses, and consideration of other evidence-based reviews or existing reports, including the 2008 Physical Activity Guidelines for Americans. The 2005 Dietary Guidelines for Americans were the starting place for most reviews. If little or no scientific literature had been published on a specific topic since the 2005 Report was presented, the DGAC indicated this and established the conclusions accordingly. A third distinctive feature of this Report is the introduction of two newly developed chapters. The first of these chapters considers the total diet and how to integrate all of the Report's nutrient and energy recommendations into practical terms that encourage personal choice but result in an eating pattern that is nutrient dense and calorie balanced. The second chapter complements this total diet approach by integrating and translating the scientific conclusions reached at the individual level to encompass the broader environmental and societal aspects that are crucial to full adoption and successful implementation of these recommendations....

Part B. Section 3: Translating and Integrating the Evidence: A Call to Action

The data clearly document that America is experiencing a public health crisis involving overweight and obesity. Particularly alarming is the further evidence that the obesity epidemic involves American children and youth, as nearly one in three are classified as overweight or obese. Childhood obesity and overweight is a serious health concern in the United States (US) because of immediate health consequences, as well as because it places a child at increased risk of obesity in adulthood, with all its attendant health problems such as cardiovascular diseases (CVD) and type 2 diabetes (T2D). All adults—parents, educators, caregivers, teachers, policy makers, health care providers, and all other adults who work with and care about children and families—serve as role models in some capacity and share responsibility for helping the next generation prevent obesity by promoting healthy lifestyles at all ages. Primary prevention of obesity, starting in pregnancy and early childhood, is the single best strategy for combating and reversing America's obesity epidemic for current and future generations. While there is also an urgent need to improve the health and well-being of children and adults who are already overweight and obese, primary prevention offers the strongest universal benefits. Solving the obesity problem will take a coordinated system-wide, multi-sectoral approach that engages parents as well as those in education, government, healthcare, agriculture, business, advocacy and the community. This approach must promote primary prevention among those who are not yet overweight and address weight loss and fitness among those who are overweight.

Disparities in health among racial and ethnic minorities and among different socioeconomic groups have been recognized as a significant concern for decades. Several subgroups of the population (Native Americans, Blacks, Hispanics, and segments of the population with low income) have a strikingly high prevalence of overweight and obesity. Dietary patterns vary among different ethnic and socioeconomic groups. Individuals of lower education and/or income levels tend to eat fewer servings of vegetables and fruits than do those with more education and/or higher income. According to national surveys, Blacks tend to have the lowest intakes of vegetables and fruits among ethnic groups, but also have a higher prevalence of hypertension and related diseases, such as stroke. Although the reasons for these differences are complex and multifactorial, this report addresses research indicating that certain dietary changes can provide a means to reduce health disparities. If we are successful in changing dietary intake patterns of all Americans through a systematic approach, we will go along way in narrowing the gap in health disparities.

Although obesity is related to many chronic health conditions, it is not the only diet-related public health problem confronting the nation. Nutritionally suboptimal diets with or without obesity are etiologically related to many of the most common, costly, and yet preventable health problems in the US, particularly CVD (atherosclerosis, stroke) and related risk factors (T2D, hypertension, and hyperlipidemia), some cancers, and osteoporosis. Improved nutrition and appropriate eating behaviors have tremendous potential to enhance public health, prevent or reduce morbidity and mortality, and decrease health care costs.

The science is not perfect; evidence is strong in some areas and limited or inconsistent in other areas. Nevertheless, this report is an urgent call to action to address a major public health crisis by focusing on helping all Americans achieve energy balance through adoption and adherence to current nutrition and physical activity guidelines.

After reviewing its entire report, the Dietary Guidelines Advisory Committee (DGAC) recognized a need to not only document the evidence, but translate and integrate major findings that have cross-cutting public health impact and provide guidance on how to implement the changes necessary to enhance the health and well being of the population. Below are the four major cross-cutting findings from the 2010 DGAC Report, followed by suggestions for implementation.

Four Main Integrated Findings to be Used in Developing the 2010 Dietary Guidelines for Americans

1. Reduce the incidence and prevalence of overweight and obesity of the US population by reducing overall calorie intake and increasing physical activity.

A focus on life-stage approaches (pregnant women, children, adolescents, adults, and older adults) is necessary nationwide to help Americans meet nutrient needs within appropriate calorie intake. To achieve this, Americans should:

- Know their calorie needs. In other words, individuals need to know how many calories they should consume each day based on their age, sex, and level of physical activity.

- Significantly lower excessive calorie intake from added sugars, solid fats, and some refined grain products.

- Increase their consumption of a variety of vegetables, fruits, and fiber-rich whole grains.

- Avoid sugar-sweetened beverages.

- Consume smaller portions, especially of high-calorie foods.

- Choose lower-calorie options, especially when eating foods away from home.

- Increase their overall physical activity.

- Have access to improved, easy-to-understand labels listing calorie content and portion size on packaged foods and for restaurant meals (especially quick service [i.e., fast food] restaurants, restaurant chains, and other places where standardized foods are served).

Collectively, these measures will help Americans manage their body weight and improve their overall health. In order to achieve this goal, the public and private sectors must be committed to assisting all Americans to know their calorie needs at each stage of life and help them recognize how to manage and/or lower their body weight. Simple but effective consumer-friendly tools for self-assessment of energy needs and self-monitoring of food and beverage intake are urgently needed and should be developed. These strategies will enable everyone to recognize and implement, both inside and outside the home, dietary recommendations that have been consistent for decades.

2. Shift food intake patterns to a more plant-based diet that emphasizes vegetables, cooked dry beans and peas, fruits, whole grains, nuts, and seeds. In addition, increase the intake of seafood and fat-free and low-fat milk and milk products, and consume only moderate amounts of lean meats, poultry, and eggs.

This approach will help Americans meet their nutrient needs while maintaining energy balance. Importantly, this will assist Americans to increase their intake of shortfall nutrients, such as potassium and fiber. These goals can be attained through a range of food patterns—from omnivore to vegan—that embrace cultural heritage, lifestyle, and food preferences. These flexible patterns of eating must encompass all foods and beverages that are consumed as meals and snacks throughout the day, regardless of whether they are eaten at home or away from home.

3. Significantly reduce intake of foods containing added sugars and solid fats because these dietary components contribute excess calories and few, if any, nutrients. In addition, reduce sodium intake and lower intake of refined grains, especially refined grains that are coupled with added sugar, solid fat, and sodium.

The components of the American diet that are consumed in excess are solid fats and added sugars (SoFAS), refined grains, and sodium. SoFAS alone contribute approximately 35 percent to total energy intake of Americans. Collectively, the consumption of foods containing SoFAS, refined grains, and sodium lead to excessive calorie intake, resulting in weight gain and health consequences such as hypertension, CVD, and T2D. Reducing the intake of these over-consumed components will require much more than individual behavior change. A comprehensive approach is needed. The food industry will need to act to help Americans achieve these goals. Every aspect of the industry, from research and development to production and retail, needs to contribute healthful food solutions to reduce the intake of SoFAS, certain refined grain products, and sodium. Sound health and wellness policies at the local, state, and national level also can help facilitate these changes.

4. Meet the 2008 Physical Activity Guidelines for Americans.

A comprehensive set of physical activity recommendations for people of all ages and physical conditions was released by the US Department of Health and Human Services in 2008 (HHS, 2008). The 2008 Physical Activity Guidelines for Americans were developed to help Americans to become more physically active. By objective measures, large portions, indeed the majority, of the US population are sedentary (Metzger, 2008). In fact, Americans spend most of their waking hours engaged in behaviors that expend very little energy (Matthews, 2008). To increase the public's participation in physical activity, compelling multi-sector approaches are needed to improve home, school, work, and community environments to promote physical activity. These changes need to surpass planned exercise and foster greater energy expenditure throughout the day. Improved exposure to recreational spaces, increased use of active transportation, and encouraging development of school and worksite policies that program physical activity throughout the day can help enable Americans to develop and maintain healthier lifestyle behaviors. Special attention and creative approaches also are needed to help Americans reduce sedentary behaviors, especially television viewing and video game use, among children and adolescents.

A Call to Action

Dietary Guidelines for Americans have been published since 1980. During this time obesity rates have escalated and dietary intake patterns have strayed from the ideal. The 2010 DGAC recognizes that several of its recommendations have been made repeatedly in prior reports with little or no demonstrable impact. For example, recommended intakes of vegetables and fruit remain woefully unchanged, despite continuing advice to markedly increase intake of these foods. Substantial, high-level barriers appear to impede achievement of these goals, including certain government regulations and policies. Chief among these are land use policy and economic incentives for food manufacturers. The food supply and access to it has changed dramatically over the past 40 years, contributing to an overall increased calorie intake by many individuals. Since the 1970s, the number of fast food restaurants has increased 147 percent. The portions that are served in restaurants and the serving sizes of foods sold in packages at stores have increased as well. Moreover, the number of food items at the supermarket has increased from 10,425 in 1978 to 46,852 in 2008, and most of these contribute SoFAS, refined grains, and sodium to the American diet … This has far-reaching effects such that the average child now consumes 365 calories per day of added sugars and 433 calories per day of solid fat for a combined total of 798 calories, or more than one-third of total calorie intake … Conversely, Americans spend 45 percent less time preparing food at home … or eating food at the family table than previously, and this behavioral trend is associated with increased risk of weight gain, overweight and obesity. **In this context, the DGAC concluded that mere repetition of advice will not effectively help Americans achieve these evidence-based and often-repeated goals for a healthy diet.** (emphasis in original)

Ensuring that all Americans consume a health-promoting dietary pattern and achieve and maintain energy balance requires far more than individual behavior change. A multi-sectoral strategy is imperative. For this reason, the 2010 DGAC strongly recommends that HHS and USDA convene appropriate committees, potentially through the Institute of Medicine (IOM), to develop a strategic plan focusing on the behaviors and actions needed to successfully implement the four key 2010 DGAC recommendations highlighted above.

A coordinated strategic plan that includes all sectors of society, including individuals, families, educators, communities, allied health professionals, public health advocates, policy makers, scientists, and small and large businesses (e.g., farmers, agricultural producers, food scientists, food manufacturers, and food retailers of all kinds), should be engaged in developing and implementing the plan to help all Americans eat well, be physically active, and maintain good health. It is important that any strategic plan be evidence-informed, action-oriented, and focused on changes in systems (IOM, 2010a). This systems approach is already underway in countries such as the United Kingdom for obesity prevention (Butland, 2007) with promising results. Recent examples of this approach in the US include an IOM committee convened by HHS and USDA and charged with developing strategies for gradually but dramatically reducing sodium intake, which remains persistently high even after more than 40 years of advice. This IOM committee recently issued its report (IOM, 2010b), providing a comprehensive strategy to reduce dietary sodium intake in the general population by focusing on the food supply and targeting industry to partner in systematic reductions in sodium content of foods. Already there is encouraging evidence that food manufacturers are responding positively and are committed to reducing the sodium content in their food products. Similarly, the US National Physical Activity Plan, released in May, 2010, was developed by multiple stakeholders and provides a comprehensive, realistic implementation framework intended to promote physical activity in the American population. Most recently, the May, 2010, White House Task Force on Childhood Obesity Report, Solving the Problem of Childhood Obesity Within a Generation, also calls for a multi-sector, systems approach to solving this important public health issue.

An Urgent Need to Focus on Children

Any and all systems-based strategies must include a focus on children. Primary prevention of obesity must begin in childhood. This is the single most powerful public health approach to combating and reversing America's obesity epidemic over the long term. Trends for childhood overweight and obesity are alarming, with obesity prevalence rates tripling between 1980 and 2004. Although rates for children appear to be leveling off, they remain high, with one-third currently overweight or obese, defined as at or above the 85th percentile on body mass index (BMI)-for-age growth charts (Ogden, 2010). These numbers represent more than 25 million children in the US. In order to reverse this trend, we will need to work together as a Nation to improve the food environment to which children are exposed at home, school, and the community. Efforts to prevent childhood obesity need to start very early, even in utero. Increasing evidence indicates that maternal obesity before conception and excessive gestational weight gain represent a substantial risk of childhood obesity in the offspring ... Thus, addressing maternal nutrition, physical activity, and body weight before conception and during pregnancy as well as emphasizing early childhood nutrition is paramount for preventing the onset of childhood obesity. Areas targeting childhood obesity prevention that should be addressed include, but are not limited to:

- Improve foods sold and served in schools, including school breakfast, lunch, and after-school meals and competitive foods so that they meet the recommendations of the IOM report on school meals (IOM, 2009) and the key findings of the 2010 DGAC. This includes all age groups of children, from preschool through high school.

- Increase comprehensive health, nutrition, and physical education programs and curricula in US schools and preschools, including food preparation, food safety, cooking, and physical education classes and improved quality of recess.

- Develop nationally standardized approaches for health care providers to track BMI-for-age and provide guidance to children and their families to effectively prevent, monitor, and/or treat childhood obesity.

- Develop nationally standardized approaches for health care providers to improve nutrition, physical activity participation, healthy weight gain during pregnancy and the attainment of a healthy weight postpartum.

- Increase safe routes to schools and community recreational areas to encourage active transportation and physical activity.

- Remove sugar-sweetened beverages and high-calorie snacks from schools, recreation facilities, and other places where children gather.

- Develop and enforce responsible zoning policies for the location of fast food restaurants near schools and places where children play.

- Increase awareness and promote action around reducing screen time (television and computer or game modules) and removing televisions from children's bedrooms.

- Develop and enforce effective policies regarding marketing of food and beverage products to children. Efforts in this area are underway through a government interagency committee comprised of the Federal Trade Commission, Centers for Disease Control and Prevention, USDA, and Food and Drug Administration, as well as some self-regulation from industry (Omnibus Appropriations Act, 2009).

- Develop affordable summer programs that support children's health, as children gain the most weight during the out-of-school summer months (von Hippel, 2007).

Challenges and Opportunities for Change

Change is needed in the overall food environment to support the efforts of all Americans to meet the key recommendations of the 2010 DGAC (Story, 2009). The 2010 DGAC recognizes that the current food environment does not adequately facilitate the ability of Americans to follow the evidence-based recommendations outlined in the 2010 DGAC Report. Population growth, availability of fresh water, arable land constraints, climate change, current policies, and business practices are among some of the major challenges that need to be addressed in order to ensure that these recommendations can be implemented nationally. For example, if every American were to meet the vegetable, fruit, and whole-grain recommendations, domestic crop acreage would need to increase by an estimated 7.4 million harvested acres (Buzby, 2006). Furthermore, the environment does not facilitate the ability of individuals to follow the 2008 Physical Activity Guidelines for Americans. Most home, school, work, and community environments do not promote engagement in a physically active lifestyle. To meet these challenges, the following sustainable changes must occur:

- Improve nutrition literacy and cooking skills, and empower and motivate the population to prepare and consume healthy foods at home, especially among families with children.

- For all Americans, especially those with low-income, create greater financial incentives to purchase, prepare, and consume vegetables and fruit, whole grains, seafood, fat-free and low-fat milk and milk products, lean meats, and other healthy foods. Currently, individuals have an economic disincentive to purchase healthy foods.

- Improve the availability of affordable fresh produce through greater access to grocery stores, produce trucks, and farmers' markets.

- Increase environmentally sustainable production of vegetables, fruits, and fiber-rich whole grains.

- Ensure household food security through measures that provide access to adequate amounts of foods that are nutritious and safe to eat.

- Develop safe, effective, and sustainable practices to expand aquaculture and increase the availability of seafood to all segments of the population. Ensure that consumers have access to user-friendly benefit/risk information to make informed seafood choices.

- Encourage restaurants and the food industry to offer health-promoting foods that are low in sodium; limited in SoFAS and refined grains; and served in smaller portions.

- Implement the US National Physical Activity Plan, a private-public sector collaborative promoting local, state, and national programs and policies to increase physical activity and reduce sedentary activity (National Physical Activity Plan, 2010). Through the Plan and other initiatives, develop efforts across all sectors of society, including health care and public health; education; business and industry; mass media; parks, recreation, fitness, and sports; transportation, land use and community design; and volunteer and non-profit. Reducing screen time, especially television, for all Americans also will be important.

The 2010 DGAC recognizes the significant challenges involved in implementing the goals outlined here. These challenges go beyond cost, economic interests, technological and societal changes, and agricultural limitations. Over the past several decades, the value of preparing and enjoying healthy food has eroded, leaving instead the practices of eating processed foods containing excessive sodium, solid fats, refined grains, and added sugars. As a Nation, we all need to value and adopt the practices of good nutrition, physical activity, and a healthy lifestyle. The DGAC encourages all stakeholders to take actions to make every choice available to Americans a healthy choice. To move toward this vision, all segments of society—from parents to policy makers and everyone else in between—must now take responsibility and play a leadership role in creating gradual and steady change to help current and future generations live healthy and productive lives. A measure of success will be evidence that meaningful change has occurred when the 2015 DGAC convenes.

---

3. Food Deserts

Related to the problem of food insecurity as well as the problem of obesity is the problem of access to healthy food. The following excerpt is a summary of a Congressionally mandated report on this issue.

**Michele Ver Ploeg, Vince Breneman, Tracey Farrigan,
Karen Hamrick, David Hopkins, Phil Kaufman, Biing-Hwan Lin,
Mark Nord, Travis Smith, Ryan Williams, Kelly Kinnison,
Carol Olander, Anita Singh, and Elizabeth Tuckermanty**
*Access to Affordable and Nutritious Food—Measuring and
Understanding Food Deserts and Their Consequences*
USDA Economic Research Service, Report No. AP-160 (June 2009)

Report to Congress

Increases in obesity and diet-related diseases are major public health problems. These problems may be worse in some U.S. communities because access to affordable and nutritious foods is difficult. Previous studies suggest that some areas and households have easier access to fast food restaurants and convenience stores but limited access to supermarkets. Limited access to nutritious food and relatively easier access to less nutritious food may be linked to poor diets and, ultimately, to obesity and diet-related diseases. Congress, in the Food, Conservation, and Energy Act of 2008, directed the

U.S. Department of Agriculture (USDA) to conduct a 1-year study to assess the extent of the problem of limited access, identify characteristics and causes, consider the effects of limited access on local populations, and outline recommendations to address the problem.

This report presents the findings of the study, which include results from two conferences of national and international authorities on food deserts and a set of commissioned research studies done in cooperation with the National Poverty Center at the University of Michigan. It also includes reviews of existing literature, a national-level assessment of access to supermarkets and large grocery stores, analysis of the economic and public health effects of limited access, and a discussion of existing policy interventions. A variety of analytical methods and data are used to assess the extent of limited access to affordable and nutritious food and characteristics of areas with limited access.

Findings

Access to a supermarket or large grocery store is a problem for a small percentage of households. Results indicate that some consumers are constrained in their ability to access affordable nutritious food because they live far from a supermarket or large grocery store and do not have easy access to transportation. Three pieces of evidence corroborate this conclusion:

- Of all U.S. households, 2.3 million, or 2.2 percent, live more than a mile from a supermarket and do not have access to a vehicle. An additional 3.4 million households, or 3.2 percent of all households, live between one-half to 1 mile and do not have access to a vehicle.

- Area-based measures of access show that 23.5 million people live in low-income areas (areas where more than 40 percent of the population has income at or below 200 percent of Federal poverty thresholds) that are more than 1 mile from a supermarket or large grocery store. However, not all of these 23.5 million people have low income. If estimates are restricted to consider only low-income people in low-income areas, then 11.5 million people, or 4.1 percent of the total U.S. population, live in low-income areas more than 1 mile from a supermarket.

- Data on time use and travel mode show that people living in low-income areas with limited access spend significantly more time (19.5 minutes) traveling to a grocery store than the national average (15 minutes). However, 93 percent of those who live in low-income areas with limited access traveled to the grocery store in a vehicle they or another household member drove.

These distance and time-based measures are national estimates that do not consider differences between rural and urban areas in terms of distance, travel patterns, and retail market coverage.

Urban core areas with limited food access are characterized by higher levels of racial segregation and greater income inequality. In small-town and rural areas with limited food access, the lack of transportation infrastructure is the most defining characteristic.

These area- or distance-based results are in line with a nationally representative survey of U.S. households conducted in 2001. Responses to direct questions about food access show that nearly 6 percent of all U.S. households did not always have the food they wanted or needed because of access-related problems. More than half of these households also lacked enough money for food. It is unclear whether food access or income constraints were relatively greater barriers for these households.

Supermarkets and large grocery stores have lower prices than smaller stores.

A key concern for people who live in areas with limited access is that they rely on small grocery or convenience stores that may not carry all the foods needed for a healthy diet and that may offer these foods and other food at higher prices. This report examines whether prices of similar foods vary across retail outlet types and whether the prices actually paid by consumers vary across income levels.

These analyses use proprietary household-level data that contain information on food items purchased by approximately 40,000 demographically representative households across the United States. Results from these analyses show that when consumers shop at convenience stores, prices paid for similar goods are, on average, higher than at supermarkets.

Low-income households shop where food prices are lower, when they can.

Findings also show that food purchases at convenience stores make up a small portion of total food expenditures (2 to 3 percent) for low-income consumers. Low- and middle-income households are more likely to purchase food at supercenters, where prices are lower. Administrative data on SNAP benefit redemptions from 2008 show that 86 percent of SNAP benefits were redeemed at supermarkets or large grocery stores. Research that considers the prices paid for the same food across household income levels indicates that while some of the very poorest households—those earning less than $8,000 per year—may pay between 0.5 percent and 1.3 percent more for their groceries than households earning slightly more, households earning between $8,000 and $30,000 tend to pay the lowest prices for groceries, whereas higher income households pay significantly higher prices.

The study also examined food shopping behavior and the types of food purchased for SNAP participants and other low-income households. Data from the 1996/1997 NFSPS show that SNAP participants were, on average, 1.8 miles from the nearest supermarket. However, the average number of miles both SNAP participants and eligible nonparticipants traveled to the store most often used was 4.9 miles. These same data show that SNAP participants who did not shop at supermarkets purchased less noncanned fruit, noncanned vegetables, and milk than SNAP participants who shopped frequently at a supermarket.

Easy access to all food, rather than lack of access to specific healthy foods, may be a more important factor in explaining increases in obesity.

Many studies find a correlation between limited food access and lower intake of nutritious foods. Data and methods used in these studies, however, are not sufficiently robust to establish a causal link between access and nutritional outcomes. That is, other explanations cannot be eliminated as the cause of lower intake. A few studies have examined food intake before and after healthy food options become available (either within existing stores or because new stores opened). The findings are mixed—some show a small but positive increase in consumption of fruits and vegetables, while others show no effect.

The causal pathways linking limited access to nutritious food to measures of overweight like Body Mass Index (BMI) and obesity are not well understood. Several studies find that proximity of fast food restaurants and supermarkets are correlated with BMI and obesity. But increased consumption of such healthy foods as fruits and vegetables, low-fat milk, or whole grains does not necessarily lead to lower BMI. Consumers may not substitute away from less healthy foods when they increase their consumption of healthy foods. Easy access to all food, rather than lack of access to specific healthy foods, may be a more important factor in explaining increases in BMI and obesity.

Understanding the market conditions that contribute to differences in access to food is critical to the design of policy interventions that may be effective in reducing access limitations.

Access to affordable and nutritious food depends on supply (availability) and consumer demand. Consumer behavior, preferences, and other factors related to the demand for some foods may account for differences in the types of foods offered across different areas. Food retailer behavior and supply-side issues such as higher costs to developing stores in underserved areas may also explain variation across areas in which foods are offered and what stores offer them.

If high development costs serve as a barrier to entry for supermarkets in some areas with low access, then subsidy programs or restructured zoning policies may be effective solutions. If consumer demand factors, such as inadequate knowledge of the nutritional benefits of specific foods, contribute to differences in access by reducing demand, then a public health campaign may be a preferred strategy. Several local and State-level efforts are underway that could provide the basis for a better understanding of the types of interventions that may work best.

Food has been used as a tool for community development.

Projects such as farmers' markets, community gardens, promotion of culturally specific foods for ethnic minorities and Native Americans, local food production and promotion, youth agricultural and culinary training programs, and many other types of programs have all been implemented in a variety of settings, both urban and rural. USDA's Community Food Projects Competitive Grant program has much experience in funding and nurturing such programs.

The current state of research is insufficient to conclusively determine whether some areas with limited access have inadequate access.

Future research should consider improved methods to measure access levels, availability, and prices of foods faced by individuals and areas. More research is needed to understand how access, availability and price affect the shopping and consumption behaviors of consumers.

Data linking information on the types of foods consumers purchase and eat with measures of consumers' levels of access and the prices they face could help explain the economic consequences of food access. Studies that use improved methods and data to determine how food access affects diet, obesity, and other health outcomes are also needed to help explain the health consequences of food access.

Notes

1. The full *Access to Affordable and Nutritious Food* report is available on the USDA website at http://www.ers.usda.gov/Publications/AP/AP036/.

2. The Wallace Center at Winrock International, a nonprofit organization that "supports entrepreneurs and communities in building a food system that is healthier for people,

the environment, and the economy, provides leadership through the National Good Food Network." According to their website, "[t]he Network seeks to 'scale up' supply, by facilitating aggregation and distribution of healthy, green, fair, affordable food—a market-based approach to issues of health food access." In response to the USDA study, they called for a "set of coordinated, community based activities across the country, including outreach to existing corner stores, incentives for locating new retail stores, public transportation improvements, farmers market development, nutrition education, and other activities to improve food access." *See* http://wallacecetner.org/our-values/level-1-folder-1/experts-react-to-usda-food-desert-study/.

3. One of the five key initiatives of First Lady Michele Obama's *Let's Move* campaign to address the problem of childhood obesity is the elimination of food deserts.

> Lack of access is one reason why many children are not eating recommended levels of fruits, vegetables, and whole grains. And food insecurity and hunger among children is widespread.... The Administration, through new federal investments and the creation of public private partnerships will:

> **Eliminate Food Deserts:** As part of the President's proposed FY 2011 budget, the Administration announced the new Healthy Food Financing Initiative—a partnership between the U.S. Departments of Treasury, Agriculture, and Health and Human Services that will invest $400 million a year to help bring grocery stores to underserved areas and help places such as convenience stores and bodegas carry healthier food options. Through these initiatives and private sector engagement, the Administration will work to eliminate food deserts across the country within seven years.

> **Increase Farmers Markets:** The President's 2011 Budget proposes an adeditional $5 million investment in the Farmers Market Promotion Program at the U.S. Department of Agriculture which provides grants to establish, and improve access to, farmers markets.

First Lady Michele Obama Launches Let's Move: America's Move to Raise a Healthier Generation of Kids, The White House Office of the First Lady (February 9, 2010).

4. In June 2010, Walmart announced its participation in the "Chicago Community Investment Partnership" as part of an effort to "eradicate food deserts and stimulate local economic development." Included in the plan is the opening of several dozen stores of varying sizes, providing "access to affordable groceries especially to those 600,000 residents living within Chicago's three, self-identified food deserts." *Walmart Announces Goal to Work with the City to Increase Store Growth Over Five Years*, http://walmartstores.com/pressroom/news/10020.aspx.

4. The Role of Agriculture and the Way Forward

Neil Hamilton writes optimistically of a new "food democracy, "and his belief that "a powerful transformation, a food revival, is underway in our nation, one that promises to create new opportunities for anyone taking part in it." Yet with any transformation, he acknowledges, there is controversy.

> The issues implicated in the debate over a food democracy are truly monumental: our rights as consumers to be informed and to have more satisfying food choices and alternatives in the market; the rights of farmers, chefs and marketers

to produce and market foods reflecting their diversity and creative potential; and our nation's ability to have a food system that promotes good health, confidence, understanding, and enjoyment as well as economic opportunity. The outcome of this struggle is unknown but the stakes are clear. Clear also are the responsibilities of people who care about what they eat, who want food they believe is more satisfying and not just less expensive, who want to have confidence in the foods they buy and to know and trust the farmers and businesses who produce it. If you want the right to make choices in the market, in your community, and in your kitchen about the food you buy and eat, if you want to be informed and know more about how your food is raised, or want to support the farmers and companies producing food in ways you trust, then you are involved in the fight to build a food democracy in America. You deserve to know more about our food system and to be challenged to make it better.

Neil D. Hamilton, *Essay—Food Democracy and the Future of American Values*, DRAKE J. AGRIC. L. 9 (2004).

The USDA's "Know Your Farmer, Know Your Food" program has been well received by many, but clearly not by all. In April 2010, Republican Senators Saxby Chambliss (Georgia), John McCain (Arizona), and Pat Roberts (Kansas) wrote a letter to Secretary Vilsack complaining about the program and demanding an itemized accounting as to how funds had been spent under the program.

> Launched in September 2009, the Department describes the initiative as a way to help Americans eat healthier by "knowing where your food comes from and how it gets to your plate." In addition to organizing college campus lectures and Facebook chats with USDA bureaucrats, the Department's strategy for reconnecting farmers with consumers also involves subsidizing the so-called locavore niche market. Last year alone, the Administration released over $65 million under the Know Your Farmers banner and has pledged to deliver millions more in Fiscal Year 2011. Unfortunately, this spending doesn't appear geared toward conventional farmers who produce the vast majority of our nation's food supply, but is instead aimed at small, hobbyist and organic producers whose customers generally consist of affluent patrons at urban farmers markets.

Letter to Secretary Vilsack from Senators Saxby Chambliss, John McCain, and Pat Roberts (April 27, 2010). Commentary and posted reactions to the letter are available at http://aglaw.blogspot.com/2010/04/senators-challenge-know-your-farmer.html.

On July 16, 2010, Iowa Public Television's *Market to Market* series featured a debate between Michael Pollan and Blake Hurst, a Missouri farmer who has challenged Pollan's criticism of our food system. The topic of the debate: *The Future of Agriculture*. The segment is available at http://www.iptv.org/mtom/story.cfm/feature/600. It illustrates the controversy between those, like Pollan and Hamilton, who advocate for a new agriculture and much of traditional commercial agriculture.

Robert Paarlberg wrote a stinging editorial, *Attention Whole Foods Shoppers*, in FOREIGN POLICY MAGAZINE (May/June 2010) with the introduction: "Stop obsessing about arugula. Your "sustainable" mantra—organic, local, and slow—is no recipe for saving the world's hungry billions." He issued a strong defense of industrialized, capital-intensive agriculture and sharp criticism of organic farming, arguing that only the former could provide sufficient food for the world's population.

The following month, Anna Lappe responded with an equally stringing critique of Paarlberg's analysis, challenging his assumptions, data, and his understanding of organic farming. *Food Fight*, FOREIGN POLICY MAGAZINE (July/August 2010). *See* http://www.foreign policy.com/articles/2010/06/21/food_fight for a direct link to *Food Fight* and the Lappe response along with a direct link to the Paarlberg essay.

> 'Eating is an agricultural act,' as Wendell Berry famously said. It is also an ecological act, and a political act, too. Though much has been done to obscure this simple fact, how and what we eat determines to a great extent the use we make of the world—and what is to become of it. To eat with a fuller consciousness of all that is at stake might sound like a burden, but in practice few things in life can afford quite as much satisfaction.

Michael Pollan, OMNIVORE'S DILEMMA, 11 (2006).

There is much to think about, and perhaps more people talking about food and agriculture than ever before. Those discussions, in particular those between consumers and farmers, will make the food system of the future.

Index

Note: *f* designates footnotes, *t* designates tables.